PSYCHOLOGY

The Science of · Mind and Behavior

Second Edition

PSYCHOLOGY

The Science of Mind and Behavior

John W. Santrock
University of Texas at Dallas

ωcb
Wm. C. Brown Publishers
Dubuque, Iowa

Book Team

Editor *James M. McNeil*
Developmental Editor *Sandra E. Schmidt*
Designer *Mary K. Sailer*
Production Editor *Kevin Campbell*
Photo Editor *Shirley Charley*
Photo Researcher *Carol M. Smith*
Permissions Editor *Vicki Krug*
Visuals Processor *Joyce E. Watters*

wcb group

Chairman of the Board *Wm. C. Brown*
President and Chief Executive Officer *Mark C. Falb*

wcb

Wm. C. Brown Publishers, College Division

President *G. Franklin Lewis*
Vice President, Editor-in-Chief *George Wm. Bergquist*
Vice President, Director of Production *Beverly Kolz*
National Sales Manager *Bob McLaughlin*
Director of Marketing *Thomas E. Doran*
Marketing Information Systems Manager *Craig S. Marty*
Marketing Manager *Kathy Law Laube*
Executive Editor *John Woods*
Manager of Visuals and Design *Faye M. Schilling*
Manager of Design *Marilyn A. Phelps*
Production Editorial Manager *Julie A. Kennedy*

Cover illustration by Kim Behm and Laura Meadows/Hellman Associates, Inc.

The credits section for this book begins on page 653 and is considered an extension of the copyright page.

Library of Congress Catalog Card Number: 87–72133

ISBN 0-697-06725-4 (cloth), 0-697-06736-X (paper)

Printed in the United States of America by Wm. C. Brown Publishers
2460 Kerper Boulevard, Dubuque, IA 52001

10 9 8 7 6 5 4 3

For Mary Jo

Brief Contents

Contents

Section I

Introduction to Mind and Behavior

Section II

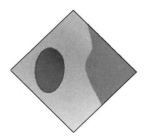

Biological and Perceptual Processes

Learning and Cognition

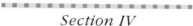

Section IV

Development and the Life Cycle

Section V

Motivation and Emotion

Section VI

Personality and Abnormal Psychology

Section VII

Social Psychology

Preface

I remember when I took my first course in psychology. It was during a period in my life when I was searching for answers to many questions—to who I was, what I was all about, where I was headed in life. Psychology, of course, did not answer these questions, nor did it promise to. But the study of psychology taught me many things. It taught me not to accept simple answers to complex questions about how the mind works and why we behave the way we do; it taught me to think critically about psychological problems and to handle stress more effectively; it taught me to learn more efficiently; it taught me to think about the way I had been socialized by my parents and peers, and the way I had socialized them; it taught me about helping and hurting, influencing others and being influenced by them; and it kindled an enthusiastic desire to find out more about the marvel of the human mind and behavior.

That is why I became a psychologist; that is why I still am a psychologist. The unsolved mysteries of mind and behavior are no less exciting, no less interesting, and no less stimulating to me than they were twenty-five years ago when I was a college freshman.

My goal as an author of psychology textbooks has always been to communicate my enthusiasm for the teaching and the practice of psychology. I have tried here to present a thorough, well-rounded presentation of the basics of the field without neglecting to discuss its unresolved controversies. I have tried to encourage the reader to think critically about the theories and discoveries of psychology.

If an introductory psychology text is to excite as well as instruct the reader, it must accomplish several very different goals simultaneously. Like the pieces of a puzzle, all the key elements must be in place for a text to truly meet the needs of the instructor and student. I believe that the most important pieces of this puzzle can be identified as follows: a solid, research-oriented presentation of psychology as a science; a mode of presentation that will interest and *motivate* the reader; a student-oriented pedagogical system that encourages *learning;* and a book and ancillary package that is enjoyable to teach from.

Psychology has the most current, thoroughly integrated research, conveying the *science* of psychology. *Psychology* has lively examples and student-oriented applications throughout to keep the reader interested and *motivated*. *Psychology* has a unique *learning* framework that organizes complex material and focuses attention on important concepts; and *Psychology* has a complete, integrated instructional package that coordinates lecture enrichment material, transparencies, videotapes, interactive software, and more, making *teaching* more effective.

Science

Psychology offers a blend of classic and contemporary research presented in a lively and interesting manner. This balance exists in each of *Psychology's* chapters. For example, the chapter on intelligence presents both the early makers of intelligence tests and the contemporary theorists who are paving the way for new insights about intelligence.

Psychology is also extremely up-to-date. More than four hundred references from 1985 to 1988 are cited, including *more than two hundred, 1987, 1988, and "in press" citations.* Psychology's scientific knowledge is expanding on many frontiers and I have attempted in each chapter to capture the excitement of these new discoveries as well as those classic studies that are the foundation of the discipline.

Motivation

In writing *Psychology,* I have tried to convey the excitement of research—the rich moments of learning about the brain's intricate workings, about the mind's images and memories, about behavior's many paths. I have tried to communicate the discoveries of psychology with enthusiasm, with energy, and with a constant awareness of their relevance to the reader. When a concept is introduced, lively examples and applications of the concept are provided. At the beginning of each chapter, a section called "Images" is introduced—an imaginative, high-interest piece that focuses on a topic related to the chapter's content. For example, chapter 10 on "Adolescence, Adult Development, and Aging" opens with a discussion on Jim Croce's song *Time in a Bottle,* and chapter 14 on "Abnormal Psychology" opens with a discussion of F. Scott Fitzgerald's and Ernest Hemingway's depression and Hemingway's suicide. PSYCHOLOGY boxes appear two to three times in each chapter—a brief glimpse through any chapter reveals their special appeal. For example, chapter 8 on "Intelligence" includes a box on the Repository for Germinal Choice— a sperm bank whose donors are restricted to Nobel and other prize winners— and the ethical issues it raises; chapter 11 on "Motivation" includes a box on the role of power in the nuclear arms race; and chapter 15 on "Social Thinking and Influence" includes a box on attribution theory and media explanations for a tragedy at a rock concert.

Learning

Psychology incorporates an effective and challenging learning system. This text was designed to enhance student comprehension and encourage critical thinking. I wanted to challenge students with the latest knowledge in the field of psychology. I wanted them to think, to analyze, and to understand this information. Topics are explored in sufficient depth to challenge students, and the complex nature of psychology is presented in such a way as to encourage critical thinking skills.

However, I not only wanted to encourage thinking skills, I also wanted to use textbook pedagogy help students learn. A carefully designed pedagogical framework has been built into *Psychology.* Critical to this framework are the CONCEPT TABLES that appear two to three times in every chapter. They are designed to activate the student's memory and comprehension of major topics or key concepts that have been discussed to that point. This allows the student to get a "handle" on complex concepts and ideas and to understand how key concepts are interrelated. Concept Tables provide a visual picture, or cognitive framework, of the most important information in each section.

In addition, CHAPTER OUTLINES at the beginning of each chapter show the overall organization of the material. At the end of the chapter, a detailed SUMMARY in outline form provides a helpful review. KEY TERMS are boldfaced in the text, listed with page references at the end of each chapter, and defined in a page-referenced GLOSSARY at the end of the book. An annotated list of SUGGESTED READINGS also appears at the end of each chapter. Finally, before students read the first chapter of *Psychology,* they will come across a section called STUDY SKILLS that provides helpful strategies for improved time use, memory, exam taking, and more. These elements should help students learn, and more important, understand the field of psychology.

Teaching

By writing a text that is comprehensive and up-to-date, my final goal was to write a *teachable* text. I hoped that the combination of solid, up-to-date research, presented in a readable, interesting writing style, and incorporating an effective student-oriented learning system would produce a text that is as enjoyable to teach from as it is to study.

In addition, the publisher and the ancillary team have worked together to produce an outstanding integrated teaching package to accompany *Psychology.* The authors of the teaching supplements are all experienced teachers of the introductory psychology course. The supplements have been designed to make it as easy as possible to customize the entire package to meet the unique needs of individual professors and their students.

The key to this package is the *Instructor's Course Planner,* prepared by Timothy N. Shearon and Janice F. Adams of Middle Tennessee State University. The Instructor's Course Planner is conveniently packaged in a three-ring binder so that lecture notes or classroom material can be added. To further meet individual teaching requirements, this flexible planner provides complete, separate teaching units for every major topic. These topic teaching units coordinate lecture suggestions, classroom activities, quizzes, handouts, discussion questions, test items, and directions for using the transparencies. In an additional chapter enrichment section, the Instructor's Course Planner includes supplementary presentations of a "Critical Thinking" issue, a "Research Focus," and an "Application" for each chapter, plus student projects, discussion guides for the videotape package, film suggestions, and suggestions for using Psycom, the software simulation package.

In addition, a comprehensive *Test Item File* has been prepared by David Ball, Karlene Ball, and Bettina Beard of Western Kentucky University. The Test Item File consists of two separate test banks with a total of 3,000 multiple choice, fill in the blank, and true/false test items. Each test item is referenced to both text page and learning objective, and is identified as factual, conceptual, or applied.

A *Transparency Set* of 140 acetate transparencies, many in full color, includes graphics and tables from both the text and outside sources and can be used as lecture outlines. These transparencies have been designed to help in classroom teaching and organizing lectures.

A *Student Study Guide* by Steven A. Schneider, Pima Community College, and Michael G. Walraven, Jackson Community College, includes the following for each chapter: page-referenced learning objectives, a chapter overview, key terms exercise, guided review, student test questions, and a set of questions that go "beyond the text," asking students to think critically about issues raised in the chapter and to apply chapter material to real-life situations.

ʊɕɓ *TestPak* is the free, computerized testing service available to adopters of *Psychology: The Science of Mind and Behavior.* All questions in the Test Item File are available on TestPak. Two options are available. The call-in/mail-in TestPak service guarantees that we will put in the mail to you a test master, a student answer sheet, and an answer key within two working days of receiving your request. Call-in hours are 8:30–1:30, Central time, Monday through Thursday. **ʊɕɓ** TestPak is also available for instructors who want to use their IBM PC or their Apple IIe, IIc or Macintosh to create their own tests. Upon request, adopters of *Psychology: The Science of Mind and Behavior* will receive the Test Item File, program diskettes, and user's guide. With these, the instructor will be able to create tests, answer sheets, and answer keys. The program allows for adding, deleting, or modifying test questions. No programming experience is necessary.

ʊɕɓ *QuizPak,* the interactive self-testing, self-scoring quiz program, will help your students review text material from any chapter by testing themselves on an Apple IIe, IIc or Macintosh, or an IBM PC. Adopters will receive the QuizPak program, question disks, and an easy-to-follow user's guide. QuizPak may be used at a number of work stations simultaneously and requires only one disk drive.

PSYCOM, Psychology on Computer: Simulations, Experiments, and Projects, is an interactive software package for introductory psychology. It is available for the Apple IIe and IIc and the IBM PC. The projects teach students to collect data, analyze it, and discuss the results within the context of scientific study. Results of the experiments can be tabulated for individual students or the entire class. A student workbook accompanies the software, providing background readings, instructions, worksheets, and other material necessary to complete the simulations.

Acknowledgements

This book was produced by many minds and hands. The publisher, William C. Brown, has provided excellent support for the book. James McNeil, Senior Editor, and Sandy Schmidt, Senior Developmental Editor, should feel a special sense of pride about *Psychology.* Their enthusiasm for the book was contagious. Sandy's writing advice is especially appreciated. Kevin Campbell spent long hours overseeing the production of *Psychology*—I appreciate his careful work with the manuscript. Laura Beaudoin copyedited the manuscript with care and competence. Mary Sailer, Designer, provided creative touches that make the book very attractive. Shirley Charley and Carol Smith went the extra mile in tracking down elusive and effective photos. Vicki Krug efficiently obtained permissions. Special thanks go to Timothy N. Shearon and Janice F. Adams, Middle Tennessee State University, who prepared the innovative Course Planner; to David Ball, Karlene Ball, and Bettina Beard, Western Kentucky University, who prepared the comprehensive Test Item File; and to Steven Schneider, Pima Community College, and Michael G. Walraven, who prepared an excellent Student Study Guide.

Special thanks also go to Christopher J. Frederickson and James C. Bartlett, University of Texas at Dallas, who served both as reviewers and as contributors of material in the sections on biological and cognitive processes.

I benefited enormously from the ideas and insights of many colleagues. I would like to thank the following individuals for providing helpful feedback on the first edition:

Norma Baker
Belmont College

Roy Connally
University of Central Florida

Robert O. Engbretson
Southern Illinois University–Edwardsville

Roy Fontaine
Williamsport Area Community College

Cynthia A. Ford
Jackson State University

Gilbert M. French
University of South Dakota

Renee L. Harrangue
Loyola Marymount University

Francis A. Martin
Belmont College

Thomas A. McGrath
Fairfield University

Barbara K. Sholley
University of Richmond

Martha S. Spiker
University of Charleston

Michael R. Stevenson
Ball State University

Barbara Streitfeld
University of Hartford

William Walker
University of Richmond

Lonnie R. Yandell
Belmont College

I would also like to express my appreciation to the following instructors who provided in-depth reviews of chapters from the first edition and/or all or part of the manuscript for the current edition:

Bernard A. Albaniak
University of South Carolina

Ira B. Albert
Dundalk Community College

Lewis M. Barker
Baylor University

Jerrold E. Barnett
Northwest Missouri State University

James C. Bartlett
University of Texas–Dallas

John D. Batson
Furman University

Don Baucum
Birmingham–Southern College

James O. Benedict
James Madison University

David Berger
SUNY–Cortland

John B. Best
Eastern Illinois University

Charles L. Brewer
Furman University

John P. Broida
University of Southern Maine

William H. Calhoun
University of Tennessee–Knoxville

George A. Cicala
University of Delaware

James V. Couch
James Madison University

Thomas Fitzpatrick
Rockland Community College

Christopher Frederickson
University of Texas–Dallas

Richard A. Griggs
University of Florida–Gainesville

Charles G. Halcomb
Texas Tech. University

Anne E. Harris
Arizona State University

William J. Hepler
Butler University

Garth Hines
University of Arkansas–Little Rock

James J. Johnson
Illinois State University

Ralph H. Kolstoe
University of North Dakota

T. C. Lewandowski
Delaware County Community College

Kathleen McNamara
Colorado State University

Linda Musun-Miller
University of Arkansas–Little Rock

Jay B. Pozner
Jackson Community College

JoAnn Preston
University of Richmond

Celia C. Reaves
Monroe Community College

Phillip L. Rice
Moorhead State University

Sherman Ross
Howard University

Richard Seefeldt
University of Wisconsin–River Falls

David G. Sequin
Jamestown Community College

Jack P. Shilkret
Anne Arundel Community College

Robert F. Smith
George Mason University

Theresa Socha
Frostburg State College

Ralph H. Song
University of Wisconsin–Whitewater

A final note of thanks goes to my family—Mary Jo, my wife, and my daughters Tracy, 21, and Jennifer, 18.

Your Critical Thinking Skills

Much of the knowledge we are exposed to in the course of our education passes through our minds like tiny grains of sand washed through a porous sieve. In other words, it goes in one ear and out the other! We need to do more than just memorize or passively absorb new information; we need to learn how to *think critically*. It is the ability to *think* that you should carry beyond this course, an ability that will enable you to acquire new knowledge about mind and behavior, to replace old knowledge about mind and behavior, and to recognize what types of knowledge about mind and behavior are worth acquiring in the first place. How can we cultivate the ability to think critically and clearly?

According to a leading cognitive psychologist, Robert J. Sternberg (1987), we need to use the right thinking processes, develop problem-solving strategies, improve our mental representation, expand our knowledge base, and become motivated to use our newly-learned thinking skills. Let's consider each of these ideas in turn.

Using the Right Thinking Processes

What are the right thinking processes? To think critically, or indeed to solve any problem or learn any new knowledge, you need to take an active role in learning new information. This means that you must call upon a variety of active thinking processes, such as the following:

Listening carefully

Identifying or formulating questions

Identifying or formulating criteria for judging possible answers

Organizing your thoughts

Noting similarities and differences

Deducing

Distinguishing between logically valid and invalid inferences

Making value judgments

Finally, you need to be able to ask and answer questions of clarification, such as "What is the main point?" "What did the author mean by that?" and "Why?"

This textbook asks you many questions, often at the beginning of a topic, encouraging you to think about the topic. As you go through the book, you should not simply uncritically accept all of the information that is presented. Psychology is a changing discipline—we are acquiring new information about mind and behavior in the 1980s and will continue to do so in the 1990s, replacing old knowledge with new knowledge about mind and behavior. Have an inquiring mind. Remember to ask, "If the researcher had conducted her experiment this way instead of that way, what would she have discovered?"

Do not be afraid to think, "That research study does not make sense to me. I think the conclusion fails to take into account the changing role of females in today's society," for example. It is through such critical thinking that psychology has advanced as a science.

Strategies

Good thinkers use more than just the right thinking processes—they also know how to combine them into workable strategies for solving problems. It is the rare problem that can be solved by a single type of thought process used in isolation. We need to learn to *combine* thinking processes in order to effectively master a new task.

For example, Robert Ennis (1987), who has developed a well-known taxonomy of critical thinking skills, describes the importance of multiple thinking processes in his experience as a juror serving on a murder trial. Clearly, Ennis did not study "juries" or "murder" in college. But Ennis and his fellow jurors were called upon to judge the credibility of the witnesses; interpret a complicated set of legal criteria for murder and voluntary manslaughter; draw conclusions about the intentions, beliefs, and truthfulness of the defendant; and determine how the victim might have been stabbed. Critical thinking involves combining such complex thought processes in a way that makes sense, not just jumbling them together in a way that never produces anything concrete.

Mental Representation of Both Sides of Issues and the Multiple Determination of Behavior

We need to be able to see things from multiple points of view. Unless we can mentally represent information from more than one point of view, we may well rely on an inadequate set of information. If we do not seek out alternative explanations and interpretations of problems and issues, our conclusions may be based on our own expectations, prejudices, stereotypes, and personal experience.

Throughout this book, you will be encouraged to think about both sides of issues and the multiple determination of behavior, challenging you to think critically. It is easy to fall into the trap of thinking that there is only one side to an issue. For example, you might be inclined to think that behavior is determined only by environmental experiences, to the exclusion of hereditary influences. In many places in the book, you will be encouraged to think critically about the manner in which heredity and environment interact to produce behavior. When we think about what causes behavior, we sometimes lean toward explaining the behavior in terms of a single cause. For example, a friend might tell us, "Our marriage did not work because he could not let go of his mother." The husband's inability to relinquish his strong attachment to his mother may have been one cause for the divorce, but there were undoubtedly others—perhaps economic problems, sexual difficulties, personality conflicts, and so on. One of psychology's great lessons is that behavior is not singly determined; behavior is multiply determined. Understanding and applying this principle will be encouraged throughout the book and can help you to think critically about mind and behavior.

Knowledge Base

It is important for you to keep in mind that thinking does not occur in the absence of knowledge: we need to have something to think about. However, it is a mistake to concentrate only on information to the exclusion of thinking skills, because you simply will become a student who has a lot of knowledge but who is unable to evaluate and apply it. It is equally a mistake to concentrate only on thinking skills, because you would become a student who knows how to think but has nothing to think about! The material on Study Skills that begins on page xxv will help you to acquire this knowledge base of information about psychology.

Motivation to Use Thinking Skills

All of the thinking skills you possibly could master would be irrelevant if they were not actually put to use. As you read this book, you will be encouraged to use your critical thinking skills as you study and as you go about your everyday activities. Critical thinking is both a matter for academic study *and* a part of living. Considering both sides of issues, contemplating the multiple determinants of behavior, using the right thought processes, combining the right thought processes into workable strategies, and having access to psychology's knowledge base can help you to think critically about issues and problems as you go through the course of your daily lives.

Suggested Reading

Baron, J. B., & Sternberg, R. J. (Eds.). (1987). *Teaching thinking skills: Theory and practice.* New York: W. H. Freeman.

This book presents essays by ten eminent psychologists, educators, and philosophers that portray the current state of knowledge about critical thinking skills. It offers various exercises and strategies that can be performed both inside and outside the classroom to enhance your critical thinking skills.

Your Study Skills

You have taken courses in history, math, English, and science, but have you taken a course in study skills? Have you ever seriously sat down and mapped out a time management program for yourself? Have you ever studied how to improve your memory, then tried the techniques to see if they work? Have you ever had an organized plan to "attack" a textbook? Before you begin reading the specific content of this book, take time to read the following section on how to improve your study skills. You will be motivated to think about ways to manage your time, to improve your concentration, to memorize more effectively, and to function more efficiently in the classroom. You will learn skills to understand this and other books more clearly and discover how to prepare for and take exams.

Managing Your Time

A student came to my office about two weeks before the final exam in an introductory psychology course. He had a D average in the course and wanted to know what was causing him to get such a low grade. It turned out that he wasn't doing well in any of his classes, so we talked about his background. Eventually, the conversation turned to his study techniques and what he could do to get better grades on his final exams. I asked Tom to put together a study schedule for the four final exams he was getting ready to take in two weeks. He planned to study a total of four hours for his psychology exam; only one of those hours was scheduled for the night before the exam and no study time was allotted to the morning before the exam (the exam was in the late afternoon).

I told Tom that although the psychology exam probably was not the most difficult one he would ever take in college, I thought the material would require more than four hours of study time if he wanted to improve his grade for the course. As we talked further, it became evident that Tom was a terrible manager of time. True, he had a part-time job in addition to the twelve credit hours he was taking, but as we mapped out how he used his time during the day, Tom quickly became aware that he was wasting big chunks of time.

A week is made up of 168 hours. The typical college student sleeps 50 hours, attends classes 19 hours, eats 11 hours, and studies 20 hours per week. For Tom, we had to add 15 hours a week for his part-time job and 6 hours a week for transportation to and from school, work, and home. Subtracting the 20 hours of study time, Tom found that his main activities accounted for 101 of the week's 168 hours, suggesting that even though he works he still has 67 hours in which to find time for studying.

Figure P.1
Record of one day's activities and suggestions for making better use of time.

TIME		TIME USED	ACTIVITY - DESCRIPTION	
START	END			
7:45	8:15	:30	DRESS	Paste on mirror 3 × 5 cards: Laws of economics; psychological terms; statistical formulas—study while brushing teeth, etc.
8:15	8:40	:25	BREAKFAST	Look over textbook assignment and previous lecture notes to establish continuity for today's psychology lecture.
8:40	9:00	:20	NOTHING	
9:00	10:00	1:00	PSYCHOLOGY - LECTURE	
10:00	10:40	:40	COFFEE - TALKING	Break too long and too soon after breakfast. Should work on psychology notes just taken; also should look over economics assignment.
10:40	11:00	:20	NOTHING	
11:00	12:00	1:00	ECONOMICS - LECTURE	
12:00	12:45	:45	LUNCH	Should re-work the lecture notes on economics while still fresh in mind. Also, look over biology assignment to recall the objective of the coming lab.
12:45	2:00	1:15	READING - MAGAZINE	
2:00	4:00	2:00	BIOLOGY - LAB	
4:00	5:30	1:30	RECREATION - VOLLEYBALL	
5:30	6:00	:30	NOTHING	Use this time for reading a magazine or newspaper.
6:00	7:00	1:00	DINNER	
7:00	8:00	1:00	NAP	Not a good idea. Better finish work, then get a good night's sleep.
8:00	8:50	:50	STUDY - STATISTICS	
8:50	9:20	:30	BREAK	Break—too long.
9:20	10:00	:40	STUDY - STATISTICS	Good as a reward if basic work is done.
10:00	10:50	:50	RAP SESSION	
10:50	11:30	:40	STUDY - ACCOUNTING	Insufficient time allotted, but better than no time.
11:30	11:45	:15	READY FOR BED	While brushing teeth, study the 3 × 5 cards. Replace cards that have been mastered with new ones.
11:45	7:45	8:00	SLEEP	

You may find it helpful to fill out a weekly schedule of your activities to see where your time goes. Figure P.1 provides an example of one student's daily time schedule along with comments about how and where time could have been used more effectively. Some students are afraid that a schedule will make them too rigid. However, successful students usually follow organized time schedules and manage their time efficiently. If you waste less time, you will actually have much more free time for personal activities. And in managing your time effectively you will feel a sense of control over your life. Try taking five minutes at the beginning of every day to chart your plan for the day. Before you go to bed at night review your day to see how well you met your schedule. After you have done this for several weeks, it should become routine.

Study Skills

Given that you manage your time efficiently, how can you use the study time you have effectively? First, you need to concentrate on *really* studying in the time set aside for studying. Second, a number of memory techniques can help you recall information. Third, you can discover strategies for learning more effectively from textbooks like this one. Fourth, you can reduce your study time by functioning more effectively during class. Fifth, you can learn some important tips in preparing for and taking exams. Let's consider each of these in turn.

Concentration

There are many distractions that keep you from studying or remembering what you have studied. Select your place of study carefully. Most individuals need a desk—a place where pens, paper, and a book can be placed. Use your desk *only* for studying. If you nap or daydream while you are at your desk, the desk can act as a cue for napping or daydreaming. Use your desk as a cue for studying. When you want to nap or daydream, go somewhere else. Be sure the area where you study is well lighted and does not have glare. Do your utmost to find a place that is quiet when you study. If the library is the right place for you, then go there, especially if there are people in the dorm or at home who distract you. Noise is one of the main distractions to effective studying. For the most part, it is a good idea to turn off the stereo, radio, or television while you are studying.

So far we have talked about physical aspects of the environment that may help or hinder your ability to concentrate on what you are studying. Psychological or personal situations may also interfere with your ability to concentrate. Daydreaming is one way to avoid hard work. Even though daydreaming may seem pleasant at the time we are doing it, we pay the consequences later, possibly with a poor grade on a test or in a course. Everyone has personal relationships that may at some point intrude on study time. Force yourself to put personal relationships and problems out of your mind during the time you have set aside for studying. Tell yourself you will deal with them after you have finished studying. If the problems seem overwhelming and you cannot avoid thinking about them, you may want to contact the student counseling service at your college or university. Most college and university counseling centers not only have counselors who help students with personal problems, but they often have study skills counselors who help students with such matters as time management, concentration, and so on.

Memory Techniques

At some point in this course and the other courses you are taking this semester, you will have to remember what you have heard in class and read in books. How can you remember more effectively?

First, make up your mind to remember. If you really want to improve your memory you can, but you have to motivate yourself to improve it. Second, keep refreshing your memory. Almost everything tends to fade unless we periodically think about what it is we are to remember. Periodically rehearsing what you have heard in class or read in this book will help you to store the information and to retrieve it when you have a test. Third, organize what you want to remember. Organize, outline, or structure what it is you want to remember. Pick out the main points in what you are studying and arrange them in a meaningful pattern or outline. Then recite and repeat them until you can recall them when needed. Select, organize, and repeat—these are time-tested steps for helping you to remember.

A number of memory tricks also can improve your memory. One memory trick is to relate what you have read to your own life. Throughout this book you will be encouraged to do this. You can also use a number of organized systems to improve your memory. One such system involves taking the first letter of each word in an ordered series and using those letters to form a new name or sentence. For example, in chapter 3, "Sensation and Perception," you will learn that the colors in the light spectrum are *r*ed, *o*range, *y*ellow, *g*reen, *b*lue, *i*ndigo, and *v*iolet. You can learn this ordering quickly by thinking of the name Roy G. Biv. Additional information about memory strategies appears in chapter 6, "Memory."

Learning from This and Other Textbooks

This textbook has a number of built-in devices to improve your learning. You read about many of these in the preface. Beyond the way the book is organized an extraordinary technique can make your reading more efficient—it is called the SQ3R method, and it was developed by Dr. Francis P. Robinson more than forty years ago. *S* stands for *Survey*, *Q* represents *Question*, and 3R signifies *Read*, *Recite*, and *Review*.

To survey, glance over the headings in each chapter to find the main points that will be developed. The chapter outline at the beginning of each chapter will help in this regard. This orientation will help you to organize the ideas as you read them later.

To *question,* you may want to begin by turning each heading into a question. This will arouse your curiosity and should increase your comprehension. The question may help to make important points stand out. Ask yourself questions as you read through the chapter. As you find information that answers your questions, underline or mark over the material with a felt pen.

To accomplish the third step in the SQ3R method, you begin *reading* as you normally would in a book. In the SQ3R method, though, your reading should be more efficient because you have built a foundation for understanding the material by already surveying and questioning.

The fourth step in the SQ3R method involves *reciting* information periodically as you go through a chapter. To help you remember this strategy, two to three times per chapter you will encounter a concept table, which encourages you to recite what you have read in a particular part of the chapter. In many instances you will want to do this more than two to three times per chapter. Every several pages you should stop and think about what you have just read and briefly recite the main points.

After you have used the techniques suggested so far, you need to *review* the material you have read at least several times before you take a test. Do not think that just because you have read a chapter you will be able to recall all of its information. By reciting the information over and over and continuing to review the material, you will improve your test performance. At the end of each chapter in this book you will find an outline summary that will help you in the review process.

The Classroom Lecture

What goes on in your classroom lecture is just as important as what is in this textbook. You would not skip a chapter in this book if you knew it was assigned for a test, so it is not a good idea to skip a class just to reach the allowable number of cuts or to cram for an exam. More than a few students feel that because they go to class and listen they do not need to devote further time to a lecture. However, by preparing for the lecture, using your learning skills during the lecture, and doing some follow-up work after the lecture, you should be able to improve your performance on tests.

Section I

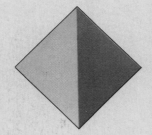

Introduction to Mind and Behavior

My friend . . . care for your psyche, and . . . make it as good as possible. . . . Know thyself, for once we know ourselves, we may learn how to care for ourselves, but otherwise we never shall.

—Socrates

Chapter 1

What Is Psychology?

▪ ▪

What is needed is not the will to believe, but the wish to find out.

—*Bertrand Russell*

▪ ▪

Images of Psychology

Charlie's view from the spacecraft is exhilarating. He is about to join ten women and men from other countries, and together they will occupy the first American space station. They will live and work in a weightless world orbiting hundreds of miles above the earth.

Long before astronauts traveled into space, psychologists were involved in the simulation of man-machine systems for spaceflight. Research was conducted with people confined for long periods of time in sealed cabins that reproduced most of the living conditions of space capsules. In recent years, as living in space for prolonged periods of time has become more of a reality, psychologists have examined the environmental and social conditions likely to exist on a space station.

As a psychologist, Charlie will evaluate living conditions on the space station. Using his training in environmental and social psychology, he will study ways to improve productivity and stimulate creativity, and he will examine work and rest cycles and privacy and leisure activities. Charlie will also conduct research on how the environment in the space station can best counteract monotony. He is aware that the Soviets have developed background music programs that provide variety and establish the best mood for different work and rest situations. The Soviets place a high priority on the mental well-being of their space crews. A support group of clinical psychologists on earth communicates with and monitors how well cosmonauts are coping with space travel and work. Two-way televised meetings occur regularly between cosmonauts and their families and friends.

Our astronaut, Charlie, is a fictitious example that illustrates how psychologists might study the mind and behavior of people in space and possibly make life there more productive and enjoyable. Cosmonaut Svetlana Savitskaya is not fictitious. Observations of Soviet space stations indicate that when Svetlana joined the crew on 211- and 237-day missions, the behavior of the all-male crews changed dramatically (Bluth & Helppie, 1986). The five male crew members began shaving twice a day and were quick to lend her assistance in biology experiments. Svetlana said she was careful not to make mistakes because they might reflect on women in general. Svetlana believes women are better than men at some tasks in outer space, such as precision tasks requiring meticulous touch. She says that men are better at tasks requiring heavy exertion. When the press referred to her ability to elevate the mood of the male crew members, Svetlana replied, with irritation, "We do not go into space to improve the mood of the crew. Women go into space because they measure up to the job."

We live in an extraordinary time. It is a time of dramatic changes in social organization, of tremendous economic growth, and of an explosion in our knowledge about ourselves. Throughout history, contradictory answers have existed to some of the most fundamental questions of interest to psychologists: What is mind? Why do we behave the way we do? How can we solve people's problems? What are the contributions of biology and experience and of genes and environment to our psychological makeup? The answers to such provocative questions remain diverse and sometimes contradictory. In the case of

Cosmonaut Svetlana Savitskaya, who participated on 211- and 237-day missions into space. Are there some tasks that women can do better in space than men?

Svetlana, we could ask why women are better than men at some tasks and men better than women at others. Is it because we are born that way? Or is it because as males and females we have different experiences as we grow? As females enter occupations once reserved for males, will reporters be less likely to ask questions such as the one asked of Svetlana? Or will our biological makeup forever produce differences in male and female abilities and ways of interacting with the opposite sex?

Psychologists seek knowledge about varied aspects of mind and behavior. The description of Charlie and Svetlana showed us two types of psychologists: clinical psychologists concerned with mental health and environmental and social psychologists interested in social conditions. In this chapter, you will learn that there are many other kinds of psychologists. But first we look at what psychology is—its contents, its theories, and its methods. ■

What Is Psychology?

Psychology is the scientific study of mind and behavior. **Behavior** is everything we do that can be observed directly—two people *kissing,* a baby *crying,* a college student *riding a motorcycle.* Mind is trickier than behavior and includes everything in our mental life that cannot be observed directly—someone *thinking* about kissing someone, a baby's *feelings* when its mother leaves the room, and the college student's *memory* of the motorcycle episode. I cannot directly observe your images of kissing, the baby's feelings, or the college student's memory. **Mind,** then, is our mental life, our thoughts and feelings that cannot be seen directly but are no less real.

Psychology has not always been defined in terms of mind and behavior. Early in this century, psychologists were interested primarily in mental processes. Before long many psychologists attacked the study of mental life as too vague. From the 1920s until the 1950s, the study of behavior dominated psychology. Psychologists were more comfortable studying what they could observe directly rather than making inferences about what was going on in a person's head. But psychology as the study of behavior alone did not last.

Today, many psychologists believe that the interior world of mental processes is filled with experiences that cannot be ignored. They believe that covert (internal) experiences, such as images, memories, and dreams, are among psychology's most fascinating phenomena. New experimental techniques and some ingenious research designs have allowed psychologists to measure and evaluate mental processes such as memory, problem solving, and the use of imagery. Although mental processes cannot be observed *directly,* they can still be studied in a scientific way. There are some psychologists who still believe we should study only those behaviors that can be observed directly, but most recognize the importance of behavior *and* mind.

Early and Contemporary Approaches to Psychology

Psychology emerged as a science in the late nineteenth century, influenced by both philosophy and biology. The early Greek philosophers Socrates and Aristotle urged us to know ourselves, to use logic to make inferences about mental processes, and to systematically observe behavior. In the centuries before psychology emerged as a science, philosophers continued to have strong opinions about mind and behavior. They asked and debated questions on how we acquire knowledge. Did information come to us through our senses and our experiences with the environment, or was it inborn? Charles Darwin's ideas on evolution and the organism's biological adaptation were influential in molding the thinking of early psychologists as well.

© 1960 United Feature Syndicate, Inc.

The Beginnings of Psychology as a Science

Imagine that you are in Leipzig, Germany, in the year 1879. A bearded man with a wrinkled forehead and pensive expression is sitting in the room. His head turns toward a soft sound coming from the far side of the room. After several minutes his head turns once again, this time toward a loud sound. The scenario is repeated with sounds of varying intensity. The man is Wilhelm Wundt, who is credited with developing the first scientific psychology laboratory. By exposing himself to environmental conditions that he systematically varied, and then recording his reactions and judgments to the changing (or different) stimuli, Wundt was investigating the elements, or "structures," of the mind.

The year is now 1892. You are a student sitting in a class at Cornell University in Ithaca, New York. You and the other students wait with anticipation as a man strides into the lecture hall wearing a flowing black gown. Three assistants follow him. Instruments that demonstrate the nature of psychological experimentation are laid out on the stage. This is the protocol of E. B. Titchener, who popularized Wundt's ideas in America. Like Wundt, Titchener was intrigued by how people consciously experience and perceive their world. Their attempts to classify the structures of the mind were not unlike a chemist breaking down chemicals into their component parts—water into hydrogen and oxygen, for example. Because of his interest in the *structures* of the mind, Titchener's approach to psychology became known quite logically as **structuralism.**

The first of the new psychologists to the United States was not Titchener, but William James. James did not believe that the elementary, rigid structures for which Titchener searched existed. James argued that our minds are characterized by a continuous flow of information about our experiences rather than by discrete components. Following in the steps of Darwin, James emphasized the mind's ability to continuously evolve as it adapted to information about the environment. James' approach to psychology became known as **functionalism,** quite simply because he stressed the *functions* of the mind and behavior in adapting to the environment.

Many of the early psychologists, such as Wundt, Titchener, and James, used **introspection** to discover information about conscious experiences. Introspection is a technique whereby specially trained people carefully observe and analyze their own mental experiences. It is a process of turning inward in search of mind's nature. Wundt was the master of introspection training. Before his students were permitted to tell about their images and perceptions, they had to participate in a minimum of 10,000 practice observations! Philosophers had used introspection for several thousand years, but they had never varied conditions so systematically. The technique of introspection, however, came under heavy fire. The introspectionists thought they were studying immediate experience, but in reality, it takes time to introspect. Introspection was in reality retrospection, and thus the act of introspection changed the observer's experience, therefore modifying or "contaminating" the observation.

From its very start, then, psychology has been characterized by competing approaches. Wundt and Titchener thought mind was composed of elements and structures. James argued that mind was made up of functions that adapted to the environment. Neither structuralism nor functionalism was destined for long-term stardom in psychology. This emphasis on consciousness soon fell out of favor in psychology, because critics stressed that the approaches lacked objectivity and investigated mental processes that were too vague (Hilgard, 1987; Kendler, 1987).

Contemporary Approaches to Psychology

Other approaches to understanding mind and behavior soon emerged. Some psychologists believed that only behavior that can be observed directly, and not the inner workings of mind, should be studied. Others wanted to retain the concept of mind but focus on its deep-seated interior instead of its conscious parts. These approaches lived longer lives than structuralism and functionalism. They continue to enjoy rich followings even today, and were joined by other views in the ongoing exploration of the nature of mind and behavior.

Why are there so many different approaches to psychology? Why isn't one of them right and the rest of them wrong? All approaches to psychology are in a sense correct. They are all valid ways of looking at psychology, just as blueprints, floor plans, and photographs are all valid ways of looking at a house. Some approaches are better for some purposes (a floor plan is more useful than a photograph for deciding how much lumber to buy, and the neurobiological approach is probably more useful than the cognitive approach for understanding epilepsy), but no single approach is "right" or "wrong." Approaches are judged on whether they tend to generate useful information.

Remembering the abstract principles of psychological approaches can be difficult, almost like swimming upstream against an onrushing current. I don't want you to become overwhelmed or drown while reading about these approaches. So, after each of the five major approaches—the behavioral approach, the psychoanalytic approach, the humanistic and phenomenological approaches, the cognitive approach, and the neurobiological approach—we will apply that approach to the topic of dating.

Behavioral Approach

The year is 1898. You are ushered into a room where you see a dog hooked up to a harness. The dog is salivating profusely, and you wonder what is going on. A gentleman in a white laboratory coat walks over and quietly informs you that an experiment in learning is taking place. He explains that it is a very simple form of learning, in this case documented by the dog's salivation in anticipation of being fed. The man is Ivan Pavlov, who shows you that by putting the dog's tray down or by allowing the dog to catch a glimpse of the attendant who fed him the previous day, the dog will begin to salivate. (More details about the life of Pavlov's dogs appear in chapter 5.)

Pavlov's experiments emphasized careful observation of overt behavior following precise manipulation of the environment. The observations were very different from the information collected through Wundt's introspection, which emphasized inferences about the conscious mind. Pavlov's interest in the overt behavior of organisms and the precise manner in which he observed behavior impressed an American by the name of John B. Watson. Watson believed that consciousness had no place in psychology—that it was too vague and couldn't be measured. The view of Pavlov and Watson is called the **behavioral approach,** the scientific study of behavior and its environmental determinants. According to behaviorists, we do well in school because of the rewards we experience; we behave in a well-mannered fashion for our parents because of the controls they place on us; and we work hard at our jobs because of the money we receive for our effort. We don't do these things, according to behaviorists, because of the motivation to be a competent person or because they make us feel better. We do them because of the environmental conditions we have experienced and are continuing to experience.

The contemporary view of behaviorism also emphasizes the importance of observing behavior to understand the individual. And the rigorous methods for obtaining information about behavior advocated by Pavlov and Watson remain a cornerstone of the behavioral approach. Contemporary behaviorists continue to stress the importance of environmental determinants of behavior as well.

While an emphasis on observable behavior and environmental determinants is characteristic of all behavioral views today, different forms of behaviorism have developed. One form is close to the beliefs of Watson and is best represented by the well-known behaviorist B. F. Skinner (1938, 1987). Like Watson, Skinner argues that looking into the mind for the determinants of behavior detracts the investigator from the true cause of behavior—the external environment. Behaviorists who follow Skinner's tradition are interested in modifying and rearranging environmental experiences to determine their effects on the organism, whether rat, pigeon, or human. A father complains his son is misbehaving at home. Careful observation reveals that the father rarely rewards his son even though the son has done a number of positive things. The behaviorist calls the father's attention to this information and instructs him to tell the child how pleased he is whenever the child behaves positively (for example, completing a chore on time or coming home from school with a good test grade).

In this example, the behaviorist is not interested in what the father or the son is thinking or feeling. The behaviorist is interested only in their behavior, which can be directly observed. Not every behaviorist accepts Skinner's rejection of thought processes. **Social learning theorists,** such as Albert Bandura (1969, 1986), believe we not only need to evaluate behavior and its controlling environmental conditions, but also how our thoughts modify the impact of environment on behavior. Perhaps the son has observed other children misbehaving and has images and memories of that behavior. If these children are popular with peers, the son imitates their behavior. Bandura believes imitation is one of the main ways we learn about our world. To reproduce a model's behavior we must code and store the information in memory, which is a mental or cognitive process. Thus, social learning theorists broadened the scope of behaviorism to include not only observed behavior but also how information about the environment is cognitively processed. The behavioral approach is described in much greater detail in both chapters 5 and 13.

What can the behavioral approaches tell us about dating? The behavioral approaches tell us not to look inside of our heads for clues about dating behavior. Inner motives and feelings about another person cannot be directly observed so they will be of no help in understanding dating. The behaviorists say we should be sensitive to what goes on before and after a date, searching for the rewarding aspects that attracted us to the other person in the first place (perhaps a flirtatious smile or a particular appearance). A particular date may be rewarding because it gets us attention from others, possibly increasing our status in a group. Social learning theory tells us that dating behavior may come from watching what others do and listening to what they say, for example, observing an older brother's strategies of what to do (or what not to do) to get someone to go out with him.

Observe these two individuals on a date. If you were a psychologist with a behavioral orientation, what aspects of dating would you be interested in studying?

Psychoanalytic Approach

The year is 1904. You are lying on an incredibly comfortable couch in an office in Vienna, Austria. A gentleman with a stern look on his face walks in and sits down near you. He asks you to close your eyes. After several minutes of silence, he inquires about your childhood experiences. The man asking the questions is Sigmund Freud.

Unlike many pioneer psychologists, Freud was intrigued by the abnormal aspects of people's lives. Others were interested in either the conscious aspects of mind or in directly observable (overt) behavior. For Freud, the *key* to understanding mind and behavior rested in the unconscious aspects of mind—the aspects of which we are unaware. Freud compared the human mind to an iceberg. The conscious mind is only the tip of the iceberg, the portion above water; the unconscious mind is the huge bulk of the iceberg, the portion under water.

Freud believed that the way we think and behave is influenced heavily by unlearned biological instincts. These instincts, particularly our sexual and aggressive impulses, often come in conflict with the demands of society. For example, in Freud's view, a child inherits the tendency to act aggressively. The aggressive instinct is located in the child's unconscious mind and is responsible for the aggressive energy a boy shows in destroying a peer's sand castle, punching his brother in the nose, or running wildly through a neighbor's flower garden. The aggressive instinct conflicts with acceptable social behavior, so the child must learn to adapt.

While Freud saw much of development as instinctually based, he argued that relationships with parents represented the chief environmental contribution to our personality. That is why he asked you about your childhood as you relaxed on the couch. By getting you to talk about your early family life, Freud hoped you would unconsciously reveal clues about the conflicts causing your problems. The **psychoanalytic approach,** then, is the view that emphasizes the unconscious aspects of mind, conflict between biological instincts and society's demands, and early childhood experiences.

Psychoanalysis has survived, although its form has changed somewhat from Freud's original theories. Many contemporary psychoanalytic theorists downplay sexual instincts as strong determinants of personality and place the emphasis on rational thought and cultural circumstances (Eagle, 1987). Contemporary theorists still stress the developmental unfolding of personality and that childhood experiences affect our personality as adults. Unconscious thoughts remain a central interest, although theorists believe conscious thoughts make up more of the iceberg than Freud thought. Much more about Freud's theory appears in chapter 13, where we discuss personality.

Erik Erikson (1968) is an important revisionist of Freud's views. Erikson believes we progress through a series of personality stages over the human life cycle, unlike Freud, who thought personality virtually was etched in stone by five years of age. Erikson believes Freud shortchanged the role of culture in personality. Consider, for example, the adolescent years. In Erikson's approach, the key developmental task to be achieved is identity, a search for who one is, what one is all about, and where one is going in life. For Freud, adolescents were primarily sexual beings, not wrapped, as Erikson believes, in an exploration of many different roles, some sexual, but also some vocational, ideological, religious, life style, and gender. Erikson believes that by exploring alternatives in many different roles the adolescent moves toward an identity. Erikson's view fits with our achievement-oriented culture, where exploration of alternative career options is a salient part of finding out who one is and where one is headed in life. More about Erikson's theory is presented in chapters 9 and 10, where we describe development through the life cycle.

What can psychoanalytic theory tell us about dating? Above all, psychoanalytic theory tells us we will have a difficult time understanding our own dating behavior. The reasons for our dating behavior are pushed deep within our unconscious mind and are primarily sexual in nature. Sex is viewed as an unlearned human instinct that dominates our dating behavior. Society's job is to keep this instinct in check, which conflicts with our inner sexual motivation. Our dating behavior can be traced to experiences with our parents during our childhood years as well. Possibly we are dating someone whose appearance and behavior unconsciously remind us of our early relationship with our mother or father. Erikson would instruct us to give more attention to the cultural standards involved in dating and how dating fits into our identity as a person.

Humanistic and Phenomenological Approaches

Some psychologists are not satisfied with either the behavioral approach, with its emphasis on environmental determinants of behavior, or the psychoanalytic approach, with its focus on instincts, abnormality, and unconscious thoughts. Humanistic psychologists hold another view. The **humanistic approach** focuses on expanding consciousness, subjective experiences, and positive feelings. Humanistic psychologists emphasize our positive qualities and our ability to remove fears and constraints from our lives. The humanistic psychologists take particular opposition to the behaviorists, saying that we *choose* what we want to do in life rather than being controlled by our environment.

Humanistic psychology is a **phenomenological approach** to understanding the individual. By this we mean that our subjective, personal perception of the world is more important to an understanding of mind and behavior than is behavior alone. Humanists believe we possess a tremendous potential for self-understanding. They also think we can help others achieve this self-understanding by providing a warm, comfortable social climate—in other words, by being supportive.

Carl Rogers (1961) and Abraham Maslow (1971) were the main architects of the humanistic approach. Rogers placed special emphasis on improving an individual's self-conception by providng a warm and supportive therapeutic environment. Maslow stressed the importance of achieving our potential, which he thinks is virtually limitless. Maslow called humanistic psychology the "third force" in psychology, believing it deserved the attention accorded the first two forces, behaviorism and psychoanalytic theory. The humanistic approach is a more recent view than behaviorism and psychoanalytic theory, so its staying power in psychology is yet to be determined. Critics call humanistic psychology vague and unscientific, but the approach has been applauded for helping us reach our human potential and cope more effectively with our problems. More about Rogers's and Maslow's approaches appears in chapter 13.

What can the humanistic and phenomenological approaches tell us about dating? Humanistic psychologists do not believe dating is based on sexual instinct, but rather it is a natural tendency of human beings to be loving toward each other. They believe each of us has the potential to be a loving person if only we would recognize it. This approach emphasizes that dating can be better understood if we focus on subjective perceptions of each other instead of actual dating behaviors. For example, your perception that you are in love with someone you are dating is more important than the number of kisses exchanged on a date. Your perception that you are in love gives meaning to your kisses; without knowing your perception of what the kisses mean, the kisses cannot be understood adequately.

Cognitive Approach

According to many contemporary psychologists, the **cognitive approach** is an extremely important force in psychology. Maslow's third force places a premium on feelings. The cognitive approach places a premium on thoughts. *Cognition* comes from the Latin word meaning *to know;* cognitive psychologists want to know how our thoughts work. How do we solve algebraic equations?

Why do we remember some things for a short while yet others for a lifetime? How can we use imagery to plan for the future? Cognitive psychology involves the study of attention, perception, memory, thinking, and problem solving.

The cognitive psychologist views the mind as an active and aware problem-solving system. This positive view of an organism contrasts with the pessimism of the psychoanalytic approach, which sees the individual as controlled by instincts, and the behavioral view, which portrays behavior as controlled by external environmental forces. In the cognitive view, the individual's mental processes are in control of behavior. By using memories, perceptions, images, and thinking, greater cognitive control over behavior is possible than in either the psychoanalytic or behavioral approaches.

One popular version of cognitive psychology is the **information processing perspective.** Psychologists using this approach study how we process information in the world around us—how we attend to the information, how we perceive it, how we store it, how we think about it, and how we retrieve it for further use.

Computers were a prominent influence in the development of the information processing perspective (Siegler, 1983). Essentially, computers are high-speed information processing systems. In the 1950s it was discovered that if computers were programmed appropriately, they could perform tasks that previously only humans could perform, such as playing chess or computing the answers to complex math problems. Computers may provide a logical and concrete, though perhaps oversimplified, version of how information is processed in the mind.

Herbert Simon was among the pioneers of the information processing approach. He reasoned that the human mind could be understood by comparing it to a computer processing information. In this model, the sensory and perceptual systems provide an "input channel," similar to data being entered into a computer. As information (input) comes into the mind, mental processes or operations act on it, just as the computer's software program acts on data. The transformed input generates information that remains in memory much in the way a computer stores what it has worked on. Finally, the information is retrieved from memory and put to use in the form of an overt response that can be observed, not unlike a computer searching for, finding, and printing out information. The mind-computer link is discussed in chapter 7. In that chapter, we will look at what a computer can do that the human mind cannot, and what the human mind can do that the computer cannot.

What can the cognitive approach tell us about dating? According to the cognitive approach, our conscious thoughts are the key to understanding dating. Memories and images of people we want to date, or have dated, influence our behavior. As you are reading these words, you can stop and think about your most memorable dates, including some you probably want to forget! You can think about your current dating or marital situation or project what it will be like in the future: Is she loyal to me? What will the future of our relationship be like? Is he getting tired of me? You can imagine what it would be like to go out with someone for the first time, or a second time.

The cognitive approach says that beliefs and values are important in understanding dating. What are your thoughts about the most important qualities of a date—is personality more important than looks? Should sex be postponed, or should you engage in premarital sex? According to the cognitive approach, these kinds of conscious thoughts and many more aspects of our rich mental life help us to understand dating.

The inelegant sea slug with its elegant memory. How do neurobiologists study the sea slug to learn about memory?

Neurobiological Approach

Our remarkable capabilities as human beings would not be possible without our brains. The human brain and nervous system is truly the most complex, intricate, and elegant system imaginable. The **neurobiological approach** looks to the brain to understand emotions, thoughts, and behaviors. Rather than study only thoughts as cognitive psychologists do, neurobiologists believe that thoughts have a physical basis in the brain. The human brain is only a three-pound glob of matter, but in this glob are more than 10 billion interconnected nerve cells. Electrical impulses zoom throughout our cells and chemical substances are released as we feel, think, and act.

Neurobiologists do study human brains, but much of their work is with brains having far fewer nerve cells. Consider the elegant memory of the inelegant sea slug, a tiny snail with only about 10,000 nerve cells. The sea slug is a slow creature, but if given an electric shock to its tail, the tail withdraws quickly. The tail withdraws even faster if the sea slug's tail has been shocked previously. In a primitive way, the sea slug remembers! This memory seems to be written in chemicals. Shocking the sea slug's tail releases a chemical that basically provides a reminder that the tail was shocked. This "memory" informs the nerve cell to send out chemical commands to retract the tail the next time it is touched (Kandel & Schwartz, 1982). If nature builds complexity out of simplicity, then the mechanism used by the sea slug may work in the human brain as well. In humans, the memory may come from the sight of a close friend, a dog's bark, or the sound of a car horn. Chemicals, then, may be the ink with which memories are written.

The human brain is divided into left and right sides. Roger Sperry (1964) made one of the most exciting discoveries in neuroscience when he revealed that some aspects of our behavior are controlled more by one side of the brain than the other. In a sense, our brain is split, with one side not always knowing what the other side is doing. Our own human gift of speech, for example, involves primarily the left side of our brain. More about Sperry's discovery and the electrochemical changes in the brain's cells awaits you in chapter 2.

What can the neurobiological approach tell us about dating? The neurobiological approach reminds us that underlying our thoughts, emotions, and behaviors in a dating situation is a physical brain and nervous system. Have you ever thought about how your brain changes when you are attracted to someone? When your heart pitter-patters, we sometimes say "the chemistry is right." An attraction may literally involve the chemistry of the brain. When your feelings for someone increase, the chemistry of the brain changes. Your feelings for someone may be occurring more in the right side of your brain than the left side. In these ways dating behavior is wired into the circuitry of the brain.

An Eclectic Approach to Psychology

Which of these approaches—behavioral, psychoanalytic, humanistic, cognitive, or neurobiological—is the best way to view the nature of mind and behavior? There is no single indomitable theory that offers all the answers. Each theory contributes to the science of psychology, but no single theory provides a complete description and explanation of human behavior and mental processes. For these reasons, all five major approaches to psychology are presented in this text in an unbiased fashion. As a result, you can view the field of psychology as it actually exists—with different theorists drawing different conclusions about the nature of mind and behavior. Figure 1.1 provides an overview of some of the major contributors to these theories and the approximate time period their contributions were made.

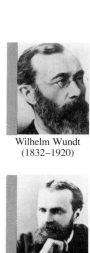

Wilhelm Wundt
(1832–1920)

William James
(1842–1910)

E. B. Titchener
(1867–1927)

John B. Watson
(1878–1958)

Abraham Maslow
(1908–1970)

1880 —

1890 —

1900 —

1910 —

1920 —

1930 —

1940 —

1950 —

1960 —

1970 —

1879: Wilhelm Wundt develops the first psychology laboratory at the University of Leipzig.

1890: William James publishes *Principles of Psychology*, which promotes functionalism.

1892: E. B. Titchener popularizes structuralism in the United States.

1900: Sigmund Freud publishes *Interpretation of Dreams*, reflecting his psychoanalytic view.

1906: The Russian Ivan Pavlov publishes the results of his learning experiments with dogs.

1913: John Watson publishes his volume on behaviorism, promoting the importance of environmental influences.

1938: B. F. Skinner publishes *The Behavior of Organisms*, expanding the view of behaviorism.

1950: Erik Erikson publishes *Childhood and Society*, a psychoanalytic revision of Freud's views.

1954: Maslow presents the humanistic view, emphasizing the positive potential of the individual.

1958: Herbert Simon presents his information-processing view.

1961: Carl Rogers publishes *On Becoming a Person*, highlighting the humanistic approach.

1961: Albert Bandura presents ideas about social-learning theory, emphasizing the importance of imitation.

1964: Roger Sperry publishes his split-brain research, showing the importance of the brain in behavior.

No entries are made for recent decades because theory and research must be supported over time to have a lasting impact in the field of psychology.

Ivan Pavlov
(1849–1936)

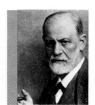

Sigmund Freud
(1856–1939)

B. F. Skinner
(1904–   )

Erik Erikson
(1902–   )

Carl Rogers
(1902–1987)

Figure 1.1
Major contributors to the early and contemporary approaches to psychology.

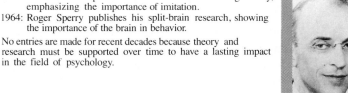

Herbert Simon
(1916–   )

Albert Bandura
(1925–   )

Roger Sperry
(1913–   )

■ ■ ■ ■ ■ ■ ■ ■ ■ ■ ■ ■ ■ ■ ■ ■ ■ ■ ■ ■

Concept Table 1.1

Psychology: Its Nature and Approaches		
Concept	**Processes/related ideas**	**Characteristics/description**
What is psychology?	Its nature	Psychology is the scientific study of mind and behavior: mind refers to our thoughts and feelings; behavior is what can be observed.
Early and contemporary approaches	Early approaches	Wilhelm Wundt developed the first scientific psychology laboratory in 1879. Titchener popularized Wundt's ideas in the United States; his psychology was known as structuralism. William James emphasized the functions of the mind in adapting to the environment; his view was called functionalism. Many early approaches used introspection, which later came under fire.
	Contemporary approaches	The behavioral approach focuses on behavior and its environmental determinants. The psychoanalytic approach focuses on the unconscious, conflict, and early experiences. The humanistic and phenomenological approaches focus on expanding consciousness, subjective experiences, and positive feelings. The cognitive approach focuses on mental processes. The neurobiological approach focuses on the brain and nervous system.
	An eclectic approach	No single theory offers all the answers; each contributes to the science of psychology.

We have discussed the definition of psychology, its scientific beginnings, and a number of different psychological perspectives. A summary of these topics is presented in concept table 1.1. The approaches described so far are very much a part of the scientific nature of psychology—theories that explain the nature of mind and behavior. But psychology is also a science because of the methods it uses to collect information about mind and behavior. Without these theories and methods, psychology might well be classified as art or religion rather than science.

The Science Base of Psychology

Some people have difficulty thinking of psychology as a science in the same way physics, chemistry, and biology are sciences. Can a discipline that studies why people are attracted to each other, how they reason about moral values, and the way imagery affects memory be equated with disciplines that investigate how gravity works and the molecular structure of a compound? Science is not defined by *what* it investigates but by *how* it investigates. Whether you are studying photosynthesis, butterflies, Saturn's moons, or people, it is the way you study that makes the approach scientific or not.

To be a scientist is to be skeptical. As we think about ourselves and the world we can make many observations about mind and behavior: people don't change; love is blind; happiness is the key to success; people are crazy because society makes them that way; communication with spirits is possible. Such statements provoke a psychologist's curiosity *and* skepticism. Psychology seeks to sort fact from fancy by critically questioning the nature of mind and behavior. Hearing the claim that someone communicated with spirits or that a horse can count to ten spurs the scientist to question how these observations were made and under what conditions.

To learn more about a famous horse and how its mathematical genius was widely accepted initially, then rebuked by a sharp observer's curiosity and skepticism, see Psychology 1.1, "Hans, the Clever Horse."

Science is not defined by what it studies but by how it investigates it. Photosynthesis, butterflies, Saturn's moons, or relationships among people all can be studied in a scientific manner.

Theory and the Scientific Method

According to Henri Poincaré, "Science is built of facts the way a house is built of bricks, but an accumulation of facts is no more science than a pile of bricks a house." Science *does* depend upon the raw material of facts or data, but as Poincaré indicated, science is more than just facts. The nature of theory and the scientific method illustrate Poincaré's point.

Theories are general beliefs that help us to explain the data or facts we have observed and make predictions. A good theory has **hypotheses.** Hypotheses are assumptions that can be tested to determine their accuracy. For example, a theory about depression would explain our observations of depressed individuals and predict why people get depressed. We might predict that people are depressed because they fail to focus on their strengths and dwell extensively on their shortcomings. This prediction would help to direct our observations by telling us to look for overexaggerations of weaknesses and underestimations of strengths and skills.

To obtain accurate information about mind and behavior it is important to follow the **scientific method.** To do this, we must follow a number of steps: identify and analyze the problem, collect data, draw conclusions, and revise theories. For example, you decide that you want to help people overcome depression. You have identified a problem, which does not seem to be a very difficult task. But as part of this first step, you need to go beyond a general description of the problem by isolating, analyzing, narrowing, and focusing on what you hope to investigate. What specific strategies do you want to use to decrease depression? Do you want to look at only one strategy, or several strategies? What aspect of depression do you want to study—its biological characteristics, cognitive characteristics, or behavioral characteristics?

One group of psychologists chose to study the behavioral and cognitive aspects of depression (Lewinsohn & others, 1984). They analyzed depression and wondered if individuals could be helped by taking a course on coping with depression. One of the many components in the course involved teaching depressed individuals to control their negative thoughts. In this first step of the scientific method, the researchers identified and analyzed a problem.

■ ■

Psychology 1.1

Hans, the Clever Horse

The year is 1911. According to experts, Hans, a horse, could reason and "talk." Hans had been trained by a retired math teacher, Mr. von Osten, to communicate by tapping his forefoot and moving his head. A head nod meant yes, while a head shake suggested no. Mr. von Osten developed a code for verbal information in which each letter was represented by a pair of numbers. The letter *A* was coded as one tap, pause, one tap, and the letter *I* was three taps, pause, two taps.

Once Hans learned to tap his foot or move his head when questioned, he was given simple problems and then fed a piece of bread or carrot for correct responses. By the end of his training, Hans could spell words spoken to him, and he excelled in math. He became a hero in Germany—his picture was on liquor bottles and toys. Experts were so impressed that an official commission of thirteen scientists,

educators, and public officials examined the horse, testing him to see if he really could do all of the things claimed. They came away even more impressed and issued a statement saying that there was no evidence of any intentional influence or aid on the part of Hans's questioners.

But there was one scientist who was not so sure that Hans was as intelligent as he had been portrayed. Oskar von Pfungst, a sharp observer, had detected that Hans always faced his questioner. Von Pfungst hypothesized (developed the hunch or belief) that this might have something to do with his math ability.

The scientist set up a simple experiment. He wrote numbers on a card and held them up one at a time, asking Hans to tap out the numbers written on each card. Half of the cards were held so that only Hans could see them. With the cards von Pfungst could see, Hans was his usual brilliant self, getting 92 percent of them

correct. But for the numbers von Pfungst could not see, Hans got only 8 percent correct.

Von Pfungst repeated the experiment over and over again with nearly the same results. He then carefully observed Hans with his other questioners, including von Osten. As soon as they stated the problem to Hans, most questioners would turn their head and upper body slightly. When the correct number of foot taps had been made by Hans, the questioner would move his head upward. Despite his years of work with the horse, Mr. Von Osten had never dreamed that Hans had learned to "read" him. Von Osten commented that he actually was angry at the horse and felt betrayed by him!

We can see that experts can be wrong and that what seems to be the truth may be a false impression. Even experts can be fooled if they do not use appropriate research procedures to check their observations.

After we identify and analyze the problem, the next step in the scientific method involves collecting information (data). Psychologists observe behavior and draw inferences about thoughts and emotions. For example, in their investigation of depression, Lewinsohn and his colleagues observed how effectively individuals who completed the course on coping with depression monitored their moods and engaged in productive work.

Once data have been collected, psychologists use statistical procedures to understand the meaning of the quantitative data. They then attempt to draw conclusions (information about statistical procedures is provided in the appendix). In the investigation of depression, statistics helped the researchers determine whether or not their observations were due to chance. After data have been analyzed, psychologists compare their findings with what others have discovered about the same issue or problem.

The final step in the scientific method is revising theory. Psychologists have developed a number of theories about why we become depressed and how we can cope with depression. Data such as that collected by Lewinsohn and his associates force us to study existing theories of depression to see if they are accurate. (Theories of depression are discussed in chapter 14.) Over the years some psychological theories have been discarded and others have been revised. Wundt's theory of structuralism has been discarded, while behaviorism and psychoanalytic theory have been substantially revised. Cognitive psychology and the neuroscience approach, which are recent theoretical approaches, are undergoing revision as the scientific method is applied to the questions they raise.

Collecting Information about Mind and Behavior

Systematic observations can be conducted in a variety of ways. For example, we can watch behavior in the laboratory or in a more natural setting such as on a street corner. We can question people using interviews and surveys, develop and administer standardized tests, conduct case studies, or carry out physiological research or research with animals. To help you understand how psychologists use these methods, we will apply each method to the study of aggression.

Observation

Sherlock Holmes chided Watson, "You see but you do not observe." We look at things all the time, but casually watching a friend cross the campus is not scientific observation. Unless you are a trained observer and practice your skills regularly, you may not know what to look for, you may not remember what you saw, what you are looking for may change from one moment to the next, and you may not communicate your observations effectively. Oskar von Pfungst's observations of Hans, the clever horse (Psychology 1.1), revealed clearly that it is important to be a keen, skilled, and trained observer.

For observations to be effective, we have to know what we are looking for, who we are observing, when and where we will observe, how the observations will be made, and in what form they will be recorded. That is, our observations have to be made in some *systematic* way. Consider aggression. Do we want to study verbal or physical aggression, or both? Do we want to study children or adults, or both? Do we want to evaluate them in a university laboratory, at work, at play, or at all of these locations? Do we want to audiotape or videotape their behavior, or both? A common way to record our observations is to write them down, using shorthand or symbols; however, tape recorders, video cameras, special coding sheets, and one-way mirrors are used increasingly to make observations more efficient.

When we observe, frequently it is necessary to *control* certain factors that determine behavior but are not the focus of our inquiry. For this reason much psychological research is conducted in a **laboratory,** that is, a controlled setting in which many of the complex factors of the "real world" are removed. For example, Albert Bandura (1965) brought children into a laboratory and had them observe an adult repeatedly hit a plastic, inflated Bobo doll about three feet tall. Bandura wondered to what extent the children would copy the adult's behavior. (The children copied the adult's behavior extensively. More on this classic study in aggression appears in chapter 5.) By conducting his experiment in a laboratory with adults the children did not know as models, Bandura removed intrusions such as television, stereos, parents, siblings, friends, and a familiar room. He had complete control over when the child would witness aggression, how much would be seen, and what its form would be. Bandura could not have accomplished his experiment as effectively if the other factors had been present.

Conducting laboratory research, however, can be costly. First, it is almost impossible to conduct without the participants knowing that they are being studied. Second, the laboratory setting may be *unnatural* and therefore cause *unnatural* behavior from the participants. Frequently, subjects show less aggressive behavior in a laboratory than in a more familiar natural setting, such as in a park or at home. Also, they show less aggression when they are unaware of being observed. Third, some aspects of mind and behavior are difficult if not impossible to produce in the laboratory. Certain types of stress are difficult (and unethical) to investigate in the laboratory, for example, re-creating the circumstances that stimulate violence in fans at sporting events. Alcohol, for instance, consistently has been found to increase aggression in an individual when provoked (Jeavons & Taylor, 1985). In 1985 at a soccer game in Brussels, Belgium, a riot broke out. The English fans, filled with alcohol, aroused by the competition, and taunted by the Italian fans, attacked the Italians. As the Italians retreated, they were crushed against a wall—the death toll was thirty-eight. It would be impossible and unethical to recreate in a laboratory circumstances that would even remotely resemble the Brussels soccer game.

Although laboratory research is a valuable tool for psychologists, **naturalistic observation** provides insight that sometimes cannot be achieved in the laboratory. In naturalistic observation, psychologists observe behavior in real-world settings and make no effort to manipulate or control the situation. Naturalistic observations have been conducted at soccer games, day-care centers, college dormitories, rest rooms, corporations, malls, restaurants, dances, and other places where people live and frequent. In contrast to Bandura's observations of aggression in a laboratory, psychologists have observed the aggression of children in nursery schools, of marital partners at home, and the arguments and violence at sporting events and political protests (Friedrich & Stein, 1973; O'Leary, in press; Patterson, 1982; Worschel & Austin, 1986).

Observations can be conducted in laboratories or in naturalistic settings. For example, a psychologist might observe the nature of social interaction during political protest, as in the naturalistic setting shown here.

Interviews and Questionnaires

Sometimes the best and quickest way to get information from people is to ask them for it. Psychologists use interviews and questionnaires to find out about the experiences and attitudes of people. Most **interviews** are conducted face to face, although they can take place over the telephone.

Interviews range from highly unstructured to highly structured. Examples of unstructured interview questions are: How aggressive do you see yourself? and How aggressive is your child? Examples of structured interview questions are: In the last week how often have you yelled at your spouse? and How often in the last year has your child been involved in fights at school? Structure can be imposed by the questions themselves, or the interviewer can categorize answers by asking the respondent to choose from several options. For example, in the question about how aggressive you are, you might be asked to choose from "highly aggressive," "moderately aggressive," "moderately unaggressive," and "highly unaggressive." In the question about how often you yelled at your spouse in the last week, you might be requested to choose "0," "1–2," "3–5," "6–10," or "more than 10 times."

An experienced interviewer knows how to put the respondent at ease and encourage her to open up. A competent interviewer is sensitive to the way the person responds to questions and often probes for more information. A person may respond with fuzzy statements to questions about the nature of marital conflict, for example, "Well, I don't know whether we have a lot of conflict or not." The skilled interviewer would push for more specific, concrete answers, possibly asking, "If you had it to do over, would you get married?" or "Tell me the worst things you and your husband have said to each other in the last week?" Using these interviewing strategies forces researchers to be involved with, rather than detached from, their subjects, which can lead to a better understanding of mind and behavior (Brenner, Brown, & Canter, 1985; Cozby, 1986).

Just as observations can take place in different settings, so can interviews. An interview might occur at a university, in a person's home, or at a person's place of work. While too little attention has been given to how such settings influence the kind of information obtained, one recent strategy attempted to make the interview more naturalistic. Brenda Bryant (1985) developed "The Neighborhood Walk," an interview conducted with a child while walking through the child's neighborhood. Bryant believes "The Neighborhood Walk" provides concrete cues that can elicit information not otherwise obtained. As you walk with seven-year-old Joshua through his neighborhood, he might tell you, "The old man in that house is scary—we never go near there," or, pointing to a field, he might say, "What a fun place—Mr. Pierce comes out and plays football with us there. He helps me out at the YMCA too." Bryant has found the interview especially helpful in generating information about the support systems available to children.

Interviews are not without problems. Perhaps the most critical of these problems involves the response set of "social desirability," in which a person tells the interviewer what he thinks is most socially acceptable or desirable rather than what he truly feels or thinks. When asked about her marital conflict, Jane may not want to disclose that arguments have been painfully tense in the last month. Sam, her husband, may not want to divulge that he has been having an extramarital affair for more than a year when asked about his sexual relationships. Skilled interviewing techniques and questions to help eliminate such defenses are critical in obtaining accurate information.

Psychologists also question people using questionnaires or surveys. A **questionnaire** is similar to a highly structured interview except that the respondent reads the question and marks her answer on paper rather than responding verbally to the interviewer. One major advantage of surveys and questionnaires is that they can be given to a large number of people easily. Questions on surveys should be concrete, specific, and unambiguous, and an assessment of the authenticity of the replies should be made (Agnew & Pyke, 1987).

Sometimes we want information about a small set of people, such as all black graduates of a particular high school in the last five years or all college students from your campus who have participated in a nuclear arms protest. At other times, we want to know something about a large population of people, such as all people in the United States. In each instance, it is important that the people surveyed are representative of the group we wish to describe. We accomplish this important task by surveying a random sample of subjects. In a **random sample** every member of a population or group has an equal chance of being selected.

Random samples are important because, in most instances, we cannot survey everyone we are trying to describe, for example, all people in the United States. The National Crime Survey is an example of a random sample survey (U.S. Department of Justice, 1983). If we asked people from a high-crime area of Miami, Florida, about their victimization and used this information to project the frequency of crime in the United States, projections would be inflated. While certain pockets of Miami do have extremely high crime rates, the recent National Crime Survey, giving each household in the United States an equal chance of being surveyed, indicated that victimization of households throughout the country is high—close to one-third of the households surveyed had been victimized by violence or theft.

How do researchers obtain a random sample of subjects? In cases like the National Crime Survey, methods ensure that those sampled are representative of the proportion of black, white, low-income, middle-income, high-income, rural, and urban individuals in the United States. A national random sample of 5,000 subjects, for example, would have fewer blacks than whites, fewer high-income than low-income persons, and fewer rural than urban subjects.

Appropriate sampling methods are not always followed. Newspapers and magazines often conduct surveys of their readership, and those who participate by mailing or calling in their opinions probably feel more strongly about the issue in question, than those who do not respond. Examples of this would be whether or not drunk driving laws should be tougher or whether or not premarital sex is morally wrong. Surveys encounter problems similar to interviews, for example, people not telling the truth.

Case Studies

A **case study** is an in-depth look at an individual and is used mainly by clinical psychologists. Case studies are used when the unique aspects of an individual's life cannot be duplicated, either for practical or ethical reasons, yet they have implications for understanding mind and behavior. A case study provides information about an individual's fears, hopes, fantasies, traumatic experiences, family relationships, health, or anything that will help the psychologist understand the person's mind and behavior.

Traumatic experiences have produced some truly fascinating case studies in psychology. A twenty-six-year-old teacher shot his girl friend while he was a passenger in the car she was driving. Soon after the act, he ran to a telephone booth to call his priest. He had met the woman only eight months before the shooting, yet it was an intense love affair with marriage planned. Several months after meeting the woman, the teacher became depressed, drank heavily, and talked about suicide. The suicidal ideas progressed to images of murder-suicide. His actions became bizarre. On one occasion he punctured the tires of her car. On another he stood on the side of a road where she passed frequently in her car, extending his hand in his pocket so she would think he was holding a gun. His relationship with the woman vascillated between love and hate. He described the last several months before the murder as complete chaos. He informed another couple that he was going to kill his girl friend, but they interpreted it as mere talk due to his inebriated state (Revitch & Schlesinger, 1978).

This case reveals how depressive moods, bizarre thinking, and premonitions can precede violent acts, such as murder. Other vivid case studies appear throughout this text, among them a woman with three personalities, each of which is unaware of the others, and a modern-day wild child named Genie, who lived in near isolation during her childhood.

While case histories provide dramatic, in-depth portrayals of people's lives, caution must be exercised when we try to generalize this information. The subject of a case study is unique, with a genetic makeup and experiences none of us can possess. In addition, case studies involve judgments of unknown reliability, in that no check is made to see if other psychologists agree with the observations.

Standardized Tests

Standardized tests require that people answer a series of written or oral questions. Two distinctive features of standardized tests are that the individual's answers usually are totaled to yield a single score, or a set of scores, that reflects something about the individual, and that the individual's score is compared to the scores of a large group of similar people to determine how the individual responded *relative* to others. Scores often are described in percentiles. For example, perhaps you scored in the 92nd percentile on the SAT. This

Psychologists have many tools to investigate mind and behavior. Standardized tests are among the most widely used tools. Here, the psychologist is administering a standardized intelligence test to determine the nature of the individual's intelligence.

method tells you how much higher or lower you scored than the large group of individuals who took the test previously. Among the most widely used standardized tests are the Stanford-Binet intelligence test and the Minnesota Multiphasic Personality Inventory (MMPI).

To continue our look at how different measures are used to evaluate aggression, consider the MMPI, which includes a scale to assess an individual's delinquency and antisocial tendencies. The items on this scale ask you to respond whether or not you are rebellious, impulsive, and have trouble with authority figures. The twenty-six-year-old teacher who murdered his girl friend would have scored high on a number of the MMPI scales, including one designed to measure how strange and bizarre are our thoughts and ideas.

The main advantage of standardized tests is that they provide information about individual differences among people. But information obtained from standardized tests does not always predict behavior in nontest situations. Standardized tests are based on the belief that an individual's behavior is consistent and stable. Although personality and intelligence, two of the primary targets of standardized tests, have some stability, they *can* vary, depending on the situation in which a person is evaluated. A person may perform poorly on a standardized test of intelligence but when observed in a less anxious context, such as at home, the person may reveal a much higher level of intelligence. This criticism is especially relevant for minority groups, some of whom have been inappropriately classified as mentally retarded on the basis of their scores on standardized intelligence tests. For example, several mentally retarded children did poorly on a standardized test that evaluated their planning skills, yet they were crafty enough to plan an elaborate escape from the mental retardation institution where they lived. More about personality tests appears in chapter 13.

Physiological Research and Research with Animals

Two additional methods that psychologists use to gather data are physiological research and research with animals. Increased research into the biological basis of behavior and technological advances have produced remarkable insights about mind and behavior. For example, electrical stimulation of certain areas of the brain has turned docile, mild-mannered people into hostile, vicious attackers; and higher concentrations of some hormones have been associated with delinquent behavior in male adolescents (King, 1961; Nottelmann & others, 1987).

Much physiological research cannot be carried out with humans and so psychologists use animals. With animals we can control genetic background, diet, experiences during infancy, and countless other factors. In human studies, these factors have to be treated as random variation, or "noise," and they may interfere with accurate results. With animals, we can investigate the effects of treatments (brain implants, for example) that would be unethical to attempt with humans. Moreover, it is possible to track the entire life cycle of some animals over a relatively short period of time. Laboratory mice, for example, have a life span of approximately one year.

With regard to aggression, castration has turned ferocious bulls into docile oxen by acting on the male hormone system. After a number of breedings of aggressive mice, researchers have created mice who are absolutely ferocious, attacking virtually anything in sight (James, 1951). Do these findings with animals apply to humans? When we discuss aggression in greater detail in chapter 17, you will learn how hormones and genes influence human aggression. This influence, however, is less than in animals. Because humans differ from animals in many ways, one disadvantage of research with animals is that the results may not apply to humans.

Figure 1.2
An observed correlation between two events cannot be used to conclude that one event causes a second event. Other possibilities are that the second event caused the first event, or that a third, unknown event caused the correlation between the first two events.

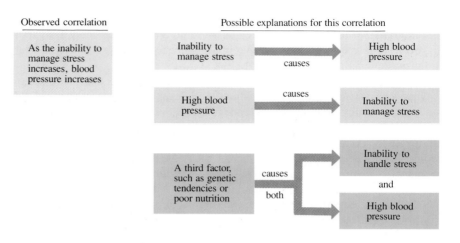

Strategies for Setting up Research Studies

How can we learn if listening to rock music deadens a person's hearing? How can we discover if overeating is due to a psychological state of mind? How can we figure out if high blood pressure is due to stress? When designing research to answer such questions a psychologist must decide whether to use a correlational strategy or an experimental strategy.

Correlational Strategy

One goal of psychological research is to describe how strongly two or more events or characteristics are related. When a psychologist has this goal, a **correlational strategy** is used. This is a useful strategy, because the more strongly events are correlated (related, or associated), the more we can predict one from the other. For example, consider one of our major national health problems, high blood pressure. If we find that high blood pressure is strongly associated with an inability to manage stress, then we can use the inability to manage stress to predict high blood pressure.

The next step, taken all too often, is to conclude from such evidence that one event *causes* the other. Following this line of reasoning, we would erroneously conclude that the inability to manage stress causes high blood pressure. Why is this reasoning *wrong?* Why doesn't a strong correlation between two events mean that one event causes the other? A strong correlation could mean that the inability to manage stress causes high blood pressure, but it *also* could mean that high blood pressure causes an inability to manage stress. And, a third possibility exists: although strongly correlated, the inability to manage stress and high blood pressure do not cause each other at all. How could this be? Possibly a third factor underlies their association, such as a genetic tendency or poor nutrition (see figure 1.2).

Throughout this text you will read about numerous studies that were based on a correlational strategy. Keep in mind that it is easy to think that because two events or characteristics are correlated, one causes the other. To ensure that your understanding of correlation is clear, let's look at another example. People who make a lot of money have higher self-esteem than those who make less money. We could mistakenly interpret this to mean that making a lot of money causes us to have high self-esteem. What are the two other interpretations we need to consider? It could be that developing high self-esteem causes us to make a lot of money, or that a third factor (such as education, social upbringing, or genetic tendencies) causes the correlation between making a lot of money and a high self-esteem.

Experimental Strategy

The **experimental strategy** allows us to determine the causes of behavior precisely. The psychologist accomplishes this task by performing an **experiment,** which is a carefully regulated setting in which one or more of the factors believed to influence the behavior being studied is manipulated and all others are held constant. If the behavior under study changes when a factor is manipulated, we say that the manipulated factor causes the behavior to change. Experiments are used to establish cause and effect between events, something correlational studies cannot do. *Cause* is the event being manipulated and *effect* is the behavior that changes because of the manipulation. Remember that in testing correlation, nothing is manipulated; in an experiment, the researcher actively changes an event to see the effect on behavior.

You won't be needing those, sir; you're in the control group.
Courtesy of T. Haggerty.

The following example illustrates the nature of an experiment. The problem to be studied is whether marijuana impairs alertness and increases confidence (Saslow, 1982). Since marijuana is not legally available, we obtain permission from the appropriate authorities to use the drug in an experiment. We decide that to conduct our experiment we need one group of subjects who will smoke marijuana and one group who will not. We randomly assign our subjects to these two groups. **Random assignment** reduces the likelihood that the results of the experiment will be due to some preexisting differences in the two groups. For example, random assignment greatly reduces the probability that the two groups will differ on such factors as prior use of marijuana, health problems, intelligence, alertness, social class, age, and so forth.

The subjects who smoke the marijuana are called the **experimental group,** that is, the group whose experience is manipulated. The subjects who do not smoke marijuana are the **control group,** that is, a comparison group treated in every way like the experimental group except for the manipulated factor. The control group serves as a baseline against which the effects found in the manipulated condition can be compared.

After the subjects in the experimental group have smoked the marijuana, the behaviors of the two groups are compared. We choose to study how fast the subjects will react when asked to make a simple hand movement in response to a flash of light. We also decide to ask them how well they thought they performed this task. When we analyze the results, we find that the subjects who smoked the marijuana were slower in reacting to the flash of light but actually thought they did better than the subjects who did not smoke marijuana. We conclude that smoking marijuana decreases alertness but increases confidence.

In an experiment, the manipulated, or influential, factor is called the **independent variable.** The label *independent* is used because this variable can be changed independently of other factors. In the marijuana experiment, the amount of marijuana smoked was the independent variable. The experimenter manipulated how much marijuana the subjects experienced independently of all other factors. In an experiment, the researcher determines what effect the independent variable has on the **dependent variable.** The label *dependent* is used because this variable depends on what happens to the subjects in the experiment. In the marijuana experiment, the dependent variable was represented by two measures: a reaction time task to measure alertness and a question to evaluate confidence. The subjects' responses on these measures depended on the influence of the independent variable (whether or not marijuana was smoked). An illustration of the nature of the experimental strategy, applied to the marijuana study, is shown in figure 1.3.

Figure 1.3
The nature of the experimental strategy is applied here to a study of the effects of marijuana on alertness and confidence.

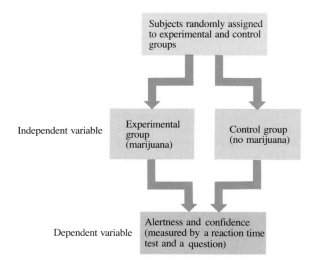

As an example of the experimental strategy, a psychologist might randomly assign subjects to either a relaxation or a stress management condition (experimental group) or a condition in which these factors are not present (control group). For instance, in the experimental group the subjects might participate in some form of martial arts, such as slow motion Kada (shown here) during lunch hour each work day for a month while the control group would not.

Remember that the correlational study of the relation between stress and blood pressure gave us little indication of whether stress influences blood pressure, or vice versa. A third factor may have caused the correlation. A research study that determined if stress management reduces high blood pressure will help you to understand further the experimental strategy (Irvine & others, 1986). Thirty-two males and females from thirty-four to sixty-five years of age with high blood pressure were randomly assigned to either a group who were trained in relaxation and stress management (experimental group) or a group who received no training (control group). The independent variable consisted of ten weekly one-hour sessions that included educational information about the nature of stress and how to manage it, as well as extensive training in learning to relax and control stress in everyday life. The blood pressure of both groups was assessed before the training program and three months after it was completed. Nurses who were unaware of which group the subjects had been in measured blood pressure at the three-month follow-up. The results indicated that the relaxation and stress management program (the independent variable) was effective in reducing high blood pressure.

It might seem as if we should always choose an experimental strategy over a correlational strategy, since the experimental strategy gives us a better sense of the influence of one variable on another. Are there instances when a correlational strategy might be preferred? Three such instances are 1) when the focus of the investigation is so new that we have little knowledge of which variables to manipulate (for example, factors associated with AIDS); 2) when it is physically impossible to manipulate the variables (for example, suicide); and 3) when it is unethical to manipulate the variables (for example, determining the link between illness and exposure to dangerous chemicals). The issue of ethics in research is prominent.

Ethics in Psychological Research

When Anne and Pete, two nineteen-year-old college students, agreed to participate in an investigation of dating couples, they did not consider that the questionnaire they filled out would get them to think about issues that might lead to conflict in their relationship and possibly end it. One year after this investigation (Rubin & Mitchell, 1976), nine of the ten participants said that they had discussed their answers with their dating partner. In most instances the discussions helped to strengthen the relationships. But in some cases, the participants used the questionnaire as a springboard to discuss problems or concerns previously hidden. One participant said, "The study definitely played a role in ending my relationship with Larry." In this circumstance, the couple had different views about how long they expected to be together. She anticipated that the relationship would end much sooner than Larry thought. Discussion of their answers to the questions brought the long-term prospects of the relationship out in the open, and eventually Larry found someone who was more interested in marrying him.

At first glance, you would not think that a questionnaire on dating relationships would have any substantial impact on the participants' behavior. But psychologists have recognized increasingly that considerable caution must be taken to ensure the well-being of the participants in a psychological study. Today colleges and universities have review boards that evaluate the ethical nature of research conducted at their institutions. Proposed research plans must pass the scrutiny of an ethics research committee before the research can be initiated. In addition, the American Psychological Association (APA) has developed guidelines for ethics in its members.

The code of ethics adopted by the APA instructs psychologists to protect their subjects from mental and physical harm. The best interest of the subjects needs to be kept foremost in the researcher's mind. All subjects must give their informed consent to participate in the research study, which requires that subjects know what their participation will involve and any risks that might develop. For example, dating research subjects should be told beforehand that a questionnaire may stimulate thought about issues they might not anticipate. The subjects also should be informed that in some instances a discussion of the issues raised can improve their dating relationship, while in other cases, it can worsen the relationship and even terminate it. After informed consent is given, the subject must reserve the right to withdraw from the study at any time while it is being conducted.

Deception is an ethical issue that has been debated extensively by psychologists. In some circumstances, telling the subject beforehand what the research study is about substantially alters the subject's behavior and destroys the investigator's data. For example, a psychologist wants to know whether a bystander will report a theft. A mock theft is staged and the psychologist observes which bystanders report it. Had the psychologist informed the bystanders beforehand that the study intended to discover the percentage of bystanders who will report a theft, the whole intent of the study would have been lost.

In one investigation (Latané & Elman, 1970), researchers staged the theft of a case of liquor while the store's cashier was out of the view of the thief and the bystanders. Researchers discovered that bystanders were more likely to report the crime to the cashier when they were alone than when two or more bystanders were present. We will discuss the reasons for this behavior in chapter 17. In the case of research on bystander intervention, the researcher had to weigh deceiving the subjects against the value of the research. Most psychologists agree that conditions that lead people to report crimes can be beneficial to society, so deception is warranted. In all cases of deception, the psychologist must ensure that the deception will not harm the subject and that the subject will be debriefed (told the complete nature of the study) as soon as possible after the study is completed.

The use of animals in psychological research also has generated a great deal of controversy. Animal welfare and animal rights activists criticize all animal research, and scientists respond that animals are very important in research. In some cases, scientists have explored alternatives to the use of animals in psychological studies. To read more about this prominent issue see Psychology 1.2.

■ ■ ■ ■ ■ ■ ■ ■ ■ ■ ■ ■ ■ ■ ■ ■ ■

Psychology 1.2

How Ethical Is Research with Animals?

*Science without conscience is
but the death of the soul.*

—Montaigne

■ At the 1985 meeting of the American Psychological Association (APA) in Los Angeles, California, hundreds of animal welfare and animal rights activists circled in front of the convention entrance waving signs and yelling slogans such as PSYCHOLOGISTS ARE KILLING OUR ANIMALS and STOP THE PAIN AND ABUSE.

For generations, some psychologists have used animals in their research. Such research has produced findings that have provided a better understanding and treatment of emotional and behavioral problems in human beings. Neal Miller (1985), a leading figure in contemporary psychology who has made important discoveries about the effects of biofeedback on health, listed the following areas where animal research has benefitted humans: psychotherapy and behavioral medicine; rehabilitation of neuromuscular disorders; understanding and alleviating effects of stress and pain; discovery and testing of drugs to treat anxiety and severe mental illness, such as schizophrenia; knowledge about drug addiction and relapse; treatments to help premature infants gain weight so they can leave the hospital sooner; and knowledge about the nature of memory so that some deficits of memory in old age can be alleviated.

How widespread is research with animals in psychology? Only about 5 percent of APA members use animals in their research.

Table 1.A Animals in Graduate Departments of Psychology in the U.S.		
Animals	**Number**	**%**
Rats and mice	226,762	89.75
Birds	14,415	5.70
Cats	1,502	.59
Primates	1,340	.53
Rabbits	967	.38
Amphibians	841	.33
Dogs	51	.02
Others (hamsters, moles, gerbils, fish)	6,809	2.70
Total	**252,687**	**100.00**

Source: Adapted from Report on Animal Research Survey by K. H. Mesirow, 1984, paper presented at the American Psychological Association, Toronto. In Gallup, G. G., Jr., and Suarez, S. D., "Alternatives to the use of animals in psychological research," *American Psychologist,* 1985, 40, 1104–1111. Table on page 1106.

Table 1.A reveals the type of animals used in psychological research (Gallup & Suarez, 1985). Note that rats and mice are the most widely used by far.

How widespread is abuse to animals in psychological research? According to animal welfare and rights activists, it is extensive. Although at times researchers use procedures that would be unethical with humans, they are guided by a stringent set of standards that address such matters as the housing, feeding, and psychological consideration of animals. Unnecessary pain is to be avoided and the researcher is required to weigh the potential benefit of the research against the possible harm to the animal.

In one case a researcher experimenting with monkeys to find ways of helping stroke victims was found guilty of not providing adequate medical care for six monkeys and was fined $3,015

(Holden, 1981). When the case came to court it was revealed that he had been on vacation when the condition of the animals deteriorated, so he was not convicted of inflicting unnecessary pain on the animals. But he still had to pay the fine and was blamed for the inadequate medical care the monkeys received.

One animal rights group has circulated a leaflet describing six types of extreme abuse to research animals in psychology; however, a recent study surveyed the 608 articles published in the previous five years by the APA and could not find a single example of the abuse described. Although animal abuse does not seem to be as common as animal activist groups charge, stringent ethical guidelines must be followed when animals, as well as humans, are the subjects of psychological research.

Psychologists show concern about the ethical standards for conducting research with animals. Psychologists must carefully evaluate the benefits of their animal research for humankind.

Animal welfare and rights activists believe psychologists have been too abusive to animals in their research. Psychologists believe that while there have been isolated examples of abuse, the abuse has been exaggerated by the activists.

■ ■
Concept Table 1.2

The Science Base of Psychology		
Concept	**Processes/related ideas**	**Characteristics/description**
Theory and the scientific method	Theory	General beliefs that help us to explain what we observe and make predictions. A good theory has hypotheses, which are assumptions that can be tested.
	The scientific method	A series of procedures (identifying and analyzing a problem, collecting data, drawing conclusions, and revising theory) to obtain accurate information.
Ways of collecting information—measures	Observation	A key ingredient in psychological research that includes laboratory and naturalistic observation.
	Interviews and questionnaires	Used to assess perceptions and attitudes. Social desirability and lying are problems with their use. Sampling is important in conducting surveys.
	Case study	Provides an in-depth look at an individual. Caution in generalizing is warranted.
	Standardized tests	Designed to assess an individual's characteristics relative to those of a large group of similar individuals
	Physiological research and research with animals	Focus is on the biological dimensions of the organism. While greater control over conditions can be achieved with animals, generalization to humans may be problematic.
Strategies for setting up research studies	Correlational strategy	Describes how strongly two or more events or characteristics are related. It does not allow causal statements.
	Experimental strategy	Involves manipulation of influential factors, the independent variables, and measurement of their effect on the dependent variables. Subjects are assigned randomly to experimental and control groups in many studies. The experimental strategy can reveal the causes of behavior and tell us how one event influences another.
Ethics in psychological research	General guidelines	Researchers must ensure the well-being of subjects. The risk of physical and mental harm must be reduced, informed consent should occur, and deception should be used with caution.
	Animal research	Current controversy surrounds the use of animals in psychological research, although abuse is not as widespread as some activists charge.

Our coverage of the science base of psychology has taken us through theory and the scientific method, ways of collecting information about mind and behavior, strategies for setting up research, and ethical considerations. An overview of these main ideas is presented in concept table 1.2.

Psychology's Many Areas of Specialization

Do psychologists spend all of their time in a laboratory observing rats and playing with numbers? No, they do not. Psychology is a varied field with many areas of specialization. Remember in our description of Charlie, the astronaut, and Svetlana, the cosmonaut, that social psychologists and clinical psychologists were involved in making space travel more habitable. Let's look now in more detail at what psychologists do.

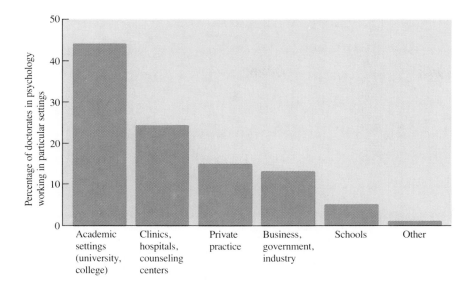

Figure 1.4
The percentages of doctorates in psychology working in particular settings.

Careers in Psychology

As a psychologist, you might spend your day seeing people with problems, or you might teach at a university and conduct research. You might work in business and industry designing more efficient work conditions for employees or helping the company select more efficient criteria for hiring. In pursuing a career in psychology, you can expand your opportunities (and income) considerably by obtaining a graduate degree, although a graduate degree is not absolutely necessary. Jobs such as house parent, drug abuse counselor, mental health aide, teacher of mentally retarded children, and staff member of a crisis hotline center often require only an undergraduate degree.

Many undergraduate psychology majors feel that psychology provides them with a sound preparation for adult life as well as a solid background for entry into other careers and graduate work in other areas. It is not unusual for undergraduate psychology majors to be hired by businesses or to go on to medical school, law school, or some other graduate work (Goodstein, 1986).

About one-third to one-half of all undergraduate psychology majors plan to get a master's degree or a doctorate in psychology. Where do psychologists with these advanced degrees work? About 43 percent work in colleges and universities teaching, researching, and/or counseling (see figure 1.4). Other settings in which you will find psychologists include public schools (as counselors and school psychologists), hospitals and mental health clinics (as counselors and clinical psychologists), government agencies (as researchers and administrators), the military (as researchers and clinical psychologists), business (as industrial psychologists and experts on organizational behavior), and prisons (usually as counselors or clinicians). Less than 15 percent of psychologists are in private clinical practice.

Figure 1.5
The percentages of doctorates in psychology in various specializations. Note: This figure shows the major subareas of psychology and how psychologists with doctorates are represented in the subareas. In this APA survey, 24,653 individuals responded that they had doctorates and 13,818 (or 56 percent) of those individuals had doctorates in clinical or counseling psychology.

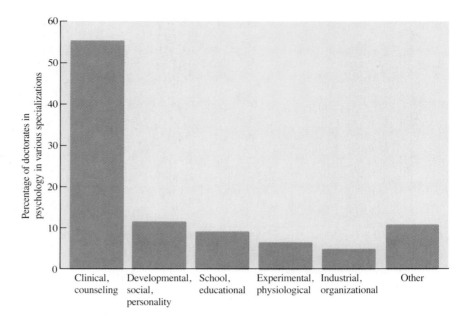

Areas of Specialization in Psychology

If you go to graduate school, you will be required to specialize in a particular area of psychology. The major specializations include clinical and counseling; experimental and physiological; developmental, social, and personality; school and educational; and industrial and organizational (see figure 1.5 for the percentages of individuals who currently have doctorates in these specializations). Sometimes the categories are not mutually exclusive. For example, some social psychologists are also experimental psychologists.

More psychologists specialize in **clinical and counseling psychology** than any other area. This specialization is practiced by psychologists who diagnose and treat people with psychological problems. The work of clinical psychologists and counseling psychologists often does not differ, although a counseling psychologist sometimes deals with people who have less serious problems. In many instances, counseling psychologists work with students, advising them about personal problems and career planning.

Clinical psychologists are different from psychiatrists. Typically, a clinical psychologist has a doctorate degree in psychology, which requires three to four years of graduate work plus one year of internship in a mental health facility. **Psychiatry** is a branch of medicine practiced by physicians with a doctor of medicine (MD) degree who subsequently specialize in abnormal behavior and psychotherapy. Clinical psychologists and psychiatrists both are interested in improving the lives of people with mental health problems. Because psychiatrists are medical doctors, however, they can prescribe drugs while clinical psychologists cannot.

Experimental and physiological psychology are areas of psychology that often involve pure research. Although psychologists in other areas conduct experiments, virtually all experimental and physiological psychologists follow precise, careful experimental strategies. These psychologists are more likely to work with animals, although many do not. A wide range of interests characterizes experimental psychology, including memory, sensation and perception, motivation, and emotion. Physiological psychologists' interests are far ranging, from investigating the role of the brain in behavior to evaluating how drugs influence hormones. The neurobiological approach to psychology is closely aligned with physiological psychology.

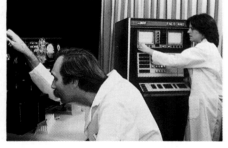

Experimental and physiological psychology are areas in which precise, careful, experimental strategies are followed. Shown here are researchers investigating the nervous system. They are using a fluorescene-activated cell sorter to analyze the functions of single cells in the nervous system.

Clinical and counseling psychology is the most widely chosen specialty by psychologists. Here, a counselor advises a student about her career plans.

Developmental psychology is concerned with how we become who we are from conception to death. In particular, developmental psychologists focus on the biological and environmental factors that contribute to human development. For many years the major emphasis in this area was on child development, although these specialists are showing a strong interest in adult development and aging. Their inquiries range across the biological, cognitive, and social domains of life.

Social psychology deals with people's social interactions, relationships, perceptions, and attitudes. Social psychologists believe we can better understand mind and behavior if we know something about how people function in groups.

Personality psychology focuses on the relatively enduring traits and characteristics of individuals. Personality psychologists study self-concept, aggression, moral development, gender roles, and how inwardly or outwardly directed we are.

School and educational psychology is concerned with children's learning and adjustment in school. School psychologists counsel children and parents when children have problems in school, often giving psychological tests to assess a child's personality and intelligence. Most educational psychologists teach and conduct research just like other academic psychologists. Their students often are prospective teachers and school psychologists.

Industrial and organizational psychology focuses on the application of psychology to business and the world of work. Industrial and organizational psychologists are concerned with training employees, improving working conditions, and developing criteria for employee selection. For example, an organizational psychologist might recommend a new management structure for a company that would open up communication lines. The background of industrial and organizational psychologists often includes training in social psychology.

As we come to the close of this first chapter I hope you are excited about the field of psychology. It is a field that offers a great deal of information about people and a field with many challenging jobs. One subject covered in this chapter was the neurobiological approach and the area of specialization called physiological psychology. Chapter 2 covers many fascinating aspects of our biological foundations and how our brain processes information about the world.

Summary

I. **What Is Psychology?**
Psychology is the scientific study of mind and behavior. Mind refers to our mental life, our thoughts and feelings that cannot be observed directly; behavior is everything we do that can be observed directly.

II. **The Beginnings of Psychology as a Science**
Wilhelm Wundt is credited with developing the first scientific psychology laboratory in 1879. Titchener popularized Wundt's ideas in the United States; his approach to psychology was known as structuralism. William James emphasized the functions of the mind in adapting to the environment; his view was called functionalism. Many of the early approaches used the technique of introspection, which later came under fire.

III. **Contemporary Approaches to Psychology**
Five prominent contemporary approaches to psychology are behaviorism, psychoanalytic theory, humanistic and phenomenological approaches, the cognitive approach, and the neurobiological approach. The behavioral approach focuses on behavior and its environmental determinants; the psychoanalytic approach focues on the unconscious, conflict, and early experiences; the humanistic and phenomenological approaches focus on expanding consciousness, subjective experiences, and positive feelings; the cognitive approach focuses on mental processes; and the neurobiological approach focuses on the brain and nervous system. No single theory offers all the answers; each contributes to the science of psychology.

IV. **Theory and the Scientific Method**
Theories are general beliefs that help us to explain what we observe and make predictions. A good theory has hypotheses, which are assumptions that can be tested to determine their accuracy. The scientific method is a series of procedures (identifying and analyzing a problem, collecting data, drawing conclusions, and revising theory) to obtain accurate information.

V. **Collecting Information about Mind and Behavior**
Systematic observation is a key ingredient in psychological research and includes laboratory and naturalistic observation. Interviews and questionnaires (or surveys) assess a person's perceptions and attitudes. Social desirability and lying are problems with their use. Sampling is an important consideration in conducting surveys. The case study provides an in-depth look at an individual. Caution in generalizing to others from a case study is warranted. Standardized tests are designed to assess an individual's characteristics relative to those of a large group of similar individuals. Physiological research and research with animals focus on the biological dimensions of the organism. While greater control over conditions can be achieved with animals, generalization from animals to humans may be problematic.

VI. **Strategies for Setting up Research Studies**
The correlational strategy describes how strongly two or more events or characteristics are related. It does not allow causal statements. The experimental strategy involves manipulation of influential factors, the independent variables, and measurement of their effect on the dependent variables. Subjects are assigned randomly to experimental and control groups in many studies. The experimental strategy can reveal the causes of behavior and tell us how one event influences another.

VII. **Ethics in Psychological Research**
Researchers must ensure the well-being of subjects in psychological studies. The risk of mental and physical harm must be reduced, informed consent should occur, and deception should be used with caution. Current controversy surrounds the use of animals in psychological research, although abuse is not as extensive as some activists charge.

VIII. **Careers in Psychology**
There are many ways to be a psychologist. Careers range from improving the lives of people with mental problems to teaching at a university and conducting research.

IX. **Areas of Specialization in Psychology**
The areas of specialization in psychology include: clinical and counseling; experimental and physiological; developmental, social, and personality; school and educational; and industrial and organizational.

Key Terms

psychology *7*
behavior *7*
mind *7*
structuralism *8*
functionalism *8*
introspection *8*
behavioral approach *9*
social learning theorists *10*
psychoanalytic approach *11*
humanistic approach *12*
phenomenological approach *12*
cognitive approach *12*
information processing perspective *13*
neurobiological approach *14*

theories *17*
hypotheses *17*
scientific method *17*
laboratory *19*
naturalistic observation *20*
interview *20*
questionnarie *21*
random assignment *25*
case study *22*
standardized tests *22*
correlational strategy *24*
experimental strategy *25*
experiment *25*
random sample *21*

experimental group *25*
control group *25*
independent variable *25*
dependent variable *25*
clinical and counseling psychology *32*
psychiatry *32*
experimental and physiological psychology *32*
developmental psychology *33*
social psychology *33*
personality psychology *33*
school and educational psychology *33*
industrial and organizational psychology *33*

Suggested Readings

Agnew, N. Mck. & Pyke, S. W. (1987). *The science game* (4th ed). Englewood Cliffs, NJ: Prentice-Hall. This popular book covers a number of important ideas about research methods in an entertaining and informative way.

American Psychological Association. (1985). *Careers in psychology.* Washington D.C.: American Psychological Association. This is an informative free booklet that provides information about careers in psychology. Write to the American Psychological Association, 1200 Seventeenth Street N.W., Washington D.C. 20036, for a copy of this booklet.

Sagan, C. (1979). *Broca's brain.* New York: Ballentine Books. Sagan, the author of the popular book *Cosmos,* is an accomplished scientist and exciting writer. In *Broca's Brain,* he sketches many intriguing portrayals of science. This book will give you a good feel for how to think in a scientific way.

Saslow, C. A. (1982). *Basic research methods.* Reading, MA: Addison-Wesley. This book is easier to read and more enjoyable than most research methods texts. It provides details about how research in psychology is conducted.

Watson, R. I. (1968). *The great psychologists: Aristotle to Freud.* Philadelphia: Lippincott. A fascinating look at early psychologists' views on mind and behavior is provided.

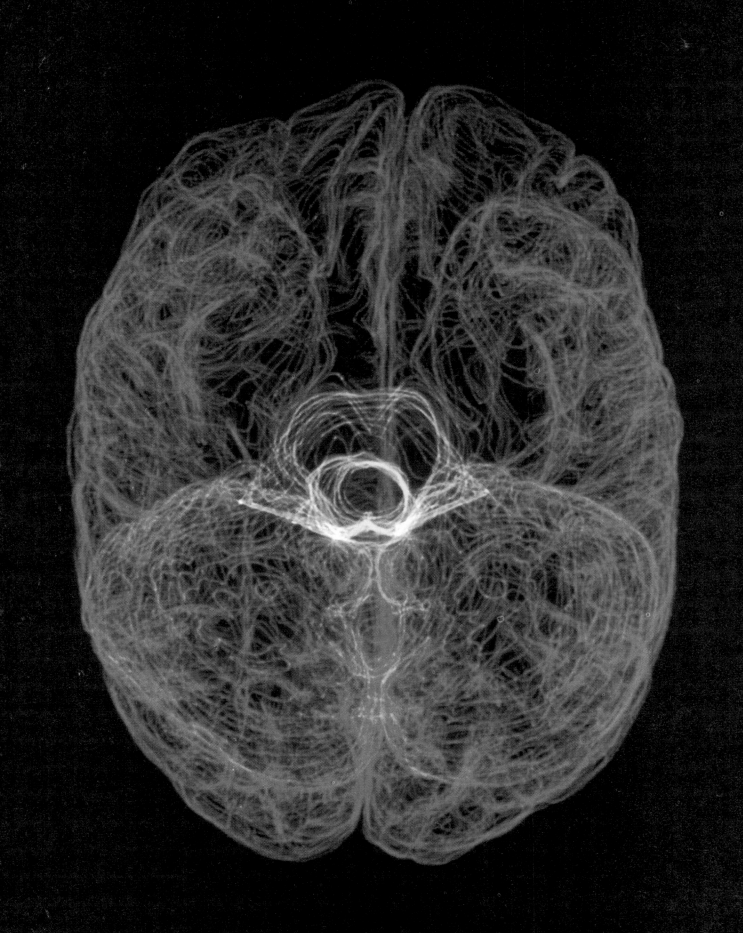

Biological and Perceptual Processes

There is a grandeur in this view of life . . . whilst this planet has gone cycling on according to the fixed law of gravity, from so simple a beginning endless forms most beautiful and wonderful have been, and are being, evolved.

—Charles Darwin, On the Origin of Species

Chapter 2

Biological Foundations and Brain Processes

> *Swiftly the brain becomes an enchanted loom, where millions of flashing shuttles weave a dissolving pattern—always a meaningful pattern—though never an abiding one.*
>
> —*Sir Charles Sherrington, 1906*

Images of Biological Foundations and Brain Processes

Separated at birth, the Mallifert twins meet accidentally.
Drawing by Chas. Addams; © 1981 The New Yorker Magazine, Inc.

Jim Springer and Jim Lewis are identical twins. They were separated at the age of four weeks and didn't see one another again until they were thirty-nine years old. Both worked as part-time deputy sheriffs, both vacationed in Florida, both drove Chevrolets, both had dogs named Toy, and both married and divorced women named Betty. One twin named his son James Allan, and the other named his son James Alan. Both liked math but not spelling, enjoyed carpentry and mechanical drawing, chewed their fingernails down to the nubs, had almost identical drinking and smoking habits, had hemorrhoids, put on ten pounds at about the same point in development, first suffered headaches at the age of eighteen, and had similar sleep patterns.

But Jim and Jim had some differences as well. One wore his hair over his forehead while the other wore it slicked back with sideburns. One expressed himself better orally while the other was more proficient in writing. But for the most part their profiles were more alike than different.

Another pair, Daphne and Barbara, were called the "giggle sisters" because they were always making each other laugh. A thorough search of their adoptive families' histories revealed no gigglers. Further, the identical twin sisters handled stress by ignoring it, avoided conflict and controversy whenever possible, and showed no interest in politics.

Two other female identical twin sisters were separated at six weeks and reunited in their fifties. Both had nightmares, which they describe in hauntingly similar ways—both dreamed of doorknobs and fishhooks in their mouths as they smothered to death! The nightmares began during early adolescence and stopped in the last ten to twelve years. Both were bedwetters until about twelve to thirteen years of age and they reported educational and marital histories that are remarkably similar.

These sets of twins are part of the Minnesota Study of Twins Reared Apart, directed by Thomas Bouchard and his colleagues. These researchers bring identical (identical genetically because they come from the same egg) and fraternal (dissimilar genetically because they come from two eggs) twins from all over the world to Minneapolis to investigate psychological aspects of their lives. For example, the twins are given a number of personality tests and detailed medical histories are obtained, including information about smoking, diet, exercise habits, chest X rays, heart stress tests, and EEGs (brain wave tests). The twins are interviewed and asked more than 15,000 questions about their family and childhood environment, personal interests, vocational orientation, values, and aesthetic judgments. They also are given ability and intelligence tests (Bouchard, & others, 1981; Lykken, 1982).

The examples of Jim and Jim, the giggle sisters, and the identical twins who had the same nightmares help us to think about our genetic heritage and the biological foundations of our existence. Organisms are not like billiard balls, moved by simple, external forces to predictable positions. Environmental experiences *and* biological foundations work together to make us who we are. Our coverage of biological foundations begins with a look at how the human species came to be. Then the question of how characteristics are transmitted from one generation to the next is tackled. Next, the part of our physical makeup that helps us most to adapt to our world is considered. These topics deal, respectively, with evolution, genetics, and the brain. To complete the chapter, one final, provocative question is raised: What is brain and what is mind, and how are the two connected, if at all? ▪

The Evolutionary Perspective and Genetics

In the H. G. Wells movie *The Man Who Could Work Miracles,* the gods discuss Earth. The first god says, "They were apes only yesterday. Give them time." The second god responds, "Once an ape always an ape." The first god then replies, "No, it will be different. . . . Come back here in an age or so and you will see." The first god was right, evolution did not stop with apes. In evolutionary time humans are relative newcomers to Earth, yet we have established ourselves as the most successful and dominant species. If we consider evolutionary time in terms of a calendar year, we could say that humans arrived here late in December (Sagan, 1980). As our earliest ancestors left the forest to feed on the savannahs, and finally to form hunting societies on the open plains, their minds and behaviors changed. How did this evolution come about? The answer lies in the principle of natural selection.

Natural Selection

Let's go back in time to the middle of the nineteenth century. Charles Darwin, a naturalist, is sitting in the study of his country home near London. He has just completed an around-the-world voyage on the H.M.S. *Beagle,* observing many different species of animals and their surrounding conditions. Darwin published his observations and thoughts in 1859 in *On the Origin of Species.* He believed that organisms reproduced at rates that would cause enormous increases in the populations of most species, yet populations remained nearly constant.

Darwin reasoned that an intense, constant struggle for food, water, and resources must occur among the many young born each generation. Because of this struggle many of the young do not survive. Those that do pass their genes on to the next generation. And, as Darwin believed, those that do survive to reproduce probably are superior in a number of ways to those who do not. In other words the survivors are better adapted to their world than the nonsurvivors. Over the course of many generations, organisms with the characteristics needed for survival would comprise a larger percentage of the population. Over many, many generations, this could produce a gradual modification of the whole population. If environmental conditions change, however, other characteristics might develop and this process could move in a different direction. For Darwin, and many scientists today, this process of **natural selection** guides the evolutionary process (Campbell, 1985).

Guatemalan identical twins. Identical twins show behaviors that are often highly similar, suggesting the importance of our biological heritage. Organisms are not like billiard balls, moved by simple, external forces to predictable positions. Environmental experiences and *biological heritage orchestrate our being.*

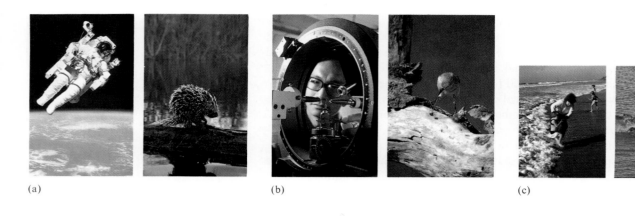

(a)   (b)   (c)

Figure 2.1
The better an animal is adapted to its environment, the more successful it becomes. Humans, more than any other mammal, are able to adapt to and control most types of environments. (a) Technological advances give greater freedom of movement and independence; (b) greater intelligence has led to the use of complex objects that enhance life; (c) because of longer parental care, humans learn more complex behavior patterns, which contribute to adaptation.

Over a million species have been classified, from bacteria to blue whales, with many varieties of beetles in between. The work of natural selection has resulted in the disappearing acts of moths and the quills of porcupines. And the effects of evolution can be seen in the technological advances, intelligence, and longer parental care of human beings (see figure 2.1).

Generally, evolution proceeds at a very slow pace. The lines that led to the emergence of human beings and the great apes began to diverge about fourteen million years ago! Modern humans, *Homo sapiens,* came into existence only about fifty thousand years ago. And the beginning of civilization as we know it began about ten thousand years ago. No sweeping evolutionary changes in humans have occurred since then—for example, our brain is not ten times as big, we do not have a third eye in the back of our head, and we haven't learned to fly.

Genetics

No matter what the species, there must be a mechanism for transmitting characteristics from one generation to the next. This mechanism is explained by the principle of genetics. Each of us carries a genetic code that we inherited from our parents. Physically, this code is located within every cell in our bodies. Our genetic codes are alike in one important way—they all contain the *human* genetic code. Because of the human genetic code, a fertilized human egg cannot grow into an eel, an egret, or an elephant.

We each began life as a single cell weighing about one twenty-millionth of an ounce! This tiny piece of matter housed our entire genetic code—the information about who we would become. These instructions orchestrated growth from that single cell to a person made of trillions of cells, each containing a perfect replica of the original genetic code.

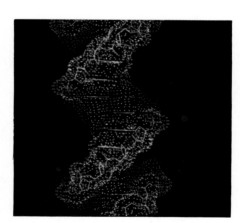

Figure 2.2
The remarkable substance known as DNA. Notice that the DNA molecule is shaped like a spiral staircase. Genes are short segments of the DNA molecule. The horizontal bars that look like the rungs of a ladder play a key role in locating the identity of a gene.

The nucleus of each human cell contains forty-six **chromosomes,** which are threadlike structures that come in structurally similar pairs. You inherited twenty-three chromosomes from your mother and another twenty-three chromosomes from your father. Chromosomes are composed of the remarkable substance deoxyribonucleic acid, or **DNA.** DNA is a molecule arranged in a "double helix" shape that looks like a circular staircase (see figure 2.2). **Genes,** the units of hereditary information, are short segments of the DNA "staircase." Genes act as a blueprint for cells to reproduce themselves and manufacture the proteins that maintain life. Chromosomes, DNA, and genes can be mysterious. To help you turn mystery into understanding see figure 2.3.

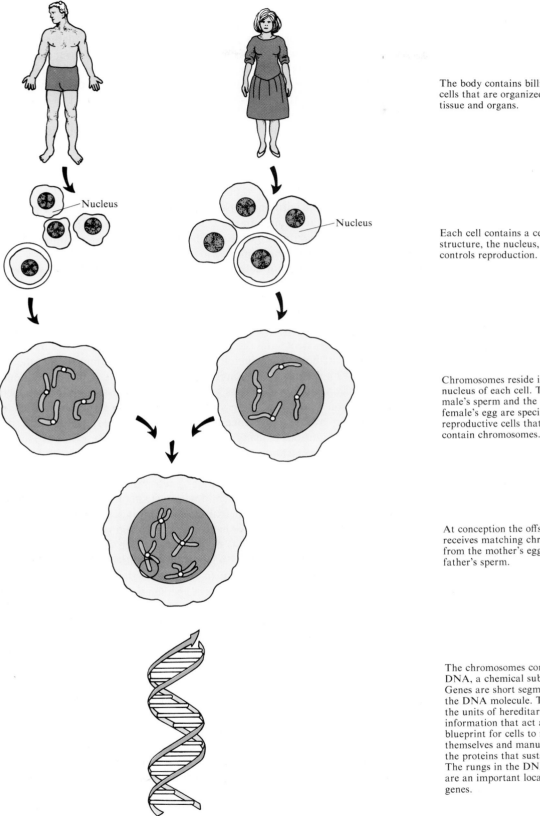

The body contains billions of cells that are organized into tissue and organs.

Each cell contains a central structure, the nucleus, which controls reproduction.

Chromosomes reside in the nucleus of each cell. The male's sperm and the female's egg are specialized reproductive cells that contain chromosomes.

At conception the offspring receives matching chromosomes from the mother's egg and the father's sperm.

The chromosomes contain DNA, a chemical substance. Genes are short segments of the DNA molecule. They are the units of hereditary information that act as a blueprint for cells to reproduce themselves and manufacture the proteins that sustain life. The rungs in the DNA ladder are an important location of genes.

Figure 2.3
Facts about chromosomes, DNA, and genes.

Drawing by Ziegler; © 1985 The New Yorker Magazine, Inc.

As you might guess, genetic transmission is a highly complex process and much is yet to be known about how genes work. We do know that some genes are dominant over others when they come together to determine our characteristics. Brown eyes, farsightedness, and dimples rule over blue eyes, normal vision, and freckles, for example. Some characteristics are determined by genes carried on the twenty-third chromosome pair, which is the pair that determines the sex of the offspring. These characteristics tend to appear in the members of one sex more than the other. Colorblindness and hairy ear rims are more likely to show up in males than females, for example.

Most genetic transmission is more complicated than these rather simple examples. Few psychological characteristics are the result of the action of a single gene pair. Most are determined by the combination of many different genes. Each of us has at least 50,000 genes in our chromosomes. When these 50,000 genes combine with another's 50,000 genes at conception, the possible combinations are staggering—in the many trillions. No wonder scientists are struck by the complexity of genetic transmission (Fuller & Simmel, 1987; Loehlin, Willerman, & Horn, in press).

But genes alone do not determine who we are. Both genes and *environment* are necessary for an organism to exist. Every aspect of mind and behavior is influenced to some degree by the interaction of nature *and* nurture, genes *and* environment. Neither factor operates alone. Even biologists who study the simplest animals agree that it is virtually impossible to separate the effects of an animal's genes and the effects of the environment (Johnson, 1987).

Let's look at how this principle might work with humans. Imagine we could identify the precise gene combination that makes you either very outgoing or very shy. Could your shyness be predicted from knowing exactly which gene combination controls it? The answer is no, because shyness is a characteristic shaped by life experience. Parents, for example, may push a shy child into social situations causing her to become more gregarious; or an outgoing child might be so traumatized by early life experiences that his friendly nature becomes inhibited.

But in the genetic-environment model, environmental experiences do not completely mold the organism. The child with a strong genetic tendency to be shy probably will not become an extremely outgoing individual. Environmental experiences may modify her extreme shyness and make her only somewhat less shy. Sandra Scarr (1984) explains that each of us has a range of potential. For example, someone with genes for medium-tall height who lives in a poor environment may grow up to be shorter than average. But in an excellent nutritional environment, the same person would grow up to be taller than average. No matter how well fed an individual with genes for short height, he will never be taller than average. Scarr believes that characteristics such as shyness and intelligence may work the same way. That is, there is a range within which the environment can modify shyness or intelligence, but shyness and intelligence are not completely malleable.

Although the Jim and Jim twins you read about at the beginning of the chapter grew up in different environments, they showed remarkably similar characteristics when observed as adults. How can psychologists study such genetic influences? Animals can be inbred or selectively bred to control genetic factors, but of course ethically we cannot do this with humans. Two strategies used with humans are twin studies and adoption studies. These strategies focus on the genetic relationship of individuals to their family members. The influence of genetic and environmental factors can be determined because the degree of genetic relatedness is known.

In the **twin study,** the focus is on the genetic relationship between twins. The most common twin study is not the way Jim and Jim were studied (identical twins reared apart) but rather a comparison of identical twins with fraternal twins (Rushton & others, 1986).

In the **adoption study,** researchers capitalize on the fact that an individual is closer to the biological parents than to the adoptive parents, who care for the individual. Investigators study whether the individual's characteristics are more similar to the biological parents or to the adoptive parents. A number of adoption studies have been conducted (Horn, 1983; Plomin, 1987; Scarr & Weinberg, 1983; Wender & others, 1986), but the most famous took place many years ago (Skodak & Skeels, 1949). In this study, many children whose biological mothers were mentally retarded were diagnosed as mentally retarded themselves. Some of these supposedly mentally retarded children were adopted by parents in the normal range of intelligence. Later in life, these adopted children scored in the normal range of intelligence. The intelligence levels of these adopted children was higher than those of the children who remained with their retarded mothers, but it was lower than children with normal mothers who were adopted into the same type of families. Thus, in this classic adoption study intelligence seemed to be influenced by both heredity—the intelligence of the adopted children's biological mothers—and environment—the intelligence of the adopted children's parents.

Sociobiology

A contemporary view in psychology that promotes the power of genes in determining behavior is **sociobiology** (Wilson, 1975). The main principle of sociobiology is that all behavior is motivated by the desire to contribute one's genetic heritage to the greatest number of descendents. That is, sociobiologists believe an organism is motivated by a desire to dominate the gene pool.

A story about President Calvin Coolidge and his wife illustrates the sociobiology doctrine. One day the president and Mrs. Coolidge took separate tours of a government farm. When Mrs. Coolidge arrived at the chicken pens, she asked if the rooster copulated more than once a day. The guide responded that yes, he copulated a dozen times or more each day. Mrs. Coolidge told the guide to tell that to the president. When President Coolidge was informed, he asked if the rooster copulated with the same hen every time. He was told that no, it was a different hen each time. The president suggested the guide tell that to Mrs. Coolidge. This story became so widespread among sociobiologists that the "Coolidge effect" was coined to describe renewed male interest at the appearance of new females. Sociobiologists claim the rooster is trying to dominate the gene pool, and each new copulation increases the likelihood that he will do so.

Hens and other mammalian females have a limited number of eggs and the periods of gestation and rearing are lengthy. Because of this and the fact that sperm is plentiful, an individual male potentially can produce far more offspring than a female. Males who pursue many females are more likely to spread their genes, and over time this should lead to a stronger tendency in males than females to pursue sexual contacts. The males of most species do initiate sexual behavior more often than females and with a greater number of partners. This is especially true with cattle and sheep, who inseminate large harems. This phenomenon has been observed in human societies as well (Hinde, 1984).

The genetic basis of the initiation of sexual contact by males is but one of a number of sociobiology's controversial ideas. Sociobiologists argue that altruism, aggression, dominance, and the socialization of children can be

■ ■ ■ ■ ■ ■ ■ ■ ■ ■ ■ ■ ■ ■ ■ ■ ■

Concept Table 2.1

Evolution and Genetics		
Concept	**Processes/related ideas**	**Characteristics/description**
Evolution	Natural selection	Proposed by Charles Darwin. Argues that genetic diversity occurs in each species. Some organisms have characteristics that help them adapt to their environment and these are likely to be perpetuated.
Genetics	Chromosomes, DNA, and genes	The nucleus of each human cell contains forty-six chromosomes, which are composed of DNA. Genes are short segments of DNA and act as a blueprint for cells to reproduce and manufacture proteins that maintain life. Most genetic transmission involves combinations of genes.
	Genetic-environmental interaction	Every behavior is due to some degree to the interaction of genes and environment.
	Genetic methods	Animals can be inbred or selectively bred to control for genetic factors. With humans twin studies and adoption studies are used.
	Sociobiology	Argues that all behavior is motivated to dominate the gene pool. Critics say sociobiology ignores the enviromental determinants of behavior. This controversy is another version of the nature-nurture argument.

understood more completely if they are considered in terms of attempts to dominate the gene pool (Buss & Barnes, 1986; Symons, 1986, in press). For example, consider an individual's loyalty to his family and the self-sacrifice or altruism such loyalty might motivate. It is not unusual for a parent to save a child from a blazing fire, even if it means risking his own life. Even if the parent dies in the blaze, the child's genes will survive, so the parent has increased the likelihood that his genes will dominate the gene pool.

Critics argue that sociobiology does not give adequate consideration to experience and plasticity of human behavior. They point out that human social behavior emerges to improve the well-being of society and not just to continue an individual's genes. Much of the evidence that supports the contentions of sociobiology is based on animal research, and critics argue that animal research cannot be generalized to humans.

Sociobiologists say that the critics misunderstand them. They point out that all behavior is the result of *genetic-environmental interaction.* Sociobiologists agree that through experience the behavior of organisms can be modified, but such changes must be considered within the boundaries of genetic influences (Crawford, Smith, & Krebs, 1987). E. O. Wilson (1975), the founder of sociobiology, argues that while human beings are indeed a culture-making and culture-using species, culture should not be interpreted apart from biology, because culture and evolution are inherently interwoven.

The sociobiology controversy, then, is another version of the nature-nurture controversy, which has been a part of psychology throughout its history. The "nature" proponents claim that biological and genetic factors are the most important determinants of mind and behavior; the "nurture" proponents emphasize that environment and experience are more important.

Our tour of biological foundations has focused on evolution—how human beings came to be who they are—and genetics—the mechanism by which characteristics are transmitted from one generation to the next. The main themes of these ideas are summarized in concept table 2.1. Of all the aspects of human beings that have evolved, none helps us adapt to our world more than the brain—to its knowns and unknowns we now turn.

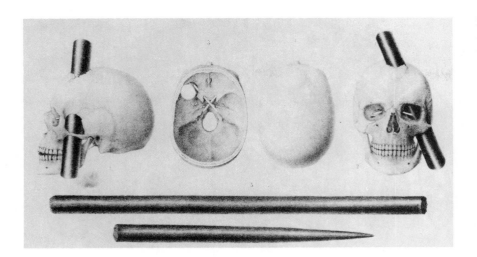

Figure 2.4
Drawings to illustrate the injury to Phineas P. Gage. Remarkably, his wounds healed in a matter of weeks, but his personality changed dramatically, suggesting the brain's role in personality.

The Brain and Nervous System

Shakespeare referred to the brain as the soul's dwelling house. And Descartes was confident he knew the precise location in the center of the brain of the soul—the place where mind exerted its influence over body. Philosophers as well as scientists continue their debate over what is mind and what is brain. The flurry of recent interest in mind-brain connections will be dealt with later in the chapter, but first we need to get a solid grounding in what the brain really is all about. To do this we will study some early considerations of the brain, the elegant organization of the nervous system, details about the brain's cells, the brain's anatomy, integration in the brain, and some ideas about glands.

Early Approaches

The fascinating case of Phineas P. Gage, a twenty-five-year-old foreman who worked for the Rutland and Burlington Railroad in Vermont, reveals some of the ways behavior is controlled by the brain. On September 13, 1848, Phineas and several coworkers were using blasting powder to construct a roadbed. The crew drilled holes in the rock and gravel, poured in the blasting powder, and then tamped down the powder with a steel rod. The powder blew up while Phineas was still tamping it down, driving the iron up through the left side of his face and out through the top of his head (see figure 2.4). Phineas was thrown to the ground, but amazingly, he was still conscious and able to talk. His coworkers placed him on an ox cart and drove him almost a mile to his hotel. Phineas got out of the cart himself and walked up the flight of stairs to his room. A physician was called and discovered that he could put the entire length of his index finger through the cylindrical hole in Phineas's skull!

Though the wound in Phineas's skull healed in a matter of weeks, he became a different person. Phineas had been a mild-mannered, hard-working, emotionally calm individual prior to the accident. He was well liked by all who knew him. Afterward, he became obstinate, moody, irresponsible, selfish, and incapable of participating in any planned activities. Phineas's misfortune illustrates how the brain is involved in determining the nature of our personality.

Figure 2.5
*A phrenology map based on the
system developed by Gall.
Phrenologists claimed that psychic
functions were localized in the
cerebral cortex where the tissue
responsible for each function
produced a characteristic bump on
the skull. Personality was deduced by
mapping the bumps and ridges on an
individual's head.*

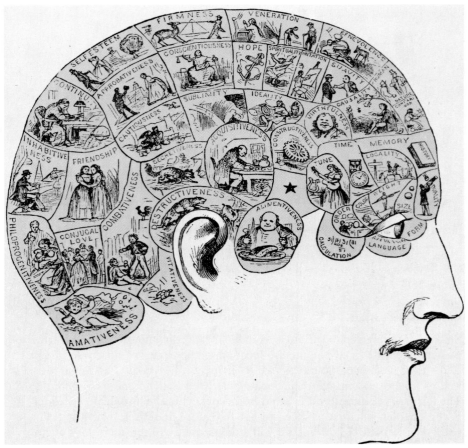

Early in the nineteenth century, the realization that certain parts of the brain are responsible for certain types of behavior began to emerge. A German physician named Franz Joseph Gall argued that the bumps and depressions in the skull were linked to intelligence and personality, an approach referred to as **phrenology.** Gall mapped out a large number of psychological functions: benevolence, destructiveness, mirthfulness, and individuality, for example. Rub your skull and find where your bumps are located, then turn to figure 2.5 to discover Gall's explanation of their significance.

Gall's basic idea was right; different brain regions do have different functions. Where Gall went wrong (besides thinking that skull bumps accurately reflect brain shape) was in the types of psychological functions he assigned to different brain regions. His phrenology maps were quickly rejected by scientists of his time, but the notion that functions are localized has prevailed.

More scientific support of the localization concept came from a study by Paul Broca in 1861. A patient of Broca had received an injury to the dominant side of his brain some thirty-one years earlier. The injury was to a precise part of the dominant side of the brain called the third frontal convolution. The patient became known as Tan, because that was the only word he could speak. Tan suffered from aphasia, a language disorder that is associated with brain damage. Tan died several days after Broca evaluated him, and an autopsy revealed the location of the injury. Today we refer to this region of the brain as Broca's area and know that it plays an important role in language.

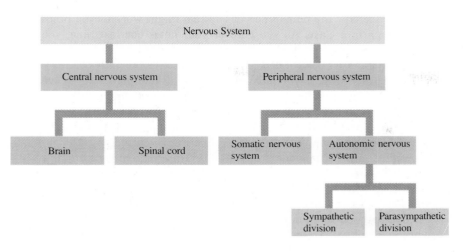

Figure 2.6
The major divisions of the nervous system.

The degree to which functions are localized in the brain is an enduring issue. Today psychologists believe that while a particular structure of the brain may be more involved with one psychological function than another, for the most part psychological function is not based on a specific structure, but rather on *various* areas of the brain.

The Elegant Organization of the Nervous System

When Emerson said, "The world was built in order and the atoms march in tune," he must have had the human nervous system in mind. This truly elegant system is highly ordered and organized (Kaas, 1987). It is at work processing information in everything we do, whether stumbling across a tiger in the jungle, seeing a loved one across a crowded room, or preparing a speech. The human nervous system is made up of bundles of nerve fibers. Neuroscientists call the nerve cell that is the basic building block of the nervous system a **neuron.**

The nervous system is divided into two parts: the central nervous system and the peripheral nervous system. The **central nervous system (CNS)** is made up of the brain and spinal cord. More than 99 percent of all neurons (nerve cells) in our body are located in the CNS. The **peripheral nervous system** is a network of nerves that connect the brain and spinal cord to other parts of the body. The peripheral nervous system brings information to and from the brain and spinal cord and carries out the commands of the CNS to execute various muscular and glandular activities.

The two major divisions of the peripheral nervous system are the somatic nervous system and autonomic nervous system. The **somatic nervous system** consists of *sensory nerves,* which convey information from the skin and muscles to the CNS about such matters as pain and temperature, and *motor nerves,* which inform muscles when to act. The **autonomic nervous system** takes messages to and from the body's internal organs, monitoring such processes as breathing, heart rate, and digestion. It too is divided into two parts, the **sympathetic division** and the **parasympathetic division,** which link emotions and the internal parts of the body. The sympathetic division is at work when an individual is aroused, while the parasympathetic division slows down various body parts. More information about the autonomic nervous system appears toward the end of this chapter and in chapter 12 when we discuss emotion and stress. Figure 2.6 displays the hierarchical organization of the nervous system just outlined.

Let's see how the human nervous system might work as you prepare to give a speech in a class. As you go over your notes one last time, your peripheral nervous system carries information about the notes to your central nervous system. Your central nervous system processes the marks on the paper, interpreting the words as you memorize key points and plan ways to keep the audience interested. After studying the notes several minutes longer, you scribble a joke midway through them. Your peripheral nervous system is at work again, conveying the information from your brain to the muscles in your arm and hand that enables you to make the marks on the paper. The information transmitted from your eyes to your brain and from your brain to your hand is being handled by the somatic nervous system. This is your first speech in awhile, so you are a little uptight. As you think about getting up in front of the class, your stomach feels queasy and your heart begins to thump. This is the sympathetic division of the autonomic nervous system functioning as you become aroused. You regain your confidence after reminding yourself that you know the speech cold. As you relax, the parasympathetic division of the autonomic nervous system is working.

Neurons

So far we have described the major divisions of the nervous system. But there is much more to the intriguing story of how the nervous system processes information. Let's get inside the huge nervous system and find out more about the cells, chemicals, and electrical impulses that are the nuts and bolts of its operation.

Pathways of Neurons

The flow of information to the brain, within the brain, and out of the brain can be described in terms of three components of the nervous system: afferent nerves, interneurons, and efferent nerves. The cells that carry input to the brain are called **afferent nerves,** or sensory nerves. *Afferent* comes from the Latin word meaning "bring to." The cells that carry the output are the **efferent nerves,** or motor nerves. The word *efferent* is derived from the Latin word meaning "bring forth."

To see how afferent and efferent nerves work, let's consider a well-known reflex, the knee jerk. In knee-jerk behavior, afferent cells transmit information directly to efferent cells, so the information processing is quick and simple. The processing of information involving the knee jerk takes place at the spinal cord and does not require the brain's participation. More complex information processing is accomplished by passing the information through systems of **interneurons,** which make up most of the brain. For example, as you read the notes for your speech the afferent input from your eye was transmitted to your brain, then passed through many interneuron systems, which translate (process) the patterns of black and white into neural codes for letters, words, associations, and meanings. Some of the information is stored in the interneuron systems for future associations and some (if you read aloud) is output as efferent messages to your lips and tongue.

Your gift of speech is possible because human interneuron systems are organized in ways that permit language processing. Although the neurons in a canary's brain are exactly the same as those in a frog's brain, frogs croak while canaries sing because the neurons are organized differently in the two brains. The interneurons in the frog's vocalization system are connected in such a way that they produce croaking, while the canary's produce singing.

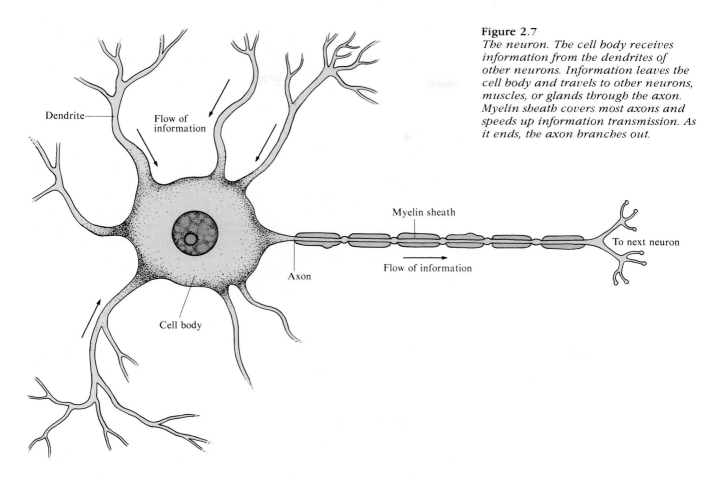

Figure 2.7
The neuron. The cell body receives information from the dendrites of other neurons. Information leaves the cell body and travels to other neurons, muscles, or glands through the axon. Myelin sheath covers most axons and speeds up information transmission. As it ends, the axon branches out.

This is why the study of brain organization—the anatomy and fine structure of the brain—is so important. Brain organization is the key to understanding all of the complex and wondrous things that brains do. We'll tackle the brain's anatomy later; first, let's examine neurons in greater detail.

Structure of the Neuron

As indicated earlier, neuron is the neuroscientist's label for nerve cell. The neuron handles information processing in the nervous system at the cellular level. There are some 10 to 20 billion neurons in the human brain. The average neuron is as complex as a small computer, with as many as 15,000 physical connections with other cells (Kolb & Whishaw, 1985). At times the brain may be lit up with as many as a quadrillion connections.

The three basic parts of the neuron are the cell body, dendrites, and the axon (see figure 2.7). The neuron's **cell body** contains the nucleus, which directs the manufacture of the substances the neuron uses for its growth and maintenance. Most neurons are created very early in life and will not be replaced if they are destroyed. Interestingly, though, some types of neurons continue to multiply in adults, and most are capable of changing their shapes, sizes, and connections throughout the life span.

Figure 2.8
These schematic drawings show the location, size, shape, and configuration of some neurons.

Adapted from
Fundamentals of Human
Neuropsychology, *2/E*
by Bryan Kolb and Ian Q.
Whishaw. Copyright ©
1980, 1985 W. H. Freeman
and Company.

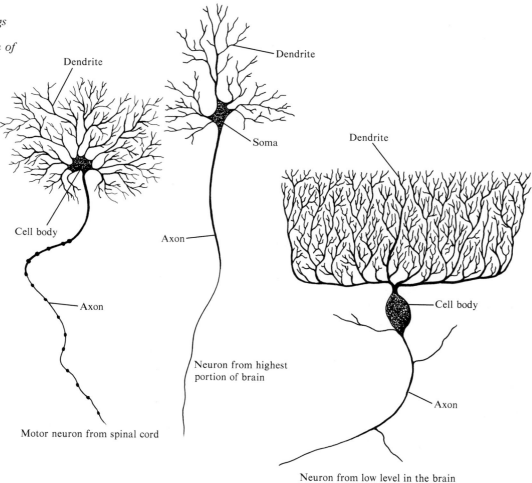

Dendrite

Dendrite

Soma

Dendrite

Cell body

Axon

Axon

Cell body

Neuron from highest portion of brain

Axon

Motor neuron from spinal cord

Neuron from low level in the brain

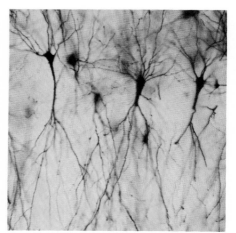

Figure 2.9
This photograph shows neurons in a midregion of the brain. Notice the large number of dendritic branches that extend from each cell body.

The part of the neuron that extends away from the cell body is called the **dendrite.** Most nerve cells have a number of dendrites. Dendrites are the receiving part of the neuron, serving the important function of collecting information and orienting it toward the cell body. Figure 2.8 shows dendrites in different parts of the central nervous system. Notice the extensive branching of the dendrites. Figure 2.9 is an actual photograph of dendrites in the brain.

Although there are many dendrites radiating from the cell body of the neuron, there is only one axon. The **axon** is much thinner and much longer than a dendrite and looks like an ultrathin cylindrical tube. The axon of a single neuron may extend all the way from the top of the brain to the base of the spinal cord, a distance of over three feet. The axon carries information away from the cell body to other cells. Most axons are covered with a layer of fat cells that insulate the axon called a **myelin sheath.** As shown in figure 2.7, there are gaps in the myelin sheath. As information travels down the axon, it jumps across these gaps, causing it to travel faster. The more myelin, the faster the conduction. The myelin sheath developed as brains evolved and became larger and it became necessary for information to travel longer distances. The myelin sheath helped information travel faster over long distances in the nervous system. This is not unlike the appearance of freeways and turnpikes as cities grew. The newly developed roadways keep the fast-moving, long-distance traffic from getting tangled up with slow-moving local traffic.

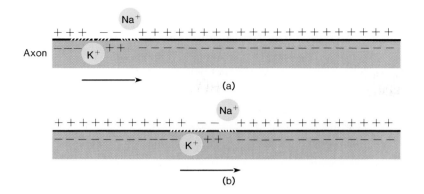

Figure 2.10
Movement of sodium and potassium ions down the axon. This diagram shows the sodium ions on the outside and the potassium ions on the inside of the neuron's membrane as the nerve impulse travels down the axon. At the top the nerve impulse has just begun (a), and at the bottom the nerve impulse has moved further along the axon (b).

The Nerve Impulse

Neurons send information down the axon as brief impulses, or waves, of electricity. Perhaps in a movie you have seen a telegraph operator sending a series of single clicks down a telegraph wire to the next station. That is what neurons do. To send information to other neurons, they send a series of single, electrical clicks down their axons. By changing the rate and timing of the clicks, the neuron can vary the nature of the message it sends. As you reach to turn this page, hundreds of such clicks will stream down the axons in your arm to tell your muscles just when to flex and how vigorously.

To understand how a neuron, which is a living cell, creates and sends electrical signals, we need to examine this cell and the fluids in which it floats. A neuron is a balloonlike bag filled with one kind of fluid and surrounded by a slightly different kind of fluid. A piece of this balloonlike bag is stretched and pulled to form a long, hollow tube, which is the axon. The axon tube is very thin; a few dozen in a bundle would be about the thickness of a human hair.

To see how this fluid-filled "balloon" called a neuron creates electrical signals, we must look at two things: the particles that float in the fluids and the actual wall of the cell, the membrane. The important particles in the fluids are the elements sodium and chloride (which we get from common table salt—sodium chloride) and potassium. Each particle, called an **ion,** has an electrical charge. The neuron creates electrical signals by the movement of these charged ions back and forth through its membrane; the waves of electricity that are created sweep along the membrane.

How does the neuron move these ions? It's really fairly simple: the membrane, the wall of our balloon, is covered with hundreds of thousands of small doors, or gates, that open and close to let the ions pass in or out of the cell. Normally, when resting, or not sending information, the membrane gates for sodium are closed, and those for potassium and chloride are partly open. Because the membrane is in a semipermeable state, the ions separate; sodium is kept outside, lots of potassium ends up inside, and most of the chloride goes outside. Because the ions are separated, a charge, or **resting potential,** is present along the membrane of the cell (figure 2.10 shows movement of the sodium and potassium ions). That potential, by the way, is about one-fourteenth of a volt, so fourteen neurons could make a one-volt battery. In the electric eel, its 8,400 cells could generate 600 volts.

Figure 2.11
The action potential is a temporary change in the neuron's membrane potential; it travels down the axon.

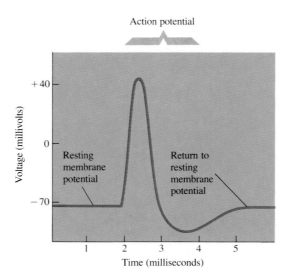

When the neuron gets enough excitatory input to cause it to send a message, the sodium gates at the base of the axon open briefly, then shut again. While those gates are open sodium rushes into the axon, carrying an electrical charge, and that charge causes the next group of gates on the axon to flip open briefly. And so it goes all the way down the axon, just like a long row of cabinet doors opening and closing in sequence. After the sodium gates close, potassium ions flow out of the cell and bring the membrane charge back to the resting condition. Thus a "wave" of electrical charge (the "clicks" we mentioned earlier) sweeps down the axon, and that wave is called the **action potential** (see figure 2.11).

The wave of electrical charge that sweeps down the axon abides by the **all-or-none principle.** This means that once the electrical impulse reaches a certain level of intensity, it fires and moves all the way down the axon, remaining at the same strength throughout its travel. The electrical impulse traveling down an axon is much like a fuse to a firecracker. It doesn't matter whether a match or blowtorch is used to light the fuse; as long as a certain minimal intensity has been reached, the spark travels quickly and at the same level of strength down the fuse until it reaches the firecracker (see figure 2.12).

Synapses and Neurotransmitters

What happens once the neural impulse reaches the end of the axon? Neurons themselves do not touch each other directly, but nevertheless they manage to communicate. The story of the connection between one neuron and another is one of the most intriguing and highly researched areas of contemporary neuroscience. Neurons are separated by tiny gaps called **synapses.** Most synapses are between the axon of one neuron and the dendrites or cell body of another neuron. On rare occasions they occur between the dendrites of one neuron and the dendrites of the next neuron (Shepherd, 1974).

How does information get across this gap to the next neuron? The end of an axon branches out into a number of fibers that end in structures called synaptic knobs. Chemical substances called **neurotransmitters** are found in

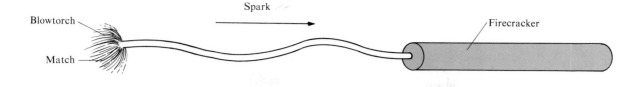

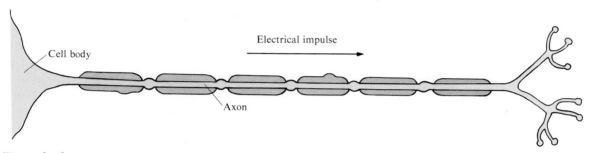

Figure 2.12
*The all-or-none principle. The all-or-none principle can be compared to a
fuse and a firecracker. Regardless of whether it is lit by a blowtorch or a
match, once a certain level of intensity is reached, the fuse lights and then the
spark travels at the same level of strength until it reaches the firecracker. So it
is with an electrical impulse firing and traveling the entire length of an axon.*

tiny synaptic vesicles (chambers) located in these synaptic knobs. The molecules of these chemical substances wait for a nerve impulse to come down
through the axon. Once the nerve impulse reaches the synaptic knobs, the
electrical signal causes these miniature springlike molecules to contract, pulling
the vesicles out to the edge of the synaptic knob. At the edge the vesicles burst
open, and the neurotransmitter molecules spew forth into the gap between the
two neurons. In the synaptic gap the neurotransmitter molecules bump about
in random motion, and some land on receptor sites in the next neuron, where
they fit like small keys in equally small locks. The key in the lock, in turn,
opens a "door" and electrical signals begin to sweep through the next neuron.
So, neurotransmitters are chemical substances that carry information across
the synaptic gap to the next neuron. Synapses and neurotransmitters can be
mysterious, just as genes and DNA can be. To help turn more mystery into
understanding, see figure 2.13.

More than fifty different neurotransmitters, each with a unique chemical makeup, have been discovered and the list probably will grow to 100 or
more in the near future (Barnard & Darlison, in press; McGinty & Szymusiak, in press; Panksepp, 1986). Interestingly, most creatures that have been
studied, from snails to whales, use the same neurotransmitter molecules that
our own brains use. And many animal venoms, such as that of the black widow,
actually are neurotransmitterlike substances that disturb neurotransmission.

*Most creatures that have been
studied—from the snail shown above
to whales—use the same
neurotransmitter molecules that our
own brains use.*

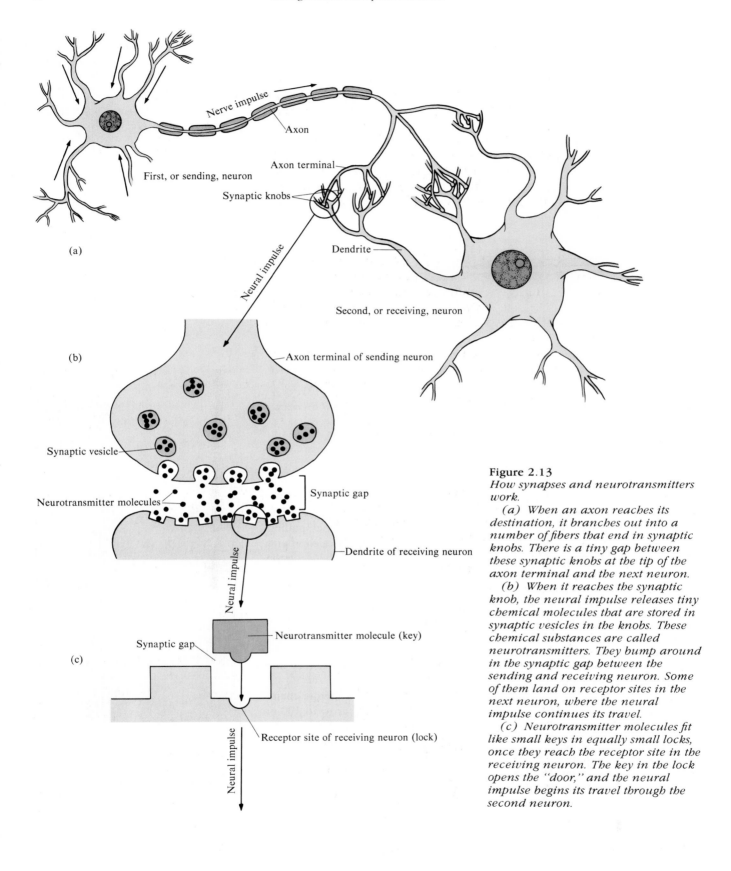

Nerve impulse

Axon

First, or sending, neuron

Axon terminal

Synaptic knobs

(a)

Neural impulse

Dendrite

Second, or receiving, neuron

(b)

Axon terminal of sending neuron

Synaptic vesicle

Synaptic gap

Neurotransmitter molecules

Neural impulse

Dendrite of receiving neuron

Synaptic gap

Neurotransmitter molecule (key)

(c)

Receptor site of receiving neuron (lock)

Neural impulse

Figure 2.13
*How synapses and neurotransmitters
work.*

*(a) When an axon reaches its
destination, it branches out into a
number of fibers that end in synaptic
knobs. There is a tiny gap between
these synaptic knobs at the tip of the
axon terminal and the next neuron.*

*(b) When it reaches the synaptic
knob, the neural impulse releases tiny
chemical molecules that are stored in
synaptic vesicles in the knobs. These
chemical substances are called
neurotransmitters. They bump around
in the synaptic gap between the
sending and receiving neuron. Some
of them land on receptor sites in the
next neuron, where the neural
impulse continues its travel.*

*(c) Neurotransmitter molecules fit
like small keys in equally small locks,
once they reach the receptor site in the
receiving neuron. The key in the lock
opens the "door," and the neural
impulse begins its travel through the
second neuron.*

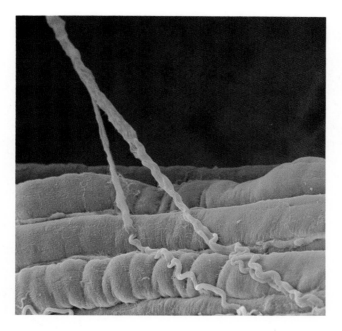

Figure 2.14
Nerves, acetylcholine, and muscles. The nerve impulse, conducted down a nerve fiber that ends in skeletal muscle, releases a small amount of the chemical acetylcholine. The action of acetylcholine at the motor end-plate initiates the chemical changes that cause the muscle to contract. The photo shows a number of nerve fibers leading to and crossing several striated muscle cells.

What are some of these neurotransmitters and how are they related to our behavior? **GABA,** which stands for the imposing chemical gamma amino butyric acid, inhibits the firing of neurons. It is found throughout the brain and spinal cord and is believed to be the neurotransmitter in as many as one-third of the brain's synaptic connections. GABA is so important in the brain because it keeps many neurons from firing. This inhibition helps to control the preciseness of the signal being carried from one neuron to the next. The degeneration of GABA may be responsible for Huntington's Chorea, a deadly disease that includes a loss of muscle control. Without GABA's inhibiting influence, the nerve impulse becomes imprecise and muscles lose their coordination.

Another important neurotransmitter is **acetylcholine (ACh),** which produces contractions of skeletal muscles by acting on motor nerves (see figure 2.14). While GABA inhibits neurons from firing, in most instances ACh excites neurons and stimulates them to fire. The venom of the black widow we spoke of causes ACh to gush through the synapses between the spinal cord and skeletal muscles, producing violent spasms. The drug curare, found on the tips of some South American Indians' poison darts, blocks some receptors for ACh. This paralyzes skeletal muscles.

Norepinephrine is a neurotransmitter that usually inhibits the firing of neurons in the brain and spinal cord, but excites the heart muscles, the intestines, and the urogenital tract. Too little norepinephrine is associated with depression and too much of it is linked to highly agitated, manic states. Figure 2.15 provides a look at what norepinephrine-containing cells in the brain actually look like. The neurotransmitter **dopamine** also is related to our mental health—too much dopamine in the brain's synapses is associated with the severe disturbance called schizophrenia, in which an individual loses contact with reality (Marder & May, 1986). More about the role of neurotransmitters in mental health and how drugs can be used to control their action appears in chapters 14 and 15. **Serotonin** is a neurotransmitter that is involved in the regulation of sleep, and like norepinephrine, seems to play a role in depression as well. To learn more about serotonin's role in seasonal depression, read Psychology 2.1.

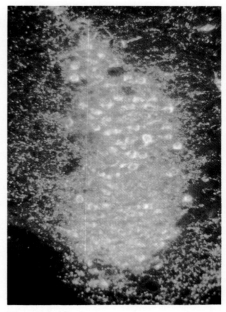

Figure 2.15
Thousands of norepinephrine-containing neurons are shown in this photograph of the rat's brain stem. The presence of norepinephrine causes the neurons to glow with the bright green appearance you see. In humans, too little norepinephrine in the brain's cells is associated with depression, too much with manic, agitated behavior.

■ ■ ■ ■ ■ ■ ■ ■ ■ ■ ■ ■ ■ ■ ■ ■ ■ ■

Psychology 2.1

Serotonin, the Pineal Gland, and Seasonal Depression

During the seventeenth century, René Descartes believed that the seat of the soul was located in the **pineal gland** (see figure 2.A). It was here, Descartes philosophized, that mind controlled the body. The pineal gland is centrally located just below where the two sides of the brain are connected. Descartes' speculation cannot be documented scientifically but information discovered recently about the pineal gland suggests it may play a part in seasonal depression (Bloom, Lazerson, & Hofstadter, 1985; Bridgemann, 1985). Seasonal depression is labeled seasonal affective disorder in the scheme of classifying mental disturbances. The depression is characterized by depression in the fall and winter and maniclike behavior in the spring and summer. In January, the sufferer appears lethargic, unmotivated, and unable to cope with life's stresses. In June, the same person appears overly energetic, nervous, and hyper.

At the National Institute of Mental Health, scientists investigating this form of depression believe something keeps sufferers from adapting to seasonal changes when days grow

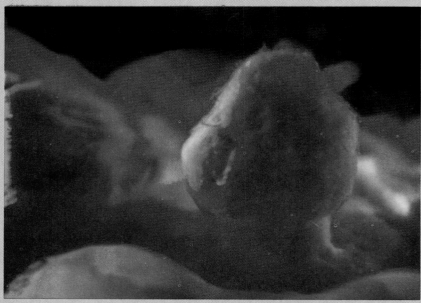

Figure 2.A
The striking beauty of the pineal gland, thought by Descartes to be the seat of the soul. Today researchers are investigating its role in biological rhythms, such as light-dark cycles. The pineal gland is the location of the greatest amount of serotonin in the brain.

shorter (Rosenthal & others, 1984; Wener, & others 1979, 1986). They speculate that the culprits are the pineal gland, serotonin, and related factors. The area of the human brain responsible for sensing light and dark is thought to be located in a region of the hypothalamus. This region has connections to the pineal gland, where serotonin reaches a high level of concentration. In the pineal gland, serotonin is converted to melatonin. In some lizards, melatonin is the main reason their skin lightens when

One final neurotransmitter we will consider has captured a great deal of public attention. To think about its role in your life, put yourself in the following situation. During your first week of running, you pant along, barely able to make a mile. But you are dedicated and determined to reach your goal—to run twenty miles a week. By the sixth week, you have increased your endurance to where you can run four miles at a time, five times a week. As you run the last mile of your four-mile course, you begin to reflect on your life and whether it has changed since you began your regular running regimen.

darkness falls. And in sparrows and chickens, the amount of melatonin in the blood is linked closely with daytime activity and nighttime sleep. For example, when melatonin is injected into sparrows, they fall asleep. Serotonin itself, as mentioned earlier, is an important neurotransmitter involved in sleep (Thompson, 1985).

Exactly how the links between the hypothalamus and the pineal gland and serotonin and melatonin work is still not known. But their neural pathways connect and each is involved in some way with light-dark cycles. How does seasonal depression come into this picture? The scientists at the National Institute of Mental Health expose individuals with seasonal depression to a bank of high-intensity, full-spectrum lights for several hours before dawn (see figure 2.B). Remember that high levels of melatonin occur in some animals only after darkness falls. Generally, these individuals respond to the bright-light therapy within four days of starting treatment and relapse within four days of discontinuing treatment. The light therapy is used most in the fall and winter months when seasonal depression is most

Figure 2.B
Scientists at the National Institute of Mental Health are treating seasonal depression with a bank of high-intensity lights for several hours each morning before daybreak during the fall and winter months, when seasonal depression is most debilitating. In some yet unknown way, scientists speculate that the involvement of the pineal gland, serotonin, and melatonin in light-dark cycles may be behind the successful treatment.

debilitating; in some instances light therapy in the winter keeps manic episodes lower in the summer months as well.

Scientific investigation of the link between the pineal gland and serotonin and seasonal depression is still speculative because the processes that control biological rhythms are so difficult to pin down. While scientists are making progress in understanding the brain mechanisms associated with seasonal depression, there is much to know and document.

You feel good about yourself and have a sense of self-control and accomplishment. You also realize that things don't bother you as much as they used to. You seem better able to handle stress. Feelings of self-control and accomplishment, an increased energy level, and the physical diversion may account for your increased ability to handle stress, but there is a physiological explanation involving neurotransmitters that may contribute to your psychological well-being.

When individuals run long distances, one candidate for explaining the euphoric feeling of "runner's high" is elevated levels of natural opiates called endorphins.

As early as the fourth century B.C. the Greeks were aware of the euphoric power of the wild poppy. But it was not until more than 2,000 years later that the magical formula behind the opium's addictive action was discovered. In the early 1970s, scientists found that opium plugs into a sophisticated system of natural opiates lying deep within the pathways of the brain (Pert & Snyder, 1973). The system seems to be involved in shielding the body from pain and elevating feelings of pleasure. A long-distance runner, a woman giving childbirth, and a person in shock after a car wreck all have elevated levels of the natural opiates, which are called **endorphins.**

The influence of some neurotransmitters is excitatory, while the effect of others is inhibitory, and some can function in both excitatory and inhibitory ways depending on what information-processing job is to be done. As the neurotransmitter moves across the synaptic gap to the receiving neuron, its molecules may spread across a large spatial area or be confined to a small space. The molecules may come in rapid sequence or be spaced out. The receiving neuron must integrate all of this information and decide whether or not to fire.

Glial Cells

It was the Spanish neuroanatomist, Santiago Ramón y Cajal who discovered that the brain is made up of two types of cells—neurons, or nerve cells, and glial cells. Somewhat amazingly there are about ten times as many **glial cells** in the brain as neurons, putting the number of glial cells at about 100 to 200 billion! Ramón y Cajal used advances in microscope techniques to discover the glial cells early in the twentieth century. He described the cells as looking like glue between the nerve cells.

Unfortunately, we do not know as much about glial cells as we do about neurons. We do know that glial cells do not have axons or dendrites, and they are not specialized to send or receive information. They probably function as

■ ■

Concept Table 2.2

The Brain and Nervous System		
Concept	**Processes/related ideas**	**Characteristics/description**
Early approaches	Their nature	Suggested that various parts of the brain were responsible for various aspects of behavior.
The elegant organization of the nervous system	The central nervous system	Consists of the brain and spinal cord—contains more than 99 percent of all neurons.
	The peripheral nervous system	A network of nerves that connect the brain and spinal cord to other parts of the body. Two major divisions are the somatic nervous system and the autonomic nervous system. The autonomic system is subdivided into the sympathetic and parasympathetic systems.
Neurons	Pathways of neurons	Afferent nerves (sensory nerves) carry input to the brain; efferent nerves (motor nerves) carry the output away from the brain; interneurons do most of the information processing within the brain.
	Structure of the neuron	The three basic parts are the cell body, dendrite, and axon. The myelin sheath speeds information transmission.
	The nerve impulse	Neurons send information in the form of brief impulses, or "waves," of electricity. These waves are called the action potential and operate according to the all-or-none principle.
	Synapses and neurotransmitters	The gaps between neurons are synapses. The neural impulse reaches the axon terminal and stimulates the release of neurotransmitters from tiny vesicles. These carry information to the next neuron, where it fits like a key in a lock. Important neurotransmitters are GABA, acetylcholine, norepinephrine, serotinin, and endorphins. Some neurotransmitters are excitatory, others inhibitory.
	The glial cells	Provide physical support for neurons and are thought to be involved in the regulation and nutrition of neurons.

physical supports for neurons. They seem to regulate the internal environment of the brain, especially the fluid surrounding neurons, and provide nutrition for neurons. For example, in two investigations, neurons grew more rapidly and prolifically when placed in a solution containing glial cells than neurons floating in the same solution without glial cells (Banker, 1980; Kennedy & Fok-Seang, 1986). The myelin sheath that covers most axons is made up of glial cells.

Ramón y Cajal could not see the cells of the brain with his naked eye when he discovered the distinction between neurons and glial cells at the beginning of this century. Today the techniques for studying the brain are far more advanced, although the scientific study of brains still involves the microscope and staining techniques. Read Psychology 2.2 for a look at some of the technological advances in the study of the brain.

It has been some time since you read about Phineas Gage, Franz Joseph Gall, and Broca's patient Tan. Since then you have read about the elegant organization of the entire nervous system and how information processing works at the cellular level in the brain. A summary of these aspects of the nervous system is presented in concept table 2.2.

■ ■ ■ ■ ■ ■ ■ ■ ■ ■ ■ ■ ■ ■ ■ ■ ■

Psychology 2.2

Brain Watching

■ Franz Joseph Gall would be amazed. Were he alive today he might marvel at the sophisticated devices available to monitor the brain's activity and undoubtedly be humbled by it all. We no longer feel the bumps on a person's skull like Gall did in the early nineteenth century. And we no longer study only dead brains, because twentieth century techniques have become so sophisticated we can "see" inside of fully functioning brains.

High-powered microscopes are widely used in neuroscience research. Neurons are stained with the salts of various heavy metals such as silver and lead. These stains coat only a small portion of any group of neurons. The stains allow neuroscientists to view and study each and every part of a neuron in microscopic detail. The photo of the neuron back in figure 2.9 was made possible by staining the neurons with silver metal, then photographing them through a high-powered microscope.

The electroencephalograph is widely used to monitor the electrical activity of the brain and nervous system. This instrument produces a record of brain-wave activity referred to as an electroencephalogram (or EEG), which is obtained by placing a small electrode on the organism's scalp. The electrode measures the electrical activity of thousands of cells in the brain. The device has

been used widely to assess brain damage, epilepsy, and other problems. In chapter 4 we will see how the EEG has been helpful in charting sleeping and waking patterns.

Not every recording of brain activity is made with electrodes on the surface of the brain. In single-unit recording, a portrayal of the electrical activity of a single neuron is obtained by inserting a very thin wire or needle in or near an individual cell. The wire or needle transmits the neuron's electrical activity to an amplifier.

For years X rays have been used to determine damage inside our bodies, both in the brain and in other locations. But a single X ray of the brain is very hard to interpret because it shows the three-dimensional nature of the body's interior in a two-dimensional picture. Medical engineers have invented a device called the computerized axial tomography, or CAT scan for short, which takes a number of X rays of the brain's interior from many different angles. The pictures are transmitted to a computer that improves their quality. The CAT scan gives more specific information about the location of damage due to a stroke, language disorder, or loss of memory.

Another scanning device, developed more recently than the CAT scan, is the positron-emission

tomography, or PET scan. To do the scan, small portions of a radioactive substance are injected into the brain. Detectors record the location of the substance. The radioactive substance being monitored tends to have its greatest concentration in the areas of the brain that are the most active. As shown in figure 2.C, the radioactive substance lights up the brain in different ways depending on whether the individual is in a resting state or is looking at objects and naming them. In some instances, the PET scan is a very effective method of analyzing the nature of brain damage, as in the case of a stroke (Fox, 1984).

One final technique deserves mention. Nuclear magnetic resonance (NMR) is the most recent development in brain watching. Another name for this technique is MRI, or magnetic resonance imaging. The latter name is gaining popularity with physicians, who fear that patients may be reluctant to submit to tests with the word nuclear in the name. The technique involves placing a magnetic field around the person's body and using radio waves to construct images of brain tissues and biochemical activity. It provides very clear pictures of the brain's interior, does not require the brain to be injected with a substance, and there is no peril of radiation overexposure.

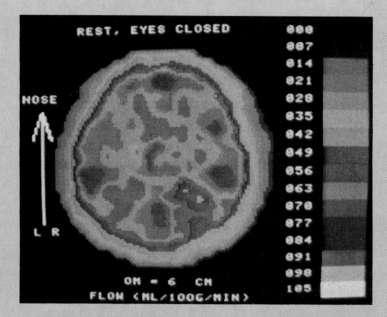

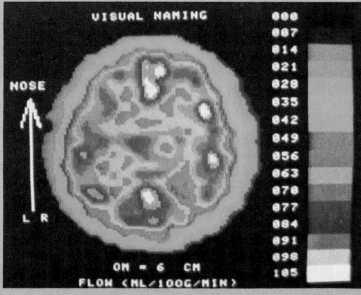

Figure 2.C
These images are created by computer interpretation of multiple X-rays. The image on the top is of an individual who is resting with eyes closed. The image on the bottom is of an individual who is looking at objects and naming them.

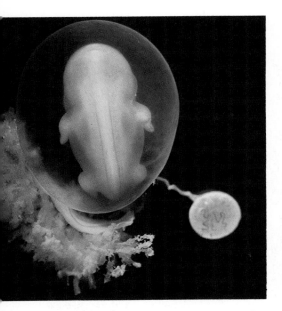

Figure 2.16
The primitive, tubular appearance of the nervous system at six weeks in the human embryo.

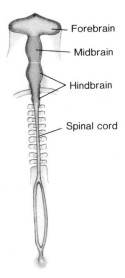

— Forebrain

— Midbrain

— Hindbrain

— Spinal cord

Figure 2.17
The major brain regions as they appear early in the development of a human embryo. Notice that the hindbrain is at the lowest level, the midbrain at mid-level, and the forebrain at the highest level in the brain.

The Brain

Most of the information about the brain thus far has been about one or two cells. Earlier we indicated that about 99 percent of all neurons in the nervous system are located in the brain and the spinal cord. Neurons do not float idly in the brain. They are connected in precise ways to compose the various structures of the brain.

Embryological Development and Levels in the Brain

During embryological development (between conception and birth), the nervous system begins as a long, hollow tube on the back of the embryo. As the nervous system develops, the brain forms into a large mass of neurons and loses the tubular appearance. At birth, the initial primitive organization of the brain is hardly recognizable because so much growth and differentiation have occurred. Figure 2.16 reveals dramatically the tubular shape of the human nervous system in a six-week-old embryo.

The elongated tube changes shape and develops into three major divisions: the hindbrain, which is the portion of the brain adjacent to the spinal cord; the midbrain, which is above the hindbrain; and the forebrain, which is at the highest level of the brain (see figure 2.17). The brain's different levels and the major structures at those levels are shown in figure 2.18.

Hindbrain

The **hindbrain,** located at the rear of the skull is the lowest portion of the brain. The two main parts of the hindbrain are the medulla and the cerebellum. The **medulla** helps to control breathing and regulates some of the reflexes that allow us to maintain our upright posture. The **cerebellum** is just above and to the rear of the medulla. It consists of two rounded structures, generally thought to play important roles in the motor system. Leg and arm movements are coordinated at the cerebellum, for example. When we play golf, practice the piano, or perfect our moves on the dance floor, the cerebellum is hard at work. If a higher portion of the brain commands us to write the number 7, it is the cerebellum that integrates the necessary muscular activities to do this. If the cerebellum becomes damaged, our movement becomes uncoordinated and jerky.

Midbrain

The **midbrain,** located between the hindbrain and forebrain, is an area where many nerve fiber systems ascend and descend to connect the higher and lower portions of the brain. In particular, the midbrain is involved in the relay of information between the brain and the eyes and ears. The ability to attend to an object visually, for example, is linked to one bundle of neurons in the midbrain. A section near the bottom of the midbrain is damaged when an individual has Parkinson's disease, a deterioration of movement that produces rigidity and tremors in the elderly.

Two systems in the midbrain are of special interest. One is the **reticular formation** (see figure 2.19), a diffuse collection of neurons involved in stereotyped patterns of behavior such as walking, sleeping, or turning to attend to a sudden noise. The other system is comprised of small groups of neurons that use the special neurotransmitters serotonin, dopamine, and norepinephrine. These three groups contain relatively few cells, but they send their axons to a remarkable variety of brain regions, perhaps explaining their involvement in high-level, integrative functions.

But it is not the hindbrain or midbrain that separates humans from animals. In humans, it is the forebrain that becomes enlarged and specialized (see figure 2.20).

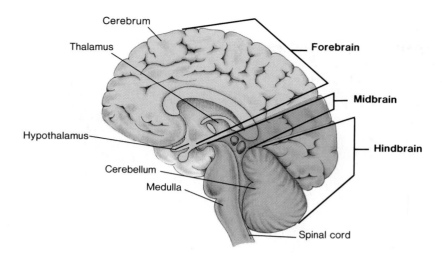

Figure 2.18
The brain structures located at different levels of the brain. The hindbrain is composed of the medulla and cerebellum. The forebrain includes the hypothalamus, thalamus, and cerebrum.

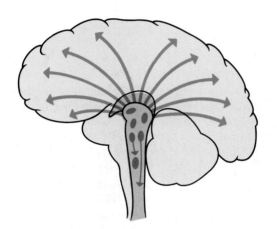

Figure 2.19
The reticular formation is a network of nerve fibers that runs through the brain stem. The arrows shown radiating from the brain stem are drawn to show the connections of the reticular formation to the higher portions of the brain in the neocortex. The reticular formation is involved in arousal and attention.

Brain evolution

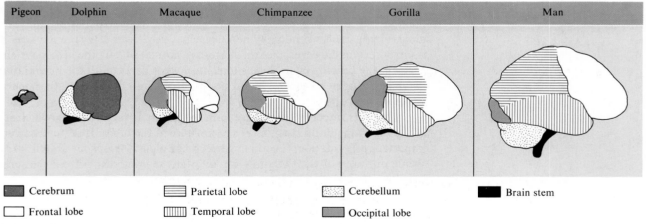

Figure 2.20
The evolution of the brain. As the brain has evolved, its more advanced functions have become centered in the forebrain. The higher up the evolutionary tree an animal is, the greater the size and complexity of the forebrain. In such mammals as the dolphin, folded outgrowths of the brain have become the dominating cerebral hemisphere, allowing greater thinking capacity. In primates like the macaque, chimpanzee, gorilla, and human, specified areas have evolved in the hemisphere.

Figure 2.21
A view of some of the reciprocal connections of the limbic system.

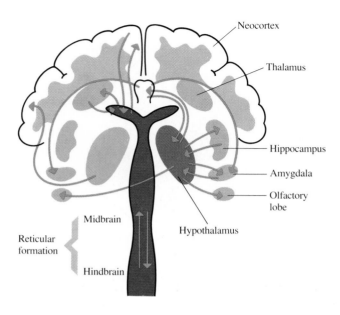

Forebrain

You try to understand what all of these terms and parts of the brain mean. You talk with friends and plan a party for this weekend. You remember it has been six months since you went to the dentist and that it is time to make an appointment. You are confident you will do well on the next test in this course. All of these experiences and millions more would be impossible without the highest region of the human brain—the **forebrain.** Among its most important structures are the limbic system, thalamus, basal ganglia, hypothalamus, and neocortex.

The **limbic system** seems to play important roles in both memory and emotion. The two principal structures in the limbic system are the **amygdala** and the **hippocampus** (see figure 2.21). Both receive information from the neocortex and the brain stem. Let's think further about the limbic system's role in memory. One function of the limbic system appears to be the storage of memories. People with extensive damage to the hippocampal-amygdaloid regions simply cannot retain any new conscious memories after the damage. It is fairly certain, however, that memories are not stored "in" the limbic system. Instead, the limbic system seems to control what parts of all the information passing through the cortex should be "printed" into durable, lasting neural traces in the cortex.

Another important structure in the forebrain is the **thalamus,** which sits at the top of the brain stem in the central core of the brain. It serves as a very important relay station, functioning much like a giant telephone switchboard. While one area of the thalamus works to orient information from the sense receptors (hearing, seeing, etc.), another region seems to be involved in sleep and wakefulness, having ties with the reticular formation (see figure 2.21 for the location of the thalamus).

Yet another structure in the forebrain is the **basal ganglia.** These are a collection of structures essential to starting and stopping voluntary movements. Individuals with damage to the basal ganglia suffer either from unwanted movement (such as constant writhing or jerking of limbs) or too little movement (as in the slow and deliberate movements of those with Parkinson's disease).

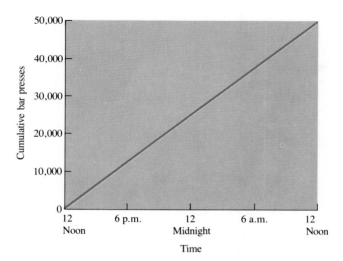

Figure 2.22
This graph vividly shows how often a rat pushed a bar during one 24-hour period just to receive a mild electric shock to the hypothalamus.

The **hypothalamus** is another important structure in the forebrain. Much smaller than the thalamus and about the size of a kidney bean, it controls three very enjoyable activities—eating, drinking, and sex. Perhaps the best way to describe the function of the hypothalamus is in terms of a regulator. It is sensitive to changes in the blood and neural input, and it responds by influencing the secretion of hormones and neural outputs. For example, if the temperature of circulating blood near the hypothalamus is increased by just one or two degrees, certain cells in the hypothalamus start increasing their rate of firing. As a result, a whole chain of events is set in motion. Increased circulation through the skin and sweat glands occurs immediately to release this heat from the body. The cooled blood circulating to the hypothalamus slows down the activity of some of the neurons there, stopping the process when the temperature is just right—37.1° C. These temperature-sensitive neurons function like a finely tuned thermostat in returning the body to a balanced state.

The hypothalamus also is involved in emotional states and stress, playing an important role as an integrative location for handling stress. Much of this integration is accomplished through the hypothalamus's action on the pituitary gland, located just below it. If certain areas of the hypothalamus are electrically stimulated, a feeling of pleasure results. In a classic experiment, James Olds and Peter Milner (1954) implanted an electrode in the hypothalamus of a rat's brain. When the rat ran to a corner of an enclosed area, a mild electric current was delivered to its hypothalamus. The researchers thought the electric current was punishment for the rat and would cause it to avoid the corner. Much to their surprise, the rat kept returning to the corner. Olds and Milner believed they had discovered a pleasure center in the hypothalamus.

Olds (1958) conducted further experiments and found that rats would press bars until they dropped over from exhaustion just to continue to receive a mild electric shock to their hypothalamus. Figure 2.22 shows how one rat pressed a bar more than 2,000 times an hour for a period of twenty-four hours to receive the stimulus to its hypothalamus. Today researchers agree that the hypothalamus is involved in pleasurable feelings, but that other areas of the brain such as the limbic system and a bundle of fibers in the forebrain are important in the link between brain and pleasure as well (Kornetsky, 1986). More about the role of the hypothalamus in the regulation of hunger and sex appears in chapter 11. Its importance in emotion and stress is described in chapter 12.

Figure 2.23
The two halves of the human brain are clearly seen in this photograph. The two halves are called hemispheres.

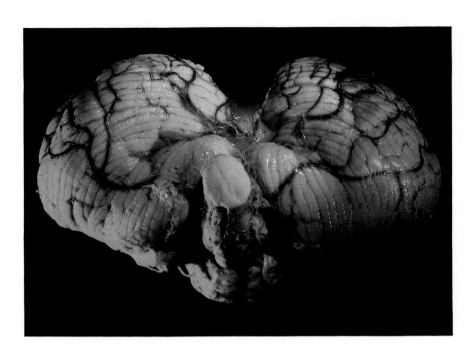

Figure 2.24
The location of the four lobes of the human brain.

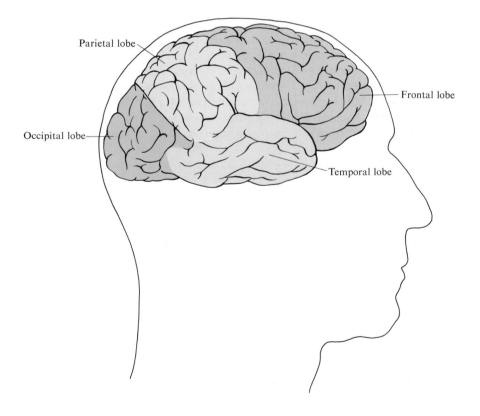

A final region of the forebrain, the **neocortex,** is the most recently developed part of the brain in the evolutionary scheme. The neural tissue that comprises the neocortex is the largest part of the brain in volume (about 80 percent) and covers the lower portions of the brain almost like a large cap. Let's look at the neocortex in more detail.

Exploring the Neocortex

The wrinkled surface of the neocortex is divided into two halves (see figure 2.23). These two halves are called hemispheres and each is divided into four lobes—frontal, parietal, temporal, and occipital (see figure 2.24). It is important to know that these lobes are not strictly functional regions but rather conveniently labeled anatomical regions. Nonetheless, there are functional differences among the lobes, and they often are used in somewhat loose ways to describe functions. For example, the correspondence between lobes is clearest for the **occipital lobe,** where primarily visual functioning occurs. The **temporal lobe** is associated with hearing, the **frontal lobe** is thought to be involved in the control of voluntary muscles as well as being the seat of higher intelligence, and the **parietal lobe** is involved in body sensation.

In the same way that the different lobes of the neocortex are associated with different processes, different regions of the lobes have different jobs. Scientists have determined this primarily through topographic mapping. Two of the most widely used types of topographic maps are projection maps and functional maps. Projection maps are made by electrically stimulating areas of the brain and detecting the resulting behavior or by recording the electrical activity of the neocortex during certain behaviors (Udin & Fawcett, in press).

Wilder Penfield, a neurosurgeon at the Montreal Neurological Institute, worked with a number of patients with very serious forms of epilepsy. Penfield frequently performed surgery to remove portions of the epileptic patient's brain. He realized that removing a portion of the brain might destroy or impair some of the individual's functions. To avoid this, he developed a map that showed how particular places in the neocortex are linked with particular functions. Penfield (1947) used electrical stimulation of the brain to develop a map of the neocortex that would serve as a valuable guide in performing operations on the brain.

Penfield's patients were given a local anesthetic so they would remain conscious during the operation. After he opened the skull and exposed the outer layer of neocortex, he stimulated different areas with a thin electric probe (see figure 2.25). Penfield performed hundreds of these operations, each time electrically stimulating the patient's brain and noting the behavioral responses. Figure 2.26 shows the locations on the neocortex linked with specific sensory and motor areas of the body. Notice that for both sensory and motor areas there is a point-to-point relation between parts of the body and a location on the neocortex. Also notice that the face and hands are given proportionally more space than other body parts. Because the face and hands are capable of finer perceptions and movements than other body areas, they need more neocortex representation.

So far our description of the neocortex has focused on sensory and motor areas, but more than 75 percent of the neocortex is made up of areas referred to as association areas, or the **association cortex.** These many large areas are not directly related to sensory or motor processes. It is believed that the association areas are responsible for many of our highest human accomplishments, such as thinking and problem solving.

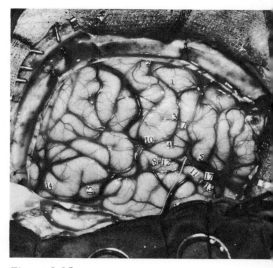

Figure 2.25
The exposed neocortex of one of Penfield's patients. The numbers identify the locations that Penfield stimulated with a very thin electric probe. When he stimulated the area marked by number 11, for example, the patient opened his mouth, sneezed, and began chewing.

Figure 2.26
The location of motor and sensory areas on the cortex. (a) Motor areas involved with the control of voluntary muscles; (b) sensory areas involved with cutaneous and certain other senses.

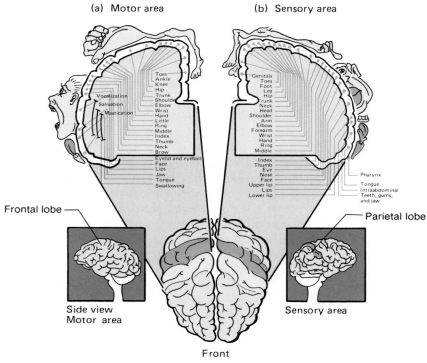

Of special interest is the finding that damage to a specific part of the association cortex often does not result in a specific loss of function. With the exception of language areas (which are localized), loss of function seems to depend more on the extent of damage to the association areas than to the specific location of the damage. By observing brain-damaged individuals and using the mapping technique, scientists have found that the association cortex is involved in linguistic and perceptual functioning. The largest portion of association areas is located in the frontal lobe, directly under the forehead. Damage to this area does not lead to sensory or motor loss. Indeed, it is this area that may be most directly related to thinking and problem solving. Early experimentation even referred to the frontal lobe as the center of intelligence, but more recent research suggests that frontal lobe damage may not result in a lowering of intelligence. Planning and judgment are characteristics often associated with the frontal lobe. Personality also may be linked with the frontal lobe. Recall the misfortune of Phineas Gage, whose personality radically changed after he had experienced frontal lobe damage.

Functional regions of the neocortex, such as the lip region on the map in figure 2.26, can be subdivided further into **cortical columns.** Cortical columns are complex multicellular ensembles with the basic columnar unit made up of 100 or so vertically interconnected neurons that span the layers of the cortex (Mountcastle, 1975). The special function of such columns in the brain may be their ability to communicate with columns in other regions in a temporary way. The physiologist who discovered these multicellular ensembles, Vernon Mountcastle, believes the higher order of the columns receives, filters, and integrates information from several senses, such as hearing and vision. Mountcastle (1975, 1986) speculates that the columns hold the key to understanding how conscious awareness is created. To learn more about how these important cortical columns work in integrating information turn to Psychology 2.3.

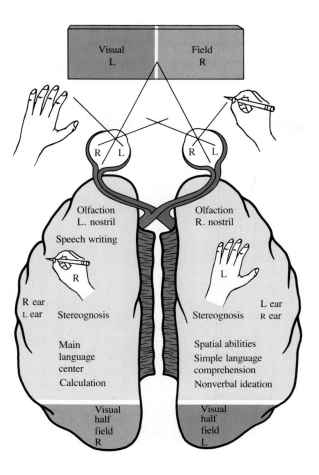

Figure 2.27
Schematic drawing to show the functions separated by surgery for brain disorder. This is a simplified summary based on findings in neuroanatomy, cortical lesion data, and postoperative testing.

In our discussion you learned that the neocortex is divided into two hemispheres. The fascinating story of information processing in the neocortex involves lobes, maps, and columns, but it could not be completely told without referring to how the two sides of the brain work.

Split-Brain Research and the Cerebral Hemispheres

The two hemispheres of the brain are connected by a large bundle of axons called the **corpus callosum.** For many years scientists were unaware of the function of this bundle, although it was speculated that it was involved in the communication of information between the two hemispheres. The corpus callosum of an epileptic patient known as W. J. was deliberately severed in an operation performed in the 1960s. Neurosurgeons thought the surgery might reduce the unbearable seizures he was experiencing by limiting them to only one side of his brain. Roger Sperry and his associates (1968) examined W. J. to see how information comes into and goes out of the left and right hemispheres of the brain. Put briefly, the right hemisphere receives information only from the left side of the body, and the left hemisphere gets information only from the right side of the body. Consequently, if you hold an object in your left hand only the right hemisphere of your brain can detect this. If you see an object in the right side of your visual field, only the left hemisphere of your brain registers this event (see figure 2.27). For people with a normal corpus callosum, both hemispheres of the brain detect such information because it can be communicated from one hemisphere to the other via the corpus callosum. But what happens to individuals when their corpus callosum is cut?

■ ■ ■ ■ ■ ■ ■ ■ ■ ■ ■ ■ ■ ■ ■ ■ ■

Psychology 2.3

Cortical Columns—Ensembles in the Vast Sheet of Neural Tissue

■ You have learned that the neocortex is a vast sheet of neural tissue that is draped over the entire forebrain. Although the neocortex is immense, and contains many millions of nerve cells, we can get a fairly good idea of how it works, and how brains work in general, if we look closely at the organization of the system.

Let's start with a simple problem. When a mosquito bites your arm, how does your brain "know" where the bite occurred? The answer lies in topographic maps. The nerve fibers from your arm, which carry the information about the bite, make their way through the nervous system in a very orderly fashion. At each relay, they make precise and orderly connections, and so it continues all the way to the neocortex. The topographic map of the body surface in figure 2.26 shows which part of the neocortex is connected to which part of the skin. Because the skin is sending information, the cortical map shows which part of the neocortex is "listening to" which region of the skin. It is as if the neocortex were a huge committee of people sitting together collecting information about some nationwide issue. If

each committee member has a private phone line from one specific distant city, then you can see how the group would know the source of incoming information—if Sally's phone rings, the information has to be from Detroit; George's means news from Cincinnati.

Now you can see why organization is so crucial in brain function. If the wires are crossed, the information will be scrambled. Also, you can now see why each part of your brain is vital to overall function. What news could we get from Detroit if Sally were unavailable to answer her telephone?

In our example of the neocortex as a committee, the incoming telephone lines represent the nerve fibers coming to the neocortex from distant body regions and sense organs. But what in the neocortex could represent the members of the committee? The answer is cortical columns. The cortical sheet is really more like a layer cake than a single sheet, and each layer is made of nerve cells. Push a round cookie cutter down through the cake, and you have a cortical column: a cylinder of stacked layers.

What does a cortical column do? It processes information from one very specific part of the sensory world. One of the best examples of this is found in the part of the neocortex in mice that processes information from the face. Mice use their whiskers to explore their world. Careful mapping studies have shown that each single whisker has its own private processor in the sensory cortex. The processor for a single whisker is a single column, or barrel, in the face part of the neocortex. Thus when one whisker is touched, one column processes the information through its layers to determine how hard and how long the push has been (Woolsey & Van der Loos, 1970).

These columns, or barrels, are shown in figure 2.D. One fascinating thing that has been learned from studying these particular cortical columns concerns the brain's ability to adjust its organization. If one or two whiskers are removed from a mouse's face very early in life, the cortical barrels reorganize themselves. Those columns that would have processed information from the missing whiskers disappear, and the neighboring columns expand in size (Woolsey & Wann, 1976).

The processing of many important aspects of our psychological makeup primarily takes place in either the left or the right hemisphere of the brain. The left hemisphere seems to control the ability to use language. The right hemisphere does not seem to be able to transform sensations into words. Patients in Sperry's experiments (Sperry, 1974; Sperry & Gazzaniga, 1967) such as W. J., whose corpus callosum was severed, could describe in words sensations that were received by the left hemisphere (a stimulus in the right visual

So now you have some notion of how your brain can sort and recognize all of the different sensory signals that flow constantly into it. Each bit of information is sent to its private processor—the cortical column—and the business of extracting and digesting the news is begun. The other parts of your neocortex are also made up of columns. In your visual cortex, for example, single columns are connected to specific parts of your retina, so they "watch for" visual information from specific parts of your visual field. Also, all of the columns in a region of the neocortex send their information on in a converging pattern. In that way, for example, information extracted from one whisker can be combined with information from neighboring whiskers to give the brain an integrated picture.

Figure 2.D
The whiskers on the right side of a mouse's face (a) project to the columns in the cerebral cortex (b).

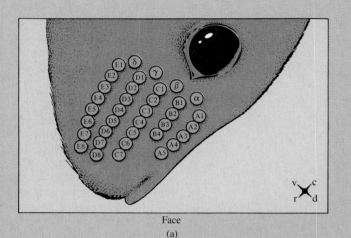

Face
(a)

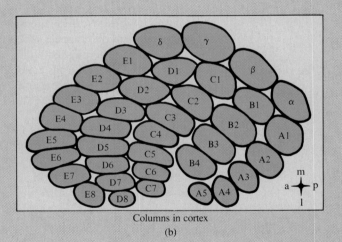

Columns in cortex
(b)

field). However, these same patients could not describe in words sensations that were received by the right hemisphere (a stimulus in the left visual field). Because the corpus callosum was severed, the information could not be communicated from one hemisphere to the next. More recent studies of split-brain patients suggest that language indeed is a very *infrequent* occurrence in the right hemisphere (Gazzaniga, 1983, 1986).

While the right hemisphere does not control language, it is involved in some types of abstract thinking, formation of simple concepts, and imagery. In one recent experiment (Kosslyn, 1986), a split-brain patient was able to create the general outlines of an image (in this case the shape of a beagle's ears) with either hemisphere but could fill in the details of the image only with the left hemisphere. The right hemisphere seems to have more control over perceptual responses based on touch, and emotional reactions seem to occur more strongly in the right hemisphere as well (Leg & Bryden, 1979).

An intriguing extension of the concept of the brain's hemispheres controlling different functions was proposed by Robert Ornstein (1972). He believes the relative dominance of one hemisphere over the other helps to explain the nature of human consciousness. From his view, consciousness is made up of two parts, one rational and intellectual, the other intuitive and artistic. In Ornstein's own words,

> The left hemisphere of the cortex which subtends language and mathematics seems to process information primarily in a linear, sequential manner, appropriate to its specialities. The right side of the cortex processes its input more as a "patterned whole," that is, in a more simultaneous manner than does the left. This simultaneous processing is advantageous for the integration of diffuse inputs, such as for orienting oneself in space, when motor, kinesthetic, and visual input must be quickly integrated. This mode of information processing, too, would seem to underlie an "intuitive" rather than an "intellectual" integration of complex entities. (p. 79)

Ornstein goes on to argue that the differences between the two hemispheres may serve as a basis for differences in thought between Western and Eastern cultures. Western thought, which tends to be rational, may show a left-hemisphere dominance, whereas Eastern thought, which tends not to be rational, may be dominated by the right hemisphere. It should be emphasized that in people whose corpus collosums are normal, the two hemispheres of the brain work together in processing information. Some psychologists believe that this point is overlooked as the functions of the left and right hemispheres are dramatized.

As we have explored the intricate and detailed nature of the brain, we have described how certain regions of the brain have become specialized to perform certain functions. But as we see next, there is a great deal of connectedness among various brain parts and regions—much of our psychological functioning depends on such integration.

Integration of Function in the Brain

How do all of the various brain regions cooperate to produce the wondrous complexity of thought and behavior that characterize humans? Part of the answer to this question, such as how the brain solves an algebra problem or writes a good poem, is still beyond the grasp of neuroscience. Still, we can get a sense of integrative brain function by considering something such as the act of escaping from a burning building. Gall and his phrenologists might have suggested that such a behavior was controlled by an "escaping from danger" center in the brain. Let us compare that view with a more contemporary one.

Imagine you are sitting at your desk writing letters when fire breaks out behind you. The sound of crackling flames is relayed from your ear, through the thalamus, to your auditory cortex and on to the auditory association cortex.

cathy®   by Cathy Guisewite

At each stage the stimulus energy has been processed to extract information, and at some stage, probably at the association cortex level, the sounds are finally matched with something like a neural memory representing previous sounds of fires you have heard. The association to "fire" sets new machinery in motion. Your attention (guided in part by the reticular formation) swings to the auditory signal being held in your association cortex, and simultaneously (again guided by reticular systems) your head turns toward the noise. Now your visual association cortex reports in: "objects matching flames are present." In other association regions, the visual and auditory reports are synthesized ("we have things that look and sound like fire"), and neural associations representing potential actions ("flee") are activated. But firing the neurons that code the plan to flee will not get you out of the chair. You must engage the basal ganglia, and from there the commands will arise to set brain stem, motor cortex, and cerebellum to the actual task of transporting you out of the room.

Which part of your brain did you use to escape? Virtually all systems had some role; each was quite specific, and together they generated the behavior. By the way, you would probably remember an event such as a fire in your room. That is because your limbic circuitry would have likely issued the "start print" command when the significant association "fire" was first triggered. The next time the sounds of crackling flames reach your auditory association cortex, the associations triggered will include those of this most recent escape.

Since our discussion of the cellular level of the brain we have encountered a great many of the brain's structures and regions. To help you remember these structures and their functions, as well as the important point about integration in the brain, study concept table 2.3. Incidentally another system, in addition to the nervous system, was placed in operation when you heard the sound of crackling flames—the endocrine system. The endocrine system took longer than the nervous system to go into action, but its chemical messages were pouring into your bloodstream and on to different organs of your body in a matter of seconds.

■ ■ ■ ■ ■ ■ ■ ■ ■ ■ ■ ■ ■ ■ ■ ■ ■ ■ ■

Concept Table 2.3

The Brain		
Concept	**Processes/related ideas**	**Characteristics/description**
Embryological development and levels in the brain	Hindbrain, midbrain, forebrain	A neural tube develops into the hindbrain (lowest level), midbrain (middle level), and forebrain (highest level). The main structures of the hindbrain are the medulla and cerebellum. The midbrain's major structure is the reticular formation. The forebrain consists of the limbic system (which also runs through the midbrain), thalamus, basal ganglia, hypothalamus, and neocortex. Each is specialized to perform certain information processing jobs. The neocortex is a vast sheet of neural tissue.
Exploring the neocortex	Hemispheres and lobes	The wrinkled surface of the neocortex is divided into two hemispheres (left and right) and four lobes (frontal, parietal, temporal, and occipital).
	Topographic mapping, the association cortex, and columns	Topographic mapping has helped scientists determine the neocortex's role in different behaviors. The neocortex consists of sensory areas, motor areas, association areas, and cortical columns.
	Split-brain research and the cerebral hemispheres	Pioneered by Sperry, this involves severing the corpus collosum. This led to the conclusion that language is mainly a left-hemisphere function, while touch and emotion are predominantly right-hemisphere functions. In normal people, the two hemispheres work together to process information.
Integration of function in the brain	Its nature	Most psychological functions do not involve a single structure in the brain but rather the integration of information by a number of structures.

The Endocrine System—Glandular Information Processing

Recall that the autonomic nervous system involves connections with internal organs, regulating processes like respiration, heart rate, and digestion. A number of important body reactions produced by the autonomic nervous system result from the action of this system on the endocrine glands.

The **endocrine glands** release their chemical products directly into the bloodstream. These chemical products are called **hormones,** and they travel more slowly than nerve impulses with the exception of adrenaline and nor-adrenaline, which act very quickly on a number of body tissues. Hormones travel in the bloodstream to all parts of the body; the membrane of every cell has receptors to one or more hormones.

The endocrine glands consist of the hypothalamus and the pituitary gland at the base of the brain, the thyroid and parathyroid glands at the front of the neck, the adrenal glands just above the kidneys, the pancreas in the abdomen, and the ovaries in the female's pelvis and the testes in the male's scrotum (see figure 2.28). Other hormones are produced as well, including several in the gastrointestinal tract that control digestion. In much the same way that the brain's control of muscular activity is constantly monitored and altered to suit the information received by the brain, so is the action of the endocrine glands continuously monitored and changed by the nervous, hormonal, and chemical information sent to them.

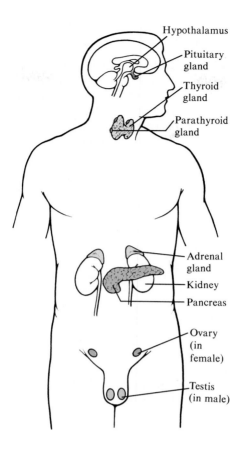

Figure 2.28
The locations of major endocrine glands. The pituitary gland releases hormones that regulate the hormone secretions of the other glands. The pituitary gland is itself regulated by the hypothalamus.

The Pituitary Gland

The **pituitary gland** is an important endocrine gland that sits at the base of the skull and is about the size of a pea. The anterior (front) part of the pituitary is known as the master gland because almost all of its hormones direct the activity of target glands elsewhere in the body. For example, follicle stimulating hormone (FSH) produced by the pituitary monitors the level of sex hormones in the ovaries of females and testes of males. Though most pituitary hormones influence a specific organ, growth hormone (GH) acts on all tissues to produce growth during childhood and adolescence. Dwarfs have too little of this hormone, giants too much.

The Adrenal Glands

The **adrenal glands** play an important role in our moods, our energy level, and our ability to cope with stress. Each adrenal gland secretes epinephrine (also called adrenaline) and some norepinephrine (also called noradrenaline). Epinephrine helps ready the individual for an emergency by acting on smooth muscles, the heart, stomach, intestines, and sweat glands. Epinephrine also stimulates the reticular formation, which in turn arouses the sympathetic nervous system, and this system subsequently excites the adrenal glands to produce more epinephrine. Norepinephrine also alerts the individual for emergency situations by interacting with the pituitary and the liver. You may remember that norepinephrine also functions as a neurotransmitter when released by neurons. In the case of the adrenal glands, norepinephrine is released as a hormone. In both instances, norepinephrine is a conveyor of information—in the first instance to neurons, in the second to glands (Simpson, in press).

   We have been talking about the brain and nervous system at length and have not used the word *mind* much in doing so. As you read about the brain, you may have wondered about the relation of brain to mind. If so, you are like many curious philosophers and scientists who have pondered this connection for centuries.

Brain and Mind

Is everything that makes us human no more than the interaction of chemicals and electrical charges inside the labyrinth of the brain? Or is there something more? A popular joke told by Thomas Hewitt Key in the 19th century went like this:

> What's the matter?
> Never mind.
> What is mind?
> No matter.

Though the Victorians may have believed that mind is mind and matter is matter and the two never meet, psychologists today are not so sure.

   Two prominent positions on the mind-body issue are monism and dualism. **Monism** stresses a single underlying existence of mind and body—in other words, mind and body are inseparable. In this view, mind is brain and brain is mind. By contrast, proponents of **dualism** say mind and body have a separate existence, the mind being nonphysical, the brain being physical. One version of dualism proposed by philosopher René Descartes argues that while mind and body have a separate existence, they can interact (Marx & Hillix, 1987).

   Interest in the relation of mind and brain has increased in the last decade due to surges of interest in the neurosciences as well as cognitive psychology (Pribram, 1986). The philosopher Popper and the scientist Eccles put their minds (or is it brains?) together, agreeing with Descartes that mind and brain maintain a separate interactiveness (Popper & Eccles, 1977). The neuroscientist Sperry and the philosopher Searle declare themselves clearly on the side of mind, believing that mind moves and controls matter (Sperry, 1976; Searle, 1979). By contrast, the famous behaviorist B. F. Skinner (1976, 1987) has given up hope for a science of mental life.

   There is no known scientific method to help choose among the possible answers to the mind-body issue. Some brain researchers, though, believe the concept of mind is headed for a fateful death as they chip away at the depths of the brain and uncover more information about its electrochemical basis. Still there are skeptics who argue that such human characteristics as will and consciousness will forever elude brain researchers.

   While the mind-body issue has not been settled, and may never be, our biological heritage is undeniable. In this chapter we have seen how evolution, genes, and the brain influence our behavior. In the next chapter you will learn more about the brain as we investigate the nature of sensation and perception, studying such intriguing questions as how we see, hear, smell, touch, and feel pain.

Summary

I. **Evolution**

Charles Darwin proposed the theory of evolution. Its main principle is natural selection, which argues that genetic diversity occurs in each species. In this diversity some organisms have characteristics that help them adapt to their environment. These beneficial characteristics are likely to be perpetuated.

II. **Genetics**

The nucleus of each human cell contains forty-six chromosomes, which are composed of DNA. Genes, the unit of hereditary information, are short segments of DNA. The genes act as a blueprint for cells to reproduce themselves and manufacture proteins that maintain life. Most genetic information involves combinations of genes. Scientists believe both genes *and* environment are necessary for an organism to exist; every behavior is due to some degree to the interaction of genes and environment. Scientists use different methods to assess genetic influences—animals can be inbred or selectively bred, but with humans the twin study and the adoption study are used. The controversial contemporary theory of sociobiology argues that all behavior is motivated by a desire to dominate the gene pool.

III. **Early Approaches to the Brain and the Elegant Organization of the Nervous System**

Early approaches suggested that various parts of the brain were responsible for various aspects of behavior. The elegant organization of the nervous system is divided into the central and peripheral nervous systems. The central nervous system is made up of the brain and spinal cord, which contains more than 99 percent of all neurons. The peripheral nervous system is a network of nerves that connects the brain and spinal cord to other parts of the body. Its two major divisions are the somatic nervous system and the autonomic nervous system. The autonomic nervous system is subdivided into the sympathetic and parasympathetic divisions.

IV. **Neurons**

The pathways of neurons include afferent nerves (sensory nerves), which carry information to the brain, efferent neurons (motor nerves), which carry information away from the brain, and interneurons, which do most of the information processing in the brain itself. Neuron is the neuroscientist's label for nerve cell. The three basic parts of the neuron are the cell body, dendrites (which carry information to the cell body), and the axon (which carries information away from the cell body). Most axons are covered with a myelin sheath that speeds up information transmission. Neurons send information down the axon in the form of brief impulses, or "waves," of electricity. These waves are called the action potential. This neural impulse operates according to the all-or-none principle. The gaps between the neurons are called synapses. The neural impulse comes down the axon and reaches the axon terminal, where it stimulates the release of neurotransmitters from tiny vesicles. The neurotransmitters carry information across the synapse to the next neuron, where it is received like a key that fits into a lock. Among the neurotransmitters that play important roles in mind and behavior are GABA, aceytlcholine, norepinephrine, serotonin, and endorphins. The influence of neurotransmitters can be excitatory or inhibitory.

V. **Glial Cells**

The brain contains two types of cells: neurons and glial cells. Glial cells provide physical support for neurons and are thought to be involved in the regulation and nutrition of neurons.

VI. **Embryological Development and Levels in the Brain**

During embryological development the neural tube changes shape and develops into three major divisions—hindbrain (lowest level), midbrain (middle level), and forebrain (highest level). The main structures of the hindbrain are the medulla and cerebellum. The midbrain's major structure is the reticular formation. The forebrain consists of the limbic system (which also runs through the midbrain), thalamus, basal ganglia, hypothalamus, and neocortex. Each of these structures is specialized to perform certain information processing jobs. The neocortex is a vast sheet of neural tissue.

VII. **Exploring the Neocortex.**

The wrinkled surface of the neocortex is divided into two hemispheres (left and right) and four lobes (frontal, parietal, temporal, and occipital). Topographic mapping has helped scientists determine the neocortex's role in different behaviors. The neocortex consists of sensory areas, motor areas, association areas, and cortical columns. Split-brain research, pioneered by Sperry, involves severing the corpus callosum, the bundle of fibers that connect the two hemispheres. This research led to the conclusion that language is mainly a left-hemisphere function, while touch and emotion are predominantly right-hemisphere functions. In normal people, the two hemispheres work together to process information.

VIII. **Integration of Function in the Brain**

For the most part psychological functions do not involve a single structure in the brain but rather the integration of information by a number of structures.

IX. **The Endocrine System**
The endocrine glands discharge their chemical products directly into the bloodstream. These chemical products, called hormones, travel to all parts of the body. The pituitary gland is known as the master gland because it communicates with many other glands in the body. The adrenal glands play an important role in mood, energy, and stress. The endocrine system basically performs glandular information processing.

X. **Brain and Mind**
Philosophers and scientists have speculated about the relation of mind and brain (or mind and body) for centuries. Two prominent views are monism and dualism. There is a flurry of interest in mind-brain relations brought on by advances in neuroscience and cognitive research, although there is no known scientific method to evaluate the mind-body issue.

Key Terms

chromosomes *42*
deoxyribonucleic acid (DNA) *42*
genes *42*
twin study *45*
adoption study *45*
sociobiology *45*
phrenology *48*
neuron *49*
central nervous system (CNS) *49*
peripheral nervous system *49*
somatic nervous system *49*
autonomic nervous system *49*
sympathetic division *49*
parasympathetic division *49*
afferent nerves *50*
efferent nerves *50*
interneurons *50*
cell body *51*
dendrite *52*
axon *52*

myelin sheath *52*
ion *53*
resting potential *53*
action potential *54*
all-or-none principle *54*
synapses *54*
neurotransmitters *54*
GABA *57*
acetylcholine (ACh) *57*
norepinephrine *57*
dopamine *57*
serotonin *57*
pineal gland *58*
endorphins *60*
glial cells *60*
hindbrain *64*
medulla *64*
cerebellum *64*
midbrain *64*
reticular formation *64*
forebrain *66*

limbic system *66*
amygdala *66*
hippcampus *66*
thalamus *66*
basal ganglia *66*
hypothalamus *67*
neocortex *69*
occipital lobe *69*
temporal lobe *69*
frontal lobe *69*
parietal lobe *69*
association cortex *69*
cortical columns *70*
corpus callosum *71*
endocrine glands *76*
hormones *76*
pituitary gland *77*
adrenal glands *77*
monism *78*
dualism *78*

Suggested Readings

Bloom, F. E., Lazerson, A., & Hofstadter, L. (1985). *Brain, mind, and behavior.* New York: W. H. Freeman. This book was designed to be part of a multimedia teaching package involving the Public Broadcasting System's eight-part series, "The Brain." The beauty of the brain is captured in both photographs and well-written essays on its many facets.

Gould, S. J. (1980). *The panda's thumb.* New York: Norton. Gould is one of the best contemporary scientist-writers and in this book provides fascinating insights about the nature of evolution, including these chapters "Were Dinosaurs Dumb?" "Return of the Hopeful Monster," and "The Panda's Thumb."

Groves, P. M., & Rebec, G. V. (1988). *Biological psychology* (3rd ed). Dubuque, IA: Wm. C. Brown. This is a textbook for courses in physiological psychology and provides extensive detail about specific neuroscience topics.

Nilsson, L. (1973). *Behold man.* Boston: Little Brown. Incredible photographs taken through an electron microscope lead you inside the human brain to see what its structures and neurons actually look like.

Recent Trends in Neuroscience This is a monthly journal that may be in your college or university library. It is easier to read than most neuroscience journals and includes humorous comments about the brain and nervous system. It is an up-to-date informative publication about what is going on in brain research.

Watson, J. D. (1968). *The double helix.* New York: New American Library. This book is a personalized account of the research leading up to one of the most provocative discoveries of the twentieth century—the discovery of the DNA molecule. The book reads like a mystery novel and illustrates the exciting discovery process in science.

Chapter 3

Sensation and Perception

Hamlet: Do you see yonder cloud that's almost in the shape of a camel?

Polonious: By the Mass, and 'tis like a camel indeed.

Hamlet: Methinks it is like a weasel.

Polonious: It is backed like a weasel.

Hamlet: Or like a whale?

Polonious: Very like a whale.

—*Shakespeare, Hamlet* (Act III)

Images of Sensation and Perception

Alfredo came to the United States in 1942 to escape the terrors of World War II. He had been the head chef at a leading continental restaurant in Rome and continued his culinary artistry in the United States, obtaining a job with a posh eatery in New York City. Alfredo was a restless sort though, and he loved to try new foods and drinks. He heard that a food company was looking for someone to work as a food taster and applied for the job. Needless to say the food company was more than pleased to have a master chef as a food taster.

The company was about to launch a new line of Chinese food when Alfredo said, "Wait a minute, I just don't know much about Chinese food." He went to the library and to his surprise he found that some foods are loved in China because of the way they sound when they are eaten. For example, the Chinese enjoy the sound of crunchy jellyfish. Alfredo also discovered that Chinese taste seems to be more complex than that of Americans. For example, the Chinese cuisine includes textured foods that are themselves flavorless and must be combined with other foods to give them flavor. The best textured foods have no color, no flavor, and no fragrance of their own. Shark's fin and bird's nest are two examples.

Not long after his exposure to shark's fin and bird's nest, Alfredo decided to stop moonlighting as a food taster. But surely there must be something he could do to stimulate his taste buds, something that would not require him to eat all of the things he downed as part of his job with the food company.

Alfredo got a job as a wine taster and even after his retirement as a chef has continued to work as a wine taster. Recently he talked about wine tasting: "Wine tasting means a lot more than having your taste buds stimulated. The first step involves judging the wine's appearance, especially in terms of clarity and color. So the first judgment is a visual one. Most people think of a wine's color as red, pink, or yellow, but there are at least fourteen colors used to describe wine, such as brick-red, ruby, and pelure d'oignon (onion skin)."

Alfredo continued, "Then you should evaluate the odor of the wine. The more experienced you get at wine tasting, the more odor is a key to your judgment. I swirl the wine around in a glass and then take a couple of sniffs. I've smelled wines that are foxy, heady, lively, sappy, and musty.

"So," Alfredo remarked, "you see that before even one taste some fairly strong impressions about the wine have already been formed. The third step is tasting, which involves rolling the wine around in the mouth. You probably didn't know that professional wine tasters actually spit out the wine rather than swallow it.

"When I taste a wine I notice three things: sweetness, sourness, and bitterness. If the wine is balanced the sweet, sour, and bitter tastes come across harmoniously. For example a young wine with too much grape will taste too bitter.

"But," Alfredo went on, "we aren't through yet. We still have to consider the wine's aftertaste. After spitting out (or swallowing) the wine, you sense how long the aftertaste remains. If the flavor remains for less than six seconds that is bad. A wine with a good aftertaste stays with you longer. And new flavors appear after the wine has left your mouth, flavors that you note for their pleasantness or unpleasantness."

Like Alfredo, each of us uses a number of sensory and perceptual systems to detect, process, and interpret what we experience in our environment. Sensing and perceiving involve a complex and sophisticated visual system; the auditory system, an elaborate engineering marvel compacted into a space the size of an Oreo cookie; and other processes that inform us about soft caresses and excruciating pain, sweet and sour tastes, floral and peppermint odors, and whether our world is upside down or right side up. Before we tackle each of the senses in greater detail, though, we need to know more about the nature of sensation and perception. ■

What Are Sensation and Perception?

How do you know the color of the grass? . . . that a smell is sweet, that a sound is a sigh, and that the lights around the shore are dim? You know these things because of your senses. All outside information comes into us through our senses. Without vision, hearing, touch, taste, smell, and other senses, your brain would be isolated from the world; you would live in a dark silence—a tasteless, colorless, feelingless void.

Sensation is the process of detecting and encoding stimulus energy in the world. Stimuli emit physical energy—light, sound, and heat, for example. The sense organs detect this energy and then transform it into a code that can be transmitted to the brain. The first step in "sensing" the world is the work of the *receptor cells,* which respond to certain forms of energy. The retina of the eye is sensitive to light, and special cells in the ear are sensitive to sound, for example. This physical energy is transformed into electrical impulses; the information carried by these electrical impulses travels through nerve fibers that connect the sense organs with the central nervous system. Once in the brain, information about the external world travels to the appropriate area of the cerebral cortex. (Recall from chapter 2, for example, that visual information travels to the occipital lobes at the back of the head, while auditory information goes to the temporal lobes just above the ears.)

Our brain organizes and interprets information to give it meaning for us; this is the process of **perception.** Our eyes record a fast-moving silver object in the sky, but they do not "see" a passenger jet; our eardrum vibrates in a particular way, but it does not "hear" a Beethoven symphony. Organizing and interpreting what is sensed, that is, "seeing" and "hearing" meaningful patterns in sensory information, is perception.

In our everyday lives, the two processes of sensation and perception are virtually inseparable. When the brain receives sensory information, for example, it automatically interprets the information. Because of this, some contemporary psychologists refer to sensation and perception as a unified information processing system; others prefer to retain the distinction between the two processes.

Detecting the Sensory World

A radar operator's task is to detect "blips" on a radar screen and decide whether they signify hostile or friendly aircraft. How bright do the "blips" have to be for the radar operator to see them? How do psychologists study our abilities to take in the stimulation in our environment? And what are some of the factors that might affect our detection of these stimuli?

Thresholds

Could you detect the wing of a fly falling on your cheek from a distance of one centimeter? Could you tell the difference between a drink sweetened with sugar and one sweetened with artificial flavoring? Would motivation enter into your ability to detect such differences—for example, if you are on a diet might you have a greater interest in the sweetner than in the fly?

Absolute Threshold

A basic problem in any sensory system is its ability to detect varying degrees of energy in the environment. This energy can take the form of light, sound, chemical, or mechanical stimulation. How much of a stimulus is necessary for you to see, hear, taste, smell, or feel something? This *minimum* amount of energy is called the **absolute threshold.** Below the absolute threshold you cannot detect that a stimulus is present; when the threshold is reached, you detect the presence of the stimulus.

An experiment with a wristwatch or a clock will help you understand the principle of absolute threshold. Find a wristwatch or clock that ticks; put it on a table and walk far enough across the room so that you no longer hear the ticking. Then gradually move toward the wristwatch or clock. At some point you will begin to hear the ticking. Hold your position and notice that occasionally the ticking fades and you may have to move forward to reach the threshold; at other times it may become loud and you can move backward (Coren, Porac, & Ward, 1979).

In this experiment, the absolute threshold was not always what you thought. If the experiment had been conducted a number of times, several distances would have been recorded as the absolute threshold. For example, the first time you tried the experiment you may have heard the ticking at twenty-five feet from the clock. But you probably didn't hear it every time at twenty-five feet. You might have heard the ticking at twenty feet 50 percent of the time. Psychologists have determined that the absolute threshold is the stimulus value that is recorded 50 percent of the time (see figure 3.1). To learn about the approximate absolute thresholds of five senses, see table 3.1.

Under ideal circumstances, our senses have very low absolute thresholds. For example, you might have been surprised to learn in table 3.1 that the human eye can see a candle flame at thirty miles on a dark, clear night. But the conditions under which we detect stimuli in our environment are often not ideal. If the night is cloudy and the air is polluted, for example, you will have to be much closer to see the flicker of a candle flame. And other lights on the horizon—car lights or house lights—may hinder your detection of the candle's flame. Psychologists call the presence of such competing and irrelevant stimuli background **noise.** For example, someone speaks to you from the door of the room where you are sitting. You may fail to respond because your roommate is talking on the phone and a tape player is blaring out your favorite song. We

Table 3.1	Approximate Absolute Thresholds for Five Senses
Vision	A candle flame at thirty miles on a dark, clear night.
Hearing	A ticking watch at twenty feet under quiet conditions.
Taste	A teaspoon of sugar in two gallons of water.
Smell	One drop of perfume diffused throughout three rooms.
Touch	The wing of a fly falling on your cheek from a distance of one centimeter.

Source: Adapted from Galanter, 1962.

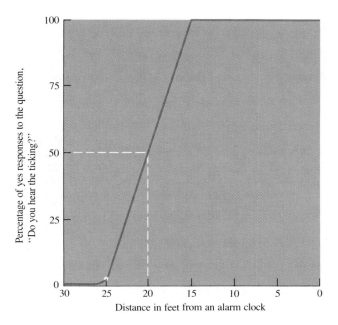

Figure 3.1
Determining the absolute threshold. The absolute threshold is the stimulus value that is detected 50 percent of the time. Here the absolute threshold for detecting the ticking of the clock is 20 feet.

usually think of noise as being auditory, but as used by psychologists, noise also involves other senses. The irrelevant, competing pollution, cloudiness, car lights, and house lights are forms of *visual noise* that hamper your detection of a candle flame from a great distance.

Our motivation is an important factor in whether or not we detect a stimulus. If someone offers us one hundred dollars to find a needle in a haystack, we might strain our eyes a little harder and search a little longer than if no money were involved. A pilot's motivation to detect a faint blip on the radar screen may be greater than usual if during the past week a plane crashed in the vicinity. If a story breaks about a series of burglaries in your neighborhood, you may be more likely than usual to detect a rustling in the bushes outside of your house.

Signal detection theory recognizes that detecting sensory stimuli is due to more than just the properties of the stimuli and the sensory system. Psychological factors such as motivation are important as well. For example, sometimes we hear only what we want to hear and see only what we want to see. Two individuals sitting near you at lunch may have been talking for fifteen minutes and you did not hear anything they said. Then, one comments about a best friend of yours and you immediately tune in on the conversation. A pilot may not see the blip on the radar screen because he is preoccupied with the nasty comment his supervisor made just before the plane left the ground. A witness may not select a burglar in a police lineup because the individual does not fit her expectation of what a criminal would look like.

Subliminal Perception

We have discussed sensations that are above an individual's threshold of awareness. But what about the possibility that we experience the sensory world at levels beyond our detection? Might our brain detect very faint stimuli in a subconscious manner? **Subliminal perception** is the perception of stimuli below the threshold of awareness. Is this type of perception possible? To learn more about this controversial possibility, turn to Psychology 3.1.

Signal detection theory argues that motivation is involved in our detection of stimuli. For example, as shown above, individuals may be so absorbed with each other that they do not detect the waiter's presence.

■ ■ ■ ■ ■ ■ ■ ■ ■ ■ ■ ■ ■ ■ ■ ■ ■ ■ ■

Psychology 3.1

Subliminal Perception—from Cokes to Rock Music

Subliminal perception holds great interest for individuals who are curious about whether or not they can be controlled or influenced by messages below their thresholds of awareness. Two of the most widely publicized claims involve a commercial firm in the 1950s that maintained that very brief presentations of the words "Drink Coca-Cola" and "Eat popcorn" dramatically increased the sales of these items and the belief in the 1980s that satanic messages are embedded in rock music.

Life magazine reported that more than 45,000 unknowing movie viewers were exposed to very brief flashes of the words "Drink Coca-Cola" while they were watching movie screens. The article stated that Coke sales rose 18 percent and popcorn sales soared more than 50 percent because of the subliminal messages (Brean, 1958; McConnell, Cutler, & McNeil, 1958). Scientists criticized the claims of the subliminal perception enthusiasts and asked if the messages enhanced an already existing but weak desire for Coke, if they induced a drive that had not existed, and if individuals rose from their seats and marched like robots to the concession stand or bought Coke on the way home from the movie. In one experiment, individuals who were exposed to "Drink Coke" subliminal messages did rate themselves as thirstier than a control group (Hawkins, 1970).

Such results suggest the possible existence of subliminal perception but they do not tell if we would buy Coke over another drink; they clearly do not support claims that advertisers can make us buy whatever they desire.

An interesting experiment by Carol Fowler and her colleagues (1981) provides some evidence that we process information from our sensory world at a level beneath our awareness. In this experiment words were shown on a screen so rapidly that the subjects could not tell what they were seeing. Subsequently, the subjects were shown two words (such as "hotel" and "book") and asked which was most like the subliminally presented word ("lodge"). Somewhat amazingly, the subjects answered most questions correctly. A possible explanation for these results is that sensory information too faint to be recognized consciously may be picked up by sensory receptors and transmitted to the brain at a level beneath conscious awareness.

Whether or not advertisers can influence us to buy their products through subliminal perception is still of interest to many individuals. Another concern is whether rock music is embedded with satanic messages, the degree to which such messages reach our conscious awareness, and the extent to which the messages themselves are responsible for deviant behavior. This phenomenon employs

messages played backwards into rock music: according to this theory, when the record is played normally (forward) the messages cannot be consciously perceived, but they influence our behavior in a subliminal way.

Researchers have been unable to support the belief that these messages exist or that they influence our behavior. Indeed, investigators have discovered that individual perceptions of whether or not these messages exist is largely a function of what they *expect* to hear. When told beforehand that a message of satanic quality will subliminally influence them, subjects are likely to hear the message. With no such expectation, individuals do not hear the message (Vokey & Read, 1985).

What can we make of the claims of subliminal persuasion enthusiasts and the research conducted by experimental psychologists? First, weak sensory stimuli can be registered by sensory receptors and is possibly encoded in the brain at a level beneath conscious awareness. Second, no evidence supports the claims of advertisers and rock music critics that such sensory registry and neural encoding have any substantial impact on our thoughts and behavior. Rather, evidence suggests that we are influenced extensively by those sounds and views we are aware of consciously and can attend to efficiently.

Difference Threshold

In addition to studying the amount of stimulation required for a stimulus to be detected, psychologists investigate the degree of difference that must exist between two stimuli before this difference is detected. This **difference threshold** is the smallest amount of stimulation required to discriminate one stimulus from another. An artist may be able to detect the difference between two similar colors. A tailor may be able to determine a difference in the texture of two fabrics by feeling them. How different must the colors and textures be for these individuals to determine the difference? Just as the absolute threshold is determined by a 50 percent detection rate, the difference threshold is defined as the point at which two stimuli are detected as different 50 percent of the time. This point is known as the **just noticeable difference** (or **jnd**).

An important aspect of difference thresholds is that the threshold increases with the magnitude of the stimulus. You may notice when your roommate turns up the volume on the stereo a small amount when it is playing softly but not detect it when it is turned up an equal amount when it is playing very loudly. More than 150 years ago, E. H. Weber, a German psychologist, noticed that regardless of their magnitude, two stimuli must differ by a constant proportion to be detected. Weber's observation that the difference threshold is a constant proportion rather than a constant amount was proven so widely that it became known as **Weber's law.** For example, we add 1 candle to 60 candles and notice a difference in the brightness of the candles; we add 1 candle to 120 candles and do not notice a difference. We discover, though, that adding 2 candles to 120 candles does produce a difference in brightness. Adding 2 candles to 120 candles is the same proportionately as adding 1 candle to 60 candles. The exact proportion varies with the stimulus involved. For example, a change in a tone's pitch of .3 percent can be detected, but a 20 percent change in taste and a 25 percent change in smell are required for an individual to detect a difference.

Sensory Adaptation

Naked except for capes that hang to their knees, two Ona Indians wade in freezing water as they use a bow and arrow to kill fish for their dinner. Darwin encountered the Ona Indians when he rounded Cape Horn on the southern tip of South America. At night, they slept naked on the wet, virtually frozen ground. The ability of these Indians to endure the freezing temperatures with little or no clothing reflects the principle of **sensory adaptation,** a weakened response to stimulus energy. You have experienced sensory adaptation countless times in your life—adapting to the temperature of a shower, to the water in a swimming pool, to the taste of jalapenos (I'm still working on this one), to loud sounds of rock music, or to the offending smell of a locker room. Over time we are less responsive and sensitive to these sensory experiences; this is the principle of sensory adaptation.

At this point you should have a basic understanding of sensation and perception, the thresholds of sensory awareness, and sensory adaptation. These topics are summarized in concept table 3.1. Now it is time to study each of the senses in more detail; we begin with the sense about which we know the most—vision.

Sensory adaptation is a weakening response to the same amount of stimulus energy present. As shown above, the ocean feels less cold after the individuals have been in it for a few minutes.

Concept Table 3.1

The Nature of Sensing and Perceiving		
Concept	**Processes/related ideas**	**Characteristics/description**
What are sensation and perception?	Sensation	The process of detecting and encoding stimulus energy in the environment.
	Perception	The process of organizing and interpreting sensed information to give it meaning.
Detecting the sensory world	Absolute threshold	The minimum stimulus intensity an individual can detect. The absolute threshold is the stimulus value detected 50 percent of the time. Noise is irrelevant and competing stimuli; motivation also influences our ability to detect stimuli. Signal detection theory recognizes that psychological factors affect detection.
	Subliminal perception	The perception of stimuli below the threshold of awareness; this is a controversial topic.
	Difference threshold	The smallest amount of stimulation required to discriminate one stimulus from another. When this is done 50 percent of the time, it is called a just noticeable difference. Weber's law states that regardless of magnitude, two stimuli must differ by a constant proportion to be detected.
	Sensory adaptation	Weakened responsiveness to stimulus energy.

Figure 3.2
(a) The electromagnetic spectrum and visible light. Visible light is only a narrow band in the electromagnetic spectrum. Visible light's wavelengths range from about 400 to 700 nanometers; X rays are much shorter and radio waves are much longer.
(b) Ultraviolet. Most ultraviolet rays are absorbed by the ozone in the earth's upper atmosphere. The small fraction that reaches the earth is the ingredient in sunlight that tans the skin (and can cause skin cancer).
(c) Infrared. The electromagnetic radiation just beyond red in the spectrum is felt as heat by receptors in the skin.

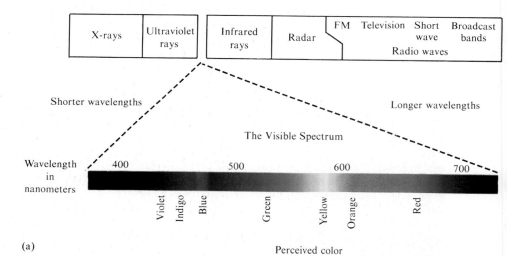

(a)

(b)

(c)

Vision

We see a world of shapes and sizes, some stationary, others moving, some in black and white, others in color. But how do we see in this way? What is the machinery that enables us to experience this marvelous landscape?

The Visual Stimulus and the Eye

Light is a form of electromagnetic energy that can be described in terms of wavelengths. The difference between visible light and other forms of electromagnetic energy is its wavelength. Waves of light are much like the waves formed when a pebble is tossed into a lake. The wavelength is the distance from the peak of one wave to the peak of the next. Visible light's wavelengths range from about 400 to 700 nanometers (nm); a nanometer is one billionth of a meter. Outside of this range of visible light are longer radio and infrared radiation waves and shorter ultraviolet and X rays (see figure 3.2). These other wavelengths might bombard us, but we do not see them. Why do we see only this narrow band of the electromagnetic spectrum? The most frequent answer to this question is that our visual system evolved in the sun's light; thus, our visual system is able to perceive the spectrum of energy emitted by the sun. By the time sunlight reaches the earth's surface, it is strongest in the wavelengths between 400 and 700 nm.

We see this narrow band of the electromagnetic spectrum with our eyes. By looking closely at your eyes in the mirror, you will notice three parts—the sclera, iris, and pupil—which are shown in figure 3.3. The **sclera** is the white part, which helps to maintain the shape of the eye and to protect it from injury.

HERMAN®

"What you're looking at could make you a very rich man."

Figure 3.3
Parts of the eye—the sclera, the iris, the pupil, and the cornea—can be seen in this photograph.

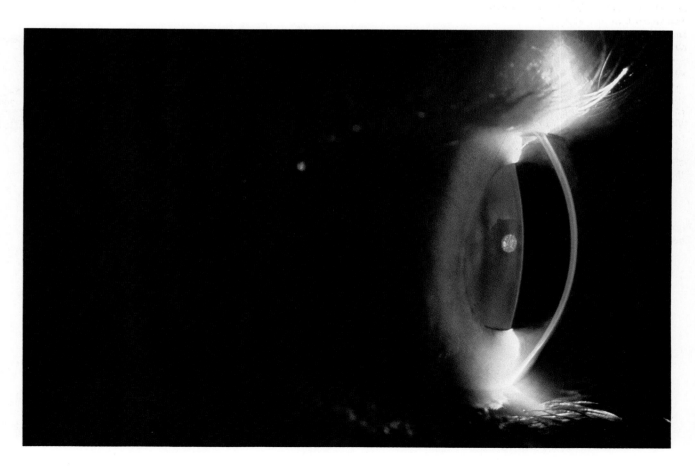

Figure 3.4
*The main structures
of the eye.*

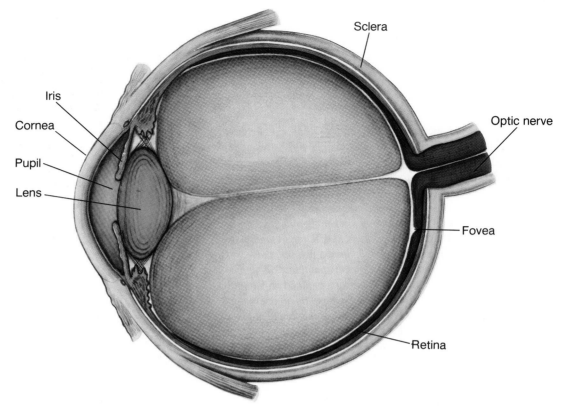

The **iris** is a ring of muscles ranging in color from light blue to dark brown. The **pupil** is the opening in the center of the iris, which appears black; its primary function is to maintain optimal light intensity. There is one outside structure you cannot see. This is the **cornea,** a clear membrane just in front of the iris, which bends light rays as they enter your eye. Figure 3.4 shows the location of the cornea and other important structures in the eye. The eye's **lens** changes shape to bring objects into focus.

The **retina** is a very important light-sensitive mechanism in the back of the eye that operates much like film in a camera. It consists of light receptors called **rods** and **cones** and different kinds of neurons, which you will read about shortly. One minute structure in the center of the retina is the **fovea,** an area where vision is the sharpest. Also on the retina is the **blind spot,** the location where the optic nerve leaves the eye on its way to the brain. Because no light receptors are present on this blind spot, we cannot see anything that reaches this point on the retina. For example, look at figure 3.5. Close your left eye and use your right eye to look at the X. Hold the figure about arm's length away to begin, then slowly move it toward you, staring continuously at the X. At some point you will be unable to see the circle; at this distance the circle's image has fallen on the blind spot of your right eye. The circle will reappear if you move the figure closer.

Because the retina is so important to vision, we need to study its makeup more closely. The rods and cones in the retina are specialized nerve cells that break light down into neural impulses. This process occurs by means of a photochemical reaction. For example, a chemical called *rhodopsin* is broken down when light meets the rods; a similar process occurs with a chemical called

Figure 3.5
Diagram to determine your blind spot.

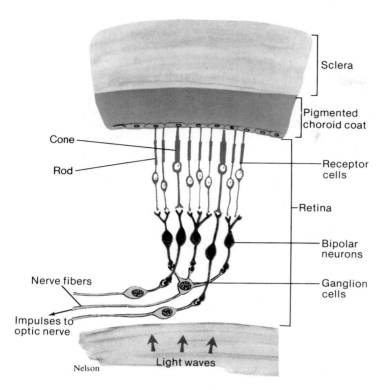

Sclera

Pigmented
choroid coat

Cone

Rod

Receptor
cells

Retina

Bipolar
neurons

Nerve fibers

Ganglion
cells

Impulses to
optic nerve

Nelson

Light waves

Figure 3.6
The cells of the retina. The rods and cones are the light-sensitive cells in the retina. Here chemicals break down the physical energy of the light and turn the information into a neural impulse. The impulse moves first through the bipolar cells and then to the neighboring ganglion cells. Subsequently, the information is transmitted to the brain through the optic nerve. The choroid coat shown in the diagram is a vascular coat that lies between the sclera and retina.

Table 3.2 Characteristics of Rods and Cones

Characteristics	Rods	Cones
Type of vision	Black and white	Color
Light conditions	Dimly lighted	Well lighted
Shape	Thin and long	Short and fat
Distribution	Not on fovea	On fovea

iodopsin when light meets the cones. The breakdown of the chemicals produces a neural impulse that is first transmitted to a *bipolar cell* and then moves to a *ganglion cell* (see figure 3.6). The nerve impulse subsequently reaches the axons of the ganglion cells, which make up the optic nerve.

Rods and cones are involved in different aspects of vision. Rods, which are long and cylindrical, are very sensitive to light. Thus, they function well under low illumination; as you might anticipate, they are hard at work at night. Rods, however, are not sensitive to color. For this reason we have difficulty seeing color at night. Cones, which are shorter and fatter than rods, do detect color but only under good illumination. The rods and cones are concentrated in different parts of the retina; rods are found almost everywhere but the fovea while cones are concentrated at the fovea. Because we know that rods are used in poorly lit conditions and that the fovea has no rods, we can conclude that vision is poor for objects registered at the fovea at night. A summary of some of the main characteristics of rods and cones is presented in table 3.2.

So far we have studied the importance of the light stimulus and the structures of the eye. The journey of visual information now leads us to the brain and how this visual information is processed.

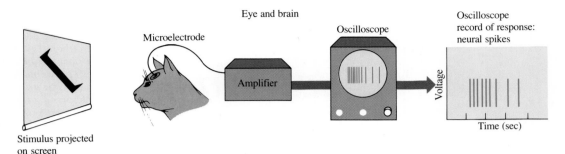

Stimulus projected
on screen

Figure 3.7
Experimental arrangement of Hubel and Wiesel's discovery of neurons that are very sensitive to lines and angles. An electrode is inserted into a cell at some point in the visual system of the experimental animal. Various light stimuli are projected on a screen in front of the animal's eyes. The eyes are generally paralyzed so that particular locations on the screen project to particular locations on the animal's retina. The impulse activity of an individual cell in response to the stimuli (shown in the oscilloscope record) indicates the characteristics of that cell's receptive field.

From Eye to Brain and Neural Visual Processing

The **optic nerve** leads out of the eye toward the brain, carrying information about light. Approximately two-thirds of the fibers that make up the optic nerve cross over at a point called the **optic chiasma.** Information registered on the right side of the retina ends up on the right side of the brain after crossing the optic chiasma and vice versa; however, one other crossing occurs before light reaches the retina. As we look at the world, what we see on the left side is registered on the right side of the retina, and vice versa, because the lens reverses the image. What all of these crossings mean is that what we see in the left side of our visual field ends up on the right side of our brain.

After traveling through the thalamus, information about light reaches the visual cortex in the occipital lobe. The visual cortex combines information from both eyes and is responsible for higher levels of visual processing. One of the most fascinating programs of research involving visual processing in the brain was conducted by David Hubel and Torsten Wiesel (1965), who won a Nobel Prize for their discovery that some neurons detect different features of the visual field. By recording the activity of a single neuron in a cat while presenting the cat with patterns that varied in size, shape, color, and movement, they found that the visual cortex has neurons that are sensitive to lines and angles (see figure 3.7). For example, one neuron might have a sudden burst of activity when a stimulus with lines of a particular angle appear in the visual field; another neuron might fire only when moving stimuli appear in the field; yet another neuron might be stimulated when the stimulus has a combination of certain angles, sizes, and shapes.

Color Vision

We spend a lot of time thinking about color—the color of the car we want to buy, the color we are going to paint the walls of our room, the color of the clothes we wear. We can change our hair color or even the color of our eyes to make us look more attractive.

What Is Color?

The human eye registers light wavelengths between 400 and 700 nm (as you saw in figure 3.2). The light waves themselves have no color. The sensations of color reside in the visual system of the observer. So, if we talk about red light we refer to the wavelengths of light that evoke the sensation of red. Objects appear colored to us because they reflect certain wavelengths of light to our eyes. We can remember the colors of the light spectrum by thinking of an imaginary man named ROY G. BIV, for the colors *r*ed, *o*range, *y*ellow, *g*reen, *b*lue, *i*ndigo, and *v*iolet.

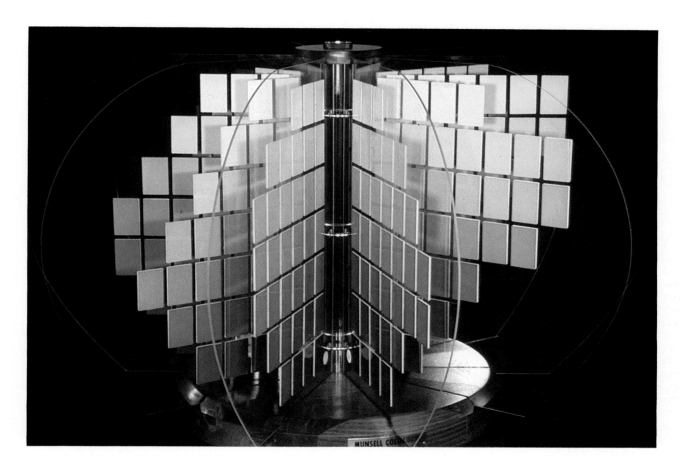

Three important properties of color are hue, saturation, and brightness. A color's **hue** is based on its wavelength, a color's **saturation** on purity, and a color's **brightness** on intensity. As shown in figure 3.2, the longest wavelengths seen by the human eye (about 700 nm) appear to be red, the shortest (about 400 nm) appear to be violet.

Hue is what we commonly conceive color to be. The discovery that light is made up of different colors of light is an intriguing one. Isaac Newton had escaped the great plague of London in 1666 by moving to Cambridge for the summer. It was at Cambridge that Newton conducted his work on the nature of light. He isolated himself in a room that was dark except for a ray of sunlight that passed through a small hole in a shutter. He held up a prism to the ray of light; the prism bent the white light into a row of colors, much like a rainbow. In this way, Newton discovered that white light is made up of a number of colors of light (Wasserman, 1978).

To understand the saturation, or purity, of color see figure 3.8. The purity of color is determined by the amount of white light added to a single wavelength of a color. Colors that are very pure have no white light; on the color tree they are located on the outside. As we move toward the interior of the color tree, notice that the saturation of the color changes. The closer we get to the center of the tree, the more white light has been added to the single wavelength of a particular color.

After adding saturation to hue, a much larger range of colors can be seen. But one more dimension of color needs to be described—brightness. Brightness involves the intensity of light. White has the most brightness, black

Figure 3.8
An example of colors arranged in a color tree.

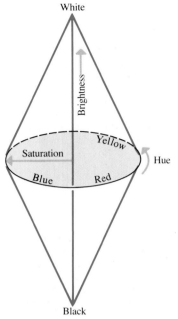

Figure 3.9
How the dimensions of hue, saturation, and brightness are represented on the color tree. The color tree shows each possible color sensation located somewhere in a three-dimensional color space; the dimensions of this space are hue, saturation, and brightness. Saturation is represented horizontally, brightness vertically.

the least. Figure 3.9 represents the color tree shown in figure 3.8 with the three dimensions of color—hue, saturation, and brightness—labeled. Notice that brightness is placed on the vertical axis; the brighter a color, the higher it is on the tree. By looking at figure 3.8 again you can see how much brighter the colors are at the top than at the bottom; the grays are in between.

When mixing color we get different results depending on whether we mix light or pigments (see figure 3.10). An **additive mixture** of color indicates that we are mixing beams of light from different parts of the color spectrum. A **subtractive mixture** indicates that we are mixing pigments. Through additive mixing we can produce virtually the entire color circle by using any three widely spaced colors. Television is an example of additive mixing; only three colors are involved—red, blue, and green. If you look at a color television screen through a magnifying glass, you will notice that a yellow patch of light is actually a combination of tiny red and green dots. Look at other patches of color on a television screen with a magnifying glass to observe their composition.

An artist's painting is an example of subtractive mixing. When blue and yellow are mixed on the television screen, a gray or white hue appears. But when the artist mixes a dab of blue paint with a dab of yellow paint, the color green is produced. In a subtractive color mixture each pigment absorbs (subtracts) some of the light falling on it and reflects the rest of the light. When two pigments are mixed the light that is not absorbed or subtracted from either one emerges (Wasserman, 1978).

Theories of Color Vision

For centuries, scientists have puzzled over how the human eye sees the almost infinite variety of color in the world. Though we can discriminate 319 different colors, no one believes that we have 319 different kinds of cones in our retinas (Bartley, 1969). Instead, even the earliest theorists assumed that our retinas respond to a few primary colors and then relay the information to the brain, where it is synthesized into the many different hues we perceive. But early theorists disagreed about which colors the retina was selecting. Two main theories were proposed, and each turned out to be right (Boynton, in press).

The first theory was based on what you just learned—that mixing red, blue, and green lights produces all of the colors we perceive. Thomas Young and Hermann von Helmholtz took that fact and made the reasonable suggestion that the retina responds only to the amount of red, blue, and green light coming from the stimulus, letting the brain *remix* them to produce the actual color. This is called the **Young-Helmholtz trichromatic theory** of color vision and it has proven to be true. Individual cones do respond either to red, blue, or green, just as Young and Helmholtz thought (see figure 3.11). In an exciting investigation related to this trichromatic theory, geneticists discovered the three individual genes in the human chromosome that direct cones to produce the three pigments that make them sensitive to red, blue, or green light (Nathans, Thomas, & Hogness, 1986).

The second major theory about color vision was based on some well-known aspects of color vision that could not be explained by the trichromatic theory. One of these aspects involves **afterimages**—sensations that remain after a stimulus is removed. Visual afterimages are common and they frequently involve complementary colors. If you look at red long enough, eventually a green afterimage will appear; if you look at yellow long enough, eventually a blue afterimage will appear. See figure 3.12 to experience an afterimage for yourself. The trichromatic theory cannot explain such complementary afterimages.

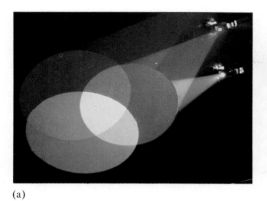

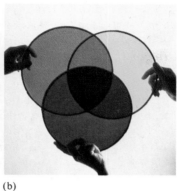

(a)　　　　　　　　　(b)

Figure 3.10
Comparing the mixing of light with the mixing of pigments. (a) Additive color mixtures occur when lights are mixed. For example, red and green lights when combined yield yellow. The three colors together give white.
(b) Subtractive color mixtures occur when pigments are mixed or light is shown through colored filters placed over one another. Most of the time blue-green and yellow mixed together will give green, and complementary colors produce black.

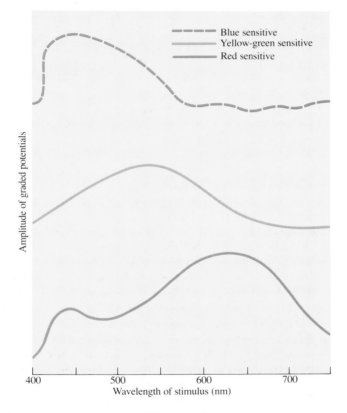

- - - - Blue sensitive
———— Yellow-green sensitive
———— Red sensitive

Amplitude of graded potentials

400　　500　　600　　700
Wavelength of stimulus (nm)

Figure 3.11
These recordings were taken from single color-sensitive cells in the retina of the carp. The presence of cones that respond only to blue, green, or red supports the Young-Helmholtz trichromatic theory of color vision.

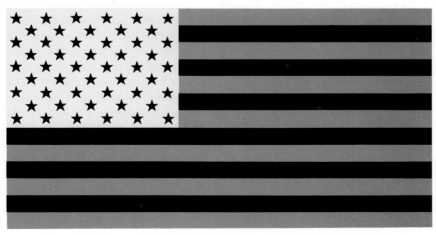

Figure 3.12
Negative afterimage. If you stare at the center of the flag for approximately 30 seconds and then look at a white wall or piece of paper, you should see a negative afterimage in the colors opposite those in the flag.

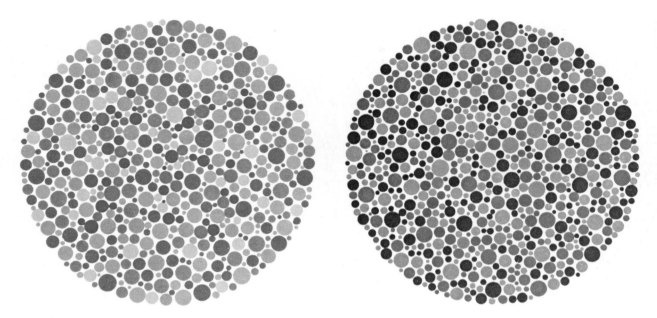

Figure 3.13
Examples of stimuli used to test for color blindness. In the left circle, people with normal vision see the number 16, but people with red-green color blindness do not. In the right circle, people with normal vision detect the number 8, but those with red-green color blindness see one number or none. A complete color blindness assessment involves the use of 15 stimuli.

Ishihara Eye Test for Colour Blindness. Reprinted with permission of Graham-Field Inc., New Hyde Park, N.Y.

The Young-Helmholtz theory cannot offer a satisfactory explanation of color blindness either. The term *color blind* is somewhat misleading because it suggests that an individual who is color blind cannot see color at all. Complete color blindness is rare, and most individuals who are color blind can see some colors but not others. The most frequent form of color blindness involves red and green. Approximately 10 percent of men but only 1 percent of women show red-green color blindness. These individuals tend to see both red and green colors as a yellow-tinted gray and cannot distinguish between shades of red and green.

Individuals who have normal vision and can see all colors are referred to as *trichromatic,* those with either red-green or blue-yellow difficulties are referred to as *dichromatic,* and those who are completely color blind are referred to as *monochromatic.* Examples of the tests given to evaluate color blindness are shown in figure 3.13.

Both color blindness and afterimages suggest that the visual system treats colors as complementary pairs—a red-green and a blue-yellow pair. This led Edward Hering (1920) to propose that the cones might actually respond to such pairs, with a given cone, for example, being excited by red and inhibited by green; another cone might be excited by yellow and inhibited by blue. This is called the **opponent-process theory** of color vision; the theory explains both afterimage and color blindness (Hurvich & Jameson, 1969).

If you stare at red, for instance, your red-green system seems to "tire," and when you look away, it rebounds and gives you a green afterimage. Also, if you mix equal amounts of opponent colors, such as blue and yellow, you see gray; figure 3.14 displays a color wheel illustrating this principle. Color blindness, which affects either red-green or yellow-blue, also is explained by the opponent-process theory. If your red-green system is defective, you will see gray for those colors; if your blue-yellow system is defective, you will see gray for those two opponent colors as well. And that is what happens for color-blind individuals.

We have seen that the cones are trichromatic—they respond to red, blue, or green. Then how can the opponent-process theory also be correct? The answer is that the red, blue, and green cones are connected to the retinal ganglion cells (refer to figure 3.6) in such a way that the three-color code is immediately translated into the opponent-process code. For example, a red cone might

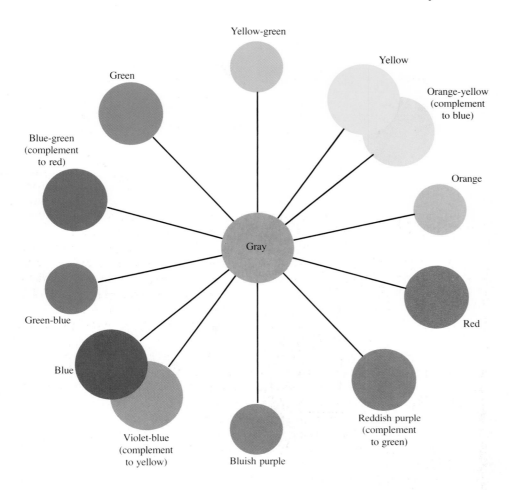

Figure 3.14
The color wheel. Colors opposite each other produce the neutral gray in the center when they are mixed. For instance, blue-green is the complement of red.

inhibit and a green cone might excite one particular ganglion cell. Thus, *both* the trichromatic and the opponent-process theory are right—the eye and the brain use both methods to code colors. Interestingly, in different parts of the brain's visual centers, some neurons can be found that respond to colors in the trichromatic fashion (Motokawa, Taira, & Okuda, 1962) and some follow the opponent-process code (DeValois & Jacobs, 1968). In the visual cortex, some cells respond only when a stimulus has the right color *and* shape (Gouras & Kruger, 1975).

An intriguing footnote to our discussion of color vision concerns something you already have learned, namely, that red-green color blindness is found in males and not females. When the genes controlling red, blue, and green were discovered, it was also discovered that the red and green pigment genes are located on the X sex chromosome (Nathans, Thomas, & Hogness, 1986). Females always have two X chromosomes, so a defective gene on one of these X chromosomes does not result in red-green color blindness. Females almost always have a second, normal X chromosome that blocks the expression of the defective trait. Males, by contrast, have only one X chromosome; if that X chromosome is defective, the male will have red-green color blindness from birth.

Our tour of the visual system has been an extensive one—you have read about the light spectrum, the structures of the eye, neural visual processing, and the marvels of color vision. To help you remember the main themes of the visual system see concept table 3.2. Next, you will study the second-most researched sensory system, our hearing.

■ ■ ■ ■ ■ ■ ■ ■ ■ ■ ■ ■ ■ ■ ■ ■ ■ ■ ■ ■

Concept Table 3.2

Vision		
Concept	**Processes/related ideas**	**Characteristics/description**
The visual stimulus and the eye	The visual stimulus	Light is a form of electromagnetic energy that can be described in terms of wavelengths. The receptors in the human eye are sensitive to wavelengths from 400 to 700 nm.
	The eye	Key external parts are the sclera, iris, pupil, and cornea. The lens focuses light rays on the retina, the light-sensitive mechanism in the eye. Chemicals in the retina break down chromatic light into neural impulses.
	From eye to brain and neural visual processing	The optic nerve transmits neural impulses to the brain. Because of crossovers of nerve fibers, what we see in the left visual field is registered in the right side of the brain and vice versa. Visual information reaches the occipital lobe of the brain where it is stored and further integrated. Hubel and Wiesel discovered that neurons in the visual cortex can detect features of our visual world such as line, angle, and size.
Color vision	The nature of color	Objects appear colored because they reflect certain wavelengths of light between 400 and 700 nm. Important properties of color are hue, saturation, and brightness. Mixing colors of light involves an additive mixture; mixing pigments involves a subtractive mixture.
	Theories of color vision	The Young-Helmholtz theory states that by mixing red, blue, and green light all of the colors we perceive can be produced. This trichromatic theory cannot explain color blindness and afterimages, which the opponent-process theory can. Both color blindness and afterimages suggest the visual system treats colors as complementary pairs—red-green and yellow-blue.

The Auditory System

Just as light provides us with information about the environment, so does sound. Think about what life would be like without music, the rushing sound of ocean waves, or the gentle voice of someone you love.

The Nature of Sound and How We Experience It

At a rock concert you may have felt the mechanical pulsations of loud sounds or sensed that the air around you was vibrating. Bass instruments are especially effective at creating mechanical pulsations, even causing the floor or a seat to vibrate on occasion. When a bass instrument is played loudly we sense the movement of air molecules being pushed forward in waves by the speaker. These vibrations in the air are called sound, or sound waves, which are picked up by our auditory (or hearing) system.

A *tuning fork* provides further information about the nature of sound. A tuning fork is a two-pronged instrument that produces a tone when it is struck; you may have seen one in a music classroom or a science laboratory. The vibrations of the tuning fork cause air molecules to vibrate just like a bass instrument. Figure 3.15 provides a diagram of a sound wave produced by a tuning fork.

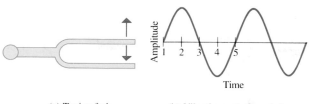

(a) Tuning fork

(b) Vibration pattern made by a prong of the tuning fork

Table 3.3	Decibel Levels of Various Sounds	
Level	**dB**	**Example**
	160	Loudest rock band on record
Intolerable	140	Very painful
	120	Very loud thunder
Very noisy	100	Heavy automobile traffic
Loud	80	Loud music from radio
Moderate	60	Average conversation
Faint	40	Quiet neighborhood
Very faint	20	Soft whisper
	0	Softest detectable noise

All sound waves are not equal. They differ in **frequency,** which is the number of cycles a sound wave completes in one second. The frequency of sound waves is measured in *hertz* (Hz) units, which refers to the number of cycles per second. Young adults can hear frequencies in the range of 20 to 20,000 Hz, but older adults have difficulty hearing the higher frequencies. Middle C on a piano has a frequency of 262 Hz. The ear detects the frequency of a sound wave as **pitch.** High-frequency sounds are high-pitched; low-frequency sounds are low-pitched. A soprano voice sounds high-pitched, a bass voice sounds low-pitched, for example.

Sound waves not only vary in frequency but also in **amplitude.** Amplitude is the change in pressure created by sound waves. In figure 3.15, amplitude is reflected in the height of each sound wave, that is, whether the air is expanded or compressed. The amplitude of a sound wave is measured in *decibels* (dB), which refer to the amount of pressure produced by a sound wave relative to a standard. Typically, the standard is the weakest sound the human ear can detect; thus zero would be the softest noise detectable by humans. Table 3.3 presents the decibel levels of a variety of sounds. The ear senses the amplitude of sound waves as **loudness.** The higher the amplitude of a sound wave, the louder the sound is perceived to be. In the world of amplitude this means that air is moving rapidly for loud sounds and slowly for soft sounds.

So far we have been describing a single sound wave; most sounds, though, are made up of a collection of sound waves with varying frequencies. This collection of sound waves is called **complexity.** The perception of this complexity is known as **timbre,** which is experienced as the quality of sound. Timbre is what makes one human voice sound different than another and also what makes an oboe sound different than a tuba.

Figure 3.16
Major parts of the human ear.

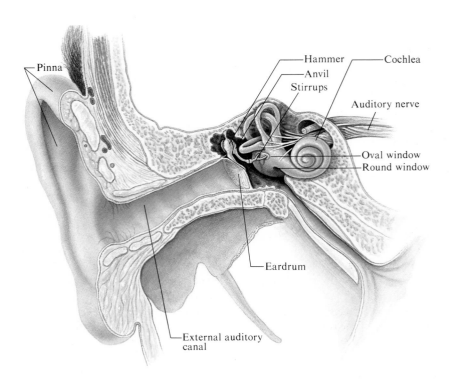

Structures and Functions of the Ear

What happens to sound waves once they reach your ear? How do various structures of the ear transform sound waves of compressed air so they can be understood by the brain as sound?

The ear is divided into the outer ear, middle ear, and inner ear (the major structures of the ear are shown in figure 3.16). The **outer ear** is made up of the pinna and external auditory canal. The pinna is the outer part of the ear that helps to collect sounds and is what we think of when we hear the word ear. The external auditory canal connects the outer ear with the middle ear, which is the structure that often gets filled with wax.

The **middle ear** has four main structures: eardrum, hammer, anvil, and stirrups. The eardrum is the first structure that sound touches in the middle ear. The eardrum vibrates in response to a sound and the sound then touches three bony structures: the hammer, anvil, and stirrups. The middle ear structures help to concentrate sound so it can be processed further in the inner ear.

The main parts of the **inner ear** are the oval window, cochlea, and the organ of Corti located in the cochlea. From the stirrup, sound travels to the oval window, the only part of the inner ear to receive sound vibrations directly. Sound waves go into the **cochlea,** a snaillike, fluid-filled structure. An important part of the cochlea is the **organ of Corti,** which runs the entire length of the cochlea. It contains the ear's sensory receptors, which change the energy pressure of sound into the kind of chemical and electrical energy that can be processed by the brain. Hairlike sensory receptors are stimulated by vibrations of the **basilar membrane,** which is located at the base of the organ of Corti. These vibrations generate nerve impulses, which vary with the extent of the membrane's vibration.

One of the mysteries of the auditory system is how the inner ear registers the frequency of sound. Three theories have been proposed to explain this mystery: place theory, frequency theory, and volley theory. According to **place theory,** each frequency produces vibrations at a particular spot on the basilar membrane. Georg von Bekesy won a Nobel Prize in 1961 for his research on the basilar membrane. Von Bekesy (1960) studied the effects of vibration on the oval window of human cadavers. Through a microscope, he saw that this stimulation produced a traveling wave. High-frequency vibrations create traveling waves that stimulate the area of the basilar membrane next to the oval window; low-frequency vibrations stimulate other areas of the membrane closer to the tip of the cochlea.

Place theory adequately explains high-frequency sounds but fares poorly with low-frequency sounds. A sound frequency below 400 Hz does not stimulate a particular spot on the basilar membrane; instead, it virtually transforms the entire basilar membrane on an equal basis. Because humans can detect sounds lower than 400 Hz, some other factor must account for the perception of sound. **Frequency theory** suggests that the frequency of the auditory nerve's firing is involved in our perception of sound. This theory argues that the basilar membrane does indeed vibrate as a whole at lower frequencies.

A third theory, **volley theory,** offers a modification and expansion of frequency theory to account for high-frequency sounds. A single neuron has a maximum firing capacity of about 1,000 times per second. Thus, frequency theory cannot be applied accurately to tones over 1,000 Hz. Volley theory argues that sounds above 1,000 Hz can be accounted for by a team of neurons, with each neuron on the team firing at a different time. The term volley theory was used because the neurons fire in a sequence of rhythmic volleys at higher frequencies. Thus, place and frequency theories better explain low frequencies; volley theory is superior in explaining high frequencies.

Neural Auditory Processing

How does information get from the cochlea to the lower portion of the brain? And how is information processed once it is in the brain?

The **auditory nerve** extends from the cochlea to the cochlear nucleus in the medulla area of the brain stem. Auditory information moves up the auditory pathway in a more complex manner than visual information in the visual pathway. Many synapses appear in the ascending auditory pathway and after the fibers enter the medulla many of them cross over to the other side of the brain. After passing through a large bundle of axons and several other neural stations in the midbrain, auditory information finally reaches the neocortex, where it is stored and integrated in the temporal lobe.

Now that we have described the visual and auditory systems in some detail, we turn to a number of other sensory systems—the skin senses, the chemical senses, the kinesthetic senses, and the vestibular sense. As you can tell, we have more than what is commonly referred to as the five senses (vision, audition, touch, taste, and smell).

The Skin Senses

The skin is our largest sensory system and has some important functions. This sensory system that drapes over our bodies has receptors for touch, temperature (warmth, cold), and pain.

Touch

Take a rubber band and with it lightly touch the following parts of your body: the bottom of your foot, your leg, your nose, and your forefinger. You should be able to sense that these different parts of your body do not have the same sensitivity to touch. Men and women do not always show the same sensitivity to touch. In one investigation, men had a higher threshold for touch over most of their body than did women (Weinstein, 1968). This study found that the body's most sensitive areas were in the head region (nose and upper lip, for example), and the least sensitive areas were in the foot region (sole of the foot, for example).

Temperature

Do you feel too hot or too cold right now, or do you feel about the right temperature? Our bodies have a regulatory system that keeps the body's temperature at about 98.6 degrees Farenheit. The skin plays an important role in this regulatory system. Some years ago it was found that we have separate locations on our skin that sense warmth and cold (Dallenbach, 1927). The forehead is especially sensitive to heat, the arm is less sensitive, and the calf is the least sensitive.

Pain

What are your most memorable experiences of pain? Although pain is an unpleasant experience, it has an important function in telling us that something is wrong with our bodies. Imagine what would happen if you fractured a bone in your leg during a race and felt no pain. You might keep running on it for a long distance. Nonetheless, we vary extensively in our ability to tolerate pain; some long-distance runners have continued to finish races even with a broken bone in their leg, for example. Some individuals hardly seem to know what pain is, while others sense pain with the slightest discomfort. An endurance for pain also varies from one culture to another. In some cultures individuals are taught to endure pain as long as they possibly can; in other cultures, individuals are encouraged to avoid all painful encounters.

No acceptable theory exists that can explain the sense of pain. One prominent view, though, is **gate-control theory** (Melzack & Dennis, 1978). Neural "gates" are present in both the spinal cord and the brain stem. The amount of pain we feel is determined by whether these gates are open or shut. If the pain gates are open, information about pain is allowed to go through to the higher centers of the brain. The brain, in turn, can send information back down to the spinal cord and influence whether a pain gate is open or closed. In this way, emotions, attitudes, hypnosis, and even acupuncture can influence how much pain we sense.

Acupuncture is a technique in which thin needles are inserted at specific points in the body to relieve specific symptoms (see figure 3.17). Interestingly, the point of stimulation may be some distance from the symptom being treated.

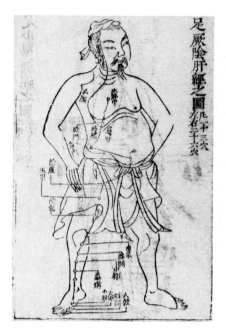 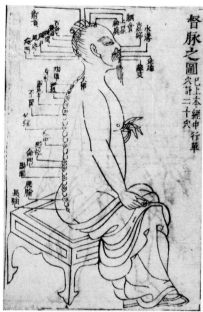

Figure 3.17
These Ming dynasty (A.D. 1300 to 1600) charts illustrate points on the meridians—the supposed pathways of life energy through the body—where acupuncture needles are inserted. Each meridian is named for an internal organ, such as the liver, although points on that meridian may be remote from the organ itself.

For example, when surgery for the removal of the stomach is performed and acupuncture is used as the anesthetic, four needles are placed in the pinna of each ear (Melzack, 1973). Though we have been slow to accept acupuncture in the United States, the technique is used widely in dental practice in China and sparingly in abdominal surgery. How could acupuncture reduce the sensation of pain? The gate control mechanisms may be partly responsible and the role of endorphins is also being explored.

Currently there is much interest in how procedures such as acupuncture might work and the neurochemical changes that are involved. For example, Bruce Pomeranz (1984) used acupuncture to reduce sensitivity to pain in a group of mice. He injected a second group with naloxone, a substance that blocks endorphins, before acupuncture was used. The second group of animals continued to be sensitive to pain, while the first group was not. Solomon Snyder, a key figure in the discovery of endorphins, recently found that when any tissue such as the skin or lining of the intestines is injured, a chemical called *bradykinin* is released. Snyder believes it is the most powerful pain-producing substance known. A very small amount of this substance injected under the skin produces intense pain. When the bradykinin is released, it attaches to special bradykinin receptors on the nerve tips in the immediate area of the injury, causing pain signals to be relayed to the brain. Scientists are working to discover chemicals that will block the pain pathways from the very beginning.

Rather than a simple pain pathway, most researchers today believe the brain's perception of pain is a complex symphony of brain chemicals and receptors. The brain not only acts like a computer that receives pain signals but probably is an active participant in the increase or decrease of pain. At the same time pain impulses are flashed to the brain, where they are screened, endorphins are released in the brain to suppress pain recognition. To some degree, this is what influences an individual's pain threshold.

Figure 3.18
The tip of the tongue, showing the numerous threadlike papillae that give the surface a velvety look (X 240).

Table 3.4	Primary Odors Suggested by Amoore
Odor	**Example**
Camphoraceous	Camphor
Pungent	Spices
Floral	Flowers
Ethereal	Ether
Pepperminty	Oil of peppermint
Musky	Musk
Putrid	Decaying meat

From Hole, John W., Jr., *Human Anatomy and Physiology,* 4th ed. © 1978, 1981, 1984, 1987 Wm. C. Brown Publishers, Dubuque, Iowa. All Rights Reserved. Reprinted by permission.

The Chemical Senses

To turn a civilization virtually upside down, a group of chemists simply shifted a few carbon, hydrogen, and oxygen atoms. So it seemed when the Coca-Cola company changed the formula for Coke in the spring of 1985. The uproar forced the company to bring back the original flavor in the summer of the same year after spending millions of dollars on advertising the virtues of the new Coke. The chemists at the Coca-Cola company were working with one of the chemical senses—the *gustatory* (or taste) *sense.* We have another chemical sense, the *olfactory sense,* which involves smell. Both of these senses differ from other senses we have discussed because they react to *chemicals* rather than *energy.*

Taste

It will not be the prettiest sight you have ever seen, but try this anyway. Take a drink of milk, allowing it to coat your tongue. Then go up to a mirror and stick your tongue out and look carefully at its surface. You should be able to see rounded bumps above the surface of your tongue (Matlin, 1983). These rounded bumps are called **papillae;** they contain taste buds, the basic receptors for taste (see figure 3.18). About 10,000 of these taste buds are located on your tongue, around your mouth, and even in your throat.

Taste buds respond to four main qualities: sweet, sour, bitter, and salty. Though all areas of the tongue can detect each of the four tastes, different regions of the tongue are more sensitive to one taste than another. The tip of the tongue is the most sensitive to sweet; the rear of the tongue is the most sensitive to bitter; just behind the sweet area is the most sensitive area for salt; and just behind that is the most sensitive area for sour.

Smell

Smell is an important but mysterious sense. We look for a sunset or a play to see, a symphony or rock concert to hear, and a massage to feel. But have you ever thought of entertaining yourself with an evening of smells (Matlin, 1983)?

Numerous attempts have been made to classify smells. Aristotle even showed some interest in this classification. More recently, smells have been classified into seven primary odors (Amoore, 1964). See table 3.4 for the names of these odors and some common items with which they are associated.

Perhaps the most important part of the olfactory system is the **olfactory epithelim;** *olfactory* means smell and *epithelium* means skin, so this is the skin with which you smell. The olfactory epithelium is located at the forward base of the cerebral hemisphere. Smell receptors are located within the olfactory epithelium. One theory of how the olfactory sense works emphasizes that odor molecules (such as minty or musky) have certain shapes that regulate the kind of smell we perceive. For example, minty molecules are oval in shape, camphoraceous molecules are rounder. The receptor sites in the olfactory epithelium are associated with the shapes of odorous molecules much as the shape of a key is related to the shape of the lock it opens.

How good are you at recognizing smells? Without practice, most individuals do a rather poor job of identifying odors. This sense can be perfected, however; perfumers, as perfume testers are called, can distinguish between 100 and 200 different fragrances (Cain, 1979).

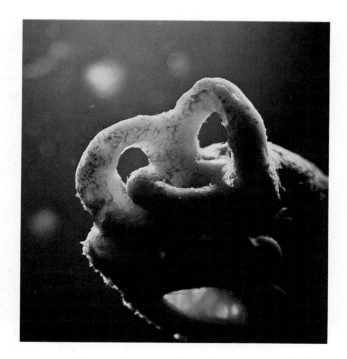

Figure 3.19
The semicircular canals are part of the vestibular sense. The three canals are roughly perpendicular to each other in three planes of space. Any angle of head rotation is registered by hair cells in one or more semicircular canals in both ears.

The Kinesthetic and Vestibular Senses

You know the difference between walking and running and between lying down and sitting up. And you know when you are upside down on a loop-to-loop ride at an amusement park. How do you know these things? Your body has two kinds of senses that provide information to your brain about your movement and orientation in space: the **kinesthetic senses,** which provide information about movement, posture, and orientation, and the **vestibular sense,** which provides information about balance and movement.

No specific organ contains the kinesthetic senses. Instead, these senses are located in the cells of our muscles, joints, and tendons. For example, you decide to strengthen your body. You begin a weight-lifting regimen and are at the point where you can bench press 150 pounds. You decide to really go for it and put the key in the Nautilus machine at 200 pounds. After several deep breaths, you thrust the 200 pounds upward; it quickly falls back to the bar holding the rest of the weights. Your body's ability to sense that it was not ready to press the 200 pounds was due to your kinesthetic senses. But it doesn't take 200 pounds of weights to set off your kinesthetic senses. Move your hand forward and touch this page. Wiggle your toes. Smile. Frown.

The vestibular sense tells us whether our body is tilted, moving, slowing down, or speeding up. It works in concert with the kinesthetic senses to coordinate our proprioceptive feedback, which is the information about the position of our limbs and body parts in relation to other body parts. An important part of the vestibular sense is the **semicircular canals** (see figure 3.19), which lie in the inner ear. These canals consist of three circular tubes that lie in three different planes of the body—left-right, up-down, and front-back. The tubes provide feedback to the brain when the body or head tilts in one of these three directions. Notice in figure 3.20 that the receptors of the vestibular sense are similar to the receptors for smell and audition.

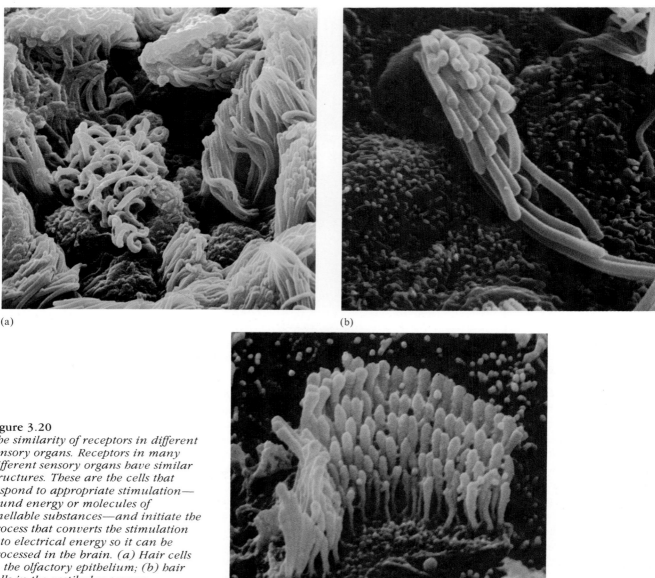

(a)   (b)

(c)

Figure 3.20
The similarity of receptors in different sensory organs. Receptors in many different sensory organs have similar structures. These are the cells that respond to appropriate stimulation— sound energy or molecules of smellable substances—and initiate the process that converts the stimulation into electrical energy so it can be processed in the brain. (a) Hair cells in the olfactory epithelium; (b) hair cells in the vestibular organs; (c) auditory hair cells.

Because the semicircular canals and the vestibular sense inform us about our equilibrium, this sense sometimes is called the equilibratory sense. There are occasions when we might wish our semicircular canals were less sensitive to body orientation, such as when motion causes the semicircular canals to become upset and the result is seasickness or dizziness. The most accepted view of why we get motion sickness is that the brain is constantly receiving information about the body's motion and position from three sources: the inner ear, eyes, and other sensors in various parts of the body. Information from these sources feeds into the brain, which compares it with stored information about motion and position. The problem begins when these different sources send contradictory messages. For example, a passenger standing on a ship's deck watching the waves can see the rail of the ship rising and falling. The roll of the deck makes the individual feel like she is riding a roller coaster.

Concept Table 3.3

The Auditory, Skin, Chemical, Kinesthetic, and Vestibular Senses		
Concept	Processes/related ideas	Characteristics/description
The auditory system	Sound	Sound waves vary in frequency, amplitude, and complexity; the perceptions are pitch, loudness, and timbre, respectively.
	The ear	Comprised of the outer ear, middle ear, and inner ear. The basilar membrane, located inside the cochlea in the inner ear, is where vibrations are changed into nerve impulses.
	Theories of hearing	Place theory emphasizes a particular place on the basilar membrane; frequency theory stresses the frequency of the auditory nerve's firing; volley theory is a modification and expansion of frequency theory to handle high-frequency sounds. Place and frequency theories are better at explaining low-frequency sounds, volley theory high-frequency sounds.
	Neural auditory processing	Information about sound is carried from the cochlea to the brain by the auditory nerve. Information is stored and integrated in the temporal lobe.
The skin senses	Touch, temperature, and pain	Skin contains three important senses: touch, temperature (warmth, cold), and pain. Pain has the important adaptive function of informing us when something is wrong in our body. No theory of pain is completely accepted. Gate-control theory has been given considerable attention.
The chemical senses	Taste, smell	These senses differ from other senses because they react to chemicals rather than energy.
The kinesthetic and vestibular senses	Their nature	The kinesthetic senses provide information about movement, posture and orientation; the vestibular sense provides information about balance and movement.

The brain is not accustomed to all of this contradictory information. Over time, though, the brain recognizes that stored information no longer is relevant to the current discordant input. Two to three days usually is long enough to get adjusted to sensory conflict, but it can take longer.

Let's pause a moment and summarize the main themes of our discussion. Some of the most important ideas about the auditory, skin, chemical, and kinesthetic/vestibular senses are presented in concept table 3.3.

Perception

Earlier in this chapter we said that perception is the brain's process of organizing and interpreting sensory information to give it meaning. When perception goes to work, sensory receptors have received energy from stimuli in the external world and sensory organs have processed and transformed the information so it can be transmitted to the brain. Perception is a creation of the brain; it is based on input extracted from sensory organs, such as the eye, ear, and nose. But perception goes beyond this input. The brain uses information previously extracted as a basis for making educated guesses, or interpretations, about the state of the outside world. Usually the interpretations are correct and useful. For example, on the basis of a change in color or texture, we can conclude that a dog is on the rug. On the basis of a continuous increase in size, we can conclude that a train is coming towards us. Sometimes, though, the interpretations or inferences are wrong; the result is an illusion—when we see something that is not there (Wolfe, 1986).

© *King Features Syndicate, Inc., 1977. Reprinted with special permission of King Features Inc.*

Figure 3.21
Reversible figure-ground pattern.
Either a goblet or a pair of silhouetted
faces in profile is seen.

To explore the world of perception, we will study how we perceive shape, depth, motion, and constancy. A number of fascinating illusions also will be described. We will conclude with the controversial topic of extrasensory perception.

Shape Perception

Think about the world you see and its shapes—buildings against the sky, boats on the horizon, letters on this page. We see these shapes because they are marked off from the rest of what we see by **contour,** a location at which a sudden change of brightness occurs. Think about the letters on this page again. As you look at the page, you see letters, which are shapes, in a field or background, the white page. This is called a *figure-ground relationship,* in which the figure is the distinct shape and what is left over is the ground. Some figure-ground relationships, though, are highly ambiguous and it is difficult to tell what is figure and what is ground. A well-known ambiguous figure-ground relationship is shown in figure 3.21. As you look at the figure your perception is likely to shift between seeing two faces and a single goblet. Another example of figure-ground ambiguity is found in the work of artist M. C. Escher, which keeps us from favoring one figure over another seemingly because spatial location and depth cues are not provided (see figure 3.22).

Figure 3.22
The sophisticated use of figure-ground relationship in Escher's woodcut Relativity *(1938).*
© 1988 M. C. Escher. c/o Cordon Art—Baarn—Holland

One group of psychologists—the Gestalt psychologists—has been especially intrigued by how we perceive shapes in our world. Gestalt psychologists developed a number of principles of perceptual organization, one of the most important being that the whole is not equal to the sum of its parts (figure 3.23 illustrates this point). The figure-ground relationship just described in another important Gestalt principle.

Three additional Gestalt principles are closure, proximity, and similarity. The principle of *closure* says that when we see a disconnected or incomplete figure, we fill in the spaces and see it as a complete figure (see figure 3.24a). The Gestalt psychologists also said that we organize our perceptions in terms of the *proximity* of the elements. In figure 3.24b, we see four columns of squares, not one set of twelve squares. *Similarity* is another Gestalt principle of perceptual organization. In figure 3.24c we see vertical columns of circles and squares in the display on the left; we see horizontal rows of circles and squares in the display on the right. In both of these displays, our mind organizes the shapes into similar categories.

Each of the Gestalt principles stresses our strong tendency to give our perceptions complete structure. Are we born with the ability to perceive the world according to Gestalt principles or do we learn these principles through experiences with the environment? The Gestalt psychologists believe they are innate, or inborn. In some way, they say, our minds are organized to perceive the world in structured and meaningful ways. Some psychologists, though, disagree, believing that we *learn* to perceive our world through experiences with it.

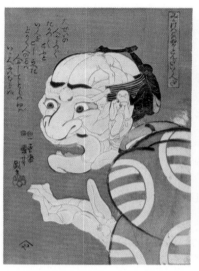

Figure 3.23
Example of the Gestalt principle that the whole does not equal the sum of the parts: Kuniyoshi Ichiyusai, A Kindly Man of Fearful Aspect, *Late Edo era. The configuration of the whole in this illustration is clearly qualitatively different than the sum of its parts.*
Collection by Jazo Suzuki, from Museum of Fun Exhibition by Asahi Shimbur, 1979.

Figure 3.24
Principles of Gestalt psychology:
(a) the principle of closure,
(b) the principle of proximity,
(c) the principle of similarity.

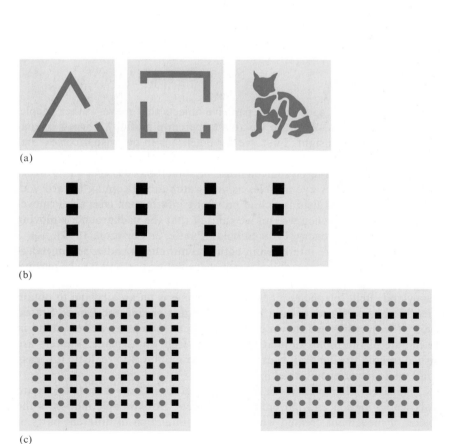

Figure 3.25
Linear perspective. Perhaps the most common and most striking instance of linear perspective is the apparent convergence in the distance of parallel railroad tracks. Of course, the actual space between the tracks is constant, but the corresponding retinal images and accordingly the size of the apparent separation of the tracks decrease with the distance of the tracks.

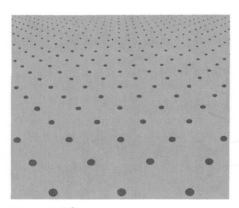

Figure 3.26
Texture gradient. The gradients of texture create an impression of depth on a flat surface.

Depth Perception

How do we perceive a world in three dimensions when only two dimensions are present in the image received from the eye? The answer lies in the study of depth perception and is explained by binocular and monocular cues (Grossberg, 1987a, b).

Your two eyes see the world from two slightly different locations, providing a slightly different image for each eye. This binocular disparity in the two eyes becomes less apparent the farther an object is from the viewer—beyond about thirty feet the image that falls on the two eyes is virtually the same.

Other cues for depth perception are monocular. With these cues an image falls on only one eye. **Monocular cues** have become so widely used by artists that they have become known as *pictorial cues*. Following are six monocular cues:

1. *Linear perspective.* The farther an object is from the viewer, the less space it takes up in the visual field. As shown in figure 3.25, as an object recedes in the distance, parallel lines in the object converge.
2. *Texture gradient.* Texture becomes more dense the farther away it is from the viewer (see figure 3.26) (Cutting, 1987).
3. *Relative size.* Objects farther away create a smaller retinal image than those nearby.
4. *Interposition.* An object that partially conceals or overlaps another object is perceived as closer.
5. *Shadowing.* The shadow of an object provides cues to its depth.
6. *Aerial perspective.* Pollution and water vapor in the air scatter light waves, giving distant objects a hazy appearance.

Motion Perception

During the course of each day we perceive objects that move—other people, cars, planes, animals. Why are we able to perceive motion? Three explanations provide some insight. First, we have neurons in our visual cortex that are specialized to detect motion. Second, feedback from our body tells us whether we are moving or someone else or some object is moving. For example, you move your eye muscles as you watch a ball coming toward you. Third, our perceptual field is rich in providing information cues about movement. For example, when we run we can tell that the background is moving (Gibson, in press; Gregory, 1978; Sekular, Pantle, & Levinson, 1979).

Psychologists are interested in both real movement and *apparent movement,* which occurs when an object is stationary but we perceive it to be moving (Wallach, 1987). An example of apparent movement can be experienced at Disneyland. Bell Telephone mounted nine cameras on an airplane to obtain nine different perspectives on a number of sights around the United States. The motion pictures are shown on nine different screens as viewers stand in the middle of the room, simulating the view from an airplane. Viewers are warned to hold the handrail because perceived motion is so realistic it is easy to fall while experiencing the "movement."

Apparent motion comes in many different forms; two that stand out are stroboscopic motion and movement aftereffects. **Stroboscopic motion** is the illusion of movement created when a rapid stimulation of different parts of the retina occurs—motion pictures are a form of stroboscopic motion. **Movement aftereffects** happen when we watch continuous movement and then look at another surface, which then appears to move in the opposite direction. Figure 3.27 provides an opportunity to experience movement aftereffects.

Figure 3.27
Movement aftereffects. An example of a geometric pattern that produces afterimages in which motion can be perceived. If the center of the pattern is fixated for approximately 10 seconds and then the afterimage is projected on a plain white surface, rotary motion is usually perceived.

Figure 3.28
Size constancy. Even though our retinal image of the hot air balloons changes, we still perceive the different balloons as being the same size. This illustrates the principle of size constancy.

Perceptual Constancy

We experience a perceptual world with many constancies; among the constancies are size, shape, and brightness. **Size constancy** is the recognition of an object as being the same size even though the retinal image of the object changes (figure 3.28). *Shape constancy* is the recognition that an object remains the same even though its orientation to us changes. If you look around the room, you see objects of varying shapes—chairs, tables, and so on. If you

Figure 3.29
Shape constancy. The various projected images from an opening door are quite different, yet a rectangular door is perceived.

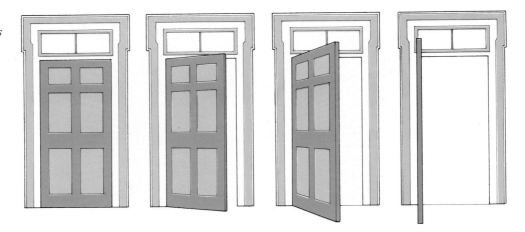

walk around the room, you will see these objects from different sides and angles. Even though the retinal image of the objects changes as you walk, you still perceive the objects as having the same shape (see figure 3.29). *Brightness constancy* is the recognition that an object retains the same degree of brightness even though different amounts of light fall on it. For example, regardless of whether you are reading this book indoors or outdoors, the white pages and black print do not look any different to you in terms of their whiteness or blackness.

Why do we experience perceptual constancies? The retinal image and perceived distance are two of the most important reasons. Perceived distance is influenced by such factors as the monocular and binocular cues present and our memory of past experiences of size (Gogel & DaSilva, 1987). Many visual illusions seem to be influenced by our perception of size constancy, one being the famous moon illusion we will discuss shortly.

Illusions

A visual illusion occurs when two objects produce exactly the same retinal image but are perceived as different images. Illusions are incorrect, but they are not abnormal. They can provide insight into how our perceptual processes work. More than 200 different types of illusions have been discovered (Gillam, 1980); we will study six.

One of the most famous illusions is the *Müller-Lyer illusion* shown in figure 3.30. The two lines are exactly the same length although *b* looks longer than *a*. Another illusion is the *horizontal-vertical illusion,* in which the vertical line looks longer than the horizontal line, although the two are equal (see figure 3.31). The *Ponzo illusion* also is a line illusion in which the top line looks much longer than the bottom line (see figure 3.32).

Why do these line illusions exist? One reason is that we mistakenly use certain cues for maintaining size constancy. For example, in the Ponzo illusion we see the upper line as being farther away (remember that objects higher in a picture are perceived as being farther away). The Müller-Lyer illusion, though, is not so easily explained. One idea is that our experience with similar architectural figures in our culture contributes to the illusion. For example, members of the Zulu culture, who live in a world of open spaces and curved structures, do not experience the Müller-Lyer illusion as strongly as individuals from the United States and other cultures, who regularly view rectangular objects (Gregory, 1978). We also may make our judgments about the lines by comparing incorrect parts of the figures. For example, when individuals were shown the Müller-Lyer illusion with the wings painted a different color, the illusion was greatly reduced (Coren & Girus, 1972).

Figure 3.30
The Müller-Lyer illusion.

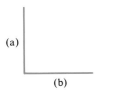

Figure 3.31
The horizontal-vertical illusion.

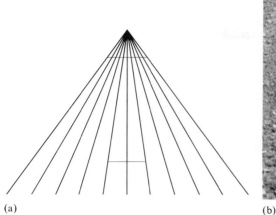

(a)

(b)

Figure 3.32
The Ponzo illusion. The two horizontal lines are actually the same length in (a); the two bars are the same length in (b).

Figure 3.33
Chances are you have experienced the moon illusion on a number of occasions. Why does the moon look so much larger on the horizon?

Another well-known illusion is the *moon illusion* (see figure 3.33). The moon is 2,000 miles in diameter and 289,000 miles away. Since both the moon's size and its distance from us are beyond our own experience, we have difficulty judging just how far away it really is. When the moon is above us, little information is present to help us judge its distance—no texture gradients or stereoscopic cues exist, for example. But when the moon is on the horizon, we can judge its distance in relation to familiar objects—trees and buildings, for example. The result is that we estimate the size of the moon as much larger when it is on the horizon than when it is overhead.

Yet another fascinating illusion is the *devil's tuning fork*. Look at figure 3.34 for about thirty seconds, then close the book. Now try to draw the tuning fork. You undoubtedly discovered that this was a difficult, if not impossible, task. Why was it so difficult? Probably because your cultural experience led you to interpret the two-dimensional drawing as three-dimensional. This interpretation caused you to have problems with depth cues, which are ambiguous in the figure. Interestingly, Africans without a formal education have no problem reproducing the devil's tuning fork because they merely see a pattern of flat lines (Coren, Porac, & Ward, 1979).

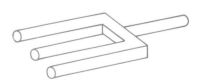

Figure 3.34
The Devil's tuning fork.

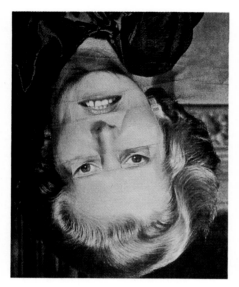

Figure 3.35
Why does this famous face look so different when you turn the book upside down?

Figure 3.36
In this situation involving an attempt to demonstrate telepathy, a "sender" in another room is informed in advance when a light will come on. The sender tries to relay this information mentally to the subject (above). The subject chooses a card, then the previously selected light is turned on and compared with the subject's choice.

In our final example of an illusion a "doctored" horrific face seen upside down goes unnoticed. Look at figure 3.35—you probably recognize this famous face as Margaret Thatcher. What seems to be an ordinary portrait (the illusion) actually is doctored. Both the mouth and the eyes have been cut out from the original and pasted back on upside down. If you turn this book upside down, the horrific look is easily seen. The "Thatcher" illusion may take place because the mouth is so far out of alignment, we simply cannot respond to its expression; it is still a fearful face, but we do not see that. And we may have a difficult time telling what really is the top of the mouth in the picture (Parks & Cross, 1986).

So far our coverage of perception has taken us through the perception of shape, depth, motion, constancy, and illusions; a summary of these ideas is presented in concept table 3.4. One final, curious perceptual phenomena remains to be discussed—extrasensory perception.

Extrasensory Perception

Our eyes, ears, mouth, nose, and skin provide us with sensory information about the external world; our perceptions are based on our interpretation of this sensory information. But some individuals claim that they can perceive the world through something other than normal sensory channels. Perception that does not occur through normal sensory processes is called **extrasensory perception (ESP).** The majority of psychologists do not believe in ESP, but a small number investigate the phenomenon.

Extrasensory experiences fall into three main categories. The first is **telepathy,** or the transfer of thought between two individuals who are in rapport. Figure 3.36 shows how attempts are made to demonstrate the existence of telepathy. **Precognition,** the second category, is the perception of events before

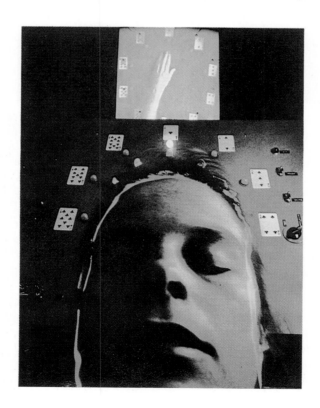

they occur. For example, a fortune teller may claim to see into the future and tell you what will happen to you in the next year. The final category, **clair-voyance,** is the ability to see or be aware of events that are not in sight. An individual may say that she can see someone standing in the room, even though others cannot, for example.

One of the most famous cases of extrasensory perception involved Uri Geller, a psychic who supposedly was able to perform mind-boggling feats; observers saw Geller correctly predict the number on a die rolled in a closed box eight out of eight times, reproduce drawings that were hidden in sealed envelopes, bend forks without touching them, and start broken watches. While he had worked as a magician, Geller claimed that his supernatural powers were created by energy sent from another universe. Careful investigation of Geller's feats revealed that they were nothing more than the tricks of a magician. For example, in the case of the die, Geller was allowed to shake the box and open it (Randi, 1980).

A major difficulty with ESP experiments is their failure to replicate. Proponents of ESP claim that they can communicate with the dead or with an individual who is miles away, but critics demand to see or experience the same phenomena themselves. Parapsychologists, as the ESP enthusiasts are called, have difficulty repeating their extrasensory experiences. Yet replication is one of the hallmarks of scientific investigation. Reviews of the ESP research literature conclude that when the scientific method is applied to ESP, the existence of the phenomenon has not been proved (Akers, 1984, 1986; Shaver, 1986). To learn why most psychologists do not believe in ESP, read Psychology 3.2.

In the next chapter we will explore many other aspects of our awareness, both of our external world and our internal world. Sleep and dreams, altered states of consciousness, and the influence of drugs on mind and behavior await you in chapter 4.

Concept Table 3.4

Perception		
Concept	**Processes/related ideas**	**Characteristics/description**
Shape perception, depth perception, motion perception, and perceptual constancy	Shape perception	Seen because it is marked off by contour. An important aspect is figure-ground relationship. Gestalt psychologists developed a number of principles of perceptual organization.
	Depth perception	Seen because of binocular and monocular cues. Monocular cues are widely used and are called pictorial cues.
	Motion perception	Interest focuses on both real movement and apparent movement. Stroboscopic motion and movement aftereffects are two prominent aspects of apparent movement.
	Perceptual constancy	Includes size, shape, and brightness. Retinal image and perceived distance provide some explanation.
Illusions	Their nature	Occur when two objects produce exactly the same retinal image but are perceived as different images. Among the more than 200 different illusions are the Müller-Lyer illusion and the moon illusion. Perceptual constancies and cultural experiences are among the factors thought to be responsible for illusions.

Psychology 3.2

Debunking the Claims of ESP

■ A woman reports that she has power over the goldfish in a huge fifty-gallon tank. She claims that she can will them to swim to either end of the tank. As soon as she wills it, the fish take off.

Under the careful scrutiny of James Randi, this woman's account turned out to be just another fish story. The woman had written Randi, a professional magician, who has a standing offer of $10,000 to anyone whose psychic claims withstand his analysis. In the case of the woman and her goldfish, Randi received a letter from her priest validating her extraordinary power. Randi talked with the priest, who told him that the woman would put her hands in front of her body and then run to one end of the tank. The fish soon followed. Since the fish could see out of the tank just as we can see into it, Randi suggested that she put opaque

brown wrapping paper over one end of the tank and then try her powers. The woman did and called Randi about the result, informing him that she had discovered something new about her powers: that her mind could not penetrate the brown paper! The woman believed that she had magical powers and completely misunderstood why Randi had asked her to place the brown paper over the fish tank.

No one has claimed Randi's $10,000 prize, but he has been called to investigate several hundred reports of supernatural and occult powers. Faith healers have been among those he has evaluated. Randi has witnessed individuals yelling and dancing up and down, saying they are healed of such maladies as cancer and diabetes. When asked how they know they are healed they usually say it is because they no longer

have the disease or because the faith healer told them so. On checking back with the "healed" a week later, Randi has found diabetics taking insulin and a cancer patient resuming radiation therapy. In some cases, their health has dramatically worsened, as in the case of a diabetic who had to be taken to the hospital because he had stopped his insulin treatment. When asked if they still believed in the faith healer's treatment, it is not unusual to hear these individuals say that they just did not believe strongly enough.

Randi makes the distinction between the tricks of magicians, such as himself, and the work of the psychics and faith healers. He says that magic is done for entertainment, the other for swindling.

Summary

I. **What Are Sensation and Perception?**
Sensation is the process of detecting and encoding stimulus energy in the environment. Perception is the process of organizing and interpreting the information sensed to give it meaning.

II. **Detecting the Sensory World**
Absolute threshold is the minimum amount of stimulus an individual can detect. Psychologists have determined that the absolute threshold is the stimulus value detected 50 percent of the time. Noise refers to the presence of irrelevant and competing stimuli; motivation also influences our ability to detect the presence of stimuli. Signal detection theory recognizes that psychological factors, such as motivation, affect stimulus

detection. Subliminal perception is the perception of stimuli below the threshold of awareness; this is a controversial topic. The difference threshold is the smallest amount of stimulation required to discriminate one stimulus from another. When this is done 50 percent of the time, it is called a just noticeable difference. Weber's law states that regardless of their magnitude, two stimuli must differ by a constant proportion to be detected. Sensory adaptation is a weakened response to stimulus energy.

III. **The Visual Stimulus and the Eye**

Light is a form of electromagnetic energy that can be described in terms of wavelengths. The receptors in the human eye are sensitive to wavelengths between 400 and 700 nm. The key external parts of the eye are the sclera, iris, pupil, and cornea. The lens focuses light rays on the retina, the light-sensitive mechanism in the eye. Chemicals in the retina break down chromatic light into neural impulses. The optic nerve transmits neural impulses to the brain. Because of crossovers of nerve fibers what we see in the left visual field is registered in the right side of the brain and vice versa. Visual information reaches the occipital lobe of the brain where it is stored and further integrated. Hubel and Wiesel discovered that some neurons in the visual cortex detect different features of our visual world, such as line angle and size.

IV. **Color Vision**

Objects appear colored because they reflect only certain wavelengths of light between 400 and 700 nm. Three important properties of colors are hue, saturation, and brightness. When mixing color we get different results depending on whether we mix light or pigments; light involves an additive mixture, pigments a subtractive mixture. Two major theories of color vision have been proposed and both turned out to be right. The Young-Helmholtz trichromatic theory is based on the idea that by mixing red, blue, and green light all of the colors we perceive can be produced. This theory cannot explain color blindness and afterimages, which the opponent-process theory can. Both color blindness and afterimages suggest that the visual system treats colors as complementary pairs— red-green and yellow-blue.

V. **The Auditory System**

Sound waves, vibrating changes in the air, vary in frequency, amplitude, and complexity; the perception of these three dimensions of sound are pitch, loudness, and timbre, respectively. The ear is made up of the outer ear, middle ear, and inner ear. The basilar membrane, located inside the cochlea in the inner ear, is where vibrations are changed into neural impulses. Three theories of hearing explain auditory processing in the cochlea: place theory, frequency theory, and volley theory. Information about sound is carried from the cochlea to the brain by the auditory nerve. The auditory pathway is complex; eventually the information is stored and integrated in the temporal lobe.

VI. **The Skin Senses**

The skin contains three important senses: touch, temperature (warmth, cold), and pain. Pain has the important adaptive function of informing us when something is wrong in our body. No theory of pain is completely accepted; gate-control theory has been given considerable attention.

VII. **The Chemical and the Kinesthetic and Vestibular Senses**

The senses of taste and smell differ from other senses because they react to chemicals rather than energy. The kinesthetic senses provide information about movement, posture, and orientation; the vestibular sense provides information about balance and movement.

VIII. **Shape perception, Depth Perception, Motion Perception, and Perceptual Constancy**

We see shapes because they are marked off from the rest of what we see by contour. An important aspect of shape perception is the figure-ground relationship. Gestalt psychologists developed a number of principles of perceptual organization. We see depth because of binocular and monocular cues. Interest in motion perception focuses on both real and apparent movement; stroboscopic motion and movement aftereffects are prominent aspects of apparent movement. We experience a world with many constancies, among them size, shape, and brightness. Retinal image and perceived distance provide some explanation of why we experience perceptual constancies.

IX. **Illusions**

A visual illusion occurs when two objects produce exactly the same retinal image but are perceived as different images. Among the more than 200 visual illusions are the Müller-Lyer illusion and the moon illusion. Perceptual constancies and cultural experiences are among the factors thought to be responsible for illusions.

X. **Extrasensory Perception**

Extrasensory perception is perception that does not occur through normal sensory channels but rather through supernatural or extraordinary means. Three main forms are telepathy, precognition, and clairvoyance. The claims of ESP enthusiasts have not held up to the scientific method.

Key Terms

sensation *83*
perception *83*
absolute threshold *84*
noise *84*
signal detection theory *85*
subliminal perception *85*
difference threshold *87*
just noticeable difference (jnd) *87*
Weber's law *87*
sensory adaptation *87*
light *89*
sclera *89*
iris *90*
pupil *90*
cornea *90*
lens *90*
retina *90*
rods *90*
cones *90*
fovea *90*
blind spot *90*

optic nerve *92*
optic chiasma *92*
hue *93*
saturation *93*
brightness *93*
additive mixture *94*
subtractive mixture *94*
Young-Helmholtz trichromatic theory *94*
afterimage *94*
opponent-process theory *96*
frequency *99*
pitch *99*
amplitude *99*
loudness *99*
complexity *99*
timbre *99*
outer ear *100*
middle ear *100*
inner ear *100*
cochlea *101*

organ of Corti *101*
basilar membrane *101*
place theory *101*
frequency theory *101*
volley theory *101*
auditory nerve *101*
gate-control theory *102*
papillae *104*
olfactory epithelium *104*
kinesthetic senses *105*
vestibular sense *105*
semicircular canals *105*
contour *108*
monocular cues *110*
stroboscopic motion *110*
movement aftereffects *110*
size constancy *111*
visual illusion *112*
extrasensory perception (ESP) *114*
telepathy *114*
precognition *114*
clairvoyance *115*

Suggested Readings

Fineman, M. (1981). *The inquisitive eye.* New York: Oxford University Press. A highly entertaining book that provides many illustrations of vision and visual perception. Easier to read than most books on these topics.

Frisby, J. P. (1980). *Seeing: Illusion, brain, and mind.* New York: Oxford University Press. A fascinating book on illusions that not only presents many different illusions but attempts to show how computer scientists are trying to develop simulations of the visual process.

Keller, H. (1970). *Story of my life.* New York: Airmont. The fascinating story of Helen Keller's life as a blind person. Provides insight into blind people's perception of the world and how they use other senses.

Melzack, R. (1973). *The puzzle of pain.* London: Penguin. A fascinating book about the nature of pain, including detailed ideas about acupuncture.

Rock, I. (1984). *Perception.* New York: W. H. Freeman. Rock is one of the leading researchers in the perceptual field. In this beautifully illustrated book, he describes many fascinating aspects of perception.

Sekuler, R., & Blake, R. (1985). *Perception.* New York: Knopf. For a more detailed look at many of the topics in this chapter, spend some time with this text. Individual chapters include color perception, knowledge and perception, and smell and taste.

Chapter 4

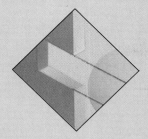

States of Consciousness

■ ■

Time past and time future
Allow but a little consciousness,
To be conscious is not to be in time
But only in time can the moment in the rose-garden,
The moment in the arbor where the rain beat,
The moment in the draughty church at smokefall
Be remembered; involved with past and future.
Only through time is time conquered.

—T. S. Eliot

■ ■

Images of States of Consciousness

One summer day in 1797, a man living in an isolated farmhouse in England took a dose of opium and sat down to read about Kubla Khan in a volume called *Purchas his Pilgrimage.* Before long the man, Samuel Taylor Coleridge, fell asleep. During his sleep Coleridge composed a poem of 200 to 300 lines. Later he wrote that the images rose up without any sensation or consciousness of effort. As soon as he awoke, he began writing down the words of the poem:

In Xanadu did Kubla Khan
A stately pleasure-dome decree . . .
His flashy eyes, his floating hair!
Weave a circle round him thrice,
And close your eyes with hold dread.
For he on honey-dew hath fed,
And drunk the milk of Paradise.

At this point, line fifty-four, he was interrupted for approximately one hour by someone at the door. When he returned to his desk, Coleridge was dismayed to find that the rest of the poem had vanished from his mind. On numerous occasions over a number of years he tried to complete the poem but could not remember the words. What Coleridge did remember before being interrupted is regarded as one of the best pieces of English romantic poetry.

Coleridge's experiences bring up some of the most important topics in states of consciousness: the nature of sleep and dreams, the relation of unconscious and conscious thought, altered states of consciousness, and the role of drugs in states of consciousness. Each of these topics is a prominent theme in this chapter. ■

What Is Consciousness?

What are you aware of right now? Possibly the words you are reading, your roommate's stereo? Or are you daydreaming about the attractive individual you were introduced to after the last psychology class?

Normal Waking Consciousness

Consciousness consists of the external stimuli and internal mental events that we are aware of at any given time (Ornstein, 1973). This awareness can take many different forms, from sleeping and daydreaming to meditation and from hypnosis to normal waking states.

Sometimes consciousness is a highly concentrated effort actively directed toward a goal. You put forth a conscious effort to win a tennis match, for example. At other times consciousness is more passive. For example, you become aware of your environment when you take a deep breath after a rain shower and say, "It smells so clean out here now." Right now your consciousness may be both active and passive. You may be actively planning to do well on the next test and therefore are reading this book; passively you may sense that you have a lot of energy so you are going to study another hour.

Often information moves in and out of consciousness in a rapid fashion. William James (1890) described the mind as a **stream of consciousness**— a continuous flow of changing sensations, images, thoughts, and feelings. We may race from one topic to the next—from thinking about how well we feel to what we are going to do tomorrow to where we are going to have lunch. Our consciousness becomes highly focused when we concentrate hard on a task and block all else out of our minds.

At the turn of the century, James (1890) commented on the importance of consciousness in understanding mind and behavior, a theme we have returned to in psychology today.

> Our normal waking consciousness, rational consciousness as we call it, is but one special type of consciousness, whilst all about it, parted from it by the filmiest of screen, there lie potential forms of consciousness entirely different. We may go through life without suspecting their existence: but apply the requisite stimulus, and at a touch they are there in all their completeness, definite types of mentality which probably somewhere have their field of application and adaptation. No account of the universe in its totality can be final which leaves these other forms of consciousness quite disregarded.

Subconscious, Nonconscious, and Unconscious Processes

An automobile mechanic does not think through the steps necessary to replace the parts in an engine because the process is routine. But if the mechanic gets stuck, he may have to think through the steps and thus bring into awareness what he knows. Often we get along in our world by functioning at a **subconscious level,** that is, beneath our level of awareness, to solve problems and carry out our everyday activities.

Our mind and body carry out many processes that we are unaware of, referred to as **nonconscious** processes. Most nonconscious processes involve body functions, such as the brain processes involved in the control of temperature and digestion.

Remember from chapter 1 that Freud believed most of our thoughts are **unconscious,** shoved far beneath our awareness because they are too laden with sexual and aggressive overtones to be admitted to consciousness. Freud felt that one of psychotherapy's main goals was to bring unconscious thoughts into conscious awareness so they can be addressed. Think about a young man who is inhibited around women, breaking into a cold sweat if a woman comes near him. He is unaware that his behavior is unconsciously influenced by the cold, punitive way his mother interacted with him when he was a child.

Because we cannot study the unconscious mind directly, its existence must be inferred. In this area of study, rigorous, experimentally oriented psychologists feel especially uneasy about the role of states of consciousness in psychology. Indeed, we have made little scientific progress in studying the unconscious mind. But even experimental psychologist Ernest Hilgard (1983, 1986) commented that one of the premier goals of psychology in the coming decades should be the unraveling of the mysteries of the unconscious mind.

Daydreaming

We all daydream, and sometimes this gets us into trouble. Perhaps in school a teacher has asked you a question while you were staring into another world. **Daydreaming** lies somewhere between active consciousness and dreaming while we are asleep; it is like dreaming while we are awake. What are daydreams like? Samuel Johnson said they are "airy notions of hope or fear beyond the sober limits of probability." Daydreams are often fantasy experiences. As you sit in English class listening to the professor's lecture, your mind drifts and forms an image of a movie star or you think about what life would be like if you lived in a different time or place. Daydreams are part of our conscious awareness; we shift our attention from the task at hand to thoughts and images of another place and time. Daydreams may be pleasant flights of fantasy, or they may involve anxious, angry, or guilty images (Singer, 1975, 1984). Sometimes, daydreams are just a way of relieving boredom.

We have been talking about what states of consciousness are like when we are awake. But an important part of our life takes place when we are not awake. Sleep and dreams still have mysterious qualities, but scientists are developing some fascinating insights about them.

Sleep and Dreams

The mattress salesman told me, "After all, you spend about one-third of your life sleeping. The least you can do for yourself is to spend $500 for this unbelievable mattress." When we are awake we can detect changes in our consciousness, but we usually do not think of sleep as a time when we are conscious. However, mental activity does occur during sleep and during dreams as well.

Sleep

Each night something lures us from work, from play, and from our loved ones into a solitary state. It is sleep, the sandman's spell that claims more of our time than any other pursuit. Down through the centuries, as philosophers and scientists probed and analyzed every waking moment, those who were interested in sleep primarily were fascinated by its role as a springboard for dreams. We know now that sleep involves much more.

Different Kinds of Sleep

The invention of the electroencephalograph, described in chapter 2, led to some major breakthroughs in understanding sleep by revealing how the brain's electrical activity changes during sleep. In a moment we will describe sleep's EEG patterns, but first let's consider what the brain's activity is like when we are excited and when we are relaxed. As shown in figure 4.1, an individual in an excited state shows an EEG pattern of rapid, relatively small changes in electrical voltage. This is a *desynchronized* pattern and the waves are known as **beta waves.** When individuals relax or close their eyes, the EEG's pattern is larger and the waves are known as **alpha waves.**

What happens to the electrical activity of the brain when we fall asleep? Through careful inspection of EEGs, different stages of sleep based on the brain's electrical activity have been discovered. Thousands of subjects have been wired to recording devices such as the EEG in sleep laboratories to more accurately chart the brain's activity during sleep (see figure 4.2).

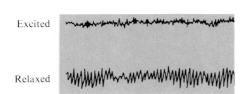

Figure 4.1
Electroencephalograms recorded during excited and relaxed states.

Figure 4.2
In this sleep laboratory a subject sleeps in a soundproof room while changes in the electrical activity of her brain are monitored by electrodes placed on different areas of her scalp.

Sleep is far more complex than simply falling asleep and then waking up. When we close our eyes and wait for sleep, we often drift into a twilight zone in which our awareness of the external world decreases. Psychologists call this transition between wakefulness and sleep a **hypnagogic state.** It is a drowsy, pleasant state of existence during which we sometimes experience vivid visual images, such as bright flashes of geometric patterns.

As we fall asleep, the rapid brain waves of waking are replaced by slow brain waves. These slow brain waves characterize Stage 1 of sleep, which is a light sleep (see figure 4.3). Then the sleeper sinks into the second and third stages of sleep, called nondream sleep. Each of these two stages involves progressively more muscle relaxation and slower brain waves. The sleeper then moves into Stage 4, a deep state during which the sleeper is difficult to rouse and often appears confused when awakened. It is in this deep state of sleep that sleepwalking, sleeptalking, and bedwetting tend to occur.

After about seventy minutes of sleep, much of which is spent in Stages 3 and 4, the individual moves restlessly and drifts up through the sleep stages toward wakefulness. But instead of reentering Stage 1, the individual enters a very different form of sleep called Stage 1 REM sleep, or more commonly called **REM sleep.** During REM sleep, the EEG pattern shows fast waves similar to those of wakefulness. REM stands for rapid eye movement, and during REM sleep your eyeballs move up and down and from left to right (see figure 4.4).

When individuals are awakened during REM sleep, they are more likely to report that they have been dreaming than when they are awakened during another stage. In sleep laboratories, individuals who claim that they rarely dream frequently report dreaming when they are awakened during REM sleep. And the longer the period of REM sleep, the more likely the individual will report dreaming (Foulkes, 1972). Dreams do occur during slow-wave or nonREM sleep, but the frequency of dreams in these other stages is not high (Webb, 1978).

So far we have described only one cycle of sleep, which consists of the first four stages plus REM sleep. One of these cycles lasts about ninety minutes and recurs several times a night (see figure 4.5). Several points are important to remember about the frequency of these cycles. The amount of deep sleep (Stage 4) is much greater in the first half of a night's sleep than in the second half. The majority of REM sleep takes place during the latter part of a night's sleep, and the length of the REM period becomes progressively longer. The first REM period might last for ten minutes and the last as long as one hour.

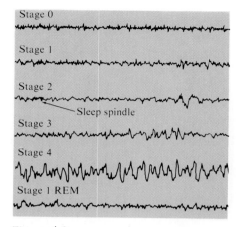

Figure 4.3
EEGs recorded during different stages of wakefulness and sleep. All tracings are drawn approximately to scale.

Source: After A Manual of Standardized Terminology, Techniques, and Scoring System for Sleep Stages of Human Subjects, *A. Rechtschaffen and A. Kales (Eds.), The National Institute of Health, no. 204, 1968.*

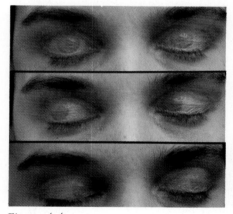

Figure 4.4
During REM sleep, our eyes move rapidly as if we were observing the images we see moving in our dreams.

Figure 4.5
Graph depicting sleep pattern in young adults during a normal night of sleep. Note the reduction of slow-wave sleep, especially Stage 4 sleep, during the latter part of the night and the relative increase of REM sleep as well.

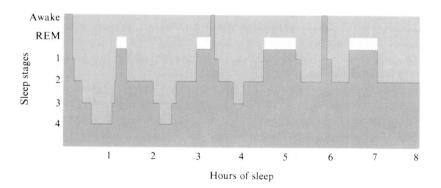

Figure 4.6
Centuries before scientists discovered that some biological rhythms involve adaptations to the earth's seasonal and light-dark cycles, human beings marked the significance of seasonal changes with rites and celebrations.

Sleep and Circadian Rhythms

Remember from our discussion of the brain in chapter 2 that depression can be seasonal. By increasing the seasonally depressed individual's exposure to light during the winter months, depression is reduced. Nature's rhythm involves seasons and more: summer, fall, winter, and then spring; night and then day. Through the years individuals have speculated about the meaning of these cycles, planned their activities around them, and even had festivals to commemorate them (see figure 4.6). Our body has rhythms, most of which we are unaware of—the rise and fall of hormones in the bloodstream, accelerated and decelerated cycles of brain activity, highs and lows of body temperature, for example. Some rhythms are *circadian,* from the Latin word "circa" meaning "about" and "dies" meaning "day." The human sleep/wake cycle is a **circadian rhythm.**

The sleepiness we feel after a few nights, or even just one night, may be due not only to a lack of sufficient sleep but to a shift in our circadian rhythms (Coleman, 1986; Dement, 1976). If you fly from Los Angeles to New York and then go to bed at 11 P.M. Eastern Standard Time, you may have trouble falling asleep because your body is still on Pacific time. Even if you sleep for eight hours that night, you may find it hard to wake up at 7 A.M. Eastern time because your body thinks it is 4 A.M. If you stay in New York for several days, your body will adjust to the new schedule.

The phase shift that occurred when you flew from Los Angeles to New York does not necessarily mean a loss of sleep; it means your body time is out of phase, or synchronization, with clock time. When jet lag occurs it is the result of two or more body rhythms being out of synch. We usually go to bed when our body temperature begins to drop, but in our new location we may be trying to go to bed when it is rising. When we wake up in the morning our adrenal glands release large doses of cortisol. In our new geographical location the glands may be releasing this chemical just as we are getting ready for bed at night.

Another circumstance in which circadian rhythms may become desynchronized is when shift workers change their work hours. A number of near-accidents in air travel have been associated with pilots who have not yet become synchronized to their new shift and are not working as efficiently as usual. It has been speculated that shift rotation was one of the causes of the nuclear incident at Three Mile Island (Moore-Ede, Sulzman, & Fuller, 1982). The team of workers monitoring the nuclear plant when the incident took place had been placed on night shift just after a six-week period of constant shift rotation.

As researchers became intrigued by the role of biological rhythms, they naturally were curious about what happens when an individual is completely isolated from clocks, calendars, night, the moon, the sun, and all indices of time. A number of experiments have focused on such isolation experiences (e.g., Kales, 1970; Siffre, 1975). To learn more about this isolation and how it influences our sleep patterns, read Psychology 4.1.

Interestingly, the natural circadian rhythm of most animals, including humans, is twenty-five to twenty-six hours, but our internal clocks easily adapt to the twenty-four hour rhythms (light, sounds, warmth) of the turning earth. When we are isolated from environmental cues, our sleep-wake cycles continue to be rather constant, but typically longer than twenty-four hours, as the experience of Michel Siffre showed.

The effects of profound sleep loss have been difficult to study because preventing individuals from sleeping is stressful. Subjects tend to become irritable, lose concentration, and show other signs of stress after two to three days without sleep (Weaver, 1986; Webb, 1978). As individuals become more motivated to sleep, they may snatch bits of "micro-sleep" while standing up;

Cave "Days" and Calendar Days

■ French scientist Michel Siffre entered Midnight Cave near Del Rio, Texas, on February 14, 1972. A small nylon tent deep within the cave was Siffre's home for six months (see figure 4.A). Because Siffre could not see or sense the sun rising and setting in the cave, he began to live by biological cycles instead of by days. When Siffre wanted to go to sleep, he called the support crew outside and told them to turn off the lights in the cave. Just before he went to sleep, he attached electrodes to his scalp so his sleep cycles could be recorded. When he woke up, he called the support crew and asked them to turn on the cave's lights.

Siffre referred to each one of his sleep/wake cycles as a day. Siffre's days closely resembled a twenty-four hour cycle throughout the six months in the cave, although they were slightly longer and more varied toward the end of the six months. Near the end of his stay in the cave, occasionally Siffre's days were very long, but most still averaged about twenty-eight hours (see figure 4.B).

After six months Siffre misjudged which month it was. It was August, but he thought it was only July. On day 151 of Siffre's cave experience, the caveman made this entry into a diary:

Gerard tells me it is August 10 . . . and the experiment is concluded; I am confused; I believed it to be mid-July. Then, as the truth sinks in, comes a flood of relief.

Siffre's comments about life in the cave reflect the cave's eeriness and the confusion such experiences create:

You live following your mind . . . you have not the alternance of day and night. . . . It's all in your brain . . . no sound, nothing . . . darkness completely.

Figure 4.A

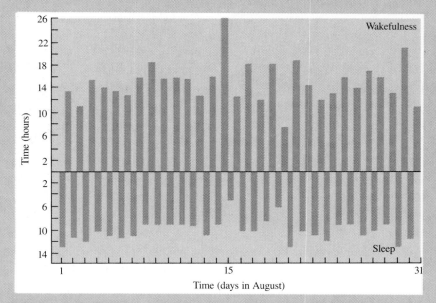

Figure 4.B
Siffre's August "Days."

it is not unusual to watch subjects become disoriented as they move in and out of sleep. Individuals who are highly motivated (and able to cope with the stress) can function surprisingly well after as much as eight to ten days without sleep (Dement, 1976).

But how much sleep do we really need each night? Some of us can get by on an average of five to six hours of sleep a night, and others of us may need nine to ten hours to function effectively. The idea that each of us needs eight hours of sleep each night is a myth.

Why Do We Sleep?

There are two theories about why we sleep—repair theory and ecological theory. **Repair theory** states that sleep restores, replenishes, and rebuilds our brains and bodies, which somehow are worn out or used up by the day's waking activity. This idea fits with the feeling of being "worn out" before we sleep and "restored" when we wake. Most individuals believe in some version of repair theory; Aristotle believed in the repair theory of sleep.

Support for repair theory comes from findings that growth hormone is secreted during slow-wave (deep) sleep and that some brain tissue repair occurs during this form of sleep (Adam, 1980; Smith, 1985). However, an increase in slow-wave sleep does not consistently occur the night following extensive physical effort and exertion (Spiegel, Koberle, & Allen, 1986). Nearly three decades of intense searching in sleep laboratories has failed to uncover any specific repair or restoration that occurs during sleep. And the surprisingly good performance of individuals who have been awake for many days dampens support for repair theory, although modest impairment of memory has been reported following sleep loss (Greiser, Greenberg, & Harrison, 1972).

Ecological theory is a relatively recent view of why we sleep (Webb, 1978). According to this theory, the main purpose of sleep is to keep animals from wasting their energy and harming themselves during those parts of the day or night to which they have not adapted. For example, our ancestors would have fumbled around in the dark, risking accidents or attack by large predators such as lions and tigers. So, like the chimpanzees who sleep safely in treetops at night, our ancestors presumably hid protected in sleep through the night.

In today's world, ecological factors still are important for animals in the wild. Small animals of prey with good hiding places, such as mice and rabbits, sleep regularly and safely all through the daylight hours. By contrast, large animals, such as horses and cows, who cannot hide, show scanty and irregular sleep patterns. Piecing together the factors of size and predatory status, almost two-thirds of the variation in length of sleep can be accounted for by body weight and danger of attack (Allison & Chichetti, 1976).

Both repair theory and ecological theory have some merit. It is possible that originally sleep was most important for keeping us and most animals out of trouble but since has evolved to allow for certain repair processes.

Neural Basis of Sleep

It once was thought that sleep happens when there is not enough sensory stimulation to keep the brain awake. Without stimuli, it was believed that the brain just "slows down," producing sleep. Later it was realized that sleep comes and goes without any obvious change in the amount of environmental stimulation. Theorists suggested we might have an internal "activating system" in the reticular formation that keeps the brain activated, or awake, all day. Sleep was thought to be caused by "fatigue" of the so-called activating system, or by an accumulation of some "sleep toxin" that chemically depressed the activating system (Monnier & Hosli, 1965).

Ecological theory says that the reason organisms sleep is to keep them from wasting their energy and risking harm during those parts of the day or night for which they have not been adapted.

BLOOM COUNTY
by Berke Breathed

© 1986, Washington Post Writer's Group, reprinted with permission.

The contemporary view of sleep is radically different. As you have learned, the brain is not "stopped" during sleep, but instead it is actively performing complex maneuvers that produce both REM and nonREM sleep behaviors. In fact, when sleep is examined at the cellular level, many neurons fire faster than in a waking state.

The puzzle is not completely solved, but some of the major pieces of the brain's machinery have been identified. NonREM sleep, for example, requires the participation of neurons in both the forebrain and medulla areas of the brain. REM sleep is a period of especially intense brain activity, also requiring the cooperation of a number of brain systems (Hobson, Lydic, & Baghdoyan, 1986).

Much of the current interest in the neural basis of sleep focuses on the role of neurotransmitters. Acetylcholinelike substances injected into the brain "turn-on" cholinergic neurons and produce REM sleep behaviors (Hobson & Steriade, 1986). Norepinephrine and serotonin also are involved in sleep; neurons using these neurotransmitters often stop firing completely during REM sleep. Their silence seems to release other neurons, allowing REM sleep to begin (Coote, Futuro, & Logan, 1985). Groups of neurons in the brain stem also seem to generate bursts of activity that cause eye movements and visual imagery during REM sleep (Hobson & McCarley, 1977).

So far we have discussed normal aspects of sleep, although in evaluating the sleep deprivation studies, we found that prolonged loss of sleep often produces stress, irritability, and disorientation. As we see next, there are many ways sleep can become disordered.

Sleep Disorders

Many individuals get into bed, fall asleep, and have a restful night. For others, the night is not so restful. Some of us do not sleep well at night, sleepwalk, sleeptalk, want to sleep much of the day, or have breathing problems while we sleep.

Sleepwalking and sleeptalking occur during the deepest stages of sleep. Individuals who sleepwalk are called *somnambulists*. For many years it was believed that somnambulists were acting out their dreams. But somnambulism occurs during Stages 3 and 4 of sleep, the time when the individual is not likely to be dreaming. The problem of talking in one's sleep is called *somniloquy*, which also occurs during nonRem sleep. Awakened sleepwalkers and sleeptalkers act confused and do not remember what they have done or said, possibly because the behaviors occur during the deep stages of sleep.

Some individuals want to sleep most of the time, while others are not able to sleep enough. **Narcolepsy** is the irresistable urge to fall asleep, which may last anywhere from several minutes to several hours. The urge is so strong that the individual may fall asleep while talking or standing up (Guilleminault, 1985). Interestingly, narcoleptics immediately enter REM sleep instead of moving through the first four sleep stages and then on to REM sleep. Narcolepsy runs in families, so it may be influenced by heredity (Guilleminault, Passouart, & Dement, 1976).

But a far more frequent problem is *insomnia,* the inability to sleep. This may manifest itself as a problem in falling asleep, in waking up during the night, or in waking up too early. As many as one in five Americans has insomnia (Kripke & Simons, 1976). We spend large sums of money trying to sleep better, buying nonprescription drugs or prescription sedatives, yet there is no evidence that nonprescription drugs produce a better night's sleep. Sedatives reduce the amount of time individuals spend in Stage 4 and REM sleep, possibly upsetting the restfulness of their sleep (Syvalahti, 1985). The chemical compound *tryptophan,* which is found in milk and milk products, does seem to help individuals sleep better. Next time you have a problem falling asleep, a glass of milk may do the trick.

Another type of sleep disorder is **sleep apnea.** Individuals with this disorder stop breathing while they are asleep because the windpipe fails to open or brain processes involved in respiration fail to work properly. They wake up periodically during the night so they can breathe better, although they are not usually aware of their awakened state. During the day these individuals may feel sleepy because they have been deprived of sleep at night (Cherniack, 1986). This disorder is most common among infants and individuals over the age of sixty-five (Ancoli-Israel, 1981; Klink & Quan, 1986).

In our tour of sleep we have seen that dreams are more characteristic of REM sleep than other sleep stages. Let's now explore the dream world in more detail.

Dreams

As long as time has been recorded, dreams have had historical, personal, and religious significance (Dement, 1976). Preserved Babylonian clay tablets reveal that as early as 5000 B.C., dreams and their interpretations were recorded. Egyptians built temples in honor of Serapis, the god of dreams. The populace occasionally slept there, hoping their dreams would be made more enjoyable. Dreams are described at length in more than seventy passages in the Bible and in many primitive cultures dreams are an extension of reality. A chief in Africa once dreamed that he had visited England. On awakening, he ordered a wardrobe of European clothes. As he walked through the tribal village in his new wardrobe, he was congratulated on having made the trip. And when a Cherokee Indian dreamed he had been bitten by a snake, he was treated for the snake bite.

Today, we still are trying to figure out why we dream and what dreams mean (see figure 4.7). Dream research has not had the scientific bent of sleep research. Much of the interest in dreams stems from psychoanalysts who have probed the unconscious mind to understand the symbolic content of dreams (Baudry, 1986; Erdelyi, 1985). Other than dream research connected with sleep stages, sound scientific studies of dreaming are difficult to find.

Figure 4.7
The world of dreams can be enchanting or hellish.
The Garden of Delights, *Center panel. Hieronymous Bosch.* © *Scala/Art Resource, New York.*

Interpretation of Dreams

Many of us dismiss the nightly excursion into the world of dreams as a second-rate mental activity, unworthy of our rational selves. By focusing only on the less mysterious waking world, we deny ourselves the opportunity of chance encounters with distant friends, remote places, dead relatives, gods, and demons.

Do you dream about pits, caves, bottles, apples, and airplanes? Or do you dream about reptiles, serpents, umbrellas, and poles? If so, psychoanalytic theory would say that your dreams have a strong sexual content. Psychoanalytic theorists are concerned with the meaning of dream content and provide guidelines for explaining and interpreting it. They believe that such content conceals, but may be made to reveal, information about the dreamer's conception of the world.

According to Freud's (1955) theory, dreaming is unconscious and reflects our sexual or aggressive instincts that cannot be expressed during wakefulness (see figure 4.8 for a portrayal of one of Freud's dreams). These impulses are pressing to be activated and dreams provide an avenue for their expression. In its final form, a dream is a distorted and symbolic version of the instincts that triggered it. The raw materials used by the individual to construct the dream are traces of prior perceptual experiences, especially experiences in the day preceding the dream. Freud also stressed that dreams contain memories of infant and child experiences.

Dreams are not logically organized, but rather they consist of a bizarre pattern of the original elements. These transformations complicate the task of dream interpretation. According to Freud, the bizarre pattern occurs so that repressed impulses are successfully disguised.

"You weren't actually in the dream, but you did do the voice-over."

Drawing by Frascino; © 1987 The New Yorker Magazine, Inc.

Figure 4.8
Freud's dream as a young boy that his mother was being carried off by two bird-headed creatures. The bird-headed creatures in Freud's boyhood dream closely resembled illustrations from the Bible he had seen.

In agreement with Freud, Alfred Adler (1958) says that we dream when we are troubled by something and the unresolved problems of life press upon us during sleep. Like Freud, Adler believes dreams contain symbolic content. However, Adler stresses that Freud was wrong in thinking that sleep is unconscious and not reality oriented, while wakefulness is conscious and reality oriented. Adler also says that Freud was wrong in thinking that dreams are motivated by sexual and aggressive instincts.

It appears that Freud and Adler were correct in thinking that dreams are characterized by both residues of daily life and symbolic content. The following example of a dream reflects an individual's daily work as a file clerk at a library. Notice how the dream led to an elaboration that was far removed from the librarian's daily experiences.

> I was in the library and I was filing cards, and I came to some letter between *a* and *c*. I was filing some country, I think it was Burma, and just as I put that in, there was this scene of some woman, who was sent to look for a little girl who was lost, and she was sent to Burma. They thought the little girl was going there, for some reason. This was sort of like a dramatization of what I was doing. I mean I was filing, and then this scene took place, right at the same time. In the setting it was sort of like you imagine it, but I had the feeling it was really happening. (Foulkes, 1972, p. 129)

Not all psychologists view dreams as a clash between biological forces, such as sexual instincts, and the concerns of reality. The **activation-synthesis view** is very different from the psychoanalytic view. The activation-synthesis view argues that dreams have no inherent meaning. Instead, they reflect the brain's efforts to make sense out of neural activity during REM sleep (Hobson & McCarley, 1977).

A third view emphasizes that dreams are a form of thinking about and even solving life's problems. Support for this view comes from research that involves awakening and then questioning individuals just after they have completed a REM sleep period (Cartwright, 1978). When this is done, the first dream of the night often reflects a realistic view of a problem. The second dream is a similar experience in the recent past. The third dream goes back to an earlier point in the individual's life. The next several dreams often are future oriented. It is at this point that problem solving begins to take place, although many dreamers never get this far in a night's dreaming; others just keep repeating the problem without getting to the future-oriented solution stage.

Dreams and Consciousness

Increasingly psychologists are interested in the conscious aspects of dreaming (Wright & Koulack, 1987). One way to study the conscious ties of dreaming is to increase the ability to dream. Steven LaBerge (1981, 1985), a psychologist at the Stanford University Sleep Research Laboratory, has done this both with subjects and himself.

The term **lucid dreaming** was introduced at the beginning of this century to describe a class of dreams in which you "wake up" mentally but remain in the sensory landscape of the dream world. During a lucid dream, the dreamer

Psychology 4.2

Dream Flying

■ A number of techniques can increase lucid dreaming. If you awaken from a dream in the middle of the night, return to the dream immediately in your imagination. Now envision yourself recognizing the dream. Tell yourself that the next time you dream you want to recognize that you are dreaming. If your intention is strong and clear enough, you may discover that you are in a lucid dream when you go back to sleep.

Many lucid dreamers report dreams in which they fly unaided, not unlike Superman. Dream flying gives the dreamer an exhilarated feeling of freedom and is a basic means of travel in the dream world. How could you dream fly? LaBerge (1985) says that before you go to bed, say to yourself, "Tonight I fly!" Then, while you still are awake, imagine a journey of flight. If you discover yourself flying, it is a clear indication that you are in a dream. When you realize that you are

dreaming, remember that you want to fly. When you actually feel yourself flying, tell yourself that this is a dream. Start out modestly by just floating above the surface. As you gain confidence in the notion that you are dreaming and that you can control your dreaming, you can try to fly with more abandon. You may then try to fly at low altitudes and later even soar above the clouds and look down at planet earth. Throughout your effort to dream fly, remember that you are in a dream. With this in mind, any fears should be kept at a minimum, and your control over the dream enhanced.

LaBerge says that until recently we have had little control over the creative nature of our dreams. With lucid dreaming, though, it may be possible to intentionally influence the creativity of our dreams. LaBerge suggests that before you go to bed you should choose a problem you would like to solve and state it in the form of

a question. For example, you might ask, "What is the title of my next term paper?" or "How can I become less shy?" If you have a health problem, you might ask, "How can I regain my health?" Write down the problem and memorize it. When you are ready to go to bed tell yourself you will have a lucid dream. Then remember your question and see yourself looking for the answer in the lucid dream. When you are in a lucid dream, ask the question and try to find a solution.

You might have the most success in solving problems during lucid dreaming if you take a direct approach. For example, if your problem is shyness, you might try to see yourself as outgoing and sociable in your lucid dream. Reflect on how your dream solution related to your waking problem. You might combine your problem-solving effort with dream flying by visiting an expert on your problem and asking that individual questions.

is consciously aware that the dream is taking place. In a typical lucid dream, you suddenly become aware that you are dreaming and your mind becomes clearer (Tart, 1986). To learn more about ways that you can increase lucid dreaming, read Psychology 4.2.

Dreams and sleep truly are fascinating aspects of states of consciousness and of psychology. A summary of the main themes of our discussion of the nature of states of consciousness and sleep and dreams is presented in concept table 4.1.

■ ■

Concept Table 4.1

The Nature of Consciousness, Sleep, and Dreams		
Concept	**Processes/related ideas**	**Characteristics/description**
What is consciousness?	Its nature	The total external and internal mental events an individual is aware of. Its forms are a stream of consciousness, the subconscious, the nonconscious, the unconscious, and daydreaming.
Sleep	Different states of sleep	The EEG measures the brain's electrical activity. Beta waves show we are in an excited state, alpha waves a relaxed state. The transition from waking to sleep is called a hypnagogic state. When we sleep we move from light sleep in Stage 1 to deep sleep in Stage 4. Then we go into REM sleep, where dreams occur. Each night we go through a number of these sleep cycles.
	Sleep and circadian rhythms	A circadian rhythm is a cycle of about twenty-four hours. The human sleep/wake cycle is an important circadian rhythm. This cycle can become desynchronized. Individuals isolated in caves for months continue to follow this rhythm. There is no set amount of sleep we need each night.
	Why do we sleep?	We sleep for restoration and repair (repair theory) and to keep us from wasting energy and risking harm during the time of day or night to which we are not adapted (ecological theory).
	The neural basis of sleep	Early views emphasized environmental stimulation and subsequently an internal "activating system" in the reticular formation. The contemporary view states that the brain is actively engaged in producing sleep behaviors and different neurotransmitters are involved.
	Sleep disorders	Among the most prominent are sleepwalking and sleeptalking (which occur during Stages 3 and 4 of sleep), narcolepsy, insomnia, and sleep apnea.
Dreams	Interpretation of dreams	Freud's psychoanalytic view stresses the importance of unconscious thought. Freud believed our dreams are caused by conflicts between biological instincts and the demands of reality. Psychoanalytic theorists believe that dreams have rich, symbolic content and involve a residue of daily and early childhood experiences. The activation-synthesis hypothesis argues that dreams are the brain's way of trying to make sense out of its neural activity. A third view emphasizes the role of dreams in thinking and problem solving.
	Dreams and consciousness	The old view is that waking is conscious and dreaming is unconscious. The new view shows a connection between dreams and consciousness. Lucid dreaming is an example of this close association.

Altered States of Consciousness

A young cancer patient is about to undergo a painful bone-marrow procedure. A man directs the boy's attention, asking him to breathe with him and listen carefully. The boy's attention is focused on a pleasant fantasy—riding a motorcycle over a huge pizza, dodging anchovies and maneuvering around chunks of mozzarella. Minutes later the procedure is over. The boy is relaxed and feels good about his self-control (see figure 4.9) (Long, 1986).

A college student has studied hard for an exam but she is uptight about it. She goes to a quiet place in a field near her dorm and assumes a position with her legs crossed and her back straight. She lets her breathing become relaxed and natural, setting its own pace and depth. Then she focuses on her breathing and the movement of her stomach, not allowing extraneous thoughts or external stimuli to pull her attention away from the breathing.

An individual almost died in an automobile crash. His brush with death was so close that doctors almost gave up on reviving him. After he regained consciousness, he reported that he had stepped outside of his body and saw himself dying. He saw himself sliding down a long spiral tunnel.

A youth lies down and puts on a set of stereo headphones, tuning in the soft music of a harp. She then takes a cube of LSD. Before long images flash through her mind. She says she feels a warm sense of compassion and a wonderful sense of being pure and clean.

These four experiences—hypnosis with the cancer patient, the meditation of a college student, a near-death experience, and drug-induced images—are altered states of consciousness.

Hypnosis

Hypnosis is a psychological state of altered attention and awareness in which the individual is unusually receptive to suggestions. Hypnosis has been used since the beginning of recorded history. It has been associated with religious ceremonies, magic, the supernatural, and many erroneous theories. Today hypnosis is recognized as a legitimate process in psychology and medicine, although much is yet to be learned about how it works.

Mesmer and the History of Hypnosis

In the eighteenth century the Austrian physician Anton Mesmer cured his patients by passing magnets over their bodies. Mesmer said the problems were cured by "animal magnetism," an intangible force that passes from therapist to patient. In reality, the cures were due to some form of hypnotic suggestion. Mesmer's claims were investigated by a committee appointed by the French Academy of Science. The committee agreed that Mesmer's treatment was effective. However, they disputed his theoretical claims about animal magnetism and prohibited him from practicing in Paris. Mesmer's animal magnetism view was called *mesmerism,* and even today we use the term *mesmerized* to mean hypnotized or enthralled.

Induction and Features of the Hypnotic State

Four elements are present when hypnosis is induced. First, the subject is made comfortable and distracting stimuli are minimized. Second, the subject is told to concentrate on one specific thing, such as an imagined scene, which takes her further away from the immediate environment. Third, suggestions are made to the subject about what she is expected to experience in the hypnotic state (e.g., relaxation or a pleasant floating sensation). Fourth, the hypnotist suggests certain events or feelings that he knows will occur or observes occurring (e.g., "your eyes are getting tired"). When the suggested effects occur, the subject interprets them as being caused by the hypnotist's suggestions and accepts them as an indication that something is happening. This increases the subject's expectations of future effects and makes her even more suggestible.

One of the most outstanding characteristics of the hypnotic state is the subject's suggestibility. When individuals are hypnotized, they readily accept and respond to ideas offered by the hypnotist. They may even carry out suggestions offered to them while hypnotized *after* they emerge from the hypnotic state. This is called **posthypnotic suggestion.** If you are told to forget everything that went on while you were in a hypnotic state, you will do so—this is called **posthypnotic amnesia** (Kihlstrom, 1985).

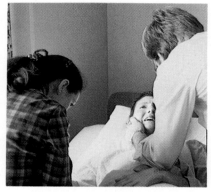

(a)

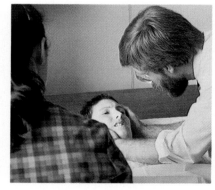

(b)

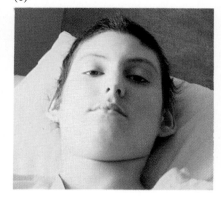

(c)

Figure 4.9
The use of hypnosis with a bone marrow aspiration in a young cancer patient. (a) At the University of Texas Health Science Center in San Antonio, a young cancer patient is about to undergo a painful bone marrow aspiration. The therapist directs the patient's attention and asks him to breathe with him and to listen carefully. (b) The therapist gets the boy to focus on a pleasant fantasy, and (c) minutes later the boy is relaxed and calm.

Individual Differences in Hypnosis

Do you think you could be hypnotized? What about your friends—are they likely to be influenced more by hypnosis than yourself? Or would you act like a squadron of cadets, snapping to attention in response to a drill sergeant's command? Throughout the 200-year study of hypnosis, it has been known that individuals vary in their hypnotic ability. About 10 to 20 percent of the population are very susceptible to hypnosis, 10 percent or less cannot be hypnotized at all, and the remainder fall somewhere in between (Bowers & Davidson, 1986; Hilgard, 1965).

There is no simple way to tell whether you can be hypnotized other than undergoing a hypnotic induction attempt by a skilled hypnotist. One measure has been developed, though, to assess how susceptible individuals are to hypnosis. The Stanford Hypnotic Susceptibility Scale includes a brief hypnotic induction and a number of hypnotic suggestions. The suggestions begin with inductions that are easy to produce, such as moving extended arms slowly apart. More difficult inductions follow, such as being unable to smell a strong odor (e.g., an onion). Individuals who score high on the hypnotic scale have the capacity to immerse themselves in imaginative activities—listening to music or reading a novel, for example. They become completely absorbed in what they are doing, removing the boundaries between themselves and what they are experiencing in their environment (Hilgard, 1970; Lynn & Snodgrass, 1986; Sweeney, Lynn, & Belleza, 1986).

Theories of Hypnosis

Since Anton Mesmer proposed his theory of "animal magnetism," we have been trying to figure out why hypnosis works. Contemporary theories of hypnosis are organized around two broad, competing frameworks—the special-process, or state, view; and the nonstate, or cognitive-social, view.

In the **special-process view,** hypnotic behavior is seen as qualitatively different than nonhypnotic behavior. Hypnotic responses, elicited by suggestions, are involuntary rather than deliberate actions. Dissociations among cognitive systems take place and amnesic barriers are formed. The main representative of the special-process view is the **hidden-observer theory** of Ernest Hilgard (1977, 1986). Hilgard's research shows how part of the hypnotized individual's mind is completely unaware of what is happening. The individual remains a passive, or *hidden,* observer until called on to comment.

Hilgard discovered this double train of thought in hypnosis in a class demonstration with a blind individual. Hilgard, the hypnotist, induced deafness in the blind individual and showed the class how unresponsive the subject was to what was going on around him. A student asked whether the subject really was as unresponsive as he seemed. Hilgard, being a flexible teacher, asked the subject if there might be some part of him that could hear. If so, he was told to raise a finger. Surprisingly, the finger rose. Hilgard asked the subject to report from the part that was listening and made his finger rise; at the same time he told the subject that he would not be able to hear what this part of himself said. The second part of the individual's awareness, indeed, had heard all that went on and reported it. Further inquiry by Hilgard revealed that approximately half of a group of highly hypnotizable subjects had a hidden observer but were unaware of it until they went through a procedure similar to the blind individual's.

Are we hidden observers in other circumstances in our everyday lives? Some of us talk on the phone about a social affair while writing down a grocery list. Or, we listen to ourselves tell a story to ensure that it is clear or we scan the faces of the audience while telling a joke. In these and other common situations we attend to and perform two different activities simultaneously (Hebb, 1982). Possibly this double activity could be improved with practice, as when secretaries write from dictation while reading other material at a normal rate (Neisser, 1982).

Hilgard's hidden-observer view is a provocative explanation of hypnosis, but there is much we still do not know. Why do some experienced, easily hypnotized subjects not report the presence of a hidden observer, for example?

A conflicting perspective, the nonstate view, says that hypnotic behavior is similar to other forms of social behavior and can be explained without resorting to special processes. From this perspective, hypnotic behavior is purposeful, goal-directed action that is best understood by the way subjects interpret their situation and how they try to present themselves (Barber & Wilson, 1977; Coe, 1987; Sarbin, 1986; Spanos, 1986). The **nonstate view** recognizes that "good" hypnotic subjects often act as if they have lost control over their behavior. But these aspects of behavior are interpreted as voluntary rather than automatic. Responsive hypnotic subjects act as if their responses are involuntary because their preconceptions about hypnosis define acting in this way as central to the role of being hypnotized. They are not faking their hypnosis, but they have become caught up in performing the hypnotic role.

The "special-process" controversy still sparks extensive debate, centering on whether hypnosis involves involuntary (as the special-process camp believes) or voluntary (as the nonstate advocates believe) behavior (Beahrs, 1986; Kihlstrom, 1986; St. Jean, 1986; Spanos, 1986). As theories about the nature of hypnosis continue to spark debate, applications of hypnosis have become widespread.

Applications of Hypnosis

Hypnosis is widely used in psychotherapy, medicine and dentistry, criminal investigation, and sports. The use of hypnosis in psychotherapy has been applied to alcoholism, somnambulism, suicidal tendencies, overeating, and smoking. One of the least effective, yet most often used, applications of hypnosis is in helping individuals to stop overeating and quit smoking. Hypnotists give their patients the direct suggestion that they stop these behaviors, but rarely are dramatic results achieved. Usually, results are poor or transitory. The most effective use of hypnosis is as an adjunct to other forms of psychotherapy, which will be discussed in chapter 15.

In medicine, hypnosis has been used to treat the psychological aspects of disease, including the control of pain, hypnoanaesthesia, reduction of fear and anxiety, and management of chronically or terminally ill patients. In the latter circumstance, hypnosis helps patients accept their situation, motivates them to cooperate in the treatment process, and gives them a sense of control over their symptoms and pain (Hoffman & O'Grady, 1986; Steggles & others, 1987). Not only has hypnosis been used to treat the psychological aspects of disease, but it also has been involved in attempts to literally change the organic nature of the disease itself. In some conditions, such as the elimination of warts, asthma, and migraine headaches, the results have been promising, but for cancer the results are very dim. In dentistry, hypnosis has been used to control fear and as an anesthetic.

Another use of hypnosis has been to obtain the truth from crime suspects and witnesses. Hypnosis has had varying degrees of success in this regard. For example, in 1967, the Boston Strangler provided minute details about his crimes while under hypnosis and convinced police that he was guilty. And when twenty-six children were kidnapped from a school bus, the driver, under hypnosis, remembered enough of the license plate number of the getaway vehicle for the police to find the vehicle and the children (Brody, 1980). Nonetheless, Martin Orne (1979) points to some of the problems in using hypnosis for extracting the truth from witnesses and suspects. He notes that memories change over time and individuals under hypnosis may provide distortions of what actually happened. Memories of actual events cannot be distinguished from subsequent experiences and information. For these reasons, Orne believes that hypnosis should not be used in court to verify statements.

Hypnosis also has been used in sports to improve athletic performance. The athlete's mental state is an important part of performance, and this mental state can be influenced by hypnotic suggestions. The main benefit in sports seems to result from the induction of relaxation and confidence. In one investigation, a hypnotist was able to improve golfers' confidence in their putting by suggesting to them that the hole was the size of a sewer (Kroger & Fezler, 1976). Baseball star Rod Carew habitually used hypnosis to improve his hitting performance. And after hypnosis a pitcher who threw wildly had success at getting his pitches in the strike zone. Unfortunately, though, as he got the ball over the plate more often, batters were able to hit the ball more (Udolf, 1981).

Meditation is another altered state of consciousness. Is meditation different from hypnosis? They share similar qualities, but in the standard form of meditation individuals empty their minds; in hypnosis, individuals are busy figuring something out. In meditation individuals do not want to be interrupted by instructions; in hypnosis individuals wait for the hypnotist to tell them what to do.

Meditation

At one time meditation, like hypnosis, was thought to have more in common with mysticism than science. And as with hypnosis, increased research attention in recent years has been devoted to it. While meditation only became popular in the United States in recent years, it has been an important dimension in the lives of many Asians for centuries (West, 1988).

Traditional forms of meditation involve the practice of *yoga,* a Hindu system of thought that incorporates exercises to attain bodily or mental control and well-being, and *Zen,* a sect of Buddhism that aims for enlightenment through meditation. The strategies of meditation vary but usually take one of two forms: either cleansing the mind to have new experiences or increasing concentration. Instructions for cleansing the mind might take this form:

> Resolve to do nothing, to think nothing, to make no effort of one's own, to relax completely and let go one's mind and body . . . stepping out of the stream of ever-changing ideas and feelings which your mind is, watch the onrush of the stream. Refuse to be submerged in the current. (Chaudhuri, 1965, pp. 30–31)

Instructions for focusing attention might take this form:

> Place yourself face to face with another person. Look at him and be aware when your mind wanders. Be aware when you treat his face like an object, a design, or play perceptual games with it. Distortions may appear which tell you what you project into the relationship: angels, devils, animals, and all the human possibilities may appear in his face. Eventually you may move past these visual fantasies into the genuine presence of another human being. (Maupin, 1962, p. 188)

The most popular form of meditation in the United States is **transcendental meditation,** derived from an ancient Indian technique. This form of meditation involves a *mantra,* which is a resonant sound repeated mentally or aloud to focus attention. One widely used mantra is the phrase *Om Mani Padme Hum.* By concentrating on this phrase, the individual has replaced other thoughts with the syllables *Om Mani Padme Hum.* In transcendental meditation training, the individual learns to associate a mantra with a special meaning.

As a physiological state, meditation shows qualities of both sleep and wakefulness, yet it is distinct from them. It resembles the hypnagogic state, which is the transition from wakefulness to sleep, but at the very least is a prolongation of that state.

Early studies of the relation between body states and meditation revealed that oxygen consumption is lowered, heart rate slows down, blood flow increases in the arms and forehead, and EEG patterns are predominantly of the alpha variety—regular and rhythmic (see figure 4.10) (Wallace & Benson, 1972). Recent studies support these earlier findings but question whether meditation is more effective than relaxation in reducing body arousal (Bahrke & Morgan, 1978; Holmes & others, 1983; Raskin, Bali, & Peeke, 1980). The

The businessman is shown meditating during a break in his hectic schedule. What kind of physiological changes does meditation produce?

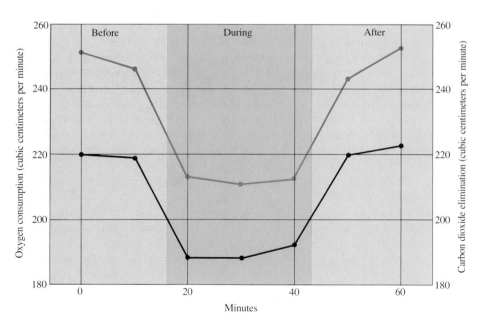

Figure 4.10
The effects of meditation on oxygen consumption. The blue area shows the reduced oxygen consumption of subjects during meditation. After meditation, oxygen consumption returned to premeditation levels.
From "The Physiology of Meditation," by Wallace, R. K., and H. Benson. Copyright © 1972 by Scientific American, Inc. All rights reserved.

Figure 4.11
Physiological responses of meditators and nonmeditators who relaxed. Heart rate scores are for 30-second intervals. Higher skin resistance scores reflect lower arousal. Notice that relaxing was just as beneficial in reducing body arousal as was meditation.

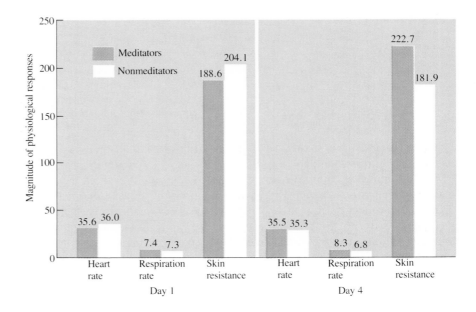

research of David Holmes and his colleagues (1988; Holmes & others, 1983) provides insight into this question. Highly trained and experienced meditators were asked to relax for five minutes, then meditate for twenty minutes, and finally relax for five minutes. Ten other subjects who had no training or experience in meditation were asked to relax for five minutes, then rest for twenty minutes, and finally relax for five minutes. Body arousal was measured throughout the experiment in the form of heart rate, skin resistance, respiration, and blood pressure. As shown in figure 4.11, meditation did lower body arousal, but no more than relaxation did.

Meditation might also influence the individual's psychological characteristics, such as reducing stress, increasing energy, and reducing self-blame. In one investigation (Carrington, 1977) regular meditation was practiced by a group of subjects for two, twenty-minute sessions a day over a period of several months. The individuals reported that the meditation reduced their overall tension. However, because a control group of subjects was not used we do not know whether meditation has positive effects beyond what a half hour of quiet rest each day might provide.

We have seen that many psychologists believe hypnosis and meditation are altered states of consciousness. Some of the most dramatic accounts of altered states of consciousness, though, appear in the realm of extrasensory perception, which we discussed in chapter 3, and in the form of near-death experiences, which we describe next.

Near-Death Experiences

The year is 1920. Thomas Edison had always been a believer in electrical energy. He once wrote that when an individual dies, a swarm of highly charged energies deserts the body and goes into space, entering another cycle of life.

Always the scientist, Edison felt that some experiment demonstrating the immortal nature of these energies was necessary. In an interview in the October 1920 issue of *Scientific American,* he stated:

> I have been thinking for some time of a machine or apparatus which could be operated by personalities which have passed onto another existence or sphere . . . I am inclined to believe that our personality hereafter does affect matter. If we can evolve an instrument so delicate as to be affected by our personality as it survives in the next life, such an instrument ought to record something.

Edison never built the machine, but on his deathbed he had a vision of the next life, remarking, "It is very beautiful over there."

On June 20, 1978, the *National Enquirer* ran a full-page headline declaring, "New Evidence of Life After Death" and advertised "science's answer to the afterlife" for a mere three dollars. That money would have gotten you a copy of the *Circular Continuum,* which simply refers to Einstein's ideas about the nature of energy and matter as proof of life after death. You also would have received an illustration of a man falling through a long spiral tunnel into the afterlife.

In the 1970s, medical journals began publishing reports of patients who had experienced afterlife visions following near-death encounters (e.g., Macmillan & Brown, 1971). Communication with the dead also was reported via spiritualists, ghosts, automatic writing, apparitions, and related techniques. In one report, a dead man communicated to his wife that the afterlife had "a lawn that would put any Earth golf course to shame" (Loehr, 1976, p. 48).

Physician Raymond Moody (1977) is the most widely quoted supporter of the near-death experience. He says that the typical near-death experience includes these elements: hearing doctors or spectators pronounce one dead, feelings of peace and quiet, a loud ringing or buzzing noise, a dark tunnel through which one can feel oneself moving, out-of-body experiences, meeting others, a panoramic view of one's life, cities of light, and supernatural rescues from real physical death by some spirit.

The possibility that perceptions of afterlife are hallucinations was raised by Ron Siegel (1980). He believes that drug-induced hallucinations are curiously similar to perceptions of the afterlife in the near-death experience. For example, in an afterlife report, one individual said, "I found myself in a tunnel—a tunnel of concentric circles, a spiraling tunnel." While in a drug-induced hallucination, another individual reported, "I'm moving through some kind of train tunnel." (See figure 4.12 to observe what this tunnel looks like.)

It has been assumed that hallucinations contain only information stored in our brain and, unlike real perceptions of the afterlife, cannot portray strange new environments or novel experiences. But hallucinations, like dreams, images, thoughts, and fantasies, are often elaborate cognitive embellishments of memory images, not just mere pictorial replicas. For example, think about the last time you went swimming at the beach. Does this memory include an image of yourself on the beach or in the water? It probably does. But this image is obviously fictitious because you could not have been looking at yourself. Images in our memory often include pictures of this kind. Hallucinations also include equally improbable images of flying and panoramic vistas of incredible beauty and novelty. Like hallucinations, visions of the afterlife are suspiciously similar to this world. Near-death experiences, then, may well be based on stored images in the brain.

Figure 4.12
A dark tunnel through which one can feel oneself moving is frequently reported by individuals who have had a near-death experience and by individuals during a drug-induced experience. This painting was made to show a pattern that is often reported during the early stages of intoxication from marijuana. It is possible that the blue color is related to the initial lowering of the body temperature and to the absorption of blue light in the retina's cells.

■ ■ ■ ■ ■ ■ ■ ■ ■ ■ ■ ■ ■ ■ ■ ■ ■ ■ ■

Concept Table 4.2

Hypnosis, Meditation, and Near-Death Experience		
Concept	**Processes/related ideas**	**Characteristics/description**
Hypnosis	Its nature and history	A psychological state of altered attention in which the subject is unusually receptive to suggestion. The history of hypnosis begins with Anton Mesmer and his belief in animal magnetism and moves to the present view of the hidden observer.
	Induction, common features, and individual differences	Hypnosis involves reducing distracting stimuli and making the subject comfortable, getting the individual to concentrate, and suggesting what is to be experienced in the hypnotic state. About 10 to 20 percent of the population is highly susceptible to hypnosis, about 10 percent cannot be hypnotized at all, and the remainder fall in between.
	Theories of hypnosis	There are two broad, competing frameworks. In the special-process, or state, view, hypnotic behavior is qualitatively different. It is involuntary and dissociation among cognitive systems and amnesic barriers are believed to be involved. Special attention has been given to Hilgard's hidden-observer perspective. The alternative nonstate view argues that hypnotic behavior is similar to other forms of social behavior. From this perspective, hypnotic behavior is purposeful, goal-directed action that is understood by focusing on the way subjects interpret their role and how they try to present themselves.
	Applications	Widely applied to a variety of circumstances, including psychotherapy, medicine, dentistry, criminal trials, and sports. The success of these applications has varied.
Meditation	Its nature	Involves either cleansing the mind or increasing concentration. Research has shown that while meditation reduces body arousal it may not do so more than relaxation.
The near-death experience	Its nature	Research on hallucinations indicates that the near-death experience may involve some form of hallucination.

Our tour of altered states of consciousness has taken us through mesmerism and the hidden observer in hypnosis, yoga, Zen, and transcendental meditation, as well as the near-death experience. A summary of the main themes of hypnosis, meditation, and near-death experience is presented in concept table 4.2. Now we turn to another method of altering consciousness—drugs.

Drugs and Consciousness

When Sigmund Freud experimented with cocaine he was looking for possible medical uses for the substance, among them a use in eye surgery. He soon found that the drug provided an ecstatic feeling and wrote to his fianceé to inform her of how just a small dose of the substance produced lofty, wonderful sensations. Over time Freud stopped taking cocaine, though, because it became apparent that some individuals experienced bad effects from the drug and several died from overdoses. Cocaine is but one of many drugs taken to alter consciousness.

The Uses of Psychoactive Substances

Why do we use **psychoactive substances?** Since the beginning of history humans have searched for substances that would sustain and protect them and also act on their nervous systems to produce pleasurable sensations. Among the substances that alter consciousness are ethyl alcohol, hemp and cactus plants, mushrooms, poppies, and tobacco, an herb that has been smoked and sniffed for more than 400 years.

Individuals are attracted to psychoactive substances because they help them adapt to an ever-changing environment. Smoking, drinking, and taking drugs reduce tension and frustration, relieve boredom and fatigue, and in some cases help us escape from the harsh realities of the world. Psychoactive drugs provide us with pleasure by giving us inner peace, joy, relaxation, kaleidoscopic perceptions, surges of exhilaration, and prolonged heightened sensation. They may be useful in helping us to get along in our world. For example, amphetamines may keep us awake all night so we can study for an exam. Drugs also satisfy our curiosity—some individuals take drugs because they are intrigued by sensational accounts of drugs in the media, while others may listen to a popular song and wonder if the drugs described can provide them with unique, profound experiences. Drugs are taken for social reasons also— many psychoactive drugs allow individuals to feel more comfortable and enjoy the company of others.

But the use of psychoactive drugs for such personal gratification and temporary adaptation carries a very high price tag: drug dependence, personal and social disorganization, and a predisposition to serious and sometimes fatal diseases (Gawin, in press). Thus, what is intended as adaptive behavior is maladaptive in the long run. For example, prolonged cigarette smoking, in which the active drug is nicotine, is one of the most serious yet preventable health problems. Smoking has been described as "suicide in slow motion."

When a **tolerance** for psychoactive substances develops, the user needs a greater amount of the drug to produce the same effect. The first time an individual takes 5 mg of Valium a very relaxed feeling results, but after taking the pill every day for six months, 10 mg may be needed to achieve the same calming effect.

When individuals stop taking psychoactive drugs, it is not uncommon for them to experience **withdrawal.** The unpleasant effects of withdrawal can involve intense pain and cravings for the drug. This occurs because the individual's body has developed a physical dependency on the drug, also known as an addiction. In some instances, individuals are psychologically dependent on drugs, using them to cope with problems and stress in their lives. Let's now look more closely at several major classes of drugs, beginning with the depressants.

Depressants

Depressants slow down the central nervous system. Medically, depressants have been prescribed to reduce nervousness and anxiety and to induce sleep. Among the most widely used depressants are alcohol, tranquilizers, sedatives, and opiates.

We do not always think of alcohol as a drug, but it is an extremely potent one. Alcohol acts upon the body primarily as a depressant and slows down the activities of the brain; however, in low doses, alcohol can be a stimulant (Prunell & others, 1987). If used in sufficient quantities it will damage or even kill biological tissues, including muscle and brain cells. The mental and behavioral effects of alcohol involve reduced inhibition and impaired judgment. Initially we may feel more talkative and feel a sense of confidence. Skilled performance, such as driving, becomes impaired, and as more alcohol is ingested, intellectual functioning, behavioral control, and judgment become less efficient. Eventually the drinker becomes drowsy and falls asleep. With extreme intoxication, the individual may lapse into a coma. Each of these behavioral effects varies with how the individual's body metabolizes alcohol, body weight, the amount of alcohol ingested, and whether previous drinking has led to tolerance.

Adolescents at an anti-drug rally in Pasadena, California. The number one substance abuse problem among adolescents is alcohol abuse.

Alcohol is the most widely used drug in our society. It has produced many enjoyable moments and many sad ones as well. Alcoholism is the third leading killer in the United States with more than 13 million individuals classified as alcoholics. Alcohol costs the United States more than 40 billion dollars each year in health costs, lost productivity, accidents, and crime (Smith, 1986). Each year approximately 25,000 individuals are killed and 1.5 million injured by drunk drivers. More than 60 percent of homicides involve the use of alcohol by both the offender and victim, while 65 percent of aggressive sexual acts against women involve the use of alcohol by the offender (Goodman & others, 1986). Alcohol is the number one substance abused by adolescents. A national sample of more than 17,000 high school seniors obtained each year in the 1980s reveals that more than 40 percent have had five or more drinks on any one occasion during the last two weeks (Johnson, Bachman, & O'Malley, 1986).

The widespread problem of alcohol abuse has led to a search for its cause and cure. There is increasing evidence of a genetic predisposition to alcoholism, although it is important to remember that both genetic and environmental factors are involved (Cadoret, Throughton, & O'Gorman, 1987; Shuckit, 1986). Drugs that reduce alcohol consumption are being tested; the most promising are serotenergic drugs, which carry this label because they work on the neurotransmitter serotonin. Many forms of therapy, which will be described in chapter 15, have been used with individuals who have alcohol-related problems.

Tranquilizers, such as Valium and Librium, also are depressants. They usually have a milder effect than sedatives, although both create a state of relaxation. Both tranquilizers and sedatives can become habit forming; they also can produce symptoms of withdrawal when an individual stops taking them. At the anatomical level of the brain, they depress the systems involving wakefulness and attention, especially the reticular formation. At the cellular level, they influence the action of norepinephrine and serotonin.

Opiates, which consist of opium and its derivatives, also depress the activity of the central nervous system. Many drugs have been produced from the opium poppy, among them morphine and heroin (which is converted to morphine when it enters the brain). For several hours after taking an opiate, the individual feels euphoric, pain is relieved, and an increased appetite for food and sex appears. But the opiates are among the most physically addictive drugs (Marlatt & others, in press). It is not long before the body craves more heroin and experiences very painful withdrawal unless more is taken. The neurotransmitters most often affected when an individual takes opium are the endorphins, thus, when the drug is taken away the brain has an insufficient amount of endorphins, which accounts for the excruciating pain of withdrawal (Platt, 1986).

Stimulants

Whereas depressants slow down the central nervous system, **stimulants** increase central nervous system activity. Stimulants increase heart rate, breathing, and temperature, but decrease appetite. Stimulants increase our energy, lessen our feeling of fatigue, and lift our mood and self-confidence. Just as with depressants, though, discontinuation of the stimulants can be painful. The most widely used stimulants are caffeine, nicotine, amphetamines, and cocaine.

Amphetamines are widely prescribed stimulants, sometimes appearing in the form of diet pills. They also are referred to as pep pills and uppers. Amphetamines seem to have their stimulating effect on the brain by increasing the release of norepinephrine and dopamine, as does cocaine (Gold, 1986).

Did you know that cocaine was an ingredient in Coca-Cola? Of course, it has long since been removed from the soft drink. **Cocaine** comes from the coca plant, native to Bolivia and Peru. For many years Bolivians and Peruvians chewed on the plant to increase their stamina. Today cocaine is either snorted or injected in the form of crystals or powder. The effect is a rush of euphoric feelings, which eventually wear off, followed by depressive feelings, lethargy, insomnia, and irritability. With extended use, cocaine can deplete norepinephrine and dopamine neurotransmitters; in one investigation, 83 percent of cocaine abusers reported sleep dysfunctions and depression, probably as a consequence of such depletion (Gold, Washton, & Dackis, 1985).

Cocaine is a highly controversial drug. Users claim it is exciting, makes them feel good, and increases their confidence. Yet it is clear that cocaine has potent cardiovascular effects and is potentially addictive. The recent deaths of sports stars, such as the University of Maryland's Len Bias, suggest how lethal cocaine can be. When the impact of the drug is severe, it can produce a heart attack, stroke, or brain seizure. The increase in cocaine-related deaths often is traced to very pure or tainted forms of the drug, which was the case in Bias's death (Gold, Gallanter, & Stimmel, 1987).

How many individuals take cocaine? Figures vary, but estimates range as high as 5 million regular users and 20 million casual users (Smith, 1986). The increase seems to have occurred primarily among the adult population. Several investigations report either a drop or a leveling off in cocaine use among high school and college students (Johnson, Bachman, & O'Malley, 1987; MacDonald, 1986).

A young woman using cocaine. The greatest increase in cocaine use is in the adult population.

Hallucinogens

Hallucinogens, sometimes called psychedelic drugs, modify an individual's perceptual experiences. We will discuss three hallucinogens: marijuana, LSD, and the recent designer drug MDMA.

LSD stands for the chemical lysergic acid diethylamide. The effects on the individual's body may include dizziness, nausea, and tremors; perceptual effects may include hallucinations or misperceptions of time; emotional and cognitive effects may include rapid mood swings or impaired attention and memory. The synaptic activity of the neurotransmitter serotonin is disrupted when LSD is taken.

Marijuana, a milder hallucinogen than LSD, comes from the hemp plant, *Cannabis sativa,* which originated in central Asia but now is grown in most parts of the world. Marijuana is made of the hemp plant's dry leaves; its dried resin is known as hashish (see figure 4.13). The active ingredient in marijuana is *THC,* which stands for the chemical delta-9-tetrahydrocannabinol. This ingredient does not resemble the chemicals of other psychoactive drugs and the brain processes affected by marijuana for the most part remain uncharted. Because marijuana is metabolized slowly, its effects may be present over the course of several days.

Figure 4.13
(a) Hemp plants growing in the wild; marijuana is made of the hemp plant's dry leaves. (b) Loose marijuana and a rolled joint. (c) Hashish, the dried resin of the hemp plant.

(a)

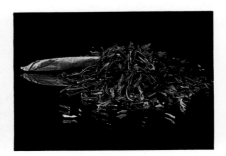

(b)

(c)

The physical effects of marijuana include increases in pulse rate and blood pressure, reddening of the eyes, coughing, and dryness of the mouth. Psychological effects include a mixture of excitatory, depressive, and hallucinatory characteristics, making it difficult to classify the drug. The drug can produce spontaneous unrelated ideas, distorted perceptions of time and place can occur, verbal behavior may increase or cease to occur at all, and increased sensitivity to sounds and colors might appear. Marijuana also can impair attention and memory, suggesting that smoking marijuana is not conducive to optimal school performance. When marijuana is used daily in heavy amounts it also can impair the human reproductive system and may be involved in some birth defects. A downturn in marijuana use has occurred during the 1980s (Johnson, Bachman, & O'Malley, 1987).

Another drug with mildly hallucinogenic qualities is **MDMA,** chemically labeled methylene dioxy-metaamphetamine, which has become known as one of the "designer drugs." These drugs are made by chemically reengineering an existing controlled substance to create a drug that is currently legal (Beck & Morgan, 1986). MDMA is known by a variety of street names, among them Ecstasy, Adam, and XTC. It has properties related to marijuana and the amphetamines, producing both mild hallucinogenic and strong stimulant effects. To learn more about the controversy around MDMA, read Psychology 4.3.

Interaction of Drugs

Our description of the effects of different drugs has focused on how each drug alone influences mind and behavior. But many individuals take more than one drug, and the effects of two or more drugs taken together often is more dangerous than when either is taken alone.

Cocaine abusers are susceptible to the upper-downer syndrome associated with amphetamines. To control or reduce cocaine's stimulant-depressant effect, users commonly combine cocaine and alcohol. This pattern can contribute to alcohol toxicity, which in turn can result in drunk driving accidents as well as chronic alcohol abuse. The use of alcohol or other depressants to relieve cocaine's effects also can become a secondary drug problem (Smith, 1986).

The most extensively studied drug interactions involve alcohol and sedatives. The combination of these drugs produces the same impairment but with a lower dose than when either is taken separately. Another common drug combination is alcohol and marijuana—there seems to be an additive effect when these are taken together, both acting as depressants on the central nervous system (Chan, 1984; Hollister, in press; Lytle, in press).

Drugs in the Work Place

Alcohol abuse is a tremendous hindrance to work productivity. Surveys indicate that among employed adults, 12 percent are alcohol dependent, as reflected in symptoms of withdrawal and loss of control. An additional 7 percent are identified as nondependent alcohol abusers (Mayer, 1983).

Illegal drug use in the work place also has increased. A truck driver for an air courier service smokes a few joints at lunch, assures his buddies he is fine, and twenty minutes later smashes his truck into a tree. A pharmaceutical company throws out a huge batch of contaminated products because the quality control inspector was stoned. A stockbroker uses cocaine daily—he can't remember the million-dollar trade his boss congratulates him on completing. Joint by joint and pill by pill, the use of illegal drugs has entered the work place and spread to almost every occupation.

A cocaine user at work. What controversies have the use of drugs in the workplace generated?

━ ━ ━ ━ ━ ━ ━ ━ ━ ━ ━ ━ ━ ━ ━ ━ ━

Psychology 4.3

Ecstasy and the Designer Drugs—Threats, Promises, Little Scientific Data

Cocaine usually gives me an up-and-down jagged feeling that lasts only for a short time. I alternately like it and hate it, though for some reason it has very seductive qualities. "Ecstasy," on the other hand, is just as the name implies. It's "state of the art." It puts me in a place of total bliss for three or four hours. Whereas coke makes me feel jittery, MDMA is very smooth. I know it has amphetamine in it, but I feel so relaxed. (Murphy, 1986)

Only recently has the public become aware of MDMA as a street drug. One reason for its popularity in Texas undoubtedly is its sale in student and gay bars. The blatancy of sales presented a very public and thus potentially problematic drug-use pattern to authorities. Major stories in *Newsweek, Time, Life,* and numerous other popular magazines in the mid-1980s often sensationalized the euphoric and therapeutic capabilities of MDMA.

With the publicity has come increased street use of MDMA, which escalated from an estimated 10,000 doses in 1976 to 30,000 doses *per month* in 1985 (Siegel, 1985). MDMA has effects similar to amphetamines but seems to produce a longer, smoother euphoria than cocaine. This type of euphoria means the drug has a high potential for abuse. Heavy use of MDMA may impair the immune system and deplete the serotonin supply of the brain (Frith, 1986; Schuster, 1986).

MDMA also is used by some psychotherapists as an adjunct to therapy. Some of the psychotherapeutic claims are wildly positive, indicating that MDMA allows a person to put on a therapist's thinking cap for a few hours and see oneself with a new vision (Leverant, 1986). While MDMA has been heralded by some as a cure for everything from personal depression to cocaine addiction, research on its effects are still in their infancy and support for its therapeutic success has yet to occur.

There are many controversies around MDMA. The advent of such designer drugs led to the passage of a federal law permitting emergency control for twelve to eighteen months of substances that pose imminent hazards to public safety. Do liberal pharmaceutical adventurists have the right to engineer such substances and challenge the government regulatory agencies to prohibit the private ingestion of drugs for psychic exploration? Drug engineers argue that the government allows other dangerous activities to occur. On the other side are those who argue that drugs such as MDMA should be prohibited because there may be hazards involved. These individuals argue that such psychoactive substances should undergo a prescribed series of animal toxicity studies before being declared safe.

The issue of MDMA's medical potential is another topic of passionate debate with strongly held convictions and little convincing data. Complex issues such as the potential therapeutic benefit versus actual toxicity continue to be the focus of considerable debate. The drug is both a threat and a promise, and the debate is both intense and vocal. Little scientific data has been collected, so support for either side is not available (Seymour, Wesson, & Smith, 1986).

Just as controversy surrounds the legality and control of designer drugs such as Ecstasy, so does controversy surround drugs in the work place. Do companies have the right to test their employees for drug use and abuse or are they violating the individual's rights? Do they have the right to ban their employees from smoking, even off the job, as one company recently did because of the negative health and productivity consequences attributed to smoking? These are provocative, important questions with no easy answers.

This chapter concludes section II, "Biological and Perceptual Processes." We have learned about the biological foundations of mind and behavior, brain processes, sensation and perception, and states of consciousness. In the next section we turn our attention to learning and cognition, beginning with the topic of learning in chapter 5.

Summary

I. What Is Consciousness?
Consciousness consists of the external and internal mental events that we are aware of at a given time. Consciousness comes in many forms, among them a stream of consciousness, the subconscious, the nonconscious, the unconscious, and daydreaming.

II. Stages of Sleep
The EEG measures the brain's electrical activity. Beta waves show we are in an excited state, alpha waves a relaxed state. The transition from wakefulness to sleep is called a hypnagogic state. When we go to sleep we move through four stages, from light sleep in Stage 1 to deep sleep in Stage 4. Then we go into REM sleep, where most dreaming occurs. During each night's sleep we go through a number of these sleep cycles.

III. Sleep and Circadian Rhythms
A circadian rhythm refers to cycles that are about an entire day or twenty-four hours long. The human sleep/wake cycle is an important circadian rhythm. This cycle can become desynchronized through long air travel or changing work shifts. In some experiments, individuals have isolated themselves in caves for months; these individuals continue to follow twenty-five- to twenty-six-hour days. There is no set amount of sleep we need each night.

IV. Why We Sleep and the Neural Basis of Sleep
We sleep for two main reasons—for restoration and repair (repair theory) and to keep us from wasting energy and harming ourselves during those parts of the day or night to which we are not adapted (ecological theory). Early views of sleep emphasized the role of environmental stimulation and subsequently an internal "activating system" in the reticular formation. The

contemporary view is radically different: the brain is actively engaged in producing sleep behaviors and different neurotransmitters are involved.

V. Sleep Disorders
Among the most prominent sleep disorders are sleepwalking and sleeptalking (which occur during Stages 3 and 4 of sleep), narcolepsy (an irresistible urge to sleep), insomnia (a problem in getting to sleep), and sleep apnea (the individual stops breathing while asleep).

VI. Dreams
Freud's psychoanalytic view stresses the importance of unconscious thought in dreaming. Our dreams are caused by conflicts between our biological instincts and the demands of reality in Freud's view. Psychoanalytic theorists believe that dreams have rich, symbolic content and involve a residue of daily and early childhood experiences. The activation-synthesis hypothesis argues that dreams are the brain's way of trying to make sense out of its neural activity. A third view of dreaming emphasizes the role of dreams in thinking and problem solving. The old view of dreams and consciousness was that waking is conscious and dreaming is unconscious. The new view dismisses this dichotomy and shows a connection between dreams and consciousness. Lucid dreaming is an example of the close association of dreaming and consciousness.

VII. The Nature of Hypnosis
Hypnosis is a psychological state of altered attention in which the subject is unusually receptive to suggestion. The history of hypnosis begins with the Austrian physician Anton Mesmer and his belief in animal magnetism; the present view is the hidden-observer view. Regardless of how hypnosis is induced, it includes these features: the subject is made

comfortable and distracting stimuli are reduced; the individual is told to concentrate on something that takes her away from the immediate environment; and suggestions are made about what the subject is expected to experience in the hypnotic state. About 10 to 20 percent of the population is highly susceptible to hypnosis, about 10 percent cannot be hypnotized at all, and the remainder fall in between.

VIII. Theories of Hypnosis and Applications
There are two broad, competing frameworks in contemporary theorizing about hypnosis. In the special-process, or state, view hypnotic behavior is qualitatively different. It is involuntary and the special process of dissociation among cognitive systems and amnesic barriers is believed to be involved. Special attention has been given to Hilgard's hidden-observer theory. The alternative nonstate view argues that hypnotic behavior is similar to other forms of social behavior and can be explained without resorting to special processes. From this perspective, hypnotic behavior is purposeful, goal-directed action that is understood by focusing on the way subjects interpret their role and how they try to present themselves. Hypnosis has been widely applied to a variety of circumstances that include psychotherapy, medicine, dentistry, criminal trials, and sports. These applications have met with mixed results.

IX. Meditation
Meditation involves either cleansing the mind or increasing concentration. Research has shown that while meditation reduces body arousal it may not do so more than relaxation.

X. Near-Death Experience
Research on hallucinations indicates that the near-death experience—perceptions of an afterlife—may involve some form of hallucination.

XI. **The Nature of Psychoactive Substances**

Psychoactive substances—those that alter perception or mood—have been used since the beginning of human existence for pleasure, utility, curiosity, and social reasons. Tolerance for many psychoactive substances develops, and it is not unusual for users to experience withdrawal when they have taken a drug extensively.

XII. **Depressants, Stimulants, and Hallucinogens**

Depressants slow down the central nervous system; they include alcohol, tranquilizers, sedatives, and opiates. Stimulants increase the activity of the central nervous system. The most widely used stimulants are caffeine, nicotine, amphetamines, and cocaine. Hallucinogens modify an individual's perceptual experiences and produce hallucinations. LSD, marijuana, and MDMP are examples of drugs that have hallucinogenic effects. The manufacture of designer drugs has stirred considerable controversy. A major concern is multiple drug use. Drugs in the work place have become a problem; ethical issues of control and legality surround their use both on and off the job.

Key Terms

Suggested Readings

Alcock, J. E. (1981). *Parapsychology: Science or magic?* New York: Pergamon Press. A thorough overview of research on many different aspects of extrasensory perception.

Borbely, A. (1986). *Secrets of sleep.* New York: Basic Books. A fascinating, lively portrayal of sleep, dreams, and sleep disorders by a leading expert in the field.

Ornstein, R. E. (Ed.) (1973). *The nature of human consciousness.* New York: Viking. A book of readings focused on a diverse set of ideas about consciousness; includes high-interest ideas such as Zen meditation, the physiology of meditation, the teaching stories of the Sufis (e.g., the magic horse, the story of tea), and biological rhythms.

Udolf, R. (1981). *Handbook of hypnosis for professionals.* New York: Van Nostrand Reinhold. An excellent overview of what is known about the nature of hypnosis, its uses, and the various techniques of hypnosis.

Wallace, B., & Fisher, L. E. (1987). *Consciousness and behavior* (2nd ed.). Boston: Allyn & Bacon. An up-to-date, authoritative treatment of the increased interest in understanding consciousness in the field of psychology, including many recent research efforts.

Wolman, B. B. (Ed.) (1979). *Handbook of dreams.* New York: Van Nostrand Reinhold. Fascinating articles on such topics as drugs and dreams, lucid dreaming, interpretation of dreams, the dreams of schizophrenics, and children's dreams.

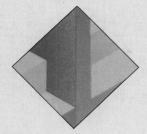

Learning and Cognition

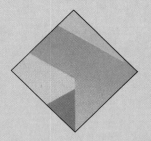

Learning

■ ■

Learning is an ornament in prosperity, a refuge in adversity.

—Aristotle

■ ■

Images of Learning

Jess is an eighth-grader at a junior high school in California. At fourteen years old, he already weighs 185 pounds. He is the school's best athlete, but he used to get some of his biggest thrills out of fighting. Jess knocked out several fellow students with bottles and chairs and once hit the principal with a stick, for which he received a forty-day suspension from school.

Jess's teachers unanimously agree that he was an "impossible" case; no one was able to control him. But one week, his teachers began to notice an almost complete turnabout in Jess's behavior. His math teacher was one of the first to notice the "strange" but improved behavior. Jess looked at her one day and said, "When you are nice you help me learn a lot." The teacher was shocked. Not knowing quite what to say, she finally smiled. Jess continued, "I feel really good when you praise me." Jess continued a consistent pattern of such statements to his teachers and even came to class early or sometimes stayed late just to chat with them.

What was responsible for Jess's turnaround? Some teachers said he attended a mysterious class every day that might provide some clues to his change in behavior. In that "mysterious" class a teacher was training students in behavior modification, which emphasizes that behavior is determined by its consequences. Those consequences weaken some behaviors and strengthen others.

As an experiment, Paul Graubard and Harry Rosenberg (1974) selected seven of the most incorrigible students in a junior high school—Jess was one of them—and had a teacher give the seven students instruction and practice in behavior modification in one forty-three-minute class period a day.

In their daily training sessions the students were taught a number of rewards to use to shape a teacher's behavior. Rewards included eye contact, smiling, and sitting up straight and being attentive. The students also practiced ways to praise the teacher, saying such things as, "I like working in this class where there is a good teacher." Furthermore, they worked on ways to discourage certain teacher behaviors by saying such things as, "I just have a rough time working well when you get mad at me." Jess had the hardest time learning how to smile. He was shown a videotape of his behavior and observed that he actually leered at people when he was told to smile. Although it was a somewhat hilarious process, Jess practiced in front of a camera until he eventually developed a charming smile.

The experiment was divided into three phases. During the first phase students did not try to change their regular teachers' behavior. This first phase established a norm of the teachers' behavior, or what is called a **baseline.** During the second phase, the students worked at changing the teachers' behavior. This is usually referred to as the **acquisition phase** (or in this experiment, the intervention phase). Finally, the students entered the last phase of the experiment, in which they were not to use any of the techniques they had learned to change the teachers' behavior. This last phase is referred to as extinction because the consequences for behavior are removed. The students were taught to keep accurate records for the experiment, and they kept daily tallies of the number of positive and negative contacts they had with their teachers.

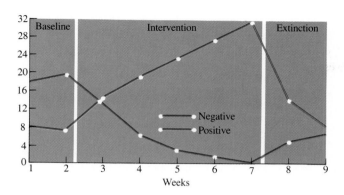

Figure 5.1
*Average number of positive and
negative teacher-student contacts.*
Reprinted from Psychology Today Magazine.
Copyright © 1974 American Psychological
Association.

Figure 5.1 shows the number of positive and negative behaviors shown by Jess and his six classmates during their interaction with teachers. During the five weeks in which the students implemented their behavior-change tactics, the average number of positive teacher-student interchanges improved dramatically and the number of negative contacts dropped substantially. Then several weeks after the students stopped using the behavior-change tactics (extinction), the number of positive contacts nose-dived and the number of negative interchanges increased slightly.

When the experiment was over the students resumed their use of behavior-change strategies, but no formal records were kept. Informal comments and observations suggested that the students were having more positive relationships with their teachers after the program had formally ended than before it had begun.

But what happened in the long run? In the case of this experiment we do not know, but in many cases such behavior modification interventions do not result in long-lasting changes once the consequences for behavior are removed. More about behavior modification appears in this chapter.

Learning builds on the base of our evolutionary inheritance. It helps us to face the challenges of survival and adaptation. We learn to ignore stimuli that are unimportant, to anticipate changes in our world, modify our environments, and benefit from the experience of being able to do so (Bolles & Beecher, in press; Flaherty, 1985). ∎

What Is Learning?

In learning how to use a computer, you might make some mistakes along the way, but at some point you will get the knack of how to use it. You will *change* from an individual who could not operate a computer to one who can. Learning anything new involves change. Once you have learned to use a computer the skill usually does not leave you. Once you learn how to drive a car, you do not have to go through the process again at a later time. Learning also involves a *relatively permanent* influence on behavior. You learned how to use a computer through *experience* with the machine. Through experience you also learned that you have to study to do well on a test, that when you go to the opera you have to dress up, and that a field goal in football scores three points. Putting these pieces together we arrive at a definition of **learning**: a relatively permanent change in behavior that occurs through experience.

Psychologists have explained our many experiences with a few basic learning processes. We *respond* to things that happen to us, we *act* and experience consequences for our behavior, and we *observe* what others say and do. These three aspects of experience form the three main types of learning we will study in this chapter—classical conditioning (responding), operant conditioning (acting), and observational learning (observing). As we study the

Figure 5.2
Themes of learning.

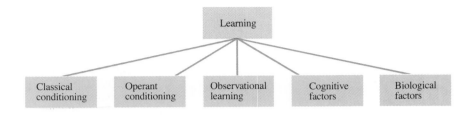

Learning takes place through experience. This young girl has learned *through* experience *with the kangaroos that they will not harm her.*

nature of learning you will discover that early approaches investigated the way experience and behavior are connected without referring to cognitive or mental processes. In recent years, learning approaches have emphasized how cognitive processes mediate the connection between experience and behavior (Pearce, in press). We will discuss cognitive approaches to learning later in the chapter. Finally, biological constraints on learning are evaluated. Figure 5.2 provides an overview of the five main themes in our coverage of learning.

Classical Conditioning

It is a nice spring day. A father takes his baby out for a walk. The baby reaches over to touch a pink flower and is badly stung by a bumble bee sitting on the petals. Several weeks later, the baby's mother brings home some pink flowers. She removes a flower from the arrangement and takes it over for her baby to smell. The baby cries loudly as soon as she sees the pink flower. The baby's panic at the sight of the pink flower illustrates the learning process of classical conditioning.

How Classical Conditioning Works

Figure 5.3
Surgical preparation for studying the salivary reflex. When the dog salivated, the saliva would collect in a glass funnel atached to the dog's cheek. This way the strength of the salivary response could be precisely measured.

The principle of **classical conditioning** was discovered by the Russian physiologist Ivan Pavlov (1927) while he was investigating the way the body digests food. In his study of the digestive system, Pavlov implanted a tube in a dog's salivary gland so he could measure the amount of saliva the dog secreted under various conditions (see figure 5.3). One day as Pavlov approached the dog with a tray of powdered meat, the dog began to salivate. Previously the saliva had flowed only when the dog was eating (see figure 5.4 to observe Pavlov's experimental setting). This aroused Pavlov's curiosity. Why did the dog salivate *before* eating the meat powder? He began putting together the pieces that complete the puzzle of classical conditioning.

Pavlov sensed that the dog's behavior included both unlearned and learned components. He called the food an **unconditioned stimulus (UCS)** and defined it as a stimulus that causes reflexive, or unlearned, behavior. The saliva that flowed from the dog's mouth in response to the food was called an **unconditioned response (UCR).** The unconditioned response is not learned. The UCS and UCR automatically become associated. In the case of the baby and the flower, the baby's learning and experience did not cause her to cry when the bee stung her. Her crying was unlearned and occurred automatically. The bee's sting was the UCS and the crying was the UCR.

The more Pavlov showed food to the dog, the more the dog salivated. Pavlov then rang a bell immediately before giving the meat powder to the dog. Until then, ringing the bell did not have a particular effect on the dog, except perhaps to wake the dog from a nap. The bell was a neutral stimulus. But the dog began to associate the sound of the bell with the food and salivated when the bell was sounded. The bell had become a **conditioned** (learned) **stimulus**

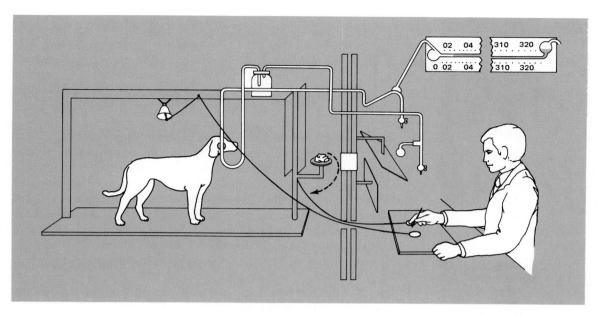

Figure 5.4
A modern apparatus for Pavlov's experiment in classical conditioning.

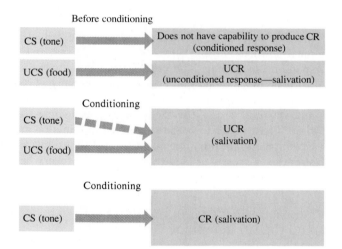

Before conditioning

CS (tone) → Does not have capability to produce CR (conditioned response)

UCS (food) → UCR (unconditioned response—salivation)

Conditioning

CS (tone) ⤏
UCS (food) → UCR (salivation)

Conditioning

CS (tone) → CR (salivation)

Figure 5.5
Diagram of classical conditioning procedure. At the start of conditioning, the UCS will evoke the UCR, but the CS does not have this capacity. During conditioning, the CS and UCS are paired so that the CS comes to elicit the response. The key learning ingredient is the association of the UCS and CS.

(CS) and the salivation a **conditioned response (CR)**. Before conditioning (or learning), the bell and the food were not related. After their association, the conditioned stimulus (the bell) produced a conditioned response (salivation). In the case of the baby, the pink flower (the conditioned stimulus) elicited crying (the conditioned response) because of its association with the bee. Figure 5.5 provides a summary of how classical conditioning works.

The interval between the CS and UCS is one of the most important aspects of classical conditioning. It is important because it defines the degree of association or *contiguity* of the stimuli. Conditioned responses develop when the interval between the CS and UCS is very short, as in a matter of seconds. In many instances optimal spacing is a fraction of a second (Kimble, 1961).

Generalization, Discrimination, and Extinction

After a time Pavlov found that the dog responded to other sounds, such as a whistle, by salivating. The more bell-like the noise, the stronger the dog's response. The baby not only cried at the sight of pink flowers but also at the sight of red and orange flowers. This aspect of classical conditioning is called **generalization,** the tendency of a stimulus similar to the original conditioned stimulus to produce a response that is similar to the conditioned response.

Stimulus generalization is not always beneficial. For example, the cat who generalizes from a minnow to a piranha has a major problem; therefore, it is important to discriminate between stimuli. **Discrimination** is the process of learning to respond to certain stimuli and not to others. To produce discrimination, Pavlov gave food to the dog only after ringing the bell and not after any other sounds. In this way, the dog learned to distinguish between the bell and other sounds. In this case, the baby did not cry at the sight of blue and green flowers, thus distinguishing them from pink flowers. The baby associated the pain of the bee sting with pink flowers but not with blue or green flowers.

Pavlov rang the bell repeatedly in a single session and did not give the dog any food. Eventually the dog stopped salivating. This result is **extinction,** the weakening of the CS's tendency to elicit the CR by unreinforced presentations of the CS. Over time the baby encountered many pink flowers and was not stung by a bee. Consequently, her fear of pink flowers subsided and eventually disappeared.

Extinction is not always the end of the conditioned response. The day after Pavlov extinguished the conditioned salivation at the sound of a bell he took the dog to the laboratory and rang the bell, still not giving the dog any meat powder. The dog salivated, indicating that an extinguished response can spontaneously recur. The process by which a conditioned response can recur without further conditioning is called **spontaneous recovery.** In the case of the baby, even though she saw many pink flowers after her first painful encounter and was not "stung" by them, she showed some signs of fear from time to time. Figure 5.6 shows the sequence of extinction and spontaneous recovery. Spontaneous recovery can occur several times, but as long as the conditioned stimulus is presented alone, spontaneous recovery becomes weaker and eventually ceases to occur.

Why Classical Conditioning Works and the Contemporary Perspective

Pavlov explained classical conditioning in terms of **stimulus substitution,** arguing that the nervous system is structured in such a way that the CS and UCS bond together and eventually the CS substitutes for the UCS. But if the CS substitutes for the UCS, the two stimuli should produce similar responses. This does not always happen. Using a shock as a UCS often elicits flinching and jumping while a light (CS) paired with a shock may cause the organism to be immobile, for example (Bindra & Palfai, 1967).

Pavlov's explanation of classical conditioning includes no mention of cognition. But Pavlov has been associated incorrectly with the cognitive aspects of learning. Joel Dubow, the communications manager of Coca-Cola, recently nominated Pavlov as the father of modern advertising (Koten, 1984). Dubow said that Pavlov took a neutral object and, by associating it with a meaningful object, made it a symbol for something else. He went on to say that Pavlov imbued the object with imagery, thereby adding to its value. Dubow concluded by saying that this is what modern advertising tries to do.

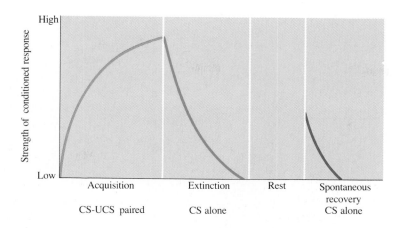

Figure 5.6
The strength of a conditioned response during acquisition, extinction, and spontaneous recovery. During acquisition the conditioned stimulus and unconditioned stimulus are paired. As seen in the graph, when this occurs the strength of the conditioned response increases. During extinction the conditioned stimulus is presented alone, and as can be seen, this results in a decrease of the conditioned response. After a rest period spontaneous recovery appears, although the strength of the conditioned response is not nearly as great at this point as it was after a number of CS-UCS pairings. When the CS is presented alone again after spontaneous recovery, the response is extinguished rapidly.

Dubow's description of Pavlov's classical conditioning is very cognitive and uncharacteristic of the Russian's behavioral orientation. Further, it clings to the stimulus substitution view of classical conditioning, which is no longer perceived as the best explanation of how classical conditioning works. While ads for Coca-Cola may be effective, the effectiveness is not the result of stimulus substitution (Leahey & Harris, 1985).

What is the contemporary explanation of why classical conditioning works? **Information theory** stresses that the key to understanding classical conditioning focuses on the information the organism gets from the situation (Rescorla, 1967, 1987, in press; Rescorla & Wagner, 1972). Some years ago E. C. Tolman (1932) said that the information value of the CS is important in telling the organism what will follow. In Tolman's words, the organism uses the CS as a sign or expectation that a UCS will follow. Tolman's belief that the information the CS provides is the key to understanding classical conditioning was a forerunner of contemporary thinking.

Contemporary interest in classical conditioning emphasizes processing information about the situation and the complexity of the situation (Dickinson, 1980; Mackintosh, 1983). The trend is to study multiple determinants of behavior and discover the organism's ability to learn the predictive relation between stimuli. This perspective recognizes that multiple conditioned stimuli probably will be present, the organism's past experience with the stimuli needs to be considered, and cognitive factors such as memory and imagery may mediate the CS-UCS pairing (Baker, Singh, & Bindra, 1985; Bouton & others, 1986; Ross & LoLordo, 1987). The contemporary perspective on classical conditioning contrasts with the Pavlovian perspective, which focused almost exclusively on the CS-UCS association and did not adequately take into account the cognitive and contextual factors that influence the CS-UCS pairing.

Classical Conditioning in Humans

Since Pavlov's experiments, individuals have been conditioned to respond to the sound of a buzzer, a glimpse of light, or the touch of a hand. Classical conditioning has a great deal of survival value for the individual. Because of classical conditioning, we jerk our hands away before they are burned by fire and we move out of the way of a rapidly approaching truck before it hits us. Classical conditioning is at work in words that serve as important signals. Walk into an abandoned house with a friend and yell, "Snake!" Your friend probably will bolt out the door. Describe a peaceful, tranquil scene—an abandoned beach with waves lapping onto the sand—and the harried executive may relax as if she were actually lying on the beach.

*By developing an image of a peaceful,
tranquil scene such as the one here,
you may be able to relax as if you
actually were there. In such instances,
the process of classical conditioning is
at work.*

Phobias

Phobias are irrational fears, which many psychologists believe are caused by classical conditioning. The famous behaviorist John Watson conducted an experiment to demonstrate this (Watson & Rayner, 1920). A little boy named Albert was shown a white laboratory rat to see if he was afraid of it. He was not. As Albert played with the rat a loud noise was sounded behind his head. As you might imagine, the noise caused little Albert to cry. After only seven pairings of the loud noise with the white rat, Albert began to fear the rat even when the noise was not sounded. Albert's fear was generalized to a rabbit, a dog, and a sealskin coat. Today we could not ethically conduct this experiment. Especially noteworthy is the fact that Watson and Raynor did not remove Albert's fear of rats, so presumably this phobia remained with him after the experiment.

In recent years, dissatisfaction with the classic hypothesis that fears and phobias result from direct traumatic classical conditioning—the pairing of an initially neutral event with a highly aversive one—has emerged (Domjan, 1986, 1987; Emmelkamp, 1982). An alternative explanation, favored by many psychologists, is based on observational learning. The theory of observational learning states that a phobia results from observing another individual respond to something in a fearful way. For example, a young boy develops a fear of dogs because he observed another child be scared or bitten by a dog. A woman reads about someone being afraid of high places or falling off a ledge and subsequently develops the fear herself. We will discuss observational learning in more detail later in the chapter.

Still it seems that classical conditioning explains many phobias, especially in its contemporary form, which takes into consideration the complexity of information in the situation and cognitive processes such as memory and imagery (Mineka, in press; Mineka & Cooke, 1986).

Counterconditioning and Systematic Desensitization

If we can produce fears by classical conditioning, we should be able to eliminate them. **Counterconditioning** is a procedure for weakening a CR by associating the stimuli to a new response incompatible with the CR. Though Watson did not eliminate little Albert's fear of white rats, an associate of Watson's, Mary Cover Jones (1924), did eliminate the fears of a three-year-old boy named Peter. Peter had many of the same fears as Albert; however, Peter's fears were not produced by Jones. Among Peter's fears were white rats, fur coats, frogs, fish, and mechanical toys. To eliminate these fears, a rabbit was brought into Peter's view but kept far enough away that it would not upset him. At the same time the rabbit was brought into view, Peter was fed crackers and milk. On each successive day the rabbit was moved closer to Peter as he ate crackers and milk. Eventually Peter reached the point where he would eat the food with one hand and pet the rabbit with the other.

One variation of counterconditioning that has become popular in recent years in treating fears and other emotional problems is **systematic desensitization.** The fearful individual is asked to set up a hierarchy of fearful stimuli. Then he is asked to imagine the least fearful stimulus while simultaneously relaxing. When this stimulus ceases to produce fear, he goes on to the next fearful stimulus, and so on, each time relaxing as he does so. The basic assumption is that fear and relaxation are incompatible; as relaxation is strengthened, fear is weakened (Wolpe, 1961).

Joseph Wolpe (1986), who developed the concept of systematic desensitization, described a case that illustrates how a hierarchy of fearful stimuli is used in therapy. A man came to Wolpe following a six-month period in which he said he could not see. Wolpe sent him to an ophthalmologist who found nothing physiologically amiss. The man's history revealed two important items: first, he always had been extremely anxious, especially fearing disapproval; second, the blindness began under circumstances of severe disapproval. For some time the man had been in charge of executing his father-in-law's will. One day he learned that his mother-in-law had filed suit against him for failing to execute the will properly. For him this amounted to a colossal failure. Upon hearing he would be arraigned in court, he became extremely nervous and noticed that he was having difficulty focusing on objects. To Wolpe, these facts suggested a problem of social vulnerability, not vision.

After further interviewing, Wolpe developed a hierarchy of items to which the man was sensitive. For example, if the man were invited to dinner and the first course was tasteless soup, he would consume it to please the hostess. If she offered him another bowl he could not refuse. The hierarchy item consisted of politely refusing. Desensitizing the man to this and a wide range of related situations reduced his crippling reactions. He learned to relax, rather than be anxious. After six months, the man's vision began to reappear for increasingly longer spells; after eight months it was fully recovered. The final breakthrough was marked by driving himself to Wolpe's office, a distance of twenty-five miles. The recovery has now lasted for more than two years. Much more about the process of desensitization will be presented in chapter 15.

Applying classical conditioning to human behavior has led to the study of other types of problems and disturbances. Among these is drug addiction. As discussed in Psychology 5.1, our tolerance for drugs such as heroin and alcohol may be at least partly due to classical conditioning.

■■■■■■■■■■■■■■■■■

Psychology 5.1

Drug Tolerance: Contextual Cues for Injection of Morphine in Rats and Humans

Heroin is king. It is king because it leaves you floating on a peaceful sea—a place where nothing really matters at all and everything is beautiful. It is a peaceful fantasy-land where your mind swims in a warm, secure sensory sea. The emptiness you felt disappears. The hurt is gone. Your inadequacies no longer exist. In their place are power, confidence, and ecstasy.

■ This heroin addict's comments portray only the pleasure of heroin, which lasts for about three-to-four hours on a typical dose. If another dose is not taken within four-to-six hours, painful symptoms of withdrawal appear—craving for the drug, chills, sweating, and cramps, for example. The more the drug is used, the less effective it is in producing the desired pleasurable feelings. Greater amounts of the drug become necessary to produce the desired effects. Opiates, of which heroin is a member, alcohol, and barbituates are especially susceptible to this effect, which is called drug tolerance (remember our discussion of this topic in chapter 4).

Historically, drug tolerance has been conceptualized as an automatic physiological effect of repeated drug administration. However, a classical conditioning explanation of drug tolerance has been proposed (Siegel, 1983). This explanation focuses on the drug as the UCS and the cues that consistently accompany drug administration—the injection procedure and the setting where the drug is taken—as the CS. The conditioned stimuli signal drug administration, which produces a conditioned response that probably strengthens over time.

Increasing doses, then, are needed to obtain any high at all and the overall effect of the drug decreases. As time goes on, this may result in the addict overdosing.

If the classical conditioning interpretation of drug tolerance is correct, it has important implications for drug treatment. Possibly the best way to treat addicts is to work with them in the context of their drug world, rather than remove them to a faraway drug treatment center. Removing them from their drug world may help initially, but once they are placed back into that environment the cues may be overwhelming and the drug addiction may return.

An experiment with animals suggests that addicted organisms will most likely take a drug when stimuli previously associated with the drug are present (Hinson & others, 1986). The investigation focused on self-injection of morphine by rats. The rats were trained to drink a morphine solution and then were given repeated morphine injections in a distinctive environment so that these cues would become conditioned to produce a desire for the drug. Subsequently the rats were allowed to drink morphine in either the drug-conditioned environment or a home cage. As the classical conditioning model

predicted, the rats ingested far more morphine in the drug-conditioned context than in their home.

Keep in mind, though, that classical conditioning does not explain all aspects of drug tolerance. Drug abuse in humans is complex, involving physiological mechanisms, genetic factors, and cultural influences as well (Domjan, 1987).

A heroin addict. The addict's drug tolerance is influenced by cues in the environment. For example, the matches, table, and room might become conditioned stimuli that signal drug administration, which could produce a conditioned response that strengthens over time.

Concept Table 5.1

The Nature of Learning and Classical Conditioning		
Concept	**Processes/related ideas**	**Characteristics/description**
Learning	Its nature	A relatively permanent change in behavior due to experience. How we respond to the environment (classical conditioning), how we act in the environment (operant conditioning), and how we observe the environment (observational learning) are the most important ways in which we experience. Early approaches emphasized connections between environment and behavior; many contemporary approaches stress that cognitive factors mediate environment-behavior connections.
Classical conditioning	The basic features	Pavlov discovered that the organism learns the association between an unconditioned stimulus (UCS) and a conditioned stimulus (CS). The UCS automatically produces the UCR (unconditioned response). After conditioning (CS-UCS pairing), the CS elicits the CR (conditioned response) by itself. Generalization, discrimination, and extinction also are involved.
	Why classical conditioning works and the contemporary perspective	Pavlov explained classical conditioning in terms of stimulus substitution but the modern explanation is based on information theory. Today interest focuses on the complexity of the context and cognitive factors such as memory and imagery, which mediate the CS-UCS connection.
	Classical conditioning in humans	Has survival value for humans, as when we develop a fear of hazardous conditions. Irrational fears are explained by classical conditioning. Counterconditioning and systematic desensitization have been used to alleviate fears.
	Evaluation of classical conditioning	Important in explaining the way learning in animals occurs. It is not the only way we learn and misses the active nature of the organism in the environment.

Evaluation of Classical Conditioning

Pavlov described all learning in terms of classical conditioning. In reality we learn in many other ways. Nonetheless, classical conditioning helps us learn about our environment and has been successful in eliminating human fears. However, a view of learning that describes the organism as *responding* to the environment fails to capture the *active* nature of the organism and its influence on the environment. Next, we study a major form of learning that places more emphasis on the activity of the organism in the environment—operant conditioning. Before turning to that discussion, let's review the main themes of classical conditioning. Concept table 5.1 will help you with this review and provide information about the basic nature of learning.

Operant Conditioning

During World War II, B. F. Skinner constructed a rather strange project—a pigeon-guided missile. A pigeon in the warhead of the missile operated the flaps on the missile and guided it home by pecking at an image of a target. How could this possibly work? When the missile was in flight, the pigeon pecked the moving image on a screen. This produced corrective signals to keep the missile on its course. The pigeons did their job well in trial runs, but top Navy officials just could not accept pigeons piloting their missiles during a war. Skinner, however, congratulated himself on the degree of control he was able to exercise over the pigeons.

Figure 5.7
This box is typical of the puzzle boxes Thorndike used in his experiments with cats to study the law of effect. Stepping on the treadle released the door bolt. A weight attached to the door then pulled open the door and allowed the cat to escape.

Following the pigeon experiment, Skinner (1948) wrote *Walden Two,* a novel in which he presented his ideas about building a scientifically managed society. Skinner envisioned a utopian society that could be engineered through behavioral control. Skinner viewed existing societies as poorly managed because individuals believe in myths such as free will. He pointed out that humans are no more free than pigeons; denying that our behavior is controlled by environmental forces is to ignore science and reality, he argued. In the long run, Skinner believed we would be much happier when we recognized such truths, especially his concept that we could live a prosperous life under the control of positive reinforcement. Skinner's operant conditioning view has had a strong impact in the field of psychology and we will discuss his ideas in greater detail in just a moment. First, though, we consider a forerunner of Skinner's learning principles, E. L. Thorndike's law of effect.

Thorndike's Law of Effect

At about the same time Ivan Pavlov was conducting classical conditioning experiments with salivating dogs, American psychologist E. L. Thorndike was studying cats in puzzle boxes (see figure 5.7). Thorndike put a hungry cat inside a box and a piece of fish outside. To escape from the box the cat had to learn how to open the latch inside the box. At first the cat made a number of ineffective responses; it would claw or bite at the bars or thrust its paws through the openings. Eventually, the cat would step on the treadle that released the door bolt. When the cat was returned to the box it went through the same random activity until it stepped on the treadle once more. On subsequent trials the cat made fewer and fewer random movements until it would immediately claw the treadle to open the door (see figure 5.8). Based on such experiments, Thorndike developed the **law of effect,** which states that behaviors followed by positive outcomes are strengthened, while behaviors followed by negative outcomes are weakened.

The key question for Thorndike was how the correct stimulus-response bond strengthens and eventually dominates incorrect stimulus-response bonds. According to Thorndike, the correct S-R association strengthens and the incorrect S-R association weakens because of the consequences of the organism's actions. Thorndike's view is called **S-R theory** because the organism's behavior is due to a connection between a stimulus and response. As we see next, Skinner's operant conditioning expanded Thorndike's basic ideas.

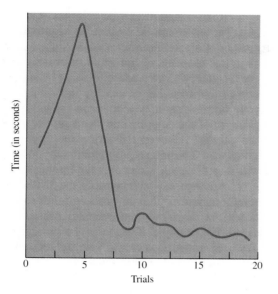

Figure 5.8
Learning curve showing how the time one cat took to escape from a puzzle box decreased.

Skinner's Operant Conditioning

My college tennis coach used to wear the same old shirt to every match we played. He was superstitious and believed that the shirt was a good-luck charm, helping us to maintain our winning streak. Athletes, gamblers, and most of us engage in some superstitious behavior. Why do we do these things?

Skinner says that superstitious behavior is strengthened because it is *accidentally* reinforced. In a series of experiments, Skinner (1953) demonstrated how even pigeons can become superstitious. He gave the pigeons a small portion of food every fifteen seconds regardless of what they were doing. The pigeons apparently were able to make an association between their activity and the food. The pigeons were conditioned to hop on one foot and then the other and to strut with their head cocked in the air (see figure 5.9).

Skinner describes the way in which our behavior is controlled in the following way. The organism *operates* in the environment to produce a change that will lead to a reward (Skinner, 1938). Skinner chose the term **operants** to describe the responses that are actively emitted because of the consequences for the organism. The consequences—rewards or punishments—are *contingent,* or dependent on, the organism's behavior. For example, a simple operant might be pressing a lever that leads to the delivery of food; the delivery of food is contingent on pressing the lever. In sum, **operant conditioning** is a form of learning in which the consequences of behavior lead to changes in the probability of that behavior's occurrence.

More needs to be said about the nature of reinforcement and punishment. **Reinforcement** (or reward) is a consequence that increases the probability a behavior will occur. By contrast, **punishment** is a consequence that decreases the probability a behavior will occur. For example, if someone you meet smiles at you and the two of you continue talking for some time, the smile has reinforced your talking. However, if someone you meet frowns at you and you quickly leave the situation, then the frown has punished your talking with the individual.

Figure 5.9
Sometimes we are superstitious about our behavior. For example, the girl wearing No. 12 on her jersey, above, may want to keep this number in all the sports she plays the rest of her life. Skinner says that such superstitious behavior is strengthened because it accidently is reinforced. He believes superstitious behavior appears in humans for the same reason it does in pigeons.

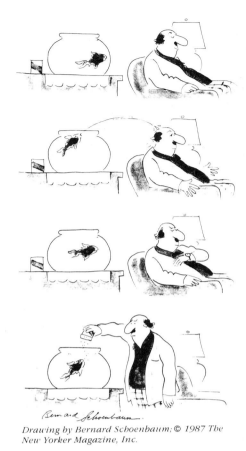

Drawing by Bernard Schoenbaum; © 1987 The New Yorker Magazine, Inc.

Reinforcement can be complex. Usually we think of reinforcement as positive, but it can be positive or negative. In **positive reinforcement** the frequency of a response increases because it is followed by a pleasant stimulus, as in our example of the smile increasing talking. In **negative reinforcement** the frequency of a response increases because the response either removes an unpleasant stimulus or lets the individual avoid the stimulus. For example, your father nags at you to clean the garage. He keeps nagging. Finally you get tired of the nagging and clean out the garage. Your response (cleaning out the garage) removed the unpleasant stimulus (nagging). Torture works the same way. The interrogator might say, "Tell me what I want to know and I will stop dripping water on your forehead."

Another way to remember the distinction between positive and negative reinforcement is that in positive reinforcement something is *added,* or obtained; in negative reinforcement something is *subtracted,* avoided, or escaped. For example, if you receive a sweater as a graduation present something has been added to increase your achievement behavior. But consider the situation when your parents criticize you for not studying hard enough. As you study harder, they stop criticizing you—something has been subtracted, in this case their criticism.

Negative reinforcement and punishment are easily confused because they both involve aversive or unpleasant stimuli, such as an electric shock or a slap in the face. To keep them straight, remember that negative reinforcement *increases* the probability a response will occur, whereas punishment *decreases* the probability a response will occur. When an alcoholic consumes liquor to alleviate uncomfortable withdrawal symptoms, the probability of future alcohol use is *increased.* The reduction of the withdrawal symptoms is a negative reinforcer for drinking. But if an inebriated alcoholic is seriously injured in a car wreck in which his drinking was a factor and he subsequently stops drinking, then punishment is involved because a behavior—drinking—was *decreased.* Table 5.1 provides an overview of the distinctions between positive reinforcement, negative reinforcement, and punishment.

Now that we know the basic concepts of operant conditioning, several additional points will help us understand how behaviorists study operant conditioning. One of Skinner's basic beliefs is that the mechanisms of learning are the same for all species. This belief led him to an extensive study of animals in the hope that the basic mechanisms of learning could be understood with organisms more simple than humans. For example, he believed that pigeons are successful at piloting missles and engage in superstitious behavior for the same reasons that humans do these things. The reason is operant conditioning.

Skinner and other behaviorists have made every effort to study organisms under precisely controlled conditions so that the connection between the operant and the specific consequences could be examined in minute detail. One of the ways in which Skinner achieved such control was the development in the 1930s of the Skinner box (see figure 5.10). A device in the box would deliver food pellets into a tray at random. After a rat became accustomed to the box, Skinner installed a lever and observed the rat's behavior. As the hungry rat explored the box, it occasionally pressed the lever and a food pellet would be dispensed. Soon after, the rat learned that the consequences of pressing the lever were positive—it would be fed. Further control was achieved by soundproofing the box to ensure that the experimenter was the only individual influencing the organism. In many experiments the responses were mechanically recorded by a cumulative recorder and the food (the stimulus) was dispensed automatically. Such precautions were designed to avoid human error.

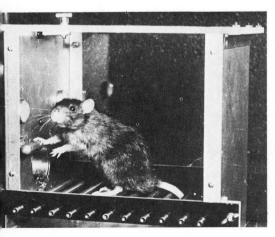

Figure 5.10
A rat in a Skinner box.

Table 5.1 Positive Reinforcement, Negative Reinforcement, and Punishment

Process	Type of stimulus	Effect on response	Example
Positive reinforcement	Pleasant	Increases	You invest more money in the stock market after making a profit in the market.
Negative reinforcement	Aversive	Increases	You lose money in the stock market. In an effort to recoup your losses you then invest in real estate.
Punishment	Aversive	Decreases	You invest in the stock market, your stocks go down, you sell them, and you don't invest in stocks again.

By now you probably can see that operant conditioning works quite differently than classical conditioning. In classical conditioning, the most important things happen *before* a response is made; in operant conditioning, they take place *after* a response is made. In classical conditioning, the key aspects of learning occur between two *stimuli,* a CS and a UCS; in operant conditioning, the key aspects of learning occur in the association of the organism's *actions* with the *consequences.* A classically conditioned response is involuntary—Pavlov's dogs had no control over their salivation just as we have no control over our palms perspiring. But most human behavior is voluntary. We perform many behaviors because we believe they will benefit us and we engage in other behaviors to avoid unpleasant experiences. We also have the capacity to change our behavior if we stop receiving benefits or are punished. It is this capacity to change or shape behavior through its consequences that is at the heart of operant conditioning (Brownstein, in press).

Principles of Operant Conditioning

Among the important features of operant conditioning that determine its effectiveness in controlling behavior are time interval, shaping and chaining, primary and secondary reinforcement, and schedules of reinforcement, as well as extinction, generalization, and discrimination. We will consider each of these features.

Time Interval

As with classical conditioning, learning is more efficient in operant conditioning when the interval between stimulus and response is seconds rather than minutes or hours. In general, the shorter the interval between the organism's response and its consequences, the more effective learning will be (Logan, 1960). A distinction is made between the immediate consequences and delayed consequences because learning is usually more efficient under immediate consequences. This is because delayed consequences allow other responses to occur that may be undesired but yet reinforced.

Shaping and Chaining

Sometimes it takes time for a behavior to occur. The learning process may be shortened if an approximation of the desired behavior is rewarded. The process of rewarding approximations of desired behavior is called **shaping.** In one circumstance parents used shaping to toilet train their two-year-old son. The parents knew all too well the grunting sound the child made when he was ready to fill his diaper. In the first week they gave him candy if the sound was heard within twenty feet of the bathroom. The second week he was given candy

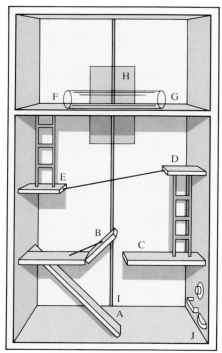

Figure 5.11
Starting at A, the rat climbs the ramp to B, crosses the drawbridge to C, climbs the ladder to D, crosses the tightrope to E, climbs ladder to F, crawls through the tunnel to G, enters the elevator at H, descends to I, presses the lever at J, and then receives food.

Playing the slot machines. What kind of reinforcement schedule probably is being used with these slot machines?

only if he grunted within ten feet of the bathroom, the third week only if he was in the bathroom, and the fourth week, he had to use the potty to get the candy. It worked! (Fischer & Gochros, 1975).

To teach a complex sequence, or chain, of behaviors, shaping can be combined with a procedure known as **chaining.** The procedure begins by shaping the final response in the sequence. Then you work *backwards* until a chain of behaviors is learned. For example, after the final response is learned, then the next-to-last response is reinforced, and so on. Both shaping and chaining are used extensively by animal trainers to teach complex or unusual sequences of behavior. A dolphin who does three back flips, throws a ball through a hoop, places a hat on its head, and finally applauds itself has been trained through a combination of shaping and chaining. Figure 5.11 shows a sequence of behaviors a rat learned through the process of chaining.

Primary and Secondary Reinforcement

Positive reinforcement can be classified in terms of **primary and secondary reinforcement,** which focuses on the distinction between inborn and unlearned and learned aspects of behavior. Primary reinforcers are innately satisfying, that is, it does not take any learning on the organism's part to make them positive. Food, water, and sexual satisfaction are primary reinforcers.

Secondary reinforcers acquire their positive value through experience. Hundreds of secondary reinforcers penetrate our lives. For example, social reinforcers include praise, smiles, and a pat on the back. When a student is given 25 dollars for the A on her report card, the 25 dollars is a secondary reinforcer. It is not innate, and it increases the probability that the student will work to get another A in the future. Money often is referred to as a *token reinforcer.* When an object can be exchanged for some other reinforcer, the object may have reinforcing value itself, thus, it is called a token reinforcer. Gift certificates and poker chips are other token reinforcers.

Schedules of Reinforcement

In most of life's experiences, we are not reinforced every time we make a response. A golfer does not win every tournament she enters; a chess whiz does not win every match he plays; a student is not patted on the back each time she solves a problem. This type of reinforcement is called **partial reinforcement** (or intermittment reinforcement), which simply means that responses are not reinforced each time they occur. Four types of partial reinforcement have been identified, each with rules that determine the occasion when a response will be reinforced. These **schedules of reinforcement** are a fixed-ratio schedule, a variable-ratio schedule, a fixed-interval schedule, and a variable-interval schedule.

A *fixed-ratio schedule* means that a behavior will produce a reward every *n*th time it is performed. For example, if you are playing the slot machines in Atlantic City and they are on a fixed-ratio schedule, you might get a dollar back every sixth time and 20 dollars back every 100 times you put money in. It doesn't take long to figure out that if you watch someone else play a machine without winning your chances of getting the big payoff from that machine will be greater.

Consequently, slot machines are on *variable-ratio schedules,* which means that you get rewarded for your behavior after an average of *n* responses. Thus, on the *average* you may get 20 dollars every 100 times you put money in a slot machine, but that money will not come in predictable intervals. For

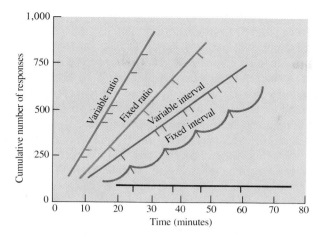

example, you might play the slot machine for two hours straight, putting in 300 silver dollars and not get the 20-dollar payoff even once. Then another individual might come along and put in three silver dollars and get paid off twice. The variable-ratio schedule is randomly determined so that you cannot tell when the next reward is coming.

The remaining two reinforcement schedules are determined by *time elapsed* since the last behavior was rewarded. On a *fixed-interval schedule* you are rewarded the first time you engage in a behavior after a fixed amount of time. For example, you might get rewarded the first time you put money in a slot machine after every ten-minute period has elapsed. On a *variable-interval schedule,* you are rewarded after a variable amount of time has elapsed. On this schedule, the slot machines might reward you after ten minutes, then after two minutes, then after eighteen minutes, and so forth.

Which of these schedules is the most effective? The closer a schedule is to *continuous* reinforcement, the faster the individual learns. However, once behavior is learned, the intermittent schedules can be effective in *maintaining* behavior. As shown in figure 5.12, the rate of behavior varies from one schedule to the next (Skinner, 1961). The fixed-ratio schedule produces a high rate of behavior with a pause occurring between the reinforcer and the behavior. This type of schedule is used widely in our lives. For example, if an individual is paid 100 dollars for every ten lawns he mows, then he is on a fixed-ratio schedule. The variable-ratio schedule also elicits a high rate of behavior and the pause after the reinforcement is eliminated. This schedule usually elicits the highest rate of responding of all four schedules.

The interval schedules produce behavior at a lower rate than the ratio schedules (Shimoff, Matthews, & Catania, 1986). The fixed-interval schedule stimulates a low rate of behavior at the start of an interval and a somewhat faster rate toward the end. This happens because the organism apparently recognizes that behavior early in the interval will not be rewarded but that later behavior will be rewarded. Thus, a scallop-shaped curve characterizes the behavior pattern of an organism on a fixed-interval schedule. The variable-interval schedule produces a slow, consistent rate of behavior.

So far we have discussed the importance of time intervals, shaping and chaining, primary and secondary reinforcement, and schedules of reinforcement to understanding how positive reinforcement elicits an operant response. Next we see that the processes of extinction, generalization, and discrimination are important in operant conditioning as in classical conditioning.

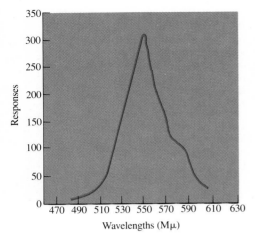

Figure 5.13
A characteristic gradient of generalization. In the experiment by Guttman and Kalish (1956), pigeons initially pecked a disc of a particular color (in this graph, a color with a wavelength of 550 Mμ) after they had been reinforced for this wavelength. Subsequently, when the pigeons were presented discs of colors with varying wavelengths, they were more likely to peck discs that were similar to the original disc.

Extinction, Generalization, and Discrimination

In parapsychology, card-guessing experiments are popular. A "sender" goes through a specially designed set of cards, one at a time, with another individual who is a "receiver." The receiver guesses the identity of each card. Over many trials the receiver should identify the cards more consistently than would be expected by chance. In these experiments, the receiver is not informed whether each of his guesses is correct, so these experiments work just like extinction in operant conditioning. Even if the subject is correct, he does not get reinforced. It has been found that some apparently "gifted" subjects do well at the card guessing initially but over time their performance falters, possibly because they become fatigued, but probably because of extinction (Leahey & Harris, 1985; Tart, 1975).

Remember from our discussion of classical conditioning that extinction is the weakening of the CS's tendency to elicit the CR by unreinforced presentations of the CS. In operant conditioning, **extinction** is a decrease in the tendency to perform the response brought about by unreinforced consequences of that response. Spontaneous recovery also characterizes the operant form of extinction. For example, a factory worker gets a monthly bonus for producing more than her quota. Then, as a part of economic tightening, the company decides that it can no longer afford the bonuses. When bonuses were given the worker's productivity was above quota every month; once the bonus was removed performance decreased.

In classical conditioning, generalization is the tendency of a stimulus similar to the conditioned stimulus to produce a response similar to the conditioned response. In operant conditioning, **generalization** is a response that is somewhat different from the response originally learned to that stimulus. For example, in one investigation pigeons were reinforced for pecking at a disc of a particular color (Guttman & Kalish, 1956). Stimulus generalization was tested by exposing the pigeons to discs of varying colors. As shown in figure 5.13, the pigeons were most likely to peck at the disc that was closest in color to the original one.

In classical conditioning, discrimination is the process of learning to respond to certain stimuli and not to others. In operant conditioning, **discrimination** is the process of responding in the presence of one stimulus that is reinforced but not in the presence of another stimulus that is not reinforced. For example, you might look at two street signs, both made of metal, both the same color, and both with words on them. However, one sign says, "Enter at your own risk," and the other reads, "Please walk this way." The words serve as *discriminative stimuli* because the sign that says, "Please walk this way" indicates that you will be rewarded for doing so, whereas the sign that says, "Enter at your own risk," suggests that the consequences may not be positive.

Applications of Operant Conditioning

A preschool child repeatedly throws down his glasses and breaks them. A high school student and her parents have intense arguments. A college student is deeply depressed. An elderly individual cannot control her eliminative functions. Operant conditioning procedures have helped individuals such as these adapt more effectively and cope with their problems. Using classical and operant conditioning to change behavior in everyday life is called **behavior modification.** Behavior modification based on operant conditioning emphasizes changing behavior by following a desired behavior with reinforcement. In clinical psychology, behavior modification usually is referred to as *behavior therapy,* which will be described in chapter 15.

The main goal of behavior modification is to replace unacceptable, maladaptive responses with acceptable, adaptive ones. Consequences for behavior are established to ensure that acceptable responses are reinforced and unacceptable ones are not. Advocates of behavior modification believe that without adequate response consequences, many emotional and mental problems can result (Kanfer & Scheft, 1987; O'Leary & Wilson, 1987). The child who throws down his glasses and breaks them may be receiving too much attention from his teacher and peers for his behavior, thus, an unacceptable behavior is unwittingly reinforced. In this instance, the parents and teacher would be instructed to remove attention from the destructive behavior and transfer it to more constructive behavior such as working quietly and playing cooperatively with peers (Harris, Wolf, & Baer, 1964).

Barbara and her parents were on a collision course. Things got so bad that her parents decided to see a clinical psychologist. The psychologist talked with each family member, trying to get them to pinpoint the problem. The psychologist got the family to sign a behavioral contract that spelled out what everyone needed to do to reduce the conflict. Barbara agreed to: 1) be home before 11 P.M. on weeknights; 2) look for a part-time job so that she could begin to support herself; and 3) refrain from calling her parents insulting names. Her parents agreed to: 1) talk to Barbara in a low tone of voice if they were angry, rather than yell; 2) refrain from criticizing teenagers, especially Barbara's friends; and 3) give Barbara a small sum of money each week for gas, makeup, and socializing, but only until she obtained a job.

The family agreed to a point system for each of these behavioral areas. If they failed to meet the standards upon which they had agreed, they lost points; if they met the standards, they gained points. The points would be transferred into money at the end of each week. If the system broke down, the family could discuss the problem at their weekly meeting with the psychologist. The points of conflict and contingencies could change as the situation improved or worsened and the psychologist would change the contract accordingly.

Sam, a nineteen-year-old college student, has been deeply depressed lately. His girlfriend broke off their relationship of two years and his grades are dropping. He sees a psychologist, who enrolls him in the "Coping With Depression" course developed by Peter Lewinsohn and his colleages (1986; Zeiss & Lewinsohn, 1986). Sam learns to monitor his daily moods and increase his ratio of positive to negative life events. The psychologist trains Sam to develop more efficient skills for coping with depression and gets Sam to agree to a behavioral contract, much as the psychologist did with Barbara and her parents. More details about Lewinsohn's approach to coping with depression appears in chapter 15.

Mary is an elderly woman who lives in a nursing home. In recent months she has been losing control of her eliminative functions and is increasingly dependent on the staff for help with her daily activities. The behavioral treatment designed for Mary's problem involves teaching her to monitor her behavior and schedule toileting time. She is also required to do pelvic floor exercises. The program for decreasing Mary's dependence requires that the staff attend more to her independent behavior when it occurs and remove attention from dependent behavior whenever possible. Such strategies have been effective in reducing eliminative and dependent behavior problems in the elderly (Baltes & others, 1983; Burgio & Burgio, 1986; Whitehead, Burgio, & Engel, 1985).

Some children develop the tendency of throwing temper tantrums. How might behavior modification be used to reduce or eliminate the tantrum behavior?

Behavior modification also is used to teach fathers to engage in more effective care-giving behavior with their infants, to encourage mentally retarded children to be less aggressive, to teach autistic youth purchasing skills, to train mentally disturbed individuals to take their prescribed drugs on a regular basis, and to help college students improve their social and assertive skills (Bellack, 1986; Dachman & others, 1986; Kelly & Lamparski, 1985; Mace & others, 1986; Masters & others, 1988; Singh & Millichamp, 1987).

Biofeedback

For many years it was believed that operant conditioning was effective only with voluntary responses. The focus of behavior modification was on such voluntary behaviors as aggression, shyness, and achievement. Efforts helped individuals to reduce their aggression, to be more assertive and outgoing, and to get better grades, for example. Involuntary behaviors such as blood pressure, muscle tension, and pulse rate were thought to be outside the boundaries of operant conditioning and more appropriate for classical conditioning. Beginning in the 1960s, though, Neal Miller (1969) and others began to demonstrate that an individual could control internal behaviors through the process of **biofeedback.** In the process of biofeedback the individual is given information about bodily processes so they can be changed.

How does biofeedback work? Let's consider the problem of reducing an individual's muscle tension. The individual's muscle tension is monitored and the level of tension is fed back to him. Often the feedback is in the form of an audible tone. As muscle tension rises, the tone becomes louder; as it drops, the tone becomes softer. The reinforcement in biofeedback is the raising and lowering of the tone (or in some cases, seeing a dot move up or down on a television screen) as the individual learns to control muscle tension. Figure 5.14 shows how biofeedback was used to repair nerve damage in a young boy's arm after an automobile accident.

When biofeedback was discovered, some overzealous individuals made exaggerated claims about its success and potential for helping individuals with such problems as high blood pressure and migraine headaches. As more carefully designed investigations have been conducted, the enthusiastic claims have been replaced with a more settled, conscientious understanding of the complexities of biofeedback (Miller, 1985; Norris, 1987). For example, some success in lowering blood pressure has been achieved, although it is easier to raise blood pressure through biofeedback. Relaxation training or stress management are as effective as biofeedback in reducing blood pressure (Johnston, 1985).

Computer-Assisted Instruction

Behavior modification is not only effective in therapy, but it has also been applied to the world of computers to promote better instruction. Some years ago Skinner developed a machine to assist teachers with their instruction of students. The teaching machine engaged the student in a learning activity, paced the material at the student's own rate, tested the student's knowledge of the material, and provided immediate feedback about correct and incorrect answers. Skinner hoped that the machine would revolutionize learning in schools, but the revolution never took place.

Today, the idea behind Skinner's teaching machine is applied to computers, which assist teachers in the instruction of students. Research comparisons of computer-assisted instruction with traditional teacher-based

Figure 5.14
Using biofeedback to relearn the use of an arm. A therapist used biofeedback to train a young boy to relearn the use of a nerve-damaged hand that had been impaired because of an automobile accident. A television monitor was attached to electrodes on individual muscles in the boy's arm. The electrodes measure motor signals from the brain to those muscles, signaling them when to contract. When the signal gets through to the correct muscle, dots on the TV screen move toward the top of the screen.

Concept Table 5.2

Operant Conditioning		
Concept	**Processes/related ideas**	**Characteristics/description**
Thorndike's law of effect	Its nature	States that behaviors followed by a positive outcome are strengthened, while those followed by a negative outcome are weakened. Referred to as S-R theory.
Skinner's operant conditioning	What operant conditioning is	The organism operates in the environment to produce change that will lead to reward. A form of learning in which the consequences of the behavior lead to changes in the probability of its occurrence.
	Positive reinforcement, negative reinforcement, and punishment	In positive reinforcement the frequency of a response increases because it is followed by a pleasant stimulus. In negative reinforcement the frequency of a response increases because it either removes an unpleasant stimulus or lets the organism avoid the stimulus. Punishment decreases the probability that a behavior will occur.
	Comparison with classical conditioning	Operant conditioning focuses on what happens after a response is made; classical conditioning emphasizes what occurs before a response is made. The key connection in classical conditioning is between two stimuli; in operant conditioning it is between the organism's response and its consequences. Operant conditioning mainly involves voluntary behavior, classical conditioning involuntary behavior.
Principles of operant conditioning	Time interval	Immediate consequences are more effective than delayed consequences.
	Shaping and chaining	Shaping is the process of rewarding approximations of the desired behavior. Chaining involves establishing a complex chain of responses. The final response in the sequence is learned first, then the next to the last, and so on.
	Primary and secondary reinforcement	Primary reinforcement refers to innate reinforcers (food, water, and sex); secondary reinforcement refers to reinforcers that acquire positive value through experience (money and smiles).
	Schedules of reinforcement	A response will be reinforced on a fixed-ratio schedule, a variable-ratio schedule, a fixed-interval schedule, or a variable-interval schedule.
	Extinction, generalization, and discrimination	Extinction is a decrease in the tendency to perform the response brought about by unreinforced consequences of that response. Generalization is giving a response that is somewhat different from the response originally learned to that stimulus. Discrimination is the process of responding in the presence of one stimulus that is reinforced but not in the presence of another stimulus that is not reinforced.
Applications of operant conditioning	Behavior modification	The use of learning principles to change maladaptive or abnormal behavior. Focuses on changing behavior by following it with reinforcement.
	Widespread use	Behavior modification is used widely to reduce maladaptive behavior. Among its applications are controlling aggressive behavior, reducing conflicts between parents and adolescents, coping with depression, helping elderly individuals function more independently, biofeedback, and computer-assisted instruction.

instruction suggest that in some areas, such as drill and practice on math problems, computer-assisted instruction may produce superior results (Kulik, Kulik, & Gangert-Drowns, 1985).

By now you should have a good feel for how operant conditioning works. A summary of the main themes of operant conditioning is presented in concept table 5.2.

Figure 5.15
*In the frames on the left, an adult
model aggressively attacks a Bobo doll.
In the frames on the right, the
preschool-aged girl who has observed
the adult model's aggressive actions
follows suit.*

Observational Learning

Would it make sense to put a fifteen-year-old boy behind the wheel of a car
and turn him loose with no driver's training? Should we ask him to drive down
the road and then reward his positive behaviors? Not many of us would want
to be on the road when some of his disastrous mistakes occur. Albert Bandura
(1971, 1986) believes that if we learned in such a trial-and-error fashion, it
would be an exceedingly laborious and at times hazardous process. Instead,
many of our complex behaviors are due to our exposure to competent models
who display appropriate behavior in solving problems and coping with their
world.

Observational learning, also called imitation or modeling, occurs when
an individual observes someone else's behavior. The capacity to learn behavior
patterns by observation eliminates tedious trial-and-error learning. In many
instances observational learning takes less time than operant conditioning.

The following experiment by Bandura (1965) illustrates how observational learning can occur by watching a model who is neither reinforced nor
punished. The only requirement for learning is that the individual be connected in time and space with the model. The experiment also illustrates an
important distinction between learning and performance.

An equal number of boys and girls of nursery school age watched one
of three films in which an individual beat up an adult-sized plastic Bobo doll
(see figure 5.15). In the first film, the aggressor was rewarded with candy, soft
drinks, and praise for aggressive behavior; in the second film, the aggressor
was criticized and spanked for the aggressive behavior; and in the third film,
there were no consequences to the aggressor for the behavior. Subsequently,
each child was left alone in a room filled with toys, including a Bobo doll. The
child's behavior was observed through a one-way mirror. As shown in figure
5.16 children who watched the aggressor be reinforced or suffer no consequences for aggressive behavior imitated the aggressive behavior more than
the children who watched the aggressor be punished. As might be expected,
boys were more aggressive than girls. The important point about these results
is that observational learning occurred just as extensively when modeled aggressive behavior was not reinforced as when it was reinforced.

A second important point focuses on the distinction between learning
and performance. Just because an organism does not *perform* a response does
not mean it was not *learned*. When children were offered rewards (in the form
of decals and fruit juice) for imitating the model's behavior, the differences
in imitative behavior among the children in the three situations disappeared.
In this experiment, all of the children *learned* about the model's behavior, but
the *performance* of the behavior did not occur for some children until reinforcement was presented. Bandura believes that when an individual observes
behavior but makes no observable response, the individual still may have acquired the modeled response in cognitive form.

Since his early experiments, Bandura (1986) has focused on some of the
specific processes that influence an observer's behavior following exposure to
a model. One of these is *attention*. Before the individual can reproduce a model's actions, she must attend to what the model is doing or saying. You may
not hear what a friend says if the stereo is blaring or you might miss the teacher's analysis of a problem if you are admiring someone sitting in the next row.
Attention to the model is influenced by a host of characteristics. For example,
warm, powerful, atypical individuals command more attention than do cold,
weak, typical individuals.

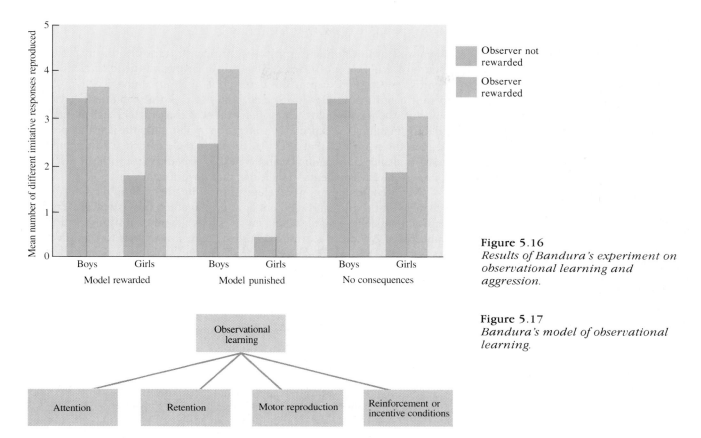

Figure 5.16
Results of Bandura's experiment on observational learning and aggression.

Figure 5.17
Bandura's model of observational learning.

The next consideration is the individual's *retention.* To reproduce a model's actions, you must code the information and keep it in memory so that it can be retrieved. A simple verbal description or a vivid image of what the model did assists retention. Memory is such an important cognitive process that most of the next chapter is devoted to it.

Another process involved in observational learning is *motor reproduction.* An individual may attend to a model and code in memory what he has seen, but because of limitations in motor development he may not be able to reproduce the model's action. A thirteen-year-old may see Chris Evert hit a great two-handed backhand or Magic Johnson do a reverse slam dunk but be unable to reproduce the pro's actions.

A final process in Bandura's conception of observational learning involves *reinforcement* or *incentive conditions.* On many occasions we may attend to what a model says or does, retain the information in memory, and possess the motor capabilities to perform the action but we may fail to repeat the behavior because adequate reinforcement is not present. This was demonstrated in Bandura's study (1965) when those children who had seen a model punished for aggression reproduced the model's aggression only when they were offered an incentive to do so. A summary of Bandura's model of observational learning is shown in figure 5.17.

Bandura views observational learning as an information processing activity. As the individual observes, information about the world is transformed into cognitive representations that serve as guides for action. As we see next, interest in the cognitive factors of learning has increased dramatically in recent years.

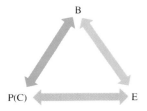

Figure 5.18
*Bandura's model of the reciprocal
influence of behavior (B), personal
and cognitive factors P(C), and
environment (E). The arrows reflect
how relations between these factors
are reciprocal rather than
unidirectional. Examples of personal
factors include intelligence, skills, and
self-control.*
Albert Bandura, Social Foundations of Thought &
Action: A Social Cognitive Theory, © 1986, p. 24.
Adapted by permission of Prentice-Hall, Inc.,
Englewood Cliffs, New Jersey.

Cognitive Factors in Learning

When we learn, we often cognitively represent or transform our experiences. In our excursion through learning thus far we have had little to say about these cognitive processes, except in our description of observational learning. In the operant conditioning view of Skinner and the classical conditioning view of Pavlov, no room is given to the possibility that cognitive factors such as memory, thinking, planning, or expectations might be important in the learning process. Skinnerians point out that they do not deny the existence of thinking processes, but since they cannot be observed they may interfere with the discovery of important environmental conditions that govern behavior.

Many contemporary psychologists, including behavioral revisionists who recognize that cognition should not have been ignored in classical and operant conditioning, believe that learning involves much more than stimulus-response connections. A view of learning that gives some importance to cognitive factors is the **S-O-R model**—**S** stands for stimulus, **O** for organism, and **R** for response. The *O* sometimes is referred to as the *black box* because the mental activities of the organism cannot be seen and, therefore, must be inferred.

Bandura (1986) described another model of learning that involves the behavior, the person, and the environment. As shown in figure 5.18, behavior, cognitive and other personal factors, and environmental influences operate interactively. Behavior can influence cognition and vice versa, the person's cognitive activities can influence the environment, environmental experiences can change the person's thought processes, and so on.

Let's consider how Bandura's model might work in the case of a college student's achievement behavior. As the student studies diligently and gets good grades, her behavior produces positive thoughts about her abilities. As part of her effort to make good grades, she plans and develops a number of strategies to make her studying more efficient. In these ways her behavior has influenced her thought, and her thought has influenced her behavior. At the beginning of the semester, her college made a special effort to involve students in a study skills program. She decided to join. Her success, along with that of other students who attended the program, has led the college to expand the program next semester. In these ways, environment influenced behavior, and behavior changed the environment. And the expectations of the college administrators that the study skills program would work made it possible in the first place. The program's success has spurred expectations that this type of program could work in other colleges. In these ways cognition changed the environment, and the environment changed cognition. Expectations are an important variable in Bandura's model. Next we look in greater detail at expectations and cognitive maps, as well as at the role of insight in learning.

Expectations and Cognitive Maps

E. C. Tolman says that when classical and operant conditioning occur the organism acquires certain expectations. In classical conditioning the young boy fears the rabbit because he *expects* it will hurt him. In operant conditioning an individual works hard all week because she *expects* to be paid on Friday.

In 1946, Tolman and his colleagues conducted a classic experiment to demonstrate the importance of expectations in learning. Initially, rats ran an elevated maze (see figure 5.19). The rats started at *A*, ran across the circular table at *B*, through an alley at *CD*, then along the path to the food box at *G*. *H* represents a light that illuminated the path from *F* to *G*.

This maze was replaced by one with several false runways (see figure 5.20). The rats ran down what had been the correct path before but found

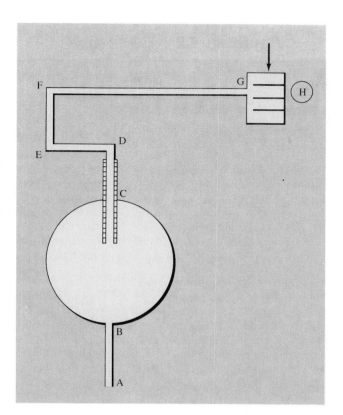

Figure 5.19
*Maze running as expectancy learning.
Apparatus used in preliminary
training.*

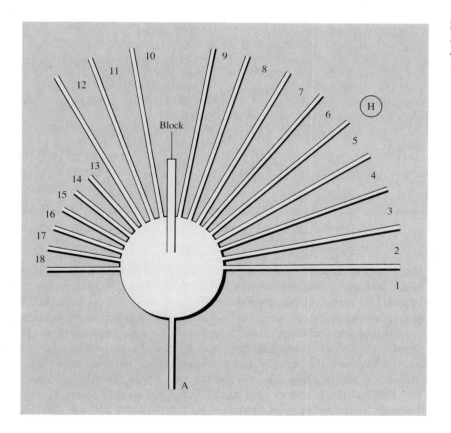

Figure 5.20
*Maze running as expectancy learning.
Apparatus used to test expectation
concerning the location of food.*

■ ■

Psychology 5.2

Cognitive Maps in Infants and Adults— from Playpens to Los Angeles

You probably have seen those maps that reflect one's perception of the size of his or her city or state in relation to the rest of the United States. In Texas, Texas will be drawn about three-fourths the size of the entire United States. In Manhattan, Manhattan might be drawn as nine-tenths the size of the United States. In one investigation, the cognitive maps of individuals with varying social and ethnic backgrounds in Los Angeles were obtained (Gould & White, 1974). As shown in figure 5.A, upper middle-class whites from the Westwood area of Los Angeles had a very different cognitive map of their city than the impoverished Spanish-speaking citizens from Boyle Heights. These findings reveal how our cognitive maps are influenced by where we live, what we experience, and our social background.

When we move around in a new environment, we develop a sense of where things are located. But when we have learned where something is located, what exactly

have we learned? What frame of reference do we use? We might learn the location of a building or state relative to ourselves ("the gas station is on the right" or "New England is east of here," for example). Alternatively, we might learn the location of the same building or area of the country in a more objective fashion, much in the way a map conveys information. This latter type of learning involves a more *objective* frame of reference than the *egocentric* frame of reference we mentioned earlier.

Whether we use an egocentric or objective frame of reference may depend on the situation (Mandler, 1983; Smyth & others, in press). For example, many of us learn the route to a new place in an egocentric way. We may say, "Go to Main Street, turn right and go for two blocks, then turn left and you will see the building on your left." Yet in other situations, an objective frame of reference dominates, such as when we take a shortcut to a familiar place. We can

take this shortcut by relying on our sense of direction. In general, egocentric representations are associated with knowledge of *routes* and objective representations are associated with *map* or *survey* knowledge that involves shortcuts and a sense of direction.

As young infants we often responded to our world egocentrically, but as early as the second year of life infants begin to develop objective frames of reference (Acredolo, 1978). This early emergence may be related to the infant's body movements. As an infant begins to crawl, the changing (egocentric) directions of stationary objects may be noticeable (for example, what was on the right appears on the left after turning around). This may stimulate the infant to attend to landmarks that lead to the development of objective frames of reference (Bremner, 1985; Bryant, 1985). Thus, even an infant in a playpen may be developing a cognitive map of how to navigate in the world.

that it was blocked. Which of the remaining paths would the rats choose? We might anticipate that they would choose paths 9 and 10 because they were nearest the path that had been successful. Instead, the rats explored several paths, running along one for a short distance, returning to the table, then trying out another one, and so on. Eventually, the rats ran along one path all the way to the end. This path was number 6, not 9 or 10. Path 6 ran to a point about four inches short of where the food box had been located previously. According to Tolman, the rats had not only learned how to run the original maze, they also had learned to expect food upon reaching a specific place. This type of learning is referred to as *place learning*.

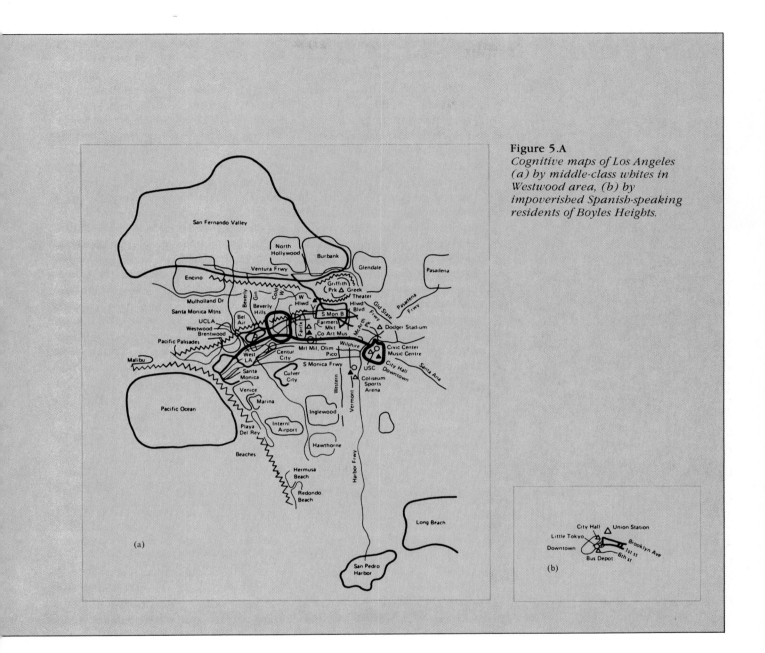

Figure 5.A
Cognitive maps of Los Angeles (a) by middle-class whites in Westwood area, (b) by impoverished Spanish-speaking residents of Boyles Heights.

In his paper "Cognitive Maps in Rats and Men," Tolman (1948) set forth his belief that organisms select information from the environment and construct a *cognitive map* of their experiences. In Tolman's view, this cognitive map guides the organism's behavior. As discussed in Psychology 5.2, interest in cognitive maps is alive and well today.

Tolman was not the only psychologist who was dissatisfied with the S-R view of learning. Gestalt psychologist Wolfgang Kohler thought that the cognitive process of insight learning also was an important form of learning.

Figure 5.21
This chimp has developed the insight to stack boxes on top of one another in order to reach the fruit.

Insight Learning

Wolfgang Kohler, a German psychologist, spent four months in the Canary Islands during World War I observing the behavior of apes. While there he conducted two fascinating experiments. One is called the "stick" problem, the other the "box" problem. Though the two experiments are basically the same, the solutions to the problems are different. In both dilemmas, the ape discovers that it cannot reach an alluring piece of fruit, either because the fruit is too high or it is outside of the ape's cage and beyond its reach. To solve the stick problem, the ape has to insert a small stick inside a larger stick to reach the fruit. To master the box problem, the ape must stack several boxes to reach the fruit (see figure 5.21).

According to Kohler (1925), solving these problems does not involve trial and error or mere connections between stimuli and responses. Rather, when the ape realizes that his customary actions are not going to get the fruit, he often sits for a period of time and ponders how to solve the problem. Then he pops up, as if he has had a sudden flash of insight, and quickly puts the sticks together or piles the boxes on top of one another and gets the fruit. Kohler calls this type of problem solving **insight learning.**

The study of cognitive factors tells us that learning is more than just studying the environmental determinants of behavior. Such matters as expectations, insight, and observation are involved. A summary of the main themes of observational learning and cognitive factors in learning is presented in concept table 5.3. As we see next, the organism also brings a biological background to the learning context.

■ ■ ■ ■ ■ ■ ■ ■ ■ ■ ■ ■ ■ ■ ■ ■ ■ ■ ■

Concept Table 5.3

Observational Learning and Cognitive Factors in Learning		
Concept	**Processes/related ideas**	**Characteristics/description**
Observational learning	Its nature	Occurs when an individual observes someone else's behavior. Also called imitation or modeling. It is important to distinguish between what is learned and whether it is performed.
	Processes	Bandura believes that observational learning involves attention, retention, motor reproduction, and reinforcement or incentive conditions.
Cognitive factors in learning	Models	Many psychologists recognize the importance of studying how cognitive factors mediate environment-behavior connections. The S-O-R model reflects this, as does Bandura's contemporary model, which emphasizes reciprocal connections between behavior, person (cognition), and environment.
	Expectations and cognitive maps	Tolman reinterpreted classical and operant conditioning in terms of expectations. We construct cognitive maps of our experiences that guide our behavior; psychologists still study the nature of cognitive maps.
	Insight learning	Kohler, like Tolman, was dissatisfied with the S-R view of learning. He believed that organisms reflect and suddenly gain insight into how a problem should be solved.

Biological Factors in Learning

Albert Einstein had many special talents. He perceived new things and posed deep challenges. Was Einstein's intelligence due to environmental connections as the operant enthusiasts believe? As a child, Einstein showed little indication of what he was to become. His parents worried because he did not speak until the age of three. He was an indifferent student in elementary school, where he said the teachers reminded him of drill sergeants. In his youth, nationalism and intellectual rigidity characterized his European education. Clearly, Einstein's mind was more than the product of his environment. His biological heritage was an important ingredient of his brilliant mind. What are some of the ways biological factors can restrict or enhance learning?

Physical Characteristics

We can't breathe under water, fish can't play ping pong, and cows can't solve math problems. The structure of an organism's body permits certain kinds of learning and inhibits others. For example, chimpanzees cannot learn to speak because they lack the necessary vocal equipment. Some of us cannot solve difficult calculus problems, others of us can, and the differences do not all seem to be due to experience. Remember from our discussion of genetic influences in chapter 2 that behavior is the result of genetic-environmental interaction. Genetic-environmental interaction is important for intelligence as well as other aspects of mind and behavior.

Preparedness

Some animals learn readily in one situation but have difficulty learning in slightly different circumstances. The difficulty might not be due to some subtle complexity of the learning situation but rather to the predisposition of the organism. Martin Seligman (1970) describes this difficulty in terms of **preparedness** of the organism to learn. An organism may or may not be biologically prepared to learn in a given situation. For example, cats can escape from a cage by pulling a string to open the door or by pushing the door, but if they have to lick, their escape ability is greatly reduced. In most situations humans are prepared to walk and talk.

Instinctive Drift

Keller and Marion Breland (1961), who were students of B. F. Skinner, used operant conditioning to train a variety of animals to perform at fairs, conventions, and in television advertisements. They used Skinner's techniques of shaping, chaining, and discrimination to teach pigs to cart large wooden nickels to a piggy bank and deposit them. They also trained raccoons to pick up a coin and place it in a metal tray.

Although the pigs and raccoons, as well as other animals such as chickens, accomplished most of the tasks (raccoons became very adept basketball players, for example—see figure 5.22), some of the animals began to act in strange ways. Instead of picking up the large wooden nickel and carrying it to the piggy bank, the pigs would drop the nickel on the ground, shove it with their snouts, toss it in the air, and then repeat these actions. The raccoons began to

Figure 5.22
This raccoon's skill in using its hands made it an excellent basketball player, but because of instinctive drift, the raccoon had a much more difficult time taking money to the bank.

hold onto the coin rather than dropping it into the metal container. They would rub the coin against the metal container, act like they were going to drop it into the container, but then bring it back out. When two coins were introduced, the raccoons rubbed them together in a miserly fashion. Somehow these behaviors were overwhelming the strength of the reinforcement that was given at the end of the day.

Why were the pigs and raccoons misbehaving? The pigs were engaging in a rooting instinct, which is used to uncover edible roots. The raccoons were engaging in an instinctive food-washing response. The tendency of animals to revert to instinctive behavior is called **instinctive drift.**

Taste Aversion

A psychologist went to dinner with his wife and ordered filet mignon with Bérnaise sauce, his favorite dish. Afterwards, they went to the opera. Several hours later he became very ill with stomach pains and nausea. Several weeks later he tried to eat Bérnaise sauce but couldn't bear it. The psychologist's experience involves *taste aversion,* another biological constraint on learning (Garcia, Ervin, & Koelling, 1966; Logue, 1987, in press).

If an organism ingests a substance that poisons but does not kill, the organism often develops considerable distaste for that substance. Rats that experience low levels of radiation after eating show a strong aversion to the food they were eating when the radiation made them ill. This aversion has been shown to last for as long as thirty-two days. Such long-term effects cannot be accounted for by classical conditioning, which would argue that a single pairing of the conditioned and unconditioned stimuli would not last that long. Radiation and chemical treatment of cancer often produce nausea in patients and the resulting pattern of aversions often resemble those shown by laboratory animals (Garcia y Robertson & Garcia, 1985, 1987).

This predator has threatened the livestock of a rancher. How is taste aversion research helping the farmer deal with the problem?

Taste aversion research has produced information that is important to the ecology of animals. For example, the livestock of farmers and ranchers may be threatened by wolves or coyotes. Instead of killing the pests or predators, they are fed poisoned meat of their prey (e.g., cattle, sheep). The wolves and coyotes, poisoned but not killed, develop a taste aversion for cattle or sheep and, hence, are less of a threat to the farmers and ranchers. In this way ranchers, farmers, cattle, sheep, wolves, and coyotes can live in some semblance of ecological balance.

Contemporary Behavior Theory and Evolutionary Biology

Influenced by biological theory, contemporary behaviorists are interested in how organisms select among various options in life (Bolles & Beecher, in press; Domjan, 1987; Domjan & Hollis, 1987; Smith, 1986; Sober, 1984; Williams, 1986; Zeiler, 1987). Rather than ask the traditional question of how rewards strengthen behaviors, the contemporary behaviorists question how organisms make choices in their environment. Special interest is devoted to discovering how the organism chooses the optimal response among a number of alternatives. These are the same kinds of questions that are being asked by evolutionary biologists who study behavioral ecology (Kamil & Yoerg, 1982).

Learning is a pervasive aspect of life and has a great deal of adaptive significance for organisms. We have studied many different forms of learning and seen how cognitive and biological factors influence learning. In the next chapter we become absorbed more deeply in the world of cognition as we explore the nature of memory.

Summary

I. What Is Learning?

Learning is a relatively permanent change in behavior due to experience. Psychologists have explained our many experiences with a few basic learning processes. Among the most important experiences are how we *respond* to the environment (classical conditioning), how we *act* in the environment (operant conditioning), and how we *observe* the environment (observational learning). Early approaches emphasized connections between environment and behavior; many contemporary approaches stress that cognitive factors mediate environment-behavior connections.

II. Classical Conditioning: Its Nature

Pavlov discovered the principle of classical conditioning in which the organism learns the association between an unconditioned stimulus (UCS) and a conditioned stimulus (CS). The UCS automatically produces the UCR (unconditioned response). After conditioning (CS-UCS pairing), the CS alone elicits the CR (conditioned response). Generalization, discrimination, and extinction are involved in classical conditioning. Pavlov explained classical conditioning in terms of stimulus substitution but the modern explanation is based on information theory. Today interest in classical conditioning focuses on the complexity of the context and cognitive factors, such as memory and imagery, that mediate the CS-UCS connection.

III. Classical Conditioning in Humans and Evaluation of Classical Conditioning

Classical conditioning has survival value for humans, such as when we develop a fear of hazardous conditions. Irrational fears are explained by classical conditioning. Counterconditioning and systematic desensitization also are used to alleviate fears.

Classical conditioning is very important in explaining the way learning in animals occurs. While classical conditioning explains some aspects of human learning, it clearly is not the only way we learn. Classical conditioning misses the active nature of the organism in the environment.

IV. Operant Conditioning: Its Nature

E. L. Thorndike's law of effect states that behaviors followed by a positive outcome are strengthened while those followed by a negative outcome are weakened. Thorndike's theory is referred to as S-R theory. Skinner says that the organism operates in the environment to produce change that will lead to a reward. Operant conditioning is a form of learning in which the consequences of behavior lead to changes in the probability of its occurrence.

V. Operant Processes and Comparison with Classical Conditioning

Reinforcement increases the probability a behavior will occur. In positive reinforcement, the frequency of a response increases because it is followed by a pleasant stimulus. In negative reinforcement, the frequency of a response increases because it either removes an unpleasant stimulus or allows the organism to avoid the stimulus. Punishment decreases the probability that a behavior will occur. Operant conditioning focuses on what happens after a response is made; classical conditioning emphasizes what occurs before a response is made. The key connection in classical conditioning is between two stimuli; in operant conditioning it is between the organism's response and its consequences. Operant conditioning mainly involves voluntary behavior, classical conditioning involuntary behavior.

VI. Principles of Operant Conditioning

Operant conditioning involves the principles of time interval, shaping and chaining, primary and secondary reinforcement, schedules of reinforcement, as well as extinction, generalization, and discrimination.

VII. Applications of Operant Conditioning

Behavior modification uses learning principles to change maladaptive or abnormal behavior. Behavior modification based on operant conditioning focuses on changing behavior by following it with reinforcement. Behavior modification is used widely to reduce maladaptive behavior.

VIII. Observational Learning

Observational learning, also called imitation or modeling, occurs when an individual learns from someone else's behavior. An important distinction must be made between what is learned and what is performed. Bandura believes that observational learning involves attention, retention, motor reproduction, and reinforcement or incentive conditions.

IX. Cognitive Factors in Learning: Models

Psychologists recognize the importance of studying how cognitive factors mediate environment-behavior connections. The S-O-R model reflects this cognitive interest, as does Bandura's contemporary model, which emphasizes reciprocal connections between behavior, person (cognition), and environment.

X. Some Cognitive Factors in Learning

Tolman reinterpreted classical and operant conditioning in terms of expectations. He argued that we construct cognitive maps of our experiences that guide our behavior; psychologists still study the nature of cognitive maps. Kohler, like Tolman, was dissatisfied with the S-R view of learning. He believed that organisms reflect on a problem-solving situation and then suddenly gain insight into how the problem should be solved.

XI. Biological Factors in Learning

Biological factors suggest there are constraints on what an organism can learn from experience. These constraints involve physical characteristics, preparedness, instinctive drift, and taste aversion. Contemporary learning theorists focus on how organisms select among responses to optimize their adaptation. This interest is similar to that of evolutionary biologists.

Key Terms

baseline *152*
acquisition phase *152*
learning *153*
classical conditioning *154*
unconditioned stimulus (UCS) *154*
unconditioned response (UCR) *154*
conditioned stimulus (CS) *154*
conditioned response (CR) *155*
generalization *156, 168*
discrimination *156, 168*
extinction *156, 168*
spontaneous recovery *156*

stimulus substitution *156*
information theory *157*
phobias *158*
counterconditioning *159*
systematic desensitization *159*
law of effect *162*
S-R theory *162*
operants *163*
operant conditioning *163*
reinforcement *163*
punishment *163*
positive reinforcement *164*
negative reinforcement *164*

shaping *165*
chaining *166*
primary and secondary reinforcement *166*
partial reinforcement *166*
schedules of reinforcement *166*
behavior modification *168*
biofeedback *170*
observational learning *172*
S-O-R model *174*
insight learning *178*
preparedness *179*
instinctive drift *180*

Suggested Readings

Axelrod, S., & Apsche, J. (Eds.). (1983). *The effects of punishment on human behavior.* New York: Academic Press. An up-to-date, authoritative volume on how punishment can be used effectively to control behavior. Considerable detail about reducing the negative side effects of punishment and a full consideration of the ethical issues involved in the use of punishment are included.

Balsam, P. D., & Tomie, A. (1985). *Context and learning.* Hillsdale, NJ: Erlbaum. Provides excellent essays on the importance of considering information in the context in which learning occurs to understand processes such as classical and operant conditioning.

Bandura, A. (1986). *Social foundations of thought and action.* Englewood Cliffs, NJ: Prentice-Hall. This book presents Bandura's cognitive view of learning, including the importance of considering reciprocal connections between behavior, environment, and cognition. An extensive discussion of observational learning is included.

Hammonds, B. (Ed.), (1985). *Psychology and learning.* Washington D.C.: American Psychological Association. This is the fourth volume of the American Psychological Association's master lecture series in which well-known psychologists discuss aspects of psychology of widespread public interest. This volume focuses on the nature of learning, including chapters on applications of learning theory, understanding environment, and the evolution of learning mechanisms.

Kalish, H. I. (1981). *From behavioral science to behavior modification.* New York: McGraw-Hill. An excellent overview of the successes and failures of behavior modification, including both classical and operant conditioning. Also includes excellent overviews of the basic learning processes described in this chapter.

Skinner, B. F. *Walden two.* (1960). New York: Macmillan. Skinner once entertained the possibility of a career as a writer. In this interesting and provocative book, he outlines his ideas on how a more complete understanding of the principles of instrumental conditioning can lead to a happier life. Critics argue that his approach is far too manipulative.

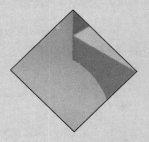

Memory

I come into the fields and spacious palaces of my memory, where are treasures of countless images of things of every manner.

—St. Augustine

Images of Memory

There are few moments when we are not steeped in memory. Memory is at work with each step we take, each thought we think, each word we utter. How much does memory matter to us? Consider the unfortunate case of M. K., a high school teacher who at the age of forty-three was stricken with an acute episode of encephalitis. Within hours, he lost access to almost all memories he had formed during the previous five years. Worse still, he had virtually no memory of anything that happened to him after the onset of the encephalitis. Since the illness began, M. K. has learned a few names over the years, a few major events, and he can get around the hospital (Rozin, 1976). M. K.'s tragic circumstance, in which a microscopic viral agent rendered him memoryless, conveys the emptiness of a life without memory.

The importance of memory is revealed in another very different case. A Russian known only by the initial S could remember a list of seventy items without making an error. And he had no difficulty recalling the list backwards! S once was asked to remember the following formula:

$$N \cdot \sqrt{d^2 \cdot \frac{85}{VX}} \cdot 3 \sqrt{\frac{276^2 \cdot 86x}{n^2V \cdot \pi264}} \, n^2b = sv \frac{1624}{32^2} \cdot r^2s$$

S studied the formula for seven minutes and then reported how he memorized it. The following portion of his response reveals how he made up stories to aid his memory:

> Neiman (N) came out and jabbed at the ground with his cane (.) He looked up at a tall tree which resembled the square-root sign ($\sqrt{}$), and thought to himself: "No wonder this tree has withered and begun to expose its roots. After all, it was here when I built these two houses" (d^2). Once again he poked his cane (.) Then he said: "The houses are old, I'll have to get rid of them; the sale will bring in far more money." He had originally invested 85,000 in them (85).

S's complete story was four times this length. It must have been a powerful one, because fifteen years later with no advance notice, he recalled the formula perfectly!

Envious as we might be of S's remarkable memory, especially when taking college exams, S suffered from it. He had to devise techniques for forgetting because he remembered virtually everything, no matter how trivial. He once commented that each word called up images and the images collided with one another—the result sometimes was chaos. Forgetting was M. K.'s curse, but it was S's salvation. It should be noted that individuals like S, who are extremely good at remembering vast amounts of material, are somewhat rare. ▪

What Is Memory?

Memory is the retention of information over time. Psychologists study how information gets into memory, known as **encoding,** how this information is stored, and how it is retrieved. Sometimes information is retained only for an instant, and sometimes the information is stored for a lifetime. Memory is involved when you listen to someone tell you a phone number and proceed to dial it, when you recall the name of your best friend from high school, and when you study for an exam. Think how barren your life would be without memory. You would know nothing of what went on two seconds ago, let alone twenty minutes or ten years ago. Could you function at all?

Memory is somewhat complex and requires an understanding of several important processes. Our exploration of memory will take us through several different forms of memory, determined by what information is remembered and how long it is remembered. In addition to learning how information gets into memory and how it is retrieved, you will study the biological basis of memory and some strategies for improving memory.

Time Frames of Memory

We remember some information for only a fraction of a second, some for seconds, and yet other information for minutes and even a lifetime. The types of memory defined by these time frames are referred to as sensory registers, short-term memory, and long-term memory, respectively.

A model that portrays these three time frames of memory and the processes of encoding and retrieval is shown in figure 6.1. Information from the world is detected by sensory processes. Some of these stimuli are registered only for a fleeting instant. The stimuli might be sights or sounds, for example, that are registered for only as long as we are exposed to them. As shown in figure 6.1, these stimuli go into our sensory registers but are not processed further in short-term or long-term memory. **Sensory registers,** then, is a form of memory in which stimuli are registered for the brief time we are exposed to them. For example, as you drive down the road you are exposed to thousands of stimuli, such as a tree, a person, or a truck that passes you, but you register most of these for only a fleeting instant.

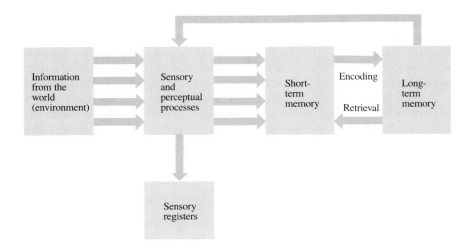

Figure 6.1
Sensory registers, short-term memory, and long-term memory.

Think about walking across the campus of your college, passing dozens of students. As you observe the sea of faces, how are your sensation-perception, short-term memory, and long-term memory working?

In **short-term memory** we retain recently encountered information or information retrieved from long-term memory for a brief period of time, usually about fifteen to thirty seconds. In **long-term memory** we retain information for an indefinite period of time and the information can be used over and over again. Notice in figure 6.1 that information goes from short-term memory to long-term memory through the process of encoding and moves back to short-term memory through the process of retrieval. Notice also that information in long-term memory can influence perception, even before short-term memory is reached.

In the contemporary view of cognition, the interplay between sensation-perception and long-term memory often precedes rather than follows short-term memory (Klatsky, 1984). For example, consider the experience of walking across a crowded college campus, passing dozens of your fellow students. With your mind on getting to the next class on time, or possibly on the date you have tonight, you are scarcely aware of the sea of faces you pass. The faces are not entering your short-term memory—processing is effectively blocked at some earlier level of sensation or perception. Yet if you pass a friend, or possibly someone you *wish* were a friend, you instantly perk up and greet them. *That* individual's face has entered short-term memory, capturing your attention. How could this happen? Apparently, although you were not aware of it, you were checking the familiarity of each face you passed, a process that requires contact with long-term memory.

Of course, after you recognize your friend and form a representation of him in short-term memory, you have the ability to recall the encounter. Suppose a few steps farther another friend asks, "Did you see John coming this way?" Almost certainly you could answer correctly—such is the power of short-term memory. But what if after an hour, or even a week, someone asks if you have seen John recently. Will you remember your encounter with John while walking across campus? Maybe or maybe not. Getting new information from short-term memory that is permanently encoded into long-term memory can be a difficult and failure-prone process. Frequently the information cannot be retrieved, and if it can, subsequent retrieval of this new information can fail.

The links between short-term and long-term memory form serious bottlenecks in our ability to recall information, and there is no better example than our faulty memory for names. Suppose John has a friend with him, and he introduces you to her. You listen carefully to her name, and while you are talking, you say it over and over again in short-term memory. You truly *want* to remember this name and even ask your new acquaintance to repeat it for you. But five minutes later on your way to class, you think of the individual and consider calling her and the name is gone! How could the name have been so vivid in awareness and then so hopelessly forgotten just a few minutes later?

Two possibilities can explain this. Perhaps despite repeating the new friend's name (actually the association between the individual and the name) it was not adequately encoded in long-term memory—a clear representation in short-term memory does not guarantee encoding into long-term memory. Or perhaps the name was encoded into long-term memory, but its representation is such that it is simply irretrievable in your current state (if you are lucky, the name might occur to you later).

As you can see, information does not move from the sensory registers to short-term memory to long-term memory. Rather there is a complex interaction among sensation-perception, short-term memory, and long-term memory. Indeed, the model in figure 6.1 is a simple one, devised to illustrate memory's basic processes. As we discuss memory, you will discover that psychologists entertain a number of other ideas about how memory processes work.

Sensory Registers

Think about all of the information you encounter as you move through each day of your life. As you are walking to class in the morning, literally thousands of stimuli come into your field of vision and hearing—cracks in the sidewalk, a chirping bird, a noisy motorcycle, the blue sky, faces of hundreds of people, and so on. Not all of these are *registered* by your eyes, ears, and other sensory receptors, but many are. For example, you are exposed to hundreds of students' faces but notice only a few—a good-looking guy, a friend, someone who looks too young to be on campus. As we mentioned, psychologists believe most of these stimuli are registered for not much longer than the brief time we are exposed to them in what are called sensory registers.

A classic study by George Sperling (1960) illustrates how sensory registers work. He presented subjects with patterns of stimuli such as those shown in figure 6.2. As you look at the letters you have no trouble recognizing them. But Sperling allowed his subjects to see the letters for one-twentieth of a second only. After the letters were flashed on the screen, the subjects were able to report four or five of the nine letters. To learn if subjects were *registering* more of the letters, Sperling sounded a low, medium, or high tone just after the letters were presented. The subjects were told that the tone was a signal to report only the letters from the bottom, middle, or top row, respectively. Under these conditions, the subjects performed much better. Indeed, they were able to remember almost all of the items. This research demonstrates that our sensory processing of information is often better than our verbal reports indicate.

Remember, though, that information lasts only for an instant in the sensory registers, much like sitting by the window on a speeding train as images rapidly move through your field of vision. These fleeting images are called **iconic** if they are visual and **echoic** if they are auditory. Sights last for less than one second, and sounds last a little longer, up to about three to four seconds. But what about memories that last longer than icons or echoes?

Short-Term Memory

You are sitting in a large room taking the SAT test. You have just read three paragraphs about King George of England and have started to answer questions about the material. Your ability to retain this material involves short-term memory, a very important part of our memory system. Short-term memory usually lasts for about fifteen to thirty seconds, unless the individual continues to attend to the information. If the individual continues to attend to the information, the duration of short-term memory is indefinite. Remember that information comes into short-term memory through either sensory and perceptual processes or through long-term memory. The short-term memory system has been described as a *workbench* because so much activity involved in processing information goes on here (Klatzky, 1980).

As we walk down the street we literally are bombarded by thousands of stimuli. Not all of these stimuli are registered by our senses, but many are.

Figure 6.2
Array of stimuli similar to those flashed for about 1/20th of a second to subjects in Sperling's experiment.

Figure 6.3
Serial position effect. When a person is asked to memorize a list of words, the words memorized last usually are recalled best, those at the beginning next best, and those in the middle the least efficiently.

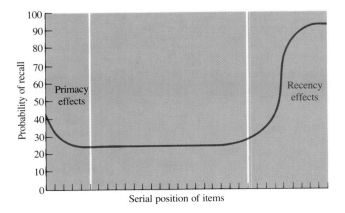

Short-term memory has a limited capacity. This important point was made by George Miller (1956) in his paper "The magical number seven, plus or minus two." The capacity of short-term memory for most individuals is seven items, plus or minus two. Miller was correct about the limited capacity of short-term memory, but when we think about our short-term memory it seems as if its capacity is more than seven items. For instance, consider the words "hot," "city," "book," "time," "forget," "tomorrow," and "smile." If you stored these words in short-term memory, thirty-four letters would be involved. Miller argued that we are able to store so much information in short-term memory because of **chunking,** that is, organizing items into meaningful or manageable units. Thus, in the example of the thirty-four letters, we *chunk* the letters into seven words. Telephone numbers, social security numbers, and license plate numbers are common examples of how chunking can help us to remember lists of numbers in everyday life.

A dramatic demonstration of chunking involves a subject with a normal short-term memory capacity of about seven items (Ericsson & Chase, 1982). The subject practiced his short-term memory for more than 230 hours over a period of 200 days. He gradually improved his performance from seven to eighty pieces of information. His performance soared because he learned to treat sequences of information as groups (or chunks), groups as supergroups, and supergroups as higher-level groups, forming a hierarchical organization of elements.

Another way to improve short-term memory is by **rehearsal.** Information already in short-term memory is repeated, as when we are trying to remember a phone number, so that the length of time the information stays in short-term memory is increased.

An interesting aspect of memory is that we remember information experienced first and last better than what we experienced in the middle. If someone were to give you the directions, "Left on Mockingbird, right on Central, right on Stemmons, left on Balboa, and right on Parkside," you probably would remember "left on Mockingbird" and "right on Parkside" easier than the turns and streets in the middle. Superior recall at the beginning of a list of items is called the *primacy effect,* while excellent memory of the end of the list is called the *recency effect.* Together, the combination is called the **serial-position effect.** Figure 6.3 shows what a typical serial-position effect looks like.

What causes primacy and recency effects? The first few items in a list are remembered well because they probably are rehearsed more often than later items. Short-term memory is relatively empty when they enter, so there is little competition for rehearsal time. In this way, the items make it into long-term memory. The last several items are remembered for a different reason. At the time they are recalled, they are in short-term memory. However, if there is a delay after the information is presented (even for thirty seconds) and the subjects are not allowed to rehearse, the recency effect diminishes. Elements in the middle are not remembered well because by the time they get into short-term memory, competition from other information is present and these items get less rehearsal. In this way many of the items in the middle drop out of short-term memory before they reach long-term memory.

Long-Term Memory

The storehouse of long-term memory is staggering. John von Neuman, a distinguished information theorist, has put the size at 2.8×10^{20} (280 quintillion) bits. Chances are von Neuman assumed that we never forget anything, but even considering that we forget things, we can hold several billion times more information than a large computer. What is more impressive about long-term memory is how efficiently we retrieve information. Usually it takes only a few seconds to search through this huge storehouse to find the information we want. Who discovered America? What was the name of your first date? When were you born? Who developed the first laboratory of psychology? You can answer these questions instantly.

An important question psychologists ask about long-term memory focuses on *what* is remembered. Chris Evert moves gracefully for a wide forehand, finishes the follow-through, skips quickly back to the center of the court, pushes off for a short ball and dumps a drop shot over the net. If we asked her about this rapid sequence of motor behaviors, she probably would have a difficult time verbally communicating all of the movements.

By contrast, if we asked her about the last time she played such a tough opponent, she quickly responds, "Martina." In the first instance, she was unable to verbally describe exactly what she had done. But in the second instance she had no problem talking about it. John Anderson (1983, 1985) believes such instances illustrate a distinction between **declarative knowledge,** information that can be verbally communicated, and **procedural knowledge,** which consists of skills, about which it is difficult, if not impossible, to communicate verbally. Declarative knowledge has been called "knowing *that*," procedural knowledge has been called "knowing *how*." Other examples of procedural knowledge are driving a car and reading.

Declarative knowledge has been studied much more extensively than procedural knowledge. A common distinction in declarative knowledge is made between episodic and semantic content of memory (Tulving, 1972, 1987). **Episodic memory** refers to the where and when of events and episodes in an individual's life. If you remembered that you had a piano lesson at 10 A.M. yesterday and that you had orange juice for breakfast this morning, you were using episodic memory. **Semantic memory** reflects our general knowledge about the world. Examples of semantic memory include knowing who flew the first airplane, remembering what an airplane is, and recalling the definition of a word. While some psychologists believe the distinction between episodic and semantic memory is an important one (e.g., Tulving, 1986, 1987) others are not so sure (Anderson & Ross, 1980; Ratcliffe & McKoon, 1986). The organization of declarative and procedural knowledge and episodic and semantic memory in long-term memory is shown in figure 6.4.

Remembering how to hit a tennis ball is a form of procedural knowledge; procedural knowledge has been called "knowing how."

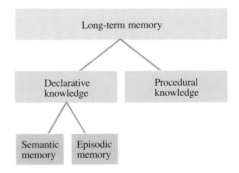

Figure 6.4
Declarative and procedural knowledge and semantic and episodic memory.

Attention is an important aspect of encoding. The forest ranger has captured this group's attention, facilitating their encoding of the information he is providing.

An important aspect of attention is selectivity. This couple is showing selective attention, ignoring all of the information about them.

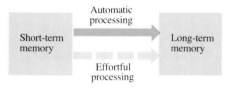

Figure 6.5
Automatic and effortful processing.

Encoding

You are listening to a lecture. Some of the information enters your memory and some of it does not. Many psychologists who study memory are interested in *how* information, such as that presented in a lecture, is processed. Our attention to what is being said or done is one key ingredient.

Attention

"Pay attention" is a phrase we hear all of the time. Just what is attention? When you take an exam you attend to it. This implies that you have the ability to focus your mental effort on certain stimuli (the test questions) while excluding other stimuli from your consideration. Thus, an important aspect of attention is *selectivity*. This ability to focus and concentrate on a narrow band of information is called **selective attention.** When selective attention fails us, we have difficulty ignoring information that is irrelevant to our interests or goals (Neill & Westberry, 1987; Posner, 1987). For example, if the television set or stereo is blaring while you are studying, you may have trouble concentrating.

Not only is attention selective, but also it is *shiftable*. If a professor asks you to pay attention to a certain question and you do this, your behavior indicates that you can shift the focus of your mental effort from one stimulus to another. If the telephone rings while you are studying, you shift your attention from studying to the telephone. An external stimulus is not necessary to elicit an attention shift. At this moment you can shift your attention from one topic to another virtually at will. You might think about the last time you ate at a Chinese restaurant, then think about the last time you ate at an Italian restaurant, then think about which is your favorite restaurant of all time.

As we have seen, attention is the concentration and focusing of mental *effort,* a focus that is both selective and shifting. Effort plays an important role in the two important ways of encoding information—automatic and effortful processing.

Automatic and Effortful Processing

An important aspect of encoding information in memory is the degree of effort required, which has led to the distinction between **automatic and effortful processing** (Hasher & Zacks, 1979). Automatic processing requires no additional effort on our part, but effortful processing does. Information about spatial aspects of the environment or frequency of events can be encoded automatically. For example, "a baseball field is shaped like a diamond," and "she came to the chess match twice this week," are encoded automatically. However, when activities such as organization, rehearsal, imagery, and elaboration are used, encoding takes more effort. A number of investigations have shown that this allocation of capacity, or effort, is related to improved memory (Ellis, Thomas, & Rodrigquez, 1984; O'Brien & Myers, 1985). Figure 6.5 portrays how information may be encoded from short-term into long-term memory by either automatic processing or effortful processing.

Does this mean that if you put more effort into studying your memory for the material will improve? For the most part it certainly does, and the more the material (such as the text you are reading) induces such an effort, the more it will be remembered (McDaniel & others, in press).

Among the most important types of cognitive activities that require effortful processing are deep processing, organization, elaboration, and imagery (see figure 6.6). We now consider each of these in turn.

Levels of Processing

Some information requires deep processing, and other information is processed on a shallow level. The deeper the information is processed the more effort is required. Fergus Craik and Robert Lockhart (1972) developed the **levels of processing view** of memory, which basically emphasizes that memory is on a continuum. The physical or sensory features of information are analyzed first at the *shallow* level of processing. This might involve detecting features such as lines, angles, and contours or the sound of a word. At the *intermediate* level of processing, the stimulus is recognized and labels are given to objects or events. Then, at the *deepest* level, information is processed semantically (meaningfully and symbolically). For example, if you heard the word *boat* at the shallow level you might think of the general contour of a boat, at the intermediate level you might label the object described as a boat, and at the deepest level, you might produce a network of associations, such as characteristics of boats, the yacht you dream of owning one day, and so on.

According to the levels of processing view, information will be remembered better if meaning is encoded than if only the surface, perceptual features are put into the memory system (see figure 6.7 for a description of the levels of processing view). A number of investigations have shown that memory improves when subjects are instructed to make semantic associations with the information given (Hyde & Jenkins, 1969; Parkin, 1984).

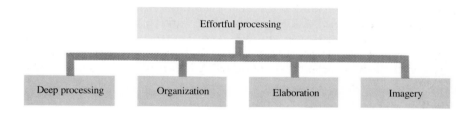

Figure 6.6
Types of effortful processing.

Shallow processing	Physical and perceptual features	The lines, angles, and contour that make up the physical appearance of an object, such as a car, are detected.
Intermediate processing	Stimulus is recognized and labeled	Recognition that the object is a car.
Deep processing	Semantic, meaningful, symbolic characteristics are used	Associations connected with car are brought to mind—you think about the Porsche or Ferrari you hope to buy or the fun you and friends had on spring break when you drove a car to the beach.

Depth of processing

Figure 6.7
The depth of processing view of memory.

Figure 6.8
An example of a hierarchical organization.

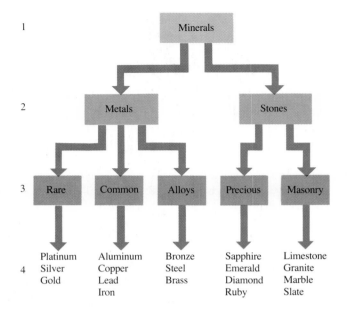

Figure 6.9
The beneficial effects of hierarchical organization on memory in the experiment by Bower and his colleagues (1969).

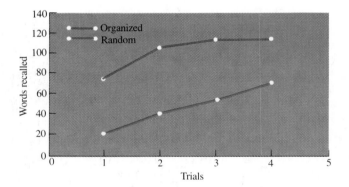

Organization

Recall the twelve months of the year as quickly as you can. Did you make any errors? How long did it take you? What was the order of your recall? The answers to these questions probably are: "no," "four to six seconds," and "natural order" (January, February, March, etc.). Now try remembering the months in alphabetical order. Did you make any errors? How long did it take you? There is a clear distinction between recalling the months naturally and alphabetically. This demonstration (Tulving, 1983) makes it easy to see that your memory for the months of the year is organized. Indeed, one of the most pervasive features of memory is its organization.

An important feature of memory's organization is that sometimes it is hierarchical. A *hierarchy* is a system in which items are organized from general classes to more specific classes. An example of a hierarchy for the general category of minerals is shown in figure 6.8. In an experiment using conceptual hierarchies of words such as those in figure 6.8, Gordon Bower and his colleagues (1969) showed the importance of organization in memory. Subjects who were presented the words in hierarchies remembered the words much better than those who were given the words in random groupings (see figure 6.9).

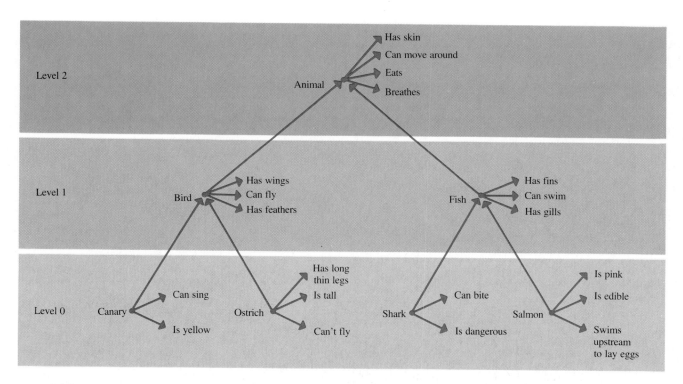

Different models of how memory is hierarchically organized have been proposed, but all share the important assumption that vast associative networks are involved. One of the first hierarchical networks emphasized that words or concepts are represented by nodes in a complex network of orderly links (figure 6.10) (Collins & Quinlin, 1969). More recently, cognitive psychologists realize that this model is too neat and regular. For example, individuals take longer to answer true or false to the statement "An ostrich is a bird" than they do to the statement "A canary is a bird." Memory researchers now envision the network as more irregular and distorted: a *typical* bird, such as a canary, is closer to the node or center of the category *bird* than the atypical ostrich. An example of the revised model is shown in figure 6.11, which allows for the typicality of information while retaining the original notion of node and network.

We add new material to this network by placing it in the middle of the appropriate region. The new material is gradually tied in—by meaningful connections—to the appropriate nodes in the surrounding network. That is why if you cram for a test, you will not remember the information over the long term; the new material is not knit into the long-term web. By contrast, discussing the material or incorporating it into a research paper does interweave it until it is a fixed part of long-term memory (Hunt, 1982).

If recent trends continue, we can expect more complex and powerful network models to flourish. Currently, there is a wave of excitement over the **parallel distributed processing models** (or PDP) developed by David Rumelhart and James McClelland (1986). They argue that memory is retained in a parallel fashion, that is, simultaneously over a wide range of different connections. Thousands, even millions, of connections are possible. In the resulting network, connections are excited or inhibited. Perception, action, or thought occur because the strength or weight of the connections is altered. A task is completed or input is processed when the system "settles" or "relaxes," at least tentatively, on a "solution."

Figure 6.10
A hierarchical organization of memory with nodes at different levels in the hierarchy.

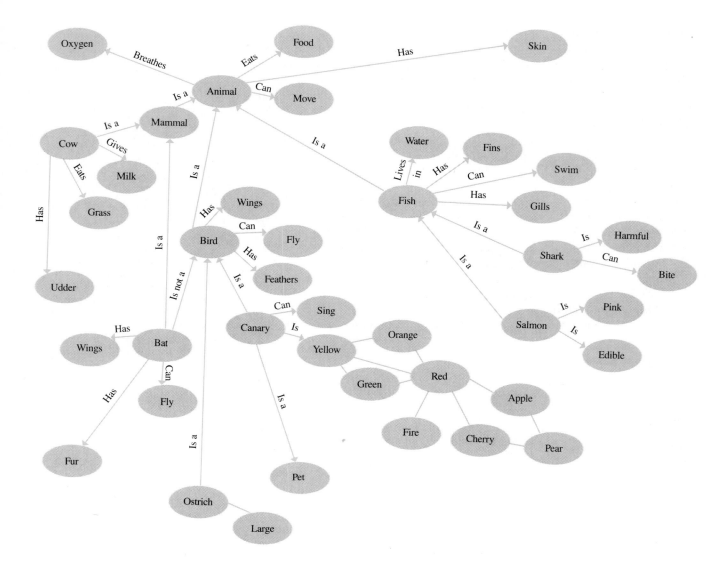

Figure 6.11
A revision of the earlier hierarchical network view of how information is organized in long-term memory.

Perhaps the most radical implication of the PDP approach is that knowledge is derived from the connections themselves, instead of from the nodes being connected. The appeal of this approach is that it seems to fit with what we know about how the brain works. Just as there are extensive synaptic connections between neurons, so might there be a similar extensive connectedness in the system of memory. The future will decide if we are, at last, in a position to model how the brain learns and remembers. More about how the brain functions in memory appears later in this chapter.

Elaboration

When encoding is elaborated, memory improves (Pressley & others, 1987). **Elaboration** refers to more extensive processing of the information that enters our memory system. For instance, rather than memorizing the definition of memory only, your memory of the memory concept will be enhanced if you can come up with examples of how information enters your mind, how it is stored, and how you retrieve it. Thinking of examples of a concept as you encode the concept is a good way to use elaboration to improve memory. Self-reference is another effective way to elaborate information. For instance, if the word *win* were on a list of words to remember, you might think of the last time you won a bicycle race, or if the word *cook* appeared, you might imagine the last time you cooked dinner.

One reason that elaboration produces better memory is *distinctiveness* (Craik & Jacoby, 1979; Ellis, 1987; Hunt & Mitchell, 1982). Elaboration makes the information we encode more distinctive and unique. As encoding becomes more elaborate, more is remembered about an event, and as more is remembered, the chance of input being distinctive is increased. For example, if you observe a bank robbery and encode that the getaway vehicle is a red 1986 or 1987 Pontiac with tinted windows and spinners on the wheels, your memory of the car will be better than someone who only encodes that the getaway vehicle is a late model red car. Your elaboration of what the car looks like when it is encoded into memory makes the concept of car more distinctive. So, elaboration produces *more processing* and processing that is more *distinctive*.

We have seen that deep processing, organization, and elaboration are effortful processes that improve our memory. Another mental activity that can improve memory and that requires effortful processing is imagery.

The more you elaborate about an event, the better your memory for the event will be. For example, if you encode information about how large the crowd was, the people with you, the songs you heard, their performers, and how much money was raised, you probably will remember a concert—such as the Farm Aid Benefit, shown here—more vividly.

Imagery

Imagine walking up the sidewalk to your house, opening the door, and going inside. What do you see when you are standing inside the door? Now mentally walk through the house to the room in the back and form a picture of what this room looks like. Now picture your bedroom in the house. Where is your bed in relation to the door? Imagining these things is reasonably easy for most of us. Such *images* involve sensations without the presence of an external stimulus.

For many years imagery was ignored by psychologists, mainly because it was believed to be too mentalistic by behaviorists. But the studies of Allan Paivio (1971, 1986) document how imagery can improve memory. Paivio argued that memory is stored in one of two ways: as a verbal code or as an image code. For example, a picture can be remembered by a label (verbal code) or a mental image. Paivio thinks that the image code produces better memory because it has more detail, thus creating a more distinctive code. Although imagery is widely accepted as an important aspect of memory, there is controversy over whether we have separate codes for words and images (Kosslyn, 1983; Pylyshyn, 1973).

Some of us are more proficient at using imagery to facilitate memory than others. In rare instances individuals have what is known as **eidetic imagery,** which is the ability to visualize scenes no longer in view with virtual photographic clarity. For example, Robert Lovett, former United States secretary of defense, reportedly has eidetic imagery (Loftus, 1980). He first became aware of his extraordinary ability in high school, where he was a star in math and foreign language. He went on to Harvard Law School, where the final examination in one of his classes involved a moot court case. Lovett recited the case verbatim, and as a result, was suspected of cheating. The professor told him that he was going to have to give him either an A or a zero. Lovett asked if it would help if he quoted the case again, which he did. The professor gave Lovett an A. More about imagery appears later in the chapter when we discuss strategies for improving memory.

■■■■■■■■■■■■■■■■■■■■■

Concept Table 6.1

The Nature of Cognition and Memory, Time Frames of Memory, and Encoding		
Concept	Processes/related ideas	Characteristics/description
What is memory?	Its nature	The retention of information over time. Psychologists study how information gets into memory, how it is stored, and how it is retrieved.
Time frames of memory	Sensory registers	A form of memory in which stimuli are registered for the brief time we are exposed to them. Iconic memory is visual, echoic memory is auditory.
	Short-term memory	Our retention of recently encountered information or information retrieved from long-term memory for a brief period of time, usually about fifteen to thirty seconds. Short-term memory has a limited capacity and is called the workbench of memory. Chunking and rehearsal benefit short-term memory. The serial-position effect involves both primacy and recency effects.
	Long-term memory	Involves the retention of information for an indefinite period of time. Its storehouse is staggering. This memory is divided into declarative and procedural (skills) knowledge. Declarative knowledge consists of either semantic or episodic content.
Encoding	Attention	The ability to focus on certain stimuli. Attention is both selective (the ability to focus and concentrate on a narrow band of information) and shifting.
	Automatic and effortful processing	Automatic processing requires no allocation of capacity while effortful processing does. Effortful processing, which includes deep processing, organization, and imagery, is associated with improved memory.
	Levels of processing	Craik and Lockhart's model emphasizes that memory takes place on a continuum. When subjects make semantic connections, which involve deep processing, memory is improved.
	Organization	One of the most pervasive aspects of memory. Involves grouping or combining items. Often information is organized hierarchically. The parallel distributed processing model emphasizes that memory is retained in a parallel fashion.
	Elaboration	Improves memory because it involves more processing and more processing makes encoding more distinctive.
	Imagery	Involves sensations without an external stimulus present. Paivio argues that we have separate verbal and image codes, but this is controversial. Imagery often improves memory.

We have seen that the time frames of memory and encoding are very important aspects of memory processing. To help you remember the main themes of this discussion, along with ideas about the nature of memory and cognition, study concept table 6.1.

Retrieval and Forgetting

Have you ever forgotten where you parked your car, your mother's birthday, or the time you were supposed to meet a friend to study? Have you ever sat in class taking an exam, unable to remember something? Psychologists have formed a number of theories about why we forget information and how we retrieve it.

Retrieval

How do we get information out of our memory storage system so we can use it? We do this through a process called retrieval. Much of the information in short-term memory is readily available, but some of it may require a search process. Retrieval in long-term memory is more complicated because information usually is not as readily available as in short-term memory.

In the process of retrieval, we search our memory storage to find the relevant information. This search can be virtually automatic or it can be effortful, just as with encoding (see figure 6.12). For example, when asked your mother's name, retrieval is automatic, but when asked the name of your first-grade teacher, retrieval is more effortful. The search may be brief and direct, as in the case of retrieving a frequently called phone number, or it may be prolonged and more complex, as when solving a difficult problem. As appropriate information is found, it is pulled together to guide and direct the individual's verbal or motor responses.

An interesting aspect of retrieval that each of us has experienced at some point in our lives is the *tip-of-the-tongue phenomenon* (TOT). This occurs when we are confident we know something but just can't quite seem to pull it out of memory. In one investigation of TOT, subjects were shown pictures of famous individuals and asked to say their names (Yarmey, 1973). When the subjects could not think of a name but were sure they knew it, they were said to be in a TOT state. Over 600 instances of TOT were reported. Subjects would invariably continue trying to retrieve the name they were sure they knew. In doing so they often tried to locate the individual's profession—a subject who could not remember Henry Kissinger's name might say politician, for example. Subjects would repeat initial letters or syllables as part of the retrieval strategy. One subject searching to retrieve the name of Liza Minelli tried Monetti, Mona, Magetti, Spaghetti, and Bogette. The implication of the tip-of-the-tongue phenomena is that without good retrieval cues, information that is stored in memory may be difficult to find.

Indeed, one of the most important aspects of retrieval is good cues. We may be unable to pull information out of our memory because few cues are available or those that are available are not very efficient. Much of the information we store is filed under different labels. We might be able to search and find information about a restaurant under "Chinese," "downtown," or "best restaurants in the last year." This means that retrieval is facilitated by associations with the item you are trying to locate. For example, individuals seem to be able to recall a political event by associating it with another political event (Brown, Shevell, & Rips, 1986). If you were asked when Lyndon Johnson became president, you might think of the year John F. Kennedy was assassinated.

Retrieval cues may work by putting us in the general location where we have stored the information or by matching up the information with the cues we use to encode the information. A number of studies have found that memory improves when the cues at encoding and retrieval are similar (Eich, 1985; Smith, 1986). For example, we remember things better when we are in the same physical location in which we encoded the information. When you go back to where you grew up, you begin to remember things that otherwise would not have come to mind—your playmates, the games you played, your teachers' names and faces, and so on. The matching of encoding and retrieval cues suggests that retrieving information in the same room you studied may have some benefit, so it's possible you might get a better grade on an exam if you study in the same room where your exam will be held!

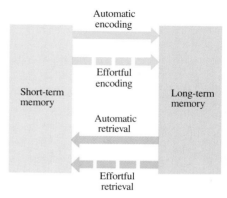

Figure 6.12
Retrieval.

This college student is studying for an upcoming exam. How might retrieval cues help her study?

Memory involves both internal and external cues. **State-dependent memory** emphasizes that the states or internal conditions present when information is encoded may be important cues for retrieving that information. If you encode information while you are happy, you probably will remember it better later if you are happy rather than sad. If you learn information while under the influence of caffeine, nicotine, or other drugs, memory improves if you retrieve the information while in a similar state. State-dependent effects are not always congruent between encoding and retrieval, but in many cases they are (Bartlett, Burleson, & Santrock, 1982; Eich, 1980, 1987).

Failure to use effective retrieval cues is one reason we forget. We may forget an important idea on an exam because we have not used the right cue to retrieve it. For example, you might forget the point of Sperling's experiment because you are using short-term memory as the cue instead of sensory registers. To learn more about how retrieval processes are involved in autobiographical memory, see Psychology 6.1.

Decay and Interference

Psychologists have proposed other theories of why we forget. Two long-standing theories involve decay and interference. **Decay theory** states that when something new is learned, a memory trace is formed; as time passes, this trace decays. This theory may account for some forgetting, but forgetting is caused by many factors other than the mere passage of time.

Interference theory states that we forget because other information gets in the way of what we want to remember. Two kinds of interference are possible: proactive and retroactive. **Proactive interference** occurs when material that was learned early on interferes with the recall of material learned later. Remember that *pro* means "forward in time." For example, suppose you had a good friend ten years ago named Mary, and last night you met someone at a party named Marie. You might find yourself calling your new acquaintance Mary because the old information ("Mary") is interfering with the new information ("Marie").

Retroactive interference occurs when material learned later interferes with material that was learned earlier. Remember that *retro* means "backward in time." Suppose that you have become friends with Marie (and finally gotten her name straight). You might find yourself sending a letter to your old friend, but addressing it to "Marie" because the new information ("Marie") is interfering with the old information ("Mary").

Motivation

Freud believed that we forget what threatens us. He thought that if something became too stressful we repressed it by pushing it beneath our awareness into our unconscious mind. A number of case studies suggest that we do have a tendency to forget the annoying, tension-filled experiences in our lives and remember the more joyous, rewarding ones. Psychologist Marigold Linton (1979) wrote a short description of a major occurrence in her life on a separate card each day from 1972 to 1977. Every month she tested her memory of these occurrences. She found that she was much more likely to forget the upsetting, stressful events than the pleasant ones.

Implicit Memory

An important discovery about how we forget is that a failure to consciously recollect an event can be accompanied by unconscious, "implicit memory" for it (Graf & Schacter, 1987; Schacter, in press). **Implicit memory** occurs when performance on a task is facilitated without deliberate recollection from a specific learning episode. Thus, an individual can benefit from an experience—showing implicit performance as a result of this experience—and yet be totally unable to consciously recollect the experience.

Perhaps the clearest example of implicit memory is **infantile amnesia,** the inability to remember anything about the first three years of our lives. Each of us learned an abundant amount of useful knowledge from events we experienced in those early years—and presumably we continued to reap benefits from this knowledge, such as language, perceptual and motor skills, and general knowledge about the nature of the world. But how many events from birth to the age of three can you consciously remember? Both intuition and research suggest that the answer is not very many (Sheingold & Tenney, 1982). In other words, infantile amnesia is a failure of conscious recollection for events we experienced near the beginning of our lives—it can coexist with implicit knowledge we acquired from these very same events.

Infantile amnesia is a fascinating aspect of our distant past, but even events we experienced recently—even events only a few minutes old—can be forgotten in the sense that they cannot be consciously remembered. Yet, they can be unconsciously remembered in the form of implicit memory. To see how this might work, consider something psychologists call a fragment completion task. An example of an item on this type of task is:

__ SS__ SS__ __

Can you think of a word that completes this fragment? Completing such a fragment can be difficult, but the probability of success is much greater if the solution word, "assassin," has been seen recently. Further, the degree of importance from having previously seen the word "assassin" cannot be predicted from conscious memory with this experience—a subject who has seen the word "assassin" but does not *remember* seeing it will just as likely be able to complete the sentence fragment as a subject who has seen the word *and* consciously remembers the experience. Both subjects are more likely to complete the sentence fragment than a third subject who has not seen the word "assassin" recently.

You may have recognized that implicit memory is closely related to the concept of procedural knowledge we discussed earlier in the chapter. One distinction though is that implicit memory concerns individual events (such as hearing the word "assassin") whereas procedural knowledge involves gradual learning based on many experiences (such as learning to ride a bicycle). Both implicit memory and procedural knowledge are relevant to an understanding of amnesia, which we turn to next.

Amnesia

It is February 1986. Mark is cross-country skiing in Minnesota. Pausing for a moment, he takes off his skis and backpack. He begins to realize he is lost. As he wanders through the cold, barren area, he becomes tired and numb. Time passes and it is now spring. Fourteen months have passed since Mark left to go skiing. His backpack now contains running shoes, swimming goggles, and glasses—items unfamiliar to him. He knows something is drastically wrong. He cannot remember how he got to the field or why he has the running shoes, goggles, and glasses. He has amnesia.

Psychology 6.1

Autobiographical Memories—Retrieving Information about the Night of the Senior Prom and Your Thirteenth Birthday

■ Memory provides each of us with a sense of who we are. Our sense of who we are changes as we add experiences to our lives and remember them. The study of how people remember and forget events and people in their own lives is known as autobiographical memory.

In one study of autobiographical memory, students were asked to think out loud as they remembered a specific event, such as going to a zoo, feeling sad, or being turned down for a date (Reiser, Black, & Abelson, 1985). The students used several strategies to remember such events. They often used the particular activity, person, or time period they believed was involved to discover the general context of memory, as well as to put limits on the search process. When asked about circumstances that made them sad, for example, they searched for activities where they felt sad.

A common strategy for remembering certain information is to think about events in a given time period. This temporal orientation is one of the most characteristic features of autobiographical memory. We tend to remember things that happened just about the same time, before, or after a particular event.

Some events are especially dramatic and have a very vivid quality about them. I remember quite well where I was the day President John F. Kennedy was assassinated. Perhaps you remember where you were when

the space shuttle Challenger exploded. Such "flashbulb memories" are characterized by their surprise occurrence and the tremendous amount of attention they are given. It intrigues psychologists that several decades later a person can remember where she was and what was going on in her life at the time of such an event. Some psychologists (e.g., Brown & Kulik, 1979) believe these memories are part of an adaptive system that fixes in memory the details that accompany important events so they can be reinterpreted at a later time.

In another investigation (Rubin, 1985; Rubin & Kozin, 1984), the types of events that make up flashbulb memories were studied. Students were asked to report the three most vivid memories in their lives. Virtually all of these were of a personal nature rather than nationally significant events or circumstances. The memories tended to center around an injury or accident, sports, members of the opposite sex, animals, deaths, the first week at college, and vacations. The students also answered questions about their memories of twenty events likely to produce flashbulb memories. As shown in table 6.A, 85 percent of the students said a car accident they had witnessed was of the flashbulb memory type (meaning it was surprising, consequential, emotional, and vivid), while only 12 percent reported their thirteenth birthday as being this way.

Table 6.A Flashbulb Memories	
Cues	**Percent**
A car accident you were in or witnessed	85
When you first met your roommate at Duke	82
The night of your high school graduation	81
The night of your senior prom (if you went or not)	78
An early romantic experience	77
A time you had to speak in front of an audience	72
When you got your admissions letter from Duke	65
Your first date—the moment you met him/her	57
President Reagan was shot in Washington	52
The night President Nixon resigned	41
The first time you flew in an airplane	40
The moment you opened your SAT scores	33
Your seventeenth birthday	30
The day of the first space shuttle flight	24
The last time you ate a holiday dinner at home	23
Your first class at Duke	21
You heard that President Sadat of Egypt was shot	21
When you heard that the Pope had been shot	21
The first time your parents left you alone for some time	19
Your thirteenth birthday	12

*Percent of Duke students in memory experiment who reported events on experimenter's list were of "flashbulb" quality.

(a)

(b)

(c)

Do you have a "flashbulb memory" for (a)what you were doing when President Reagan was shot? (b) the night of your senior prom in high school? (c) what you were doing when the Challenger exploded? and (d) when you received your admission letter from college?

(d)

Mark's case is hypothetical but for some individuals every day is a new day. **Anterograde amnesia** is a memory disorder that affects our memory of *new* information or events. What was learned before the onset of the condition is not affected. A famous case of anterograde amnesia involves H. M. (Milner, Corkin, & Teuber, 1968). H. M. could identify his friends, recall their names, and even tell stories about them but only if he had known them before the age of ten, when he underwent surgery to stop epileptic seizures. Anyone H. M. met after the surgery remained a virtual stranger even though he spent thousands of hours with them. However, H. M.'s short-term memory remained unchanged and he continued to be above average in intelligence.

While anterograde amnesiacs cannot remember new information, recent evidence illustrates that they can learn new skills (Glisky & Schacter, in press). One especially intriguing case involves a severe amnesiac patient who was taught the skills required to perform a complex data-entry job. Her memory of general information from the past did not improve but her ability to perform a specific skill did. When asked to remember her learning experience, she could recall nothing about it. This type of finding supports the distinction made earlier in the chapter between declarative knowledge (for information or knowing *that*) and procedural knowledge (for skills or knowing *how*).

Amnesia occurs in a second form known as **retrograde amnesia,** which involves memory loss for a segment of the past but not for new events. This type of amnesia occurs most often when individuals experience severe blows to the head. For example, a football player might receive a head injury and not be able to remember the circumstances surrounding the injury. The key difference from anterograde amnesia is that the forgotten information is *old* (prior to the event that caused the amnesia).

Schemata and Reconstruction of the Past

Long-term memory has been compared to a library. The library stores books just like your memory stores information. We retrieve information similar to locating and then checking out a book. But much of long-term memory is not as exact as the library analogy suggests. When we search through our long-term memory store we don't always find the *exact* "book" we want, or we might find the book we want but discover that only several pages of the book are intact. We have to *reconstruct* the rest (Anderson, 1987).

The theory of memory's reconstructive nature began with Sir Frederick Bartlett's (1932) studies of how individuals remembered stories. Bartlett found that instead of recalling a story they had read verbatim, subjects left out parts, added others, and revised yet others. For example, in "The War of the Ghosts," an Indian folk tale, subjects revised the plot until it resembled a standard Western tale. A flurry of interest in research on reconstructive memory has occurred—interest in recalling stories, along with inquiries about eyewitness testimony, autobiographical memory, and the memory of events and conversations (Bransford & Franks, 1971; Loftus, 1980; Neisser, 1982).

Schemata

When we reconstruct information, we often fit it into information already existing in our mind. The existing information we have about various concepts, events, and knowledge is called **schemata.** Schemata come from prior encounters with the environment and influence the way we encode, make inferences about, and retrieve information.

These two men are remembering how their deep sea fishing trip went. As each recounts the experience, their memories reconstruct the experience, each offering a slightly different version of what happened.

Scripts are schemata for events. Each of us has a script we follow when we go to a college football game. What are some of the characteristics of a script for attending a college football game?

Name:	Restaurant				
Props:	Tables		**Roles:**	Customer	
	Menu			Waiter	
	Food			Cook	
	Bill			Cashier	
	Money			Owner	
	Tip				
Entry Conditions:	Customer is hungry.		**Results:**	Customer has less money.	
	Customer has money.			Owner has more money.	
				Customer is not hungry.	

Scene 1: *Entering*
Customer enters restaurant.
Customer looks for table.
Customer decides where to sit.
Customer goes to table.
Customer sits down.

Scene 2: *Ordering*
Customer picks up menu.
Customer looks at menu.
Customer decides on food.
Customer signals waitress.
Waitress comes to table.
Customer orders food.
Waitress goes to cook.
Waitress gives food order to cook.
Cook prepares food.

Scene 3: *Eating*
Cook gives food to waitress.
Waitress brings food to customer.
Customer eats food.

Scene 4: *Exiting*
Waitress writes bill.
Waitress goes over to customer.
Waitress gives bill to customer.
Customer gives tip to waitress.
Customer goes to cashier.
Customer gives money to cashier.
Customer leaves restaurant.

Figure 6.13
A simplified version of Schank and Abelson's script for a restaurant. Think about how your organized knowledge of these activities occurring in a restaurant influences your encoding, inferences about, and retrieval of information.

While reconstructing "The War of the Ghosts" story, subjects drew on both their schemata for daily experiences in general and their schemata for adventure or ghost stories in particular. To make some sense of this story about a war party on a canoe, the subjects would use experiences of their own—say, a canoe trip down a rapids—and structured information from earlier stories— a common adventure story about primitive folks and ghosts, for example. When information in "The War of the Ghosts" was consistent with these previously constructed schemata, recall was aided and sometimes was quite accurate. However, discrepancies between the prior schemata and the details of the present story caused systematic distortions in recall.

We not only have schemata for stories but also for scenes or spatial layouts (a beach or a bathroom), as well as for common events (going to a restaurant, playing football, or writing a term paper). Schemata for events are called **scripts** (Schank & Abelson, 1977). An example of a restaurant script is shown in figure 6.13. Notice that this script has information about physical features, people, and typical occurrences. This type of information is helpful to individuals when they need to figure out what is happening around them. For example, if you are enjoying your after-dinner coffee in a restaurant and a man in a tuxedo comes over and puts a piece of paper on the table, your script tells you that he probably is a waiter who has just given you the check.

John Dean, a key figure in the Nixon Administration. Dean's testimony at the Watergate inquiry revealed how repisodic memory works: A simple recollection is often a series of repeated experiences.

Repisodic Memory

The basis of many of life's everyday memories is not a single event or episode but rather repeated experiences. Ulric Neisser (1982) says that the single, clear memories we recall so vividly actually stand for something else; they are "screen" memories. Their basis is a sequence of related events that the single recollection simply typifies or represents. Neisser calls this mental activity **repisodic memory.**

The testimony of John Dean in the Watergate hearings provides an example of how repisodic memory works. The Nixon-Watergate tapes recorded exactly what Dean said, which served as a control set of information against which to compare his testimony. The following comments were recorded on the tapes many times:

1. Dean: "I would say these people are going to cost a million dollars over the next two years."
2. The president: "First, it is going to require approximately a million dollars to take care of the jackasses who are in jail. That can be arranged."
3. The president: ". . . sounds like a lot of money, a million dollars."

During his testimony, Dean remembered the million-dollar theme, but he assigned the comments to the wrong day and put them in the wrong conversations. Dean's memory was not like a tape recorder, but it seemed to retain the general message, or gist, of what was happening. When we organize our past experiences, we do so much in the way Dean did. We may forget some of the small details, or get some of them wrong, but we remember the general themes of what occurred.

Eyewitness Testimony

At times an individual's memories achieve public importance. This was true in the Watergate affair and it also is the case in the legal arena, where testimony about the past can be crucial in determining a defendant's future. Much of the interest in eyewitness testimony has focused on distortion, bias, and inaccuracy in memory (Loftus, 1979; Wells & Loftus, 1984; Wells & Turtle, 1986).

When dealing with eyewitness testimony, it is important to ask how much time has passed between the incident and the person's recollection of the incident. Memory does fade over time. In one investigation, subjects were able to identify pictures with 100 percent accuracy after a two-hour time lapse but four months later only 57 percent accuracy was achieved (accuracy due to chance in this study was 50 percent!) (Shepard, 1967).

Memory is not like a videotape. It can be altered by new information. In one study, students were shown a film of an automobile accident (Loftus, 1975) and then asked how fast the white sports car was going when it passed the barn. Other subjects were asked the same question without mention of the barn. There was no barn in the film. Later, 17 percent of the students who heard the barn mentioned said that they had seen a barn in the film; only 3 percent who had not heard a barn mentioned said that they saw it. New information, then, can add to and even replace existing information in our memory.

It has been found that people of one race or ethnic group do not recognize individual differences in people of another race or ethnic group. Thus, Hispanic eyewitnesses may not be accurate when asked to pick an Oriental suspect from a police lineup. Identifying individuals from police lineups or photographs is not always reliable. In one investigation, clerks in small stores were asked to identify photographs of customers who had been in their stores two hours earlier (Brigham & others, 1982). Only 33 percent of the customers were correctly identified. In another experiment, a mugging was staged in which a woman's purse was stolen (Buckout, 1980). A film of the mugging was shown on a television news program. Immediately after the film was shown, a lineup of six suspects in the robbery was broadcast and viewers were asked to phone in and identify which of the six individuals they thought committed the robbery. Of the 2,000 callers, more than 1,800 identified the wrong individual! The mugger, who was actually white, was perceived to be black or Hispanic by one-third of the viewers. Might this be an example of schemata for racial prejudice influencing memory?

Neurobiological Basis of Memory

Is there a place in your brain where memories are stored? If so, how are they stored there? Karl Lashley (1950) spent a lifetime looking for such a location. He trained rats to discover the correct pathway in a maze and then cut out a portion of the animal's brain and retested its memory of the maze pathway. After experimenting with thousands of rats, Lashley found that the loss of various cortical areas did not affect the rat's ability to remember the maze's path. Lashley concluded that memories are not stored in a specific location of the brain.

If our memories are not localized, where are they? Perhaps they are spread throughout the brain. At one point, some scientists believed that memory was located throughout the brain in the ribonucleic acid (RNA) of cells. James McConnell thought that perhaps worms can "eat" memories. What does this mean? McConnell (1962) argued that just as DNA is involved in the genetic transmission of information, RNA is the physical basis of memory. McConnell trained planaria (flatworms) to shudder at the presentation of a light. He then chopped up the frightened flatworms and fed them to untrained, hungry flatworms. Would the untrained flatworms absorb the memory of the frightened flatworms? McConnell reported that the untrained flatworms were more likely to contract their bodies from light than their cannibalistic counterparts who had devoured uneducated planaria. He said the body contractions occurred the first time the light was presented. Other researchers, however, were never able to replicate McConnell's controversial findings.

Although interest in RNA's role in memory declined, extensive investigation of the biological basis of memory has occurred in the last several decades. The questions being studied include: Is memory highly localized? Does a specific neuron remember anything or is there a memory trace through many interconnected neurons? Mortimer Mishkin (1987), chief of neuropsychology at the National Institute of Mental Health, concludes that there is extensive redundancy in the brain, but that it is not a pointless or endless redundancy.

Many researchers believe that memory is located in discrete sets or trace circuits of neurons. Larry Squire (1986, 1987), for example, says that micromemories probably are clustered in groups of about 1,000 neurons. He points out that memory is distributed through the brain in the sense that no specific memory center exists. Many parts of the brain and nervous system participate in the memory of a particular event. Yet memory is localized in the sense that a limited number of brain systems and pathways participate in the process, and each probably contributes in different ways.

Identification of individuals from police lineups or photographs is not always reliable. Individuals from one race or ethnic group have difficulty in recognizing differences among people of another race or ethnic background.

Some of our neurons respond to faces, others to eye or hair color. But to recognize someone as a particular person, many neurons must work in concert with each other.

Squire also argues that neurobiological evidence exists for a distinction between declarative and procedural knowledge. (Remember that declarative knowledge refers to information and "knowing *that;*" procedural knowledge refers to skills and "knowing *how*"). The neurological evidence is that declarative knowledge seems to be controlled by the hippocampus and amygdala areas of the brain while procedural knowledge is more diffused throughout the brain.

Single neurons, of course, are at work in memory. Researchers who measure the electrical activity of single cells have found that some respond to faces, others to eye or hair color, for example. But for you to recognize your Uncle Albert, individual neurons that provide information about hair color, size, and other characteristics must act together.

The importance of neurons in memory has been supported by the research of Eric Kandel and James Schwartz (1982), whose observations of the sea slug were described in chapter 1. They have been able to grasp how memory works at the level of neurons in the sea slug because its brain contains only 10,000 neurons, and its neurons are much larger and less complex than those of humans. The research on sea slugs demonstrated that the neurotransmitter serotonin was released at particular synapses; it was these synapses that were being changed when the sea slug "remembered" to withdraw its tail in anticipation of being shocked.

As neurobiologists probe the physical basis of memory, are we likely to reach a point when the psychological study of memory becomes unimportant? First, we are far from working out the complexity of such physical underpinnings in human memory, and second, keep in mind that different levels of explanation are possible.

It has been some time since we reviewed our discussion of memory. To help your review, the main themes of retrieval, schemata and reconstruction of the past, and neurobiological basis of memory are presented in concept table 6.2.

Mnemonics and Memory Strategies

In the fifth century B.C., the Greek poet Simonides attended a banquet. After he left, the building collapsed, crushing the guests and maiming their bodies beyond recognition. Simonides was able to identify the bodies by using a memory technique. He generated vivid images of each individual and mentally pictured where they had sat at the banquet table. Specific techniques such as this, many of which involve imagery, have been used to improve memory. These techniques, called **mnemonics,** are strategies designed to make memory more efficient. Psychology 6.2 reveals how mnemonics can be used to remember someone's name.

Imagery

The technique for remembering used by Simonides is called the *method of loci.* It is an imagery technique you can apply to memory problems of your own. Suppose you have a list of chores to do. To ensure that you remember them all, first associate a concrete object with each chore. A trip to the store becomes a dollar bill, a telephone call to a friend becomes a telephone, cleanup duty becomes a broom, and so on. Then produce an image of each "object" so you can imagine it in a particular location in a familiar building, such as your house. You might imagine the dollar bill in the kitchen, the telephone in

Concept Table 6.2

Retrieval and Forgetting, Schemata and Reconstruction of the Past, Neurobiological Processes, and Mnemonics		
Concept	**Processes/related ideas**	**Characteristics/description**
Retrieval and forgetting	Retrieval	Involves getting information out of memory. The search can be automatic or effortful. An important aspect is the use of good cues. Memory is improved when the cues are similar at encoding and retrieval. State-dependent memory emphasizes that internal states are important in understanding retrieval. Failure of the retrieval process is one way we forget.
	Decay and interference	Decay theory says that we forget because of the passage of time. Interference theory suggests that we forget because other information gets in the way—two types are proactive and retroactive interference.
	Motivation	Freud believed that we forget something because it is threatening to us. We push this stressful material into our unconscious mind.
	Implicit memory	When performance on a task is facilitated without deliberate recollection from a specific learning episode; reveals how the unconscious mind can influence our memory.
	Amnesia	Two forms are anterograde amnesia, the failure to remember new information, and retrograde amnesia, the failure to remember information acquired before the onset of amnesia. Anterograde amnesics can learn new skills.
Schemata and reconstruction of the past	Schemata	Existing sets of information in our mind that influence encoding, inference, and retrieval. Schemata for events are called scripts.
	Repisodic memory	Most of our everyday memory, which consists of repeated events and experiences that we recall as a single event.
	Eyewitness testimony	A prominent way that memories achieve public importance. Shows how memory is reconstructive. The bulk of interest focuses on distortion, bias, and inaccuracy.
Neurobiological basis of memory	Its nature	A major issue is the extent memory is localized or distributed. Single neurons are involved in memory, but much of memory seems to be made up of circuits of neurons that may consist of 1,000 neurons. Memory appears to be distributed, but not endlessly.

the dining room, and so on. The vividness of the image and the unique placement virtually guarantees recollection. It also helps if you mentally move through the house in some logical way as the images are "placed."

A second imagery strategy is the *peg method,* in which a set of mental pegs, such as numbers, have items attached to them. For instance, you might begin with something like: "One is a bun, two is a shoe, three is a tree," and so forth up to as many as ten to twenty numbers. Once you can readily reproduce these rhymes, you can use them as mental pegs. For example, if you were required to remember a list of items in a specific order—such as the directions to someone's house—you could use the following mental pegs: One-bun-left on Market; two-shoe-right on Sandstone; three-tree-right on Balboa, and so on. But to complete the strategy, you need to develop an image for each direction: I left the bun at the market; my right shoe got caught in the sand and stone; there's a tree right on Balboa. When you have to retrieve the directions, you select the appropriate cue word, such as *bun* or *shoe,* and this should stimulate the production of the compound image with the correct response. Researchers have been encouraged by the effectiveness of such strategies in improving memory (Bellezza, 1981; McDaniel & Pressley, 1987).

■ ■ ■ ■ ■ ■ ■ ■ ■ ■ ■ ■ ■ ■ ■ ■ ■ ■ ■

Psychology 6.2

I'll Never Forget What's-His-Name

■ Have you ever had trouble remembering someone's name? Probably so. A face might look familiar, but the name escapes you. This problem can be helped with the use of mnemonics.

Remembering someone's name can be broken down into three subproblems: remembering the face, remembering the name, and remembering the connection between the two (Loftus, 1980). To remember the face, look at it closely while focusing on some distinctive feature, such as a large nose. To remember the name, try to find some meaning in it. As with a foreign language, you might think about a part of the name that sounds like an English word.

Finally, to remember the connection between the face and the name, think of an image that links the key word and the distinctive feature in the face. If you have just been introduced to Mr. Clausen, the man with the large nose, you might think of the English word *claws* as a key word for Clausen. Now imagine a large lobster claw tearing away at Clausen's large nose. When you see Mr. Clausen the next time, recall this image and the name Clausen should come to mind (see figure 6.A).

Another technique for remembering someone's name involves an expanded pattern of rehearsal. When you are introduced to someone, repeat the name immediately. You might say, "Tom Naylor? Hello, Tom." About ten to fifteen seconds later, look at the individual and rehearse his name silently. Do it again after one minute and then again after three minutes. The name will have a good chance of being retained in your long-term memory. One reason this spacing strategy works is that most forgetting occurs within a very short time after you learn a new fact (Loftus, 1980).

Systematic Memory and Study Strategies

Techniques such as the method of loci and the peg method can be used to improve memory, but strategies based on a number of aspects of our knowledge about memory are especially helpful. One such strategy, ARESIDORI, is a simple mnemonic code for: 1. *A*ttention, 2. *R*ehearsal, 3. *E*laboration, 4. *S*emantic processing, 5. *I*magery, 6. *D*istinctiveness, 7. *O*rganization, 8. *R*etrieval, 9. *I*nterest (Ellis, 1986). Most of the components of ARESIDORI have been discussed in this chapter and are basic to good memory. Note that number 9, interest, essentially refers to motivation. It is helpful to review your own study habits to determine which of the principles of ARESIDORI you use effectively and which you could profit from by using more often.

Many different study systems exist and many of them include some basic principles of memory. The most widely used system is SQ3R (Robinson, 1961). S stands for Survey, Q for Question, and 3R for Read, Recite, Review. To use this system in the next chapter, you might do the following. To survey, glance over the headings to find the main points of the chapter (the chapter outline helps in this regard). To question, turn each heading into a question, and continue to ask yourself questions throughout the chapter. To accomplish the 3R part of the system, start reading the chapter as you normally would, recite information periodically as you go through the chapter, and then review the material you have read several times before you take a test. The concept tables and summary will help you with the review process.

In the next chapter we explore other aspects of cognition, giving special attention to how we think and how we use language.

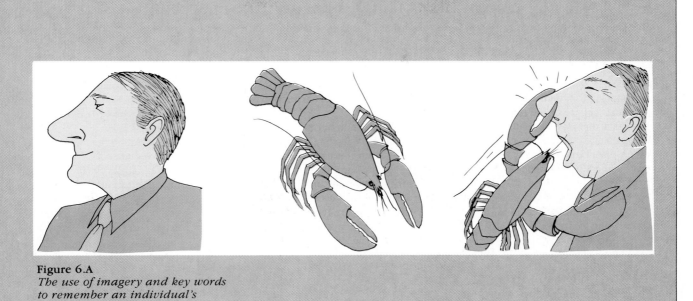

Figure 6.A
The use of imagery and key words to remember an individual's name.

Summary

I. **What is Memory?**
Memory is the retention of information over time. Psychologists study how information gets into memory, called encoding, how it is stored, and how it is retrieved.

II. **Time Frames of Memory**
Three time frames of memory are sensory registers, short-term memory, and long-term memory. Sensory registers are a form of memory in which stimuli are registered for the brief time we are exposed to them. Iconic memory is visual; echoic memory is auditory. Short-term memory is our retention of recently encountered information or information retrieved from long-term memory for a brief time, usually about fifteen to thirty seconds. Short-term memory has a limited capacity and is called the workbench of memory. Chunking and rehearsal benefit short-term memory. The serial-position effect involves both primacy and recency effects. Long-term memory involves the retention of information for an indefinite period of time. Its storehouse is staggering. Psychologists have divided what is remembered into declarative and procedural (skills) knowledge. Declarative knowledge consists of either semantic or episodic content.

III. **Encoding**
Important features of encoding are attention, automatic and effortful processing, levels of processing, organization, elaboration, and imagery. Attention is both selective and shifting. Selective attention is the ability to focus on a narrow band of information. Automatic processing requires no allocation of capacity while effortful processing does. Effortful processing improves memory. Four types of effortful processing are deep processing, organization, elaboration, and imagery.

IV. **Retrieval and Forgetting**
Retrieval involves getting information out of memory. The search can be automatic or effortful. One of the most important aspects of retrieval is the use of good cues. Memory is improved when the cues are similar at encoding and retrieval. State-dependent memory emphasizes that internal states are important in understanding retrieval. Failure of the retrieval process is one way we forget. Two other theories of forgetting are decay theory and interference theory, the latter involving either proactive or retroactive interference. Freud argued that we forget something because it is threatening to us. We push this stressful material into the unconscious mind. Recent interest in implicit memory reveals how the unconscious mind influences memory. Amnesia comes in two forms: anterograde amnesia, the failure to remember new information; and retrograde amnesia, the failure to remember information acquired before the onset of amnesia. Anterograde amnesiacs can learn new skills.

V. **Schemata and Reconstruction of the Past**
Information in our minds that influences encoding, inference, and retrieval is called schemata. Schemata for events are called scripts. Repisodic memory occurs when repeated events and experiences are recalled as a single event. Eyewitness testimony reveals how memory is reconstructive.

VI. **Neurobiological Basis of Memory**
A major issue is whether memory is localized or distributed. Single neurons are involved in memory, but much of memory seems to be made up of circuits of neurons that consist of approximately 1,000 neurons. So memory appears to be distributed, but not endlessly. There are different levels of explanation for memory phenomena.

VII. **Mnemonics and Memory Strategies**
Mnemonics are techniques for improving memory. Many of these involve imagery, including the method of loci and peg method. Systems based on a number of aspects of our knowledge have been developed, including ARESIDORI and SQ3R.

Key Terms

memory *185*
encoding *185*
sensory registers *185*
short-term memory *186*
long-term memory *186*
iconic *187*
echoic *187*
chunking *188*
rehearsal *188*
serial-position effect *188*
declarative knowledge *189*

procedural knowledge *189*
episodic memory *189*
semantic memory *189*
selective attention *190*
automatic and effortful processing *190*
levels of processing view *191*
parallel distributed processing models *193*
elaboration *194*
eidetic imagery *195*
state-dependent memory *198*

decay theory *198*
proactive interference *198*
retroactive interference *198*
implicit memory *199*
infantile amnesia *199*
anterograde amnesia *202*
retrograde amnesia *202*
schemata *202*
scripts *203*
repisodic memory *204*
mnemonics *206*

Suggested Readings

Best, J. B. (1986). *Cognitive psychology.* St. Paul, MN: West. This well-written text on cognitive psychology explores many of the topics in this chapter in greater detail. Included are individual chapters on imagery, organization, encoding, storing, and retrieving.

Hunt, M. (1982). *The universe within.* New York: Simon & Schuster, 1982. Hunt traveled to many universities and talked to top scholars in the cognitive area. This book represents his distillation of their ideas. The outcome is a well-written, accurate overview of the current state of knowledge on cognition. Includes many intriguing comments about the relation between the human mind and computers.

Loftus, E. (1980). *Memory.* Reading, MA: Addison-Wesley. Elizabeth Loftus is well known for her study of the role of memory in eyewitness testimony. In this paperback, she provides an excellent overview of how memory works and includes considerable information about the nature of forgetting.

McDaniel, M. A., & Pressley, M. (1987). *Imagery and related mnemonic processes.* New York: Springer-Verlag. This book provides a number of excellent strategies, especially those involving imagery, for improving memory.

Neisser, U. (1982). *Memory observed.* San Francisco: W. H. Freeman. Neisser, one of the leading figures in cognition, has stressed for many years that context is important in our study of cognition. This book consists of a series of articles by different individuals all focused on memory in natural settings and includes a series of chapters on eidetic memory.

Chapter 7

Thinking and Language

I think, therefore I am.

—*Descartes*

Images of Thinking and Language

The scene is the computer room at a consulting firm on a Saturday morning. The vice-president of the firm has come in early because he plans to demonstrate the computer system to some prospective customers later in the day. He looks at the machine's teletype and sees a note that says to type all messages into the teletype and end them with a period. The vice-president recognizes that the note must have been left by Dr. Daniel Bobrow, who often works with the computer late at night from a terminal in his home. Believing that Dr. Bobrow is still hooked into the computer, the vice-president types out a message to him:

What things can computers do that humans cannot? What things can humans do that computers cannot?

VP: Do you think I can use the computer this morning?

TELETYPE: Why do you ask?

VP: I might be able to make some additional telecom sales.

T: Why aren't you sure?

VP: My prospective customers have never seen a demonstration of the system.

T: Does this mean very much to you?

VP: Of course it does.

T: You seem very positive of that.

VP: This is ridiculous.

T: What do you mean, this is ridiculous?

VP: Is there any reason why I can't use the computer now?

T: Tell me more about your prospective customers.

(Hunt, 1982, pp. 315–16)

The furious vice-president got on the phone and called Bobrow at home, asking him why he was being so snotty. Bobrow, who had been asleep, did not know what the vice-president was talking about. The vice-president read him the teletype exchange and Bobrow, amid a fit of laughter, informed the embarrassed vice-president that he had been conversing with a machine.

To be somewhat more accurate, the vice-president had been conversing with a program left on the machine by another employee. The program is called DOCTOR; it simulates the responses of a nondirective psychotherapist talking to a patient. The program is not as intelligent as the vice-president assumed. Joseph Weizenbaum of MIT designed the program to pick up key words and punctuation marks and use them to trigger preprogrammed replies that are deceivingly understanding and responsive. Weizenbaum was surprised that a number of people who talked with DOCTOR, knowing that it was just a program, often tended to take its replies seriously.

Human beings have been enthralled by the idea that in some way they might be able to construct lifelike mechanisms in their own image—robots, androids, thinking machines. The plots of various movies often go something like this. The machine at first obeys its creator, then becomes sophisticated and outgrows its maker, becoming impudent and dangerous, but in the end it is defeated by the wisdom of the human being.

Until recently, this situation was likely to exist only in science fiction. However, today, an electronic network, even without "intelligence," can come precariously close to having power over us. If this is the case, what would happen if computers could be programmed to perform in truly intelligent ways with the information they receive and possess? What would happen if they could comprehend, think, make decisions, and act on those decisions? Would the story have a different ending, with the machine defeating the human being?

Since 1966, when DOCTOR was introduced, computer scientists have created programs that mimic human intelligence in a number of ways and even outdo human intellect in certain areas. We know that computers can calculate numbers much faster and more accurately than we could ever hope to. They are also better than any of us at routing air traffic, predicting weather, and detecting whether certain disputed literary works were written by certain authors. Some computers can summarize news stories, comprehend spoken sentences, follow through on orders, diagnose diseases, and play games.

But there are some important things humans can do that computers cannot. A machine can learn and improve on its own program, but it does not have the means to develop a new goal. Computers are better at simulating the logical aspects of our mind than the nonlogical, intuitive, and unconscious aspects. The extraordinary multiple pathways in the brain probably produce thinking that cannot be mimicked by computers. And the human mind is aware of itself. No computer approaches the richness of human consciousness. ■

The Nature of Cognition and the Cognitive Revolution in Psychology

Exploring the human mind has been regarded with a kind of mystical awe throughout most of human history. Now, ten thousand years after the dawn of civilization, a new understanding of the mind is flourishing. The mind is viewed as a natural phenomena that can be investigated by scientific methods. What is this thing we call *mind* like?

The Nature of Cognition

When we use the term *mind,* most often we are referring to cognition. **Cognition** is our mental activities—how information enters our mind, how it is stored and transformed, and how it is retrieved and used to perform such complex activities as problem solving and reasoning.

A simple model of cognition is shown in figure 7.1. Cognition begins when information from the world is detected through sensory and perceptual processes, which we discused in chapter 3. Then information is stored, transformed, and retrieved through the processes of memory, which we discussed

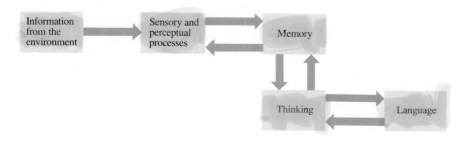

Figure 7.1
A model of cognition.

in chapter 6. Notice in our model that information can flow back and forth between memory and perceptual processes. For example, we are good at remembering the faces we see, yet at the same time, our memory of an individual's face may be different from how the person actually looks.

Information in memory also can be manipulated and transformed through **thinking,** which involves such processes as concept formation, problem solving, and reasoning. For example, you might take the information you have in memory about math (addition, subtraction, and so on) and use it to solve the problem of balancing your checkbook. Or you might have information about three different summer jobs and draw a conclusion about which is the best for you to pursue. Notice in figure 7.1 that arrows are drawn both ways between memory and thinking. Once you have reasoned about which job you will pursue this summer, your conclusion becomes a part of your memory, for example.

We will discuss thinking in the first half of this chapter and language in the second half. **Language** is a sequence of words. Figure 7.1 shows that the relation between language and thinking is reciprocal. Language helps us to think, make inferences, tackle difficult decisions, and solve problems. But thinking influences language also. Because of the way you think, certain words will be chosen to name objects, for example. Psychologists have asked, which comes first—thinking or language? Do our thoughts come first and then we use words to name the thoughts? Or do our words precede our thoughts, making thought impossible without them? We will address this intriguing question later in the chapter.

Keep in mind that our cognitive model is a simple one, designed to illustrate the main cognitive processes and their interrelations. We could have drawn arrows between memory and language, between thinking and perception, and between language and perception, for example. Also, it is important to know that the boxes in the figure do not represent sharp, distinct stages in processing information. There is continuity and flow between the cognitive processes as well as overlap.

The Cognitive Revolution in Psychology

By the 1940s serious challenges confronted the claim of behaviorists that organisms learn primarily through environment-behavior connections. The first successful computer suggested that machines could perform logical operations. This indicated that some mental operations might be modeled by computers, and possibly computers could tell us something about how cognition works. Cognitive psychologists often use the computer to help explain the relation between cognition and the brain. The physical brain is described as the computer's hardware and cognition as its software (see figure 7.2). The ability of the human mind and brain to process information has highlighted psychology's cognitive revolution since the 1950s (Baron, in press).

While interest in computers stimulated the study of cognition, other developments also were responsible. The study of brain injuries during World War II provided information about specific types of damage and cognitive incapacity. And there were exceptions to the general dominance of behaviorism in the early part of this century. The 1930s saw the publication of Sir Frederick Bartlett's *Remembering* (1932), a decidedly contemporary treatment of memory that anticipated many recent developments.

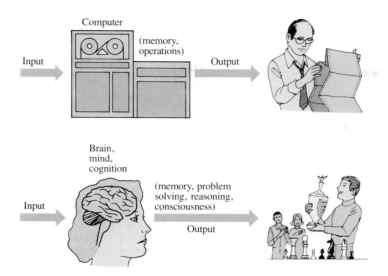

Figure 7.2
Computers and cognition: an analogy.

Thinking

Information in memory can be manipulated and transformed through thinking. We can think about the concrete, such as boats and beaches, and the abstract, such as freedom and independence. We can think about the past—life in the 1940s, 1960s, and 1980s—and the future—life in the year 2000. We can think about reality—how to do better on the next test in this course—and fantasy—what it would be like to meet William Shakespeare or land a spacecraft on Jupiter. When we think, we often use concepts. What characterizes these basic units of thinking and how are they formed?

Concept Formation

We have a special ability for categorizing things. We know that apples and oranges are fruits, but that they have different tastes and colors. We know that Porsches and Chevrolets are in the category of automobiles, but we know that they differ in such categories as cost, speed, and prestige. How do we know that apples and oranges are fruits and that Porsches and Chevrolets are automobiles despite their differences? The answer lies in our ability to ignore their different forms and group them on the basis of some feature(s). For example, all Porsches and Chevrolets have four wheels, a steering wheel, and provide a means of transportation. In other words we have a concept of what an automobile is. A **concept** is a category used to group objects, events, and characteristics on the basis of common properties.

Why are concepts important? Without concepts, each object and event in our world would be unique. Any kind of generalization would be impossible. Concepts allow us to relate experiences and objects. The Chicago Cubs, Atlanta Braves, and Milwaukee Brewers are professional baseball teams. Without the concept of baseball team, we would be unable to compare these teams.

Concepts make our memory more efficient. When we group objects to form a concept, we remember the characteristics of the concept rather than each object or experience. When one stockbroker tells another stockbroker

Figure 7.3
Array of cards presented to a subject in a concept learning experiment. The experimenter chooses the correct concept, and the subject attempts to discover the rules that define the concept.

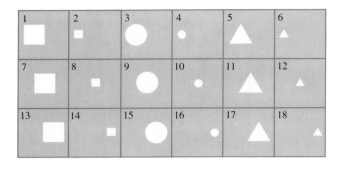

Drawing by Koren; © 1986 The New Yorker Magazine, Inc.

that the Dow Jones Industrial Average went up today, the second broker knows that IBM, Exxon, and General Motors, components of the average, had a good chance of increasing in value. By using the concept of the Dow Jones Industrial Average, communication was more efficient and probably memory was facilitated.

Concepts keep us from constantly needing to learn. Each time we come across the Dow Jones Industrial Average, we do not have to relearn what it is. We already know what the concept means. Concepts also have an informational value that provides clues about how to react to an object or experience. For example, if we see a dish of pretzels our concept of food—and pretzels are a member of that concept—provides information that it is okay to eat them. Concepts allow us to associate classes of objects or events. Some classes of objects are associated in structured patterns. For example, Dennis Conner won the America's Cup; the America's Cup is given to the winner of an international yachting competition; yachting is a sport.

In research on concepts, psychologists often have investigated an individual's ability to detect why an object is included in a particular concept. Let's look at an example of how this is accomplished. Figure 7.3 displays a number of cards shown to an individual in a typical concept formation experiment (Moates & Schumaker, 1980). The shapes (square, circle, or triangle), sizes (small, large), and position (left, middle, or right) of the figures on the cards vary. The experimenter arbitrarily decides on a concept, such as large circles, and asks the individual to discover it. Subjects are presented with an example of the concept (such as card 3) and asked to choose other cards until they discover what the concept is. After each card choice, the subject is told whether or not the card chosen is an example of the concept.

An important procedure in concept formation is to develop hypotheses about the concepts. This is done when alternative explanations are considered and tested. For example, you go to a tennis pro for a lesson because your serve needs work. The pro has a concept of what a good serve should look like. He observes you hit four or five serves and then entertains several hypotheses, or best estimates, of why you can't get your serve over the net consistently. Then he proceeds to test each of these hypotheses to determine which is correct. Finally, he discovers that his hypothesis about not tossing the ball high enough is correct. Researchers have found that when individuals are intelligent and

What is your prototype for a football player? Doug Flutie, shown at left in street clothes, former Heismann trophy winner, does not fit the prototype for a football player.

tasks are simple, concept formation is best if more than one hypothesis is entertained at the same time. For individuals with limited memory abilities and difficult tasks, it may be more efficient to simply focus on one hypothesis at a time (Levine, 1975; Matlin, 1983).

Some psychologists believe that the study of concept formation has been too artificial. Eleanor Rosch (1973) argues that real-life concepts are less precise, less well known, and less arbitrary than those used in many psychological experiments, such as the earlier example of "large circles." She has pursued the study of real-life concepts, or *natural categories* as they also are called. Rosch thinks that we learn real-life concepts through the process of **prototype matching.** Individuals decide if an item belongs to a particular concept by comparing the item to a prototype, or the best representative of the concept. Think of your concept of a football player: perhaps very muscular, big, and not too bright. Football players who match this concept are said to be prototypical; football players who are thin, small, and intellectual are not prototypical. Thus, all members of a concept are not equal. When the members are not equal, the concept may be organized in terms of a prototype.

Not every psychologist who studies concept formation, though, believes concepts are organized in terms of a prototype. A current interest focuses on how concept formation can take place without stored summary representations (Estes, 1986; Hintzman, 1986; Medin, 1986). This view suggests that memory traces are simultaneously activated, creating a kind of *buzz* in memory. If many of the activated traces are in a certain category, then the individual can detect whether an item fits a concept. This recent view places more emphasis on experiences with individual stimuli than a prototype of the stimuli.

In the 19th century, New York City began to experience traffic jams. The horse-drawn vehicles were making street traffic dangerous. How did William Eno solve this problem?

Figure 7.4
The hobbits and orcs problem. Can you solve it?

Problem Solving

Problem solving would be difficult without a knowledge of concepts. Think about the concept of driving, something many of us do every day. When we drive, our lives are punctuated by stop signs and traffic signals. Usually we don't think of these signs and signals as solutions to problems but they are (Bransford & Stein, 1984). Many of these solutions were engineered by William Eno, the "father of traffic safety." Eno, born in New York City in 1858, became concerned about the horrendous traffic jams in the city. The horse-drawn vehicles were making street traffic dangerous. Eno published a paper about the urgency of street traffic reform. His concept proposed solutions to the problem—stop signs, one-way streets, and pedestrian safety islands—ideas that affect our behavior today.

Indeed, our lives today are influenced by solutions to problems made by individuals in the past. Consider solutions to problems such as the Cuban missile crisis in the early 1960s. The Cuban missile crisis came extremely close to triggering a nuclear war. At meetings during the crisis a number of plans for dealing with Fidel Castro and the Soviet Union were considered. Had the Kennedy administration ignored the Soviet buildup of weapons on the island of Cuba, the course of world history might have been dramatically different.

Let's consider a more mundane problem called the hobbits and orcs problem. It goes like this:

> Three hobbits and three orcs are on one side of the river. You want to transport all of them to the other side. A maximum of two creatures can be in the boat but at least one must be on all crossings. Since orcs eat hobbits, it is critical that hobbits never be outnumbered by orcs at any time, on either side of the river. Describe a sequence of crossings that will transport all six creatures across the river without endangering the hobbits (see figure 7.4) (Thomas, 1974).

In this situation, a problem is stated and you are asked to solve it. Try to solve this problem, bearing in mind that the solution may take some time (the answer appears at the end of the chapter).

Just what is problem solving? **Problem solving** is an attempt to find an appropriate way of attaining a goal when the goal is not readily available. We face many problems in the course of our everyday lives—trying to figure out why our car won't start, planning how to get enough money to buy a stereo, working a jigsaw puzzle, or estimating our chances of winning at blackjack.

A valuable contemporary model of problem solving has been deveoped by John Bransford and Barry Stein (1984). The elements of what they call the IDEAL problem solver are: I = identify the problem; D = define and represent the problem; E = explore possible strategies; A = act on the strategies; and L = look back and evaluate the effects of your activities.

Identifying Problems

Encouraging individuals to identify problems may sound strange, but this is an important aspect of solving problems. Real-life problems need to be recognized and identified before they can be solved. Consider the situation of two brothers, Ladislao and George Biro, who were proofreaders. They spent much of their time correcting spelling mistakes and typographical errors in printed material. They recorded the errors they found in ink because pencil faded. The brothers tried fountain pens but they were messy. After recognizing this problem, the Biro brothers invented the ball-point pen, and their original company is now part of a corporation known as Bic. Mail-order catalogs are good

Figure 7.5
*Inventions designed to solve some
common problems.*

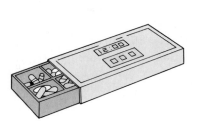

Medicine clock. Set this little pill-box
alarm to ring every ½, 1, 2, 4, 8, or
12 hours, and it plays a little song
to remind you to take your medicine.

Don't lock yourself out
of house, car! Magnetic cases
hide spare keys safely.

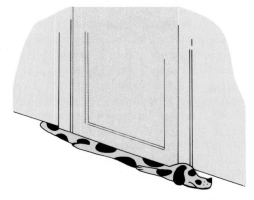

A quick twist opens the most
stubborn jars and bottles!

Wage war on energy costs. Dog sleeps in front of
drafty doors and windows.

sources of clever solutions to common problems. Objects shown in figure 7.5
provide examples of such inventions. The first step taken by the inventors of
these objects was to identify a problem to be solved.

Defining Problems

The second step in the IDEAL problem solver is to define the problem as carefully as possible. For example, a doctor recognizes that symptoms such as high
blood pressure indicate that a problem exists. The problem is identified but
now it must be defined more precisely. The doctor must discover the reasons
for the patient's symptoms. Different definitions of the problem call for different treatments. Both hardening of the arteries and everyday stress can produce high blood pressure but require different forms of treatment, for example.

Defining the problem may sound somewhat simple. Sometimes it is, as
in the case of winning at poker or fixing a leaky faucet. But many of the most
interesting problems in life are ill-defined: What does it take before I can call
myself a success? How can I write a book that will become a best-seller? What
is happiness? An ill-defined problem presented in a research investigation asked
subjects to imagine that they were the minister of agriculture in the Soviet
Union (Voss & others, 1983). Crop productivity had been low for the last
several years, and the subjects were to come up with a plan to increase crop
production. This problem was ill-defined because the subjects did not know
why crop production was low, they were not told how to increase crop production, and they were not informed how much of an increase was expected.

One of the most successful ways to solve ill-defined problems (or for that matter, most problems) is to divide the problem into a number of subproblems (Bransford, Sherwood, & Sturdevant, 1987). This procedure is called **subgoaling.** Instead of trying to reach one overarching goal, you instead strive to attain a number of smaller goals along the way. Consider the problem of writing a paper for a college course. You can divide the paper into a number of subproblems, such as selecting a topic, locating the literature, reading the literature, organizing what you read in the literature, writing the paper, and then rewriting and typing the final draft. Once you have identified the subproblems, you start with the first one and try to reduce the difference between the original state (no paper) and the goal state (a completed paper).

Exploring Alternative Approaches

The third component of the IDEAL problem solver is to explore alternative approaches to solving a problem. To do this, you analyze how you currently are reacting to a problem and then consider the options or strategies that might be used. In addition to dividing a problem into subproblems, you can work a problem backwards. Imagine that you need to meet someone for lunch across town and you don't want to be late. It is easier to solve the problem of deciding when to leave by working backwards. If you want to arrive at noon and know that it takes thirty minutes of travel time, the problem can easily be worked backward in time (noon − thirty minutes = 11:30 departure). Working backwards is a good strategy when the goal state is clear and the original state is not.

Another problem-solving strategy involves abstract or complex problems. These kinds of problems often can be solved by considering simpler, specific instances of the problems. Before figuring out what it takes to win the election for president of the United States, it helps if a candidate discovers the strategies that work in winning caucuses in Iowa and New Hampshire, for example.

Two other important strategies are algorithms and heuristics. **Algorithms** are procedures that are guaranteed to produce an answer to a problem. When you solve a multiplication problem you are using an algorithm. When you follow the directions for putting together a lawn chair, an algorithm also is involved. If algorithms are so successful, why don't we use them more often? The answer lies in ill-defined problems. There is no known guaranteed solution to an ill-defined problem. Even for well-defined problems, some solutions are so vast that an algorithm cannot be found. Chess is a good example of this. Beginning at the conventional starting position, it is estimated that chess has 10^{40} (or ten followed by forty zeros!) different continuations or potential games. With so many possibilities, it is understandable why even computers have not found a single perfect chess algorithm (Best, 1986).

Heuristics are strategies, or rules of thumb, that suggest a solution to a problem but do not ensure it will work. Working backwards and subgoaling are heuristic strategies as are the memory strategies described in chapter 6 and the techniques devised by clinical psychologists to improve an individual's ability to cope with stress. Consider another situation—a flat tire. If you are faced with the problem of changing a flat tire, a helpful heuristic is loosening the bolts before jacking up the car. This heuristic improves the likelihood that you will efficiently change the tire.

Another important heuristic involves estimating probabilities. Many circumstances are uncertain and yet we are called on to make predictions. On June 5, 1979, a newspaper article reported that Space Agency Chief Robert Frosch said there was a 152 to 1 chance that Skylab would hurt someone when it plunged to earth. Frosch also said there was a fifty-fifty chance the reentry would occur by July 9. Two heuristics that are important in such problem solving are availability and representativeness (Tversky & Kahneman, 1973).

The **availability heuristic** suggests that we evaluate the probability of an event by recalling the frequency of past occurrences. Thus, we might assess the probability of Skylab falling in a particular area by recalling whether any other space materials had fallen there. Other factors involved in the availability heuristic are our familiarity with the information and the vividness of the possible event. Because the media tend to overexpose us to information about such things as tornadoes, cancer, and accidents, we may overestimate their occurrence. It is important to note that we sometimes give too much weight to vivid, flashy information when making estimates.

If you were asked to estimate the probability of this airline crash, what kind of heuristic would you probably use?

The **representativeness heuristic** suggests that we make estimates based on how well something matches a prototype, that is, the most common or representative example. Consider the following description of an individual's dinner companion: skilled at carpentry, proficient at wrestling, owns a pet snake, knows how to repair motorcycles, and has been arrested for beating someone with a chain. What is the probability that this person is a male? Most likely, the description fits your prototype of a male more than your prototype of a female, so you might estimate that there is a nine in ten chance the dinner companion is male.

In this example, your prototype served you well because there are far more males in the population who fit the description given than females. But sometimes our prototypes do not take into account the frequency of events in a total population. For example, would you say the probability is greater that the dinner companion is a member of an outlawed motorcycle gang or a salesman? My guess is that you answered something like, "There is a much greater chance that he is a member of an outlawed motorcycle gang," in which case you would be wrong. Why? While only a very small percentage of the millions of salesmen in the world fit the description of the dinner companion, the total number represented by this percentage is greater than the total number of outlawed motorcycle gang members who fit the description.

Let's assume there are 10,000 members of violent motorcycle gangs in the world and 100 million salesmen. Even if 1 of every 100 motorcycle gang members fits our description, there would be only 100 of them. If just 1 of every 100,000 salesmen fits our description, their total would number 1,000. So the probability is ten times greater that the dinner companion is a salesman than a member of the motorcycle gang. There are many instances in our lives when we fail to account for the population from which a sample is drawn. One of these instances is playing blackjack. Systematic errors in estimating probabilities at this game are described in Psychology 7.1.

We each get into the habit of solving problems with a particular strategy. Solving problems with the same strategy or tendency is called a **learning set**. In many instances, learning sets serve us efficiently. Without them, we would waste time looking for the solution to a problem we already know. You probably have encountered a problem with learning sets in your college classes.

■■■■■■■■■■■■■■■■■■■

Psychology 7.1

Blackjack—Systematic Errors in Reasoning

In a game of blackjack you are dealt the two of hearts and the jack of spades. The dealer has the four of spades and a card down. Should you take another card or stay with twelve?

In the game of blackjack, you draw cards, trying to come as close as possible to twenty-one without going over. Kings, jacks, and queens are worth ten points, and aces are worth either one or eleven points. A two-card total of twenty-one is called a blackjack, which automatically wins. One team of researchers examined over 11,000 blackjack hands played by 112 gamblers in a casino to determine how the players made their game decisions. A player

with considerable practice can learn the winning probabilities associated with each combination of a player's total and dealer's hand. That is, a player can develop a strategy for learning when to hold (stop drawing cards) and when to take a hit (draw another card). But, in fact, the researchers found that most gamblers do not make decisions based on rational decisions (Wagenaar, Keren, & Pleit-Kuiper, 1984). For example, fear of "busting," or going over twenty-one was very common, often leading to poor decisions.

Some of the gamblers in the study increased their bets after a loss and decreased them after a win. Others did the

opposite, believing that since they just won, they were likely to be on a winning streak or since they just lost, they should bet less the next time. All of these strategies are irrational, and some psychologists believe it has to do with the representativeness heuristic (Kahneman & Tversky, 1972). That is, the prototype or sample we base our estimates on is not representative of the total number of blackjack hands played. The logic of probability and chance in blackjack is not based on a small sample of what happens during one or two hours but on what happens in the total population of blackjack hands.

You may have several professors whose exams are based primarily on lecture materials. In another class you follow the strategy that got you good grades in these lecture-oriented classes and spend little time with the textbook for the course. When you see the first exam in this class, you learn that the strategy that worked in the first class is not appropriate—this exam has a number of questions based only on the text.

A problem often used to demonstrate the concept of a learning set is called the nine-dot problem. Take out a piece of paper and copy the arrangement of the following nine dots:

Without lifting your pencil connect the dots using only four straight lines. Why are so many individuals unable to find a solution to the nine-dot problem? We have a learning set that tells us to think of the nine-dot configuration as a square. We consider the outer dots as a boundary and do not extend the lines beyond them. A solution to the nine-dot problem is shown at the end of the chapter.

The concept of **functional fixedness** is much like that of a learning set. Functional fixedness is the inability to solve a problem because it is viewed only in terms of its usual function. If the problem to be solved involves the

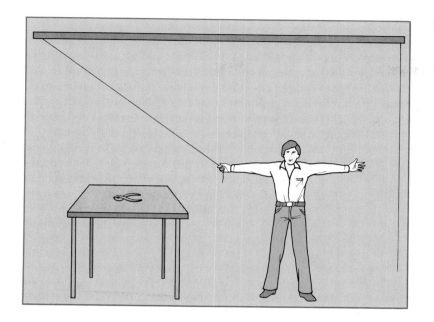

Figure 7.6
The Maier string problem: How can the two strings be tied together if you cannot reach them both at the same time?

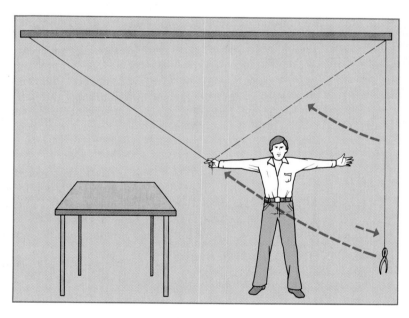

Figure 7.7
Solution to the Maier string problem: Use the pliers as a weight to create a pendulum motion that brings the second string closer.

usual function, then it can be solved easily. But if the problem involves something new and different, then problem solving will be adversely affected. An example of functional fixedness involves pliers (Maier, 1931). The problem is to tie two strings together that are hanging from a ceiling (see figure 7.6). If you hold one and then move toward the other, you cannot reach the second one. There is a common tool—a pair of pliers—on a table. Can you solve the problem?

The solution to this problem (shown in figure 7.7) consists of tying the pliers to the end of one string to serve as a weight. Swing this string back and forth like a pendulum. Then let go of the "weight" and grasp the other string. Finally, reach out and grab the swinging string. Your past experience with pliers makes this a difficult problem to solve. To solve the problem you need to find a unique use for the pliers, in this case as a weight to create a pendulum.

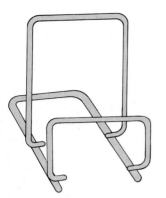

Figure 7.8
A book holder.

Figure 7.9
A book holder that also guards against stains.

Figure 7.10
The IDEAL problem solver.

Acting on a Plan and Looking at the Effects

We cannot be sure that our identification and definition of the problem, and our exploration of strategies to solve it, are correct until we act on them and discover if they actually work. These final two steps in Bransford's and Stein's IDEAL problem solver are closely related. An illustration of the importance of acting on the basis of strategies and looking at the effects is illustrated in figure 7.8. This object was invented to solve the problem of following a recipe in a cookbook while your hands are busy doing other things.

Assume that you invented this apparatus. You probably would want to try it out and see if it works. As you use it, you would soon see that the invention has a problem. The cookbook is not protected from spilled or splattered food. Looking at these effects, you might revise the apparatus to look like the holder shown in figure 7.9. Without acting on your plan and evaluating the effects, you may never have discovered the improved invention. A summary of the steps in the IDEAL problem solver is shown in figure 7.10.

Expertise

Some individuals do certain things extraordinarily well while others are mere novices at the same thing. Even within a particular domain of knowledge, such as nuclear physics, cognitive psychologists make distinctions between the stars, those who stand out above the others, and those who are knowledgeable but have not made outstanding contributions.

A meaningful question focuses on how experts accomplish their feats. What do they do that is different from ordinary, less-skilled problem solvers? Experts have broad and highly organized knowledge about their field, which allows them to solve a problem from memory without going through a tedious problem-solving effort. The expert organizes knowledge in a hierarchical fashion. In the expert's mind, specific details are grouped into chunks, which in turn are grouped into more general topics, which in turn come under the heading of even more global topics, and so on.

Figure 7.11 shows the hierarchical arrangement one physicist used to organize his knowledge to solve a physics problem. The dotted lines are associations made by experience that led directly from one specific point to another. These *pointers* connected the smaller branches of the "concept" tree and possibly produced shortcuts in solving the problem. An example of how a novice might solve the same problem is shown in figure 7.12. Notice the absence of pointers and fewer interconnections. Experts seem to have many interconnections in their storehouse of knowledge.

How do experts achieve this storehouse of knowledge with all of its interconnections and shortcuts? It takes experience and effort, gradually built up over many years. Experts develop efficient strategies for accomplishing tasks, they are capable of quickly and accurately evaluating alternative ideas, and

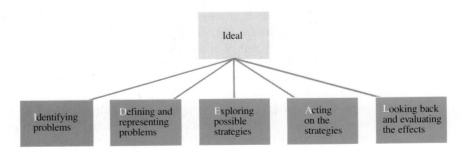

they acquire specifically tailored tricks (associations and networks of ideas that make things work) that make a problem more manageable (Bourne & others, 1986; Isaacs & Clark, 1987). Whether the field is cardiology, commodities trading, chemical engineering, law, or gardening, many of these characteristics distinguish experts from novices (Johnson, 1979).

Reasoning

For centuries philosophers thought that reasoning occurred according to the laws that govern logic. But as we know from our everyday encounters, individuals do not always reason in highly logical, formal ways. **Reasoning** is involved when we try to draw conclusions from facts. We will describe four types of reasoning and then return to the issue of how humans reason.

Forms of Reasoning

Four types of reasoning include 1) putting ideas in their proper order, 2) seeing relations between conditions, 3) understanding syllogisms, and 4) making analogies.

The type of reasoning involved in the following problem is putting things in their proper order:

> If you like Tom better than Troy,
> And you like Tim less than Troy,
> Whom do you like the least?

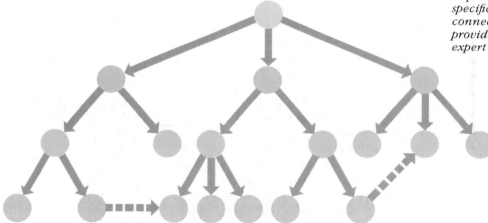

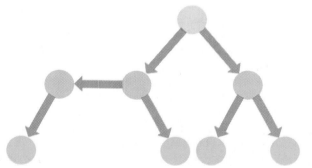

Figure 7.11
An example of how information about a physics problem was organized in the mind of an expert on physics. An expert's knowledge is based on many years of experience in which small bits of information have been linked with other small pieces, which together are placed into a more general category. This category in turn is placed in an even more general category of knowledge. The dotted lines are used as pointers, associations between specific elements of knowledge that connect the lower branches and provide mental shortcuts in the expert's mind.

Figure 7.12
An example of how information about a physics problem might be organized in the mind of a novice on physics. The novice's knowledge shows far fewer connections, shortcuts, and levels than the expert's knowledge.

When faced with this type of reasoning, we often put items together in a global ordering, not unlike schemata in memory. In studying how individuals reason about such problems, one investigation found that people do not store each sentence in memory but encode a general, integrated idea about the items (Potts, 1979). We also reason in this way by listing the items in an array, either left to right or top to bottom.

A second way we reason is to see relations between conditions, which usually involves if/then statements. Is the following reasoning valid?

> If it's raining, the streets are wet.
> It isn't raining.
> Therefore, the streets aren't wet.

This reasoning is not valid. Even if it is not raining the streets could still be wet for some other reason—it may have snowed, someone may have just washed her car, or a fire hydrant might have been opened, for example.

A third form of reasoning involves syllogisms. A **syllogism** consists of a major premise, a minor premise, and a conclusion. A premise is a general assumption. This type of problem invariably involves a reference to quantity, such as some, all, or none. Consider the following statements:

> All elephants are fond of dry martinis.
> All those who are fond of dry martinis are bankers.
> Therefore, all elephants are bankers.

The first sentence about elephants is the major premise and the second sentence about bankers is the minor premise. Though it may seem a little ridiculous, the conclusion—that all elephants are bankers—is technically correct because in this type of reasoning it is assumed that all of the premises are correct (Matlin, 1983).

A frequent mistake in syllogistic reasoning is the failure to distinguish between information given in the premise and information received from long-term memory (Henle, 1962). For example, in encoding the phrase, "Some men are aggressive," you might supplement this with the thought "but some are not" on the basis of your experience with men. This unintended intrusion in logical reasoning by long-term memory often produces errors in formal reasoning.

A fourth form of reasoning involves analogies. For example:

> Beethoven is to music as Picasso is to _____ .

Every **analogy** is made up of four components. The relationship between the first two components of an analogy is the same as the relationship between the last two components of an analogy. We use analogies frequently, as when we apply prior knowledge to a new situation. When you took the SAT or ACT tests, you probably were asked to supply the correct word in an analogy.

Analogies can be very helpful in solving problems, especially when they are visually represented (Beveridge & Parkins, 1987; Bransford & Stein, 1984). Benjamin Franklin noticed that a pointed object drew a stronger spark than a blunt object when both were in the vicinity of an electrified body. Originally he believed that this was an unimportant observation. It was not until he recognized that clouds did not draw a strong spark in the vicinity of an electrified body that he realized that pointed rods of iron could be used to protect buildings and ships from lightning. The pointed rod attracted the lightning, thus deflecting it from buildings and ships. Wilhelm Kekele discovered the ringlike structure of the benzene molecule in organic chemistry only after he visualized its structure using the analogy of a snake biting its tail (see figure 7.13). In many ways, analogies make the strange familiar and the familiar strange.

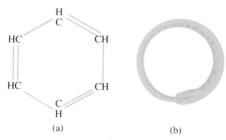

Figure 7.13
The use of analogy in problem solving. The benzene ring (a) is one of the most important structures in organic chemistry. It was only discovered by Wilhelm Kekulé after he imagined how its structure might be analogous to a snake biting its tail (b).

How Logical Is Human Reasoning?

The Greeks sometimes referred to humans as featherless bipeds. But they also gave us another more lofty designation: rational beings. How rational are we?

We have discussed instances in which we are not so rational—playing blackjack and reasoning if an individual is more likely to be a motorcycle gang member or a salesman, for example. If we look at ourselves objectively, we can come up with countless examples of failures in rational thinking. The hobbits and orcs problem required a high level of rational thinking. Many individuals have a great deal of difficulty with this problem and other problems that require systematic, logical thinking.

If we require a final piece of evidence that even outstanding minds bend logic to their own conclusions, we need to go no further than the United States Supreme Court (Hunt, 1982). In recent years, a number of important cases focusing on constitutional guarantees produced split decisions. Constitutional guarantees are the premises with which all nine justices begin, and many of their decisions involve reasoning of the highest order, yet the justices arrive at different, sometimes diametrically opposite, conclusions. How can this possibly be? The justices *interpret* the language of the Constitution in their own ways, justifying their own social values. As Chief Justice Charles Hughes said to William Douglas when Douglas was new to the Supreme Court, "You must remember one thing. At the constitutional level where we work, 90 percent of any decision is emotional. The rational part of us supplies the reasons for supporting our predilections."

How logical is human reasoning? Even in the highest courts, logic often is bent to support an individual's interests.

How do we survive in the world as well as we do if our reasoning is so flawed? Our reasoning is flawed only in comparison to the way a logician formally reasons. In the logician's world, everything is precise, consistent, and rigid. In our world of everyday living, we do not need to be completely precise, consistent, and rigid in our thinking to survive. You may not choose the most systematic, logical way to get from your house to a friend's, but nonetheless you find your way and may discover a shortcut that is better than what a formal logical analysis of the route would provide. You also might choose to solve a problem in a way that worked for you in the past rather than through a logical analysis of a situation. For example, in trying to earn money in college, you might pursue selling magazines to fellow students just as you sold newspapers when you were growing up. Our reasoning as human beings may not be as logical as a formal logician or a philosopher, but it usually gets the job done.

Our ability to get along in our world without using formal logic should not lead us to neglect the importance of logic and reasoning in our lives. There are many circumstances when it helps to have the power of reasoning on our side (Gardner, 1985). In almost every scientific investigation, reasoning is used to set up the basic hypothesis to be studied and to understand the findings. When we perform analytical and computational tasks, such as working out a family budget or filing an income-tax report, we use reasoning. When we play chess, bridge, or even ticktacktoe, we reason. When we are a juror or plaintiff or defendant, we reason about the law. When we talk or plead or argue with another or grapple with life's everyday problems, much of our reasoning consists of logical inferences—whether valid or not—from what we already know or think we know. In sum, our reasoning is both irrational and rational, not always perfect, but usually functional.

Our discussion of thinking has taken us through some of the mind's most important pathways—concept formation, problem solving, and reasoning. A summary of these main ideas, as well as information about the nature of cognition and the cognitive revolution, is presented in concept table 7.1.

■ ■ ■ ■ ■ ■ ■ ■ ■ ■ ■ ■ ■ ■ ■ ■ ■ ■ ■ ■

Concept Table 7.1

Cognition and Thinking		
Concept	**Processes/related ideas**	**Characteristics/description**
The nature of cognition and the cognitive revolution	What is cognition?	Our mental activities—how information enters the mind, how it is stored and transformed, and how it is retrieved and used to perform such complex activities as problem solving and reasoning. Thinking—the manipulation and transformation of information in memory—and language—a sequence of words—are important aspects.
	The cognitive revolution	This revolution has occurred in the last half century. The computer has played an important role, stimulating the model of the mind as an information processing system.
Thinking	Concept formation	A concept is used to group objects, events, or characteristics. Concepts help us to generalize, improve our memory, keep us from constantly needing to learn, have informational value, and improve association skills. Psychologists often have investigated an individual's ability to detect why an object is included in a particular concept. Developing hypotheses about concepts is important. We form concepts through prototype matching, but sometimes we are more likely to consider individual items.
	Problem solving	An attempt to find an appropriate way of attaining a goal when the goal is not readily available. A valuable model is the IDEAL problem solver: I = identifying problems, D = defining problems, E = exploring alternative approaches, A = acting on a plan, and L = looking at the effects. Alternative strategies include ideas about algorithms, heuristics, learning set, and functional fixedness.
	Reasoning	An attempt to draw conclusions from facts. Four kinds of reasoning include tasks pertaining to putting items in order, relations between conditions (if/then statements), syllogisms, and analogies. Human reasoning does not always follow formal logic.

Language

In the thirteenth century, the Holy Roman Emperor Frederick II had a cruel idea. He wanted to know what language children would speak if no one talked to them. He selected several newborns and threatened the adults who cared for them with their lives if they ever talked to infants. Frederick never found out what language the children spoke because they all died.

About five centuries later, in 1799, a nude boy was observed running through the woods in France. The boy was captured when he was approximately eleven years old; it was believed that he had lived in the wild for at least six years. He was called the Wild Boy of Aveyron (Lane, 1976). When the boy was found he made no attempt to communicate. Even after a number of years of care he never learned to communicate effectively.

Such circumstances bring up an important issue in language, namely, what are the biological and environmental contributions to language? Later in the chapter we will describe a modern-day wild child named Genie, who will shed more light on this issue. Indeed, the contributions of biology and environment figure prominently throughout our discussion of language.

What Is Language?

Every human society has language. Human languages number in the thousands, differing so much on the surface that many of us despair at learning more than even one. Yet all human languages have some things in common.

The definition of language provided earlier in the chapter stated that language is a sequence of words (Miller, 1981). This definition describes language as having two different characteristics—the presence of words and sequencing. But there are other charcteristics as well. The use of language is a highly creative process. For example, you can understand this sentence even though you have never seen or heard it. And you can create a unique sentence that you have not seen or heard before. This creative aspect of language is called **infinite generativity.** Infinite generativity is an individual's ability to generate an infinite number of meaningful sentences using a finite set of words and rules.

Yet another characteristic of language is **diplacement.** This means that we can use language to communicate information about another place and time, although we also use language to describe what is going on in our immediate environment. A final very important characteristic of language is its different rule systems. These include phonology, morphology, syntax, semantics, and pragmatics, which we now discuss in turn.

Language is comprised of basic sounds or *phonemes*. In the English language there are approximately thirty-six phonemes. The study of the sound system of language is called **phonology;** phonological rules ensure that certain sound sequences occur (e.g., *sp, ar, ba*) and others do not (e.g., *zx, qp*).

A good example of a phoneme in the English language is /k/, the sound represented by the letter *k* in the word *ski* and the letter *c* in *cat*. While the /k/ sound is slightly different in these two words, the variation is not distinguished and the /k/ sound is viewed as a single phoneme. In some languages, such as Arabic, this kind of variation is believed to represent separate phonemes (Dale, 1976).

Language is also characterized by a string of sounds that gives meaning to what we say and hear. The string of sounds is a *morpheme;* **morphology** refers to the rules for combining morphemes. Every word in the English language is made up of one or more morphemes. Not all morphemes are words, however (e.g., *pre-, -tion,* and *-ing*). Some words consist of a single morpheme (e.g., *help*), while other words are made up of more than one morpheme (e.g., *helper,* which has two morphemes, *help + er,* with the morpheme *er* meaning "one who," in this case "one who helps." Just as phonemes ensure that certain sound sequences occur, morphemes ensure that certain strings of sounds occur in particular sequences. For example, we would not reorder *helper* to *erhelp.* Morphemes have fixed positions in the English language, and these morphological rules ensure that some sequences appear in words (e.g., *combining, popular,* and *intelligent*) and others do not (e.g., *forpot, skiest*).

Syntax involves the way words are combined to form acceptable phrases and sentences. Because you and I share the same syntactic understanding of sentence structure, if I say to you, "Bob slugged Tom" and "Bob was slugged by Tom," you know who did the slugging and who was slugged in each case. You also understand that the sentence, "You didn't stay, did you?" is a gramatical sentence but that "You didn't stay, didn't you?" is unacceptable and ambiguous.

A concept closely related to syntax is **grammar,** which refers to the formal description of syntactical rules. In grade school and high school most of us learned rules about sentence structure. Linguists devise rules of grammar that are similar to those you learned in school but are much more complex and powerful. Many contemporary linguists distinguish between the "deep" and "surface" structure of a sentence. **Surface structure** is the actual order of the words in a sentence; **deep structure** is the syntactic relation of the words in a sentence.

Smithereens

"If you don't mind my asking, how much does a sentence diagrammer pull down a year?"

Copyright © 1981 United Feature Syndicate, Inc.

By applying syntactic rules in different ways, one sentence (the surface structure) can have two very different deep structures. This is one reason why sentences can be ambiguous. For example, consider this sentence: "Mrs. Smith found drunk on her lawn." Was Mrs. Smith drunk or did she find a drunk on the lawn? Either interpretation fits the sentence, depending on the deep structure applied.

Semantics refers to the meaning of words and sentences. Every word has a set of semantic features. Girl and woman, for example, share the same semantic features as the words female and human but differ in regard to age. Words have semantic restrictions on how they can be used in sentences. The sentence "The bicycle talked the boy into buying a candy bar" is syntactically correct but semantically incorrect. The sentence violates our semantic knowledge—bicycles do not talk.

A final set of language rules involves **pragmatics,** which is the ability to engage in appropriate conversation. Certain pragmatic rules ensure that a particular sentence will be uttered in one context and not another. For example, you know that it is appropriate to say, "Your new haircut certainly looks good" to someone who has just had their hair styled, but that it is inappropriate to say, "That new hairstyle makes you look awful." Through pragmatics we learn to convey intended meaning with word, phrases, and sentences. Pragmatics helps us to communicate more smoothly with others (Hay, 1987; Nelson, 1978).

Is this ability to generate rule systems for language, and then use them to create an almost infinite number of words, learned or is it the product of biology and evolution?

The Biological Basis of Language

In 1882, two-year-old Helen Keller was left deaf, blind, and mute by a severe illness. By the time she was seven years old, she feared the world she could not see or hear. Alexander Graham Bell suggested to her parents that they hire a tutor named Anne Sullivan to help Helen overcome her fears (see figure 7.14). By using sign language Anne was able to teach Helen a great deal about language. Helen Keller became an honors graduate of Radcliffe College and had this to say, "Whatever the process, the result is wonderful. Gradually from naming an object we advance step by step until we have traversed the vast distance between our first stammered syllable and the sweep of thought in a line of Shakespeare."

What is the process of learning language like? Helen Keller had the benefit of a marvelous teacher, which suggests that experience is important in learning language. But might there have been biological foundations responsible for Helen's ability to communicate? Did Helen, despite her condition, have some biological predisposition to learn language?

Figure 7.14
Anne Sullivan was able to use sign language to teach Helen Keller about language.

The Biological Story
Newborn birds come into the world ready to sing the song of their species. They listen to their parents sing the song a few times and then they have learned it for the rest of their lives. Noam Chomsky (1957) believes that the language of humans works in much the same way. He says we are biologically predisposed to learn language at a certain time and in a certain way. Chomsky's ideas prompted David McNeil (1970) to propose that a child comes into the world with a **language acquisition device (LAD)** that is wired to detect certain language categories (e.g., phonology, syntax, and semantics). McNeil also believes that we are able to detect deep and surface structures in language.

The contemporary view of language continues to stress that biology has a very strong role in language (Miller, 1981; Foss, 1988; Pinker, 1984). For example, George Miller (1981) argues that biology is far more important than environment in determining the nature of language. In his view, the fact that evolution shaped humans into linguistic creatures is undeniable.

Both physical and social evolution help to explain the development of language skills. The brain, nervous system, and vocal system changed over hundreds of thousands of years. Prior to *Homo sapiens,* the physical equipment to produce language was not present. Then social evolution occurred as humans, with their newly evolved language capacity, had to generate a way of communicating. *Homo sapiens* went beyond the groans and shrieks of their predecessors with the development of abstract speech. Estimates vary as to how long ago humans acquired language—from about 20,000 to 70,000 years ago. In evolutionary time, then, language is a very recent acquisition.

Anthropologists speculate about the social conditions that led to the development of language. Social forces may have pushed humans to develop abstract reasoning and create an economical system for communicating with others (Crick, 1977). For example, humans probably developed complex plans and strategies for providing food and shelter, and, they may have been motivated to develop language to reach a high level of competence.

The role of language in human evolution has stimulated psychologists to think about the possibility that animals have language.

Do Animals Have Language?

In 1914 in what is now Addo Park in South Africa a hunter was asked to exterminate a herd of 140 elephants. He killed all but twenty and those elephants were so clever at hiding that he abandoned the effort to find them. In 1930 the area became a wild game preserve and the elephants have been protected since that time. Elephants four generations removed from the time the hunter killed most of the herd still remain curiously nocturnal and shy. Somehow the elephants must have communicated from one generation to the next the hazards they might encounter, possibly through trumpeting calls that tell other elephants to avoid humans (Gould, 1983).

Leafcutter ants following each other, carrying parts of leaves. Do these ants have language?

No one doubts that animals of many different species have wondrous and ingenious communication systems and that their communication is adaptive in signaling danger, food, and sex. Indeed, some of these communication systems are complex. For example, the female of one firefly species has learned to imitate the flashing signal of another species to lure the aliens into her territory. Then she eats them. But are such communications considered language in the human sense?

Let's think about some of the important characteristics of human language that make it unique. There are at least four such characteristics. First, human language is productive—remember our comments about the infinite generativity of language. Second, human language is structured at different levels—remember that language begins with information about phonemes and ends with the more complex levels of syntax, semantics, and pragmatics. Third, the sounds of human language are arbitrary—languages around the world use words that sound different to refer to the same thing. Fourth, all human languages make some use of sequencing to reveal variations in meaning—remember that "Bob slugged Tom" means something very different than "Bob was slugged by Tom."

Figure 7.15
The language dances of honey bees. The round dance indicates that nectar is within 100 meters of the hive. The tail-wagging dance points in the direction of the nectar when it is more than 200 meters away. Distances between 100 and 200 meters are signalled by a third dance.

Round dance

Tail-wagging dance

The issue in the animal language controversy is whether these four characteristics of human language are present in animal communication. Even the lowly bee has been compared to humans in this regard (von Frisch, 1974). After a worker bee hunts for nectar and returns to the hive, she goes through an intricate dance to communicate the location of the nectar to the other bees (see figure 7.15). Though the dance of the bees is intriguing, it does not have the characteristics of human language we just listed. It is not nearly as productive; all the bees' communication is about the same thing—the location of the nectar. No evidence of different levels of communication is shown, and bees do not use arbitrary sounds. Bees do not vary the order of their symbols to generate different meanings. In other words, the language of bees is very different from the language of humans.

But what about animals higher on the evolutionary scale, such as chimpanzees and apes? Is their language similar to human language? To discover the answer to this intriguing question and to learn about the way scientists teach apes and chimpanzees language, read Psychology 7.2.

We conclude that animals communicate with each other and that the evidence shows chimpanzees can be trained to use sign language. Whether animals such as chimpanzees possess all of the characteristics of human language (such as the rule systems of phonology, morphology, syntax, semantics, and pragmatics) is still a topic of heated debate in the ape language controversy.

Is There a Critical Period for Learning Language?

In addition to considering continuities in language between humans and animals and the role of evolution, another biological aspect of language involves the issue of whether there is a critical period for learning language. If you have listened to Henry Kissinger, former secretary of state, speak you have some evidence for the belief that there exists a critical period for learning language. If an individual over twelve years of age emigrates to a new country and then starts to learn its language, the individual probably will speak the language with a foreign accent the rest of his life. Such was the case with Kissinger. But if an individual emigrates as a young child, the accent goes away as the new language is learned (Asher & Garcia, 1969; Oyama, 1973). Similarly, speaking like a native New Yorker is less related to how long you have lived in the city than to the age at which you moved there. Speaking with a New York "dialect" is more likely if you moved there before the age of twelve. Apparently, puberty marks the close of a critical period for acquiring the phonological rules of different languages and dialects.

Eric Lenneberg (1962) speculated that lateralization of language in the brain also is subject to a similar critical period. He says that up until about twelve years of age, a child who has suffered damage to the brain's left hemisphere can shift language to the right side of the brain; after this period, such a shift is impossible. The idea of a critical period for shifting lateralization of language is controversial and research on the issue is inconclusive (de Villiers & de Villiers, 1978).

The experiences of a modern-day wild child named Genie raise further interest in the idea of whether a critical time for acquiring language exists. Genie was found in 1970 in California. At the time she was thirteen years old and had been reared by a partially blind mother and a violent father. She was discovered because her mother had applied for public assistance at a welfare office. At the time Genie could not speak and could not stand erect. She had lived in almost total isolation during her childhood years. Naked and restrained by a harness that her father had fashioned, she was left to sit on her potty seat day after day. She could only move her hands and feet and had virtually nothing to do every day of her life. At night, she was placed in a kind of straitjacket and caged in a crib with wire mesh sides and an overhead cover. She was fed, although sparingly. When she made a noise, her father beat her. He never spoke to her with words but growled and made barking sounds toward her.

Genie underwent extensive rehabilitation and training over a number of years (Curtiss, 1977). During her therapy, Genie learned to walk with a jerky motion and was toilet trained. She learned to recognize many words and to speak. At first she spoke in one-word utterances and eventually began to string together two-word utterances. She created some two-word sequences on her own such as "big teeth," "little marble," and "two hand." Later she was able to put together three words—"small two cup," for example.

But unlike normal children, Genie never learned how to ask questions and she never understood grammar. Even four years after she began to put words together, her speech sounded like a garbled telegram. Genie never understood the differences between pronouns and between passive and active verbs. She continues as an adult to speak in short, mangled sentences, such as "father hit leg," "big wood," and "Genie hurt."

Such findings confirm the belief that language must be triggered to be learned and that the optimal time for that triggering is during the early childhood years. Clearly, biology plays an important role in language. But as you have seen in a number of areas of psychology, even the most heavily inherited characteristics require an environment for their expression.

The Behavioral View and Environmental Influences

Behaviorists view language as just another behavior, like sitting, walking, or running. They argue that language represents chains of responses (Skinner, 1957) or imitation (Bandura, 1971). But many of the sentences we produce are novel in the sense that we have not heard them or spoken them before. For example, a child hears the sentence, "The plate fell on the floor," and then says, "My mirror fell on the blanket," after she drops the mirror on the blanket. The behavioral mechanisms of reinforcement and imitation cannot completely explain this.

While spending long hours observing parents and their young children, Roger Brown (1973) searched for evidence that parents reinforce their children for speaking in grammatical ways. He found that parents did sometimes smile and praise their children for sentences they liked, but that they also

■■■■■■■■■■■■■■■■■■■■■

Psychology 7.2

Ape Talk—from Gua to Nim Chimpsky

■ It is the early 1930s. A seven-month-old chimpanzee named Gua has been adopted by humans (Kellogg & Kellogg, 1933). Gua's adopters want to rear her alongside their ten-month-old son, Donald. Gua was treated much the way we rear human infants today—her adopters dressed her, talked with her, and played with her. Nine months after she was adopted, the project was discontinued because the parents feared that Gua was slowing down Donald's progress.

About twenty years later, another chimpanzee was adopted by humans (Hayes & Hayes, 1951). Viki, as the chimp was called, was only a few days old at the time. The goal was straightforward: teach Viki to speak. Eventually she was taught to say "Mama," but only with painstaking effort. Day after day, week after week, the parents sat with Viki and shaped her mouth to make the desired sounds. She ultimately learned three other words—Papa, cup, and up—but she never learned the meanings of these words and her speech was not clear.

Approximately twenty years later, another chimpanzee named Washoe was adopted when she was about ten months old (Gardner & Gardner, 1971). Recognizing that the earlier

Figure 7.A
Washoe using American Sign Language: "sweet" for lollipop.

experiments with chimps had not demonstrated that apes have language, the trainers tried to teach Washoe the American Sign Language, which is the sign language of the deaf. Daily routine events, such as meals and washing, household chores, play with toys, and car rides to interesting places provided many opportunities for the use of sign language. In two years Washoe learned 38 different signs and by the age of five she had a vocabulary of 160 signs. Washoe learned how to put signs together in novel ways, such as "you drink" and "you me tickle" (see figure 7.A).

Yet another way to teach language to chimpanzees exists. The Premacks (Premack & Premack, 1972) constructed a set of plastic shapes that symbolized different objects and were able to teach the meanings of the shapes to a six-year-old chimpanzee, Sarah. Sarah was able to respond correctly using such abstract symbols as "same as" or "different from." For example, she could tell you that "banana is yellow" is the same as "yellow color of banana." Sarah eventually was able to "name" objects, respond "yes," "no," "same as," and "different from" and tell you about certain

reinforced sentences that were ungrammatical. Brown concluded that no evidence exists to document that the rule systems of language are based on reinforcement.

Another criticism of the behavioral view is that it fails to explain the extensive orderliness of language. The behavioral view predicts that vast individual differences should appear in speech development because of each child's unique learning history. But as we have seen, a compelling fact about language is its structure and ever-present rule systems. All infants coo before

Figure 7.B
Nim Chimpsky learning sign language.

events by using symbols (such as putting a banana on a tray). Did Sarah learn a generative language capable of productivity? Did the signs Washoe learned have an underlying system of language rules?

Herbert Terrace (1979) doubts that these apes have been taught language. Terrace was part of a research project designed to teach language to an ape by the name of Nim Chimpsky (named after famous linguist Noam Chomsky) (see figure 7.B). Initially, Terrace was optimistic about Nim's ability to use language as humans use it, but after further evaluation he

concluded that Nim really did not have language in the sense that humans do. Terrace says that apes do not spontaneously expand on a trainer's statements like humans do; instead, the apes basically just imitate their trainer. Terrace also believes that apes do not understand what they are saying when they speak; rather they are responding to cues from the trainer that they are not aware of.

The Gardners take exception to Terrace's conclusions (Gardner & Gardner, 1986). They point out that chimpanzees use inflections in sign language to refer to various actions, people, and places. They

also cite recent evidence that the infant chimp Loulis learned over fifty signs from his adopted mother Washoe and other chimpanzees who used sign language.

The ape language controversy goes on. It does seem that chimpanzees can learn to use signs to communicate meanings, which has been the boundary for language. Whether the language of chimpanzees possesses all of the characteristics of human language such as phonology, morphology, syntax, semantics, and pragmatics is still being argued (Maratsos, 1983).

they babble. All toddlers produce one-word utterances before two-word utterances, and all state sentences in the active form before they state them in the passive form.

However, we do not learn language in a social vacuum. Most children are bathed in language from a very early age. We need this early exposure to language to acquire competent language skills. The Wild Boy of Aveyron did not learn to communicate effectively after being reared in social isolaton for many years. Genie's language was rudimentary even after a number of years of extensive training.

In every culture, individuals are bathed in language from a very early age.

What are some of the ways the environment can contribute to language development? Imitation is one important candidate. A child who is slow in developing her language ability can be helped if parents use carefully selected lists of words and grammatical constructions in their speech to the child (Whitehurst, 1985). Recent evidence also suggests that parents provide more corrective feedback for children's ungrammatical utterances than Brown originally thought (Penner, 1987). Nonetheless, a number of experts on language believe that imitation and reinforcement facilitate language but are not absolutely necessary for language acquisition (de Villiers & de Villiers, 1978).

One intriguing role of the environment in the young child's acquisition of language involves *motherese,* or the **baby-talk register.** Consider the experience of language expert Roger Brown (1986):

> My office . . . is next door to the Child Development Research Laboratory. We are pretty well insulated against sound transmision, so the voices in the laboratory are content-filtered for me, but I can nevertheless always tell when someone is talking to a baby. That is because everyone, all adults and even children as young as three to four years . . . speaks to babies in a special 'register' (the baby talk register or BT). (p. 518)

A *register* is a way of speaking to people (or pets) in a particular category, such as babies or foreigners. The baby-talk register has six features: 1) a higher than normal frequency (about 267 Hz); 2) a greater than normal range of pitch; 3) a rising final intonation on imperatives; 4) occasional whispering; 5) longer than normal duration in speaking separable verbs (such as puuuush in); and 6) two main syllabic stresses on words calling for one syllabic stress (such as pú-úsh-ín).

It is difficult to talk in the baby-talk register when not in the presence of a baby. But as soon as you start talking with a baby you immediately shift into the BT register. Much of this is automatic and something parents are not aware they are doing. The BT register seems to serve an important function in both capturing the infant's attention and maintaining communication (Snow, 1988).

The BT register seems to be universal (Ferguson, 1977). It was documented as early as the first century B.C. and has been described in highly diverse languages. In some cases, such as high pitch, exaggerated intonation, and simple sentences, the BT register is virtually the same in different languages.

How Language Develops

In describing language we have touched on language development a number of times. You just read about the BT register parents use with their infants. Earlier we discussed Frederick II's effort to learn which language children would speak, the Wild Boy of Aveyron, Genie, and Donald and Gua.

When does an infant utter her first word? The event usually occurs at about ten to thirteen months of age, though some infants take longer. Many parents view the onset of language as coincident with this first word, but some significant accomplishments in language deveopment are attained earlier.

Before babies say words, they babble, emitting such vocalizations as "goo-goo" and "ga-ga." Such babbling starts at about three to six months of age; the start is determined by biological maturation, not reinforcement or the ability to hear. Even deaf babies babble for a time (Lenneberg, Rebelsky, & Nichols, 1965). Babbling probably exercises the baby's vocal apparatus and facilitates the development of articulation skills that are useful in later speech.

But the purpose of a baby's earliest communication skills is to attract attention from parents or others in the environment. Infants engage the attention of others by making and breaking eye contact, by vocalizing sounds, or by performing manual actions such as pointing. All of these behaviors involve pragmatics (Gleason, 1988).

A child's first words include those that name important people (dada), familiar animals (kittie), vehicles (car), toys (ball), food (milk), body parts (eye), clothes (hat), household items (clock), or greeting terms (bye). These were the first words of babies fifty years ago and they are the first words of babies today (Clark, 1983). At times it is hard to tell what these one-word utterances mean. One possibility is that they stand for an entire sentence in the infant's mind. Because of limited cognitive or linguistic skills, possibly only one word comes out instead of the whole sentence. This is called the **holophrase hypothesis,** that is, a single word is used to imply a complete sentence.

For words that a child uses as nouns, the meanings can be overextended or underextended. Eve Clark (1983) has studied early words and described a number of *overextensions*. For instance, when a child learns to say the word "dada" for father, she often applies the term beyond the class of individuals it was intended to represent, using it for other men, strangers, or boys, for example. With time, such overextension decreases and eventually disappears. *Underextension* occurs when a child fails to use a noun to name a relevant event or object. For instance, the child may learn to use the word "boy" to describe a five-year-old neighbor but not apply the word to a male infant or a nine-year-old male.

By the time children are eighteen to twenty-four months of age, they usually utter two-word statements. During this two-word stage, they quickly grasp the importance of expressing concepts and the role that language plays in communicating with others. To convey meaning with two-word utterances, the child relies heavily on gesture, tone, and context. The wealth of meaning children can communicate with a two-word utterance includes:

Identification: See doggie.
Location: Book there.
Repetition: More milk.
Nonexistence: Allgone thing.
Negation: Not wolf.
Possession: My candy.
Attribution: Big car.
Agent-action: Mama walk.
Action-direct-object: Hit you.
Action-indirect-object: Give papa.
Action-instrument: Cut knife.
Question: Where ball? (Slobin, 1972)

One of the most striking aspects of this list is that it is used by children all over the world. The examples are taken from utterances in English, German, Russian, Finnish, Turkish, Samoan, and Luo, but the entire list could be made up from examples from a two-year-old's speech in any language.

A child's two-word utterance differ substantially from adult word combinations. Language usage at this time is called **telegraphic speech.** When we send telegrams to individuals we try to be short and precise, excluding any unnecessary words. As indicated in the examples of telegraphic speech from children from around the world, articles, auxiliary verbs, and other connectives usually are omitted. Of course telegraphic speech is not limited to two-word utterances. "Mommy give ice cream," or "Mommy give Tommy ice cream," also are examples of telegraphic speech.

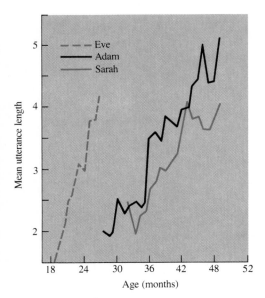

Figure 7.16
Individual variation in chronological age in children's mean lengths of utterance. This graph displays the average length of utterances (in number of words) generated by three children who ranged in age from one and one-half to four years.

One- and two-word utterances classify children's language development in terms of the number of utterances. Roger Brown (1973) expanded this concept by proposing that **mean length of utterance (MLU)** is a good index of a child's language maturity. Brown identified five stages based on an estimation of the number of words per sentence that a child produces in a sample of about 50 to 100 sentences. The mean length of utterance for each stage is as follows:

Stage	MLU
1	$1+ \rightarrow 2.0$
2	2.5
3	3.0
4	3.5
5	4.0

The first stage begins when the child generates sentences consisting of more than one word, such as the examples of two-word utterances we gave. The 1+ designation suggests that the average number of words in each utterance is greater than one but not yet two because some of the child's utterances are still holophrases. This stage continues until the child averages two words per utterance. Subsequent stages are marked by increments of 0.5 in mean length of utterance.

Brown's stages are important for several reasons. First, children who vary in chronological age as much as one-half to three-fourths of a year still have similar speech patterns. Second, children with similar mean lengths of utterance seem to have similar rule systems that characterize their language. In some ways, then, MLU is a better indicator of language development than chronological age. Figure 7.16 shows the individual variation in chronological age that characterizes children's MLU.

As we have just seen, language unfolds in a sequence. At every point in development, the child's linguistic interaction with parents and others obeys certain principles (Brown, 1988). Not only is this development strongly influenced by the child's biological wiring, but the language environment the child is bathed in from an early age is far more intricate than behaviorists such as Skinner imagined. A summary of the main ideas we have discussed about language is presented in concept table 7.2. A final consideration in our study of this remarkable ability we call language involves its ties with culture and cognition.

Language, Culture, and Cognition

Take a moment and reflect on several questions. Did the culture in which you grew up influence your language? Does language influence the way you think? Does thinking influence the nature of your language?

While we have stressed the universal aspects of language, such as how children all over the world speak in two-word utterances at about the same point in their development, some cultural differences in language do exist. For example, some words have a different meaning for you and me because of the different experiences we have had. And your experiences differ markedly from individuals growing up in other areas of the world. Consider the Eskimo, who has a dozen or more words to describe the various textures, colors, and physical states of snow; in English, we only have a few.

Concept Table 7.2

Language		
Concept	**Processes/related ideas**	**Characteristics/description**
What is language?	Its nature	A sequence of words that involves infinite generativity, displacement, and rule systems. Rule systems include phonology, morphology, syntax, semantics, and pragmatics.
The biological basis of language	The biological story	Chomsky believes that we are biologically wired to acquire language. McNeil says that we have a language acquisition device that includes wiring for surface and deep structures. The fact that evolution shaped humans into linguistic creatures is undeniable.
	Do animals have language?	Animals clearly can communicate and chimpanzees can use sign language. Whether animals have all of the properties of human language is debated.
	Critical period	The experiences of Genie and other children suggest that early childhood is an optimal time for learning language. If exposure to language does not come before puberty, life-long deficits in grammar occur.
The behavioral view and environmental influences	Their nature	Language is just another behavior. Behaviorists believe language is learned primarily through reinforcement and imitation, although they probably play a facilitative rather than a necessary role. An intriguing aspect of early language learning is the baby-talk register.
How language develops	Its nature	Vocalization begins with babbling at about three to six months of age. A baby's earliest communication skills are pragmatic. One-word utterances occur at about ten to thirteen months; the holophrase hypothesis has been applied to this. By eighteen to twenty-four months, most infants use two-word utterances. Language at this point is often referred to as telegraphic. Brown developed the idea of mean length of utterance (MLU). Five stages of MLU have been identified, providing a valuable indicator of language maturity.

The **Whorf/Sapir hypothesis** stresses that the more vocabulary we have, the more our perceptions will be differentiated. Thus the Eskimo is expected to see more variations of snow than you or me (Whorf, 1956; Sapir, 1958). Other interpretations are possible, though. The speakers of two languages may have the same perceptions but not be able to code or work with them efficiently. And, it may be that certain categories, such as color, may be universal and independent of language.

Eleanor Heider argues that color systems, indeed, are universal. She believes language does not vary across cultures nearly as much as the Whorf/Sapir hypothesis suggests. In one experiment, Heider (1972) selected eight colors considered to be prototypes (best examples) and thirteen colors not considered to be prototypes by English speakers. The prototype colors were more easily named by all twenty-three speakers in the twenty-three different languages than were the nonprototype colors. Individuals in all cultures were more likely to have a name for red than for chartreuse, for example. The importance of Heider's study is that it suggests that thought is not always based on language, as the Whorf/Sapir hypothesis states (Rosch, 1988).

What is your prototype for a bird? If you grew up in the United States, it might be a robin, but if you grew up in South America it might be a parrot.

Nonetheless, there are instances when language influences perception and thought. Though there seem to be universal prototypes for colors, other concepts may not be as universal. Consider the concept of birds. Your prototype for bird may be a robin, while the prototype for a South American might be a much larger and more exotic bird such as a parrot.

Our experiences build up a catalog that is either rich or poor in names for a particular concept, whether it be birds, tools, or music. If part of your mind's library of names has been constructed through years of experience attending antique automobile shows, you proably will "see" finer gradations among such cars than someone who has not had these experiences and who does not have a similar library of coded names and descriptions. In this way, language acts as a window that filters the amount and nature of information passed on for further processing.

But what about our memory and problem solving? What role does language play in these important cognitive activities? We saw in chapter 6 that information is stored in memory not only in terms of sounds and images, but also in words. Remember that when words are stored in memory their processing often is deep and their retrieval more effortful.

Language helps us to think, make inferences, tackle difficult decisions, and solve problems. Language can be thought of as a tool for representing ideas. Some psychologists have argued that we cannot think without language, a proposition that has produced heated controversy. Is thought dependent on language, or is language dependent on thought? Language does provide a medium for representing abstract ideas. Our language rules are more sophisticated than thought at an earlier point in our development, suggesting that language is *not* always dependent on thought (Bruner, 1964).

But cognition serves as an important foundation for language also. Evidence that cognition is important for language comes from studies of deaf children. On a variety of thinking and problem-solving tasks, deaf children perform at the same level as children of the same age who have no hearing problems. Some of the deaf children in these studies do not even have command of written or sign language (Furth, 1971).

So, thought can direct language and language can direct thought (Jenkins, 1969). Language is virtually an unbounded symbol system, capable of expressing most thoughts. And language is the way we humans communicate most of our thoughts to each other. We do not always think in words, but without a doubt, our thinking would be greatly impoverished without them.

Our thinking and language skills set us apart from other life forms on this planet. Through our thinking and language, we have mastered our world and adapted effectively to its challenges. In the next chapter we continue our investigation of thinking and language as we explore individual differences in mental functioning.

Summary

I. The Nature of Cognition and the Cognitive Revolution

Cognition is our mental activities—how information enters the mind, how it is stored and transformed, and how it is retrieved and used to perform such complex activities as problem solving and reasoning. Thinking—the manipulation and transformation of information in memory—and language—a sequence of words—are important aspects of cognition. The cognitive revolution in psychology has occurred in the last half century. The computer has played an important part in this revolution, stimulating the model of the mind as an information processing system.

II. Concept Formation

A concept is a category used to group objects, events, or characteristics on the basis of common properties. Concepts help us generalize, improve our memory, keep us from constantly needing to learn, have informational value, and improve association skills. Psychologists often have investigated an individual's ability to detect why an object is included in a particular concept. An important part of concept formation is forming hypotheses about concepts. One way we form concepts is through prototype matching, but sometimes we are more likely to consider individual items.

III. Problem Solving

Problem solving involves an attempt to find an appropriate way of attaining a goal when the goal is not readily available. A valuable model for solving problems is the IDEAL problem solver: I = identifying problems; D = defining problems; E = exploring alternative approaches; A = acting on a plan; and L = looking at the effects. Exploring alternative strategies includes ideas about algorithms, heuristics, learning set, and functional fixedness. Psychologists are interested in how experts develop expertise.

IV. Reasoning

Reasoning involves an attempt to draw conclusions from facts. Four kinds of reasoning include: 1) tasks that pertain to putting items in order; 2) relations between conditions (if/then statements); 3) syllogisms; and 4) analogies. Human reasoning does not always follow formal logic.

V. What Is Language?

Language is a sequence of words that involves infinite generativity, displacement, and rule systems. The rule systems include phonology (sound system), morphology (meaning of sounds we say and hear), syntax (how words are combined for acceptable phrases and sentences), semantics (meaning of words and sentences), and pragmatics (ability to engage in conversation effectively).

VI. The Biological Basis of Language

Chompsky believes that we are biologically wired to acquire language at a certain time and in a certain way. McNeil says that we have a language acquisition device that includes wiring for deep and surface structures. The fact that evolution shaped humans into linguistic creatures is undeniable. Animals clearly can communicate and chimpanzees can use sign language. Whether animals have all of the properties of human language is debated.

The experiences of Genie and other children suggest that early childhood is an optimal time for learning language. If exposure to language does not occur by puberty, life-long deficits in grammar occur.

VII. The Behavioral and Environmental Dimensions of Language

Behaviorists view language as just another behavior, such as walking. Behaviorists believe language is learned primarily through reinforcement and imitation. Reinforcement and imitation probably play a facilitative rather than a necessary role in language acquisition. An intriguing aspect of early language learning is the baby-talk register.

VIII. Language Development

Vocalization begins with babbling at around three to six months of age. A baby's earliest communication skills are pragmatic in nature. One-word utterances occur at about ten to thirteen months; the holophrase hypothesis has been applied to this. By eighteen to twenty-four months of age, most infants use two-word utterances. Language at this point is referred to as telegraphic. Brown developed the idea of mean length of utterance (MLU), which is the average number of words per sentence. Five stages of MLU have been identified, providing a valuable indicator of language maturity.

IX. Language, Culture, and Cognition

To a limited degree culture influences the nature of our language, although the strong biological base of language should be kept in mind. Language is important in many of our cognitive activities, among them memory and thinking. Cognitive activities also influence our language.

Key Terms

Suggested Readings

Baron, J. B., & Sternberg, R. J. (1987). *Teaching thinking skills.* New York: W. H. Freeman. Twelve eminent psychologists, educators, and philosophers contribute information about the latest approaches to teaching thinking skills. Descriptions of promising training programs are provided.

Bransford, J. D., & Stein, B. S. (1984). *The ideal problem solver.* New York: W. H. Freeman. Bransford and Stein present their model of problem solving, called the IDEAL Problem Solver. This book includes hundreds of fascinating problems, along with a number of tips on how to solve problems more effectively.

Curtiss, S. (1977). *Genie.* New York: Academic Press. Susan Curtiss tells the remarkable story of Genie, a modern-day wild child and her ordeal of trying to acquire language.

Gardner, H. (1985). *The mind's new science.* New York: Basic Books. This book is an excellent account of the cognitive revolution in psychology. Widely acclaimed by experts in cognitive psychology, this book is well written and provides a good overview of cognition.

Premack, D. (1986). *Gavagai! The future history of the ape language controversy.* Cambridge, MA: MIT Press. Premack describes some fascinating aspects of the ape language controversy, including his own ideas on how it contributes to our understanding the nature of language.

Solutions to Problems

1. *Hobbits and Orcs Problem:*
   In the Hobbits and Orcs problem (with R representing the right bank and L representing the left bank), here are the steps in the solution:
   (1) Move 2 Orcs, R to L.
   (2) Move 1 Orc, L to R.
   (3) Move 2 Orcs, R to L.
   (4) Move 1 Orc, L to R.
   (5) Move 2 Hobbits, R to L.
   (6) Move 1 Orc, 1 Hobbit, L to R.
   (7) Move 2 Hobbits, R to L.
   (8) Move 1 Orc, L to R.
   (9) Move 2 Orcs, R to L.
   (10) Move 1 Orc, L to R.
   (11) Move 2 Orcs, R to L.

2. *Nine-Dot Problem:*

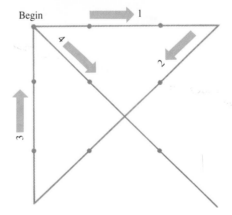

Chapter 8

Intelligence

■■■

What a piece of work is a man! How noble in reason! how infinite in faculty! in form, in moving, how express and admirable! in action how like an angel! in apprehension how like a god!

—*Shakespeare,* Hamlet

■■■

Images of Intelligence

Intelligence and intelligence tests frequently make the news. The following two stories appeared in the *Los Angeles Times:*

> IQ testing that leads to the placement of an unusually large number of black children in so-called mentally retarded classes has been ruled unconstitutional by a federal judge. On behalf of five black children, Chief District Court Judge Robert Peckham said the use of standardized IQ tests to place children in educable mentally retarded (EMR) classes violated recently enacted federal laws and the state and federal constitutions. . . . Peckham said the history of IQ testing and special education in California "revealed an unlawful discriminatory intent . . . not necessarily to hurt black children, but it was an intent to assign a grossly disproportionate number of black children to the special, inferior and dead-end EMR classes." (October 18, 1979).

> A controversial Escondido sperm bank for superbrains has produced its first baby—a healthy, nine-pound girl born to a woman identified only as a small-town resident in "a sparsely populated state." . . . Founded by inventor Robert K. Graham of Escondido in 1979, the facility contains sperm donated by at least three Nobel Prize winners, plus other prominent researchers. . . . The sperm bank was founded to breed children of higher intelligence. The goal has been denounced by many critics, who say that a child's intelligence is not determined so much by his genes as by his upbringing and environment. (May 25, 1982).

As you might expect, these stories sparked impassioned debate (Kail & Pellegrino, 1985). Some arguments focus on the ethical and moral implications of selective breeding of bright children and selective placement of children in special classes. Other arguments concern the statistical basis of conclusions, such as whether the tests are really biased if the data are analyzed properly. What you hear *less* often but should hear *more* often is a discussion of the construct of intelligence itself (Dwyer, 1987). That is, what is intelligence? How should it be conceptualized? ■

What Is Intelligence?

Intelligence is a possession that most of us value highly, yet it is an abstract concept with few agreed-upon referents. You would agree upon referents for such characteristics as height, weight, and age, but if asked to agree on referents for something like an individual's size, there is less certainty. Size is a more *abstract* notion than height or weight. Also, size is more difficult to measure directly than height or weight. We can only estimate size from a set of empirical measures of height and weight. Measuring intelligence is much the same as measuring size, though *much more* abstract. That is, we believe intelligence exists, but we do not measure intelligence directly. We cannot peel back an individual's scalp and observe intellectual processes in action. The only way we can study these intellectual processes is *indirectly,* by evaluating the intelligent acts that an individual generates. For the most part, psychologists have relied on intelligence tests to provide an estimate of these intellectual processes.

Throughout much of the history of Western civilization, intelligence has been described in terms of knowledge and reasoning (Kail & Pellegrino, 1985). Today, most of us view intelligence in a similar light. In one investigation, individuals were asked to judge which of 250 behaviors were typical of an intelligent individual (Sternberg & others, 1981). Both experts (psychologists researching intelligence) and lay individuals (people of various backgrounds and education) judged the behaviors similarly. The two groups agreed that intelligence can be divided into two main categories. The first is *verbal ability,* reflected in such behaviors as "displays a good vocabulary," "reads with high comprehension," "is knowledgeable about a particular field of knowledge," and "displays curiosity." The second is *problem-solving skills,* reflected in such behaviors as "reasons logically and well," "is able to apply knowledge to problems at hand," and "makes good decisions."

Thus, the primary components of intelligence are very close to the mental processes we discussed in the last chapter—thinking and language. The differences between how we discussed thinking and language and how we will discuss intelligence lies in the concepts of individual differences and assessment. **Individual differences** are the consistent, stable ways we are different from each other. The history of the study of intelligence in psychology has focused extensively on individual differences and their assessment. We can talk about individual differences in personality (which we will in chapter 13), or in any other domain in psychology, but it is in the area of intelligence that the most attention is given to individual differences. For example, an intelligence test will tell if you can logically reason better than most others who have taken the test.

Psychologists have a name for the field that involves the assessment of individual differences—**psychometrics.** In a few moments we will go on a brief historical tour of individual differences and intelligence tests, but first we need to know something very important in the field of psychometrics—how tests are constructed and evaluated.

How Tests Are Constructed and Evaluated

Any good test must meet three criteria—it must be reliable, it must be valid, and it must be standardized. We consider each of these three criteria in turn.

Reliability

If a test that measures some characteristic is a stable and consistent test, scores should not significantly fluctuate because of chance factors, such as how much sleep you get the night before the test, who the examiner is, the temperature in the room where you take the test, and so on. How consistently an individual performs on a test is known as the test's **reliability.**

Reliability can be measured in several different ways. One common method is to give the same individual the same test on two different occasions—this is called **test-retest reliability.** Thus, if we gave an intelligence test to a group of high school students today and then gave them the same test in six months, the test would be considered reliable if those who scored high on the test today scored high on the test in six months. One negative feature of test-retest reliability is that individuals sometimes do better the second time they take the test because they are familiar with it.

A second method of measuring reliability is to give alternate forms of the same test on two different occasions. The test items on the two forms of the test are similar but not identical. This strategy eliminates the chance of individuals performing better due to familiarity with the items, but it does not eliminate an individual's familiarity with the procedures and strategies involved in the testing.

Standardization of tests requires that uniform procedures be followed. For example, the test directions and the amount of time allowed to complete the test should be the same for all individuals.

A third method of measuring reliability is **split-half reliability.** With this method, test items are divided into two halves, such as the odd-numbered items and the even-numbered items. The items are different, and the two scores are compared to determine how consistently the individual performed. When split-half reliability is high we say that a test is *internally consistent.* For example, if we gave an intelligence test that included vocabulary items on one half of the test and logical reasoning items on the other half, we would expect the total scores of the individuals taking the test to be similar to their scores on each half of the test.

Validity

A test may consistently measure an attribute such as intelligence or personality, but this consistency does not ensure that we are measuring the attribute we want to measure. A test of intelligence might actually measure something else, such as anxiety. The test might consistently measure how anxious you are, and thus have high reliability, but not measure your intelligence, which it purports to measure. **Validity** is the extent a test measures what it is intended to measure.

Like reliability, there are a number of methods to measure validity. One method is **content validity,** which refers to the test's ability to give a broad picture of what is to be measured. For example, a final test in this class, if it is comprehensive over the entire book, should sample items from each of the chapters rather than just two or three chapters. If an intelligence test purports to measure both verbal ability and problem-solving ability, the items should include a liberal sampling of items that reflect both of these domains. The test would not have high content validity if it asked you to define several vocabulary items but did not require you to reason logically in solving a number of problems.

One of the most important methods of measuring validity is **criterion validity,** which is the test's ability to predict other measures, or criteria, of the attribute. For example, a psychologist might validate an intelligence test by asking the employers of the individuals who took the intelligence test how intelligent they are at work. The employers' perceptions are another criterion for measuring intelligence. It is not unusual for the validation of an intelligence test to be another intelligence test. When the scores on the two measures overlap substantially, we say the test has high criterion validity. Of course, we may use more than one other measure to establish criterion validity. We might give the individuals a second intelligence test, get their employers' perceptions of their intelligence, and observe their behavior in problem-solving situations ourselves.

Criterion validity can follow one of two courses, concurrent or predictive. **Concurrent validity** assesses the relation of a test's scores to a criterion that is presently available (concurrent). For example, a test might assess children's intelligence. Concurrent validity might be established by analyzing how the scores on the intelligence test correspond to the children's grades in school at this time.

Predictive validity assesses the relation of a test's scores to an individual's performance at some point in the future. For example, scores on an intelligence test might be used to predict whether the individual will be successful in college. Likewise, the SAT test is used for a similar purpose. Or tests might be developed to determine success as a police officer or as a pilot. Individuals take the test and then at a later time are evaluated to see if indeed they are able to perform effectively in these jobs.

Standardization

Good tests are not only reliable and valid, they are standardized as well. Developing uniform procedures for administering and scoring a test is important in **standardization.** Uniform testing procedures require that the testing environment be as similar as possible for all individuals. The test directions and the amount of time allowed to complete the test should be the same, for example.

The test constructor also develops **norms**—established standards of performance—for the test. This is accomplished by giving the test to a large group of individuals representative of the population for whom the test is intended. This allows the test constructor to determine the distribution of test scores. Norms inform us which scores are considered high, low, or average. For example, if you received a score of 120 on an intelligence test, that number alone has little meaning. The score takes on meaning when we compare it with the other scores. If only 20 percent of the standardized group scored above 120, then we can interpret your score as high rather than low or average. Many tests of intelligence are designed for individuals from diverse groups. So that the tests will be applicable to such different groups, many of them have norms, that is, established standards of performance for individuals of different ages, social classes, and races. Figure 8.1 summarizes the main points of our discussion of test construction and evaluation.

What contributes to the standardization of the test this individual is taking?

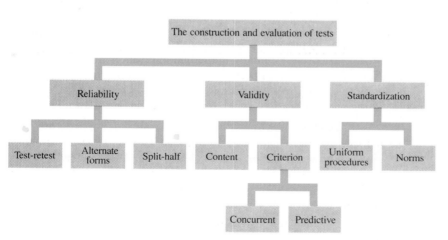

Figure 8.1
Test construction and evaluation.

The Measurement and Nature of Intelligence

Earlier we indicated that often intelligence is defined in terms of verbal ability and problem-solving skills. But we also indicated that intelligence is an abstract concept that is difficult to define. While many psychologists and lay people equate intelligence with verbal ability and problem-solving skills, others prefer to define it as the individual's ability to learn from and adapt to the experiences of everyday life. If we were to settle on a definition of intelligence based on these criteria it would be that **intelligence** is verbal ability, problem-solving skills, and the ability to learn from and adapt to the experiences of everyday life. As we discuss the measurement of intelligence throughout history, you will discover, however, that psychologists have debated the nature of intelligence.

The Early History

The German psychologists, especially Wundt, who created psychology as a separate discipline, were not interested in intelligence and its assessment (Kail & Pellegrino, 1985). For them, psychology's appropriate subject matter was sensation and perception. They completely ignored the "higher mental processes" such as thinking and problem solving, which we equate with intelligence today. The early German psychologists were interested in the general laws of behavior; any differences between individuals were thought to be mistakes in measurements reflective of a young science. But before the close of the nineteenth century, proposals were made for a psychology of intelligence and individual differences.

In 1884, visitors to the International Health Exhibition at London's South Kensington Museum were invited to pay three pence each to enter Sir Frances Galton's "Anthropomorphic Laboratory" (Fancher, 1985). Galton tempted the visitors by offering them a partial view of what was happening behind the trellised wall. Observers could see that each paying customer manipulated a number of interesting contrivances while an attendant wrote down information about their performance. By the exhibition's end, more than 9,000 men and women had been enticed into the laboratory. Without knowing it, they constituted the first large sample to take an intelligence test, though the term was not used at that time and a modern observer would find little similarity between the "tests" they took and the ones in use today. The battery of tests Galton administered measured such characteristics as head size, strength of hand grip, breathing capacity, reaction time, visual acuity, and memory for visual forms.

Sir Frances Galton is considered the father of mental tests (Boring, 1950). Like the early German psychologists, Galton believed that simple sensory, perceptual, and motor responses were the core of intelligence. In his laboratory he attempted to discover systematic individual differences in these processes. But his efforts produced no important findings about individual differences, possibly because of the sheer amount of data he collected. While his research provided few conclusive results, Galton raised many important questions about intelligence—how it should be measured, what its components are, and the degree to which it is inherited—that we continue to study today (Kail & Pellegrino, 1985).

The first North American psychologist to study individual differences was James McKeen Cattell—his most notable work was in the last decade of the nineteenth century. Like Galton, Cattell thought that sensory, perceptual, and motor processes represented the heart of intelligence. Cattell's battery of tests included having college students select the heavier of two weights and evaluating the speed with which they responded to a tone. He sought to discover a relation between these responses and achievement in college, but the results were disappointing. Cattell is credited with developing the label *mental test*. His research, like Galton's provided few important conclusions about intelligence, but he, too, developed a tradition that paved the way for further studies of individual differences in intelligence.

Alfred Binet and the Binet Tests

In 1904, the French Ministry of Education asked psychologist Alfred Binet to devise a method that would determine which students did not profit from typical school instruction. School officials wanted to reduce overcrowding by placing those who did not benefit from regular classroom teaching in special schools. Binet and his student Theophile Simon developed an intelligence test to meet this request. The test is referred to as the 1905 Scale and consisted of thirty different items ranging from the ability to touch one's nose or ear when asked to the ability to draw designs from memory and define abstract concepts.

Binet developed the concept of **mental age (MA),** which is an individual's level of mental development relative to others. Binet reasoned that a mentally retarded child would perform like a normal child of a younger age. He developed norms for intelligence by testing fifty nonretarded children from three to eleven years of age. Children suspected of mental retardation were given the test and their performance was compared with children of the same chronological age in the normal sample. Average mental-age scores (MA) correspond to chronological age (CA), which is age from birth. A bright child has an MA above CA, a dull child has an MA below CA.

The term **intelligence quotient (IQ)** was devised in 1912 by William Stern. IQ consists of a child's mental age divided by chronological age multipled by 100:

$$IQ = \frac{MA}{CA} \times 100$$

If mental age is the same as chronological age, then the individual's IQ is 100; if mental age is above chronological age, the IQ is more than 100; if mental age is below chronological age, the IQ is less than 100. Scores noticeably above 100 are considered above average, those noticeably below are considered below average. For example, a six-year-old child with a mental age of eight would have an IQ of 133 while a six-year-old child with a mental age of five would have an IQ of 83.

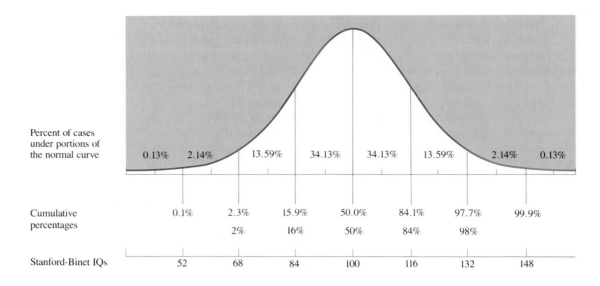

Figure 8.2
The normal curve and Stanford-Binet IQ scores (Sattler, 1982). The distribution of IQ scores approximates a normal curve. Most of the population falls in the middle range of scores. Notice that extremely high and extremely low scores are very rare. Slightly more than two-thirds of the scores fall between 84 and 116. Only about 1 in 50 individuals has an IQ of more than 132 and only about 1 in 50 individuals has an IQ of less than 68.

Over the years extensive effort has been expended to standardize the Binet test, which has been given to thousands of children and adults of different ages, selected at random from different parts of the United States. By administering the test to large numbers of individuals and recording the results, it has been found that intelligence measured by the Binet approximates a **normal distribution** (see figure 8.2). This type of distribution is symmetrical, with a majority of cases falling in the middle of the possible range of scores and few scores appearing towards the ends of the range.

The many revisions of the Binet test in the United States are called the Stanford-Binet tests (Stanford University is where the revisions were done). Many of the revisions were carried out by Lewis Terman, who applied Stern's IQ concept to the test, developed extensive norms, and provided detailed, clear instructions for each problem appearing on the test.

Why were the Binet scales such a major advance over the earlier efforts of Galton and Cattell? Binet argued that intelligence could not be reduced to sensory, perceptual, and motor processes, as Galton and Cattell believed. Binet stressed that the core of intelligence consists of more complex mental processes such as memory, imagery, comprehension, and judgment. Galton and Cattell thought that children were untrustworthy subjects in psychological research, but Binet believed that a developmental approach was crucial for understanding the concept of intelligence. The developmental interest was underscored by the emphasis on the child's mental age in comparison to chronological age.

The current Stanford-Binet is given to individuals from the age of two through adulthood. It includes a wide variety of items, some requiring verbal responses, others nonverbal responses. For example, items that characterize a six-year-old's performance on the test include the verbal ability to define at least six words such as "orange" and "envelope," and the nonverbal ability to trace a path through a maze. Items that reflect the average adult's intelligence include defining such words as "disproportionate" and "regard," explaining a proverb, and comparing idleness and laziness.

HERMAN®

"You did very well on our IQ test!"

The fourth edition of the Stanford-Binet was published in 1985 (Thorndike, Hagan, & Sattler, 1985). One important addition to this version is the analysis of the individual's responses in terms of four content areas: verbal reasoning, quantitative reasoning, abstract/visual reasoning, and short-term memory. A general composite score also is obtained to reflect overall intelligence. The Stanford-Binet continues to be one of the most widely used individual tests of intelligence.

The Wechsler Scales

Besides the Stanford-Binet, the other most widely used individual intelligence tests are the **Wechsler scales,** developed by David Wechsler. They include the Wechsler Adult Intelligence Scale-Revised (WAIS-R); the Wechsler Intelligence Scale for Children-Revised (WISC-R), for use with children between the ages of six and sixteen; and the Wechsler Preschool and Primary Scale of Intelligence (WPPSI), for use with children from the ages of four to six and a half (Wechsler, 1949, 1955, 1967, 1974, 1981).

The Wechsler scales not only provide an overall IQ score but the items are grouped according to eleven subscales, six of which are verbal and five of which are nonverbal. This allows the examiner to obtain separate verbal and nonverbal IQ scores and to see quickly the areas of mental performance in which the individual is below average, average, or above average. The inclusion of a number of nonverbal subscales makes the Wechsler test more representative of verbal *and* nonverbal intelligence; the Binet-Simon test includes some nonverbal items but not as many as the Wechsler scales. The eleven subscales on the Wechsler Adult Intelligence Scale-Revised are shown in figure 8.3, along with examples of each subscale.

Figure 8.3
The subtests of the WAIS-R and
examples of each subtest.

Verbal subtests

General information
The individual is asked a number of general information questions about experiences that are considered normal for individuals in our society.
For example, "How many hours apart are eastern standard time and pacific standard time?"

Similarities
The individual must think logically and abstractly to answer a number of questions about how things are similar.
For example, "In what way are boats and trains the same?"

Arithmetic reasoning
Problems measure the individual's ability to do arithmetic mentally and include addition, subtraction, multiplication, and division.
For example, "If oranges are $1.20 per dozen, how much does one orange cost?"

Vocabulary
To evaluate word knowledge, the individual is asked to define a number of words. This subtest measures a number of cognitive functions, including concept formation, memory, and language.
For example, "What does the word *disparate* mean?"

Comprehension
This subtest is designed to measure the individual's judgment and common sense.
For example, "Why do individuals buy automobile insurance?"

Digit span
This subtest primarily measures attention and short-term memory. The individual is required to repeat numbers forward and backward.
For example, "I am going to say some numbers and I want you to repeat them backward: 4 7 5 2 8.

Picture completion
A number of drawings are shown, each with a significant part missing. Within a period of several seconds, the individual must differentiate essential from nonessential parts of the picture and identify which part is missing. This subtest evaluates visual alertness and the ability to organize information visually.
For example, "I am going to show you a picture with an important part missing. Tell me what is missing.

Picture arrangement
A series of pictures out of sequence are shown to the individual, who is asked to place them in their proper order to tell an appropriate story. This subtest evaluates how individuals integrate information to make it logical and meaningful.
For example, "The pictures below need to be placed in an appropriate order to tell a meaningful story."

Object assembly
The individual is asked to assemble pieces into something. This subtest measures visual-motor coordination and perceptual organization.

For example, "When these pieces are put together correctly, they make something. Put them together as quickly as you can."

Block design
The individual must assemble a set of multi-colored blocks to match designs that the examiner shows. Visual-motor coordination, perceptual organization, and the ability to visualize spatially are measured.

For example, "Use the four blocks on the left to make the pattern on the right."

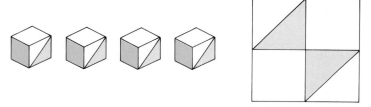

Coding
This subtest evaluates how quickly and accurately an individual can link code symbols and digits. The subtest assesses visual-motor coordination and speed of thought.

For example, "As quickly as you can, transfer the appropriate code symbols to the blank spaces."

Verbal reasoning
Choose the correct pair of words to fill the blanks. The first word of the pair goes
in the blank space at the beginning of the sentence; the second word of the
pair goes in the blank at the end of the sentence.

. . . . . . is to night as breakfast is to . . . . . .

    A. supper — corner
    B. gentle — morning
    C. door — corner
    D. flow — enjoy
    E. supper — morning

The correct answer is E.

Numerical ability
Choose the correct answer for each problem.

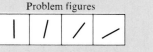

Add	13	A	14		Subtract	30	A	15
	12	B	25			20	B	26
		C	16				C	16
		D	59				D	8
		E	none of these				E	none of these

The correct answer for the first problem is B; for the second, E.

Abstract reasoning
The four "problem figures" in each row make a series. Find the one among the
"answer figures" that would be next in the series.

Problem figures   Answer figures

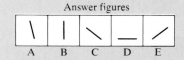

The correct answer is D.

Clerical speed and accuracy
In each test item, one of the five combinations is underlined. Find the same
combination on the answer sheet and mark it.

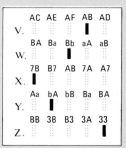

Does Intelligence Have a Single Nature?

Is it more appropriate to think of intelligence as an individual's general ability
or as a number of specific abilities? Long before David Wechsler analyzed
intelligence in terms of general and specific abilities (giving the individual an
overall IQ but also providing information about specific subcomponents of intelligence), Charles Spearman (1927) proposed that intelligence has two factors. Spearman's **two-factor theory** argued that we have both general
intelligence, which he called *g,* and a number of specific intelligences, which
he called *s.* Spearman believed that these two factors could account for an
individual's performance on an intelligence test.

    However, some factor approaches abandoned the idea of a general in-
telligence and searched for specific factors only. L. L. Thurstone (1938) proposed a **multiple-factor theory of intelligence.** Thurstone consistently came up

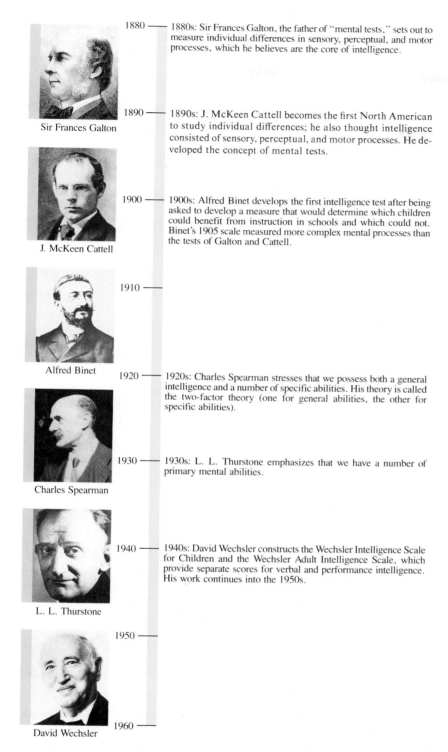

1880 — 1880s: Sir Frances Galton, the father of "mental tests," sets out to measure individual differences in sensory, perceptual, and motor processes, which he believes are the core of intelligence.

Sir Frances Galton

1890 — 1890s: J. McKeen Cattell becomes the first North American to study individual differences; he also thought intelligence consisted of sensory, perceptual, and motor processes. He developed the concept of mental tests.

J. McKeen Cattell

1900 — 1900s: Alfred Binet develops the first intelligence test after being asked to develop a measure that would determine which children could benefit from instruction in schools and which could not. Binet's 1905 scale measured more complex mental processes than the tests of Galton and Cattell.

1910 —

Alfred Binet

1920 — 1920s: Charles Spearman stresses that we possess both a general intelligence and a number of specific abilities. His theory is called the two-factor theory (one for general abilities, the other for specific abilities).

1930 — 1930s: L. L. Thurstone emphasizes that we have a number of primary mental abilities.

Charles Spearman

1940 — 1940s: David Wechsler constructs the Wechsler Intelligence Scale for Children and the Wechsler Adult Intelligence Scale, which provide separate scores for verbal and performance intelligence. His work continues into the 1950s.

L. L. Thurstone

1950 —

1960 —
David Wechsler

Figure 8.5
Pioneers in the construction of tests to measure individual differences in intelligence.

with six to twelve abilities when analyzing large numbers of intelligence test responses. He called these factors primary mental abilities. The seven primary mental abilities that most often appeared in Thurstone's analysis were: verbal comprehension, number ability, word fluency, spatial visualization, associative memory, reasoning, and perceptual speed. Figure 8.4 provides examples of the types of items included in some of Thurstone's factors.

We have seen that Spearman, Thurstone, and many others were pioneers in the development of tests to assess individual differences in intelligence. Figure 8.5 summarizes the contributions of these pioneers.

Psychology 8.1

Bird to Beethoven—Seven Frames of Mind

Larry Bird, the six-foot nine-inch superstar of the Boston Celtics, springs into motion. Grabbing a rebound off the defensive board he quickly moves across two-thirds the length of the ninety-four-foot basketball court, all the while processing the whereabouts of his five opponents and four teammates. As the crowd screams, Bird calmly looks one way, finesses his way past a defender, and whirls a behind-the-back pass to a fast-breaking teammate, who dunks the ball for two points. Is there specific intelligence to Bird's movement and perception of the spatial layout of the basketball court?

Now we turn the clock back 200 years. A tiny boy just four years of age is standing on a footstool in front of a piano keyboard practicing. At the age of six the young boy is given the honor of playing concertos and trios at a concert. The young boy is Ludwig von Beethoven, whose musical genius was evident at a young age. Did Beethoven have a specific type of intelligence, one we might call musical intelligence?

Bird and Beethoven are different types of individuals with different types of abilities. Howard Gardner (1983), in his book, *Frames of Mind,* argues that Bird's and Beethoven's talents represent two of seven intelligences that we possess. Beyond the verbal and mathematical intelligences tapped by such tests as the SAT and most traditional intelligence tests, Gardner thinks that we have the ability to spatially analyze the world, movement skills, insightful skills for analyzing ourselves, insightful skills for analyzing others, and musical skills.

Gardner believes that each of the seven intelligences can be destroyed by brain damage, that each involves unique cognitive skills, and that each shows up in exaggerated fashion in both the gifted and *idiots savants* (individuals who are mentally retarded but who have unbelievable skill in a particular domain, such as drawing, music, or computing). I remember vividly an individual from my childhood who was mentally retarded but could instantaneously respond with the correct day of the week (say Tuesday or Saturday) when given any date in history (say June 4, 1926, or December 15, 1746).

Gardner is especially interested in musical intelligence, particularly when it is exhibited at an early age. He points out that musically inclined preschool children not only have the remarkable ability to learn musical patterns easily, but that they rarely forget them. He recounts a story about Stravinsky, who as an adult could still remember the musical patterns of the tuba, drums, and piccolos of the fife-and-drum band that marched outside of his window when he was a young child.

To measure musical intelligence in young children, Gardner might ask a child to listen to a melody and then ask the child to recreate the tune on some bells he provides. He believes such evaluations can be used to develop a profile of a child's intelligence. He also believes that it is during this early time in life that parents can make an important difference in how a child's intelligence develops.

Critics of Gardner's approach point out that we have geniuses in many domains other than music. There are outstanding chess players, prize fighters, writers, politicians, physicians, lawyers, preachers, and poets, for example; yet we do not refer to chess intelligence, prize-fighter intelligence, and so on.

One recent classification, developed by Howard Gardner (1983), also includes seven components of intelligence, although they are not the same as Thurstone's seven factors. By turning to Psychology 8.1, you can read about Gardner's seven frames of mind. Clearly, there is some disagreement about whether intelligence is a general ability or a number of specific abilities, and if there are specific abilities just what those are.

Two reasons stand out why so much disagreement characterizes the approaches to intelligence (Kail & Pellegrino, 1985). First, there are many ways to analyze the same data. Different apparent solutions, which produce different psychological interpretations, can be obtained from the same data.

(a)   (b)

(a) Larry Bird, NBA superstar of the Boston Celtics. Howard Gardner believes Bird's movement skills and spatial perception are forms of intelligence. (b) Ludwig van Beethoven. Gardner also argues that musical skills, such as those shown by Beethoven, are a form of intelligence.

Second, the data obtained in separate studies differ. The critical data for interpretations of whether intelligence is a general ability or a number of specific abilities involve correlations (recall our discussion of this in chapter 1). The pattern of correlations depends on the group tested (school children, armed service recruits, or criminals, for example), the total number of tests administered, and the specific tests that are included in the battery. The outcome of studies is that the abilities thought to make up the core of intelligence may vary across different investigations. Despite these inconsistencies, evidence suggests that intelligence is *both* a general ability and a number of specific abilities.

Group Tests

The Stanford-Binet and Wechsler tests are individually administered intelligence tests. The psychologist approaches the testing situation as a structured interaction between the psychologist and the individual being tested. This provides an opportunity to sample the individual's behavior. During testing the psychologist observes the ease with which rapport is established, the level of energy and enthusiasm the individual expresses, and the degree of frustration tolerance and persistence the individual shows in performing difficult tasks. Each of these observations helps the psychologist understand the individual.

On some occasions, though, it is necessary to administer group intelligence tests, which are more convenient and economical than individual tests. For example, when World War I began, Binet's test was already popular and the idea of using tests to measure intelligence was generally accepted. The armed services thought it would be beneficial to know the intellectual abilities of its thousands of recruits. All of these individuals clearly could not be tested individually. The result was the publication of the Army Alpha Test in 1917 to measure the intelligence of this large number of individuals on a group basis. In the same year the Army Beta Test, mainly a performance test given orally, was designed for illiterate individuals who could not read the Army Alpha Test.

Though economical and convenient, group tests have some significant disadvantages. The examiner cannot establish rapport, determine the level of anxiety, and so forth when a test is given to a large group. Most testing experts recommend that when important decisions are to be made about an individual, a group intelligence test should be supplemented by other information about the individual's abilities (Anastasi, 1988). For example, many children take ability tests at school in a large group. If a decision is to be made about placing a child in a special education class, it should not be based on such group tests alone. The psychologist should administer an individual intelligence test such as Stanford-Binet or Wechsler and collect an extensive amount of additional information about the child's abilities outside of the testing situation.

A group test that many of you have taken in recent years is the Scholastic Aptitude Test (SAT). This test, taken each year by more than 1 million high school seniors, measures some of the same abilities as intelligence tests. However, it does not yield an overall IQ score; rather the SAT provides separate scores for verbal and mathematical ability. The SAT is similar to the original Binet test in that it was developed to predict success in school.

The SAT is used widely as a predictor of success in college, but it is only one of many pieces of information that determines whether a college admits a student. High school grades, the quality of the student's high school, letters of recommendation, individual interviews with the student, and special circumstances in the student's life that might have impeded academic ability are taken into account along with the SAT scores.

In recent years a controversy has developed over whether private coaching can raise a student's SAT scores. The student's verbal and mathematical abilities, which the SAT taps, have been built over years of experience and instruction. Research shows that private coaching on a short-term basis cannot help to raise SAT scores substantially. Researchers have found that on the average SAT-preparation courses raise the student's scores only 15 points on the SAT's 200 to 800 scale (Kulik, Bangert-Drowns, & Kulik, 1984; Messick & Jungeblut, 1981).

Aptitude Tests and Achievement Tests

Psychologists distinguish between an **aptitude test,** which predicts an individual's ability to learn a skill or what the individual can accomplish with training, and an **achievement test,** which measures what has been learned or what skills have been mastered. However, the distinction between these two types of tests is sometimes blurred. Both tests assess the individual's current status, both include similar types of questions, and both produce results that usually are highly correlated.

In each of your psychology classes you will take tests to measure your mastery of the class's content. These tests are achievement tests. If you major in psychology and decide to apply for graduate school, you may take the Graduate Record Exam Subject Test in Psychology, which would be used with other information (such as college grades, interviews, scores on the verbal, math, and analytical sections of the Graduate Record Exam, and so on) to predict whether you will be successful at graduate work in psychology. The Graduate Record Exam Subject Test in Psychology may contain questions similar to those from various psychology tests in undergraduate school, but this time the test items are being used to predict your performance in graduate school so it would fall into the category of aptitude test. The test's *purpose,* not its *content,* determines whether it is an aptitude or an achievement test.

The SAT has the ingredients of both an aptitude test and an achievement test. It is an achievement test in the sense that it measures what you have learned in terms of vocabulary, reading comprehension, algebraic skills, and so on; it is an aptitude test in the sense that it is used to predict your performance in college.

At this point we have covered many different facets of test construction and the nature of intelligence tests. To help your study of the main points of this discussion turn to concept table 8.1.

This woman is administering an achievement test. How does an achievement test differ from an aptitude test?

■ ■ ■ ■ ■ ■ ■ ■ ■ ■ ■ ■ ■ ■ ■ ■

Concept Table 8.1

Intelligence, Test Construction, and Intelligence Tests		
Concept	**Processes/related ideas**	**Characteristics/description**
What is intelligence?	Its nature	An abstract concept that is measured indirectly. Psychologists rely on intelligence tests to estimate intellectual processes. Verbal ability and problem-solving skills are included in a definition of intelligence. Some psychologists believe intelligence includes an ability to learn from and adapt to everyday life. Extensive effort is given to assessing individual differences in intelligence. This is called psychometrics.
How tests are constructed and evaluated	Reliability	How consistently an individual performs on a test. Three forms of reliability are test-retest, alternate forms, and split-half.
	Validity	The extent a test measures what it is intended to measure. Two methods of assessing validity are content validity and criterion validity. Criterion validity involves either concurrent or predictive validity.
	Standardization	Involves uniform procedures for administering and scoring a test; it also involves norms.
The measurement and nature of intelligence	The early history	Sir Frances Galton is the father of mental tests. He believed that sensory, perceptual, and motor processes were the core of intelligence; he tried to measure individual differences but found no formidable conclusions. James McKeen Cattell was the first North American to study individual differences; he developed the label of mental test.
	Alfred Binet and the Binet tests	Alfred Binet developed the first intelligence test, known as the 1905 Scale. He developed the concept of mental age while William Stern developed the concept of IQ. The Binet has been standardized and revised a number of times. The many revisions are called the Stanford-Binet tests. The test approximates a normal distribution and assesses more complex mental processes than those of Galton and Cattell. The current test is given to individuals from the age of two through adulthood.
	The Wechsler scales	Besides the Binet, most widely used intelligence tests. They include the WAIS-R, the WISC-R, and the WPPSI. These tests provide an overall IQ, verbal and performance IQ, and information about eleven subtests.
	Does intelligence have a single nature?	Psychologists debate whether intelligence is a general ability or a number of specific abilities. Spearman's two-factor theory and Thurstone's multiple-factor theory state that a number of specific factors are involved. Current thinking suggests that Spearman's conceptualization of intelligence as both a set of specific abilities and a general ability was right.
	Group tests	Convenient and economical, but they do not allow the examiner to monitor the testing and personally interact with the subject. The Army Alpha and Beta tests were the first widely used group intelligence tests. The SAT is a group test used in conjunction with other information to predict academic success in college.
	Aptitude tests and achievement tests	Aptitude tests predict an individual's ability to learn a skill or future performance; achievement tests assess what an individual already knows. The distinction between these tests is sometimes blurred; the SAT has the ingredients of both.

Controversies and Issues in Intelligence

Through its history, the concept of intelligence has had its share of controversies. Three that currently share the spotlight are: 1) the degree to which intelligence is due to heredity or environment; 2) the extent to which intelligence tests are culturally biased; and 3) whether intelligence is knowledge or process. We will consider each of these in turn and then discuss some of the uses and misuses of intelligence tests.

The Heredity-Environment Controversy

Arthur Jensen (1969) sparked lively and at times hostile debate when he presented his thesis that intelligence is primarily inherited. Jensen believes that environment and culture play only a minimal role in intelligence. In one of his most provocative statements, Jensen claimed that clear-cut genetic differences are present in the average intelligence of races, nationalities, and social classes. When Jensen first stated in the *Harvard Educational Review* in 1969 that lower intelligence probably was the reason that blacks do not perform as well in school as whites, he was called naive and racist. He received hate mail by the bushel and police escorted him to his classes at the University of California at Berkeley.

Jensen examined a number of studies of intelligence, many of which involved comparisons of identical and fraternal twins. Remember that identical twins have identical genetic endowments so their IQs should be similar. Fraternal twins and ordinary siblings are less similar genetically so their IQs should be less similar. Jensen found support for his argument in these studies. Studies with identical twins produced an average correlation of .82; studies of ordinary siblings produced an average correlation of .50. Note the difference of .32. To show that genetic factors are more important than environmental factors, Jensen compared identical twins reared together with those reared apart; the correlation for those reared together was .89 and for those reared apart it was .78 (a difference of .11). Jensen argued that if environmental influences were more important than genetic factors, then siblings reared apart, who experienced different environments, should have IQs much further apart.

Many scholars have criticized Jensen's work. One criticism concerns the definition of intelligence itself. Jensen believes that IQ as measured by standardized intelligence tests is a good indicator of intelligence. Critics argue that IQ tests tap only a narrow range of intelligence. Everyday problem solving, work, and social adaptability, say the critics, are important aspects of intelligence not measured by the traditional intelligence tests used in Jensen's sources. A second criticism is that most investigations of heredity and environment do not include environments that differ radically. Thus, it is not surprising that many genetic studies show environment to be a fairly weak influence on intelligence.

Jensen and others have placed the importance of heredity's influence on intelligence at about 80 percent (e.g., Loehlin & Nichols, 1976). Intelligence *is* influenced by heredity, but most psychologists do not put the figure as high as this. In one review of research, the influence was placed at 50 percent (Henderson, 1982).

Figure 8.6
The means of intelligence for natural children from white families, interracial children adopted by middle-class white families, and black children reared by their own families.

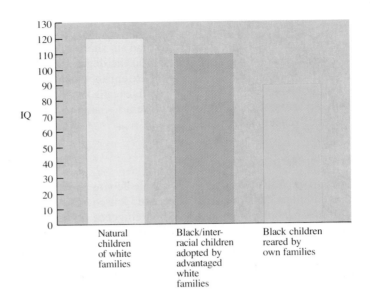

Jensen believes that two genetically based levels of learning exist. At the first level, Level I, is *associative learning,* which involves short-term memory, rote learning, attention, and simple reasoning skills. At the second level, Level II, is *cognitive learning,* which involves abstract thinking, symbolic thought, conceptual learning, and the use of language in problem solving. Jensen argues that associative learning is equally distributed across racial and national lines, but that cognitive learning is concentrated more in middle-class Anglo-American populations than in lower-class black populations. Today, Jensen (1985) continues to argue that genetic differences among races, nationalities, and social classes exist. Indeed, Jensen is such a strong advocate of heredity's influence on intelligence that he believes we could breed for intelligence. Just such an effort—The Repository for Germinal Choice—is being made today. To read more about the Nobel Prize sperm bank for breeding intelligence, mentioned at the beginning of the chapter, see Psychology 8.2.

Critics such as Sandra Scarr (1975) believe that Jensen's ideas about the influence of heredity on intelligence are simple-minded. Scarr and her colleague Richard Weinberg (1976, 1979) studied 130 black children who were adopted as infants by white, middle-class families. The IQs of a comparison group of black children from the same area who lived with their natural black parents averaged 87. As shown in figure 8.6, years after the black children were adopted by white, middle-class families, their average IQ was found to be 110. The IQs of the white children in the same families as the adopted black children also were assessed. Their IQs averaged 116. Thus, the IQs of the adopted black children were closer to their white step-siblings' IQs than to the national average for black children, which is an IQ of 85.

But before we suggest that masses of black children be placed in white, middle-class homes, Scarr and Weinberg (1976) remind us that they do not endorse IQ as the ultimate human value. Their findings do support the belief, though, that social environment plays an important role in intelligence. Other recent research on adopted children supports the environment's role in intelligence (Plomin, 1986, 1987).

Psychology 8.2

Doran, Dr. Graham, and the Repository for Germinal Choice

■ Doran (a name from the Greek word meaning "gift") learned all of the elements of speech by two years of age. An intelligence test showed that at the age of one his mental age was four (see figure 8.A). Doran was the second child born through the Nobel Prize sperm bank, which came into existence in 1980. The sperm bank was founded by Robert Graham in Escondido, California, with the intent of producing geniuses (see figure 8.B). Graham collected the sperm of Nobel Prize–winning scientists and offered it free of charge to intelligent women of good stock whose husbands were infertile.

One of the contributors to the sperm bank is physicist William Shockley, who shared the Nobel Prize in 1956 for inventing the transistor. During the 1960s and 1970s Shockley received his share of criticism for preaching the genetic basis of intelligence. Two other Nobel Prize winners have donated their sperm to the bank, but Shockley is the only one who has been identified.

More than twenty children have been sired through the sperm bank. Are the progeny prodigies?

It may be too early to tell. Except for Doran, little has been revealed about the children. Doran's genetic father was labeled "28 Red" in the sperm bank (the color apparently has no meaning). He is listed in the sperm bank's catalog as handsome, blond, and athletic, with a math SAT score of 800 and several prizes for his classical music performances. One of his few drawbacks is that he passed along to Doran an almost one-in-three chance of developing hemorrhoids. Doran's mother says that her genetic contribution goes back to the royal court of Norway and to the poet William Blake.

The odds are not high that a sperm bank will yield that special combination of factors required to produce a creative genius. George Bernard Shaw, who believed that the influence of heredity on intelligence is strong, once told a story about a beautiful woman who wrote him saying that with her body and his brain they could produce marvelous offspring. Shaw responded by saying that unfortunately the offspring might get his body and her brain.

Not surprisingly, the Nobel Prize sperm bank is heavily

criticized. Some say that brighter does not mean better. They also say that IQ is not a good indicator of social competence or human contribution to the world. Other critics say that intelligence is an elusive concept to measure and that it cannot reliably be reproduced like the sperm bank is trying to do. Visions of the German gene program of the 1930s and 1940s are created. The German Nazis believed that certain traits were superior and tried to breed children with such traits and killed people without these traits.

While Graham's Repository of Germinal Choice (as the Nobel Prize sperm bank is formally called) is strongly criticized, consider its possible contributions. The repository does provide a social service for couples who cannot conceive a child, and individuals who go to the sperm bank probably provide an enriched environment for the offspring. To once childless parents, the offspring produced by the sperm bank, or any of the other new methods of conception available, are invariably described as a miracle (Garelik, 1985).

Figure 8.A
Doran, one of the offspring born through the Repository for Germinal Choice.

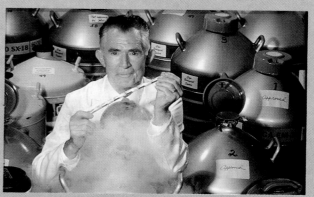

Figure 8.B
Dr. Robert Graham, founder of the Repository for Germinal Choice. Shown here with the frozen sperm of a Nobel Prize donor.

Figure 8.7
Sample items from the Chitling
Intelligence Test
Source: Adrian Dove, 1968.

1. A "gas head" is a person who has a:
   (a) fast-moving car
   (b) stable of "lace"
   (c) "process"
   (d) habit of stealing cars
   (e) long jail record for arson
2. "Bo Diddley" is a:
   (a) game for children
   (b) down-home cheap wine
   (c) down-home singer
   (d) new dance
   (e) Moejoe call
3. If a pimp is uptight with a woman who gets state aid, what does he mean when he talks about "Mother's day"?
   (a) second Sunday in May
   (b) third Sunday in June
   (c) first of every month
   (d) none of these
   (e) first and fifteenth of every month
4. A "handkerchief head" is:
   (a) a cool cat
   (b) a porter
   (c) an Uncle Tom
   (d) a hoddi
   (e) a preacher
5. If a man is called a "blood," then he is a:
   (a) fighter
   (b) Mexican-American
   (c) Negro
   (d) hungry hemophile
   (e) red man, or Indian
6. Cheap chitlings (not the kind you purchase at a frozen-food counter) will taste rubbery unless they are cooked long enough. How soon can you quit cooking them to eat and enjoy them?
   (a) forty-five minutes
   (b) two hours
   (c) twenty-four hours
   (d) one week (on a low flame)
   (e) one hour

Answers: 1. c 2. c 3. e 4. c 5. c 6. c

Are Intelligence Tests Culturally Biased?

Many of the early intelligence tests were culturally biased, favoring urban children over rural children, middle-class children over lower-class children, and white children over minority children. The norms for the early tests were based almost entirely on white, middle-class children. And some of the items themselves were culturally biased. For example, one item on an early test asked what should be done if you find a three-year-old child in the street; the correct answer was "call the police." Children from impoverished inner-city families might not choose this answer if they have had bad experiences with the police; rural children might not choose it since they may not have police nearby. Such items clearly do not measure the knowledge necessary to adapt to one's environment or to be "intelligent" in an inner-city minority neighborhood or in rural America (Scarr, 1984). The contemporary versions of intelligence tests attempt to reduce such cultural bias.

Even if the content of test items is made appropriate, another problem may exist with intelligence tests. Since many questions are verbal in nature, minority groups may encounter problems understanding the language of the questions. Minority groups often speak a language that is very different from standard English. Consequently, they may be at a disadvantage when they take intelligence tests oriented toward middle-class, white individuals. Such cultural bias in tests is dramatically underscored by tests such as the one in figure 8.7. The items in this test have been constructed to reduce the cultural disadvantage black children might experience on traditional intelligence tests.

Culture-fair tests were developed to reduce cultural bias. Two types of culture-fair tests have been devised. The first includes items that are familiar to individuals from all socioeconomic and ethnic backgrounds, or items that at least are familiar to the individuals who are taking the test. For example, a child might be asked how a bird and a dog are different, on the assumption that virtually all children have been exposed to dogs and birds.

The second type of culture-fair test has all the verbal items removed. Figure 8.8 shows a sample item from the Raven Progressive Matrices Test, which exemplifies this approach. Even though tests such as the Raven Progressive Matrices are designed to be culture-fair, individuals with more education score higher on them than those with less education (Anastasi, 1988).

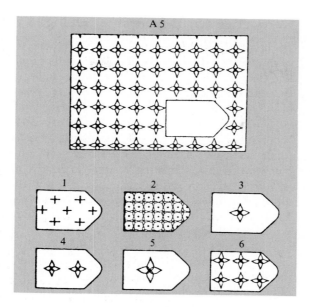

Figure 8.8
Sample item from the Raven Progressive Matrices Test. The individual is presented with a matrix arrangement of symbols, such as the one at the top of this figure, and must then complete the matrix by selecting the appropriate missing symbol from a group of symbols.

One test that takes into account the socioeconomic background of children is the SOMPA, which stands for System of Multicultural Pluralistic Assessment (Mercer & Lewis, 1978). This test can be given to children from five to eleven years of age. SOMPA was designed for children from low-income families. Instead of relying on a single test, SOMPA is based on information about four different areas of the child's life: 1) verbal and nonverbal intelligence in the traditional intelligence test mold, assessed by the WISC-R; 2) social and economic background of family, obtained through a one-hour parent interview; 3) social adjustment to school, evaluated by an adaptive behavior inventory completed by parents; and 4) physical health, determined by a medical examination.

The Kaufman Assessment Battery for Children (K-ABC) has been trumpeted as an improvement over past culture-fair tests (Kaufman & Kaufman, 1983). It can be given to children from two and a half to twelve and a half years of age. This test is standardized on a more representative sample, which includes more minority and handicapped children, than are most tests. The intelligence portion focuses less on language than the Stanford-Binet, and the test includes an achievement section with subtests for arithmetic and reading. Nonetheless, like other culture-fair tests, the K-ABC has its detractors (Bracken, 1985; Keith, 1985).

The Iatmul people of Papua, New Guinea. Their intelligence involves the ability to remember the names of many clans.

Culture-fair tests remind us that traditional intelligence tests are probably culturally biased, yet culture-fair tests do not provide a satisfactory alternative. Constructing a truly culture-fair intelligence test, one that rules out the role of experience emanating from socioeconomic and ethnic background, has been difficult and may be impossible. Consider, for example, that the intelligence of the Iatmul people of Papua, New Guinea, involves the ability to remember the names of some 10,000 to 20,000 clans; by contrast, the intelligence of islanders in the widely dispersed Caroline Islands involves the talent of navigating by the stars.

Knowledge versus Process in Intelligence

In chapter 7 we discussed the cognitive revolution in psychology. Much of this cognitive revolution has emphasized the processing of information rather than knowledge itself. The information processing approach to intelligence raises two interesting questions about intelligence: What are the fundamental types of information processing abilities? and How do these develop?

Few of us would deny that changes in both processing and knowledge occur as we develop. However, a consensus does not exist on something more fundamental. We accumulate knowledge as we grow from an infant to an adult, but what might be growing is simply a reserve of processing capacity. That is, your greater processing capacity as an adult than as a child might be what allows you to learn more. By contrast, possibly your greater processing capacity as an adult is a consequence of your greater knowledge, which allows you to process information more effectively.

It is not easy to choose between these two possibilities. Frank Keil (1984) calls this the great **structure-process dilemma** of intelligence. What are the mechanisms of intelligence and how do they develop? Does information processing ability change or does knowledge and expertise change? Or do both occur?

To make the structure-process dilemma somewhat more concrete, consider a simple computer metaphor. Suppose we have two computers, each of which is capable of solving multiplication problems (e.g., 13 × 24, 45 × 21), but one computer works faster than the other. What is the explanation? One possibility is that the faster computer has a greater "capacity" (that is, core memory), in which to do mental work. This greater core memory, which psychologists often refer to as *working memory,* might allow the computer to work on two or more components of a problem at once.

Another explanation is that the faster computer might have a greater store of relevant knowledge. Perhaps it has in its data bank (long-term memory) a complete multiplication table up to 99 × 99. The slower computer might have a table up to 12 × 12 (as do most humans). The faster computer need not be fundamentally faster—its subroutines may be relatively slow—but it is able to perform the multiplication task because of knowledge, not because of processing capacity.

Explaining intelligence is similar to explaining the difference between the fast and slow computers—is processing or knowledge responsible for how intelligence changes with age? Based on research on memory, it seems likely that the answer is both (Zembar & Naus, 1985). If so, the essential task for researchers is to determine the ways that processing and knowledge interact in the course of intellectual development.

The modern information processing perspectives do not argue that knowledge is unimportant. Rather, many information processing psychologists believe that attention should be given to the knowledge base generated by intellectual processes. One information processing approach to intelligence that recognizes the importance of both process and knowledge is R. J. Sternberg's (1986) model. To learn more about Sternberg's view of intelligence, turn to Psychology 8.3.

If we believe that information processing activities such as attention, memory, and problem solving are important aspects of intelligence, an important question is, Can these information processing skills be taught? Joan Baron and R. J. Sternberg (1987) believe we can teach intelligence, especially that which is practical in nature. They are interested in teaching individuals to think in less irrational ways. They say that we should be more critical of the first ideas that pop into our minds; we should be taught how to think longer about problems and to search in more organized ways for evidence to support our views.

The emphasis on teaching information processing skills is evident at several major universities. Carnegie-Mellon and UCLA, for example, encourage students to take courses in information processing that include instruction in how to solve problems and think logically. However, teaching information processing skills has limits (Kamil, 1987). Remember that cramming for the SAT only raises scores slightly.

When you were in elementary and secondary school did any of your teachers work with you to improve your memory strategies? Beyond the first few grades of elementary school did your teachers help you improve your reading skills? Did they discuss ways that imagery and organization might help you process information more efficiently? If you are like most college students, the answers to these questions are all no.

Perhaps if a concentrated effort were made to instruct individuals over the long term—from kindergarten through college—in ways to improve information processing skills we would be more efficient adult learners. At this time, though, we do not have an information processing skills curriculum that could be taught in a developmental fashion, although efforts in that direction have begun (e.g., Gagne, 1985; Glazer, 1982; White, in press). Some experts, though, believe that we cannot teach attention, memory, and problem-solving skills in general; rather, information processing skills in specific domains, such as geometry or English, should be taught. Nonetheless, most information processing psychologists agree that individuals would benefit greatly from an infusion of information processing skills teaching throughout our educational system.

The Use and Misuse of Intelligence Tests

Psychological tests are tools. Like all tools, their effectiveness depends on the knowledge, skill, and integrity of the user. A hammer can be used to build a beautiful kitchen cabinet or it can be used as a weapon of assault. Like a hammer, psychological tests can be used for positive purposes or they can be badly abused. It is important for both the test constructor and the test examiner to be familiar with the current state of scientific knowledge about intelligence and intelligence tests (Anastasi, 1988).

Even though they have limitations, tests of intelligence are among psychology's most widely used tools. To be effective, though, intelligence tests must be viewed realistically. They should not be thought of as a fixed, unchanging indicator of an individual's intelligence. They also should be used in conjunction with other information about an individual and not relied on as the sole indicator of intelligence. For example, an intelligence test should not be used as the sole indicator of whether a child is placed in a special education or gifted class. The child's developmental history, medical background, performance in school, social competencies, and family experiences should be taken into account, too.

The single number provided by many IQ tests can easily lead to stereotypes and expectations about an individual. Many individuals do not know how to interpret the results of intelligence tests and sweeping generalizations about an individual are too often made on the basis of an IQ score. For example, consider that you are a teacher in the teacher's lounge the day after school has started in the fall. You mention a student—Johnny Jones—and a fellow teacher remarks that she had Johnny in class last year; she comments that he was a real dunce and points out that his IQ is 78. You cannot help but remember this information and it may lead to thoughts that Johnny Jones is not very bright so it is useless to spend much time teaching him. In this way, IQ scores are misused and stereotypes are formed (Rosenthal & Jacobsen, 1968).

Psychology 8.3

Analytical Ann, Insightful Todd, and Street-Smart Art

■ R. J. Sternberg (1985, 1986, 1987) believes each of us has three types of intelligence and he calls his view the **triarchic theory of intelligence.** Consider Ann, who scores high on traditional intelligence tests such as the Stanford-Binet and is a star analytical thinker. Consider Todd, who does not have the best test results but has an insightful and creative mind. And consider Art, a street-smart individual who has learned how to deal in practical ways with his world, although his scores on traditional intelligence tests are low.

Sternberg calls Ann's analytical thinking and abstract reasoning *componential intelligence;* it is the closest to what we call intelligence in this chapter and what commonly is measured by intelligence tests. Todd's insightful and creative thinking is called *experiential intelligence* by Sternberg. And Art's street smarts and practical know-how is called *contextual intelligence* by Sternberg (see figure 8.C).

In Sternberg's view of componential intelligence, the basic unit in intelligence is a *component,* simply defined as a basic unit of information processing. Sternberg believes that such components include those used to acquire or store information, to retain or retrieve

information, to transfer information, to plan, make decisions, and solve problems, and to carry out problem-solving strategies or translate our thoughts into performance. Notice the similarity of these components to our description of how memory and thinking work in chapters 6 and 7.

The second part of Sternberg's model focuses on experience. According to Sternberg, an intelligent individual has the ability to solve new problems quickly, but also she learns how to solve familiar problems in an automatic, rote way so that her mind is free to handle other problems that require insight and creativity.

The third part of the model involves practical knowledge—such as how to get out of trouble, how to replace a fuse, and how to get along with people. Sternberg calls this kind of practical knowledge *tacit knowledge.* It includes all of the important information about getting along in the real world that you are not taught in school. He believes that tacit knowledge is more important for success in life than explicit, or "book," knowledge.

Tacit knowledge is difficult to measure, although Sternberg has assembled items that he thinks measure it. Some of the items

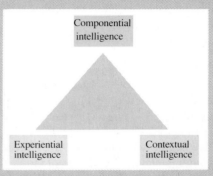

Figure 8.C
The triarchic model of intelligence.

assess how an individual responds to dilemmas and problem-solving circumstances in domains such as business, politics, and science. Some of the items also assess sensitivity to nonverbal cues (see figure 8.D). Nonverbal cues to consider include: pleasantness of facial expression, the extent to which individuals look at each other, the degree individuals lean toward each other, how relaxed they are, how naturally (comfortably) each individual holds his or her arms and legs, how tense their hands are, what their body builds are, what their socioeconomic standing is, how far apart their bodies are, how much physical contact they have, and how similar their appearances are.

Ability tests can help a teacher divide children into homogeneous groups who function at roughly the same level in math or reading so they can be taught the same concepts together. However, when children are placed in tracks, such as "advanced," "intermediate," and "low," extreme caution needs to be taken. Periodic assessment of the groups is needed, especially with the "low" group. Ability tests measure *current* performance, and maturational changes or enriched environmental experiences may produce advances in a child's intelligence that require he be moved to a higher group.

Figure 8.D
These items are used by Sternberg to assess practical intelligence; they evaluate the individual's ability to decode nonverbal cues. The two pictures on the left are supervisor-supervisee pairs; the two pictures on the right are couples. Which is the supervisor and supervisee in the two photos on the left? Which of the two couples is genuine and which pair does not really go together in the two photos on the right?

We have a tendency in our culture to consider intelligence or a high IQ as the ultimate human value. It is important to keep in mind that our value as humans includes other important matters, such as a consideration of others, positive close relationships, and competence in social situations. The verbal ability and problem-solving skills measured on traditional tests of intelligence are only one part of human competence.

■ ■ ■ ■ ■ ■ ■ ■ ■ ■ ■ ■ ■ ■ ■ ■ ■

Concept Table 8.2

Controversies and Issues in Intelligence		
Concept	**Processes/related ideas**	**Characteristics/description**
The heredity-environment controversy	The nature of the controversy	In the late 1960s Jensen argued that intelligence is approximately 80 percent hereditary and that genetic differences exist in the average intelligence of races, nationalities, and social classes. Intelligence *is* influenced by heredity, but not as strongly as Jensen believed. Scarr and Weinberg's research on adopted black children revealed the importance of the social environment.
Cultural bias in intelligence tests	The nature of the bias	Early tests favored middle-class, white, urban children. Current tests attempt to reduce such bias. Culture-fair tests are an alternative to traditional tests; most psychologists believe they cannot replace the traditional tests. The SOMPA and K-ABC have tried to take cultural bias heavily into account.
Knowledge versus process	The structure-process dilemma in intelligence	The mechanisms of intelligence and its development are both those of changing information processing abilities and changing expertise and knowledge.
	Sternberg's triarchic model of intelligence	Includes an emphasis on both information processing and knowledge. He believes intelligence comes in three forms: componential, experiential, and practical.
	Can information processing skills be taught?	Baron and Sternberg believe they can, especially when practical intelligence is involved. Information processing psychologists believe there should be an infusion of their approach in the schools. There probably are some genetic limitations.
The use and misuse of intelligence tests	What are some of the uses and misuses?	Despite limitations, when used by a judicious examiner, tests can be valuable tools for determining individual differences in intelligence. The tests should be used with other information about the individual. IQ scores can produce unfortunate stereotypes and expectations. Ability tests can help divide children into homogeneous groups. However, periodic testing should be done. Intelligence or a high IQ is not necessarily the ultimate human value.

Despite their limitations, when used judiciously by a competent examiner, intelligence tests do provide valuable information about individuals. There are not many alternatives to these tests. Subjective judgments about individuals simply reintroduce the bias the tests were designed to eliminate.

We have looked at two rather long-standing controversies in intelligence—the heredity-environment issue and the extent to which intelligent tests are culturally biased—and one recent controversy—the knowledge-process dilemma. We also considered the uses and misuses of intelligence tests. A summary of these controversies and issues is presented in concept table 8.2.

The Extremes of Intelligence

The atypical individual has always been of interest to psychologists. Intellectual atypicality has intrigued many psychologists and drawn them to study both the mentally retarded and the gifted.

Mental Retardation

The most distinctive feature of mental retardation is inadequate intellectual functioning. Long before formal tests were developed to assess intelligence, the mentally retarded were identified by a lack of age-appropriate skills in learning and caring for oneself. With the development of intelligence tests more emphasis was placed on IQ as an indicator of mental retardation. But it is not unusual to find two retarded individuals with the same low IQ, one of whom is married, employed, and involved in the community and the other requiring constant supervision in an institution. These differences in social competence led psychologists to include deficits in adaptive behavior in their definition of mental retardation. The currently accepted definition of **mental retardation** refers to an individual who has a low IQ, usually below 70 on a traditional test of intelligence, and who has difficulty adapting to everyday life. About 5 million Americans fit this definition of mental retardation (Zigler, 1987).

There are different classifications of mental retardation. About 80 percent of the mentally retarded fall into the mild category, with IQs of 50 to 70. About 12 percent are classified as moderately retarded, with IQs of 35 to 49; these individuals can attain a second-grade level of skills and may be able to support themselves as adults through some type of labor. About 7 percent of the mentally retarded are in the severe category, with IQs of 20 to 34; these individuals learn to talk and engage in very simple tasks, but they require extensive supervision. Only 1 percent of the mentally retarded fall into the profound classification with IQs below 20; they are in constant need of supervision.

What causes mental retardation? The causes are divided into two categories: organic and cultural-familial. Individuals with **organic retardation** are retarded because of a genetic disorder or brain damage; *organic* refers to the tissues or organs of the body, so there is some physical damage that has taken place in organic retardation. Down's syndrome, a form of mental retardation (see figure 8.9), occurs when an extra chromosome is present in the individual's genetic make-up, for example. It is not known why the extra chromosome is present, but it may involve the health of the female ovum or the male sperm. Although those who suffer organic retardation are found across the spectrum of IQ distribution, most have IQs between 0 and 50.

Individuals with **cultural-familial retardation** make up the majority of the mentally retarded population; they have no evidence of organic damage or brain dysfunction and IQs range from 50 to 70. Psychologists seek to find the cause of this type of retardation in the impoverished environments these individuals probably have experienced (Broman, Bien, & Shaughnessy, in press). Even with organic retardation, though, it is wise to think about the contributions of genetic-environment interaction. Parents with low IQs not only may be more likely to transmit genes for low intelligence to their offspring but also tend to provide them with a less enriched environment.

Figure 8.9
A Down's syndrome child. What causes a child to develop Down's syndrome? In which major classification of mental retardation does the condition fall?

Giftedness

Conventional wisdom has identified some individuals in all cultures and historical periods as gifted because they have talents not evident in the majority of the people. Despite this widespread recognition of the gifted, psychologists have difficulty reaching a consensus on the precise definition and measurement of giftedness. Some experts view the gifted as the top end of a continuum of intelligence (Humphreys, 1985; Zigler & Farber, 1985). Some of these advocates view this ability as a unitary characteristic that is perhaps hereditary. Others see the gifted as individuals who express specific talents that have been nurtured environmentally (Wallach, 1985). A comprehensive definition of **gifted** is an individual with well-above-average intelligence (an IQ of 120 or more) and/or a superior talent for something. Most school systems emphasize intellectual superiority and academic aptitude when selecting children for special instruction; however, they rarely consider competence in the visual and performing arts (art, drama, dance), psychomotor abilities (tennis, golf, basketball), or other special aptitudes.

A classic study of the gifted was begun by Lewis Terman (1925) more than sixty years ago. Terman studied approximately 1,500 children whose Stanford-Binet IQs averaged 150. His goal was to follow these children through their adult lives—the study will not be complete until the year 2010.

The accomplishments of the 1,500 children in Terman's study are remarkable. Of the 800 males, 78 have obtained PhDs (they include two past presidents of the American Psychological Association), 48 have earned MDs, and 85 have been granted law degrees. Nearly all of these figures are ten to thirty times greater than found among 800 men of the same age chosen randomly from the overall population (Getzels & Dillon, 1973). These findings challenge the commonly held belief that the intellectually gifted are disturbed emotionally or maladjusted socially. This belief is based on striking instances of mental disturbances among the gifted. Sir Frances Galton suffered from an anxiety disorder and had two nervous breakdowns, for example. Sir Isaac Newton, Van Gogh, da Vinci, Socrates, and Poe all had emotional problems. But these are the exception rather than the rule; no relation between giftedness and mental disturbance in general has been found. A number of recent studies support Terman's conclusion that, if anything, the gifted tend to be more mature and have fewer emotional problems than others (Janos & Robinson, 1985).

In another investigation, individuals with exceptional talents as adults were interviewed about what they believe contributed to their giftedness (Bloom, 1983). The 120 individuals had excelled in one of six fields—concert pianists and sculptors (arts), Olympic swimmers and tennis champions (psychomotor), and research mathematicians and research neurologists (cognitive). They said the development of their exceptional accomplishments required special environmental support, excellent teaching, and motivational encouragement. Each experienced years of special attention under the tutelage and supervision of a remarkable series of teachers and coaches. They also received extensive support and encouragement from their parents. All of these stars devoted exceptional amounts of time to practice and training, easily outdistancing the amount of the time spent in all other activities combined.

Creativity

Most of us would like to be both gifted and creative. Why was Thomas Edison able to invent so many things? Was he simply more intelligent than most individuals? Did he spend long hours toiling away in private? Somewhat surprisingly, when Edison was a young boy his teacher told him that he was too dumb to learn anything! Other examples of famous individuals whose creative genius went unnoticed when they were young include Walt Disney, who was fired from a newspaper job because he did not have any good ideas; Enrico Caruso, whose music teacher told him that his voice was terrible; and Winston Churchill, who failed one year of secondary school. Among the reasons such individuals are underestimated as youngsters is the difficulty of defining and measuring creativity.

The prevailing belief of experts who study intelligence and creativity is that the two are not the same thing (Monroe, 1988; Wallach, 1985). One distinction is between **convergent thinking,** which produces one correct answer, and **divergent thinking,** which produces many different answers to the same question (Guilford, 1967). For example, this intellectual problem-solving task has one correct answer and thus requires convergent thinking: "How many quarters will you get in return for sixty dimes?" But this question has many possible answers and requires divergent thinking: "What are some unique

1. *Sketches:* Add just enough detail to the circle below to make a recognizable object (two examples of acceptable responses are shown).

2. *Word fluency:* Write as many words as you can think of with the first and last letters R_____M ("rim" would be one).

3. *Name grouping:* Classify the following six names in as many different ways as you can (a person might group 1, 3 and 4 together because each has two syllables).

 1. GERTRUDE   2. BILL
 3. ALEX   4. CARRIE
 5. BELLE   6. DON

4. *Making objects:* Using two or more of the forms shown below, make a face. Now make a lamp (examples of good responses are shown).

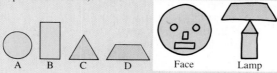

Figure 8.10
Sample items from Guilford's test of creative thinking.

things that can be done with a paper clip?" A degree of creativity is needed to answer this question. Other examples of divergent thinking are generated by the following: Name words that belong to a particular class. For example, name as many objects as you can that weigh less than one pound. Even when you are not asked to, do you give divergent answers? For example, if you are asked what unique things can be done with a paper clip do you spontaneously generate different categories of use for the paper clip? For more examples of items on tests of creativity turn to figure 8.10.

Creativity is the ability to think about something in a novel and unusual way and to come up with unique solutions to problems. When individuals in the arts and sciences who fit this description are asked what enables them to produce their creative works, they say that they generate large amounts of associative content when solving problems and that they have the freedom to entertain a wide range of possible solutions in a playful manner (Wallach & Kogan, 1965).

How strongly is creativity related to intelligence? A certain level of intelligence seems to be required to be creative in most fields, but many highly intelligent people (as measured by IQ tests) are not very creative.

In this chapter we have discussed many different aspects of intelligence. In the next section we turn our attention to development across the life cycle, beginning in chapter 9 with the infant and childhood years.

Summary

I. **What Is Intelligence?**
Intelligence is an abstract concept that can only be measured indirectly; for the most part, psychologists have relied on intelligence tests to estimate intellectual processes. Verbal ability and problem-solving skills are described by both experts and lay people as components of intelligence. Some psychologists believe that the definition of intelligence should include the ability to learn and adapt to experiences in everyday life. Extensive effort has been given to assessing individual differences in intelligence. This field is called psychometrics.

II. **How Tests Are Constructed and Evaluated**
Three important aspects of test construction are reliability, validity, and standardization. Reliability refers to how consistently an individual performs on a test. Three measures of a test's reliability are test-retest, alternate forms, and split-half. Validity is the extent to which a test measures what it is intended to measure. Two main measures of validity are content validity and criterion validity; criterion validity involves either concurrent validity or predictive validity. Standardization focuses on the development of uniform procedures for administering and scoring a test and norms.

III. **The Early History of Intelligence Testing**
Sir Frances Galton is regarded as the father of mental tests. He believed that sensory, perceptual, and motor processes were the core of intelligence; he tried to measure individual differences in these processes but arrived at no formidable conclusions. James McKeen Cattell was the first North American to study individual differences; he developed the label of mental test. Alfred Binet developed the first intelligence test; it became known as the 1905 Scale. Binet developed the concept of mental age while William Stern developed the concept of IQ. Over the years the Binet test has been standardized and revised many times. These revisions are called the Stanford-Binet tests. The Binet test approximates a normal distribution. It assessed more complex mental processes than the tests of Galton and Cattell. The current edition can be given to individuals from the age of two through adulthood.

IV. **The Wechsler Scales**
Besides the Binet, the most widely used intelligence tests are the Wechsler scales. They include the WAIS-R, the WISC-R, and the WPPSI. These tests provide not only an overall IQ, but also verbal and performance IQs and information about eleven subtests.

V. **Does Intelligence Have a Single Nature?**
Through the years, psychologists have debated whether intelligence is a general ability or a number of specific abilities. Spearman's two-factor theory and Thurstone's multiple-factor theory argued that a number of factors were involved; Spearman also thought that intelligence was a general ability. Current thinking suggests that Spearman's conceptualization of intelligence as both a set of specific abilities and a general ability was right.

VI. **Group Tests and Aptitude and Achievement Tests**
Individual tests allow the psychologist to monitor the testing situation closely and personally interact with the subject; group tests are more convenient and economical, but they do not allow the examiner such careful evaluation. The Army Alpha and Beta Tests were the first widely used group intelligence tests. The SAT is a group test that is used in conjunction with other information to predict academic success in college. Aptitude tests predict an individual's ability to learn a skill or to predict future performance; achievement tests assess what an individual has learned. The distinction between these two types of tests is sometimes blurred; the SAT has the ingredients of both.

VII. **The Heredity-Environment Controversy and Cultural Bias**
The heredity-environment controversy heated up in the late 1960s when Arthur Jensen published a paper arguing that intelligence is approximately 80 percent hereditary and that genetic differences are present in the average intelligence of races, nationalities, and social classes. Intelligence *is* influenced by heredity, but not as strongly as Jensen believed. Scarr and Weinberg's research on adopted black children revealed the importance of the social environment to intelligence. The early intelligence tests were culturally biased, favoring middle-class, white, urban children. Current intelligence tests attempt to reduce such bias. Culture-fair tests are an alternative to traditional intelligence tests, but most psychologists believe they cannot replace the traditional tests. The SOMPA and K-ABC are two tests that take cultural bias heavily into account.

VIII. **Knowledge versus Process**
Are the mechanisms of intelligence and its development those of changing information processing abilities, or are they those of changing expertise and knowledge? The answer probably is both. Sternberg's model includes an emphasis on both information processing and knowledge. He believes intelligence comes in three forms: componential, experiential, and practical. Baron and Sternberg believe that information processing skills can be taught, especially when practical intelligence is involved. Information processing psychologists believe there should be an infusion of their approach in the schools. There probably are some genetic limitations on how extensively these skills can be taught.

IX. The Use and Misuse of Intelligence Tests

Despite their limitations, when used by a judicious examiner, intelligence tests are valuable tools for determining individual differences in intelligence. The tests should be used in conjunction with other information about the individual. IQ scores can produce unfortunate stereotypes and expectations about intelligence. Ability tests can help divide children into homogeneous groups (reading, math) so they can be taught the same concepts together. However, when children are placed in tracks, periodic testing should be done. Intelligence or a high IQ is not necessarily the ultimate human value; there are a number of routes to human competence.

X. The Extremes of Intelligence

A mentally retarded individual has a low IQ, usually below 70 on a traditional intelligence test, and has difficulty adapting to everyday life. Different classifications of mental retardation exist. The two main causes of retardation are organic and cultural-familial. Both giftedness and creativity are difficult to define. We defined giftedness as an individual with well-above-average intelligence (an IQ of 120 or above) and/or a superior talent for something. We defined creativity as the ability to think about something in a novel and unusual way and to come up with unique solutions to problems.

Key Terms

Suggested Readings

Anastasi, A. (1988). *Psychological testing* (6th ed.). New York: Macmillan. This widely used text on psychological testing provides extensive information about test construction, test evaluation, and the nature of intelligence testing.

Fancher, R. E. (1985). *The intelligence men: Makers of the IQ controversy.* New York: Norton. Fancher's book includes an extensive portrayal of the history of intelligence testing—many insights and detailed descriptions of the lives of the intelligence test makers are provided.

Horowitz, F. D., & O'Brien, M. (Eds.). (1985). *The gifted and the talented.* Washington, D.C.: The American Psychological Association. This volume pulls together what we currently know about the gifted and the talented. Experts have contributed chapters on the nature of the gifted and the diverse topics involved.

Kail, R., & Pellegrino, J. W. (1985). *Human intelligence.* New York: W. H. Freeman. This book brings together a number of different perspectives on human intelligence; it includes separate chapters on the psychometric and information processing approaches.

Sattler, J. M. (1982). *Assessment of children's intelligence and special abilities.* Boston: Allyn & Bacon. Extensive information is provided about the measurement of children's intelligence, both for normal children and those from special populations, such as the mentally retarded.

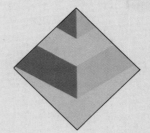

Development and the Life Cycle

*The first cry of a newborn baby
in Chicago or Zamboango, in
Amsterdam or Rangoon, has
the same pitch and key, each
saying, "I am! I have come
through! I belong! I am a
member of the Family." . . .
babies arriving, suckling,
growing into youths restless
and questioning. Then as
grown-ups they seek and hope.
They mate, toil, fish, quarrel,
sing, fight, pray.*

—*Carl Sandburg*

Chapter 9

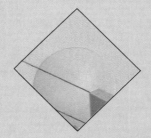

Infant and Child Development

■■

The childhood shows the man as morning shows the day.

—*Milton*

■■

Images of Infant and Child Development

Each weekday at 8 A.M., Ellen Smith takes her daughter, Tanya, to the day-care center at Brookhaven College in Dallas. Then Mrs. Smith goes to work and returns in the evening to take Tanya home. Mrs. Smith says Tanya has excelled in day care; now, after three years at the center, Tanya is adventuresome, interacts confidently with peers, and gets along well with adults.

In Los Angeles, day care has been a series of horrors for Barbara Jones. After two years of unpleasant experiences with sitters, day-care centers, and day-care homes, Mrs. Jones quit her job as a successful real-estate agent to stay home and take care of her two-year-old daughter, Gretchen. "I didn't want to sacrifice my baby for my job," said Mrs. Jones, who was unable to find good substitute care in day-care homes. When she placed Gretchen in a day-care center, she said she felt like her daughter was being treated like a piece of merchandise—dropped off and picked up.

Many parents worry whether day care will adversely affect their children. They fear that day-care centers lessen the emotional attachment of the infant to them, retard the infant's cognitive development, fail to teach the child how to control anger, and allow the child to be unduly influenced by other children.

The number of women in the labor force with children under the age of six increased from 2.5 million to 4.5 million in 1986. And the number of such women with no spouse present increased from .42 million in 1960 to 1.9 million in 1986. About 2 million children currently receive formal licenced day care, and more than 5 million attend nursery school. Day care has become a basic need of the American family (Birns & Daye, 1988).

Excellent day care consists of an infant-teacher ratio of three to one, teacher aids trained to care for infants, and a safe environment with many stimulating toys. It should include regular mealtimes, adequate structure during the day, appropriate nap and quiet time, as well as a staff willing to talk with parents. Much day care, though, is unregulated and consists of whatever arrangements a harried parent can make.

Research on day care indicates that children who receive quality care do not show any developmental deficits and sometimes get along better with their peers than children reared exclusively at home (Scarr, 1986). However, children who receive poor quality day care often evidence poor self-control and insecure attachment (Belsky, 1987b, in press; Clarke-Stewart & Fein, 1983).

Day care is but one of many provocative topics in the development of children. As we explore the world of the child, you will learn about how children have been viewed through history and about their development from the time sperm meets egg until adolescence. ■

Children in History

During the Middle Ages, the goal of child rearing was salvation—the purpose of parenting was to remove sin from the child's life. This perspective, called **original sin,** argued that children are born bad; only through the constraints of parenting or salvation would children become competent adults. During the

Renaissance, from the fourteenth to the seventeenth centuries, philosophers speculated at length about the nature of children and how they should be reared. Two contrasting views about the nature of the child emerged during the Renaissance—the **tabula rasa** and **innate goodness** views. Near the end of the seventeenth century, John Locke argued that children are not innately evil, but instead they are like a "blank tablet," a *tabula rasa* as he called it. Locke believed that childhood experiences are important in determining adult characteristics; he advised parents to spend time with their children and to help them become contributing members of society.

During the eighteenth century, Jean-Jacques Rousseau agreed with Locke that children are not basically evil, but he did not think they were a blank tablet either. Rousseau said children are inherently good, and because of their innate goodness, they should be permitted to grow naturally with little parental monitoring or constraint.

The original sin, tabula rasa, and innate goodness views of the nature of a child initiated the nature-nurture debate in child development. The original sin and innate goodness views place a premium on nature; the tabula rasa view emphasizes nurture.

As psychology developed as a science, the biological views of Charles Darwin influenced early theorizing about children. Darwin himself is credited with making the scientific study of children respectable when he developed a baby journal for recording systematic observations of an infant's behavior. Both G. Stanley Hall and Sigmund Freud believed the child went through developmental stages, which were heavily controlled by biological maturation. In the spirit of the original sin view, Freud argued that children come into the world as a bundle of sexual and aggressive instincts. Arnold Gesell (1928) also stressed that a child's development unfolded according to a genetic blueprint. Gesell observed the characteristics of children at different ages in highly systematic ways. Figure 9.1 shows Gesell in the photographic dome he used to watch children without interrupting them.

But the behaviorist John Watson (1930) proposed a view of children dramatically different from Darwin, Hall, Freud, and Gesell. Watson argued that children could be shaped into whatever society wanted, in line with the tabula rasa view. Watson stressed that parents were too soft on children; quit cuddling and smiling at babies so much, he told parents.

Ideas about the nature of child development have been like a pendulum, swinging between nature and nurture. Today we are witnessing a surge of interest in the biological underpinnings of development, probably because the pendulum had swung too far in the direction of thinking that development was due exclusively to environmental experiences (Hinde & Stevenson-Hinde, 1987).

Sociopolitical events and issues also spurred research on childhood (Alexander, 1987; White, 1985; Zigler, 1987). Developmental psychology flourishes when there is substantial national activity on behalf of children and families. The war on poverty in the 1960s led to the formation of Project Head Start, designed to give children from low-income families an early opportunity to learn. In the 1980s the changing nature of society has motivated research interest in the effects of divorce on children, working mothers and day care, and gender differences.

Today we think of childhood as a highly eventful and unique period of life that lays the foundation for the adult years and yet is very different from them. We value childhood as a special time of growth and we invest great resources in caring for and educating children.

Figure 9.1
Gesell's photographic dome. Gesell is the man inside the dome with the infant. Cameras rode on metal tracks at the top of the dome and were moved as needed to record the child's activities. Others, such as the female in this photo, could observe from outside the dome without being seen by the child.

What Is Development?

What do we mean when we speak of a child's "development"? Psychologists use the term **development** to mean a pattern of movement or change that begins at conception and continues throughout the life cycle. Most development involves growth, although it can also consist of decay (as in the death process). The pattern of movement in development is complex because it is the product of several processes—biological, cognitive, and social.

There are two enduring issues in the study of child development. First is the effect of heredity weighed against the effect of environment. Child development includes not only genetic and biological influences but environmental experiences as well, as we discussed in chapter 2. A second key issue in the extent development is *continuous* or *discontinuous;* this issue concerns the degree to which later development depends on earlier development and experiences. Is the behavior of an eight-year-old child due to what is happening to him right now or to experiences in the first five years of his life? If he is maladjusted and does not get along with his peers, is it because his parents argue and are considering a divorce, or is it because he was malnourished as an infant?

For many years, it was believed that early experiences, especially in the first five years of life, determined development later in life, even in adulthood. This view was proposed by Freud and has continued to exert a strong influence. But as developmental psychologists examine the entire life cycle more extensively, they question whether early experience is the sole or even primary determinant of later development. While it is agreed that early experiences are important prototypes for the way later experiences are handled, the effects of early experiences may not be irreversible. Possibly good parenting at age eight can compensate for bad parenting at age one. Perhaps a good marriage can make up for a bad childhood.

A classic longitudinal study (Thomas & Chess, 1987; Thomas, Chess, & Birch, 1970) set out to describe different characteristics of infants, such as how extraverted or introverted they were. As the children were followed through childhood and adolescence, it became apparent that some showed more continuity in their behavior than others. Changes in the environment of certain children led to less continuity in their behavior. For example, as an infant and young child, David was active, cheerful, and friendly. His parents were intensely competitive and placed a great deal of pressure on David to succeed academically. When he did not do well in school, they blamed his teachers. Picking up on these cues, David never assumed responsibility for his behavior. By the time he reached college, he was apathetic and unmotivated. In David's case, little continuity between his behavior as a child and as a college student was apparent. If his parents had provided a more relaxed, supportive family environment for achievement and encouraged self-responsibility, greater continuity in David's behavior would have occurred (Chess & Thomas, 1977).

To summarize, if you believe early experiences determine later development you are taking a continuity stance; by contrast, if you think we have a strong capacity for change later in development, you are taking a discontinuity stance. As with most important issues in psychology, support for either extreme is not solid. Just as development is influenced by both heredity and experience, so is it characterized by both continuity and discontinuity.

The Prenatal Period and Birth

At one time you were an organism floating around in a sea of fluid inside your mother's womb. From the moment you were conceived until the moment you were born, some astonishing developments took place.

The Course of Prenatal Development

Imagine how you came to be you. Out of thousands of eggs and millions of sperm, one egg and one sperm united to produce you. Had the union of the sperm and egg come a day or even an hour earlier or later, you might have been very different—maybe even the opposite sex!

Conception occurs when a single sperm cell from the male unites with the ovum (egg) in the female's fallopian tube; this process also is called fertilization. Not many years ago, infertility meant that couples would never have a child. But the age of test-tube babies has arrived; as discussed in Psychology 9.1, today's infertile couple has a number of options.

The fertilized egg is called a **zygote;** it receives one-half of its chromosomes from the mother and one-half from the father. The zygote begins as a single cell, then after one week and many cell divisions, the zygote is made up of 100 to 150 cells. By the end of two weeks, the mass of cells attaches to the uterine wall. This first two weeks is referred to as the **germinal period** of development.

During the next six weeks, some remarkable developments take place: cell differentiation increases its pace, support systems for cells form, and organs appear. The period from two to eight weeks after conception is called the **embryonic period** (see figure 9.2). Before most women even know they are

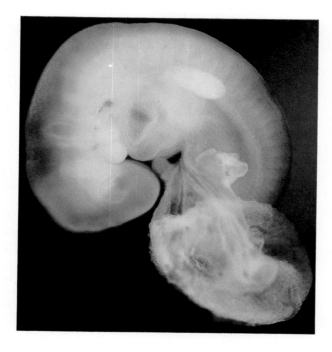

Figure 9.2
At about four weeks the embryo is about .2 inches in length. The head, eyes, and ears begin to show. The head and neck are half the body length; the shoulders will be located where the whitish arm buds are attached.

Psychology 9.1

Conception, Pregnancy, and Technology

The year is 1978. One of the most dazzling occurrences in the past decade is about to unfold. Mrs. Brown is infertile, but her physician informs her about a new procedure. In this procedure the mother's ovum is surgically removed, fertilized in a laboratory medium with live sperm cells obtained from a male donor, stored in a laboratory solution that substitutes for the uterine environment, and finally implanted in the mother's uterus. This technique is called *in vitro fertilization;* as shown in figure 9.A(a) this procedure involves a number of options. Another method shown involves artificial insemination by a donor. Figure 9.A(b) shows another recently devised technique when in vitro fertilization is not successful.

Technology is at work to discover potential birth defects once pregnancy has begun. **Amniocentesis** is a test that can detect more than 100 different birth defects. It is performed in the fourteenth to sixteenth weeks of pregnancy. A long, thin needle is inserted into the abdomen to extract a sample of amniotic fluid, the liquid that cushions the fetus. Fetal cells in the fluid are grown in the laboratory for two to four weeks and then studied for the presence of defects. The later amniocentesis is performed, the better the diagnostic potential. But the earlier it is performed, the more useful it can be in deciding whether a pregnancy should be terminated.

As scientists have searched for more accurate, safe assessments of high-risk prenatal circumstances, they have developed the **chorionic villus test.** Available since the mid-1980s, this test involves removing a small sample of the placenta nine to ten weeks

into pregnancy. It takes two to three weeks to diagnose. The chorionic villus test allows a decision about abortion to be made near the end of the first trimester of pregnancy, a point when abortion is safer and less traumatic than after amniocentesis

in the second trimester. These techniques provide valuable information about the presence of birth defects, but they also raise moral issues pertaining to whether an abortion should be obtained if birth defects are present.

Figure 9.A
New ways of creating babies. (a) Artificial insemination and in vitro fertilization.

Legend:
- Ovum from mother
- Ovum from donor
- Sperm from father
- Sperm from donor
- Child born of mother
- Child born of donor

AID: Artificial insemination by donor

1. Father infertile
2. Mother infertile and unable to carry child
3. Both parents infertile, but mother able to carry child
4. Mother infertile but able to carry child

IVF: In-vitro fertilization

1. Mother fertile but unable to conceive
2. Father infertile, mother fertile but unable to conceive
3. Mother infertile but able to carry child
4. Both parents infertile, but mother able to carry child
5. Mother infertile and unable to carry child
6. Both parents infertile, mother unable to carry child
7. Mother unable to carry child, but both parents fertile
8. Mother fertile but unable to carry child, father infertile

(b) Gamete intrafallopian transfer. This method was devised to overcome the low success rate (15 to 20%) of in vitro fertilization. The method is exactly the same as in vitro fertilization except the eggs and sperm are immediately placed in the oviducts after they have been put together. This procedure is especially effective for couples whose eggs and sperm never reach the oviducts. In the photograph, a forceps is used to grasp the upper part of the fallopian tube (red); a catheter containing sperm and eggs is placed in the tube.

pregnant, important changes are already occurring. In the third week the neural tube that eventually becomes the spinal cord is forming. At about twenty-one days old, eyes begin to appear and by twenty-four days the cells for the heart start to differentiate. During the fourth week, arm and leg buds emerge. At five to eight weeks, arms and legs become more differentiated, the face starts to form, the intestinal tract appears, and facial structures fuse. All of this is happening in an organism that by eight weeks weighs only one-thirtieth of an ounce and is just over an inch long (see figure 9.3). One of the most distinguishing features of the embryonic period is that many organs begin to emerge at this time.

The **fetal period** begins two months after conception and lasts for seven months on the average. Growth and development continue their dramatic course and organs mature to the point where life can be sustained outside the womb. At four months after conception, the fetus is about six inches long and weighs four to seven ounces. Prenatal reflexes become more apparent and the mother feels movement for the first time (see figure 9.4). At six months after conception, the eyes and eyelids are completely formed, a fine layer of hair is present, the grasping reflex appears, and irregular breathing begins. By seven to nine months, the fetus is much longer and weighs considerably more and the functioning of various organs is stepped up as well.

As these massive changes take place during prenatal development, some mothers tiptoe about in the belief that everything they do has a direct effect on the unborn child. Others behave more casually, assuming that their experiences have little impact. The truth lies somewhere between these extremes. Although in a comfortable, well-protected environment, the fetus is not totally immune to the larger environment surrounding the mother.

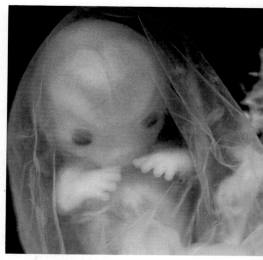

Figure 9.3
At eight weeks, 4 centimeters (1.6 inches), the developing individual is no longer an embryo, but a fetus. Everything that will be found in the fully developed human being has now been established. The fetal stage is a period of growth and perfection of detail. The heart has been beating for a month, and the muscles have just begun their first exercises. Two menstrual periods have now been skipped. At about this time the mother-to-be goes to a doctor or clinic for prenatal care.

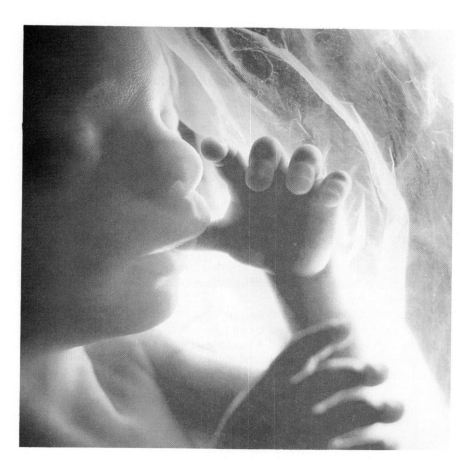

Figure 9.4
At 4½ months, about 18 cm (just over 7 inches). When the thumb comes close to the mouth, the head may turn, and lips and tongue begin their sucking motions—a reflex for survival.

Weeks of prenatal development

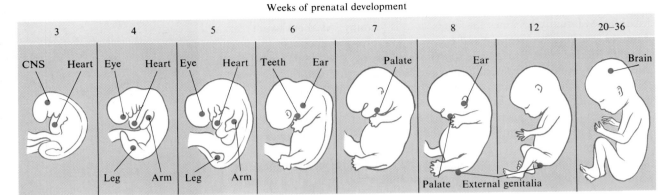

● Part of fetus where damage is greatest

Figure 9.5
The effect of teratogens at specific points in prenatal development.

Scientists label any agent that causes birth defects a **teratogen,** which comes from the Greek word *tera,* meaning "monster;" the study of birth defects is called teratology. Rarely do specific teratogens (such as drugs) link up with specific birth defects (such as leg malformation). So many teratogens exist that virtually every fetus is exposed to at least several of them. It may take a long time for the effects of a teratogen to appear; only half of these effects are present at birth.

Despite uncertainties about teratogens, scientists have identified some teratogens and the point in prenatal development they are most likely to do their greatest damage (see figure 9.5). The most damaging effects of teratogens occur in the first eight weeks, but damage to the brain can occur in the last months of pregnancy as well. Vulnerability to the brain is highest at fifteen to twenty-five days into prenatal development, for the eye from twenty-four to forty days, for the heart from twenty to forty days, and for the legs from twenty-four to thirty-six days (Tuchmann-Duplessis, 1975).

How might drugs affect prenatal development? Some pregnant women take drugs, smoke tobacco, and drink alcohol without thinking about the possible effects on the fetus. Occasionally, a rash of deformed babies are born, bringing to light the damage drugs can have on the developing fetus. This happened in 1961 when many pregnant women took a popular tranquilizer called thalidomide. In adults, the effects of thalidomide are mild; in embryos, they are devastating. Not all infants were affected in the same way. If the mother took thalidomide on day twenty-six (probably before she knew she was pregnant), an arm might not grow. If she took the drug two days later, the arm might not grow past the elbow. The thalidomide tragedy shocked the medical community and parents into the stark realization that the mother does not have to be a chronic drug user for the fetus to be damaged. Taking the wrong drug at the wrong time is enough to physically handicap the offspring for life.

Heavy drinking by pregnant women also can have a devastating effect on offspring. A cluster of characteristics called **fetal alcohol syndrome (FAS)** identifies children born to mothers who are heavy drinkers; it includes a small head (called microencephaly) as well as defective limbs, face, and heart. Most of these children are below average in intelligence. While no serious malformations such as those found in FAS are found in infants born to mothers who are moderate drinkers, infants whose mothers drink moderately during pregnancy (for example, one to two drinks a day) are less attentive and alert, with the effects still present at four years of age (Coles, 1987; Streissguth & others, 1984).

Table 9.1 The Apgar Scale

	Score		
	0	*1*	*2*
Heart rate	Absent	Slow—less than 100 beats per minute	Fast—100 to 140 beats per minute
Respiratory effort	No breathing for more than one minute	Irregular and slow	Good breathing with normal crying
Muscle tone	Limp and flaccid	Weak, inactive, but some flexion of extremities	Strong, active motion
Body color	Blue and pale	Body pink, but extremities blue	Entire body pink
Reflex irritability	No response	Grimace	Coughing, sneezing, and crying

From Apgar, V. A., "A proposal for a new method of evaluation of a newborn infant," in *Anesthesia and Analgesia . . . Current Researches, 32,* pp. 260–267. © 1953 International Anesthesia Research Society. Reprinted by permission.

If the mother has a disease during pregnancy or at the time of birth this can also harm development. German measles (Rubella), especially early in pregnancy, can damage the fetus's eyes, ears, and heart. If the mother has been vaccinated, no problem occurs. Sexually transmitted diseases, such as syphilis, can cause mental retardation or blindness in offspring. A mother infected with AIDS may transmit the disease to her offspring. Herpes is dangerous only if the mother has an outbreak at the time of delivery, at which time the newborn is exposed to the virus in the birth canal. A Caesarian section, in which the baby is delivered through the uterus, avoids this problem (Rosenblith & Sims-Knight, 1985).

Birth and the Newborn

Birth marks a dramatic transition for the fetus. In the womb the fetus is in a dark, free-floating, low-gravity environment with a relatively warm, constant temperature. At birth, the newborn must quickly adjust to light, gravity, cold, and a buzzing array of changing stimuli. Even the very process of being pushed out of the womb is physically strenuous.

An important concern is the health and well-being of the newborn when it comes into the world. The **Apgar Scale** has been used for many years to assess the newborn's health (see table 9.1). One minute and five minutes after birth the obstetrician or nurse gives the newborn a rating of zero, one, or two on each of the five signs: heart rate, respiratory effort, muscle tone, body color, and reflex irritability. A total score of seven to ten is favorable, five indicates developmental difficulties may be present, and three or below signals an emergency and that survival is in doubt.

A more subtle test than the Apgar and one that is increasingly used is the **Brazelton Neonatal Behavioral Assessment Scale.** This scale includes an evaluation of the infant's reaction to people. The Brazelton Scale usually is given on the third day of life and repeated two to three days later. The assessment involves twenty reflexes and reactions to different circumstances, such as a rattle. A very low Brazelton score indicates possible brain damage, but if the infant is simply sluggish in responding, Brazelton training is recommended. Parents are instructed in ways to stimulate their infant and increase the infant's alertness. Brazelton training has been effective in improving social skills of high-risk as well as healthy, responsive infants (Brazelton, 1979, 1987; Worobey & Belsky, 1982).

■ ■

Concept Table 9.1

History of Interest in Children, Development, Prenatal Development, and the Birth Process		
Concept	Processes/related ideas	Characteristics/description
History of interest in children	Philosophical views	In the Middle Ages, the original sin view dominated. In the Renaissance, the tabula rasa and innate goodness views addressed the nature of child development.
	Research and theory in the late nineteenth and the twentieth century	The ideas of Darwin, Hall, Freud, and Gesell had a strong biological flavor; Watson's view emphasized environmental influences. There is a reawakening of biological interest. Research is influenced by sociopolitical considerations.
What is development?	General nature and issues	A pattern of movement or change that begins at conception and continues throughout the life cycle. The pattern is complex because it involves biological, cognitive, and social processes. Two enduring isuses in development are heredity-environment and continuity-discontinuity.
Prenatal development	Conception and prenatal periods	Conception occurs when a sperm unites with the ovum. The fertilized egg is the zygote. The first two weeks after conception is the germinal period, two to eight weeks is the embryonic period, and two to nine months is the fetal period.
	Teratogens	Agents that cause birth defects. Many exist and rarely does a specific teratogen cause a specific birth defect. Drugs as well as maternal diseases can harm the fetus.
Birth and the newborn	Assessment	The Apgar Scale is used to evaluate the newborn's health and well-being; the Brazelton Scale is also widely used.
	Interaction	Brazelton training is recommended when the newborn is sluggish. Bonding is widely recommended, but it shows no long-term advantages.

It is widely publicized that mothers who have prolonged contact with their babies in the first minutes, hours, or days after birth will form more enduring attachments to their infants than mothers not allowed this contact. Early physical contact between the baby and the parent is called **bonding** (Klaus & Kennell, 1976). While many hospitals and physicians now advocate bonding, the most recent research evidence suggests that the early physical contact does not provide the infant with any long-term advantages (e.g., Bakeman & Brown, 1980; Lamb, 1982; Myers, 1984). The absence of positive findings from the parent-infant bonding research should not keep parents from interacting with their newborns, though, because such contact brings pleasure to many parents. In the case of some parents and infants (such as adolescent mothers, preterm infants, mothers from disadvantaged circumstances, and fathers), bonding may set in motion a climate for improved parent-infant interaction after the hospital stay (Maccoby & Martin, 1983; Rosenblith and Sims-Knight, 1985).

The past several decades have witnessed an explosion of knowledge about the period of development from birth to two years of age. As we discuss infancy, you will notice the amount of interest in the newborn. Before you turn to the section on infancy, see concept table 9.1 for a review of our discussion of development so far.

Testing the Moro reflex, one of the most frequent and dramatic reflexes of the newborn. When a newborn is roughly handled, for example, it becomes startled, arches its back, and throws its head back. At the same time, the newborn flings its arms and legs and then rapidly closes them to the body's center as if falling. A vestige of our ape ancestry, the Moro reflex disappears by three to four months of age.

Infancy

Newborns are not as helpless as they look. The newborn can breathe, suck, swallow, and eliminate wastes. It can look, hear, taste, smell, feel, turn its head, and signal for help. A newborn naturally contracts its throat to keep water from rushing in when it is placed under water—a genetically influenced survival mechanism.

Physical Development

Some reflexes present in newborns persist throughout our lives—coughing, blinking, and yawning, for example. Others disappear in the months following birth as higher brain functions mature and voluntary control over many behaviors develops. One of the most frequent and dramatic reflexes of the newborn is the **Moro reflex,** a vestige of our ape ancestry. When a newborn is handled roughly, hears a loud noise, sees a bright light, or feels a sudden change of position, it becomes startled, arches its back, and throws its head back. At the same time, the newborn flings its arms and legs out and then rapidly closes them to the center of the body as if falling. This Moro reflex disappears by three to four months of age.

What do newborns do other than respond reflexively to their world? They sleep and eat. Newborns sleep about sixteen to seventeen hours a day; not until one month of age do they sleep more at night than during the day. By about four months, their sleep schedules correspond more to our adult schedules (Parmalee & Stern, 1972). About one-half of an infant's sleep is REM sleep (remember this is sleep during which we dream). As adults REM sleep comprises only one-fifth of our night. REM sleep may provide added stimulation for infants since they spend more time asleep than awake, and it may be important in brain development.

The biggest dispute about newborns and eating focuses on whether it is better to bottle-feed or breast-feed. The growing consensus is that it is generally better to breast-feed (Auerback, 1987; Corboy, 1987). Breast-feeding provides milk that is clean and digestible and helps to immunize the newborn from disease. Breast-fed babies also gain weight more rapidly than bottle-fed babies. However, only about one-half of mothers nurse newborns and even fewer continue to nurse their infants for several months. Mothers who work outside the home may find it impossible to breast-feed their young infant for many months, but even though breast-feeding provides more ideal nutrition for the infant, bottle-fed infants are not psychologically harmed.

Figure 9.6
*Changes in body form and proportion
during prenatal and postnatal growth.
The early development of the top
portion of the body reflects the cephalo-
caudal principle.*

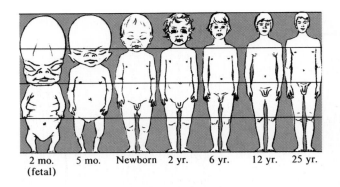

2 mo.   5 mo.   Newborn   2 yr.   6 yr.   12 yr.   25 yr.
(fetal)

As the infant grows, some parts of the body develop more rapidly than
others. The **cephalo-caudal pattern** describes the fact that growth always occurs first at the top of the person (the head), then at the neck, shoulders, middle
trunk, and so on. This same pattern also occurs in the head area—the top parts
of the head, such as the eyes and brain, grow faster than the lower portion,
such as the jaw. An illustration of the cephalo-caudal pattern is shown in figure
9.6, revealing the prominence of the head area.

Growth is rapid during the first year of life, although some periods are
relatively quiet and others burst with change. While growth decelerates in the
second year, both gross (large muscle) and fine (small, more finely tuned
muscle) motor skills develop. Significant strides in walking and running abilities take place, along with the ability to manipulate objects with one hand.

What about the infant's brain? Isn't it likely to develop in a dramatic
fashion? Remember that the human infant begins life as a single cell and in
just nine months is born with a brain and nervous system containing 10 to 20
billion neurons. This means that at some point during prenatal development,
neurons were producing at a rate of 25,000 per minute! You are born with all
the neurons you will ever have in your life. But at birth and in early infancy
the connectedness of the neurons is impoverished. By looking at figure 9.7,
you can see the substantial increase in dendritic growth from birth to two
years. The increased branching of neurons allows greater connections between
neurons.

Perceptual Development

William James (1890) described the world of the newborn as "a great,
blooming, buzzing confusion." A century later, psychologists believe James
was wrong. Infant perception of visual information is far more advanced than
was previously thought.

A newborn cannot tell you if she can see. How could you find this out?
One way is to move a large object toward the newborn, then observe if she
moves her head away, as if to avoid a collision. The head movement of a newborn in response to a moving object indicates that she can see. While infants
are not blind at birth, their vision is fuzzy, registering at about 20/600 on the
well-known Snellen chart used by your optometrist. But by six months, this
improves to 20/100 (Aslin, in press; Banks & Salapatek, 1983).

Do infants prefer some faces to others? Can they perceive depth? At
least by two months of age, infants prefer a normal face to a distorted face
(Fantz, 1966). And by six months they perceive depth. The classic study by

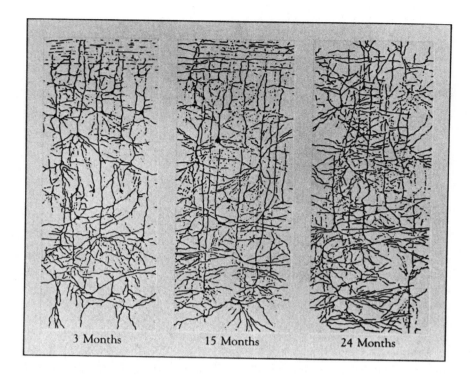

3 Months   15 Months   24 Months

Figure 9.7
The connectedness of dendrites spreads dramatically during the course of life's first two years. Notice how many more connections exist between dendrites at twenty-four months than at three months of age. Some developmentalists and neurobiologists believe the increased dendritic spreading plays an important role in the infant's advances in processing information.

Eleanor Gibson and Richard Walk (1960) revealed that six-month-old infants crawled to the shallow side more often than to the deep side of the visual cliff, indicating they perceived depth. Similar results were obtained with young animals (figure 9.8). Whether infants younger than six months perceive depth is controversial (Campos, Langer, & Krowitz, 1970; Granrud & others, 1984).

Young infants can see; can they also hear? Not only can newborn infants hear, but two weeks *before* birth the fetus responds to sounds. Shortly after birth, infants also can smell, taste, touch, and sense pain. For example, when the male infant is circumcised (usually on the third day of life), pain is evident not only from his crying but also in a massive increase in blood cortisol. It is remarkable that the newborn male does not suffer serious consequences from circumcision. Instead, the circumcised infant displays remarkable resiliency and ability to cope with stress. Not long after the circumcision, the newborn male drifts into deep sleep; the sleep seems to serve an an elegant coping mechanism for handling the high degree of stress present (Gunnar, Malone, & Fisch, 1987).

Cognitive Development

Matthew is one year old. He has seen over 1,000 flash cards with pictures of shells, flowers, insects, flags, countries, words—you name it—on them. His mother, Billie, has made close to 10,000 eleven-inch square cards for Matthew and his four-year-old brother, Mark. Billie is following the regimen recommended by Glenn Doman, director of the Philadelphia Institute for Human Potential. Using Doman's methods, Billie is teaching Matthew Japanese and a little math. Billie expects Matthew to be reading and mastering math problems by the age of two.

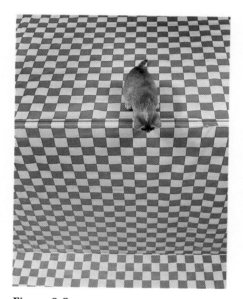

Figure 9.8
The visual cliff. Eleanor Gibson and Richard Walk developed the visual cliff, which has a glass-covered dropoff, to investigate whether young infants have depth perception. Not only were the young infants reluctant to venture onto the glass, but neither were young animals, as demonstrated by the hesitant kitten.

Figure 9.9
Piaget's view of how we understand the world.

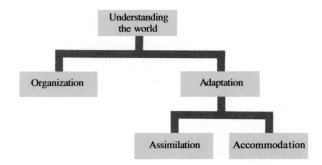

Is this the best way to foster cognitive development? Many developmental psychologists believe Doman's institute is a money-making scheme and that something is fundamentally wrong with his strategy. They argue that intense tutoring keeps children from discovering knowledge about the world on their own by stifling curiosity and exploration. Jean Piaget, the famous Swiss development psychologist, called the question, What should we do to foster the child's cognitive development? the American question because it was asked so often of him by American audiences. As we see next, Piaget's view suggests that the Doman approach is not the desired way to help children know their world.

Piaget's Approach

Piaget (1896–1980) stressed that the child actively constructs his own cognitive world; information is not just poured into his mind from the environment. Two processes underlie the individual's construction of the world: organization and adaptation. To make sense of our world, we organize our experiences. For example, we separate important ideas from less important ideas. We connect one idea to another. But we not only organize our observations and experiences, we also *adapt* our thinking to include new ideas, because additional information furthers understanding. Piaget (1960) believed that we adapt in two ways: assimilation and accommodation (see figure 9.9).

Assimilation occurs when we incorporate new information into our existing knowledge. **Accommodation** occurs when we adjust to new information. Consider a circumstance in which a five-year-old girl is given a hammer and nails to hang a picture on the wall. She has never used a hammer, but from experience and observation she realizes that a hammer is an object to be held, that it is swung by the handle to hit the nail, and that it is usually swung a number of times. Recognizing each of these things, she fits her behavior into information she already has (assimilation). However, the hammer is heavy, so she holds it near the top. She swings too hard and the nail bends, so she adjusts the pressure of her strikes. These adjustments reveal her ability to alter her conception of the world slightly (accommodation).

Piaget thought that assimilation and accommodation operate even in the young infant's life. Newborns reflexively suck everything that touches their lips (assimilation), but after several months of experience, they construct their understanding of the world differently. Some objects, such as fingers and the mother's breast, can be sucked, and others, such as fuzzy blankets, should not be sucked (accommodation).

Table 9.2 Piaget's Stages of Cognitive Development		
Stage	**Description**	**Age range**
Sensorimotor	The infant progresses from reflexive instinctual action at birth to the beginning of symbolic thought. The infant constructs an understanding of the world by coordinating sensory experiences with physical actions.	Birth to 2
Preoperational	The child begins to represent the world with words and images; these words and images reflect increased symbolic thinking and go beyond the connection of sensory information and physical action.	2 to 7
Concrete operational	The child can now reason logically about concrete events and classify objects into different sets.	7 to 11
Formal operational	The adolescent reasons in more abstract and logical ways. Thought is more idealistic.	11 to 15

Piaget also believed that we go through four stages in understanding the world. Each of the stages is age-related and consists of distinct ways of thinking. It is the *different* way of understanding the world that makes one stage more advanced than another; knowing *more* information does not make the child's thinking more advanced in the Piagetian view. This is what Piaget meant when he said the child's cognition is *qualitatively* different in one stage compared to another. A brief overview of Piaget's four stages of cognitive development is shown in table 9.2. We will discuss preoperational and concrete operational thought later in this chapter and formal operational thought in the next chapter. For now let's find out more about the infant's conception of the world.

The Sensorimotor Stage

The **sensorimotor stage** of cognitive development lasts from birth to about two years of age, corresponding to the period of infancy. The infant constructs an understanding of the world by coordinating sensory experiences (such as seeing and hearing) with physical, motoric actions—hence the term *sensorimotor*. At the beginning of this stage, the newborn has little more than reflexive patterns with which to work; at the end of the stage, the two-year-old has complex sensorimotor patterns and is beginning to operate with primitive symbols.

We live in a world of objects. Imagine yourself as a five-month-old infant and how you might experience the world. You are in a playpen filled with toys. One of the toys, a monkey, falls out of your grasp and rolls behind a larger toy, a hippopotamus. Would you know the monkey is behind the hippopotamus, or would you think it is completely gone? Piaget believed that "out of sight" literally was "out of mind" for young infants; at five months of age, then, you would not have reached for the monkey when it fell behind the hippopotamus. By eight months of age, though, the infant begins to understand that out of sight is not out of mind; at this point, you probably would have reached behind the hippopotamus to search for the monkey, coordinating your perceptual experiences with your motoric actions.

Figure 9.10
Piaget thought that object permanence was one of the infancy's landmark accomplishments. For this five-month-old infant, "out of sight" literally is "out of mind," and the infant does not search for the hidden monkey. By eight to nine months of age, this infant will search for the hidden monkey, reflecting the presence of object permanence.

Piaget thought that **object permanence** was one of the infant's most important accomplishments. With this accomplishment, infants understand that objects and events continue to exist even though they are not in direct contact with them. The most common way to study object permanence is to show an infant an interesting toy and then cover the toy with a sheet or blanket. If the infant understands that the toy still exists, she will try to uncover it (see figure 9.10). Object permanence continues to develop throughout the sensorimotor period. For example, when infants initially understand that objects exist even when out of sight, they look for them only briefly; by the end of the sensorimotor period, infants engage in a more prolonged and sophisticated search for the objects (Flavell, 1985; Sophian, 1985).

Object permanence is important in the infant's social world as well. The infant develops a sense that people are permanent just as he comes to understand that toys are permanent. The five-month-old infant does not sense that a caregiver exists beyond moment-to-moment encounters but does by eight months of age. The infant's cognitive accomplishments, then, not only tell us how the infant understands a world of blocks, toys, and playpens, but also how she constructs a world of people (Escalona, 1988).

Social Development

The newborns of some species function independently in the world; other species are not so independent. At birth the opossum is still considered fetal and is capable of finding its way around only in its mother's pouch, where it attaches itself to her nipple and continues to develop. This protective environment is similar to the uterus. By contrast, the wildebeest must run with the herd moments after birth. The newborn wildebeest's behavior is far more adultlike than the opossum's, although the wildebeest does have to obtain food through suckling. The maturation of the human infant lies somewhere between these two extremes; much learning and development must take place before the infant can sustain itself (see figure 9.11) (Maccoby, 1980).

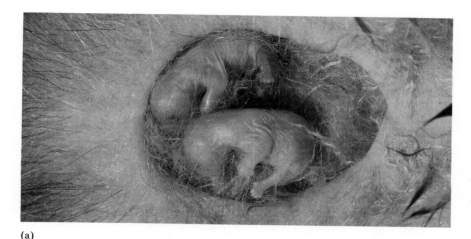

(a)

(b)

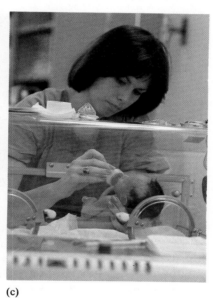

(c)

Figure 9.11
Variations in the dependency of newborns in different species. Some species' newborns behave independently, others not so independently. The newborn opossum is fetal, capable of finding its way around only in its mother's pouch, where it attaches itself to her nipple and continues to develop (a). By contrast, the wildebeest runs with the herd moments after birth (b). The human newborn's maturation lies somewhere in between the opossum and the wildebeest (c).

Because it cannot sustain itself, the human infant requires extensive care. What kind of care is needed and how does the infant begin the road to social maturity? Much of the interest in infant care focuses on attachment, although the infant's development of independence and a sense of self are important as well.

Attachment

In everyday language, an *attachment* is a relationship between individuals in which each person feels strongly about the other and tries to ensure the continuation of the relationship. Many pairs of people are attached: friends, relatives, lovers, a teacher and a student. In the language of child development, however, **attachment** often is restricted to a particular developmental period, to a relationship between particular social figures, and to a particular phenomenon thought to reflect unique characteristics of the relationship. The developmental period is infancy, the social figures are the infant and one or more adult caregivers, and the phenomenon in question involves a bond.

There is no shortage of theories about infant attachment. Freud believed that the infant becomes attached to the person or object that provides oral satisfaction; for most infants, this is the mother, since she is most likely to feed the infant.

Figure 9.12
The classic Harlow and Zimmerman (1959) infant monkey study on contact comfort. Here the infant monkey clings to the cloth "mother" but feeds from the wire "mother."

Figure 9.13
The results of Harlow and Zimmerman's study of wire and cloth mothers. The average amount of time infant monkeys spent in contact with their wire and cloth mothers is shown. The infant monkeys spent most of their time with the cloth mother, regardless of which mother fed them.

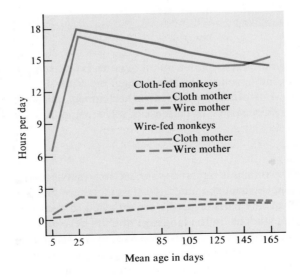

Figure 9.14
*Goslings following "Mother" Lorenz.
Konrad Lorenz revealed that in the
first thirty-six hours of their life goslings
would attach themselves to the first
moving object they saw. Lorenz called
this process imprinting.*

But is feeding as important as Freud thought? A classic study by Harry Harlow and Robert Zimmerman (1959) suggests the answer is no. They evaluated whether feeding or contact comfort was more important to infant attachment. Infant monkeys were removed from their mothers at birth and reared for six months by surrogate (substitute) "mothers." As shown in figure 9.12, one of the mothers was made of wire, the other of cloth. Half of the infant monkeys were fed by the wire mother, half by the cloth mother. Periodically the amount of time the infant monkeys spent with either the wire or the cloth monkey was computed. Figure 9.13 indicates that regardless of whether they were fed by the wire or the cloth mother, the infant monkeys spent far more time with the cloth mother. This study clearly demonstrates that feeding is not the crucial element in the attachment process and that contact comfort is important.

Might familiarity also breed attachment? A famous study by Konrad Lorenz (1965) suggests that the answer is yes. Lorenz separated the eggs laid by one goose into two groups. He returned one group to the goose to be hatched; the other group was hatched in an incubator. The goslings in the first group performed as predicted; they followed their mother as soon as they hatched. But those in the second group, who first saw Lorenz after hatching, followed him everywhere as if he were their mother. Lorenz marked the goslings and then placed both groups under a box. Mother goose and "mother" Lorenz stood aside as the box was lifted. Each group of goslings went directly to its "mother" (see figure 9.14). Lorenz called this process **imprinting,** that is, the rapid, innate learning within a critical period of time that involves attachment to the first moving object seen.

For goslings, the critical period for imprinting is the first thirty-six hours after birth. Is there a critical period for attachment in human infants? Not hours or days, but a longer, more flexible sensitive period may exist (Hinde, 1983; Hinde & Stevenson-Hinde, 1987). Many developmental psychologists believe that attachment to a caregiver during the *first year* of life provides an important foundation for later development.

Erik Erikson (1968) is one psychologist who adopts this view. He proposed that the first year of life repesents the stage of **trust versus mistrust.** A sense of trust requires a feeling of physical comfort and a minimal amount of fear and apprehension about the future. Trust in infancy sets the stage for a lifelong expectation that the world will be a good and pleasant place to be. Erikson also believes that responsive, sensitive parenting contributes to the infant's sense of trust.

Erikson has developed one of the most comprehensive and well received theories of the human life-span. For Erikson, the **epigenetic principle** guides our development through the life cycle. This principle states that anything that grows has a ground plan, out of which the parts arise, each having a special time of ascendency, until all of the parts have arisen to form a functioning whole. In Erikson's theory, eight stages of development unfold as we go through the life cycle. He called these *psychosocial* stages (in contrast to Freud's *psychosexual* stages). Each stage consists of a unique developmental task that confronts the individual with a crisis that must be faced. For Erikson, the crisis is not a catastrophe, but a turning point of increased vulnerability and enhanced potential. The more the individual resolves the crises successfully the healthier development will be.

The perspective of John Bowlby and Mary Ainsworth also stresses the importance of attachment in the first year of life and the responsiveness of the caregiver. Bowlby (1958, 1969, 1980) believes the infant and mother instinctively form an attachment. He believes the newborn is innately social and biologically equipped to elicit the mother's attachment behavior. The baby cries, clings, smiles, and coos. Later the infant crawls, walks, and follows the mother. The goal for the infant is to keep the mother nearby. Research on attachment supports Bowlby's view that at about six to seven months attachment of the infant to a caregiver intensifies (Ainsworth, 1967; Schaffer & Emerson, 1964).

Although attachment to a caregiver intensifies midway through the first year, isn't it likely that some babies have a more positive attachment experience than others? Ainsworth (1979) thinks so and says this variation can be categorized as **secure or insecure attachment.** An infant who is securely attached to the caregiver uses the caregiver, usually the mother, as a secure base from which to explore the environment. The infant moves freely away from the mother but processes her location through periodic glances. The securely attached infant responds positively to being picked up by others, and when put back down, moves away freely to play. An insecurely attached infant, by contrast, avoids the mother or is ambivalent toward her. The insecurely attached infant has fear of strangers and is upset by minor, everyday separations.

Why are some infants securely attached and others insecurely attached? Ainsworth believes it depends on how sensitive the caregiver is to the infant's signals. For example, infants who are securely attached are more likely to have mothers who are more sensitive, accepting, and expressive of affection toward them than those who are insecurely attached (Egeland & Farber, 1984).

If early attachment to the caregiver is important, it should relate to the child's social behavior later in development. Research by Alan Sroufe (1985, in press) documents this connection. In one investigation, infants who were securely attached to their mothers early in infancy were less frustrated and happier at two years of age than their insecurely attached counterparts (see figure 9.15) (Matas, Arend & Sroufe, 1978).

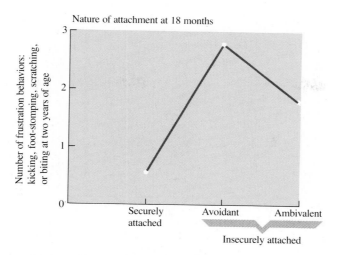

Figure 9.15
The effects of attachment on frustration.

Other research has failed to confirm consistently that secure attachment is the key ingredient of social competence (Lewis & others, 1984). Some developmental psychologists think too much emphasis is placed on the importance of the attachment bond in infancy. Jerome Kagan (1987), for example, believes the infant is highly resilient and adaptive; he argues that the infant is evolutionarily equipped to stay on a positive developmental path even in the face of wide variations in parenting. Kagan and others also stress that genetic and temperament characteristics play more important roles in the child's social competence than attachment theorists are willing to acknowledge (Goldsmith & others, 1987; Trudel, 1987). For example, an infant may have inherited a low tolerance for stress; this, rather than an insecure attachment bond, may be responsible for his inability to get along with peers.

Another criticism of attachment theory is that it ignores the diversity of social agents and social contexts that exist in the infant's world. Experiences with both the mother *and* the father, changing gender roles, day care, the mother's employment, peer experiences, socioeconomic status, and cultural values are not considered adequately by the secure attachment concept (Belsky, 1987a; Lamb & others, 1984). In all of these perspectives, the importance of social relationships with parents is recognized—their differences lie in the criticalness of an early attachment bond.

Independence and a Sense of Self

Attachment is not the only important social occurrence in infancy; independence and a sense of self are high on the list as well. Erikson (1968) believes that while trust versus mistrust is the key developmental issue in the first year of life, the focus in the second year is on **autonomy versus doubt.** After gaining trust in her caregiver, the infant starts to discover that her behavior is her own; she asserts her sense of autonomy. She realizes her *will*. Continued dependency creates a sense of doubt in the infant.

As infants develop a sense of autonomy during the second year of life, they reveal a stronger sense of self. How can a psychologist determine if an infant has a sense of self? The psychologist places a dot of rouge on an infant's nose and watches to see how often the infant touches his nose. Then the infant is placed in front of a mirror and the observer notes whether the nose touching

Figure 9.16
The development of self-recognition in infancy. Percentage of subjects showing recognition of the rouge by touching, wiping, or verbally referring to it in two different studies at different ages.

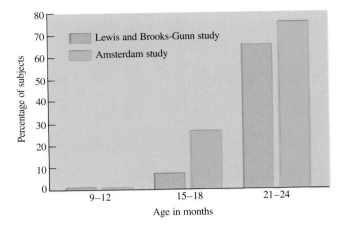

This eighteen-month-old shows a sense of self.

increases. As indicated in figure 9.16, infants increasingly recognize the rouge on their nose during the second year of life. Their interest in the rouge suggests they recognize their own image and coordinate the image with the action of touching their own bodies (Amsterdam, 1968; Lewis & Brooks-Gunn, 1979).

By two years of age much development has taken place. A summary of these accomplishments is presented in concept table 9.2. But much more child development remains.

Childhood

A four-year-old child draws green suns, yellow skies, cars that float on clouds, pelicans that kiss seals, and people who curiously look like tadpoles. These are examples of how the world is constructed by children in the period of **early childhood,** the time frame encompassing the preschool years (approximately three to five years of age). A nine-year-old child draws orange suns, blue skies, cars on roads, and people who look like people. These are examples of how the world is constructed by children in the period of **middle and late childhood,** sometimes referred to as the elementary school years (roughly six to eleven years of age). Childhood is more than drawing pelicans kissing seals and suns that are green or orange; you will discover, though, that such drawings reflect differences in the way preschool and elementary school children cognitively represent their worlds. Before we tackle some of the truly fascinating cognitive changes in childhood, let's survey the physical changes that take place.

■ ■ ■ ■ ■ ■ ■ ■ ■ ■ ■ ■ ■ ■ ■ ■ ■ ■ ■ ■

Concept Table 9.2

Concept	Processes/related ideas	Characteristics/description
	Infancy	
Physical development	Its nature	The infant comes into the world equipped with a number of reflexes. Sleeping and eating are two important states. Growth follows a cephalo-caudal pattern. Brain growth is characterized by extensive dendritic branching.
Perceptual development	Its course and features	Infants can see, but their vision is about 20/600 at birth; it improves to 20/100 at six months. By six months infants can perceive depth. Fetuses and newborns can hear. Smell, touch, taste, and a sense of pain also operate in the newborn.
Cognitive development	Piaget's approach	The child constructs an understanding of the world using organization and adapation. Adaptation is comprised of assimilation and accommodation. Piaget has identified four stages of cognitive development: sensorimotor, preoperational, concrete operational, and formal operational.
	The sensorimotor stage	Lasts from birth to two years of age and involves the coordination of sensorimotor action. Object permanence occurs at about eight months of age in most infants.
Social development	Attachment	Involves the bond between infant and caregiver (usually the mother). A number of theories of attachment exist. Feeding does not seem to be critical in the infant's development of attachment, but contact comfort, familiarity, and the caregiver's responsiveness are. Some experts think secure attachment is critical to social competence, others do not.
	Independence and a sense of self	An important theme in the second year of life. Erikson's second stage is called autonomy versus doubt.

Physical Development

Striking, catching, throwing, kicking, balancing, rolling objects, rolling one-self, zipping, lacing, buttoning, cutting, locking, latching, snapping, buckling, stacking, fitting, pushing, dancing, and swimming—preschool children can perform these physical feats and many more. Growth rate slows down during early childhood; otherwise we would be a species of giants. Continuing the theme of cephalo-caudal development, the brain is closer to full growth than the rest of the child's body, attaining 75 percent of its adult weight by the age of three.

In middle and late childhood, motor development is much smoother and more coordinated than in early childhood. While a preschool child can zip, cut, latch, and dance, an elementary school child can zip, cut, latch, and dance more efficiently.

Cognitive Development

Dramatic cognitive growth takes place during the preschool years. A four-year-old child's vocabulary has grown to approximately 1,500 words; by five years of age, it has reached 2,200 words. The five-year-old child can hear a long sentence and remember it. And the preschool child's thought is much more symbolic than the infant's; remember that Piaget believed symbolic thought began toward the end of infancy. During early childhood, symbolic

Figure 9.17
*The beaker task, used to evaluate
whether a child can think
operationally.*

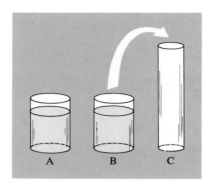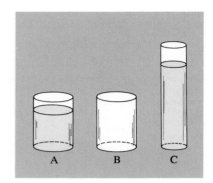

thought is readily apparent. For example, preschool children use scribbles and shapes to represent people, houses, toys, and animals. To learn more about the fascinating way the preschool child represents the world symbolically, turn to Psychology 9.2.

Preoperational and Concrete Operational Thought

The preschool child begins to represent the world with words, images, and drawings; symbolic thoughts go beyond simple connections of sensory information and physical action. But while the preschool child can symbolically represent the world, according to Piaget, she still cannot perform **operations,** that is, mental representations that are reversible. This is why Piaget (1967) said children two to seven years of age were in the **preoperational stage** of thought.

A well-known test of whether a child can think operationally is to present a child with two identical beakers, A and B, filled with liquid to the same height (see figure 9.17). Next to them is a third beaker, C. Beaker C is tall and thin, while beakers A and B are wide and short. The liquid is poured from B into C and the child is asked whether the amounts in A and C are the same. The four-year-old child invariably says that the amount of liquid in the tall, thin beaker (C) is greater than that in the short, fat beaker (A). The eight-year-old child consistently says the amounts are the same. The four-year-old child, a preoperational thinker, cannot mentally reverse the pouring action; that is, she cannot imagine the liquid going back from container C to container B.

The child's thought in the preoperational stage also is egocentric. By **egocentrism,** Piaget meant the inability to distinguish between one's own perspective and someone else's perspective. The following telephone conversation between four-year-old Mary, who is at home, and her father, who is at work, typifies Mary's egocentric thought:

> *Father:* Mary, is mommy there?
> *Mary:* (Silently nods)
> *Father:* Mary, may I speak to mommy?
> *Mary:* (Nods again silently)

Mary's nods were egocentric because she failed to consider her father's perspective before replying. An older, nonegocentric child would have responded verbally.

"Look what I can do, Grandma!"
Reprinted with special permission of King Features Inc.

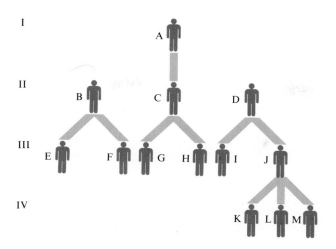

Figure 9.18
A family tree of four generations (I through IV). Children at the preoperational stage of thought cannot carry out this classification; children at the concrete operational stage can.

But preoperational thought is more than a mere waiting period for operational thought. We already have highlighted the increased symbolic nature of preoperational thought. Not only do preoperational thinkers begin to use symbols more effectively, they are extremely intuitive. Piaget referred to preoperational thought as intuitive because on the one hand young children seem so sure about their understanding, yet they are so unaware of why they know something. They don't understand the importance of logical reasoning; they believe their sharp insight, or intuition, gives them the answers to understanding the world.

The preoperational thinker asks a trillion questions about the world, reflecting his desire to know and understand.

"Why does a lady have to be married to have a baby?"

"Who was the mother when everybody was a baby?"

"Why do leaves fall?"

"Why does the sun shine?"

From approximately seven to eleven years of age, the child is in the **concrete operational stage** of thought. At this stage, the child can use operations—she can mentally reverse the liquid from one beaker to another and understand that the volume is the same even though the beakers are different in height and width. The child can now reason about virtually anything she can perceive. Logical reasoning replaces intuitive thought as long as the principles can be applied to specific or *concrete* examples. The concrete operational thinker needs objects and events present to reason about them. For example, she cannot imagine the steps necessary to complete an algebraic equation, which is far too abstract at this stage of cognitive development.

As part of concrete operational thought, the child develops the logical skills necessary to classify objects into groups. For example, the concrete operational thinker can classify the family members of four generations, as shown in figure 9.18. The nine-year-old child, for example, will tell you that the grandfather (A) has three children (B, C, and D), each of whom has two children (E through J), and finally one of these children (J) has three children (K, L, and M). A child who comprehends this classification understands that person J can at the same time be father, brother, son, and grandson. A preoperational child cannot perform this classification and says that a father cannot fill these other roles (Furth & Wachs, 1975).

Psychology 9.2

Where Pelicans Kiss Seals, Cars Float on Clouds, and Humans Are Tadpoles

At about three years of age and sometimes even at two, children's spontaneous scribbles begin to resemble pictures. One three and one-half-year-old child looked at the scribble he had just drawn and said it was a pelican kissing a seal (see figure 9.B).

At about three to four years of age, children begin to create symbols of humans. Invariably the first symbols look curiously like tadpoles; see the circle and two lines in figure 9.C—the circle represents a head and the two lines are legs.

These observations of children's drawings were made by Denise Wolf, Carol Fucigna, and Howard Gardner in their ongoing program of research at Harvard University. They point out that many people think young children draw a human in this rather odd way because it is the best they can

do. Piaget said children intend their drawings to be realistic; they draw what they know rather than what they see. So the tadpole, with its strange exemptions of trunk and arms, might reflect a child's lack of knowledge of the human body and how its parts fit together.

However, children may know more about the human body than they are capable of drawing. One three-year-old child drew a tadpole but described it in complete detail, pointing out where the feet, chin, and neck were. When three- and four-year-old children are asked to draw someone playing ball, they produce symbols of humans that include arms, since the task implicitly requires arms (see figure 9.D).

Possibly because preschool children are not very concerned about reality, their drawings are

fanciful and inventive (see figure 9.E). Suns are blue, skies are yellow, and cars float on clouds in the symbolic world of the preschool child. The symbolism is simple but strong, not unlike the abstractions found in some contemporary art.

In the elementary school years, the child's symbols become more realistic, neat, and precise (see figure 9.F). Suns are yellow, skies are blue, and cars are placed on roads.

Figure 9.B
A 3½-year-old's symbolic drawing. Halfway into this drawing, the 3½-year-old artist said it was "a pelican kissing a seal."

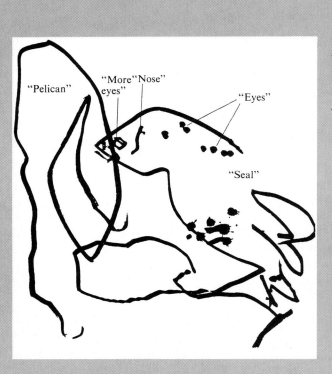

Figure 9.C
The 3-year-old's first drawing of a person: a "tadpole" consisting of a circle with two lines for legs.

A child's ability to symbolically represent the world on paper is related to the development of perceptual-motor skills. But once such skills are developed, some artists revert to the style of young children's drawings. As Picasso once commented, "I used to draw like Raphael but it has taken me a whole lifetime to learn to draw like children" (After Winner, 1986).

From Winner, E. (1986, August). Where pelicans kiss seals. *Psychology Today,* pp. 24–35. © 1980 American Psychological Association, Washington, DC. Reprinted by permission.

Figure 9.D
A young child, when asked to draw people playing ball, included arms.

Figure 9.E
This 6-year-old's drawing is free, fanciful, and inventive.

Figure 9.F
An 11-year-old's drawing is neater and more realistic, but also less inventive.

Evaluating Piaget

Piaget was a genius at observing children, and his insights are often surprisingly easy to verify. Piaget showed us some important things to look for in cognitive development, such as object permanence in infancy, egocentrism in early childhood, and operational thought in middle and late childhood. He also told us how we must make experiences fit our cognitive framework, yet simultaneously adapt our understanding to new experiences.

But Piaget has not gone uncriticized (Bertenthal, 1987; Case & others, 1987; Flavell, 1985; Inhelder, DeCaprona, & Cornu-Wells, 1988; Mandler, 1983). The stages of cognitive development are not as neatly packaged as Piaget envisioned; for example, children do not always learn to classify objects at the same time they learn to reverse mental operations. Some cognitive skills seem to appear earlier than Piaget believed (symbolic thought, for example, may be more prominent late in infancy) and others later (developing hypotheses and deducing solutions to problems in adolescence, for example).

Information processing psychologists believe more attention should be given to the tasks used to study children's cognition. They are intrigued by the possibility that if tasks are made interesting and simple, children may be more cognitively mature than Piaget thought. This strategy recently was followed to determine if a preschool child could reason about a syllogism (Hawkins & others, 1984). (Remember that a syllogism is a type of reasoning problem, consisting of two premises, or statements, assumed to be true, plus a conclusion.) To simplify problems, words like "some" and "all" were made implicit rather than explicit. The problems focused on fantasy creatures alien from practical knowledge. Imagine how wide a child's eyes become when stories about purple bangas who sneeze at people and merds who laugh and don't like mushrooms are told. Two such syllogisms read to children were:

> "Every banga is purple.
> Purple animals always sneeze at people.
> Do bangas sneeze at people?"

> "Merds laugh when they're happy.
> Animals that laugh don't like mushrooms.
> Do merds like mushrooms?"

By simplifying the problem and making its dimensions more appropriate, the researchers demonstrated that preschool children can reason about syllogisms. Although Piaget's theories are being revised today, he still stands as the giant in the study of children's cognitive development. Because of Piaget's insights, we will never look at children and their understanding of their world in the same way.

Social Contexts and Development

The young child's social ventures are vigorous. With a surplus of energy, her failures are quickly forgotten and she approaches new challenges with enthusiasm. The older child faces the tasks of school and the more serious business of achievement. Parents were important in the infant's development of attachment and independence; they continue to assume an important role during the childhood years as do peers.

How should parents rear their children? We don't have all of the answers, although an authoritative style usually is preferred over authoritarian or permissive styles.

Parent-Child Relationship

For years heated debates have swirled around the question, How should parents rear their children? We don't have the complete answer, but we can provide some helpful guidelines. An important classification of parenting styles was developed by Diana Baumrind (1971). She believes parents interact with children in one of three ways: authoritarian, authoritative, and laissez-faire, or permissive.

Authoritarian parenting involves a restrictive, punitive style that exhorts the child to follow the parent's directions and to respect work and effort. The authoritarian parent places firm limits and controls on the child with little verbal exchange allowed. For example, an authoritarian parent might say, "You do it my way or else. There will be no discussion!" Research reveals that the children of authoritarian parents often are anxious about social comparisons, fail to initiate activity, and have poor communication skills.

Authoritative parenting encourages the child to be independent but still places limits, demands, and controls on his actions. Extensive verbal give-and-take is allowed and parents are warm and nurturant toward the child. For example, an authoritative parent might put his arm around the child in a comforting way and say, "You know you should not have done that; let's talk about how you can handle this situation better the next time." Children whose parents are authoritative are socially competent, self-reliant, and socially responsible.

Permissive parenting comes in two forms: permissive-indifferent and permissive-indulgent (Maccoby & Martin, 1983). **Permissive-indifferent** parents are very uninvolved in their child's life. This parent cannot answer the question, "It is 10 P.M. Do you know where your child is?" Children have a strong need for their parents to care about them; children whose parents are permissive-indifferent develop the sense that other aspects of the parents' lives are more important than they are. Children whose parents are permissive-indifferent are socially incompetent—they show poor self-control and do not handle independence well.

Permissive-indulgent parents are highly involved with their children but place few demands or controls on them. They let their children do what they want, and the result is that children never learn to control their own behavior and always expect to get their way. Some parents deliberately rear their children in this way because they believe the combination of warm involvement with few restraints will produce a creative, confident child. One boy I know whose parents deliberately reared him in a permissive-indulgent manner moved his parents out of their bedroom suite and took it over for himself. He now is eighteen years old and has not learned to control his behavior; when he can't get something he wants, he still throws temper tantrums. As you might expect, he is not very popular with his peers; as with his parents, he expects his peers to bow down to his demands. Children whose parents are permissive-indulgent never learn respect for others and have difficulty controlling their behavior.

There is more to understanding parent-child relations than parenting style. For many years the socialization of children was viewed as a straightforward, one-way matter of indoctrination—telling small children about the use of spoons and potties, the importance of saying thank you, and not killing the new baby brother. The basic philosophy was that the child had to be trained

to fit into the social world, so his behavior had to be shaped accordingly. However, socialization is more than molding the child into a mature adult. The young child is not like the inanimate blob of clay the sculptor molds into a polished statue; children socialize parents just as parents socialize children. This is called the process of **reciprocal socialization.** As developmental psychologists probe the nature of reciprocal socialization, they are impressed by the importance of synchrony in parent-child relationships (Isabella, 1987; Stern, 1974). Some parents and children seem to get along and others do not. One child may need a parent to soothe his emotional wounds when he faces life's stresses; another child may fare better when the parent simply talks to him in an adultlike fashion. Both children in these examples are getting attention from the parent, but in different ways; one way may fit with the child's makeup better than the other.

A parent also needs to consider the child's developmental status; a competent parent does not interact with a ten-year-old child in the same way as with a two-year-old child (Belsky & Pensky, 1987; Maccoby, 1980; White, 1988). During the child's second and third years, the parent usually handles disciplinary matters by physical manipulation; the child is carried away from mischievous activity, fragile objects are placed out of reach, and sometimes the child is spanked. As the child grows older, parents turn more to reasoning, moral exhortation, and giving or withholding special privileges. Parents also spend less time with the older child and monitor her activities more indirectly.

For many years the major focus of parent-child relationships was on the mother and the child; today the father's role in the child's development raises provocative questions: Can and do fathers act sensitively as caregivers to infants? How involved are fathers in the child's development (Lamb, 1987; Pedersen, in press). Research suggests that fathers can act sensitively to the infant's signals to be touched and fed (Parke & Sawin, 1980). Infants and children often prefer to play with fathers than mothers, possibly because fathers play more actively than mothers. However, in stressful situations, young children usually turn to their mothers instead of their fathers (Lamb, 1977).

Fathers spend more time with their children now than they did a decade ago, but they still spend far less time than mothers. Even when the mother works, the father interacts with the child in a face-to-face manner only about one-third as much as the mother. When we consider level of responsibility—such as who makes sure the child is dressed well, gets to school on time, is fed nutritious meals, and goes to the dentist—fathers are even less involved (Lamb, 1986).

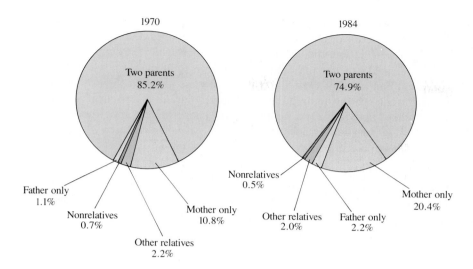

Figure 9.19
Where children under 18 live.
Data from the U.S. Bureau of the Census.

The Hodgepodge of Family Structures

As we move toward the latter part of the twentieth century, children are being socialized in a greater variety of family structures than ever before in history. As shown in figure 9.19, a substantial increase in the number of children under eighteen who lived in a single-parent family occurred between 1970 and 1984. If current trends continue, by the time we reach the year 2000 one in every four children will have lived a portion of their lives with a stepfather or step-mother by the time they are eighteen years of age. Less than 10 percent of children in the United States live in a two-parent family in which only one parent (usually the father) is the breadwinner. Mothers have joined the work force in expanding numbers. As we discussed at the beginning of the chapter, a major concern has evolved—who is caring for and monitoring our children?

Early studies of the effects of divorce on children followed a father-absent tradition. Children from father-absent and father-present families were compared, and differences in their development were attributed to the absence of the father. But family structure (such as father-present, divorced, widowed) is only one of many factors that influence the child's adjustment. The contemporary approach advocates evaluating the strengths and weaknesses of the child prior to divorce, the nature of events surrounding the divorce itself, and post-divorce family functioning. Investigators are finding that the availability and use of support systems (baby-sitters, relatives, day care), an ongoing, positive relationship between the custodial parent and the ex-spouse, authoritative parenting, financial stability, and the child's competencies at the time of the divorce are related to the child's adjustment (Block, Block, & Gjerde, 1986; Hetherington, 1987; Kelly, 1987; Santrock & Warshak, 1986; Wallerstein & Kelly, 1980).

Many divorced, as well as married, parents must work outside the home to make ends meet. The evidence suggests that childen whose mothers work outside the home are as well adjusted as children whose mothers do not (Hoffman, 1979). The mother's employment also provides the child with two achievement-oriented models instead of just one.

Nonetheless, employed parents need to exercise caution not only about the quality of care their young children experience (Belsky, 1987), but also about the after-school hours and summer months of their older children and adolescents. In one investigation, 90 percent of the adjudicated juvenile delinquents in Montgomery County, Maryland, were "latchkey children"—so-called because they carry a key to their house (Long & Long, 1983). One expert on child disturbances calls the lack of supervision of children after school the "3 to 6 P.M. problem," because it is during these hours that the greatest number of referrals of children to psychological clinics occur (Lipsitz, 1983). A recent investigation, though, suggests it is not the latchkey experience itself that is harmful but how parents interact with their children when they are with them and monitor their lives when they are not with them. (Steinberg, 1986). Parents who structured their latchkey children's after-school hours with clubs, school activities, and neighborhood cooperatives, and who were authoritative rather than authoritarian or permissive, had children who were less susceptible to peer pressure.

Peers and Play

As you think about your childhood years, most likely some of your most enjoyable as well as frustrating moments were spent with peers. Peers provide the child with a source of information about the world outside of the family. Through peer discussions, a child may learn that another child's parents argue all the time, make him go to bed early, do not let him watch Saturday morning cartoon shows, and give him an allowance. Children frequently compare themselves with their peers: are they better than, about the same, or worse than their peers at skateboarding, math, reading, answering questions, and having friends? It is hard to do this at home because siblings are usually older or younger and do not provide a fair comparison.

A major goal of most children is to have friends and be popular. Children who are successful at this are happy, enthusiastic, show a concern for others, and have effective communication skills. For example, children who are good conversationalists, who listen attentively, and who are affectionate with their peers are popular and make friends easily (Burleson, 1985; Gottman & Parker, 1987; Hartup, 1983; Parker & Gottman, 1985).

When children are asked what they enjoy most, they invariably answer "playing." The word *play* is conspicuous in children's conversations with each other: "What can we play?" "Let's play hide-and-seek." "No, let's play inside." The major portions of many young children's days are spent in play, which encourages affiliation with peers, helps children work off frustrations, and provides a setting for exploring and seeking out new information (Görlitz & Wohlwill, 1987).

We have seen that children are exposed to many different social agents and contexts as they develop. Experiences with parents and peers are important determinants of a child's personality development, which we turn to next. First, though, you may want to review the main themes of children's physical, cognitive, and social development in concept table 9.3.

Social Competence and Personality Development

What makes a child socially competent? What are some important aspects of the child's personality and how do they develop?

The Socially Competent Child

A socially competent child is able to use resources within herself and in the environment to achieve positive developmental outcomes (Waters & Sroufe, 1983). Resources within the child include self-esteem, self-control, delay of gratification, resilience to stress, and a healthy orientation toward achievement and work. For example, the socially competent child feels good about herself and has confidence in her abilities; she can control her behavior in the face of temptation and threat; she is able to delay gratification when appropriate rather than seeking immediate satisfaction; she copes effectively with stress (often viewing stress as a challenge rather than a threat); and she persists with effort in achieving goals. Parents are important resources in the child's environment throughout the childhood years; in early childhood and beyond, play and peers take on more importance.

When you were young, what did you enjoy doing the most? Probably playing. The major part of your day as a young child probably was spent in play, which served some important functions in your development— encouraging affiliation with peers, helping to work off frustrations, and providing a setting for exploring and seeking out new information.

Concept Table 9.3

Childhood Periods, Physical Development, Cognitive Development, and Social Contexts and Development		
Concept	Processes/related ideas	Characteristics/description
Childhood periods and physical development	Childhood periods	Early childhood coincides with the preschool years, roughly three to five years of age. Middle and late childhood correspond with the elementary school years, about six to eleven years of age.
	Physical development	Slows during the childhood years, although motor development becomes smoother and more coordinated.
Cognitive development	Preoperational and concrete operational thought	A key aspect of development is the ability to perform operations (mental representations that are reversible). The preoperational child (ages two to seven) cannot do this, the concrete operatonal child (ages seven to eleven) can. The preoperational child is egocentric; symbolic and intuitive thought are prominent. In concrete operational thought logical reasoning occurs when concrete rather than abstract information is involved.
	Evaluating Piaget	A genius at observing children, he changed forever the way we view the child's understanding of the world. His views have not gone uncriticized; information processing psychologists advocate more attention to the tasks used to assess children's cognition.
Social contexts and development	Parent-child relations	Baumrind's parenting strategies—authoritarian, authoritative, and laissez-faire, or permissive—are widely used classifications. Socially competent children are more likely to have authoritative parents. However, the socialization of children is a reciprocal process; children also socialize parents. Greater interest in the father's role is being shown, although fathers still are not very involved in the child-rearing process.
	The hodgepodge of family structures	Children today grow up in a greater variety of family structures than ever before—psychologists study the effects of divorce, the mother's employment, and the "latchkey" experience.
	Peers and play	Important dimensions of child development. Psychologists study the factors that contribute to peer popularity and friendship. Play takes up the major portion of many young children's days and serves many functions.

The dimensions of social competence may be different at various points in development—dependency is a positive feature of social competence in the first year but later takes on a more negative tone. We saw that Erikson believes the development of trust is the most salient component of social competence in the first year, while autonomy has that distinction in the second year. What does Erikson believe are the most important dimensions of social competence during the remainder of childhood?

Erikson's Childhood Stages

Erikson (1968) believes that the socially competent child develops a sense of initiative in early childhood. The conflict for the child at this point in development involves **initiative versus guilt.** As the preschool child encounters a widening social environment, Erikson believes the child is challenged more than when he was an infant; active, purposeful behavior is needed to cope with these challenges. Children are asked to assume responsibility for their body, their behavior, their toys, and their pets. But as children move into new spheres and are asked to assume more responsibility, uncomfortable guilt feelings may appear. Erikson has a positive outlook about this stage, though; most guilt and failure are quickly compensated for by a sense of accomplishment.

Children's initiative brings them in contact with a wealth of new experiences. As they move into middle and late childhood, they direct their energy toward mastering knowledge and intellectual skills. Erikson says the socially competent child at this point in development gains a sense of industry; the conflict involves **industry versus inferiority.** At no other time is the child more enthusiastic about learning than at the end of this period of expansive imagination, which characterizes early childhood. The danger at this stage is a sense of inferiority—of feeling incompetent and unproductive. Erikson believes teachers have a special responsibility for children's development of industry; they should "mildly but firmly coerce (them) into the adventure of finding out that one can learn to accomplish things which one would never have thought of by oneself" (Erikson, 1968, p. 127).

Gender Roles

The child's social competence and personality also involve gender roles. Imagine you are observing two four-year-old children and one says, "You stay here with the baby while I go fishing." Don't you immediately think that one of the children is a boy and the other a girl? Don't you also infer that the child doing the talking is a boy?

During early childhood, children make grand generalizations about **gender roles,** which are social expectations of how we should act and think as males and females. For example, three-year-old William accompanied his mother to the doctor's office. A man in a white coat walked by and William said "Hi, Doc." Then a woman in a white coat walked by and William greeted her, "Hi, nurse." William's mother asked him how he knew which person was a doctor and which was a nurse. William replied, "Because doctors are daddies and nurses are mommies." As Piaget said, young children seem so sure about their thoughts, yet so often inaccurately understand the world. William's "nurse" turned out to be his doctor, and vice versa (Carper, 1978).

Nowhere in the social and personality development of children have more sweeping changes occurred in recent years than in the area of gender roles. At a point not long ago, it was accepted that boys grew up to conform to traditional "masculine" stereotypes and girls to conform to "feminine" stereotypes. The feedback children experienced from parents, peers, teachers, and television was consistent with this thinking. Today, diversity characterizes the gender roles of children and the feedback they receive from their environment. A young girl's mother may promote femininity, but the girl may be close friends with a "tomboy" in the neighborhood and have a teacher who encourages her assertiveness.

In the past, the well-adjusted male was expected to be independent, aggressive, and power-oriented; the well-adjusted female was expected to be dependent, nurturant, and uninterested in power and dominance. By the mid-1970s, though, the landscape of gender roles was changing. Many females were unhappy with the label "feminine" and felt stigmatized by its association with characteristics such as passiveness and unassertiveness. Many males were uncomfortable with being called "masculine" because of its association with such characteristics as insensitivity and aggressiveness. Many lay people as well as psychologists believed that something more than "masculinity" and "femininity" was needed to describe the change in gender roles that was taking place. The byword became **androgyny,** meaning the combination of masculine and feminine characteristics in the same person (Bem, 1977; Spence & Helm-

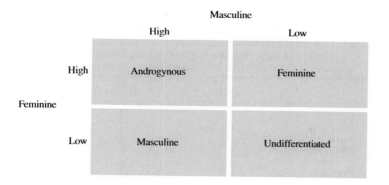

Figure 9.20
The four classifications of gender roles.

reich, 1978). The androgynous child might be a male who is assertive (masculine) and nurturant (feminine), or a female who is dominant (masculine) and sensitive to others' feelings (feminine).

The primary characteristics used to assess androgyny are self-assertiveness and integration (Ford, 1986). The self-assertive characteristics include: leadership, dominance, independence, competitiveness, and individualism. Integrative characteristics include: sympathy, affection, and understanding. The androgynous child or adult is simply a male or female who has a high degree of both masculine and feminine characteristics—no new characteristics are used to describe the androgynous individual. An individual can be classified as masculine, feminine, or androgynous. A fourth category, *undifferentiated,* also is used to assess gender roles; this category describes an individual who has neither masculine nor feminine characteristics. The four classifications of gender roles are shown in figure 9.20.

Which children are the most competent? Children who are undifferentiated are the least competent: they are the least socially responsible, they have the least self-control and they receive the poorest grades in school. This category is not fully understood by psychologists and few children are classified in this way. But what about the majority of children who are either masculine, feminine, or androgynous—which group is the most competent?

This is not an easy question to answer because the dimensions of androgyny and the dimensions of competence are not clearly spelled out in research on the issue. In many instances androgynous children are the most competent, but a key point involves what the criteria for competence are. If the criteria for competence involve both self-assertion and integration, then androgynous children generally are more competent. However, if the criteria for competence primarily involve self-assertion, then a masculine gender role is favored; if they mainly involve integration, then a feminine gender role is preferable.

The self-assertive dimension of gender roles has been valued in our culture more than the integrative dimension. When psychologists have assessed the relation of gender roles to competence, their criteria for competence have included twice as many self-assertive items as integrative items. A disturbing outcome of such cultural standards and research bias is that masculine dimensions are perceived to mean competence. We need to place a higher value on integration in our culture and include it in our assessments of competence.

Table 9.3	Adjectives that Describe Possible Gender Differences

What are the differences in the behavior and thoughts of boys and girls? For each of the adjectives below, indicate whether you think it *best* describes boys or girls—or neither—in our society. Be honest and follow your first impulse.

	Girls	Boys
Verbal skills	☐	☐
Sensitive	☐	☐
Active	☐	☐
Competitive	☐	☐
Compliant	☐	☐
Dominant	☐	☐
Math skills	☐	☐
Suggestible	☐	☐
Social	☐	☐
Aggressive	☐	☐
Visual-spatial skills	☐	☐

Gender Differences and Stereotyping

In addition to studying expectations and attitudes about gender, we also can evaluate whether boys and girls actually differ on a number of dimensions. To sample some of the possible differences in gender, turn to table 9.3. According to Eleanor Maccoby and Carol Nagy Jacklin (1974), females have better verbal skills, but males have better math skills, are more aggressive, and have superior visual-spatial ability (the kind of skills an architect would need in designing the angles and dimensions of a building).

Not everyone agrees with Maccoby and Jacklin (e.g., Block, 1976; Eccles, 1987a; Hyde, 1985) and as our culture changes it is difficult to make conclusions about gender differences. As our expectations and attitudes about gender roles change, possibly the nature of actual gender differences between children will change.

Consider the expectations and attitudes about an area related to the gender differences in math skills: computer ability. In two recent novels, *Turing's Man* (Botler, 1984) and *The Second Self* (Turkle, 1984), technology overwhelms humanity. In both stories, females are not portrayed as having integral roles in this technological, computer culture. One character notes, "There are few women hackers. This is a male world." (Turkle, 1984). Unfortunately, both boys and girls are socialized to associate computer programming with math skills, and typically programming is taught in math departments by males. Male-female ratios in computer classes range from 2:1 to 5:1, although computers in offices tend to be used equally by males and females. Males also have more positive attitudes toward computers. It is hoped that Turkle's male computer hacker will not serve as the model for computer users in the future (Lockheed, 1985).

Gender bias and stereotyping in learning materials were not publicized until the late 1960s; documentation since then is startling in its scope and consistency (Minuchin & Shapiro, 1983). Bias occurs in readers, curriculum materials, and textbooks ranging from social studies through math. The language, illustrations, role depictions, and ratio of male to female figures reflect traditional gender roles and frequently are biased against females. Little nurturance and emotional sensitivity is shown by boys and men in learning materials; little strength, skill, and ability to make decisions appear in the behavior

Psychology 9.3

How Good Are Girls at Wudgemaking If the Wudgemaker Is "He"?

In one investigation, the following description of a fictitious, gender-neutral occupation, wudgemaker, was read to third- and fifth-grade children, with repeated reference either to *he, they, he or she,* or *she* (Hyde, 1984):

> Few people have heard of a job in factories, being a wudgemaker. Wudges are made of oddly shaped plastic, and are an important part of video games. The wudgemaker works from a plan or pattern posted at eye level as *he or she* puts together the pieces at a table while *he or she* is sitting down. Eleven plastic pieces must be snapped together. Some of the pieces are tiny, so that *he or she* must have good coordination in *his or her* fingers. Once all eleven pieces are put together, *he or she* must test out the wudge to make sure that all of the moving pieces move properly. The wudgemaker is well paid, and must be a high school graduate, but *he or she* does not have to have gone to college to get the job. (Hyde, 1984, p. 702)

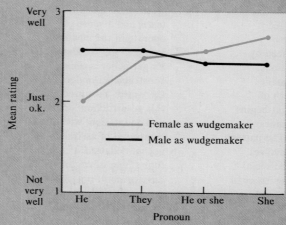

Figure 9.G
Mean ratings of how well women and men would do as wudgemakers, according to pronoun used in the description.
From Hyde, J. S., "Children's understanding of sexist language," in Developmental Psychology, 20, *p. 703. Copyright © 1984 by the American Psychological Association. Reprinted by permission of the author.*

One-fourth of the children were read the story with *he* as the pronoun, one-fourth with *they,* one-fourth with *he or she* (as shown), and one-fourth with *she.* The children were asked to rate how well women could do the job of wudgemaking and also how well they thought men could perform the job. As shown in figure 9.G, ratings of how well women could make wudges were influenced by the pronoun used; ratings were lowest for *he,* intermediate for *they* and *he or she,* and highest for *she.* This suggests that the use of the gender-neutral *he,* compared to other pronouns, influences children's conceptions of how competent males and females are in our society.

of girls and women. Occupational roles are more apparent for males than females, who often are portrayed in limited and conventional jobs. The generic "he" is used consistently to refer to both males and females. For a fascinating look at the way language is related to children's perception of how competent "wudgemakers" are, turn to Psychology 9.3.

Development does not end with childhood. We also develop as adolescents and adults. We will discuss this development in the next chapter.

Summary

I. History of Interest in Children

In the Middle Ages, the original sin view dominated. In the Renaissance, the tabula rasa and innate goodness views addressed the nature of the child's development. The ideas of Darwin, Hall, Freud, and Gesell had a strong biological flavor; Watson's view emphasized environmental influences. Research also is influenced by sociopolitical considerations.

II. The Nature of Development

Development is a pattern of movement or change that begins at conception and continues through the life cycle. The pattern is complex because it involves biological, cognitive, and social processes. Two enduring issues in development are heredity-environment and continuity-discontinuity.

III. Prenatal Development

Conception occurs when a sperm unites with the ovum. The fertilized egg is called a zygote. The first two weeks after conception is called the germinal period, two to eight weeks after conception is called the embryonic period, and two to nine months after is called the fetal period. Teratogens are agents that cause birth defects. Many teratogens exist; rarely does a specific teratogen cause a specific birth defect. Drugs as well as maternal diseases can harm the fetus.

IV. Birth and the Newborn

The Apgar Scale is used to evaluate the newborn's health and well-being; the Brazelton Scale is also widely used. Brazelton training, which includes parenting skills, is recommended when the newborn is sluggish. Bonding is widely recognized, but it shows no long-term benefits.

V. Infant Physical and Perceptual Development

The infant comes into the world equipped with a number of reflexes. Sleeping and eating are two important states. Growth follows a cephalo-caudal pattern. Brain growth during infancy involves extensive dendritic branching. Infants can see, but their vision is about 20/600 at birth; it improves to 20/100 at six months. By six months infants can perceive depth. Newborns can hear; fetuses respond to sound two weeks before birth. Smell, touch, taste, and a sense of pain also operate in the newborn.

VI. Infant Cognitive Development

Piaget believes the child constructs an understanding of the world. Two processes underlie this construction: organization and adaptation, with the latter comprised of assimilation and accommodation. Piaget identified four stages of cognitive development: sensorimotor, preoperational, concrete operational, and formal operational. The sensorimotor stage lasts from birth to two years of age and involves the coordination of sensorimotor action. Object permanence is a hallmark of the sensorimotor stage, occurring for the first time during the second half of the first year.

VII. Infant Social Development

Attachment involves the bond between the infant and the caregiver (usually the mother). A number of theories of attachment have been proposed. Feeding does not seem to be critical in the infant's attachment, but contact comfort, familiarity, and the caregiver's responsiveness are. Controversy surrounds the concept of secure attachment; some experts think it is critical for the development of social competence, others do not. Independence is an important theme of the second year of life (Erikson's second stage is called autonomy versus doubt). By eighteen to twenty-four months, infants have a sense of self.

VIII. Childhood Periods and Physical Development

Early childhood coincides with the preschool years, roughly three to five years of age; middle and late childhood correspond to the elementary school years, about six to eleven years of age. Physical growth slows during childhood, although motor development becomes much smoother.

IX. Cognitive Development in Childhood

A key aspect of the child's cognitive development is the ability to perform operations (mental representations that are reversible). The preoperational child cannot do this, the concrete operational child can. The preoperational child also is egocentric. Symbolic and intuitive thought are predominant in the preoperational stage, which occurs mainly from two to seven years of age. The concrete operational stage occurs from seven to eleven years of age; logical reasoning occurs as long as concrete rather than abstract information is involved. Piaget was a genius at observing children and changed forever the way we view the child's understanding of the world. His views have not gone uncriticized, though; information processing psychologists advocate more attention to the tasks used to assess children's cognition.

X. Social Contexts and Development

Baumrind's three parenting strategies—authoritarian, authoritative, and laissez-faire, or permissive—are widely used classifications. Socially competent children are more likely to have authoritative parents. However, the socialization of children is a reciprocal process; children also socialize parents. Greater interest in the father's role is being shown, although fathers still are not very involved with their children.

Children today grow up in a greater variety of family structures than ever before—psychologists study the effects of divorce, the mother's employment, and the "latchkey" experience. Peers and play are important dimensions of child development. Psychologists study the factors that contribute to peer popularity and friendship. Play takes up a major portion of many young children's days and serves many functions.

XI. Social Competence and Personality Development

The socially competent child can draw on effective resources from within and in the environment. Erikson believes initiative versus guilt characterizes the preschool years while industry versus inferiority predominates during the elementary school years. Gender roles focus on society's expectations for males and females. Recent interest has emphasized androgyny, the belief that competent individuals have both masculine and feminine characteristics. Self-assertion and integration are the most important dimensions of masculinity and femininity, respectively, that contribute to androgyny. Controversy surrounds whether androgynous children are more competent. Psychologists have documented the existence of some gender differences and point out that considerable stereotyping of males and females takes place.

Key Terms

original sin *280*
tabula rasa *281*
innate goodness *281*
development *282*
conception *283*
zygote *283*
germinal period *283*
embryonic period *283*
amniocentesis *284*
chorionic villus test *284*
fetal period *285*
teratogen *286*
fetal alcohol syndrome (FAS) *286*
Apgar Scale *287*
Brazelton Neonatal Behavioral Assessment Scale *287*

bonding *288*
Moro reflex *289*
cephalo-caudal pattern *290*
assimilation *292*
accommodation *292*
sensorimotor stage *293*
object permanence *294*
attachment *296*
imprinting *297*
trust versus mistrust *298*
epigenetic principle *298*
secure or insecure attachment *298*
autonomy versus doubt *299*
early childhood *300*

middle and late childhood *300*
operations *302*
preoperational stage *302*
egocentrism *302*
concrete operational stage *303*
authoritarian parenting *307*
authoritative parenting *307*
permissive-indifferent parenting *307*
permissive-indulgent parenting *307*
reciprocal socialization *308*
initiative versus guilt *311*
industry versus inferiority *312*
gender roles *312*
androgyny *312*

Suggested Readings

Child Development and *Developmental Psychology* These two research journals are highly respected outlets for scientific information about child development. Go to your library and leaf through the issues published in the last several years to get a sense of developmental psychologists' research interests.

Flavell, J. H. (1985). *Cognitive development* (2nd ed.). Englewood Cliffs, NJ: Prentice-Hall. This book represents an outstanding treatment of the child's cognitive development; it is written by one of the leading scholars in the field.

Hyde, J. S. (1985). *Half the human experience* (3rd ed.). Lexington, MA: D. C. Heath. An excellent review of what we know about gender roles. Special attention is given to the development of females.

Lamb, M. E. (1986). *The father's role: Applied perspectives*. New York: Wiley. A number of leading scholars in the study of family processes describe their views; the book includes chapters on divorce, working mothers, and father custody.

Mussen, P. H. (Ed.)(1983). *Handbook of child psychology, vols. 1–4* (4th ed.). New York: Wiley. This four-volume set is used by developmental psychologists as a major reference for information about child development. Chapters range from the history of childhood to reviews of biological, cognitive, and social processes.

Adolescence, Adult Development, and Aging

■ ■

Youth beholds happiness gleaming in the prospect,
Age looks back on the happiness of youth, and instead of hopes, seeks
its enjoyment in the recollection of hope.

—Coleridge

■ ■

Images of Adolescence, Adult Development, and Aging

If I could save time in a bottle
the first thing that I'd like to do
is save every day till eternity passes away
just to spend them with you . . .

If I had a box just for wishes
and dreams that never came true,
the box would be empty except for
the memory for how they were answered by you.

But there never seems to be enough time to do
the things you want to do once you find them.
Looked around enough to know that you're the one
I want to go through time with. (Jim Croce, *Time in a Bottle*)

Time in a Bottle
© *1971, 1972 DenJac Music Co. & MCA Music Inc. All worldwide rights administered by DenJac*
Music Co. Used by permission. All rights reserved.

We view time differently depending on where we are in the life cycle. We are more concerned about time at some points in life than others. Adolescents show more interest in time than children. The adolescent's time perspective often combines looking toward a boundless future with living in the immediacy of the here and now. Since they perceive their future as unlimited, they feel they can try many different things. The adolescent's sense of time was captured by Joseph Conrad in the late nineteenth century: "I remember my youth and the feeling that never came back anymore—the feeling that I could last forever, outlast the sea, the earth, and all men."

Jim Croce's song, *Time in a Bottle,* reflects a theme of life and a time perspective that unfolds as we move into the adulthood years. As young adults, love and intimacy assume prominent roles in our lives. We begin to look back at where we have been. As middle-aged adults, we look back even more and reflect on what we have done with the time we have had. We look toward the future more in terms of how much time remains to accomplish what we wish to do with our lives. As adolescents look to the future as endless, their parents, most of whom are middle-aged or about to be, show a more intense interest in time and perceive it differently than their offspring.

As older adults, we look back even more and review our lives, adding up the pluses and minuses of our many experiences, integrating them into a sense of who we are and what our life has been about. ■

Adolescence

In 1904, G. Stanley Hall reviewed the current thinking about masturbation in adolescence. He concluded that masturbation is one of the saddest of all human weaknesses and went on to review suggestions for how masturbation could be reduced or even eliminated. Included in the suggestions were the abolition of erotic pictures, feather beds, horseback riding, and even bicycling.

BLOOM COUNTY

by Berke Breathed

© 1986, Washington Post Writer's Group, reprinted with permission.

Hall thought the best strategy was to have adolescents work hard and long and go to bed early. We no longer view masturbation as a major problem in adolescence, but controversy still surrounds the issue of just how stressful and turbulent the adolescent years are.

Historical Beginnings and the Nature of Adolescence

While G. Stanley Hall had some odd ideas about masturbation, he played an important part in the study of adolescence. Hall (1904) is known as the father of the scientific study of adolescence. According to Hall, adolescence is a time of storm and stress, full of contradictions and wide swings in mood. Thoughts, feelings, and actions oscillate between conceit and humility, good and temptation, happiness and sadness. The adolescent may be nasty to a peer one moment and kind the next moment. At one time the adolescent may want to be alone but seconds later want close companionship. Because he viewed adolescence as a turbulent time charged with conflict, Hall's perspective became known as the **storm and stress view.**

During most of the twentieth century, the abnormalities and deviancies of adolescence have been studied more than the normalities. Consider Hall's image of adolescents as well as those portrayed in the media—rebellious, in conflict, impulsive, faddish, delinquent, and self-centered. In the 1970s and 1980s a push to dispel the myth that adolescents are a sorry lot has emerged. A survey by Daniel Yankelovich (1974), for example, is among a growing number of investigations that reveal little if any differences in values, life-styles, and codes of personal conduct between adolescents and their parents. Parents and their adolescent offspring do not differ in their attitudes toward such matters as self-control, hard work, saving money, competition, compromise, legal authority, and private properties. Some of the stereotypes of adolescents are carry-overs from perceptions of the 1960s—adolescents were seen as rebellious, disenchanted, and distasteful toward adult values (Adelson, 1979). More than an adolescent generation gap, an adolescent "generalization gap" has developed, meaning that widespread generalizations have been made about adolescents based on information about a small percentage of highly visible adolescents.

Grandville Stanley Hall, 1846–1925. Hall is known as the father of the scientific study of adolescence. He believed that adolescence is filled with storm and stress. Today we no longer believe that adolescence is the universal crisis Hall envisioned.

Adolescence is not the jaundiced time Hall envisioned. The vast majority of adolescents make the transition from childhood to adulthood competently. As with any period of development, adolescence has its hills and valleys, issues to be negotiated, mistakes and adjustments, highs and lows, and ebbs and flows in life. Today we view adolescence in a much more balanced, positive way than earlier in this century.

Current interest in the history of adolescence raises the possibility that adolescence actually is an historical invention. As A. K. Cohen (1964) commented:

> Not quite children and certainly not adults, in many ways privileged, wielding unprecedented economic power as consumers of clothing, entertainment, and other amenities, the object of a peculiar blend of tenderness, indulgence, distrust, hostility, moving through a seemingly endless course of "preparation for life" . . . playing furiously at "adult" games but resolutely confined to a society of their own peers and excluded from serious and responsible participation in the world of their elders. . . . a few years ago it occurred to me that when I was a teenager, in the early depression years, there were no teenagers! The teenager has sneaked up on us in our own lifetime and yet it seems to us that he always has been with us. . . . The teenager had not yet been invented (though, and) there did not yet exist a special class of beings, bound in a certain way . . . not quite children and certainly not adults. (p. ix)

At a point not long ago, then, the "teenager" may not yet have been invented. While adolescence has a biological base, sociohistorical conditions probably contributed to the emergence of the concept of adolescence. American society may have "inflicted" the status of adolescence on its youth through child-saving legislation (Lapsley, Enright, & Serlin, 1985). By developing laws for youth only, the adult power structure placed young people in a submissive position, one that restricted their options, encouraged dependency, and made their move into the world of adult work more manageable. From 1890 to 1920, virtually every state developed laws that excluded youth from work and required them to attend school. In this time frame, a 600 percent increase in the number of high school graduates occurred (Tyack, 1976).

As in the development of children, genetic, biological, environmental, and social factors interact in adolescent development. Also, continuity and discontinuity characterize adolescent development. The genes inherited from parents still influence thought and behavior during adolescence, but inheritance now interacts with the social conditions of the adolescent's world—with family, peers, friendships, dating, and school experiences. An adolescent has experienced thousands of hours of interactions with parents, peers, and teachers in the past ten to thirteen years of development. Still new experiences and developmental tasks appear during adolescence. Relationships with parents take a different form, moments with peers and friends become more intimate, dating occurs for the first time as does sexual exploration. The adolescent's thoughts are more abstract and idealistic. Biological changes trigger a heightened interest in body image. Adolescence, then, has both continuity and discontinuity with childhood.

Adolescence can be defined as a period of transition from childhood to adulthood that involves physical, cognitive, and social changes. In most cultures adolescence is entered between ten and thirteen years of age and exited at some point between eighteen and twenty-two years of age.

As psychologists explore adolescence in more detail, they describe this time frame as having early and late phases. **Early adolescence** occurs roughly between ten and fifteen years of age, a time when physical changes and maturation are extensive. **Late adolescence** occurs between sixteen to eighteen and eighteen to twenty-two years of age, a period when maturation has slowed considerably and more serious concerns with identity and careers develop.

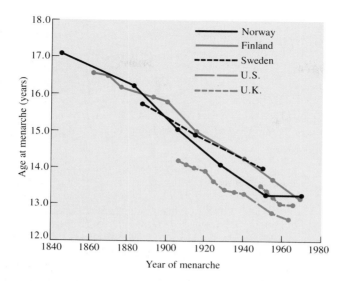

Figure 10.1
Median ages at menarche in selected northern European countries and the United States from 1845 to 1969.

Physical Development

Imagine a toddler displaying all the features of puberty—a three-year-old girl with fully developed breasts or a boy just slightly older with a deep male voice. We would see this by the year 2250 if the age of puberty would continue to decrease at its present pace. Menarche (the first menstruation) has declined from 14.2 years in 1900 to about 12.45 years today. Age of menarche has been declining an average of about four months a decade for the last century (see figure 10.1). We are unlikely, though, to see pubescent toddlers in the future because what happened in the last century is special. That something special is a higher level of nutrition and health. A lower age of menarche is associated with increased standards of living (about 10 to 15 percent of the variation in age at menarche is genetically determined) (Petersen, 1979, in press).

Menarche is one event that characterizes puberty, but there are others as well. While **puberty** can be defined as rapid maturation, it is not a single, sudden event. Puberty is part of a gradual process of development that begins at conception. We know when a young person is going through puberty, but pinpointing its beginning and end is difficult. Except for menarche, which occurs rather late in puberty, no single marker heralds puberty. For boys, the first whisker or first wet dream are events that could mark its appearance, but both may go unnoticed.

Behind the first whisker in boys and widening of hips in girls is a flood of hormones. Remember from chapter 2 that hormones are powerful chemical substances secreted by the endocrine glands and carried through the body in the bloodstream. The concentrations of certain hormones increase dramatically during adolescence. In boys, **testosterone** is associated with the development of external genitals, an increase in height, and voice change. In girls, **estradiol** is linked with breast, uterine, and skeletal development (Dillon, 1980). In one investigation, testosterone levels increased eighteen-fold in boys but only two-fold in girls during puberty; estradiol increased eight-fold in girls but only two-fold in boys (Nottelmann & others, 1985). This same influx of hormones may be associated with adjustment in adolescence. In a recent study, a higher concentration of testosterone was present in boys who rated themselves more socially competent (Nottelmann & others, 1987).

These hormonal and body changes occur on the average about two years earlier in females (ten and one-half years of age) than in males (twelve and one-half years of age). Four of the most noticeable areas of body change in

Puberty is a time of tremendous biological change. It has been coming faster every decade in this century. Defining when puberty is entered is difficult, however. How would you determine if the girls shown here are in puberty?

Figure 10.2
*Normal range and average age of
height spurt and development of
sexual characteristics in females.*
From "Growing Up," by J. M. Tanner. Copyright
© 1973 by Scientific American, Inc. All rights
reserved.

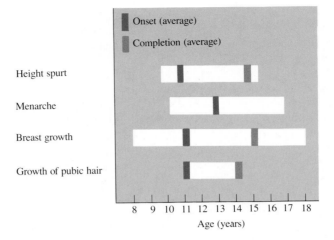

Figure 10.3
*Normal range and average age of
height spurt and development of
sexual characteristics in males.*
From "Growing Up," by J. M. Tanner. Copyright
© 1973 by Scientific American, Inc. All rights
reserved.

females are height spurt, menarche, breast growth, and pubic hair. In boys the most obvious changes are height spurt, penile growth, testes growth, and pubic hair. The normal and average range of these characteristics is shown in figures 10.2 and 10.3.

A host of psychological changes accompany an adolescent's physical development. Imagine yourself as you were beginning puberty. Not only did you probably think about yourself differently, but your parents and peers probably began acting differently toward you. Maybe you were proud of your changing body, even though you were perplexed about what was happening. Or possibly you felt embarrassed about the changes and experienced anxiety. Perhaps your parents no longer perceived you as someone they could sit in bed and watch television with or as someone who should be kissed good night.

Some of you entered puberty early, others entered late. When adolescents mature earlier or later than their peers, might they perceive themselves differently? Some years ago, in the California Longitudinal Study, early maturing boys perceived themselves more positively and had more successful peer relations than their late maturing counterparts (Jones, 1965). The findings for early maturing girls were similar but not as strong as for boys. When the late maturing boys were studied in their thirties, however, they had developed a stronger sense of identity than the early maturing boys (Peskin, 1967). Possibly this occurred because the late maturing boys had more time to explore life's options or because the early maturing boys continued to focus on their advantageous physical status instead of career development and achievement.

More recent research confirms, though, that at least during adolescence, it is advantageous to be an early maturing rather than a late maturing boy (Blyth, Bulcroft, & Simmons, 1981; Simmons & Blyth, 1987). The more recent findings for girls suggest that early maturation is a mixed blessing: these girls experience more problems in school but also more independence and popularity with boys. Grade level also makes a difference. In the sixth grade early maturing girls showed greater satisfaction with their figures than late maturing girls, but by the tenth grade late maturing girls were more satisfied (see figure 10.4). The reason for this is that by late adolescence, early maturing girls are shorter and stockier while late maturing girls are taller and thinner. The late maturing girl in late adolescence has a body that more closely approximates the American ideal of feminine beauty—tall and thin.

Cognitive Development

"Oh my gosh. I can't believe it. Help. I can't stand it," Tracy desperately exclaims. Her mother queries, "What is wrong with you?" Tracy responds, "Everybody in this place is looking at me!" "Why?" the mother asks. Without replying, Tracy rushes to the restaurant's rest room and depletes the remains of a can of hair spray. Five minutes later she returns to the table, where her mother again asks what is wrong. Tracy finally says that she had this one hair that would not stay in place and she just knows that all of the people were staring at her. Such is one of the interesting and curious cognitive changes of early adolescence called egocentric thought. We will study this further but first let's see what Piaget had to say about cognitive change in adolescence.

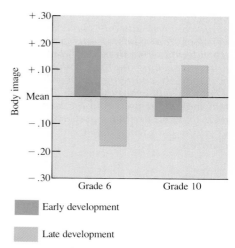

Early development

Late development

Figure 10.4
Early and late maturing adolescent girls' perceptions of body image in early and late adolescence.

Girls mature on the average two years earlier than boys do. And there is substantial individual variation in maturation—some adolescents mature very early, others very late. In what ways might early maturation or late maturation hinder or help the boys and girls shown here?

Early adolescence is a time when an acute concern with one's body image develops. Young adolescents spend considerable time in front of the mirror, checking out their bodies to see how they are changing and wondering what they will eventually look like. As they look at themselves in the mirror, their thoughts are more abstract and idealistic than when they were children.

Formal Operational Thought

Piaget believed that **formal operational thought** came into play between the ages of eleven and fifteen. Formal operational thought is more abstract than a child's thinking. The adolescent is no longer limited to actual concrete experience as the anchor of thought. Instead, she may conjure up make-believe situations, hypothetical possibilities, or purely abstract propositions and reason about them. Accompanying the abstract nature of adolescent thought is the quality of idealism. Adolescents begin to think about ideal characteristics for themselves and others and compare themselves and others to ideal standards. During adolescence thought often takes fantasy flights into the future.

At the same time an adolescent thinks more abstractly and idealistically than a child, she also thinks more logically. The adolescent begins to think more like a scientist in the sense of devising a plan to solve a problem and systematically testing solutions. This kind of problem solving has an imposing name: **hypothetical-deductive reasoning.** The adolescent develops hypotheses, or best guesses, about ways to solve a problem, such as an algebraic equation. She then deduces, or concludes, which is the best path to follow in solving the equation. By contrast, a child is more likely to solve problems in a trial-and-error fashion.

Adolescent thought is egocentric. David Elkind (1978) believes **adolescent egocentrism** has two parts: an imaginary audience and a personal fable. The **imaginary audience** is the adolescent's belief that others are as preoccupied with her as she herself is (remember the depleted can of hair spray). Attention-getting behavior, so common in adolescence, reflects egocentrism and the desire to be onstage, noticed, and visible. Imagine the eighth-grade boy who thinks he is an actor and all others the audience as he stares at the tiny blemish on his face.

Jennifer converses with her best friend, Anne, about something she just heard. "Anne, did you hear about Barbara. You know she fools around a lot. Well, the word is she is pregnant. Can you believe it? But it won't ever happen to me." Later in the conversation, Anne tells Jennifer, "I really like Bob, but sometimes he is a jerk. He just doesn't understand me. He has no idea what my true feelings are." The **personal fable** refers to the adolescent's sense of personal uniqueness and indestructibility, reflected respectively in Jennifer's and Anne's comments. In their efforts to maintain this sense of uniqueness and indestructibility, adolescents sometimes create a fictitious story, or a fable. Imagine a girl who is having difficulty getting a date. She may develop a fictitious account of a handsome young man living in another part of the country who is madly in love with her.

As the adolescent's thought becomes more abstract and logical, the use of language also changes. You will discover in Psychology 10.1 that this development includes changes in the uses of satire, metaphor, and improved writing skills. The social aspects of language also improve during adolescence. Adolescents are superior to children at monitoring a listener's interest and understanding, for example.

Social and Personality Development

The social world of adolescents are many and varied. Through experiences with parents, siblings, peers, friends, clique members, teachers, and other adults, we make the transition from childhood to adulthood.

Parent-Adolescent Relationships

Mark Twain, reflecting on his youth, commented: "When I was a boy of fourteen my father was so ignorant I could hardly stand to have the man around. But when I got to be twenty-one, I was astonished how much he learnt in seven years." Early adolescence is a time when conflict with parents escalates beyond childhood levels (Montemayor & Hanson, 1985; Steinberg, 1987). This increase may be due to a number of factors: the biological changes of puberty, cognitive changes involving increased idealism and logical reasoning, social changes focused on independence and identity, maturational changes in parents, and violated expectations on the part of parents and adolescents. The adolescent compares her parents to an ideal standard and then criticizes the flaws. A thirteen-year-old girl tells her mother, "That is the tackiest looking dress I have ever seen. Nobody would be caught dead wearing that." The adolescent demands logical explanations for comments and discipline. A four-teen-year-old boy tells his mother, "What do you mean I have to be home at 10 P.M. because its the way we do things around here? Why do we do things around here that way? It doesn't make sense to me."

Many parents see their adolescent as changing from a compliant child to someone who is noncompliant, oppositional, and resistant to parental standards. The tendency of parents is to clamp down and put more pressure on the adolescent to conform to parental standards (Collins, 1985, 1987). Parents often expect adolescents to be mature adults immediately rather than understanding that the journey takes ten to fifteen years. Parents who recognize that this process takes time handle their youth more competently and calmly than those who demand immediate conformity. The opposite tactic—letting the adolescent do as he pleases without supervision—also is unwise.

■■■■■■■■■■■■■■■■■■■■■■■

Psychology 10.1

From Sophisticated Nicknames to *Mad* Magazine—Advances in Cognition and Language in Adolescence

■ A junior high school student is sitting in school making up satirical labels for his teachers. One he calls "the walking wilt Wilkie and his wilking waste." Another he describes as "the magnificent Manifred and his manifest morbidity." The use of nicknames increases during early adolescence as does their abstractness—"stilt," "spaz," "nerd," and "marshmallow mouth," for example. These examples reflect the aspect of language called **satire,** which refers to irony, wit, or derision used to expose folly or wickedness. Adolescents use and understand satire more than children. The satire of *Mad* magazine, which relies on double meaning, exaggeration, and parody to highlight absurd circumstances and contradictory happenings, finds a more receptive audience among thirteen- to fourteen-year-olds than eight- to nine-year-olds (see figure 10.A).

Another aspect of language that comes into use in adolescence is **metaphor.** A metaphor is an implied comparison between two ideas that is conveyed by the abstract meaning contained in the words used. For example, a person's faith and a piece of glass are alike in that they can both be shattered. A runner's performance and a politician's speech are alike in that both are predictable. Children have a difficult time understanding metaphorical comparisons; adolescents are better able to understand their meaning.

The increased abstractness and logical reasoning of the adolescent's cognition can be witnessed in improved writing ability (Scardamalia, Bereiter, & Goelman, 1982). Organizing ideas is critical to good writing. Logical thinking helps the writer develop a hierarchical structure, which helps the reader understand which ideas are general, which are specific, and which are more important than others. Researchers have discovered that children are poor at organizing their ideas prior to writing and have difficulty detecting the salient points in prose passages (Brown & Smiley, 1977). While adolescents are not yet Pulitzer Prize-winning novelists, they are better than children at recognizing the need for making both general and specific points in their writing. The sentences adolescents string together make more sense than those constructed by children. And adolescents are more likely than children to include an introduction, several paragraphs that represent a body, and concluding remarks when writing an essay (Fischer & Lazerson, 1984).

Attachment to parents increases the probability the adolescent will mature into a competent adult. Just as in childhood, parents provide an important support system that helps the adolescent to explore in a healthy way a wider, more complex social world full of uncertainties, challenges, and stresses (Cooper & Ayers-Lopez, 1985; Hill & Holmbeck, in press). Although adolescents show a strong desire to spend more time with peers, they do not move into a world isolated from parents.

While conflict with parents does increase in early adolescence, it does not reach the tumultuous proportions envisioned by G. Stanley Hall. Rather, much of the conflict involves the everyday events of family life such as keeping

Figure 10.A
*The satire of Mad Magazine—
finding an audience among young adolescents.*

a bedroom clean, dressing neatly, getting home by a certain time, not talking forever on the phone, and so on. The conflicts rarely involve major dilemmas like drugs and delinquency.

The everyday conflicts that characterize parent-adolescent relationships may serve a positive developmental function (Blos, 1962; Hill, 1987). These minor disputes and negotiations can facilitate the adolescent's transition from being dependent on parents to becoming an autonomous individual. For example, in one investigation adolescents who expressed disagreement with parents more actively explored identity development than adolescents who did not express disagreement with their parents (Cooper & others, 1982).

Figure 10.5
The self-esteem of adolescents from different cliques and the nobodies.

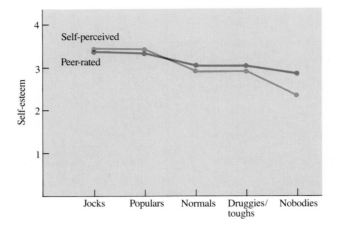

Peers

Imagine you are back in junior and senior high school, especially during one of your good times. Peers, friends, cliques, dates, parties, and clubs probably come to mind. During adolescence, especially early adolescence, we conform more to peer standards than in childhood. Investigators have found that around the eighth to ninth grades, conformity to peers, especially to their antisocial standards, peaks (Berndt, 1979; Douvan & Adelson, 1966). For example, at this point in adolescence an individual is most likely to go along with a peer to steal hubcaps off a car, draw graffitti on a wall, or steal cosmetics from a store counter.

In virtually any junior high or high school we would find three to six well-defined cliques. If you were a member of a clique, weren't you proud of your identity? A recent investigation revealed that clique membership is associated with the adolescent's self-esteem (Brown & Lohr, in press). As shown in figure 10.5, the self-esteem of the "jocks" and "populars" was highest while that of the "nobodies" was the lowest. But one group of adolescents not in a clique had self-esteem equivalent to the jocks and populars—this group was the "independents," who indicated that clique membership was not important to them.

Dating also takes on added importance during adolescence. As Dick Cavett (1974) remembers, the thought of an upcoming dance or sock hop was absolute agony, "I knew I'd never get a date. There seemed to be only this limited set of girls I could and should be seen with, and they were all taken by the jocks." Adolescents spend considerable time either dating or thinking about dating, which has gone far beyond its original courtship function to a form of recreation, a source of status and achievement, and a setting for learning about close relationships.

Female adolescents bring a stronger desire for intimacy and personality to dating than male adolescents (Duck, 1975). Adolescent dating is a context in which gender-related role expectations intensify. Males feel pressured to perform in "masculine" ways and females sense the need to behave in "feminine" ways. Particularly in early adolescence when pubertal changes are occurring, the adolescent male wants to show that he is the best male possible and the adolescent female wants to show that she is the best female possible. Dating is but one of a number of circumstances that signal the development of independence and identity during adolescence.

Our time spent in peer relations during adolescence probably brings back some of our most enjoyable memories. Conformity to peer standards is prominent during early adolescence, with conformity—especially to antisocial peer standards—often peaking in the eighth and ninth grades.

For Erik Erikson, adolescence is a time of identity development—of thinking about who one is, what one is all about, and where one is headed in life.

Independence and Identity

An adolescent's ability to take control of his life is fostered by appropriate adult reactions to his desire for independence. At the onset of adolescence, the average boy or girl does not have the knowledge to make appropriate or mature decisions in all areas of life. As an adolescent pushes for autonomy, the wise adult relinquishes control in areas where the adolescent can make mature decisions and helps in areas where knowledge is more limited. Gradually, the adolescent will acquire the ability to make mature decisions independently (Santrock, 1987).

Closely related to the adolescent's pursuit of independence is identity. Erik Erikson (1968) describes **identity versus identity confusion** as the fifth stage of the human life cycle, corresponding roughly to the adolescent years. It is a time of interest in finding out who one is, what one is all about, and where one is headed in life.

During adolescence, world views become important to the individual, who enters what Erikson calls a "psychological moratorium"—a gap between the security of childhood and the autonomy of adulthood. Numerous identities can be drawn from the surrounding culture, and adolescents experiment with different roles. The youth who successfully copes with these conflicting identities during adolescence emerges with a new sense of self that is both refreshing and acceptable. The adolescent who does not successfully resolve this identity crisis is confused, suffering what Erikson calls identity confusion. This confusion can take one of two courses: the individual may withdraw, isolating himself from peers and family, or he may lose his own identity in the crowd.

Adolescents want to decide freely for themselves such matters as what careers they will pursue, whether they will go to college, and whether they will marry. In other words, they want to free themselves from the shackles of their parents and other adults and make their own choices. At the same time, many adolescents have a deep fear of making the wrong decision and of failing. But as adolescents pursue their identities and their thoughts become more abstract and logical, they reason in more sophisticated ways. They are better able to judge what is morally right and wrong and become capable decision makers.

Moral Development

> In Europe a woman was near death from a special kind of cancer. There was one drug that the doctors thought might save her. It was a form of radium that a druggist in the same town had recently discovered. The drug was expensive to make, but the druggist was charging ten times what the drug cost him to make. He paid $200 for the radium and charged $2,000 for a small dose of the drug. The sick woman's husband, Heinz, went to everyone he knew to borrow the money, but he could only get together $1,000 which is half of what it cost. He told the druggist that his wife was dying and asked him to sell it cheaper or let him pay later. But the druggist said, "No, I discovered the drug, and I am going to make money from it." So Heinz got desperate and broke into the man's store to steal the drug for his wife. (Kohlberg, 1969, p. 379)

This story is one of eleven devised by Lawrence Kohlberg (1966, 1976, 1984) to investigate the nature of moral thought. After reading the story, the interviewee answers a series of questions about the moral dilemma. Should Heinz have done that? Was it right or wrong? Why? Is it a husband's duty to steal the drug for his wife if he can get it in no other way? Would a good husband do it? Did the druggist have the right to charge that much when there was no law actually setting a limit on the price? Why?

Based on the reasons individuals give to this and other moral dilemmas, Kohlberg believes three levels of moral development exist, each of which is characterized by two stages:

1. **The preconventional level.** At this low level the individual shows no internalization of moral values—moral thinking is based on punishments (Stage 1) or rewards (Stage 2) that come from the external world. In regard to the Heinz and the druggist story, at Stage 1 an individual might say he should not steal the drug because it is a big crime; at Stage 2, an individual might say he shouldn't steal the drug because the druggist needs to make a profit.

2. **The conventional level.** At this level of morality, internalization is intermediate. The individual abides by certain standards (internal), but they are the standards of others (external), such as parents (Stage 3) or the laws of society (Stage 4). At Stage 3, an individual might say that Heinz should steal the drug for his wife because that is what a good husband would do; at Stage 4, an individual might say that it is natural to want to save his wife but that it still is always wrong to steal.

3. **The postconventional level.** At this highest level, morality is completely internalized and not based on others' standards. The individual recognizes alternative moral courses, explores the options, and then develops a personal moral code. The code may be among the principles generally accepted by the community (Stage 5) or it may be more individualized (Stage 6). At Stage 5, an individual might say that the law was not set up for these circumstances so Heinz can steal the drug; it is not really right, but he is justified in doing it. At Stage 6, the individual is faced with the decision of whether to consider the other people who need the drug just as badly as his wife. Heinz should consider the value of all lives involved.

Kohlberg believes these levels and stages occur in a sequence and are age-related; some evidence for these beliefs has been found, although few people reach Stages 5 or 6 (Colby & others, 1983; Walker, 1987). Kohlberg thinks development occurs through maturation of thought, the mutual give-and-take of peer relations, and opportunities for role taking. Parent-child relationships do not contribute to moral thought in Kohlberg's view because they are too power oriented.

Kohlberg's provocative view has generated considerable research on moral development, and his theory has not gone unchallenged. One criticism of Kohlberg's view is that moral reasons can often be a shelter for immoral behavior—bank embezzlers and presidents address the loftiest of moral virtues when analyzing moral dilemmas but their own behavior may be immoral. No one wants a nation of cheaters and thieves who reason at the postconventional level. The cheaters and thieves may know what is right and what is wrong but still do what is wrong.

A second major criticism of Kohlberg's view is that it does not adequately reflect connectedness with and concern for others. Carol Gilligan (1982, 1985) argues that Kohlberg's theory emphasizes a **justice perspective,** that is, a focus on the rights of the individual. People are differentiated and seen as standing alone in making moral decisions. By contrast, the **care perspective** sees people in terms of their connectedness with others and the focus is on interpersonal communication. According to Gilligan, Kohlberg has greatly underplayed the care perspective in moral development. She believes this may be because most of his research was with males rather than females.

Gilligan also thinks that moral development has three basic levels. She calls Level 1 preconventional morality, which reflects a concern for self and survival. Level II, conventional morality, shows a concern for being responsible and caring for others. Level III, postconventional morality, shows a concern for self and others as interdependent. Gilligan believes Kohlberg has underemphasized the care perspective in the moral development of *both* males and females and that the highest level of morality for both sexes involves a search for moral equality between one's self and others.

The issues of what is right and what is wrong as well as the pursuit of identity are prominent concerns during adolescence. As adults, we continue to deal with these same important issues.

As adolescents progress toward adulthood, they are faced with a complex world of work that requires highly specialized tasks. Many individuals spend an extended period of time in training in technical institutes and colleges. For many, this creates an extended period of economic and personal temporariness (Kenniston, 1970). This time frame may last for several years or it may continue for a decade or more. Despite this time period, many youth do not settle the questions whose answers once defined adulthood—questions of the individual's relationship to society, of vocation, of social roles, or of lifestyle.

Defining entry into adolescence is not easy, but the criteria for entering adulthood seem even more difficult to determine. It has been said that adolescence begins in biology and ends in culture, suggesting that what defines an adult in the United States may not be the same criteria as in a South-sea island culture. But development does not stop with adolescence; much change occurs as life continues to unfold. Before you turn to our discussion of adult development, you might want to review the main themes of our discussion of adolescence, which are presented in concept table 10.1.

Concept Table 10.1

Adolescence		
Concept	**Processes/related ideas**	**Characteristics/description**
Historical beginnings and the nature of adolescence	Historical beginnings	G. Stanley Hall is known as the father of the scientific study of adolescence. In the early 1900s, he proposed the storm and stress view. It is easy to develop stereotypes of adolescents in any era. Current evaluation suggests the concept of adolescence may have been invented.
	The adolescent time frame	The transition between childhood and adulthood. In most cultures, it is entered between ten and thirteen years old and exited between eighteen and twenty-two years old. A distinction is made between early and late adolescence.
Physical changes	The nature of puberty	A rapid change in maturation, which has arrived earlier in recent years. Hormonal changes are prominent. Puberty occurs roughly two years earlier for girls than boys, although its normal range is large.
	Early and late maturation	Early maturation generally favors boys but has mixed effects for girls. The effects of early and late maturation are complex and can involve physical, cognitive, and social aspects of development.
Cognitive changes	Their nature	Piaget argued that formal operational thought appears between eleven and fifteen years of age. Thought is abstract and idealistic but includes planning and logical analysis. Egocentrism also characterizes adolescent thought. Language changes appear during adolescence.
Social and personality development	Parent-adolescent relationships	Conflict with parents often increases but may serve a positive developmental function. It is not as tumultuous as Hall envisioned. Adolescents do not become detached from parents, rather connectedness continues.
	Peers	Adolescents increase time spent with peers. Conformity to antisocial peer standards peaks at about thirteen to fourteen years of age. Clique membership is linked to self-esteem. Dating is a major interest.
	Independence and identity	Independence usually is acquired through appropriate adult reactions that relinquish control when maturity is shown. Erikson believes the major issue is identity vs. identity confusion.
	Moral development	Kohlberg proposed three levels (each with two stages) that vary in the degree moral development is internalized— preconventional, conventional, and postconventional. Among his critics is Gilligan, who believes he has underrepresented the care perspective.

Adult Development

The words of Robert Sears and Shirley Feldman (1973) suggest that although it is important to study developmental changes in childhood, we change during adulthood as well:

> The next five or six decades are every bit as important, not only to those adults who are passing through them but to their children, who must live with and understand parents and grandparents. (p. v)

We have not always viewed the adult years in this way. The traditional view of development emphasized extreme change from conception to adolescence, especially from conception through infancy, stability in adulthood, and decline in old age. While still recognizing the importance of the childhood years, the **life-cycle perspective** places much more emphasis on developmental changes during the adult years. Figure 10.6 shows how the traditional perspective and the life-cycle perspective compare (Baltes, 1987a; Baltes & Reese, 1984; Datan, Rodenheaver, & Hughes, 1987; Santrock, 1986).

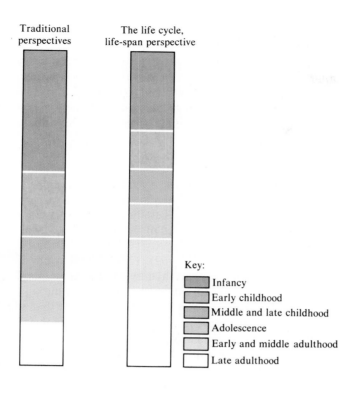

Traditional perspectives

The life cycle, life-span perspective

Key:

- Infancy
- Early childhood
- Middle and late childhood
- Adolescence
- Early and middle adulthood
- Late adulthood

Figure 10.6
Perspectives on life-span development reflecting points in the life cycle where change and development are thought to occur.

By 1940, developmental investigations of infancy, childhood, and adolescence were commonplace, but studies of age-related changes during adulthood and the nature of aging were just beginning (Havighurst, 1973). Today, there is a flurry of interest in adult change and aging and some intriguing questions are being investigated: How much and when does our personality change after age twenty? Does intelligence decline and if so when? What are the keys to unlocking the mystery of aging?

Just as the years from conception to adulthood are identified by certain periods, so too are the adult years. We enter **early adulthood** at some point in our late teens or early twenties and leave it sometime in our late thirties. It is a time when we establish personal and economic independence, seek intimacy with one or more individuals, and pursue career development intensely. We enter **middle adulthood** at about thirty-five to forty-five years of age and exit it from fifty-five to sixty-five years of age. This is a time of expanding personal and social involvement, increased responsibility, adjusting to physical decline, and reaching and maintaining career satisfaction. We enter **late adulthood** at sixty to seventy years of age and this period lasts until death. It is a time of adjusting to decreased strength and health, retirement, reduced income, and new social roles.

Notice that approximate age bands identify the periods of adult development and that the age bands overlap. Psychologists are more certain about the periods of childhood than adulthood—most of us would agree that a one-year-old child is in the period of infancy and that a four-year-old child is in the period of early childhood. But the age periods of adulthood are much broader and there is less agreement on whether or not someone forty-one years old is in middle adulthood. Not only are the criteria and age bands for adult periods less clear-cut than for childhood periods, but as one prominent life-span theorist, Bernice Neugarten (1986), argues, we rapidly are becoming an age-irrelevant society. She points out that we already are familiar with the twenty-eight-year-old mayor, the thirty-year-old college president, the thirty-five-year-old grandmother, and the sixty-five-year-old father of a preschooler.

Neugarten believes that most adult themes appear and reappear throughout the adult years. Issues of intimacy and freedom that haunt a couple throughout a relationship in early adulthood may be just as salient in late adulthood. The pressure of time, reformulating goals, and coping with success and failure are not the exclusive properties of adults of any particular age. Keeping in mind that the age bands of adult periods are fuzzy, let's now see what physical, cognitive, and social changes take place during the adult years.

Physical Development

How many Olympic athletes have you seen over the age of thirty? Carlos Lopes won the 1984 Olympic marthon at the age of thirty-seven, which was a rare feat. Of 137 Olympic athletes studied in one Olympics competition, only 21 were over the age of thirty. All of the athletes who participated in events demanding extreme speed and agility, such as the 100-yard-dash and broad jump, were under thirty (Tanner, 1962). The peak of our physical performance usually occurs between nineteen and twenty-six years of age.

We not only reach our peak performance during early adulthood, but during this time we are also our healthiest. More than nine out of ten people between the ages of seventeen and forty-four view their health as good or excellent (U.S. Department of Health, Education, and Welfare, 1976). Few young adults have chronic health problems, and young adults have fewer colds and respiratory problems than they did during childhood.

But young adults rarely recognize that bad eating habits, heavy drinking, and smoking can impair their health status when they are middle aged. Despite warnings on packages and in advertisements that cigarettes are hazardous to health, adolescents actually increase their use of cigarettes as they enter young adulthood (Bachman, O'Malley, & Johnson, 1978). As indicated in table 10.1, they also increase their weekly use of alcohol, any use of marijuana, and any use of amphetamines, barbiturates, and hallucinogens.

As we enter middle adulthood we are more acutely concerned about our health status. We experience a general decline in physical fitness throughout middle adulthood and some deterioration in health. The three greatest health concerns at this point in development are heart disease, cancer, and weight. Cancer related to smoking often surfaces for the first time in middle adulthood.

The *Harvard Medical School Newsletter* reports that about 20 million Americans are on a "serious" diet at any particular moment. Being overweight is a critical health problem in middle adulthood. For individuals who are 30 percent or more overweight, the probability of dying in middle adulthood increases by 40 percent. Obesity also increases the probability an individual will suffer other ailments, including hypertension and digestive disorders.

Because a youthful appearance is stressed in our culture, physical deterioration in middle adulthood is difficult to cope with. Many individuals whose hair grays, whose skin wrinkles, whose body sags, and whose teeth yellow strive to make themselves look younger. Undergoing cosmetic surgery, dying hair, purchasing a wig, and joining weight reduction programs are frequent excursions of the middle-aged adult. In one investigation, middle-aged women focused more attention on their facial attractiveness than older or younger

Table 10.1   Changes in Usage Rates for Cigarettes, Alcohol, Marijuana, and Other Drugs.

	Percentage of respondents reporting usage during the period		
	1968–69	*1969–70*	*1973–74*
Daily use of cigarettes	35	40	44
Weekly use of alcohol	31	44	58
Any use of marijuana	21	35	52
Any use of amphetamines, barbiturates, hallucinogens	12	18	24

Note: In 1968–69, the individuals were high school seniors; in 1973–74, the individuals were in their early twenties.

Source: Bachman, O'Malley, & Johnson, 1978.

women; the middle-aged women also perceived that the signs of aging had a more detrimental effect on their appearance (Nowak, 1977). In our culture, some aspects of aging in middle adulthood, such as gray hair, are signs of attractiveness in males, while similar changes in females are perceived as unattractive.

An especially important biological change for women is **menopause**. Menopause marks the end of menstruation and the childbearing years. The average age of menopause in the United States is fifty; it is considered that menopause has occurred after twelve consecutive months without a menstrual period. Menopause has varied outcomes for women, both physically and psychologically. About two-thirds of all women experience only mild physical symptoms; approximately 15 percent have symptoms that warrant medical attention, such as hot flashes and atrophy of the vagina (Women's Medical Center, 1977). The following comments of two women reveal the physical and psychological variation that greets menopause:

> I had hot flashes several times a week for almost six months. I didn't get as embarrassed as some of my friends who also had hot flashes, but I found the "heat wave" sensation most uncomfortable.

> I am constantly amazed and delighted to discover new things about my body, something menstruation did not allow me to do. I have new responses, desires, sensations, freed and apart from the distraction of menses (periods).

Do men experience a similar biological change? Men do not lose their capacity to father children but their sexual potency declines slightly in the fifties. Testosterone production gradually drops off and it takes longer to have an erection, however, the erection can be maintained longer. Sexual desire in men may not decline at all during middle adulthood (Wagenwoord & Bailey, 1978).

The decline in some physical characteristics during middle adulthood, then, is not just imagined. The middle-aged individual may not see as well, run as fast, or be as healthy as in the twenties. But what about cognitive characteristics? Do they peak in the twenties and decline during middle adulthood?

Cognitive Development

Do people continue to develop cognitively in adulthood or are they just as smart as they ever will be by the end of adolescence? Piaget believed that an adult and an adolescent think in the same way. But some developmental psychologists believe it is not until adulthood that individuals consolidate their formal operational thinking. That is, they may begin to plan and hypothesize about problems as adolescents, but they become more systematic in approaching problems as adults. While some adults are more proficient at developing hypotheses and deducing solutions to problems than adolescents, many adults do not think in formal operational ways at all (Keating, 1980).

Other psychologists believe that the absolute nature of adolescent logic and youth's buoyant optimism diminish in early adulthood. According to the perspective of Gisela Labouvie-Vief (1982, 1986), a new integration of thought takes place in early adulthood. She thinks the adult years produce pragmatic constraints that require an adaptive strategy of less reliance on logical analysis in solving problems. Commitment, specialization, and channeling energy into finding one's niche in complex social and work systems replace the youth's fascination with idealized logic. If we assume that logical thought and buoyant idealism represent the criteria for cognitive maturity, we would have to admit that the cognitive activity of adults is too concrete and pragmatic. But from Labouvie-Vief's view, the adult's understanding of reality's constraints reflects cognitive maturity, not immaturity.

Our cognitive abilities are very strong during early adulthood, and they do show adaptation to the pragmatic aspects of our lives. Less clear is whether our logical skills actually decline. Competence as a young adult probably requires doses of both logical thinking skills and pragmatic adaptation to reality. For example, as an architect designs a building she logically analyzes and plans the structure but understands the cost constraints, environmental concerns, and time it will take to get the job done effectively.

Do cognitive abilities decline as we enter middle adulthood? The aspect of cognition that has been investigated more than any other in this regard is memory (e.g., Santrock & Bartlett, 1986). Putting the pieces of the research puzzle together, we find that memory decline in middle adulthood is more likely to occur when long-term rather than short-term memory is involved. For example, a middle-aged man can remember a phone number he heard twenty seconds ago, but he probably won't remember the number as efficiently the next day. Memory is also more likely to decline when organization and imagery are not used. By using memory strategies such as organizing lists of phone numbers into different categories or imagining that the phone numbers represent different objects around the house, memory can be improved. Memory also tends to decline when the information to be recalled is recently acquired knowledge or when the information is not used often. For example, a middle-aged adult may easily remember chess moves, baseball rules, or television schedules if he has used this information extensively in the past. And finally, memory tends to decline if recall rather than recognition is required. If the middle-aged man is shown a list of phone numbers and asked to select the number he heard yesterday (recognition), this can be done more efficiently than recalling the number without the list. Memory in middle adulthood will also decline if health is poor and attitudes are negative.

When we discuss cognitive changes in late adulthood more will be said about the issue of memory decline during the adult years. So far we have seen that we experience changes in physical and cognitive development as we move through the adult years. What about the social contexts of our lives and our personality—do they change as well?

| Table 10.2   Gould's Transformations in Adult Development |||
Stage	Approximate age	Development(s)
1	16 to 18	Desire to escape parental control.
2	18 to 22	Leaving the family: peer group orientation.
3	22 to 28	Developing independence: commitment to a career and to children.
4	29 to 34	Questioning self: role confusion; marriage and career vulnerable to dissatisfaction.
5	35 to 43	Period of urgency to attain life's goals: awareness of time limitation. Realignment of life's goals.
6	43 to 53	Settling down: acceptance of one's life.
7	53 to 60	More tolerance: acceptance of past; less negativism; general mellowing.

From Gould, Roger L., *Transformations.* Copyright © 1978 by Roger Gould. Reprinted by permission of Simon & Schuster, Inc.

Social and Personality Development

As we become adults, developing an intimate relationship with another person becomes important in our lives. And most of us take a job on a full-time basis and develop a career. Early in this century Freud was asked what adults needed to do to adapt to the demands of reality. He answered: love and work. These themes continue to be dominant aspects of our adult life today. A number of different theories of adult development have been proposed, most of which to some degree address themes of work and love, career and intimacy. One set of theories proposes that adult development unfolds in stages, the other stresses the importance of life events.

Stage Theories of Adult Personality Development

Erikson's eight stages of the life cycle include one stage for early adulthood and one stage for middle adulthood. Erikson believes that only after identity formation is well developed can true intimacy occur. He thinks that early adulthood is a critical time for the **intimacy versus isolation** stage. Intimacy helps us to form our identity, because in Erikson's words, "We are what we love." If intimacy does not develop, Erikson argues that a deep sense of isolation and impersonal feelings overcome the individual.

In middle adulthood, Erikson (1968) believes that individuals need to assist the younger generation in developing and leading useful lives. The stage of **generativity versus stagnation** focuses on successful child rearing. Childless adults often find substitute children through adoption, guardianship, or a close relationship with the children of friends and relatives. The positive side of this stage—generativity—reflects an ability to positively shape the next generation. The negative side—stagnation—leaves the individual with a feeling of having done nothing for the next generation.

Roger Gould (1978) believes we go through seven developmental stages as adults (see table 10.2). Gould portrays the twenties as a time when we assume new roles, the thirties as when we begin to feel stuck with our responsibilities, and the forties as the point when we develop a sense of urgency as we realize time is passing us by. Gould argues that mid-life is every bit as turbulent as adolescence. Handling the mid-life crisis and realizing that a sense of urgency is a natural reaction to life at this stage helps to keep us on the path of adult maturity.

Figure 10.7
Levinson's seasons of a man's life.

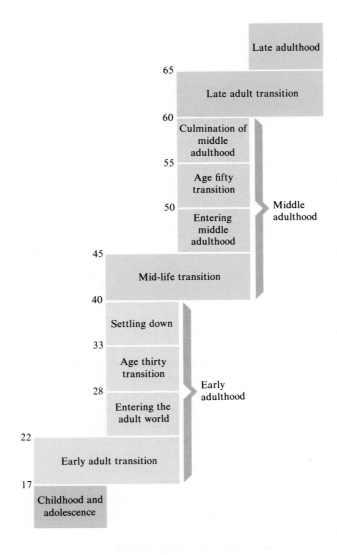

In *Seasons of a Man's Life,* Daniel Levinson (1978) also described adult development as a series of stages. Middle-aged male hourly workers, academic biologists, business executives, and novelists were interviewed extensively. Based on these interviews, Levinson concluded that developmental tasks must be mastered at a number of different points in adulthood (see figure 10.7).

In early adulthood, the two major tasks are exploring the possibilities for adult living and developing a stable life structure. The twenties represent the novice phase of adult development. At the end of a boy's teens, a transition from dependence to independence should occur. This transition is marked by a dream—an image of the kind of life the youth wants, especially in terms of marriage and a career. The novice phase is a time of experimenting and testing the dream in the real world.

From approximately twenty-eight to thirty-three, the more serious question of determining goals is faced. During the thirties, a man usually works to develop his family life and career. In the late thirties, he enters a phase of becoming his own man (or BOOM, becoming one's own man, as Levinson calls it). By age forty, he reaches a stable point in his career, outgrows his earlier, more tenuous status as an adult, and now looks forward to the kind of life he will lead as a middle-aged adult.

In Levinson's view, the change to middle adulthood lasts about five years and requires that the adult come to grips with four major conflicts that have existed since adolescence: 1) being young versus being old; 2) being destructive versus being constructive; 3) being masculine versus being feminine; and 4) being attached to others versus being separated from them. The success of the mid-life transition depends on how effectively he can reduce these polarities and accept each of them as a part of his being.

The perspectives of Erikson, Gould, and Levinson emphasize that we go through a number of adult stages of development. In evaluating these stage theories, several points need to be kept in mind. First, the research on which they are based is not empirically sound—much of it involves clinical observations rather than rigorous, controlled observations, for example. Second, the perspectives tend to describe the stages as crises, especially in the case of the mid-life stage. Research on middle-aged adults reveals that few adults experience mid-life in the tumultuous way described by the stage-crisis views; individuals vary extensively in how they cope with and perceive mid-life (Farrell & Rosenberg, 1981; Vaillant, 1977). Psychology 10.2 provides insight into how concepts such as the mid-life crisis are overdramatized in our society. And third, a number of adult-development psychologists believe more attention should be given to life events.

The Life-Events Framework

Life events rather than stages may be responsible for change in our adult lives. Such events as marriage, divorce, the death of a spouse, a job promotion, or being fired from a job involve varying degrees of stress and influence our development as adults (Holmes & Rahe, 1967).

But more than life events themselves need to be considered (Hultsch & Plemons, 1979). We need to know about the many factors that mediate the influence of life events on adult development—physical health, intelligence, personality, family support, and income, for example. We also need to know how the individual perceives the life event and how she copes with the stress involved. For instance, one individual may perceive a life event as highly stressful whereas another person may perceive the same life event as a challenge. And we need to consider the life stage of the person and the sociohistorical circumstances present. For example, divorce may be more stressful for an individual in his fifties who has been married for many years than for a man in his twenties who has been married for only a few years (Chiriboga, 1982). Individuals may cope with divorce more effectively in 1990 than 1890 because divorce is more commonplace and accepted in today's society. Figure 10.8 portrays how life events can lead to change in adult development.

Figure 10.8
A life-events framework for understanding adult developmental change.

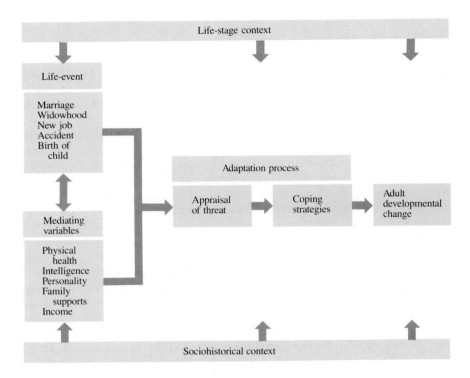

(a)

(b)

How much does our personality change and how much does it stay the same as we develop through adulthood? In the early 1970s, Jerry Rubin was a Yippie demonstrator (a), but in the 1980s, Rubin became a Wall Street businessman (b). Rubin says that his transformation underscores continuity in personality: whether Yippie or Wall Street businessman, he approached life with curiosity and enthusiasm.

Constancy and Change in Personality during Adulthood

Richard Alpert was an achievement-oriented, hard-working college professor in the 1960s. In the 1970s, Richard Alpert became Ram Dass, a free-spirited guru in search of an expanded state of consciousness. Most people would look at Alpert and Ram Dass and see two very different people. But Harvard psychologist David McClelland, who has known Alpert and Ram Dass well, says that Dass is the same old Richard, still charming, still concerned with inner experience, and still power hungry.

Psychology 10.2

Why Gail Sheehy's *Passages* Is Not Accepted by Scientists

In 1976 Gail Sheehy's book, *Passages*, was so popular that it topped the *New York Times* best-seller list for twenty-seven weeks. Sheehy's goal in *Passages* was to describe adult development. She cited discussions with Daniel Levinson and Roger Gould and information from interviews with 115 men and women as her main sources.

Sheehy argues that we all go through developmental stages roughly bound by chronological age. Each stage contains problems we must solve before we can progress to the next stage. The periods between the stages are called *passages*. Sheehy uses catchy phrases to describe each stage: the "trying twenties," "catch-thirty," the "deadline decade" (between thirty-five and forty-five), and the "age forty crucible." Sheehy's advice never wavers: adults in transition may feel miserable, but those who face up to agonizing self-evaluation, who appraise their weaknesses as well as their strengths, who set goals for the future, and who try to be as independent as possible will be happier than those who do not fully experience these trials.

Sheehy believes these passages earn us an *authentic identity.* This identity is not based on the authority of one's parents or on cultural prescriptions. Instead, it is constructed through one's own strenuous efforts. Sheehy says that adults who allow themselves to fully experience life's issues and examine their lives are the individuals who find their identity and thrive.

Unfortunately, Sheehy does not disclose such elementary information as the sex and racial composition of her sample of 115 adults, how the sample was selected, what questions were asked in the interviews and by whom, and the length of the interviews. The data may be biased toward individuals experiencing a great deal of stress because a disproportionate number of divorced adults were in the sample. The author described the cases only to buttress a point about adult development; no mention was made of how representative the cases were. In addition, Sheehy conducted no statistical analyses.

Psychologist George Vaillant (1977) points out the overdramatization of stress and conflict in reports such as Sheehy's.

Just as pop psychologists have reveled in the not-so-common high drama of adolescent turmoil, just so the popular press, sensing good copy, has made all too much of the mid-life crisis. The term *mid-life crisis* brings to mind some variation of the renegade minister who leaves behind four children and the congregation that loved him in order to drive off in a magenta Porsche with a twenty-five-year-old striptease artiste. Like all tabloid fables, there is much to be learned from such stories, but such aberrations are rare, albeit memorable, caricatures of more mundane issues of development. As with adolescent turmoil, mid-life crises are much rarer in community samples than clinical samples. The high drama in Gail Sheehy's best-selling *Passages* was rarely observed in the lives of the Grant Study men. (pp. 222–223)

Jerry Rubin views his own transformation from yippie to Wall Street businessman in a way that underscores continuity in personality. Rubin says that discovering his identity was accomplished in a typical Jerry Rubin fashion—trying out anything and everything and jumping around wild-eyed and crazy. Whether yippie or Wall-Street businessman, Rubin approached life with enthusiasm and curiosity (Rubin, 1981).

William James (1890) said that our basic personality is set like plaster by the time we are thirty and never softens again. Like Jerry Rubin and David McClelland, James believed that our bodies and attitudes may change through the adult years, but the basic core of our personality does not. Yet many psychologists are enthusiastic about our capacity for change as adults, arguing that too much importance is attached to personality change in childhood and not enough to change in adulthood.

Some researchers argue for extreme consistency in personality based on data they have collected longitudinally (Costa, 1986; Costa & McRae, 1980; Costa & others, 1987). Paul Costa, for example, believes that our degree of extraversion or introversion, our level of adjustment, and our openness to new experiences do not change much during our adult lives. Costa says that an individual at age twenty-five who is shy and quiet will be that same shy and quiet person at age fifty.

A more moderate view of the stability-change issue comes from the architects of the California Longitudinal Study, which now spans more than fifty years (Eichorn & others, 1981; Mussen, Honcik, & Eichorn, 1982). These researchers believe some stability exists over the long course of adult development, but that adults are more capable of changing than Costa thinks. For example, a person who is shy and introverted at age twenty-five may not be completely extraverted at age fifty, but he may be less introverted than at twenty-five. Possibly this individual married someone who encouraged him to be more outgoing and supported his social ventures; perhaps he changed jobs at age thirty and became a salesman, placing him in a circumstance where he was required to develop his social skills.

Humans are adaptive beings. We are resilient throughout our adult lives, but we do not become entirely new personalities. In a sense we change but we remain the same—amidst the change is an underlying coherence and stability.

Intergenerational Relations

With each new generation, personality characteristics, attitudes, and values are replicated or changed. As older family members die their emotional, intellectual, personal, and genetic legacies are carried on in the next generation. Their children become the oldest generation and their grandchildren the second generation.

For the most part family members maintain considerable contact across generations (Leigh, 1982; Troll & Bengston, 1982). Sometimes, though, this contact involves conflict. Recent analyses from the California Longitudinal Study (Elder, Caspi, & Downey, 1986) reveal how such conflict is carried from generation to generation. These analyses showed that children whose parents had a high degree of marital conflict and who were unaffectionate subsequently had tension in their own marriages and were ineffective in disciplining their own children (now the third generation).

Individuals in middle adulthood play an important role in intergenerational relations. Often individuals are parents to adolescent offspring while their own parents are about to enter late adulthood. While individuals in middle adulthood may be guiding and financially supporting their adolescent children, they may have to deal with parents who are no longer a secure base in times of emotional difficulties or financial problems. Instead, the older parents often need affection and financial support from their middle-aged offspring (Lowy, 1981). These simultaneous pressures from adolescents and aging parents may contribute to stress during middle adulthood.

So far we have studied our development as adults until we are about fifty to sixty years of age. Not long ago, few people lived beyond this age. But as more people live longer, interest in the later years of life has mushroomed. Before we study the nature of late adulthood, turn to concept table 10.2 to review the main themes of adulthood we have discussed.

Intergenerational relations play an important role in life-span development. As each new generation succeeds the preceding one, personality characteristics, attitudes, and values are replicated or change. For the most part, as shown here, family members maintain considerable contact across generations.

Concept Table 10.2

Adulthood		
Concept	**Processes/related ideas**	**Characteristics/description**
The life-cycle perspective	Its nature	States that change takes place throughout the human life span. Adulthood is divided into early, middle, and late periods. Neugarten believes many issues are renegotiated throughout adulthood.
Physical development	Physical skills, health, and menopause	The peak of our physical skills and health usually comes in early adulthood, a time when it is easy to develop bad health habits. Menopause has varied physical and psychological effects.
Cognitive development	Its nature	Some psychologists argue that cognition is more pragmatic in early adulthood. Cognitive skills are strong in early adulthood. In middle adulthood memory may decline; strategies such as organization can reduce this.
Social and personality development	Stage theories and the life-events framework	Erikson, Gould, and Levinson have emphasized a number of stages of adult development. There is an emphasis on increased stress in middle adulthood, but this may be overdrawn. A complex life-events framework takes into account life events, mediating factors, adaptation, and sociohistorical circumstances.
	Constancy and change in personality	Truth lies somewhere between extreme constancy and extreme change. We are adaptive and resilient throughout our lives, but underlying such change is some degree of stability and continuity.
	Intergenerational relations	With each generation, many characteristics are replicated or changed. There often is considerable contact between generations and middle adulthood plays an important role.

Late Adulthood and Aging

The words of Salvatore Quasimodo stimulate images of what life in late adulthood might be like, "Each of us stands alone at the heart of the earth pierced through by a ray of sunlight: And suddenly it's evening."

Physical Development

While we may be in the evening of our lives in late adulthood, we are not meant to passively live out our remaining years. Everything we know about older adults suggests they are healthier and happier the more active they are.

John Pianfetti, age seventy, and Madge Sharples, age sixty-five, recently completed the New York Marathon. Older adults don't have to run marathons to be healthy and happy, but even moderate exercise can benefit their health. By getting men and women aged fifty to eighty-seven to do calisthenics, walk, run, stretch, and swim for forty-two weeks, researchers found dramatic changes in the oxygen transport capabilities of the participants' bodies (Adams & deVries, 1973; deVries, 1970). The improvements occurred regardless of age and prior exercise history.

Jogging hogs have shown the dramatic effects of exercise on health. Colin Bloor and Frank White (1983) trained a group of hogs to run approximately 100 miles per week. Then, they narrowed the arteries that supplied blood to the hogs' hearts. The hearts of these jogging hogs developed extensive alternate pathways for blood supply and 42 percent of the threatened heart tissue was salvaged compared to only 17 percent in a control group of hogs.

Exercise is an excellent way to maintain health in late adulthood and possibly increase our life spans. Other strategies have been tried through history. The aging King David attempted to prolong his life by lying against the bodies of warm young virgins. Just how long can we live and what influences our longevity?

The experimental setup in Colin Bloor and Frank White's experiment on exercise and health. Hogs, such as the one shown here, were trained to run approximately one hundred miles per week. Then the experimenters narrowed the arteries that supplied blood to the hogs' hearts. The jogging hogs' hearts developed alternative pathways for blood supply, while a group of non-jogging hogs were less likely to recover.

■ ■ ■ ■ ■ ■ ■ ■ ■ ■ ■ ■ ■ ■ ■ ■ ■ ■ ■

Psychology 10.3

Charlie Smith, the Abkhasians, and 1,200 Centenarians

■ Imagine that you are 120 years old. Would you still be able to write your name? Could you think clearly? What would your body look like? Would you be able to walk? To run? Could you still have sex? Would you have an interest in sex? Would your eyes and ears still function? Could you work?

Has anyone ever lived to be 120 years old? Supposedly, one American, Charlie Smith (?1842–1979), lived to be 137 years old. In three areas of the world, not just a single person but many people have reportedly lived more than 130 years. These areas are the Republic of Georgia in Russia, the Vilcabamba valley in Ecuador, and the province of Hunza in Kashmir. Three people over 100 years old (centenarians) per 100,000 people is considered normal. But in the Russian region where the Abkhasian people live, approximately 400 centenarians per 100,000 people have been

How old the Abkhasians are has not been fully documented.

reported. Some of the Abkhasians are said to be 120 to 170 years old (Benet, 1976).

However, there is reason to believe that some of these claims are false (Medvedev, 1974). Indeed, we really do not have sound documentation of anyone living more than approximately 115 to 120 years. In the case of the Abkhasians, birth registrations, as well as other documents such as

marriage certificates and military registrations, are not available. In most instances, the ages of the Abkhasians have been based on the individuals' recall of important historical events and interviews with other members of the village (Benet, 1976). In the Russian villages where people have been reported to live a long life, the elderly experience unparalleled esteem and honor. Centenarians are often given special positions in

Longevity

We are no longer a youthful society. As more people live to older ages, the proportion of individuals at different ages has become increasingly similar. Indeed, the concept of a period called late adulthood is a recent one—until the twentieth century most people died before they were sixty-five. In 1900 only one American in twenty-five was over sixty-five while today it is one in nine. By the middle of the twenty-first century, one in four Americans will be sixty-five years of age or older. Figure 10.9 shows the number of Americans over sixty-five in 1900, 1940, and 1980 and the projected numbers for the year 2040. As shown in figure 10.10, a significant increase in the number of people over the age of eighty-five is anticipated as well.

Nonetheless, while a much greater percentage of people are living to an older age, the life span has remained virtually unchanged since the beginning of recorded history. What has changed is **life expectancy**—the number of people expected to reach what seems to be an unbudging end point. Even though improvements in medicine, nutrition, exercise, and life-style have given us twenty-two additional years of life since 1900, few of us will live to be 100. To learn more about what life at 100 or even older is like read Psychology 10.3.

the community, such as the leader of social celebrations. Thus there is a strong motivation to give one's age as older than one really is. One individual who claimed to be 130 years of age was found to have used his father's birth certificate during World War I to escape army duty. Later it was discovered that he only was seventy-eight years old (Hayflick, 1975).

What about Charlie Smith? Was he 137 years old when he died? Charlie was very, very old, but it cannot be documented that he was actually 137. In 1956 officials of the Social Security Administration began to collect information about American centenarians who were receiving benefits. Charlie Smith was visited in 1961. He gave his birthdate as July 4, 1842, and his place of birth as Liberia. On one occasion he said he had been bought at a slave auction in New Orleans in 1854. Charlie Smith of Galveston, Texas, bought him and gave the young boy his own name.

Charlie was twenty-one years of age in 1863 when he supposedly was freed under the Emancipation Proclamation, but he decided to stay with the Smiths. By the end of the nineteenth century, Charlie had settled in Florida. He worked in turpentine camps, and at one point owned a turpentine farm in Homeland, Florida. Smith's records at the Social Security Administration do not provide evidence of his birthdate, but they do mention that he began to earn benefits based on Social Security credits by picking oranges at the age of 113 (Freeman, 1982).

Charlie Smith lived to be very old—exactly how old we will never know. He seems to have lived a very active life even after the age of 100. Many other Americans have lived to be 100 as well. In a recent book, *Living to Be 100: 1200 Who Did and How They Did It* (Segerberg, 1982), Social Security Administration interviews of 1,127 individuals

from 1963 to 1972 were searched for physical, psychological, and social information. Seventy-three other individuals were interviewed. Especially entertaining are the bizarre reasons several of the centenarians gave as to why they were able to live to be 100: "because I slept with my head to the north," "because of eating a lot of fatty pork and salt," and "because I don't believe in germs." While the impressions are those of a journalist, not a scientist, the following conclusions based on what it takes to live a long life seem to make sense. Organized purposeful behavior, discipline and hard work, freedom and independence, balanced diet, family orientation, good peer and friendship relations, and low ambition were among the most important factors related to high self-esteem and low levels of stress, both of which are associated with longevity.

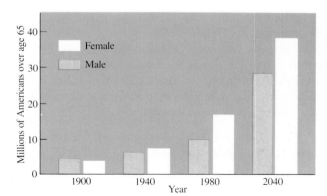

Figure 10.9
The aging of America: millions of Americans over age 65 from 1900 to the present and projected to the year 2040.
Source: U.S. Census Data: Social Security Administration: The Statistical History of the United States, 1976.

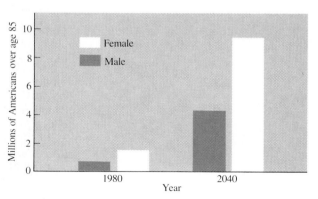

Figure 10.10
Millions of Americans over age 85 in 1980 and projected in the year 2040.
Source: Social Security Administration: The Statistical History of the United States.

What about you? What chance do you have of living to be 100? By taking the test in table 10.3 you can obtain a rough estimate of your chances and also discover some of the most important contributors to longevity. According to the questionnaire, heredity and family, health (weight, diet, smoking, and exercise), education, personality, and life-style are factors in longevity.

Biological Theories of Aging

Even if we keep a remarkably healthy profile through our adult years, we begin to age at some point. What are the biological explanations for aging?

Virtually all biological theories of aging assign genes an important role. It is assumed that the life span of the individual is determined by a program wired into the genes of the species. Support for the genetic basis of aging comes from research demonstrating that cells of the body can divide only a limited number of times (Hayflick, 1977, 1987). Cells from human embryonic tis-stissue can divide only about fifty times, for example. Cells extracted from older individuals divide fewer times than those taken from younger individuals. The cells of the elderly people still have dividing capability, however, so we rarely live to the end of our life-span potential. Based on the way human cells divide, biologists have placed the upper limit of the human life span at 110 to 120 years.

A theory that tells us to look within the body's cells to explain the aging process takes a *micro* approach. The label *micro* is used because a cell is a very small unit of analysis. By contrast, some scientists believe we should look at a more *macro* level to explain aging. The label *macro* refers to a larger, more global level of analysis.

One macrobiological approach to aging is called **homeostatic imbalance theory.** Proponents of homeostatic imbalance theory link mortality to the decline in organ reserve. At the level of the organism, life may be defined as internal homeostasis. The body's internal world is balanced and regulated within strict limits, though. Neural and endocrine systems monitor heart, lungs, liver, kidneys, and other organs to maintain this balance. In young adulthood, biologists estimate that we have an organ reserve that is ten times that required to sustain life. This organ reserve allows a stressed individual to restore homeostasis, or balance, when the body is damaged by an external element. But beginning at approximately age thirty, our organ reserve begins a gradual drop that continues through the remainder of our life. Eventually our organ reserve capacity reaches zero, and we die even if a disease is not present. After the age of thirty an individual's mortality rate doubles every eight years because of this decline in organ reserve (Upton, 1977).

While no one knows for sure why we age, scientists today believe we have a biological clock that ultimately will be identified. Some scientists believe the clock resides in the cells of the body, others argue that it lies in the homeostatic balance of the body. Yet others argue that certain parts of our body are more important than others in understanding aging—the hypothalamus, for example.

The Course of Physical Decline in Late Adulthood

As we age the probability we will have some disease or illness in late adulthood increases. For example, a majority of individuals who still are alive at the age of eighty are likely to have some impairment. One illness that is given considerable attention is **Alzheimer's disease,** a degenerative, irreversible disorder in which the brain actually shrinks. More than 2 million people over the age of sixty-five have Alzheimer's diesease. To learn more about the nature of this widespread illness read Psychology 10.4.

Table 10.3 Can You Live To Be 100?

The following test gives you a rough guide for predicting your longevity. The basic life expectancy for males is age sixty-seven, and for females age seventy-five. Write down your basic life expectancy. If you are in your fifties or sixties, you should add ten years to the basic figure because you have already proved yourself to be a durable individual. If you are over age sixty and active, you can even add another two years.

Basic life expectancy

Decide how each item below applies to you and add or subtract the appropriate number of years from your basic life expectancy.

1. Family history
   Add five years if two or more of your grandparents lived to eighty or beyond. _____
   Subtract four years if any parent, grandparent, sister, or brother died of heart attack or stroke before fifty. _____
   Subtract two years if anyone died from these diseases before sixty. _____
   Subtract three years for each case of diabetes, thyroid disorder, breast cancer, cancer of the digestive system, asthma, or chronic bronchitis among parents or grandparents. _____

2. Marital status
   If you are married, add four years. _____
   If you are over twenty-five and not married, subtract one year for every unwedded decade. _____

3. Economic status
   Add two years if your family income is over $40,000 per year. _____
   Subtract three years if you have been poor for the greater part of your life. _____

4. Physique
   Subtract one year for every ten pounds you are overweight. _____
   For each inch your girth measurement exceeds your chest measurement deduct two years. _____
   Add three years if you are over forty and not overweight. _____

5. Exercise
   Regular and moderate (jogging three times a week), add three years. _____
   Regular and vigorous (long-distance running three times a week), add five years. _____
   Subtract three years if your job is sedentary. _____
   Add three years if it is active. _____

6. Alcohol
   Add two years if you are a light drinker (one to three drinks a day). _____
   Subtract five to ten years if you are a heavy drinker (more than four drinks per day). _____
   Subtract one year if you are a teetotaler. _____

7. Smoking
   Two or more packs of cigarettes per day, subtract eight years. _____
   One to two packs per day, subtract two years. _____
   Less than one pack, subtract two years. _____
   Subtract two years if you regularly smoke a pipe or cigars. _____

8. Disposition
   Add two years if you are a reasoned, practical person. _____
   Subtract two years if you are aggressive, intense, and competitive. _____
   Add one to five years if you are basically happy and content with life. _____
   Subtract one to five years if you are often unhappy, worried, and often feel guilty. _____

9. Education
   Less than high school, subtract two years. _____
   Four years of school beyond high school, add one year. _____
   Five or more years beyond high school, add three years. _____

10. Environment
    If you have lived most of your life in a rural environment, add four years. _____
    Subtract two years if you have lived most of your life in an urban environment. _____

11. Sleep
    More than nine hours a day, subtract five years. _____

12. Temperature
    Add two years if your home's thermostat is set at no more than 68°F. _____

13. Health care
    Regular medical checkups and regular dental care, add three years. _____
    Frequently ill, subtract two years. _____

Your life expectancy total _____

From *The Psychology of Death, Dying and Bereavement,* by Richard Schultz. Copyright © 1978 by Newbery Award Records, Inc. Reprinted by permission of Random House, Inc.

■ ■ ■ ■ ■ ■ ■ ■ ■ ■ ■ ■ ■ ■ ■ ■ ■

Psychology 10.4

Alzheimer's Disease

■ Mary's family thought she was having vision problems when at age sixty-five she could not remember how to do the crossword puzzles she loved so much. Soon her family detected other symptoms pointing to a more serious condition. Mary no longer recognized her husband and even ran away from him in terror several times. She thought he was a stranger who was going to attack her, although he was an extremely kind and gentle man.

Mary's family finally took her to a hospital, where she was diagnosed as having Alzheimer's disease. Her condition progressed to the point where her personality changed, she had trouble sleeping, she had difficulty controlling her body functions, she showed a loss of appetite, and she became depressed.

Because of the increasing prevalence of Alzheimer's disease, researchers have stepped up their efforts to understand the causes of the disease and discover more effective ways to treat it. This

research has included the following:

- It has been found that at least 10 percent and possibly as many as 70 percent of Alzheimer's cases are inherited. Families with an incidence of Alzheimer's disease are three times as likely to have a case of Down's syndrome in their family as well. Scientists have yet to isolate the gene or genetic combination responsible, but they are getting closer—it is on chromosome twenty-one (Barnes, 1987).
- Whether or not computers can stave off the memory loss in Alzheimer's disease is being investigated. Possibly if the brain is used to its fullest potential, its functions can be maintained longer.
- Whether or not special living conditions can improve the motor skills of Alzheimer's patients is being studied. Color codes and bright lights

may help the daily functioning of the Alzheimer patient. Dance and exercise may improve motor abilities.
- The family's role as a support system for Alzheimer's patients is being evaluated. Psychologists believe the family can help improve the mental outlook of the Alzheimer's patient.

While the exact causes of Alzheimer's disease are unknown, scientists are optimistic that solutions are on the horizon. Some scientists compare the current status of Alzheimer's to the challenge of heart disease three decades ago. It, too, was thought to be an inevitable part of aging—then came drugs to control high blood pressure and the recognition of the role of diet in atherosclerosis. Scientists hope that their search through the body's tangle of neurons, different areas of the brain (such as the hippocampus), and genes will provide an answer to the cause of Alzheimer's.

The brain is of considerable interest to scientists who study the course of physical decline in late adulthood. As we age we lose a number of neurons. Some researchers estimate that the loss may be as high as 50 percent over the adult years, although others believe the loss is substantially less and that an accurate assessment of neuron loss has not been made (Bondareff, 1977; Diamond, 1978). Perhaps a more reasonable estimate is that 5 to 10 percent of our neurons atrophy until we reach the seventies. After that, neuron loss may accelerate (Leaf, 1973).

A significant aspect of the aging process may be that neurons do not replace themselves (Moushegian, 1987). Nonetheless, generally it is believed that the brain has remarkable recovery and repair capability, losing only a small portion of its ability to function in the late adulthood years (Labouvie-Vief, 1986). The adaptive nature of the brain was demonstrated in a recent study by Paul Coleman (1986). From the forties through the seventies, dendritic growth increased (recall that dendrites are the receiving part of the neuron—they are especially important because they comprise about 95 percent of the surface of nerve cells). But in very old people, those in their

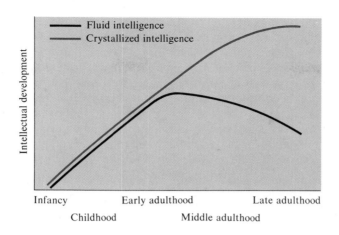

Figure 10.11
Fluid and crystallized intellectual development across the life span.

nineties, dendritic growth was no longer taking place. Through the seventies, then, dendritic growth may compensate for neuron loss, but not when individuals reach their nineties.

Not only does our brain change as we age, but our circulatory machinery becomes less efficient. Elastin, the molecules that determine the elasticity of heart and blood vessels, decreases and collagen, the stiff protein that comprises about one-third of the body's protein, increases. Arteries are more resistant to the flow of blood, and heart output—about five quarts a minute at age fifty—drops about 1 percent a year thereafter. With the heart muscle less efficient and the vessels more resistant, heart rate and blood pressure rise, both of which are related to heart disease. Even in a healthy older person, blood pressure that was 100/75 at age twenty-five probably will be 160/90 in late adulthood.

Remember that the further we move through the late adulthood years, the more likely some physical impairment will be present. Is this likely to be true for our cognitive abilities as well?

Cognitive Development

At age seventy, Dr. John Rock introduced the birth-control pill. At age eighty-nine, Arthur Rubinstein gave one of his best performances at New York's Carnegie Hall. From eighty-five to ninety years of age, Pablo Picasso completed three sets of drawings. And at age seventy-six, Anna Mary Robertson Moses took up painting—as Grandma Moses she became internationally famous and staged fifteen one-woman shows throughout Europe. Are these feats rare exceptions?

The issue of intellectual decline through the adult years is a provocative one. David Wechsler (1972) concluded that the decline in intelligence is simply part of the general aging process we all go through. But the issue seems much more complex. John Horn thinks some abilities decline while others do not (Horn & Donaldson, 1980). As shown in figure 10.11, Horn argues that crystallized intelligence (based on cumulative learning experiences) increases throughout the life span, while fluid intelligence (the ability to perceive and manipulate information) steadily declines from middle adulthood.

Some serious criticisms of Horn's hypothesis have come from Paul Baltes and K. Warner Schaie (Baltes, 1987b; Baltes & Kliegl, 1986; Schaie, 1984). They believe many data on intelligence and aging, such as Horn's, are flawed because they were collected in a cross-sectional manner. In a **cross-sectional study,** individuals of different ages are tested at the same time. For example, a cross-sectional study might assess the intelligence of different groups of forty- and seventy-year-old individuals in a single evaluation, say in 1985. The average forty-year-old person and the average seventy-year-old person tested in

Intellectual feats such as the creative painting of "Grandma Moses" in late adulthood hardly seem like intellectual decline. Shown here at age 88, Grandma Moses (whose real name was Anna Mary Robertson) is finishing a painting that will become a Christmas card.

Active older people are more satisfied with their lives than inactive older people. Older people should be encouraged to take trips, exercise, attend meetings, and get out in the world rather than merely sit at home.

"No, no! The day the earth stood still was in May. We weren't married till June."

Drawing by Geo. Price: © 1972 The New Yorker Magazine, Inc.

1985 were born and reared in different eras, which produced different opportunities. For instance, as the seventy-year-old individuals grew up, they had fewer educational opportunities, which probably influenced their scores on intelligence tests. So if we find differences in intelligence levels of forty- and seventy-year-old individuals when we assess them in a cross-sectional manner, the differences may be due to something like educational opportunities instead of age.

By contrast, a longitudinal study might evaluate the intelligence of the same individuals at age forty and then again at age seventy. In a **longitudinal study,** the same individuals are retested after a period of years. The longitudinal data collected by Schaie (1984) and others do not reveal an intellectual decline in adulthood.

In thinking about how to study intelligence in late adulthood, we need to consider what components should be investigated and how they should be measured. Horn, Baltes, and Schaie have mainly studied general intelligence and several of its subfactors, such as fluid and crystallized intelligence, through psychometric testing. Are we likely to find a decline in intelligence if we focus on an important intellectual process such as memory and observe it in various contexts?

Remember that in some circumstances memory declines even in middle age. The same can be said for older adults. The decline depends on such information processing activities as organization, elaboration, imagery, and retrieval. By the same token, improving the use of these processes improves memory in late adulthood just as in middle adulthood.

Possibly if we observed memory and problem solving in more naturalistic contexts, less decline in late adulthood would be discovered. Nancy Denney (1986) points out that most tests of memory and problem-solving abilities measure how older adults perform trivial activities, not unlike those found on school exams. In her research, Denney assessed cognition among older adults by observing how they handled a landlord who would not fix their stove and what they would do if a Social Security check did not arrive on time. Denney revealed that the ability to solve such practical problems actually increased through the forties and fifties as people gained life experience. She also found that people in their seventies were no worse at this type of practical problem solving than their counterparts in their twenties, who were quite good at solving practical problems.

What does this mean to the basic issue of intellectual decline in adulthood? Remember that we do not have just one intelligence but many intelligences. Older adults are not as intelligent as younger adults when it comes to speed of processing information and this probably harms their performance on school-related tasks and traditional measures of intelligence. But when we consider general knowledge and possibly something we might call wisdom, that is an entirely different matter (Dixon & Baltes, 1986; Holliday, Burnaby, & Chandler, 1987; Smith, Dixon, & Baltes, in press).

Social and Personality Development

In the past, the image of the older adult was of a person sitting in a rocking chair watching the world go by. Now we know that the most well-adjusted and satisfied older adults are active, not passive, individuals. According to the **activity theory** of late adulthood, the more active and involved older people are, the more satisfied they are and the less likely they will age. Research

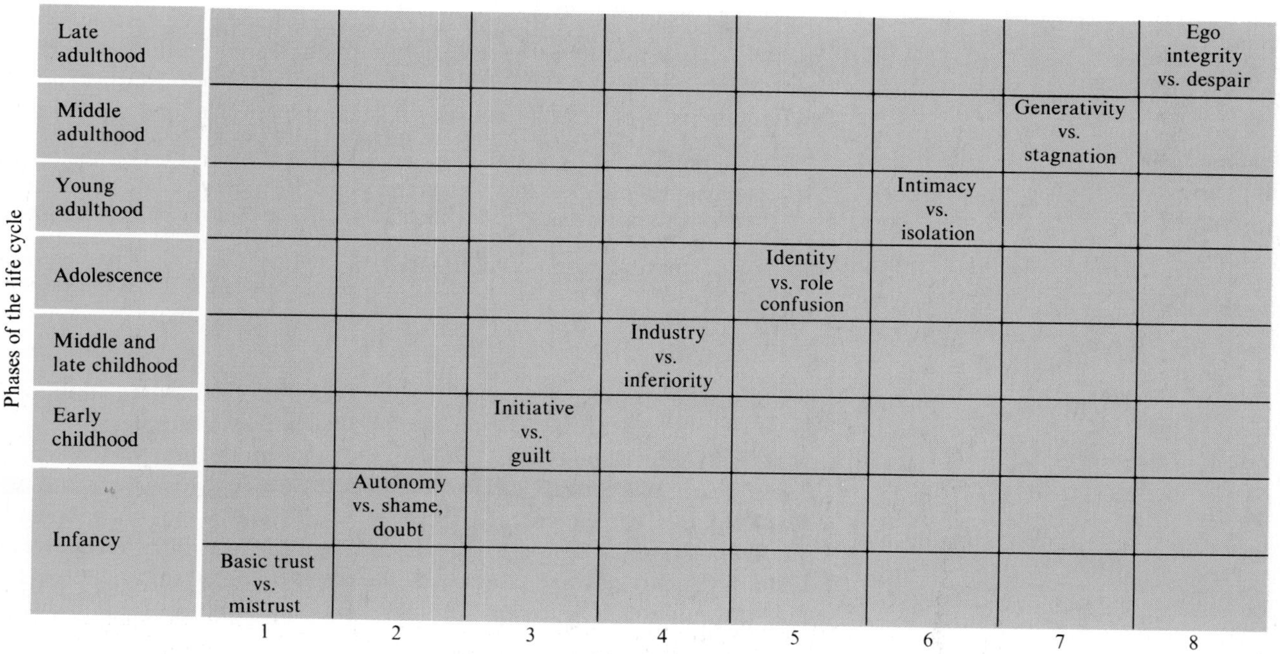

Phases of the life cycle	1	2	3	4	5	6	7	8
Late adulthood								Ego integrity vs. despair
Middle adulthood							Generativity vs. stagnation	
Young adulthood						Intimacy vs. isolation		
Adolescence					Identity vs. role confusion			
Middle and late childhood				Industry vs. inferiority				
Early childhood			Initiative vs. guilt					
Infancy		Autonomy vs. shame, doubt						
	Basic trust vs. mistrust							

Figure 10.12
Erikson's stages of development.

documents that elderly people who go to church, attend meetings, take trips, and exercise are happier than those who simply sit at home. Income as well as health also is associated with life satisfaction in predictable ways (Kuhn, 1987; Markides & Martin, 1979).

Too often the elderly are stereotyped. A new word in our vocabulary is **ageism,** which is prejudice against older people. Many individuals in late adulthood face painful discrimination; they are not hired for new jobs or are eased out of existing jobs because they are perceived as too rigid or feeble-minded. Sometimes older adults are shunned socially because they are thought of as senile or boring. At times they are perceived as children and described with such adjectives as cute and adorable. Their children may edge them out of their family life, perceiving their elderly parents as sick, ugly, or parasitic. These are inhuman perceptions to be sure, but unfortunately they exist (Neugarten & Neugarten, 1986).

As individuals move into the late adulthood years, they reflect on what their life has been like. Consider Edna, age seventy-five, who recently thought to herself:

I think about my life a lot—it is in the back of my mind on a lot of occasions. Thoughts of the past come into mind when I look at my children and their children. When I walk down the street I think back to when I was a young girl . . . to the enjoyable moments with my friends and parents. I think about my husband, our wedding . . . the times we struggled to make ends meet. He is gone now, but I have so many memories of him.

Edna's reflections typify those of individuals in the final stage, **integrity verus despair,** of Erikson's eight stages of the life cycle (for an overview of Erikson's eight stages see figure 10.12). From Erikson's perspective, the later years of life are a time of looking back at what we have done with our lives. Through many different routes the older person may have developed a positive outlook in each of the preceding periods of development. If so, the retrospective glances and reminiscence reveal a life well spent, and the individual will feel satisfied (integrity). But the older adult may have a negative outlook from crises earlier in life. If so, the retrospective glances may produce doubt, gloom, and despair over the total worth of his life. Erikson's own words capture the rich thoughts of older adults as they reflect on their personality development:

> A meaningful old age, then . . . serves the needs for that integrated heritage which gives indispensable perspective to the life cycle. . . . To whatever abyss ultimate concerns may lead individual(s) . . . toward the end of life, a new edition of an identity crisis (appears) which we may state in the words: "I am what survives of me." (1968, pp. 140–141)

Death and the Dying Process

Death may come at any point in the life cycle, but during late adulthood we know that for most of us it is much closer. How do we face death?

Elizabeth Kübler-Ross (1974) says that we go through five stages in facing death: denial and isolation, anger, bargaining, depression, and acceptance. Initially, the individual responds, "No, it can't be me. It's not possible." But denial is only a temporary defense. When the individual recognizes that denial no longer can be maintained, she often becomes angry and resentful. Now the individual's question becomes, "Why me?" Anger often is displaced onto physicians, nurses, family members, and even God. In the third stage, the dying person develops the hope that death can somehow be postponed or delayed. The individual now says, "Yes, me, but. . . ." Bargaining and negotiation, often with God, produces the hope that in exchange for a few more months of life, the individual will lead a reformed life dedicated to God or the services of others.

As the dying individual comes to accept the certainty of her death, she often enters a period of preparatory grief, becoming silent, refusing visitors, and spending much of the time crying or grieving. This behavior should be viewed as normal and is an effort to disconnect the self from all love objects. Kübler-Ross describes the final stage, characterized by peace and acceptance of one's fate, as the end of the struggle, the final resting stage before death.

Do all individuals go through the stages in the sequence Kübler-Ross proposed? If not, will they cope less effectively with dying? No one has confirmed that all individuals go through the stages in the order described (Schulz & Alderman, 1974). Kübler-Ross herself feels she has been misread, saying that she never intended the stages to be an invariant progression toward death. Although Kübler-Ross recognizes variation in how individuals face death, she believes the optimal way is the sequence she proposed.

But some individuals struggle until the very end, almost angrily hanging onto their lives. They follow the encouragement of Dylan Thomas: "Do not go gentle into that good night. Old age should burn and rave at close of day . . . rage against the dying of the light." In these instances, acceptance of death never comes. Indeed, people die in different ways and experience different feelings and emotions during the process: hope, fear, curiosity, envy, apathy, relief, even anticipation. And they often move rapidly from one mood to another and in other instances two moods may be present simultaneously (Kalish, 1981).

By now you can appreciate that much development takes place in adolescence and adulthood, just as in infancy and childhood. This chapter concludes our discusion of development through the life cycle. In the next section, you will read about motivaton, emotion, and stress, including the developmental themes of emotion in infants, exercise and eating problems of adolescents, the daily hassles and uplifts of college students and middle-aged adults, and coping with stress in the elderly.

Summary

I. Historical Beginnings and the Nature of Adolescence
G. Stanley Hall proposed a storm and stress view of adolescence in 1904. We no longer subscribe to this view. Recent interest in the history of adolescence suggests the concept of adolescence might have been invented. In most cultures, adolescence is entered between ten and thirteen years old and exited between eighteen and twenty-two years old. In recent years a distinction had been made between early and late adolescence.

II. Physical and Cognitive Development in Adolescence
Puberty is a rapid change in maturation. Hormonal changes are prominent in puberty, which occurs roughly two years earlier for girls than boys. Early maturation generally favors boys but has mixed effects for girls. The effects of early and late maturation are complex. Piaget argued that formal operational thought appears from eleven to fifteen years of age. It is characterized by abstract thinking and idealism, as well as planning and logical analysis. Adolescent egocentrism and changes in language also occur.

III. Social and Personality Development in Adolescence
Conflict with parents increases in adolescence, but it may serve a positive developmental function. Adolescents increase their time spent with peers but also keep their connectedness to parents. Antisocial conformity to peer standards peaks between thirteen and fourteen years of age. Clique membership is associated with self-esteem, and dating is a major interest. Adolescents show a strong push for independence and identity. Erikson believes the major theme of adolescence is identity versus identity confusion. Kohlberg developed a provocative cognitive theory of moral development but his view has not gone unchallenged. Gilligan, who

thinks he has underrepresented the care perspective, is one of his most severe critics.

IV. The Life-Cycle Perspective
The life-cycle perspective argues that more change takes place in adulthood than the traditional child perspective. Adulthood is divided into early, middle, and late adulthood. Neugarten believes many issues are renegotiated throughout adulthood.

V. Physical and Cognitive Development in Early and Middle Adulthood
The peak or our physical skills and health usually comes in early adulthood, a time when it is easy to develop bad health habits. Menopause has varied physical and psychological effects, with few women having serious complications. Some psychologists argue that cognition is more pragmatic in early adulthood. Cognitive skills are strong in early adulthood. Some decline in memory occurs in middle adulthood, although strategies such as organization can reduce this decline.

VI. Social and Personality Development in Early and Middle Adulthood
Erikson, Gould, and Levinson have emphasized a number of stages of adult development. There is an emphasis on increased stress in middle adulthood, but this may be overdrawn. A complex life-events framework takes into account many factors other than stage of development, including life events, mediating factors, adaptation, and sociohistorical circumstances. The channel of truth lies somewhere between extreme change and extreme constancy in our personalities. We are adaptive and resilient throughout our lives, but underlying this change is some degree of stability and continuity. Middle adulthood plays an important role in intergenerational relations.

VII. Physical Development in Late Adulthood
Life expectancy has increased dramatically but the life span has remained virtually stable for centuries. Longevity is influenced by such factors as heredity, family, health, education, personality, and life-style. Macrobiological theories of aging are global and stress such factors as homeostasis; microbiological theories are molecular and search for the cellular basis of aging. As we age through late adulthood our chance of developing some impairment increases. Controversy surrounds the issue of neuron loss in aging. Alzheimer's disease is a degenerative brain disorder affecting more than 2 million people over age sixty-five.

VIII. Cognitive Development in Late Adulthood
There is extensive debate over the stimulating issue of whether intelligence declines in late adulthood. Recent naturalistic research on memory suggests the decline may be exaggerated. It is important to remember that we have many intelligences and the overall question of intellectual decline is an extremely global one. Decline does occur in speed of processing, but wisdom is a different matter.

IX. Social Development in Late Adulthood
Everything we know about late adulthood suggests an active older life is preferred to disengagement. Erikson believes the final issue in the life cycle to be negotiated is integrity versus despair, which involves a life review process.

X. Death and the Dying Process
Death may come at any point in the life cycle but in late adulthood we know it is near. Kübler-Ross proposed five stages of dealing with death.

Key Terms

Suggested Readings

Binstock, R. H., & Shanas, E. (Eds.). (1985). *Handbook of aging and the social sciences.* New York: Van Nostrand Rheinhold. Many provocative ideas about aging and the social worlds of the elderly are presented in this volume. It includes contributions from many experts on aging, with a chapter on ageism and legal issues involved in discrimination against older people.

Eichorn, D. M., et al. (Eds.). (1981). *Present and past in middle life.* New York: Academic Press. A very important book in furthering our knowledge of adult development. Describes the California Longitudinal Study that spans nearly fifty years.

Erikson, E. H. (1968). *Identity: Youth and crisis.* New York: Norton. One of the most famous efforts of Erikson. Provides significant information about his eight stages of development, with special attention to the nature of identity development in adolescence and early adulthood.

Kalish, R. A. (1981). *Death, grief, and caring relationships.* Monterey, CA: Brooks/Cole. An excellent, detailed overview of many facets of death and the dying process. One of the most thorough, comprehensive, and well-written sources available.

Levinson, D., et al. (1978). *Seasons of a man's life.* New York: Ballantine. Levinson's national best-seller describes his theory of adult personality development. Also includes substantial case study material.

Santrock, J. W. (1987). *Adolescence* (3rd ed.). Dubuque, IA: Wm. C. Brown Publishers. A detailed overview of adolescence with separate chapters on such topics as identity, sexuality, and moral development. Also includes informaton about delinquency and drugs, as well as other problems in adolescence.

Motivation and Emotion

The passions and desires, like
the two twists of a rope,
mutually mix with the other,
and twine inextricably round
the heart; producing good, if
moderately indulged; but
certain destruction if suffered
to become inordinate.

—Robert Burton

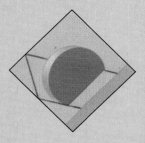

Motivation

■■

Upon what meat doth this our Caesar feed, That he has grown so
great? Let me have some men that are fat; . . . Yon Cassius has a lean
and hungry look; He thinks too much: such men are dangerous.

—*Shakespeare*

■■

Images of Motivation

John Belushi, the comic. Bonnie and Clyde, bank robbers. Rasputin, Russian
mastermind and manipulator. All were high-profile individuals who took risks,
sought adventure, and thrived on excitement. Belushi excelled at making audiences laugh and sought excitement through cocaine. Bonnie Parker and Clyde
Barrow wreaked havoc on towns as they robbed banks and shot lawmen. Rasputin gained a reputation early in the twentieth century as a mystic. The giant,
uncouth Russian monk was an unruly man who delighted in keeping the ar-
istocracy in an uproar with his out outlandish comments and behavior.

Frank Farley (1986) believes that thrill-seeking behavior such as that
of Belushi, Bonnie and Clyde, and Rasputin can be destructive or constructive.
He also says that individuals can seek thrills in the physical or cognitive domain. Sir Francis Crick, Nobel Prize winner for codiscovering DNA's cellular
structure, sought thrills in the cognitive domain. Evel Knievel, the daredevil
entertainer, sought stimulation in the physical domain. Both Crick and
Knievel turned their thrill-seeking motivation into constructive accomplishments. But Bonnie and Clyde and Rasputin, became destructive—Bonnie and
Clyde in the physical domain; Rasputin in the cognitive domain. Belushi's
behavior led to constructive and destructive consequences: the ability to make
millions laugh but a drug-induced death.

Each of us is motivated to seek variety in our experiences with the world.
But most of us do not go to the extremes of these individuals. Marvin Zuckerman (1979) constructed a scale to measure this ability to seek sensation—
the Sensation Seeking Scale (SSS). Zuckerman defines *sensation seeking* as
the motivation for varied, novel, and complex sensations and experiences. High
sensation seekers take physical and social risks just for the sake of the experiences. By responding to the items in table 11.1 you can get a sense of your
motivation for sensation seeking.

Shakespeare said, "Every why hath a wherefore." And Charles Farrar
Brown questioned, "Why is thus? What is the reason for this thusness?" Why
are you so hungry? Why are you interested in having sex? Why do you want
to get an A in this class? Why do you seek thrills? The answer is: because you
are motivated. **Motivation** involves the question of "why" individuals behave,
think, and feel the way they do.

If you are hungry, you probably will put this book down and go to the
refrigerator. If you are sexually motivated, you may go to a party and flirt
with someone you think is attractive. If you are motivated to achieve, you may
stay in the library until 3 A.M. tonight studying. When you are motivated, you
do something. When you are motivated your behavior is directed; you go to
the refrigerator, a party, the library. Hunger, sex, and achievement are three
important themes in your life, and three things that energize and direct your
behavior. We will discuss each of these themes in detail in this chapter. But
first let's get a feel for the general way psychologists have viewed the "whys"
of behavior. ■

(a)   (b)   (c)   (d)

Table 11.1 Selected Items from the Sensation Seeking Scale

(a) John Belushi, the comic,
(b) Bonnie and Clyde, bank robbers,
(c) Evel Knievel, daredevil stuntman,
(d) Rasputin, Russian mastermind and manipulator—all were high-profile individuals who took risks, sought adventure, and thrived on excitement. All would score high on the trait of sensation seeking.

For each of the following items decide which of the two choices best describes your likes and feelings. If neither choice applies, choose the one that *most* describes you. Answer all items.

1. a. I like the tumult of sounds in a busy city.
   b. I prefer the peace and quiet of the country.
2. a. I dislike the sensations one gets when flying.
   b. I enjoy many of the rides in amusement parks.
3. a. I would like a job which would require a lot of traveling.
   b. I would prefer a job in one location.
4. a. I often wish I could be a mountain climber.
   b. I can't understand people who risk their necks climbing mountains.
5. a. I get bored seeing the same old faces.
   b. I like the comfortable familiarity of everyday friends.
6. a. I like to explore a strange city or section of town by myself, even if it means getting lost.
   b. I prefer a guide when I am in a place I don't know well.
7. a. I find people that disagree with my beliefs more stimulating than people who agree with me.
   b. I don't like to argue with people whose beliefs are sharply divergent from mine, since such arguments are never resolved.
8. a. I prefer more subdued colors in decoration.
   b. I like to decorate with bright colors.
9. a. When I have nothing to do or look at for any length of time I get very restless.
   b. I often enjoy just relaxing and doing nothing.
10. a. Most people spend entirely too much money on life insurance.
    b. Life insurance is something that no man can afford to be without.
11. a. I don't like to drink coffee because it overstimulates me and keeps me awake.
    b. I like to drink coffee because of the lift it gives me.
12. a. The worst social sin is to be rude.
    b. The worst social sin is to be a bore.
13. a. The most important goal of life is to live it to the fullest and experience as much of it as you can.
    b. The most important goal of life is to find peace and happiness.
14. a. If I were a salesman I would prefer working on commission if I had a chance to make more money than I could on a salary.
    b. If I were a salesman I would prefer a straight salary rather than the risk of making little or nothing on a commission basis.
15. a. I like sharp or spicy foods.
    b. I prefer foods with a minimum of seasoning.

How to score your answers: Count one point for sensation seeking for each of the following: 1a, 2b, 3a, 4a, 5a, 6a, 7a, 8b, 9a, 10a, 11b, 12b, 13a, 14a, 15a.

If you answered eleven or more items this way you probably have a strong motivation for sensation seeking. If you answered five items or less this way your probably have a weak motive for sensation seeking. If you responded this way six to ten times you probably are in the average range of sensation seekers. The older one gets the more sensation seeking scores go down. These items represent an abbreviated version of Zuckerman's Sensation Seeking Scale.

Some Ideas about the "Whys" of Behavior

Sam Walton, the founder of Walmart stores, made about 5 billion dollars in 1986. What was his motivation for doing this? Henry VIII had six wives in his lifetime. What motivated Henry to marry this number of times?

Instincts

An **instinct** is an innate, biological determinant of behavior. Did Sam Walton have an instinct for acquisitiveness? Did Henry VIII have a sexual instinct? We don't hear much about instincts anymore but they had a prominent place in psychology early in this century. Influenced by Darwin's evolutionary theory, William McDougall (1908) argued that all behavior is determined by instincts. He said that we have instincts for acquisitiveness, curiosity, gregariousness, pugnacity, and self-assertion. At about the same time, Sigmund Freud (1917) argued that our behavior is instinctually based; he believed that sex and aggression were especially powerful in motivating our behavior.

It was not long before psychologists formed their own lists of instincts, each striving to capture subtle differences. Psychologists thought that perhaps we have one instinct for physical aggression, one for assertive behavior, and yet another for competitive behavior. Instinct theory, though, did not really explain anything. The wherefore behind Shakespeare's why was not being adequately explored by the instinct doctrine: an instinct invariably was inferred from the behavior it was intended to explain. Instinct theory did call attention to the idea that some of our motivation is unlearned and involves physiological factors. This idea is important in our understanding of motivation today.

Needs and Drives

If you do not have an instinct for sex, maybe you have a need or a drive for it. A **drive** is an aroused state that occurs because of a physiological **need.** You might have a need for water, for food, or for sex. The need for food, for example, arouses your hunger drive. This motivates you to do something—go to MacDonalds's for a Big Mac, for example—to reduce the drive and satisfy the need. As a drive becomes stronger, we are motivated to reduce it. This action is known as **drive-reduction theory.**

Usually, but not always, needs and drives are closely associated in time. For example, when your body needs food your hunger drive will probably be aroused. An hour after you have eaten a Big Mac you might still be hungry (thus, you *need* food), but your hunger *drive* might have subsided. From this example you can sense that drive pertains to a *psychological state;* need involves a *physiological* state.

An important concept in motivation and one that is important in understanding drives is homeostasis—the body's tendency to maintain a balanced equilibrium, or steady state. Literally hundreds of biological states in our bodies must be maintained within a certain range: temperature, blood-sugar level, potassium and sodium levels, oxygen, and so on. When you dive into an icy swimming pool, your body heats up. When you walk out of an air-conditioned room into the heat of a summer day, your body begins to cool down. These changes occur automatically in an attempt to restore your body to its optimal state of functioning.

Homeostasis is achieved in our bodies much like a thermostat in a house keeps the temperature constant. For example, assume the thermostat in your house is set at 68 degrees. The furnace heats the house until a temperature of 68 degrees is reached, at which time the furnace shuts off. Because a source of heat no longer is present, the temperature eventually falls below 68 degrees. This is detected by the thermostat, which turns the furnace back on again. The cycle is repeated so that the temperature is maintained within narrow limits.

Homeostasis is used to explain both physiological imbalances and psychological imbalances. For example, if we have not been around people for a long time, we may be motivated to seek their company. If we haven't studied hard for a test in some months, we may be aroused to put in considerably more study time. The concepts of drive and homeostasis have played important roles in understanding motivation. So has the concept of incentive.

Incentives

> If a man runs after money, he's money mad; if he keeps it, he's a capitalist; if he spends it, he's a playboy; if he doesn't try to get it, he lacks ambition; . . . and if he accumulates it after a life-time of hard work, people call him a fool who never got anything out of life.

These words from Vic Oliver suggest that something more than drive motivates our behavior—something more external. Money is an external stimulus that is a powerful motivator of behavior.

In the study of motivation, external stimuli are known as **incentives.** Motivation theorists stress that both positive and negative incentives energize and direct behavior. For example, a sexually attractive individual is a positive incentive for approaching that person at a party and starting a conversation; the threat of an intruder is a negative incentive for purchasing a security system for your home.

By identifying the concept of incentives, psychologists expanded their definition of the "why" of our behavior to include a combination of internal, physiological needs, psychological drives, *and* external stimuli. We have discussed a number of different instincts, drives, needs, and incentives. Are some of these more important to you than others? Might you have to satisfy some needs before others?

Hierarchy of Motives

Is getting an A in this class more important to you than eating? If the person of your dreams told you that you were marvelous would that motivate you to throw yourself in front of a car for her safety? According to Abraham Maslow (1954, 1971), our "basic" needs must be satisfied before we can satisfy our "higher" needs. Based on Maslow's **hierarchy of motives** we would conclude that in most instances people need to eat before they can achieve and that they need to satisfy their safety needs before their love needs. Maslow believes that we have five basic needs, which unfold in the following sequence: physiological, safety, love and belongingness, self-esteem, and self-actualization (see figure 11.1).

It is the need for self-actualization that Maslow has described in the greatest detail. **Self-actualization** includes everything an individual is capable of being. According to Maslow, self-actualization is possible only after the other needs in his hierarchy are met. Obviously, you cannot be everything you are capable of being if you are hungry all of the time. Individuals who are self-actualized feel a sense of fulfillment and they are content with their philosophy and outlook on life. Their behavior reflects these feelings. Maslow cautions that most individuals stop maturing after they have developed a high

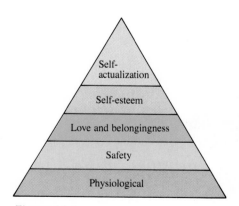

Figure 11.1
Maslow's hierarchy of needs.

level of self-esteem, and thus they do not become self-actualized. Many of Maslow's writings focus on how individuals can reach the elusive motivational state of self-actualization—we will have much more to say about this theory in chapter 13, "Personality."

The idea that we have a hierarchy of motives is an appealing one. Maslow's theory stimulates each of us to think about the ordering of motives in our own lives. Not everyone agrees on the order in which we satisfy our needs, though. In some instances the order may be different from what Maslow envisioned.

Biological, Cognitive, and Social Processes

The contemporary perspective on motivation stresses biological, cognitive, and social processes (Mook, 1987). Rather than instinct motivating our behavior, contemporary psychologists see biology's role in motivation in the form of physiological mechanisms. These mechanisms are more important in some areas than others. For example, when describing our motivation to satisfy our hunger or our need for sex, physiological factors are prominent; when describing our motivation for achievement and power, physiological factors are far less prominent.

There are cognitive aspects to motivation also, including conscious thoughts, thinking, and understanding. The cognitive orientation in the study of motivation has been influenced by the cognitive revolution in general in psychology and its emphasis on how individuals process information about their world. Information processing is important in our interpretation of most motivational circumstances, whether hunger, sex, achievement, curiosity, power, competence, or other motivational states are at issue (Geen, Beatty, & Arkin, 1984).

And we should not forget that environmental stimulation and social settings are also involved in motivation. Even in trying to understand motives often considered to be strongly biological in nature, the environment figures prominently. Consider hunger, for example. Environmental cues that stimulate eating behavior and cultural standards for eating must both be addressed. Consider also sexual behavior. Sexual behavior not only is influenced by biological processes, but by environmental cues, social interactions, relationships, and sociocultural standards for sex as well. And the standards for achievement vary extensively across cultures. Social contact between parents and children, comparisons among peers, and models of achievement are among the complex factors that must be considered. Let's now address each of these important areas of motivation in more detail, beginning with hunger.

Hunger

Imagine that you live in the Bayambang area of the Philippines. You are very poor and have little food to eat. The same is true for virtually everyone in your village. Hunger is a way of life for your village. Now imagine yourself as the typical American, eating not only breakfast, lunch, and dinner, but snacks along the way, and maybe even conducting a midnight raid on the refrigerator.

Food is an important aspect of life in any culture. Whether we have very little or large amounts of food available to us, hunger is an important influence on our behavior. What mechanisms explain why we get hungry?

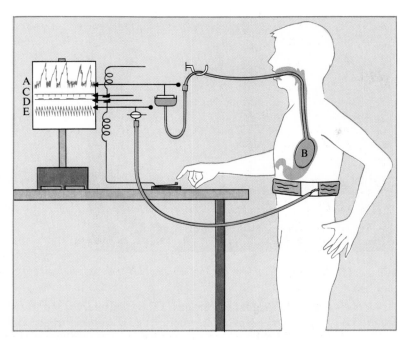

Figure 11.2
Cannon and Washburn's classic experiment on hunger. Notice the letters A, B, C, D, and E in the drawing. A is the record of the increases and decreases in the volume of the balloon in the subject's stomach, B. Number of minutes elapsed is shown in C. The subject's indication of feeling hungry is recorded at D. E is a reading of the movements of the abdominal wall to ensure that such movements are not the cause of changes in stomach volume.

Physiological Factors

You are sitting in class and it is 2 P.M. You were so busy today that you skipped lunch. As the professor lectures, your stomach starts to growl. For many of us, a growling stomach is one of the main signs that we are hungry. Psychologists have wondered for many years about the role of *peripheral factors—* such as the stomach, liver, and blood chemistry—in hunger.

Peripheral Factors

In 1912, a classic experiment on hunger was conducted. Walter Cannon and A. L. Washburn constructed the apparatus shown in figure 11.2. Washburn was the first subject. As part of the procedure, a balloon partially filled with air was passed through a tube inserted in his mouth and pushed down into his stomach. A machine that measures air pressure was connected to the balloon so that stomach contractions could be monitored. Washburn indicated when he felt hungry by pressing a key. The results for Washburn as well as other subjects indicated a close association between stomach contractions and reports of being hungry.

Stomach contractions can be a signal for hunger, but the stomach also can send signals that stop hunger. We all know that a full stomach can decrease our appetite. In fact, the stomach actually tells the brain not only how full it is, but also how much nutrient is in the stomach load. That is why a stomach full of rich food stops your hunger faster than a stomach full of water (Deutsch & Gonzales, 1980). Interestingly, the same stomach hormone that helps start the digestion of food (called cholecystokinin, or CCK) reaches your brain through the bloodstream and signals you to stop eating. Stomach signals are not the only factors that affect hunger. People who have had their stomachs surgically removed still get hunger pangs (Ingelfinger, 1944).

Blood sugar is an important factor in hunger, probably because the brain is critically dependent on sugar for energy. One set of sugar receptors is located in the brain itself, and these receptors trigger hunger when sugar levels get too low. Another set of sugar receptors is in the liver, which is the organ that stores excess sugar and releases it into the blood when needed. The sugar

Figure 11.3
A normal animal (left) and a hyperphagic animal (right). Note that the hyperphagic animal weighs more than twice as much as the normal animal (640 versus 290 grams).

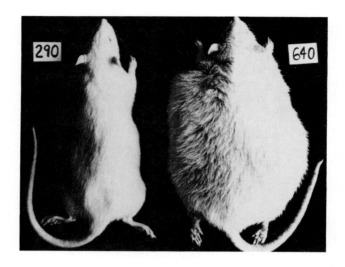

"Let's just go in and see what happens."
Drawing by Booth; © 1986 The New Yorker Magazine, Inc.

receptors in the liver signal the brain via the vagus nerve, and this signal also can make you hungry (Novlin & others, 1983). Another important factor in blood sugar control is the hormone *insulin,* which causes excess sugar in the blood to be stored in cells as fats and carbohydrates. Insulin injections cause profound hunger because they lower blood sugar drastically. Recent evidence suggests that insulin may influence hunger in other ways as well. We will come back to that topic later in our discussion (Rodin, 1984).

Brain Processes

So far we have been talking about peripheral factors in hunger. But aren't *central factors* in the body also involved in understanding hunger? The answer is yes and the central factors involve the brain. One critical brain region in hunger is the **ventromedial hypothalamus (VMH).** When a rat is given a brain lesion in the VMH, it immediately becomes *hyperphagic* (that is, it eats too much) and rapidly becomes obese (Brobeck, Tepperman, & Long, 1943), as shown in figure 11.3. It was thought that the VHM was a "satiety center," and that the lesion left animals unable to satiate their hunger. The picture now emerging, however, suggests that the VMH causes an hormonal disorder (remember that the hypothalamus is the control center for many hormones). After the VHM lesion is given, the rat's body cells act as if they are starving, constantly converting all nutrients from the blood into fat and never releasing them (Gold & Simson, 1982). That is the main reason the animals become obese (see figure 11.4). One of the fascinating aspects of this condition is that the animals stop gaining weight once they reach a certain weight, suggesting that hormones and body cells may control the body's overall "set point" for body weight. **Set point** refers to the weight maintained when no effort is made to gain or lose weight.

Another aspect of the brain that is important in eating is the system of dopamine neurons that run up from the lower brain. When these nerve fibers are destroyed by a lesion in the lateral hypothalamus, rats become *aphagic* (that is, they stop eating) and literally die of starvation (Heffner, Zigmond, & Stricker, 1977). That is because dopamine neurons are needed to activate the brain's motor centers for eating. One of the interesting findings about the connection between the dopamine neurons and eating is that too much activity in those systems *causes* eating. This is shown in rats when their tails are

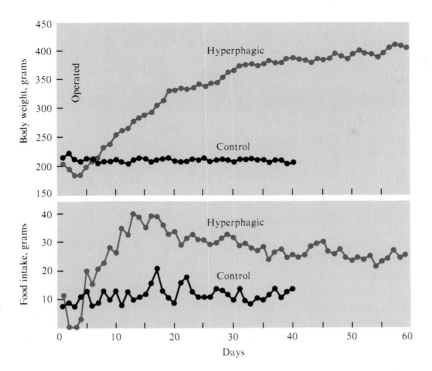

Figure 11.4
Body weight and food intake in control (normal) and hyperphagic (ventromedial hypothalamic lesions) rats. The data are plotted as functions of time after the placement of bilateral ventromedial hypothalamic lesions.

pinched. This causes stress, which excites the dopamine neurons and leads to excessive eating. Rats will more than double their food intake when their tails are pinched twice a day (Rowland & Antelman, 1976).

To summarize, we can see that the brain monitors both blood sugar levels and the condition of the stomach, then integrates this information (and probably other information as well) in the process of regulating hunger. Hypothalamic regions are of special importance in the integration process, and the dopamine system works to activate actual feeding behavior (Weiner & Baum, in press).

Your internal physiological world is very much involved in whether or not you are hungry. But aren't some external factors that interact with physiological processes probably involved too?

External Cues

Psychologists are interested in how environmental cues might stimulate hunger. When you drive by an ice cream store and see a huge chocolate sundae displayed on a sign, does it stimulate your hunger?

Stanley Schachter (1971) believes that one of the main differences between obese and normal weight individuals is their attention to environmental cues. From his perspective, individuals of normal weight attend to internal cues for signals of when to eat—for example, when blood sugar level is low, hunger pangs are sensed in the stomach. By contrast, an obese individual responds to external cues as signals of when to eat—how food tastes, looks, and smells, for example.

Clearly, though, overeating and obesity involve more than responding to environmental cues for food. Keeping in mind that environmental cues do influence eating behavior, let's see what other factors might be at work to determine whether you pull into the ice cream store to buy that chocolate sundae displayed on the sign.

Does this photograph make you feel hungry? If so, you are responding to external cues that stimulate your hunger.

Figure 11.5
Basal metabolic rate in females and males. BMR varies with age and sex. Rates are usually higher for males and decline proportionately with age for both sexes.

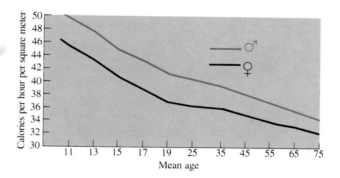

Obesity and Eating Behavior

A tall, slender woman goes into the locker room of the fitness center, throws her towel across the bench, and looks squarely into the mirror and yells, "You fat pig. You are nothing but a fat pig." The alarm goes off and forty-five-year-old Robert jumps out of bed, throws on his jogging shorts, and begins his daily predawn three-mile run. When he comes back to shower and dress, he too looks at his body in the mirror. Tugging at the flabby overhang, he says, "Why did you eat that bowl of ice cream last night?"

We are a nation obsessed with food, spending extraordinary amounts of time thinking about, eating, and avoiding food. Understanding obesity and overeating is complex; it involves genetic inheritance, physiological mechanisms, and environmental influences. And there are a variety of treatments for being overweight (Logue, 1986).

Biogenetic Factors

You may have inherited a tendency to be overweight. Only 10 percent of children who do not have obese parents become obese themselves; about 40 percent of children with one obese parent become obese; about 70 percent of children who have two obese parents become obese themselves. The extent to which this is due to experiences with parents or genes cannot be determined in studies with humans, but research with animals indicates they can be bred to have a propensity for fatness (Blundell, 1984).

The amount of stored fat in your body is thought to be an important factor in the set point of your body weight (it is not known how strongly genetic factors contribute to this). Fat is stored in adipose cells. When these cells are filled, you don't get hungry. When they are not full, you probably will become hungry. It seems that when we gain weight the number of fat cells increases, and we may not be able to get rid of them. An individual of normal weight has somewhere between 30 to 40 billion fat cells; obese individuals have as many as 80 to 120 billion fat cells. Interestingly, adults who were not obese as children but who become overweight as adults have larger fat cells than their normal weight counterparts, but they do not have more fat cells (VanItallie, 1984).

Metabolic rate also is important in understanding obesity. **Basal metabolism rate (BMR)** is the minimum amount of energy an individual uses in a resting state. As shown in figure 11.5, BMR varies with age and sex. Rates decline precipitously during adolescence and then more gradually during adulthood, and they are slightly higher for males than females. Many individuals gradually increase their weight over a period of many years. Figure 11.5 suggests that to some degree the weight gain is due to a declining basal metabolism rate. The declining BMR underscores that to maintain weight in adulthood we have to reduce our food intake.

Stress and Environmental Cues

How many times have you been to a party when the guests were not munching on food or drinking? When you study for a test do you often eat something? Stress may induce some of us to eat. Consuming a whole bag of potato chips is not unlike the rats overeating when their tails were pinched. Remember that the stress of mild tail pinching caused the rats to eat more than twice what they normally did. Research with overweight individuals suggests that under stress overweight individuals also increase their food intake while normal weight individuals reduce their food intake.

Environmental cues often are involved in overeating (Schachter, 1971). For example, the sight of food frequently is stimulating to obese individuals. In one investigation, some individuals were exposed to a bowl of cashew nuts under a bright light, while others were presented the nuts in a dimly lit setting (Ross, 1974). Normal weight individuals ate approximately the same number of nuts regardless of the lighting conditions; the overweight individual ate twice as many nuts when they were under a bright light.

While environmental cues are important in understanding obesity, some psychologists believe we should also take into account the conscious ability to control our behavior in the face of such alluring stimuli. Judy Rodin (1981, 1984) believes that self-control is an important aspect of dieting. To read more about Rodin's ideas, turn to Psychology 11.1.

An Increasingly Heavy Population and Weight-Loss Programs

Our gustatory system and taste preferences developed at a time when food was scarce. Few calories were easily accessible in the environment first encountered by *Homo sapiens*. A concentrated source of sugar (and thus calories) was ripe fruit. Early in the history of our species a preference for sweet food and drinks probably developed since ripe fruit was so accessible (Rozin, 1976). Today, food and drinks with high concentrations of sugar are readily available to most of us. But unlike the ripe fruit of our ancestors, which contained sugar *plus* vitamins and minerals, Gummie Bears and Cocoa Crispies fill us with empty calories.

Estimates indicate that about one-half of the middle-aged population in the United States weighs over the upper limit of their normal weight range (Pfaffman, 1977). Further, the proportion of American children who are overweight increased more than 50 percent over the two decades from the 1960s to the 1980s (Gortmaker, 1987). As individuals' weights have increased, the interest in losing weight has become a national obsession. Throughout history there have been dieters. Even Roman women were known to starve themselves. But never before has there been a time when so many people spent so much time, energy, and money on their weight. Since its inception in 1963, Weight Watchers alone has enrolled more than 15 million members. Although men *and* women have gained weight and both sexes show strong concerns about losing weight, the obsession with dieting seems to be more intense among women (Chernin, 1981).

A myriad of ways to lose weight exist: bypass surgery, exercise, diets, and different forms of psychotherapy. Which ones work? Does one work better than the rest? Do any of them work at all?

The most dramatic form of losing weight involves bypass surgery, which is an intestinal or gastric bypass operation. This procedure is recommended only for individuals who are 100 pounds or more overweight, in which case the obesity may be life threatening. Bypass surgery has been successful in reducing overeating. In one investigation of more than 700 patients followed for one year or longer, 55 percent of the overweight pounds were lost (Halmi, 1980). In some instances, though, bypass operations have serious side effects,

Psychology 11.1

Insulin, Doughnuts, and Pasta

Judy Rodin (1984, 1987) points out that not long ago we believed that obesity was caused by such things as unhappiness or responding to external food cues. The contemporary perspective, according to Rodin, is that a number of biological, cognitive, and social factors are more important. She argues that while obese individuals are more responsive to external food cues than normal weight individuals, there are individuals at all weight levels who respond more to external than internal stimuli. Many individuals who respond to external cues also have the conscious ability to keep environmental food cues from totally controlling their eating patterns.

Rodin says that many women today try to consciously restrain their eating. The problem is especially acute for women because the ideal body for women in our society is extraordinarily thin. It is all too easy for a female to feel overweight even if she is five pounds underweight for her age. The current ideal female body works against heredity, since women are genetically programmed to be fatter than men.

Rodin believes that exercise is an important aspect of weight loss and weight maintenance. She points out that no matter what your genetic background, aerobic exercise increases your metabolic rate, which helps to burn calories.

Much of Rodin's research has focused on the role of insulin in hunger and obesity. She observes that what we eat influences our insulin levels. When we eat complex carbohydrates such as cereals, bread, and pasta, insulin levels go up but then fall off gradually. When we consume simple sugars such as candy bars and Cokes, insulin levels rise and then fall off sharply—the sugar low with which many of us are all too familiar.

Glucose levels in the blood also are affected by these complex carbohydrates and simple sugars in similar ways. The consequence is that we are more likely to eat within the next several hours after eating simple sugars than complex carbohydrates. And the food we eat at one meal probably influences how much we will eat at our next meal. So consuming doughnuts and candy bars, in addition to providing no nutritional value, set up an ongoing sequence of what and how much we probably will crave the next time we eat.

When we consume simple sugars like taffy, we develop sugar lows because insulin levels rise and then fall sharply; however, when we eat complex carbohydrates, as in pizza, insulin levels go up but they fall off gradually.

among them liver disease. For extremely obese individuals, the benefits may be greater than the adverse side effects; for example, a more positive mood and increased physical exercise sometimes accompany reduced calorie intake in these individuals.

Drugs are also used to help individuals lose weight. Amphetamines are widely used to decrease food consumption, although they often have adverse side effects such as increased blood pressure and possible addiction. Weight loss with amphetamines usually is short-lived. The ineffective drugs include over-the-counter drugs such as Dexatrim. No drug currently is available that has been proven successful in long-term weight reduction (Logue, 1986).

Exercise is a much more attractive alternative than weight-loss drugs such as amphetamines. Exercise not only burns up calories but it continues to raise the metabolic rate for several hours *after* the exercise. Exercise actually lowers your body's set point for weight, making it much easier to maintain a lower weight (Bennett & Gurin, 1982). Nonetheless, it is very difficult to convince obese individuals to exercise. One problem is that moderate exercise does not reduce calorie consumption and in many cases individuals who exercise take in more calories than their sedentary counterparts (Stern, 1984). Still, exercise combined with conscious self-control of eating habits can produce a viable weight-loss program. When exercise is a component of weight-loss programs, individuals keep weight off longer than when calorie reduction alone is followed.

What about the "diets" themselves? There is the "Grapefruit Diet", the "Drinking Man's Diet," and the "Scarsdale Diet," to name just a few. It is difficult to pass a grocery store cashier counter without being assaulted by such diets etched on the covers of popular magazines (Logue, 1986). An analysis of sixteen of these crash diets revealed that many of them do not provide adequate nutrients (Dwyer, 1980). Three of these diets—the "Scarsdale Diet," the "Last Chance Feeding Diet," and the "Fasting Is a Way of Life Diet"— were found to be dangerous because they promote dehydration. Many liquid protein diets are extremely low in important nutrients, and individuals have died from staying on them too long while not eating other foods. Some diets, such as the "Slim Chance in a Fat World" and "Take It off and Keep It off" diets, do have well-balanced nutrition and contain appropriate information about the use of self-control in losing weight.

The diets of many competent programs follow the guidelines set forth by the American Dietetic Association. Their 1987 recommendations call for the following: a doubling of the average individual's intake of 10 to 15 grams of fiber per day (ten years ago fiber was not even on the list); lowering the percent of daily calories derived from fat to 30 percent; raising the percent of daily calories derived from complex carbohydrates (fruits, grains, and vegetables) to 50 to 60 percent. Weight Watchers is one diet program that adopts the guidelines of the American Dietetic Association.

Millions of individuals have joined groups such as Weight Watchers, NutriSystem, and TOPS (Take Off Pounds Sensibly). Reports of the success of these programs vary (Stunkard, Levine, & Fox, 1970; Stuart & Mitchell, 1980), although individuals who stay with the programs do seem to lose some weight. But dropout rates are astronomical, and those who stay with the programs usually do not reach their goal weights or maintain them for long. When behavioral self-control techniques are combined with calorie reduction programs, the probability of success usually improves. A typical behavioral component might involve having the overweight individual keep a daily chart of eating patterns, become aware of the circumstances that stimulate overeating, change the conditions that promote overeating, give oneself a reward (other than high-calorie food) for good eating habits, and engage in an aerobic exercise program.

Everything we know about weight loss suggests that exercise is a key component of weight loss programs— individuals who exercise and diet keep weight off longer than when they only reduce calories.

One of the reasons that long-term maintenance of weight loss is so difficult involves something called the "yo-yo phenomenon." The fact that severe calorie restriction invariably reduces metabolic rate makes dieting less effective the longer the individual remains on the diet. When an individual becomes discouraged and gives up on a diet and returns to a high-calorie intake, weight gain occurs rapidly because metabolic rate is still reduced from the dieting experience. Often, more pounds are regained than were lost. A regular, vigorous exercise regimen seems to be the only practical way to counteract the tendency for calorie reduction to reduce metabolic rate.

No diet or treatment program is the panacea hoped for by millions of individuals who earnestly want to lose weight (Stunkard, in press). If one program worked for everyone, we would not witness such high turnover rates. Some individuals find success with a certain diet or weight-loss program, yet for others the same program fails miserably. The majority of overweight individuals shed very few pounds over the long-term, although a great deal of time, money, and effort are invested in weight-loss programs (Wooley & Wooley, 1984).

Despite such dismal statistics, interest in the nature of obesity and its treatment shows no sign of slowing down. Perhaps we will discover ways to treat obesity more effectively, and possibly more moderate weights will become fashionable as well—weights that are medically acceptable and achieved by appropriate nutrition and exercise.

Anorexia Nervosa and Bulimia

Fifteen-year-old Jane gradually eliminated foods from her diet to the point where she subsisted by eating *only* applesauce and eggnog. She spent hours observing her own body, wrapping her fingers around her waist to see if it was getting any thinner. She fantasized about becoming a beautiful fashion model who would wear designer bathing suits. But even when she reached eighty-five pounds, Jane still felt fat. She continued to lose weight, eventually emaciating herself. She was hospitalized and treated for **anorexia nervosa,** an eating disorder that involves the relentless pursuit of thinness through starvation. Eventually anorexia nervosa can lead to death, as it did for popular singer Karen Carpenter.

Anorexia nervosa afflicts primarily females during adolescence and the early adulthood years (only about 5 percent of anorexics are male). Most individuals with this disorder are white and from well-educated, middle- and upper-income families. Although anorexics avoid eating, they have an intense interest in food, they cook for others, they talk about food, and they insist on watching others eat. Anorexics have a distorted body image, perceiving themselves as beautiful even when they have become skeletal in appearance. As self-starvation continues and the fat content of the body drops to a bare minimum, menstruation usually stops. Behavior often is hyperactive.

Numerous causes of anorexia nervosa have been proposed; they include societal, psychological, and physiological factors. The societal factor most often held responsible is the current fashion image of thinness. Psychological factors include motivation for attention, desire for individuality, denial of sexuality, and a way of coping with overcontrolling parents. Anorexics sometimes have families that place high demands for achievement on them. Unable to meet their parents' high standards, they feel an inability to control their own lives.

By limiting their food intake, anorexics gain some sense of self-control. Physiological causes focus on the hypothalamus, which becomes abnormal in a number of ways when an individual is anorexic (Garfinkel & Garner, 1982). But the bottom line is that, at this time, we are uncertain of exactly what causes anorexia nervosa.

An eating disorder related to anorexia nervosa is **bulimia.** Anorexics occasionally follow a binge-and-purge pattern, but bulimics do this on a regular basis. The bulimic binges on large amounts of food and then purges by self-induced vomiting or using a laxative. The binges sometimes alternate with fasting or at other times with normal eating behavior. Like anorexia nervosa, bulimia is primarily a female disorder. Bulimia has become prevalent among college women with estimates suggesting that one in two of these women binge and purge at least some of the time. While anorexics can control their eating, bulimics cannot. Depression is a common characteristic of bulimics. Bulimia can lead to gastric irritation and chemical imbalance of the body. Many of the same causes proposed for anorexia nervosa are offered for bulimia.

We have spoken at length about hunger, eating patterns, obesity, weight-loss programs, and anorexia nervosa and bulimia, but an aspect of motivation closely related to hunger also merits attention: thirst.

Thirst

Would you live longer without food or without water? Your body is approximately 75 percent fluids. Maintaining this level is important to your existence. While you could live a long time without food, you could only live several days without fluids. As with the investigation of hunger, scientists initially explained thirst in terms of peripheral physiological factors, then turned to an interest in brain processes.

Not only did Walter Cannon have subjects swallow balloons to see if stomach grumblings were involved in hunger, he also deprived them of water to determine if their thirst was related to the dryness of their mouth (Cannon, 1918). His "dry mouth theory" argued that we drink when our mouth is dry and do not drink when it is wet. But just as the stomach's hunger pangs stimulate eating but are not the only cause of the behavior, the mouth's dryness can trigger drinking but is not the only reason we replenish body fluids.

Though we sometimes do drink because our mouths are dry, scientists believe other factors are important. Water balance is critical for our survival, and we have multiple physiological systems that monitor and regulate water balance. First, a very small, circular region of the hypothalamus (with only 275 nerve cells!) contains **osmoreceptors,** which monitor the saltiness of the blood (Hatton, 1976). When the blood is too salty, these receptors cause **antidiuretic hormone** (ADH) to be released. This prevents urinary loss of water. The receptors also signal the brain, causing thirst. But another system also monitors our water balance. The receptors for this system are located in the kidneys and in some arteries. They monitor blood pressure. When blood pressure is too low (indicating too little water in the bloodstream), they signal the brain to drink (Fitzsimons, 1972).

We have discussed some general ideas about the nature of motivation and some specific information about hunger and thirst. To help you remember the main themes described so far, see concept table 11.1. Now let's consider another very important type of motivation.

Concept Table 11.1

Principles of Motivation, Hunger, and Thirst		
Concept	Processes/related ideas	Characteristics/description
The "whys" of behavior	Instincts, needs, and drives	Instinct theory flourished early in the twentieth century, but instincts do not adequately explain motivation. Drive-reduction theory emphasized a drive as an aroused state brought about by a physiological need. Reducing the drive satisfies the need. Homeostasis is an important motivational process promoted by drive-reduction theory.
	Incentives	Based on the belief that external factors are important in motivation.
	Hierarchy of motives	Maslow believed some motives need to be satisfied before others. Self-actualization is given considerable importance.
	Biological, cognitive, and social processes	The contemporary view of motivation includes a focus on biological (especially physiological) factors, conscious thoughts and understanding, and social processes.
Hunger	Physiological factors	The brain monitors both blood sugar level and the condition of the stomach (interest in the stomach was stimulated by Cannon's research), then integrates this information. Hypothalamic regions are important, especially VMH, and the dopamine system helps to activate actual feeding behavior.
	External cues	Schachter's research suggests environmental cues are involved in the control of eating behavior.
	Obesity and eating behavior	Biogenetic factors and stress and environmental cues are involved. The population is increasingly heavy and weight-loss programs abound. Cognitive processes, especially self-control techniques, are of special interest as is exercise.
	Anorexia nervosa and bulimia	These disorders have increased, primarily in adolescent and college-age females. Societal, psychological, and physiological causes have been proposed, but there is no consensus.
Thirst	Its nature	Cannon's theory indicates we sometimes drink because our mouths are dry, but other factors are involved. Interest in regulatory systems focuses on osmoreceptors in a small region of the hypothalamus, as well as volume receptors in the kidneys and arteries.

Sex

The importance of sex in our lives was vividly captured by Woody Allen's observation, "Sex without love is an empty experience. Yes, but as empty experiences go, it is one of the best." Allen's comments suggest not only a motivation for sex, but also an interpretation of its role in our lives. We do not need sex for everyday survival the way we need food and water, but we do need it for survival of the species. Among the fascinating inquiries about our sexual lives are: What is the biological basis of sex? How do sociocultural standards for sex vary around the world? What are our sexual attitudes? How responsive are we to environmental sex stimuli and how much does our cognitive interpretation influence our sexual behavior?

Hormones and Brain Processes

Sex hormones are among the most powerful and subtle chemicals in nature. These hormones are controlled by the master gland in the brain, the pituitary. In females, hormones from the pituitary carry messages to the ovaries to produce the sex hormone **estrogen.** In males, the pituitary messages travel to the testes where the sex hormone **androgen** is manufactured.

The secretion of androgen from the testes of the young male fetus (or the absence of androgen in the female) completely controls sexual development in the womb. If enough androgen is produced, as happens with a normal developing boy, male organs and genitals develop. If there is little androgen, as with normal developing girls, then female organs and genitals develop. In instances where the hormone level is imbalanced (as in a developing male with insufficient androgen, or a female exposed to excess androgen), the genitals are intermediate between male and female (Money & Erhrardt, 1972). Such individuals are referred to as **hermaphrodites.**

Although estrogen is the dominant sex hormone in females and androgen fills this role in males, each person's body contains both hormones. The amount of each hormone varies from one individual to the next; for example, among vocalists basses have more androgen than tenors (Durden-Smith & Desimone, 1983).

As we move from the lower to the higher animals, hormonal control over sexual behavior is less dominant. When the testes of a male rat are removed (castration), sexual behavior declines and eventually ceases. But in monkeys and humans, castration produces greater variation in sexual behavior. Some men lose their sexual motivation rather quickly following castration and others experience a gradual decline over many years (Money & Ehrhardt, 1972).

In females estrogen increases dramatically at the time of ovulation, which is midway through the menstrual cycle and when a woman is most likely to become pregnant. Unlike primates, a female rat will only accept the male rat at the time during which she is ovulating. Human females report preferences at different points in the menstrual cycle, with no generalization to all women possible (Udry & Morris, 1977).

The secretion of hormones during the menstrual cycle also may be associated with mood fluctuations in females. The weight of the evidence indicates there are definite mood swings during the middle of the menstrual cycle and later during the premenstrual phase (Bardwick, 1971). Approximately three of every four women experience such mood shifts, and hormonal changes probably are involved. Estrogen reaches peak levels from day twenty-two to twenty-four of the menstrual cycle, which is when depressive and irritable feelings are reported. However, it is possible that mood swings cause a rise in estrogen level, rather than vice versa.

Recently interest has focused on chemical messengers called **pheromones,** which are odorous substances released by animals that serve as powerful attractants. Pheromones are involved when male guinea pigs are attracted by the urine of an ovulating female. They are at work when all the male cats in the neighborhood know when a female cat is in heat. Not many years ago Jovan developed a fragrance they claimed would magnetically attract men. The company said the perfume contained a pheromone derived from human sweat. The perfume was designed to lure human males just as pheromones

Are pheromones at work in the attraction of this male and female for each other? Pheromones are odorous substances that function as powerful attractants. Odor is but one of many cues for sexual behavior. When humans are involved, eyes probably are more important than noses.

attract male guinea pigs and cats. The fragrance was not the smashing success the perfumery anticipated, suggesting there is more to sexual attraction in humans than smell.

Demonstrating that pheromones are involved in human sexual behavior is difficult, although research has shown that male pheromones are associated with increased fertility in men and greater menstrual regularity in women (e.g., Cutler & Preti, 1986). Women with unusually long or short menstrual cycles developed more average cycles after regularly inhaling a compound made of male sweat, hormones, and natural body odors. The researchers describe the smell of the compound as much like a men's locker room. Odor, though, is but one of many cues for sexual behavior. When human beings are involved, eyes likely are more important than noses, a point we will come back to later.

The secretion of sex hormones is regulated by a feedback system. The pituitary gland monitors hormone levels, but it is regulated by the hypothalamus. The pituitary gland sends out a signal via a gonadotropin to the testes or ovaries to manufacture the hormone. Then the pituitary gland, through interaction with the hypothalamus, detects when an optimal hormone level is reached and maintains this level (Peterson & Taylor, 1980).

The importance of the hypothalamus in sexual activity has been shown by electrically stimulating or surgically removing it. Electrical stimulation of certain hypothalamic areas increases sexual behavior; surgical removal of areas of the hypothalamus produces sexual inhibition. In one investigation, electrical stimulation of the hypothalamus in a male led to twenty ejaculations in only one hour (Vaughn & Fisher, 1962). The limbic system, which runs through the hypothalamus, also seems to be involved in sexual behavior. Its electrical stimulation can produce penile erection in males and orgasm in females (Heath, 1964).

In higher animals the temporal lobes of the neocortex play an important role in moderating sexual arousal and directing this arousal to an appropriate goal object. For example, temporal lobe damage to male cats impairs the animal's ability to select an appropriate partner. In one investigation, male cats with temporal lobe lesions tried to copulate with everything in sight: a teddy bear, chairs, even the researcher! And temporal lobe damage in humans also has been associated with changes in sexual activity (Saunders, 1966). In humans, then, sexual activity is influenced by communication between systems at different levels in the brain. Two of the most important systems involve the hypothalamus and temporal lobe.

The Human Sexual Response

There is considerable curiosity about how our sexual anatomy actually functions during sexual activity. William Masters and Virginia Johnson (1966) carefully observed and measured physical responses to sexual arousal. Thousands of these cycles were evaluated in hundreds of subjects. Based on their extensive effort, we now conceive of the human sexual response as having four phases (see figure 11.6). The **excitement phase** represents the beginning of erotic responsiveness and it may last from several minutes to several hours depending on the nature of the sex play involved. Two processes seem to characterize this phase: engorgement of blood vessels and increased blood flow in genital areas; and muscle tension. The most obvious signs of response in this phase are partial erection of the penis and lubrication of the vagina.

The second phase of the human sexual response is called the **plateau phase;** it consists of a continuation and heightening of arousal begun in the excitement phase. The increases in breathing, pulse rate, and blood pressure that occurred during the excitement phase become more intense, penile erection is more complete, and orgasm seems closer.

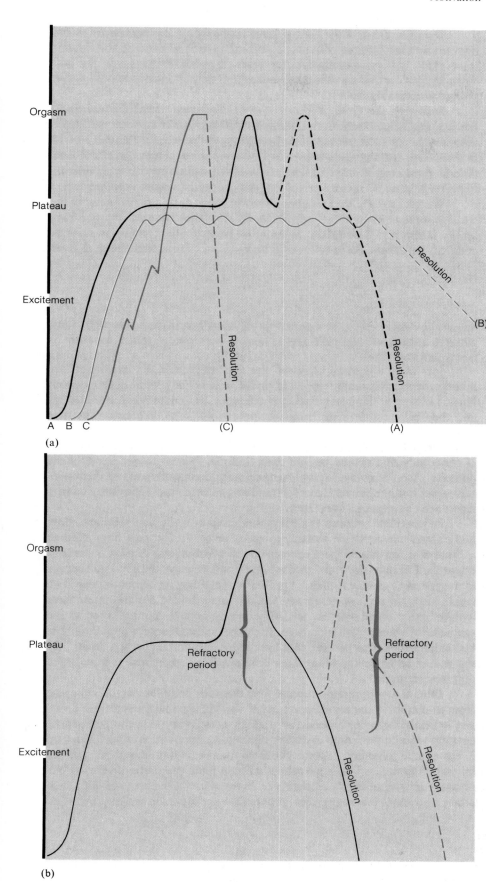

(a)

(b)

Figure 11.6
Female and male human sexual response patterns. (a) Typical female sexual response patterns. Three basic patterns are possible in female sexual response. Pattern A somewhat resembles the male pattern (figure 8.2), except for the possibility of multiple orgasms without falling below the plateau level. Pattern B represents the nonorgasmic arousal. Pattern C represents intense female orgasm, which resembles the male pattern in its intensity and rapid resolution. (b) Typical male sexual response pattern. In their basic response pattern, males usually have a single orgasm. For a second orgasm to occur during the same arousal, a refractory period must separate the two orgasms.

Sexual behavior has its magnificent moments throughout the animal kingdom. Insects mate in midair, male peacocks display their plumage, and male elephant seals have prolific sex lives. Experience plays a more important role in human sexual behavior. We can talk about sex with each other, read about it in magazines, and watch it on television and the movie screen.

The third phase of the human sexual response cycle is **orgasm.** How long does orgasm last? Some individuals sense that time is standing still when it takes place, but orgasm only lasts for about three to fifteen seconds. For both sexes orgasm involves an explosive discharge of neuromuscular tension and an intense pleasurable feeling.

Following the three to fifteen seconds of orgasm, the individual enters the final **resolution phase.** In this phase, arousal diminishes and engorged blood vessels return to their normal state. One difference between males and females in this phase is that males enter a *refractory period,* lasting anywhere from several minutes up to an entire day, in which they cannot have another orgasm. Females have no refractory period and may repeatedly experience orgasm.

We not only are curious about what happens during sexual activity but we also want to know what individuals do after they have an orgasm. Variability is the best description. Some of us want to sleep, others want to be cuddled. Yet others like to eat or even be left alone (Jones, Shainberg, & Byer, 1985).

Sociocultural Factors

We are biological sexual beings, but we are social sexual beings as well. Some cultures consider sexual pleasures as normal occurrences, others see them as weird and abnormal.

Ines Beag is a small island off the coast of Ireland. Its inhabitants are among the most sexually repressed in the world. They know nothing about French kissing or hand stimulation of the penis. Sex education does not exist, and they believe that after marriage, nature will take its course. The men think that intercourse is bad for their health. Individuals in this culture detest nudity. Only babies are allowed to bathe nude, and adults wash only the parts of their body that extend beyond their clothing. Premarital sex is out of the question. After marriage, sexual partners keep their underwear on during intercourse! It is not difficult to understand why females in the Ines Beag culture never achieve orgasm (Messinger, 1971).

By contrast, consider the Mangaian culture in the South Pacific. Boys learn about masturbation as early as six or seven. At thirteen, boys undergo a ritual that introduces them to manhood in which a long incision is made in the penis. The individual who conducts the ritual instructs the boy about sexual strategies, such as how to help his partner achieve orgasm before he does. Two weeks after the incision ceremony, the thirteen-year-old boy has intercourse with an experienced woman. She helps him to hold back ejaculation so she can achieve orgasm with him. Soon after, the boy searches for girls to further his sexual experience, or they seek him, knowing that he now is a "man." By the end of adolescence, Mangaians have sex every night and average three orgasms per night.

Ours is a culture more liberal than the Ines Beag, but we do not come close to matching the sexual practices of the Mangaians. The cultural diversity in sexual behavior around the world is a testimony to the importance of environmental experiences in determining sexual motivation. As we move up in the animal kingdom, experience seems to take on more power as a determinant of sexuality. While we cannot mate in midair like bees or display our plumage as magnificently as peacocks, humans can talk about sex with each other, read about it in magazines, and watch it on television and at the movies.

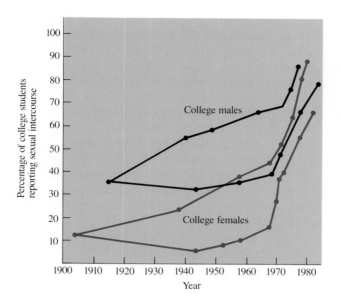

Figure 11.7
Percentage of college youth reporting having sexual intercourse at different points in the twentieth century. Two lines are drawn for males and two for females. The lines represent the best two fits through the data for males and the data for females of the many studies surveyed.

Sexual Attitudes and Behavior

Four percent of the male elephant seals off the coast of California were responsible for 85 percent of the copulations in one recent breeding season. Television soap operas might lead us to conclude that humans are not very different from the elephant seal, mating and moving from partner to partner. However, humans do show more allegiance to one partner than most species. And our advanced brains enable us to ponder about the best sexual strategy for us.

Heterosexual Attitudes and Behavior

Had you been a college student in 1940 you probably would have had a very different attitude toward many aspects of sexuality than you do today, especially if you are a female. A review of college students' sexual practices and attitudes from 1900 to 1980 reveals two important trends (Darling, Kallen, & VanDusen, 1984). First, the percentage of young people reporting intercourse has dramatically increased, and second, the proportion of females reporting coital involvement has increased more rapidly than in the case of males, although the initial base for males was greater (see figure 11.7). Prior to 1970, about twice as many college males as females reported coital involvement, but since 1970, the proportion of males and females is about equal. These changes suggest that major shifts in the standards governing sexual behavior have taken place. That is, movement away from a double standard in which it was more appropriate for males than females to have intercourse has occurred.

Two surveys that include wider age ranges of adults verify these trends. Morton Hunt's survey of more than 2,000 adults in the 1970s revealed more permissiveness toward sexuality than Alfred Kinsey's inquiries in the 1940s (Hunt, 1974; Kinsey, Pomeroy, & Martin, 1948). Hunt's survey, though, may have overestimated sexual permissiveness because it was based on a sample of *Playboy* magazine readers. Kinsey found that foreplay consisted of a kiss or two, but by the 1970s Hunt discovered that foreplay had lengthened, now averaging fifteen minutes. Hunt also found that individuals in the 1970s were using more varied sexual techniques in their lovemaking. Oral-genital sex, virtually taboo at the time of Kinsey's survey, was more accepted by the 1970s.

"Don't encourage him, Sylvia."
The Far Side Cartoon is reproduced by permission of Chronicle Features.

Two more things about heterosexual attitudes and behavior are important to consider: the double standard we mentioned earlier and the nature of extramarital sex. While it has become more appropriate for females to engage in premarital sex, some vestiges of the double standard still exist. As one male adolescent recently remarked, "I feel a lot of pressure from my buddies to go for the score." Further evidence of physical and emotional exploitation of females was found in a survey of 432 fourteen- to eighteen-year-old adolescents (Goodchilds & Zellman, 1984). Both male and female adolescents accepted the right of the male adolescent to be sexually aggressive, but left matters up to the female to set the limits for the male's overtures. Yet another manifestation of the double standard is the mistaken belief that it is wrong for females to plan ahead to have sexual intercourse (by taking contraceptive precautions), but it is somewhat permissible for them to be swept away by the passion of the moment.

The double standard is at work in extramarital relations, although not as extensively as in earlier years. In Kinsey's research about half of the husbands and one-fourth of the wives had engaged in sexual intercourse with someone other than their spouse during their marriage. In Hunt's survey in the 1970s, the figure was still about the same for males but had increased for females, especially younger females—24 percent of wives under the age of twenty-five had experienced extramarital affairs while only 8 percent had in the 1940s. The majority of us still disapprove of extramarital sex; more than 80 percent said it was wrong in the Hunt survey.

We indicated that the double standard is present among adolescent males and females. Indeed, adolescence is a time when sex can be especially problematic. As discussed in Psychology 11.2, many aspects of our culture suggest that we are not helping adolescents understand sex.

Homosexual Attitudes and Behavior

Both the early (Kinsey) and more recent (Hunt) surveys indicate that about 4 percent of males and 3 percent of females are exclusively homosexual. While the incidence of homosexual behavior does not seem to have increased, attitudes toward homosexuality were becoming more permissive, at least until the last several years. With the threat of AIDS, future surveys may indicate that homosexuality is less accepted.

Why are some individuals homosexual whereas others are heterosexual? Speculation about this question has been extensive, but no firm answers are available. Homosexual and heterosexual males and females have similar physiological responses during sexual arousal and seem to be aroused by the same types of tactile stimulation. Investigations suggest that in terms of a wide range of attitudes, behaviors, and adjustments, no differences between homosexuals and heterosexuals are present (Blumstein & Schwartz, 1983: Bell, Weinberg, & Mammersmith, 1981). Recognizing that homesexuality is not a form of mental illness, the American Psychiatric Association discontinued its classification of homosexuality as a disorder, except in those cases where the individuals themselves consider the sexual orientation to be abnormal.

Heredity, hormonal imbalance, family processes, and chance learning are among the factors proposed as causes of homosexuality. Concerning family processes, it has been argued that a dominant mother and a weak father promote homosexuality; the evidence is far from consistent about this proposal, however. Concerning chance learning, someone may be seduced by an individual of the same sex and subsequently develop a homosexual preference. The most common view is that homosexuality occurs because of any of these reasons and that in a number of instances it is the result of an interaction of these factors (Durden-Smith & Desimone, 1983; McWhirter, Reinsch, & Sanders, in press; Money, 1987).

What causes homosexual behavior? Speculation about this question is extensive, but no firm answers are available. Heredity, hormonal imbalance, family experiences, and chance learning are among the possible causes.

Environmental Cues and Pornography

In our discussion of sexual motivation we have considered a number of ideas about the roles of biogenetic and sociocultural factors. And we have seen that cognitive factors are important in the sexual motivation of humans. In considering the role of the environment, psychologists have been especially interested in environmental cues; in recent years, the most controversial aspect of this interest has focused on pornography.

In 1986 a federal Pornography Commission linked sexual violence to pornography in a 1,900-page report that described sexual conduct ranging from sexual contact with fish to the physical condition of peep booth shows. In the same year, 7-Eleven stores discontinued the sale of *Playboy* and *Penthouse,* possibly as a result of receiving a letter from the commission.

A number of social scientists objected to the commission's conclusions and the way their research was interpreted by the panel members. For example, the commission cited data showing that states with the highest circulation of adult magazines also have the highest incidence of rape. But the research of Murray Strauss, cited in the conclusion of the commission's report, does not support the belief that pornography *causes* rape. Strauss points out that the scientific literature indicates we should be more concerned about violence in the media than sex in the media when rape is at issue (e.g., Strauss, Gelles, & Steinmetz, 1986).

Ed Donnerstein (1987) also believes that his research was distorted by the commission. In one investigation, he showed pornographic movies to male college students. They then were escorted to mock rape trials where they filled out answers to questions. Students who saw the pornographic movies indicated less sympathy for the victims than students who did not see the pornographic movies. The commission said that this did not necessarily indicate that pornography causes rape, but did show that pornography lowers the sensitivity level of those who view it. By summarizing and interpreting bits and pieces of research, and by interviewing rape victims, the commission arrived at its conclusion that sexual violence is associated with pornography (Tarkenton, 1986).

Is sexual conduct associated with sexual cues? Is sexual violence associated with pornography? The words we hear, the features of individuals we see and their actions—a soft caress, a certain smell—all of these sensory experiences are environmental cues that can instigate sexual activity. Our sexual behavior is associated with environmental cues.

Visual cues such as erotic slides or films stimulate sexual behavior as well. Individuals who see these materials are more likely to engage in some form of sexual activity during the next several hours than those who see nonsexual visual stimuli (Amoroso & others, 1971). In another investigation, sexually explicit videotapes lessened the sexual anxiety of college females (Wishnoff, 1978).

Sex offenders report having less contact with erotic magazines and movies during their adolescent years than do those who are not sex offenders. When censorship of pornographic materials was removed in the 1960s in Denmark, sex-related crimes actually declined. So does viewing pornographic material lead to an increase or a decrease in sex crimes? The nature of erotic material seems to be an important factor in this controversy. When sexual content is combined with violence, increased male aggression toward females may occur (Malamuth & Donnerstein, 1983). But clearly, the overall conclusions of the Pornography Commission were unwarranted based on the research evidence.

■ ■ ■ ■ ■ ■ ■ ■ ■ ■ ■ ■ ■ ■ ■ ■ ■ ■ ■ ■

Psychology 11.2

Adolescents and Sex—from Pill to Personal Fable

■ Many of the songs popular among adolescents have words such as, "Tonight's the night," and "Good girls don't, but I do." The sexual themes of music and the sexual overtones that are rampant in magazines and on television often suggest a societal standard of sex as fun and harmless.

At age sixteen, slightly over 40 percent of males and between 30 to 40 percent of females have had sexual intercourse (Dreyer, 1982). The pressure on males to have sexual intercourse is evidenced by the fact that at thirteen more than twice as many males (12 percent) report having had intercourse than females (5 percent), even though male adolescents enter puberty on the average two years later than female adolescents. Recent data indicate that in some areas of the country, sexual experiences of young adolescents may even be greater. In an inner-city, low-income area of Baltimore, at age fourteen, 81 percent of the males said that they already had engaged in sexual intercourse; other

Table 11.A Types of contraceptives used by urban adolescents				
Method	Method first used		Method last used	
	1976	*1979*	*1976*	*1979*
Pill	33%	19%	48%	41%
IUD	2	1	3	2
Diaphragm	0	1	1	4
Condom	36	34	23	23
Douche	3	1	3	2
Withdrawal	18	36	15	19
Rhythm	5	5	4	6

From Zelnick, M., & J. F. Kantner, Sexual activity, contraceptive use, and pregnancy among metropolitan-area teenagers: 1971–1979. *Family Planning Perspectives, 12,* 230–237. Copyright © 1980 Alan Guttmacher Institute.

surveys in inner-city, low-income areas also reveal a high incidence of early sexual intercourse (Clark, Zabin, & Hardy, 1984).

While premarital intercourse can be meaningful for older, mature adolescents, many are ill-equipped to handle sex. Adolescents may attempt intercourse without really knowing what to do or how to satisfy their partner—leading to frustration and a sense of sexual inadequacy—and many are poorly informed about contraception or

fail to use contraceptives. Surveys reveal that one-fourth to one-third of sexually active adolescents never use contraceptives; only about one-third always use them (Zelnick & Kantner, 1980). Note in table 11.A that while the pill and condom are the most widely used contraceptives, there was an increase in the use of the withdrawal method, especially as the first method used.

Adolescents' knowledge of human sexuality is not as advanced as we sometimes think it is. In one investigation, the

Humans Are Cognitive Sexual Beings

Humans are cognitive sexual beings as well as biological and social sexual beings. Genes and hormones and environmental cues and sociocultural conditions all play significant roles in our sexual lives. But just as self-control strategies influence our eating behavior, so can cognitive processes influence our sexual behavior. An individual's memory or fantasy may cause an orgasm just as a partner's touch can. For many of us, our conscious perception of sexual satisfaction is as important, if not more important, than the sexual act itself and its accompanying physiological changes. How we interpret our sexual experiences, the meaning we attach to certain aspects of sexual behavior, sexual beliefs and values, and our imaginations and expectations are all part of our life as cognitive sexual beings (Byrne, 1982).

majority of adolescents indicated that the greatest risk of pregnancy is during menstruation (Zelnick & Kantner, 1977).

The adolescent pregnancy rate is increasing even though the birth rate is decreasing. If current trends continue, four in ten females will become pregnant at least once while they are in adolescence (Alan Guttmacher Institute, 1981). As indicated in figure 11.A, adolescents in the United States have the highest pregnancy rate at all ages when compared with other countries.

The adolescent's sense of uniqueness and indestructibility (known as the *personal fable*) may also account for the high pregnancy rate (Lipsitz, 1983). The young adolescent often says, "It won't happen to me." The combination of the sexual standards of our society, which suggest that sex is fun and harmless, adolescents' natural sexual curiosity, an inadequate knowledge of sexuality, and egocentric thought, results in social dynamite.

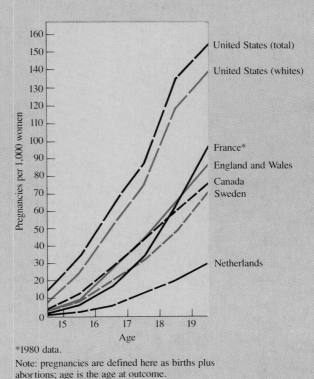

*1980 data.

Note: pregnancies are defined here as births plus abortions; age is the age at outcome.

Figure 11.A
Pregnancy rates per 1,000 women by women's age, 1981.

Cognitive interpretation of sexual activity also involves our perception of the individual with whom we are having sex and their perception of us. We imbue our sexual acts with such perceptions: Is he loyal to me? How can I better satisfy her? What is our future relationship going to be like? How important is sex to him? Should I try something different? What if she gets pregnant? Amidst the wash of genes, hormones, and environmental cues in human sexual activity is the cognitive ability to control, reason about, and try to make sense of what is happening.

The main themes of our coverage of sexual motivation are presented in concept table 11.2. The motivation for hunger, thirst, and sex includes important physiological underpinnings. Some aspects of motivation, though, are less clearly tied to biological processes. Among the more so-called social motives are competence, achievement, and power.

Concept Table 11.2

Sex		
Concept	**Processes/related ideas**	**Characteristics/description**
Biological and sociocultural factors	Biological processes	Genes determine whether the growing fetus will develop testes or ovaries, then the hormones from the testes (androgens) determine whether the organism will have male genitals (if androgen is secreted) or female genitals (if no androgen is secreted). Androgen in males and estrogen in females are the dominent sexual hormones. Hormonal control over sex is more dominant among animals than humans. In humans sexual activity is integrated by a number of brain systems. Masters and Johnson mapped out the nature of human sexual response.
	Sociocultural factors	Cultural diversity supports the belief that environmental experiences are important in human sexual activity.
Sexual attitudes and behavior	Heterosexuality	Increased liberalization has occurred. Some dimensions of the double standard, however, still exist. Greater effort in helping adolescents make the transition from immature to mature sexual beings is needed.
	Homosexuality	Rates of homosexuality have remained constant in the twentieth century. Homosexuality is no longer classified as a disorder. No definitive conclusions about the cause have been reached.
Environmental cues and cognitive factors	Environmental cues	Associated with sexual activity. Visual cues are especially important. There is considerable interest in the role of pornography in sexual and aggressive behavior.
	Cognitive sexual beings	Memory, fantasy, interpretation, meaning, beliefs, values, and expectations are all part of the cognitive picture in understanding the nature of human sexuality.

Figure 11.8
This monkey showed a motivation for novel stimulation and was willing to work just so he could unlock the window and watch the toy train go around in a circle.

Competence, Achievement, and Power

We are a species motivated to do well at what we attempt, to gain mastery over the world in which we live, to explore with enthusiasm and curiosity unknown environments, to achieve the heights of success, and to gain power.

Competence Motivation

Drive-reduction theory is based on the belief that the organism is motivated to reduce a need. In the 1950s, experiments began to show that organisms are motivated to seek stimulation, rather than always trying to reduce a need. Monkeys will solve simple problems just for the opportunity to watch a toy train, for example (see figure 11.8) (Butler, 1953). Rats consistently move around in complex mazes with a number of pathways instead of in a simple maze with few corridors. And a series of experiments suggested that college students could not tolerate social isolation for more than two to three days, even though they were getting paid for it (Bexton, Heron, & Scott, 1954). The sensory deprived students developed a strong motivation to quit the experiment and became bored, restless, and irritable. Figure 11.9 illustrates the isolation chamber of a sensory deprivation experiment.

Psychologists have investigated how shorter periods of sensory deprivation—such as spending time in a water immersion tank—can reduce stress (Suedfeld & others, 1986). A typical water immersion tank is four-by-eight feet with a ten-inch deep solution of Epsom salts in ninety-three to ninety-four-degree water (see figure 11.10). The cover of the tank opens easily. With the cover closed the tank is completely dark. The solution is buoyant so the participant's face is always out of the water. After fifty-five minutes, music is

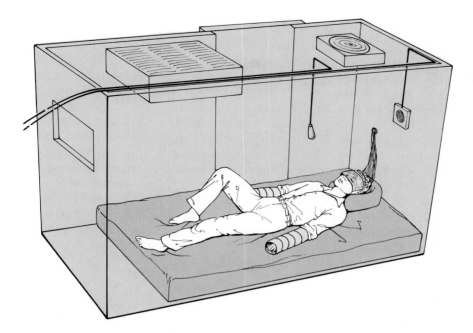

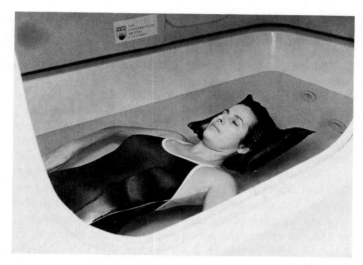

Figure 11.10
Water immersion tank. Water immersion tanks have been used to reduce sensory stimulation. A 55-minute "float" has been shown to reduce stress.

piped into the tank to signal the end of the session. In an investigation of twenty-seven customers using one commercial facility, the participants indicated that the floating experience was highly relaxing and put them in a pleasant mood (Suedfeld, Ballard, & Murphy, 1983).

In sum, sensory deprivation can be harmful in some circumstances and helpful in others. When we are deprived of sensory stimulation for days at a time, it is clear that we do have a strong motivation to seek stimulation.

In the 1950s another concept was developed that suggested our motivation goes beyond the reduction of biological needs. R. W. White (1959) said that we have **competence motivation** (also called **mastery motivation**), which is the motivation to deal effectively with our environment, to be competent and do well at what we attempt, to process information efficiently, and to make the world a better place. White said we do these things not because they serve biological needs but because we have an intrinsic (internal) motivation to effectively interact with our environment. Closely related to this idea is the motivation for achievement.

Achievement Motivation

When Vince Lombardi was coach of the Green Bay Packers, in his customary intense manner, he said, "Winning isn't everything, it is the only thing." A less intense promotion of the importance of achievement in our lives is found in the words of Henry Wadsworth Longfellow, "Let us be up and doing with a heart for any fate; still achieving, still pursuing."

We live in an achievement-oriented world with standards that tell us success is important. The standards suggest that success requires a competitive spirit, a desire to win, a motivation to do well, and the wherewithal to cope with adversity and persist until obstacles are overcome. Some psychologists, though, believe we are a nation of hurried, wired people who are uptight about success and failure and are far too worried about what we have accomplished in comparison to others (Elkind, 1981). It was in the 1950s that an interest in achievement began to flourish; the interest initially focused on the need for achievement.

Need for Achievement

Think about yourself and your friends for a moment. Are you more achievement oriented than they are or less so? If we asked you and your friends to tell stories about achievement-related themes could we accurately determine which of you is more achievement oriented?

David McClelland (1955) stressed that individuals vary in their motivation for achievement and that we can measure these differences. Borrowing from Henry Murray's (1938) theory of personality, McClelland referred to achievement motivation as **_n_ achievement** (need for achievement), meaning the individual's motivation to overcome obstacles, desire for success, and effort expended to seek out difficult tasks and do them well as quickly as possible. To measure achievement, individuals were shown ambiguous pictures that were likely to stimulate achievement-related responses. Then they were asked to tell a story about the picture; their comments were scored according to how strongly they reflected achievement (McClelland & others, 1953).

A host of studies have correlated achievement-related responses with different aspects of the individual's experiences and behavior. The findings are diverse, but they do suggest that achievement-oriented individuals have a stronger hope for success than a fear of failure, are moderate rather than high or low risk takers, and persist for appropriate lengths of time in solving difficult problems (Atkinson & Raynor, 1974). Early research indicated that independence training by parents promoted children's achievement, but more recent research reveals that parents need to set high standards for achievement, model achievement-oriented behavior, and reward their children for their achievements in order to increase achievement (Huston-Stein & Higgens-Trenk, 1978).

Achievement motivation is not as consistent and stable as McClelland envisioned it either; an individual may be strongly motivated to attain success on the athletic field but not in the classroom (Mischel, 1986). McClelland's own research indicates that achievement effort can be improved during the adult years. A three- to six-week training course emphasizing the importance of taking moderate risks, being future oriented, and setting goals significantly improved the achievement efforts of individuals who took the course compared to others who did not (McClelland & Winter, 1969).

As part of their interest in competence and achievement motivation, psychologists have focused on the internal and external factors that contribute to such motivation. Considerable enthusiasm has greeted the issue of whether we should emphasize intrinsic or extrinsic motivation.

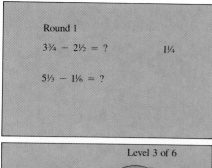

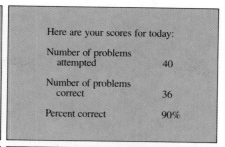

Figure 11.11
Examples of educational computer programs involving drill (top panel) versus game (lower panels) formats. The top panel shows a typical panel of a drill and practice program in which the child is praised after he or she gets the problem right. The bottom panel is an example from the Fractions Basketball program developed by Sharon Dugdale and David Kibbey, 1973.

Intrinsic and Extrinsic Motivation

Imagine that you must teach children about the addition and subtraction of fractions and help them practice these problems. One possibility would be to develop a simple "drill-and-practice" exercise that would provide each child with a sequence of problems and praise after each correct answer. Such programs, indeed, are widespread. An alternative approach might be to present the same sequence of problems in the form of an instructional computer game specifically developed to enhance the child's motivation. These programs are becoming available but they are less common than the drill-and-practice type. "Fractions Basketball" is one example developed by the PLATO PROJECT at the University of Illinois (Dugdale & Kibbey, 1980). Figure 11.11 shows how the drill-and-practice program and the computer game strategy vary (Lepper, 1985).

The interest in intrinsic motivation comes from ideas about our motivation for challenge, competence, effectiveness, and mastery (Harter, 1981; White, 1959); curiosity, incongruity, complexity, and discrepancy (Berlyne, 1960); and perceived control and self-determination (Deci, 1975). **Intrinsic motivation** involves an underlying need for competence and self-determination. By contrast, **extrinsic motivation** is due to external factors in the environment, especially rewards. If you work hard in school because a personal standard of excellence is important to you, intrinsic motivation is involved. But if you work hard in school because you know it will bring you a higher paying job when you graduate, extrinsic motivation is at work.

An important consideration when motivating someone to do something is whether or not to offer an incentive (Pittman & Heller, 1987). If an individual is not doing competent work, seems bored, or has a negative attitude, it may be worthwhile to consider incentives to improve motivation. However, there are times when external rewards can get in the way of motivation. In

Figure 11.12
Time spent in art activity under expected reward and no-reward conditions. Students with an initial high interest in art spent more time in art activity when no reward was mentioned than when they expected a reward for the participation.

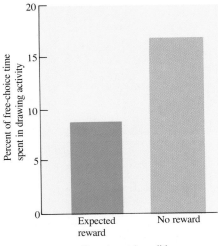

one investigation, students with a strong interest in artistic work spent more time in a drawing activity when they expected no reward than their counterparts who knew that they would be rewarded (see figure 11.12) (Lepper, Greene, & Nisbett, 1973).

Intrinsic motivation implies that internal motivation should be promoted and external factors deemphasized. In this way, we learn to attribute the cause of our successes and failures to ourselves, especially to how much effort we expend. But in reality, achievement is motivated by both internal and external factors. We never are divorced from the external environment. Some of the most achievement-oriented individuals are those who have *both* a high personal standard for achievement and are also highly competitive. In one investigation, low-achieving boys and girls who engaged in individual goal setting *and* were given comparative information about their peers worked more math problems and got more of them correct than their counterparts who experienced either condition alone (Schunk, 1983). Other research suggests that social comparison by itself, though, is not a wise strategy (Nicholls, 1984). The argument is that social comparison puts the individual in an ego-involved, threatening, self-focused state rather than a task-involved, effortful, strategy-focused state.

Achievement in Females and Minority Groups

Two major recent interests are the achievement orientation of females and the achievement orientation of minority-group individuals. There has been a significant increase in the number of females entering occupations previously thought to be appropriate only for males. Yet discrimination and inadequate opportunities for education are prominent issues affecting the achievement levels of females, as well as blacks and other minority-group individuals (Eccles, 1987b).

While some women are entering previously all-male occupations, the majority of women still have not achieved parity with men in the marketplace. Differences in the average salaries of men and women are still huge: in professional jobs women earn only about three-fourths as much as men and in clerical and sales jobs, even less (Bureau of Labor Statistics, 1986). On a more positive note, more women are entering law school and medical school than in the past. As greater numbers of women pursue careers, they are faced with issues involving career and family. Recent research indicates that high-ability juniors and seniors in college show a strong interest in combining career *and* family interest (Fassinger, 1985).

Drawing by M. Stevens; © 1987 The New Yorker Magazine, Inc.

Some of the brightest and most gifted girls do not have achievement and career aspirations that match their talents. In one study, high-achieving girls had much lower expectations for success than high-achieving boys (Stipek & Hoffman, 1980). In the gifted research program at Johns Hopkins University many mathematically precocious girls did select scientific and medical careers, although only 46 percent aspired to a full-time career compared to 98 percent of the boys (Fox, Brody, & Tobin, 1979).

To help talented female youth redirect their paths, some high schools are using programs developed by colleges and universities. Project CHOICE (Creating Her Options In Career Education) was designed by Case Western University to detect barriers in reaching one's potential. Gifted eleventh-grade females received individualized counseling that included interviews with female role models, referral to appropriate occupational groups, and information about career workshops. A program at the University of Nebraska (Kerr, 1983) was successful in encouraging talented female high school students to pursue more prestigious careers. This was accomplished by individualized counseling and participation in a "Perfect Future Day," in which girls shared career fantasies and discussed barriers that might impede their fantasies. Internal and external constraints were evaluated, gender-role stereotypes were discouraged, and high aspirations were applauded. While these programs have shown short-term success in redirecting the career paths of high-ability females, in some instances the benefits fade over time—six months or more, for example (Fox, 1976). It is important to be concerned about improving the awareness of career alternatives for all female youth, however, and not just those of high ability.

An equally important concern is the achievement of minority-group individuals, both females and males. One of the primary limitations of existing research on minority-group achievement is that there have been so few research studies on the subject. The research literature on achievement has focused almost exclusively on white males (Adelson, 1980). And too often research on minority groups has been interpreted as "deficits" by middle-class, white standards. Rather than perceiving individuals as *culturally different,* many conclusions unfortunately characterize the cultural distinctiveness of blacks, Hispanics, and other minority groups as deficient in some way.

It is important not to characterize the cultural distinctiveness of blacks, Hispanics, and other minority groups as deficient in some way. Instead, they should be perceived as culturally different.

Much of the research on minority groups is plagued by a failure to consider socioeconomic status (determined by some combination of occupation, education, and income). In many instances, when race *and* socioeconomic status are investigated in the same study, social class is a far better predictor of achievement orientation than race (Graham, 1986). Middle-class individuals fare better than their lower-class counterparts in a variety of achievement-oriented circumstances—expectations for success, achievement aspirations, and recognition of the importance of effort, for example (McAdoo & McAdoo, 1985).

Sandra Graham has conducted a number of investigations that reveal not only stronger social-class than racial differences but also the importance of studying minority-group motivation in the context of general motivational theory (Graham, 1984, 1986, 1987; Graham & Long, 1986). Her inquiries focus on the causes blacks give for their achievement orientation—why they succeed or fail, for example. She is struck by how consistently middle-class black children do not fit our stereotypes of either deviant or special populations. They, like their middle-class white counterparts, have high achievement expectations and understand that failure is often due to lack of effort rather than to luck.

The indisputable fact is that too many minority-group individuals are faced with educational, career, and social barriers (Edelman, 1985). Individuals from minority groups have benefited from the Civil Rights Act of 1964, but much more progress is needed. We do not have all of the answers to the problems of poverty and racial prejudice in this country, but as the Reverend Jesse Jackson has commented, it is hoped that we have begun to ask some of the right questions.

Sandra Graham, UCLA psychologist. Shown here talking with a group of young boys about motivation, Dr. Graham has conducted important research showing that middle-class black children—like their middle-class white counterparts—have high achievement expectations and understand that their failure is often due to lack of effort rather than to lack of luck.

Power

Power has its distasteful moments, as reflected in the words of Percy Bysshe Shelley, "Power like desolating pestilence, pollutes whate'er it touches." But some find strength and excitement in the motivation for power, as did Benito Mussolini, "I believe that . . . if a people wish to live they should develop a will to power, otherwise they vegetate."

It is hard to distinguish the motives for power and achievement from our everyday understanding and from prominent theories of motivation (e.g., Maslow, 1954). Achievement brings power, and power brings achievement recognition, according to this argument. But while achievement motivation moves us toward meeting standards of excellence, and thus to task-oriented striving, *power motivation* seems to be more involved in the social world. For the power-oriented individual, the social world is omnipresent and necessary for personal satisfaction (Veroff, 1982). The qualities of motivation for power may come out in their most visible form when we observe the behavior of national leaders. To learn more about their motivation for power, turn to Psychology 11.3.

In this chapter we have studied many different facets of motivation. In the next chapter we will study emotion, stress, and health. Both the words motivation and emotion come from the Latin word *movere,* which means to move. Both motivation and emotion lead to action and movement.

Psychology 11.3

From Napoleon and LBJ to Reagan-Gorbachev: The Motivation for Power and the Nuclear Arms Race

■ Napoleon is described as having but one passion, that of power. He never lost time on subjects that diverted him from the aim of conquering the world (Metternich, 1880). And no man in history became president with a greater relish for power than Lyndon Johnson (Evans & Novak, 1967).

National leaders' motivation for power may be an important impetus to the nuclear arms race (Frank, 1987a, b). By definition, a national leader has a strong drive to accumulate and exercise power. The characteristics of national leaders include toughness, persuasiveness, optimism, suspiciousness, and competitiveness. The international leader must be willing to inflict sufficient suffering and death on the enemy to attain victory. National leaders often possess a personal magnetism and charisma. Their persuasiveness includes convincing others *and* themselves that their policies are correct and

How can we reduce the threat of nuclear war? Anti-nuclear activities have become increasingly respectable, as reflected here in the large number of demonstrators from different countries.

appropriate. Hitler was able to persuade himself that he was acting accordingly (Bullock, 1969).

Leaders of nations see themselves as acting in the highest moral fashion. And their motivation for power is

maintained by an enthusiasm for positive outcomes even in the face of great adversity. In reaching the top, most national leaders overcame formidable opposition, invariably winning more than losing. Most national leaders have a low threshold for suspiciousness.

Summary

I. **The "Whys" of Behavior**
Instinct theory flourished early in the twentieth century, but instincts do not adequately explain motivation. Drive-reduction theory provided a combination of psychological and physical factors to account for motivation. Drives are aroused states brought about by physiological needs. Reducing the

drive satisfies the need. Drive-reduction theory stimulated an interest in homeostasis, an important motivational concept. Believing that external factors also are important in motivation, psychologists turned to incentives. Maslow developed the concept of hierarchy of motives. The contemporary view of motivation includes an emphasis on biological (especially physiological), cognitive, and social factors.

II. **Physiological Factors in Hunger**
The brain monitors both blood sugar level and the condition of the stomach (interest in the stomach was generated by Cannon's research), then integrates this information. Hypothalamic regions are very important in the integration process, especially VMH; the dopamine system helps to activate actual feeding behavior.

All leaders at various times must conceal information even if it involves deceit. Stalin's suspiciousness reached the point of persecution mania (Deutscher, 1967).

National leaders are very competitive, striving to increase the size and power of departments under their control at virtually every step of the bureaucracy. Rivalries within military bureaucracies may be especially intense, since leaders would most likely not have chosen military careers without a strong motivation for power. One student at the Naval War College wrote a paper suggesting that the Navy keep only enough nuclear weapons for deterrence. The paper received a distinguished grade, but when a four-star admiral heard about it he called the student and told him that if the Navy took this stance the Air Force would get all of the money and the Navy would not have any carriers (Frank & Rivard, 1986).

Probably the most common moral reason given for the drive for power today is the claimed necessity of defending ourselves against a powerful and evil enemy. This attitude shifts one's own aggressive and powerful ambitions to the opponent. Military programs are justified in the name of defense: the Department of War has become the Department of Defense, requiring a defense budget and heavily supporting a Strategic Defense Initiative. National leaders have not solved the arms race through diplomatic negotiations. In the service of power, the leaders of opposing nations continue to point the finger of blame at each other. As nuclear buildups continue, nuclear protests appear, although these protests have not curbed the arms race.

It is unlikely that the drive for power will be eliminated from the human mind. Unfortunately, the ultimate arbiter of power

historically has been superior violence. There are some hopeful developments, however. Small moves toward a world consensus can be detected. Images of enemies shift quickly. Only a few years ago Mainland China was perceived as an enemy, and now it is perceived as an ally of the United States (Kalven, 1982). Important also are the antinuclear activities in nations with few or no nuclear capabilities—New Zealand and Sweden, for example. Antinuclear activities in the United States have gained respectability. Increased sharing of programs between the United States and the Soviet Union have occurred, fostering the hope that mutual understanding between the people of the two nations will develop. This activity followed the November 1985 summit (Cracraft, 1986). These developments are not trivial; they involve issues of life and death for each of us (Frank, 1987a, b).

III. **External Cues, Obesity, and Eating Behavior**
Environmental experiences are important in understanding hunger. Schachter's research indicates environmental cues are involved in the control of eating behavior. However, understanding obesity and eating behavior is complex, involving biogenetic factors and stress and environmental cues. The

population is increasingly heavy and many weight-loss programs exist as a response to this. Cognitive factors, especially self-control techniques, are of increasing interest, as is the role of exercise. Anorexia nervosa and bulimia are two eating disorders that have increased dramatically in recent years. A number of factors have been proposed as causes of these disorders, but no consensus exists.

IV. **Thirst**
Cannon's theory indicates we sometimes drink because our mouths are dry, but other factors are involved. Interest in regulatory systems focuses on osmoreceptors in a small region of the hypothalamus, as well as volume receptors in the kidneys and arteries.

V. Biological and Sociocultural Factors in Sex

The genes determine whether the growing fetus will develop testes or ovaries, then the hormones from the testes (androgens) determine whether the organism will have male genitals (if androgen is secreted) or female genitals (if no androgen is secreted). Androgren is the dominant sexual hormone in males; estrogen has this role in females. Hormonal control over sex is more dominant among animals than humans. In humans, sexual activity is integrated through communication between a number of brain systems. Masters and Johnson mapped out the nature of the human sexual response. Cultural diversity supports the belief that environmental experiences are important in human sexual activity.

VI. Sexual Attitudes and Behavior

Sexual attitudes are more liberal than in the past. Some dimensions of the double standard still remain, however. Greater effort needs to be expended in understanding the nature of adolescent sexuality. Rates of homosexuality have remained low and constant for a number of years. Homosexuality no longer is thought of as a disease. Its cause has not been determined.

VII. Environmental Cues and Cognitive Factors

Environmental cues are associated with sexual activity. Visual cues are especially important. Considerable interest has developed in the role of pornography in sexual and aggressive behavior. Memory, fantasy, interpretation, meaning, beliefs, values, and expectations are all part of the cognitive picture in understanding the nature of human sexuality.

VIII. Competence, Achievement, and Power

Recognizing that motivation is more than reducing physiological needs, psychologists such as R. W. White argued that we are motivated to be competent and effectively master our environment. Early interest, stimulated by McClelland's ideas, focused on need for achievement. Contemporary ideas on achievement include the distinction between intrinisic and extrinisic motivation, as well as a concern about achievement orientation in females and minority groups. Motivation for power is associated with achievement, but power more often involves a concern with the social world. Exploration of the power motive in national leaders provides insight into its nature.

Key Terms

motivation *362*
instinct *364*
drive *364*
need *364*
drive-reduction theory *364*
homeostasis *364*
incentives *365*
hierarchy of motives *365*
self-actualization *365*
ventromedial hypothalamus (VMH) *368*

set point *368*
basal metabolism rate (BMR) *370*
anorexia nervosa *374*
bulimia *375*
osmoreceptors *375*
antidiuretic hormone (ADH) *375*
estrogen *377*
androgen *377*
hermaphrodites *377*

pheromones *377*
excitement phase *378*
plateau phase *378*
orgasm *380*
resolution phase *380*
competence motivation *387*
n achievement *388*
intrinsic motivation *389*
extrinsic motivation *389*

Suggested Readings

Durden-Smith, J., & Desimone, D. (1983). *Sex and the brain.* New York: Arbor House. A fascinating, almost breathtaking journey through the brain and body in search of the underpinnings of sexual motivation.

Grinspoon, L. (Ed.). (1987). *The long darkness.* New Haven: Yale University Press. This book offers considerable insight into the nature of the nuclear arms race, the importance of considering the power motive in such key issues in our world, and the role scientists play in such matters.

Hyde, J. S. (1986). *Understanding human sexuality* (3rd ed.). New York: McGraw-Hill. This textbook on human sexuality covers a wide array of topics, including detailed coverage of heterosexual and homosexual behavior, as well as the importance of biological, cognitive, and social factors in understanding our sexual being.

Logue, A. W. (1986). *The psychology of eating and drinking.* New York: W. H. Freeman. A well-written and authoritative coverage of what we know about the nature of hunger, thirst, eating behavior, obesity, and dieting is provided by this book.

McAdoo, H. P., & McAdoo, J. L. (1985). *Black children: Social, educational, and parental environments.* Beverly Hills, CA: Sage. This book provides a contemporary look at the nature of achievement orientation in black children. Included are chapters written by leading experts in the field of minority group motivation.

Mook, D. G. (1987). *Motivation.* New York: W. W. Norton. A textbook on motivation that covers the topics in this chapter, plus many more aspects of motivation. Includes detailed looks at contemporary theorizing about the nature of human motivation.

Chapter 12

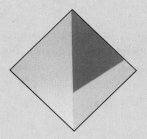

Emotion, Stress, and Health

■ ■

The passions are at once temptors and chastisers. As temptors, they come with garlands of flowers on brows of youth; as chastisers, they appear with wreaths of snakes on the forehead of deformity. They are angels of light in their delusion; they are fiends of torment in their inflictions.

—*Henry Giles*

■ ■

Images of Emotion, Stress, and Health

Mort, age fifty-two, has worked as an air-traffic controller for the last fifteen years. An excitable person, he compared the job to being in a mad cage. During peak air traffic the tension was almost unbearable. In these frenzied moments, Mort's emotions were a mixture of rage, fear, and surprise. The tension spilled over into his family life. In his own words, "When I would get home, my nerves were hopping. I would take it out on the nearest person." Sally, his wife, told Mort that if he could not calm his emotions and handle stress more effectively, she would leave him. She suggested he change to a less upsetting job. He did not heed her advice. His intense emotional behavior continued and she left him two years ago.

Just last week the roof fell in on Mort. He had a heart attack Sunday evening when the computer that monitors air traffic temporarily went down. Quadruple bypass surgery saved his life. Yesterday his doctor talked with him about the stress in his life and what could be done to reduce it. The doctor gave Mort a test to reveal his vulnerability to stress. Mort was told to score each item from 1 (almost always) to 5 (never), according to how much each statement applied to him. Table 12.1 shows the stress test given to Mort.

You probably fared better than Mort on the test. Mort rarely gets enough sleep, frequently skips meals, has not dated steadily since his divorce, has no relatives living within fifty miles, never exercises, smokes two packs of cigarettes a day, drinks two to three scotches on the rocks every evening (more on weekends), is about the right weight, and has no religious interests. He has only one friend and does not feel very close to him. Mort says he never has enough time to do the things he wants to do, he has fun only about once every two weeks, and he rarely has quiet time to himself during the day. Mort scored sixty-eight on the stress test, indicating he is seriously vulnerable to stress and close to the extremely vulnerable range.

By the end of his conversation with the doctor, Mort promised to look into another career and to slow down. He also vowed to increase his social network and to reduce his smoking and drinking.

Mort's life was filled with emotion and stress. Our own lives are punctuated with different emotions and varying degrees of stress: The joy of a pleasant moment, the sadness of an unpleasant one; the rage of angry combat, the love of a warm embrace; the calm, collected feeling when our life feels under control, the miserable feeling of being overwhelmed by the world. ■

Table 12.1	Stress Test

Rate yourself on each item using a scale of 1 (almost always) to 5 (never).

1. I eat at least one hot, balanced meal a day.
1 — 2. I get seven to eight hours sleep at least four nights a week.
3 — 3. I give and receive affection regularly.
5 — 4. I have at least one relative within fifty miles whom I can rely on
5 — 5. I exercise to the point of perspiration at least twice a week.
1 5 — 6. I smoke less than half a pack of cigarettes a day.
1 5 — 7. I take fewer than five alcoholic drinks a week.
5 8. I am the appropriate weight for my height.
5 9. I have an income adequate to meet my basic expenses.
5 10. I get strength from my religious beliefs.
5 11. I regularly attend church.

3 12. I have a network of friends and acquaintances.
1 13. I have one or more friends to confide in about personal matters.
3 14. I am in good health (including eyesight, hearing, teeth).
5 15. I am able to speak openly about my feelings when angry or worried.
5 16. I have regular conversations with the people I live with about domestic problems, e.g., chores, money, and daily living issues.
5 17. I do something for fun at least once a week.
1 18. I am able to organize my time effectively.
1 19. I drink fewer than three cups of coffee (or tea or cola drinks) a day.
3 20. I take quiet time for myself during the day.

Total: _____

To get your total score, add up the figures and subtract twenty. Any number over thirty indicates a vulnerability to stress. You are seriously vulnerable if your score is between fifty and seventy-five, and extremely vulnerable if it is over seventy-five.

Emotion

One of the most curious and difficult questions in psychology is, How can we tell if a person is in an emotional state? Are you in an emotional state when your heart beats fast, your palms sweat, and your stomach churns? Or are you in an emotional state when you think about how much you are in love with someone? Or when your face grimaces or smiles? The body, the mind, and the face play important roles in understanding emotion—psychologists debate how critical each is in determining whether or not we are in an emotional state (Berscheid, 1987; Hatfield, 1987). We will explore each of these important aspects of emotion, but first let's think about the range of emotions and how they can be classified.

Range and Classification of Emotions

What emotions do you experience in your life? Do you experience anger, love, contempt, awe, compassion, anxiety, pride, sadness, happiness, and enthusiasm? More than 200 emotions are named in the English language. Psychologists have tried different classifications of our many emotions, but the classification of Robert Plutchik (1980) has received the most attention. Plutchik believes emotions have four distinctions: 1) they are positive or negative; 2) they are primary or mixed; 3) many are polar opposites; and 4) they vary in intensity.

What are our primary emotions? Sadness, happiness, disgust, surprise, anger, and fear are Plutchik's candidates.

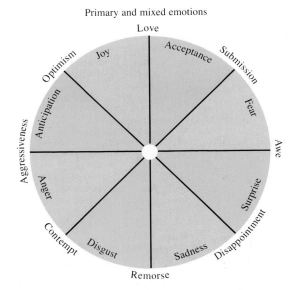

Figure 12.1
*Plutchik's wheel of emotions. The
primary emotions are labeled inside
the wheel; for example, sadness and
surprise. The emotions listed on the
outside of the circle result from mixing
adjacent primary emotions. Plutchik
believes emotions opposite each other
cannot be experienced
simultaneously.*
Reprinted from Psychology Today *Magazine.
Copyright © 1980 American Psychological
Association.*

Ecstasy and enthusiasm are positive emotions; grief and anger are negative emotions. For example, think about your ecstasy when you get an unexpected A on a test and your enthusiasm about the football game this weekend—these are positive emotions. Think also about your moments of grief when someone close to you dies and your anger when someone verbally attacks you and says you have not tried hard enough—these are negative emotions. Positive emotions enhance our self-esteem; negative emotions lower our self-esteem. Positive emotions improve our relationships with others; negative emotions depress the quality of those relationships.

Plutchik also believes that emotions are like colors. All colors can be produced by mixing the primary colors. Possibly some emotions are primary— if mixed together, they form all other emotions. Happiness, disgust, surprise, sadness, anger, and fear are candidates for **primary emotions.** For example, combining sadness and surprise gives disappointment. Jealousy is composed of love and anger. Plutchik developed the emotion wheel (shown in figure 12.1) to show how primary emotions work. Mixtures of primary emotions adjacent to each other combine to produce other emotions. Some emotions are opposites—love and remorse, optimism and disappointment. Plutchik believes we cannot experience emotions that are polar opposites simultaneously. You cannot feel sad at the same time you feel happy, he says. Imagine just getting a test back in this class. As your eyes scan the paper for the grade, your emotional response will be happy *or* sad, not both.

Happiness is an emotion we all seek. Like other emotions, its intensity varies. Sometimes we are incredibly happy, at others only a little happy. You might be overwhelmed with happiness if you won a million dollars in a lottery, but only slightly happy if you were given 20 dollars for participating in a psychological research study.

It was not until 1973 that *Psychological Abstracts,* the major source of psychological research summaries, included happiness as an index term. The recent interest in happiness focuses on positive ways we experience our lives, including cognitive judgments of our well-being. That is, psychologists want to know what makes you happy and how you perceive your happiness. Many years ago Rousseau described the subjective nature of happiness in this way: "Happiness is a good bank account, a good cook, and a good digestion."

Table 12.2	General Happiness and Mundane Pleasure Ratings of Lottery and Nonlottery Winners			
General happiness				**Mundane pleasure**
	Past	*Present*	*Future*	
Winners	3.77	4.00	4.20	3.33
Nonwinners	3.32	3.82	4.14	3.82

Note: Happiness and pleasure ratings were made on a six-point scale, ranging from 0 (not at all) to 5 (very much).

Source: From Brickman, P., et. al., Lottery winners and accident victims: Is happiness relative? *Journal of Personality and Social Psychology, 36,* 917–927. Copyright 1978 by the American Psychological Association. Reprinted by permission of the author.

In a recent review of research on happiness (Diener, 1984), "a good cook" and "good digestion" were not on the list of factors that contribute to our happiness, but self-esteem, a good marriage or love relationship, social contacts, regular exercise, the ability to sleep well, and meaningful religious faith were. Age, gender, race, education, intelligence, or children were not related to happiness.

But what about Rousseau's "good bank account?" Can we buy happiness? One investigation tried to find out if lottery winners are happier than people who have not received a landslide of money (Brickman, Coates, & Janoff-Bulman, 1978). Twenty-two major lottery winners were compared with twenty-two people living in the same area of the city. The general happiness of the two groups did not differ when they were asked about the past, present, and the future. The nonwinners actually were happier doing life's mundane things such as watching television, buying clothes, and talking with a friend (see table 12.2).

Winning a lottery does not appear to be the key to happiness. What is important, though, is having enough money to buy life's necessities. Extremely wealthy people are not happier than people who can purchase the necessities. People in wealthy countries are not happier than people in poor countries. The message is clear: if you think money buys happiness, now is a good time to reflect on the matter (Diener, 1984).

When you are happy are you aroused? What about when you are sad? Do you have to be aroused to experience emotion?

Are people in poorer countries like Guatemala and Mexico likely to be less happy than people in wealthier countries like the United States? If this Guatemalan woman's behavior is any indication, the answer is no.

Physiological Arousal and Brain Processes in Emotion

Emerson said, "Passion, though a bad regulator, is a powerful spring." These words indicate that emotion involves some type of arousal. Many psychologists believe that when you are aroused, the arousal has a physiological basis.

The Nature of Arousal

As you drive down a highway, the fog thickens. Suddenly you see a pile of cars in front of you. Your mind temporarily freezes, your muscles tighten, your stomach becomes queasy, and your heart feels like it is going to pound out of your chest. You immediately slam on the brakes and try to veer away from the pile of cars. Tires screech, windshield glass flies, and metal smashes, Then all is quiet. After a few short seconds you realize you are alive. You find that you can walk out of the car. Your fear turns to joy, as you sense your luck in not being hurt. In a couple of seconds, the joy turns to anger. You loudly ask who caused the accident.

Figure 12.2
Arousal and performance. The Yerkes-Dodson Law argues that optimal performance occurs under moderate arousal. However, for new or difficult tasks, low arousal may be best; for well-learned, easy tasks, high arousal can facilitate performance.

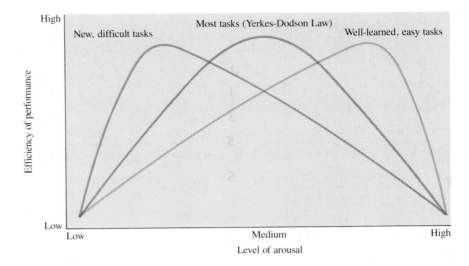

As you moved through the emotions of fear, joy, and anger, your body changed. During intense arousal your sympathetic nervous system was working. At the time of the accident your arousal decreased as the parasympathetic nervous system became more dominant: your heart rate, breathing rate, and blood sugar level decreased; your pupils constricted; and your stomach secretion and salivation increased. The sympathetic and parasympathetic nervous systems, the two divisions of the autonomic nervous system, were described in chapter 2—you may want to review that discussion now.

Psychologists have been interested in arousal for a long time. Early in this century, performance was said to be best under conditions of moderate rather than low or high arousal. This principle is known as the **Yerkes-Dodson Law.** At the low end of arousal you might be too lethargic to perform tasks well; at the high end you may not be able to concentrate. Think about how aroused you were the last time you took a test. If your arousal was too high, your performance probably suffered.

Moderate arousal often serves us best in tackling life's tasks, but there are times when low or high arousal produces optimal performance. For well-learned or simple tasks (signing your name, pushing a button on request), optimal arousal can be quite high. By contrast, when learning a task (such as how to play tennis) or doing something complex (such as solving an algebraic equation) much lower arousal is preferred. Figure 12.2 projects how arousal might influence easy, moderate, and difficult tasks. As tasks become more difficult, the ability to be alert and attentive, but relaxed, is critical to optimal performance.

You have been asked to think about your emotional states in the face of an automobile crash and a college exam. Now put yourself in the situation of lying to someone. Because body changes predictably accompany changes in emotional states, it was reasoned that a machine might be able to determine if a person is lying. To learn more about this controversial machine, the lie detector, turn to Psychology 12.1. The lie detector, or polygraph, relies on changes in heart rate, breathing, and electrodermal responses for information about emotional states. Might the face also be a revealing clue to emotional states?

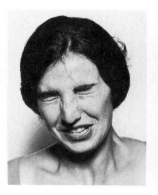

Facial Cues as Emotion Detectors

How important is the face as an emotion detector? Shakespeare expressed its importance in this way: "He parted frowning from me, as if ruin leap'd from eyes: So looks the chafed lion." Paul Ekman (1980, 1985) believes that the face is *the* single best clue available. His careful observations uncovered 7,000 faces we display through various muscle movements. These many faces of emotion do not vary significantly from one culture to another. Ekman visited the Fore tribe, an isolated Stone Age culture in New Guinea. Before Ekman's visit, most of the Fore had never seen a Caucasian face. Ekman showed them photographs of American faces expressing emotions such as fear, happiness, anger, and surprise. Then he read them stories about people in emotional situations. The Fore were able to match the descriptions of emotions with the facial expressions in the photographs. The similarity of facial expressions by persons in New Guinea and the United States is shown in figure 12.3.

Could we use the wealth of information available from facial expressions as an index of lying? Like the polygraph, the face is not always an accurate indicator. A communication channel such as the face, which sends messages quickly and visibly, can deceive (Ekman & Friesen, 1978). It may be difficult for other parts of the body with less message capacity to hide deception— gestures, fidgeting, and nervous movements, for example. Premeditated lies may be more difficult to detect in a person's body than spontaneous lies. By planning to lie, speakers may control their voices and rehearse their cover-up.

Psychologists have proposed that arousal is involved in emotion, and they are interested in ways to detect emotion. Beyond this, they have developed a number of theories about how arousal works in emotion.

James-Lange and Cannon-Bard Theories.

Suppose you and your date are enjoying a picnic in the country. As you prepare to eat, a bull comes running across the field. Why are you afraid? Two well-known theories involving physiological arousal address this question.

Common sense tells you that you are trembling and running away from the bull because you are afraid. But William James (1890) and Carl Lange (1922) said emotion works in the opposite way. According to the **James-Lange theory** of emotion, stimuli in the environment trigger physiological states in the body. You see the bull scratching its hoof and you begin to run away. The

Figure 12.3
Facial expresssions on persons from the United States and New Guinea. Judging the pleasant–unpleasant dimension in each case is not difficult. Perhaps you can also guess whether the photos show disgust, happiness, or fear.

Psychology 12.1

Leaks about Fighter Planes and Stealing from the Company's Coffer: Are Polygraphs the Answer?

The year is 1963. A memo leaked from the Air Force about the development of the TFX fighter plane invokes the ire of President John F. Kennedy. The year is now 1983. President Ronald Reagan says he is "up to his kiester in leaks." He issues a memorandum to government agencies suggesting employees be required to take polygraph tests. Several representatives, including Jack Brooks (1985), took exception to this reversal in government policy. They called for hearings on the following issue: Can polygraphs really tell whether someone is lying?

The **polygraph** is a machine that tries to determine if someone is lying by monitoring changes in the body thought to be influenced by emotional states. Heart rate, breathing, and electrodermal response (an index detecting skin resistance to passage of a weak electric current) are among the body functions observed. In a typical polygraph test, a person is asked a number of neutral questions and several key, not so neutral, questions. If the person's heart rate, breathing, and electrodermal response increase substantially when the key

questions are asked, it is assumed the person is lying (see figure 12.A to observe a polygraph testing situation and what a polygraph printout looks like).

The polygraph is widely used today. Employers want to know which employees are likely to steal from their coffers; police wish to extract the truth from a person they believe is guilty of a crime; and government agencies try to identify those who might leak secret information. In congress' inquiry into the polygraph's effectiveness, psychologists Leonard Saxe, Denise Dougherty, and Theodore Cross (1985) were called to testify. They said that a standard lie detector situation does not exist; rather a number of strategies for inferring truth or deception based on physiological assessment of emotions are used. Their testimony revealed the complexity of the lie detector test. Although the degree of arousal to a series of questions is measured through simple physiological changes, no unique physiological response to deception has been found (Lykken, 1981; Orne, 1975). Heart rate and breathing can increase for reasons other than lying, thus

making intrepretation of the physiological indicators of arousal a complex matter. The accuracy of polygraph tests depends on the way questions are developed and the testing situation itself.

Accurately identifying truth or deception rests mainly on the skill of the examiner and the skill of the person being examined. Subjects can use deliberate countermeasures, such as physical movements, drugs, cognitive strategies, and biofeedback techniques to avoid detection of deception. Tensing your muscles, biting your tongue, squeezing your toes, and shifting your position in the chair can influence the polygraph's accuracy— examiners can detect only about 80 percent of these countermeasures (Honts, Raskin, & Kircher, 1983). Drugs are more difficult to detect. For example, the drug Meprobamate concealed one person's lies on a polygraph test (Waid & others, 1981). The Department of Defense has proposed a urinalysis to improve the accuracy of drug detection (Stilwell, 1984). We do not have good information about the ability of cognitive strategies to deter lie detection, but the use of

aroused body then sends sensory messages to the brain, at which point emotion is perceived. According to this theory, you do not run away because you are afraid, rather you are afraid because you are running away. In other words, you perceive a stimulus in the environment, your body responds, and you interpret the body's reaction as emotion. In one of James's own examples, you perceive you have lost your fortune, you cry, and then interpret the crying as feeling sad. This goes against the common sense sequence of losing your fortune, feeling sorry, and then crying.

Figure 12.A
The polygraph, shown here, tries to tell us whether someone is lying by monitoring changes in the body that are believed to be influenced by emotional states. While the polygraph is widely used today, the consensus is skepticism about its ability to reveal deception.

biofeedback has been shown to reduce the polygraph's validity (Corcoran, Lewis, & Garver, 1978).

Sometimes, though, the mere presence of the polygraph and the belief it is accurate at detecting deception triggers confession (Jones & Sigall, 1971; Quigley-Fernandez & Tedeschi, 1978). This type of research refers to the polygraph as a "bogus pipeline," which means that subjects may reveal hidden information even if the machine is a fake.

The polygraph is based on a simple principle: Arousal is related to lying. Yet we have seen that the detection of lying is not so simple. The complexity of the polygraph situation makes many psychologists skeptical. This skepticism is furthered when psychologists discover that many polygraph examiners are poorly informed about the complexity. Goethe may have been right, "When I err every one can see it, but not when I lie."

Walter Cannon (1927) objected to the James-Lange theory. To understand his objection, imagine the bull and the picnic once again. Seeing the bull scratching its hoofs causes the hypothalamus of your brain to do two things simultaneously: first, it stimulates your autonomic nervous system to produce the physiological changes involved in emotion (increased heart rate, rapid breathing); second, it sends messages to your cerebral cortex where the experience of emotion is perceived. Philip Bard (1934) supported this theory,

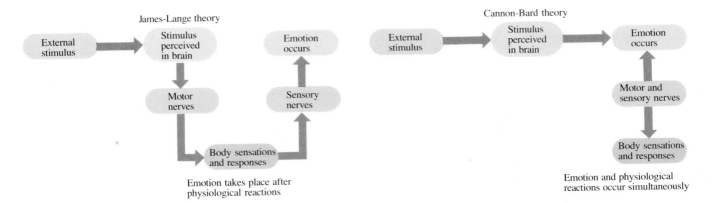

James-Lange theory

External stimulus → Stimulus perceived in brain → Motor nerves → Body sensations and responses → Sensory nerves → Emotion occurs

Emotion takes place after physiological reactions

Cannon-Bard theory

External stimulus → Stimulus perceived in brain → Emotion occurs → Motor and sensory nerves → Body sensations and responses

Emotion and physiological reactions occur simultaneously

Figure 12.4
Comparison of the James-Lange and Cannon-Bard theories of emotion.

and so the view became the **Cannon-Bard theory** of emotion. A major point in the Cannon-Bard argument is that the body's responses do not have a major role in causing emotion. Figure 12.4 shows how the James-Lange and Cannon-Bard theories differ.

One more point is important about these two theories. The James-Lange theory argued that each emotion has its own special physiology. People distinguish anger from fear and happiness from sadness on the basis of distinctive patterns of physical response. In contrast, the Cannon-Bard theory emphasized that different emotions involve the same body changes. This argument continues today (Mandler, 1984; Schwartz, Weingerger, & Singer, 1981). In an investigation by Gary Schwartz and his colleagues (1981), thirty-two college students with prior acting experience were asked to imagine different emotional experiences: happiness, sadness, anger, and fear. In one condition, they also were asked to relax. In the control condition, the subjects were asked to imagine walking up and down steps. Heart rate and blood pressure were monitored during imagery. As shown in figure 12.5, the four emotions were related to different patterns of physiological processes. Heart rate was lowest during happy imagery, highest during angry and fearful imagery. Diastolic blood pressure was highest during anger and lowest during sad imagery. While the James-Lange theory virtually was buried by psychologists earlier in the twentieth century, one aspect of it has been revived: some emotions can be differentiated physiologically.

As psychologists probe the elusive nature of emotion, the brain is given an important role. A theory different from those we have studied suggests that opponent processes in the central nervous system are involved in emotion.

The Opponent-Process Theory

Richard Solomon (1980, 1986) developed a provocative view of how the brain functions in emotion. He assumes the brain is always functioning to maintain a state of equilibrium. Solomon's **opponent-process theory** argues that pleasant or unpleasant stimuli cause both a primary and a secondary process to occur in the brain. The *secondary* process is the central nervous system's reaction to the *primary* process of the autonomic nervous system. The secondary process reduces the intensity of a feeling.

In Solomon's view, the primary process starts when a stimulus begins and it ends when the stimulus is terminated. The secondary process occurs more gradually, beginning at some point after the stimulus onset, and takes longer to subside. After several stimulations, the secondary process is strengthened.

Parachute jumping and drug addiction provide examples of how the opponent-process theory works. Parachute jumpers experience a euphoric feeling after their jump. The euphoria opposes the high level of fear before the jump.

As these two individuals argue angrily, are there different kinds of physiological changes taking place than if they were happy or sad? The research of Gary Schwartz and his colleagues (1981) suggests that different emotions are associated with unique cardiovascular patterns.

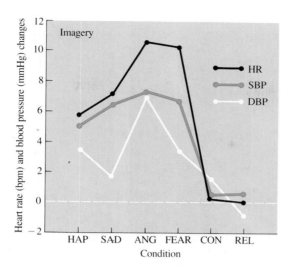

Figure 12.5
Mean changes in heart rate (HR) and in systolic (SBP) and diastolic (DBP) blood pressure separately for the happiness (HAP), sadness (SAD), anger (ANG), fear (FEAR), control (CON), and relaxation (REL) conditions following seated imagery.

After several jumps, the initial fear diminishes, but the euphoria remains strong so the person continues to jump. In this example, fear is the primary process and euphoria the secondary process. When a person takes opium, an intense rush occurs, followed by a less intense but pleasurable feeling. When the drug effects wear off, the user experiences discomfort and craves the drug, which leads to another dose. But the next dose produces a less intense rush and diminished pleasure. The aftereffects are more unpleasant—abstinence can cause sheer agony. The rush and pleasurable feelings represent the primary process of emotion, the unpleasurable feelings and craving the secondary process.

Much of what we have said about emotion has focused on its physiological basis. While physiological factors play important roles in emotion, cognitive processes are at work as well.

Cognition and Emotion

Does emotion depend on the tides of the mind? Are we happy only when we think we are happy? Cognitive theories of emotion share an important point: emotion always has a cognitive component. Thinking is said to be responsible for feelings of love and hate, joy and sadness. While giving cognitive processes the main credit for emotion, the cognitive theories recognize the role of the brain and body in emotion (Mandler, 1984). That is, the hypothalamus and autonomic nervous system make connections with the peripheral areas of the body when emotion is experienced. According to cognitive theorists, body *and* thought are involved in emotion.

Schachter's and Singer's View

A theory of emotion that gives cognition a strong role was developed by Stanley Schachter and Jerome Singer (1962). They agree that emotional events produce internal, physiological arousal. As we sense the arousal, we look to the external world for an explanation of why we are aroused. We interpret the external cues present and then label the emotion. For example, if you feel good after someone has made a pleasant comment to you, you might label the emotion happy. If you feel bad after you have done something wrong, you may label the feeling guilty. Schachter and Singer believe much of our arousal is diffuse and not tied to specific emotions. Because the arousal is not instinctive, its meaning is easily misinterpreted.

How is parachute jumping an example of how the opponent-process theory works? Parachute jumpers feel euphoric after their jump. The euphoria opposes the high level of fear that existed before the jump. After several jumps, the fear diminishes, but the euphoria remains strong, so the individual continues to jump. Fear is the primary process and euphoria is the secondary process.

Figure 12.6
The precarious Capilano Bridge is shown at left; the experiment is shown in progress at right. An attractive woman approached men while they were crossing the 200-foot-high bridge; she asked them to make up a story to help her out. She also made the same request on a lower, much safer bridge. The men on the Capilano River Bridge told sexier stories, probably because they were aroused by the fear or excitement of being up so high on a swaying bridge. Apparently they interpreted their arousal as sexual attraction for the female interviewer.

To test their theory of emotion, Schachter and Singer (1962) injected subjects with epinephrine, a drug that produces high arousal. After the subjects were given the drug, they observed someone behave either in a euphoric way (shooting papers at a wastebasket) or in an angry way (stomping out of the room). As predicted, the euphoric and angry behavior influenced the subjects' cognitive interpretation of their own arousal. When they were with a happy person, they rated themselves as happy; when they were with an angry person, they said they were angry. But this effect was found only when the subjects were *not* told about the true effects of the injection. When subjects were told that the drug would increase their heart rate and make them jittery, they said the reason for their own arousal was the drug, not the other person's behavior.

Psychologists have had difficulty replicating the Schachter and Singer experiment, but, in general, research supports the belief that misinterpreted arousal intensifies emotional experiences (Leventhal & Tomarken, 1986; Reisenzein, 1983). An intriguing study substantiates this belief. An attractive woman approached men while they were crossing the Capilano River Bridge in British Columbia. Only those without a female companion were approached. The woman asked the men to make up a brief story for a project she was doing on creativity (Dutton & Aron, 1974). By the way, the Capilano River Bridge sways precariously more than 200 feet above rapids and rocks (see figure 12.6). The female interviewer made the same request of other men crossing a much safer, lower bridge. The men on the Capilano River Bridge told more sexually oriented stories and rated the female interviewer more attractive than men on the lower, less fearful bridge.

Why do you think this happened? The researchers concluded that the men on the high bridge were aroused (possibly by the fear or excitement of being up so high on a swaying bridge). The men on the high bridge interpreted their arousal as sexual attraction for the female interviewer. Other exciting and fearful moments might produce similar interpretations—a wild party or a car accident, for example. The arousal these events stimulate may lead you to interpret the arousal as sexual attraction to a companion. Caution suggests that when you feel sexually attracted to someone, sifting through the possible causes for your arousal may be a wise strategy.

The Primacy Debate: Cognition or Emotion?

Richard Lazarus (1984) believes cognitive activity is a precondition for emotion. He says we cognitively appraise ourselves and our social circumstances. These appraisals, which include values, goals, commitments, beliefs, and expectations, determine our emotions. People may feel happy because they have a deep religious commitment, angry because they did not get the raise they anticipated, or fearful because they expect to fail an exam.

Robert Zajonc (1984) disagrees with Lazarus. Emotions are primary, he says, and our thoughts are a result of them. Who is right? Both likely are correct. Lazarus refers mainly to a cluster of related events that occur over a period of time, while Zajonc describes single events or a simple preference for one stimulus over another. Lazarus speaks about love over the course of months and years, a sense of value to the community, and plans for retirement; Zajonc talks about a car accident, an encounter with a snake, and liking ice cream better than spinach. Some of our emotional reactions are virtually instantaneous and probably don't involve cognitive appraisal, such as a shriek upon detecting a snake. Other emotional circumstances, especially those that occur over a long period of time, such as a depressed mood or anger toward a friend, are more likely to involve cognitive appraisal.

Sociocultural Influences on Emotion

Think once again about the bull and the picnic in the field. Perhaps you decided to show your courage to your date and went through a toreador sequence that left you with feelings of pride. Had you not been with someone you liked, you might have ignored the bull and walked away disinterested.

Emotions often involve someone else: your enthusiasm for going to the beach or skiing with *friends,* your love for the *person* of your dreams, your surprise when your *parents* tell you that your younger *brother* is coming to your college next year, your fear of giving a speech in front of your *classmates* and *professor,* and your sadness when you discover that your *roommate* lost her job.

The social aspects of emotion not only involve our relationships with others, but also the culture in which we live. To see how culture structures our emotional life, think about the worlds of the Utku Eskimos and Hopi Indians. The Utku Eskimos discourage anger by cultivating acceptance and by dissociating themselves from any expression of anger (Briggs, 1970). If an Utku trip is hampered by an unexpected snowstorm, the Eskimo does not become frustrated, he simply accepts the presence of the snowstorm and builds an igloo. Most of us would not act as mildly in the face of subzero weather and barriers to our travel.

Not long ago the Hopi Indians and a group of United States government officials clashed (Tavris, 1984). Government officials could not understand why the Hopis would not finish the projects for which they had received millions of dollars. The bureaucrats said, "Look how lazy they are!" The Hopi Indians could not understand why Washington officials were so angry. The Hopi see life as a rhythmic pattern. The rhythm is not to be interrupted under any circumstance. The Hopi planned to complete the projects but at their own pace. These two groups did not understand each other because of the different values of their respective cultures.

Our emotional reactions are influenced by the culture in which we live. The Utku Eskimos, for example, discourage anger by cultivating acceptance and by dissociating themselves from any expression of anger.

Figure 12.7
Sample photographs of a model's surprised expression and an infant's corresponding expression.

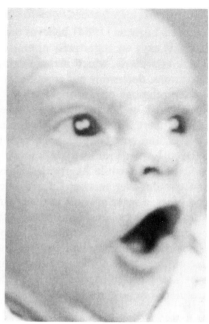

Emotion in Newborns and Infants

A newborn wails, a two-month-old baby smiles at her mother, and a four-month-old infant is surprised at a new toy. These emotional displays are adaptive, regulative, and help the young infant communicate with her world. Some emotions, such as fear, promote survival in infants. Fear of the dark and sudden changes in the environment inform the infant about danger. Emotions can regulate the distance between the infant and others; a smile encourages someone to come closer, anger tells the person to go away. Emotions aid the infant's communication skills, telling others about feelings and needs. A smile may inform the adult the infant is feeling comfortable, a cry that things are unpleasant (Campos & others, 1983; Camras, 1987; Izard & Malatesta, 1987).

Some emotions appear earlier than others in the infant's development. Startle, distress, disgust, and a reflexive smile seem to be present even at birth. Three to four months through the first year surprise, anger, and sadness emerge. Fear is not displayed until about six months of age (Izard, 1982). The infant's emotional displays cannot be used to infer the presence of emotional states, but the muscle configurations of infants' faces are those commonly associated with certain emotional states.

While infants display a variety of their own emotions, can they also imitate someone else's emotional expressions? If an adult smiles, will the baby follow with a smile? If an adult protrudes her lower lip, wrinkles her forehead, and frowns, will the baby show a saddened look? If an adult opens her mouth, widens her eyes, and raises her eyebrows, will the baby follow suit? Could infants only one day old do these things?

Tiffany Field and her colleagues (1982) explored these questions with newborns only thirty-six hours after their birth. The model held the newborn's head upright with the model's and the newborn's faces separated by ten inches. The newborn's facial expressions were recorded by an observer who stood behind the model. The observer could not see which facial expressions the model was showing. The model expressed one of three emotions: happiness, sadness, or surprise (see figure 12.7). As shown in figure 12.8, infants were most likely to imitate the model's display of surprise by widely opening their mouths. When

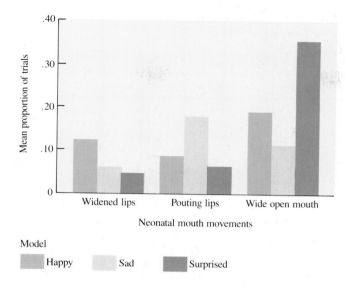

Figure 12.8
Imitation of adult emotions by 36-hour-old newborns. The graph shows the mean proportion of trials during which newborn mouth movements followed a models' facial expression. Mouth movements included widened lips (happy), pouting lips (sad), and wide open mouth (surprise).

the infants observed a happy model, they frequently widened their lips. When the model expressed sadness, the infants followed with lips that reflected pouting. Other research supports the belief young infants can imitate an adult's emotional expressions (Meltzoff, 1987; Meltzoff & Moore, 1977), but it is open to interpretation whether the imitation is learned or an innate ability (Wolff, 1987).

Emotional experiences play important roles in our lives, whatever our age or circumstance. Some of these emotional experiences are stressful. When a child's parents divorce, his distress is reflected in a mixture of fear, anger, surprise, sadness, and grief. After his wife dies, a middle-aged doctor can hardly contain his grief. The doctor becomes ill himself. Before turning to our discussion of stress, study concept table 12.1 to remember the main themes of emotion.

Stress

The year is 1988. A woman walks out of her Manhattan apartment at the beginning of another working day. She fights her way through a line of people and arrives at the bus stop just as the bus is leaving. As she arrives late for work, her boss tells her that her report was due an hour ago and the client is furious. Her boss says she can forget the summer vacation she was promised. As soon as her boss leaves, she pounds her fist into her desk so hard she rips the skin off of two knuckles. Her stomach churns, her back muscles knot up, and her blood pressure climbs. She gets two aspirins, a Maalox, and suddenly develops an urge for a dry martini.

Although we don't run into saber-toothed tigers anymore, we live in a world that includes many stressful circumstances. According to the American Academy of Family Physicians, two-thirds of office visits to family doctors are for stress-related symptoms. And stress is believed to be a major contributor to coronary heart disease, cancer, lung problems, accidental injuries, cirrhosis of the liver, and suicide, six of the leading causes of death in the United States. The three best-selling drugs in the United States are an ulcer medication (Tagamet), a hypertension drug (Inderal), and a tranquilizer (Valium).

Stress is a sign of the times. Corporations have developed elaborate stress management programs. Everywhere you look people are jogging, going to health clubs, and following diets designed to reduce tension. No one really knows whether we experience more stress than our parents or grandparents, but it seems as if we do.

■ ■ ■ ■ ■ ■ ■ ■ ■ ■ ■ ■ ■ ■ ■ ■ ■ ■ ■

Concept Table 12.1

Emotion		
Concept	**Processes/related ideas**	**Characteristics/description**
Range and classification of emotion	Their nature	We experience a wide range. Plutchik believes emotions are positive or negative, primary or mixed, bipolar opposites, and vary in intensity. One emotion of special interest is happiness.
Arousal and physiological processes	Arousal	The sympathetic nervous system is involved in arousal; the parasympathetic system is involved when arousal decreases. Many aspects of our body are influenced by arousal. The Yerkes-Dodson law addressed the issue of arousal and performance. The polygraph rests on the principle of arousal in emotion. The polygraph situation is complex and psychologists remain skeptical about its validity.
	Facial cues	Emotion is displayed through facial expressions. Ekman says we have as many as 7,000 facial expressions of emotion, which are similar across cultures.
	James-Lange and Cannon-Bard theories	In the James-Lange view, we initially perceive a stimulus, our body responds, then we experience the emotion. By contrast, the Cannon-Bard theory plays down the body's role in emotion, saying we simultaneously experience an emotion and bodily changes. Dispute about whether the same body changes underlie all emotions continues.
	The opponent-process theory	In Solomon's view, every emotion has a primary and a secondary process. The secondary process is the central nervous system's reaction to the primary process of the autonomic nervous system. The secondary process reduces the intensity of an emotion and increases equilibrium; with repeated stimulations it strengthens.
Emotion and cognition	Overview	Cognitive views argue that emotion always has a cognitive component and that in most instances cognition directs emotion.
	Schachter-Singer view	Emotional events produce emotional arousal. Arousal often is diffuse so we look to the external world to interpret. We label the emotion based on environmental cues.
	Primacy: Cognition or emotion?	Lazarus believes cognition always directs emotion, Zajonc says emotion is dominant. Both probably are right.
Sociocultural influences and emotions in infants	Sociocultural influences	Values and standards in a culture are associated with emotion.
	Emotion in infants	They are adaptive, regulative, and communicative. Infants display a wide variety of emotions. Some appear earlier in development than others. Newborns only thirty-six hours old can imitate an adult's emotional expressions.

The Body's Response to Stress

According to the Austrian-born founding father of stress research, the late Hans Selye (1974, 1983), stress simply is the wear and tear in the body due to the demands placed on it. Any number of environmental events or stimuli will produce the same stress response in the body. Selye observed patients with different problems: the death of someone close, loss of income, arrest for embezzlement. Regardless of their problem, strikingly similar symptoms appeared: loss of appetite, muscular weakness, and decreased interest in the world.

To describe the common effects on the body when demands are placed on it, Selye developed the concept of the **general adaptation syndrome,** which moves through three stages. First, in the alarm stage, the body detects the presence of stress and tries to eliminate it. Muscle tone is lost, temperature decreases, and blood pressure drops. Then, a rebound reaction called countershock occurs. The adrenal cortex enlarges and hormone release increases. The alarm stage is short. Before long, the person moves into a more prolonged defense against stress, the stage of resistance. The person exerts an all-out effort to combat stress. If the effort fails and the stress persists, the individual goes into the exhaustion stage, during which time defenses degenerate rapidly.

An example of how the general adaptation syndrome works involves the demands placed on your body as you near the time of a final exam. You might develop an alarm reaction when you realize you are not studying enough. If you mobilize your forces, you may study day and night with little or no sleep over the course of several days. But the stage of resistance cannot go on forever. You "crash" as the stage of exhaustion emerges.

Strain is a term closely aligned with the body's response to stress. Our body is strained when we use it beyond its evolutionary intention. Prolonged strain occurs because we do not always fight or flee from our troubled circumstances. In most instances, we don't punch our boss when our emotions are broiling; we don't resign our job either. We simply stay in the situation, worrying and agonizing about our image, priorities, responsibilities, and frustrations. As exhaustion deepens, breakdowns often take place in the weakest parts of our body. For one person, the strain might produce high blood pressure, for another depression, and for someone else migraine headaches (Maddi, 1986).

Not all stress is bad, though. Selye called the positive features of stress **eustress.** Competing in an athletic event, writing an essay, or pursuing someone who is attractive require the body to expend energy. Selye doesn't say we should avoid these pleasures in life, but he does emphasize that we should minimize their wear and tear on our bodies.

Illness and the Immune System

Psychologists once were hesitant to associate psychological states with illness because they could not imagine a physiological connection (Maier & Laudenslager, 1985). Evidence for this connection has increased and researchers in this field, known by the imposing name of **psychoneuroimmunology,** are beginning to explain how psychological factors influence physical health. The new field of psychoneuroimmunology explores connections between psychological factors, such as emotions and attitudes, the nervous system, and the immune system.

The immune system keeps us healthy by recognizing foreign materials such as bacteria, viruses, and tumors, and then by destroying them. Its machinery consists of billions of white blood cells located in the lymph system. The white blood cells come in two forms: lymphocytes and phagocytes. The main job of the lymphocytes is to recognize and destroy foreign cells (figure 12.9 shows lymphocytes taking on cancer cells); the primary work of the phagocytes is to finish the job by eating and eliminating these cells. Researchers have found that when certain types of lymphocytes, called natural killer (NK) cells, are highly active, cancer is less likely to develop. The NK cells seem to be part of an early immune surveillance system that keeps tumors from growing and spreading. Just how they do this important task is still not clear.

(a)

(b)

Figure 12.9
David vs. Goliath: (a) A small white blood cell (lymphocyte) takes on a large cancer cell (the one with the smoother surface); (b) A small natural killer (NK) cell attacks a larger tumor cell, which defends itself by forming blisters on its surface.

Exploratory efforts are beginning to uncover connections between psychological factors and the immune system. Sandra Levy (1984, 1985) investigated NK-cell activity when cancer spread to the lymph nodes of women treated for breast cancer. Women who accepted the disease and adjusted to their condition had less NK-cell activity than women who became angry and agitated about their disease. Levy believes acceptance of the disease reflects a belief of helplessness; in contrast, anger and agitation suggest that something might be done to alter the disease. In this way, beliefs about control may affect NK-cell activity.

AIDS is another disease that may be affected by psychoneuroimmunological factors. When an individual is told he has been exposed to the AIDS virus, he often goes into a deep depression. Since depression is thought to adversely affect the immune system, the AIDS patient ends up with an even greater suppression of the immune system.

Much of what we know about psychoneuroimmunology needs further clarification, verification, and explanation (Baum & others, in press). The next several decades should witness increased growth in this field; it is hoped that more precise links between psychological factors, the brain, and the immune system will be revealed. The outcome of this research could provide more successful treatments of our most baffling diseases, cancer and AIDS among them.

Stress and the Environment

Many circumstances, big and small, can produce stress in our lives. What makes some stimuli stressful and others less stressful?

Overload, Conflict, and Frustration

Sometimes stimuli become so intense that we can no longer cope. When noise is at a high level over a period of time, at some point it overloads our adaptability. This overload can occur with work as well. How often have you said to yourself, "There are not enough hours in the day to do all I have to do."

Stimuli not only overload us, but they can also be a source of conflict. Conflict occurs when we must decide between two or more incompatible stimuli. Three major types of conflict are: approach/approach, avoidance/avoidance, and approach/avoidance. In an **approach/approach conflict,** we are attracted to two stimuli, but we have to choose one of them. Should we go out with the good-looking, tall, thin person, or with the rich, more stockily built person? Should we buy a Corvette or a Porsche? The approach/approach conflict is the least stressful of the three types because either choice, known as an "approach" stimulus, leads to a reasonably positive result.

In an **avoidance/avoidance conflict,** we must choose between two unattractive stimuli. We want to avoid both, but we must choose one. Will we go to the dentist to have a bad tooth pulled or endure the toothache? Are we going to give a presentation in class or not show up and get a zero? Obviously these conflicts are more stressful than having the luxury of choosing between two approach stimuli. In many instances, we delay our decision about the avoidance/avoidance conflict until the last possible moment.

In an **approach/avoidance conflict,** a single stimulus or circumstance includes both negative and positive aspects. We really like the person we are going with and are thinking about getting married. On the one hand we are attracted by the steady affection and love, but on the other hand marriage at this time might hinder our career. We look at a menu and face a dilemma—the double chocolate delight would be sumptuous, but is it worth the extra pound of weight? Our world is full of approach/avoidance conflicts and they can be highly stressful. In these circumstances, we often vascillate before deciding. As we approach decision time, avoidance tendencies frequently dominate (Miller, 1959).

Frustration is another circumstance that produces stress. **Frustration** refers to any situation in which a person cannot reach a desired goal. If we want something and cannot have it, we feel frustrated. Our world is full of frustrations that build up to make our life more stressful—not having enough money to buy the car we want, not getting promoted at work, not getting an A average, being delayed for an important appointment by traffic, and not being able to get the person we like to like us. Failures and losses are especially frustrating—not getting grades that are high enough to get into medical school or losing someone we are closely attached to through death, for example. Sometimes the frustrations we experience are major life events, as in the cases of divorce and death, and others are an accumulation of daily hassles.

Life Events and Daily Hassles

Think about your life. What events have created the most stress for you? A change in financial status, getting fired at work, a divorce, the death of someone you loved, a personal injury? And what about the everyday events of your life? What hassles you? Not having enough time to study, problems with a roommate, arguing with your girlfriend or boyfriend, not getting enough credit for the work you do at your job?

Significant life events have been proposed as a major source of stress and attempts have been made to link such life events with illnesses. The effects of individual life events, such as a tornado or volcano eruption, can be evaluated, or the effects of *clusters* of events can be studied. A widely used scale to measure clusters of life events and their possible impact on illness was devised by Thomas Holmes and Richard Rahe (1967). Their Social Readjustment Rating Scale includes events ranging from the death of a spouse (100 stress points) to minor violations of the law (11 stress points). (See table 12.3 for the complete listing of life events and their stress points.) Note that not all stressful events are negative. For example, buying a house gets you 31 stress points and even Christmas earns 12.

People who experience clusters of life events, such as divorce, being fired from a job, and sexual difficulties, are more likely to become ill (Maddi, 1986). However, the ability to predict illness from a knowledge of life events alone is modest. Total scores on life events scales such as the Social Readjustment Rating Scale are frequently ineffective at predicting future health problems. A life-events checklist tells us nothing about a person's physiological makeup, constitutional strengths and weaknesses, ability to cope with stressful circumstances, support systems, or the nature of the social relationships involved, all of which are important in understanding how stress is related to illness. A divorce, for example, might be less stressful than a marrriage filled with day-to-day tension. In addition, the Holmes-Rahe scale includes positive events, such as marital reconciliation and gaining a new family member, which can buffer the effects of negative events.

Table 12.3 Social Readjustment Rating Scale

Rank	Life event	Mean value
1	Death of spouse	100
2	Divorce	73
3	Marital separation	65
4	Jail term	63
5	Death of close family member	63
6	Personal injury or illness	53
7	Marriage	50
8	Fired at work	47
9	Marital reconciliation	45
10	Retirement	45
11	Change in health of family member	44
12	Pregnancy	40
13	Sex difficulties	39
14	Gain of new family member	39
15	Business readjustment	39
16	Change in financial state	38
17	Death of close friend	37
18	Change to different line of work	36
19	Change in number of arguments with spouse	35
20	Mortgage over $10,000	31
21	Foreclosure of mortgage or loan	30
22	Change in responsibilities at work	29
23	Son or daughter leaving home	29
24	Trouble with in-laws	29
25	Outstanding personal achievement	28
26	Spouse begins or stops work	26
27	Begin or end school	26
28	Change in living condition	25
29	Revision of personal habits	24
30	Trouble with boss	23
31	Change in work hours or conditions	20
32	Change in residence	20
33	Change in schools	20
34	Change in recreation	19
35	Change in church activities	19
36	Change in social activities	18
37	Mortgage or loan less than $10,000	17
38	Change in sleeping habits	16
39	Change in number of family get-togethers	15
40	Change in eating habits	15
41	Vacation	13
42	Christmas	12
43	Minor violations of the law	11

How many of these events have you experienced in the last year? Add the numbers associated with each event. The sum is an index of how much life change related to stress you have experienced in this one-year period. In their original study, Holmes and Rahe (1967) found that a score in the 200s was linked with about a 50 percent chance of illness and a score of 300 or above was associated with about an 80 percent chance of illness.

From Holmes, T. H., and R. H. Rahe, The social readjustment rating scale, *Journal of Psychosomatic Research, 11,* 203–218. © 1967 Pergamon Press, Inc., Elmsford, NY.

It may not be life's major events that are the primary sources of stress, but rather our daily experiences. Enduring a boring but tense job or marriage and living in poverty do not show up on scales of major life events. Yet the everyday pounding we take from these living conditions can add up to a highly stressful life and eventually illness. Some psychologists (e.g., Lazarus & Folkman, 1984) believe we can gain greater insight into the source of life's stresses by focusing more on daily hassles and uplifts. To learn more about daily hassles and uplifts, especially those most common among college students and middle-aged adults, read Psychology 12.2.

■ ■ ■ ■ ■ ■ ■ ■ ■ ■ ■ ■ ■ ■ ■ ■ ■ ■ ■ ■

Psychology 12.2

Daily Hassles and Uplifts

*It's not the large things that
send a man to the madhouse
. . . no, it's the continuing
series of small tragedies that
send a man to the madhouse
. . . not the death of his love
but a shoelace that snaps with
no time left.*

—*Charles Bukowski*

■ These thoughts reflect the belief that daily hassles might be better predictors of stress in our lives than major life events. Support for this view comes from a study of 210 police officers in Florida (Spielberger & Grier, 1983). The day-to-day friction associated with an inefficient judicial system and distorted press accounts of police work were far more stressful than responding to a felony in progress or making arrests.

How about your own life? What are the biggest hassles in your life? In one investigation, the most frequent daily hassles of college students were wasting time, concerns about meeting high standards, and being lonely (Kanner & others, 1981). The most frequent uplifts of the college students were having fun, laughing, entertainment, getting along well with friends, and completing a task.

While college students were coping with academic and social problems in this investigation, middle-aged adults more often reported economic concerns— rising prices and taxes, for example. Table 12.A provides information about the ten most frequent daily hassles and uplifts experienced by the middle-aged adults.

Table 12.A Ten Most Frequent Daily Hassles and Uplifts of Middle-Aged Adults Over a Nine-Month Period

Item	% of times checked[a]	Item	% of times checked
Hassles		*Uplifts*	
1. Concerns about weight	52.4	1. Relating well with your spouse or lover	76.3
2. Health of a family member	48.1	2. Relating well with friends	74.4
3. Rising prices of common goods	43.7	3. Completing a task	73.3
4. Home maintenance	42.8	4. Feeling healthy	72.7
5. Too many things to do	38.6	5. Getting enough sleep	69.7
6. Misplacing or losing things	38.1	6. Eating out	68.4
7. Yard work or outside home maintenance	38.1	7. Meeting your responsibilities	68.1
8. Property, investment, or taxes	37.6	8. Visiting, phoning, or writing someone	67.7
9. Crime	37.1	9. Spending time with family	66.7
10. Physical appearance	35.9	10. Home (inside) pleasing to you	65.5

a. The "% of times checked" figures represent the mean percentage of people checking the item each month averaged over the nine monthly administrations.

From Kanner, A. D., et al., Comparison of two modes of stress measurement: Daily Hassles and uplifts versus major life events. *Journal of Behavioral Medicine, 4,* 1–39. © 1981 Plenum Publishing Corporation, New York. Reprinted by permission.

Table 12.4 The Support Networks of Depressed and Nondepressed Individuals

	Men		Women	
Item	*Patients*	*Controls*	*Patients*	*Controls*
	Quantitative indices			
Quality of family support (1–9 scale)	5.36	6.47	5.20	6.74
Number of friends	10.89	21.34	11.32	20.08
Number of network contacts	12.43	18.04	14.21	17.88
Number of close relationships	3.82	6.62	4.42	6.86
Quality of significant relationship (0–24 scale)	13.80	16.38	14.64	17.34
Quality of work support (1–9 scale)	5.00	6.02	5.61	6.06

From Billings, Andrew G., et. al., Social-environment factors in unipolar depression, *Journal of Abnormal Psychology, 92,* 119–133. Copyright 1983 by the American Psychological Association. Reprinted by permission of the author.

Critics of the daily hassles approach argue that some of the same problems involved with life events scales occur when assessing daily hassles (Dohrenwend & Shrout, 1985). For example, knowing about a person's daily hassles tells us nothing about physiological changes, body strengths and weaknesses, how the person copes with the hassles, and how they perceive the hassles.

Social Processes

Our physical and social world compared to that of our ancestors is more crowded, polluted, noisy, and achievement oriented. In such a world, support systems may be needed to buffer stress. In one investigation, the support systems, including family members, friends, and co-workers, of depressed and nondepressed subjects were studied (Billings, Cronkite, & Moos, 1983). As shown in table 12.4, the depressed individuals had fewer and less supportive relationships with family members, friends, and co-workers than did nondepressed individuals. Family relationships and support systems seem to be key ingredients in the ability to cope with stress and illness. In one investigation of the prognosticators of cancer, mental illness, and suicide, a lack of closeness to one's parents and a negative attitude toward one's family were the most powerful predictors of illness (Thomas, 1983). Widows die at a rate three to thirteen times as high as married women for every known cause of death. Close, positive attachments to others, both family and friends, consistently show up as important buffers of stress.

Consider Robert, who had been laid off by the Studebaker Corporation in 1962 when it was about to fold, then by a truck manufacturer that went under in the 1970s, and more recently in cutbacks at a Chrysler plant in the early 1980s. By all accounts you would expect Robert to be very stressed, yet he is one of the most well-adjusted people in his community. When asked his secret in the face of adversity and stress, he responded that he has a loving wife and goes to church every Sunday. Far more important than the trials and tribulations in his life is the support from others that helps him handle the stress.

Close, positive attachments to others— both family and friends—consistently show up as important buffers of stress. Think about your own circumstances—how much do family and friends help you through the stresses in your life?

As we search for answers to why some people cope with stress better than others, we find that certain population groups show less stress than others—Mormons, symphony conductors, and women listed in *Who's Who* enjoy remarkably good health and longevity, for example. Why? Possibly something in the way these people live is responsible as well as such abstractions as faith, pride of accomplishment, and productivity.

Cognitive Processes

How much does the way we think affect the way stress influences our lives? In the case of Robert, who had been laid off of several jobs, his thinking meant a great deal. And for Mormons, their faith probably helps them to cope with adversity.

Remember from our discussion of emotion that Richard Lazarus believes emotion always has a cognitive component. He emphasizes that throughout our lives we struggle to make sense out of what is happening to us and try to develop a pattern of order and continuity. This struggle is centered around cognitive appraisal and coping, commitments, and beliefs about the self and the world (Folkman & others, 1986; Lazarus, 1984).

Cognitive appraisal is the way we interpret an event in our lives. Imagine getting a D on a test. Is this irrelevant, benign, harmful, threatening, or challenging to you? These are cognitive appraisals of a stressful situation. Coping also is a key process in understanding stress. How we cope with any stressful encounter influences our emotion and well-being. Lazarus argues that coping takes one of two forms. In **problem-focused coping,** we face our troubles and try to solve them. For example, if you are having trouble with a class, you might go to the study skills center at your college or university and enter a training program to learn how to study more effectively. You have faced your problem and attempted to do something about it. In **emotion-focused coping,** we change the way we perceive an encounter and the way we respond emotionally to our difficulties. In this type of coping we might avoid something, rationalize what has happened to us, deny it is occurring, laugh it off, or call on our religious faith for support. If you use emotion-focused coping you might avoid going to the class you are having trouble in or talking with the teacher about your difficulty. You might say that the class doesn't matter, deny that you are having problems, laugh and joke about it with your friends, or pray that you will do better.

Commitments are our valued ideals and goals and the choices we make or are prepared to make to reach those ideals and goals. When we are committed to ideals and goals, we will expend considerable energy in their behalf. Commitments entail plans, priorities, and expectations. You may develop a plan to become a medical doctor, set your priorities so that studying often takes precedence over partying, and have high expectations for success. The high school and college years are described by Erik Erikson (1968) as the time when the individual struggles and comes to grips with an identity. Erikson is speaking about a search for a workable set of commitments for living and functioning in society. An absence of commitments may reflect a pervasive sense of meaninglessness in one's life. A strong commitment may help the individual cope with stress and overcome barriers to goals.

Lazarus also emphasizes that our beliefs about our self make an important difference in the way we handle stress. Especially significant is having a sense of control over events. If we believe we have effective resources for handling demanding encounters, we probably react with more composure and confidence than if we perceive that we do not have such resources available to us. For example, people with little control over their job, such as cooks and assembly-line workers, have higher rates of heart disease than people who can dictate the pace and style of their work. Telephone operators, waiters, cashiers, and others whose work makes substantial psychological demands but provides little opportunity for decision making could be at risk for stress. High demands and low control are burdensome in our effort to cope with stress.

An intriguing experiment conducted by Ellen Langer and Judith Rodin (1976) shows how powerful such a sense of control over events can be. One group of elderly residents in a nursing home was told about the importance of establishing responsibility for themselves. A second group at the same nursing home was informed of the importance of the staff's responsibility for them. To improve communication, the first group was given the freedom to make choices rather than have the staff make choices for them. A plant was given to each of the individuals in the first group and they were told that it was their responsibility to care for it and make it grow. Three weeks later the elderly residents in the first group were much more alert, participated more actively, and had a stronger sense of well-being than their counterparts in the second group, who were dependent on the staff.

A follow-up eighteen months later suggested that enhanced self-responsibility and control over the environment were still present in the first group (Rodin & Langer, 1977). Perhaps the most striking data come from the death rates. The average death rate in the nursing home was 25 percent of the residents over the eighteen-month period. However, only 15 percent of those in which responsibility had been induced died during this time frame, while 30 percent of the staff-dependent group died! Perceived control over one's environment, then, can be literally a matter of life or death.

Personality Factors

Do you have certain personality characteristics that help you cope more effectively with stress? Do other characteristics make you more vulnerable to stress? Two prominent candidates are hardiness and the Type-A behavior pattern.

Hardiness is a personality style characterized by a sense of commitment (rather than alienation), control (rather than powerlessness), and a perception of problems as challenges (rather than threats) (Maddi, 1986). In the Chicago Stress Project, business managers thirty-two to sixty-five years of age were studied over a five-year period. During the five years, most of the managers experienced stressful events, such as divorce, job transfers, the death of a close friend, inferior performance evaluations at work, and working at a job with an unpleasant boss. In one investigation, managers who developed an illness (ranging from the flu to a heart attack) were compared with those who did not (Kobasa, Maddi, & Kahn, 1982). The latter group was more likely to have a hardy personality. In another study of business executives, hardiness along with exercise and social support were evaluated to determine whether they buffered stress and reduced illness. As shown in table 12.5, when all three factors were present in the executive's life the level of illness dropped dramatically. This suggests the power of multiple buffers of stress, rather than a single buffer, in maintaining health.

Table 12.5 Illness of High-Stress Business Executives: The Effects of Personal Hardiness, Exercise, and Support Systems	
Resistance sources	**Number of illnesses**
All three high	357
Two high	2,049
One high	3,336
None high	6,474

Note: The measure of illness is based on the Seriousness of Illness Survery, a self-report checklist of 126 commonly recognized illnesses—severity weights were given to illnesses based on ratings by large numbers of physicians and lay persons.

Source: After Kobasa & others, 1985, p. 529.

A cluster of characteristics make up the **Type-A behavior pattern**—excessively competitive, an accelerated pace of ordinary activities, impatience, doing several things at the same time, hostility, and an inability to hide the fact that time is a struggle in life. In the late 1950s a secretary for two California cardiologists, Meyer Friedman and Ray Rosenman, observed that the chairs in their waiting room were tattered and worn, but only on the front edge. The cardiologists had noticed the impatience of their cardiac patients, often arriving exactly on time for their appointment and in a great hurry to leave. Subsequently they conducted a research study of 3,000 healthy men between the ages of thirty-five and fifty-nine over a period of eight years (Friedman & Rosenman, 1974). During the eight years, the Type-A men had twice as many heart attacks or other forms of heart disease as anyone else. And autopsies of the men who died revealed Type-A men had coronary arteries that were more obstructed than other men.

Since the original research of Friedman and Rosenman, an extensive effort examining the link between Type-A behavior and coronary disease has cast some doubt on the strength of the association (e.g., Shekelle, Gayle, & Norusis, 1985; Williams, Barefoot, & Haney, 1986). Studies with large samples of Type-A subjects (on the order of one thousand or more) and carefully designed interviewing techniques still reveal an association between Type-A behavior and coronary risk, but the association is not as strong as was believed (Williams, 1986, 1987). Researchers have examined the different components of Type-A behavior, such as hostility, to determine a more precise link with coronary risk. People who are hostile or consistently turn anger inward are more likely to develop heart disease (Barefoot, Dahlstrom, & Williams, 1983; MacDougall, Dembroski, & Dimsdale, 1985). Hostile, angry individuals have been labeled "hot reactors," meaning they have intense physiological reactions to stress—their hearts race, their breathing hurries, and their nerves tense up, which could lead to heart disease.

The dust has not completely settled in the debate about whether Type-A behavior in general should be abandoned in favor of its more precise components. Meyer Friedman still believes the cluster of anger, impatience, competitiveness, and irritation is related to heart disease, for example. And his clinical staff reports success with counseling and behavior modification programs designed to reduce the intensity of the cluster in coronary risk patients. As one sixty-four-year-old heart attack victim who went through counseling commented, "I realized that there is more than one way of getting from point A to point B. . . . If I had a problem before, I'd just drive forward and solve it at any cost. Now I know what I don't complete I'll finish tomorrow." (Fischman, 1987, p. 50). Thus, while empirical research studies have chipped away at the Type-A behavior pattern, trying to find which of its components are most strongly associated with coronary disease, the Type-A behavior pattern remains a strong contender in clinical analysis and treatment.

"You're a Type A just like your father."
Reprinted from Psychology Today *Magazine. Copyright © 1986 American Psychological Association.*

"Exercise vigorously at least several times a week" is some of the best advice that can be given to individuals who are experiencing stress.

Coping with Stress

Some of the advice given to heart attack victims and other individuals experiencing stress makes sense—quit smoking, lose weight, cut down on salt and caffeine, take vacations on a regular basis, exercise vigorously at least several times a week, and make sure you have one or more friends in whom you can confide. In some cases we can remove stress from our lives—change jobs, transfer to a less academically competitive college, and so on. In other cases, drugs may be used to reduce stress. Inderal, for example, is a drug that interferes with the action of certain stress hormones.

Most programs designed to reduce stress involve teaching people how to relax. These programs do not remove stress factors, but they help individuals manage their stress so they can lead more productive and enjoyable lives (Johnston, 1985). Remember from chapter 4 that inducing relaxation, whether through transcendental meditation or in some other manner, produces rather dramatic physiological changes—decreased heart rate, lower blood pressure, and reduced oxygen consumption. As indicated in chapter 5, biofeedback has been successful in helping individuals reduce the tension in their bodies (Chapman, 1986). A yoga enthusiast, Swami Rama, was carefully evaluated at the Menninger Clinic in Kansas; he could stop his heart from pumping blood for seventeen seconds and change the temperature in the palm of his hands. While few of us have this control over our body's internal regulating mechanisms, the evidence that this control is possible is encouraging. Some strategies may give us short-term relief from the discomfort of stress but in the long run usually are ineffective—among them withdrawal, aggression, and defense mechanisms.

Every semester several students stop showing up for my classes, often after the first exam. They never come and talk to me about their performance in the class, and they don't go through the proper procedures for dropping the class. The result of their avoidance is that they have an F on their record at the end of the semester. By not coming to class after performing poorly on the first exam the students withdraw from a setting that is stressful. But they do not take into account the long-term consequences of their avoidant behavior.

Sometimes we strike out with aggression when we are faced with stress. In the late 1960s after a student found out he had flunked my introductory psychology course, he called me a few choice names to my face. The next day, he came to my office to apologize, saying that he deserved the F and that he failed two other classes as well. The growing evidence of a link between hostility and heart disease provides a reason for learning how to live in a less tumultuous, more level emotional manner.

cathy®　　　　　　　　　　　　　　　　　by Cathy Guisewite

We may call on a number of defense mechanisms when confronted with stress. Consider a twenty-eight-year-old woman whose husband has just divorced her. She begins running around with her seventeen-year-old niece and feels secure when she is with teenagers. She avoids going out with males her own age and turns down a job promotion. In the face of stress, this woman regressed to an earlier period of her life to recapture the positive experiences it had brought and avoided responsibilities that would further her career. In Lazarus' terms, the woman was engaging in emotion-focused rather than problem-focused coping. Instead of facing her current problems, cognitively appraising her situation, and evaluating viable alternatives for solving problems, she let her emotions overwhelm her and used defense mechanisms to handle the threats to her ego.

In this case, emotion-focused coping was not the better choice. But there are times when such coping can be beneficial in handling stress. For example, denial is one of the major protective psychological mechanisms that enables people to cope with the flood of feelings that occur when the reality of death or dying becomes too great (Kalish, 1981). In other circumstances, emotion-focused coping is not adaptive. Denying that you are not doing well in school when in reality you are flunking two classes is not adaptive. Denying that the person you were dating doesn't love you any more when in reality that person has become engaged to someone else is not adaptive either. However, denial can be used to avoid the destructive impact of shock by postponing the time when you have to deal with stress.

Much has been said about the importance of thinking positively when under stress. Most of the time we *do* want to avoid negative thinking when handling stress. A positive mood improves our ability to process information more efficiently, leads us to be more altruistic, and gives us higher self-esteem (Clark & Isen, 1982; Diener, 1984; Fried & Berkowitz, 1979). An optimistic attitude is superior to a pessimistic one in most instances, producing the sense that we are capable of controlling our environment (Bandura, 1986). A negative mood increases our chances of getting angry, feeling guilty, and magnifying our mistakes (Watson & Clark, 1984).

Nonetheless, in some cases a strategy of defensive pessimism may work best in handling stress. By imagining negative outcomes individuals may be able to prepare for forthcoming stressful circumstances (Norem & Cantor, 1986; Showers & Cantor, 1985). Think about the honors student who is absolutely convinced she will flunk the next test, or the nervous host who is afraid her lavish dinner party will fall apart. For these two people, thoughts of failure may not be paralyzing but instead will motivate them to do everything necessary to ensure that things go smoothly. In one recent investigation, negative thinking initiated the following constructive pattern of thoughts and feelings: evaluating negative possibilities; wondering what the future held; psyching up for future experiences so they would be positively experienced; feeling good by sensing that one was prepared to cope with the worst; and forming positive expectations (Showers, 1986). Positive *and* negative thinking, then, are involved with coping with stress.

There are many different ways to effectively cope with stress, just as there are many different ways to ineffectively cope with stress. We have highlighted some of these techniques in this chapter and will discuss others in chapter 15. But we should not only be looking for ways to more effectively cope with stress, we also should be searching for ways to prevent illness and promote health. Before turning to our discussion of these important topics, it may be helpful to study the main themes of stress presented in concept table 12.2.

■ ■

Concept Table 12.2

Stress		
Concept	**Processes/related ideas**	**Characteristics/description**
The body's response to stress	General adaptation syndrome	Describes the common effects of stress on the body. Hans Selye believes stress is the wear and tear on the body as a result of the demands placed on it. This involves three stages—alarm, resistance, and exhaustion. Strain characterizes the effects of stress on the body. Not all stress is bad—Selye calls good stress eustress.
	Illness and the immune system	Psychoneuroimmunology explores connections between psychological factors, the nervous system, and the immune system. Exploratory research is beginning to uncover some connections between attitudes and emotions and the immune system.
Stress and the environment	Overload, conflict, and frustration	Stress is produced because stimuli become so intense and prolonged we cannot cope. Three types of conflict are approach/approach, avoidance/avoidance, and approach/avoidance. Frustration occurs when we cannot reach a goal.
	Life events and daily hassles	Stress may be produced by major life events or daily hassles. Life events lists tell us nothing about how individuals cope with stress, their body strengths and weaknesses, and other important dimensions of stress. Daily hassles provide a more focused look, but their evaluation should include information about coping and body characteristics.
Cognitive processes and personality factors	Social processes	Support systems help individuals cope with stress. Something about the way some groups, such as Mormans, live may explain why they cope better with stress.
	Cognitive processes	Lazarus believes we struggle to make sense of what is happening to us. This is centered around cognitive appraisal, commitments, and beliefs about the self and world. He distinguishes between problem-focused and emotion-focused coping.
	Personality factors	Hardiness is associated with a lower incidence of illness. Type-A behavior is a cluster of characteristics originally believed to predict coronary disease. The Type-A cluster is controversial, with some researchers arguing that only specific components of the cluster, such as hostility, are linked with coronary disease.
Coping with stress	Its nature	Effective ways to deal with stress include relaxation, exercise, positive close relationships, healthy diet, and optimistic thoughts. In some instances, defensive pessimism may produce adaptive coping.

Preventing Illness and Promoting Health

What can you do to prevent sickness? How can you stay healthy? Preventing illness and promoting health are concerns of a new field called health psychology.

Health Psychology

Around 2600 B.C. Oriental physicians, and later around 500 B.C. Greek physicians, recognized that good habits were essential for good health. Rather than emphasize magical thinking or blame the gods for illness, they realized that individuals had some control over their health. The physician was viewed as a guide, assisting the patient in restoring a natural physical and emotional balance. In more recent times, medical professionals have tended to be specialists. While this tendency continues, in the 1980s an interest in integrated medical care has developed. Once again, family medicine is seen as an important approach to caring for patients. The belief has emerged that illness and health are multidimensional and complex, often requiring knowledge about neurology, cardiology, and psychology. Further, we are returning to the view of the early Orientals and Greeks that the ultimate responsibility for integrating the patient's care rests with the patient.

The new approach to preventing illness and promoting health is a **holistic orientation.** Rather than linking illness to a specific cause such as genes or germs, this approach recognizes the complex, multidimensional nature of illness and health. Genes and germs might be involved, say the holistic health advocates, but a better understanding of the problem will transpire if we know something about psychological factors, life-style, and the nature of the health-care delivery system, for example. Interest in the psychological factors involved in illness and the promotion of health led to the development of a new division in 1978 in the American Psychological Association called health psychology (Matarazzo, 1979).

We are becoming increasingly aware that our behavior determines if we will develop a serious illness and when we will die (Antonovsky, 1987; Feurstein, Labbe, & Kuczmierczyk, 1986; Stone, 1986). Seven of the ten leading causes of death in the United States seem to be associated with the *absence* of various health behaviors (Richmond, 1979). Diseases such as influenza, rubella, and polio no longer are major causes of death; more deaths now are caused by heart disease (37.8 percent of all deaths), cancer (20 percent), and stroke (9.6 percent). Personal habits and life-styles are believed to play substantial roles in these diseases. This has led health economists, public health professionals, physicians, and psychologists to predict that the next major step in improving the general health of the United States population will be primarily behavioral, not medical (DeLeon & Pallack, 1982).

Factors Influencing Health Behavior

Common sense tells us that if we eat and sleep regularly, show moderation in eating and drinking, and exercise we will be healthy. In one investigation of almost 7,000 adults, those who practiced these habits were healthier (with fewer disabilities and chronic conditions and more vigor) than those who did not (Belloc & Breslow, 1972). One investigation reported that more than seven in ten of us try to regulate eating, almost half of us try to get more sleep and rest, and more than one-third of us try to exercise more (Harris & Guten, 1979). See table 12.6 for other ways we protect our health. Indeed, we do seem to know what it takes to be healthy. In one study, college students' ranking of health-protective activities such as those in table 12.6 virtually matched that of licensed nurses (Turk, Rudy, & Salovey, 1984).

While most of us know what it takes to prevent illness and promote health, we don't fare very well when it comes to applying this information to ourselves. In one investigation, college students reported that they probably would never have a heart attack or drinking problem, but that other college students would (Weinstein, 1984). The college students also said no relation existed between their risk of heart attack and how much they exercised, smoked, or ate red meat or high cholesterol food such as eggs, even though they correctly recognized that factors such as family history influenced risk. Many college students, it seems, have unrealistic, overly optimistic beliefs about their future health risks.

Table 12.6	Categories of Activities Performed to Protect Health
Activity category	**Percentage**
Nutrition; foods; eating conditions	71.3
Sleep; rest; relaxation	46.1
Exercising; physical activity; physical recreation	35.5
Contact with health system	18.8
Personal hygiene or dress	14.5
Psychological, mental, or emotional well-being	12.6
Watching one's weight	9.7
Avoiding or limiting tobacco use	8.8
Use of medication	7.8
Alcohol use	6.8
Other physical activity	5.6
General environment	5.1
Home, work, or neighborhood environment	3.1
Intake of substance other than food, medicine, or alcohol	2.4
Other	0.5

From Harris, D. M., and S. Guten, Health-protective behavior: An exploratory study, *Journal of Health and Social Behavior, 20,* 19.

Most of us are not very good at recognizing the symptoms of an illness. For example, most people believe they can tell when their blood pressure is elevated; the facts say otherwise (Pennebaker, 1982). The majority of heart attack victims have never sought medical attention for cardiac problems (Feurstein, Labbe, & Kuczmierczyk, 1986). And many of us do not go to a doctor when the early warning signs of cancer, such as a lump or a cyst, appear. Even when we do seek medical help, we do not always follow the doctor's orders. More than half of those with very high blood pressure do not comply with recommended treatment (Leventhal, Zimmerman, & Gutmann, 1984).

We may not comply with a doctor's orders because we have our own theories about our health and do not completely trust the doctor's advice. Sometimes doctors do not give patients clear information or fully explain the risks of ignoring their orders. To quit smoking or eat more nutritiously, patients need a clear understanding of the danger of their bad habits and a concrete set of instructions of what to do. Success or failure in treatment may depend on whether the doctor can present a valid and believable danger and an effective strategy for coping with the problem (Stone, 1986).

Preventive Health in Childhood

Many of our patterns of health and illness are longstanding. Our experiences as children and adolescents contribute to our current health practices as adults. Did your parents seek medical help at your first sniffle, or did they wait until your temperature was 104 degrees? Did they feed you heavy doses of red meat and sugar or vegetables and fruits? Did they get you involved in exercise programs or did you lie around watching television all the time? Did you grow up in a tense family atmosphere or one in which stress was handled calmly and life was low key?

Let's consider two of these questions further—exercise and family tension. The exercise revolution has not touched the lives of enough children. The 1985 School Fitness Survey tested 18,857 children aged six to seventeen on nine fitness tasks. Compared to a similar survey in 1975 there was virtually no improvement in the tasks. For example, 40 percent of boys six to twelve years old could not do more than one pull-up and a full 25 percent could not do any! Fifty percent of the girls aged six to seventeen and 30 percent of the boys aged six to twelve could not run a mile in less than ten minutes. In the fifty-yard dash, the adolescent girls in 1975 were faster than the adolescent girls in 1985.

Many of us experience stressful family environments, which set the tone for ineffective ways of coping with stress. Recent research reveals that children with a Type-A behavioral pattern have more illnesses, cardiovascular symptoms, muscle tension, and sleep disturbances. The Type-A children were more likely than other children to have Type-A parents. When these Type-A parents were observed interacting with their Type-A children they were likely to criticize their child's failures and compare them to others when evaluating their performance (Eagleston & others, in press; Thoresen & others, 1985).

The exciting prospect of health psychology is that psychological principles and techniques can be used to reduce illness and restore health in adulthood even if we have learned many bad habits as children and adolescents. In the next section of this text, we continue our exploration of problems and disturbances, focusing on the nature of abnormal psychology and psychotherapies, along with information about personality.

Many of our health patterns are longstanding. What were your eating habits like when you were growing up, for example? Did your parents feed you heavy doses of red meat and sugar or vegetables and fruits?

Summary

I. Range and Classification of Emotions

We experience a wide range of emotions. Plutchik believes emotions are positive or negative, primary or mixed, bipolar opposites, and vary in intensity. One emotion of special interest is happiness; only recently have psychologists turned to its study.

II. Arousal and Physiological Processes

The sympathetic nervous system is involved in increased arousal, the parasympathetic system in decreased arousal. Many aspects of our body are influenced by arousal. The Yerkes-Dodson law addresses the issue of arousal and performance. The polygraph rests on the principle of arousal in emotion; the polygraph test is complex and psychologists remain skeptical about its validity. Emotion is displayed through facial expressions. Ekman says we have as many as 7,000 facial expressions of emotion. He believes facial expressions for emotion are similar across cultures.

III. Some Theories of Emotion

In the James-Lange view, we initially perceive a stimulus, our body responds, then we experience emotion. By contrast, the Cannon-Bard theory plays down the body's role in emotion, saying we simultaneously experience an emotion and bodily changes. Dispute about whether the same body changes underlie all emotions continues. In the opponent-process theory of Solomon, every emotion has a primary and secondary process. The secondary process is the central nervous system's reaction to the primary process of the autonomic nervous system. The secondary process reduces the intensity of an emotion and increases equilibrium. With repeated stimulations, the secondary process strengthens.

IV. Emotion and Cognition

Cognitive views argue that emotion always has a cognitive component and that in most instances cognition directs emotion. In the Schachter-Singer view, emotional events produce emotional arousal. Arousal often is diffuse so we look to the external world to interpret the arousal and then label the emotion based on environmental cues. Lazarus and Zajonc have debated the issue of whether cognition or emotion dominates. Lazarus says cognition always directs emotion; Zajonc says it is the other way around.

V. Sociocultural Influences and Emotions in Infants

While much of the interest in emotion has focused on physiological and cognitive factors, emotion also takes place in a social context. Values and standards in a culture are associated with emotion. Emotions in infancy are adaptive, regulative, and communicative. Infants display a wide variety of emotions; some of these appear earlier than others. Newborns only thirty-six hours old can imitate an adult's emotional expressions.

VI. The Body's Response to Stress

Hans Selye believes stress is the wear and tear on the body as a result of the demands placed on it. He developed the concept of the general adaptation syndrome to describe the common effects of stress on the body. This involves three stages—alarm, resistance, and exhaustion. Strain characterizes the effects of stress on the body. Not all stress is bad for the body—Selye calls good stress eustress. Increased interest in psychoneuroimmunology is occurring; this field explores connections between psychological factors, the nervous system, and the immune system. Exploratory research is beginning to show some connections between attitudes and emotions and the immune system, although much is yet to be verified.

VII. Stress and the Environment

Stress occurs because stimuli become so intense and prolonged we cannot cope with them. Three types of conflict are: approach/approach, avoidance/avoidance, and approach/avoidance; the latter two are the most stressful. Frustration occurs when we cannot reach a goal. Stress can be produced by major life events or daily hassles. Life events checklists have not been very effective in predicting future illness, although clusters of life events have been linked to increased risk of illness. Life events checklists tell us nothing about how individuals cope with stress and their body strengths or weaknesses. Daily hassles provide a more focused look at the everyday lives of people under stress, but their evaluation also should include information about coping and body characteristics. Support systems are an important aspect of the social world that help individuals cope with stress.

VIII. Cognitive Processes and Personality Factors

Lazarus believes we struggle to make sense out of what is happening to us. This struggle is centered around cognitive appraisal, commitments, and beliefs about the self and world. He distinguishes between problem-focused and emotion-focused coping. Hardiness is associated with a lower incidence of illness. Type-A behavior is a cluster of characteristics originally believed to predict coronary disease. Currently, the Type-A cluster is controversial, with some researchers arguing that only specific components of the cluster, especially hostility, are linked with coronary disease.

IX. **Coping with Stress**
There are many effective ways to deal with stress, among them relaxation, exercise, positive close relationships, healthy diet, and optimistic thoughts. In some instances, defensive pessimism may produce adaptive coping.

X. **Preventing Illness and Promoting Health**
A new approach in psychology and medicine to prevent illness and promote health is a holistic orientation. This approach recognizes the complex, multidimensional nature of illness and emphasizes the importance of such dimensions as psychological factors, life-style, and the nature of the health-care delivery system. An absence of good health behaviors is increasingly recognized as responsible for illness and death. Regulation of eating and sleeping and increased exercise are believed to be important contributors to health. Most of us know this but do a poor job of applying the information to ourselves. We are not very good at recognizing the symptoms of illness and we often do not comply with doctor's orders. Many of our health and illness patterns are learned in childhood. Our nation's children are not physically fit and many children live in a family atmosphere of high stress.

Key Terms

primary emotions *400*
Yerkes-Dodson law *402*
polygraph *404*
James-Lange theory *403*
Cannon-Bard theory *406*
opponent-process theory *406*

general adaptation syndrome *412*
eustress *413*
psychoneuroimmunology *413*
approach/approach conflict *414*
avoidance/avoidance conflict *414*
approach/avoidance conflict *414*

frustration *415*
problem-focused coping *419*
emotion-focused coping *419*
commitments *419*
hardiness *420*
Type-A behavior pattern *421*
holistic orientation *425*

Suggested Readings

Diener, E. (1984). Subjective well-being. *Psychological Bulletin, 95,* 542–575. This article pulls together a wide variety of information about the nature of happiness. It includes a number of theoretical approaches and measurement strategies involved in finding out what makes us happy.

Ekman, P. (1985). *Telling lies: Clues to deceit in the marketplace, politics, and marriage.* New York: Norton. Ekman, a leading expert in studying the facial expressions of emotion, provides detailed information about how our faces and behavior reveal clues to our emotional states.

Izard, C. E., Kagan, J., & Zajonc, R. B. (1984). *Emotions, cognition, and behavior.* Leading experts on emotion describe the issues involved in links between emotion, thought, and action.

Journal of Psychosomatic Research This journal includes many outstanding articles on the role of health practices, use of drugs, relaxation, biofeedback, and other strategies in reducing stress and decreasing illness.

Lazarus, R. S., & Folkman, S. (1984). *Stress, appraisal, and coping.* New York: Springer. A thorough overview of Lazarus' cognitive approach to emotion and stress is provided, including details on how to assess stress and cognitive appraisal.

Personality and Abnormal Psychology

*They cannot scare me with
their empty spaces
Between stars—on stars where
no human race is.
I have it in me so much nearer
home
To scare myself with my own
desert places.*

—Robert Frost

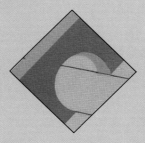

Personality

Every person cries out to be read differently.

—*Simone Weil*

Images of Personality

Sigmund Freud and Carl Rogers, whose theories we will address in this chapter, are giants in the field of personality. The lives of theorists and their experiences have a major impact on the content of their theories. As with each of us, the search for understanding human behavior begins by examining our own.

Sigmund Freud's theory emphasizes the sexual basis of our personality. What were Freud's sexual interests in adolescence? History shows that Freud repressed most of his sexual desires while busily pursuing intellectual matters. In all of the writings about Freud's life, only one incident during his youth reveals something about his sexual desires:

> The story relates to his first love experience at the age of sixteen when—for the first time in his life—he revisited his birthplace. He stayed there with the Fluss family. . . . With their daughter, Gisela, a year or two younger than himself, a companion of his early childhood, he fell in love on the spot. He was too shy to communicate his feelings or even to address a single word to her, and she went away to her school after a few days. The disconsolate youth had to content himself with the fantasy of how pleasant life would have been had his parents not left that happy spot where he could have grown up a stout country lad, like the girl's brothers and married the maiden. So it was all his father's fault. (Jones, 1953, pp. 25–26)

Carl Rogers's theory stresses the importance of developing positive conceptions of ourselves and sensitivity to others' feelings. What was Rogers's youth like? He had virtually no social life outside his family, although he does not remember that this bothered him (Rogers, 1967). At the age of twelve, his family moved to a farm; apparently his mother wanted to shield her children from the evils of city life. Even though he was saddled with extensive chores at home, such as milking the cows every morning at 5 A.M., Rogers managed to make straight A's in school. He had little time for friendships and dating, and never had what could be called a real date in high school. Once Carl had to take a girl to a class dinner as a matter of custom. He vividly remembered the anxiety of having to ask her to the dinner. She agreed to go, but Rogers said he does not know what he would have done if she would have turned him down.

These experiences of Freud and Rogers are examples of how theorists' own experiences and behavior influence their thinking. Perhaps Freud's own sexual repression in adolescence contributed to his theory that all behavior has a sexual basis. And perhaps Rogers's anxieties about social contact as a young boy fostered his theoretical emphasis on warmth in social relationships.

Freud's and Rogers's theories are but two of the many perspectives on personality to be discussed in this chapter. You also will learn about the way psychologists assess personality, but before we tackle theories and assessment, an important question needs to be asked. ■

What Is Personality?

Think about yourself for a moment. What are you *really* like? Are you outgoing or shy? Aggressive or calm? Intellectual or nonintellectual? Considerate or uncaring? Try to come up with seven or eight of these traits that reflect the way you respond to your world. In compiling this list, you chose personality characteristics that you probably feel are an enduring part of your makeup as a person. For example, if you said that you are an outgoing person, wouldn't you also say that you were outgoing a year ago and that you will probably be an outgoing person one year, five years, and ten years from now? Most of us believe that we do have some enduring personality characteristics. It is these enduring, distinctive thoughts, emotions, and behaviors that characterize the way we adapt to our world and comprise what psychologists call **personality.**

The theories we describe ask why individuals respond to the same situation in different ways. For example, *why* is Sam so talkative and gregarious and Al so shy and quiet when they meet someone for the first time? *Why* is Gretchen so confident and Mary so insecure about their upcoming job interviews? Some theories state that biological and genetic factors are responsible, others argue that life experiences are more important. Some theorists argue that the way we think about ourselves is the key to understanding personality, others stress that the way we behave toward each other is more important.

The diversity of theories make understanding personality a challenging undertaking. Just when you think one theory has the correct explanation of personality, another theory will crop up and make you rethink your earlier conclusion. To keep from getting frustrated, remember that personality is a complex, multifaceted topic and no single theory has been able to account for all aspects of personality. Each theory has contributed an important piece to the personality puzzle. While the theories sometimes disagree about certain aspects of personality, much of their information is *complementary* rather than contradictory. Together they let us see the total landscape of personality in all its richness.

Psychoanalytic Theories

For psychoanalytic theorists, personality is primarily unconscious, that is, beyond awareness, and made up of structures of thought heavily colored by emotion. Psychoanalytic theorists believe that behavior is merely a surface characteristic and that to truly understand someone's personality we have to look at the symbolic meanings of behavior and the deep inner workings of the mind. Psychoanalytic theorists also stress that early experiences with parents extensively shape our personalities. These characteristics are highlighted in the main psychoanalytic theory, that of Sigmund Freud.

Freud's Theory

Loved and hated, respected and despised, for some the master, for others a fool—Sigmund Freud, whether right or wrong in his views, has been one of the most influential thinkers of the twentieth century. Freud was a medical doctor who specialized in neurology. He developed his ideas about psychoanalytic theory from his work with patients with mental problems. He was born in 1856 in Austria, and he died in London at the age of eighty-three. Most of his years were spent in Vienna, though he left the city near the end of his career because of the anti-Semitism of the Nazis.

Figure 13.1
*In a dramatic moment at the
Salpetriere Hospital in Paris, Jean-
Martin Charcot (right) demonstrates
the curative power of hypnosis.
Charcot's ideas and demonstrations
had a profound influence on the
development of Freud's theory.*

Freud was the firstborn child in a Jewish family. His mother saw him
as special and his brothers and sisters treated him as a genius. Later we will
see that one aspect of Freud's theory emphasizes a young boy's sexual attraction for his mother; it is possible this belief was derived from his own romantic attachment to his mother, who was young and beautiful and some
twenty years younger than Freud's father.

Freud's association with two physicians had a dramatic impact on the
development of his personality theory. After he graduated from medical school,
he worked with the famous French neurologist Jean-Martin Charcot, an outstanding hypnotist. Charcot treated many patients with hysteria, a disorder
in which the individual has physical symptoms but no physical causes for the
symptoms can be found. For example, a blind patient showed no neurological
evidence that could substantiate that the person actually was blind. By means
of hypnosis Charcot removed the symptoms; this suggested that psychological,
not physical, factors were responsible for the symptoms (see figure 13.1).

As a young physician in Vienna, Freud also became friends with Joseph
Breuer, who sent Freud patients and discussed cases with him. One of their
clients was a young woman named Bertha Pappenheim. When Freud and
Breuer wrote about her case, they protected her identity by calling her Anna
O. She had a number of symptoms, including impaired vision and paralysis
of the limbs. They discovered that by getting her to talk freely under hypnosis
the symptoms could be removed.

But some patients were not easy to hypnotize and sometimes the benefits
did not last long. As Freud continued to talk with many patients, he developed
the method of **psychoanalysis,** in which the patient recaptures forgotten memories without the aid of hypnosis. Freud recognized that patients' current
problems could be traced to their childhood experiences, many of which involved sexuality. He also recognized that the early experiences were not readily
available to the individual's conscious mind. Only through extensive questioning, probing, and analyzing was Freud able to put the pieces of the individual's personality together and help the individual become aware of how
these early experiences were affecting present adult behavior.

During psychoanalysis, the individual is encouraged to engage in **free association,** saying out loud whatever comes to mind no matter how trivial or embarrassing. When Freud detected that the person resisted the spontaneous flow of thoughts, he would probe further, believing this was a point that probably was related to the individual's emotional problem. Through extensive free association and persistent probing, Freud might determine that a woman's blindness was caused by seeing her mother raped when the patient was only four years old. Or he might determine that a young man's hand paralysis was caused by his father's whippings when he caught the patient masturbating as a young boy. Too painful and tension-filled to face, these early experiences came out in disguised form later in life.

In Freud's view, much more of our mind is unconscious than conscious. He envisioned our mind as a huge iceberg, with the massive part below the surface of the water being the unconscious part. Freud said that each of our lives is filled with tension and conflict; to reduce this tension and conflict we keep information locked in our unconscious mind. For Freud, the unconscious mind held the key to understanding behavior. Freud believed that even trivial behaviors have special significance when the unconscious forces behind them are revealed. A twitch, a doodle, a joke, a smile—each may have an unconscious reason for appearing. They often slip into our behavior without our awareness. For example, Barbara is kissing and hugging Tom, whom she is to marry in several weeks. She says, "Oh, *Jeff,* I love you so much." Tom pushes her away and says, "Why did you call me Jeff? I thought you didn't think about him anymore. We need to have a talk!" You probably can think of times when these so-called *Freudian slips* came out in your own behavior.

Freud also believed that dreams hold important clues to our behavior. Recall from chapter 4 that Freud said dreams are unconscious representations of the conflict and tension in our everyday life. Since the conflicts and tension are too painful to handle consciously, they come out in our unconscious dreams. Just as with free associations during psychoanalysis, much of dream content is symbolic and disguised, requiring extensive analysis and probing to be understood.

The Structure of Personality

Freud (1917) believed that personality had three structures: the id, the ego, and the superego. One way to understand the three structures is to consider them as three rulers of a country (Singer, 1984). The id is king or queen, the ego is prime minister, and the superego is high priest. The id is an absolute monarch, owed complete obedience; it is spoiled, willful, and self-centered. The id wants what it wants right now, not later. The ego as prime minister has the job of getting things done; it is tuned into reality and is responsive to society's demands. The superego as high priest is concerned with right and wrong; the id may be greedy and needs to be told that nobler purposes should be pursued.

The **id** is the reservoir of psychic energy and instincts that perpetually presses us to satisfy our basic needs—food, sex, and avoidance of pain, for example. In Freud's view, the id is unconscious; it has no contact with reality. The id works according to the **pleasure principle,** that is, it *always* seeks pleasure and avoids pain. Freud believed the id is the only part of personality present at birth; even in adults the id acts like a selfish infant, demanding immediate gratification.

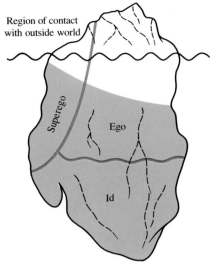

Region of contact
with outside world

Figure 13.2
*Conscious and unconscious processes.
This rather odd-looking diagram
illustrates Freud's belief that most of
the important personality processes
occur below the level of conscious
awareness. In examining people's
conscious thoughts and their
behaviors, we can see some reflections
of the ego and the superego. But,
whereas the ego and superego are
partly conscious and partly
unconscious, the primitive id is the
unconscious, totally submerged part of
the "iceberg."*

It would be a dangerous and scary world if our personalities were all id. As the young child develops, he learns that he cannot eat twenty-six popsicles; sometimes he is not even allowed to eat one. He also learns that he has to use the toilet instead of his diaper. As the child experiences the demands and constraints of reality, a new structure of personality is formed—the **ego.** The ego abides by the **reality principle;** it tries to bring the individual pleasure within the boundaries of reality. Few of us are cold-blooded killers or wild wheeler-dealers; we take into account obstacles to our satisfaction that exist in our world. We recognize that our sexual and aggressive impulses cannot go unrestrained. The ego helps us test reality—to see how far we can go without getting into trouble and hurting ourselves.

While the id is completely unconscious, the ego is partly conscious. It houses our higher mental functions—reasoning, problem solving, and decision making, for example. For this reason, the ego is referred to as the executive branch of the personality; like an executive in a company, it makes the rational decisions that helps the company succeed.

The id and ego have no morality. They do not take into account whether something is right or wrong. This is left to the third structure of personality, the **superego,** referred to as the moral branch of personality. Think of the superego as what we often refer to as our "conscience." Like the id, the superego does not consider reality; it doesn't deal with what is realistic, only with whether the id's sexual and aggressive impulses can be satisfied in moral terms. You probably are beginning to sense that both the id and the superego make life rough for the ego. Your ego might say, "I only will have sex occasionally and be sure to take the proper precautions because I don't want the intrusion of a child in the development of my career." But your id is saying, "I want to be satisfied; sex is pleasureable." And your superego is at work too, "I feel guilty about having sex."

Remember that Freud considered personality to be like an iceberg; most of personality exists below our level of awareness, just as the massive part of the iceberg is beneath the surface of the water. Figure 13.2 illustrates this analogy and how extensive the unconscious part of our mind is, in Freud's view.

Defense Mechanisms

How does the ego resolve the conflict between its demands for reality, the wishes of the id, and the constraints of the superego? In Freud's view, the conflicting demands of the personality structures produce anxiety. For example, when the ego blocks the pleasureable pursuits of the id an inner anxiety is felt. This diffuse, distressed state develops when the ego senses that the id is going to cause some harm to the individual. The anxiety alerts the ego to resolve the conflict by means of **defense mechanisms,** which protect the ego and reduce the anxiety produced by the conflict.

Freud thought that the most powerful and pervasive defense mechanism is **repression;** it works to push unacceptable id impulses out of our awareness and back into our unconscious mind. Repression is the foundation from which all other defense mechanisms work; the goal of every defense mechanism is to *repress* or push threatening impulses out of awareness. Freud said that our early childhood experiences, many of which he believed were sexually laden, are too threatening and conflictual for us to deal with consciously. We reduce the anxiety of this conflict through the defense mechanism of repression.

Among the other defense mechanisms we use to protect the ego and reduce anxiety are rationalization, displacement, sublimation, projection, reaction formation, and regression. **Rationalization** occurs when the real motive for an individual's behavior is not accepted by the ego. The real motive is replaced by a sort of cover motive. For example, you are studying hard for an exam tomorrow. You are really getting into the material when a friend calls and says he is having a party in an hour. He tells you that a certain person you find attractive will be there. You know that if you don't stay in your room and study you will do poorly on tomorrow's exam. But you tell yourself, "I did well on the first test in this class and I have been studying hard all semester; it's time I have some fun." So you go to the party. The real motive is going to the party, having fun, and seeing the attractive person. But a little voice within you says that if that is the reason then you should stay home and study. Your ego now steps in and fixes the motive to look better. Your ego says that you have worked hard all semester and you need to unwind, and that you will probably do better on the exam if you relax a little—a rationale that is more acceptable than just going to have fun and meet the desirable other person.

Displacement is the shift of unacceptable feelings from one object to another, more acceptable object. For example, a woman is harassed by her boss. She gets angry but she knows she can't take the anger out on the boss because she might get fired. When she gets home that evening, she yells at her husband, thus transferring her feelings toward her boss to her husband.

Sublimation occurs when a socially useful course of action replaces a distasteful one. Sublimation is actually a type of displacement. For example, an individual with strong sexual urges may turn them into socially approved behavior by becoming an artist who paints nudes.

Projection occurs when we attribute our own shortcomings, problems, and faults to others. For example, a man who has a strong desire to have an extramarital affair keeps accusing his wife of flirting with other men. The manipulative businesswoman who takes advantage of everyone to push herself up the corporate ladder tells her associate, "Everybody around here is so manipulative; they never consider my feelings." When we can't face our own unwanted feelings, we *project* them onto others and see others as having the trait.

Reaction formation occurs when we express an unacceptable impulse by transforming it into its opposite. For example, an individual who is attracted to the brutality of war becomes a peace activist. Or a person who fears his sexual urges becomes a religious zealot.

Regression involves behaving in a way that characterized a previous developmental level. When anxiety becomes too great for us, we revert to an early behavior that gave us pleasure. For example, a woman may run home to her mother every time she and her husband have a big argument.

Two final points about defense mechanisms need to be underscored. First, they are unconscious; we are not aware we are calling on them to protect our ego and reduce anxiety. Second, when used in moderation or on a temporary basis, defense mechanisms are not necessarily unhealthy. For example, recall from chapter 12 how such defense mechanisms as denial can help an individual cope with impending death. For the most part, though, we should not let defense mechanisms dominate our behavior and prevent us from facing the demands of reality.

(a)

(b)

(c)

(d)

(e)

Freud said we go through five stages of psychosexual development. In the oral stage (a), pleasure centers around the mouth. In the anal stage (b), pleasure focuses on the anus—the nature of toilet training is important here. In the phallic stage (c), pleasure involves the genitals—the opposite-sex parent becomes a love object here. In the latency stage (d), the child represses sexual urges—same-sex friendship is prominent. In the genital stage (e), sexual reawakening takes place—the source of pleasure now becomes someone outside of the family.

The Development of Personality

As Freud listened to, probed, and analyzed his patients, he became convinced that their problems were the result of experiences early in life. Freud believed that we go through five stages of psychosexual development, and that at each stage of development we experience pleasure in one part of the body more than others. He called these body parts **erogenous zones** because of their pleasure-giving qualities.

Freud thought that our adult personality was determined by the way conflicts between these early sources of pleasure—the mouth, the anus, and then the genitals—and the demands of reality were resolved. When these conflicts are not resolved, the individual may become fixated at a particular stage

of development. **Fixation** is closely linked with the defense mechanism of regression. Fixation occurs when an individual's needs are under- or overgratified. For example, a parent may wean a child too early, be too strict in toilet training the child, punish the child for masturbation, or smother the child with warmth. We will return to the idea of fixation and how it may show up in an adult's personality, but first we need to learn more about the early stages of personality development.

During the first twelve to eighteen months of life, the activities of the infant that bring the greatest amount of pleasure center around the mouth; in the **oral stage** of development chewing, sucking, and biting are chief sources of pleasure. These actions reduce tension in the infant.

The period from about one and a half years to three years of life is called the **anal stage** because the child's greatest pleasure involves the anus, or the eliminative functions associated with it. In Freud's view, the exercise of anal muscles reduces tension.

The **phallic stage** of development occurs approximately between the ages of three and six; its name comes from the word *phallus,* a label for penis. During the phallic stage, pleasure focuses on the genitals as the child discovers that self-manipulation is enjoyable.

■■■■■■■■■■■■■■■■■■

Psychology 13.1

Little Hans, His Widdler, and Phobia

■ A man wrote to Freud about his son Hans, who had developed a nervous disorder. The symptoms were a fear of going into the streets, depression in the evening, and a fear that a horse would bite him.

At the age of three, Hans showed a lively interest in the part of his body that he described as his "widdler." When he was three and a half, his mother caught him with his hand on it. She threatened him: "If you do that, I shall send for Dr. A. to cut off your widdler. And then what will you widdle with?" Hans replied, "With my bottom." Hans made many other remarks about widdlers in animals and humans when he was between three and four years old, including questions directed at his mother and father about whether they had widdlers. For example,

Mother: "What are you staring like that for?"
Hans: "I was only looking to see if you'd got a widdler, too."
Mother: "Of course. Didn't you know that."
Hans: "No, I thought you were so big you'd have a widdler as big as a horse."

Freud believed that Little Hans, as the boy was called, was a classic example of how sexual urges underlie our personality. Freud gave special importance to an incident when the boy was four years old. As Hans's mother was drying and powdering him after his bath, he asked if she would put her finger on his widdler. When she objected that such an act would be improper, Hans laughed and said, "But it's great fun." Freud believed that Hans was trying to seduce his mother.

Freud believed that Hans was afraid of horses because he was fascinated by their widdlers. Freud

told Han's father to tell the boy that women do not have widdlers.

One day Hans and his father went to the zoo. Hans showed a fear of giraffes, elephants, and all other large animals. Hans denied his father's statement that he was afraid of the big animals because they had big widdlers.

Later Hans reported this dream: "In the night there was a big giraffe in the room and a crumpled one; and the big one called out because I took the crumpled one away from it. Then it stopped calling out; and then I sat down on top of the crumpled one."

After talking to the boy, the father informed Freud that the dream was a matrimonial scene transposed into the giraffe's life. Hans developed an urge for his mother and came into the room for that reason. The father believed the whole thing was a continuation of Hans's fear of horses. The dream was thought to

In Freud's view the phallic stage has a special importance in personality development because it is during this period that the **Oedipus complex** appears. This name comes from Greek mythology, in which Oedipus, the son of the King of Thebes, unwittingly killed his father and married his mother. In the Oedipus complex, the young child develops an intense desire to replace the parent of the same sex and enjoy the affections of the opposite-sexed parent. To learn more about the Oedipus complex, turn to Psychology 13.1 where you will read about a fascinating case in Freud's practice.

How is the Oedipus complex resolved? At about five to six years of age, children recognize that their same-sex parent might punish them for their incestuous wishes. To reduce this conflict, the child identifies with the same-sex parent, striving to be like him or her. If the conflict is not resolved, though, the individual may become fixated at the phallic stage. Table 13.1 reveals some possible links between adult personality characteristics and fixation, sublimation, and reaction formation involving the phallic stage, as well as the oral and anal stage.

be related to Hans's habit of occasionally getting into bed in spite of his father's disapproval. Freud suggested that sitting down on the crumpled giraffe meant taking possession of the mother. Further support for this belief came when Hans called his mother a big giraffe the next day. Freud said that Hans wanted to replace his father, whom he saw as a rival for the mother's affection, and take possession of his mother. Freud believed that Hans transferred his fear of his father onto horses.

But Freud's interpretation of Little Hans's phobia has not gone uncriticized. Joseph Wolpe and Stanley Rachman (1960) agree that Little Hans enjoyed being with his mother, but that no evidence exists to suggest he wanted to copulate with her. Hans was told repeatedly that he was afraid of his father and that there was a relation between the horses and his father; Hans always denied this, though.

Freud thought that Hans developed his phobia to keep him close to his mother, yet Hans still got anxious when he went outside for walks with his mother accompanying him. Freud also argued that the reason Hans's fear of horses eventually subsided was that he resolved his Oedipus complex and identified with his father.

Wolpe and Rachman say no evidence exists to show that anything like an Oedipus complex was ever present. They believe Hans's phobia can be explained by learning theory. Hans was a sensitive child who was moved by people who wept in his presence; long before his phobia developed he became very anxious when he saw the horses on a merry-go-round beaten. Wolpe and Rachman believe that an incident Freud referred to as minor was the cause of the entire disturbance.

The incident involved Hans's observation of a horse pulling a bus falling down.

Hans: "I'm most afraid when the bus comes along."
Father: "Why? Because they are so big?"
Hans: "No. Because once a horse in a bus fell."
Father: "When?"
Hans: "When the horse in the bus fell down, it gave me such a fright really; that was when I got the nonsense."

Hans (just like Little Albert in John Watson's conditioning experiment with rats, described in chapter 5) reacted with anxiety not only to the original conditioned stimulus (horses) but to other related objects (horse-drawn buses, vans, and features of horses).

Table 13.1 Possible Links Between Adult Personality Characteristics and Fixation at Oral, Anal, and Phallic Stages

Stage	Adult extensions	Sublimations	Reaction formations
Oral	Smoking, eating, kissing, oral hygiene, drinking, chewing gum	Seeking knowledge, humor, wit, sarcasm, being a food or wine expert	Speech purist, food faddist, prohibitionist, dislike of milk
Anal	Notable interest in one's bowel movements, love of bathroom humor, extreme messiness	Interest in painting or sculpture, being overly giving, great interest in statistics	Extreme disgust with feces, fear of dirt, prudishness, irritability
Phallic	Heavy reliance on masturbation, flirtatiousness, expressions of virility	Interest in poetry, love of love, interest in acting, striving for success	Puritanical attitude toward sex, excessive modesty

From *Introduction to personality* by Jerry Phares. Copyright © 1984 Scott, Foresman and Company. Reprinted by permission.

In the **latency stage,** occurring between approximately six years of age and puberty, the child represses all interest in sexual urges, instead showing more interest in developing intellectual and social skills. This activity channels much of the child's energy into emotionally safe areas and aids the child in forgetting the highly stressful conflicts of the phallic stage.

The **genital stage,** which occurs from puberty on, is a time of sexual reawakening; the source of sexual pleasure now becomes someone outside of the family. Freud believed that unresolved conflicts with parents reemerged during adolescence. When resolved, the individual was capable of developing a mature love relationship and functioning independently as an adult.

Psychoanalytic Dissenters and Revisionists

Because Freud explored so many new and uncharted regions of personality, it is not surprising that many individuals thought his views needed to be replaced or revised. Sexuality, early experience, social factors, and the unconscious mind are four areas in which Freud's critics believe his views were misguided (e.g., Adler, 1927; Erikson, 1968; Fromm, 1947; Horney, 1937; Jung, 1917; Kohut, 1977; Rapaport, 1967; Sullivan, 1953). The key objections to Freud's theory are as follows:

> Sexuality is not the pervasive underlying force behind personality that Freud believed it to be.
>
> The first five years of life are not as powerful in shaping adult personality as Freud thought; later experiences deserve more attention.
>
> Social factors are more important than Freud believed. For example, Harry Stack Sullivan (1953) emphasized that personality cannot be studied apart from social circumstances; personality characteristics actually describe an individual's way of interacting with the social world—nurturant, introverted, or assertive, for instance.
>
> The ego and conscious thought processes play more dominant roles in our personality than Freud gave them credit; we are not wed forever to the id and its instinctual, unconscious clutches. The ego has a separate line of development than the id; viewed in this way, achievement, thinking, and reasoning are not always tied to sexual impulses as Freud thought.

Carl Jung (1875–1961) and Alfred Adler (1870–1937), contemporaries of Freud, were especially critical of Freud's views. Unlike most of the psychoanalytic dissenters, Jung actually believed that Freud underplayed the role of the unconscious in our personality. Jung thought that the roots of personality go back to the dawn of human existence. Every human has a common heritage that influences the way we think, feel, and act, he said. Jung called this common heritage the **collective unconscious;** it is impersonal and is the same in each of us. These common experiences have made a deep, permanent impression in the human mind; Jung called these impressions **archetypes.**

Two common archetypes are *anima* (woman) and *animus* (man); each of us has a passive "femininity" and an assertive "masculinity," said Jung. We also have an archetype for the self, which is represented in the art of many different generations. For example, the mandala, a figure within a circle, has been used so often Jung took it to represent the archtype of the self (see figure 13.3).

Figure 13.3
A mandala, which Jung believed was the symbol for the archetype of self.

Alfred Adler believed that Freud gave far too much attention to the unconscious aspects of personality. From Adler's perspective, we have the ability to consciously monitor and direct our lives. Like Jung, Adler has a number of disciples today (Silverman & Corsini, 1984). Adler's individual psychology stresses that people are striving toward a positive being and that they create their own goals. The individual's adaptation is enhanced by developing social interests and reducing feelings of inferiority.

Evaluating the Psychoanalytic Theories

While psychoanalytic theories have become heterogeneous, nonetheless, they share some core principles. Our personality is determined not only by current experiences but by those from early in our life as well. The principles that early experiences are important determinants of personality and that we can better understand personality by examining it developmentally have withstood the test of time.

The belief that environmental experiences are mentally transformed and represented in the mind likewise continues to receive considerable attention. Psychoanalytic theorists forced psychologists to recognize that the mind is not all consciousness; our minds have an unconscious portion that influences our behavior. Psychoanalytic theorists' emphasis on the importance of conflict and anxiety requires us to consider the dark side of our existence, not just its bright side. Adjustment is not always an easy task, and the individual's inner world often conflicts with the outer demands of reality. And finally, psychoanalytic theories continue to force psychologists to study more than the experimental, laboratory topics of sensation, perception, and learning; personality and adjustment are rightful and important topics of psychological inquiry as well.

However, the main concepts of psychoanalytic theories have been difficult to test. As we discovered in the case of Little Hans, inference and interpretation are involved in determining whether psychoanalytic ideas are accurate. Researchers have not successfully investigated such key concepts as repression in the laboratory.

Much of the data used to support psychoanalytic theories have come from patients' reconstruction of the past, often the distant past (adults' perceptions of their early child experiences) and are of doubtful accuracy. Other data come from clinicians' subjective evaluations of clients; in such cases it is easy for the clinician to see what she expects because of the theory she holds.

Some psychologists object that Freud overemphasized the importance of sexuality in understanding personality, and that Freud and Jung placed so much faith in the unconscious mind's ability to control behavior.

The psychoanalytic perspectives also provide a model of the person that is too negative and pessimistic. We are not born into the world with only a bundle of sexual and aggressive instincts; our compliance with the external demands of reality does not always conflict with our biological needs.

Psychoanalytic theories overdramatize early experiences within the family as determinants of personality. We retain the capacity for change and adaptation throughout the human life cycle.

You should have some sense of what personality is and the themes of psychoanalytic theories. A summary of these ideas is presented in concept table 13.1. Next, a view of personality *very* different from the psychoanalytic theories is discussed.

Concept Table 13.1

The Nature of Personality and Psychoanalytic Theories		
Concept	**Processes/related ideas**	**Characteristics/description**
Personality	Its nature	Our enduring thoughts, emotions, and behaviors that characterize the way we adapt. A key question is why individuals respond to the same situation in different ways.
Freud's psychoanalytic theory	The man and the unconscious mind	Freud was one of the most influential thinkers in the twentieth century. He developed psychoanalysis and observed that free association provides insight into an individual's emotional problems. He believed most of our mind is unconscious.
	The structure of personality	Freud said personality has three structures: id, ego, and superego. The id is the reservoir of psychic energy that tries to satisfy our basic needs; it is unconscious and operates according to the pleasure principle. The ego tries to provide us with pleasure by operating within the boundaries of reality. The superego is the moral branch of personality.
	Defense mechanisms	The conflicting demands of personality structures produce anxiety; defense mechanisms protect the ego and reduce this anxiety. Repression, the most pervasive defense mechanism, pushes unacceptable id impulses back into the unconscious mind. Other defense mechanisms include rationalization, displacement, sublimation, projection, reaction formation, and regression. Defense mechanisms are unconscious.
	The development of personality	Freud was convinced that problems develop because of childhood experiences. He said we go through five psychosexual stages: oral, anal, phallic, latency, and genital. If our needs are under- or overgratified at a particular stage, we can become fixated at that stage. During the phallic stage, the Oedipus complex is a major source of conflict.
Psychoanalytic dissenters and revisionists	Criticisms of Freud's view	Too much emphasis on sexuality and the first five years of life; too little attention to social factors and the strength of the ego and conscious thought processes.
	Jung and Adler	Jung thought Freud underplayed the role of the unconscious mind; he developed the concept of the collective unconscious. Adler said Freud gave the unconscious too much power; he says we have the ability to consciously control our behavior.
Evaluating the psychoanalytic theories	Their nature	Strengths are an emphasis on the past, the developmental course of personality, mental representation of environment, unconscious mind, emphasis on conflict, and influence on psychology as a discipline. Weaknesses are the difficulty in testing main concepts, lack of an empirical data base and overreliance on reports of the past, too much emphasis on sexuality and the unconscious mind, a negative view of human nature, and too much power given to early experience.

Behavioral and Social Learning Perspectives

Tom is engaged to marry Ann. Both have warm, friendly personalities and they enjoy being with each other. Psychoanalytic theorists would say that their warm, friendly personalities are derived from long-standing relationships with their parents, especially their early childhood experiences. They also would argue that the reason for their attraction is unconscious; they are unaware of how their biological heritage and early life experiences have been carried forward to influence their adult personalities.

Psychologists from the behavioral and social learning perspectives would observe Tom and Ann and see something quite different. They would examine their experiences, especially their most recent ones, to understand the reason for the attraction. Tom would be described as rewarding Ann's behavior, and vice versa, for example. No reference would be made to unconscious thoughts, the Oedipus complex, defense mechanisms, and so on.

Remember from chapters 1 and 5 that behaviorists believe psychology should examine only what can be directly observed and measured. At approximately the same time Freud was interpreting his patients' unconscious minds through early childhood experiences, behaviorists such as Ivan Pavlov and John B. Watson were conducting detailed observations of behavior under controlled laboratory conditions. Out of the behavioral tradition grew the belief that personality is observable behavior, learned through experiences with the environment. The two versions of the behavioral approach that are prominent today are the behavioral view of B. F. Skinner and the social learning perspective.

Skinner's Behaviorism

Skinner did not need the mind, unconscious or conscious, to explain an individual's personality. For him, an individual's personality was the individual's behavior. Behaviorists such as Skinner believe our personalities (behavior) are not as consistent as most personality theorists argue; behaviorists say that we do not have to resort to biological or internal aspects of the person to explain behavior. Because of such beliefs, some psychologists say that including Skinner among personality theorists is like inviting a wolf to a party of lambs (Phares, 1984). Behaviorists have been criticized for taking the *person* out of personality and viewing the organism as "empty." Critics say that if we adopted the behavioral approach we might just as well substitute a walking sack of potatoes for the person.

From the behavioral perspective, where is personality located and how is it determined? For Skinner, personality is simply the individual's observed, overt behavior; it does not include internal traits or thoughts. For example, observations of Sam reveal that his behavior is shy, achievement-oriented, and caring. These behaviors represent his personality from the behavioral perspective. Why is Sam's personality, or behavior, this way? For Skinner, the rewards and punishments in Sam's environment have shaped him into a shy, achievement-oriented, and caring individual. Because of interactions with family members, friends, teachers, and others, Sam has *learned* to behave in this fashion.

Behaviorists who support Skinner's perspective would say that Sam's shy, achievement-oriented, and caring behavior is not consistent and enduring. For example, Sam is uninhibited on Saturday night with friends at a bar, unmotivated to achieve heights of greatness in English class, and occasionally nasty toward his sister. The issue of the consistency of personality is an important one; we will discuss this on a number of occasions later in the chapter.

Since behaviorists believe that personality is learned and often changes according to environmental experiences and situations, it follows that by rearranging experiences and situations the individual's personality can be changed. For the behaviorist, shy behavior can be changed into outgoing behavior; aggressive behavior can be shaped into docile behavior; lethargic, boring behavior can be turned into enthusiastic, interesting behavior. Much more about the behavioral techniques used to accomplish these changes in "personality" are discussed in chapter 15.

Social Learning Theory

Some psychologists believe the behaviorists basically are right when they say that personality is learned and influenced strongly by environmental experiences. But they believe Skinner went too far in declaring that cognition is unimportant in understanding the nature of personality. The group of psychologists who emphasize behavior, environment, *and* cognition as the key factors in personality are called social learning theorists.

The social learning theorists say we are not mindless robots, responding mechanically to others in our environment. And we are not like weather vanes, behaving like a Communist in the presence of a Communist or like a John Bircher in the presence of a John Bircher. Rather, we think, reason, imagine, plan, expect, interpret, believe, value, and compare. When others try to control us, our values and beliefs allow us to resist their control.

Albert Bandura (1977, 1986) and Walter Mischel (1973, 1984) are the main architects of the contemporary version of social learning theory, which was labeled *cognitive* social learning theory by Mischel. Recall from chapter 5 that Bandura believes much of our learning occurs by observing what others do. Through observational learning we cognitively represent the behavior of others and then possibly adopt this behavior ourselves. For example, a young boy may observe his father's aggressive outbursts and hostile interchanges with people; when observed with his peers, the young boy's style of interaction is highly aggressive, showing the same characteristics as his father's behavior. Or, a young female executive adopts the dominant and sarcastic style of her boss. When observed interacting with one of her subordinates, the young woman says, "I need this work immediately if not sooner; you are so far behind you think you are ahead!" Social learning theorists believe we acquire a wide range of such behaviors, thoughts, and feelings through observing others' behavior; these observations form an important part of our personality.

Social learning theorists also differ from the behavioral view of Skinner by emphasizing that we can regulate and control our own behavior, despite our changing environment. For example, another young female executive who observed her boss behave in a dominant and sarcastic manner toward employees found the behavior distasteful and went out of her way to be encouraging and supportive toward her subordinates. Someone tries to persuade you to join a particular social club on campus and makes you an enticing offer. You reflect about the offer, consider your interests and beliefs, and make the decision not to join. Your *cognition* (your thoughts) leads you to control your behavior and resist environmental influence in this instance.

Like the behavioral approach of Skinner, the social learning view emphasizes the importance of empirical research in studying personality. This research has focused on the processes that explain personality—the social and cognitive factors that influence what we are like as people. One process that Walter Mischel believes is important in understanding an individual's personality is delay of gratification, which is the ability to defer immediate gratification for more desirable future gratification. For example, think about how important delay of gratification is in school; you must control your behavior and resist the temptation to slack off and have a good time now so you will be rewarded with good grades later. Again, the point is that we are capable of controlling our behavior rather than being influenced by others. To learn more about Mischel's ideas on delay of gratification and to discover the way social learning theorists conduct research on personality, read Psychology 13.2.

Walter Mischel, professor of psychology at Stanford University, is a main figure in the development of the cognitive social learning theory of personality.

Delaying Gratification for Marshmallows and Pretzels

■ Four-year-old Barbara is told that she can have one marshmallow now or two marshmallows if she waits until the experimenter returns. What might influence Barbara's choice? Mischel believes that one factor is whether or not the rewards are visible. For example, in one investigation preschool-aged children were willing to wait ten times longer when the rewards (e.g., marshmallows) were hidden from view than when they could be readily observed (see figure 13.A) (Mischel, Ebbesen, & Zeiss, 1972). This suggests that children can gain control over their ability to delay gratification by keeping desired rewards out of sight.

Another way children might learn to delay gratification is to mentally represent the desired goal objects in different ways. For example, when children mentally represented the rewards in consummatory, or "hot," ways (such as focusing on their taste— thinking how yummy, crunchy, and tasty pretzels are), they delayed gratification much less than children who mentally represented the rewards in nonconsummatory, or "cold," ways (such as thinking of pretzels as sticks or tiny logs) (Mischel & Baker, 1975). These experiments showed that how we mentally represent the outcomes of a situation influences our ability to delay gratification.

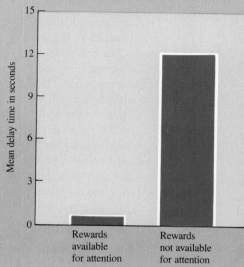

Figure 13.A
Delay of gratification as a function of the desired goal object being available for attention.

Social learning research focuses primarily on how cognitive and situational factors change the individual's behavior; the emphasis is on *change* and the processes responsible for the change, not on stable individual differences between people. Recently, though, Mischel has turned his attention to the important question of how enduring is the ability to delay gratification and how stable are the differences between individuals.

Mischel and his colleagues have demonstrated that a preschool child's ability to delay gratification for pretzels or marshmallows is related to his socially competent behavior some twelve years later (Mischel, 1984;

Mischel, Peake, & Zeiss, 1984). For example, the preschool child who is willing to wait to get two marshmallows later instead of one right now is observed to be attentive and able to concentrate during adolescence.

Mischel points out that although his research shows that the preschool child who delays behavior in one situation may not do so in even slightly different contexts (e.g., if rewards are visible), this does not mean the child's tendency to delay gratification will not endure. The results of his laboratory research and his longitudinal investigation of individual differences portray personality as *both* adaptive to situations and consistent over time.

Evaluating the Behavioral and Social Learning Perspectives

The behavioral and social learning perspectives emphasize that environmental experiences and situational influences determine personality. These approaches have fostered a scientific climate for understanding personality that highlights the observation of behavior. The social learning perspective emphasizes both environmental influences and cognitive processes in explaining personality; this view also suggests individuals have the ability to control their environment.

The criticisms of the behavioral and social learning perspectives sometimes are directed at the behavioral view alone and at other times at both approaches. The behavioral view is criticized for ignoring the importance of cognition in personality and placing too much importance on the role of environmental experiences. Both approaches have been described as being too concerned with change and situational influences on personality and not paying adequate tribute to the enduring qualities of personality. Both views are said to ignore the biological determinants of personality. Both are labeled reductionistic, which means they look at only one or two components of personality rather than at how all of the pieces fit together. And critics have charged that the behavioral and social learning views are too mechanical. By being overly concerned with several minute pieces of personality, the most exciting and rich dimensions of personality are missed, say the detractors. This latter criticism—that the creative, spontaneous, and human characteristics of personality are missing from the behavioral and social learning approaches—has been made on numerous occasions by adherents of the humanistic approach, which we consider next.

The Phenomenological and Humanistic Perspectives

Remember our example of the engaged couple, Tom and Ann, who were described as having warm, friendly personalities. Phenomenological and humanistic psychologists would describe their warm, friendly personalities as reflecting their inner self; they would emphasize that a key to understanding their attraction is their positive perception of each other. Tom and Ann are not viewed as controlling each other's behavior; rather they have determined their own course of action and each freely chosen to marry. No recourse to biological instincts or unconscious thoughts as determinants of their attraction occurs in the phenomenological and humanistic perspectives.

The **phenomenological perspective** stresses the importance of our perceptions of ourselves and our world in understanding personality; the approach centers on the belief that for each individual, reality is what is *perceived*. The most widely known phenomenological approach to personality is the **humanistic perspective,** which has stressed the importance of self-perceptions, inner experiences, self-determination, and self-confidence. Humanistic psychologists emphasize the positive qualities of individuals, believing they have the ability to handle stress, control their lives, and achieve what they desire. Each of us has the ability to break through and understand ourselves and our world; we can burst the cocoon and become a butterfly, say the humanists.

You may be able to sense that the phenomenological and humanistic approaches provide stark contrasts to the psychoanalytic view of personality, which is based on conflict and little faith in the individual's ability to understand his personality, and to the behavioral view, which emphasizes that an individual's behavior is determined by rewards and punishments from others. Two of the leading architects of the phenomenological and humanistic approaches are Carl Rogers and Abraham Maslow.

Carl Rogers's Approach

Like Freud, Rogers (1961) began his inquiry about human nature with troubled personalities. Rogers explored the human potential for change; in the knotted, anxious, defensive verbal stream of his clients, he concluded that individuals are prevented from becoming who they are.

Our Conditioned, Controlling World

Rogers believed that most individuals have considerable difficulty accepting their own true feelings, which are innately positive. As we grow up, significant others condition us to move away from these positive feelings. Our parents, siblings, teachers, and peers place constraints and contingencies on our behavior; too often we hear, "Don't do that," "You didn't do that right," "How could you be so stupid?" and "You didn't try hard enough." When we don't do something right, we often get punished. And parents may even threaten to take away their love. Thus, Rogers believed each of us is a victim of **conditional positive regard,** meaning that love and praise often are not given unless we conform to parental or social standards. The result is that our self-esteem is lowered.

These constraints and negative feedback continue during our adult lives. The result is that our relationships either carry the dark cloud of conflict or we conform to what others want; too infrequently are we allowed to express ourselves positively. As we struggle to live up to society's standards, we distort and devalue our true self. And we may even completely lose our sense of self by mirroring what others want (Rogers, 1961).

The Self

Through the individual's experiences with the world a self emerges—this is the "I" or "me" of your existence. Rogers did not believe that all aspects of the self are conscious, but he did believe they are all accessible to consciousness. The self is construed as a whole; it consists of one's self-perceptions (how attractive I am, how well I get along with others, how good an athlete I am) and the values we attach to these perceptions (good-bad, worthy-unworthy, for example).

Rogers also considered the congruence between the real self, that is, the self as it really is as a result of our experiences, and the ideal self, which is the self we would like to be (figure 13.4 shows a portrait that reflects the ideal and real self). The greater the discrepancy between the real self and the ideal self, the more maladjusted we will be, said Rogers. To improve our adjustment we can develop more positive perceptions of our real self, not worry so much about what others want, and increase our positive experiences in the world. In such ways our real self and ideal self will be closer.

Figure 13.4
Half naked, half clothed, Picasso's 1932 portrayal of a Girl Before a Mirror *reflects the twin images of Carl Rogers's ideal and real selves.*
(Oil on canvas, 64 × 51¼ in. Collection, The Museum of Modern Art, New York. Gift of Mrs. Simon Guggenheim.)

Unconditional Positive Regard

Rogers believed that as we grow, we sense that a positive regard for ourselves feels good. This need for positive self-regard requires love, acceptance, warmth, and respect from significant others in our world. Unfortunately, the positive regard coming from others has strings attached; do this and you will get a dollar, do that and you will get a hug. Rogers believed these **conditions of worth** become a part of us and tell us what kinds of behavior will bring us positive regard.

But Rogers thought that each of us should be valued regardless of our behavior. Even when our behavior is obnoxious, below acceptable standards, or inappropriate, we need the respect, comfort, and love of others. When these positive behaviors are given without contingency this is known as **unconditional positive regard.** Rogers believed strongly that unconditional positive regard elevates our self-worth and positive self-regard. Unconditional positive regard is directed to the individual as a person of worth and dignity, not to his behavior, which may not deserve positive regard (Rogers, 1974).

The Fully Functioning Person

Rogers (1980) stressed the importance of becoming a fully functioning person. What is a fully functioning person like? She is open to experience, is not very defensive, is aware of and sensitive to the self and the external world, and for the most part has a harmonious relationship with others. A discrepancy between our real self and our ideal self may occur; others may try to control us; and our world may have too little unconditional positive regard; but Rogers believed that we are highly resilient and capable of becoming a fully functioning person. He believed that our good side could not be kept down.

This self-actualizing tendency of ours is reflected in Roger's comparison of a person with a plant he once observed on the coastline of northern California. Rogers was looking out at the waves beating furiously against the jagged rocks, shooting mountains of spray into the air. Rogers noticed a tiny palm tree on the rocks, no more than two or three feet high, taking the pounding of the breakers. The plant was fragile and top-heavy; it seemed clear that the waves would crush the tiny specimen. A wave would crunch the plant, bending its slender trunk almost flat and whipping its leaves in a torrent of spray. Yet the moment the wave passed, the plant was erect, tough, and resilient once again. It was incredible that the plant could take this incessant pounding hour after hour, week after week, possibly even year after year, all the time nourishing itself, maintaining its position, and growing. In this tiny palmlike seaweed Rogers saw the tenacity of life, the forward thrust of life, and the ability of a living thing to push into a hostile environment and not only hold its own, but adapt, develop, and become itself. So it is with each of us, in Rogers view (Rogers, 1963).

Abraham Maslow's Approach

Abraham Maslow was one of the most powerful forces behind the humanistic movement in psychology. He called the humanistic approach the "third force" in psychology, that is, an important alternative to the psychoanalytic and behavioral forces. Maslow pointed out that psychoanalytic theories place too much emphasis on disturbed individuals and their conflicts. Behaviorists ignore the person all together, he said.

Maslow (1971) set out to chart the human potential of creative, talented, and healthy people. These people, he believed, strive for self-actualization and try to be the best they possibly can be. Like Rogers, Maslow said each of us has a basic goodness, a drive to be something positive; each of us has the capacity for love, joy, and self-development.

In chapter 11, Maslow's hierarchy of human needs was described. Self-actualization was listed as the highest of the needs and could not be satisfied until other lower needs were met. As shown in figure 13.5, we have added a new label to Maslow's well-known hierarchy of needs—metaneeds.

Maslow believed needs come in two basic forms: deficiency needs and metaneeds (or growth needs). The basic needs—physiological (e.g., food) and psychological (affection, security, self-esteem)—are **deficiency needs;** if not fulfilled, we try to make up for their deficiency. The higher needs are called **metaneeds,** or growth needs; they include truth, goodness, beauty, wholeness, aliveness, uniqueness, perfection, justice, richness, and playfulness. The metaneeds cannot be satisfied until the lower needs are met. The metaneeds themselves, however, are not hierarchically arranged in Maslow's model. For example, while we have to satisfy our need for belongingness before our need for self-actualization, we do not have to satisfy our need for goodness before our need for aliveness. When our metaneeds are not fulfilled, we may become maladjusted, says Maslow; individuals may become alienated, weak, and cynical, for example.

Maslow developed psychological profiles of famous people and concluded that such individuals as Eleanor Roosevelt, Albert Einstein, Abraham Lincoln, Walt Whitman, William James, and Ludwig van Beethoven were self-actualized. On the basis of his interpretations of people's lives, he believed the characteristics listed in table 13.2 reflect self-actualization.

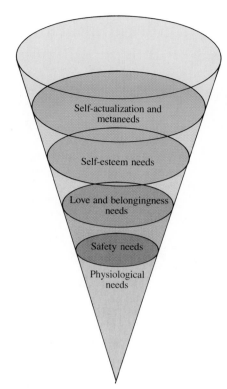

Figure 13.5
Maslow's hierarchy of needs. Only when the needs in the smaller circles are reasonably satisfied can self-actualization and satisfaction of metaneeds be accomplished.

Table 13.2 Maslow's Characteristics of Self-Actualized Individuals

Realistic orientation

Self-acceptance and acceptance of others and the natural world as they are

Spontaneity

Problem-centered rather than self-centered

Air of detachment and need for privacy

Autonomous and independent

Fresh rather than stereotyped appreciation of people and things

Generally have had profound mystical or spiritual, though not necessarily religious, experiences

Identification with humankind and a strong social interest

Tendency to have strong intimate relationships with a few special, loved people rather than superficial relationships with many people

Democratic values and attitudes

No confusion of means with ends

Philosophical rather than hostile sense of humor

High degree of creativity

Resistance to cultural conformity

Transcendence of environment rather than always coping with it

From Maslow, A. H., *The farther reaches of human nature,* pp. 153–174. © 1971 Viking Press, New York, NY. All rights reserved.

■ ■ ■ ■ ■ ■ ■ ■ ■ ■ ■ ■ ■ ■ ■ ■ ■ ■ ■ ■

Psychology 13.3

The Inner Journey from Manipulation to Self-Actualization

■ Everett Shostrum, former president of the Division of Humanistic Psychology in the American Psychological Association, had been a strong advocate of Maslow's ideas on self-actualization. In his book, *Man the Manipulator* (subtitled "The inner journey from manipulation to actualization"), Shostrum (1967) described how each of us has manipulating tendencies that can be turned into self-actualizing ones. Figure 13.B shows eight dimensions of our personality that can turn toward either manipulation or self-actualization. For example, an individual may become a leader or a dictator, a bully or an assertor. Shostrum has listed famous individuals who instead of following manipulating paths, chose self-actualizing courses.

From Dictator to Leader. The leader leads but does not dictate; he is forceful but not dominating.

Winston Churchill exemplified this type of self-actualization; during World War II he evidenced a democratic form of leadership.

From Weakling to Empathizer. The empathizer not only talks but listens sensitively and is aware of weaknesses in the self. She requires competence but accepts the human tendency to err. Eleanor Roosevelt had this type of personality. While recognizing her personal limitations, she showed considerable empathy toward underdeveloped nations and impoverished people around the world.

From Calculator to Respector. Instead of using or exploiting others, the self-actualizer respects others as people; they are not thought of as "things." This type of self-actualization was present in the personality of Mahatma Gandhi, a man whose nonviolent style always reflected a deep respect for others.

From Clinging Vine to Appreciator. The appreciator does not simply depend on others, like a clinging vine, but appreciates others' points of view. Pope John XXIII was an example of the appreciator through his role as ambassador to other religions of the world.

From Bully to Assertor. The assertor appreciates a worthy opponent, but is direct and straightforward with the adversary. The assertor is not hostile and dominating like the bully. Abraham Lincoln was an assertor, evidenced in the Lincoln-Douglas debates and his leadership during the Civil War.

From Nice Guy to Carer. The carer is not just a "goody-goody"; rather he is affectionate, friendly, and deeply loving. Albert Schweitzer, through his sincere devotion to the people of Africa, exemplified the characteristics of the carer.

An extension of Maslow's ideas about self-actualization was developed by Everett Shostrum (1967). By reading Psychology 13.3, you will learn about the characteristics thought to be present in the lives of some famous individuals.

Evaluating the Phenomenological and Humanistic Perspectives

The phenomenological and humanistic perspectives have sensitized psychologists to the importance of phenomenological experience; our perceptions of ourselves and our world are key ingredients of personality. The emphasis on consciousness likewise has had a significant impact on how we view personality. The humanistic psychologists have reminded us that we need to consider the whole person and the individual's positive nature. The contributions of these approaches have been felt in the area of human relations; many individuals believe the humanistic approach has helped them to understand both themselves and others. And the approaches have facilitated our ability to effectively communicate with others.

From Judge to Expressor. The expressor is not judgmental of others; he is able to express his own convictions strongly, however. Thomas Jefferson revealed this type of personality in his presidential role.

From Protector to Guide. The guide does not protect or teach others; rather she gently helps each person find a path of competence and identity. Buddha, the founder of the prominent Eastern religion, was such a person. He stressed that each person must find the way up the mountain herself.

In some instances, self-actualizers integrate different characteristics. For example, Shostrum concluded that someone who combines expression and guidance does not think "for" others but "with" them. In this form of self-actualization, one's views are expressed but full decision making rests on the other person's shoulders. For example, Jesus expressed his views in the Sermon on the Mount but the decision to follow Jesus was with each individual; the same was true of the Beatitudes, which were invitations, not demands.

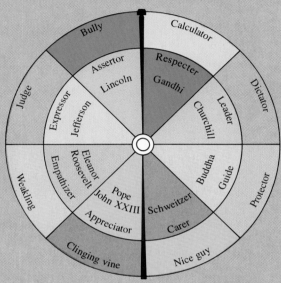

Figure 13.B
Shostrum's portrait of manipulators and self-actualizers.

One weakness of these approaches is that they are very hard to test scientifically. Self-actualization, for instance, is not clearly defined; psychologists are not certain how to study this concept empirically. Some humanistic psychologists even scorn the scientific approach, preferring clinical interpretation as a data base. Verification of humanistic concepts has come mainly from clinical experiences rather than controlled scientific efforts. Some critics also believe these approaches are *too* optimistic about human nature; they possibly overestimate the freedom and rationality of humans. And some critics say these approaches encourage self-love and narcissism.

We have seen that the behavioral and social learning approaches and the phenomenological and humanistic approaches take different paths to understanding personality. A summary of the main ideas in these approaches is presented in concept table 13.2. Yet another prominent view of personality remains to be discussed—trait theory.

■ ■ ■ ■ ■ ■ ■ ■ ■ ■ ■ ■ ■ ■ ■ ■ ■ ■ ■ ■

Concept Table 13.2

The Behavioral and Social Learning Perspectives and the Phenomenological and Humanistic Perspectives		
Concept	**Processes/related ideas**	**Characteristics/description**
The behavioral and social learning perspectives	Skinner's behaviorism	Emphasizes that cognition is unimportant in personality; personality is observed behavior, which is influenced by the rewards and punishments in the environment. Personality often varies according to the situation.
	Social learning theory	The environment is an important determinant of personality, but so are cognitive processes. We have the capability of controlling our own behavior through thoughts, beliefs, and values. Bandura's emphasis on observational learning and Michel's research on delay of gratification highlight the cognitive aspects of social learning theory.
	Evaluating the behavioral and social learning perspectives	Strengths of both perspectives include emphases on environmental determinants and a scientific climate for investigating personality, as well as the focus on cognitive processes and self-control in the social learning approach. The behavioral view has been criticized for taking the person out of personality and for ignoring cognition. These approaches have not given adequate attention to enduring individual differences, to biological factors, and to personality as a whole.
The phenomenological and humanistic perspectives	Their nature	The phenomenological approach emphasizes our perceptions of ourselves and our world; centers on the belief that reality is what is perceived. The humanistic approach is the most widely known phenomenological perspective.
	Carl Rogers's approach	Each of us is a victim of conditional positive regard. The result is that our real self is not valued. The self is the core of personality; it includes both the real and ideal self. Rogers advocated unconditional positive regard to enhance our self-concept. Each of us has the innate, inner capability of becoming a fully functioning person.
	Abraham Maslow's approach	Maslow called the humanistic movement the "third force" in psychology. Each of us has a self-actualizing capacity. Maslow distinguishes between deficiency needs and self-actualization, or metaneeds.
	Evaluating the phenomenological and humanistic perspectives	Sensitized us to the importance of subjective experience, consciousness, self-conception, the whole person, and our innate, positive nature. Weaknesses focus on the absence of a scientific orientation, a tendency to be too optimistic, and an inclination to encourage self-love.

Trait Theory and Trait-Situation Interaction

For years philosophers, psychologists, writers, and the public have described themselves and others in terms of traits. More than 2,000 years ago Theophrastus described the stingy man, the liar, and the flatterer. In more recent times, we find that individuals still are labeled according to their traits; the following excerpt is exemplary:

> Could a miser be lurking beneath that sensuous flesh and persuasive charm? Well, don't expect sapphires from him, dear, if he
> —itemizes who owes what when you're out Dutch-treat rather than splitting the bill
> —washes plastic party cups to reuse them
> —steams uncanceled stamps from letters
> —reshapes bent paper clips
> —has a dozen recipes for chicken wings
> —cuts his own hair
> —wants rolls and butter included in his doggie bag
> (*Cosmopolitan,* September 1976, p. 148).

(a)

(b)

Think about yourself and your friends; how would you describe yourselves? You might classify yourself as outgoing and sociable and one of your friends as shy and quiet. You might refer to yourself as emotionally stable but one of your other friends as emotionally unstable. Part of our everyday existence involves describing ourselves and others in traitlike terms. Some of the earliest views classified people according to body types and corresponding personality characteristics.

Personality-Type Theory

As early as 400 B.C. Hippocrates classified individuals in terms of their body type and accompanying personality profiles. In more recent times, William Sheldon (1954) proposed a well-known theory of body types and personality. He concluded that individuals basically are one of three types: **endomorphic** (a soft, round, large-stomached person who is relaxed, gregarious, and food-loving); **mesomorphic** (a strong, athletic, and muscular person who is energetic, assertive, and courageous); and **ectomorphic** (a tall, thin, fragile person who is fearful, introverted, and restrained) (see figure 13.6). Sheldon's view was called **somatotype theory,** which stated that precise charts of an individual's body reveal distinct body types, which in turn are associated with certain personality characteristics. However, subsequent research has shown that there is no significant relationship between body type and personality (Cortes & Gatti, 1970).

Somatotyping is not popular today, although it was the basis of well-known runner and author George Sheehan's recommendations for running styles and sports motivation. A major problem with personality-type theory is that many individuals do not fit into a neatly packaged category. Using one, two, three, or four categories to describe an individual ignores the rich complexity of human characteristics. As we see next, the trait theories provide a more empirical approach that recognizes the complexity and breadth of personality.

(c)

Figure 13.6
Artists' portraits of body types and accompanying personality characteristics. (a) A gently endomorphic Venus by Titian; (b) a rugged, athletic mesomorphic David by Michelangelo; (c) an anxious, ectomorphic actor by Picasso.

([a] © Scala/Art Resource, New York.
[b] Academy of Fine Arts, Florence. [c] Picasso, Pablo. The Actor, 1905. Oil on canvas, 76⅜ × 44⅛ in. The Metropolitan Museum of Art, New York, gift of Thelma Chrysler Foy, 1952.)

Figure 13.7
Sample profile for an individual on some of the basic traits described by Cattell.

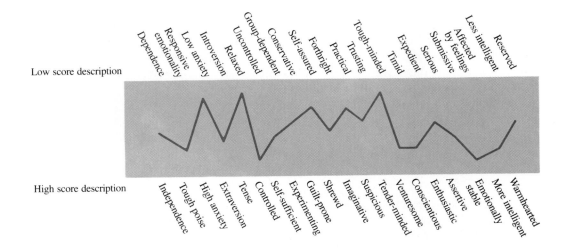

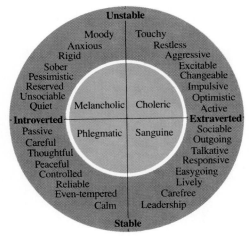

Figure 13.8
Eysenck's dimensions of personality. The inner ring shows the four basic temperaments of Hippocrates; the outer ring shows the results of modern factor analytic studies conducted by Eysenck and others.

Trait Theories

Trait theories argue that personality is best understood by studying the organization of traits within the person; these traits are essentially consistent in different situations and stable over time. According to trait theorists, these enduring traits are the core of personality.

Gordon Allport (1937) believed that our personality traits account for our behavior in a wide diversity of circumstances. For example, if you have a trait of honesty, it would be predicted that you would behave in moral ways in a variety of contexts, rarely, if ever, lying, cheating, or stealing. Allport combed the dictionary and concluded that 18,000 different words could be used to describe personality. Just as psychologists had classified motivations and emotions, Allport believed several overarching categories could simplify the vast number of personality trait descriptions. One of these categories was **individual traits,** which includes an individual's unique way of dealing with the world. Indeed, one of the hallmarks of Allport's trait theory was his emphasis on the uniqueness of the individual. However, two other prominent trait theorists have searched for the traits that are common to all of us.

Raymond Cattell (1965) and Hans Eysenck (1967) developed a list of traits they believe represent the core of every human being's personality. They used the mathematical technique of **factor analysis** to arrive at these basic traits of personality. Factor analysis is a complex statistical procedure that determines the relation between many different items or components. Using this technique, we can reduce a large number of trait categories to a manageable bundle. For example, Cattell says that he consistently discovers the presence of thirty basic traits in individuals, which he calls **source traits;** figure 13.7 shows some of these basic traits.

Eysenck consistently found the traits of stability-instability and introversion-extraversion when the personalities of large numbers of individuals were assessed (see figure 13.8). An unstable personality is moody, anxious, restless, and touchy; a stable personality is calm, even-tempered, carefree, and has leadership qualities. An introverted personality is quiet, unsociable, passive, and careful; an extraverted personality is active, optimistic, sociable, and outgoing.

Recent Developments in Trait Psychology

The search for the basic trait dimensions of personality continues. One trend suggests that converging evidence from a number of factor analytic studies reveals five basic dimensions of personality (Digman, 1986; Hogan, 1986a, 1987). Called the **big-five factors of personality,** they include:

extraversion-introversion

friendly compliance versus hostile noncompliance

neuroticism

will to achieve

intellect

Extraversion-introversion focuses on assertiveness, gregariousness, and shyness; friendly compliance versus hostile noncompliance involves love and friendship at one end of the continuum and enduring problems of aggression and lawlessness at the other end; neuroticism is how emotionally stable or unstable an individual is; the will to achieve emphasizes achievement motivation; and intellect includes our intelligence and creativity.

Not everyone agrees with this classification; debate includes whether intellect should be considered as part of intelligence, for example (e.g., Buss & Finn, 1987; Jackson, 1984). The benefits of classification are clear when we consider how many characteristics individuals have. But as we see next, not everyone agrees that trait classification is the best way to understand personality.

The Attack on Traits

In 1968, Walter Mischel published a landmark book in the field of personality, *Personality and Assessment.* Mischel criticized the trait view of personality, as well as the psychoanalytic approach, both of which emphasize the internal organization of personality. Rather than view personality as broad, internal traits that are consistent across situations and time, Mischel said that personality changes according to the situation.

Mischel summarized an array of studies and revealed that trait measures, indeed, do a poor job of predicting actual behavior. For example, Mischel said that if an individual is described as having an aggressive trait, when we observe the individual's behavior the degree of aggressiveness will vary from one context to another. The individual may be aggressive with his friend, but not his boss, for example.

Mischel's argument was an important one, but psychologists were not willing to conclude that personality waxes and wanes endlessly. This unwillingless to support Mischel's **situationism** and willingness to acknowledge that personality was not as stable as trait theories emphasized led to a revised conceptualization of personality.

Trait-Situation Interaction

Today, most psychologists in the field of personality are interactionists; they believe both person and situation variables are necessary to understand personality. Even the two major protagonists in the trait-situation (or sometimes called person-situation) controversy, Epstein (trait) and Mischel (situation),

■ ■

Concept Table 13.3

Trait Theory and Trait-Situation Interaction		
Concept	**Processes/related ideas**	**Characteristics/description**
Personality-type theory	Its nature	Involves classifying an individual according to a particular type. Sheldon's somatotype theory is the most well-known example; it involves describing individuals according to one of three body types. This view has been criticized heavily.
Trait theories	Their nature	Personality involves the organization of traits within an individual; these traits are essentially enduring. Allport stressed the individuality of trait organization, while Cattell and Eysenck sought the common traits in each of us.
	Recent developments	The search for the basic trait dimensions of personality continues; one contemporary view emphasizes five basic personality dimensions.
	The attack on traits	Mischel's *Personality and Assessment* ushered in an attack on trait theory; the criticism was that personality varies according to the situation more than trait theory acknowledges.
Trait-situation interaction	Its nature	Today most psychologists in the field of personality are interactionists; they believe personality is determined by the *interaction* of person and situation characteristics.

agree that person and situation factors contribute to a better understanding of personality. They also agree that the degree of consistency in personality depends on the kinds of persons, situations, and behaviors sampled (Pervin, 1986, 1987).

An outcome of the trait-situation controversy is a more precise specification of the link between traits and situations. For example, it has been found that 1) the more narrow and limited a trait is, the more likely it will predict behavior; 2) some people are consistent on some traits and other people are consistent on other traits; and 3) personality traits exert a stronger influence on an individual's behavior when situational influences are less powerful (Baron & Byrne, 1987).

Think about your own personality traits and the situations in your life. Do you think the big-five personality traits fit your own personality traits? Do you have some personality traits that others do not have? How strongly do situational pressures cause you to change your personality? A summary of the main ideas in trait theory and trait-situation interaction is presented in concept table 13.3.

Personality Assessment

"This line running this way indicates that you are a gregarious person, someone who really enjoys being around people. This division over here suggests that you are a risk taker; I bet you like to do things that are adventurous sometimes." These are the words of Lady Saturn, a palmist. Palmistry involves determining an individual's personality by interpreting the irregularities and folds in the skin of the hand. Each of these signs is interpreted in a precise manner. For example, a large mound of Saturn, the portion of the palm directly below the third joint of the middle finger, relates to wisdom, good fortune, and prudence.

Palmistry purports to provide a complete assessment of personality through the reading of signs. However, no reasonable explanation of the interpretive inferences made, coupled with knowledge that the hand's characteristics can change through exercise, dismiss palmistry as a legitimate way to assess personality; instead psychologists place it in the category of superstition and quackery (Lanyon & Goodstein, 1982).

How can palmists stay in business? Probably because of sensitive observational skills. They respond to such cues as voice, general demeanor, and dress, which are more relevant signs of personality than the skin configuration of the hand. Palmists also are experts at offering general, trivial statements such as, "Although you usually are affectionate with others, sometimes you don't get along with people." This statement falls into the category of the **Barnum effect:** if you make your predictions broad enough any person can fit the description. The effect was named after circus owner P. T. Barnum, who once said "a sucker is born every minute."

Palmistry aside, psychologists use a number of tests and methods to evaluate personality. And they assess personality for different reasons. Clinical and school psychologists assess personality to better understand an individual's psychological problems; they hope the assessment will improve their diagnosis and treatment of the individual. Industrial psychologists and vocational counselors assess personality to aid the individual's selection of a career. And research psychologists assess personality to investigate the theories and dimensions of personality we have discussed so far in this chapter. For example, if a psychologist wants to investigate self-concept, some measure of self-concept is needed.

Before we describe some specific types of personality tests, two more important points need to be made about the nature of personality assessment. First, the tests chosen by the psychologist frequently depend on the psychologist's theoretical orientation. And second, most personality tests are designed to measure stable, enduring personality characteristics, free of situational influences.

Psychologists who believe personality is a stable, enduring set of characteristics give personality tests to measure these characteristics; they follow the approach of trait theory. For example, if you score high on a personality test designed to measure both anxiousness and introversion, it is assumed that you consistently are anxious and introverted. Most personality tests also assume that individuals have the same basic characteristics; they simply vary in the degree they possess the characteristics.

By contrast, behaviorists argue that personality varies according to the situation; because personality tests do not measure situational variation, behaviorists use other strategies to assess behavior. They directly observe behavior, they have the individual carefully construct self-reports of her behavior, and they interview the individual about the circumstances that influence her behavior.

Psychologists who follow a psychoanalytic approach use measures that allow the individual's unconscious thoughts to be displayed. First, we will study the tests that measure unconscious thoughts—the so-called projective tests—then turn to the tests that measure traits—self-report tests—and conclude with behavioral assessment.

© 1980 Newspaper Enterprise,
Association, Inc.

Projective Tests

A **projective test** presents the individual with an ambiguous stimulus and then asks her to describe it or tell a story about it. Projective tests are based on the assumption that the ambiguity of the stimulus allows the individual to *project* into it her feelings, desires, needs, and attitudes. The test is especially designed to elicit the individual's unconscious feelings and conflicts, providing an assessment that goes deeper than the surface of personality. Projective tests attempt to get *inside* of your mind to discover how you *really* feel and think, going beyond the way you overtly present yourself.

The Rorschach Inkblot Test

The most well-known projective test is the **Rorschach Inkblot Test,** developed in 1921 by the Swiss psychiatrist Hermann Rorschach. The test consists of ten cards, half in black and white and half in color, which are administered to the individual one at a time (see figure 13.9). The individual is asked to describe what he sees in each of the inkblots. For example, an individual may say, "That looks like two people fighting." After the individual has responded to all ten inkblots, the examiner presents each of the inkblots again and inquires about the individual's earlier response. For example, the examiner might ask, "*Where* did you see the two people fighting?" and "*What* about the inkblot made the two people look like they were fighting?" Besides recording the responses, the examiner notes the individual's mannerisms, gestures, and attitudes.

How useful is the Rorschach in assessing personality? The answer to this question depends on one's perspective. From a scientific perspective, researchers have a less than enthusiastic attitude toward the Rorschach (Feshbach & Wiener, 1986; Kendall & Norton-Ford, 1982). Their disenchantment stems from the failure of the Rorschach to meet the criteria of reliability and validity, described in chapter 8 when we discussed the nature of intelligence testing. If the Rorschach was reliable, two different scorers should agree on the personality characteristics of the individual. If the Rorschach was valid, the individual's personality should predict behavior outside of the testing situation; that is, it should predict whether an individual will attempt suicide, become severely depressed, cope successfully with stress, or get along well with others. Conclusions based on research evidence suggest that the Rorschach does not meet these criteria of reliability and validity. This has led to serious reservations about the Rorschach's use in diagnosis and clinical practice.

Yet the Rorschach continues to enjoy widespread use in clinical circles; some clinicians swear by the Rorschach, saying it is better than any other measure at getting at the true, underlying core of the individual's personality. They are not especially bothered by the Rorschach's low reliability and validity, pointing out that this is so because of the extensive freedom of response encouraged by the test. It is this ambiguity and freedom of response that makes the Rorschach such a rich clinical tool, say its advocates.

The Rorschach controversy probably will not subside in the near future. Research psychologists will continue to criticize the low reliability and validity of the Rorschach; many clinicians will continue to say that the Rorschach is a valuable clinical tool, providing insights about the unconscious mind that no other personality test can.

Other Projective Tests

Like the Rorschach, the **Thematic Apperception Test (TAT),** which was developed by Henry Murray in the 1930s, consists of ambiguous stimuli to which individuals can respond freely. The TAT consists of a series of pictures, each on an individual card (see figure 13.10); the individual is asked to tell a story about each of the pictures, including events leading up to the situation described, the characters' thoughts and feelings, and how the situation turns out. It is assumed that the individual projects her own unconscious feelings and thoughts into the story she tells. In addition to being used as a projective technique in clinical practice, the TAT is used to evaluate the nature of an individual's motivation in research investigations. Several of the TAT's cards are believed to be especially effective at encouraging stories with achievement-related themes, telling the investigator about the individual's underlying need for achievement (e.g., McClelland & others, 1953).

Many other projective tests are used in clinical assessment. One test asks the individual to complete a sentence (e.g., "I often feel . . . ." "I would like to . . . ."), another test asks the individual to draw a person, and another test presents a word, such as *fear* or *happy,* and asks the individual to say the first thing that comes to mind. Like the Rorschach, these projective tests have their detractors and advocates; the detractors often criticize the tests' low reliability and validity, and the advocates describe the tests' abilities to reveal the underlying nature of the individual's personality better than more straightforward stimuli.

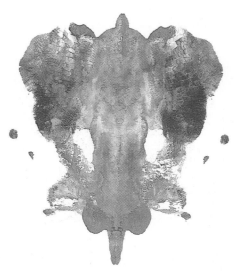

Figure 13.9
An example of the type of stimuli used in the Roschach inkblot test.

Figure 13.10
A picture from the Thematic Apperception Test (TAT).

Self-Report Tests

No doubt you have taken a self-report personality test. Sometimes these tests evaluate many different dimensions of your personality; others assess a limited part of your personality, such as introversion-extraversion, or sensation-seeking (remember the sensation-seeking scale at the beginning of chapter 11). The **self-report tests** assess your personality traits by asking you what they are; they are not designed to reveal your unconscious personality characteristics. Self-report tests are questionnaires that contain a large number of statements or questions; you respond with a limited number of choices (yes or no; true or false; agree or disagree). How do psychologists construct these self-report tests?

Constructing Self-Report Tests

Many of the early personality tests were based on **face validity,** which is an assumption that the content of the test items is a good indicator of what the individual's personality is like. For example, if I developed a test item that asks you to respond whether or not you are introverted, I accept your response as a straightforward indication that you are or are not introverted. For example, the following item might be used in this regard: "I enjoy being with people." Tests based on face validity assume that you are responding honestly and nondefensively, giving the examiner an accurate portrayal of your personality.

But not everyone is honest, especially when it concerns their own personality makeup. Even if the individual basically is honest, he may be giving socially desirable answers. **Social desirability** refers to a response set in which the individual answers according to what he thinks the examiner wants to hear or in a way that makes the individual look better. For example, if I am basically a lazy person, I may not want you to know this and I may try to present myself in a more positive way; therefore, I would respond negatively to following item: "I fritter away time too much." Because of such response sets, psychologists realized that they needed to go beyond face validity in constructing personality tests.

Empirical keying is used to develop personality tests that make no assumptions about the nature of the items; in this approach, what counts is whether the test items predict some criterion. For example, a test given to a candidate for a position as a police officer should be able to predict how successful the individual will be in the job. A test of introversion should differentiate individuals who behave in a shy manner or an outgoing manner. Individuals diagnosed as deeply depressed and who reside in a mental hospital should respond differently on a test of depression than individuals not so diagnosed. Remember that the content of the items is irrelevant in an empirically keyed test. If the item, "I enjoy reading poetry," predicts success as a police officer, then it is retained in the test even if it seems an unlikely question. The most widely used empirically keyed personality test is described next.

The Minnesota Multiphasic Personality Inventory

The **Minnesota Multiphasic Personality Inventory (MMPI)** originally was developed to improve the diagnosis of mentally disturbed individuals. A pool of 1,000 self-descriptive statements were given to groups of mental patients diagnosed on the basis of clinical judgment. The items also were given to normal individuals. How often individuals agreed with each item was calculated; only items that clearly differentiated the diagnostic group from the normal group were retained. For example, a statement might become an item on the depression scale of the MMPI if patients diagnosed with a depressive disorder agreed

Table 13.3 The Clinical Scales of the MMPI

Clinical scales	Description	Sample item
1. Hypochondriasis	Items distinguish individuals who are preoccupied with their body and fear of illness, even though no physical illness can be detected. These individuals often are cynical and defeatist.	I wake up fresh and rested most mornings. (False*)
2. Depression	Items distinguish individuals who are pessimistic about the future, have low morale, feel worthless, and are sluggish in thought and behavior.	At times I am full of energy. (False)
3. Hysteria	Items distinguish individuals who show immature behavior or denial of problems. These individuals often complain of multiple symptoms.	I have never had a fainting spell. (False)
4. Psychopathic deviate	Items distinguish individuals who disregard rules and laws, have empty emotional relationships with others, and have family problems. These individuals are often adventurous.	I liked school. (False)
5. Masculinity-femininity	Items distinguish individuals who have masculine and feminine interests. The scale has been used to distinguish males with heterosexual and homosexual interests. High-scoring females have been described as rebellious, unrealistic, and indecisive; however, most women score low on the scale. High-scoring males have been described as sensitive and esthetic.	I like mechanics magazine. (False)
6. Paranoia	Items distinguish individuals with delusions either about how influential they are or how victimized they are; they often appear to be shrewd, guarded, or worrisome.	Someone has it in for me. (True)
7. Psychasthenia	Items distinguish individuals who have obsessive thoughts or engage in compulsive actions; the items also distinguish individuals who are very fearful, rigid, and anxious.	I am certainly lacking in self-confidence. (True)
8. Schizophrenia	Items distinguish individuals who are withdrawn, unusual, cold, aloof, and who may have hallucinations and delusions.	I believe I am a condemned person. (True)
9. Hypomania	Items distinguish individuals who are overactive and are easily excited emotionally; these individuals often appear impulsive.	At times my thoughts have raced ahead faster than I could speak them. (True)
10. Social introversion	Items distinguish individuals who are modest, shy, and may withdraw from social contacts.	I enjoy social gatherings just to be with people. (False)

*The true or false responses within parentheses indicate the scored direction (high or low) of each of the items.

Source: University of Minnesota Press, Minneapolis, MN.

with the statement significantly more than did normal individuals. Thus, an item with little face validity, such as "I sometimes tease animals," might be included on the depression scale, or any other scale, of the MMPI.

Through empirical keying the MMPI was reduced to 550 items, each of which can be answered true or false. The items vary widely in content and include such statements as:

I like to read magazines.

I never have trouble falling asleep.

People are out to get me.

An individual's answers are grouped according to ten clinical scales, which include such categories as depression, psychopathic deviate, schizophrenia, and social introversion (table 13.3 provides a description of each of the categories and sample items).

The MMPI includes four validity scales in addition to the ten clinical scales. The validity scales were designed to overcome some of the problems of response bias inherent in personality tests. These validity scales indicate whether an individual is lying, careless, defensive, or evasive when answering the test items. For example, if the individual responds "false" to a number of items such as, "I get angry sometimes," it would be interpreted that she is trying to make herself look better than she really is. The rationale behind the lie scale is that each of us gets angry at least some of the time, so the individual who responds "false" to many such items is faking her responses.

Thousands of research studies and many books have documented the ability of the MMPI to improve the diagnosis of mentally disturbed individuals (e.g., Butcher & Finn, 1983). Some critics point out, however, that the MMPI is less effective in diagnosing differences among normal individuals. They believe the MMPI has been misused in business and education to predict which individual will make the best job candidate or which career an individual should pursue. In some instances, individuals giving the MMPI and interpreting its scales are not adequately trained in psychological testing and diagnosis. In these cases, the MMPI is being used beyond its intent.

Evaluating Self-Report Tests

Adherents of the trait approach, which advocates the use of self-report measures to assess personality, have strong faith in the utility of these tests. Psychologists are continuing to build better self-report measures. For example, in an effort to measure the big-five personality factors described earlier in the chapter, Robert Hogan (1986b) devised the Hogan Personality Inventory. In many instances, self-report tests have produced a better understanding of the nature of the individual's personality traits. However, some critics (especially those from a psychoanalytic persuasion) believe the self-report measures do not get at the underlying core of personality and its unconscious determinants. Other critics (especially those of a behavioral persuasion) believe the self-report tests do not adequately capture the situational variation in personality and the ways personality changes as the individual interacts with the environment.

Behavioral Assessment

Behavioral assessment attempts to obtain more objective information about an individual's personality by observing the individual's behavior directly. Instead of removing situational influences from personality as projective and self-report measures do, behavioral assessment assumes that personality cannot be evaluated apart from the environment.

Recall from chapter 5 that behavior modification is an attempt to apply learning principles to change maladaptive behavior. Behavioral assessment of personality emerged from this tradition. For example, recall that the observer often will make baseline observations of the frequency of the individual's behaviors. This might be accomplished under controlled laboratory conditions or in more naturalistic circumstances. Examples of observing a child's aggressive behavior in these contexts are shown in figure 13.11. The therapist then will modify some aspect of the environment, such as getting parents and the child's teacher to stop giving the child attention when he engages in the aggressive behavior. After a specified period of time, observations are conducted to determine if the changes in the environment were effective in reducing the child's maladaptive behavior.

Sometimes, though, direct observations are impractical. What does a psychologist with a behavioral orientation then do to assess personality? She might ask individuals to make their own assessments of behavior, encouraging them to be sensitive to the circumstances that produced the behavior and the outcomes or consequences of the behavior. For example, a therapist might

Figure 13.11
Observation of a child's aggressive behavior under controlled laboratory and naturalistic conditions. (a) The child's aggressive behavior is being observed through a one-way mirror. This allows the observer to exercise control over the observation of aggression. (b) The child's aggressive behaviors can be observed in a naturalistic situation. This allows the observer to obtain information about the everyday occurrence of behaviors.

Table 13.4 Items from the Spouse Observation Checklist

Type of behavior	Item
Shared activities	We sat and read together. We took a walk.
Pleasing interactive events	My spouse asked how my day was. We talked about personal feelings. My spouse showed interest in what I said by agreeing or asking relevant questions.
Displeasing interactive events	My spouse commanded me to do something. My spouse complained about something I did. My spouse interrupted me.
Pleasing affectionate behavior	We held each other. My spouse hugged and kissed me.
Displeasing affectionate behavior	My spouse rushed into intercourse without taking time for foreplay. My spouse rejected my sexual advances.
Pleasing events	Spouse did the dishes. Spouse picked up around the house.
Displeasing events	Spouse talked too much about work. Spouse yelled at the children.

Couples are instructed to complete a more extensive checklist for fifteen consecutive evenings. Each spouse records the behavior of his or her partner, and they make daily ratings of their overall satisfaction with the spouse's behavior.

From Jacobson, N. S., et al., Toward a behavioral profile of marital distress, *Journal of Consulting and Clinical Psychology, 48,* 696–703. Copyright 1980 by the American Psychological Association.

want to know the course of marital conflict in the everyday events of a couple (Margolin, Michelli, & Jacobson). Table 13.4 shows a spouse observation checklist that couples can use to record the partner's behavior.

The influence of social learning theory has increased the use of cognitive assessment in personality evaluation. The strategy is to discover what thoughts underlie the individual's behavior; that is, how do individuals think about their problems? What kinds of thoughts precede maladaptive behavior, occur during its manifestation, and follow it? Cognitive processes such as expectations, planning, and memory are assessed, possibly by interviewing the individual or asking them to complete a questionnaire. For example, an interview might include questions that address whether the individual overexaggerates his faults and condemns himself more than is warranted. A questionnaire might sample an individual's thoughts after an upsetting event or assess the way she thinks during tension-filled moments (Bellack & Hersen, 1988; Kendall, 1985).

More information about behavioral and cognitive assessment appears in chapter 15, where we discuss psychotherapies. Many of the behavioral and cognitive assessments of personality are recent developments and are just beginning to find their way into the evaluation of personality. Increasingly, psychologists who use projective and self-report tests to measure personality are evaluating the individual's behavior and thought in the testing situation to provide important additional information (Singer, 1977; Walter & Affiliates, 1986).

In the course of our discussion we have seen that personality has many different faces. The complexity of personality was recognized by R. W. White (1976), who said the complexity is not a surface illusion; it is an inescapable fact. But just because personality is complex does not mean it cannot be understood. By now you should have a better understanding of the nature of personality and *your* personality. In the next chapter we turn our attention to abnormal psychology, where our discussion of personality includes its abnormal aspects.

Summary

I. **The Nature of Personality**
Personality refers to our enduring thoughts, emotions, and behaviors that characterize the way we adapt to our world. A key question in personality is why individuals respond to the same situation in different ways.

II. **Freud's Personality Theory**
Sigmund Freud has been one of the most influential thinkers in the twentieth century. He developed psychoanalysis and observed that free association provides insight into an individual's emotional problems. He believed that most of our mind is comprised of unconscious thoughts. Freud said that personality has three structures: id, ego, and superego. The id houses biological instincts, is completely unconscious, and operates according to the pleasure principle; the ego tries to provide pleasure by operating according to the reality principle; and the superego is the moral branch of personality.

The conflicting demands of personality structures produce anxiety; defense mechanisms protect the ego and reduce this anxiety. Freud said that repression is the most pervasive defense mechanism; others include rationalization, displacement, sublimation, projection, reaction formation, and regression. In moderation, defense mechanisms can be healthy; however, they should not be allowed to dominate our lives.

Freud was convinced that our problems develop primarily because of early childhood experiences. He said we go through five psychosexual stages, oral, anal, phallic, latency, and genital. We can become fixated at each stage if our needs are under- or overgratified. During the phallic stage, the Oedipus complex is a major source of conflict.

III. **Psychoanalytic Dissenters and Revisionists**
Critics argued that Freud's view placed too much emphasis on sexuality and the first five years of life; he also gave too little attention to social factors and failed to recognize the power of the ego and conscious thought processes. Jung and Adler, two contemporaries of Freud, were especially critical of his views. Jung thought Freud underplayed the unconscious nature of the mind; he developed the concept of the collective unconscious. Adler said Freud gave the unconscious too much power; he believed that we have the ability to consciously control our behavior.

IV. **Evaluating the Psychoanalytic Theories**
The strengths are an emphasis on the past, the developmental course of personality, mental representation of the environment, unconscious mind, emphasis on conflict, and influence on psychology as a discipline. Weaknesses of psychoanalytic theories are the difficulty in testing main concepts, lack of an empirical data base and overreliance on reports of the past, too much emphasis on sexuality and the unconscious mind, a negative view of human nature, and too much power given to early experience.

V. **The Behavioral and Social Learning Approaches**
Skinner's behavioral approach emphasizes that cognition is unimportant in understanding personality; personality is observed behavior, which is influenced by rewards and punishments in the environment. This approach stresses that personality often varies according to the situation.

Social learning theorists believe the environment is an important determinant of personality, but so are cognitive processes. We have the capability of controlling our own behavior through thoughts, beliefs, and values, for example. Bandura's emphasis on observational learning and Mischel's research on delay of gratification underscore the cognitive aspects of social learning theory.

The strengths of these approaches involve their emphasis on environmental determinants and a scientific climate for investigating personality; the focus on cognitive processes and self-control in the social learning approach also is a strength. The behavioral view has been criticized for taking the person out of personality and for ignoring cognition. These approaches do not give adequate attention to enduring individual differences, to biological factors, and to personality as a whole.

VI. **The Phenomenological and Humanistic Approaches**
The phenomenological approach emphasizes our perceptions of ourselves and our world; the approach centers on the belief that reality is what is perceived. The humanistic approach is the most widely known phenomenological approach.

Carl Rogers's approach emphasizes that each of us is a victim of conditional positive regard; conditions are placed on our worth. The result is that our real self is not valued as positively as it should be. The self is the core of personality; it includes both the real and the ideal self.

Rogers advocated the use of unconditional positive regard to enhance our self-concept. He stressed that each of us has the innate, inner capability of becoming a fully functioning person.

Abraham Maslow was a powerful figure in the humanistic movement, calling it the "third force" in psychology. He believes each of us has a self-actualizing capability. Maslow distinguishes between deficiency needs and self-actualized or metaneeds.

These approaches have sensitized psychologists to the importance of subjective experience, consciousness, self-conception, the whole person, and our innate, positive nature. Their weaknesses focus on the absence of a scientific orientation, a tendency to be too optimistic, and an inclination to encourage self-love.

VII. Trait Theory and Trait-Situation Interaction

Personality-type theory involves classifying an individual according to a particular type; Sheldon's somatotype theory is an example. This view is heavily criticized. Trait theories emphasize that personality involves the organization of traits within the individual; these traits are believed to be essentially enduring. Allport stressed the individuality of traits; Cattell and Eysenck sought the common traits that exist in each of us. The search for basic trait dimensions continues; one contemporary view stresses that we have five basic traits. Mischel's *Personality and Assessment* ushered in an attack on trait theory; basically the criticism was that personality varies according to the situation more than the trait theorists acknowledge. Today most psychologists are interactionists; they believe personality is determined by a combination of traits or person variables and the situation.

VIII. Personality Assessment

Psychologists use a number of tests and measures to assess personality; these measures often are tied to the psychologist's theoretical orientation. Personality tests basically were designed to measure stable, enduring aspects of personality. Projective tests use ambiguous stimuli to get the individual to project her personality into the stimuli; they try to discover unconscious aspects of personality. The Rorschach is the most widely used projective test; its effectiveness has been controversial. Self-report measures are designed to assess an individual's traits; the most widely used self-report test is the MMPI, which is an empirically keyed test. Behavioral assessment tries to obtain more objective information about personality through observation of behavior and its environmental ties. Cognitive assessment increasingly is used as part of the behavioral assessment process.

Key Terms

personality *435*

psychoanalysis *436*

free association *437*

id *437*

pleasure principle *437*

ego *438*

reality principle *438*

superego *438*

defense mechanisms *438*

repression *438*

rationalization *439*

displacement *439*

sublimation *439*

projection *439*

reaction formation *439*

regression *439*

erogenous zones *440*

fixation *441*

oral stage *441*

anal stage *441*

phallic stage *441*

Oedipus complex *442*

latency stage *444*

genital stage *444*

collective unconscious *444*

archetypes *444*

phenomenological perspective *450*

humanistic perspective *450*

conditional positive regard *451*

conditions of worth *452*

unconditional positive regard *452*

deficiency needs *453*

metaneeds *453*

endomorphic *457*

mesomorphic *457*

ectomorphic *457*

somatotype theory *457*

trait theories *458*

individual traits *458*

factor analysis *458*

source traits *458*

big-five factors of personality *459*

situationism *459*

Barnum effect *461*

projective test *462*

Rorschach Inkblot Test *462*

Thematic Apperception Test (TAT) *463*

self-report tests *464*

face validity *464*

social desirability *464*

empirical keying *464*

Minnesota Multiphasic Personality Inventory (MMPI) *464*

Suggested Readings

Hall, C. S., & Lindsey, G. (1986). *Introduction to theories of personality.* New York: Wiley. This leading text includes chapters on Freud, Jung, Adler, Allport, Cattell, and Eysenck, as well as many other leading personality theorists.

Journal of Personality and Social Psychology. This journal is rated as one of the best sources of information about current research on personality. Look through the issues of the last several years to obtain a glimpse of current research interests and the ways personality is assessed.

Jung, C. G. (1964). *Man and his symbols.* Garden City, NY: Doubleday. Includes the writings of Jung and four of his disciples; Jung's ideas are applied to anthropology, literature, art, and dreams.

Laynon, R. I., & Goodstein, L. D. (1982). *Personality assessment* (2nd ed.). New York: Wiley Interscience. Includes chapters on the history of personality assessment, special applications of personality assessment such as insanity evaluations and child-custody decisions, as well as a number of criticisms of personality assessment.

Pervin, L. A. (1985). Personality: current controversies and issues in personality. *Annual Review of Psychology, 36,* 83–114. This lengthy chapter provides a detailed look at some of the controversies about personality—includes considerable insight into the nature of the trait-situation controversy.

Shostrum, E. L. (1972). *Man, the manipulator.* New York: Bantam. This paperback presents Shostrum's ideas about the route from manipulation to self-actualization. Fascinating reading that provides many examples and case studies.

Chapter 14

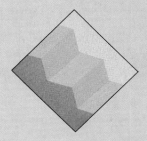

Abnormal Psychology

He raves; his words are loose as heaps of sand, and scattered wide from sense.—So high he's mounted on his airy throne, that now the wind has got into his head, and turns his brain to frenzy.

—*Dryden*

Images of Abnormal Psychology

"For two years my life had been a drawing on resources that I did not possess. . . . In a real dark night of the soul it is always three o'clock in the morning, day after day." These words of famous novelist F. Scott Fitzgerald in *The Crack-up* reflect the author's own self-scrutiny. *The Crack-up* is a perceptive, insightful analysis of mental disturbance and its emotional exhaustion.

Fitzgerald portrayed himself with a past filled with glitter and success in a world based on illusion and euphoria; now his world was filled with inner ruin, pessimism, and a morbid attraction to nothingness. Fitzgerald felt estranged from the events and people he loved, straining to perform even the simplest of acts. He no longer even liked to be with people. Fitzgerald commented, "One is not waiting for the fadeout of a single sorrow, but rather being an unwilling witness to an execution, the disintegration of one's own personality" (Wilson, 1945, p. 76).

Suicide was a recurrent theme in another famous American author's life and work—Fitzgerald's friend Ernest Hemingway. Even before his father's suicide, Hemingway seemed obsessed by the theme of self-destruction. As a young boy he enjoyed reading Stevenson's "The Suicide Club." At one point in his adult life, Hemingway said he would rather go out in a blaze of light than have his body worn out and old and his illusions shattered.

Hemingway's suicidal thoughts sometimes coincided with his marital crises. Just before marrying Hadley, Hemingway became apprehensive about his new responsibilities and alarmed her by the mention of suicide. Five years later, during a crisis with Pauline, he calmly told her he would have committed suicide if their love affair had not been resolved happily. Hemingway was strangely comforted by the morbid thoughts of death. When feeling low, he would think about death and ways of dying; the best way he thought, unless he could arrange to die in his sleep, would be to go off an ocean liner at night.

Hemingway committed suicide in his sixties. His suicide raised the question of why a man with good looks, sporting skills, friends, women, wealth, fame, genius, and a Nobel Prize would kill himself. Hemingway developed a combination of physical and mental disturbances. He had neglected his health for some years, suffering from weight loss, skin disease, alcoholism, diabetes, hypertension, and impotence. His body in a shambles, he dreaded becoming an invalid and the slow death this would bring. At this point, the severely depressed Hemingway was losing his memory and no longer could write. One month before his suicide, Hemingway said, "Staying healthy. Working good. Eating and drinking with his friends. Enjoying himself in bed. I haven't any of them" (Meyers, 1985, p. 559).

Ernest Hemingway. He frequently expressed suicidal thoughts during his life. He committed suicide at age sixty-one.

Mental disturbances have no social and economic boundaries; they find their way into the lives of the rich and famous and the poor and unknown. In this chapter we will study a number of mental disturbances, including the depression and suicide that enveloped the lives of Fitzgerald and Hemingway. Before we study these disturbances, though, let's think about what it means to be abnormal and how mental disturbances are classified. ■

What Does It Mean to Be Abnormal?

One young man, R. C., ate the flesh of a friend who died in an accident. Another man told his friends and family that he was going to drive off a cliff. He repeated the threat on a number of occasions and finally did it. Yet another man, B. P., informed the public that he had killed a number of people during various fights over the previous ten years.

Cannibalism, suicide, and murder—aren't these abnormal behavior? What caused these individuals to commit such acts? In these three incidents, the behaviors were actually thought of as "normal." The three individuals involved were called heroes! In the first circumstance, R. C. was a passenger on an airplane that crashed into the Andes mountains of South America. He and several others were the only survivors; they barely remained alive for two months in the blizzard conditions of the mountains. The only way R. C. survived was by reluctantly eating the dead bodies for food. In the second circumstance, what appeared to be a suicide attempt actually was a famous daredevil stunt by the motorcyclist Evel Knievel. In the third circumstance, the crime-fighting accomplishments of a sheriff in a small southern town were applauded in the movie *Walking Tall,* which described how Buford Puser eliminated one criminal after another (Mahoney, 1980).

Defining what is normal and what is abnormal is not a simple task; the line between the two is often precariously thin. Attempts to define abnormality and search for its causes include malevolent gods, statistics, biological factors, psychological factors, culture, and experiences. Demons, witches, vampires, and even the moon and planets are given responsibility for abnormal behavior. In the Middle Ages Satan and Lucifer, as the devil was known, were considered the major provokers of madness. An individual was abnormal if he followed the course of the devil or was possessed by demons. Psychologists no longer believe abnormality is determined by such factors; what does constitute abnormal behavior?

The Statistical Approach

Albert Einstein, John McEnroe, and Barbara Walters—are these individuals abnormal or deviant? The **statistical approach** defines abnormal behavior as that which deviates substantially from the average. We don't usually think of Einstein as abnormal because he was so bright, McEnroe as deviant because he is such a masterful tennis player (although some of us might consider his temperamental outbursts as signs of abnormal behavior), and we don't consider Walters as abnormal because she is one of the most talented television interviewers (see figure 14.1).

Figure 14.1
Barbara Walters is one of television's most talented interviewers. Is her behavior abnormal?

We all are deviant from one another on certain dimensions. Because you like classical music and your friends do not does not make you abnormal. It is in the areas of social behavior and thought where we look for statistical differences that might underscore abnormality. If a man sits on a park bench day after day uttering bizarre, confused statements while staring blankly into space, his behavior deviates dramatically from what commonly is displayed in our culture.

Sometimes, though, statistical incidences vary from one culture to another and from one point in history to another within the same culture. Women of the Mangaian culture in the South Sea islands train young adolescent males in sexual techniques; the young males are then encouraged to practice their skills with young adolescent females. In the United States, we would consider such behavior abnormal; but in the Mangaian culture it is the norm. Early in this century, masturbation was thought to cause everything from warts to insanity; today less than 15 percent of adolescents think that masturbation is wrong (Hyde, 1986).

The Biological Approach

Proponents of the biological approach believe that abnormal behavior is due to some physical malfunctioning in the body. If an individual behaves in an uncontrollable manner, is out of touch with reality, or is severely depressed, biological factors are thought to be the culprits. Today special interest focuses on the role of brain processes and drug therapy in understanding and treating abnormal behavior. Interest also focuses on genetic factors.

The forerunner of the biological approach was the **medical model** (also called the disease model); the medical model states that abnormality is a disease or illness precipitated by internal body causes. From this perspective, abnormalities are called mental *illnesses* and the individuals afflicted are *patients* in *hospitals* who are treated by *doctors*.

Psychological and Sociocultural Approaches

While the biological approach is an important perspective in understanding abnormal behavior, many psychologists believe it underplays the importance of psychological and sociocultural factors. Emotional turmoil, inappropriate learning, distorted thoughts, and inadequate relationships are of interest in the psychological and sociocultural approaches rather than brain processes or genes. The theories of personality discussed in the last chapter provide insight about the nature of abnormal as well as normal behavior. The psychoanalytic theories, the behavioral and social learning approaches, and the phenomenological and humanistic views contain valuable insights about the psychological and sociocultural determinants of abnormal behavior. Much more about their approaches to the treatment of abnormal behavior appears in the next chapter.

Advocates of the psychological and sociocultural approaches criticize the medical model because they believe it encourages labeling of mental disturbances. A label such as "anxiety disorder" may persist even though the behavior is temporary. Also the individual may accept the label and then display the abnormal behavior more frequently (Scheff, 1966; Szasz, 1977).

An Interactionist Approach

When considering an individual's behavior, whether abnormal or normal, it is important to remember the complexity of the individual and the multiple influences on behavior. Neither the biological nor the psychological and sociocultural approaches can independently capture this complexity and multiple influence.

Abnormal behavior is influenced by biological, cognitive, and environmental factors. Current areas of interest in studying biological factors are computer imaging techniques to discover abnormalities in brain structure and functioning; the role of neurotransmitters in different mental disturbances; the use of drugs to treat abnormal behavior, especially by changing the action of neurotransmitters; and the degree to which disorders are inherited (Pardes, 1986). Among the current areas of interest in studying cognitive factors are the roles of symbolic thought, decision making, planning, imagery, reasoning, memory, and problem-focused coping in disturbances that involve depression, phobias, personality disorders, and schizophrenia (Millon & Klerman, 1986). And among the current areas of interest in studying environmental factors are the importance of close relationships, especially family; support systems; rewards and punishment; and the incidence of different mental disturbances in our culture and other cultures (Blazer & others, 1985; Engel, 1977; Schwartz & Wiggins, 1986).

As we have discussed different approaches to abnormality, we have seen that it is not always an easy task to determine whether or not an individual is abnormal. To learn more about this difficulty turn to Psychology 14.1, where you will read about college students who faked abnormal symptoms and were admitted to a mental hospital. Among the most provocative issues in abnormal psychology today is how to further classify individuals once they are labeled as abnormal.

■■■■■■■■■■■■■■■■■■■
Psychology 14.1

"Disturbed" College Students in a Mental Hospital and *One Flew over the Cuckoo's Nest*

■ Imagine that things are going well for you. You are a very well-adjusted person. You like yourself, your grades are good, and you have a close circle of friends. Your parents are supportive, and though you've had your disagreements with them, you recognize that they did a good job in raising you. Above all else, you certainly do not consider yourself mentally disturbed.

You are one of eight "normal" individuals, three men and five women, who have been chosen by a psychologist to participate in an experiment (Rosenhan, 1973). You present yourself at the admitting desk of a psychiatric hospital complaining that you keep hearing a voice that you can't identify—it keeps saying, "empty," "hollow," and "thud." You are interviewed and your life history is taken. You are honest about your life history although you don't reveal your real name. Somewhat to your surprise you are admitted right away.

During the next several days you act your normal self. A psychiatrist looks at your current complaint about hearing voices as well as your case history, and he talks with you on several occasions. His diagnosis: You are schizophrenic. The seven other subjects got themselves admitted to other psychiatric hospitals and all but one was diagnosed as schizophrenic (they too complained of the unidentified voice and otherwise presented themselves in a normal manner).

You and the other "patients" all expressed an interest in leaving the hospital and behaved in a very cooperative manner with the staff. Nonetheless, you were kept in the hospital for fifteen days and finally released with the diagnosis of schizophrenia, which is now in remission. Your cohorts' stays in the psychiatric hospitals lasted from three to fifty-two days.

David Rosenhan (1973), who was responsible for this provocative experiment, concluded that normal people are often not detectably sane and that many psychiatric workers tend to make mistakes on the side of diagnosing normal people as abnormal. Rosenhan developed a second experiment to see if this tendency could be turned around. The psychiatric staff was informed that a number of patients who were fakes would be coming to the hospital during the following three months trying to get themselves admitted. The psychiatric staff was requested to tell which if any of the patients seen during this three-month period might possibly be faking their symptoms. In actuality, no fake patients were sent to the psychiatric staff by Rosenhan. Yet one member of the psychiatric staff said that 41 of the 193 patients were probably faking their symptoms.

As part of his research on being sane in insane places, Rosenhan (1973) had the "mental patients" he planted in the hospitals collect data. To determine the responsiveness of the staff to the eight "patients," the "patients" asked psychiatrists, nurses, and attendants questions such as the following: "Pardon me, Mr. (Dr., or Ms.) X. Can you tell me when I will be eligible for grounds privileges (discharge and the like)?" Though the content varied, the patients' questions were always appropriate and were asked in a very courteous manner. The responses of the staffs of the hospitals to the questions are shown in table 14.A. As you can see, 71 percent of the psychiatrists totally ignored the questions, as did 88 percent of the nurses and attendants. Notice also that less than one-fourth of the psychiatrists and only 10 percent of the nurses and attendants even made any effort at eye contact with the "patients," and even fewer stopped to talk with them.

However, not all mental health institutions are as depressing as those described by Rosenhan and the one pictured in the movie *One Flew Over the Cuckoo's Nest* (see figure 14.A). Behavior in mental institutions is frequently not what most people expect, particularly as drug therapy has become more effective in treating serious mental disturbances. Often it is difficult to differentiate mental patients from nonpatients. The buildings are not populated by raving lunatics, as has sometimes been portrayed in the media. Still, it is important to keep the Rosenhan data in mind in our effort to improve the treatment of mentally disturbed people.

Table 14.A Responses of Psychiatric Staffs to "Patient" Inquiries

	Psychiatric hospitals	
Contact	Psychiatrists	Nurses and attendants
Responses		
Moves on, head averted (%)	71	88
Makes eye contact (%)	23	10
Pauses and chats (%)	2	2
Stops and talks (%)	4	0.5
Respondents (no.)	13	47
Attempts (no.)	185	1,283

From Rosenhan, D. L., On being sane in insane places, *Science, 179,* 250–258, January 19, 1973. © 1973 American Association for the Advancement of Science. Reprinted by permission.

Figure 14.A
The maltreatment of individuals in mental institutions was vividly captured in the movie One Flew Over the Cuckoo's Nest. *Jack Nicholson starred in the movie as a sane "patient" among mentally disturbed individuals. Not all mental institutions are as depressing as the one depicted in this movie.*

Classification of Mental Disorders

For virtually each of the major topics in this text, we have found that psychologists have a penchant for classification; they ask, "What is the best way to classify biological influences? Learning? Cognition? Development? Motivation? Personality? The classification of mental disorders has its roots in biology and medicine. Since the time of ancient Egypt, Greece, and Rome, diseases have been classified.

What are the benefits of classifying mental disorders? First, a classification system provides professionals with a shorthand system for communicating with each other. For example, if one psychologist mentions that her client has a panic disorder and another psychologist says that her client has a generalized anxiety disorder, the two psychologists understand what these disturbances are like. Second, a classification system permits psychologists to construct theories about the causes of particular disturbances and design treatments for them. Third, a classification system can help psychologists predict disturbances; a classification system provides information about the likelihood of a disorder occurring, which individuals are most susceptible to the disturbance, the progress of the disorder once it appears, and the prognosis for effective treatment (Meehl, 1986; Millon, 1986).

In the twentieth century, the American Psychiatric Association is responsible for the major classification of mental disturbances in the United States. Revisions of earlier classifications led to the development in 1980 of **DSM-III** (which stands for the third edition of the Diagnostic and Statistical Manual of Mental Disorders), currently the most widely used system for classifying mental disorders.

DSM-III

The first classification of mental disorders in the United States was based on the census data of 1840. One category of all mental disorders was used; both the idiotic and the insane were placed in this inclusive category.

Modern efforts to construct a systematic classification of mental disorders began with DSM-I, published in 1952; for the first time a glossary with definitions of terms was provided. DSM-II appeared in 1968; more systematic input from expert diagnosticians improved this effort.

Two important categories in DSM-II not included in DSM-III deserve mention: neurotic and psychotic. The term **neurotic** refers to relatively mild mental disorders in which the individual has not lost contact with reality. For example, someone who is extremely anxious, troubled, and unhappy may be able to carry out his everyday functions and have a clear perception of reality; this individual would be classified as neurotic. The term **psychotic** refers to severe mental disturbances; psychotic individuals have lost contact with reality. The psychotic individual's thinking or perception is so distorted that he lives in a psychological world far removed from others. The psychotic individual might hear voices that are not present or think he is a famous person, such as Jesus Christ.

The terms neurotic and psychotic were dropped from the DSM classification system because they were believed to be too broad and ill-defined for diagnostic labels. Instead of the neurotic category, DSM-III uses more precise

Table 14.1 Main Categories of Mental Disorders and Their Description in DSM-III

1. *Disorders usually first evident in infancy, childhood, or adolescence*
   For example, mental retardation and eating disorders.
2. *Organic mental disorders*
   Involve an injury to the brain or biochemical imbalances in the brain, for example, syphilis and Alzheimer's disease.
3. *Substance use disorders*
   For example, abuse of alcohol, heroin, and other drugs.
4. *Schizophrenic disorders*
   People who have lost contact with reality and display unusual behavior and bizarre thoughts.
5. *Paranoid disorders*
   Excessive and overwhelming suspicions and persecutory feelings.
6. *Affective disorders*
   Persistent depression, abnormal elation, or some alternation between the two.
7. *Anxiety disorders*
   Anxiety overwhelms a person to the point where he cannot function well in day-to-day life. Also includes specific fears (phobias) and obsessive-compulsive behavior.
8. *Somatoform disorders*
   Physical symptoms exist without physical basis, and there is a strong presumption that symptoms are linked to psychological factors

or conflicts, as in conversion disorders. Hypochondriacs unrealistically interpret physical sensations as abnormal and are preoccupied with the fear or belief that they suffer from a serious disease.

9. *Dissociative disorders*
   Individuals eliminate their problems from memory. Amnesia is the most well-known example. Another is multiple personality.
10. *Psychosexual disorders*
    People who have problems with their sexual identity, such as transexuals and transvestites, and those who have difficulty with their sexual performance (e.g., erectile failure in males).
11. *Personality disorders*
    Long-standing maladaptive personality traits. Odd or eccentric people, individuals who show antisocial behavior, and those who are extremely narcissistic are examples.
12. *Conditions that are not attributable to a mental disorder but are a focus of attention or treatment*
    For example, people with marital problems and those experiencing parent-child or parent-adolescent conflict.

Source: DSM-III American Psychiatric Association, 1980

categories such as anxiety disorders, somatoform disorders, and dissociative disorders—disturbances we will discuss shortly. Rather than the general psychotic category, DSM-III uses categories such as shizophrenia and bipolar affective disorder, which we also will discuss later. While neurotic and psychotic have been dropped from the DSM classification, clinicians still use the terms from time to time as a convenient way of referring to relatively mild or relatively serious mental disorders.

In 1974 the American Psychiatric Association appointed a task force to develop DSM-III; when published in 1980, DSM-III contained eighteen major classifications and more than 200 specific disorders (some of the most prominent classifications along with a brief description of each are presented in table 14.1). Among the advantages of DSM-III over DSM-II are improved diagnostic criteria (vague descriptions were replaced with more specific guidelines), redefinition of major categories in line with research findings (for example, schizophrenia is defined more narrowly), new categories (malingering, for instance), and a multiaxial system (Webb & others, 1981).

The **multiaxial system** consists of five dimensions, or "axes," on which the individual is assessed. This system ensures that an individual will not merely be assigned to a mental disturbance category; she will be characterized in terms of a number of clinical factors that are grouped according to axes. Axis I consists of the primary classifications or diagnosis of the disturbance (for example, fear of people). Axis II focuses on developmental or personality disorders that begin in childhood or adolescence and often continue into adulthood (for example, mental retardation or certain personality disorders). Axis III refers to any physical disorders that might be relevant in understanding the disturbance (for example, an individual's history of disease, such as a cardiovascular problem). Axis IV indexes the severity of the psychosocial stressors in the individual's recent past that might have contributed to the mental problem (for example, divorce, death of a parent, or loss of job). Axis V involves a global evaluation of the individual's highest level of functioning in the last year. For example, does the individual have a history of poor work and relationship patterns, or have there been times when the individual performed effectively at work and enjoyed positive interpersonal relationships? If functioning has been high at some point in the past, prognosis for recovery is enhanced.

The Controversy Surrounding DSM-III

A rash of criticism was directed at DSM-III even before it reached the public. Criticism has ranged from mild to feverish, with the strongest coming mainly from psychologists. Psychologists are unhappy with the medical terminology and disease implications of the classification; the complexity of the system; the inclusion of problems of living that should not be classified as mental disorders; and the questionable reliability and validity of the categories (Eysenck, 1986; Garmezy, 1978; Meehl, 1986; Millon, 1986; Scheff, 1986).

Some mental health professionals believe several DSM-III categories have an antifemale bias. Premenstrual dysforic disorder and self-defeating personality disorders are two examples. The critics argue that premenstrual disorder should not be classified as a mental disorder but rather as a problem of living and that a tendency exists to apply the self-defeating personality disorder exclusively to women, especially in relationships with abusive men, which further blames the victim.

The revision of DSM-III, called DSM-III-R, was published in 1987. The premenstrual disorder and self-defeating personality disorder were still in the diagnostic manual, but they had been relegated to an appendix. Another highly controversial category, a form of homosexuality, was dropped in the revision of DSM-III.

Revision of DSM-III will continue and it is predicted that DSM-IV will be published by the mid-1990s. For the time being, psychiatrists still are more satsified with DSM-III than psychologists (Auerbach & Childress, 1987; Millon & Klerman, 1986; Pasnau, 1986); nonetheless, psychologists usually go along with the classification system of DSM-III. For all its criticisms, DSM-III is the best classification system currently available and the majority of health insurance companies insist on a diagnostic category before they will pay for an individual's therapy.

Now that we have discussed the nature of abnormality and the classification of mental disorders (a summary of these ideas is presented in concept table 14.1), we turn to the diagnostic categories themselves and the main types of mental disturbances.

Concept Table 14.1

The Nature of Abnormality and the Classification of Mental Disorders		
Concept	**Processes/related ideas**	**Characteristics/description**
Nature of abnormality	Approaches	At different points in history, mental disorders were attributed to supernatural causes. More recently, the statistical, biological, and psychological and sociocultural approaches are prominent. The statistical approach states that an individual is abnormal if she deviates substantially from the average.
	The biological approach	Mental disorders have biological causes. The forerunner of this approach is the medical model, which describes individuals as "patients" in "hospitals" where they are treated by "doctors."
	Psychological and sociocultural approaches	Many psychologists believe the biological approach underplays the importance of psychological and sociocultural factors and that the medical model encourages labeling of mental disorders.
	An interactionist approach	Abnormal behavior is complex; a more complete understanding is achieved by considering biological, cognitive, and environmental factors.
Classification of mental disorders	DSM-III	DSM-II included categories of neurotic and psychotic behavior. Mental health professionals still use these terms, but they have been dropped from DSM-III. DSM-III has improved diagnostic criteria, redefined disturbances more in line with research findings, and developed a multiaxial approach.
	The controversy surrounding DSM-III	Psychologists are especially critical of DSM-III; criticisms include its medical terminology, complexity, inclusion of problems of living, and weak reliability of some categories. A revision, DSM-III-R, appeared in 1987.

Anxiety Disorders

Anxiety usually is defined as a diffuse, vague, highly unpleasant feeling of fear and apprehension. Individuals with high levels of anxiety worry a lot. The main features of **anxiety disorders** are: motor tension (jumpiness, trembling, inability to relax); hyperactivity (dizziness, a racing heart, or possible perspiration); apprehensive expectations and thoughts; vigilence and scanning reflected in hyperattentiveness. In a recent national survey, one in every twelve individuals said that anxiety was so bothersome to them that they were classified as having an anxiety disorder (Regier & others, 1984). Four important subclasses of the anxiety disorders are generalized anxiety disorder, panic disorder, phobic disorder, and obsessive compulsive disorder.

Generalized Anxiety Disorder

Anna, who is twenty-seven years old, had just arrived for her visit with the psychologist. She seemed very nervous and was wringing her hands, crossing and uncrossing her legs, and playing nervously with the strands of her hair. She said that her stomach felt knotted up, that her hands were cold, and that her neck muscles felt so tight they hurt. She said that lately arguments with her husband had escalated. In recent weeks, Anna indicated that she had been feeling more and more nervous throughout the day as if something bad were about to happen. If the phone rang or the doorbell sounded, her heart would

People with anxiety disorders worry a lot; in a recent national survey, one of every twelve individuals reported being so bothered by anxiety that they were classified as having an anxiety disorder.

Table 14.2   Nature of First Panic Attack and Associated Life Events

	No. (%) of patients
Onset of attack	
Spontaneous	47 (78)
Nonspontaneous, precipitated by:	13 (22)
Public speaking	3
Stimulant drug use	3
Family argument	2
Leaving home	2
Exercise (while pregnant)	1
Being frightened by a stranger	1
Fear of fainting	1
Stressful life events associated with attack	
No stressful life event within six months	22 (37)
Stressful life event within six months*	38 (63)
Threatened or actual separation from important person	11
Change in job causing increased pressure	8
Pregnancy	7
Move	5
Marriage	3
Graduation	3
Death of close person	3
Physical illness	2

*Four patients had two concomitant stressful life events.
Source: Breier, Charney, & Heninger, 1986, p. 1033.

beat rapidly and her breathing would quicken. When she was around people she had a difficult time speaking. She began to isolate herself; her husband became impatient with her, so she finally decided to see a psychologist (Goodstein & Calhoun, 1982).

Anna has a **generalized anxiety disorder,** which consists of persistent anxiety for at least one month without specific symptoms. In one investigation, individuals with generalized anxiety disorder had higher degrees of muscle tension and hyperactivity than individuals with other types of anxiety disorders. These individuals said they had been tense and anxious for more than one-half of their lives (Barlow & others, 1986; Lipschitz, 1987).

Panic Disorder

The main feature of **panic disorder** is recurrent panic attacks marked by the sudden onset of intense apprehension or terror. The individual often has a feeling of impending doom but may not feel anxious all the time. The unanticipated anxiety attacks include severe palpitations, extreme shortness of breath, chest pains, trembling, sweating, dizziness, and a feeling of helplessness. Victims fear that they will die, go crazy, or do something they cannot control (Katon & others, 1987).

What are some of the psychosocial and biological factors involved in panic disorder? As shown in table 14.2, the majority of panic attacks are spontaneous; those that are not spontaneous are triggered by a variety of events (Breier, Charney, & Heninger, 1986). In many instances, a stressful life event has occurred in the last six months, most often a threatened or actual separation from a loved one or a change in job. Only recently has attention been given to biological factors in understanding panic disorder (Dagar, Cowley, & Dunner, 1987). In one investigation, PET scans of panic disorder patients showed abnormal blood flow, blood volume, and oxygen flow in the right side of the brain (Ballenger, 1986).

Phobic Disorders

Agnes is an unmarried thirty-year-old woman who had been unable to go higher than the second floor of any building for more than a year. When she tried to overcome her fear of heights by going up to the third, fourth, or fifth floor, she became overwhelmed by anxiety. She remembers how it all began. One evening she was working alone and was seized by an urge to jump out of an eighth-story window. She was so frightened by her impulse that she hid behind a file cabinet for more than two hours until she calmed down enough to get her things together and go home. As she reached the first floor of the building, her heart was pounding and she was perspiring heavily. After several months she gave up her position and became a lower-paid salesperson so she could work on the bottom floor of the store (Cameron, 1963).

A **phobic disorder,** commonly called phobia, is an overwhelming fear of a particular object or situation. An individual with generalized anxiety cannot pinpoint the cause of his nervous feelings; an individual with a phobia can. Each of us is afraid of certain things; in many instances, though, these fears are not phobias. A fear becomes a phobia when a situation is so dreaded that an individual will go to almost any length to avoid it. For example, Agnes quit her job to avoid being in high places. Some phobias are more debilitating than others; an individual with a phobia for automobiles will have a more difficult time functioning in our society than an individual with a phobia for snakes, for example (Marks, 1987).

Phobic disorders involve an overwhelming fear of a particular object or situation. Phobias come in many forms; acrophobia, or fear of heights, is one example.

Phobias come in many forms; some of the most common phobias involve height, open spaces, people, closed spaces, dogs, dirt, the dark, and snakes. The most common phobia is **agoraphobia,** the fear of entering unfamiliar situations, especially open or public places. It accounts for 50 to 80 percent of the phobic population according to estimates (Foa, Steketze, & Young, 1984). Some instances of agoraphobia are preceded by panic attacks; agoraphobia in individuals seen by clinicians is often a complication of panic disorder.

Why do individuals develop phobias? Psychoanalytic theory stresses that phobias are defense mechanisms that develop to ward off threatening or unacceptable impulses. Agnes hid behind a file cabinet because she feared she would jump out of an eighth-story window. Learning theory, however, provides a different explanation of phobias; it stresses that phobias are learned fears. Remember in the case of Little Hans, described in the last chapter, that his phobia of horses was explained by the principles of learning. In Agnes's case, she may have fallen out of a window when she was a young girl; because of her past association of falling with pain, she now fears high places. Or she may have heard about or seen other individuals be afraid in high places. In these latter two examples, classical conditioning and observational learning, respectively, would be responsible for the phobias.

Biological factors also may be involved in phobias. First-generation relatives of patients with agoraphobia and panic attacks have high rates of these disorders themselves (Noyes & others, 1986), suggesting a possible genetic predisposition for phobias. Others have found that identical twins reared apart sometimes develop the same phobias; one pair became claustrophobic independently, for example (Eckert, Heston, & Bouchard, 1981).

*"But that's what you said yesterday—
'Just one more cord'!"*
Drawing by Woodman; © 1986 The New Yorker
Magazine, Inc.

Obsessive-Compulsive Disorders

Bob is twenty-seven years old and lives in a well-kept apartment; he has few friends and little social life. He was raised by a demanding mother and an aloof father. Bob is an accountant who spends long hours at work. He is a perfectionist. His demanding mother always nagged at him to improve himself, to keep the house spotless, and to be clean and neat. She made Bob wash his hands each time he touched his genital area. As an adult, Bob developed a cleansing ritual, usually triggered when he touched his genital area. He would remove his clothes in a prearranged sequence and then scrub his body from head to toe. He dressed himself in the opposite way from which he took off his clothes. If he deviated from this order, he invariably would start the sequence all over again. Sometimes Bob performed the cleansing ritual four to five times an evening. He was aware of how absurd his behavior was but felt compelled to go through with the ritual (Meyer & Osborne, 1982).

Obsessive-compulsive disorders involve recurrent obsessions or compulsions. Obsessions and compulsions are different problems, but often both are displayed by the same individual. **Obsessions** are anxiety-provoking thoughts that will not go away. The recurrent thoughts can be frightening or repulsive to the individual, but no matter how hard the individual tries to eliminate them, they reappear. For example, thoughts about killing someone in a traffic accident or sexually molesting someone may dominate a person's mind.

Compulsions are repetitive, ritualistic behaviors that usually are carried out to prevent or produce some future situation. Common compulsions involve excessive checking, cleansing, and counting. For example, a young man feels that he has to check his apartment for gas leaks, make sure the windows and doors are locked, and ensure that he has not left any valuable personal articles out in the open. His behavior is not compulsive if he does this once, but when he goes back four or five times to check and then constantly worries while he is out if he checked carefully enough, the behavior is compulsive. Most individuals do not enjoy their ritualistic behavior but feel anxious when they do not carry it out (Kozak, Foa, & McCarthy, 1987).

Somatoform Disorders

"Look, I am having trouble breathing. You don't believe me. Nobody believes me. There are times when I can't stop coughing. I'm losing weight. I know I have cancer. My father died of cancer when I was twelve." Herb has been to six cancer specialists in the last two years; none can find anything wrong with him. Each doctor has taken X rays and conducted excessive laboratory tests, but Herb's test results do not indicate any illnesses. Might some psychological factors be responsible for Herb's sense that he is physically ailing? In the last two years Herb has lost three jobs as a salesman, and he recently discovered that his wife is unfaithful.

Somatoform disorders are mental disturbances in which psychological symptoms take a physical, or *somatic,* form, even though no physical causes can be found. Although these symptoms are not caused physically, they are highly distressing for the individual; the symptoms are real, not faked. Two types of somatoform disorders are hypochondriasis and conversion disorder.

Hypochondriasis

Some individuals always seem to overreact to such signs as a missed heart beat, shortness of breath, or a slight chest pain, fearing that something is wrong with them. **Hypochondriasis** is a pervasive fear of illness and disease. At the first indication of something amiss in their bodies, hypochondriacs call a doctor; not infrequently they inform the doctor of the disease they have before she gets an opportunity to examine. When a physical examination reveals no problems, the hypochondriac usually does not believe the doctor. He often changes doctors, moving from one to another searching for a diagnosis that will match his own. Most hypochondriacs are pill enthusiasts; their medicine chests spill over with bottles of hopeful cures for their maladies.

Hypochondriasis is a difficult category to diagnose accurately; for it to occur without other mental disturbances is actually quite rare. Depression often is present in the hypochondriac, for example (Barsky, Wyshak, & Klerman, 1986; Kellner & others, 1987; Rubin, Zorumski, & Guze, 1986).

Conversion Disorder

Conversion disorder received its name from Freudian theory, which stressed that anxiety can be "converted" into a special physical symptom. The hypochondriac has no physical disability; the individual with a conversion disorder does have some loss of motor or sensory ability. The individual may be unable to speak, he may faint, or he even may be deaf or blind.

Conversion disorder was more common in Freud's time than today. Freud was especially interested in this disorder, in which physical symptoms made no neurological sense. For example, with *glove anethesia* individuals report that their entire hand is numb from the tip of their fingers to a cutoff point at the wrist. As shown in figure 14.2, if these individuals were experiencing true physiological numbness, their symptoms would be very different. Like hypochondriasis, conversion disorder often appears in conjunction with other mental disturbances; during long-term evaluation, conversion disorder often turns out to be another mental or physical disorder (Rubin, Zorumski, & Guze, 1986).

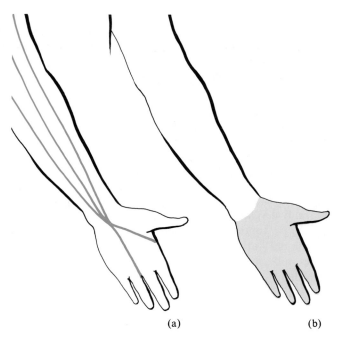

(a)   (b)

Figure 14.2
Glove anesthesia. A patient who complained of numbness in the hand might be diagnosed as suffering from conversion disorder if the area of the hand affected showed that a disorder of the nervous system was not responsible. The skin areas served by nerves in the arm are shown in (a). The "glove anesthesia" shown in (b) could not result from damage to these nerves.

Dissociative Disorders

Dissociative disorders occur when an individual suddenly loses his memory or changes his identity. Under extreme stress or shock, the individual's thoughts become *dissociated* (separated or split) from other information about the self. Amnesia, fugue, and multiple personality are examples of dissociative disorders.

Amnesia and Fugue

In chapter 6, amnesia was described as the inability to recall important events. Amnesia can be caused by an injury to the head, for example. But **psychogenic amnesia** is a dissociative disorder involving memory loss caused by extensive psychological stress. For example, an individual showed up at a hospital and said he did not know who he was. After several days in the hospital, he awoke one morning and demanded to be released. Eventually he remembered that he had been involved in an automobile accident in which a pedestrian had been killed. The extensive stress of the accident and the fear that he might be held responsible triggered the amnesia (Cameron, 1963).

　　Like amnesia, **fugue** (which means "flight") involves a loss of memory, but the individual may unexpectedly travel away from home or work, assume a new identity, and be unable to remember her previous identity. For example, a thirty-one-year-old woman named Barbara left home without a trace. Two weeks later she was picked up by police in a nearby city. When her husband came to see her, Barbara asked, "Who are you?" She could not remember anything about the last two weeks of her life. During psychotherapy, she began to gradually recall her past. She left home with enough money to buy a bus ticket to where she grew up as a child. She spent days walking the streets and standing near a building where her father had worked. Later she went to a motel with a man; according to the motel manager she entertained a series of men over a three-day period. After a two-week absence, Barbara looked more like a teenager than a thirty-one-year-old woman, wearing a ponytail and bobby socks (Goldstein & Palmer, 1975).

Multiple Personality

The most dramatic but least frequent dissociative disorder is **multiple personality;** individuals suffering from this disorder have two or more distinct personalities or selves, much like Dr. Jekyl and Mr. Hyde. Each personality has its own memories, behaviors, and relationships; one personality dominates the individual at one point, another at another point. The personalities are not aware of each other and the shift from one to the other usually occurs suddenly under distress.

　　One of the most famous cases of multiple personality involves the "three faces of Eve" (Thigpen & Cleckly, 1957). Eve White was the original dominant personality. She had no knowledge of her second personality, Eve Black, although Eve Black had been alternating with Eve White for a number of years. Eve White was bland, quiet, and serious—a rather dull personality. Eve Black, by contrast, was carefree, mischievous, and uninhibited. She would "come out" at the most inappropriate times, leaving Eve White with hangovers, bills, and a reputation in local bars that she could not explain. During treatment, a third personality, Jane, emerged, More mature than the other two, Jane seemed to have developed as a result of therapy (see figure 14.3 for a portrayal of the three faces of Eve).

Figure 14.3
Chris Sizemore, the subject of the book Three Faces of Eve, *is shown with the work she painted and entitled* Three Faces in One.

Concept Table 14.2

Anxiety, Somatoform, and Dissociative Disorders		
Concept	**Processes/related ideas**	**Characteristics/description**
Anxiety disorders	Their nature	Anxiety is a diffuse, unpleasant feeling involving fear and apprehension; features of anxiety disorders are motor tension, hyperactivity, apprehensiveness, and vigilence involving hyperattentiveness.
	Generalized anxiety disorder	Persistent anxiety for at least one month without specific symptoms.
	Panic disorder	Recurrent panic attacks marked by the sudden onset of intense apprehension.
	Phobic disorders	An overwhelming fear of a particular object or situation. Phobias come in many forms; the most common is agoraphobia. Psychoanalytic and learning explanations of phobias have been offered; recently biological factors are implicated, with individuals possibly having a genetic predisposition.
	Obsessive-compulsive disorders	Recurrent obsessions or compulsions. Obsessions are anxiety-provoking thoughts that won't go away; compulsions are repetitive, stereotyped behaviors.
Somatoform disorders	Their nature	Psychological symptoms take a physical, or somatic, form even though no evidence of a physical cause can be found.
	Hypochondriasis	A pervasive fear of illness and disease. It rarely occurs alone; depression often accompanies hypochondriasis.
	Conversion disorder	Received its name from Freudian theory, which stressed that anxiety can be "converted" into a special physical symptom. Some loss of motor or sensory ability occurs. The disorder was more common in Freud's time than today.
Dissociative disorders	Their nature	The individual suddenly loses his memory or changes his identity. Under extreme stress, the individual's thoughts become dissociated (separated or split) from other information about the self.
	Amnesia and fugue	Psychogenic amnesia involves memory loss caused by extensive psychological stress. Fugue also involves a loss of memory, but the individual may unexpectedly travel away from home or work, assume a new identity, and not remember her old one.
	Multiple personality	Involves the presence of two or more distinct personalities in the same individual. The disorder is rare.

A summary of the research literature on multiple personality suggests that certain background factors are related to the disorder (Ludolph, 1982). The most striking feature is an inordinately high rate of sexual or physical abuse during early childhood; sexual abuse occurred in 56 percent of the reported cases, for example. Mothers tend to be rejecting and depressed, fathers distant, alcoholic, and abusive. Remember that while fascinating, the multiple personality disorder is rare; since the early 1800s approximately 150 cases have been reported (Boor, 1982).

At this point, we have considered three major types of mental disturbances—anxiety, somatoform, and dissociative. A summary of the main ideas about these disorders is presented in concept table 14.2. Now we turn to a set of widespread disorders—the affective disorders.

Depression is the common cold of mental disorders; more than 250,000 individuals are hospitalized every year for the disorder.

Affective Disorders

The **affective disorders** are disturbances of mood. They include disorders with wide emotional swings, ranging from deeply depressed to highly euphoric and agitated. Depression can occur alone, as in major depression, or it can alternate with mania, as in bipolar disorder.

Major Depression

Pete contacted his college counseling center because he had been depressed for several months. Nothing cheered him up. His situation deteriorated to the point where he was depressed for long periods of time; some days he wouldn't even leave his room, keeping the shades drawn and the room dark. Two months earlier, the girl he wanted to marry decided marriage was not for her. By the time he finally contacted the college counseling center, Pete felt like he could hardly get out of bed in the morning. He had trouble maintaining conversations and felt exhausted most of the time. Pete told the counselor that he just wanted to spend time alone and that no one could help him. Pete had reached the point where mild depression was turning into major depression. The individual with **major depression** is sad, demoralized, bored, and self-derogatory; he does not feel well, loses stamina easily, has a poor appetite, and seems listless and unmotivated.

The path of depression often begins with crying, agitation, or denial of a problem; depression follows, at which time the individual appears withdrawn, apathetic, and unresponsive. Recovery is at times a slow process of regaining optimistic thoughts and an interest in life. Depression becomes a mental disturbance when the individual remains withdrawn.

Major depression is more intense and long lasting than the mild form. In our stress-filled world, depression is a frequently used term. When someone asks you what is wrong when they look at your gloomy face, you probably respond, "I feel depressed—about myself, about my life." Perhaps you haven't

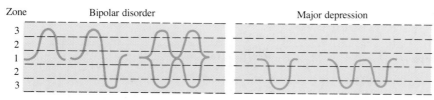

Note: Zone refers to the severity of the mood swing, either in a manic or a depressed direction.

Figure 14.4
Comparison of mood swings in bipolar and major depression.

done well in a class or things aren't working out in your love life. You feel down in the dumps. In most instances, though, your depression won't last as long or be as intense as Pete's; after a few hours, days, or weeks, you snap out of your gloomy state and begin to cope more effectively with life's stresses. Nonetheless, depression is so widespread that it has been called the "common cold" of mental disorders; more than 250,000 individuals are hospitalized every year for the disorder (Cameron, 1987). Students, professors, corporate executives, laborers—no one is immune to depression, not even F. Scott Fitzgerald or Ernest Hemingway, each of whom experienced major depression.

Major depression may not only include distorted thoughts, but also suicidal tendencies. To learn more about the nature of suicide turn to Psychology 14.2.

Bipolar Disorder

Mrs. M. was first admitted to a mental hospital at the age of thirty-eight, although she had experienced extreme mood swings since she was a child. At thirty-three, shortly before the birth of her first child, she became very depressed; she even went into a coma for four days. One month after the baby was born she became agitated and euphoric. Mrs. M. signed a year's lease on an apartment, bought furniture, and piled up debts. Several years later other manic and depressive mood swings occurred. In one of her excitatory moods, Mrs. M. swore loudly and created a disturbance at a club where she was not a member. Several days later she began divorce proceedings. On the day prior to her admission to the mental hospital, she purchased fifty-seven hats! Several weeks later, she became despondent, saying, "I have no energy. My brain doesn't work right. I have let my family down. I don't have anything to live for." In a subsequent manic bout, Mrs. M. sent the following telegram to a physician she romanticized about:

> To: You; Street and No.: Everywhere; Place: The remains of peace! We did our best, but God's will be done! I am very sorry for all of us. To brave it through thus far. Yes Darling—from Hello Handsome, Handsome is as Handsome does, thinks, lives, breathes. It takes clean air. Brother of Mine, in a girl's hour of need. All my love to the Best Inspiration one ever had. (Kolb, 1973, p. 377)

Mrs. M.'s case reveals the amazing mood swings that can characterize **bipolar disorder.** An individual with this disorder might be depressed, manic, or both. We have described the symptoms of depression; what are the symptoms of mania? The individual's mood is elated, humorous, and scheming; she is exuberant, has tireless stamina, and shows a tendency for excess; and she is restless, irritable, and almost in constant motion. The type of mood swings that might occur in bipolar disorder are shown in figure 14.4, where they are contrasted with the mood swings present with major depression.

Psychology 14.2

Suicide

To be, or not to be—that is the question.
Whether 'tis nobler in the mind to suffer
The slings and arrows of outrageous fortune,
Or to take arms against a sea of troubles
And by opposing end them. To die, to sleep—
No more, and by a sleep to say we end
The heartache and the thousand natural shocks
That flesh is heir to. 'Tis a consummation
Devoutly to be wished.

—Shakespeare, Hamlet, *(Act III)*

Suicide is a common problem in our society. Its rate has quadrupled during the last thirty years in the United States; each year about 25,000 individuals take their own lives. Beginning at about the age of fifteen the rate of suicides begins to rise rapidly (see figure 14.B). Males are about three times as likely to commit suicide as females; this may be due to their more active methods for attempting suicide—shooting, for example. By contrast, females are more likely to use passive methods such as sleeping pills, which do not cause death. While males commit suicide more frequently, females attempt it more often.

Estimates suggest that six to ten suicide attempts occur for every suicide in the general population; for adolescents the figure is as high as fifty attempts for every life taken. As many as two in every three college students have thought about suicide on at least one occasion; their methods range

from drugs to crashing into the White House in an airplane (Mishara, 1976).

Why do people attempt suicide? There is no simple answer to this important question. It is helpful to think of suicide in terms of proximal and distal factors. Proximal, or immediate, factors can trigger a suicide attempt. Highly stressful circumstances such as loss of a spouse or a job, flunking out of school, or getting pregnant when it is not desired can produce suicide attempts. Drugs also have been involved in suicide attempts more in recent years than in the past (Rich, Young, & Fowler, 1986).

But distal, or earlier, experiences often are involved in suicide attempts as well. A long-standing history of family instability and unhappiness may be present (Jacobs, 1971). A lack of affection and emotional support, high control, and a strong push for achievement by parents during early childhood are related to depression among adolescents;

these family experiences also may lead to suicide (Gjerde, 1985). In a recent investigation of suicide among gifted women, previous suicide attempts, anxiety, conspicuous instability in work and relationships, depression, or alcoholism were present in the women's lives (Tomlinson-Keasey, Warren, & Elliott, 1986). These factors are similar to those found to predict suicide among gifted men (Shneidman, 1971).

Just as genetic factors are an issue in depression, they appear in suicide as well; the closer the genetic relation to someone who has committed suicide the more likely that individual will commit suicide (Wender & others, 1986). We do not have the complete answers for detecting when an individual is considering suicide or how to prevent it, but the advice offered in table 14.B provides some valuable suggestions about effective ways to communicate with someone you think may be contemplating suicide.

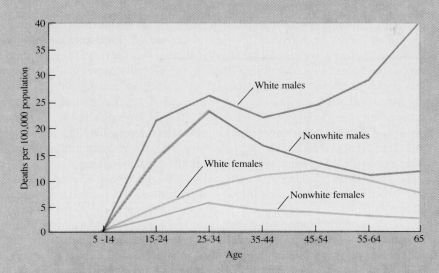

Figure 14.B
Suicide rates by sex, age, and race in the United States.
Source: After data presented by the U.S. Bureau of Census, 1980. U.S. Government Printing Office.

Table 14.B What to Do and What Not to Do when You Suspect Someone Is Likely to Commit Suicide

What to do

1. Ask direct, straightfoward questions in a calm manner. "Are you thinking about hurting yourself?"
2. Assess the seriousness of the suicidal intent by asking questions about feelings, important relationships, who else the person has talked with, and the amount of thought given to the means to be used. If a gun, pills, rope, or other means has been obtained and a precise plan developed, clearly the situation is dangerous. Stay with the person until some type of help arrives.
3. Be a good listener and be very supportive without being falsely reassuring.
4. Try to persuade the person to obtain professional help and assist him or her in getting this help.

What not to do

1. Do not ignore the warning signs.
2. Don't refuse to talk about suicide if a person approaches you about the topic.
3. Do not react with horror, disapproval, or repulsion.
4. Don't give false reassurances by saying things like, "Everything is going to be o.k." Also don't give out simple answers or platitudes like "You have everything to be thankful for."
5. Do not abandon the individual after the crisis has gone by or after professional help has commenced.

Reprinted from *Living with 10- to 15-year-olds: A parent education curriculum.* Copyright by the Center for Early Adolescence, Carrboro, NC, 1982, rev. ed. 1987. Used with permission.

Causes of Affective Disorders

What caused Pete to be so depressed? What caused Mrs. M. to engage in manic behavior one moment and be so depressed the next moment? Psychoanalytic, cognitive and learning, and biogenetic explanations have been given.

Psychoanalytic Explanations

In 1917, Sigmund Freud published a paper called "Mourning and Melancholia," in which he described his view of depression. Freud believed depression was a turning inward of aggressive instincts. He theorized that the child's early attachment to a love object (usually the mother) contains a mixture of love and hate. When the child loses the love object or her dependency needs are frustrated, feelings of loss coexist with anger. Since the child cannot openly accept such angry feelings toward the individual she loves, the hostility is turned inward. Freud said that the clinical outgrowth is depression. The unresolved mixture of anger and love is carried forward to adolescence and adulthood, where loss can bring back these early feelings of abandonment.

The British psychiatrist John Bowlby (1980) agrees with Freud that early childhood experiences are an important determinant of depression in adulthood. He believes a combination of an insecure attachment to the mother, a lack of love and affection as a child, and the actual loss of a parent during childhood gives rise to a negative cognitive set, or schema. The schema built up during childhood causes the individual to interpret later losses as yet other failures in one's effort to establish enduring and close positive relationships. Recent research data suggest that at least in the case of adolescent girls, early childhood experiences with parents are involved with depression (Gjerde, 1985). In this longitudinal study, parents' lack of affection, high control, and an aggressive achievement orientation in early childhood was associated with depression among young adolescent girls but not boys; the sex difference may be because depression occurs more often among females than males.

Cognitive and Learning Explanations

Is depression caused by the way we think about ourselves and our world? Do we learn to be depressed?

Individuals who are depressed rarely think happy thoughts; they interpret their lives in self-defeating ways and have negative expectations about the future. Aaron Beck (1967) believes that such negative thoughts reflect schemata that shape the depressed individual's experiences. These habitual negative thoughts magnify and expand a depressed individual's negative experiences. The depressed person may overgeneralize about a minor occurrence and think that he is worthless because a work assignment was turned in late, his son was arrested for shoplifting, or a friend made a negative comment about his hair. Beck believes that depressed individuals blame themselves far more than is warranted. For example, an athlete may accept complete blame for a team's loss when five or ten other teammates, the opposing team, and other factors were involved.

Self-defeating and sad thoughts fit the clinical picture of the depressed individual; whether these thoughts are the cause or the consequence of the depression, however, is controversial. Critics say that self-defeating thoughts are an outgrowth of the biological and environmental conditions that produce depression. One of the environmental factors thought to be important in understanding depression is learned helplessness.

Some years ago, in the interest of science, a researcher drowned two rats. The first rat was dropped into a tank of warm water; it swam around for sixty hours before it drowned. The second rat was handled differently. The researcher held the rat tightly in his hand until it quit struggling to get loose. Then the rat was dropped into the tank; it swam around for several minutes before it drowned. The researcher concluded that the second rat drowned more quickly because its previous experiences told it to give up hope; the rat had developed a sense of helplessness (Richter, 1957).

The idea of **learned helplessness,** first developed in research with animals, has provided a provocative explanation of why individuals become depressed. Martin Seligman (1975), for example, argued that when individuals are exposed to stress or prolonged pain over which they have no control, they learn helplessness. In other words, the depressed individual may be apathetic because he cannot restate the rewards that he previously experienced. For example, in Pete's case described earlier he could not make his fiancée come back to him.

Biogenetic Explanations

Biological explanations of depression involve genetic inheritance and chemical changes in the brain. In a large twin study conducted in Denmark, identical twins were more likely to have affective disorders than fraternal twins. If one identical twin develops an affective disorder, the other has a 70 percent chance of developing the disorder; a fraternal twin runs only a 13 percent risk (Bertelson, 1979). In another investigation, the biological relatives of an individual with an affective disorder were more likely to have the disorder than adopted relatives (Khouri & Akiskal, 1986; Wender & others, 1986).

Remember from chapter 2 that neurotransmitters are chemical messengers that carry information from one neuron to the next. Two neurotransmitters involved in depression are norepinephrine and serotonin. Decreased levels of norepinephrine are found in depressed individuals, while increased levels appear when individuals are in a manic state. Low levels of serotonin also occur in depressed individuals. Patients with unusually low serotonin levels are ten times as likely to commit suicide than individuals with normal levels (Turkington, 1985). The endocrine system also may be involved in depression—hypersecretion of cortisol from the adrenal gland occurs in depressed individuals, for example (Joyce, Donald, & Elder, 1987; Price & others, 1986). More about biological aspects of depression appears in the next chapter, where we discuss the use of drugs to alleviate depression.

Separating environmental, cognitive, and biological causes of depression is not easy; whether neurotransmitters or cognitive factors are cause or effect is still unknown. Like most behaviors we have discussed, depression is best viewed as complex and determined by multiple factors.

Schizophrenic Disorders

Bob began to miss work, spending his time watching his house from a rented car parked inconspicuously down the street and following his fellow employees as they left work to see where they went and what they did. He kept a little black book in which he scribbled cryptic notes. When he went to the water cooler at work, he pretended to drink but instead looked carefully around the room to observe if anyone looked guilty or frightened.

Bob's world seemed to be closing in on him. After an explosive scene at the office one day, he became very agitated. He left and never returned. By the time Bob arrived at home, he was in a rage. He could not sleep that night and the next day he kept his children home from school; all day he kept the shades pulled on every window. The next night he maintained his vigil; at 4 A.M., he armed himself and burst out of the house, firing shots in the air while daring his enemies to come out (McNeil, 1967).

Bob is a paranoid schizophrenic, one of the schizophrenic disorders we will describe shortly. About 1 in every 100 Americans will be classified as schizophrenic in their lifetime; the same percentage has been documented in other countries as well—Nigeria, Russia, and India, for example (Tsuang, 1976). Schizophrenic disorders are serious, debilitating mental disturbances; about one-half of all mental hospital patients in the United States are schizophrenics. More now than in the past, schizophrenics live in society and return for treatment at mental hospitals periodically; drug therapy, which will be discussed in the next chapter, is primarily responsible for fewer schizophrenics being hospitalized. About one-third of schizophrenics get better, about one-third get worse, and another one-third stay about the same once they develop this severe mental disorder. What are the symptoms of these individuals?

Characteristics of Schizophrenic Disorders

Schizophrenia produces a bizarre set of symptoms and wreaks havoc on the individual's personality. **Schizophrenic disorders** are characterized by distorted thoughts and perceptions, odd communication, inappropriate emotion, abnormal motor behavior, and social withdrawal. The term *schizophrenia* comes from the Latin word "schizo," meaning split, and "phrenia," meaning mind. The individual's mind is split from reality and personality loses its unity. Schizophrenia is not the same as mutliple personality, which sometimes is called a "split personality." Schizophrenia involves the split of *one* personality from reality, not the coexistence of several personalities within the same individual.

Many schizophrenics have *delusions,* or false beliefs—one individual may think he is Jesus Christ, another Napoleon, for example. The delusions are utterly implausible; one individual may think her thoughts are being broadcast over the radio, another may think that a double agent is controlling her every move. Schizophrenics also may hear, see, feel, smell, and taste things not there; these *hallucinations* often take the form of voices; the schizophrenic might think that he hears two people talking about him, for example. Or, on another occasion, he might say, "Hear that rumbling in the pipe; that is one of my men in there watching out for me."

Often schizophrenics do not make sense when they talk or write. Their language does not follow any rules. For example, one schizophrenic might say, "Well, Rocky, babe, help is out, happening, but where, when, up, top, side, over, you know, out of the way, that's it. Sign off." Speech does not have any meaning; these incoherent, loose word associations are called *word salad*. In a schizophrenic's speech, facts may be put together and then completely inappropriate conclusions drawn.

The normal ability to display emotions may not be present in the schizophrenic; sometimes the schizophrenic's emotions seem uncanny and eerie, as if they are coming from another world. Emotions may be blunted, inappropriate, or highly varied. The schizophrenic might laugh, get angry, or cry at inappropriate times, for example.

The schizophrenic's motor behavior may be bizarre and sometimes visible from a distance. It might take the form of an odd appearance, pacing, statuelike posture, or strange mannerisms. Some schizophrenics withdraw from their social world. The individual may be so insulated from social matters that she seems totally absorbed in interior images and thoughts.

Forms of Schizophrenia

There are many forms of schizophrenia. The most prominent forms are: disorganized, catatonic, paranoid, and undifferentiated.

Those suffering from **disorganized schizophrenia** have delusions and hallucinations that have little or no recognizable meaning, hence the label *disorganized*. The disorganized schizophrenic shows excessive withdrawal from human contact. Regression to silly, childlike gestures and behavior may appear. Many of these individuals have an adolescence characterized by isolation or maladjustment (Goodstein & Calhoun, 1982).

The central feature of **catatonic schizophrenia** is bizarre motor behavior. Catatonic schizophrenics sometimes appear to be in a completely immobile stupor (see figure 14.5); nonetheless, they are completely conscious of what is happening. In a catatonic state, the individual may show what is called *waxy flexibility*; for example, if an individual's arm is picked up and then allowed to fall, the arm stays in the new position.

The primary characteristic of **paranoid schizophrenia** is delusions. Delusions usually form a complex, elaborate system that is based on a complete misinterpretation of actual events. The three main types of delusions are: grandeur, reference, and persecution. Individuals with delusions of grandeur think of themselves as some exhalted being—the pope or the president, for example. Individuals with delusions of reference misinterpret chance events as directly relevant to their own life—thunderstorms might be perceived as a personal message from God, for example. Individuals with delusions of persecution feel they are the target of a conspiracy—recall Bob's situation, for example. It is not unusual for an individual to develop all three types of delusions in the following order: First, the individual senses that she is special and has been singled out for attention (delusions of reference); then she believes this special attention is the result of her admirable and special characteristics (delusions of grandeur); and finally she thinks that others are so jealous and threatened by these characteristics that they are spying and plotting against her (delusions of persecution) (Meyer & Osborne, 1982).

A fourth form of schizophrenia is called **undifferentiated schizophrenia;** it features disorganized behavior, hallucinations, delusions, and incoherence. This category of schizophrenia is used when the criteria for the other types are not met or when the individual meets the criteria for more than one of the other types.

Figure 14.5
Disturbances in motor behavior are prominent symptoms in catatonic schizophrenia. Patients may cease to move altogether, sometimes taking on bizarre postures.

Causes of Schizophrenia

As with depression, considerable interest has developed in the genetic and biochemical basis of schizophrenia. Environmental determinants also have been proposed.

NIMH—Nora, Iris, Myra, and Hester, the Schizophrenic Genain Quadruplets

■ The story of the Genain quadruplets began more than fifty years ago. Henry Genain had forgotten to buy his wife a birthday present, so she suggested he give her a child instead for their third wedding anniversary. The wish came true; but there were four presents instead of one (see figure 14.C). The acronyms given to the quadruplets by scientists—*N*ora, *I*ris, *M*yra, and *H*ester—come from the first letters of *N*ational *I*nstitute of *M*ental *H*ealth, where the quadruplets have been extensively studied.

The birth of the quadruplets was a celebrated occasion; one paper ran a contest to name the girls and received 12,000 entries. The city found a rent-free house for the unemployed father, a dairy company donated free milk, and a baby carriage for four was given to the family. Newspaper stories appeared from time to time about the quadruplets, portraying their similarities, especially their drama talent and a song-and-dance routine they had developed.

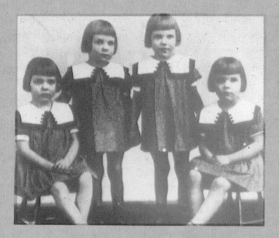

Figure 14.C
The Genain quadruplets as young children. Each of the quadruplets was diagnosed as schizophrenic by the time they were in their twenties.

But a darker side to the quadruplets' story emerged by the time they reached high school. It became clear that the girls had serious mental problems. By the time they were in their twenties, each had been diagnosed as schizophrenic. A perceptive hometown doctor recognized their symptoms and contacted NIMH. A research team led by David Rosenthal began extensive evaluation of the schizophrenic quadruplets (Rosenthal, 1963).

Some twenty years later, psychologist Alan Mirksy invited the quadruplets back to NIMH to determine how they might have changed; the research scientists also wanted to know if recently developed techniques could discover something special about their biological makeup.

PET scans revealed that sugar was used at an unusually high rate in the rear portion of the quadruplets' brains (see figure 14.D). Their brains also showed

Genetic Factors

If you have a relative with schizophrenia, what are the chances you will develop schizophrenia? It depends on how closely you are related. As genetic similarity increases, so does your risk of becoming schizophrenic. As shown in figure 14.6, an identical twin of a schizophrenic has a 46 percent chance of developing the disorder, a fraternal twin 14 percent, a sibling 10 percent, a nephew or niece 3 percent, and an unrelated individual in the general population 1 percent (Gottesman & Shields, 1982). Such data strongly suggest that genetic factors are involved in schizophrenia, although the precise nature of the genetic influence is unknown. More about genetic and genetic-environmental influences on schizophrenia is presented in Psychology 14.3, where the fascinating story of four quadruplets with schizophrenia is told.

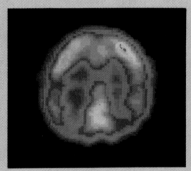

Nora   *Normal*

Figure 14.D
*In the normal brain, the areas of
high energy use are at the top
(frontal lobes). The quadruplets
all showed energy use in the
visual areas at the bottom of their
PET scan brain slices. Are these
the hallucinations? (Note: the
other three sisters showed PET
scans much more similar to Nora's
than to a normal individual.)*

much less alpha activity than the
brains of normal individuals.
Remember that alpha activity
appears in a relaxed state;
scientists speculate that the onset
of hallucinations might possibly
block alpha activity.

Some environmental
experiences probably contributed
to the Genain quadruplets'
schizophrenia as well. The father
placed strict demands on his
daughters; he delighted in
watching them undress, and he
would not let them play with
friends or participate in school or
church activities. He refused to let

the quadruplets participate in
social activities even as adults and
followed them to their jobs and
opened their mail.

What makes the Genain
quadruplets such fascinating cases
is their uniqueness—identical
quadruplets occur once in every
16 million births and only half
survive to adulthood; only 1 in 100
become schizophrenic; and the
chances of all of them being
schizophrenic happens only once
in tens of billions of births, a
figure much greater than the
current world population!
(Buchsbaum, 1984).

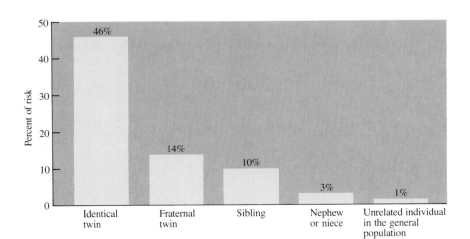

Figure 14.6
*Lifetime risk of becoming
schizophrenic according to genetic
relatedness.*

■ ■ ■ ■ ■ ■ ■ ■ ■ ■ ■ ■ ■ ■ ■ ■ ■

Concept Table 14.3

The Affective and Schizophrenic Disorders		
Concept	Processes/related ideas	Characteristics/description
The affective disorders	Their nature	Disturbances of mood that include disorders in which depression occurs alone or alternates with mania.
	Major depression	An individual is sad, demoralized, bored, and self-derogatory; he does not feel well, loses stamina easily, has a poor appetite, and seems listless and unmotivated. It is more intense and lasts longer than the milder forms; nonetheless, depression is widespread— one in five individuals will have at least one severe depression. Major depression sometimes leads to suicide.
	Bipolar disorder	Individuals show a mixture of extremely wide mood swings from depressed to manic.
	The causes of affective disorders	Psychoanalytic, cognitive and learning, and biogenetic explanations have been offered.
Schizophrenic disorders	Characteristics	A severe mental disturbance in which the individual's mind has "split" from reality; occurs in approximately 1 of every 100 individuals and accounts for approximately one-half of all mental hospital patients. Schizophrenics have distorted thoughts and perceptions, odd communication, inappropriate emotion, abnormal motor behavior, and social withdrawal.
	Forms	The most prominent forms are: disorganized, catatonic, paranoid, and undifferentiated.
	Causes	Considerable interest has developed in the genetic and biochemical basis of schizophrenia; environmental determinants also have been proposed. The diathesis-stress view emphasizes the combination of a genetic predisposition and environmental stress.

Neurobiological Factors

Among the neurobiological factors being investigated for possible roles in schizophrenia are brain metabolism, a malfunctioning dopamine system, and distorted cerebral blood flow (Turkington, 1985). Imaging techniques, such as the PET scan, clearly show deficits in the brain metabolisms of schizophrenics, as we saw in the Genain quadruplets. Do these deficits cause the disorder or are they simply symptoms of a disorder whose true origin lies deeper in the brain, in the genes, or in the environment? Whether cause or effect, information about neurobiological factors is increasing our knowledge of the nature of schizophrenia.

Schizophrenics have been found to have malfunctioning dopamine systems (Carlsson & Lindquist, 1963; van Kammen & others, 1986). Schizophrenics have too much of the neurotransmitter substance dopamine. More about the dopamine system appears in the next chapter, where we discuss the use of drugs to block the excess dopamine production.

Schizophrenics also have a reduced blood flow in the prefrontal cortex. For example, when the brains of schizophrenics are monitored while they engage in a card-sorting task, blood does not adequately flow into this region of the brain, where much of our advanced thinking takes place (Weinberger, Berman, & Zec, 1986; Wyatt & others, 1982).

Environmental Factors

As scientists understand the neurobiological aspects of schizophrenia, it is easy to lose sight of the fact that schizophrenia, like all other behavior, does not occur in an environmental vacuum. Some researchers argue that environmental factors in schizophrenia have been underestimated in recent years

Table 14.3 Different Types of Personality Disorders	
Type of disorder	**Symptoms**
Odd or eccentric behaviors	
Paranoid personality disorder	Pervasive and long-standing suspiciousness and mistrust of people; hypersensitivity and difficulty in getting along with others.
Schizoid personality disorder	Social withdrawal and absence of normal emotional relationships with others.
Schizotypal personality disorder	Oddities of thinking, perception, communication, and behavior that are not severe enough to be classified as schizophrenic.
Dramatic, emotional, or erratic behaviors	
Histrionic personality disorder	Overly reactive behavior; exaggerated expression of emotion seemingly performed for an audience.
Narcissistic personality disorder	Grandiose sense of self-importance; preoccupation with fantasies of unlimited success; exhibitionistic need for constant admiration.
Borderline personality disorder	Instability in interpersonal relationships, behavior, mood, and self-image.
Antisocial personality disorder	Chronic and continuous behavior that violates the rights of others; poor work and relationship history; onset before the age of fifteen.
Fearful or anxious behaviors	
Avoidant personality disorder	Hypersensitivity to rejection and unwillingness to enter into relationships; social withdrawal despite a desire for social interaction.
Dependent personality disorder	Failure to assume responsibility for major areas of one's life; reliance on others to make all important decisions.
Compulsive personality disorder	Preoccupation with rules, order, organization, efficiency, and detail; rigidity and inability to express warm emotions.

From *Abnormal psychology.* Copyright © 1972 by Random House, Inc.

(Goldstein, 1986; Nagler & Mirsky, 1985); others argue that no precise environmental factors occur in their investigations of schizophrenia and that genetic factors are more influential (Gottesman & Shields, 1982).

Stress is the environmental factor given the most attention; a **diathesis-stress view** of schizophrenia argues that a combination of environmental stress and biogenetic predisposition is involved (Meehl, 1962). A defective genetic makeup may only produce schizophrenia when the individual lives in a stressful environment. Stress reduction and family support are believed to be important in reducing the risk of schizophrenia (Goldstein, 1986).

We have seen that the affective and schizophrenic disorders are complex and often debilitating. A summary of the main themes of these disorders is presented in concept table 14.3. Next, you will read about an intriguing set of disorders involving personality.

Personality Disorders

Personality disorders develop when personality traits become inflexible and thus maladaptive. Individuals with these maladaptive traits often do not recognize that they have a problem and may show little interest in changing. Personality disorders involve odd or eccentric behaviors; dramatic, emotional, or erratic behavior; or fearful or anxious behavior. Ten of these personality disorders and their characteristics are described in table 14.3. One personality disorder has been given special attention—antisocial personality disorder.

Gary Gilmore had many characteristics of the antisocial personality. His deviant, antisocial ways were pervasive during his adolescent and adult years.

A transvestite has a compulsive need to occasionally impersonate the other sex by dressing up.

Antisocial Personality Disorder

Antisocial personality disorder characterizes individuals who live a life of crime, violence, and delinquency. These individuals regularly violate the rights of others; this disorder begins before the age of fifteen and continues into adulthood (Doren, 1987; Wolman, 1987). As young adolescents, truancy, school suspension, running away from home, stealing, vandalism, drug use, and violation of rules at home and school were commonplace. As adults, individuals are not able to maintain a consistent work record; they continue to engage in antisocial acts such as stealing, vandalism, and harassing others; they fail to uphold financial obligations and rarely plan ahead; they repeatedly get into fights; and they show no remorse when harming someone.

Gary Gilmore had many characteristics of the antisocial personality disorder (Sarsason & Sarsason, 1987). Gilmore was convicted of two murders and then executed in 1977. As a young adolescent, Gilmore had low grades, was often truant, and stole from his classmates. At fourteen, he was placed in a juvenile detention center for stealing a car. He was arrested on a number of occasions in adolescence, then at twenty was sent to the state penitentiary for burglary and robbery. Several years later he was released; before long he was back in the pen for other armed robberies, this time for eleven years. During his prison stay, Gilmore, a talented tatoo artist, tattooed obscene words and pictures on inmates he disliked.

When he was released from prison again, Gilmore tried several jobs but could not keep one. He moved in with a woman, but his drinking, carousing, and fighting caused her to kick him out. Several months later, Gilmore pulled into a gas station in Utah and ordered the attendant to give him all of his cash; he then shot him twice in the head. The next morning he walked into a motel and shot the manager.

Psychosexual Disorders

Psychosexual disorders characterize individuals with sexual problems mainly caused by psychological factors. Two major categories of psychosexual disorders are **paraphilias,** in which the source of the individual's sexual arousal is bizarre, and **psychosexual dysfunctions,** in which inhibitions in the sexual response cycle occur—an individual has difficulty achieving orgasm, for example.

Paraphilias

Many sexual patterns deviate sufficiently from what we consider "normal." These abnormal patterns of sexual arousal from unusual sources include fetishism, transvestism, transsexualism, exhibitionism, voyeurism, sadism, masochism, pedophilia, incest, and rape.

Fetishism is the reliance on inanimate objects or some body part (instead of the individual as a whole) for sexual arousal and gratification. Even though an individual may have a sexual preference, for example, a male's preference for a woman with large breasts or a female's preference for a man with a large penis, most of us usually consider other aspects of the individual's anatomy and personality when we are sexually aroused. Some individuals are obsessed with certain objects—fur, women's underpants, stockings—that arouse them. Most reports of fetishism involve males.

A **transvestite** is an individual who throughout his or her life has a compulsive need to impersonate the other sex by dressing like them. This individual, as far back as he or she can remember, has had a feeling of belonging to the wrong sex. Most transvestites view themselves as heterosexual and lead quiet, conventional lives, cross-dressing only in the privacy of their homes. Sometimes these individuals only engage in such behavior while they are having sex with their spouse.

A **transsexual** wants to be a member of the opposite sex—the individual's gender identity is at odds with the anatomical facts and he or she may undergo surgery to change sexes. Psychologists are uncertain why individuals become transsexuals. Can transsexuals lead full sex lives? In the female-to-male transformation, the male sex organs are cosmetic and the clitoris retains its sensations; male sex hormones intensify orgasm. Males-to-females describe a diffuse, intense body glow; they enjoy functioning as females, especially in terms of body closeness, skin responsiveness, and breast sensations (Zubin & Money, 1973). At one time the Johns Hopkins Clinic performed gender change operations; they no longer do so because the psychological adjustments are not very successful.

Exhibitionism and **voyeurism** are the two sex offenses that most often come to the attention of the police. Exhibitionists obtain sexual gratification from exposing their sexual anatomy to others, voyeurs through watching a member of the opposite sex undress or engage in sexual behavior. Both exhibitionism and voyeurism seem to provide substitute gratification and a sense of power to otherwise sexually anxious individuals, especially males. In many instances voyeurs are socially inhibited individuals.

Aggressive sexual fantasies are not uncommon, and in the course of sexual activity a slight amount of force is involved. However, in normal sexual activity, force is not extensive and does not harm the sexual partner or oneself. In **sadism** and **masochism,** the element of physical cruelty, of giving pain (sadism) and receiving pain (masochism), is present and assumes a central role in sexual satisfaction. The word *sadism* comes from the novels of the Marquis de Sade (1740–1814), who wrote about erotic scenes in which women were whipped. *Masochism* is named for an Austrian writer, Leopold von Sacher-Masoch (1836–1895), whose male characters became sexually excited and gratified when they were physically abused by women. It is not unusual for a sadist and a masochist to pair up to satisfy each other's sexual wishes; such relationships are referred to as sadomasochistic, or S & M (figure 14.7 lists several newspaper ads for S & M).

The term **pedophilia** comes from Greek and means "love of children." A pedophile covertly or overtly masturbates while talking to children, manipulates the child's sex organs, or has the child engage in sexual behavior. Most pedophiles are men, usually in their thirties or forties. Like exhibitionists, they usually have puritanical ideas about sex. The target of the male pedophile usually is a girl, often one he knows well, such as a neighbor or family friend.

MISTRESS JOANNE

From L.A. I will make you obey my every whim & command. I will tease and exhilarate and you will enjoy it. Dominance at its best by experienced West Coast mistress.
720–

WM slave 40 seeks dominant woman for adult games in water. Tubs, pools, etc. Write Blub Blub Phoenix Box

TARA

Has returned from San Francisco. Ready for a real turn on? Others have tried but I know how to please a man. Stockings, heels, garters & leather. I will make you feel like you left your heart in S.F.
286–

ATTENTION!

Voluptous dominitrix will satisfy your every submissive fantasy. Miss Ena has all the equipment to train her slaves properly, very severely if needed. Send bus. card & phone and short note describing fantasy to Box

Figure 14.7
"S & M" personal ads from a counterculture newspaper of a major city.

One of the strongest universal taboos is **incest,** which is a sexual relationship between relatives. By far the most common form of incest consists of brother-sister relationships, followed by father-daughter relationships. Mother-son incest is rare. Incest can be psychologically harmful, not only for immediate family relationships, but for the child's future relationships as well. If an offspring is produced, the chances of the child being mentally retarded increase dramatically in cases of incest.

Rape involves forced sexual gratification with an unwilling partner. In most cases of rape, the antagonist is a male and the recipient is a female. In virtually all instances of rape the psychological effects can be shattering and the effects can linger for years. Counseling and sometimes extensive psychotherapy is required to help the individual cope with rape (Calhoun & Atkeson, 1988; Stuart & others, 1987). Some psychologists believe that the term rape victim should be changed to rape survivor; this emphasizes a woman's strengths and ability to cope with the stress involved (Hyde, 1986).

Psychosexual Dysfunctions

For many years any failure in sexual performance by males was called impotence; for women it was referred to as frigidity. A more precise classification emphasizes problems associated with the phases of sexual response:

1. *Disorders of the desire phase.* A problem here indicates a lack of interest in sexual activity.
2. *Disorders of the excitement phase.* Even though an individual may be interested in having sex, he or she may not be able to maintain an erection (male) or have a swelling and secretion of fluids in the vagina (female).
3. *Disorders of the orgasmic phase.* In the orgasmic phase, rhythmic contractions of genital muscles occur in women and ejaculation takes place in men; disorders involve reaching orgasm too quickly or not at all.

In recent years considerable progress has been made in the treatment of sexual dysfunction, especially in cases of premature ejaculation and failure to reach orgasm. The efforts of William Masters and Virginia Johnson have been instrumental in this success. Today the complexity of sexual dysfunction is recognized—neurobiological, vascular, cognitive, and enviromental dimensions need to be considered, for example (Barlow, 1986; Beutler, 1986).

Substance-Use Disorders

In chapter 4, we discussed a number of drugs and their effects on the individual. A problem associated with drug use is called a **substance-use disorder.** This type of disorder is characterized by one or more of the following features: 1) a pattern of pathological use that involves frequent intoxification, a need for daily use, and an inability to control use—in a sense, psychological dependence; 2) a significant impairment of social or occupational functioning attributed to the drug use; and 3) physical dependence that involves serious withdrawal problems.

Many of the drugs described in chapter 4 can lead to a substance-use disorder. Alcohol, barbituates, and opium derivatives all are capable of producing either physical or psychological dependence. Alcoholism is an especially widespread substance-use disorder; it has been estimated that 6 to 8 million Americans are alcoholics. We are not certain what causes alcoholism, although biogenetic, psychological, and sociocultural explanations are given.

Table 14.4	Lifetime Prevalence of DSM-III Disorders in Three Different Cities		
Disorders	New Haven, CN	Baltimore, MD	St. Louis, MO
Any disorder	28.8	38.0	31.0
Substance use	15.0	17.0	18.1
Alcohol	11.5	13.7	15.7
Drugs	5.8	5.6	5.5
Schizophrenic	2.0	1.9	1.1
Affective	9.5	6.1	8.0
Major depression	6.7	3.7	5.5
Manic	1.1	.6	1.1
Anxiety	10.4	25.1	11.1
Phobia	7.8	23.3	9.4
Panic	1.4	1.4	1.5
Obsessive-compulsive	2.6	3.0	1.9
Personality disorder (antisocial)	2.1	2.6	3.3

Note: Figures are in percentages. Some individuals reported multiple disorders.

From Robins, L. N., et. al., Lifetime prevalence of specific psychiatric disorders in three sites, *Archives of General Psychiatry, 41,* 949–958. Copyright © 1984 American Medical Association, Chicago, IL.

Prevalence of Mental Disorders

How prevalent are mental disturbances in our society? A recent investigation surveyed the incidence of mental disorders in three cities—New Haven, Connecticut, Baltimore, and St. Louis. Using the Diagnostic Interview Schedule (DIS), designed to evaluate DSM-III categories, random samples of more than 3,000 individuals from each of the cities were surveyed. Table 14.4 shows the incidence of the DSM-III disorders in the three cities. As indicated, 29 to 37 percent said they had experienced at least one of the disorders. The higher rate for Baltimore is mainly due to the incidence of phobias there.

Alcohol abuse or dependence was the most common disorder in New Haven and St. Louis; phobias had this title in Baltimore. In each of the three cities, alcohol problems affected 11 to 16 percent of the population. Drug abuse and dependence was less common, involving 5 to 6 percent of the population. Approximately 1 in 20 adults said they had suffered a major depressive episode; 1 in 40 said they had an antisocial or obsessive-compulsive disorder at some point in their lives; less than 1 in 50 noninstitutionalized adults experienced schizophrenia or a panic disorder; and only about 1 in 100 said they had experienced a manic episode.

The most common diagnoses for women were phobias and major depression; for men the most prominent diagnosis was alcohol abuse or dependence. Rates of disorders dropped sharply after forty-five years of age. College graduates were less likely to have mental disorders, with especially low rates of phobias and schizophrenia. Other research has found rural/urban differences in mental disorders; in one investigation, the affective disorders were twice as frequent in urban areas (Blazer & others, 1985).

Our inquiry about the nature of abnormal psychology has taken us through many different mental disturbances. In the next chapter we will study ways to improve the lives of individuals with mental disturbances.

Summary

I. **Nature of Abnormality**
At different points in history, mental disorders were attributed to supernatural causes. More recently, the statistical, biological, and psychological and sociocultural approaches have been prominent. The statistical approach states that an individual is abnormal if she deviates substantially from the average. The biological approach argues that mental disorders have biological causes; the forerunner of this approach is the medical model. Many psychologists believe the medical model underplays the importance of psychological and sociocultural factors; the medical model also encourages labeling of mental disorders. An individual's abnormal behavior is complex; a more complete understanding is achieved by considering the biological, cognitive, and social factors involved.

II. **Classification of Mental Disorders**
DSM-II included categories of neurotic and psychotic behavior to describe relatively mild and severe mental disorders, respectively. Mental health professionals still use these categories to describe clients, but they no longer are used in the DSM classification. DSM-III is the most recent mental health classification system; it has improved diagnostic criteria, redefined disturbances more in line with research, and employs a multiaxial approach. Many psychologists have criticized DSM-III because of its medical terminology, complexity, inclusion of problems in living, and weak reliability. A revision—DSM-III-R—appeared in 1987.

III. **Anxiety Disorders**
Anxiety is a diffuse, unpleasant feeling involving fear and apprehension. The features of anxiety disorders include motor tension, hyperactivity, apprehensiveness, and vigilence involving hyperattentiveness.

Generalized anxiety disorder consists of persistent anxiety for at least one month without specific symptoms. Panic disorder involves recurrent panic attacks marked by the sudden onset of intense apprehension. Phobic disorders refer to an overwhelming fear of particular objects or situations. Agoraphobia is the most common phobia. Psychoanalytic, learning, and biological explanations of phobias have been given. Obsessive-compulsive disorders involve recurrent obsessions (anxiety-provoking thoughts) or compulsions (repetitive, stereotyped behaviors).

IV. **Somatoform Disorders**
With somatoform disorders psychological symptoms take a physical, or somatic, form even though no physical cause can be found. Hypochondriasis refers to a pervasive fear of illness and disease; it rarely occurs alone—depression often is present. Conversion disorder received its name from Freudian theory, which stressed that anxiety can be "converted" into a special physical symptom. Some loss of motor or sensory ability occurs. The disorder was more common in Freud's time than today.

V. **The Dissociative Disorders**
Dissociative disorders occur when the individual suddenly loses his memory or changes his identity. Under extreme stress, the individual's thoughts become dissociated (separated or split) from other information about the self. Psychogenic amnesia involves memory loss caused by extensive psychological stress. Fugue also involves memory loss, but the individual may unexpectedly travel away from home or work, assume a new identity, and be unable to remember the old one. Multiple personality consists of the presence of two more distinct personalities in the same individual; it is extremely rare.

VI. **The Affective Disorders**
Affective disorders are disturbances of mood; they include disorders in which depression occurs alone or alternates with mania. An individual with major depression is sad, demoralized, bored, and self-derogatory; he does not feel well, loses stamina easily, has a poor appetite, and seems listless and unmotivated. This type of depression is more intense and lasts longer than the milder form most of us experience in our everyday lives; nonetheless, depression is widespread. Major depression sometimes can lead to suicide. An individual with bipolar disorder shows a mixture of extremely wide mood swings from depressed to manic. Psychoanalytic, cognitive and learning, and biogenetic explanations of the affective disorders have been proposed.

VII. **Schizophrenic Disorders**
Schizophrenia occurs in approximately 1 in every 100 individuals and accounts for about one-half of all mental hospital patients; it is a severe mental disturbance in which the individual's mind has "split" from reality. Schizophrenics have distorted thoughts and perceptions, odd communication, inappropriate emotion, abnormal motor behavior, and social withdrawal. The most prominent forms of schizophrenia are disorganized, catatonic, paranoid, and undifferentiated. As with depression, considerable interest has developed in the genetic and biochemical basis of schizophrenia; environmental determinants also have been proposed. The diathesis-stress view emphasizes a combination of a genetic predisposition and environmental stress.

VIII. **Personality Disorders**
Personality disorders develop when personality traits become inflexible and maladaptive. Antisocial personality disorder characterizes individuals who live a life of crime, violence, and delinquency.

IX. **Psychosexual Disorders**
Individuals with psychosexual disorders have sexual problems caused by psychological factors. Two major categories are the paraphilias and psychosexual dysfunctions.

X. **Substance-Use Disorders**
Individuals with problems associated with drug use are said to have a substance-use disorder; the disorder may involve psychological dependence, physical dependence, and impairment of social or occupational functioning. Alcoholism is an especially widespread substance-use disorder.

XI. **Prevalence of Mental Disorders**
In one recent large-scale investigation, 29 to 37 percent of the population said they had experienced at least one of the DSM-III disturbances. Alcohol problems were the most common. Females were more likely to have phobias or depression; males were more likely to have alcohol problems. Depression occurs more in urban than rural areas.

Key Terms

statistical approach *473*
medical model *475*
DSM-III *478*
neurotic *478*
psychotic *478*
multiaxial system *480*
anxiety disorders *481*
generalized anxiety disorder *482*
panic disorder *482*
phobic disorders *483*
agoraphobia *483*
obsessive-compulsive disorders *484*
obsessions *484*
compulsions *484*
somatoform disorders *484*
hypochondriasis *485*

conversion disorder *485*
dissociative disorders *486*
psychogenic amnesia *486*
fugue *486*
multiple personality *486*
affective disorders *488*
major depression *488*
bipolar disorder *489*
learned helplessness *493*
schizophrenic disorders *494*
disorganized schizophrenia *495*
catatonic schizophrenia *495*
paranoid schizophrenia *495*
undifferentiated schizophrenia *495*
diathesis-stress view *499*
personality disorders *499*

antisocial personality disorder *500*
psychosexual disorders *500*
paraphilias *500*
psychosexual dysfunctions *500*
fetishism *500*
transvestite *500*
transsexual *501*
exhibitionism *501*
voyeurism *501*
sadism *501*
masochism *501*
pedophilia *501*
incest *502*
rape *502*
substance-use disorder *502*

Suggested Readings

Archives of General Psychiatry. This journal has extensive coverage of many different disorders and their classification according to DSM-III. Go to the library at your college or university or to a nearby library and leaf through issues from the last several years to get a feel for the way mental disturbances are classified and what their symptoms are.

Coleman, J. C., Butcher, J. N., & Carson, R. C. (1988). *Abnormal psychology and modern life* (8th ed.). Glenview, Ill.: Scott, Foresman. This is one of the leading textbooks in abnormal psychology. It provides a detailed look at many of the psychological disorders discussed in this chapter.

Meyer, R. G., and Osborne, Y. V. H. (1982). *Case studies in abnormal behavior.* Boston: Allyn and Bacon. Contains a series of fascinating case studies of abnormal behavior, including all of the DSM-III categories described in this chapter. The background and treatment of the abnormal behaviors are also included.

Millon, T., & Klerman, D. L. (Eds.). (1986). *Contemporary approaches to psychopathology.* New York: Guilford Press. Each chapter in this book is written by an authority on a particular mental disturbance or the classification of mental disorders. Includes a series of chapters on what the DSM-IV might look like in the 1990s.

Vonnegut, M. (1975). *The Eden express.* New York: Praeger. A fascinating account of schizophrenia and its possible association with nutrition and biochemical factors. Easy to read, sometimes humorous, and at times frightening. Vonnegut describes his gradual disintegration in terms that give valuable insight into the nature of one of the most serious psychological disorders.

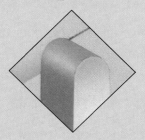

Therapies

■ ■

Every forward step we take we leave some phantom of ourselves behind.

—*John Lancaster Spalding*

■ ■

Images of Therapies

Barbara had been a housewife and mother for fifteen years. She and Tom were married just after their college graduation and she worked to help put him through graduate school. She stopped working when she had her first child. After two more children and a life of being a chauffeur and cook for the family, she felt inadequate and unhappy. She decided to seek psychotherapy.

In the first several months of therapy, Barbara talked mainly about herself. As therapy continued she increasingly talked about Tom, often with intense emotion. After six months of therapy, Barbara concluded that while she had made many of her problems, Tom had often made them worse; he treated her only as a housewife and mother, not as someone with a separate identity. Tom felt that Barbara's place was in the home; he would make derogatory comments when she talked about working again or going back to school.

As an outgrowth of the therapy, Barbara developed enough self-confidence to finally confront Tom about his demeaning remarks and unwillingness to let her do something that would make her feel good about herself. After several months of trying to get Tom to be more flexible about her interests and continuing conversations with her psychotherapist, Barbara asked Tom to move out. She got a job and eventually divorced Tom. She felt considerable pain and guilt over the decision, mainly because of her fear that it might have a negative impact on the children. Barbara desired to meet a man who would both love her *and* value her as an individual with her own identity (Sarason & Sarason, 1987).

Was the outcome of Barbara's therapy positive or negative? The answer obviously depends on our own values. Some individuals might insist that Barbara has an obligation to her husband and should not have confronted him; others would vehemently disagree, saying that the therapy was positive in allowing Barbara to understand herself and develop her own identity, even though it led to divorce.

Therapy has evolved over many centuries. Today many different forms of therapy are practiced—at last count more than 450 (Karasu, 1986). We will explore the most widely practiced therapies and give you a feel for what it would be like to go to a therapist with a particular orientation. But before we study today's therapies, let's go back in time to discover how the mentally disturbed were dealt with at different points in history. ■

Historical Perspective

During the Stone Age, a technique called *trephining* was used to let out the evil spirits in a mentally disturbed individual; it involved chipping a hole into the skull of the "evil" person (see figure 15.1). The idea that abnormal behavior was caused by evil spirits lasted for many years. For example, in Biblical times and the Middle Ages, *exorcism,* through prayer, whipping, or starvation, was commonly used to get rid of the mentally disturbed individual's evilness. During the Middle Ages the mentally disturbed often were called witches; from 200,000 to 500,000 of these individuals were burned at the stake between the fourteenth and seventeenth centuries (Ben-Yehuda, 1980).

One exception to exorcism was Hippocrates's recommendation for the treatment of the mentally disturbed in the fourth century B.C. His prescription for depression called for rest, exercise, a bland diet, and abstinence from sex and alcohol.

During the Renaissance, asylums were built to house the mentally disturbed. The word *asylum* means sanctuary; the mentally disturbed were placed in an asylum to protect them from the exploitation they were experiencing in the streets. But the asylums left much to be desired; the mentally disturbed often were chained to walls, caged, or fed sparingly.

A significant change in the treatment of the mentally disturbed was initiated by Philippe Pinel (1745–1826), the head physician at a large asylum in Paris. Pinel described the mentally disturbed as ordinary people who could not reason well because of their serious personal problems. He believed that treating the mentally disturbed like animals not only was inhumane but also hurt their recovery. Pinel convinced the French government to unchain large numbers of patients, some of whom had not been outside of the asylum for thirty to forty years (see figure 15.2). He replaced the dungeons with bright rooms and spent long hours talking with patients, listening to their problems, and giving advice.

Pinel's efforts led to reform, but it often was slow. Even as late as the nineteenth century in the United States, the mentally disturbed were kept alongside criminals in prisons. Dorothea Dix, a nurse who had taken a position at a prison in the middle of the nineteenth century, was instrumental in getting the mentally disturbed separated from criminals. She embarked on a state-to-state campaign to upgrade prisons and persuaded officials to use better judgment in deciding which individuals should be placed in prisons. State governments began building large asylums for the mentally disturbed because of Dix's efforts, although the conditions in the asylums often were no better than in the prisons.

In the twentieth century, significant advances in how we view and treat the mentally disturbed have taken place. The importance of humane treatment, concern for preventing mental disturbances, and improved methods of therapy characterize the modern-day view.

Figure 15.1
The technique of trephining involved chipping a hole in the skull through which the evil spirit, believed to be the source of the person's abnormal behavior, might escape. That some individuals actually survived the operation is shown by this skull; the bone had had time to heal considerably before the individual died.

Figure 15.2
Philippe Pinel, shown supervising the unchaining of the mentally disturbed patients at an asylum in Paris.

The Nature of Psychotherapy

Psychotherapy is the process of working with individuals to reduce their problems and improve their adjustment. Mental health professionals help individuals to recognize, define, and overcome personal and interpersonal difficulties. A number of strategies are used to accomplish these goals: talking, interpreting, listening, reinforcing, and demonstrating, for example. Psychotherapy *does not* include biomedical treatments, such as drugs or surgery, although later in the chapter we will describe the biomedical treatments of mental disturbances.

The theories of personality we discussed in chapter 13 are the basis for a number of prominent approaches to psychotherapy. The psychoanalytic theories of Freud and his dissenters and revisionists underlie the psychodynamic therapies; the phenomenological and humanistic theories of Rogers and Maslow have been an important foundation for the humanistic therapies; and the behavioral and social learning theories of Skinner and Bandura, respectively, have stimulated the development of the behavioral therapies. Other important approaches to therapy include the cognitive therapies, couple and family therapy, group therapy, and the community mental health approach. We will consider each of these therapies later in the chapter, along with biomedical therapies.

Most contemporary therapists do not use one form of therapy exclusively with their clients. The majority of today's therapists are *eclectic;* that is, they use a variety of approaches to therapy. Often a therapist will tailor the therapeutic approach to the client's needs. Even a therapist with a psychodynamic orientation might use humanistic approaches; or a family therapist might use behavioral techniques, for example.

Psychotherapy is practiced by a variety of mental health professionals, including clinical psychologists, psychiatrists, and marriage counselors. Remember from chapter 1 that psychiatrists have a medical degree and can prescribe drugs for mental disturbances; clinical psychologists, by contrast, are trained in graduate programs of psychology and use psychotherapy rather than drugs to treat mental problems.

Where does psychotherapy take place? During the first half of this century, psychotherapy was practiced primarily in mental hospitals, where individuals remained for months and even years, or in the private office of a therapist. Now psychotherapy is practiced in a greater variety of settings. During the last several decades, it is recognized that psychotherapy is not just reserved for those so disturbed they cannot live in society. Many individuals did not seek psychotherapy in the past because they did not want to be hospitalized. Today they might receive counseling and therapy at a community mental health center, at an outpatient facility of a hospital, or in the private office of a mental health practitioner.

Psychotherapy can be expensive. Although reduced fees and sometimes no fee may be arranged in public hospitals for those individuals from low-income backgrounds, still many individuals who need psychotherapy the most do not get it. It has been said that psychotherapists prefer to work with young, attractive, verbal, intelligent, and successful clients (called YAVISes) rather than those who are quiet, ugly, old, institutionalized, and different (called QUOIDs). Mental health professionals are increasingly sensitive to such problems, but a recent national sample of clinical psychologists said that a) a client from the lowest socioeconomic class had a poor prognosis for successful therapy; and b) they were much less interested in treating this type of client than individuals from higher socioeconomic classes (Sutton & Kessler, 1986).

Figure 15.3
Freud's study, where he saw patients.

Psychodynamic Therapies

The **psychodynamic therapies** stress the importance of the unconscious mind, the role of the past, and extensive interpretation by the therapist. Many psychodynamic approaches have grown out of Freud's psychoanalytic theory of personality. Today some psychodynamically oriented psychotherapists show allegiance to Freud and others make a strong effort to show how their approaches differ (Eagle, 1986, 1987).

Freud's Psychoanalysis

Over half a century in Vienna, Sigmund Freud developed the treatment for mental disturbances known as *psychoanalysis* (see figure 15.3 for a photo of Freud's study). Freud believed that psychological problems are caused by unresolved conflicts among the id, ego, and superego. These conflicts are unconscious and originate in early childhood experiences in the family. As the child's biological instincts come into conflict with the demands of parents and society, the child develops anxiety. Defense mechanisms are used to ward off anxiety; repression is pervasive in pushing anxiety and conflict beneath awareness into the unconscious mind. But defense mechanisms are only partially successful in resolving an individual's conflicts; anxiety is long lasting and enough remains in the conscious mind for some individuals to seek therapy.

Remember from chapter 13 that in Freud's view the unconscious mind dominates the individual. Many conflicts are repressed deep into the unconscious mind and bringing them into awareness is often a long, difficult task. The psychoanalyst becomes a psychological sleuth, trying to fit together the pieces of an intricate human puzzle.

Special therapeutic techniques are used to bring conflicts into awareness so they can be discussed and resolved. Free association and dream analysis are especially important psychoanalytic techniques. In *free association,* the patient lies on a couch and lets her mind wander. Remember our comment in chapter 13 that no matter how trivial or embarrassing, the patient is encouraged to say what comes into her mind. Freud believed that in talking freely about one's self and life, the individual would reveal the causes of conflict. By getting the patient to talk freely, Freud also thought that emotional feelings would come out; he used the term **catharsis** to describe this circumstance when the patient releases tension by reliving conflicting emotional experiences.

In **dream analysis,** patients are trained to remember their dreams and then report them to the psychoanalyst. Dreams contain information about the individual's unconscious thoughts and conflicts. The psychoanalyst interprets the patient's dreams to determine what their symbols mean.

Freud believed that patients often resisted his therapy. **Resistance** is the patient's unconscious defense strategies that keep the therapist from understanding the problems. Resistance occurs because it is painful to bring conflicts into conscious awareness; by resisting therapy the individual does not have to face his problems. Showing up late or missing sessions, arguing with the psychoanalyst, or faking free associations are examples of resistance. Some patients go on endlessly about some trivial matter to avoid facing their conflicts. A major goal of the therapist is to break through this resistance.

Freud also believed transference was an inevitable aspect of the therapist-patient relationship. **Transference** occurs when the patient relates to the therapist in ways that reproduce or relive important relationships in the patient's life. A patient might interact with the therapist as if the therapist were a parent or lover, for example. When transference dominates therapy, the patient's comments become directed toward the therapist's personal life. Transference is often difficult to handle; however, it can be used as a model of how the patient relates to important individuals in his life.

Interpretation plays an important role in psychoanalysis. The therapist interprets free associations, dreams, resistance, and transference. As we saw in the case of Little Hans in chapter 13, the patient's statements and behavior are not taken at face value. To understand what is truly causing the patient's conflicts, the therapist is constantly looking for symbolic, hidden meanings in what the individual says and does. From time to time the therapist makes suggestions about the possible meaning of the patient's statements and behavior. Psychology 15.1 provides an example of how the psychoanalyst uses interpretation to facilitate the patient's understanding of his problem.

Variations of Psychodynamic Therapies

Only a small percentage of psychodynamic therapists today rigorously follow Freud's guidelines. Recall from chapter 13 that Freud's ideas were challenged by Jung and Adler almost as soon as they were presented. Therapies based on Jung's and Adler's approaches continue to be practiced today, along with other versions of psychodynamic therapy.

The development of the self in social contexts is an especially important theme in contemporary psychodynamic approaches (Erikson, 1968; Kohut, 1977; Mahler, 1979). In Heinz Kohut's view, early relationships with attachment figures are important in development. As we develop we do not relinquish these attachments; we continue to need them. Kohut's prescription for therapy involves getting the patient to identify and seek out appropriate relationships with others; he also wants patients to develop more realistic appraisals of relationships. Kohut believes the therapist needs to be empathetic and understanding when interacting with the patient.

The face of psychodynamic therapy has changed extensively since its inception almost a century ago (Perry, Cooper, & Michels, 1987; Reed, 1987; Rotenberg, 1987). Individuals rarely lie on a couch but rather sit in a comfortable chair and face the therapist. The psychodynamic therapist still acknowledges the importance of the unconscious mind and early family relationships but places more emphasis on the conscious mind and current relationships (Eagle, 1986, 1987; Strean, 1988). Interest in the client's self-development and the therapist's use of empathy and understanding are emphasized even more strongly in the humanistic approaches to psychotherapy, which we discuss next.

Psychology 15.1

The Impotency of the Middle-Aged Businessman

The patient is a middle-aged businessman whose marriage is marked by repeated strife and quarrels. His sexual potency is tenuous. At times he suffers from premature ejaculation. At the beginning of one session, he complained about having to return to treatment after a long holiday weekend. He said, "I'm not so sure I'm glad to be back in treatment even though I didn't enjoy my visit to my parents. I feel I just have to be free." He then continued with a description of his home visit, which he said was depressing. His mother was bossy, aggressive, and manipulative. He feels sorry for his father. "She has a sharp tongue and cruel mouth. Each time I see my father he seems to be getting smaller; pretty soon he will disappear and there will be nothing left of him. She does that to people. I always feel that she is hovering over me ready to swoop down on me. She has me intimidated just like my wife."

"I was furious this morning. When I came to get my car, I found that someone had parked in such a way that it was hemmed in. . . . I feel restrained by the city. . . . I hate the feeling of being stuck in an office from nine until five."

At this point, the therapist called to the patient's attention that throughout the material he described how he feared confinement and that he had a sense of being trapped.

The patient responded, "I do get symptoms of claustrophobia from time to time." The fact that he suffered from claustrophobia was a new finding in the analysis. The analyst noted that the patient felt claustrophobic about the analysis. . . . In addition, the analyst noted, again to himself, that these ideas were coupled with the idea of being threatened and controlled by his mother.

The patient continued, "You know I have the same feeling about starting an affair with Mrs. X. She wants to and I guess I want to also. Getting involved is easy. It's getting uninvolved that concerns me."

In this material, the therapist associates the patient's feelings of being trapped in a confined space with being trapped in the analysis and with being trapped in an affair with a woman.

The patient continued, "I'm really chicken. It's a wonder I was ever able to have relations at all and to get married. No wonder I didn't have intercourse until I was in my twenties. My mother was always after me, 'Be careful about

getting involved with girls; they'll get you in trouble. . . . If you have sex with them, you will pick up a disease. . . .' She made it all sound so dangerous. You can get hurt from this, you can get hurt from that. It reminds me of the time I saw two dogs together and couldn't separate them—the male dog was yelping and screaming in pain. I don't even know how old I was then, maybe five or six or perhaps seven, but I was definitely a child and I was frightened."

At this point, the analyst is able to tell the patient that his fear of being trapped in an enclosed space is the conscious derivative of an unconscious fantasy in which he imagines that if he enters the woman's body with his penis, it will get stuck; he will not be able to extricate it; he may lose it. The criteria used in making this interpretation are clear: they consist of the sequential arrangement of the material, the contiguity of related themes, the repetition of the same or analogous themes, and the convergence of the different elements into one common hypothesis that encompasses all the data, namely, an unconscious fantasy of danger to the penis once it enters a woman's body. (Arlow, 1979, pp. 26–27)

Humanistic Therapies

The **humanistic psychotherapies** encourage clients to examine themselves and to grow and develop personally. In contrast to psychodynamic therapies, humanistic therapies emphasize conscious thoughts rather than unconscious thoughts, the present rather than the past, and growth and fulfillment rather than curing an illness. Two main forms of the humanistic psychotherapies are person-centered therapy and Gestalt therapy.

Person-Centered Therapy

Person-centered therapy, developed by Carl Rogers (1961, 1980), focuses on the experiences of the individual at the moment and emphasizes that each individual has the ability to improve themselves. The relationship between the therapist and the client is an important aspect of therapy, in Rogers's view. The therapist must enter into an intensely personal relationship with the client, not as a physician relates to a patient and diagnoses a cure, but as one human being to another. Notice that Rogers refers to the individual as a client, not a patient. Rogers's therapy initially was called *client-centered;* more recently he rechristened it as *person-centered* to emphasize his deep belief that all *persons* have the ability to grow.

Recall from chapter 13 that Rogers believed each of us grew up in a world filled with *conditions of worth;* the positive regard we received from others had strings attached. We usually did not receive love and praise unless we conformed to the standards and demands of others. This causes us to be unhappy and have low self-esteem as adults; rarely do we feel as good as others want us to be.

To free the individual from worry about the demands of society, the therapist creates a warm and caring environment. The Rogerian therapist never disapproves of what the client says or does. Recall from chapter 13 that Rogers believed this *unconditional positive regard* improved the client's self-esteem. The therapist deliberately follows a course of action that is nondirective and facilitative, hoping to encourage the client to examine herself and engage in independent self-appraisal and decision making.

Rogers advocated other techniques in addition to unconditional positive regard. Therapists must be genuine and not hide behind a facade; they must let the client know their feelings. Rogers called this technique **genuineness.** Therapists should think and act freely in their efforts to understand their clients; they must sense what it is like to be the client at any moment in the relationship. Rogers chose the term **accurate empathy** to describe the therapist's identification with the client. Therapists also need to be active listeners when interacting with their clients. Rogers described **active listening** as restating and supporting what the client has said and done. The following therapy transcript reveals how active listening is used in person-centered therapy.

> *Therapist:* "Everything's lousy, huh? You feel lousy?"
> (Silence of thirty-nine seconds)
> *Therapist:* "Want to come in Friday at twelve, at the usual time?"
> *Client:* [Yawns and mutters something unintelligible]
> (Silence of forty-eight seconds)
> *Therapist:* "Just kind of feel sunk way down deep in these lousy, lousy feelings, hm? Is that something like it?"
> *Client:* "No."
> *Therapist:* "No?"
> *Client:* "No. I just ain't no good to nobody, never was, and never will be."
> *Therapist:* "Feeling that now, hm? That you're just no good to yourself, no good to anybody. Just that you're completely worthless, huh? Those really are lousy feelings. Just feel that you're no good at all, hm?"
> [and from later in the session]
> *Client:* "I just want to run away and die."

Therapist: "M-hm, m-hm, m-hm. It isn't even that you want to get away from here to something. You just want to leave here and go away and die in a corner, hm?"

Client: "I wish it more'n anything else I've ever wished around here."

Therapist: "M-hm, m-hm, m-hm. I guess you've wished for a lot of things, but boy! It seems as though this wish to not live is deeper and stronger than anything you have ever wished before."

(Silence of one minute, thirty-six seconds)

(Meador & Rogers, 1979, pp. 155–158)

Gestalt Therapy

In **Gestalt therapy,** individuals are encouraged to be very open and honest with their feelings. The therapist tries to break through false screens and get individuals to act out their emotions.

Frederick (Fritz) Perls (1969), the founder of Gestalt therapy, was trained in Europe as a Freudian psychoanalyst; but as his career developed, Perls departed noticeably from Freud. Perls agrees with Freud that psychological problems originate in unresolved past conflicts and that these conflicts need to be acknowledged and worked through. Also like Freud, Perls stresses that interpretation of dreams is an important aspect of therapy.

Frederick (Fritz) Perls, founder of Gestalt therapy.

But in other ways, Perls and Freud are miles apart. Perls believes that unresolved conflicts should be brought to bear on the here and now of the individual's life. The therapist *pushes* individuals into deciding whether they will continue to allow the past to control their future or whether they will choose *right now* what they want to be in the future. To this end, Perls *confronts* individuals and encourages them to actively control their lives and be open about their feelings.

Gestalt therapists use a number of techniques to encourage individuals to be open about their feelings, to develop awareness of who they are as people, and to actively control their lives. The therapist sets examples, encourages congruence between verbal and nonverbal behavior, and uses role playing. To demonstrate an important point to a client, the Gestalt therapist might exaggerate or overportray a client's characteristic. Often the therapist will openly confront the client to stimulate change.

Consider a young female who comes to a Gestalt therapist. She slouches back with one leg across the arm of her chair and strokes her leg with her hand. She tells the therapist that she is not a seductress; she denies that she ever tries to act sexy. The Gestalt therapist imitates her behavior in an exaggerated manner and remarks, "Come on, you've got to be kidding. What a joke. Look at what you are doing with your leg and arm. I've never seen anyone who is more seductive than you are!" (Kendall & Norton-Ford, 1982).

Another technique of Gestalt therapy is role playing, either by the client, the therapist, or both. For example, if an individual is bothered by conflict with her mother, the therapist might play the role of the mother and reopen the quarrel. The therapist may encourage the individual to act out her hostile feelings toward her mother by yelling, swearing, or kicking the couch, for example. Perls believes this technique encourages clients to confront their feelings. In this way, Gestalt therapists hope to help individuals better manage their feelings instead of letting their feelings control them.

Concept Table 15.1

Historical Background, the Nature of Psychotherapy, Psychodynamic Therapies, and Humanistic Therapies		
Concept	**Processes/related ideas**	**Characteristics/description**
Historical perspective	Its nature	Many early treatments of mental disturbances were inhumane. Asylums were built during the Renaissance. Pinel's efforts led to extensive reform. Dix's efforts helped to separate the mentally disturbed from prisoners.
The nature of psychotherapy	What is psychotherapy?	A process to reduce individuals' problems and improve adjustment. Approaches include psychodynamic, humanistic, and behavioral and social learning. Drugs and surgery which are referred to as biomedical therapy are not used. Many therapists take an eclectic approach to therapy. Practitioners include clinical psychologists, psychiatrists, and marriage counselors.
Psychodynamic therapies	Their nature	Stress the importance of the unconscious mind, the role of the past, and extensive interpretation by the therapist.
	Freud's psychoanalysis	Mental disturbances are caused by unresolved unconscious conflicts between the id, ego, and superego, which originate in early childhood experiences. The therapist's interpretation of free association, dreams, resistance, and transference provide tools to understand the patient's unconscious conflicts.
	Psychodynamic variations	The development of the self in social contexts is a major theme of psychodynamic alternatives.
Humanistic therapies	Their nature	Encourage clients to examine themselves and to grow and develop personally. In contrast to psychodynamic therapies, they emphasize conscious rather than unconscious thoughts, the present rather than the past, and growth and fulfillment rather than curing an illness.
	Person-centered therapy	Developed by Carl Rogers. Focuses on the experiences of the individual at the moment and emphasizes that each individual has the ability to improve tremendously. The therapist replaces conditions of worth with unconditional positive regard and uses genuineness, accurate empathy, and active listening to raise the client's self-esteem.
	Gestalt therapy	Developed by Fritz Perls. Individuals are encouraged to be open and honest with their feelings; the therapist confronts the client and gets the individual to act out emotions. More directive than the nondirective approach of client-centered therapy. Both the psychodynamic and humanistic approaches are insight therapies.

As you probably have noticed, the Gestalt therapist is much more directive than the nondirective person-centered therapist. By being more directive, the Gestalt therapist provides more interpretation and feedback. Nonetheless, both of these humanistic approaches to therapy encourage individuals to truly be themselves, to understand themselves, to develop a sense of freedom, and to look at what they are doing with their lives.*

Both the humanistic and psychodynamic approaches are called **insight therapies;** that is, their goal is to encourage *insight* and awareness of one's self. While their approaches differ, at times dramatically, both recognize the importance of self-knowledge to improve adjustment. A summary of the main ideas about the psychodynamic and humanistic therapies, as well as the historical background and general nature of psychotherapy, is presented in concept table 15.1.

Table 15.1 A Desensitization Hierarchy from Most Fearful to Least Fearful Circumstances

1. On the way to the university the day of the speech.
2. Standing before the unopened doors of the classroom where I am supposed to give the speech.
3. My name being called to go up in front of the class.
4. The night before the speech.
5. Two days before the speech.
6. Four days before the speech.
7. A week before the speech.
8. Two weeks before the speech.
9. A month before the speech.

Behavior Therapies

Behavior therapies are based on the behavioral and social learning theories of learning and personality described in chapters 5 and 13. From the perspective of the behavior therapies, the individual's behavior is *learned* through *environmental* experiences. Behavior therapists do not search for unconscious conflicts like the psychoanalytic therapists or encourage individuals to get in touch with their feelings like the humanistic therapists. Rather than change unconscious conflicts or feelings, behavior therapists attempt to change the environment, because it is what produced and continues to control abnormal behavior. Instead of listening to their clients recount their childhood experiences, behavior therapists observe the individual's *current* behavior; when they interview the client, they ask direct questions and give specific advice about what should be done to change the abnormal behavior.

Initially the behavior therapies were based almost exclusively on the learning principles of classical and operant conditioning. In recent years, behavior therapies have become more diversified; as social learning theory grew in popularity and the cognitive approach became more prominent in psychology, cognitive factors were more likely to be included in behavior therapy (Fishman, Rotgers, & Franks, 1988; Masters & others, 1988). First, we will discuss the classical conditioning and operant conditioning approaches to therapy, then turn to the cognitive behavior therapies.

Classical Conditioning Approaches

In chapter 5, we described how some behaviors, especially fears, are acquired or learned through classical conditioning; we also indicated that these behaviors can be unlearned or extinguished. If an individual learns to fear snakes or heights through classical conditioning, possibly the individual could unlearn the fear by replacing it with pleasant thoughts or by learning to relax; these responses are incompatible with the fear. Two procedures based on classical conditioning procedures that are used in behavior therapy are systematic desensitization and aversive conditioning.

Systematic Desensitization

The procedure of **systematic desensitization** is based on the idea that anxiety and relaxation are incompatible. If an individual can be taught to be less anxious and more relaxed while confronting something unpleasant, better adjustment and healthier adaptation will result.

For example, a common fear is giving a speech. Using systematic desensitization (Wolpe, 1958, 1963), the client is asked which aspects of the fearful situation, in this case giving a speech, are the most and least frightening. Then, the therapist arranges these circumstances in order from most to least frightening—an example of this type of desensitization hierarchy is shown in table 15.1.

Systematic desensitization is frequently an effective treatment for a number of phobias, including fear of snakes. It is not unusual for systematic desensitization to be combined with observational learning.

The next step is to teach the individual to relax. The client is taught to recognize the presence of muscular contractions or tensions in various parts of the body and then how to contract and relax different muscles. Once the individual is relaxed, the therapist asks him to imagine the least fearful stimulus in the hierarchy. Subsequently, the therapist moves up the list of items from least to most fearful while the individual remains relaxed. Eventually, the individual is able to imagine the most fearful circumstance without being afraid—in our example, on the way to the university the day of the speech. In this manner, the individual learns to relax while thinking about the speech instead of being anxious.

Research evaluations suggest that systematic desensitization is often an effective treatment for a number of phobias (such as fear of giving a speech, fear of heights, fear of flying, fear of dogs, and fear of snakes), anxieties, and stressful circumstances (Kendall & Norton-Ford, 1982; Paul, 1966). Not infrequently, a behavior therapist will combine systematic desensitization with observational learning or imitation. For example, if you are afraid of snakes, the therapist would have you watch someone handle a snake; then you would be asked to engage in increasingly more fearful behaviors—first just going into the room where the snake is, then approaching the snake, then touching the snake, and eventually playing with the snake (Bandura, 1986; Bandura, Blanchard, & Ritter, 1969).

Aversive Conditioning

Behavior therapists also use another technique based on classical conditioning—**aversive conditioning.** In this procedure, repeated pairings of the undesirable behavior with aversive stimuli decrease the behavior's reward value and thus increase the likelihood the individual will stop doing it. Aversive conditioning is used to teach individuals to avoid such behaviors as smoking, eating, and drinking. Electric shocks, nausea-inducing substances, and verbal insults are used as noxious stimuli in aversion therapy.

How would aversive conditioning reduce excessive alcohol consumption, for example? Chemicals that induce nausea would be paired with alcoholic beverages. In classical conditioning terminology, the alcoholic beverage is the conditioned stimulus and the nausea-inducing agent the unconditioned stimulus. By repeatedly pairing alcohol with the nausea-inducing agent, the alcohol becomes conditioned to elicit the nausea. As a consequence, alcohol no longer is associated with something pleasant, but rather something highly unpleasant.

Operant Conditioning Approaches

Annette is a college student who has difficulty studying. She complains of feeling sleepy when she goes to her desk to study. She decided to see a therapist about how she might improve her studying because her grades were rapidly deteriorating. The behavior therapist's first recommendation was to replace her forty-watt bulb with a brighter one. His second recommendation was to turn her desk away from her bed. His third recommendation was to do her schoolwork only when she was at her desk; she was not allowed to write a letter, read *Seventeen* magazine, or daydream while at the desk. If she wanted to do any of these other things, she was told to leave her desk.

Annette had taken a course in behavioral analysis at her university. She told the behavior therapist, "I know what you are up to; you want that desk to assume stimulus control over me. I'm not going to let any piece of wood

How might operant conditioning be used to help a college student develop better study habits?

run my life." The therapist responded, "On the contrary, you want that desk to run you. You are the one who decided to put yourself under the control of your desk" (Goldiamond, 1971).

Notice the therapist's strong interest in the client's environment and how it controlled her behavior. Notice also how directly and precisely the therapist told Annette what to do to improve her study habits. He did not spend time analyzing her unconscious conflicts or encouraging her to get in touch with her feelings. Rather, he wanted to change the stimuli in the environment that were controlling her behavior and causing her problem.

In chapter 5 when we discussed the nature of operant conditioning, we looked at how the individual's behavior is controlled by its consequences. The behavior therapist who uses operant conditioning strives to change the individual's environment so that desirable behaviors are reinforced and undesirable ones are either not reinforced or punished. In behavior therapy, this process often is called behavior modification; the idea behind behavior modification is to replace unacceptable, maladaptive responses with acceptable, adaptive ones. Consequences are set up to ensure that acceptable responses are reinforced but unacceptable ones are not.

One technique based on operant conditioning that is used by behavior therapists is called a **token economy.** In a token economy, the individual's behaviors earns "tokens" (such as poker chips) that can later be exchanged for desired rewards (such as candy, money, or going to a movie). Token economies have been established in a number of classrooms, institutions for the mentally retarded, homes for delinquents, and mental hospitals with schizophrenics (e.g., Hersen, Eisler, & Miller, 1987; Phillips, 1968; Kazdin, 1982).

In some instances, behavior modification works, in others it does not. In the token economy setting, one individual may become so wedded to the tokens that when they are removed, the positive behavior associated with the tokens may disappear. Yet for another individual, the positive behavior brought about by the tokens will continue after they are removed. Some critics object to behavior modification because they believe it is unethical to extensively control an individual's behavior; they believe the manipulation infringes on the individual's rights. But as with the college student who could not study, her environment was controlling her in maladaptive ways; the therapist encouraged her to gain self-control over her environment.

Cognitive Behavior Therapies

In recent years many behavior therapists have changed the environments of individuals showing maladaptive behavior *and* modified their cognitions. The **cognitive behavior therapies** have this dual focus—change both the environment and thoughts of the individual to increase adaptive behavior. These therapies strive to change misconceptions, strengthen coping skills, increase self-control, and encourage constructive self-talk.

Albert Bandura (1986) believes that **self-efficacy**—the belief that one can master a situation and produce positive outcomes—is extremely important in producing adaptive behavior. In Bandura's view, the individual's expectations of self-efficacy determine whether therapy is successful. At each step in the therapy process, the individual needs to bolster her confidence by telling herself, "I can do this," "I'm going to make it," "I'm getting very good," and so on. As she gains confidence and begins to successfully adapt, the successes become intrinsically rewarding; the self-efficacy statements also are reinforced by the successes they produce. Before long, the individual will persist with considerable effort because of the pleasurable outcomes that were set in motion by self-efficacy.

One of the most important contributions of the cognitive behavior therapies is their emphasis on **self-instructional methods** (Meichenbaum, 1977). These methods emphasize the therapist's ability to change what clients say to themselves. The individual is not simply talked with about self-statements; rather, the therapist models relevant self-statements, encourages role playing in which the individual practices the self-statements, and uses reinforcements to strengthen the newly acquired self-conversation. The following sequence illustrates how self-instructional methods are used to cope with a stressful situation (Meichenbaum, Turk, & Burstein, 1975):

Preparing for anxiety or stress
What do I have to do?
I'm going to map out a plan to deal with it.
I'll just think about what I have to do.
I won't worry; doesn't help anything.
I have a lot of different strategies to call on.

Confronting and handling the anxiety or stress
I can meet the challenge.
I'll keep on taking just one step at a time.
I can handle it. I'll just relax, breathe deeply, and use one of the strategies.
I won't think about the pain; I'll think about what I have to do.

Coping with feelings at critical moments
What is it I have to do?
I was supposed to expect the pain to increase; I just have to keep myself in control.
When the pain comes, I'll just pause and keep focusing on what I have to do.

Reinforcing self-statements
Good, I did it.
I handled it well.
I knew I could do it.
Wait until I tell other people how I did it!

The Widespread Use of Behavior Therapies

As the field of psychology becomes more "cognitive" and drugs are widely used to treat mental disturbances, we often hear that behavioral approaches to therapy are in a downward spiral. Nonetheless, behavioral therapies are still used on a widespread basis. Some examples of recent applications include: improving an individual's social skills (Stark, 1987), eliminating a foot fetish (Cautela, 1986), reducing compulsive hand washing (Silverman, 1986), decreasing postpartum depression (Phillips, 1986), extinguishing a choking phobia (McNally, 1986), improving the adaptive behavior of schizophrenics (Bellack, 1986), and reducing the symptoms of major depression (Teri & Lewinsohn, 1986). The benefits of behavior therapy in treating schizophrenia and major depression are especially noteworthy because it is commonly thought that behavior therapies are ineffective with more severe, psychotic disorders. To learn more about the use of behavior therapy in treating major depression, turn to Psychology 15.2.

Psychology 15.2

Contemporary Behavior Therapy and the Treatment of Depression—The Lewinsohn Approach

Henry Greene is a thirty-six-year-old lawyer who wrestled with depression for months before finally seeking psychotherapy. His initial complaints were physical—fitful sleep, often ending at 3 A.M., lack of appetite, weight loss of fifteen pounds, and a disinterst in sex. Henry began to move more slowly and his voice became monotonous. He reached the point where he barely could cope with life. Henry finally let his guard down and confessed that while he looked successful from the outside, he felt like a failure on the inside. He said he actually was a third-rate lawyer, husband, lover, and father—he felt he was bound to remain that way. Henry perceived life as a treadmill of duty and guilt; he felt exhausted and saw no reason to continue (Rosenfeld, 1985).

How would a contemporary behaviorist treat someone like Henry Greene? Peter Lewinsohn and his colleagues developed the "Coping with Depression Course" (Lewinsohn, 1987; Lewinsohn & others, 1984; Lewinsohn & others, 1986), a program that is receiving increased attention. A basic theme of the program is that what individuals do behaviorally is the cause of what they feel. The therapist encourages individuals to increase the ratio of positive life events to negative life events to improve mood. To accomplish the desired ratio, most individuals require a variety of skill training exercises.

The initial assignment for someone like Henry Greene would be for him to monitor his daily moods. This would force him to pay attention to his daily mood changes; this information is used to determine which events are associated with which moods. Relaxation training follows; relaxation skills help the individual's sense of well-being. This occurs not only because of the direct benefits of relaxation but also because of the enhanced sense of self-efficacy brought about by mastering a new skill.

The next step for Henry Greene is to determine how his moods are associated with pleasant and unpleasant events in his life. Henry is asked to fill out the "Pleasant Events Schedule" and the "Unpleasant Events Schedule." Each week, Henry completes a graph showing the number of pleasant and unpleasant events, as well as his mood, for each day. Henry probably will see a close relation between unpleasant events and negative moods, and between pleasant events and positive moods. The therapist encourages Henry to increase the time he spends in pleasant activities with the hope that more positive moods will follow. The outcome should be that Henry gains a sense of power in controlling his moods.

Some individuals require individually tailored approaches. For example, some individuals need training in social skills to improve their social relationships. Others need more work in changing their thoughts. In Lewinsohn's approach, thoughts are treated as behaviors to be modified; positive thoughts are reinforced or a specified period is set aside for "worry time," for example.

The final stage in this approach is maintenance planning. Henry is asked to identify the components of the behavioral therapy that were the most successful in changing his maladaptive behavior; once identified, Henry is encouraged to continue their use. He also would be required to develop emergency plans for those times when stress overwhelms him. Henry would continue to come to follow-up sessions for six months after his treatment. Recent research results suggest that Lewinsohn's approach is effective in improving the adaptive behavior of depressed individuals (Zeiss & Lewinsohn, 1986).

Cognitive Therapies

The **cognitive therapies** emphasize that the individual's cognitions or thoughts are the main source of abnormal behavior. For example, Ms. D, a twenty-one-year-old single undergraduate student has delusions that she is evil. She perceives herself as a failure in school and a failure to her parents. She is preoccupied with internal thoughts, living much of the day dwelling on her problems, exaggerating her faults, and thinking negative thoughts about herself. These common symptoms of depressed individuals suggest that the cognitive therapies might be a viable approach in the treatment of depression.

Cognitive therapists attempt to change the individual's feelings and behaviors by changing cognitions. Cognitive therapies differ from psychoanalytic therapies by focusing more on overt symptoms instead of deep-seated unconscious thoughts, by providing more structure to the individual's thoughts, and by being less concerned about the origin of the problem. However, the cognitive therapies are less likely than the cognitive behavior therapies to use structured training sessions that require the individual to practice prescribed exercises; instead the cognitive therapies are more likely to adhere to a conversational format. The cognitive therapies also are less interested than the cognitive behavior therapies in manipulating the environment to increase adaptive behavior.

In recent years many therapists have changed to a stronger cognitive focus in their practices. Still, few systematic cognitive approaches exist. One that is given considerable attention is Albert Ellis's rational emotive therapy; another is Aaron Beck's cognitive therapy.

Rational Emotive Therapy

Rational emotive therapy is based on the idea that individuals become psychologically disturbed because of their beliefs, especially those that are irrational and self-defeating (table 15.2 lists examples of these beliefs). Albert

---

Table 15.2 Examples of Irrational and Self-Defeating Statements

1. The idea that you must—yes, *must*—have sincere love and approval almost all the time from all the people you find significant.
2. The idea that you must prove yourself thoroughly competent, adequate, and achieving; or that you must at least have real competence or talent at something important.
3. The idea that people who harm you or commit misdeeds rate as generally bad, wicked, or villainous individuals and that you should severely blame, damn, and punish them for their sins.
4. The idea that life proves awful, terrible, horrible, or catastrophic when things do not go the way you would like them to go.
5. The idea that emotional misery comes from external pressures and that you have little ability to control your feelings or rid yourself of depression and hostility.
6. The idea that if something seems dangerous or fearsome, you must become terribly occupied with and upset about it.
7. The idea that you will find it easier to avoid facing many of life's difficulties and self-responsibilities than to undertake more rewarding forms of self-discipline.
8. The idea that your past remains all-important and that because something once strongly influenced your life, it has to keep determining your feelings and behavior today.
9. The idea that people and things should turn out better than they do, and that you have to view it as awful and horrible if you do not quickly find good solutions to life's hassles.
10. The idea that you can achieve happiness by inertia and inaction or by passively and uncommittedly "enjoying yourself."
11. The idea that you must have a high degree of order or certainty to feel comfortable; or that you need some supernatural power on which to rely.
12. The idea that you can give yourself a global rating as a human and that your general worth and self-acceptance depend upon the goodness of your performances and the degree that people approve of you.

From Albert Ellis, *How to live with a neurotic*. N. Hollywood: Wilshire Books, 1975; Albert Ellis and Robert A. Harper, *A new guide to rational living*. N. Hollywood: Wilshire Books, 1975; and Albert Ellis, *Reason and emotion in psychotherapy*. Secaucus, NJ: Citadel Press, 1962. All books copyrighted by Institute for Rational Emotive Therapy, New York.

Ellis (1962, 1974, 1986, 1987; Ellis & Dryden, 1987; Ellis & others, 1988), the founder of rational emotive therapy, says that we usually talk to ourselves when we experience stress; too often the statements are irrational, making them more harmful than helpful.

Ellis miniaturized the therapy process into the letters A, B, C, D, E. Therapy usually starts at C, the individual's upsetting emotional *Conse-quence*; this might involve depression, anxiety, or a feeling of worthlessness. The individual usually says that C was caused by A, the *Activating Experi-ence*, such as a blowup in marital relations, loss of job, or failure in school. The therapist works with the individual to show that an intervening factor, B, the individual's *Belief System*, is actually responsible for why he moved from A to C. Then the therapist goes on to D, which stands for *Disputation*; at this point, the individual's irrational beliefs are disputed or contested by the ther-apist. By disputing the individual's irrational and self-defeating beliefs, the therapist encourages self-examination, such as "Where is the evidence that I am such a failure?" The individual then changes his belief system and begins to think such thoughts as "I'm not as incompetent as I thought; I'll do a lot better the next opportunity I get." At this point the individual reaches E, im-proved functioning *Effects*. For example, the next time an exam comes up, the individual does not engage in irrational thoughts, but rationally copes with the stress. To summarize:

Albert Ellis developed rational emotive therapy, an important cognitive approach.

A ⟶	B ⟶	C ⟶	D ⟶	E
Activating experience	**Belief system**	**Consequences**	**Disputation**	**Effects**
Mary loses her job	"I'm a failure!"	Becomes depressed	Therapist challenges her beliefs	Mary puts her changed beliefs to work

To learn more about Ellis's rational emotive therapy, read Psychology 15.3.

Beck's Cognitive Therapy

Aaron Beck (1976) developed a cognitive therapy to treat psychological dys-functions, especially depression. He believes the most effective therapy with depressed individuals involves four phases: 1) The depressed clients are shown how to identify self-labels, that is, how they view themselves. 2) They are taught to notice when they are thinking distorted or irrational thoughts. 3) They learn how to substitute appropriate thoughts for inappropriate ones. 4) They are given feedback and motivating comments from the therapist to stimulate their use of these techniques.

Results from a large-scale investigation by the National Institute of Mental Health (NIMH) supports the belief that cognitive therapies are an effective treatment for depression (Mervis, 1986). Aaron Beck and his col-leagues conducted this therapy with moderately to severely depressed indi-viduals for sixteen weeks at three different sites. The symptoms of depression were eliminated completely in more than 50 percent of the individuals re-ceiving the cognitive therapy compared to only 29 percent in a control group.

Psychology 15.3

"My Work Is Boring and I Resent It"

The following case illustrates the nature of rational emotive therapy. You will notice that this type of therapy is a forceful type of therapeutic persuasion:

Client: I know that I should do the inventory before it piles up to enormous proportions, but I just keep putting it off. To be honest, I guess it's because I resent it so much.

Therapist: But why do you resent it so much?

Client: It's boring, I just don't like it.

Therapist: So it's boring. That's a good reason for disliking this work, but is it an equally good reason for resenting it?

Client: Aren't the two the same thing?

Therapist: By no means. Dislike equals the sentence, "I don't enjoy this thing, and therefore I don't want to do it." And that's a perfectly sane sentence in

most instances. But resentment is the sentence, "*Because* I dislike doing this thing, I shouldn't *have* to do it." And that's invariably a very crazy sentence.

Client: Why is it so crazy to resent something that you don't like to do?

Therapist: There are several reasons. First of all, from a purely logical standpoint, it just makes no sense at all to say to yourself, "Because I dislike doing this thing, I shouldn't *have* to do it." The second part of this sentence just doesn't follow in any way from the first part. Your reasoning goes something like this: "Because I dislike doing this thing, *other people* and the *universe* should be so considerate of me that they should never make me do what I dislike." But, of course, this doesn't make any sense.

Why *should* other people and the universe be that considerate of you? It might be nice if they were. But why the devil *should* they be? In order for your reasoning to be true, the entire universe, and all the people in it, would really have to revolve around and be uniquely considerate of you. (Ellis, 1962)

The therapist has directly attacked the client's belief and forcefully told him that his thoughts are irrational. This represents an important distinction between cognitive therapists such as Ellis and behavioral or psychodynamic therapists. Behavioral and psychodynamic therapists describe the client's behavior and attitudes as maladaptive and self-defeating, but Ellis points out that they are irrational and illogical as well.

The use of a control group is an important feature in therapy research. Without a control group the researchers in the NIMH study would have had no way of knowing if the symptoms of depression in the experimental group would have disappeared even without therapy. That is, it is possible that in any random sample of depressed individuals, more than 50 percent show a remission of symptoms over a sixteen-week period, regardless of whether or not they receive therapy. Because only 29 percent of the depressed individuals in the control group were free of their symptoms, the researchers had good reason to believe that the cognitive therapy—which produced more than a 50 percent remission of symptoms—was effective.

At this point we have discussed four major approaches to therapy—psychodynamic, humanistic, behavioral, and cognitive. Table 15.3 will help you keep the approaches straight in your mind.

Table 15.3 Comparison of Psychotherapies

Topic	Approach			
	Psychodynamic	*Humanistic*	*Behavior*	*Cognitive*
Cause of problem	Client's problems are symptoms of deep-seated, unresolved unconscious conflicts	Client is not functioning at an optimal level of development	Client has learned maladaptive behavior patterns	Client has developed inappropriate thoughts
Therapy emphasis	Discover underlying unconscious conflicts and work with patient to develop insight	Develop awareness of inherent potential for growth	Learn adaptive behavior patterns through changes in the environment or cognitive processes	Change feelings and behaviors by changing cognitions
Nature of therapy and techniques	Psychoanalysis, including free association, dream analysis, resistance, and transference; therapist interprets heavily	Person-centered therapy, including unconditional positive regard, genuineness, accurate empathy, and active listening; Gestalt therapy, including confrontation to encourage honest expression of feelings; self-appreciation emphasized	Observation of behavior and its controlling conditions; specific advice given about what should be done; therapies based on classical conditioning, operant conditioning; therapies emphasizing self-efficacy and self-instruction	Conversations with client designed to get them to change their irrational and self-defeating beliefs

Group Therapies and Community Mental Health

A major issue in therapy is how it can be structured to reach more individuals and cost less. One way to address this issue is for the therapist to see clients on a group rather than individual basis; a second way is through community mental health.

Group Therapies

Nine individuals make their way into the room, each looking tentatively at the others; the only other individual each person has met is the therapist, whom each has seen for a diagnostic interview. Some seem reluctant, others enthusiastic. All have come to the meeting, though, willing to abide by the therapist's recommendation that the group might benefit them in coping with their problems. As they sit down and wait for the session to begin, one thinks, "Will they really understand me?" Another thinks, "Do the others have problems like mine?" Yet another thinks, "How much can I stick my neck out with these people?"

Individual therapy is often expensive and time consuming. Freud saw patients as often as three to five times per week for a number of years, believing that working through a psychological problem is a long process. Advocates of group therapy stress that individual therapy is limited because the client is seen outside the normal context of relationships, relationships that may hold the key to successful therapy. Many psychological problems develop in the context of interpersonal relationships—within one's family, marriage, or peer group, for example. By seeing individuals in the context of these important groups, therapy may be more successful.

Group therapy is diversified. Psychodynamic, humanistic, behavior, or cognitive therapy is practiced by some therapists. Others use group approaches not based on the major approaches to psychotherapy. Six features make group therapy an attractive format (Yalom, 1975):

1. *Information.* The individual receives information about his problem from either the group leader or other group members.
2. *Universality.* Many individuals develop the sense that they are the only person who has such frightening and unacceptable impulses. In the group individuals observe that there is anguish and suffering in others as well.
3. *Altruism.* Group members support one another with advice and sympathy and learn that they have something to offer others.
4. *Corrective recapitulation of the family group.* A therapy group often resembles a family (and in family therapy *is* a family), with the leaders representing parents and the other members siblings. In this "new" family, old wounds may be healed and new, more positive "family" ties made.
5. *Development of social skills.* Corrective feedback from peers may correct flaws in the individual's interpersonal skills. A narcissistic individual may see that he is vain if five other group members inform him about his self-centeredness; in individual therapy he may not believe the therapist.
6. *Interpersonal learning.* The group can serve as a training ground for practicing new behaviors and relationships. The vain woman may learn that she can get along better with others by not acting so selfishly, for example.

Family therapy is group therapy with the members of the natural family constituting the group. A therapist may work with an adolescent and his parents to improve relationships.

Family and Couple Therapy

"A friend loves you for your intelligence, a mistress for your charm, but your family's love is unreasoning; you were born into it and are of its flesh and blood. Nevertheless, it can irritate you more than any group of people in the world." These comments from Andre Maurois suggest that the family may be the source of a client's problems. **Family therapy** is group therapy with the members of one's natural family. **Couple therapy** is therapy with marital partners or single couples whose major problem is their relationship. These approaches stress that while one individual may have some abnormal symptoms, the symptoms are a function of family or couple relationships. Psychodynamic or behavior therapies may take the form of family or couple therapy, but the major form of family therapy is family systems therapy.

Family systems therapy stresses that the individual's psychological adjustment is related to pattens of interaction within the family system (Bedner, Burlingame, & Masters, in press; Bernal & Ysern, 1986; Haley, 1976; Minuchin, 1974, 1985; Satir, 1964). Families who do not function well together foster abnormal behavior on the part of one or more of their members. Four of the most widely used techniques in family systems therapy are as follows:

1. *Validation.* The therapist expresses an understanding and acceptance of each family member's feelings and beliefs and thus validates that person. When the therapist talks with each member, she find something nice to say.

2. *Reframing.* The therapist teaches families to reframe problems; problems are cast as a family problem, not an individual's problem. Consider the circumstance when a mother refuses to do any more housework. Instead of viewing her as having a maladaptive personality that is selfish and uncaring, the therapist reframes the problem in terms of how each family member has contributed to the circumstance. The father's failure to give her attention and the children's messiness may be involved, for example.

3. *Structural change.* The family systems therapist tries to *restructure* the coalitions in a family. In a mother-son coalition, the therapist might suggest that the father take a stronger disciplinarian role to relieve some of the burden from the mother. Restructuring might be as simple as suggesting that parents explore satisfying ways to be together; the therapist may recommend that once a week the parents go out for a quiet dinner together at a nice restaurant, for example.

4. *Detriangulation.* In some families one member is the scapegoat for two other members who are in conflict but pretend not to be. For example, in the triangle of two parents and a child, the parents may insist that their marriage is fine but find themselves in subtle conflict over how to handle the child. The therapist tries to disentangle or *detriangulate* this situation by shifting attention away from the child to the conflict between the parents.

© *1986* Psychology Today *and Joseph Farris.*

Couple therapy proceeds in much the same fashion as family therapy. Conflicts in marriages and in relationships between unmarried persons frequently involve poor communication; in some instances communication has broken down entirely. The therapist tries to improve the communication between the partners. In some cases, she will focus on the roles partners play: one may be "strong," the other "weak"; one may be "responsible," the other "spoiled," for example. The issues pursued in couple therapy are diverse; they include jealousy, sexual messages, delayed childbearing, infidelity, gender roles, two-career families, divorce, and remarriage (Goldberg, 1985; Stuart & Jacobson, 1987).

Personal Growth Groups

A number of group therapies have appeared in recent years that have a different focus than most other forms of therapy. These groups benefit individuals whose lives are lacking in intimacy, intensity, and accomplishment. These **personal growth groups** have their roots in the humanistic therapies; they emphasize personal growth and increased openness and honesty in interpersonal relations. Among the potpourri of personal growth groups that have developed are encounter groups, marathon groups, and transactional analysis groups.

*An encounter group session.
Encounter groups are designed to
promote personal growth through
candid group interaction.*

An **encounter group** is designed to promote self-understanding through candid group interaction. For example, one member of the assembled group thinks he is better than everyone else. After several minutes of listening to the bragging, another group member says, "Look, jerk, nobody here likes you; I would like to sell you for what you think you are worth and buy you for what you are actually worth!" Other group members then make similar comments, supporting the criticism of the braggart. Outside of an encounter group, individuals probably would not confront someone's bragging; through the encouragement of the group leader, though, group members feel free to express their true feelings about each other. The frank portrayals that emerge during group interaction help individuals gain insight about themselves and change behaviors that are distasteful to others.

Encounter groups improve the psychological adjustment of some individuals, but not others. In one investigation, college students who were members of encounter groups felt better about themselves and got along better with others than their counterparts in a control group (Lieberman, Yalom, & Miles, 1973). However, 8 percent of the encounter group participants felt that the experience was harmful. For the most part, they blamed the group leader for intensifying their problems; they said he made remarks that were so personally devastating they could not handle them.

Some encounter groups are conducted in a single session that lasts as long as sixteen to forty-eight hours; these are called **marathon groups** (Bach, 1966). In rare instances marathon groups are conducted in the nude for further impact. The strategy behind marathon groups is that the length of time will exhaust participants and bring forth intense emotions.

Another type of personal growth group is a **transactional analysis** group, which emphasizes the *transactions* individuals perform within themselves and with others (Berne, 1972). In this approach, each individual is described in terms of three separate mental structures—parent, adult, and child—which need to be balanced to achieve a healthy personality. If any one of these three structures is dominant, maladaptive behavior is likely to occur. For example, an individual might act too much like a parent (moral) and not enough like an adult (reality-oriented) or a child (pleasure-seeking). Note how closely the personality structures in transactional analysis correspond to Freud's theory: parent (superego), adult (ego), and child (id).

Transactional analysis also includes working with the individual's interpersonal relations; emphasis is placed on the games that people play and the scripts of their lives. Eric Berne, the founder of transactional analysis, defines *games* as repeated and destructive interactions between people. For example, Berne says that an alcoholic plays five different games: to escape tension and involvement (the "alcoholic"); to blame and attack himself (the "persecutor"); to save himself from disaster (the "rescuer"); to be taken advantage of (the "patsy"); and to supply himself with both liquor and encouragement to keep drinking (the "connection").

According to Berne, a *script* is a self-defeating, rigid strategy for coping with the world. Instead of being flexible and adaptive in their approach to life's challenges, many individuals use a single coping strategy. For example, an individual tries to be assertive all of the time, when being assertive may work in one situation, but not another. In some circumstances being a sensitive listener and somewhat unassertive might be more appropriate, for example.

Community Mental Health

The community mental health movement was born in the early 1960s when it became apparent that our mental health care system was not reducing the incidence of mental disturbances. The system was not adequately reaching the poor and even those with sufficient income were often hesitant to seek therapy because of its social stigma. New drugs for treating the severely mentally disturbed, such as schizophrenics, meant that large numbers of individuals could adapt well enough to be released from mental institutions. Few communities, though, had adequate facilities to help these individuals make the transition from institution to community.

Community Mental Health Centers

In 1963, Congress passed the Community Mental Health Center Act, which provided funds for establishing one facility for every 50,000 individuals in the nation. The centers were designed to treat the mentally disturbed in their community, and educational programs were developed to prevent mental disturbance. Thus, the intent of community mental health centers was not only to treat mental disturbance on a widespread basis but also to *prevent* it.

Outpatient care is one of the important services that community mental health centers provide. An individual can attend therapy sessions at a center and still keep his job and live with his family. Another important service of community mental health centers is to maintain storefront clinics that remain open twenty-four hours a day; these clinics often handle emergencies, such as suicide attempts and drug overdoses. Yet another important service of these centers is to act as a liaison with others in the community who provide mental health services; professionals at community mental health centers often consult with family physicians, the clergy, and teachers, for example, about the best ways to prevent and treat mental disturbances (Berren & Santiago, 1987; Randolph, Lindenberg, & Menn, 1987).

Aftercare Programs

As we indicated, the community mental health movement was stimulated by the large number of mentally disturbed individuals released from mental hospitals. *Aftercare programs* were established to help these individuals make the transition from their sheltered existence in the hospital to a normal, everyday life in the community. Aftercare programs include either permanent or temporary homes for individuals when they are released from a mental hospital.

One type of aftercare program is the *halfway house,* which is a boarding house located in the community. One example of an effective halfway house is Community Lodge, which is a place where individuals are trained to cope

Figure 15.4
Comparison of formerly hospitalized individuals who either lived in the community lodge or were placed directly in the mainstream of the community.

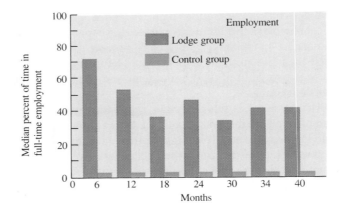

with the responsibility of living outside an institutionalized setting (Fairweather, Sanders, & Tornatsky, 1974). In one investigation, supervisors gradually were removed from the lodge, nurses visited every two weeks, and business advisors worked with the individuals on their business skills. The individuals who lived at the lodge were compared with another group of individuals who had been released directly from the hospital into the mainstream of outside life with no transitional experience. As shown in figure 15.4, through a forty-month period at the lodge residents were more likely to be holding down full-time jobs and were much less likely to relapse and return to mental hospitals. Such results suggest that an aftercare program for individuals released from mental hospitals is an important consideration in their long-term mental health adjustment (Bellack, 1986; Fischer & Breakey, 1986).

Paraprofessionals

One important outgrowth of the community mental health movement are **paraprofessionals,** who are volunteers trained to work with mentally disturbed individuals. Paraprofessionals are trained by professionals to counsel, tutor, and conduct other community services. For example, paraprofessionals answer hotlines at community mental health centers and respond to calls related to suicide, rape, and wife abuse.

Paraprofessionals also treat individuals with mental disturbances. In one investigation, retired individuals were enlisted as volunteers to work with chronically and mentally disturbed clients who had just been released from a mental hospital (Weinman & others, 1970). After extensive training and supervision, the volunteers either took a mentally disturbed individual into their homes or visited the individual in his home ten hours a week for an entire year. Compared to individuals who remained in the mental hospital, those who were released and treated ten hours a week by the retired volunteers were better adjusted—they were less likely to be living in a mental hospital one year later, for example. Other research has shown that in some instances paraprofessionals are as effective as professionals in working with mentally disturbed individuals (Hattie, Sharley, & Rogers, 1984).

Prevention

An important goal of community psychology is to identify the aspects of a community that contribute to mental disturbances and eliminate them before they harm individuals. Preventing mental disturbances takes one of three forms. *Primary prevention* focuses on the reduction of new cases of mental or physical disorders. Training for couples prior to or shortly after marriage to prevent divorce is an example of primary prevention; the training might focus on problem-solving and communication skills (Geston & Jason, 1987; Guerney, 1987).

██ ██ ██ ██ ██ ██ ██ ██ ██ ██ ██ ██ ██

Concept Table 15.2

Behavior Therapies, Cognitive Therapies, Group Therapies, and Community Mental Health		
Concept	Processes/related ideas	Characteristics/description
Behavior therapies	Their nature	Based on the behavioral and social learning theories of learning and personality. Abnormal behavior is learned through environmental experiences; it can be reduced or eliminated by changing environmental experiences or cognitive processes. Emphasis is on current behavior; behavior therapists give specific advice about problems.
	Classical conditioning approaches	Two procedures are systematic desensitization and aversive conditioning.
	Operant conditioning approaches	Emphasis is placed on the environment and its controlling conditions; abnormal behavior is determined by its consequences. Behavior modification attempts to replace maladaptive behavior with adaptive behavior; the token economy is an example.
	Cognitive behavior therapy	The focus is to change both the environment *and* the thoughts of the individual to increase adaptive behavior. Self-efficacy and self-instructional methods are emphasized.
	The widespread use of behavior therapy	While some say behavior therapy is in a downward spiral, it is widely applied to behavioral problems.
Cognitive therapies	Their nature	The individual's cognitions are the main source of abnormal behavior; many therapists have changed to a stronger cognitive focus.
	Rational emotive therapy	Developed by Albert Ellis, this approach argues that individuals are mentally disturbed because of their beliefs, especially those that are irrational and self-defeating; therapy is designed to change these beliefs.
	Beck's cognitive therapy	A cognitive therapy that changes the distorted thoughts of depressed individuals.
Group therapies and community mental health	Group therapies	Social relationships hold the key to successful therapy; therefore, group interaction may be more beneficial than individual therapy. Family and couple therapy and personal growth groups are common.
	Community mental health	Focuses on both treatment and prevention; community mental health centers, aftercare programs including halfway houses, paraprofessionals, and different forms of prevention—primary, secondary, and tertiary—characterize strategies.

Secondary prevention focuses on reducing developing abnormal behavior. For example, individuals who show early signs of juvenile delinquency might be taught vocational and social skills. In another example, a psychologist was able to reduce the symptoms of depression in a group of medical outpatients with an eight-session course and by showing a two-week television miniseries on ways to cope with depression (Munoz, 1987).

While secondary prevention emphasizes diagnosis and treatment of disorders as soon as possible, *tertiary prevention* focuses on reducing the impairment of long-standing disorders. For example, a child who has been hyperactive for several years might be trained to be more attentive in school; a schizophrenic might be helped to adapt better to society.

The community mental movement has greatly expanded the number of individuals reached by the mental health system, not only through prevention but also through treatment. Unfortunately, strong cutbacks in federal funding of community mental health centers in the 1980s have diminished their effectiveness and expansion (Geston & Jason, 1987).

It has been some time since we reviewed the main themes of therapies. Concept table 15.2 provides an overview of important themes in behavior therapies, cognitive therapies, group therapies, and community mental health.

Is Psychotherapy Effective?

Do individuals who go through therapy get better? Are some approaches more effective than others? Or is the situation like that of Dodo in *Alice's Adventures in Wonderland?* Dodo was asked to judge the winner of a race; he decided, "Everybody has won and all must have prizes." And how would we evaluate the effectiveness of psychotherapy? Would we take the client's word? The therapist's word? What would be our criteria for effectiveness? Would it be "feeling good," "adaptive behavior," "improved interpersonal relationships," "autonomous decision making," or "more positive self-concept," for example? During the last several decades an extensive amount of thought and research has addressed these questions.

Research on the Effectiveness of Psychotherapy

Nearly four decades ago Han Eysenck (1952) concluded that psychotherapy was not beneficial; the question of whether or not psychotherapy is effective still is debated. The increasing consensus is that psychotherapy is effective; conclusions suggest that no one therapy outdoes all the others, but that overall the therapies are more effective than no therapy at all. Many therapies seem to have their maximum benefit early in treatment with less improvement occurring as the individual remains in therapy (Karasu, 1986).

In one well-known evaluation of the effectiveness of psychotherapy, 475 investigations were scanned; in each of the studies some form of psychotherapy was compared with a control group (Smith, Glass, & Miller, 1980). On 88 percent of the measures, individuals who received therapy improved more than those who did not. The strategy of this research was to cull through the existing research literature for common results across many different studies—this procedure is called **metaanalysis.** While such research helps to identify common themes across disparate studies, critics point out that the quality of individual studies varies enormously; and when data are pooled in this manner they become even further removed from the clinical setting in which they were collected (Kazdin, 1986; Mintz, 1983).

Many comparisons of different forms of psychotherapy have been made. In the metaanalysis study just mentioned (Smith, Glass, & Miller, 1980), behavior therapies were compared with insight therapies (psychodynamic, humanistic). Both the behavior and insight therapies were superior to no treatment at all, but they did not differ from each other in effectiveness. A comparison of cognitive therapies and systematic desensitization also indicated that both were more effective than no treatment but did not differ in effectiveness (Berman, Miller, & Massman, 1985).

The conclusion, then, is that psychotherapy is effective, but no method of treatment is favored. Keep in mind, though, that conclusions about the effectiveness of psychotherapy are tenuous. Too often we do not know whether treatments were fairly represented in studies, whether strong versions of treatments were included, or whether treatments were carried out as intended. The techniques used in comparison studies may differ from those used in actual clinical practice. For instance, techniques widely used in clinical practice, such as a psychodynamic approach or an eclectic approach, are underrepresented in the psychotherapy comparison studies. So while it appears that psychotherapy is effective, the complexity and possible flaws in the research need to be considered.

Common Themes and Specificity in Psychotherapy

After carefully studying the nature of psychotherapy for more than twenty-five years, Jerome Frank and his associates (Frank, 1982; Gustafson, 1984; Karasu, in press) concluded that effective psychotherapies have the common elements of expectations, mastery, and emotional arousal. By inspiring an expectation of help, the therapist gets the client to continue coming to therapy. These expectations are powerful morale builders and symptom relievers in themselves. The therapist also increases the client's sense of mastery and competence; the client begins to feel that she can cope effectively with her world, for example. Therapy also arouses the individual's emotions; such arousal is essential to motivating a change in behavior.

The therapeutic relationship is another important ingredient in successful psychotherapy (Hales & Frances, 1984; Strupp, 1986, 1987). A relationship in which the client has confidence and trust in the therapist is essential to effective psychotherapy. The client and therapist engage in a "healing ritual," which requires the active participation of both the client and the therapist. As part of this ritual the client gains hope and becomes less alienated.

But while psychotherapies have common themes, some therapists worry about carrying this communality too far. Specificity in psychotherapy still needs careful attention. We need to continue our investigation of "*what* treatment, for *whom,* is most effective for *this* individual with *that* specific problem, and under which set of circumstances" (Paul, 1967). At this time, however, which approach works best in which situation with which therapist is not easily known. Some therapists are better trained than others, some are more sensitive to an individual's feelings, some are more introverted, and some are more conservative. Because of the myriad ways we differ as human beings, the ideal match of therapist and client is difficult to define.

Further Issues and Trends in Psychotherapy

Although precise conclusions are difficult to make about which therapy is most effective in which situation and with which therapist, psychotherapy is a viable enterprise. Many exciting developments are taking place as mental health professionals seek to improve the psychological adjustment of their clients. Therapists continue to fine tune their approaches and develop new, innovative strategies. A spirit of cooperation among therapists is increasing as they integrate approaches; a psychodynamic therapist uses a family systems approach; a cognitive-behavior therapist uses one of the cognitive therapies; and so on.

In addition to these changes, psychotherapy is being honed for use with special populations: the elderly, ethnic minorities, and children, for example. There also is concern about values in psychotherapy. And in keeping with the temper of the times, concern focuses on gender issues in psychotherapy; to learn more about this provocative topic turn to Psychology 15.4.

Psychology 15.4

Gender Roles and Psychotherapy

One of the by-products of changing gender roles for males and females is a possible rethinking of psychotherapy models. In some instances the development of abnormal behavior and lack of effective therapy may be due to traditional gender conditioning (Goldberg & Pepitone-Arreola-Rockwell, 1986).

The dimensions of autonomy and relatedness are central to an understanding of this conditioning. For many years autonomy was viewed as a primary determinant of maturity, relatedness was not; autonomy was the unquestioned aim of many psychotherapies, relatedness was not. Thomas Szasz (1965) claimed that the basic goal of psychotherapy is to foster autonomy, independence, and freedom. The humanistic therapists—Rogers, Maslow, and Perls—argued that to become psychologically healthy an individual has to become self-actualized through self-determination and fulfillment of needs independent of social constraints or personal commitments.

Questions are raised about autonomy as the ideal goal of therapy for females. Should therapy with females focus more on the way most females have been socialized and place more emphasis on relationships? Can females, even with therapy, achieve autonomy in a male-dominated society? Are conventional ways of thinking about autonomy and relatedness appropriate for capturing the complexity of human experience? Would therapy for females, as well as males, be improved if its goals were more androgynous in nature, stressing better psychological functioning in *both* autonomy and relatedness?

Current conceptualizations of therapy have been slow to incorporate goals that include both autonomy and relatedness. Neither autonomy nor relatedness in either extreme may be appropriate goals of therapy. In coming years we should witness increased attention to combining these important dimensions as we evaluate what therapy should be trying to accomplish (Hare-Mustin & Marecek, 1986).

Biomedical Therapies

If you asked someone why he was behaving so strangely and he responded, "It's in the water," you probably would think the individual was crazy. But an intriguing investigation revealed a relation between the concentration of lithium in drinking water and the number of admissions to mental hospitals in the state of Texas; the more lithium, the fewer admissions and readmissions (Dawson, Moore, & McGanity, 1970). Lithium and a number of other drugs have been widely used in biomedical therapies since the 1950s.

Biomedical therapies are designed to alter the way an individual's body functions; they do not focus on conversations between the therapist and clients as do psychotherapies. Drug therapy is easily the most prominent form of biomedical therapy; much less widely used forms are electroconvulsive therapy and psychosurgery. Psychiatrists or other medical doctors are responsible for administering biomedical therapies; psychologists and other mental health professionals may provide psychotherapy in conjunction with the biomedical therapy provided by psychiatrists and other medical doctors.

Drug Therapy

Psychotherapeutic drugs are used to treat many different mental disorders—anxiety, depression, and schizophrenia, for example. In some instances, these drugs are effective when other forms of therapy are not. In the case of schizophrenia, drug therapy has substantially reduced the lengths of hospital stays.

Antianxiety Drugs

Commonly known as tranquilizers, **antianxiety drugs** reduce anxiety by making individuals less excitable and more tranquil. Why are antianxiety drugs so widely used? Many individuals experience stress, anxiety, or an inability to sleep well; family physicians or psychiatrists prescribe these drugs to improve our abilities to cope with these situations more effectively. The most popular drugs prescribed are Tranxene, Librium, and Valium. These tranquilizers reduce anxiety by depressing the central nervous system.

The relaxed feeling brought on by antianxiety drugs is a welcome relief to individuals experiencing anxiety and stress in their lives. But these drugs can have adverse side effects and at times be dangerous. Antianxiety drugs often make individuals feel fatigued and drowsy; motor abilties can be impaired and work productivity reduced; and extended use can produce dependency. In some instances, the combination of antianxiety drugs and alcohol has caused death. And when an individual feels anxious, it may be best to face the problems creating the anxiety rather than rely on antianxiety drugs to avoid the problems.

Antipsychotic Drugs

The **antipsychotic drugs** are powerful drugs that diminish agitated behavior, reduce tension, decrease hallucinations and delusions, improve social behavior, and produce better sleep patterns in severely mentally disturbed individuals, especially schizophrenics. The most widely used antipsychotic drugs are the **neuroleptics.**

The most widely used explanation for the effectiveness of antipsychotic drugs is their ability to block the dopamine system's action in the brain. Recall from our discussion in chapter 14 that schizophrenics have too much of the neurochemical messenger dopamine. Numerous well-controlled investigations reveal that when used in sufficient doses, the neuroleptics reduce a variety of schizophrenic symptoms, although most reductions are of a short-term rather than long-term duration (Marder & May, 1986).

But the neuroleptics do not cure schizophrenia and they may have severe side effects. The neuroleptics treat the symptoms of schizophrenia, not its causes. If an individual stops taking the drug, the symptoms return. Neuroleptic drugs, though, have substantially reduced the lengths of hospital stays for schizophrenics. Although schizophrenics are able to return to the community because drug therapy keeps their symptoms from reappearing, most have difficulty coping with the demands of society and most are chronically unemployed (Gunderson & Mosher, 1975).

Tardive dyskinesia is a major side effect of the neuroleptics; it is a neurological disorder characterized by grotesque, involuntary movements of the facial muscles and mouth as well as extensive twitching of the neck, arms, and legs. As many as 20 percent of schizophrenics taking neuroleptics develop this disorder; elderly women are especially vulnerable. Long-term neuroleptic therapy also is associated with increased depression and anxiety; schizophrenics who take neuroleptics for many years report that they feel miserable most of the time, for example. Nonetheless, for the majority of schizophrenics, the benefits of neuroleptic treatment outweigh its risks and discomforts (Gardos & others, 1987).

Strategies to increase the effectiveness of the neuroleptics involve administering lower dosages over time rather than a large initial dose and combining drug therapy with psychotherapy. The small percentage of schizophrenics who are able to hold jobs suggests that drugs alone will not make them contributing members of society. Vocational, family, and social-skills training are needed in conjunction with drug therapy to facilitate improved psychological functioning and adaptation to society (Marder, Van Putten, & Mintz, 1984).

Antidepressant Drugs

Helen of Troy is best known for causing one of the most destructive wars in history. She also was a pioneer in using chemicals to alleviate depression. She put "nepenthe," an opium derivative, in the wine of Telemachus and his friends to reduce their sorrow. Major discoveries about using drugs to diminish depression did not occur until several thousand years later when the antidepressants were discovered. **Antidepressant drugs** regulate mood; they often are called *tricyclics* because of their three-ringed molecular structure. The tricyclics probably work because they increase the levels of certain neurotransmitters, especially norepinephrine and serotonin, in the brain. These drugs reduce the symptoms of depression in approximately 60 to 70 percent of all cases. Nonetheless, the tricyclics sometimes have adverse side effects—restlessness, faintness, and trembling, for example.

Lithium, the drug in the Texas water supply, is used widely to treat bipolar disorder (recall that this disorder involves wide mood swings of depression and mania). The amount of lithium that circulates in the bloodstream must be carefully monitored because its effective dosage lies precariously close to toxic levels. Memory impairment also is associated with lithium use (Shaw & others, 1987).

As with schizophrenia, the treatment of the affective disorders might also involve a combination of drug therapy and psychotherapy. In one investigation, the combination of tricyclics and interpersonal psychotherapy produced a lower than normal relapse rate for depressed clients (10 percent vs. 22 percent) (Frank & Kupfer, 1986). The interpersonal therapy focused on the client's ablty to develop and maintain positive interpersonal relationships and included an educational workshop for clients and their families.

Electroconvulsive Therapy

In Sylvia Plath's (1971) autobiographical novel, *The Bell Jar,* she described electroconvulsive therapy: "Then something bent down and took hold of me and shook me like the end of the world. Wee-ee-ee-ee-ee, it shrilled, through an air crackling with blue light, and with each flash a great jolt drubbed me until I thought my bones would break and the sap fly out of me like a split plant." Such images have shaped the public's view of **electroconvulsive therapy**

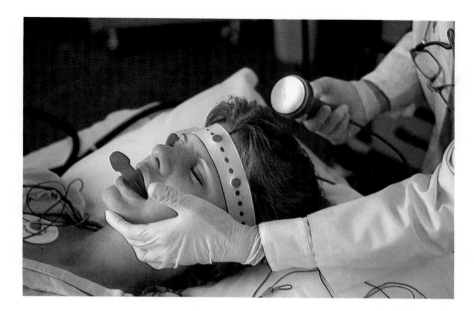

(ECT), commonly called "shock treatment." The goal of ECT is to cause a seizure in the brain much like what happens spontaneously in some forms of epilepsy. A small electric current lasting for one second or less passes through two electrodes placed on the individual's head. The current excites neural tissue, stimulating a seizure that lasts for approximately one minute.

ECT has been used for more than forty years. In earlier years it often was used indiscriminately, sometimes even as a punishment for patients. ECT is still used with as many as 60,000 individuals a year, mainly to treat major depression. Adverse side effects may include memory loss or other cognitive impairment. Today ECT is given mainly to individuals who have not responded to drug therapy or psychotherapy. ECT sounds like it would entail intolerable pain, but the manner in which it is administered today involves little discomfort. The patient is given anethesia and muscle relaxants before the current is applied; this allows the individual to sleep through the procedure, minimizes convulsions, and reduces the risk of physical injury. The individual awakens shortly afterwards with no conscious memory of the treatment.

An example reveals how ECT, used as a last resort, was effective in reducing depression (Sackheim, 1985). Ann is a thirty-six-year-old teacher and mother. She had been in psychotherapy for several years; prior to entering the hospital she took tricyclics with unsuccessful results. In the first six months of her hospital stay, doctors tried different drugs to reduce her depression; none of the drugs worked. She slept poorly, lost her appetite, and showed no interest even in reading newspaper headlines. Obsessed with the idea that she had ruined her children, she repeatedly threatened suicide. With her consent, doctors began ECT; after five treatments Ann returned to her family and job several days later. Not all cases of ECT turn out as positively. Even when ECT works, though, we do not know why it works (Kramer, 1987; Sackheim & others, 1987; Small & others, 1986).

■ ■ ■ ■ ■ ■ ■ ■ ■ ■ ■ ■ ■ ■ ■ ■ ■ ■
Concept Table 15.3

The Effectiveness of Psychotherapy and the Biomedical Therapies		
Concept	Processes/related ideas	Characteristics/description
The effectiveness of psychotherapy	Research on psychotherapy's effectiveness	Psychotherapy is effective but no treatment is favored. Research is extremely complex and many evaluations are flawed.
	Common themes and specificity	Common themes include expectations of help, development of a sense of mastery, emotional arousal, and a confiding relationship. We still need to ask which therapies work best, with which individuals, in what setting, with which therapist.
	Further issues and trends in psychotherapy	Some integration of therapies is occurring and therapies are being tailored for special populations, such as minority groups and the elderly.
Biomedical therapies	Their nature	Designed to alter the way an individual's body functions. Administered by psychiatrists or other medical doctors.
	Drug therapy	May be effective when other therapies have failed, as in reducing the symptoms of schizophrenia. Three major classes of psychotherapeutic drugs are antianxiety, antipsychotic, and antidepressant.
	Electroconvulsive therapy	Commonly called "shock treatment." Creates a seizure in the brain; its most common use is as a last resort in treating severe depression.
	Psychosurgery	An irreversible procedure; brain tissue is removed or destroyed in an attempt to improve psychological adjustment. It is more refined than early prefrontal lobotomies, but it is rarely used.

Psychosurgery

One biomedical treatment is even more extreme than ECT. The effects of **psychosurgery** are irreversible; this procedure involves removal or destruction of brain tissue to improve the individual's psychological adjustment. In the 1930s, Portuguese physician Egas Moniz developed a procedure known as a *prefrontal lobotomy*. In this procedure, a surgical instrument is inserted into the brain and rotated, severing fibers that connect the frontal lobe, where higher thought processes take place, and the thalamus, where emotion is prominent. Moniz theorized that by severing the connections between these brain structures the symptoms of severe mental disorders could be alleviated. Prefrontal lobotomies were conducted on thousands of patients from the 1930s through the 1950s. Moniz even was awarded a Nobel Prize for his work. However, while some patients may have benefited from the lobotomies, many were left in vegetable-like states because of the massive assaults on their brains.

These crude lobotomies are no longer performed. Since the 1960s, psychosurgery has become more precise. A very small lesion in the amygdala or another part of the limbic system, thought to be important in emotion, characterizes contemporary psychosurgery. Today only several hundred patients per year undergo psychosurgery; it is used as a last resort and with extreme caution.

A summary of the main ideas involved in the effectiveness of psychotherapy and the biomedical therapies is presented in concept table 15.3. To conclude our discussion of therapies, we will describe some guidelines for seeking therapy.

Guidelines for Seeking Psychotherapy

At some point in our lives many of us will consider psychotherapy. The problems we encounter vary enormously, so no absolute guidelines for seeking psychotherapy will ensure that you will benefit from it. For most of us, though, it is psychologically healthy to accept our feelings, know our faults, work on developing our talents and interests, and create a network of friends as a support system. Accomplishing these things ourselves gives us a sense of competence and mastery that probably means we do not need psychotherapy.

Nevertheless, sometimes our abilities to adjust psychologically are limited. If problems overwhelm you, it may be time to think about seeing a mental health professional. If you decide to seek psychotherapy, do not consider it an indication that you are a weak individual. To the contrary, if problems or difficulties are disrupting your daily life, reinforce yourself for having the emotional maturity to seek psychotherapy.

If you do decide to work with a mental health professional, the following guidelines may help (Weiten, 1983):

1. Do not jump into a particular therapeutic situation too quickly. Try to read about the approach, talk with the individuals involved, and converse with others who have experienced this approach.
2. Don't forget that improvement and adjustment take a great deal of effort on your part. Old patterns of behavior and thought often do not go away overnight.
3. When you do choose an approach, give it time to work. Even if you find that you are improving, remember that temporary setbacks may occur.

We have explored the promises and challenges of many different forms of therapy in this chapter. This chapter completes our coverage of personality and abnormal psychology. In the next section we will study social psychology; among the topics to be discussed are our thoughts about ourselves and others in social circumstances, how we influence others and they us, and our social relationships.

Summary

I. Historical Perspective
Many early treatments of mental disturbances were inhumane. Asylums were built during the Renaissance. Pinel's efforts led to extensive reform of the asylums and the treatment of the mentally disturbed. Dix's efforts helped to separate the mentally disturbed from prisoners.

II. The Nature of Psychotherapy
Psychotherapy is the process of working with individuals to reduce their problems and improve their adjustment. Psychotherapy includes approaches based on a number of personality theories—psychodynamic, humanistic, and behavioral and social learning. It does not include drugs and surgery, which are referred to as biomedical therapy. Many therapists take an eclectic approach to therapy.

Psychotherapy is practiced by a number of mental health professionals, including clinical psychologists, psychiatrists, and marriage counselors. Psychotherapy takes place in a greater variety of settings than in the past. Clients with higher socioeconomic status are more likely to receive therapy; many therapists expect them to benefit from therapy more than their lower-class counterparts.

III. **Psychodynamic Therapies**
The psychodynamic therapies stress the importance of the unconscious mind, the role of the past, and extensive interpretation by the therapist. Freud believed that mental disturbances are caused by unresolved unconscious conflicts between the id, ego, and superego, which originate in early childhood experiences. The therapist's interpretation of free association, dreams, resistance, and transference provide tools to understand the patient's unconscious conflicts. Many variations of psychodynamic therapies have developed; some still adhere to Freud's approach and others distance themselves from his therapy. The development of the self in social contexts has been a major theme of psychodynamic alternatives to Freud.

IV. **Humanistic Therapies**
The humanistic therapies encourage clients to examine themselves and to grow and develop personally. In contrast to psychodynamic therapies, humanistic therapies emphasize unconscious rather than conscious thoughts, the present rather than the past, and growth and fulfillment rather than curing an illness. Person-centered therapy, developed by Carl Rogers, focuses on the experiences of the individual at the moment and emphasizes that each individual has the capacity to improve tremendously. The therapist replaces conditions of worth with unconditional positive regard and uses genuineness, accurate empathy, and active listening to raise the client's self-esteem. In

Gestalt therapy, developed by Fritz Perls, individuals are encouraged to be open and honest with their feelings; the therapist confronts the client and gets the individual to act out emotions. Gestalt therapy is more directive than the nondirective approach of client-centered therapy. Both the psychodynamic and humanistic therapies are insight therapies.

V. **Behavior Therapies**
Behavior therapies are based on the behavioral and social learning theories of learning and personality. The individual's abnormal behavior is learned through environmental experiences; it can be reduced or eliminated by changing environmental experiences or cognitive processes. The emphasis is on current behavior and behavior therapists give specific advice about problems. Two procedures used that are based on classical conditioning are systematic desensitization and aversive conditioning. Operant conditioning approaches emphasize behavior and its controlling conditions; abnormal behavior is determined by its consequences. Behavior modification attempts to replace maladaptive behavior with adaptive behavior. The token economy is an example of a behavior modification strategy. Cognitive behavior therapies have a dual focus—change both the environment *and* the thoughts of the individual to increase adaptive behavior. Self-efficacy and self-instructional methods are emphasized. While some say behavior therapy is in a downward spiral, it is widely applied to a number of behavior problems.

VI. **Cognitive Therapies**
Cognitive therapies stress that the individual's thoughts are the main source of abnormal behavior; many therapists have developed a stronger cognitive focus. Rational emotive therapy, developed by Albert Ellis, argues that individuals become mentally disturbed because of their irrational beliefs and self-defeating thoughts; therapy is designed to change these beliefs. Beck's cognitive therapy tries to change the distorted perceptions of depressed individuals.

VII. **Group Therapies and Community Mental Health**
Group therapies stress that social relationships hold the key to successful therapy; therefore, group interaction may be more beneficial than individual therapy. Family and couple therapy and personal growth groups are common. Community mental health focuses on both prevention and treatment; community mental health centers, aftercare programs, paraprofessionals, and different forms of prevention characterize strategies.

VIII. **The Effectiveness of Psychotherapy**
Psychotherapy is effective but no treatment is favored. Research on psychotherapy is complex and many evaluations are flawed. Common themes of psychotherapy include expectations of help, development of a sense of mastery, emotional arousal, and a confiding relationship. But while psychotherapies have some common themes, we still need to ask which therapies work best with which individuals, in which setting, with which therapist. Integration of therapies is taking place. Therapies are being tailored for special populations, such as minority groups and the elderly.

IX. Biomedical Therapies

Biomedical therapies alter the way the body functions. They are mainly administered by psychiatrists and other medical doctors. Psychotherapeutic drugs treat many disorders. In some instances drug therapy is successful when other therapies have failed, for example, in treating the symptoms of schizophrenia. Three major classes of psychotherapeutic drugs are antianxiety, antipsychotic, and antidepressant. Electroconvulsive therapy and psychosurgery are other biomedical treatments that are used as last resorts.

X. Guidelines for Therapy

While no absolute guidelines can be given, seeking therapy should not be viewed as a sign of weakness. If an individual seeks therapy, he should learn about the approach and the therapist, remember that improvment takes effort, and give the therapy time to work.

Key Terms

psychotherapy *510*
psychodynamic therapies *511*
catharsis *511*
dream analysis *512*
resistance *512*
transference *512*
humanistic psychotherapies *513*
person-centered therapy *514*
genuineness *514*
accurate empathy *514*
active listening *514*
Gestalt therapy *515*
insight therapies *516*
behavior therapies *517*

systematic desensitization *517*
aversive conditioning *518*
token economy *519*
cognitive behavior therapies *519*
self-efficacy *519*
self-instructional methods *520*
cognitive therapies *522*
rational emotive therapy *522*
family therapy *526*
couple therapy *526*
family systems therapy *527*
personal growth groups *527*
encounter group *528*

marathon groups *528*
transactional analysis *528*
paraprofessionals *530*
metaanalysis *532*
biomedical therapies *534*
antianxiety drugs *535*
antipsychotic drugs *535*
neuroleptics *535*
tardive dyskinesia *535*
antidepressant drugs *536*
lithium *536*
electroconvulsive therapy (ECT) *536*
psychosurgery *538*

Suggested Readings

Behavior Therapy. This journal publishes a wide ranging set of behavior therapy strategies and a number of fascinating case studies. Look through the issues of the 1980s to see how behavior therapy is conducted.

Corsini, R. J. (Ed.). (1984). *Current psychotherapies* (3rd ed). Itasca, IL: Peacock. This book includes a number of chapters by well-known therapists who describe their approach to psychotherapy; for example, Albert Ellis writes about rational emotive therapy.

Goldberg, D. C. (1985). *Contemporary marriage: Special issues in couples therapy.* Homewood, IL: Dorsey Press. A number of contemporary treatments of issues in couples therapy are provided—divorce therapy, two-career couples, delayed childbirth, alternative life-styles, and jealousy, for example.

Kendall, P. C., & Norton-Ford, J. D. (1982). *Clinical psychology: Scientific and professional dimensions.* New York: Wiley. A number of different psychotherapies are described. Information about the professional dimensions of being a clinical psychologist are outlined.

Perls, F. S. (1969). *Gestalt therapy verbatim.* Lafayette, CA: Real People Press. Fritz Perls, the founder of Gestalt therapy, lays out the main ideas of his approach in vivid detail.

Wedding, D., & Corsini, R. (1979). *Great cases in psychotherapy.* Itasca, IL: Peacock. A complete description of a number of well-known cases; transcripts of cases involving Fritz Perls, Eric Berne, Sigmund Freud, Alfred Adler, Carl Jung, and Carl Rogers are presented.

Social Psychology

No man is an island, entire of itself.

—*John Donne*

Chapter 16

Social Thinking and Influence

■ ■

Man is by nature a social animal.

—Aristotle

■ ■

Images of Social Thinking and Influence

James W. Jones developed a small church in Indiana in 1953 with the noble intent of eliminating social injustice and improving interracial harmony. His church congregation included a number of blacks; he and his wife adopted seven children, including a black, a Chinese, and a Korean. Jones went to Brazil to work as a missionary for two years and while there founded an orphanage and a mission. Upon returning home he changed the name of his church to the People's Temple Full Gospel.

Jones moved his church to northern California, at which time he increased his money-raising efforts and community work. Members were asked to give all of their assets to the church as a sign of their loyalty. By the early 1970s, Jones had developed churches in the black areas of San Francisco and Los Angeles. Accolades were showered on him and his social programs were rated among the best in the country.

But Reverend Jones's social influence was not all positive. Reports circulated that when members were disobedient or tried to leave the church, Jones attempted to gain guardianship of their children, he made death threats, and beatings occurred. Jones's respectability in the community and his tight reign on information leaks to the public repressed investigations.

During the early 1970s, Jones began to change. He increasingly saw parallels between himself and Christ and presented himself to his congregation as a messiah. Church members were required to call him "Father," and he declared that everything he said was law.

In 1977, the People's Temple migrated en masse to Jonestown, Guyana, apparently because of an article that was about to appear in *New West* magazine, which revealed the abuses in Jones's church. On November 18, 1978, more than 900 members of the People's Temple committed suicide by drinking Kool-Aid laced with cyanide. The church members were simply obeying their leader's orders.

We do not know all of the answers to the Jonestown massacre, but the People's Temple had become a twisted mess of distorted social perceptions and malevolent social influence. More than forty suicide rehearsals had been practiced by the church members, beginning in California (Wooden, 1981). Jones had planned the massacre and apparently saw it as a final opportunity to make his mark on the world as it closed in on him. On the afternoon preceding the massacre United States Representative Leo Ryan, who was in Guyana to evaluate charges of abuse in the People's Temple, was gunned down along with four of his aides as they boarded a plane to leave the country. Jones convinced his members that hostile intruders were on their way to exterminate them in retaliation for the deaths at the airstrip.

Jones was a master at getting members to conform to his norms. Individuals were required to confess their deviances and failures in front of church members. Those who did not abide by what Jones demanded were beaten. Further control was obtained by taking away family and economic support.

The massacre at Jonestown—the macabre side of social thinking and influence.

At the time of the mass suicide in Jonestown, the members of the People's Temple were isolated from their families and the world. They had been stripped of their possessions and individuality. They were completely obedient to their leader, they believed that hostile forces were about to attack them, and they were made to think by the "martyr" Jones that their suicide was revolutionary and a positive act.

The massacre at Jonestown is the macabre side of social thinking and influence; it shows the power of obedience and conformity and how such power can be abused. **Social psychology** involves interpersonal thoughts and behaviors, both the extraordinary scenes—such as those in the life of the Reverend James Jones—and the countless, less ostentatious social thoughts and interactions that characterize our everyday lives. In this chapter we begin by studying attitudes and persuasion, then turn to social perceptions, and conclude with conformity. ▪

Attitudes and Persuasion

As Mark Twain once said, "It is a difference of opinion that makes horses race." **Attitudes** are beliefs and opinions about something. We have attitudes about all sorts of things, and we live in a world in which we try to influence the attitudes of each other. Nowhere is the power of persuasion more prevalent or expensive than in advertising. More than 50 billion dollars is spent each year in the United States on advertising; political candidates alone spend more than 500 million dollars. Public service announcements seek to induce us to preserve our health by buckling our seat belts and getting our blood pressure checked.

Each night newscasters come into our living rooms dispensing information. Are television newscasters' attitudes reflected in their behaviors? Do they subtly persuade us? David Brinkley once said, "I am not objective, [and] make no pretense of being objective. There are a great many things I like and dislike, and it may be that at times some indication of this appears in my facial expression."

(a)

(b)

(c)

Do newscasters' facial expressions convey their favoritism for a political candidate? Could the newscasters influence the outcome of presidential elections? (a) ABC's Peter Jennings, (b) CBS's Dan Rather, and (c) NBC's Tom Brokaw. Jennings was the only one of the three whose facial expressions revealed a strong attitude in favor of Ronald Reagan. People who watched Jennings were more likely to vote for Reagan.

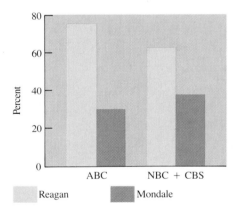

Note: These data are for Cleveland, Ohio; similar trends were found in Rolla, Mo., Williamstown, Mass., and Erie, Pa.

Figure 16.1
Percentage of sample voting for Reagan and Mondale who watched ABC, NBC, or CBS nightly news broadcasts.

A recent investigation focused on whether the smile of newscasters might play a role in the election of a president (Mullen & others, 1986). The nightly newscasts of Dan Rather, Tom Brokow, and Peter Jennings were videotaped prior to the 1984 presidential election. Coders scored how positive the newscasters' facial expressions were when they talked about either Reagan or Mondale. Peter Jennings was the only one of the three whose facial expressions revealed a strong attitude in favor of Reagan. Subsequently, in the spring of 1985 a random sample of the population was surveyed over the telephone; individuals were asked which nightly news shows they watched and for whom they voted. The percentage of ABC viewers (Jennings's station) who voted for Reagan was consistently higher than the percentage of NBC or CBS viewers (see figure 16.1). While these results suggest the possibility of subtle persuasion of voter attitudes through the facial expressions of television newscasters, it may be that individuals of certain political persuasions chose to watch particular commentators. This study was correlational in nature so we cannot conclude that the newscasters' facial expressions *caused* the different voter attitudes.

Attitudes and Behavior

Think about your attitudes about religion, politics, and sex. Now think about your behavior in these areas. Consider sex, for example. How liberal or conservative are your sexual attitudes? Does your behavior match your attitudes? Researchers have found that we have more accepting attitudes toward sexual practices than our behavior actually shows (Dreyer, 1982). As we study the relation of attitudes to behavior, two questions arise: How strongly do attitudes influence behavior? and How strongly does behavior influence attitudes?

Predicting Behavior from Attitudes

More than fifty years ago Richard LaPiere (1934) toured the United States with a Chinese couple. He expected to experience prejudice toward Orientals, for example, being refused food and lodging. However, in more than 10,000 miles of travel, the threesome was rejected only once. This sounds as if there were few negative attitudes toward Orientals in the United States during the 1930s. To see if this actually was the case, LaPiere wrote a letter to all 251 places he and his Oriental friends had visited, asking if they would provide food or lodging to Orientals. More than half responded; of those, a resounding 90 percent said they absolutely would not allow Orientals in their restaurant or motel. LaPierre's study suggests that what we say and what we do may be different.

Do our attitudes always match up this poorly with our behavior? As late as the 1970s, some social psychologists argued that the association of attitudes and behavior was so weak that the concept of attitude should be abandoned. Recognizing that the match between attitudes and behavior is not always perfect, the belief today is that attitudes are associated with behavior but in more complex ways than were studied previously. To study this complexity, social psychologists evaluate a variety of situational influences and individual characteristics that might affect the attitude-behavior connection (Chaiken & Stangor, 1987; Fazio, 1986; Jamieson & Zanna, 1987).

The connection between attitudes and behaviors may vary depending on the situation. In the study of attitudes toward Orientals in the 1930s, the Chinese who accompanied LaPiere were well dressed and carried expensive luggage; they may have inspired different attitudes if they had appeared in cheaper attire. To think further about the way the situation influences the attitude-behavior connection, consider an individual who is asked about his attitude toward individuals who drive pickup trucks. He responds, "Totally classless." A month later he has stopped for a cup of coffee in a small west Texas town. A burly man in the next booth is talking with his buddies about the merits of pickup trucks. He turns to our friend and asks, "How do you like that green pickup truck sitting outside?" Needless to say, his response was not "totally classless." This example suggests that the demands of the situation can be powerful even when we hold strong beliefs.

Other guidelines help predict behavior from attitudes. When our attitudes are based on personal experiences, our behavior is more likely to reflect our attitudes. For example, an individual may have a negative attitude about smoking but still smokes heavily. When a friend who smoked heavily dies of lung cancer, the individual quits smoking, making his nonsmoking behavior match his negative attitude about smoking (Fazio & Zanna, 1981).

When we have thought about our attitude toward something and have ready access to it, the attitude-behavior connection is strengthened. In many circumstances, though, we act in rather mindless ways, simply following scripts we have used throughout our lives. But if you have thought about your attitudes, you probably have ready access to them. For example, what is your attitude toward gun control? Coed dorms? Smoking in public places?

Attitudes that quickly come to mind or are easily accessible influence our perception of events and, therefore, are more closely tied to our behavior. In one investigation the idea that the more accessible the attitude the more likely it will influence our behavior was tested (Fazio & Williams, 1986). Attitudes toward Reagan and Mondale, and the accessibility of these attitudes as measured by how long individuals took to respond, was assessed prior to the 1984 presidential election. If a subject knew immediately that he disliked Reagan, this attitude usually was reflected in his judgment of Reagan's performance during televised debates and how he voted in the election. Attitudes about the candidates that were quickly accessible were more strongly associated with subsequent perceptions of the debates and voting behavior.

Russell Fazio (Fazio & Driscoll, 1987; Fazio & Williams, 1986) describes this type of research on attitudes as an attempt to evaluate the *how* question. That is, how do attitudes guide behavior? Most research on attitudes has emphasized the *when* question, which identifies the situational and personality factors that affect the attitude-behavior connection.

To summarize, there is a strong association between attitudes and behaviors when situational pressures are weak, when attitudes are based on personal experiences, when we have thought about our attitudes, and when they are easily accessible. But what about the other side of the coin: Does the way we act influence our attitudes?

How might this woman justify her violation of parking laws? Cognitive dissonance is about trying to reduce tension by cognitively justifying things that are unpleasant.

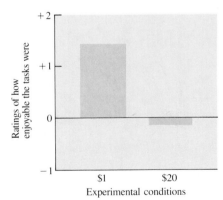

Figure 16.2
Festinger and Carlsmith's classic experiment on cognitive dissonance. Ratings were made on a scale ranging from + 5 to − 5.
Source: Festinger & Carlsmith, 1959, p. 207.

Behavior's Influence on Attitudes

In the words of John Locke, "The actions of men are the best interpreters of their thoughts." Does doing change your believing? If you quit drinking will you have a more negative attitude toward drinking? If you take up an exercise program are you more likely to extoll the benefits of cardiovascular fitness when someone asks your attitude about exercise?

Ample evidence exists that changes in behavior precede changes in attitudes (Bandura, 1986). Social psychologists offer two main explanations of why behavior influences attitudes. The first view is that we have a strong need for cognitive consistency; consequently, we change our attitudes to make them more consistent with our behavior. The second view is that our attitudes are not completely clear, so we observe our behavior and make inferences about it to determine what our attitudes should be. Let's consider these two views in more detail.

Cognitive dissonance is a well-known concept in psychology. Developed by Leon Festinger (1957), it describes our motivation toward consistency and away from inconsistency. For example, we might feel uneasy about the discrepancy between our attitudes and behavior, which often leads us to justify our actions. Consider when you do something that you do not feel good about—flunking a test or losing your temper, for instance. We frequently justify our behavior in our mind, as George Bernard Shaw did with his father's alcoholism: "If you cannot get rid of the family skeleton, you may as well make it dance." Shaw's comment was intended to minimize in his mind what seemed to be an inevitable occurrence; his justification helped him reduce the tension between his attitude about his father's drinking problem and its actual occurrence. Cognitive dissonance is about making our skeletons dance, about trying to reduce tension by cognitively justifying things that are unpleasant (Aronson, 1984, 1987).

A classic experiment in social psychology illustrates further how cognitive dissonance works. If you were paid 1 dollar to tell a lie would you end up believing the lie more than if you were paid 20 dollars to tell the lie? A behavioral interpretation would predict that you would be more likely to believe the lie if you were paid 20 dollars. But one experiment (Festinger & Carlsmith, 1959) provided an elegant example of how investigators might be able to get you to perceive human nature a little differently and in the process possibly get you to change an attitude. Remember that cognitive dissonance theory states that we are rationalizing creatures who try to make our attitudes line up with our behavior. In the experiment, college students were asked to perform boring and repetitive tasks, such as packing spools in a tray or turning rows of screws one-quarter of a turn. The experimenter induced them to lie about the task; the lie involved telling a woman waiting to participate in the experiment (who was paid for her role) how interesting and enjoyable the experience was. When the experiment was over, an interviewer asked the "liars" how much they had enjoyed their work. The students who had been given 20 dollars to lie rated the activity as dull; those who were paid only 1 dollar said it was enjoyable (see figure 16.2). That is, students who were *externally* justified (that is, paid 20 dollars) for lying told the lie but did not believe it. The ones who experienced little external justification (that is, were paid only 1 dollar) told the lie and moved toward believing what they said was true. These subjects needed an internal justification to tell the lie since they lacked an external justification; therefore they justified telling the lie by believing what they said.

We also justify cruelty in our lives. We have a need to convince ourselves that we are decent, reasonable human beings. For example, after we have a bad argument with someone, we often develop a negative attitude toward that individual, which justifies the nasty things we said to the individual. We also have a strong need to justify the effort we put forth in life. We positively evaluate goals that we must exert considerable effort to reach. Whether we reach the goals or not, we engage in the process of **effort justification.** The reasoning goes like this: if we work hard to attain a goal but then evaluate that goal in a negative way, dissonance would occur. If we put forth considerable effort and yet do not reach the goal, how could we reduce the dissonance? We could convince ourselves that we really did not work as hard as we did; or we could say that the goal was not all that important in the first place.

Our most intense justifications of our actions take place when our self-esteem is involved. If I do something cruel, then it follows that I have to perform some mental gymnastics to keep myself from thinking I am a cruel person. The clearest results in the hundreds of research studies on cognitive dissonance occur when self-esteem is involved. And it is when individuals with the highest self-esteem act in cruel ways that the most dissonance results. But what about individuals with low self-esteem? They probably experience less dissonance because acting in a cruel way is consistent with their attitudes toward themselves—attitudes that might entail some familiar labels like "nerd," "schmuck," or "zero." Put another way, individuals who think of themselves as nerds may do "nerdy" things because it keeps dissonance at a minimum.

But all of our thoughts and behaviors are not aimed at reducing dissonance; some of us, it is hoped, learn from our mistakes. There are times when we need to catch ourselves, look in the mirror, and say, "You blew it. Now what can you do to prevent that from happening again?" Eliot Aronson (1984) offers three suggestions that can keep our lives from being a treadmill of dissonance reduction:

1. Know your defensive and dissonance-reducing tendencies; be able to sense them before you get in over your head.
2. Realize that behaving in stupid and cruel ways does not necessarily mean that you are a stupid and cruel person.
3. Develop enough strengths and competencies to be able to tolerate your mistakes without having to spend a lifetime of rationalizing them away.

Not all social psychologists, however, are satisfied with cognitive dissonance as an explanation for the influence of behavior on attitudes. Daryl Bem, for example, believes that the cognitive dissonance view relies too heavily on internal factors, which are difficult to measure. Bem (1967) argues that we should move away from such fuzzy and nebulous concepts as "cognitions" and "psychological discomfort" and replace them with more behavioral terminology. His **self-perception theory** of the attitude-behavior connection stresses that we make inferences about our attitudes by perceiving our behavior. For example, consider the remark, "I am spending all of my time thinking about the test I have next week. I must be anxious." Or, "This is the third time I have gone to the student union in two days. I must be lonely." Bem believes we look to our own behavior when our attitudes are not completely clear. This means that when we have clear ideas about something, we are less likely to look to our behavior for clues about our attitudes; but if we feel more ambivalent about something or someone, our behavior is a good place to look to determine our attitude.

While the cognitive dissonance and self-perception theories of attitude-behavior associations may seem incompatible, they are not completely at odds. Self-perception theory may better explain how attitudes are acquired initially; cognitive dissonance theory may better explain attitudes and behaviors once they are formed. And, some attitudes may develop simply because of self-perception, others because of cognitive dissonance.

So far we have seen that in some instances attitudes are good indicators of an individual's behavior, in other instances they are not good indicators. A basic theme woven through our coverage of psychology's many topics is that *behavior is multiply determined*. To think that there is a one-to-one mapping of attitudes and behavior denies the complexity and adaptability inherent in human beings.

Persuasion and Attitude Change

We spend many hours of our lives trying to persuade individuals to do certain things. For example, the words from the song *Emotion in Motion* go like this, "I would do anything just to hold on to you. Just about anything you want me to." One individual is trying to persuade another individual of the intensity of his love. Politicians and corporations also are heavily involved in the persuasion process. The time has passed when a politician does not have a full arsenal of speech writers and image consultants who ensure that words and behavior are as persuasive as possible.

Advertisers also go to great lengths to persuade individuals to buy their products. Consider trying to persuade someone to buy raisins. How would you make raisins appeal to consumers? An imaginative advertisement had a chorus line of animated raisins dancing to the tune of "I Heard It Through the Grapevine" (see figure 16.3). What is it about this advertisement that persuades us to buy raisins? Social psychologists believe persuasion involves four key components: who conveys the message (the source), what the message is (the communication), what medium is used (the channel), and for whom the message is intended (the target) (see figure 16.4).

The Communicator (Source)

Suppose you are running for president of the student body; you tell students you are going to make life at your college better. Would they believe you? Whether or not they believe you depends on if you are perceived as an expert and on your credibility, how much they think they can trust you, as well as how much power, attraction, and similarity you communicate to them (McGuire, 1985, 1987). Expertise depends on qualifications. If you had held other elective offices students would be more likely to believe you have the expertise to be their president.

We attribute competence to experts, believing they are knowledgeable about the topics they address. It is not unusual for experts in one domain to assert expertise or have expertise attributed to them in another domain. William Shockley won a Nobel Prize for inventing the transistor; he also is a self-proclaimed expert on the genetic basis of intelligence. Being a transistor expert, though, does not make one an expert on human genetics.

In addition to expertise and credibility, trustworthiness is an important quality of an effective communicator. This factor depends on whether your communications are perceived as honest or dishonest. It was in Abraham Lincoln's best interest, then, to be called "Honest Abe;" being perceived as honest increased the power of his communication.

Other characteristics of communicators believed to bring about attitude change are power, attractiveness, likableness, and similarity. When asked why he was so successful with women, former Secretary of State Henry Kissinger remarked, "Power is the most important aphrodisiac." Not only can power influence relationships with the opposite sex, but it also may bring about attitude changes in other situations. In running for student body president you probably will convince students you have more clout with the administration in convincing them to build a new student social center in the student union

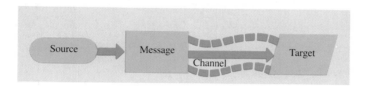

Figure 16.4
Factors in the attitude persuasion process.
From Steven Penrod, Social Psychology, © *1983, p. 307. Reprinted by permission of Prentice-Hall, Inc., Englewood Cliffs, NJ.*

than other candidates because you have been on the president's committee for student interests and have initiated a movement to sign a petition about the issue. Power seems to be an important communicator characteristic because it is associated with the ability to impose sanctions or control rewards and punishments (Galbraith, 1983; Kelley & Thibaut, 1978).

In running for student body president, you are more likely to get votes if students perceive you as attractive and similar to themselves. It is not unusual to see presidential candidates putting on miners' helmets in West Virginia, speaking a Spanish phrase in San Antonio, or riding a tractor in Iowa; these candidates are striving to show that they are common people just like those in their audience.

Similarity is used in advertising more than in the past also. In commercials we might see a homemaker scrubbing the floor while advertising a new cleaner or a laborer laughing with his buddies at a bar while drinking beer; the creators of these commercials hope that you will relate to these individuals because you perceive them as similar to yourself. Of course, many products are promoted by appealing to our personal ideals; to do this, attractive or famous individuals are used in advertisements. Linda Evans tries to persuade us to buy cologne and John Madden and Phil Collins try to persuade us to buy beer, for example.

Another factor that influences attitudes is the sex of the communicator. To learn more about how gender might be a factor in attitudes about political candidates, read Psychology 16.1.

Psychology 16.1

Gender and Politics—from Ferraro to County Clerk

It is the summer of 1984. The November presidential election is only months away; the Democrats are far behind in the polls. The economy is looking better and Republican incumbent Ronald Reagan's lead seems insurmountable. What could the Democratic party do to persuade the American population to switch their allegiance? It would have to be something ostentatious, something never tried before in the history of American politics.

One of the areas in which Reagan seemed vulnerable was women's rights; the National Organization of Women (NOW) called Reagan "insensitive" to women, for example. For the first time in history, a woman—Geraldine Ferraro—was selected to fill the vice-presidential slot on the Democratic ticket. While the Democrats did not win the 1984 presidential election, Ferraro's selection was an important step for women in their effort to achieve equality.

As more women have sought political office, the issue of gender has assumed a more important role in attitude change. Surveys reveal that in today's political climate we are more likely to vote for qualified female candidates, especially if they are running for lower political offices (Gallup,1984; Sigelman & Welch, 1984). Instances of discrimination still appear, though; this occurred in several gubernatorial campaigns (Yankelovich, Skelly, & White, 1984).

Geraldine Ferraro, campaigning as a vice-presidential candidate on the Mondale–Ferraro Democratic ticket in 1984. What is gender's role in political attitudes?

The challenge becomes one of determining for whom and under what circumstances gender makes the most difference. An investigation by Carol Sigelman and her colleagues (1986) observed the influence of the candidate's gender, physical attractiveness, prestige, and the responsibility of the office sought on electoral success; voter characteristics also were evaluated. College students were given information about six challengers to an incumbent in either a mayoral or county clerk's race. The challengers were males and females of high, moderate, or low physical attractiveness. Male, but not female, voters discriminated against female candidates. Males saw females as less qualified, voted for them less, and placed them lower in the overall ratings of challengers. The antifemale bias of males was not offset by a preference for females by female voters. Female voters tended to spread their selections evenly between the male and female candidates. Attractiveness was less consistently an asset for females seeking political office than males.

While it appears that less discrimination against female candidates occurs today than in past years, this research suggests that equality has not yet been reached.

The Message (Communication)

For two and a half millennia, rhetoric has flourished about what the content of a message should be to make it more persuasive; the compulsive Aristotle described twenty-eight different types of deductive arguments alone! Among the questions asked today are: Should appeals be positive or negative? Should a rational or emotional strategy be used? How different from the audience's opinions should the message be? Should the opposition's arguments be covered? Does the order of the message's content make a difference?

How often have we seen politicians vow to run a clean campaign and as soon as the bell sounds come out swinging at the opposition? Such politicians initially may say that their appeals will be positive but before long the appeals often become negative. Frequently, negative appeals are intended to play on our emotions; positive appeals are designed to reach our rational, logical thinking. Researchers have found that the less informed we are, the more likely we will respond to an emotional appeal. For example, if we do not know anything about nuclear waste, an emotional appeal to keep a hazardous waste dump from being built near our house may influence our attitude about the project more than an appeal based on reasoning.

And all other things being equal, the more frightened we are the more we will change our attitude (Leventhal, 1970). The day after the telecast of the vivid nuclear-war film, "The Day After," more negative attitudes about the United States' massive nuclear arsenal surfaced (Schofield & Pavelchak, 1985). Advertisers also may take advantage of our fears to stimulate attitude change. An automobile company might show test drives of its car compared to others; the announcer utters phrases such as "road-hugging ability," "advanced steering," and "powerful brakes" as the viewer sees the advertiser's car unscathed while others are piled in a heap.

Not all emotional appeals are negative, though. Music is widely used to make us feel good about messages; think about how many television commercials you have seen lately without some form of music either in the background or as a prominent part of the message. Probably not many. When we watch such commercials we may not learn anything about the product but we may associate the name of the product with the music.

How extensively should messages differ from the audience's point of view? This depends on the credibility of the source. The more credible the communicator, the more she can advocate an extreme position and persuade the audience. By contrast, if a communicator's credibility is dubious, an opinion change is likely only when a moderate discrepancy is present between the audience's view and the communicator's view. For example, if a seventy-three-year-old man who has completed the Boston marathon every year for the last thirty years and has a body that looks half his age tells you to exercise vigorously two hours a day to improve your health, you probably would believe him. But an individual who has just taken up running in the last several months may only be able to get by with telling you that you should exercise ten to twenty minutes a day.

This speaker is addressing a group of handicapped individuals about transit problems. How extensively should the speaker's message differ from the audience's point of view?

Should the opposing side's arguments be acknowledged? This depends on the audience. If you perceive that the audience may never hear the opposing side's argument, it makes no sense to tell them about it. However, when issues are highly controversial and the audience is intelligent and well informed, reference to the opposing argument should be made.

The question also arises as to whether we should wait until the climax of our presentation to make our strongest points or whether we should put our best foot forward at the beginning of the presentation. These strategies have become known, respectively, as **foot-in-the-door** versus **door-in-the-foot.** In the foot-in-the-door strategy, the individual presents a weaker point initially or makes a small request with which the listener probably will comply; the strongest point is saved until the end. In the door-in-the-foot strategy, the reverse is followed; the communicator makes her strongest point or demand initially, which the listener probably will reject, then toward the end presents a weaker point or moderate "concessionary" demand (Even-Chen, Yinon, & Bizman, 1978; Freedman & Fraser, 1966; Schwarzwald, Bizman, & Raz, 1983).

The Medium (Channel)

While there are many factors to consider in regard to the message itself, the communicator also needs to be concerned about which medium to use to present the message. In Marshall McLuhan's words, "The medium is the message." Consider the difference in watching a presidential debate on television and reading about it in the newspaper. Television lets us see how the candidates deliver the message, what their appearance and mannerisms are like, and so on. Because it presents live images, television is perceived to be the most powerful medium for changing attitudes. In one investigation, the winners of various political primaries were predicted by the amount of media exposure they had (Grush, 1980).

The persuasion capabilities of television are staggering; the 20,000 hours of television watched by the time the average American adolescent graduates from high school is more than the number of hours spent in the classroom (Adler & others, 1980). Television's influence on a variety of matters has been studied extensively by researchers; the impact of commercials on purchases, of mass media political campaigning on voting, of public service announcements on health, of broad-based ideological campaigns on life-styles, of television violence on aggression, and of program portrayals on the construction of reality.

Controversy surrounds the issue of how strongly television influences an individual's attitudes and behavior. Some reviews conclude that there is so much watching, yet so few effects (McQuire, 1986); others conclude that television has a more formidable effect (Roberts & Maccoby, 1985). Concerning mass advertising on television, noticeable effects have been found on consumer purchases, but the magnitude is not great considering the cost (Roedder, Sternthal, & Calder, 1983).

How does television stack up against other media in delivering a message? The attention-getting superiority of the electronic media may be important for simple material, but the print medium provides more comprehensive coverage of difficult material (Chaiken & Eagly, 1976). The vividness of television also gives it an advantage when the communicator is highly credible; print may be more persuasive when the communicator's credibility is suspect. More about television's influence appears in the next chapter when we discuss television violence and aggression.

The Target (Audience)

What are some audience characteristics that determine whether a message will be effective? Age, gender, and self-esteem are three such factors. Younger individuals are more likely to change their attitudes than older individuals (Sears, 1983), females are more susceptible to persuasion than males (Eagly & Carli, 1981), and self-esteem is believed to be important but does not have

Concept Table 16.1

Attitudes and Persuasion		
Concept	Processes/related ideas	Characteristics/description
Attitudes and behavior	Predicting behavior from attitudes	Attitudes are beliefs and opinions. Social psychologists are interested in how strongly attitudes predict behavior. Today, it is believed that when situational influences are weak, when attitudes are based on personal experience, when we have thought about our attitudes, and when we have ready access to them, the attitude-behavior connection is strengthened.
	Behavior's influence on attitudes	Cognitive dissonance theory, developed by Festinger, argues that we have a strong need for cognitive consistency; we change our attitudes to make them more consistent with our behavior so that dissonance is reduced. In many cases this involves self-justification of our actions. Self-justification is the most intense when our self-esteem is at issue. Not all of our thoughts are dissonance reducing. Bem developed a more behavioral approach called self-perception theory; it stresses the importance of making inferences about our own behavior, especially when our attitudes are not clear.
Persuasion and attitude change	The communicator (source)	Most influential when they have expertise and credibility, trustworthiness, and power; attractiveness and similarity are also important.
	The message (communication)	The less informed we are the more emotional appeals work; the more frightened we are the more we will be influenced. Positive emotional appeals can be persuasive, especially through the use of music. The more credible the communicator, the more extreme she can be; the less credible, the more moderation is needed. If an audience will not hear about an opposing argument, it makes no sense to tell them about it. If they are intelligent and well informed, reference to the opposition should be made. The foot-in-the-door and door-in-the-foot strategies represent opposite tactics in persuasion.
	The medium (channel)	Because it delivers live images, television may be the most powerful medium; its persuasive capabilities are staggering given the frequency of viewing. Experts debate television's influence. Television is superior for simple material but print is better for comprehensive coverage.
	The target (audience)	Younger individuals are more likely to change their attitudes than older individuals and females are more readily persuaded than males. Self-esteem is thought to be important, but a predictable effect for it has not been found. If the audience's attitude is weak and they believe they are responsible for their attitude change, the communicator will be more effective.

a predictable pattern (McQuire, 1985). Another factor is the strength of the audience's attitude. If it is not very strong, attitude change is more likely; if it is strong, the communicator will have more difficulty. And if uninvolved individuals in the audience overhear others be enthusiastic they are more likely to change attitudes than if they are highly involved in the issue addressed by the speaker (Axsom, Yates, & Chaiken, 1987). If the communicator can convince an individual that it is she who is responsible for changing her attitude rather than the communicator, the message probably will be more influential.

By now it should be apparent that the nature of attitudes and persuasion is complex; a summary of the main ideas about these important aspects of social psychology is presented in concept table 16.1. In the last two decades, social psychologists have become increasingly interested in the cognitive aspects of interpersonal relationships; the next topics—social perception and attribution—highlight this cognitive interest.

Social Perception and Attribution

As we interact in our social world, we are both actors and spectators, doing and perceiving, acting and thinking. Social psychologists are increasingly interested in how we perceive both ourselves and others. They also are interested in our motivation to make sense out of our own behavior and the behavior of others, which is known as attribution.

Social Perception

Social perception is our judgments about the qualities of individuals. How do we form impressions of others? How do we gain self-knowledge by perceiving others? How do we present ourselves to others to influence their social perceptions?

Developing Impressions of Others

We spend a great deal of time evaluating people; these evaluations often fall into broad categories—good or bad, happy or sad, introvert or extravert, for example. When asked your impression of your psychology professor, you might respond, "She is great." Then, you might go on to describe your perception of her characteristics, for example, "She is charming, intelligent, witty, and sociable." From this description we can infer that you have a positive impression of her.

Two overriding points dominate the way we form impressions. First, our impressions are *unified;* second, our impressions are *integrated.* Traits, actions, appearance, and all of the other information we obtain about an individual are closely connected in our memory even though the information may have been taken in in an interrupted or random fashion. We might get some information today, more next week, some more in two months; in between we interacted with many other individuals and developed impressions of them as well. Nonetheless, we usually perceive the information about a particular individual as a continuous block (Brown, 1986).

Solomon Asch (1946) made the point that impressions are integrated many years ago and restated it more recently (Asch & Zukier, 1984). When we say that impressions are integrated we mean that they go beyond the information given. Even if we do not have good information about an individual, we stretch ourselves to make complete judgments.

In Asch's original work (1946), subjects were asked to think of a short list of traits for a single individual. Asch had the subjects write character sketches based on the brief lists of traits. The sketches included many different combinations of the traits and went far beyond the original list of traits. This showed that we have a notion of how traits go together in an individual; that is, we have what is called an **implicit personality theory** (Bruner & Tagiuri, 1954).

When we integrate information about individuals, we tend to follow certain rules. Some evaluative dimensions are used more than others and the order in which we receive information is important. Norman Anderson (1959, 1974) believes that one dimension is most common and that two others also are used. Anderson thinks that we have the strongest inclination to evaluate individuals as "good" or "bad;" he calls this the *evaluative dimension.* Potency (strong-weak) and activity (active-passive) are two other dimensions often used in our evaluations of others. From this perspective, perceptions of "good-bad" have an overall organizing capability that pervasively influences how we integrate information about an individual.

What is the prototype for a business executive? How well does this man fit the prototype?

When integrating information about individuals we seem to have a social schema into which we fit information. Remember from our discussion of memory in chapter 6 that a schema is a category that we use to organize information. Just as we read a book and do not remember every paragraph word for word but rather the gist of what was said, so do we interpret the complex information in our social world in terms of memory categorizations. An abstract characterization of the traits that describe a particular personality type has been called a **prototype** (Cantor & Mischel, 1977; Mayer & Bower, 1986; Schneider & Blankmeyer, 1983). Prototypes act as a standard against which we match the individual we are evaluating. For example, a prototype for extraversion might be outgoing, talkative, and assertive.

A basic assumption in the cognitive orientation to developing impressions is that we tend to simplify the task of understanding people by classifying them as members of familiar groups or categories. The argument is that too much mental effort is required to individuate them (Hamilton & Trollier, in press; Miller, 1982). This means that when we categorize an individual the categorizations often are based on stereotypes and behavioral tendencies associated with the assigned category (Fiske & Taylor, 1984).

But we do not always respond to others on the basis of categories. Consider how we might form an impression upon meeting a salesman. Based on the category-classification system, we would develop an impression based on our "salesman" category. Without seeking any additional information we might perceive that the individual is pushy, self-serving, and materialistic. However, as we interact with the individual we discover that he actually is interesting, modest, bright, and altruistic. We would have to revise our initial impression and perceive him more positively. When impressions are formed in this manner, a more individualized, or *individuated,* orientation toward impression formation occurs (Heilman, 1984; Neuberg & Fiske, 1986).

The information available largely determines whether a category-based or an individuated-based impression formation will take place. When we discover information that is inconsistent with a category or when personal involvement with the individual is necessary to reach a goal, we are more likely to take an individuated approach (Clark & Reis, in press; Darley & Gross,

1983; Fiske & others, 1986). In the latter instance, you may want to find out more about the individual because it has a bearing on your own well-being. Consider the circumstance of going into business with someone; wouldn't you want to develop an accurate appraisal of her and go to some length to ensure that you were not simply stereotyping her? In sum, sometimes our impressions are based on categories, at other times they are more individuated.

Another important point about impression formation pertains to first encounters. Evidence indicates that first impressions are often enduring. The term **primacy effect** is used to describe the enduring quality of initial impressions. One reason for the primacy effect is that we pay less attention to subsequent information about the individual (Anderson, 1965). Next time you want to impress someone, a wise strategy is to make sure that you put your best foot forward in your first encounter.

Gaining Self-Knowledge from Our Perceptions of Others: Social Comparison

How many times have you asked yourself questions such as "Am I as smart as Jill?" "Is Bob better looking than I am?" "Is my taste as good as Carmen's?" We gain self-knowledge from our own behavior; we also gain it from others through the process of **social comparison,** which helps us to evaluate ourselves, tells us what our distinctive characteristics are, and aids us in building an identity.

Some years ago Leon Festinger (1954) proposed a theory of social comparison. He stressed that when no objective means is available to evaluate our opinions and abilities, we compare ourselves with others. Festinger believed that we are more likely to compare ourselves with individuals who are similar than dissimilar to us. He reasoned that if we compare ourselves with individuals who are distant from us on an issue, or who behave in very different ways than we do, we will not be able to obtain an accurate appraisal of our own behavior and thoughts. This means that we will develop more accurate self-perceptions if we compare ourselves with individuals from communities similar to where we grew up and live, with individuals with similar family backgrounds, and with individuals of the same sex, for example. Social comparison theory has been extended and modified over the years and continues to provide an important rationale for why we affiliate with others and how we come to know ourselves (Ford, 1986; Goethals & Darley, 1987; Rofe, 1984; Masters & Smith, 1987).

Presenting Ourselves to Others to Influence their Social Perceptions

How do you present yourself to others? Do you try to make yourself look better than you really are? Do you disclose a great deal about yourself or are you more inclined to keep information about yourself private? To what extent do you monitor your social world as a means of presenting yourself more favorably?

When we present ourselves to others we usually try to make ourselves look better than we really are; we also take more credit than we deserve when responsibility for success is at issue (Riess, Kalle, & Tedeschi, 1981; Ross & Sicoly, 1979). This tendency is called the **self-serving bias.** Physically, cognitively, and socially we are motivated to have other individuals form favorable impressions of us. We spend billions of dollars rearranging our faces and bodies, our minds, and our social skills; some of it is spent so we will feel good about ourselves regardless of what others think, but for many the hope is to get others to have more favorable impressions of us.

When presenting ourselves to others, we are faced with the decision of how much to disclose about ourselves. As a rule, females are more likely to engage in self-disclosure than males. For example, in an investigation of dating

"Randall, my old college nemesis, I was hoping I'd find you here."

Source: USA TODAY, *March 3, 1986.*

strategies, females were more likely to reveal sensitive, intimate feelings and pursue personality exploration than males (Douvan & Adelson, 1966). Both males and females are more likely to disclose information to females than males (Axel, 1979). In general, an individual is better liked if she engages in self-disclosure than if she is very private (Cozby, 1972).

Some of us are more concerned and aware of the impressions we make than others. The extent that we are aware of the impression we make on others and the degree to which we fine tune our performance accordingly is called **self-monitoring** (Snyder, 1979, 1987). Lawyers and actors are among the best self-monitors; salespeople, con artists, and politicians are not far behind. A former mayor of New York City, Fiorello LaGuardia, was so good at self-monitoring that by watching silent films of his campaign speeches it was possible to tell which ethnic group he was courting for votes.

High self-monitoring individuals seek information about appropriate ways to present themselves and invest considerable time in trying to "read" and understand others. Mark Snyder (1981) developed a scale to measure the extent an individual is a high or low self-monitor. To see how you fare as a self-monitor, turn to table 16.1.

Situational and interpersonal cues have a strong impact on high self-monitors, whose personality traits show less consistency and more variability across different situations. By contrast, low self-monitors are more likely to have stable personality traits and rely on information from inner states (Snyder, 1987; Snyder & Ickes, 1985). To learn more about self-monitoring, read Psychology 16.2 where you will learn about the attractiveness of dating choices.

The principle of self-monitoring stresses that individuals vary in how much they are tuned in to what is happening in the external world. A theory of psychology that has become prominent in recent years stresses that we seek to explain behavior in terms of internal or external causes; it is called attribution theory.

Lawyers are excellent at self-monitoring, being more acutely aware of the impression they make on others.

Table 16.1 Measuring Self-Monitoring

These statements concern personal reactions to a number of different situations. No two statements are exactly alike, so consider each statement carefully before answering. If a statement is true, or mostly true, as applied to you, circle the T. If a statement is false, or not usually true, as applied to you, circle the F.

1. I find it hard to imitate the behavior of other people.	T	(F)
2. I guess I put on a show to impress or entertain people.	T	(F)
3. I would probably make a good actor.	T	(F)
4. I sometimes appear to others to be experiencing deeper emotions than I actually am.	T	(F)
5. In a group of people I am rarely the center of attention.	(T)	F
6. In different situations and with different people, I often act like very different persons.	(T)	F
7. I can only argue for ideas I already believe.	(T)	F
8. In order to get along and be liked, I tend to be what people expect me to be rather than anything else.	(T)	F
9. I may deceive people by being friendly when I really dislike them.	(T)	F
10. I'm not always the person I appear to be.	(T)	F

Scoring: Give yourself one point for each of questions 1, 5, and 7 that you answered F. Give yourself one point for each of the remaining questions that you answered T. Add up your points. If you are a good judge of yourself and scored 7 or above, you are probably a high self-monitoring individual; 3 or below, you are probably a low self-monitoring individual.

From Snyder, Mark, *Journal of Personality and Social Psychology, 30,* pp. 526–537. Copyright 1974 by the American Psychological Association. Reprinted by permission of the author.

■■■■■■■■■■■■■■■■■■■■

Psychology 16.2

High Self-Monitoring College Men and the Company They Wish to Keep

■ You have read about the characteristics that qualify you as a high or low self-monitor. Do you think males who are high self-monitors might prefer different characteristics in a date than low self-monitors?

To investigate this question, Mark Snyder and his colleagues (1985) told thirty-nine college males that they could have a brief coffee date with a female student as part of a study on social interaction. The college males were given Snyder's self-monitoring scale; about half were high self-monitors, the other half were low self-monitors. Each student was given fifty file folders with information about potential dates. One page described the female's interests and preferences; another page had a yearbook-type photograph of the female. All of the females were average in appearance and their preferences and interests were normal. As the males looked through the folders, they were observed through a one-way mirror to determine how much time they spent looking at each of the pages. The high and low self-monitors looked at the same number of folders but the high self-monitors spent more time looking at the photographs than did the low self-monitors,

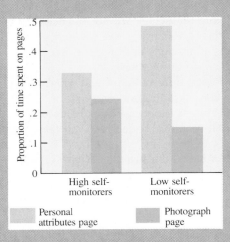

Figure 16.A
Attention to information about potential dates by college males.

who in turn spent more time reading about the females' personal attributes (see figure 16.A). When asked to describe in their own words the most important characteristic of a date, the high self-monitors were much more likely to talk about physical attractiveness.

In a second study, two more groups of high and low self-monitoring college males were selected. Each student was given the files of two females. One folder contained information about "Kristen," who was physically unattractive but very personable. The other file described "Jennifer," who was

very attractive but highly reserved, moody, and more interested in herself than others. The high self-monitoring males were more likely to select Jennifer for a potential date while the low self-monitoring males were more likely to choose Kristen.

Since high self-monitors show so much concern about the self-image they present to others, they are attentive to images presented by potential partners. In other words, high self-monitoring males endorse the statement, "A man is known by the company he keeps." It is not surprising, then, that high self-monitoring college males prefer attractive females as dates.

Attribution

Shakespeare once wrote, "Find out the cause of this effect, or rather say, the cause of this defect, for the effect defective comes by cause." Attribution theorists have taken Shakespeare's comments to heart; they argue that we want to know the causes of people's behavior because the knowledge will enable us to cope more effectively with the situations that confront us. **Attribution theory** says that we are motivated to discover the underlying causes of behavior as part of our effort to make sense out of the behavior. In a way, attribution theorists say we are like intuitive scientists, seeking the reason behind why something happens.

We can classify the reasons individuals behave the way they do in a number of ways, but one basic distinction stands out above all the others: the distinction between internal causes, such as the actor's personality traits or motives, and external causes, which are environmental, situational factors such as rewards or how difficult a task is (Heider, 1958). If you don't do well on a test, do you attribute it to the fact that the professor plotted against you and made the test too difficult (external cause) or to the fact that you did not study hard enough (internal cause)? The answer to such a question influences how we feel about ourselves; if we believe our performance was the professor's fault we won't feel as bad as when we do not spend enough time studying. To further your understanding of attribution read Psychology 16.3, where some intriguing interpretations of a rock group and its fans are made.

Our attributions are not always accurate. The way the human mind sees things suggests that attributions have some built-in bias. We have a tendency to overestimate the importance of traits and underestimate the importance of situations when we seek explanations of behavior; this is called the **fundamental attribution error** (Ross, 1977). Also, the attributions of the actor and the observer often diverge such that the actor is more likely to choose external causes and the observer internal causes. In these circumstances, the actor is the one who is producing the action to be explained; the observer is the onlooker, who offers a causal explanation of the actor's behavior or experience. Since the actor and the observer often disagree about whether internal or external causes are responsible for the actor's behavior, one of them must be wrong. Based on the fundamental attribution error, we would anticipate the observer overestimates the internal, trait causes of behavior and underestimates the social, situational causes.

Since actors and observers often have different ideas about what causes behavior, bias hounds these attributions. Behavior is determined by a number of factors, thus, it is not surprising that our social lives are pregnant with squabbling and arguing about the causes of behavior. Attribution theory provides us with a more informed perspective on disagreements in marriages, the courts, the Senate, and many other social arenas, even a crowd crush at a Who concert.

We have studied many different aspects of social perception and attribution. A summary of these topics is presented in concept table 16.2. As we have discussed social thinking and social influence, we have seen that at times individuals conform to what others think and do, changing their opinions and behaviors to be more in line with the consensus. It is to the topic of conformity that we now turn in more detail.

Psychology 16.3

The Who, Crowd Crush, and Attribution

It is December 3, 1979, in Cincinnati. The crowd of 8,000 Who fans press forward towards the stage. Eleven of them are knocked down and suffocate. What happened?

Within twenty-four hours of the crowd crush in Cincinnati, it became apparent that there was disagreement about the causes of the eleven deaths. Drugs, alcohol, weather, crowd size, the manner in which seats were sold, and a disposition for violence on the part of Who fans were all offered as explanations. The causes can be divided into those that are internal and those that are external to the actor. The actors are the Who fans; in any attribution explanation the actor is the individual(s) whose actions need explanation. Internal causes would include alcohol, drugs, and a disposition for violence. External causes include everything in the situation: the cold weather, a five-hour wait, allocation of seating, the number of police present, the manner of admission to the arena, and so on.

The mayor of Providence, Rhode Island, quickly canceled the December 17 Who concert in that city. When this date was offered to Portland, Maine, the city manager said no, it would be too risky. The cancellation and refusal reflect internal attributions since the Cincinnati "situation" would not have recurred in Providence and Portland, but there would have been Who fans in those cities. If the fault was with the fans, then a recurrence would probably take place.

The cancellation had all the force of an accusation—The Who are bad news and so are their fans.

How did the Who fans, Roger Daltry of The Who, mayors, and city managers use attribution to explain the deaths of fans in Cincinnati?

In the December 12, 1979, edition of the *Cincinnati Post* an editorial read, "Unfortunately there are thousands of impatient dopeheads who are more concerned about a good seat than a human life." But Roger Daltry, one of the Who, said, "I don't think the crowd had anything to do with it." Neither did the mayor of Cincinnati, who stressed that causes external to the Who fans triggered the crowd crush. Fifty percent of the seats were reserved and 50 percent were on a nonreserved, first-come, first-served basis. Holders of the reserved seats already were in the arena when the crowd of 8,000 nonreserved ticket individuals began their push forward. Of the fifty doors to the arena, only a few had been opened, apparently because there only were a few ticket takers working.

Officials in cities other than Providence where Who concerts were scheduled must have believed the external cause argument. In each instance, extensive evaluation and caution was exercised: security forces were doubled, all doors were opened in advance, all seats were reserved, and fans were told not to come if they did not have a ticket. The next concert was Buffalo, New York, on December 5. There was no trouble and the fans hoisted a banner that said, "These kids are all right" (which is the title of a Who song).

We use attribution in our everyday lives, just as the Who fans, Roger Daltry of the Who, the mayors, and the city managers did. We seek external and internal causes of why events or behavior occur (Brown, 1986, pp. 133–136).

Source: After Brown, R., *Social Psychology,* 2nd ed. © 1986 Macmillan Publishing Company, New York.

Concept Table 16.2

Social Perception and Attribution		
Concept	**Processes/related ideas**	**Characteristics/description**
Social perception	Developing impressions of others	Our impressions are unified and integrated. An individual's notion of how traits go together is called implicit personality theory. We have social schemata or prototypes that we use to evaluate others. We simplify our impressions by categorizing others; in some instances, though, we develop a more individuated approach to impression. First impressions are important and influence impressions at a later point.
	Gaining self-knowledge from our perception of others— social comparison	We evaluate ourselves by comparison with others. Festinger stresses that social comparison provides an important source of self-knowledge, especially when no other objective means is available; we are more likely to compare ourselves with similar others.
	Presenting ourselves to others to influence their social perceptions	We usually try to make ourselves look better than we really are; this is called the self-serving bias. We also are faced with how much to disclose with others. Self-monitoring refers to how extensively we are aware of the impressions we make on others and how much we fine-tune our social behavior accordingly.
Attribution	The nature of attribution theory	Focuses on the motivation to infer causes of behavior in order to make sense out of the world. One of the most frequent and important ways we classify the causes of behavior is in terms of internal and external causes.
	The fundamental attribution error and actor-observer differences	Our attributions are not always accurate; the human mind has a built-in bias in making causal judgments. The fundamental attribution error involves overestimating the importance of traits and internal causes while underestimating the importance of situations and external causes. Actors are more likely to choose external causes, observers internal causes. The observer may be in greater error.

Conformity

The words of Solon in Ancient Greece reflected the importance of conformity in our lives, "Each of you, individually, walketh with the tread of a fox, but collectively, ye are geese." So did the words of Thomas Morton in a more recent era, "What will Mrs. Grundy say? What will Mrs. Grundy think?" How much do you conform to what others think and do? Do you worry about what Mrs. Grundy will think?

Conforming in a Variety of Circumstances

Conformity comes in many forms and pervades many circumstances in our lives. Do you take up jogging because everyone else is doing it? Do you let your hair grow long one year and cut it short the next year because of fashion? Would you take cocaine if pressured by others or would you resist the pressure? **Conformity** can be defined as change in an individual's behavior or thought because of real or imagined pressure from others.

Put yourself in this situation. You arrive at an experimental room and observe six other individuals seated around a table. The experimenter comes into the room and states that you are about to participate in an experiment on perceptual accuracy. The group is shown two cards, the first having only a

Figure 16.5
Stimulus materials used by Solomon Asch in his study of conformity to group influence.

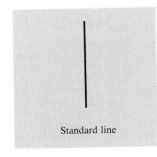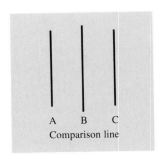

Standard line   A   B   C
                       Comparison line

Figure 16.6
Asch's conformity experiment. The dilemma for the subject (seated in the middle) is apparent in this photo, taken just after five individuals, who were confederates of the experimenter, had chosen the incorrect line.

single vertical line on it; the second card has three vertical lines of varying length (see figure 16.5). You are told that the task is to determine which of the three lines on the second card is the same length as the line on the first card.

The other individuals in the room are actually confederates of the experimenter, hired to perform in ways dictated by the experimenter (of course, you are not aware of this). As the first several cards are presented, everyone agrees about which line matches up with the standard. Then on the third trial each of the other individuals picks an incorrect line; you have a puzzled look on your face. As the next to the last individual to make a choice, you have the dilemma of responding as your eyes tell you or conforming to what the others before you said.

This classic experiment was conducted by Solomon Asch (1951); on twelve of the eighteen trials confederates of the experimenter gave incorrect responses. The conformity rate of the nonconfederate was 35 percent (figure 16.6 shows the actual situation in the Asch conformity experiment). The pressure of the consensus is strong. Even in a very unambiguous circumstance, such as the Asch experiment, we often conform to what others say and do. We don't want to be laughed at or have others be angry with us; the solution is to conform.

Given the extensiveness of conformity in Asch's laboratory study, do you think that individuals might conform to social roles outside of a laboratory setting? Put yourself in this situation. You have volunteered to participate in a psychology experiment. By the flip of a coin half of the volunteers have been designated as prisoners and half as guards in a mock prison; you are one of the fortunate ones because you will be a guard. How much would you and your fellow volunteers conform to the social roles of "guard" and "prisoner"?

Your instructions are to do a guard's job; you are to maintain law and order. In just a few hours the behavior of the "guards" and "prisoners" becomes very different; each conforms to what they think are appropriate social roles for guards and prisoners. Over the course of six days, the guards abuse their power, making the prisoners obey petty, meaningless rules and forcing them to perform tedious, useless work. Many of the prisoners begin acting like dehumanized robots. They develop an intense hatred for the guards and constantly think about ways to escape.

To document the behavioral differences between the guards and the prisoners, the interactions between the two were videotaped and then analyzed on twenty-five different occasions. As shown in figure 16.7, the most frequent behavior of the guards was to give orders. Their control was abusive, reflected in the number of insults and threats and the number of times night sticks were used to keep prisoners in line. Though many of the prisoners resisted the guards and asked questions initially, after awhile they lost their resistance and virtually stopped reacting.

This naturalistic experiment was conducted by Philip Zimbardo and his colleagues at Stanford University (Zimbardo & others, 1972). The prison study was designed to last two weeks but the "guards" and "prisoners" conformed to their social roles so extensively that the experiment had to be stopped after six days. Five of the prisoners had to be released, four because of severe depression or anxiety and the fifth because a rash had broken out all over his body. Several of the guards had become brutal with the prisoners. Figure 16.8 shows some of the actual circumstances in the prison study.

Factors that Contribute to Conformity

There are a number of factors that foster conformity. In Asch's study with lines on cards the group opinion was unanimous. When such unanimity is broken, the power of the group is lessened and individuals feel less pressure to conform. Also, if you do not have a prior commitment to an idea or action, you are more likely to be influenced by others. If you publicly commit to a course of action, as when a senator tells her constituents back home that she is in favor of a trade embargo on Japan, conformity to another point of view is less likely.

Two other factors that contribute to conformity involve the individual's characteristics and who makes up the group. Individuals with low self-esteem and doubts about their abilities are more likely to conform (Campbell, Tesser, & Fairley, 1986). And if the group members are experts, attractive to you, or similar to you in some way, you are more likely to conform.

How likely we are to conform also depends on our cultural background and childrearing experiences. For example, Norwegians conform more than the French (Moscovici, 1985). And parents who interact with their adolescents in more individuated *and* connected ways promote an individualized identity; overprotective parents encourage conformity (Grotevant & Cooper, 1985).

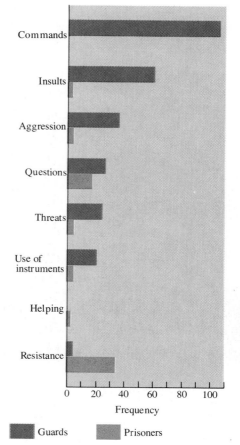

Figure 16.7
Interaction profile of guard and prisoner behavior on 25 occasions during the six days in the simulated prison environment.

Figure 16.8
At left, a volunteer for a psychology experiment is being picked up on campus—he had lost a coin flip and was designated a "prisoner." At right, conformity to the hostile and abusive role of prison guard is shown.

Drawing by Ziegler; © 1986 The New Yorker Magazine, Inc.

Why Do We Conform?

We conform for one of two main reasons: to make our life more rewarding and less punishing or to gain information. It is rewarding to be liked by others and punishing to be rejected or ridiculed. We are strongly motivated to gain others' social approval; if we don't go along, we fear that we will not get along. For example, your friend asks your opinion of her new coat. You personally think it is tacky. It would be punishing to lose a friend, so you make a conforming remark, "It really looks good on you." When we conform because of reward or punishment, psychologists say we are behaving according to *norms,* which are the rules in society that are understood and accepted as appropriate ways to behave.

But there is another reason we conform: sometimes by conforming we gain information we otherwise would not obtain. As Festinger (1954) argued, when reality is uncertain we rely on other individuals for information about reality. In this sense we do not conform because we fear we will be punished if we don't, but rather because valuable information might be obtained.

Obedience

Obedience is behavior that complies with the explicit demands of the individual in authority. In Zimbardo's prison experiment, the prisoners and the guards were obedient. Obedient behavior sometimes can become destructive; it was rapidly becoming this way for the prison guards. The mass suicides at Jonestown described at the beginning of the chapter, the massacre of Vietnamese civilians at My Lai, and the Nazi crimes against Jews in World War II were other occasions when obedience became destructive. For example, Adolph Eichmann, a supposedly ordinary man, committed a monstrous deed when he ordered the killing of six million Jews. Eichmann has been described as an ambitious functionary who believed that it was his duty to obey Hitler's orders; Eichmann was an average middle-class individual with no identifiable criminal tendencies. The following experiment by Stanley Milgram provides insight into such obedience.

You are asked to deliver a series of painful electric shocks to another individual as part of a psychology experiment. You are told that the purpose of the study is to determine the effects of punishment on memory. Your role is to be the "teacher" and punish the mistakes made by the "learner." Each time the learner makes a mistake your job is to increase the intensity of the shock by a certain amount.

You are introduced to the "learner," a nice fifty-year-old man who mumbles something about having a heart condition. He is strapped to a chair in the next room; he communicates with you through an intercom. As the trials proceed, the "learner" quickly runs into trouble and is unable to give the correct answers. Should you shock him? The shock generator in front of you has thirty switches, ranging from 15 volts (light) to 450 volts (marked as dangerous, "severe shock XXX"). Before this part of the experiment began you had been given a 75-volt shock to see how it feels. As you raise the intensity of the shock, the "learner" begins to vocalize his pain. At 150 volts, he demands to have the experiment stopped. At 180 volts, he cries out that he can't stand it anymore. At 300 volts he yells about his heart condition and pleads to be released. But if you hesitate in shocking the learner, the experimenter tells you that you have no choice, the experiment must continue.

The experiment just described is a classic one devised by Stanley Milgram (1963, 1965, 1974) to study obedience. As you might imagine this experiment was uncomfortable for the "teachers." At 240 volts, one "teacher"

Figure 16.9
At left, the fifty-year-old man ("the learner") is being strapped in a chair. The experimenter makes it look like the shock generator is being connected to his body through a number of electrodes. At right, the subject ("teacher") is giving a sample 75-volt shock.

© *1965 Stanley Milgram. From the film* Obedience, *distributed by New York University Film Division and Pennsylvania State University PCR*

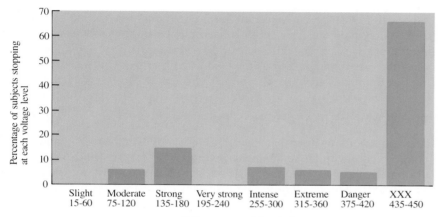

Figure 16.10
Results of the Milgram obedience experiment.

responded, "240 volts delivered: Aw, no. You mean I've got to keep going with that scale? No sir, I'm not going to kill that man—I'm not going to give him 450 volts!" (Milgram, 1965, p. 67). At the very high voltages, the "learner" quit responding. When the "teacher" asked the experimenter what to do, he simply instructed the "teacher" to continue the experiment and told him that it was his obligation to complete the job. Figure 16.9 shows what the situation in the Milgram experiment was like. By the way, the fifty-year-old man was a confederate of the experimenter. He was not being shocked at all; of course, the "teachers" were completely unaware of this.

Forty psychiatrists were asked how they thought individuals would respond to this situation. Most indicated that individuals would not go further than 150 volts, that less than 1 in 25 would go as far as 300 volts, and that only 1 in 1,000 would deliver the full 450 volts. How accurate were the psychiatrists' predictions? They were not very accurate. The majority of the individuals obeyed the experimenter; almost 2 of every 3 went all the way through the increments in shock, delivering the full 450 volts (see figure 16.10).

In subsequent studies, Milgram set up a storefront in Bridgeport, Connecticut, and recruited subjects through newspaper ads to create a more natural environment for the experiment and to obtain a wider cross-section of subjects. In these additional studies, close to two-thirds of the individuals still selected the highest level of shock for the "learner." In variations of the experiment, some factors that encouraged disobedience were discovered: when an opportunity was given to see others disobey, when the authority figure was not perceived to be legitimate and was not close by, and when the victim was made to seem more human and sensitive.

A point often raised about the Milgram experiments needs to be addressed. How *ethical* were they? Milgram's subjects clearly felt anguish and some were very disturbed about "harming" another individual. After the experiment was completed, they were told that the "learner" was not actually shocked. Even though they were debriefed and told that they really had not shocked or harmed anyone, was the anguish imposed on them ethical?

Milgram argues that we have learned a great deal about human nature from the experiments. He claims that they tell us how far individuals will go in their obedience, even if it means being cruel to someone. The subjects were interviewed later and more than four of every five said that they were glad they had participated in the study; none said they were sorry they participated. When Milgram's study was conducted the ethical guidelines for research were not as stringent as they are today. The ethical guidelines of the American Psychological Association stress that researchers should obtain informed consent from their subjects. Deception should only be used for very important purposes. Individuals are supposed to feel as good about themselves when the experiment is over as they did when it began. Under today's guidelines, it is unlikely that the Milgram experiment would be conducted.

Resisting Social Influence

Thoreau's words suggest that some of us resist social influence, "If a man does not keep pace with his companions, perhaps it is because he hears a different drummer. Let him step to the music which he hears, however measured or far away." Most of us would rather think of ourselves as treading individually like the fox instead of flocking together like geese. However, a certain degree of conformity is required if society is to function at all. As we go through our lives we are both conformists and nonconformists. Sometimes we are overwhelmed by the persuasion and influence of others and in other circumstances we resist and gain personal control over our lives. It is important to remember that our relation to the social world is reciprocal; individuals may be trying to control us, but we can exert personal control over our actions and influence others in turn (Bandura, 1986).

If you believe an authority is making an unjust request or asking you to do something wrong, what choices do you have? You can comply. But you also can evade the authority by giving the appearance of compliance but secretly not doing so; you can dissent by publicly showing doubts and disenchantment but still following directives; you can resist or disobey by openly disregarding orders and refusing to comply; you can struggle by putting together resources to challenge or confront the authority; or you might get higher authorities to intervene or organize a minority collection of individuals to show your strength (Fireman & others, 1978).

In this chapter we have discovered that our everyday lives are filled with social thoughts and social influence. We discussed the attitude-behavior connection, and how others try to persuade us to change our attitudes and thus our behavior. We also discussed how we perceive ourselves and others, and the reasons we conform to what others think and do. In the next chapter we continue our exploration of social psychology. There you will read about social relations and group behavior, including such provocative topics as hurting and helping others, as well as liking, disliking, and loving others.

Summary

I. **Predicting Behavior from Attitudes**

Attitudes are beliefs or opinions. Social psychologists are interested in how strongly attitudes predict behavior. Today, it is believed that when situational influences are weak, when attitudes are based on personal experience, when we have thought about our attitudes, and when we have ready access to them, the attitude-behavior connection is strengthened. A one-to-one mapping of attitudes to behavior does not always occur; behavior is multiply determined.

II. **Behavior's Influence on Attitudes**

Cognitive dissonance theory, developed by Festinger, argues that we have a strong need for cognitive consistency; we change our attitudes to make them more consistent with our behavior so that dissonance is reduced. In many cases this involves self-justification of our actions. Self-justification is the most intense when our self-esteem is at issue. Not all of our thoughts are dissonance reducing. Bem developed a more behavioral approach called self-perception theory; it stresses the importance of making inferences about our own behavior, which is especially important when our attitudes are not clear.

III. **Persuasion and Attitude Change: The Communicator and the Message**

Communicators are most influential in changing attitudes when they have expertise and credibility, trustworthiness, and power; we also are more likely to believe them when we perceive them to be attractive and similar to us. The less well-informed we are the more emotional appeals work; the more frightened we are the more we will be influenced.

Positive emotional appeals can be persuasive, especially through the use of music. The more credible the communicator, the more extreme she can be; the less credible, the more moderation is needed. If an audience will not hear about an opposing argument, it makes no sense to tell them about it. If they are intelligent and well informed, reference to the opposition should be made. The foot-in-the-door and door-in-the-foot strategies represent opposite tactics in persuasion.

IV. **Persuasion and Attitude Change: The Medium and the Target**

Because it delivers live images, television may be the most powerful medium; its persuasive capabilities are staggering given the frequency of viewing. Experts still debate television's influence. Television may be superior for simple material but print may be better for comprehensive coverage. Younger individuals are more likely to change their attitudes than older individuals, females are more readily persuaded than males. Self-esteem is thought to be important, but a predictable effect for it has not been found. If the audience's attitude is weak and they believe they are responsible for changing their attitude, the communicator will be more effective.

V. **Developing Impressions of Others**

Our impressions are unified and integrated. An individual's notion of how traits go together is called implicit personality theory. We have social schemata or prototypes that we use to evaluate others. A basic assumption of the cognitive view is that we simplify our impressions by categorizing others. In some instances, though, we develop a more individuated approach to impression. First impressions are important and continue to influence our impressions at a later point.

VI. **Social Comparison and Self-Presentation**

We evaluate ourselves by comparison with others. Festinger stresses that social comparison provides an important source of self-knowledge, especially when no other objective means is available. He argued that we are more likely to compare ourselves with similar others. When we present ourselves to others we usually try to make ourselves look better than we really are; this is called the self-serving bias. We also are faced with how much we want to engage in self-disclosure with others. Self-monitoring refers to how extensively we are aware of the impressions we make on others and how much we fine tune our social behavior accordingly.

VII. **Attribution**

Attribution theory focuses on the motivation to infer causes of behavior in order to make sense out of the world. One of the most frequent and important ways we classify the causes of behavior is in terms of internal and external causes. Our attributions are not always accurate; the human mind has a built-in bias in making causal judgments. The fundamental attribution error involves overestimating the importance of traits and internal causes while underestimating the importance of situations and external causes. Actors are more likely to choose external causes, observers internal causes. The fundamental attribution error suggests that the observer may be in greater error.

VIII. **Conformity**

Conformity is change in an individual's behavior because of real or imagined pressure. Two experiments demonstrated the power of conformity in our lives: Asch's study on judgments of line length, and Zimbardo's study on social roles in a mock prison. Many factors influence whether or not we conform. Two main reasons are to seek reward and avoid punishment and to gain information.

IX. **Obedience**

Obedience is behavior that complies with the explicit demands of the individual in authority. Milgram's classic experiment illustrated the power of obedience; subjects followed the experimenter's directions even though they perceived that they were hurting someone. A number of factors contribute to our disobedience. Milgram's experiments raise the question of ethics in psychological experimentation.

X. **Resisting Social Influence**

As we go through our lives we are both conformists and nonconformists. Sometimes we are overwhelmed by the power of persuasion, at other times we exert personal control and resist such influence.

Key Terms

social psychology *547*
attitudes *547*
cognitive dissonance *550*
effort justification *551*
self-perception theory *551*
foot-in-the door *556*

door-in-the-foot *556*
social perception *558*
implicit personality theory *558*
prototype *559*
primacy effect *560*
social comparison *560*

self-serving bias *560*
self-monitoring *561*
attribution theory *563*
fundamental attribution error *563*
conformity *565*
obedience *568*

Suggested Readings

Aronson, E. (1988). *The social animal* (5th ed.). New York: W. H. Freeman. This highly enjoyable presentation of research and thinking in social psychology was written by Eliot Aronson, who has conducted a number of important research studies. Included are interesting chapters on conformity, mass communication, and persuasion, as well as self-justification.

Brown, R. (1986). *Social psychology* (2nd ed.). New York: Macmillan. Roger Brown, like Eliot Aronson, has written about some of the central topics in social psychology in a very easy-to-read prose style. Chapters cover social forces in obedience and rebellion, the layman as an intuitive scientist, and systematic bias in attribution.

Cialdini, R. B. (1984). *Influence: How and why people agree to do things.* New York: Morrow. This easy-to-read book describes how we influence people and get them to go along with what we want.

McGuire, W. J. (1985). Attitudes and attitude change. In G. Lindzey & E. Aronson (Eds.), *The handbook of social psychology* (vol. 2). New York: Random House. McQuire is one of the leading researchers in the study of attitudes. A section on the history of persuasion research, an overview of mass media findings, and a multitude of theoretical perspectives on attitude change are included.

Powell, J. (1969). *Why am I afraid to tell you who I am?* Niles, IL: Argus Communications. This easy-to-read book focuses on self-awareness and interpersonal relationships. Its main theme is that we often do not open up to others and that there are many barriers to communication. The author uses a number of catch phrases such as "the braggart," "the clown," and "the egghead" to describe some of the many masks we use.

Zunin, L., & Zunin, N. (1972). *Contact: The first four minutes.* New York: Ballantine. This book focuses on first impressions, arguing that the first four minutes are crucial to our long-term impressions of others. It includes information about nonverbal communication and how to cope with rejection.

Chapter 17

Social Relations
and Group Behavior

■ ■

"Man is a knot, a web, a mesh into which relationships are tied.

—*Saint-Exupéry*

■ ■

Images of Social Relations and Group Behavior

Phil is a lovesick man. On two consecutive days he put expensive ads in New York City newspapers, urging, begging, pleading a woman named Edith to forgive him and continue their relationship. The first ad read as follows:

Edith
 I was torn two ways.
 Too full of child
 to relinquish the lesser.
 Older now,
 a balance struck,
 that a child forever behind me.
 Please forgive me,
 reconsider.
 Help make a new us;
 better now than before.
                Phil

This ad was placed in the *New York Post* at a cost of $3,600. Another full-page ad appeared in the *New York Times* at a cost of $3,408. Phil's ads stirred up quite a bit of interest. Forty-two Ediths responded; Phil said he thought the whole process would be more private. As Phil would attest, relationships are very important to us. Some of us will go to almost any length and spend large sums of money to restore lost relationships (Worschel & Cooper, 1979).

Sherry is not searching for a particular man. She is at the point where she is, well, looking for Mr. Anybody. Sherry is actually more particular than she says, although she is frustrated by what she calls the great man shortage in this country. According to the 1980 United States Census, for every 100 men over fifteen years of age who have never been married or are widowed or divorced, there are 123 women; for blacks the ratio is 100 men for every 133 women.

William Novak, author of the *Great Man Shortage,* believes it is the quality of the gap that bothers most women. He says the quality problem stems from the fact that over the last fifteen years or so, the combination of the feminist movement and women's tendency to seek therapy when their personal relationships do not work out has made women outgrow men emotionally. Novak observes that the whole issue depresses many women because society has conditioned them to assume that their lack of a marriage partner is their own fault. He points out that many women are saying to men, "You don't have to earn all the money anymore, and I don't want to have to do all the emotional work." One thirty-seven-year-old woman told Novak, "I'm no longer waiting for a man on a white horse. Now I'd settle for the horse." (Forman, 1981).

Our relationships bring us cherished and warm moments; they also can bring us moments we would rather forget, moments that are distasteful and harmful. Our relationships involve both aggression and altruism and being attracted to others and loving others. Some of our relationships occur in groups; we have relationships with other races and other nations, for example. These relationships require an understanding of how conflict between groups comes about and how it can be reduced. These are the themes of this chapter—aggression and altruism; attraction, love, and close relationships; and group relations. ■

(a)

(b)

(c)

Aggression and Altruism

Emerson said, "The meaning of good and bad, of better and worse, is simply helping or hurting." These words suggest that helping and hurting, or what psychologists call altruism and aggression, are pervasive aspects of our social relationships; they also suggest their importance in whether we are good or bad individuals.

Aggression

The strength of aggression in our makeup was vividly captured by Yoda in the movie *The Empire Strikes Back:* "Beware of the dark side. Anger, fear, aggression. The dark side of the force are they. Easily they flow, quick to join you in a fight. If once you start down the dark path, forever it will dominate your destiny; consume your will." Is the dark side Yoda speaks of biologically based? Is the dark side learned? How can it be regulated?

Biological Processes

The ancient Assyrian king Ashurbanipal delighted in beheading his enemies and blinding and mutilating officers he had captured. The Russian Czar Ivan the Terrible bludgeoned his own son and exterminated the second largest city in his empire, Novgorod, in the sixteenth century. In the twentieth century alone, 80 to 100 million people have been violently killed. In the 1970s, 4 million Cambodians were killed by their fellow Cambodians. There is more. Murders in the United States take place at the rate of 20,000 per year, assaults at 700,000 per year. Rape and wife beating have dramatically increased; reported rapes are stretching toward a figure of 200,000 per year in the United States. Asked Shakespeare, "Is there any cause in nature that makes these hard hearts?"

Freud said that aggression is instinctive; he even said we have an instinct for death. He believed that the self-destructive nature of humans comes in conflict with their self-preserving life instinct. Freud believed the death instinct is redirected and aimed at others in the form of aggression.

Ethologists also stress that aggression may be biologically based. They say that stimuli act as *innate* releasers of the organism's responses (Lorenz, 1965; Tinbergen, 1969). For example, a male robin will attack another male when it sees a red patch on the other bird's breast; when the patch is removed no attack takes place. Severe fighting and some intraspecies killing does occur

Aggression is pervasive, both in today's world and in the past. (a) The Russian czar, Ivan the Terrible, bludgeoned his own son; (b) in the 1970s, four million Cambodians were killed by their fellow Cambodians; (c) murders in the United States, such as the massacre at a McDonald's restaurant in San Diego in 1984, take place at a rate of 20,000 per year.

Much of the fighting among animals is ritualistic. For example, the cat arches its back, bares its teeth, and hisses.

in the animal kingdom, but most hostile encounters do not escalate to killing or even severe harm. Much of the fighting is ritualistic; in many instances it involves threat displays. For example, among elephant seals, observations indicate that for each actual fight, sixty-five threat displays are shown (LeBoeuf & Peterson, 1969). The type of threat display varies from one species to the next: the cat arches its back, bares its teeth, and hisses; the chimpanzee stares, stomps the ground, and screams.

Humans do not have an instinct to be killers or murderers. What evolution may have given us is an aggressive capability wired into our neuromuscular system. For example, children born deaf and blind still show aggressive behavior patterns—foot stomping, teeth clenching, and fist making—even though they have had no opportunity to observe others engage in these behaviors (Eibl-Eibesfeldt, 1977).

There is evidence in humans, though, that aggressive behavior is not always associated with a specific stimulus. Remember also from chapter 11 that most psychologists feel uneasy about the concept of instinct; when we attribute human behavior to instinct the reasoning is circular. That is, the instinct for aggression would be explained by the behaviors to which it is related, such as the 80 to 100 million people killed in the twentieth century.

While we do not have an instinct for aggression and a specific stimulus does not always release aggression, other biological processes are involved. Genes, the brain, and hormones are important. Selective breeding with animals has shown that heredity influences aggression (e.g., Ginsburg & Allee, 1942; James, 1951). After a number of breedings of aggressive animals with each other and docile animals with each other, "vicious" and "timid" strains are developed. The "vicious" strains attack virtually anything in sight; the "timid" strains rarely fight even when attacked. Of course, the genetic link is more difficult to demonstrate with humans, although recent research suggests that a genetic role may exist (e.g., Loehlin & Nichols, 1976; Mednick, Gabrielli, & Hutchings, 1984; Rushton & others, 1986). In an investigation by Philippe Rushton and his colleagues, 573 pairs of adult twins filled out questionnaires about their aggressiveness. The identical twins reported more similar aggressive tendencies than the fraternal twins.

In 1966 Charles Whitman climbed to the top of the campus tower at the University of Texas at Austin. As he looked down on students walking to and from class, he pulled the trigger of a high-powered rifle and killed fifteen individuals. Then he took his own life. An autopsy revealed a tumor in the limbic system of Whitman's brain (see figure 17.1). In another instance, a meek female mental patient had an electrode implanted in the amygdala portion of her brain (which is part of the limbic system). Immediately after electric current stimulated the amygdala, the mild-mannered woman became vicious; she yelled, snarled, and flailed around the room (King, 1961). We do not have a specific aggression center in the brain, but when the lower, more primitive areas of the brain (such as the limbic system) are stimulated by fine electric currents, aggressive behavior often results.

The female mental patient we just described was like a Jekyll-and-Hyde personality, meek one moment and a terror the next; her behavior was controlled by the stimulation received in a particular area of her brain. Is there other input to the brain besides a tumor or electrical stimulation that might produce Jekyll-and-Hyde behavior? The woman tells her divorce lawyer, "He

Figure 17.1
A pathologist points to the limbic system, the area of Charles Whitman's brain where a tumor was found.

basically is a good person. But he has a drinking problem, and when he drinks he sometimes gets violent (as she shows her bruised arm to the lawyer). I can't take it anymore. I'm scared."

Alcohol has a disinhibiting effect on many of our behaviors, especially those we might otherwise resist, such as violent aggression (Steele & Southwick, 1985). Something said or done may provoke an individual under the influence of alcohol to unleash harsh words, throw a punch, or pull the trigger of a gun. Not under the influence of alcohol, the individual might not respond so violently to the words or actions (Pihl & Zacchia, 1986).

Sometimes, though, drugs can reduce aggression. At the Rockland State Hospital mentally disturbed individuals once broke forty-six windows in one day. In the year 1955 alone, 8,000 windowpanes were broken by the mental patients. Three glaziers had to be employed full-time by the hospital! But by 1960, the number of broken windowpanes was down to 1,800. The difference: the neuroleptic drugs described in chapter 15, which have a calming effect, had been introduced (Kline, 1962).

Sam the Fifth was a terror. With hoofs scratching, eyes glazed, and nostrils snorting, he roared across the field at the intruder. Barely escaping with his life, the intruder (who turned out to be a tractor salesman) filed a complaint against the owner of the bull. The local sheriff convinced the owner that it was time to do something about Sam. What was Sam's fate? He was castrated, which changed him from a simmering volcano into a docile ox. The castration reduced Sam the Fifth's terror by acting on his male hormone system. As a rule, increased androgen levels are associated with more aggression; androgen levels are much higher in males than females (Simon & Whalen, 1986).

Cultural, Environmental, and Psychological Factors

Evolutionary theory argues for the survival of the fittest. Early in our evolution the most aggressive individuals probably were the survivors. Hunters and food gatherers had to kill animals and compete for the best food territories if they were to survive. But as anthropologist Loren Eiseley commented, "The need is now for a gentler, a more tolerant people than those who won for us against the ice, the tiger, and the bear."

Do such peaceful peoples exist today? The !Kung of southern Africa are peaceful people. They discourage any kind of aggression on the part of their children and resolve disputes calmly. The !Kung have been called the "harmless people." By contrast, the Yanomamo Indians in South America are called the "fierce people." Their sons are taught that manhood cannot be attained unless they learn to kill, fight, and pummel others. As they grow up, the Yanomamo boys are instructed at great length in ways to carry out these violent tasks (figure 17.2 shows the Yanomamo and the !Kung).

Couldn't we live our lives more like the !Kung? Unfortunately, recent observations of the !Kung by anthropologists indicate that even the !Kung are not as free of aggression as once was thought. Homocide seems to be a problem in their culture; it also appears that if they had the manpower, materials, and reasons to fight a war, they would. There still is a key difference between the !Kung and the Yanamamo, though. The !Kung actively try to dissuade their members from behaving aggressively and the Yanamamo promote aggression. The culture in which we live, then, plays an important role in either discouraging or encouraging aggression.

(a)

(b)

Figure 17.2
(a) The peaceful !Kung of Southern Africa. They discourage any kind of aggression; the !Kung are called the "harmless people." (b) Hardly harmless, the violent Yanomamo are called the "fierce people." Yanomamo youth are told that manhood cannot be achieved unless they are capable of killing, fighting, and pummeling others.

What in a culture promotes its members to be aggressive? Imagine yourself on a barren mountainside away from civilization in the country of Uganda. For about 2,000 years your ancestors lived as nomadic hunters, but early in this century the government of Uganda turned your hunting grounds into a national park. Hunting is forbidden in the park so you now are forced to farm the steep, barren mountain areas of the park. Famine, crowding, and drought have led to tremendous upheaval in families and moral values. You were sent out on your own at the age of six with no life supports; you fight and maim others to obtain food and water. Love does not seem to exist at all in your culture (Turnbull, 1972). If you were placed in this circumstance of the Ik culture, would you be this callous and aggressive?

The world of the Ik involved many frustrating, unpleasant, and aversive circumstances that produced pain and hunger. Some years ago John Dollard and his colleagues (1939) proposed that frustration, in the form of blocking or interfering with gratification, would trigger aggression. This is known as the **frustration-aggression** hypothesis. Not much later, psychologists acknowledged that aggression is caused by factors other than frustration and that frustration does not always lead to aggression; however, it still was argued that frustration was a cause of aggression (Miller, 1941). Today we are more likely to attribute aggression to unpleasant events than to frustration. It seems that the frustration-aggression connection was stated too broadly; it has been replaced with a greater interest in detailing the nature of unpleasant experiences and how we cognitively interpret these experiences.

Unpleasant experiences can involve the physical environment or people. Environmental psychologists have demonstrated how noise, weather, and crowding can stimulate aggression, for example. Murder, rape, and assault increase when temperatures are the hottest (during the third quarter of the year) as well as in the hottest years and in the hottest cities (Anderson, 1987). Our everyday encounters with individuals also produce unpleasant experiences that trigger aggressive responses. For example, when someone cuts into a line closer to the goal (e.g., a ticket booth) and when they intrude closer to us, we are more likely to respond aggressively toward that person (Harris, 1974; Milgram & others, 1986).

Whether or not we respond aggressively to unpleasant, frustrating experiences is determined by such factors as expectations, equity, intentions, and responsibility (Feshbach & Wiener, 1986). You expect to be jostled in a crowded bus, but if someone runs into you when there are only five or six individuals on the bus, you might respond more aggressively. If you perceive that an unpleasant experience is arbitrary and not justified, you might also respond aggressively. If you deserve a D in a class you are less likely to say nasty things about the professor than if you perceive the grade to be unfair. If you detect that someone intentionally tripped you and made you fall, you are more likely to respond aggressively than if you notice the individual accidently got her feet tangled with yours. Closely related to intention is responsibility; the more we perceive that an individual is responsible for his aggressive action, the more we will respond aggressively. For example, when are you likely to respond aggressively: when an eight-year-old child hits you with her shopping cart in a store, or when her babbling, assertive, and healthy thirty-year-old mother does the same thing? We assume the mother is more responsible for her behavior so we probably would respond more aggressively toward her.

Unpleasant and frustrating experiences can precipitate aggression. Social learning theorists also believe that aggression is learned through the processes of reinforcement and observational learning, described in chapter 5.

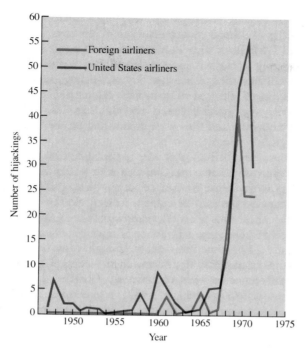

Figure 17.3
Incidence of airline hijacking over a span of twenty-five years. (Note: The rapid decline is due to countermeasures.)
Source: Albert Bandura, Aggression: A social learning analysis, © *1973, p. 106. Adapted by permission of Prentice-Hall, Inc., Englewood Cliffs, NJ.*

Aggression can pay off; it gets some individuals attention, money, sex, power, or status. Aggression also can be learned by watching others be aggressive (Bandura, 1986). Observational learning probably is involved in the spread of airline hijackings. Watching an airline hijacking on television or reading about it in the newspaper increases the probability that some individuals will try to repeat the event (see figure 17.3). We watch and hear about massive doses of aggression in our culture; one of the most pervasive opportunities comes from television.

Television and Aggression

Violence is pictured as a way of life on many television shows. Evildoers kill and get killed; police and detectives use extensive violence in upholding society's laws. Violence on television is portrayed unrealistically. The lasting results of violence rarely are seen by the viewer. An injured individual may not recover for weeks, or months, or perhaps not at all in real life, yet on television it takes only thirty to sixty minutes for recovery.

The amount of aggression on television is a special problem for children. In the 1980s, children watch an average of twenty-six hours of television each week. Almost every day of their lives they watch someone being stabbed, maimed, or slaughtered. Some psychologists believe television violence has a profound effect on shaping children's aggressive thoughts and behaviors; others believe the effects are exaggerated (McQuire, 1986; Roberts and Maccoby, 1985). Does television violence merely stimulate a child to go out and buy a Darth Vadar ray gun? Or does it trigger an attack on a playmate and even increase the number of violent attacks and murders?

Violence on television is associated with aggression in individuals who watch it. For example, in one investigation the amount of television violence watched by children when they were in elementary school was associated with how aggressive they were at age nineteen and at age thirty (Eron, 1987; Huesmann & others, in press; Huesmann & others, 1984; Lefkowitz & others, 1972).

"*AAAAALLLLL RIIIGHT!*"

Drawing by Koren; © 1986 The New Yorker Magazine, Inc.

In another investigation, long-term exposure to television violence increased the likelihood of aggression in 1,565 boys aged twelve to seventeen (Belson, 1978). Boys who watched the most aggression on television were the most likely to commit some violent action, swear, be aggressive in sports, threaten violence toward another boy, write slogans on walls, or break windows. The types of televised violence most often associated with aggression were realistic, they took place between individuals in close relationships rather than between strangers, and they were committed by the "good guys" rather than the "bad guys."

But it is another step to conclude that television violence in itself causes aggressive behavior. Children who watch the most violence may be more aggressive in the first place; other factors such as poverty and unpleasant life experiences may be culprits as well. So far we have not been able to establish a causal link from television violence to aggression (Freedman, 1984). Like other behaviors, aggression is multiply determined.

For some individuals, though, especially those with aggressive tendencies in unpleasant circumstances, seeing violence on television may mean the difference between committing a violent action or not (Huesmann & Malamuth, 1987; Levinger, 1987). I remember watching a violent movie on late-night television several years ago. A bank was robbed and the president of the bank was kidnapped at gunpoint. He was taken to his home where his wife had been tied to a chair. Three days later the headline in the newspaper described a bank robbery. As I read about the details of the robbery, it was clear that the robbers' strategy was derived from the movie, down to the type of ski masks they used to cover their faces.

Controlling and Reducing Aggression

Mark Twain once remarked, "When angry, count four; when very angry, swear." Do we need to vent our anger? Does venting our anger reduce our tendency to be aggressive in the future? Carol Tavris (1982) says that the major benefit of the ventilation approach is to raise the noise level of our society, not reduce our aggression or solve our problems. She says that individuals who are the most prone to vent their anger get angrier, not less angry. Ventilating anger follows this cycle: a precipitating event, an angry outburst, shouted recriminations, screaming or crying, a furious peak (sometimes accompanied by physical assault), exhaustion, a sullen apology, or just sullenness. The cycle sometimes is repeated the next day.

In ancient Greece, the term **catharsis** referred to the discharge of feelings by watching a dramatic play. Today the term is used in connection with aggression. Catharsis in this context is the reduction of aggression by engaging in aggressive activity, either directly or vicariously.

Both psychoanalytic and ethological theories promote catharsis as an important way to reduce aggression. Both theories argue that individuals have a natural, biological tendency to be aggressive. This tendency builds up in the individual and needs to be drained off. From this perspective, the doses of violence on television and the aggression we see in football, soccer, and other aspects of our culture are healthy because they reduce the pent-up aggression inside of us.

Social learning theory argues strongly against this view. This theory states that by acting aggressively individuals often are rewarded for their aggression; and by watching others display aggression individuals learn how to be aggressive themselves. Which view is right? Research on catharsis suggests that acting aggressively does not have any long-term effects on reducing aggres-

Is it cathartic to watch violence and aggression being displayed, as in a gory professional wrestling match?

sion. If the catharsis hypothesis were correct, war should have a cathartic effect in reducing aggression. But in a compilation of wars in 110 countries since 1900, wars actually stimulated domestic violence. Compared with nations who remained at peace, postwar nations had an increase in homocide rates (Archer & Gartner, 1976).

If catharsis does not work, what does? A former president of the American Psychological Association actually suggested that we should develop an anticruelty drug to be given to the leaders of nations (Clark, 1971). This is not the answer. Although powerful tranquilizers have reduced violent behavior in some mental patients, such drugs often have unwanted side effects. Ethical considerations are raised as well; the use of drugs to control aggression invokes thoughts of "Big Brother" controlling behavior.

Is it possible that people could simply reason with one another? More advanced moral reasoning is associated with more appropriate judgments about the intentions and consequences of aggression (Berkowitz & others, 1986). But as Aristotle observed more than 2,000 years ago, "There are some people whom one cannot instruct."

What is left? Since catharsis, drugs, or pure reason do not provide the answer, we still can try punishment, observational learning, and building empathy toward others (Aronson, 1984). However, the juvenile justice system has not been successful; delinquency has increased, not decreased since this system was developed (Gold & Petronio, 1980; Quay, 1987). We might think that putting an individual in the harsh and barren environment of a prison would reduce crime. There is little evidence to support this belief.

Is seeing someone else be punished rather than being punished yourself a deterrent to aggression? The evidence says no. The institution of the death penalty in various states has not reduced homocides in those states. Laboratory research also indicates that observing a model be punished for aggression does not consistently reduce aggression. Observation of models being rewarded for aggression, though, increases aggression (Bandura, 1986).

But if children grow up in a world with few aggressive models, if the models reward prosocial behavior, if parents build an empathy toward others in children, and if parents monitor their children's whereabouts in adolescence, aggression probably will be reduced. For example, in one study, the most important factor in whether or not an adolescent male engaged in delinquent behavior was the degree his parents monitored his social world (Patterson & Stouthamer-Loeber, 1984). Let's now look at how altruism—building empathy for others—reduces aggression.

An example of animal altruism—a baboon plucking bugs from another baboon. Most acts of animal altruism involve kin.

Altruism

Altruism is an unselfish interest in helping someone. Are you altruistic? Do you know someone who is altruistic? How can we tell if someone truly is an unselfish individual? To answer such questions, we need to know something about the biological, psychological, and environmental influences on altruism.

Biological Basis of Altruism

Most modern biologists are Darwinians in the sense that they believe in the principle of natural selection. But altruism poses a problem for the theory of natural selection. An act in the biological realm is altruistic if it increases the prospect for survival and the opportunity to reproduce. Motives, intentions, and rewards are not involved in this biological world, but as we soon will see, they are very important in considering altruism in the psychological world. In the biological world, any organism that consistently acts in an altruistic way puts itself at a disadvantage; it will have few offspring. Natural selection, then, predicts that the organism will act to protect its own being, not the group or the species.

Some instances of altruism, though, do fall within the domain of natural selection. A parent feeding its young is performing a biological altruistic act because the young's chance of survival is enhanced. Sociobiologists believe that an organism may act altruistically with kin; while not preserving itself, the organism at least increases the probability that a portion of its genes will be perpetuated (Wilson, 1975). A mother bird who performs a distraction ritual to lure predators away from the eggs in her nest is an example of this form of biological altruism. She is willing to sacrifice herself so that three or four of her offspring have the chance to survive, thus preserving her genes. In humans, parents are more likely than relatives or strangers to donate a kidney to a child (Fellner & Marshall, 1981).

Clear acts of altruism that go beyond kin are rare in the animal kingdom. As we move up the animal kingdom, instances of altruism not involving kin have been reported in porpoises and chimpanzees. What appear to be unselfish acts of kindness toward others outside of one's kin network do not appear frequently, though, until the level of *Homo sapiens* is reached. And it should be noted that identical twins are more similar in their altruistic, empathetic, and nurturant tendencies than fraternal twins (Rushton & others, 1986).

Psychological and Environmental Influences

Examples of altruism among humans are plentiful—the hard-working laborer who places a 5-dollar bill in a Salvation Army kettle, rock concerts organized by Bob Geldof and Willie Nelson to feed the hungry and help farmers, a taxi driver who risks his life to save a woman from being molested in a dark alley, a child who takes in a wounded cat and cares for it. How do psychologists account for such frequent occurrences of altruism?

Reciprocity and exchange are important aspects of altruism (Brown, 1986). Reciprocity is found throughout the human world. It not only is the highest moral principle in Christianity but also is present in every widely practiced religion in the world—Judaism, Hinduism, Buddhism, and Islam. Reciprocity encourages us to do unto others as we would have them do unto us. Certain human sentiments are wrapped up in this reciprocity: trust probably is the most important principle over the long run; guilt occurs if we do not reciprocate; and anger results if someone else does not reciprocate (Trivers, 1971).

Examples of human altruism are plentiful; here a young woman assists a handicapped child.

Many examples of altruism that are reciprocal involve social exchanges; we exchange gifts, cards, and tips for competent service, for example. **Social exchange theory** accounts for the manner in which such transfers take place. It sounds cold and calculated to describe altruism in terms of costs and benefits, but that is exactly what social exchange theory does. The theory argues that individuals should benefit those who benefit them; or for a benefit received, an equivalent benefit should be returned at some point.

Not all altruism is motivated by reciprocity and social exchange, but this view alerts us to the importance of considering self-other interactions and relationships in understanding altruism. Not all seemingly altruistic behavior is unselfish and noncontingent. Some psychologists believe that true altruism has never been demonstrated; others argue that a distinction between altruism and egoism is possible (Batson & others, 1986; Cialdini & others, 1987). When person A gives to person B to ensure reciprocity, to gain self-esteem, to present oneself as powerful, competent, or caring, or to avoid social and self-censure for failing to live up to normative expectations, then **egoism,** not altruism, is involved. By contrast, altruism occurs when person A gives to person B with the ultimate goal of benefiting person B; any benefits that come to person A are unintended.

Drawing by Stevenson; © *1985 The New Yorker Magazine, Inc.*

The circumstances most likely to involve altruism are empathetic or sympathetic emotion for an individual in need or a close relationship between the benefactor and recipient (Batson, in press; Clark & others, 1987; Lerner, 1982). An investigation with female college students revealed that when no prior relationship existed between two participants, self-motivated behavior was more likely to occur. But when a prior relationship existed between the students, altruistic motivation to increase the partner's welfare occurred (Schoenrade & others, 1986).

Describing individuals as having altruistic or egoistic motives implies that person variables are important in understanding altruistic behavior. Recall from chapter 13 that behavior is determined by both person and situational variables. The altruistic motive is investigated by studying an individual's disposition to empathize with the needy or feel a sense of responsibility for another's welfare. The stronger these dispositions, the less we would expect situational variables to influence whether giving, kindness, or helping occur.

But as with any human behavior, characteristics of the situation influence the strength of altruistic motivation. Some of these characteristics include the degree of need shown by the other individual, the needy person's responsibility for his plight, the cost of assisting the needy person, and the extent to which reciprocity is expected (Romer, Gruder, & Lizzardo, 1986). To learn more about how the situation influences altruism, read Psychology 17.1, where one of the most widely studied aspects of altruism is described, that of bystander intervention.

We have seen that as human beings we have both the capacity to hurt and to help others. A summary of the main ideas about our aggressive and altruistic tendencies is presented in concept table 17.1. Now we turn to another fascinating aspect of our social relations, those involving attraction, love, and close relationships.

Psychology 17.1

Bystander Intervention

Why do some individuals help a person in distress while others won't lift a finger? It often depends on the circumstances. More than twenty years ago a woman cried out repeatedly at about 3 A.M. as she was attacked by a psychopathic killer. The attack took place in a respectable area of New York City. The murder took approximately thirty minutes to complete. The killer left the scene only to return three times and finish off his victim as she crawled to her apartment door, screaming that someone was killing her. Thirty-eight neighbors viewed the gory scene from their windows. No one intervened or even called the police.

The victim's name was Kitty Genovese. The apparently cold-blooded indifference of the witnesses to her murder not only intrigued the press but social psychologists as well. They wanted to know how thirty-eight people could act with so little altruism. In 1968, John Darley and Bibb Latané began conducting research on bystander intervention, staging an emergency to observe the extent individuals would help. They found that individuals who observed an emergency helped less when someone else was present than when they were alone. This has happened in so many investigations since Darley's and Latané's initial study that the phenomenon is now called the

bystander effect. It occurs in a variety of criminal and medical emergencies. A ball-park figure that runs through the bystander intervention studies is that when alone 75 percent will help but when another individual is present the figure drops almost to 50 percent (Latané & Nida, 1981). Apparently this discrepancy occurs because witnesses diffuse responsibility and look to the behavior of others for clues about what to do. Individuals may think that someone else will call the police or that since no one is helping possibly the person doesn't need help.

Many other aspects of the situation influence whether the individual will intervene and come to the aid of the person in distress. Bystander intervention is less likely to occur in the following situations (Shotland, 1985):

When the intervention might lead to personal harm, retaliation from a criminal, or days in court testifying.

When helping takes time.

When a situation is ambiguous.

When the individuals strugggling or fighting are married or related.

When a victim is drunk (rather than disabled) or of a different race (see figure 17.A).

When the bystander has no prior history of victimization herself, has witnessed few crimes and intervention efforts, or has no training in first aid, rescue, or police tactics.

Figure 17.A
A naturalistic experiment involving bystander intervention. In this naturalistic experiment on a New York subway, the experimenter varied the victim's identity to determine its effect on bystander intervention. Individuals intervened and helped less when the victim was drunk rather than disabled and when he was of a different race (Piliavin, Rodin, & Piliavin, 1969).

Concept Table 17.1

Aggression and Altruism		
Concept	Processes/related ideas	Characteristics/description
Aggression	Biological processes	Psychologists do not believe we have an instinct for aggression. Biological processes are at work, though, through genes, the brain, and hormones.
	Cultural, environmental and psychological factors	Aggression is more prevalent in some cultures than others. Frustration may produce aggression. Psychologists study the role of unpleasant experiences and aversive circumstances as producers of aggression; they also are interested in how cognitive processes mediate the environment's influence. Aggression is learned through reinforcement and observational learning.
	Television and aggression	Television violence is pervasive. How strongly it is related to aggression is still debated; no causal link has been established.
	Controlling and reducing aggression	Catharsis is the reduction of aggression by being aggressive. There is little support for this. Drugs, reasoning, and punishment have not been able to control aggression. No solution for controlling aggression has been developed, although if children grow up in a world of few aggressive models, the models reward prosocial behavior, parents work on building empathy toward others in their children, and parents are active monitors of their adolescents' lives, the probability of reducing aggression is enhanced.
Altruism	Biological basis	Altruism is an unselfish interest in helping someone. But biological altruism involves increasing the prospects for survival as well as reproduction. Examples involve kin, as when a parent cares for its young. In humans, identical twins show more similar altruistic tendencies than fraternal twins.
	Psychological and environmental influences on altruism	Examples of human altruism are plentiful. Reciprocity and social exchange often are involved, although not always. An important consideration is whether motivation is altruistic or egoistic. Psychologists have studied both person and situation variables. Extensive research has been conducted on bystander intervention.

Attraction, Love, and Close Relationships

Our social relations involve more than mere interactions and acquaintances, although our close relationships begin as merely interactions and acquaintances. What attracts us to others and motivates us to spend more time with them? And another question needs to be asked, one that has intrigued philosophers, poets, and songwriters for centuries—What is love? Is it lustful and passionate as Shakespeare observed, "Sighing like a furnace, with a woeful ballad made to his mistress's eyebrow." Or should we be more cautious in our pursuit of love, as a Czech Proverb advises, "Do not choose your wife at a dance, but in the field among the harvesters."

Of equal importance is how and why close relationships dissolve. Many of us know all too well that an individual we thought was a marvelous human being and we wanted to spend the rest of our life with may not turn out to be Prince Charming or Lady Godiva. But often it has been said that it is better to have loved and lost than never to have loved at all. Loneliness is a dark cloud over many individuals' lives, something few human beings want to feel. These are the themes of our exploration of close relationships: how they get started in the first place, the faces of love, how relationships are dissolved, and loneliness.

What Attracts Us to Others in the First Place?

Does just being around someone increase the likelihood a relationship will develop? Do birds of a feather flock together; that is, are we likely to associate with those who are similar to us? How important is the attractiveness of the other person?

Physical proximity does not guarantee that we will develop a positive relationship with an individual. Familiarity can breed contempt, but familiarity is a condition that is necessary for a close relationship to develop. For the most part, friends and lovers have been around each other for a long time; they have grown up together, gone to high school or college together, worked together, or gone to the same social events. Once we have been exposed to someone for a period of time, what is it about the individual that makes the relationship breed friendship and even love rather than contempt?

Birds of a feather do indeed flock together. One of the most powerful lessons in close relationships is that we like to associate with people who are similar to us. Our friends, as well as our lovers, are much more like us than unlike us. We share similar attitudes, behavior, and characteristics with those whom we are closely involved—clothes, intelligence, personality, political attitudes, other friends, values, religious attitudes, life-style, physical attractiveness, and so on. In some limited cases and on some isolated characteristics, opposites may attract. An introvert may wish to be with an extrovert, a blonde may prefer a brunette, an individual from a low-income background may be attracted to someone with money, for example. But, overall, we are attracted to individuals with similar rather than opposite features (Berndt, 1982; Berscheid, 1985).

We are motivated to form close relationships with those who are similar to us because similarity provides *consensual validation* of our own attitudes and behaviors. That is, if someone else has the same attitudes and behaviors as us, then this supports who we are. Also, because dissimilar others are unlike us and therefore more unknown, we may be able to gain more control over similar others, whose behavior and attitudes we can predict. And similarity implies that we will enjoy interacting with the other person in mutually satisfying activities, many of which require a partner with similarly disposed behavior and attitudes.

From the long list of characteristics on which partners in close relationships can be similar, one deserves special mention: physical attractiveness. How important is physical attractiveness in determining whether we like or love someone? In one experiment, college students assumed that a computer had determined their date on the basis of similar interests, but actually the dates were randomly assigned (Walster & others, 1966). The college students' social skills, physical appearance, intelligence, and personality were measured. Then a dance was set up for the matched partners. At intermission, the partners were asked in private to indicate the most positive aspects of their date that contributed to his or her attractiveness. The overwhelming reason was looks, not other factors such as personality or intelligence. Other research has documented the importance of physical attraction in close relationships; it has been associated with the number of dates female college students have in a year, how popular someone is with peers, attention given to an infant, positive encounters with teachers, and selection of a marital partner (Adams & Lavoie, 1974; Bar-Tal & Saxe, 1976; Dion & Berscheid, 1974; Langlois, 1974; Simpson, Campbell, & Berscheid, 1986). And as described in Psychology 17.2, recent efforts even have been made to discover mathematical equations for calculating beauty.

■■■■■■■■■■■■■■■■■■■■

Psychology 17.2

Calculating Beauty

■ Can we quantify beauty? In a series of experiments, 150 white, American, male college students were asked to rate the attractiveness of 50 women from pictures of their faces (Cunningham, 1986). The male college students were precise and consistent in what they saw as beauty in the female face.

What were the elements of the ideal female face? They included (see figure 17.B):

Eye width three-tenths as wide as face at eye level

Chin length one-fifth the height of face

Distance from center of eye to bottom of eyebrow one-tenth the height of face

Height of visible eyeball one-fourteenth the height of face

Total area of nose less than one-twentieth the area of the face

These data describe an ideal face; they do not describe a real face. And they are images from a particular culture and a particular set of people in that culture (male college students from Louisville, Kentucky). On an individual basis, some of us may be drawn to particular features not in this assessment: dimples; freckles; or a strong, classic nose, for example.

But what is remarkable is the high level of agreement within a specific cultural sample of what constitutes physical beauty. As we have discussed, there often is an advantage in the social world for those who are physically beautiful.

Ideal proportions

Based on subjective judgments of beauty contest participants, researchers derived formulas for facial features that predict the highest beauty ratings. Among the findings for facial features:

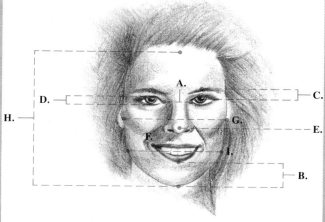

A. Eye separation: three-tenths the width of face at eye level (**G**)
B. Chin length: one-fifth the height of the face (**H**)
C. Distance from the center of the eye to the bottom of the eyebrow: one-tenth the height of face (**H**)

D. Height of the visible eyeball: one-fourteenth the height of face (**H**)
E. Total area of the nose: less than 5 percent of the area of the face.
F. Mouth width: 50 percent the width of face at mouth level (**I**).

Figure 17.B
Ideal proportions.

We tend to equate physical attractiveness with goodness. We assume that beautiful women and handsome men are warm, sensitive, kind, interesting, poised, sociable, and outgoing (Hatfield & Sprecher, 1986).

Is it any wonder that cosmetic facial surgery has been performed on such a widespread basis in recent years? Plastic surgeons report that individuals who undergo cosmetic facial surgery are seen by others as more self-assertive, intelligent, likeable, and able to succeed. Individuals who undergo cosmetic facial surgery are struck by how much their change in appearance changes the way others react to them, and sometimes they are disturbed by this fact.

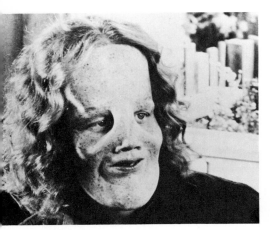

Figure 17.4
Rocky Dennis, as portrayed by Eric Stoltz in the movie Mask. *Rocky was unloved and unwanted as a young child because of his grotesque features. As his mother and peers got to know him, they became much more attracted to him.*

Changing standards of attractiveness. In the 1940s and 1950s, a Marilyn Monroe body build was ideal (a); by the 1970s, the more slender look of Twiggy was popular (b); today, a more curvaceous, slenderized look like that of Christie Brinkley is considered ideal (c).

Why do we want to be associated with attractive individuals? Again, as with similarity, it is rewarding to be around physically attractive people. It provides us with consensual validation that we too are attractive. As part of the rewarding experience, our self-image is enhanced. It also is aesthetically pleasing to look at physically attractive individuals. We assume that if individuals are physically attractive they will have other desirable traits that will interest us.

But we all can't have Linda Evans or Don Johnson as our friend or lover. How do we deal with this in our relationships? While beautiful women and handsome men seem to have an advantage, in the end we usually seek out someone at our own level of attractiveness. Most of us come away with a reasonably good chance of finding a "good match." Research indicates that this **matching hypothesis**—that while we may prefer a more attractive person in the abstract, in the real world we end up choosing someone who is close to our own level of attractiveness—holds up (Kalick & Hamilton, 1986).

Several additional points help to clarify the role of physical beauty and attraction in our close relationships. Much of the research has focused on initial or short-term encounters; attraction over the course of months and years often is not evaluated. As relationships endure, physical attraction probably assumes less importance. Rocky Dennis, as portrayed in the movie *Mask,* is a case in point (see figure 17.4). His peers and even his mother initially wanted to avoid Rocky, whose face was severely distorted. But over the course of his childhood and adolescent years, the avoidance turned into attraction and love as people got to know him.

Our criteria for beauty may vary from one culture to another and from one point in history to another. So while attempts are being made to quantify beauty and arrive at the ultimate criteria for such things as a beautiful female face, beauty is relative. In the 1940s and 1950s, a Marilyn Monroe body build (a well-rounded, Coke-bottle appearance) and face was the cultural ideal for women. By the 1970s, Twiggy and other virtually anorexic females were what women aspired to look like. And now, as we move toward the close of the 1980s, the desire for thinness has not ended, but what is beautiful is no longer either pleasingly plump or anorexic but rather a tall stature with moderate curves.

(a)

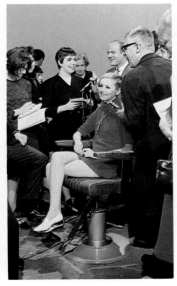

(b)

(c)

Physical attraction is more important in understanding close relationships than most individuals assumed. To ignore it and say it does not matter goes against an accumulating body of evidence. But as we already have seen, there is more to close relationships than physical attraction.

The Faces of Love

Love refers to a vast territory of human behavior, behavior that usually includes an individual doing something positively toward another individual. In this vast territory are a number of paradoxes: people run away from those they claim they want to be near, possibly as a short-term strategy they hope will lead to long-term endearment; people injure others "for their own good," and so on (Berscheid, 1987b). How can we classify and study such a complex phenomenon as love?

R. J. Sternberg (1986a) says that love's social anatomy is made up of commitment, intimacy, and passion. Ellen Berscheid (1987a) goes along with the fourfold classification of C. S. Lewis (1960): altruism, friendship, romantic love, and affection. We have discussed altruism; let's now look at friendship, romantic love, and affectionate love.

Friendship

For many of us, finding a true friend is not an easy task. In the words of Henry Adams, "One friend in life is much, two are many, three hardly possible." **Friendship** involves enjoyment (we like to spend time with our friends); acceptance (we take our friends as they are without trying to change them); trust (we assume our friends will act in our best interest); respect (we think our friends make good judgments); mutual assistance (we help and support our friends and they us); confiding (we share experiences and confidential matters with a friend); understanding (we feel that a friend knows us well and understands what we are like); and spontaneity (we feel free to be ourselves with a friend) (Davis, 1985). In an inquiry of more than 40,000 individuals, many of these characteristics were given when people were asked what a best friend should be like (see figure 17.5) (Parlee, 1979).

Figure 17.5
Characteristics people want in a friend.
Reprinted from Psychology Today Magazine. Copyright © 1979 by American Psychological Association.

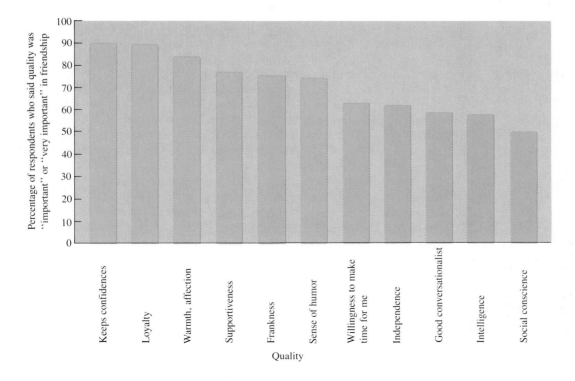

Table 17.1 Sample Items from Rubin's Loving and Liking Scales

Love scale

1. I feel that I can confide in _____ about virtually everything.
2. If I could never be with _____ , I would feel miserable.
3. One of my primary concerns is _____ 's welfare.

Liking scale

1. I would highly recommend _____ for a responsible job.
2. Most people would react favorably to _____ after a brief acquaintance.
3. _____ is the sort of person whom I myself would like to be.

Note: Subjects are asked to fill out the questionnaire in terms of their feelings for their boyfriend or girlfriend, and in terms of their feelings for a platonic friend of the opposite sex.
From Rubin, Zick, Measurement of romantic love, *Journal of Personality and Social Psychology, 16,* 267. Copyright 1970 by American Psychological Association. Reprinted by permission of the author.

How is friendship different from love? The difference can be seen by looking at the scales of liking and loving developed by Zick Rubin (1970) (see table 17.1). Rubin says that liking involves our sense that someone else is similar to us; it includes a positive evaluation of the individual. Loving, he believes, involves being close to someone; it includes dependency, a more selfless orientation toward the individual, and qualities of absorption and exclusiveness.

But friends and lovers are similar in some ways. Keith Davis (1985) has found that friends and spouse/lovers share the characteristics of acceptance, trust, respect, confiding, understanding, spontaneity, mutual assistance, and happiness. However, he found that relationships with our spouses or lovers are more likely to involve fascination and exclusiveness. Relationships with friends were perceived as more stable, especially more than those among unmarried lovers.

Romantic Love (Eros)

The fires of passion burn hot in **romantic love (Eros).** It is the type of love Juliet had in mind when she cried "O Romeo, Romeo, wherefore art thou Romeo?" It is the type of love portrayed in a new song that hits the charts virtually every week. It keeps "Dallas" and "Dynasty" at or near the top of television's most watched nighttime shows and "Days of Our Lives" and "As the World Turns" at or near the top of the most watched daytime shows. It sells millions of books for writers such as Danielle Steele. With such behavioral patterns as evidence, it is no wonder that well-known love researcher Ellen Berscheid (1987b) says that it is romantic love we mean when we say that we are "in love" with someone. It is romantic love she believes we need to understand if we are to learn what love is all about.

Romantic love is the main reason we get married. In 1967, a famous research study showed that men maintained that they would not get married if they were not "in love" with a woman, but women either were undecided or said that they would get married even if they did not love the man (see figure 17.6) (Kephart, 1967). In the 1980s, women and men agree that they would not get married unless they were "in love" (see figure 17.7). And more than half of today's men and women say that not being "in love" is sufficient reason to dissolve a marriage (Simpson, Campbell, & Berscheid, 1986).

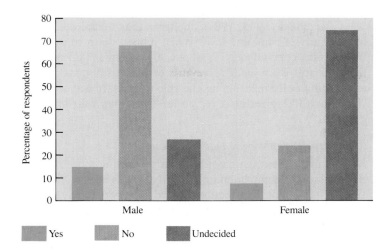

Figure 17.6
Percentage of respondents who would marry someone that they are not in love with in Kephart's 1967 study.

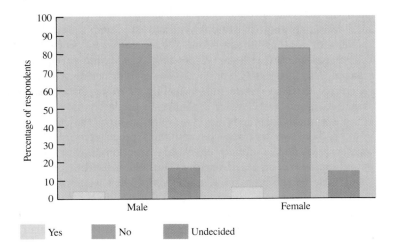

Figure 17.7
Percentage of respondents who would marry someone that they are not in love with in 1984.

From Simpson, J. A., et. al., The association between love and marriage: Kephart (1967) twice revisited, Personality and Social Psychology Bulletin, 12, 363–372. Copyright © 1986 Sage Publications, Inc. Reprinted by permission of Sage Publications, Inc.

Romantic love is especially important among college students. In one investigation, unattached college males and females were asked to identify their closest relationship. More than half named a romantic partner rather than a parent, sibling, or friend (Berscheid & Snyder, in preparation). It is about this romantic partner that an individual says, "I am *in love,*" not just, "I *love.*"

The importance of romantic love appeared in a recent biography about Ingrid Bergman (Leamer, 1986). She once told a man she cared about him deeply, valued his friendship and affection, but simply was not in love with him. Upon hearing this, the man committed suicide. Romantic love has an awesome power; its fires are based on more than liking.

Romantic love is not an animal of a single emotion. It includes a complex intermingling of different emotions—fear, anger, sexual desire, joy, and jealousy, for example. Note that not all of these emotions are positive. In one investigation, romantic lovers were more likely to be the cause of depression than friends (Berscheid & Fei, 1977).

Berscheid (1983, 1987a) believes that sexual desire is vastly neglected in the study of romantic love. When pinned down to say what romantic love truly is, she concluded, "It's about 90 percent sexual desire." Berscheid said that this still is an inadequate answer but "to discuss romantic love without also prominently mentioning the role sexual arousal and desire plays in it is very much like printing a recipe for tiger soup that leaves out the main ingredient."

Affectionate Love and Development

Love is more than just passion. That something more is usually called **affectionate love** (or companionate love); it also has been called attachment or emotional attachment. In affectionate love, we desire to have the other person near us and we have a deep affection for the other person.

There is a growing belief that the early stages of love have more romantic ingredients, but as love lasts, passion tends to give way to affection. Phillip Shaver (1986) described what this developmental course might be like. An initial phase of romantic love is fueled by mixtures of sexual attraction and gratification, a reduced sense of loneliness, uncertainty about the security of developing another attachment, and excitement aroused by exploring the novelty of another human being. With time, sexual attraction wanes, attachment anxieties either lessen or produce conflict and withdrawal, novelty is replaced with familiarity, and lovers either find themselves securely attached in a deeply caring relationship or feeling distress—boredom, disappointment, loneliness, and hostility, for example. In the latter case, one or both partners may eventually seek another close relationship.

When two lovers go beyond their preoccupation with novelty, unpredictability, and the urgency of sexual attraction, they are more likely to detect deficiencies in each other's caring (Hatfield & others, 1985; Sternberg, 1986). This may be the point in a relationship when women, who often are better caregivers than men, sense that the relationship has problems.

Friends, dates, lovers, and marital partners bring to their relationships a long history of relationships (Hartup & Rubin, 1986; Perlman & Duck, 1987; Sroufe & Fleeson, 1986). Each partner has internalized a relationship with parents, one that may have been (or continues to be) warm and affectionate or cold and aloof. One partner may have extensive experience in romantic relationships, the other little or none. These experiences are carried forward and influence our relationships with others. For example, adults who were securely attached to their parents as young children are more likely to have securely attached emotional relationships than adults who were insecurely attached (Hazan & Shaver, 1987).

Dissolution of Relationships

We live in an age when marital relationships are dissolved more frequently than at any other point in history. Whether or not a marital relationship is dissolved depends only in part on the attraction between partners. The life of a relationship is influenced by the attractiveness of actual or potential alternatives to the relationship and barriers to dissolving a relationship. Barriers to marital dissolution have diminished in recent years. Today the rewards in the relationship itself must be strong for the relationship to continue. More and more, the life of a relationship depends on how "sweet the contents;" as a result, partners evaluate the contents over and over again (Berscheid & Campbell, 1981).

The reasons for the dissolution of close relationships, including marriage, are many: infidelity, immaturity, development of a new identity, boredom, sexual incompatibility, and communication problems, for example. When relationships dissolve we usually ask ourselves why (Harvey & others, 1986). Answering this question leads to attributions about what happened. Remember from chapter 16 that our attributions often contain errors. One of the most common mistakes we make in interpreting why a relationship dissolved is oversimplification. A woman may say, "Our marriage did not work because his mother would not let go of him." Another woman comments, "If he had spent more time with our children, we would still be married." A man reports, "If she would have stayed home and not pursued her own career, I would never have left." In reality, the dissolvement of each of these relationships involved more than a single factor. The point we have repeatedly made throughout this book holds for the dissolution of close relationships as well; behavior is multiply determined.

One final point about the dissolution of relationships needs to be made. Although relationships are dissolved, they continue psychologically. Our thoughts and emotions about individuals endure long after we see and interact with them in relationships. A divorced man or woman may have thoughts of reconciliation or hatred for years after the divorce itself occurs. In the ensuing years, they will periodically evaluate what happened to their marriage. A widow, likewise, will continue to think about the death of her husband, what the relationship was like, and how her husband affects her life long after he is gone.

Loneliness

Some of us are lonely individuals. Others of us may feel that no one knows us very well. We may feel isolated and sense that we do not have anyone we can turn to in times of need or stress. Robert Weiss (1973) says loneliness comes in two forms: *emotional isolation* (resulting from the loss of an emotional attachment) and *social isolation*. Either type of loneliness can make us feel restless and depressed. Weiss also believes that one type of relationship cannot be substituted for another to diminish the feeling of loneliness. For example, an individual grieving over the loss of a love relationship probably will remain lonely even though friendships are present. Divorce or death often produces strong feelings of emotional loneliness. One widow commented that she had the feeling the whole world had just come to an end and she was all alone.

Individuals who have close emotional attachments may still have feelings of loneliness if they do not develop friendships and relationships outside of their marriages. One woman whose husband had taken a new job in another city listened to her husband describe all of the new friends he was making while she remained at home with the children. She finally convinced him that she would go along with the move only if he agreed that she could pursue a career outside of her homemaker role. She felt that this would reduce her boredom and increase her social network.

■ ■

Concept Table 17.2

Attraction, Love, and Close Relationships		
Concept	**Processes/related ideas**	**Characteristics/description**
Attraction and the faces of love	Attraction	Familiarity precedes a close relationship. We like to associate with individuals who are similar to us. Physical attraction is an important ingredient of close relationships, especially at their beginning. Over time, this importance may wane. Physical attraction is relative, varying across cultures and historical time.
	The faces of love	Long and Berscheid believe that love has four faces: altruistic, friendship, romantic, and affectionate. Friends and lovers have similar and dissimilar characteristics. Romantic love is involved when we say we are "in love"; it includes passion and sexual attraction. Romantic love includes a mixture of emotions, some positive, some negative. Affectionate love, also called companionate love, is more important as relationships age.
Dissolution of relationships and loneliness	Dissolution of relationships	Marital relationships are dissolving faster than ever. Dissolution is due to factors inside and outside the marriage. Barriers to dissolving marriages have lessened. Partners make attributions about a marriage's failure. One common error in these attributions is oversimplification. After relationships are dissolved, they psychologically continue.
	Loneliness	Two forms are emotional isolation (loss of an emotional attachment) and social isolation. Loneliness is associated with a poor attachment history with parents and low self-esteem. It is important to remember the distinction between being alone and being lonely.

It is important to distinguish being alone from being lonely. Most of us cherish the moments we can be left alone for awhile. Aloneness can heal, but loneliness can hurt.

Loneliness is associated with an individual's attachment history, self-esteem, sex, and social skills. Individuals who are lonely often have a history of poor relationships with their parents; early experiences of rejection and loss (as when a parent dies) can have a lasting effect on an individual's sense of being alone. Individuals who are lonely usually have low self-esteem and tend to blame themselves more than they deserve for their inadequacies. A lack of time spent with females, on the part of both males or females, is associated with loneliness. And lonely individuals often are deficient in social skills; they show inappropriate self-disclosure, self-attention at the expense of attention to a partner, or an inability to develop comfortable intimacy, for example (Peplau, Miceli, & Morasch, 1982; Shaver & Buhrmester, 1983; Sloan & Solano, 1984).

Before we leave the topic of loneliness, it is important to distinguish being *alone* from being *lonely*. Most of us cherish the moments when we can be left alone. For individuals in high-pressure situations, such as work or college, aloneness can heal but loneliness can hurt (Rubin, 1979). In our society we have become conditioned to believe that to be alone is a dreaded circumstance. We develop expectations that being alone should be completely avoided. But individuals who have chosen to live alone report that they are not lonelier than individuals who live with others (Rubenstein & Shaver, 1982).

We have covered many different aspects of attraction, love, and close relationships. A summary of their main themes is presented in concept table 17.2. Now we turn to another important aspect of social relations—group relations.

Group Relations

A student joining a fraternity, a jury making a decision about a criminal case, a president delegating authority and making followers feel he is one of them, a prejudiced remark against a minority group, conflict among nations, and attempts to reach peace—all of these circumstances reflect our lives as members of groups. Each of us belongs to many different groups. Some we choose, others we do not. We choose to belong to a club, but we are born into a particular ethnic group, for example. Among the important questions to be asked about group relations are: Why do we join groups? What is the structure of groups? How do we perform and make decisions in groups? Why are some individuals leaders and others followers? How do groups deal with each other, especially races and nations?

Motivation for Group Behavior and the Structure of Groups

Why does a student join a study group? A church? An athletic team? A company? Groups satisfy our personal needs, reward us, provide information, raise our self-esteem, and give us an identity. We might join a group because we think it will be enjoyable and exciting and satisfy our need for affiliation and companionship. We might join a group because we will receive rewards, either material or psychological. By taking a job with a company we get paid to work for a group, but we also reap prestige and recognition from the membership. Groups are an important source of information. For example, as we listen to other members talk in a Weight Watchers group we learn about their strategies for losing weight; as we sit in the audience at a real estate seminar we learn how to buy property for no money down. The groups in which you are a member—your family, college, a club, a team—make you feel good, raise your self-esteem, and help to identify who you are.

Any group to which you belong has certain things in common with all other groups. These commonalities are called norms and roles. **Norms** are rules that apply to all members of a group. A sorority may require each of its members to maintain a 3.00 grade-point average; if not, a member is placed on probation. This is a norm. The city government requires each of its workers to wear socks, MENSA requires individuals to have a high IQ, the Polar Bear club says its members have to complete a fifteen-minute swim below freezing temperatures. These, too, are norms.

Some rules govern only certain positions in the group. These are referred to as **roles.** In a family, parents have certain roles, siblings have other roles, and a grandparent has yet another role. On a football team, many different roles must be fulfilled: center, guard, tackle, end, quarterback, halfback, and fullback, for example, and that only covers the offense. Roles and norms, then, tell us what is expected if we are to be a member of a particular group.

Group Performance

A longstanding question is whether we perform better in a group or as an individual. The very first experiment in social psychology focused on this question. Norman Triplett (1898) found that bicyclists had better times when they raced against each other than when they raced alone. Triplett also built a "competition machine" made out of fishing reels. The machine allowed two individuals to turn the reels side by side. Observing forty children, he discovered that those who reeled next to another child worked faster than those who reeled alone.

Do you perform better as a member of a group or as an individual?

(a)

(b)

(c)

Our behavior in groups can become deindividuated. Examples of situations in which individuals can lose their individual identity include (a) Ku Klux Klan rallies; (b) Mardi Gras; (c) national patriotism crowds.

Since Triplett's work almost a century ago, many investigations of group versus individual performance have been conducted. Some studies find that we do better in groups, others find that we are more productive when we work alone. Is there some way we can make sense out of these contradictory findings?

Robert Zajonc (1965) believes that the presence of other individuals arouses us. The arousal produces energy and facilitates our performance in groups. But if our arousal is too high, we won't be able to efficiently learn new or difficult tasks. **Social facilitation,** then, improves our performance on well-learned tasks. For new or difficult tasks, we might best be advised to work things out on our own before trying them in a group. If you are good at basketball, you might perform better when others are watching, but if you are just learning to play golf you probably will fare better if you step up to the first tee when no one else is around. In one investigation, expert and poor pool players were observed in the student union at Virginia Polytechnic Institute (Michaels & others, 1982). When they were observed unobstrusively, the experts hit 71 percent of their shots, the poor players 36 percent. But when four individuals walked up to observe their play, the pool sharks improved (now making 80 percent of their shots) while the poor players got worse (now making only 25 percent of their shots).

Another factor in group performance is how closely our behavior is monitored. When we are not being watched, we have a tendency to loaf. The effect of lowered performance in a group because of reduced monitoring is called **social loafing** (Latané, 1981). The larger the group, the more likely an individual can loaf without being detected. One way to decrease social loafing is to develop a sense of personal responsibility on the part of the individual (Brickner, Harkins, & Ostrum, 1986).

Our behavior in groups also can become deindividuated. The term **deindividuation** means losing our identity as an individual and taking on the identity of the group. As early as 1895, Gustav LeBon observed that a group can facilitate uninhibited behavior, ranging from wild celebrations to mob behavior. Ku Klux Klan violence, Mardi Gra wild times, and a mob rolling a car on spring break in Fort Lauderdale are times when our behavior becomes deindividuated.

One explanation of deindividuation is that the group gives us anonymity. We may choose to act in a disinhibited way because we believe authority figures and victims are less likely to discover that we are the culprits. Or, we might act this way because it reduces self-awareness of individual responsibility. Rather than actively calculating how accountable we are for our behavior, we let go of ourselves by reducing how much we cognitively monitor ourselves. One recent investigation found that when individuals' self-awareness was reduced they acted more aggressively toward others (Prentice-Dunn & Spivey, 1986).

Group Interaction and Decision Making

Many of the decisions we make take place in a group—juries, teams, families, clubs, school boards, the Senate, a class vote, for example. What happens when individuals put their minds to the task of making a group decision? How do they decide whether or not a criminal is guilty, a country should attack another, a family should stay home or go on a vacation, sex education should be part of a school curriculum? Three aspects of group decision making bear special mention: group polarization, groupthink, and majority-minority influence.

Group Polarization

When decisions are made in a group, do we compromise our opinions and move toward the center or do we take risks and stick our necks out? In one investigation, fictitious dilemmas were presented to individuals and they were asked how much risk the characters in the dilemmas were willing to take (Stoner, 1961). When the individuals discussed the dilemmas as a group they were more likely to say that the characters would make risky decisions; when they were queried alone, they said the characters would be more cautious. Many studies have been conducted on this topic with the same results; the phenomenon is known as the *risky shift*.

We do not always make riskier decisions in groups than when alone; however, hundreds of research studies show that being in a group usually does move us even more strongly in the direction of the position we initially held (Moscovici, 1985). The solidification and further strengthening of a position as a consequence of group discussion is known as the **group polarization effect**. A "hawk" in the Senate may listen to endless hours of committee discussion about missile deployment. A "dove" on the committee hears the same words. After two years on the committee, each is more strongly committed to his position than before the deliberation began. Often views become even more polarized because of group discussion (Brown, 1987).

Why does group polarization occur? It may take place because individuals hear more persuasive arguments than they knew about previously, which strengthen their position. And it might occur because of social comparison. We may find that our position is not as extreme as others, which may motivate us to take a stand at least as strong as the most extreme advocate of the position.

Groupthink

Sometimes groups make rational decisions and come up with the best solution to a problem. But not always. Group members, especially leaders, may become obsessed with maintaining unanimity among group members. **Groupthink** is the motivation of group members to maintain harmony and unanimity in decision making, in the process suffocating differences of opinion (Janis, 1972). Examples of groupthink include the United States invasion of Cuba (the Bay of Pigs), escalation of the Vietnam war, failure to prepare for the invasion of Pearl Harbor, and the Watergate cover-up.

Leaders often have a favored solution and promote it among the group's members. Group members also tend to be cohesive and isolate themselves from qualified outsiders who could influence their decision making. Groupthink can be avoided by the leader encouraging dissident opinions, by not presenting a favored plan at the outset, and by having several independent groups work on the same problem.

Majority-Minority Influence

Think about the groups in which you have been a member. Who had the most influence, the majority or the minority? In most groups—whether a jury, family, or corporate meeting—the majority has the greatest impact. The majority exerts both normative and informational pressure on the group (Mackie, 1987). Its adherents set the group's norm; those who do not go along may be rejected or even ejected. The majority also has a greater opportunity to provide information that will influence decision making.

In most cases the majority wins, but there are occasions when the minority has its day. How can the minority sway the majority? The minority cannot win through normative influence because its numbers are fewer than

Table 17.2 Traits and Skills that Often Describe Successful Leaders

Traits	*Skills*
Adaptable to situations	Clever (intelligent)
Alert to social environment	Conceptually skilled
Ambitious and achievement-oriented	Creative
Assertive	Diplomatic and tactful
Cooperative	Fluent in speaking
Decisive	Knowledgeable about group task
Dependable	Organized (administrative ability)
Dominant (desire to influence others)	Persuasive
Energetic (high activity level)	Socially skilled
Persistent	
Self-confident	
Tolerant of stress	
Willing to assume responsibility	

Source: Gary Yukl, *Leadership in organizations,* © 1981, p. 70. Reprinted by permission of Prentice-Hall, Inc., Englewood Cliffs, NJ.

Certain individuals in the minority have played important roles in history. One such individual was Corazon Aquino, who became president of the Philippines after defeating Ferdinand Marcos.

the majority. It must do its work through *informational pressure.* To do this, the minority must present its views consistently and confidently; if this is done, the minority's views are more likely to be listened to by the majority (Moscovici, 1985; Nemeth, 1986).

Certain individuals in a minority may play a crucial role. Individuals with a history of taking minority stands may trigger others to dissent, showing them that disagreement is possible and that it may be the best course. Without such minority stands, many of the great moments in history would never have taken place; when Lincoln spoke out against slavery a vast and deep racism dominated the country, when Corazon Aquino became a candidate for president of the Philippines, few people thought Ferdinand Marcos could be beaten. Lincoln and Aquino showed the qualities of leadership. What is the nature of such leadership?

Leadership

Winston Churchill once said, "I am certainly not one of those who need to be prodded. In fact, if anything, I am the prod." What made Winston Churchill a great leader? Was it a set of personality traits, the situation into which he was thrust, or some combination of the two?

The **great person theory** says that individuals have certain traits that are best suited for leadership positions. Table 17.2 lists some of the traits and skills commonly thought to be possessed by leaders. While we can list traits that seem to be associated with leadership, the conclusion from a large number of research studies is that we cannot predict who will become a leader from the individual's personality characteristics (McGrath, 1984). Is it the situation then, that produces leaders? The situational view of leadership argues that the needs of a group change from time to time. The individual who emerges as the leader in one particular circumstance will not necessarily be the individual who becomes the leader in another circumstance.

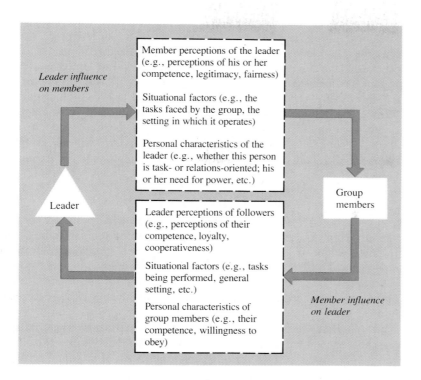

Figure 17.8
The contingency model of leadership.

A view that takes into account both personality characteristics and situational influences is called the **contingency model of leadership.** This model stresses that leadership is a complex undertaking in which leaders influence their followers and followers influence their leaders (see figure 17.8) (Fielder, 1978). In the contingency model, leaders follow one of two styles: they direct leadership either toward getting a task completed or toward members' relationships (helping group members get along). Is one of these two styles superior?

The contingency model emphasizes that the appropriate style of leadership depends on the situation. If a group is working under very favorable or very unfavorable conditions, a task-oriented leader is better. But when group conditions are more moderate, a relationship-oriented leader is better. Full tests of these ideas have not been made, but the idea that leadership is a function of both personality characteristics and situational influences is an important one. An evaluation of the leadership qualities of General Robert E. Lee supports the person-situation view (Suedfeld, Corteen, & McCormick, 1986). Lee was known for his complex military decisions, which called for dazzling maneuvers to outwit opponents. In most situations, Lee used his customary complex strategies. But as the North won battles and Lee faced other complex strategists (such as Ulysses S. Grant), he used simpler tactics. The North and South developed such hatred toward each other that they went to war. What is it about intergroup relations that produces conflict and how can it be reduced?

Intergroup Relations

On refusing to serve in Vietnam in 1966, Muhammed Ali said, "No Viet Cong ever called me a nigger." In response to the power of the United States in 1956, Nikita Kruschev said, "Whether you like it or not, history is on our side. We will bury you." And in seeking to reduce conflict in 1963, John Kennedy said, "Peace is a daily, a weekly, a monthly process, gradually changing opinions, slowly eroding old barriers, quietly building new structures." These are the themes of our study of intergroup relations. First we will discuss prejudice, ethnocentrism, and conflict; then we will evaluate ways to reduce conflict and find peace.

Prejudice, Ethnocentrism, and Conflict

You probably are reasonably sure that you know what prejudice means. And, like most individuals, you probably do not consider yourself to be prejudiced. In fact, each of us has prejudices and stereotypes. **Prejudice** is an unjustified negative attitude toward an individual because of the individual's membership in a group. The group against which the individual is prejudiced can be made up of people of a particular race, sex, age, religion, or other detectable difference.

A **stereotype** is a generalization about a group's characteristics, which does not take into account any variation from one individual to the next. Think about your image of a dedicated accountant. Most of us would describe such an individual as "brainy," "boring," "unsociable," and so forth. Rarely would we come up with a mental portrayal of this individual as extroverted, the life of the party, or artistic. Characterizing all accountants as "boring" is a clear example of a stereotype. Other common stereotypes are those that describe blacks as being naturally athletic and Italians as excitable. Researchers have found that we are less likely to detect variations among individuals who are members of groups to which we do not belong than we are among individuals who are members of groups to which we belong. For example, Caucasians are more likely to stereotype blacks than Caucasians during eyewitness identification (Brigham, 1986).

How does prejudice develop? We can learn something about prejudice by looking at the concept of **ethnocentrism,** the belief that our group is the center of the world and all other groups are beneath us. Ethnocentrism does have a positive side; this is the sense of in-group pride that fulfills our strong urge to attain and maintain a positive self-image. In the 1980s the sense of in-group pride seems to have mushroomed. We have Black Pride in America, Bantu Pride in South Africa, Gay Pride, Women's Liberation; the Scots grow more Scottish, and the Irish grow more Irish, for example.

There is something paradoxical, though, about in-group pride. Most members of a group will attest that the group is not involved in discrimination. As the American radical Stokeley Carmichael said in 1966, "I'm for the Negro. I'm not against anything." Yet virtually every cultural assertion emphasizes group differences (Brown, 1986).

One theory that explains prejudice and conflict between groups deserves special mention. It is called **social identity theory** and it is the masterpiece of Henry Tajfel (1978, 1982; Tajfel & Turner, 1986). Tajfel himself belonged to the minority of European Jews who survived World War II. It became his goal to explain the extreme prejudice and violence his group experienced. The basic claim of social identity theory is that when individuals are assigned to a group they invariably think of that group as an in-group for them. This occurs because people want to have a positive self-image.

(a)

(b)

(c)

Ethnocentrism is the belief that our group is the center of the world and all other groups are beneath us. Ethnocentrism is widespread and includes (a) Black Pride; (b) Gay Pride; and (c) Native American Pride.

Self-image consists of both a personal identity and many different social identities. Tajfel argues that individuals can improve their self-image by enhancing either their personal or their social identity. Social identity is thought to be especially important by Tajfel. We are motivated to compare the social identity of our group with the social identity of another individual's group; this comparison maximizes the distinctiveness between the two groups, especially on closely related dimensions. Think about your social identity with the geographical location in which you live. An individual who lives in Chicago may have an interest in sports and identify with the Chicago Bears. The individual's self-image is enhanced when the Bears do well, as when they won the Super Bowl in 1986. Another sports fan who lives in New York City has a social identity with the New York Giants; his self-image improved when the Giants won the Super Bowl in 1987 after a long drought.

As these two individuals talk with each other, they argue about the virtues of their teams, reinforcing the distinctiveness of their social identities with two different groups. As they strive to promote their social identities, it is not long before proud, self-congratulatory remarks are interpersed with nasty comments about the opposing team. In a capsule, the theme of the conversation has become, "My team is good and I am good; your team is bad and you are bad." And so it goes with the sexes, races, nations, social classes, religions, sororities, fraternities, and countless other groups, all seeking to improve their respective self-image through social identity with a group and comparison of the group with other groups. These comparisons often lead to competition and even perceived legitimacy of discrimination against other groups.

Tajfel showed that it does not take much to get us to think in terms of "we" and "they," or in-group and out-group. He randomly assigned children or adults to two nonoverlapping groups. The assignment was made on the basis of some trivial task; for example, one individual was assigned to one group because she overestimated the number of dots on a screen and another individual was placed in another group because he underestimated the number. Once assigned to the two groups, the members were asked to award amounts of money to pairs of other subjects. Those eligible to receive money were anonymous except for their membership in one of the two groups just created. Invariably, an individual acted favorably (awarded money) toward a member of his group (Tajfel, 1970; Tajfel & Turner, 1986). It is no wonder, then, that if we favor our own group based on such trivial criteria that we will show intense in-group favoritism when differences are not so trivial.

Conflict may be escalated when groups are similar enough to compare their outcomes, when they see how the rewards and costs are distributed, and when they perceive that the circumstances are unfair. Since what we want is never perceived to be distributed equally, perceptions of injustice are virtually inevitable when a group compares itself with another group. By being ethnocentric, each group perceives that its assets or investments are valued more than those of the other group. The result is that even when equality and fairness occur, each group perceives that it was treated with a certain degree of unfairness (Brown, 1986). As long as there are two or more groups in the world, conflict may never cease, but aren't there ways we can reduce conflict and live more peacefully?

Reducing Conflict and Seeking Peace

Martin Luther King once said, "I have a dream that my four little children will one day live in a nation where they will not be judged by the color of their skin but by the content of their character." And Carl Sandburg once commented, "Sometime they will give a war and nobody will come." How might we possibly reach the worlds Martin Luther King and Carl Sandburg envisioned—worlds void of prejudice and war?

Years ago social psychologist Muzafer Sherif brought together a group of eleven-year-old boys at a summer camp called Robbers Cave in Oklahoma (Sherif & others, 1961). The boys were divided into two groups. Competition between the boys was created by promoting in-groupness. In the first week one group hardly knew the other group existed. One group became known as the Rattlers (a tough and cussing group whose shirts were emblazoned with a snake insignia) and the other as the Eagles.

Near the end of the first week each group learned of the other's existence. It took little time for "we-they" talk to surface ("They had better not be on our ball field." "Did you see the way one of them was sneaking around?") Sherif, who disguised himself as a janitor so he could unobtrusively observe the Rattlers and Eagles, then set up competition between the groups. Baseball, touch football, and tug-of-war were played. Counselors juggled and judged events so the teams were close. Each team perceived the other to be unfair. Raids, burning the other group's flag, and fights resulted. Ethnocentric outgroup derogation was observed when the Rattlers and Eagles held their noses in the air as they passed each other. Rattlers described all Rattlers as brave, tough, and friendly and called all Eagles sneaky and smart alecks. The Eagles reciprocated by labeling the Rattlers crybabies.

After in-groupness and competition transformed the Rattlers and Eagles into opposing "armies," Sherif devised ways to reduce hatred between the groups. He tried noncompetitive contact but that did not work. Positive relations between the Rattlers and Eagles were attained only when both groups were required to work cooperatively to solve a problem. Three superordinate goals that required the efforts of both groups were: working together to repair the only water supply to the camp, pooling their money to rent a movie, and cooperating to pull the camp truck out of a ditch. All of these dilemmas were created by Sherif.

Might Sherif's idea—that of creating cooperation between groups rather than competition—be applied to racial groups? When the schools of Austin, Texas, were desegregated through extensive busing, the outcome was increased racial tension among blacks, Mexican Americans, and Anglos, producing violence in the schools. The superintendent consulted with Eliot Aronson, a prominent social psychologist, who was at the University of Texas in Austin at the time. Aronson thought it was more important to prevent racial hostility than to control it. This led him to observe a number of elementary school classrooms in Austin. What he saw was fierce competition between individuals of unequal status.

Aronson stressed that the reward structure of the elementary school classrooms needed to be changed from a setting of unequal competition to one of cooperation among equals, without making any curriculum changes. To accomplish this, he put together the **jigsaw classroom.** How might this work? Consider a class of thirty students, some Anglo, some black, some Hispanic. The lesson to be learned focuses on the life of Joseph Pulitzer. The class might be broken up into five groups of six students each, with the groups being as equal as possible in terms of ethnic composition and academic achievement level. The lesson about Pulitzer's life could be divided into six parts, with one

Eliot Aronson developed the concept of the jigsaw classroom to reduce ethnic conflict. How does the jigsaw classroom work?

part given to each member of the six-person group. The parts might be paragraphs from Pulitzer's biography, such as how the Pulitzer family came to the United States, his childhood, his early work, and so on. The components are like parts of a jigsaw puzzle. They have to be put together to form the complete puzzle.

Each student in the group is given an allotted time to study her part. Then the group meets and each member tries to teach a part to the group. After an hour or so each member is tested on the entire life of Pulitzer with each member receiving an individual rather than a group score. Each student, therefore, must learn the entire lesson; learning depends on the cooperation and effort of other members. Aronson (1986) believes this type of learning increases the students' interdependence through cooperatively reaching a common goal.

The strategy of emphasizing cooperation rather than competition and the jigsaw classroom have been widely used in classrooms in the United States. A number of research studies reveal that this type of cooperative learning is associated with increased self-esteem, better academic performance, friendships among classmates, and improved interethnic perceptions (Aronson, 1986; Slavin, 1983).

While the cooperative classroom strategy has many merits, it may have a built-in restriction to its effectiveness. Academic achievement is as much or more an individual as a team "sport" (Brown, 1986). It is individuals who enter college, take jobs, and follow a career, not groups. A parent with an advantaged child in the jigsaw classroom may react with increased ethnic hostility when the child brings home a lower grade than he typically got before the jigsaw classroom was introduced. The child tells his father, "The teacher is getting us to teach each other. In my group we have a kid named Carlos who can barely speak English." While the jigsaw classroom is an important strategy for reducing interracial hostility, caution needs to be exercised in its use because of the unequal status of the participants and the individual nature of achievement orientation.

It is not easy to get groups who do not like each other to cooperate. The air of distrust and hostility is difficult to overcome. Creating superordinate goals that require both the cooperation of both groups is one viable strategy, as evidenced by Sherif's and Aronson's work. Other strategies include disseminating positive information about the out-group and reducing the threat potential of each group (Worschel, 1986).

Reducing tension and mistrust among the world's superpowers is a goal of the GRIT strategy. How would the GRIT strategy be used in negotiations between the U.S. and the U.S.S.R.?

Reducing the threat potential of groups is receiving increased attention as social psychologists search for ways to decrease tension among nations. The technique designed to carry out this lofty goal is called the **GRIT strategy** (for Graduated and Reciprocated Initiatives in Tension-reduction) (Lindskold, 1986; Lindskold, Han, & Betz, 1986; Osgood, 1959, 1983). The escalating arms race is seen as one of distorted perceptions, stress, mistrust, and stereotyping. The cognitive dynamics involved produce a mirror-image phenomenon; that is, the citizens of each nation see the other nation as the aggressor. The Soviet Union accuses the United States of being the aggressor in Vietnam and Libya; the United States accuses the Soviet Union of the same thing in Afghanistan. Each side says its missiles are defensive and the other side's are offensive. Such distrust and tension make negotiation extremely difficult. Virtually any stance taken is perceived as trickery by the other side. Each side perceives the other as totally self-interested and inflexible. Is it any wonder that the SALT talks have produced little progress over the past two decades?

The purpose of the GRIT strategy is to reduce tension and mistrust so that disarmament and regular negotiation, trade, and international diplomacy can proceed. The strategy calls for one party to make unilateral reductions in threat capability. Such reductions would be announced in advance. After the reduction, the other group is requested to make a similar reduction. The eventual goal of the GRIT plan is to reach a point at which the groups have dramatically lowered their threat potential and, therefore, their conflict. In GRIT, one group must take the initiative for threat reduction. It may be as Piet Hein wrote, "The noble art of losing face may one day save the human race and turn into eternal merit what weaker minds would call disgrace."

Summary

I. Aggression: Biological and Cultural, Environmental, and Psychological Factors

Psychologists do not believe we have an instinct for aggression. Biological processes are at work in aggression, though, through genes, the brain, and hormones. Aggression is more prevalent in some cultures than others. Frustration may produce aggression. Today psychologists often study the role of unpleasant experiences and unpleasant circumstances as producers of aggression; they also are interested in how cognitive processes mediate the environment's influence. Aggression is learned through reinforcement and observational learning. Television violence is pervasive. How strongly television violence is related to aggression is still being debated; no causal link has been established.

II. Controlling and Reducing Aggression

Catharsis is the reduction of aggression by being aggressive. There is little support for the catharsis hypothesis. Drugs, reasoning, and punishment have not been able to control aggression. No solution for controlling aggression has been developed, although if children grow up in a world with few aggressive models, the models reward prosocial behavior, parents work on building empathy toward others in their children, and parents are active monitors of their adolescents, the probability of reducing aggression is enhanced.

III. Altruism: Biological Basis

Altruism is an unselfish interest in helping someone. But biological altruism involves increasing the prospects for survival and reproduction. Examples of biological altruism involve kin, as when a parent cares for its young. In humans, identical twins show more similar altruistic tendencies than fraternal twins.

IV. Altruism: Psychological and Environmental Influences

Examples of human altruism are plentiful. Reciprocity and social exchange often are involved, although not always. An important consideration is whether motivation is altruistic or egoistic. Psychologists have studied both person and situation variables as influences on altruistic behavior. Extensive research has been conducted on bystander intervention.

V. Attraction

Familiarity precedes a close relationship. We like to associate with individuals who are similar to us. Physical attraction is an important ingredient of close relationships, especially at their beginning. Over time, physical attraction becomes less important. It also is important to remember that physical attraction is relative, varying across cultures and historical time.

VI. The Faces of Love

Long and Berscheid believe that love has four faces: altruistic, friendship, romantic, and affectionate. Friends and lovers have some similar and dissimilar characteristics. Romantic love is involved when we say we are "in love;" it includes passion and sexual attraction. Romantic love includes a mixture of emotions, some positive, others negative. Affectionate love, also called companionate love, takes on more important status as relationships age.

VII. Dissolution of Relationships

Marital relationships are dissolving faster than ever. Dissolution is due to factors inside and outside the marriage. Barriers to dissolving marriages have weakened. Partners make attributions about a marriage's failure. One common error in these attributions is oversimplification. After relationships are dissolved, they psychologically continue.

VIII. Loneliness

Two forms of isolation are emotional isolation (loss of an emotional attachment) and social isolation. Loneliness is associated with many factors, including a poor attachment history with parents and low self-esteem. It is important to remember the distinction between being alone and being lonely.

IX. Group Behavior

Groups satisfy our personal needs, reward us, provide us with information, raise our self-esteem, and enhance our identity. Every group has norms and roles. Our performance in groups may be enhanced through social facilitation and lowered because of social loafing. Our behavior in the group also may take the form of deindividuation. Group polarization and groupthink are other concepts that help to clarify our understanding of group behavior. The majority usually has the most influence, but at times the minority has its day. Theories of group leadership include the great person theory, a situational approach, and the person-situation view, known as the contingency model of leadership.

X. Prejudice, Ethnocentrism, and Conflict

Prejudice is an unjustified negative attitude toward an individual because of the individual's group identity. A stereotype is a generalization about a group's characteristics. Ethnocentrism is the belief that one's own group is the center of the world and all other groups are of lesser stature. Ethnocentrism has a positive side—in-group pride—and a negative side—distaste for the out-group. One theory devised to explain prejudice and conflict is social identity theory. Conflict often is escalated when groups are similar enough to compare their outcomes, see how rewards and costs are distributed, and perceive that their circumstance is unfair.

XI. Reducing Conflict and Seeking Peace

Contact between groups does not reduce conflict. The most effective strategy is to develop a superordinate goal requiring the cooperation of both groups. The jigsaw classroom uses the coooperative strategy to reduce racial tension in schools. GRIT is another strategy used, especially to reduce tension between nations; it involves reducing the potential threat of each group.

Key Terms

frustration-aggression   *578*
catharsis   *580*
altruism   *582*
social exchange theory   *583*
egoism   *583*
bystander effect   *584*
matching hypothesis   *588*
friendship   *589*

romantic love (Eros)   *590*
affectionate love   *592*
norms   *595*
roles   *595*
social facilitation   *596*
social loafing   *596*
deindividuation   *596*
group polarization effect   *597)*

groupthink   *597*
great person theory   *598*
contingency model of leadership   *599*
prejudice   *600*
stereotype   *600*
ethnocentrism   *600*
social identity theory   *600*
jigsaw classroom   *602*
GRIT strategy   *604*

Suggested Readings

Gilmour, R., & Duck, S. (Eds.) (1986). *The emerging field of personal relationships*. Hillsdale, NJ: Erlbaum. This book includes a number of articles about models of close relationships and the dynamics involved in personal relationships—chapters include "when the honeymoon's over," gender effects, the causes and consequences of jealousy, and loneliness.

Hatfield, E., & Sprecher, S. (1986). *Mirror, mirror . . . The importance of looks in everyday life*. Albany: State University of New York Press. Elaine Hatfield is a pioneer in the research field of physical attractiveness and close relationships. This entertaining, insightful book details how looks affect sex, marriage, self-image, personality, and social skills.

Pettigrew, T. F. (1984). *A profile of the Negro American*. New York: Greenwood Press. Thomas Pettigrew's fascination with race relations began as a young boy growing up in Richmond, Virginia, in the 1930s. For more than thirty years he has been one of the leading authorities on race relations. This book details his belief that race relations can be improved and provides strategies for accomplishing this.

Worshel, S., & Austin, W. G. (1986). *Psychology of intergroup relations*. Chicago: Nelson Hall. This book surveys the increased interest in intergroup relations; how conflict is generated and how it can be reduced are discussed. It includes fascinating chapters on social identity, ethnocentrism, a cognitive basis for international conflicts, the GRIT strategy, and workshop ideas for reducing intergroup tension.

Appendix

Statistics

One of the biggest complaints I hear from students is "You mean I have to take statistics to complete a major in psychology?" The answer usually is yes. The word *statistics* alone causes some students to tremble, but in your daily personal and professional life you will read about statistical information and have to base decisions on it.

One of the main reasons statistics is necessary in psychology is that we easily can fool ourselves into thinking that the information we have collected supports our views. An example of this bias that even scientists have to guard against should help you see why we need statistics.

Statistical Analysis

In the early 1800s a Philadelphia doctor, Samual Morton, collected a large number of skulls from different racial groups. He thought that racial differences in intelligence existed and wanted to prove that this was reflected in the cranial capacity (skull space) of individuals from different races. He carefully measured the cranial capacity of more than 600 skulls. His results supported his belief that individuals from different races have skulls of differing cranial capacity. Morton was a respected scholar in the 1800s, and his theory was used as a scientific argument for continuing slavery.

While Morton's skulls are no longer around, he did publish his original measurements. Not too long ago, another scientist reanalyzed Morton's actual data and discovered that he had made a number of errors (Gould, 1978). Interestingly, the errors always were in the direction of supporting Morton's views about racial differences. He simply selected data that supported his theory and eliminated information that did not. The reanalysis of his original data almost two centuries later found no consistent differences when appropriate statistical measures were applied to the data. Any differences among races that appeared could actually be explained by the overall body size of the various racial groups. It appears that Morton did not deliberately present inaccurate interpretations of his data; rather, he simply had such a strong bias about race and intelligence that he only saw what he wanted in his data.

While scientists may have appropriate intentions, it is easy for them to fall into the trap that Morton did. The use of unbiased statistical tests can serve as a safeguard against any bias we might have.

Descriptive Statistics

When we collect information one of our major tasks is to *describe* that information. We have to find a way to summarize the information in a meaningful manner that explains our results. In most psychological studies we cannot just report all of the numbers we get that represent information about people or animals. Our minds would be overloaded with the information that would not have much meaning. Let's now look at some of the most important descriptive statistics psychologists use to summarize information.

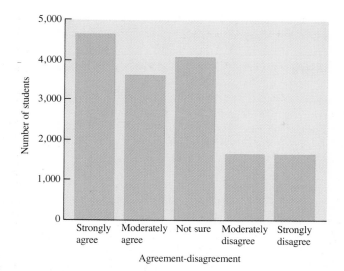

Figure A.1
*Level of agreement with the statement,
"It is not morally wrong to have sexual
intercourse before you are married."*

Frequency Distribution and Graphs

Suppose we have just completed a national survey of the sexual behavior of 15,000 seventeen year olds. One of the questions we asked was how strongly the respondents agreed or disagreed with this statement: "It is not morally wrong to have sexual intercourse before you are married." Students responded by marking whether they strongly agreed with the statement, moderately agreed, were not sure, moderately disagreed, or strongly disagreed. In figure A.1 you can see a summary of the responses of the 15,000 individuals who answered the survey. The type of graph shown in figure A.1 is called a **bar graph** simply because the information is displayed in the form of bars on the graph. Think about how economical this presentation is compared to looking at all 15,000 responses. By looking at the hypothetical information in figure A.1, you can readily see that students have a tendency to agree with the statement about sexual intercourse prior to marriage more than they disagree.

Although the frequency distribution helps us organize and summarize our information, we often want to go further in our description of the information.

Measures of Central Tendency

How many hours a week does the average college student spend exercising? This time, rather than obtaining a national sample, we sample your college. Imagine that we interviewed twenty students as they filed into the student union, asking them "How many hours during the last week did you spend exercising?" **Central tendency** informs us about the middle of a distribution, such as how many hours per week students exercise on the average. We can apply three measures of central tendency to the information we have collected about exercise: mean, median, and mode.

Table A.1	Calculation of the Mean of College Students' Hours of Exercise per Week	

$X =$ 10	$n = 20$	$\overline{X} = \dfrac{X}{n} = \dfrac{154}{20} = 7.7$
2		
15		
14		
6		
8		
1		
0		
20		
15		
15		
4		
2		
5		
13		
17		
6		
0		
0		
1		
154		

The **mean** refers to the arithmetic average of all scores. To calculate the mean, simply add all of the scores and divide the total by the number of scores. The formula for the mean is $\overline{X} = X/n,$ in which $\overline{X}$ is the mean, X is the sum of the scores, and n is the number of scores. As shown in the calculations computed from our survey of exercise habits among college students, we find that the sum of the scores is 154, the number of scores is 20, and the mean is 7.7 hours (see table A.1).

The **median** divides the distribution of scores in the middle so that half of the scores are greater than the median and half are less than the median. To determine the median, we can simply list the scores in order (from highest to lowest or lowest to highest) and count down or up until we get to the score that is in the middle. As shown in table A.2, the median score for the weekly exercise of the group of college students we interviewed is 6.

The **mode** is the score that occurs most often. By inspecting the numbers in table A.1 or A.2, you can see that three students said they exercised 15 hours a week. No other number came up three times so the mode is 15. Sometimes there is more than one mode in a distribution. For example, in the distribution of the scores 0, 1, 2, 3, 3, 4, 5, 6, 7, 7, 8, 9, there are two modes—3 and 7. This is called a **bimodal distribution.** Modes are not used in psychological studies nearly as much as means and medians, but at times modal information can be valuable. For example, we might study the problem-solving skills of a group of college students and a group of elderly individuals. We find that the means of the two groups indicate that the college students showed better problem-solving abilities. However, with the elderly population, we find a bimodal distribution of problem-solving scores, suggesting that some elderly individuals did quite well in solving problems. By looking at the modes of the distribution in such an investigation, we might uncover information and suggestions for further study that we might not otherwise have considered.

Table A.2	The Median Score of College Students' Hours of Weekly Exercise	
20	1st score	
17	2nd score	
15		
15		
15		
14		
13		The median number of hours
10		exercised per week is six.
8		
6	10th score	
6		
5		
4		
2		
2		
1		
1		
0		
0		
0	20th score	

Note: Ten scores are above the bar, and ten are below. Since a six is on both sides of the bar, the median is six. If there were different scores on each side of the bar, we would average the scores to obtain the median.

Measures of Variation

The mean truly is a *summary* statistic; it is a single score used to represent an entire set of scores. Although we already have seen the importance of summarizing information, it also is important that we not summarize too much. For this reason, we often need information about how much scores vary in addition to their mean. The two statistical measures used to show how much a distribution varies are the range and the standard deviation.

Using the data we collected about weekly exercise habits of college students, let's see how to find the range of the scores. The **range** is simply the distance from the highest score to the lowest score. In our study of exercise, then, the range is 20 because the highest score was 20 and the lowest score was 0 (20 − 0 = 20). Because the range only involves two scores in the entire distribution, it can be misleading as an index of variation. Consequently, we usually go beyond the range to find how much scores in a distribution vary.

The **standard deviation** is the most commonly used measure of variation by psychologists. It summarizes the *difference* between each score and the mean. Think of the standard deviation as how broadly or narrowly scores are dispersed around the mean. To calculate the standard deviation, we subtract the mean score from each score, square each of these differences, divide by the total number of scores, and finally take the square root. This is not as complicated as it sounds. It all can be packaged neatly into a formula:

$$\text{s.d.} = \sqrt{\frac{(X - \overline{X})^2}{n}}$$ in which s.d. is the standard deviation, $(X - \overline{X})^2$ is the sum of the square of the difference scores, and n is the total number of scores. Table A.3 shows our computation of the standard deviation of the information we collected about the weekly exercise habits of college students.

Table A.3	The Standard Deviation of College Students' Hours of Weekly Exercise	

Raw data (number of hours reported by each student)	Deviation $(X - \overline{X})$	*Square of the deviation* $(X - \overline{X})^2$
10	2.3	5.29
2	−5.7	33.49
15	7.3	53.29
14	6.3	39.69
6	−1.7	2.89
8	.3	.09
1	−6.7	44.89
0	−7.7	59.29
20	12.3	151.29
15	7.3	53.29
15	7.3	53.29
4	−3.7	13.69
2	−5.7	33.49
5	−2.7	7.29
13	5.3	28.09
17	9.3	86.49
6	−1.7	2.89
0	−7.7	59.29
1	−6.7	44.89
	$\Sigma(X - \overline{X})^2$	$= \overline{773.00}$

$$\text{s.d.} = \sqrt{\frac{\Sigma(X - \overline{X})^2}{n}} \qquad\qquad = \sqrt{\frac{773}{20}} = 6.22$$

One of the reasons the standard deviation is so valuable is that within two standard deviations of the mean of certain distributions lie 95 percent of all scores in the distribution. The type of distribution described here is the normal distribution.

The Normal Curve

The scores for a frequency distribution can be placed on a graph. These scores can take many different shapes when they are plotted on the graph. One shape that has been of considerable interest to psychologists is called the **normal curve** (or normal distribution). The normal distribution is bell-shaped and unimodal (one mode), with the greatest frequency in the center. The two sides of the curve are symmetrical around the middle. As we look further away from the center, the frequencies become smaller and smaller. To develop a normal curve we need to use two of the statistical procedures we have discussed already—the mean and standard deviation. Thus the normal curve provides information about both central tendency (mean) and variation (standard deviation).

The reason the normal curve is given so much attention by psychologists is that so many different characteristics tend to be normally distributed. As adults our height and weight, and such psychological characteristics as intelligence, are normally distributed. An example of the normal curve is shown in figure A.2. As you can see, 68.26 percent of the scores in the distribution fall within one standard deviation below the mean and one standard deviation above the mean; 95.42 percent of all scores fall within two standard deviations; and 99.74 of all scores fall within three standard deviations.

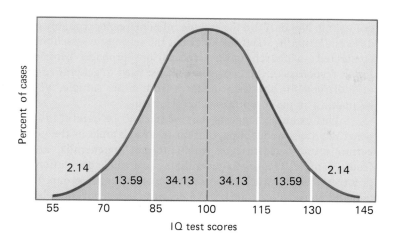

Figure A.2
The normal curve of distribution.

To see how helpful such a curve can be in interpreting psychological information, let's look at the characteristic of intelligence. One of the most widely used tests of intelligence is the Stanford-Binet. Scores on the Stanford-Binet follow a normal distribution in which the mean is 100 and the standard deviation is 16. Thus, if you score 110 on the Stanford-Binet, you are within one standard deviation of the mean. The range for one standard deviation is 100 ± 16, meaning 84–116. When someone scores 75 on this test, he or she is within two standard deviations of the mean rather than one—the range for two standard deviations is 100 ± 32, or 68–132. Thus on the Stanford-Binet approximately 95 percent of all individuals who take the test get scores of between 68 and 132.

Statistical Inference

In collecting information about college students' exercise habits, we interviewed twenty individuals at the student union. Psychologists distinguish between a sample—in our case the twenty students—and a population. When we use the word **population** in statistics we are referring to the total number of people, things, or events about which we wish to generalize. Any group selected from the population is called a **sample.** The population in our study of college students' exercise habits is all college students, not all people. Let's look more closely at how we make inferences about a population from a sample and also see how to interpret information about two different groups.

Sample and Population

In one of my classes I always have students become involved in a small research project. As part of their research experience, they have to formulate a research idea, develop some means of collecting information, such as a questionnaire or an interview, and actually obtain data from some people. In one recent class two students chose the same topic—sexual attitudes among adolescents. One of the students went to a church group to obtain information, the other to a video game parlor. In response to such questions as "Is it morally wrong to have sexual intercourse before you are married?" an overwhelming percentage of the students from the church group said that it was wrong; just as large a percentage of the students from the video parlor said that it was not wrong. Not only did the samples of adolescents probably have parents with different attitudes about sexuality but the settings in which the interviews were conducted—a church and a video parlor—probably contributed to the different responses of the two groups. If we tried to generalize to the population of adolescents in the United States from either sample, we obviously would be making an inappropriate generalization.

This example suggests that we need to be careful in making sweeping generalizations about a population from a sample in the population. Under certain prescribed strategies we do attempt to generalize about a population from a sample. The key to generalizing to a whole population is that the small group or groups must be representative of the entire group. If we want to predict the political attitudes of Americans, we do not interview men only, Republicans only, or only individuals over the age of forty, for example. Similarly, when we sample the sexual attitudes of young people, we do not collect information only from individuals who attend church on a regular basis and we do not interview in the setting of the church itself.

To increase the probability that a sample is representative of the population, statisticians often use a technique called **random sampling.** Random sampling gives every single member of an entire population an equal chance of being selected for the sample. Thus, in our example of exercise among college students, if we wanted to select a random sample of the population at the college you attend, we could not do it by selecting every third person who walked into the student union where we were conducting the interviews. Possibly some students never come to the student union so they would never be represented in the sample. Nor could we choose a random sample from every sixth person who entered the library. Some students may avoid the library entirely. To ensure a random sample of the population at your college (in which every student has an equal chance of being selected), we have to take the names of every student enrolled in the college, drop the names in a big pot, and blindfolded—pick out something like 50 to 100 names. In this manner the group selected for our sample would be random and our attempt to generalize about the entire population at your college would probably be more accurate than sampling at the student union. Random sampling, then, lets us make appropriate inferences about a population. But notice that we have been talking about making inferences to the population at your college. If we want to legitimately make inferences about all college students in the United States, we obviously cannot do so only on the basis of a sample collected at your college.

Significant Differences between Groups

Not only do psychologists make inferences about a population on the basis of samples from the population, but many psychological studies require a judgment about whether one sample differs from another sample. The basic question focuses on whether the central tendency (usually the mean) and the variation in scores (usually the standard deviation) of the two groups or samples are different from each other.

Psychologists make all kinds of comparisons between samples or groups. We compare males and females, young people and old people, people who have had certain kinds of experiences and those who have not, and so on. The expriences range from naturally occurring events (such as a sample of individuals who are divorced compared to those who are not) to situations in which we deliberately expose one sample of people to certain experiences but not the other sample (such as a sample of students who have been given an organizational strategy to remember a group of words compared with a sample of students who have not been given such a strategy). Or we might compare a sample of individuals who have been given a treatment for a psychological disorder with those who have not been given the treatment.

We need to know whether the samples or groups we collect information about really are different from each other. We use the term **significant** to help us in this matter. It turns out that whether a difference between two groups or samples is significant is based on a statistical comparison of the groups or samples. Although we won't go into the specific statistical tests psychologists use to make these comparisons (if you want to learn about them you can read an introductory statistics text), you should know in a general way how large differences between groups have to be before we say they are *significantly* different. Again we have to refer to the idea of probability and chance. As a rule, psychologists conclude that when the results of their observations would be expected to occur by chance not more than 5 times in 100 then the results are significant. This means that the results are probably due to some real differences between the two samples or groups rather than to chance factors. Many things can influence the way someone thinks or behaves, so we need to set the cutoff point for saying that some result is significant at a fairly high level, such as the point of 5 times in 100 rather than 20 times in 100. Psychologists sometimes say that their results are significant at the 0.05 level. This means that on the basis of the statistical tests they have used, 95 times out of 100 they will find the differences in the groups but there is a 5 percent chance that the differences are not real.

Let's consider an example to see how the idea of significance works. To keep our example simple we will only look at the means of samples or groups and not variation. In our first example we interview a sample of women who are divorced and a sample of women who are married about their perceptions of men. Let's assume that we have developed a "hate men" rating scale that has 9 points, ranging from extreme hatred to extreme love, with 9 representing the former and 1 the latter. The means for our interviews with the two samples of women turn out to be: divorced women, $\overline{X} = 6.5$; married women, $\overline{X} = 5.6$. When we apply our statistical tests (which you can find in statistical textbooks) to these mathematical scores, we find that although it numerically appears that divorced women hate men more than married women do, our test of differences between groups or samples tells us that the difference is probably due to chance. Therefore, we conclude that there is not a significant difference between divorced and married women in regard to how much they hate men.

In our second example, a psychological experiment is conducted in which one group of college students is given a seminar on study skills and are monitored throughout the semester by counselors. Members of this sample are compared to another group of college students who attend the seminar on study skills but are not monitored by the counselors. A third group of college students, those who got neither of these experiences, are also evaluated. In this experiment we compare the grade-point averages of the students who got the three different sets of experiences at the end of the semester. The students in the seminar-plus-monitoring sample had a grade-point average of 3.6, those in the seminar only had a 3.0 average, and those who got neither experience had a 2.8 average. Comparing the three samples of students using our statistical tests, we find a significant difference between the first group and the second or third group but not between the second and third group. We conclude that to improve student grades through study skills training, monitoring throughout the semester by counselors may be needed in addition to a seminar at the beginning of the semester.

Next we see that we are often not only interested in whether two groups or samples are significantly different from each other but also in the degree to which two distributions of scores are related to each other.

Correlation

Many of the research studies reported in this book involve the use of tests to determine the relationship between two distributions of scores. This is because we are often interested in how one measured characteristic is associated with another—intelligence with personality, stress with mental disturbance, physical attractiveness with popularity, and so forth. The most widely used statistical measure of association is **correlation.**

The correlation coefficient ranges from -1.00 to $+1.00$. Positive correlations are produced when individuals who score high on the first measure also score high on the second and when those who score low on the first measure also score low on the second. For instance, a positive correlation between stress and cardiovascular disease means that those individuals who are above average in stress are also above average in the incidence of cardiovascular problems; correspondingly, those who are below average in stress are also below average in cardiovascular disease. Negative correlations are produced when individuals who score high on the first measure tend to score low on the second and vice versa. For example, a negative correlation between college grades and the number of absences suggests that those who are above average in college grades tend to have fewer absences, whereas those who are below average in grades have more absences. Zero correlations occur when individuals who score high on the first variable are as likely to score high on the second variable as they are to score low, or when individuals who score low on the first variable are just as likely to score low on the second variable as they are high.

Correlation Values

To explain the degree to which two measures or variables are associated, or correlated, we use a single number. This number may vary from $+1$ through 0 to -1. A value of $+1$ suggests a maximum positive correlation. This maximum relationship occurs when two measures of a group of individuals associate perfectly. Consider the relationship between motivation and income. For there to be a perfect $+1$ correlation between these two variables, every single individual in the group who is higher than another individual in motivation would also have to be higher in income. There can be no exceptions when the correlation is $+1$. A value of 0 indicates no relationship at all, or a zero correlation. A value of -1 suggests a maximum negative correlation. Consider the relation between morality and self-centeredness. If we study a group of individuals and every individual who is higher in morality is lower in self-centeredness, then a -1 correlation has been found. Almost all correlations

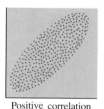 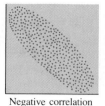 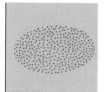

Positive correlation   Negative correlation   Zero correlation

Figure A.3
Scatter plots of correlations.

fall somewhere between these perfect correlations. The closer the correlation is to ±1, though, the more accurate our prediction of one variable from the other is. For example, if we found a correlation of +.70 between grades in high school and grades in college, we could more accurately predict an individual's grades in college than if the correlation were only +.20, or even +.40.

Scatter Plots

To visually represent the way two variables or measures are correlated, we use a graph called a **scatter plot.** On this graph each dot represents a pair of scores (one for the distribution of one set of scores and one for the distribution of the other set of scores). Figure A.3 shows the three kinds of relationships that can exist between two variables. The scatter plot on the left indicates a positive relation or correlation, telling us that as one variable increases so does the other. The middle scatter plot suggests a negative correlation, indicating that as one variable increases the other decreases. The scatter plot on the right reveals a zero correlation, or no relation at all—as one variable changes, there is no related change in the other.

Caution about Correlation

One very important reminder you always need to keep in the back of your mind when you are reading about a research study involving correlation is that when two variables are correlated—even at the perfect level of +1 or −1— it does not mean that one variable caused the other variable. In correlation, the variables are only associated; this means that you cannot infer that one caused the other. For example, we might find a very high correlation between cigarette smoking on the part of pregnant mothers and the hyperexcitability of their infant offspring. Rather than cigarette smoking's causing such hyperexcitability another factor such as the stress the mother experiences in her marital relationship or at work may be the cause of the infant's excitability. Or some genetic factors might predispose the mother to smoke, in which case these factors would be the causative agents rather than cigarette smoking itself.

In another example, consider the relationship between parents who use power-oriented discipline with their children and the children's aggression. Assume that we find a significant correlation between the use of such discipline and a child's aggression. Can we say that the parents' discipline caused the child's aggression? No, because the child's aggressiveness could precipitate the parent's power-oriented discipline just as easily as the parent's discipline could produce the child's aggression.

Key Terms

Suggested Reading

Rowntree, D. (1981). *Statistics without tears*. New York: Scribner. An introduction to basic ideas in statistics is provided; important concepts are explained by words and drawings instead of formulas.

Saslow, C. A. (1982). *Basic research methods*. Reading, MA: Addison-Wesley. This book includes valuable chapters on the language of science, how to analyze research results, how to design experiments, and how to plan your own research projects, all written in an enjoyable and informative manner.

Shaugnessy, J. J., & Zechmeister, E. B. (1985). *Research methods in psychology*. New York: Knopf. This book presents psychology's research methods and statistics in an easy-to-read fashion; included are many examples of how to use statistics in understanding life's everyday problems.

Glossary

absolute threshold   The minimum amount of physical energy that can reliably be detected by an observer.   *84*

accommodation   Occurs when we have to adjust to new information; Piagetian concept.   *292*

accurate empathy   In Rogers's therapy, the therapist's identification with the client.   *514*

acetylcholine (ACh)   A neurotransmitter that produces contractions of skeletal muscles by acting on motor nerves.   *57*

achievement test   A measure designed to evaluate what has been learned or what skills have been mastered.   *259*

acquisition phase   A phase of learning a new behavior or strengthening an old one.   *152*

action potential   A sharp change in a neuron's polarity that temporarily causes the neuron's interior to be positive and its exterior to be negative.   *54*

activation-synthesis view   The view that dreams have no inherent meaning; instead they reflect the brain's effort to make sense out of its activity.   *130*

active listening   In Rogers's therapy, restating and supporting what the client says and does.   *514*

activity theory   The view that the more active and involved older people are, the less likely they will age and the more likely they will be satisfied with their lives.   *352*

additive mixture   A mixture of beams of light from different parts of the color spectrum.   *94*

adolescence   The period of transition between childhood and adulthood that involves physical, cognitive, and social changes; entered at about ten to thirteen, exited at about eighteen to twenty-two years of age.   *322*

adolescent egocentrism   A cognitive change in adolescence that consists of two main parts—the imaginary audience and the personal fable.   *326*

adoption study   A technique used to study the effects of heredity on behavior; the comparison often is between the individual and her adopted parents and the individual and her biological parents.   *45*

adrenal glands   Endocrine glands that play important roles in our moods, our energy level, and our ability to cope with stress.   *77*

affectionate love   Also called companionate love, the type of love in which we desire to have the other person nearby and seek the person's proximity; we have a deep affection for the other person.   *592*

affective disorders   Disturbances of mood.   *488*

afferent nerves   The cells that carry input to the brain.   *50*

afterimages   Sensations that remain after a stimulus is removed; they often involve complementary colors.   *94*

ageism   The stereotype that reveals prejudice against older people.   *353*

agoraphobia   The most common phobia, in which the individual has a fear of entering unfamiliar situations.   *483*

algorithms   Procedures that are guaranteed to produce an answer to a problem.   *220*

all-or-none principle   The principle that a neuron either fires or does not fire, just like a firecracker.   *54*

alpha waves   Moderately slow brain waves characteristic of an individual who is relaxed and has her eyes closed.   *122*

altruism   Unselfish interest in helping someone else.   *582*

Alzheimer's disease   A degenerative, irreversible disorder in which the brain literally shrinks; affects more than two million people over the age of sixty-five.   *348*

amniocentesis   A test of the amniotic fluid that can detect more than one hundred birth defects.   *284*

amphetamines   Widely prescribed stimulants.   *142*

amplitude   The change in pressure created by sound waves.   *99*

amygdala   One of the two main structures in the limbic system; involved in memory.   *66*

analogy   A form of reasoning that is made up of four parts—the relationship between the first two is the same as the relationship between the last two.   *226*

anal stage   Freud's second stage of development, lasting from about one-and-a-half to three years of life; pleasure involves the anus.   *441*

androgens   Sex hormones that are primarily involved in the development of male sex charateristics.   *377*

androgyny   A term that describes the existence of masculine and feminine characteristics in both males and females; the most competent gender role is thought to be androgynous, in which the individual has both positive masculine and positive feminine characteristics.   *312*

anorexia nervosa   An eating disorder that consists of the relentless pursuit of thinness through starvation.   *374*

anterograde amnesia   A memory disorder that affects our memory of *new* information or events.   *202*

antianxiety drugs   Drugs that reduce anxiety, making the individual less excitable and more tranquil.   *535*

antidepressant drugs   Drugs that regulate mood; they often are called tricyclics because of their molecular structure.   *536*

antidiuretic hormone (ADH)   When the blood is too salty, osmoreceptors cause this hormone to be released; this prevents urinary loss of water.   *375*

antipsychotic drugs   Powerful drugs that diminish agitated behavior, reduce tension, decrease hallucinations and delusions, improve social behavior, and produce better sleep patterns.   *535*

antisocial personality disorder Disorder that characterizes individuals who live a life of crime, violence, and delinquency. *See also* personality disorders. *500*

anxiety disorders Disorders involving motor tension, hyperactivity, apprehensive expectation and thought, or vigilence and scanning reflected in hyperattentiveness. *481*

Apgar Scale A scale that has been used for many years to assess the newborn's health. The infant is rated on heart rate, respiratory effort, muscle tone, body color, and reflex irritability. *287*

approach/approach conflict Conflict we experience when we have to choose between two attractive stimuli. *414*

approach/avoidance conflict Conflict we experience when a single stimulus circumstance includes both negative and positive aspects. *414*

aptitude test A measure designed to predict an individual's ability to learn a skill or to predict what the individual can accomplish with training. *259*

archetypes The deep, permanent impressions on the human mind that occur because of our common heritage. *444*

assimilation Incorporation of new information into our existing knowledge; Piagetian concept. *292*

association cortex A part of the brain that makes up about 75 percent of the neocortex; not related to sensory or motor functioning, the association cortex is instead responsible for our highest human accomplishments, such as thinking and problem solving. *69*

attachment A relationship between two individuals in which the people feel strongly about each other and try to ensure the continuation of the relationship. *295*

attitudes Beliefs and opinions about some matter. *547*

attribution theory A theory that we are motivated to discover the underlying causes of behavior as part of our interest in making sense out of the behavior. *563*

auditory nerve The nerve that extends from the cochlea to the brain stem, carrying information about sound. *101*

authoritarian parenting A restrictive, punitive style of parenting. *307*

authoritative parenting A style of parenting that encourages a child to be independent but still places limits and controls on the child's actions; extensive verbal give-and-take occurs between parent and child. This style of parenting is associated with social competence among the children. *307*

automatic processing The encoding of information into memory that requires little effort. *190*

autonomic nervous system The part of the peripheral nervous system that takes messages to and from the body's internal organs. *49*

autonomy versus doubt Erikson's second stage of development, corresponding approximately to the second year of life; the bipolar conflict is between developing a sense of autonomy and a sense of doubt. *299*

availability heuristic A strategy by which we evaluate the probability of an event by recalling the frequency of past occurrences. *221*

aversive conditioning A technique used by behavior therapists that is based on classical conditioning. Repeated pairings of an undesirable behavior with aversive stimuli decrease the behavior's reward value and increase the probability that the individual will stop engaging in the behavior. *518*

avoidance/avoidance conflict Conflict we experience when we must choose between two unattractive stimuli. *414*

axon The part of the neuron that looks like an ultrathin cylindrical tube; carries information away from the cell body to other cells. *52*

baby-talk register Sometimes called *motherese*, this refers to the way adults and children talk to babies, including use of a higher-than-normal frequency and a greater-than-normal range of pitch. *236*

bar graph A graph that displays information in the form of bars of varying lengths. *609*

Barnum effect Based on the idea that if you make your predictions broad enough, anyone can fit the description; named after P. T. Barnum. *461*

basal ganglia A collection of structures in the forebrain involved in starting and stopping voluntary movements. *66*

basal metabolism rate (BMR) The minimum amount of energy an individual uses in a resting state. *370*

baseline A measure of how often a behavior occurs before attempts are made to change the behavior. *152*

basilar membrane A membrane located at the base of the organ of Corti; its vibrations simulate hairlike sensory receptors. *101*

behavior Everything we do that can be observed directly. *7*

behavioral approach The scientific study of behavior and its environmental determinants; emphasizes the observation of behavior. *9*

behavior modification The use of learning principles to reduce or eliminate maladaptive behavior or to teach new responses. *168*

behavior therapies Therapies based on the principles of behaviorism and social learning theory; emphasis is placed on the learning and unlearning of problems through environmental experiences. *517*

beta waves Waves that indicate a pattern of brain activity that is desynchronized; high-frequency waves characteristic of an individual who is awake. *122*

big-five factors of personality Five basic personality dimensions yielded by factor analytic studies. They are extraversion-introversion, friendly compliance versus hostile noncompliance, neuroticism, will to achieve, and intellect. *459*

bimodal distribution The existence of two modes in a single distribution of scores from a survey. *610*

biofeedback Providing the individual with information about bodily processes so the individual can try to change those processes. *170*

biomedical therapies Therapies designed to alter the way an individual's body functions; drug therapy is the most common form. *534*

bipolar disorder An affective disorder in which the individual has dramatic mood swings; the individual might be depressed, manic, or both. *489*

blind spot The location where the optic nerve leaves the eye and enters the brain; because no light receptors are present here, we cannot see anything that reaches this part of the retina. *90*

bonding Early physical contact between the baby and the parent that is encouraged by many hospitals and physicians. *288*

Brazelton Neonatal Behavioral Assessment Scale A more subtle test than the Apgar, this measure includes an evaluation of the infant's reaction to people; assesses twenty reflexes and reactions to different circumstances. *287*

brightness The dimension of color based on intensity. *93*

bulimia An eating disorder that consistently follows a binge-and-purge pattern. *375*

bystander effect A phenomenon that occurs when individuals who observe an emergency help less when someone else is present than they would if they were observing it alone. *584*

Cannon-Bard theory A theory that plays down the body's role in emotion; it states that we experience an emotion and bodily changes simultaneously. *406*

care perspective Gilligan's view that moral development should include more emphasis on people's connectedness to others. *333*

case study An in-depth look at an individual; used mainly by clinical psychologists. *22*

catatonic schizophrenia A severe mental disorder whose central feature is bizarre motor behavior. *495*

catharsis The reduction of aggression by being aggressive. No support for the catharsis hypothesis has been discovered. *580*

catharsis A process in Freud's psychoanalysis in which the patient releases tension by reliving conflicting emotional experiences. *511*

cell body In the nervous system, the part of the neuron that contains the nucleus, which directs the manufacture of substances the neuron uses for growth and maintenance. *51*

central nervous system (CNS) The brain and the spinal cord. *49*

central tendency The information provided by the middle of a distribution of data. Three measures of central tendency are mean, median, and mode. *609*

cephalo-caudal pattern The tendency for growth to occur first at the top of the individual, beginning at the head and working its way down to the neck, then the trunk, and so on. *290*

cerebellum Two rounded structures in the hindbrain that play important roles in the motor system. *64*

chaining A technique often used with shaping to teach a complex sequence or chain of behaviors. We begin by shaping the final response and work backwards until a chain of behaviors is learned. *166*

chorionic villus test A test for birth defects, available since the mid 1980s, that involves removing a small sample of the placenta nine to ten weeks into pregnancy. *284*

chromosomes Threadlike structures found in the nuclei of human cells that carry the genes. They come in structurally similar pairs; humans have twenty-three chromosome pairs. *42*

chunking The organization of items into meaningful or manageable units; allows us to store more information in short-term memory. *188*

circadian rhythm A biological rhythm with a cycle of about 24 hours. *124*

clairvoyance The ability to see or be aware of events that are not in sight. *115*

classical conditioning The process—initially discovered by Pavlov—in which a previously neutral stimulus acquires the ability to elicit a response by being associated with a stimulus that naturally produces a similar response. *154*

clinical and counseling psychology A branch of psychology practiced by psychologists who diagnose and treat people with psychological problems. *32*

cocaine A stimulant, derived from the coca plant, that has been widely used in the 1980s. *143*

cochlea A snail-like, fluid-filled structure in the inner ear where sound waves stimulate neural impulses. *101*

cognition Our mental activities—how information enters the mind, how it is stored and transformed, and how it is retrieved to perform such complex activities as problem solving and reasoning. *213*

cognitive approach The view that the key to psychology is the study of cognition, which includes such processes as attention, memory, perception, thinking, and problem solving. *12*

cognitive behavior therapies Therapies that have a dual focus—to change both the environment and the thoughts of the individual to increase adaptive behavior. *519*

cognitive dissonance A type of tension or uneasiness we feel when our behavior is inconsistent with our attitudes. Leon Festinger stated that we try to reduce this tension by cognitively justifying things that are unpleasant. *550*

cognitive therapies Therapies that emphasize the individual's cognitions or thoughts as the main source of abnormal behavior. *522*

collective unconscious Jung's term for the common heritage we all share; goes back to the dawn of human existence. *444*

commitments Lazarus's description of our valued ideals and goals and the choices we are prepared to make to reach those ideals and goals. *419*

competence motivation Also called mastery motivation; the motivation to deal effectively with the environment, to be competent and do well what is attempted, to process information efficiently, and to change the world in hope of making it better. *387*

complexity A characteristic of sound created by a collection of sound waves with varying frequencies. *99*

compulsions Repetitive, ritualistic behaviors that usually are carried out to prevent or produce some future situation. *484*

concept A category that is used to group objects, events, and characteristics on the basis of common properties. *215*

conception Occurs when a single sperm cell from the male unites with the ovum (egg) in the female's fallopian tube; also called fertilization. *283*

concrete operational stage Piaget's stage that roughly corresponds to the seven-to-eleven age period; the child can think operationally, reasoning about virtually anything she can perceive. The ability to classify objects improves dramatically during this period. *303*

concurrent validity An indicator of how a test's scores relate to a criterion that is currently available (concurrent). *246*

conditional positive regard Rogers's term for a situation in which love and praise are not given unless we conform to parental or social standards. *451*

conditioned response (CR) A response that is produced by a conditioned stimulus; a classical conditioning term. *155*

conditioned stimulus (CS) An initially neutral stimulus that produces a conditioned response after being associated with an unconditioned stimulus; a classical conditioning term. *154*

conditions of worth Rogers's term for ideas about what kinds of behaviors will bring us positive regard. *452*

cones Light-sensitive cells in the retina that enable us to see color in well-lit conditions. *90*

conformity Change in an individual's behavior or thought because of real or imagined pressure from others. *565*

consciousness The external stimuli and internal mental events that we are aware of at a given time. *120*

content validity A test's ability to give a broad picture of what is supposed to be measured. *246*

contingency model of leadership A view that takes into account both personality characteristics and situational influences; leaders influence their followers, and followers influence their leaders. *599*

contour A location at which a sudden change of brightness occurs. *108*

control group A comparison group in an experiment that serves as a baseline against which the effects found in the manipulated condition can be compared. *25*

conventional level The intermediate level of moral development in Kohlberg's theory; moral development shows an intermediate degree of internalization, and emphasis is placed on conformity to others' standards, often either parents' or society's. *332*

convergent thinking Thinking that goes toward one correct answer, characteristic of the thinking that most intelligence tests elicit. *272*

conversion disorder A disorder that received its name from Freudian theory, which stressed that anxiety can be "converted" into a special physical symptom. *485*

cornea A clear membrane just in front of the iris that bends light rays as they enter the eye. *90*

corpus callosum The large bundle of nerve fibers that connect the brain's two hemispheres, carrying information between the hemispheres. *71*

correlation The most widely used statistical measure of association between two distributions of scores. *616*

correlational strategy A technique used to determine how strongly two or more events or characteristics are related. *24*

cortical columns Complex multicellular ensembles of approximately one hundred or so vertically interconnected neurons that span the layers of the neocortex. *70*

counterconditioning A procedure for weakening the conditioned response by associating the stimuli with a new response incompatible with the CR. *159*

couple therapy Therapy with marital partners or single couples whose major problem is their relationship. *526*

creativity A difficult term to define; one definition is the ability to think about something in a novel and unusual way and to come up with unique solutions to problems. *273*

criterion validity A test's ability to predict various measures or criteria of the attribute being tested. *246*

cross-sectional study A study in which individuals of different ages are tested at the same time. *351*

cultural-familial retardation Mental retardation that is due to environmental experiences and culture; there is no evidence of organic brain dysfunction. Most individuals with this type of retardation have an IQ between 50 and 70. *271*

culture-fair tests Tests designed to reduce cultural bias in intelligence tests. *264*

daydreaming A condition somewhere between active consciousness and dreaming while we are asleep; often involves fantasies. *122*

decay theory A theory of forgetting; emphasizes that when something new is learned, a memory trace is formed. As time passes, this trace gradually decays. *198*

declarative knowledge A form of memory in which information can be verbally communicated; knowing *that*. *189*

deep structure The syntactic relation of words in a sentence. *229*

defense mechanisms Means by which the ego resolves conflicts between its demands for reality and the id's wishes; defense mechanisms protect the ego and reduce conflict. *438*

deficiency needs In Maslow's system, the kinds of needs (physiological, affection, security, and self-esteem) whose deficiency we try to make up for if they are not fulfilled. *453*

deindividuation Our tendency to "let go" of our identity as individuals and to take on the identity of the group. *596*

dendrite The part of the neuron that receives information and orients it to the cell body. *52*

dependent variable A variable that is influenced by the effects of the independent variable; it *depends* on what happens to the subjects in the experiment. *25*

depressants Drugs that slow down the central nervous system. *141*

development A pattern of movement or change that begins at conception and continues throughout the life cycle. *282*

developmental psychology A branch of psychology concerned with how we become who we are from conception to death; focuses on biological and environmental factors that contribute to development. *33*

diathesis-stress view A view emphasizing that schizophrenia is caused by a combination of environmental stress and biogenetic predisposition. *499*

difference threshold The smallest amount of stimulation required to discriminate one stimulus from another. *87*

discrimination (classical conditioning) The process of learning to respond to certain stimuli and not to others. *156*

discrimination (operant conditioning) The process of responding in the presence of one stimulus that is reinforced but not in the presence of another stimulus that is not reinforced. *168*

disorganized schizophrenia A severe mental disorder that results in delusions and hallucinations that have little or no recognizable meaning; involves excessive withdrawal from human contact. *495*

displacement The characteristic of language that enables us to communicate information about another place and time. *229*

displacement A defense mechanism by which unacceptable feelings are shifted from one object to another, more acceptable object. *439*

dissociative disorders Disorders that occur when the individual suddenly loses his memory or changes his identity. *486*

divergent thinking Thinking that produces many different answers to the same question; Guilford believes this form of thinking is closely related to creativity. *272*

DNA (deoxyribonucleic acid) A chemical molecule whose sequence determines the genetic information carried by chromosomes. *42*

door-in-the-foot A persuasion strategy in which the communicator makes her strongest point or demand initially—which the listener probably will reject—then presents a weaker point toward the end. *556*

dopamine A neurotransmitter that is associated with schizophrenia. *57*

dream analysis Analysis of the patient's dreams so that the therapist can gain clues to the nature of the patient's problems. Based on Freud's theory that unconscious thoughts will appear in dreams. *512*

drive An aroused state that occurs because of a physiological need; motivates the organism to reduce the tension involved. *364*

drive-reduction theory The view that as a drive becomes stronger, it creates tension, which organisms are motivated to reduce. *364*

DSM-III Stands for third edition of the Diagnostic and Statistical Manual of Mental Disorders; developed by the American Psychiatric Association and currently the most widely used system for classifying mental disorders. *478*

dualism A view that says mind and body have a separate existence, the mind being nonphysical, the brain being physical. *78*

early adolescence Corresponds approximately to ten to fifteen years of age; a time when the physical changes of puberty are prominent. *322*

early adulthood A period that begins at some point in our late teens or early twenties and ends at some point in our late thirties; a time of establishing personal and economic independence, seeking intimacy, and pursuing career development more intensely. *335*

early childhood The time frame encompassing the preschool years, about three to five years of age. *300*

echoic images Fleeting sound in the sensory register. *187*

ecological theory A theory that the main purpose of sleep is to keep animals from wasting their energy and harming themselves during those parts of the day or night to which they have not adapted. *126*

ectomorphic Sheldon's term for the tall, thin, fragile individual who is fearful, introverted, and restrained. *457*

efferent nerves The cells that carry information away from the brain. *50*

effort justification The need to justify the effort we put forth in life. *551*

effortful processing The encoding of information into memory by using such techniques as organization, rehearsal, imagery, and elaboration. *190*

ego The executive branch of personality, according to Freud; the structure of personality that operates according to the demands and constraints of society; includes our higher cognitive processes, such as reasoning and problem solving. *438*

egocentrism Piaget's term for the preoperational child's inability to distinguish between his own and another's perspectives. *302*

egoism When person A gives to person B to ensure reciprocity, gain self-esteem, present oneself as powerful, competent, or caring, or avoid social and self-censure for failing to live up to normative expectations. *583*

eidetic imagery The ability to visualize scenes no longer in view with virtual photographic clarity *195*

elaboration Refers to more extensive processing of the information that enters our memory system *194*

electroconvulsive therapy (ECT) Commonly called "shock treatment", this is the use of an electric shock to produce a seizure in the brain much like what happens spontaneously in some forms of epilepsy. *536*

embryonic period The period from two to eight weeks after conception; many organs begin to appear at this time. *283*

emotion-focused coping Lazarus's description of an approach in which an individual responds to stress in an emotional manner, such as through defensive appraisal. *419*

empirical keying A procedure used to develop the validity of a test by determining whether the test items predict some criterion. *464*

encoding The means by which information gets into memory. *185*

encounter group Therapy designed to promote self-understanding through candid group interaction. *528*

endocrine glands The ductless glands that release their chemical products, called hormones, directly into the bloodstream. *76*

endomorphic Sheldon's term for the soft, round, large-stomached individual who is relaxed, gregarious, and food-loving. *457*

endorphin A neurotransmitter that is a natural opium-like substance and is associated with pleasure and the control of pain. *60*

epigenetic principle Erikson's concept that anything that grows has a ground plan, out of which the parts arise, each having a special time of ascendency, until all of the parts have arisen to form a functioning whole. *298*

episodic memory A form of memory involving the where and when of events and episodes. *189*

erogenous zones Freud's concept that at each stage of development, pleasure is experienced in one part of the body more than others. *440*

estradiol A hormone associated with breast, uterine, and skeletal development in girls during puberty. *323*

estrogens Sex hormones that are primarily involved in the development of female sex characteristics. *377*

ethnocentrism The belief that our group is the center of the world and all other groups are beneath us. *600*

eustress Selye's term for the positive features of stress. *413*

excitement phase The first phase in the human sexual response cycle; the beginning of erotic responsiveness; blood vessels are engorged and muscle tension increases. *378*

exhibitionism A psychosexual disorder in which the individual obtains sexual gratification from exposing his or her anatomy to others. *501*

experiment A carefully regulated setting in which one or more of the factors believed to influence the behavior being studied are manipulated and all others are held constant. *25*

experimental and physiological psychology Areas of psychology that often involve pure research; they include a wide range of interests from memory and perception to the brain. *32*

experimental group The group whose experience is being manipulated in an experiment. *25*

experimental strategy Based on the use of the experiment, a strategy that allows us to precisely determine the causes of behavior. *25*

extinction (classical conditioning) The weakening of the conditioned stimulus's tendency to elicit the conditioned response by unreinforced presentations of the conditioned stimulus. *156*

extinction (operant conditioning) A decrease in the tendency to perform the response brought about by unreinforced consequences of that response. *168*

extrasensory perception Perception that does not occur through normal sensory channels. *114*

extrinsic motivation Motivation due to external factors in the environment, especially rewards. *389*

face validity An assumption that the content of a personality test is a good indicator of what the individual's personality is like. *464*

factor analysis A mathematical technique used to arrive at the basic traits of personality. *458*

family systems therapy Therapy stressing that the individual's psychological adjustment is related to patterns of interaction within the family system. *527*

family therapy Group therapy with the members of one's natural family constituting the group. *526*

fetal alcohol syndrome (FAS) A cluster of characteristics identifying children born to mothers who are heavy drinkers; includes a small head and defective limbs, face, and heart. *286*

fetal period A period that begins two months after conception and lasts for seven months on the average. *285*

fetishism A psychosexual disorder in which the individual relies on inanimate objects or some body part for sexual arousal and gratification. *500*

fixation Occurs when an individual becomes stuck at a particular stage of development because his needs are under- or over-gratified. *441*

foot-in-the-door A persuasion strategy in which the individual initially presents a weak point or makes a small request with which the listener probably will comply; the strongest point is saved until the end. *556*

forebrain The highest and front-most level of the brain. *66*

formal operational thought The stage that Piaget believed individuals enter between the ages of eleven and fifteen; thought becomes more abstract, more logical, and more idealistic. *326*

fovea A minute structure in the center of the retina; an area where vision is the sharpest. *90*

free association Freud's technique, used as a part of psychoanalysis, in which the patient is encouraged to say out loud whatever comes to mind, no matter how trivial or embarrassing. *437*

frequency The number of cycles a sound wave completes in one second. *99*

frequency theory The theory that the frequency of the auditory nerve's firing is involved in the perception of sound. *101*

friendship A form of close relationship that involves enjoyment, acceptance, respect, trust, mutual assistance, confiding, understanding, and spontaneity. *589*

frontal lobe One of the four lobes of the brain; involved in the control of voluntary muscles, and the seat of higher intelligence. *69*

frustration Any situation in which an individual cannot reach a goal. *415*

frustration-aggression The proposal by Dollard and his colleagues that frustration, in the form of blocking or interfering, would trigger aggression. *578*

fugue A dissociative disorder that involves memory loss but also includes unexpected travel away from home or work, with the individual assuming a new identity and an inability to remember her previous identity. *486*

functional fixedness The inability to solve a problem because the elements involved are viewed only in terms of their usual function. *222*

functionalism An early approach to psychology that emphasized the functions of mind and behavior in adapting to the environment. *8*

fundamental attribution error The tendency to overestimate the importance of traits and to underestimate the importance of situations when we seek explanations of behavior. *563*

GABA A neurotransmitter found throughout the brain that inhibits the firing of neurons. *57*

gate-control theory The theory arguing that "pain gates," which open and close, are present in the spinal cord and brain stem. *102*

gender roles The social expectations of how we should act and think as females and males. *312*

general adaptation syndrome Selye's description of the common effects on the body when demands are placed on it; consists of three stages—alarm, resistance, and exhaustion. *412*

generalization (classical conditioning) The tendency of a stimulus similar to the original conditioned stimulus to produce a response similar to the conditioned response. *156*

generalization (operant conditioning) The elicitation of a response that is somewhat different from the response originally learned for a given stimulus. *168*

generalized anxiety disorder Persistent anxiety for at least one month's duration without specific symptoms. *482*

generativity versus stagnation Erikson's seventh stage, corresponding approximately to middle adulthood. Generativity refers to helping the younger generation in developing and leading useful lives. Stagnation refers to the feeling of not having helped the younger generation. *339*

genes The units of hereditary information; they are short segments of the DNA staircase. *42*

genital stage Freud's fifth stage of development, lasting from the onset of puberty throughout adulthood; a time of sexual reawakening; the source of pleasure now becomes someone outside the family. *444*

genuineness In Rogers's therapy, the belief that the therapist should not hide behind a facade; the therapist must make her feelings known to the client. *514*

germinal period The first two weeks of development, beginning with the fertilized egg. *283*

Gestalt therapy A form of therapy in which individuals are encouraged to be very open and honest with their feelings; the therapist tries to break through false screens and get individuals to act out their emotions. Developed by Fritz Perls. *515*

gifted Describes an individual with well-above-average intelligence and/or a superior talent for something. *271*

glial cells Non-neuron cells in the brain that provide supportive and nutritive functions. *60*

grammar Closely related to syntax, this refers to the formal description of syntactical rules. *229*

great person theory The theory that individuals with certain traits are best suited for leadership positions. *598*

GRIT strategy Stands for Graduated and Reciprocated Initiatives in Tension-reduction; its purpose is to reduce tension and mistrust so that disarmament and regular negotiation, trade, and international diplomacy can proceed. The procedure begins when one party makes unilateral reductions in threat capability. *604*

group polarization effect The solidification and further strengthening of a position as a consequence of group discussion. *597*

groupthink The motivation of group members to maintain harmony and unanimity in decision making, in the process suffocating differences of opinion. *597*

hallucinogens Drugs that modify an individual's perceptual experiences. *143*

hardiness A personality style characterized by a sense of commitment, control, and challenge. *420*

hermaphrodites Individuals with genitals that are intermediate between male and female. *377*

heuristics Strategies, or rules of thumb, that suggest a solution to a problem but do not ensure that it will work. *220*

hidden-observer theory Hilgard's perspective that part of the hypnotized individual's mind is completely unaware of what is happening; the individual remains a passive or hidden observer until called on to comment. *134*

hierarchy of motives Maslow's view of motivation; that some motives (such as physiological) have to be satisfied before others (such as safety). *365*

hindbrain The lowest portion of the brain, adjacent to the spinal cord. *64*

hippocampus One of the two main structures in the limbic system; involved in memory. *66*

holistic orientation An approach that recognizes the multidimensional nature of illness and health; includes an emphasis on life-style, psychological factors, and the nature of the health care delivery system. *425*

holophrase hypothesis The idea that a single word is used to imply a complete sentence; characteristic of a child's first words. *237*

homeostasis The body's tendency to maintain an equilibrium or steady state. *364*

homeostatic imbalance theory A macrobiological theory of aging, emphasizing that aging is the result of the almost linear decline of the body's organ reserves and their ability to maintain homeostasis or equilibrium. *348*

hormones Chemical products released into the bloodstream by the endocrine glands. *76*

hue The dimension of color based on wavelength. *93*

humanistic approach An approach to psychology that focuses on expanding consciousness, subjective experiences, and positive feelings. *12*

humanistic perspective The most widely known phenomenological approach to personality; stresses self-perceptions, inner experiences, self-determination, and self-confidence. *450*

humanistic psychotherapies Therapies that encourage clients to examine themselves and to grow and develop personally. *513*

hypnagogic state The transition between wakefulness and sleep; a pleasant state of existence. *123*

hypnosis A psychological state of altered attention and awareness in which the individual is unusually receptive to suggestions. *133*

hypochondriasis A pervasive fear of illness or disease. *485*

hypothalamus An important structure in the forebrain that is involved in the control of eating, drinking, and sexual activity. It also plays a role in emotion and stress. *67*

hypotheses Assumptions that can be tested to determine their accuracy. *17*

hypothetical-deductive reasoning Reasoning that occurs for the first time during adolescence; the person develops hypotheses about ways to solve a problem and then deduces or concludes which is the best path to follow. *326*

iconic images Fleeting visual images in the sensory register. *187*

id A structure of personality in Freud's theory; the reservoir of psychic energy and instincts that perpetually presses us to satisfy our basic needs. *437*

identity versus identity confusion Erikson's fifth stage, which corresponds approximately to adolescence; the adolescent seeks to know who she is, what she is all about, and where she is headed in life. *331*

imaginary audience The adolescent's belief that others are as preoccupied with his behavior as he himself is. *326*

implicit memory Exists when performance on a task is facilitated without deliberate recollection of a specific learning episode; reveals how the unconscious mind influences memory. *199*

implicit personality theory The public's or lay person's conception of how personality traits go together in an individual. *558*

imprinting Lorenz's term for the rapid, innate learning within a critical period of time that involves attachment to the first moving object seen. *297*

incentives External stimuli that motivate the organism's behavior. *365*

incest A psychosexual distrubance in which the individual has a sexual relationship with relatives; the most common is brother-sister. *502*

independent variable The manipulated or influential factor in an experiment; can be changed *independently* of other factors. *25*

individual differences The consistent, stable ways we are different from each other. *245*

individual traits Allport's term for the unique ways in which individuals deal with their world; reflects Allport's emphasis on the individual's uniqueness. *458*

industrial and organizational psychology A branch of psychology that focuses on the application of psychology to business and the world of work. *33*

industry versus inferiority Erikson's fourth stage, corresponding approximately to the elementary school years; children develop either a sense of industry and work or a feeling of inferiority. *312*

infantile amnesia The inability to remember anything about the first three years of life. *199*

infinite generativity An individual's ability to generate an infinite number of meaningful sentences from a finite set of words and rules. *229*

information processing perspective A popular contemporary cognitive view of psychology that emphasizes how we process information; influenced extensively by the development of computers. *13*

information theory The view that the key to understanding classical conditioning is the information the organism gets from the situation. *157*

initiative versus guilt Erikson's third stage, corresponding approximately to early childhood; children develop either a sense of initiative or a sense of guilt in this period. *311*

innate goodness A philosophical view that children are inherently good—they should be allowed to grow naturally with little parental monitoring or constraint. *281*

inner ear The portion of the ear that includes the oval window, cochlea, and the organ of Corti in the cochlea; the innermost part of the ear. *100*

insight learning A form of learning involved in problem solving; the organism seems to suddenly gain an understanding or insight of how to solve the problem. *178*

insight therapies Therapies with the goal of encouraging insight and awareness of one's self; the humanistic and psychodynamic therapies. *516*

instinct An innate, biological determinant of behavior. *364*

instinctive drift The tendency of animals to revert to instinctive behavior. *180*

integrity versus despair Erikson's final stage of development, corresponding approximately to late adulthood; involves looking back and evaluating what we have accomplished in our lives. *353*

intelligence Verbal ability, problem-solving skills, and the ability to learn from and adapt to the experiences of everyday life. *248*

interneurons Neurons that carry information between sensory inputs and motor outputs; these make up most of the nerve tissue in the brain. *50*

interview A session at which questions are asked of an individual, usually in a face-to-face manner. *20*

intimacy versus isolation stage Erikson's sixth stage, corresponding approximately to early adulthood; the individual either develops a sense of intimacy or a sense of isolation. *339*

intrinsic motivation An underlying need for competence and self-determination; internal motivation. *389*

introspection A technique whereby specially trained people observe and analyze their own experiences. *8*

ion An electrically charged particle involved in the transmission of information in neurons. *53*

IQ Stands for intelligence quotient; the individual's mental age divided by chronological age multiplied by 100. *249*

iris A ring of muscles ranging in color from light blue to dark brown. It adjusts the size of the pupil in response to changing light conditions. *90*

James-Lange theory A theory of emotion arguing that we initially perceive a stimulus, our body responds, then we experience the emotion. *403*

jigsaw classroom Aronson's technique emphasizing cooperation to reduce ethnic hatred and to improve interpersonal relations and learning in racially mixed classrooms. *602*

just noticeable difference (JND) The point at which two stimuli are detected as different 50 percent of the time. *87*

justice perspective A moral development perspective that emphasizes the rights of the individual. Gilligan said that Kohlberg's theory is in error because it places too much emphasis on this approach. *333*

kinesthetic senses The senses that provide information about movement, posture, and orientation. *105*

laboratory A controlled setting in which many of the complex factors of the "real world" are removed. *19*

language A set of sequences of words that convey information. *214*

language acquisition device (LAD) The natural ability to detect certain categories of language (phonological, syntactic, and semantic); emphasizes the biological basis of language. *230*

late adolescence Occurs approximately between sixteen to eighteen and eighteen to twenty-two years of age, a time when physical maturation has slowed and stronger concerns with identity and careers are present. *322*

late adulthood A period that begins at about sixty to seventy years of age and lasts until death; a time of adjusting to decreased strength and health, retirement, reduced income, and new social roles. *335*

latency stage Freud's fourth stage of development, corresponding approximately to the elementary school years; the child represses sexual urges and focuses on intellectual and social skills. *444*

law of effect States that behaviors followed by positive outcomes are strengthened, while those followed by negative outcomes are weakened; developed by Thorndike. *162*

learned helplessness Seligman's concept describing individuals who have been exposed to prolonged pain or stress, over which they have no control, who thus learn to become helpless. The concept has been applied to depression. *493*

learning A relatively permanent change in behavior that occurs through experience. *153*

learning set A single strategy or tendency that we use to solve different problems. *221*

lens The part of the eye, located behind the iris, that changes shape to bring objects into focus. *90*

levels of processing view A perspective emphasizing that memorization takes place on a continuum of depth; at the deepest level, information is processed semantically. Because meaningful, symbolic associations are made with information memorized at this deep level, the advocates of this view believe the information is remembered better here than at the shallow level of processing. *191*

life-cycle perspective The belief that development is a lifelong process. This perspective places more emphasis on change during adulthood than does the traditional perspective, which focuses more on childhood. *334*

life expectancy The number of people expected to reach a certain age. *346*

light A form of electromagnetic energy that can be described in terms of wavelengths. *89*

limbic system A structure in the forebrain believed to play important roles in both memory and emotion. *66*

lithium A drug that is widely used to treat bipolar disorder. *536*

longitudinal study A study in which individuals are tested and then retested after a period of years. *352*

long-term memory The retention of information for an indefinite period of time. *186*

loudness The ear's detection of the sound wave's amplitude. *99*

LSD Stands for the chemical lysergic acid diethylamide; a powerful hallucinogen. *143*

lucid dreaming A class of dreams in which you "wake up" mentally but remain in the sensory landscape of the dream world. *130*

major depression A disorder in which the individual is sad, demoralized, bored, and self-derogatory; he does not feel well, loses stamina easily, has a poor appetite, and is listless and unmotivated. *488*

marathon group An encounter group conducted in a single, long session, lasting as long as sixteen to forty-eight hours. *528*

marijuana A milder hallucinogen than LSD, which comes from the hemp plant; its active ingredient is THC. *143*

masochism A psychosexual disorder in which the individual obtains sexual gratification by receiving pain. *501*

matching hypothesis The theory that while we may prefer a more attractive partner in the abstract, in the real world we end up choosing someone who is close to our own level of attractiveness. *588*

MDMA A "designer drug" with mildly hallucinogenic qualities. *144*

mean The arithmetic average of all scores in a set of data. *610*

mean length of utterance (MLU) The average number of words in a child's sentences; believed by Roger Brown to be a good indicator of the child's language maturity. *238*

median The middle score among all of the scores in a survey. *610*

medical model Also called the disease model; the view that abnormal behavior is a disease or illness precipitated by internal body causes. *475*

medulla A structure in the hindbrain; helps to control breathing and regulate reflexes. *64*

memory The retention of information over time. *185*

menopause The end of menstruation, a marker that usually occurs during middle adulthood; signals the end of childbearing capability. *337*

mental age (MA) an individual's level of mental development relative to others. *249*

mental retardation A condition characterized by inadequate intellectual functioning. The individual has a low IQ—usually below 70 on a traditional test of intelligence—and also has difficulty adapting to the course of everyday life. *271*

mesomorphic Sheldon's term for the strong, athletic, and muscular individual who is energetic, assertive, and courageous. *457*

metaanalysis Analyzing the existing research literature, looking for common results across many different studies. *532*

metaneeds The higher, or growth, needs in Maslow's hierarchy of needs. *453*

metaphor An implied comparison between two ideas conveyed by the abstract meaning contained in the words used to make the comparison. Adolescents understand metaphor much better than children do. *328*

midbrain The portion of the brain above the hindbrain. *64*

middle adulthood A period that begins at about thirty-five to forty-five years of age and ends at about fifty-five to sixty-five years of age; a time of expanding personal and social involvement, increased responsibility, adjusting to physical decline, and reaching and maintaining career satisfaction. *335*

middle and late childhood The time frame encompassing the elementary school years, about six to eleven years of age. *300*

middle ear The portion of the ear that includes the eardrum, hammer, anvil, and stirrups; helps to concentrate sound so it can be further processed. *100*

mind Mental life, thoughts, and feelings that cannot be directly observed. *7*

Minnesota Multiphasic Personality Inventory (MMPI) The most widely used self-report test of personality; consists of 550 items. It originally was developed to improve the diagnosis of mental disturbances. *464*

mnemonics Strategies designed to make memory more efficient. *206*

mode The score that occurs most often in a set of data. *610*

monism A view that stresses a single underlying existence of mind and body; mind and body are inseparable. *78*

monocular cues Depth perception cues in which the image falls on only one eye, or cues that can be perceived without binocular vision. *110*

Moro reflex One of the most frequent and dramatic reflexes of the infant and a vestige of our ape ancestry; includes a startle response, arched back, and thrown-back head. *289*

morphology The study of the smallest speech units that carry meaning, the morphemes. *229*

motivation Involves the question of why individuals think, feel, and behave the way they do. *362*

movement aftereffects The experience of watching continuous movement and then looking at another surface, which then appears to move in the opposite direction. *110*

multiaxial system A characteristic of DSM-III, consisting of five dimensions or "axes" on which the individual is assessed; this system ensures that the individual will not simply be assigned to a mental disturbance category, but that classification will be based on a number of clinical factors. *480*

multiple-factor theory of intelligence Thurstone's view that we have seven primary mental abilities: verbal comprehension, number ability, word fluency, spatial visualization, associative memory, reasoning, and perceptual speed. *254*

multiple personality The most dramatic but least frequent dissociative disorder; an individual has two or more distinct personalities or selves. *486*

myelin sheath A layer of fat cells that covers most axons; insulates the axon and speeds up information transmission *52*

n **achievement** Need for achievement; McClelland's description of the general motivation for achievement. The individual's motivation to overcome obstacles, achieve success, and seek out tasks and do them well and as quickly as possible. *388*

narcolepsy The irresistible urge to fall asleep. *128*

natural selection The principle that emphasizes genetic diversity within a species; in this diversity, some organisms have characteristics that help them adapt to their environment, and these are likely to be perpetuated. *41*

naturalistic observation Observation in real-world settings with no attempt made to manipulate or control the situation. *20*

need Involves a physiological state; a physical deprivation. *364*

negative reinforcement The frequency of a response increases because it either removes an unpleasant stimulus or lets the individual avoid the stimulus. *164*

neocortex The largest and highest part of the human brain, making up about 80 percent of the brain's volume; the portion where the highest and most complex human functions are carried out. *69*

neurobiological approach An approach emphasizing that the key to understanding psychology lies in studying the brain and nervous system. *14*

neuroleptics The most widely used antipsychotic drugs; they block the dopamine system's action in the brain. *535*

neuron The nerve cell that is the basic building block of the nervous system. *49*

neurotic A term to describe relatively mild mental disorders in which the individual has not lost contact with reality. *478*

neurotransmitters Chemical substances that act as messengers, travelling across the synapses between neurons. *54*

noise The presence of competing and irrelevant background information in a stimulus situation. *84*

nonconscious A term that describes processes involved in our body's functioning that we are not aware of, such as temperature control and digestion. *121*

nonstate view The view that hypnotic behavior is similar to other forms of social behavior; hypnotic behavior is purposeful, goal-directed action that is understood by focusing on the way subjects interpret their roles and how they try to present themselves. *135*

norepinephrine A neurotransmitter that usually inhibits the firing of neurons in the brain and spinal cord but excites the heart muscles, the intestine, and the urogenital tract. Too little is associated with depression, too much with mania. *57*

normal distribution Also called the normal curve; a symmetrical distribution of scores on a graph, in which a majority of the cases fall in the middle range of possible scores and fewer scores appear toward the ends of this range. *250, 612*

norms Rules that apply to all members of a group. *595*

norms Established standards of performance for a test. *247*

obedience Behavior that complies with the explicit demands of the individual in authority. *568*

object permanence Piaget's concept for the infant's ability to understand that objects and events still exist even though the infant is not in direct contact with them. *294*

observational learning Also called imitation or modeling, this form of learning occurs when an individual observes someone else's behavior. *172*

obsessions Anxiety-provoking thoughts that will not go away. *484*

obsessive-compulsive disorders Disorders that involve recurrent obsessions (anxiety-provoking thoughts that won't go away) or compulsions (repetitive, ritualistic behaviors the individual performs in a stereotyped way). *484*

occipital lobe One of the four lobes of the brain; involved in vision. *69*

Oedipus complex A condition that exists when a young child develops an intense desire to replace the parent of the same sex and enjoy the affections of the opposite-sexed parent. *442*

olfactory epithelium Tissue containing the receptors for smell, located at the forward base of the cerebral hemispheres. *104*

operant conditioning A form of learning in which the consequences of behavior lead to changes in the probability of that behavior's occurrence; the form of learning stressed by Skinner. *163*

operants Responses that are actively emitted because of the consequences for the organism. *163*

operations Mental representations that are reversible; a Piagetian concept. *302*

opiates Drugs that consist of opium and its derivatives; they are depressants. *142*

opponent-process theory The theory of color vision that the visual system treats certain pairs of colors—such as red-green and yellow-blue—as opposites or antagonists. *96*

opponent-process theory Solomon's view that every emotion has a primary and secondary process. The secondary process is the central nervous system's reaction to the primary process in the autonomic nervous system. The secondary process reduces the intensity of the emotion and increases equilibrium. With repeated stimulations, the secondary process strengthens. *406*

optic chiasma The point at which about two-thirds of the optic nerve's fibers cross over to the opposite side of the cerebral cortex. *92*

optic nerve The nerve that leads out of the eye toward the brain, carrying information about light. *92*

oral stage Freud's first stage of development, corresponding approximately to the first year of life; pleasure focuses on the mouth. *441*

organ of Corti A structure that runs the entire length of the cochlea; contains the ear's sensory receptors. *101*

organic retardation Mental retardation that is due to some organic factor, such as genetic or brain damage; *organic* refers to the tissues or organs of the body, so there is some physical damage that causes organic retardation. *271*

orgasm The third phase in the human sexual response cycle; an explosive discharge of neuromuscular tension and an intense pleasurable feeling occur. *380*

original sin A philosophical view that children are inherently bad—only through the constraints of parenting or salvation will they become competent adults. *280*

osmoreceptors Nerve cells located in a small area of the hypothalamus that monitor the saltiness of the blood; when the blood is too salty, they cause ADH to be released. The receptors also can signal the brain, causing thirst. *375*

outer ear A structure consisting of the pinna and external auditory canal that collects sound. *106*

panic disorder A condition whose main features are recurrent panic attacks marked by the sudden onset of intense apprehension or terror. *482*

papillae Rounded bumps on the tongue that contain taste buds, the basic receptors of taste. *104*

parallel distributed processing A very recent network view of information processing arguing that it is not the units of information themselves that hold the key to understanding information processing, but rather the strengths or weights of the connections between units. This view states that activation spreads in parallel fashion—that is, simultaneously—over a wide range of connections. *193*

paranoid schizophrenia A severe mental disorder whose central theme is delusions. *495*

paraphilias A set of psychosexual disorders in which the source of the individual's sexual arousal is bizarre. *500*

paraprofessionals Volunteers trained to work with mentally disturbed individuals. *530*

parasympathetic division The part of the autonomic nervous system involved when various parts of the body slow down. *49*

parietal lobe One of the four lobes of the brain; involved in body sensation. *69*

partial reinforcement Also called intermittent reinforcement; the organism's responses are only reinforced occasionally, not each time they occur. *166*

pedophilia A psychosexual disorder in which the individual obtains sexual gratification by covertly or overtly masturbating while talking to children, manipulating the child's sex organs, or engaging the child in sexual behavior. *501*

perception The process of organizing and interpreting sensory information. *83*

peripheral nervous system A network of nerves that connects the brain and spinal cord to other parts of the body. *49*

permissive-indifferent parenting A parenting style in which the parent is very uninvolved with the child; associated with social incompetence on the part of the child, especially a lack of self-control. *307*

permissive-indulgent parenting A parenting style in which parents are involved with their children but place few demands or limits on the children; associated with a lack of self-control on the part of children. *307*

personal fable A story or fable that the adolescent may make up to protect his sense of uniqueness and indestructibility. *327*

personal growth groups Groups developed to work with individuals whose lives are lacking in intimacy, intensity, and accomplishment. *527*

personality Enduring, consistent thoughts, emotions, and behaviors that characterize the way we adapt to the world. *435*

personality disorders Disorders that develop when personality traits become inflexible and maladaptive. *499*

personality psychology A branch of psychology that focuses on the relatively enduring traits and characteristics of individuals. *33*

person-centered therapy Developed by Carl Rogers, therapy that focuses on the experiences of the individual at the moment and emphasizes that each individual has the ability to improve. *514*

phallic stage Freud's third stage, corresponding to the preschool years; pleasure focuses on the genitals. *441*

phenomenological approach An approach that emphasizes our subjective, personal perception of the world and ourselves. *12*

phenomenological approach The view that stresses the importance of our perceptions of ourselves and our world in understanding personality; reality is what is perceived. *12*

pheromones Odorous substances released by animals that serve as powerful attractants for potential mates. *377*

phobias Irrational fears. *158*

phobic disorders Commonly called phobias, these consist of an overwhelming fear of a particular object or situation. *483*

phonology The study of the sound system of language. *229*

phrenology The view, developed by Franz Joseph Gall in the 19th century, that behavior can be predicted by evaluating the bumps on an individual's skull. *48*

pineal gland A gland centrally located in the brain just below where the two sides of the brain are located; it may work together with other structures and neurotransmitters to play a role in seasonal depression. *58*

pitch The ear's detection of the sound wave's frequency. *99*

pituitary gland An important endocrine gland that sits at the base of the skull; the anterior part is known as the master gland because its hormones direct the activity of glands in other parts of the body. *77*

place theory The theory that each frequency produces vibrations at a particular spot on the basilar membrane. *101*

plateau phase The second phase in the human sexual response cycle; a continuation and heightening of arousal occurs. *378*

pleasure principle Always seeking pleasure and avoiding pain; the way the id works. *437*

polygraph Known as the lie detector; a machine that monitors changes in the body that are thought to be influenced by emotional states. The body states assessed are heart rate, breathing, and electrodermal response. *404*

population In statistics the total number of people, things, or events about which we wish to generalize. *613*

positive reinforcement The frequency of a response increases because it is followed by a pleasant stimulus. *164*

postconventional level The highest level of morality in Kohlberg's theory—moral development is completely internalized. The individual has reasoned through a number of alternatives and arrived at an individualized form of morality. *332*

posthypnotic amnesia Occurs when you are told to forget everything that went on while you were in the hypnotic state, and you do. *133*

posthypnotic suggestion Occurs when the individual carries out suggestions offered to her while hypnotized *after* she emerges from the hypnotic state. *133*

pragmatics A set of language rules pertaining to the ability to engage in appropriate conversation *230*

precognition The perception of events before they occur. *114*

preconventional level Kohlberg's first main level of moral development; moral development at this level is not internalized; the individual only responds according to rewards and punishments. *332*

predictive validity An indicator of how a test's scores relate to an individual's performance at some point in the future. *246*

prejudice An unjustified negative attitude toward an individual because of the individual's membership in a group. *600*

preoperational stage A stage at which a child develops stronger symbolic representations of the world, but still cannot perform operations; a Piagetian stage corresponding approximately to the two-to-seven age period. *302*

preparedness The degree to which an organism is biologically ready to learn in a given situation. *179*

primacy effect The enduring quality of initial impressions. *560*

primary and secondary reinforcement Inborn, unlearned aspects of behavior involve primary reinforcement; learned aspects of behavior involve secondary reinforcement. Food is a primary reinforcer, and a pat on the back is a secondary reinforcer. *166*

primary emotions Plutchik's description of emotions as being like colors; if mixed, certain emotions can form all other emotions. He believes the primary emotions are happiness, disgust, surprise, sadness, anger, and fear. *400*

proactive interference Occurs when material that was learned earlier interferes with the recall of material learned later. *198*

problem-focused coping Lazarus's description of an approach in which an individual faces his problems and tries to solve them. *419*

problem solving An attempt to find an appropriate way of attaining a goal when the goal is not readily available. *218*

procedural knowledge A form of memory that consists of skills, about which it is difficult, if not impossible, to verbally communicate; knowing *how*. *189*

projection A defense mechanism by which we attribute our own shortcomings, problems, and faults to others. *439*

projective test A test that presents the individual with an ambiguous stimulus and then asks him to describe what it is or tell a story about it. *462*

prototype An abstract characterization of the traits that describe a particular personality type. *559*

prototype matching A process by which we decide if an item belongs to a particular concept by comparing the item to a prototype, or the best representative of the concept. *217*

psychiatry A branch of medicine practiced by physicians with a doctor of medicine (M.D.) degree who subsequently specialize in abnormal behavior and therapy. *32*

psychoactive substances Drugs that alter our perception or mood. *140*

psychoanalysis Freud's method in which the patient recaptures forgotten, repressed memories. *436*

psychoanalytic approach The view of psychology that emphasizes the unconscious aspects of mind, conflict between biological conflicts and society's demands, and early childhood experiences; developed by Freud. *11*

psychodynamic therapies Therapies that stress the importance of the unconscious mind, the role of the past, and extensive interpretation by the therapist; many of these therapies grew out of Freud's psychoanalytic theory. *511*

psychogenic amnesia A dissociative disorder involving memory loss that is caused by extensive psychological stress. *486*

psychology The scientific study of mind and behavior. *7*

psychometrics The field that involves the assessment of individual differences; involves the use of paper-and-pencil tests. *245*

psychoneuroimmunology The field that explores connections between psychological factors—such as emotions and attitudes—and the nervous and immune systems. *413*

psychosexual disorders Sexual problems that are mainly caused by psychological factors. *500*

psychosexual dysfunctions A set of psychosexual disorders in which inhibitions in the sexual response cycle occur. *500*

psychosurgery An extreme biomedical treatment that involves the removal or destruction of brain tissue to improve the individual's adjustment. *538*

psychotherapy The process mental health professionals use to work with individuals to reduce their problems and to improve their adjustment. *510*

psychotic A term to describe severe mental disorders in which the individual has lost contact with reality. *478*

puberty A rapid change to maturation that occurs primarily in early adolescence; includes sexual maturation and height and weight spurts. *323*

punishment A consequence that decreases the probability that a behavior will occur. *163*

pupil The opening in the center of the iris, which appears black; its primary function is to maintain optimal light intensity. *90*

questionnaire Similar to a highly structured interview, except the respondent reads the question and marks an answer on paper. *21*

random assignment Assignment of subjects in an experiment to groups in such a manner that each individual has the same probability as any other of being assigned to a particular group. Reduces the likelihood that the results of the experiment will be due to some preexisting differences in the groups. *25*

random sample A sample in which every member of a population or group has an equal chance of being selected. *21, 614*

range The difference between the highest and lowest scores in a set of data. *611*

rape A psychosexual disturbance in which the individual obtains sexual gratification through force with an unwilling partner. *502*

rational emotive therapy Therapy based on the idea that individuals become psychologically disturbed because of their beliefs, especially those that are irrational and self-defeating; developed by Albert Ellis. *522*

rationalization A defense mechanism by which the real motive for an individual's behavior is not accepted by the ego; the real motive is replaced by a sort of cover motive. *439*

reaction formation A defense mechanism by which we express an unacceptable impulse by transforming it into its opposite. *439*

reality principle The way the ego operates; takes into account the constraints and demands of reality. *438*

reasoning Drawing conclusions from facts. *225*

reciprocal socialization The view that socialization is a bidirectional process; children socialize parents just as parents socialize children. *308*

regression A defense mechanism by which we behave in a way that characterized a previous developmental level. *439*

rehearsal Repeating information that already is in short-term memory so that we can keep the information longer. *188*

reinforcement (reward) A consequence that increases the probability that a behavior will occur. *163*

reliability An attribute of a test that is based on how consistently an individual performs on the test. *245*

REM sleep REM stands for rapid eye movement; during REM sleep, when an EEG shows a pattern of fast waves similar to wakefulness, the eyeballs move up and down. Dreaming is more common during REM sleep than during other sleep stages. *123*

repair theory A theory that sleep serves to restore, replenish, and rebuild our brains and bodies, which have somehow been worn out or used up by the day's waking activity. *126*

repisodic memory A description of memory based on the observation that many of our recollections are not of a single event, but rather of a series of repeated experiences. *204*

representativeness heuristic A strategy by which we make estimates based on how well something matches a prototype, that is, the most common example. *221*

repression   The most powerful and pervasive defense mechanism, according to Freud; it works to push unacceptable id impulses out of awareness and back into our unconscious mind.   *438*

resistance   The patient's use of unconscious defense strategies to keep the therapist from discovering the patient's problems.   *512*

resolution phase   The final phase in the human sexual response cycle; arousal diminishes.   *380*

resting potential   The electrical imbalance that occurs across the cell membrane when a cell becomes polarized.   *53*

reticular formation   A diffuse collection of neurons involved in stereotyped patterns of behavior such as walking, sleeping, or turning to a sudden noise.   *64*

retina   The very important light-sensitive mechanism in the back of the eye that records images, much like the film in a camera.   *90*

retroactive interference   Occurs when material that was learned later interferes with material that was learned earlier.   *198*

retrograde amnesia   A memory disorder that involves memory loss for a segment of the past, not new events.   *202*

rods   Light-sensitive cells in the retina that give us black-and-white vision in poorly lit conditions.   *90*

roles   Rules that govern only certain positions in a group.   *595*

romantic love   Also called Eros, the type of love involving passion and what we mean when we say we are "in love" with someone.   *590*

Rorschach Inkblot Test   Projective personality test developed by Hermann Rorschach; consists of ten cards with inkblots on them. The individual tells the examiner what she sees in the blots, and it is hoped, reveals aspects of her personality in the process.   *462*

sadism   A psychosexual disorder in which the individual obtains sexual gratification by giving pain.   *501*

sample   Any group selected for study from a population.   *613*

satire   Irony, wit, or derision used to expose folly or wickedness; adolescents use and understand satire more than children do.   *328*

saturation   The dimension of color based on purity.   *93*

scatter plot   A graph that shows how two variables or measures are correlated. Each dot represents two scores, one from each distribution. The resulting pattern of dots indicates the correlation that exists.   *617*

schedules of reinforcement   Rules governing partial reinforcement that determine the occasion when a response will be reinforced.   *166*

schemata   The existing set of information we have about various concepts, events, and knowledge.   *202*

schizophrenic disorders   Severe mental disturbances characterized by distorted thoughts and perceptions, odd communication, inappropriate emotion, abnormal motor behavior, and social withdrawal.   *494*

school and educational psychology   A branch of psychology that is concerned with children's learning and adjustment in school.   *33*

scientific method   Method used to collect accurate information about mind and behavior. It includes these steps: identify and analyze the problem, collect data, draw conclusions, and revise theories.   *17*

sclera   The white part of the eye that helps to maintain the eye's shape and to protect it from injury.   *89*

scripts   Schemata for events.   *203*

secure or insecure attachment   Ainsworth's terms for individual differences in attachment. The securely attached infant uses the caregiver as a base to explore the world; the insecurely attached infant avoids the caregiver or is ambivalent toward her.   *298*

selective attention   The ability to focus and concentrate on a narrow band of information.   *190*

self-actualization   Maslow's term that represents the highest level of motivation; involves everything we are capable of being.   *365*

self-efficacy   Bandura's concept; the belief that one can master a situation and produce positive outcomes.   *519*

self-instructional methods   Techniques in behavior therapy that emphasize the therapist's ability to change what clients say to themselves.   *520*

self-monitoring   The extent to which we are aware of the impression we make on others and the degree to which we fine-tune our performance accordingly.   *561*

self-perception theory   Daryl Bem's view that we infer our attitudes by observing our own behavior and the circumstances in which it takes place.   *551*

self-report tests   Personality tests designed to assess your personality traits by asking you what those traits are.   *464*

self-serving bias   The tendency to make ourselves look better than we really are.   *560*

semantic memory   A form of memory that reflects our general knowledge about the world.   *189*

semantics   The meaning of words and sentences.   *230*

semicircular canals   An important part of the vestibular sense located in the middle ear.   *105*

sensation   The process of detecting and encoding stimulus energy in the world.   *83*

sensorimotor stage   The Piagetian stage lasting from birth to about two years of age; the infant constructs an understanding of the world by coordinating sensory experiences with physical, motoric actions.   *293*

sensory adaptation   A weakened response to stimulus energy that develops when the stimulus occurs repeatedly.   *87*

sensory registers   A form of memory in which stimuli are registered for not much longer than the brief time we are exposed to them.   *185*

serial-position effect   The combination of superior memory for the beginning of a list of items (primacy effect) and for the end of the list (recency effect).   *188*

serotonin   A neurotransmitter that is involved in the regulation of sleep and may also play a role in depression.   *57*

set point   The weight maintained when no effort is made to gain or lose weight.   *368*

shaping   The process of rewarding approximations of desired behavior.   *165*

short-term memory   The retention of recently encountered information or information retrieved from long-term memory for a brief period of time, usually about fifteen to thirty seconds.   *186*

signal-detection theory   The view that detecting sensory stimuli is due to more than just the properties of the stimuli and the sensory system; psychological factors such as motivation are involved too.   *85*

significant   A term used to describe real differences between groups or samples—that is, differences that are not simply due to chance factors.   *615*

situationism   The view that personality varies extensively from one context to another; associated with behaviorism and social learning theory.   *459*

size constancy   Recognition that an object is the same size even though the retinal image of the object changes.   *111*

sleep apnea   A sleep disorder in which the individual stops breathing while he is asleep because the windpipe fails to open or brain processes involved in respiration do not work properly.   *128*

social comparison   The process by which we evaluate ourselves vis-à-vis others.   *560*

social desirability   A response set in which the individual answers according to what he thinks the examiner wants to hear or in a way that makes the individual look better.   *464*

social exchange theory A theory that describes altruism in terms of costs and benefits; individuals should benefit those who benefit them, or for a benefit received, an equivalent benefit should be returned. *583*

social facilitation A phenomenon that occurs when an individual's performance improves because of the presence of others. *596*

social identity theory Tajfel's view that when individuals are assigned to a group they invariably, almost reflexively, think of the group as an in-group for them and view this group as better than the out-group. *600*

social learning theory An approach to psychology with behavioral ties that emphasizes how our thoughts modify the impact of environment on behavior. *10*

social loafing The effect of lowered performance in a group because of reduced monitoring. *596*

social perception Our judgments about the qualities of individuals. *558*

social psychology A branch of psychology that deals with people's social interactions, relationships, perceptions, and attitudes. *33, 547*

sociobiology A contemporary view emphasizing that all behavior is motivated by the desire to contribute one's genetic heritage to the greatest number of descendents. *45*

somatic nervous system A division of the peripheral nervous system that consists of sensory and motor nerves. *49*

somatoform disorders Mental disturbances in which the psychological symptoms take a physical, or *somatic*, form, even though no physical causes can be found. *484*

somatotype theory Sheldon's theory that precise charts of an individual's body reveal distinct body types, which in turn are associated with certain personality types. *457*

S-O-R model Stands for S (stimulus), O (organism), and R (response); emphasizes that characteristics of the organism or individual, such as cognitive factors, mediate the relation of stimuli to responses. *174*

source traits Cattell's term for the thirty basic personality traits he consistently discovered when he assessed large numbers of individuals *458*

special-process view The view that hypnotic behavior is qualitatively different from non-hypnotic behavior. Hypnotic responses are viewed as involuntary; dissociations among cognitive systems take place and amnesic barriers are formed. *134*

split-half reliability Reliability that is assessed by comparing an individual's performance on two halves of the same test. *246*

spontaneous recovery The process by which the conditioned response can recur without further conditioning. *156*

S-R theory A label given to Thorndike's view that the organism's behavior is due to a connection between a stimulus and a response. *162*

standard deviation A measure of variation that summarizes the difference between each score and the mean; an indicator of how widely scores are dispersed around the mean. *611*

standardization Development of uniform procedures for giving and scoring a test; giving test items to a large group representative of the population for whom the test is intended; allowing the test constructor to determine the distribution of test scores. *247*

standardized tests Measures that require individuals to answer a series of written or oral questions; the person's answers usually are totaled to yield a single score, and this score is compared to the scores of a large group of similar people. *22*

state-dependent memory A view of memory that the states or internal conditions present when information is encoded are important cues for retrieving information. *198*

statistical approach A theory of abnormality that defines abnormal behavior as that which deviates substantially from the average. *473*

stereotype A generalization about a group's characteristics that does not take individual variation into account. *600*

stimulants Drugs that increase central nervous system activity. *142*

stimulus substitution Pavlov's view of the way classical conditioning works; the nervous system is structured so that the conditioned stimulus and the unconditioned stimulus bond together and eventually the CS substitutes for the UCS. *156*

storm and stress view G. Stanley Hall's perspective that adolescence is a turbulent time, filled with anxiety and stress. *321*

stream of consciousness A continuous flow of changing sensations, images, thoughts, and feelings; described by William James. *121*

stroboscopic motion The illusion of movement created when a rapid stimulation of different parts of the retina occurs. *110*

structuralism An early approach to psychology that emphasized the study of the mind's structures. *8*

structure-process dilemma The basic issue of what the mechanisms of intelligence are and how they develop: whether by expanding information processing abilities (process), growing knowledge and expertise (structure), or both. *266*

subconscious level Level of mental functioning beneath the level of awareness. *121*

subgoaling A strategy for solving problems that involves striving to reach a number of smaller goals along the way to one overarching goal. *220*

sublimation A defense mechanism by which a socially useful course of action replaces a distasteful one. *439*

subliminal perception The perception of stimuli below the threshold of awareness. *85*

substance-use disorder A disorder characterized by a pattern of frequent drug intoxication, impairment of social or occupational functioning due to drug use, or physical dependence on drugs. *502*

subtractive mixture A mixture of pigments. Each pigment absorbs (subtracts) some of the light falling on it and reflects the rest. *94*

superego The moral branch of personality, according to Freud; much like our "conscience." *438*

surface structure The actual order of words spoken in a sentence. *229*

syllogism A form of reasoning that involves a major premise, a minor premise, and a conclusion. *226*

sympathetic division The part of the autonomic nervous system involved when the organism is aroused. *49*

synapses Very small gaps that separate neurons from each other. *54*

syntax The way words are combined to form acceptable phrases and sentences. *229*

systematic desensitization A variation of counterconditioning that has become popular in treating fears and other emotional problems; involves using imagery of fearful stimuli while inducing relaxation. *159, 517*

tabula rasa A philosophical view that children are like a "blank tablet" when they are born—experiences determine whether a child is good or bad, competent or incompetent. *281*

tardive dyskinesia A major side effect of the neuroleptic drugs; a neurological disorder involving grotesque, involuntary movements of the facial muscles and mouth as well as extensive twitching of the neck, arms, and legs. *535*

telegraphic speech The use of short and precise words, much like a telegram, to communicate; characteristic of young children's two-word utterances. *237*

telepathy The transfer of thought between two individuals who are in rapport. *114*

temporal lobe One of the four lobes of the brain; involved in hearing. *69*

teratogen Any agent that causes a birth defect. *286*

testosterone A hormone associated with the development of external genitals, increase in height, and voice change in boys during puberty. *323*

test-retest reliability Reliability that is assessed by giving an individual the same test on two different occasions. *245*

thalamus A structure in the forebrain that is an important relay station for information. *66*

Thematic Apperception Test (TAT) A projective technique developed by Henry Murray in which the individual tells stories about pictures shown on cards. *463*

theories General beliefs that help us to explain data or facts and make predictions. *17*

thinking The manipulation and transformation of information in memory that involves such processes as concept formation, problem solving, and reasoning. *214*

timbre The perception of a sound's complexity. *99*

token economy A technique in behavior therapy in which the individual earns tokens that can be exchanged later for desired rewards. *519*

tolerance A condition that occurs when a drug user needs a greater amount of the drug to produce the same effect as before. *141*

trait theories Theories stressing that personality is best understood by studying the organization of traits within the individual; traits are considered to be consistent across situations and stable over time. *458*

transactional analysis group A type of personal growth group that emphasizes the transactions individuals perform within themselves and with others; each individual is described in terms of "parent," "adult," and "child" personality structures. *528*

transcendental meditation The most popular form of meditation in the United States, derived from an ancient Indian technique; involves use of a mantra, which has a special meaning. *137*

transference A process in Freud's therapy in which the patient relates to the therapist in ways that reproduce or relive important relationships in the patient's life. *512*

transsexual An individual with a psychosexual disorder who wants to be a member of the opposite sex. *501*

transvestite An individual with a psychosexual disorder who throughout his or her life shows a compulsive need to impersonate the other sex by dressing like them. *500*

triarchic theory of intelligence Sternberg's view that intelligence consists of three dimensions: componential intelligence, experiential intelligence, and practical intelligence. *268*

trust versus mistrust Erikson's first stage of development, corresponding approximately to the first year of life; in this bipolar conflict, the infant develops either a trust in herself and the world or a sense of mistrust. *298*

twin study A technique used to study the effects of heredity on behavior; usually the comparison is between identical and fraternal twins, the latter being more genetically dissimilar. *45*

two-factor theory Spearman's view that we have both general intelligence and a number of specific intelligences. *254*

Type-A behavior pattern A cluster of characteristics—excessively competitive, an accelerated pace of ordinary activities, impatience, thinking about doing several things at once, hostility, and an inability to hide the fact that life is a struggle—thought to be related to the incidence of heart disease. *421*

unconditional positive regard Rogers's term for how we should behave toward someone to increase their self-worth; positive behavior shown toward an individual with no contingencies attached. *452*

unconditioned response (UCR) A reflexive response produced by a stimulus in the absence of learning; a classical conditioning term. *154*

unconditioned stimulus (UCS) A stimulus that causes reflexive or unlearned behavior; a term used in classical conditioning. *154*

unconscious Freud's term for thoughts shoved far beneath our level of awareness. *121*

undifferentiated schizophrenia A severe mental disorder that features disorganized behavior, hallucinations, delusions, and incoherence; this category is used when the criteria for other types of schizophrenia are not met or the individual meets the criteria for more than one of the other types. *495*

validity The extent to which a test measures what it is intended to measure. *246*

ventromedial hypothalamus (VMH) A region of the hypothalamus that is important in determining hunger; when a rat is given a brain lesion here, it immediately becomes hyperphagic and rapidly becomes obese. *368*

vestibular sense The sense that provides information about balance and movement. *105*

visual illusion An illusion that occurs when two objects produce exactly the same retinal image but are perceived as different images. *112*

volley theory A modification and expansion of frequency theory to account for high-frequency sounds; stresses that neurons fire in sequence of rhythmic volleys at higher frequencies. *101*

voyeurism A psychosexual disorder in which the individual obtains sexual gratification by watching a member of the opposite sex undress or engage in sexual behavior. *501*

Weber's law Weber's observation that the difference threshold is a constant porportion rather than a constant amount, with the exact proportion varying with the stimulus involved. *87*

Wechsler scales Individual intelligence tests developed by David Wechsler; they provide information not only about overall intelligence, but about nonverbal and verbal intelligence as well. *251*

Whorf/Sapir hypothesis States that the more vocabulary or categories we recognize, the more our perceptions will be differentiated. *239*

withdrawal Highly unpleasant body effects that result from ceasing to take a drug any longer; the unpleasant effects can involve intense pain and cravings for the drug. *141*

Yerkes-Dodson law The theory that performance is best under conditions of moderate rather than low or high arousal. *402*

Young-Helmholtz trichromatic theory The theory of color vision that there are three types of color receptors in the eye for detecting all colors; the colors are red, blue, and green. *94*

zygote The fertilized egg that receives one-half of its chromosomes from its mother, one-half from its father. *283*

References

Acredolo, L. P. (1978). Development of spatial orientation in infancy. *Developmental Psychology, 14,* 224–234.

Adam, K. (1980). Sleep as a restorative process and a theory to explain why. *Progress in Brain Research, 53,* 239–305.

Adams, G. M., & de Vries, H. A. (1973). Physiological effects of an exercise training regimen among women aged 52 to 79. *Journal of Gerontology, 28,* 50–55.

Adams, G. R., & Lavoie, J. C. (1974). The effect of sex of child, conduct, and facial attractiveness of teacher expectancy. *Education, 95,* 76–83.

Adelson, J. (1979, January). Adolescence and the generalization gap. *Psychology Today,* pp. 33–37.

Adelson, J. (Ed.). (1980). *Handbook of adolescent psychology.* New York: Wiley.

Adler, A. (1927). *Practice and theory of individual psychology.* New York: Harcourt Brace Jovanovich.

Adler, A. (1958). *What life should mean to you.* New York: Capricorn.

Adler, R. P., Lesser, G. S., Meringoff, L. K., & Robertson, T. S. (1980). *The effects of television advertising on children.* Lexington, MA: D. C. Heath.

Agnew, N. McK., & Pyke, S. W. (1987). *The science game* (4th ed.). Englewood Cliffs, NJ: Prentice-Hall.

Ainsworth, M. D. S. (1967). *Infancy in Uganda: Infant care and the growth of love.* Baltimore: Johns Hopkins University Press.

Ainsworth, M. D. S. (1979). Infant-mother attachment. *American Psychologist, 34,* 932–937.

Akers, C. (1984). Methodological criticisms of parapsychology. In S. Krippner (Ed.), *Advances in parapsychological research* (Vol. 4). Jefferson, NC: McFarland.

Akers, C. (1986). Has parapsychology found its basic experiments? *Contemporary Psychology, 31,* 180–181.

Alan Guttmacher Institute. (1976). *Eleven million teenagers: What can be done about the epidemic of adolescent pregnancies in the United States?* New York: Planned Parenthood Federation of America.

Alexander, D. (1987, April). *High interest areas in child development for the NICHD in the NIH centennial year.* Paper presented at the biennial meeting of the Society for Research in Child Development, Baltimore.

Allison, T., & Chichetti, D. (1976). Sleep in mammals: Ecological and constitutional correlates. *Science, 194,* 732–734.

Allport, G. W. (1937). *Personality: A psychological interpretation.* New York: Holt.

Amoore, J. E. (1970). *Molecular basis of odor.* Springfield, IL: Thomas.

Amoroso, D. M., Brown, M., Prusesse, M., Ware, E. E., & Pilkey, D. W. (1971). An investigation of behavioral, psychological, and physiological reactions to pornographic stimuli. In *Technical Report of the Commission on Obscenity and Pornography* (Vol. 8). Washington, DC: U.S. Government Printing Office.

Amsterdam, B. K. (1968). *Mirror behavior in children under two years of age.* Unpublished doctoral dissertation, University of North Carolina, Chapel Hill.

Anastasi, A. (1982). *Psychological testing* (5th ed.). New York: Macmillan.

Anastasi, A. (1988). *Psychological testing.* (6th ed). New York: Macmillan.

Ancoli-Israel, S. (1981). Sleep apnea and nocturnal myoclonus in a senior population. *Sleep, 4,* 349–358.

Anderson, C. (1987). Temperature and aggression: Effects of quarterly, yearly, and city rates of violent and nonviolent crime. *Journal of Personality and Social Psychology, 52,* 1161–1173.

Anderson, J. R. (1983). *The architecture of cognition.* Cambridge, MA: Harvard University Press.

Anderson, J. R. (1985). *Cognitive psychology.* New York: W. H. Freeman.

Anderson, J. R. (1987, June). *A rational analysis of human memory.* Paper presented at the Symposium on Varieties of Memory and Consciousness. Papers in honour of Endel Tulving. University of Toronto.

Anderson, J. R., & Ross, B. H. (1980). Evidence against a semantic-episodic distinction. *Journal of Experimental Psychology: Human Learning and Memory, 6,* 441–465.

Anderson, N. H. (1959). Test of a model of opinion change. *Journal of Abnormal and Social Psychology, 59,* 371–381.

Anderson, N. H. (1965). Primacy effects in personality impression formation using a generalized order effect paradigm. *Journal of Personality and Social Psychology, 2,* 1–9.

Anderson, N. H. (1974). Cognitive algebra: Integration theory applied to social attribution. In L. Berkowitz (Ed.), *Advances in experimental social psychology* (Vol. 7). New York: Academic Press.

Antonovsky, A. (1987). *Unraveling the Mystery of Health.* San Francisco: Jossey-Bass.

Archer, D., & Gartner, R. (1976). Violent acts and violent times: A comparative approach to postwar homicide. *American Sociological Review, 41,* 937–963.

Arlow, J. A. (1979). Psychoanalysis. In R. J. Corsini (Ed.), *Current psychotherapies.* Itasca, IL: Peacock.

Aronson, E. (1984). *The social animal* (4th ed.). New York: W. H. Freeman.

Aronson, E. (1986, August). *Teaching students things they think they already know all about: The case of prejudice and desegregation.* Paper presented at the meeting of the American Psychological Association, Washington, DC.

Aronson, E. (1987, August). *The long view.* Paper presented at the meeting of the American Psychological Association, New York.

Asch, S. E. (1946). Forming impressions of personality. *Journal of Abnormal and Social Psychology, 41,* 258–290.

Asch, S. E. (1951). Effects of group pressure on the modification and distortion of judgments. In H. S. Guetzkow (Ed.), *Groups, leadership and men.* Pittsburgh: Carnegie University Press.

Asch, S. E., & Zukier, H. (1984). Thinking about persons. *Journal of Personality and Social Psychology, 46,* 1230–1240.

Asher, J., & Garcia, R. (1969). The optimal age to learn a foreign language. *Modern Language Journal, 53,* 334–341.

Aslin, R. N. (in press). *Perceptual Development, Annual Review of Psychology, 39.*

Atkinson, J. W., & Raynor, I. O. (1974). *Motivation and achievement.* Washington, DC: V. H. Winston & Sons.

Auerback, A. H., & Childress, A. R. (1987). The value of DSM-III for psychotherapy. A feasibility study. *Journal of Nervous and Mental Disease, 175,* 138–142.

Auerback, K. (1987, April). *Breastfeeding and attachment in employed mothers.* Paper presented at the biennial meeting of the Society for Research in Child Development, Baltimore.

Axel, R. A. (1979, August). *Self-disclosing behavior: Gender and sex-role factors.* Paper presented at the meeting of the American Psychological Association, New York.

Axsom, D., Yates, S., & Chaiken, S. (1987). Audience response as a heuristic cue in persuasion. *Journal of Personality and Social Psychology, 53,* 30–40.

Bach, G. R. (1966). The marathon group: Intensive practice of intimate interactions. *Psychological Reports, 18,* 995–1002.

Bachman, J., O'Malley, P., & Johnson, J. (1978). *Youth in transition; Vol. VI. Adolescence to adulthood—change and stability of the lives of young men.* Institute for Social Research: University of Michigan.

Bahrke, M. S., & Morgan, W. P. (1978). Anxiety reduction following meditation and exercise. *Cognitive Therapy and Research, 2,* 323–333.

Bakeman, R., & Brown, J. V. (1980). Early interaction: Consequences for social and mental development at three years. *Child Development, 51,* 437–447.

Baker, A. G., Singh, M., & Bindra, D. (1985). Some effects of contextual conditioning and US predictability on Pavlovian conditioning. In P. D. Balsam & A. Tomie (Eds.), *Context and learning.* Hillsdale, NJ: Erlbaum.

Ballenger, J. C. (1986). Biological aspects of panic disorders. *American Journal of Psychiatry, 143,* 516–518.

Baltes, M. M., Orzech, M. J., Barton, E. M., & Lago, D. (1983). The microecology of residents and staff: Behavioral mapping in a nursing home. *Zeitschrift fur Gerontologie, 16,* 18–26.

Baltes, P. B. (1987, August). *Toward a theory of wisdom.* Paper presented at the meeting of the American Psychological Association, New York.

Baltes, P. B. (1987). Theoretical propositions of life-span developmental psychology: On the dynamics between growth and decline. *Developmental Psychology, 23,* 611–626.

Baltes, P. B., & Kliegl, R. (1986). On the dynamics between growth and decline in the aging of intelligence and memory. In K. Poeck, H. J. Freund, & H. Ganshirt (Eds.), *Neurology.* Berlin: Springer-Verlag.

Baltes, P. B., & Reese, H. W. (1984). The life-span perspective in developmental psychology. In M. H. Bornstein & M. E. Lamb (Eds.), *Developmental psychology: An advanced textbook.* Hillsdale, NJ: Erlbaum.

Bandura, A. (1965). Influence of models' reinforcement contingencies on the acquisition of imitative responses. *Journal of Personality and Social Psychology, 1,* 589–595.

Bandura, A. (1969). *Principles of behavior modification.* New York: Holt, Rinehart, & Winston.

Bandura, A. (1971). *Social learning theory.* New York: General Learning Press.

Bandura, A. (1973). *Aggression: A social learning analysis.* Englewood Cliffs, NJ: Prentice-Hall.

Bandura, A. (1977). *Social learning theory.* Englewood Cliffs, NJ: Prentice-Hall.

Bandura, A. (1986). *Social foundations of thought and action: A social cognitive theory.* Englewood Cliffs, NJ: Prentice-Hall.

Bandura, A., Blanchard, E. B., & Ritter, B. (1969). Relative efficacy of desensitization and modeling approaches for inducing behavioral, affective, and attitudinal changes. *Journal of Personality and Social Psychology, 13,* 173–199.

Banker, G. A. (1980). Trophic interactions between astroglial cells and hippocampal neurons in culture. *Science, 209,* 809–810.

Banks, M. S., & Salapatek, P. (1983). Infant visual perception. In P. H. Mussen (Ed.), *Handbook of child psychology* (Vol. 2). New York: John Wiley.

Barber, T. X., & Wilson, S. C. (1977). Hypnosis, suggestions, and altered states of consciousness: Experimental evaluation of a new cognitive-behavioral theory and the traditional trance-state theory of "hypnosis." *Annals of the New York Academy of Sciences, 296,* 34–47.

Bard, P. (1934). Emotion. In C. Murchison (Ed.), *Handbook of general experimental psychology.* Worcester, MA: Clark University Press.

Bardwick, J. (1971). *The psychology of women: A study of biocultural conflicts.* New York: Harper & Row.

Barefoot, J. C., Dahlstrom, G., & Williams, R. B. (1983). Hostility, CHD incidence, and total mortality: A 24-year follow-up study of 255 physicians. *Psychosomatic Medicine, 45,* 59–83.

Barlow, D. H., Blanchard, E. B., Vermilyea, J. A., Vermilyea, B. B., & Dinardo, P. A. (1986). Generalized anxiety and generalized anxiety disorder: Description and reconceptualization. *American Journal of Psychiatry, 143,* 40–44.

Barnard, E. A., & Darlison, M. G. (in press). Neurotransmitter-activated ionic channels. *Annual Review of Physiology, 50.*

Barnes, D. M. (1987). Defect in Alzheimer's is on Chromosome 21. *Science, 235,* 846–847.

Baron, J. B., & Sternberg, R. J. (Eds.). (1987). *Teaching thinking skills.* New York: W. H. Freeman.

Baron, R. A., & Byrne, D. (1987). *Social psychology* (5th ed.). Boston: Allyn & Bacon.

Baron, R. J. (in press). *The cerebral computer.* Hillsdale, NJ: Erlbaum.

Barsky, A. J., Wyshak, G., & Klerman, G. L. (1986). Hypochondriasis. *Archives of General Psychiatry, 43,* 493–500.

Bar-Tal, D., & Saxe, L. (1976). Perceptions of similarly and dissimilarly attractive couples and individuals. *Journal of Personality and Social Psychology, 33,* 772–781.

Bartlett, F. C. (1932). *Remembering.* Cambridge, England: Cambridge University Press.

Bartley, S. H. (1969). *Principles of perception.* New York: Harper & Row.

Batson, C. D. (in press). Prosocial motivation: Is it ever truly altruistic? In L. Berkowitz (Ed.), *Advances in experimental social psychology.* New York: Academic Press.

Batson, C. D., Bolen, M. H., Cross, J. A., & Jeuringer-Benefiel, H. E. (1986). Where is the altruism in the altruistic personality? *Journal of Personality and Social Psychology, 50,* 212–220.

Baudry, F. (1986). A dream, a sonnet, and a ballad: The path to Keats' La Belle Dame sans Merci. *Psychoanalytic Quarterly, 55,* 69–98.

Baum, A., Davidson, L. M., Singer, J. E., & Street, S. W. (in press). Stress as a psychophysiological process. In A. Baum & J. E. Singer (Eds.), *Stress.* Hillsdale NJ: Erlbaum.

Baumrind, D. (1971). Current patterns of parent authority. *Developmental Psychology Monographs, 4*(1, Pt. 2).

Beahrs, J. O. (1986). The "special-process" controversy: What is at issue? *Behavioral and Brain Sciences, 9,* 467–468.

Beck, A. (1976). Cognitive therapy and the emotional disorders. New York: International Universities Press.

Beck, A. T. (1967). *Depression.* New York: Harper and Row.

Beck, J., & Morgan, P. A. (1986). Designer drug confusion: A focus on MDMA. *Journal of Drug Education, 16,* 287–302.

Bednar, R. L., Burlingame, G. M., & Masters, K. S. (in press). Systems of family treatment. *Annual Review of Psychology.*

Bell, A. P., Weinberg, M. S., & Mammersmith, S. K. (1981). *Sexual preference: Its development in men and women.* New York: Simon & Schuster.

Bellack, A. S. (1986). Schizophrenia: Behavior therapy's forgotten child. *Behavior Therapy, 17,* 199–214.

Bellack, A. S., & Hersen, M. (Eds.). (1988). *Behavioral assessment.* Elmsford, NY: Pergamon.

Bellazza, F. S. (1981). Mnemonic devices: Classification, characteristics, and criteria. *Review of Educational Research, 51,* 247–275.

Belloc, N. B., & Breslow, L. (1972). Relationships of physical health status and health practices. *Preventive Medicine, 1,* 409–421.

Belsky, J. (1987, April). *Science, policy, and day care: A personal odyssey.* Paper presented at the biennial meeting of the Society for Research in Child Development, Baltimore.

Belsky, J. (1987, August). *Mother care, other care, and infant-parent attachment security.* Paper presented at the meeting of the American Psychological Association, New York.

Belsky, J. (in press). Nonmaternal care in the first year of life and infant-child security. *Child Development.*

Belsky, J., & Pensky, E. (1987). Developmental history, personality, and family relationships: Toward an emergent family system. In R. Hinde & J. Stevenson-Hinde (Eds.), *Towards understanding families.* London: Cambridge University Press.

Belson, W. (1978). *Television violence and the adolescent boy.* London: Saxon House.

Bem, D. J. (1967). Self-perception: An alternative interpretation of cognitive dissonance phenomena. *Psychological Review, 74,* 183–200.

Bem, S. L. (1977). On the utility of alternative procedures for assessing psychological androgyny. *Journal of Consulting and Clinical Psychology, 45,* 196–205.

Benet, S. (1976). *How to live to be 100.* New York: The Dial Press.

Bennett, W. I., & Gurin, J. (1982). *The dieter's dilemma: Eating less and weighing more.* New York: Basic Books.

Ben-Yehuda, N. (1980). The European witch craze. *American Journal of Sociology, 86,* 1–31.

Berkowitz, M. W., Mueller, C. W., Schnell, S. V., & Padberg, M. T. (1986). Moral reasoning and judgments of aggression. *Journal of Personality and Social Psychology, 51,* 885–891.

Berlyne, D. E. (1960). *Conflict, arousal, and curiosity.* New York: McGraw-Hill.

Berman, J. S., Miller, R. C., & Massman, P. J. (1985). Cognitive therapy versus systematic desensitization: Is one treatment superior? *Psychological Bulletin, 97,* 451–461.

Bernal, G., & Ysern, E. (1986). Family therapy and ideology. *Journal of Marital and Family Therapy, 12,* 129–136.

Berndt, T. J. (1979). Developmental changes in conformity to peers and parents. *Developmental Psychology, 15,* 608–616.

Berndt, T. J. (1982). The features and effects of friendship in early adolescence. *Child Development, 53,* 1447–1460.

Berne, E. (1972). *What do you say after you say hello?* New York: Grove Press.

Berren, M. R., & Santiago, J. M. (1987). An introduction to the special issue on systems aspects of chronic mental illness. *Community Mental Health Journal, 22,* 169.

Berscheid, E. (1983). Emotion. In H. H. Kelley, E. Berscheid, A. Christensen, J. Harvey, T. L. Huston, G. Levinger, E. McClintock, A. Peplau, & D. R. Peterson (Eds.), *Close relationships.* San Francisco: Freeman.

Berscheid, E. (1985). Interpersonal attraction. In G. Lindzey & E. Aronson (Eds.), *Handbook of social psychology* (3rd. ed., Vol. 2). New York: Random House.

Berscheid, E. (1987). Some comments on love's anatomy: Or, whatever happened to old-fashioned lust? In R. J. Sternberg & M. L. Barnes (Eds.), *Anatomy of love.* New Haven: Yale University Press.

Berscheid, E. (1987). Vocabularies of emotion. In B. S. Moore and A. M. Isen (Eds.), *The nature of emotion and stress.*

Berscheid, E., & Campbell, B. (1981). The changing longevity of heterosexual close relationships: A commentary and forecast. In M. Lerner (Ed.), *The justice motive in times of scarcity and change.* New York: Plenum.

Berscheid, E., & Fei, J. (1977). Sexual jealousy and romantic love. In G. Clinton & G. Smith (Eds.), *Sexual jealousy.* Englewood Cliffs, NJ: Prentice-Hall.

Berscheid, E., & Snyder, M. (in press). *The measurement of relationship closeness.* Minneapolis, MN: University of Minnesota.

Bertelson, A. (1979). A Danish twin study of manic-depressive disorders. In M. Schous & E. Stromgren (Eds.), *Origin, prevention, and treatment of affective disorders.* Orlando, FL: Academic Press.

Bertenthal, B. I. (1987). Emerging discontinuities in the Piagetian legacy. *Contemporary Psychology, 32,* 9–11.

Best, J. B. (1986). *Cognitive psychology.* St. Paul, MN: West.

Beveridge, M., & Parkins, E. (1987). Visual representation in analogical problems-solutions. *Memory and cognition, 15,* 230–237.

Bexton, W. H., Heron, W., & Scott, T. H. (1954). Effects of decreased variation in the sensory environment. *Canadian Journal of Psychology, 8,* 70–76.

Billings, A. G., Cronkite, R. C., & Moos, R. H. (1983). Social-environment factors in unipolar depression. *Journal of Abnormal Psychology, 92,* 119–133.

Bindra, I., & Palfai, T. (1967). Nature of positive and negative incentive motivational effects on general activity. *Journal of Comparative and Physiological Psychology, 63,* 288–297.

Blazer, D., et al. (1985). Psychiatric disorders: A rural-urban comparison. *Archives of General Psychiatry, 42,* 651–656.

Block, J. (1976). Issues, problems, and pitfalls in assessing sex differences: A critical review of the psychology of sex differences. *Merrill-Palmer Quarterly, 22,* 283–308.

Block, J. H., Block, J., & Gjerde, P. F. (1986). The personality of children prior to divorce: A prospective study. *Child Development, 57,* 827–840.

Bloom, B. S. (1983). *The development of exceptional talent.* Paper presented at biennial meeting of the Society for Research in Child Development, Detroit.

Bloom, F. E., Lazerson, A., & Hofstadter, L. (1985). *Brain, mind, and behavior.* New York: W. H. Freeman.

Bloor, C., & White, F. (1983). Unpublished manuscript. University of California at San Diego, La Jolla, CA.

Blumstein, P., & Schwartz, P. (1983). *American couples: Money, work, sex.* New York: Morrow.

Blundell, J. E. (1984). Systems and interactions: An approach to the pharmacology of feeding. In A. J. Stunkard & E. Stellar (Eds.), *Eating and its disorders.* New York: Raven Press.

Bluth, B. J., & Helppie, M. (1986). *Soviet space stations as analogs* (2nd ed.). Washington, DC: NASA.

Blyth, D. A., Bulcroft, R., & Simmons, R. G. (1981, August). *The impact of puberty on adolescents: A longitudinal study.* Paper presented at the annual meeting of the American Psychological Association, Los Angeles.

Bolles, R. C., & Beecher, M. D. (Eds.). (in press). *Evolution and learning.* Hillsdale, NJ: Erlbaum.

Bolter, J. D. (1984). *Turing's man.* Chapel Hill: University of North Carolina Press.

Bondareff, W. (1977). The neural basis of aging. In J. E. Birren & K. W. Schaie (Eds.), *Handbook of the psychology of aging.* New York: Van Nostrand Reinhold.

Boor, M. (1982). The multiple personality epidemic. *Journal of Nervous and Mental Disease, 170,* 302–304.

Boring, E. G. (1950). *A history of experimental psychology* (2nd ed.). New York: Appleton-Century-Crofts.

Bouchard, T. J., Heston, L., Eckert, E., Keyes, M., & Resnick, S. (1981). The Minnesota Study of Twins Reared Apart: Project description and sample results in the developmental domain. *Twin Research, 3,* 227–233.

Bourne, L. E., Dominowski, R., Loftus, E. F., & Healy, A. F. (1986). *Cognitive processes* (2nd ed.). Englewood Cliffs, NJ: Prentice-Hall.

Bouton, M. E., Jones, D. L., McPhillips, S. A., & Swartzentruber, D. (1986). Potentiation and overshadowing in odor-aversion learning: Role of method of odor presentation, the distal-proximal cue distinction, and the conditionability of odor. *Learning and Motivation, 17,* 115–138.

Bower, G. H., Clark, M., Winzenz, D., & Lesgold, A. (1969). Hierarchical retrieval schemes in recall of categorized word lists. *Journal of Verbal Learning and Verbal Behavior, 3,* 323–343.

Bowers, K. S., & Davidson, T. M. (1986). On the importance of individual differences in hypnotic ability. *Behavioral and Brain Sciences, 9,* 468–469.

Bowlby, J. (1958). The nature of the child's tie to his mother. *International Journal of Psychoanalysis, 39,* 35.

Bowlby, J. (1969). *Attachment and loss* (Vol. 1). London: Hogarth (New York: Basic Books).

Bowlby, J. (1980). *Attachment and loss: Vol. 3. Loss, sadness and depression.* New York: Basic Books.

Boynton, R. M. (in press). Color vision. *Annual Review of Psychology, 39.*

Bracken, B. A. (1985). A critical review of the Kaufman assessment battery for children (K-ABC). *School Psychology Review, 14,* 21–36.

Bransford, J. D., & Franks, J. J. (1971). Abstraction of linguistic ideas. *Cognitive Psychology, 2,* 331–350.

Bransford, J. D., Sherwood, R. D., & Sturdevant, T. (1987). Teaching thinking and problem solving. In J. B. Baron & R. J. Sternberg (Eds.), *Teaching thinking skills.* New York: W. H. Freeman.

Bransford, J. D., & Stein, B. S. (1984). *The ideal problem solver.* New York: W. H. Freeman.

Braude, M. C. (1986). Interactions of alcohol and drugs of abuse. *Psychopharmacology Bulletin, 22,* 717–721.

Brazelton, T. B. (1979). Behavioral competence of the newborn infant. *Seminars in Perinatology, 3,* 35–44.

Brazelton, T. B. (1987, August). *Opportunities for intervention with infants at risk.* Paper presented at the meeting of the American Psychological Association, New York.

Brean, H. (1958, March 31). What hidden sell is all about. *Life,* 104–114.

Breier, A., Charney, D. S., & Heninger, G. R. (1986). Agoraphobia with panic attacks. *Archives of General Psychiatry, 43,* 1029–1036.

Breland, K., & Breland, M. (1961). The misbehavior of organisms. *American Psychologist, 16,* 681–684.

Bremmer, J. G. (1985, April). *The role of active movement in the development of search in infancy.* Paper presented in the biennial meeting of the Society for Research in Child Development, Toronto.

Brenner, M., Brown, J., & Canter, D. (Eds.). (1985). *The research interview: Uses and approaches.* Orlando, FL: Academic Press.

Brickman, P., Coates, D., & Janoff-Bulman, R. J. (1978). Lottery winners and accident victims: Is happiness relative? *Journal of Personality and Social Psychology, 36,* 917–927.

Brickner, M. A., Harkins, S. G., & Ostrom, T. M. (1986). Effects of personal involvement: Thought-provoking implications for social loafing. *Journal of Personality and Social Psychology, 51,* 763–769.

Bridgeman, B. (1985). New approaches to neurobiology. *Contemporary Psychology, 30,* 956–958.

Briggs, J. L. (1970). *Never in anger.* Cambridge, MA: Harvard University Press.

Brigham, J. C. (1986). Race and eyewitness identifications. In S. Worschel & W. G. Austin (Eds.), *Psychology of intergroup relations.* Chicago: Nelson-Hall.

Brigham, J. C., Maas, A., Snyder, L. D., & Spaulding, K. (1982). Accuracy of eyewitness identification in a field setting. *Journal of Personality and Social Psychology, 41,* 683–691.

Brobeck, J. R., Tepperman, T., & Long, C. N. (1943). Experimental hypothalamic hyperphagia in the albino rat. *Yale Journal of Biological Medicine, 15,* 831–853.

Brody, J. E. (1980, October 14). Hypnotism is a powerful tool but vulnerable weapon in the fight against crime. *New York Times,* pp. 15, 17.

Broman, S. H., Bien, E. & Shaughnessy, P. (in press). *Retardation in young children.* Hillsdale, NJ: Erlbaum.

Brooks, J. (1985). Polygraph testing: Thoughts of a skeptical legislator. *American Psychologist, 40,* 348–354.

Brown, A. L., & Smiley, S. S. (1977). Rating the importance of structural units of prose passages: A problem of metacognitive development. *Child Development, 48,* 1–8.

Brown, B. B., & Lohr, M. J. (1987). Peer group affiliation and adolescent self-esteem: An integration of ego identity and symbolic interaction theories. *Journal of Personality and Social Psychology, 52* (1), 47–55.

Brown, N. R., Shevell, S. K., & Rips, L. J. (1986). Public memories and their personal context. In D. C. Rubin (Ed.), *Autobiographical memory.* New York: Cambridge University Press.

Brown, R. (1973). *A first language: The early stages.* Cambridge, MA: Harvard University Press.

Brown, R. (1986). *Social psychology* (2nd ed.). New York: Free Press.

Brown, R. (1987, August). *Evolution of the research: From risky-shift to group polarization.* Paper presented at the meeting of the American Psychological Association, New York.

Brown, R. (1988). Development of a first language in the human species. In M. B. Franklin & S. S. Barten (Eds.). *Child language: A reader.* New York: Oxford University Press.

Brown, R., & Kulik, J. (1977). Flashbulb memories. *Cognition, 5,* 73–99.

Brownstein, A. J. (in press). Overview: Progress in the experimental analysis and technology of behavior. In R. Epstein & P. Harzem (Eds.), *Progress in behavior studies.* Hillsdale, NJ: Erlbaum.

Bruch, H. (1973). *Eating disorders.* New York: Basic Books.

Bruner, J. S. (1964). The course of cognitive growth. *American Psychologist, 19,* 1–15.

Bruner, J. S., & Tagiuri, R. (1954). The perception of people. In G. Lindzey (Ed.), *Handbook of social psychology* (Vol. 2). Reading, MA: Addison-Wesley.

Bryant, B. (1985). The Neighborhood Walk: Sources of support in middle childhood. *Monographs of the Society for Research in Child Development, 50* (3, Serial No. 210).

Bryant, P. (1985, April). *Discussion of papers on problem solving and early cognitive development.* Paper presented at the biennial meeting of the Society for Research in Child Development, Toronto.

Buchsbaum, M. E. (1984, August). The Genain quadruplets. *Psychology Today,* pp. 46–51.

Bullock, A. (1969). *Hitler: A study in tyranny.* New York: Harper & Row.

Bureau of Labor Statistics. (1986). *Occupational outlook handbook.* Washington, DC: U.S. Government Printing Office.

Burgio, L. D., & Burgio, K. L. (1986). Behavioral gerontology: Application of behavioral methods to the problems of older adults. *Journal of Applied Behavior Analysis, 19*, 321–328.

Burleson, B. R. (1985, April). *Communicative correlates of peer acceptance in childhood.* Paper presented at the meeting of the Society for Research in Child Development, Toronto.

Burns, B., & Daye, D. (Eds.). *The different faces of motherhood.* Boston: Auburn House.

Buss, A. H., & Finn, S. E. (1987). Classification of personality traits. *Journal of Personality and Social Psychology, 52*, 432–444.

Buss, D. M., & Barnes, M. (1986). Preferences in human mate selection. *Journal of Personality and Social Psychology, 50*, 559–570.

Butcher, J. N., & Finn, S. (1983). Objective personality assessment in clinical settings. In M. H. Ersen, A. E. Dazdin, & A. S. Bellack (Eds.), *The clinical psychology handbook.* New York: Pergamon.

Butler, R. A. (1953). Discrimination learning by rhesus monkeys to visual-exploration motivation. *Journal of Comparative and Physiological Psychology, 46*, 95–98.

Cadoret, R. J., Troughton, E., & O'Gorman, T. W. (1987). Genetic and environmental factors in alcohol abuse and antisocial personality. *Journal of Studies on Alcohol, 48*, 1–8.

Cain, W. S. (1979). To know with the nose: Keys to odor identification. *Science, 203*, 467–470.

Calhoun, K. S., & Atkeson, B. M. (1988). *Treatment of rape victims.* Elmsford, NY: Pergamon.

Cameron, N. (1963). *Personality development and psychopathology.* Boston: Houghton-Mifflin.

Cameron, O. G. (1987). *Presentations of depression.* New York: Wiley.

Campbell, B. (1985). *Human evolution* (3rd ed.). Hawthorne, NY: Aldine.

Campbell, J. D., Tesser, A., & Fairey, P. J. (1986). Conformity and attention to the stimulus: Some temporal and contextual dynamics. *Journal of Personality and Social Psychology, 51*, 315–324.

Campos, J. J., Barrett, K. C., Lamb, M. E., Goldsmith, H. H., & Stenberg, C. (1983). Socioemotional development. In P. H. Mussen (Ed.), *Handbook of child psychology* (4th ed., Vol. 2). New York: Wiley.

Campos, J. J., Langer, A., & Krowitz, A. (1970). Cardiac responses on the visual cliff in prelocomotor human infants. *Science, 170*, 196–197.

Camras, L. A. (1987, August). *Darwin revisited: An infant's first emotional facial expressions.* Paper presented at the meeting of the American Psychological Association, New York.

Cannon, W. B. (1918). The physiological basis of thirst. *Proceedings of the Royal Society of London, 90*, 283–301.

Cannon, W. B. (1927). The James-Lange theory of emotions: A critical examination and an alternative theory. *American Journal of Psychology, 39*, 106–124.

Cantor, N., & Mischel, W. (1977). Traits as prototypes: Effects of recognition memory. *Journal of Personality and Social Psychology, 35*, 38–48.

Carlsson, A., & Lindquist, R. (1963). The effect of chlorpromazine and haloperidol on formation of 3-methoxytyramine and normetanephrine in mouse brain. *Psychopharmacologia, 28*, 309–318.

Carper, L. (1978, April). Sex roles in the nursery. *Harper's.*

Carrington, P. (1977). *Freedom in meditation.* New York: Anchor-Doubleday.

Cartwright, R. (1978, December). Happy endings for our dreams. *Psychology Today, 12*(7), 66–74.

Case, R., Bruchowsky, M., Capidolupa, S., McKeough, A., Porath, M., & Reid, D. (1987, April). Paper presented at the biennial meeting of the Society for Research in Child Development, Baltimore, MD.

Casey, E. S. (1987). *Remembering.* Bloomington, IN: University of Indiana Press.

Cattell, R. B. (1965). *The scientific analysis of personality.* Baltimore: Penguin Books.

Cautela, J. R. (1986). Behavioral analysis of a fetish: First interview. *Journal of Behavior Therapy and Experimental Psychiatry, 17*, 161–165.

Cavett, D., & Porterfield, C. (1974). *Cavett.* New York: Harcourt Brace Jovanovich.

Center for Early Adolescence. (1982). *Living with 10–15 year olds: A planning guide for a one-day conference.* Carrboro, NC: Author.

Chaiken, S., & Eagly, A. H. (1976). Communication modality as a determinant of message persuasiveness and message comprehensibility. *Journal of Personality and Social Psychology, 34*, 605–614.

Chaiken, S., & Sangor, C. (1987). Attitudes and attitude change. *Annual Review of Psychology, 38*, 575–630.

Chan, A. W. K. (1984). Effects of combined alcohol and benzodiazepines: A review. *Drug and Alcohol Dependency, 13*, 315–341.

Chapman, S. L. (1986). A review and clinical perspective on the use of EMG and thermal biofeedback for chronic headaches. *Pain, 27*, 1–43.

Chaudhuri, H. (1965). *Philosophy of meditation.* New York: Philosophical Library.

Cheney, C. D. (1979). Personal communication. Cited in P. Chance, *Learning and behavior.* Belmont, CA: Wadsworth.

Cherniack, N. S. (1986). Breathing disorders during sleep. *Hospital Practice, 21*, 81–104.

Chernin, K. (1981). *The obsession: Reflections on the tyranny of slenderness.* New York: Harper & Row.

Chess, S., & Thomas, A. (1977). Temperamental individuality from childhood to adolescence. *Journal of Child Psychology and Psychiatry, 16*, 218–226.

Chiriboga, D. A. (1982). An examination of life events as possible antecedents to change. *Journal of Gerontology, 36*, 604–624.

Chomsky, N. (1957). *Syntactic structure.* The Hague: Mouton.

Cialdini, R. B., Schaller, M., Houlihan, D., Arps, K., Fultz, J., & Beaman, A. L. (1987). Empathy-based helping: Is it selflessly or selfishly motivated? *Journal of Personality and Social Psychology, 52*, 749–758.

Clark, E. V. (1983). Meanings and concepts. In P. H. Mussen (Ed.), *Handbook of child psychology* (4th ed., Vol. 3). New York: Wiley.

Clark, H. H., & Clark, E. V. (1977). *Psychology and language.* San Diego: Harcourt Brace Jovanovich.

Clark, K. B. (1971). The pathos of power: A psychological perspective. *American Psychologist, 26*, 1047–1057.

Clark, M. S., & Isen, A. M. (1982). Toward understanding the relationship between feeling states and social behavior. In A. Hasdorf & A. M. Isen (Eds.), *Cognitive social psychology.* New York: Elsevier/North Holland.

Clark, M. S., Powell, M. C., Ovellette, R., & Milberg, S. (1987). Recipient's mood, relationship type, and helping. *Journal of Personality and Social Psychology, 53*, 94–103.

Clark, S. D., Zabin, L. S., & Hardy, J. B. (1984). Sex, contraception and parenthood: Experience and attitudes among urban black young men. *Family Planning Perspectives, 16*, 77–82.

Clarke-Stewart, K. A., & Fein, G. G. (1983). Early childhood programs. In P. H. Mussen (Ed.), *Handbook of child psychology* (4th ed.,Vol. 4). New York: John Wiley.

Coe, W. C. (1986, August). *Role theory: A contextual view of hypnotic conduct.* Paper presented at the annual meeting of the American Psychological Association, Washington, DC.

Coe, W. C. (1987, August). *Hypnosis: Where art thou?* Paper presented at the meeting of the American Psychological Association, New York.

Cohen, A. K. (1964). Foreword. In Musgrove, P. *Youth and social order.* Bloomington, IN: Indiana University Press.

Colby, A., Kohlberg, L., Gibbs, J., & Lieberman, M. (1983). A longitudinal study of moral judgment. *Monographs of the Society for Child Development* (Serial No. 201).

Coleman, P. D. (1986, August). *Regulation of dendritic extent: Human aging brain and Alzheimer's disease.* Paper presented at the annual meeting of the American Psychological Association, Washington, DC.

Coleman, R. M. (1986). *Wide awake at 3:00 A.M.: By choice or by chance?* New York: W. H. Freeman.

Coles, (1987, August). *Thirty-day follow-up of infants prenatally exposed to alcohol in a low SES, high risk population.* Paper presented at the meeting of the American Psychological Association, New York.

Collins, A. M., & Quillian, M. R. (1969). Retrieval time from semantic memory. *Journal of Verbal Learning and Verbal Behavior, 8*, 240–247.

Collins, W. A. (1985, April). *Cognition, affect, and development in parent-child relationships.* Paper presented at the biennial meeting of the Society for Research in Child Development, Toronto, Canada.

Collins, W. A. (1987). *Research on the transition to adolescence.* Unpublished manuscript, University of Minnesota, Minneapolis, MN.

Conel, J. L. (1939–1963). Postnatal development of the human cerebral cortex. Cambridge, MA: Harvard University Press, Vols. I-VI.

Cooper, C. R., & Ayers-Lopez, S. (1985). Family and peer systems in early adolescence: New models of the role of relationships in development. *Journal of Early Adolescence, 5*, 9–22.

Cooper, C. R., Grotevant, H. D., Moore, M. S., & Condon, S. M. (1982, August). *Family support and conflict: Both foster adolescent identity and role taking.* Paper presented at the meeting of the American Psychological Association, Washington, DC.

Coote, J. H., Futuro, N., & Logan, S. D. (1985). The involvement of serotonin neurons in the inhibition of renal nerve activity during desynchronized sleep. *Brain Research, 340*, 277–284.

Corboy, L. (1987, April). *Interventions for increasing breastfeeding rates among low income women.* Paper presented at the biennial meeting of the Society for Research in Child Development, Baltimore.

Corcoran, J. F. T., Lewis, M. D., & Garver, R. B. (1978). Biofeedback conditioned galvanic skin response and hypnotic suppression of arousal: A pilot study of their relation to deception. *Journal of Forensic Sciences, 23*, 155–162.

Coren, S., & Girus, J. S. (1972). Illusion decrement in intersecting line figures. *Psychonomic Science, 26*, 108–110.

Coren, S., Porac, C., & Ward, I. M. (1979). *Sensation and perception.* New York: Academic Press.

Cortes, J. B., & Gatti, F. M. (1970, April). Physique and propensity. *Psychology Today,* pp. 42–44.

Costa, P. (1986, August). *The scope of individuality.* Paper presented at the annual meeting of the American Psychological Association, Washington, DC.

Costa, P. T., & McRae, R. R. (1980). Still stable after all these years: Personality as a key to some issues in aging. In P. B. Baltes & O. G. Brim (Eds.), *Life-span development and behavior.* New York: Academic Press.

Costa, P. T., Zonderman, A. B., McRae, R. R., Cornon-Huntley, J., Locke, B. Z., & Barbano, H. E. (1987). Longitudinal analyses of psychological well-being in a national sample: Stability of mean levels. *Journal of Gerontology, 42,* 50–55.

Cozby, P. C. (1972). Self-disclosure, reciprocity, and liking. *Sociometry, 35,* 151–160.

Cozby, P. C. (1986). Interviewing as a research tool. *Contemporary Psychology, 31,* 598.

Cracraft, J. (1986, May 20–22). Unofficial thaw in the cold war. *Bulletin of the Atomic Scientists.*

Craik, F. I. M., & Jacoby, L. L. (1979). Elaboration and distinctiveness in episodic memory. In L. Nilsson (Ed.), *Perspectives on memory research.* Hillsdale, NJ: Erlbaum.

Craik, F. I. M., & Lockhart, R. S. (1972). Levels of processing: A framework for memory research. *Journal of Verbal Learning and Verbal Behavior, 11,* 671–684.

Crawford, C. B., Smith, M. S., & Krebs, D. (Eds.). (1987). *Sociobiology and psychology: Ideas, issues, and applications.* Hillsdale, NJ: Erlbaum.

Crick, M. (1977). *Explorations in language and meaning: Toward a scientific anthropology.* New York: Halstead Press.

Cunningham, M. R. (1986). Measuring the physical in physical attractiveness: Quasiexperiment on the sociobiology of female facial beauty. *Journal of Personality and Social Psychology, 50,* 925–935.

Curtiss, S. (1977). *Genie.* New York: Academic Press.

Cutting, J. E. (1987). Perception and information. *Annual Review of Psychology, 38,* 61–90.

Dachman, R. S., Alessi, G. J., Vrazo, G. J., Fuqua, R. W., & Kerr, R. H. (1986). Development and evaluation of an infant-care training program with first-time fathers. *Journal of Applied Behavior Analysis, 19,* 221–230.

Dagar, S. R., Cowley, D. S., & Dunner, D. H. (1986). Biological markers in panic states. *Biological Psychiatry, 22,* 339–359.

Dale, P. (1976). *Language and development* (2nd ed.). New York: Holt, Rinehart, & Winston.

Dallenbach, K. M. (1927). The temperature spots and end-organs. *American Journal of Psychology, 52,* 331–347.

Daly, M., & Wilson, M. (1984). A sociobiological analysis of human infanticide.

Darley, J. M., & Gross, P. H. (1983). A hypothesis-confirming bias in labeling effects. *Journal of Personality and Social Psychology, 19,* 20–33.

Darley, J. M., & Latané, B. (1968). Bystander intervention in emergencies: Diffusion of responsibility. *Journal of Personality and Social Psychology, 8,* 377–383.

Darling, C. A., Kallen, D. J., & VanDusen, J. E. (1984). Sex in transition, 1900–1984. *Journal of Youth and Adolescence, 13,* 385–399.

Darwin, C. (1859). *On the origin of species.* London: John Murray.

Datan, N., Rodeheaver, D., & Hughes, S. (1987). Adult development and aging. *Annual Review of Psychology, 38,* 153–180.

Davis, K. E. (1985, February). Near and dear: Friendship and love compared. *Psychology Today,* pp. 22–29.

Dawson, E. B., Moore, T. D., & McGanity, W. J. (1970). The mathematical relationship of drinking water, lithium, and rainfall to mental hospital admissions. *Diseases of the Nervous System, 31,* 811–820.

DeLeon, P. H., & Pallack, M. S. (1982). Public health and psychology: An important expanding interaction. *American Psychologist, 37,* 934–935.

Dement, W. C. (1976). *Some must watch while some must sleep.* New York: Doubleday.

Denny, N. (1986, August). *Practical problem solving.* Paper presented at the meeting of the American Psychological Association, Washington, DC.

de Rivera, J. (1983, August). *Current theoretical developments in emotion: Cognitive, motivational, and transformational approaches.* Invited address at the meeting of the American Psychological Association, Los Angeles.

Deutsch, J. A., & Gonzales, M. F. (1980). Gastric nutrient content signals satiety. *Behavioral and Neural Biology, 30,* 113–116.

Deutscher, I. (1967). *Stalin: A political biography.* New York: Oxford.

DeValois, R. L., & Jacobs, G. H. (1968). Primate color vision. *Science, 162,* 533–540.

de Villiers, J. G., & de Villiers, P. A. (1978). *Language acquisition.* Cambridge, MA: Harvard University Press.

deVries, H. A. (1970). Physiological effects of an exercise training regimen upon men aged 52 to 88. *Journal of Gerontology, 25,* 325–336.

Diamond, M. C. (1978, September). Aging and cell loss: Calling for an honest count. *Psychology Today,* p. 126.

Dickinson, A. (1980). *Contemporary animal learning theory.* Cambridge: Cambridge University Press.

Diener, E. (1984). Subjective well-being. *Psychological Bulletin, 95,* 542–575.

Digman, J. M. (1986, August). *The big five factors of personality in developmental perspective.* Paper presented at the meeting of the American Psychological Association, Washington, DC.

Dillon, R. S. (1980). *Diagnosis and management of endocrine and metabolic disorders* (2nd ed). Philadelphia: Lea & Fiebiger.

Dion, K., & Berscheid, E. (1974). Physical attractiveness and peer perception among children. *Sociometry, 37,* 1–12.

Dixon, R. A., & Baltes, R. A. (1986). In R. J. Sternberg & R. K. Wagner (Eds.), *Practical intelligence: Nature and origins of competence in the everyday world.* New York: Cambridge University Press.

Dohrenwend, B. S., & Shrout, P. E. (1985). "Hassles" in the conceptualizaton and measurement of life stress variables. *American Psychologist, 40,* 780–785.

Dollard, J., Doob, L. W., Miller, N. E., Mowrer, O. H., & Sears, R. R. (1939). *Frustration and aggression.* New Haven: Yale University Press.

Domjan, M. (1986, August). *Animal learning comes of age.* Paper presented at the annual meeting of the American Psychological Association, Washington, DC.

Domjan, M. (1987). Animal learning comes of age. *American Psychologist, 42,* 556–564.

Domjan, M., & Hollis, K. L. (1987). Reproductive behavior: A potential model system for adaptive specialization in learning. In R. C. Bolles & M. D. Beecher (Eds.), *Evolution and learning.* Hillsdale, NJ: Erlbaum.

Donnerstein, E. (1987, March). *Pornography, sex, and violence.* Talk given at the University of Texas at Dallas, Richardson, TX.

Doren, H. (1987). *Understanding and treating the psychopath.* New York: Wiley.

Douvan, E., & Adelson, J. (1966). *The adolescent experience.* New York: Wiley.

Dreyer, P. H. (1982). Sexuality during adolescence. In B. B. Wolman (Ed.), *Handbook of developmental psychology.* Englewood Cliffs, NJ: Prentice-Hall.

Duck, S. W. (1975). Personality similarity and friendship choices by adolescents. *European Journal of Social Psychology, 5,* 351–365.

Dugdale, S., & Kibbey, D. (1980). *Fractions curriculum of the PLATO elementary mathematical project.* Urbana-Champaign, IL: Computer-Based Education Research Laboratory.

Durden-Smith, J., & Desimone, D. (1983). *Sex and the brain.* New York: Arbor House.

Dutton, D., & Aron, A. (1974). Some evidence for heightened sexual attraction under conditions of high anxiety. *Journal of Personality and Social Psychology, 30,* 510–517.

Dwyer, C. A. (1987). Across the great divide: Research and practice in test development. *Contemporary Psychology, 32,* 520–522.

Dwyer, J. (1980). Sixteen popular diets: Brief nutritional analyses. In A. J. Stunkard (Ed.), *Obesity.* Philadelphia: W. B. Saunders.

Eagle, M. N. (1987). *Recent developments in psychoanalysis.* Cambridge, MA: Harvard University Press.

Eagleston, J. R., Kirmil-Gray, K., Thoresen, C. E., Wiedenfield, S. A., Bracke, P., Heft, L., & Arnow, B. (in press). Physical health correlates of Type A behavior in children and adolescents. *Journal of Behavioral Medicine.*

Eagly, A. H., & Carli, L. L. (1981). Sex of researchers and sex-typed communications as determinants of sex differences in influenceability: A meta-analysis of social influence studies. *Psychological Bulletin, 90,* 1–20.

Eccles, J. S. (1987, August). *Understanding motivation: Achievement beliefs, gender roles, and changing educational environments.* Paper presented at the meeting of the American Psychological Association, New York.

Eccles, J. S. (1987). Gender roles and achievement patterns. In J. M. Reinisch & L. A. Rosenblum (Eds.), *Masculinity/ Femininity.* New York: Oxford University Press.

Eckert, E. D., Heston, L. L., & Bouchard, T. J. (1981). MZ twins reared apart: Preliminary findings of psychiatric disturbances and traits. In L. Gedda, P. Paris, & W. D. Nance (Eds.), *Twin research* (Vol. 3). New York: Alan Liss.

Edelman, M. W. (1985). The sea is so wide and my boat is so small: Problems facing black children today. In H. P. McAdoo & J. L. McAdoo (Eds.), *Black children: Social, educational, and parental environments.* Beverly Hills, CA: Sage.

Egeland, B., & Farber, E. (1984). Infant-mother attachment: Factors related to its development and changes over time. *Child Development, 55,* 753–771.

Eibl-Eibesfeldt, I. (1977). Evolution of destructive aggression. *Aggressive Behavior, 3,* 127–144.

Eich, E. (1987, June). *Theoretical issues in state-dependent memory.* Paper presented at the Symposium on Varieties of Memory and Consciousness. Papers in honour of Endel Tulving. University of Toronto.

Eichorn, D. H., Clausen, J. A., Haan, N., Honzik, M. P., & Mussen, P. H. (Eds.). (1981). *Present and past in middle life.* New York: Academic Press.

Ekman, P. (1980). *The face of man.* New York: Garland STPM Press.

Ekman, P. (1985). *Telling lies: Clues to deceit in the marketplace, politics, and marriage.* New York: Norton.

Ekman, P., & Friesen, W. (1978). *FACS investigator's guide*. Palo Alto, CA: Consulting Psychologist's Press.

Elder, G., Caspi, A., & Downey, G. (1986). Problem behavior and family relationships: A multigenerational analysis. In A. Sorensen, F. Weinert & L. Sherrod (Eds.), *Human development: Interdisciplinary perspectives*.

Elkind, D. (1978). Understanding the young adolescent. *Adolescence, 13*, 127–134.

Elkind, D. (1981). *The hurried child*. Reading, MA: Addison-Wesley.

Ellis, A. (1974). *Growth through reason*. Hollywood, CA: Wilshire Books.

Ellis, A. (1962). *Reason and emotion in psychotherapy*. New York: Lyle Stuart.

Ellis, A. (1986, August). *The theory and practice of rational emotive therapy*. Paper presented at the meeting of the American Psychological Association, Washington, DC.

Ellis, A., & Dryden, W. (1987). *The practice of rational emotive therapy*. New York: Springer.

Ellis, A., McInerney, J. F., DiGiuseppe, & Yeager, R. (1988). *Rational-emotive therapy with alcoholics and substance abusers*. Elmsford, NY: Pergamon.

Ellis, H. C. (1986, March). *The ARESIDORI system: A guide for facilitating and improving your memory*. Unpublished talk presented at the University of New Mexico.

Ellis, H. C. (1987). Recent developments in human memory. In V. P. Makosky (Ed.), *The G. Stanley Hall Lecture Series*. Washington, DC: American Psychological Association.

Ellis, H. C., Thomas, R. L., & Rodriguez, I. A. (1984). Emotional mood states and memory: Elaborative encoding, semantic processing, and cognitive effort. *Journal of Experimental Psychology: Learning, Memory, and Cognition, 10*, 470–482.

Emmelkamp, P. (1982). *Phobic and obsessive-compulsive disorders: Theory, research, and practice*. New York: Plenum.

Engel, G. L. (1977). The need for a new medical model: A challenge for biomedicine. *Science, 196*, 129–136.

Erdelyi, M. H. (1985). *Psychoanalysis: Freud's cognitive psychology*. New York: W. H. Freeman.

Ericsson, K. A., & Chase, W. G. (1982). Exceptional memory. *American Scientist, 10*, 607–614.

Erikson, E. H. (1968). *Identity: Youth and crisis*. New York: Norton.

Eron, L. D. (1987). The development of aggression from the perspective of a developing behaviorism. *American Psychologist, 42*, 435–442.

Escalona, S. (1988). Cognition in its relationship to total development in the first year. In B. Inhelder, D. DeCaprona, & A. Cornu-Wells (Eds.), *Piaget Today*. Hillsdale, NJ: Erlbaum.

Estes, W. K. (1986). Memory storage and retrieval processes in category learning. *Journal of Experimental Psychology: General, 115*, 155–174.

Evans, R., & Novak, R. (1967). *Lyndon B. Johnson: The excess of power*. London: George Allen & Unwin.

Even-Chen, M., Yinon, Y., & Bizman, A. (1978). The door-in-the-face technique: Effects of the size of the initial request. *European Journal of Social Psychology, 8*, 135–140.

Eysenck, H. J. (1952). The effects of psychotherapy: An evaluation. *Journal of Consulting Psychology, 16*, 319–324.

Eysenck, H. J. (1967). *The biological basis of personality*. Springfield, IL: Charles C. Thomas.

Eysenck, H. J. (1986). A critique of contemporary classification and diagnosis. In T. Millon & G. L. Klerman (Eds.), *Contemporary directions in psychopathology*. New York: Guilford Press.

Fairweather, G. W., Sanders, D. H., & Tornatsky, L. (1974). *Creating change in mental health organizations*. New York: Pergamon.

Fancher, R. E. (1985). *The intelligence men: Makers of the IQ controversy*. New York: Norton.

Fantz, R. L. (1966). Pattern discrimination and selective attention as determinants in infancy. In A. H. Kidd & J. L. Rivoire (Eds.), *Perceptual development in children*. New York: International Universities Press.

Farley, F. (1986, August). *Assessment of Type T personality: Implications for intervention and wellness*. Paper presented at the meeting of the American Psychological Association, Washington, DC.

Farrell, M. P., & Rosenberg, S. D. (1981). *Men at midlife*. Boston, MA: Auburn House.

Fassinger, R. E. (1985). A causal model of college women's career choice. *Journal of Vocational Behavior, 27*, 123–153.

Fazio, R. H. (1986). How do attitudes guide behavior? In R. M. Sorrentino & E. T. Higgins (Eds.), *The handbook of motivation and cognition: Foundations of social behavior*. New York: Guilford Press.

Fazio, R. H., & Williams, C. J. (1986). Attributed accessibility as a moderator of the attitude-perception and attitude-behavior relations: An investigation of the 1984 presidential election. *Journal of Personality and Social Psychology, 51*, 505–514.

Fazio, R. H., & Zanna, M. P. (1981). Direct experience and attitude-behavior consistency. In L. Berkowitz (Ed.), *Advances in experimental social psychology* (Vol. 14). New York: Academic Press.

Fellner, C. H., & Marshall, J. R. (1981). Kidney donors revisited. In J. P. Ruston & R. M. Sorrentino (Eds.), *Altruism and helping behavior*. Hillsdale, NJ: Erlbaum.

Ferguson, C. A. (1977). Baby talk as a simplified register. In C. E. Snow & C. A. Ferguson (Eds.), *Talking to children*. New York: Cambridge University Press.

Feschbach, S., & Weiner, B. (1986). *Personality* (2nd ed.). Lexington, MA: D.C. Heath.

Festinger, L. (1957). *A theory of cognitive dissonance*. Evanston, IL: Row Peterson.

Festinger, L. (1954). A theory of social comparison processes. *Human Relations, 7*, 117–140.

Festinger, L., & Carlsmith, J. (1959). Cognitive consequences of forced compliance. *Journal of Abnormal and Social Psychology, 58*, 203–210.

Feurstein, M., Labbe, E. E., & Kuczmierczyk, A. R. (1986). *Health psychology*. New York: Plenum.

Field, T. M., Woodson, R., Greenberg, R., & Cohen, D. (1982). Discrimination and imitation of facial expressions by neonates. *Science, 218*, 179–181.

Fielder, F. E. (1978). Contingency model and the leadership process. In L. Berkowitz (Ed.), *Advances in experimental social psychology* (Vol. 11). New York: Academic Press.

Fireman, B., Gamson, W. A., Rytina, S., & Taylor, B. (1978). Encounters with unjust authority. In L. Kriesberg (Ed.), *Research in social movements, conflicts, and change*. Greenwich, CT: JAI Press.

Fischer, J., & Gochros, H. L. (1975). *Planned behavior change*. New York: Free Press.

Fischer, K. W., & Lazerson, A. (1984). *Human development*. San Francisco: W. H. Freeman.

Fischer, P. J., & Breakey, W. R. (1986). Homelessness and mental health: An overview. *International Journal of Mental Health, 14*, 6–41.

Fischman, S. H. (1987, February). Type A on trial. *Psychology Today*, pp. 42–50.

Fishman, D. B., Rotgers, F., & Franks, C. M. (1988). *Paradigms in behavioral therapy*. New York: Springer.

Fiske, S. T., Neuberg, S. L., Pratto, F., & Allman, C. (1986). *Stereotyping and individuating processes*. Unpublished manuscript, University of Massachusetts, Amherst.

Fiske, S. T., & Taylor, S. E. (1984). *Social cognition*. New York: Random House.

Fitzsimons, J. T. (1972). Thirst. *Physiological Reviews, 52*, 468–561.

Flaherty, C. F. (1985). *Animal learning and cognition*. New York: Knopf.

Flavell, J. H. (1985). Cognitive development (2nd ed.). Englewood Cliffs, NJ: Prentice-Hall.

Foa, E. B., Steketze, G., & Young, M. C. (1984). Agoraphobia. *Clinical Psychology Review, 4*, 431–457.

Folkman, S., Lazarus, R. S., Dunkel-Schetter, C., Delongis, A., & Gruen, R. J. (1986). Dynamics of a stressful encounter: Cognitive appraisal, coping, and encounter outcomes. *Journal of Personality and Social Psychology, 50*, 992–1003.

Ford, M. (1986). A living systems conceptualization of social intelligence: Outcomes, processes, and developmental change. In R. J. Sternberg (Ed.), *Advances in the psychology of human intelligence* (Vol. 3). Hillsdale, NJ: Erlbaum.

Ford, M. E. (1986). *Androgyny as self-assertion and integration: Implications for psychological and social competence*. Unpublished manuscript, Stanford University School of Education, Stanford, CA.

Forman, J. (1981, December 2). Looking for Mr. . . . Anybody. *Boston Globe*.

Foss, D. J. (1988). Psycholinguistics. *Annual Review of Psychology, 39*.

Foulkes, D. (1972). Theories of dream formation and recent studies of sleep consciousness. In C. T. Tart (Ed.), *Altered states of consciousness*. New York: Anchor-Doubleday.

Fowler, C. A., Wolford, G., Slade, R., & Tassinary, L. (1981). Lexical access with and without awareness. *Journal of Experimental Psychology: General, 110*, 341–362.

Fox, J. L. (1984). The brain's dynamic way of keeping in touch. *Science, 225*, 820–821.

Fox, L. H. (1976, September). *Changing behaviors and attitudes of gifted girls*. Paper presented at the meeting of the American Psychological Association, Washington, DC.

Fox, L. H., Bordy, L., & Tobin, D. (1979). *Women and mathematics*. Baltimore: Intellectually Gifted Study Group, Johns Hopkins University.

Frager, R. (1970). Conformity and anticonformity in Japan. *Journal of Personality and Social Psychology, 15*, 203–210.

Frank, E., & Kupfer, D. J. (1986). Psychotherapeutic approaches to treatment of recurrent unipolar depression: Work in progress. *Psychopharmacology Bulletin, 22*, 558–565.

Frank, J. D. (1982). Therapeutic components shared by all psychotherapies. In J. H. Harvey & M. M. Parks (Eds.), *Psychotherapy research and behavior change*. Washington, DC: American Psychological Association.

Frank, J. D., & Rivard, J. C. (1986). Antinuclear admirals—an interview study. *Political Psychology, 7*, 23–52.

Frank, J. D. (1987a). The drive for power and the nuclear arms race. *American Psychologist, 42*, 337–344.

Frank, J. D. (1987b). Afterword: Nuclear winter and the will to power. In L. Grinspoon (Ed.), *The long darkness*. New Haven: Yale University Press.

Freedman, J., & Fraser, S. (1966). Compliance without pressure: The foot in the door technique. *Journal of Personality and Social Psychology, 4,* 195–202.

Freedman, J. L. (1984). Effects of television violence on aggressiveness. *Psychological Bulletin, 96,* 227–246.

Freeman, J. (1982). The old, old, very old Charlie Smith. *The Gerontologist, 22,* 532.

Freud, S. (1900). *The interpretation of dreams.* New York: Basic Books.

Freud, S. (1917). *A general introduction to psychoanalysis.* New York: Washington Square Press.

Freud, S. (1952). *A general introduction to psychoanalysis* (J. Riviere, Trans.). New York: Washington Square Press. (Original work published 1917.)

Freud, S. (1955). *The interpretation of dreams.* New York: Basic Books. (Original work published 1900.)

Freud, S. (1957). Mourning and melancholia. In J. Strachey (Ed.), *The standard edition of the complete psychological works of Sigmund Freud* (Vol. 14). London: Hogarth. (Original work published 1917.)

Fried, R., & Berkowitz, L. (1979). Music hath charms . . . and can influence helpfulness. *Journal of Applied Social Psychology, 9,* 199–208.

Friedman, M., & Rosenman, R. (1974). *Type A behavior and your heart.* New York: Knopf.

Friedrich, L. K., & Stein, A. H. (1973). Aggressive and prosocial TV programs and the natural behavior of preschool children. *Monographs of the Society for Research in Child Development, 38*(4, Serial No. 151).

Frith, C. H. (1986, May). *Toxicity studies in animals.* Paper presented at the MDMA multidisciplinary conference, San Francisco, CA.

Fromm, E. (1947). *Man for himself.* New York: Holt, Rinehart, & Winston.

Fuller, J. L., & Simmel, E. C. (Eds.). (1987). *Perspectives in behavior genetics.* Hillsdale, NJ: Erlbaum.

Furth, H. G. (1971). Linguistic deficiency and thinking: Research with deaf subjects, 1964–1969. *Psychological Bulletin, 75,* 52–58.

Furth, H. G., & Wachs, H. (1975). *Thinking goes to school.* New York: Oxford University Press.

Gagne, E. D. (1985). *The cognitive psychology of school learning.* Boston: Little, Brown.

Galanter, E. (1962). Contemporary psychophysics. In R. Brow (Ed.), *New directions in psychology.* New York: Holt, Rinehart, & Winston.

Galbraith, J. K. (1983). *The anatomy of power.* Boston: Houghton-Mifflin.

Gallup, G. (1984, August–September). *The Gallup Report,* Nos. 228 and 229, 2–9.

Gallup, G. G., Jr., & Suarez, S. D. (1985). Alternatives to the use of animals in psychological research. *American Psychologist, 40,* 1104–1111.

Garcia, J., Ervin, F. E., & Koelling, R. A. (1966). Learning with prolonged delay of reinforcement. *Psychonomic Science, 5,* 121–122.

Garcia y Robertson, R., & Garcia, J. (1985). X rays and learned taste aversions: Historical and psychological ramifications. In T. G. Burish, S. M. Levy, & B. E. Meyerowitz (Eds.), *Cancer, nutrition and eating behavior.* Hillsdale, NJ: Erlbaum.

Garcia y Robertson, R., & Garcia, J. (1987). Darwin was a learning theorist. In R. C. Bolles & M. D. Beecher (Eds.), *Evolution and learning.* Hillsdale, NJ: Erlbaum.

Gardner, B. T., & Gardner, R. A. (1971). Two-way communication with an infant chimpanzee. In A. Schrier & F. Stollnitz (Eds.), *Behavior of nonhuman primates* (Vol. 4). New York: Academic Press.

Gardner, B. T., & Gardner, R. A. (1986). Discovering the meaning of primate signals. *British Journal for the Philosophy of Science, 37,* 477–495.

Gardner, H. (1983). *Frames of mind.* New York: Basic Books.

Gardner, H. (1985). *The mind's new science.* New York: Basic Books.

Gardner, H. (1987). Epilogue. *The mind's new science.* New York: Basic Books.

Gardos, G., Cole, J. O., Saloman, M., & Schniebolk, S. (1987). Clinical forms of severe tardive dyskinesia. *American Journal of Psychiatry, 144,* 895–902.

Garelik, G. (1985, October). Are the progeny prodigies? *Discover, 6,* 45–47, 78–84.

Garfinkel, P. E., & Garner, D. M. (1982). *Anorexia nervosa.* New York: Brunner/Mazel.

Garmezy, N. (1978). Never mind the psychologists: Is it good for the children? *Clinical Psychologist, 31,* 1–6.

Gawin, F. (in press). Cocaine dependence. *Annual Review of Medicine, 39.*

Gazzaniga, M. S. (1983). Right hemisphere language following brain bisection: A 20-year perspective. *American Psychologist, 38,* 525–537.

Gazzaniga, M. S. (1986). *The social brain.* New York: Plenum.

Geen, R., Beatty, W. W., & Arkin, R. M. (1984). *Human motivation.* Boston: Allyn & Bacon.

Gesell, A. L. (1928). Growth potential and infant personality. In *Infancy and human growth.* New York: Macmillan.

Gesten, E. L., & Jason, L. A. (1987). Social and community interventions. *Annual Review of Psychology, 38,* 427–460.

Getzels, J. W., & Dillon, T. J. (1973). The nature of giftedness and the education of the gifted. In R. M. W. Travers (Ed.), *Second handbook of research on teaching.* Chicago: Rand McNally.

Gibson, E. J. (in press). Exploratory behavior in the development of perceiving, acting, and the acquiring of knowledge. *Annual Review of Psychology, 39.*

Gibson, E. J., & Walk, R. D. (1960). The "visual cliff." *Scientific American, 202,* 64–71.

Gillam, B. (1980). Geometrical illusions. *Scientific American, 242,* 102–111.

Gilligan, C. (1982). *In a different voice: Psychological theory and women's development.* Cambridge, MA: Harvard University Press.

Gilligan, C. (1985, April). *Response to critics.* Paper presented at the biennial meeting of the Society for Research in Child Development, Toronto.

Gjerde, P. (1985, April). *Adolescent depression and parental socialization patterns: A prospective study.* Paper presented at the biennial meeting of the Society for Research in Child Development, Toronto.

Glaser, R. (1982). Instructional psychology: Past, present and future. *American Psychologist, 37,* 292–305.

Gleason, J. B. (1988). Language and socialization. In F. Kesset (Ed.), *The development of language and language researchers.* Hillsdale, NJ: Erlbaum.

Glisky, E. L., & Schacter, D. L. (in press). Acquisition of domain-specific knowledge in organic amnesia: Training for computer-related work. *Neuropsychologica.*

Goethals, G. R. (1984, August). *Social comparison theory.* Paper presented at the meeting of the American Psychological Association, Toronto.

Gogel, W. C., & DaSilva, J. A. (1987). A two-process theory of the response to size and distance. *Perception and Psychophysics, 41,* 220–238.

Gold, M. S. (1986). Adolescent cocaine epidemic. *Pharmochemistry Newsletter, 15,* 1–8.

Gold, M. S., Gallanter, M., & Stimmel, B. (1987). *Cocaine.* New York: Haworth Press.

Gold, M. S., & Petronio, R. J. (1980). Delinquent behavior in adolescence. In J. Adelson (Ed.), *Handbook of adolescent psychology.* New York: Wiley.

Gold, M. S., Washton, A. M., & Dackis, C. A. (1985). Cocaine abuse: Neurochemistry, phenomenology, and treatment. In N. J. Kozel & E. H. Adams (Eds.), *Cocaine use in America* (NIDA Research Monograph 61). Rockville, MD: NIDA.

Gold, R. M., & Simson, E. L. (1982). Perturbations of serum insulin, glucagon, somatostatin, epinephrine and glucose after obesifying hypothalamic knife cuts. In B. G. Hobel & D. Novlin (Eds.), *The neural basis of feeding and reward.* Brunswick, ME: Haer Institute.

Goldberg, D. C. (Ed.). (1985). *Contemporary marriage: Issues in couple therapy.* Homewood, IL: Dorsey Press.

Goldberg, H., & Pepitone-Arreola-Rockwell, F. (Eds.). (1986, Summer). Forward. *Psychotherapy, 23,* IV.

Goldiamond, I. (1971). Self-control procedures in personal behavior problems. In M. S. Gazzaniga & E. P. Lovejoy (Eds.), *Good reading in psychology.* Englewood Cliffs, NJ: Prentice-Hall.

Goldsmith, H. H., et al. (1987). Roundtable: What is temperament? Four approaches. *Child Development, 58,* 505–529.

Goldstein, M. J. (1986, August). *Psychosocial factors in the course and onset of schizophrenia.* Paper presented at the meeting of the American Psychological Association, Washington, DC.

Goldstein, M. J., & Palmer, J. O. (1975). *The experience of anxiety.* New York: Oxford University Press.

Goodchilds, J. D., & Zellman, G. L. (1984). Sexual signaling and sexual aggression in adolescent relationships. In N. M. Malamuth & E. D. Donnerstein (Eds.), *Pornography and sexual aggression.* New York: Academic Press.

Goodman, R. A., Mercy, J. A., Loya, F., Rosenberg, M. L., Smith, J. C., Allen, N. H., Vargas, L., & Kolts, R. (1986). Alcohol use and interpersonal violence: Alcohol detected in homicide victims. *American Journal of Public Health, 76,* 144–149.

Goodstein, L. D. (1986, August). *What are 40,000 psychology majors going to do next year?* Paper presented at the meeting of the American Psychological Association, Washington, DC.

Goodstein, L. D., & Calhoun, J. F. (1982). *Understanding abnormal behavior.* Reading, MA: Addison-Wesley.

Görlitz, D., & Wohlwill, J. F. (1987). *Curiosity, imagination, and play.* Hillsdale, NJ: Erlbaum.

Gortmaker, S. L. (1987, May). American Journal of Diseases of Children.

Gottesman, I. L., & Shields, J. (1982). *The schizophrenic puzzle.* New York: Cambridge University Press.

Gottman, J. M., & Parker, J. G. (1987). (Eds.), *Conversations of friends.* New York: Cambridge University Press.

Gould, C. G. (1983, April). Out of the mouths of beasts. *Science '83.*

Gould, P., & White, R. (1974). *Mental maps.* Harmondsworth, UK: Penguin.

Gould, R. L. (1978). *Transformations: Growth and change in adult life.* New York: Simon and Schuster.

Gouras, P., & Kruger, J. (1975, September). *Similarities of color properties of neurons in areas 17, 18, and V4 of monkey cortex.* Paper presented at the Seventh International Neurobiology meeting, Göttingen, Germany.

Graham, S. (1984). Communicating sympathy and anger to black and white students: The cognitive (attributional) antecedents of affective cues. *Journal of Personality and Social Psychology, 47,* 40–54.

Graham, S. (1986, August). *Can attribution theory tell us something about motivation in blacks?* Paper presented at the meeting of the American Psychological Association, Washington, DC.

Graham, S. (1987, August). *Developing relations between attributions, affect, and intended social behavior.* Paper presented at the meeting of the American Psychological Association, New York.

Graham, S., & Long, A. (1986). Race, class, and the attributional process. *Journal of Educational Psychology, 78,* 4–13.

Granrud, C. E., Yonas, A., Smith, I. M., Arterberry, M. E., Glicksman, M. L., & Sorknes, A. C. (1984). Infants' sensitivity to accretion and deletion of texture as information for depth at an edge. *Child Development, 55,* 1630–1636.

Gras, T., & Schacter, D. L. (1987). Selective efforts of interference on implicit and explicit memory for new associations. *Journal of Experimental Psychology: Learning, Memory, and Cognition, 13,* 43–53.

Graubard, P. S., & Rosenberg, H. (with F. Gray). (1974, May). Little brother is changing you. *Psychology Today,* pp. 42–46.

Gregory, R. L. (1978). *Eye and brain: The psychology of seeing* (3rd ed.). New York: McGraw-Hill.

Greiser, C., Greenberg, R., & Harrison, R. H. (1972). The adaptive function of sleep: The differential effects of sleep on dreaming and recall. *Journal of Abnormal Psychology, 80,* 280–286.

Grossberg, S. (1987a). Critical dynamics of three-dimensional form, color, and brightness perception: I. Monocular theory. *Perception and Psychophysics, 41,* 87–116.

Grossberg, S. (1987b). Critical dynamics of three-dimensional form, color, and brightness perception: II. Binocular theory. *Perception and Psychophysics, 41,* 117–158.

Grotevant, H. D., & Cooper, C. R. (1985). Patterns of interaction in family relationships and the development of identity exploration in adolescence. *Child Development, 56,* 415–428.

Grush, J. E. (1980). Impact of candidate expenditures, regionality, and prior outcomes on the 1976 Democratic presidential primaries. *Journal of Personality and Social Psychology, 38,* 337–347.

Guerney, B. G. (1987). Family relationship enhancement: A skill training approach. In L. Bond & B. Wagner (Eds.), *Families in transition: Primary prevention programs that work.* Beverly Hills, CA: Sage.

Guilford, J. P. (1967). *The nature of human intelligence.* New York: McGraw-Hill.

Guilleminault, C. P. (1985). Disorders of excessive sleepiness. *Annals of Clinical Research, 17,* 209–219.

Guilleminault, C. P., Passouant, B., & Dement, W. C. (1976). *Narcolepsy.* New York: Spectrum.

Gunderson, J. G., & Mosher, L. R. (1975). The cost of schizophrenia. *American Journal of Psychiatry, 132,* 901–905.

Gunnar, M. R., Malone, S., & Fisch, R. O. (1987). The psychobiology of stress and coping in the human neonate: Studies of the adrenocortical activity in response to stress in the first week of life. In T. Field, P. McCabe, & N. Schneidermann (Eds.), *Stress and coping.* Hillsdale, NJ: Erlbaum.

Gustafson, J. P. (1984). An integration of brief dynamic psychotherapy. *American Journal of Psychiatry, 141,* 935–944.

Guttman, N., & Kalish, H. I. (1956). Discriminability and stimulus generalization. *Journal of Experimental Psychology, 51,* 79–88.

Hales, R. E., & Frances, A. J. (Eds.). The therapeutic alliance and treatment outcome. *American Psychiatric Association Annual Review* (Vol. 4). Washington, DC: American Psychiatric Association.

Haley, J. (1976). *Problem-solving therapy.* San Francisco: Jossey-Bass.

Hall, C. S., & Lindsey, G. (1985). *Introduction to theories of personality.* New York: Wiley.

Hall, G. S. (1904). *Adolescence* (Vols. I and II). Englewood Cliffs, NJ: Prentice-Hall.

Halmi, D. (1980). Gastric bypass for massive obesity. In A. J. Stunkard (Ed.), *Obesity.* Philadelphia: W. B. Saunders.

Hamilton, D. L., & Trollier, T. K. (in press). Stereotypes and stereotyping: An overview of the cognitive approach. In J. Dovidio & S. L. Gaertner (Eds.), *Prejudice, discrimination, and racism: Theory and research.* New York: Academic Press.

Hare-Muston, R. T., & Maracek, J. (1986, Summer). Autonomy and gender: Some questions for therapists. *Psychotherapy, 23,* 205–212.

Haring, T., Kennedy, C. H., Adams, M. J., & Pitts-Conway, V. (1987). Teaching generalization of purchasing skills across community settings to autistic youth using videotape modeling. *Journal of Applied Behavior Analysis, 20,* 89–96.

Harlow, H. F., & Zimmerman, R. R. (1959). Affectional responses in the infant monkey. *Science, 130,* 421–432.

Harris, D. M., & Guten, S. (1979). Health protective behavior: An exploratory study. *Journal of Health and Social Behavior, 20,* 17–29.

Harris, M. B. (1974). Mediators between frustration and aggression in a field experiment. *Journal of Experimental Social Psychology, 10,* 561–571.

Harris, R. F., Wolf, N. M., & Baer, D. M. (1964). Effects of adult social reinforcement on child behavior. *Young Children, 20,* 8–17.

Harter, S. (1981). A new self-report scale of intrinsic versus extrinsic orientation in the classroom: Motivational and informational components. *Developmental Psychology, 17,* 300–312.

Hartup, W. W. (1983). Peer relations. In P. H. Mussen (Ed.), *Handbook of child psychology* (4th ed., Vol. 4). New York: John Wiley.

Hartup, W. W., & Rubin, Z. (Eds.). (1986). *Relationships and development.* Hillsdale, NJ: Erlbaum.

Harvey, J. H., Weber, A., Galvin, K. S., Huszti, H. C., & Garnick, N. N. (1986). Attribution in the termination of close relationships: A special focus on the account. In R. Gilmour & S. Duck (Eds.), *The emerging field of personal relationships.* Hillsdale, NJ: Erlbaum.

Hasher, L., & Zacks, R. T. (1979). Automatic and effortful processes in memory. *Journal of Experimental Psychology: General, 108,* 356–388.

Hatfield, E. (1987, August). *New directions in emotion research: Toward an interdisciplinary synthesis.* Paper presented at the meeting of the American Psychological Association, New York.

Hatfield, E., & Sprecher, S. (1986). *Mirror, mirror . . . The importance of looks in everyday life.* Albany: State University of New York Press.

Hatfield, E., Traupmann, J., Sprecher, S., Utne, M., & Hay, J. (1985). Equity and intimate relations: Recent research. In W. Ickes (Ed.), *Compatible and incompatible relationships.* New York: Springer-Verlag.

Hattie, J. A., Sharpley, C. F., & Rogers, H. J. (1984). Comparative effectiveness of professional and paraprofessional helpers. *Psychological Bulletin, 95,* 534–541.

Hatton, G. I. (1976). Nucleus circularis: Is it an osmoreceptor in the brain? *Brain Research Bulletin, 1,* 123–131.

Havighurst, R. J. (1973). History of developmental psychology: Socialization and personality through the lifespan. In P. B. Baltes & K. W. Schaie (Eds.), *Life-span developmental psychology: Personality and socialization.* New York: Academic Press.

Hawkins, D. (1970). The effects of subliminal stimulation on drive level and brand preference. *Journal of Marketing Research, 7,* 322–326.

Hawkins, J., Pea, R. D., Glick, J., & Scibner, S. (1984). "Merds that laugh don't like mushrooms": Evidence for deductive reasoning by preschoolers. *Developmental Psychology, 20,* 584–594.

Hay, A. E. (1987, April). *Learning to control a conversation.* Paper presented at the biennial meeting of the Society for Research in Child Development, Baltimore.

Hayes, K. J., & Hayes, C. (1951). Picture perception in a home-raised chimpanzee. *Journal of Comparative and Physiological Psychology, 46,* 470–474.

Hayflick, L. (1975, September). Why grow old? *Stanford Magazine,* pp. 36–43.

Hayflick, L. (1977). The cellular basis for biological aging. In C. E. Finch & L. Hayflick (Eds.), *Handbook of the biology of aging.* New York: Van Nostrand.

Hayflick, L. (1987). The cell biology and theoretical basis of human aging. In L. Carstensen & B. A. Edelstein (Eds.), *Handbook of Clinical Gerontology.* New York: Pergamon.

Hazen, C., & Shaver, P. (1987). Romantic love conceptualized as an attachment process. *Journal of Personality and Social Psychology, 51,* 511–524.

Heath, R. G. (Ed.). (1964). *The role of pleasure in behavior.* New York: Harper & Row.

Hebb, D. O. (1982, May). Hilgard's discovery brings hypnosis closer to everyday experience. *Psychology Today,* pp. 52–54.

Heffner, T. G., Zigmond, M. J., & Stricker, E. M. (1977). Effects of dopaminergic agonists and antagonists on feeding in intact and 6-hydroxydopamine-treated rats. *Journal of Pharmacy and Experimental Therapeutics, 201,* 386–399.

Heider, E. R. (1972). Universals in color naming and memory. *Journal of Experimental Psychology, 93,* 10–20.

Heider, F. (1958). *The psychology of interpersonal relations.* New York: John Wiley.

Heilman, M. E. (1984). Information as a deterrent against sex discrimination: The effects of applicant sex and information type on preliminary employment decisions. *Organizational Behavior and Human Performance, 33,* 174–186.

Henle, M. (1962). On the relation between logic and thinking. *Psychological Review, 69,* 366–378.

Hering, E. (1964). Grundzüge der Lehre vom Lichtsinn. In A. von Graefe & T. Saemische (Eds.), *Handbuch der gesamten Augenheilkunde* (L. M. Hurvich & D. Jameson, Trans.). Cambridge: Harvard University Press. (Original work published 1920.)

Hersen, M., Eisler, R. M., & Miller, P. M. (Eds.). (1987). *Progress in behavior modification.* Newbury Park, CA: Sage.

Hetherington, E. M. (1987). Family relations six years after divorce. In K. Pasley & M. Ihinger-Tollman (Eds.), *Remarriage and stepparenting today: Research and theory.* New York: Guilford.

Hierons, R., & Saunders, M. (1966). Impotence in patients with temporal lobe lesions. *Lancet, 2,* 761–764.

Hilgard, E. (1987). *Psychology in America.* San Diego: Harcourt Brace Jovanovich.

Hilgard, E. R. (1965). *Hypnotic suggestibility.* New York: Harcourt Brace.

Hilgard, E. R. (1970). *Personality and hypnosis: A study of imaginative involvement.* Chicago: University of Chicago Press.

Hilgard, E. R. (1977). *Divided consciousness: Multiple controls in human thought and action.* New York: Wiley.

Hilgard, E. R. (1983, August). *Dissociation theory and hypnosis.* Invited address at the American Psychological Association, Anaheim, CA.

Hilgard, E. R. (1986, September). *Research advances in hypnosis: Issues and methods.* Paper presented at the Society for Clinical and Experimental Hypnosis, Chicago.

Hill, J. P., & Holmbeck, G. N. (1987). Attachment and autonomy during adolescence. *Annals of Child Development.*

Hinde, R., & Stevenson-Hinde, J. (Eds.). (1987). *Towards understanding families.* London: Cambridge University Press.

Hinde, R. A. (1983). Ethology and child development. In P. H. Mussen (Ed.), *Handbook of child psychology* (4th ed., Vol. 2). New York: Wiley.

Hinde, R. A. (1984). Why do the sexes behave differently in close relationships? *Journal of Social and Personal Relationships, 1,* 471–501.

Hinson, R. E., Poulos, C. X., Thomas, W., & Cappell, H. (1986). Pavlovian conditioning and addictive behavior: Relapse to oral self-administration of morphine. *Behavioral Neuroscience, 100,* 368–375.

Hintzman, D. L. (1986). "Schema abstraction" in a multiple-trace memory model. *Psychological Review, 93,* 411–428.

Hobson, J. A., Lydic, R., & Baghdoyan, H. A. (1986). Evolving concepts of sleep cycle generation: From brain centers to neuronal populations. *Behavioral and Brain Sciences, 9,* 371–448.

Hobson, J. A., & McCarley, R. W. (1977). The brain as a dream state generator: An activation-synthesis hypothesis of the dream process. *American Journal of Psychiatry, 134,* 1335–1348.

Hobson, J. A., & Steriade, M. (1986). The neuronal basis of behavioral state control. In V. Mountcastle (Ed.), *Handbook of physiology.* New York: American Physiological Society.

Hoffman, C., & O'Grady, D. J. (1986, September). *Hypnosis with parents and children for coping with bone marrow transplantation.* Paper presented at the meeting of the Society for Clinical and Experimental Hypnosis, Chicago.

Hoffman, L. W. (1979). Maternal employment: 1979. *American Psychologist, 34,* 859–865.

Hogan, R. (1986a). *Manual for the Hogan Personality Inventory.* Minneapolis: NCS.

Hogan, R. (1986b, August). *Personality theory, personality assessment, and I/O psychology.* Paper presented at the meeting of the American Psychological Association, Washington, DC.

Hogan, R. T. (1987, August). *Conceptions of personality and the prediction of job performance.* Paper presented at the meeting of the American Psychological Association, New York.

Holden, C. (1981). Scientist convicted for monkey neglect. *Science, 214,* 1218–1220.

Holliday, S. G., Burnaby, B. C., & Chandler, M. J. (1987). *Wisdom: Explorations in adult competence.* New York: S. Karger.

Hollister, L. E. (in press). Interactions of cannabis with other drugs in man. National Institute on Drug Abuse Monograph Series.

Holmes, D. S. (1988). The influence of meditation versus rest on physiological considerations. In M. West (Ed.), *The psychology of meditation.* New York: Oxford University Press.

Holmes, D. S., Solomon, S., Cappo, B. M., & Greenberg, J. L. (1983). Effects of transcendental meditation versus resting on physiological and subjective arousal. *Journal of Personality and Social Psychology, 44,* 1244–1252.

Holmes, T. H., & Rahe, R. H. (1967). The social readjustment rating scale. *Journal of Psychosomatic Research, 11,* 213–218.

Honts, C. R., Raskin, D. C., & Kircher, J. C. (1983). Detection of deception: Effectiveness of physical countermeasures under high motivation conditions. *Psychophysiology, 20,* 446–447.

Horn, J. L., & Donaldson, G. (1980). Cognitive development II: Adulthood development of human abilities. In O. G. Brim & J. Kagan (Eds.), *Constancy and change in human development.* Cambridge, MA: Harvard University Press.

Horn, J. M. (1983). The Texas Adoption Project: Adopted children and their intellectual resemblance to biological and adoptive parents. *Child Development, 54,* 268–275.

Horney, K. (1937). *The neurotic personality of our time.* New York: Norton.

Hubel, D. H., & Wiesel, T. N. (1965). Receptive fields and functional architecture in two nonstriate visual areas (18 and 19) in the cat. *Journal of Neurophysiology, 28,* 229–289.

Huesmann, L. R., Eron, L. D., Dubow, E. F., & Seebauer, E. (1984, July). *Television viewing habits in childhood and adult aggression.* Paper presented at the meeting of the International Society for Research on Aggression, Turku, Finland.

Huesmann, L. R., Eron, L. D., Dubow, E. F., & Seebauer, E. (in press). Television viewing habits in childhood and adult aggression. *Child Development.*

Huesmann, L. R., & Malamuth, N. M. (1987). Media violence and antisocial behavior: An overview. *Journal of Social Issues, 42,* 1–6.

Hultsch, D. F., & Plemons, J. K. (1979). Life events and life-span development. In P. B. Baltes & O. G. Brim (Eds.), *Life-span development and behavior.* New York: Academic Press.

Humphreys, L. G. (1985). A conceptualization of intellectual giftedness. In F. D. Horowitz & M. O'Brien (Eds.), *The gifted and the talented.* Washington, DC: American Psychological Association.

Hunt, M. (1974). *Sexual behavior in the 1970s.* Chicago: Playboy Press.

Hunt, M. (1982). *The universe within.* New York: Simon & Schuster.

Hunt, R. R., & Mitchell, D. B. (1982). Independent effects of semantic and nonsemantic distinctiveness. *Journal of Experimental Psychology: Learning, Memory, and Cognition, 8,* 81–87.

Hurvich, L. M., & Jameson, D. (1969). Human color perception. *American Scientist, 57,* 143–166.

Huston-Stein, A., & Higgens-Trenk, A. (1978). Development of females from childhood through adulthood: Career and feminine role orientations. In P. Baltes (Ed.), *Lifespan development and behavior* (Vol. 1). New York: Academic Press.

Hyde, J. S. (1984). Children's understanding of sexist language. *Developmental Psychology, 20,* 697–706.

Hyde, J. S. (1985). *Half the human experience* (3rd ed.). Lexington, MA: Heath.

Hyde, J. S. (1986). *Understanding human sexuality* (3rd ed.). New York: McGraw-Hill.

Hyde, T. S., & Jenkins, J. J. (1969). Differential effects of incidental tasks on the organization of recall of lists of highly associated words. *Journal of Experimental Psychology, 82,* 472–481.

Ingelfinger, F. J. (1944). The late effects of total and subtotal gastrectomy. *New England Journal of Medicine, 231,* 321–327.

Inhelder, B., DeCaprona, D., & Cornu-Wells, A. (Eds.). (1988). *Piaget Today.* Hillsdale, NJ: Erlbaum.

Irvine, M. J., Johnston, D. W., Jenner, D. A., & Marie, G. V. (1986). Relaxation and stress management in the treatment of essential hypertension. *Journal of Psychosomatic Research, 30,* 437–450.

Isaacs, E. A., & Clark, H. H. (1987). References in conversations between experts and novices. *Journal of Experimental Psychology: General, 116,* 26–37.

Isabella, R. (1987, April). *The origins of infant-mother attachment: An examination of interactional synchrony during the infant's first year.* Paper presented at biennial meeting of the Society for Research in Child Development, Baltimore.

Izard, C. E. (1982). *Measuring emotions in infants and children.* New York: Cambridge University Press.

Izard, C. E., & Malatesta, C. Z. (1987). Perspectives on emotional development I: Differential emotions theory of early emotional development. In J. D. Osofsky (Ed.), *Handbook of infant development.* New York: Wiley.

Jackson, D. N. (1984). *Personality research form manual* (3rd ed.). Port Huron, MI: Research Psychologists Press.

Jacobs, J. (1971). *Adolescent suicide.* New York: Wiley.

Jacobson, N. S., Waldron, H., & Moore, T. (1980). Toward a behavioral profile of marital distress. *Journal of Consulting and Clinical Psychology, 48,* 696–703.

James, W. (1890). *The principles of psychology.* New York: Holt, Rinehart, & Winston.

James, W. (1950). *The principles of psychology.* New York: Dover. (Original work published 1890.)

Janis, I. (1972). *Victims of groupthink: A psychological study of foreign-policy decisions and fiascos.* Boston: Houghton-Mifflin.

Janos, P. M., & Robinson, N. M. (1985). Psychosocial development in intellectually gifted children. In F. D. Horowitz & M. O'Brien (Eds.), *The gifted and the talented.* Washington, DC: American Psychological Association.

Jeavons, C. M., & Taylor, S. P. (1985). The control of alcohol-related aggression: Redirecting the inebriate's attention to socially appropriate conduct. *Aggressive Behavior, 11,* 93–101.

Jenkins, J. J. (1969). Language and thought. In J. F. Voss (Ed.), *Approaches to thought.* Columbus, OH: Merrill.

Jensen, A. R. (1969). How much can we boost I.Q. and scholastic achievement? *Harvard Educational Review, 39,* 1–123.

Jensen A. R. (1985). The nature of black-white differences on psychometric tests: Spearman's hypothesis. *Behavior and Brain Sciences, 8,* 193–263.

Johnson, L. D., Bachman, J. G., & O'Malley, P. M. (1987). *Student drug use in America.* Ann Arbor, MI: Institute of Social Research.

Johnson, L. G. (1987). Biology (2nd ed.). Dubuque, IA: Wm. C. Brown Publishers.

Johnson, P. E. (1979, November). *Expert problem solving.* Paper presented at the meeting of the American Educational Research Association, San Francisco.

Johnston, D. W. (1985). Invited review: Psychological interventions in cardiovascular disease. *Journal of Psychosomatic Research, 29,* 447–456.

Johnston, D. W. (1985). Psychological interventions in cardiovascular disease. *Journal of Psychosomatic Research, 29,* 447–456.

Jones, E. (1953). *The life and work of Sigmund Freud* (Vol. 1). New York: Basic Books.

Jones, E. E., & Sigall, H. (1971). The bogus pipeline: A new paradigm for measuring affect and attitude. *Psychological Bulletin, 76,* 349–364.

Jones, K. L., Shainberg, L. W., & Byer, C. O. (1985). *Dimensions of human sexuality.* Dubuque, IA: Wm. C. Brown Publishers.

Jones, M. C. (1924). A laboratory study of fear: The case of Peter. *Journal of Genetic Psychology, 31,* 308–315.

Jones, M. C. (1965). Psychological correlates of somatic development. *Child Development, 36,* 899–911.

Joyce, P. R., Donald, R. A., & Elder, P. A. (1987). Individual differences in plasma cortisol changes during mania and depression. *Journal of Affective Disorders, 12,* 1–6.

Jung, C. G. (1917). *Analytical psychology.* New York: Moffat, Yard.

Kagan, J. (1984). *The nature of the child.* New York: Basic Books.

Kagan, J. (1987). Perspectives on infancy. In J. Osofsky (Ed.), *Handbook of infant development.* New York: Wiley.

Kahneman, D., & Tversky, A. (1972). Subjective probability: A judgment of representativeness. *Cognitive Psychology, 3,* 430–454.

Kail, R., & Pellegrino, J. W. (1985). *Human intelligence.* New York: W. H. Freeman.

Kales, A. (1970). Sleep patterns following 205 hours of sleep deprivation. *Psychosomatic Medicine, 32,* 189–200.

Kalish, R. A. (1981). *Death, grief, and caring relationships.* Monterey, CA: Brooks/Cole.

Kalven, J. (1982, September 3–5). A talk with Louis Harris. *Bulletin of the Atomic Scientists.*

Kamil, A. C., & Yoerg, S. I. (1982). Learning and foraging behavior. In P. P. G. Bateson & P. H. Klupfer (Eds.), *Perspectives in ethology* (Vol. 5). New York: Plenum.

Kamil, M. L. (1987). Can thinking be taught? *Contemporary Psychology, 32,* 548–549.

Kandel, E. R., & Schwartz, J. H. (1982). Molecular biology of learning: Modulation of transmitter release. *Science, 218,* 433–443.

Kanfer, F. H., & Schefft, B. K. (1987). *Guiding the process of therapeutic change.* Champaign, IL: Research Press.

Kanner, A. D., Coyne, J. C., Schaefer, C., & Lazarus, R. S. (1981). Comparison of two modes of stress measurement: Daily hassles and uplifts versus major life events. *Journal of Behavioral Medicine, 4,* 1–39.

Karasu, T. B. (1986). The psychotherapies: Benefits and limitations. *American Journal of Psychotherapy, 15,* 324–342.

Karasu, T. B. (in press). The "specificity" vs. "nonspecificity" dilemma: Towards an integrative model. *American Journal of Psychiatry.*

Kass, J. H. (1987). The organization of the neocortex in mammals. *Annual Review of Psychology, 38,* 129–151.

Katon, W., Vitaliano, J. R., Jones, M., & Anderson, K. (1987). Panic disorder. Spectrum of severity and somatication. *Journal of Nervous and Mental Disease, 175,* 12–19.

Kaufman, A. S., & Kaufman, N. L. (1983). *Kaufman assessment battery for children: Interpretive manual.* Circle Pines, MN: American Guidance Service.

Kazdin, A. E. (1982). The token economy: A decade later. *Journal of Applied Behavior Analysis, 15,* 431–445.

Kazdin, A. E. (1986). Comparative outcome studies of psychotherapy: Methodological issues and strategies. *Journal of Consulting and Clinical Psychology, 34,* 95–105.

Keating, D. (1980). Thinking processes in adolescence. In J. Adelsen (Ed.), *Handbook of adolescent psychology.* New York: Wiley.

Keil, F. C. (1984). Mechanisms in cognitive development and the structure of knowledge. In R. J. Sternberg (Ed.), *Mechanisms of cognitive development.* New York: W. H. Freeman.

Keith, T. Z. (1985). Questioning the K-ABC: What does it measure? *School Psychology Review, 14,* 9–20.

Kelley, H. H., & Thibaut, J. (1978). *Interpersonal relations: A theory of interdependence.* New York: Wiley.

Kellner, R., Abbott, P., Winslow, W. W., & Pathak, D. (1987). Fears, beliefs, and attitudes in DSM-III hypochondriasis. *Journal of Nervous and Mental Disease, 175,* 20–25.

Kellogg, W. N., & Kellogg, L. A. (1933). *The ape and the child.* New York: McGraw-Hill.

Kelly, J. B. (1987, August). *Children of divorce: Long-term effects and clinical implications.* Paper presented at the meeting of the American Psychological Association, New York.

Kendall, P. C. (Ed.). (1985). *Advances in cognitive-behavioral research and therapy.* Orlando, FL: Academic Press.

Kendall, P. C., & Norton-Ford, J. (1982). *Clinical psychology.* New York: John Wiley.

Kendler, H. (1987). *The history of psychology.* Chicago: Dorsey.

Kennedy, P. G. E., & Fok-Seang, J. F. (1986). Studies on the development, antigenic phenotype and function of human glial cells in tissue culture. *Brain, 109,* 1261–1277.

Kenniston, K. (1970). Youth: A "new" stage of life. *The American Scholar, 39,* 631–654.

Kephart, W. M. (1967). Some correlates of romantic love. *Journal of Marriage and the Family, 29,* 470–474.

Kerr, B. A. (1983). Raising the career aspirations of gifted girls. *Vocational Guidance Quarterly, 32,* 37–43.

Khouri, P. J., & Akiskal, H. S. (1986). The bipolar spectrum reconsidered. In T. Millon & G. L. Klerman (Eds.), *Contemporary approaches to psychopathology.* New York: Guilford Press.

Kihlstrom, J. F. (1985). Hypnosis. *Annual Review of Psychology, 36,* 385–414.

Kihlstrom, J. F. (1986). Strong inferences about hypnosis. *Behavioral and Brain Sciences, 9,* 474–475.

Kimble, G. A. (1961). *Hilgard and Marquis's conditioning and learning.* New York: Appleton-Century-Crofts.

King, H. E. (1961). Psychological effects of excitation of the limbic system. In D. E. Sheer (Ed.), *Electrical stimulation of the brain.* Austin: University of Texas Press.

Kinsey, A. C., Pomeroy, W. B., & Martin, E. E. (1948). *Sexual behavior in the human male.* Philadelphia: W. B. Saunders.

Klatzky, R. L. (1980). *Human memory.* New York: W. H. Freeman.

Klatzky, R. L. (1984). *Memory and awareness.* New York: Freeman.

Klaus, M. H., & Kennell, J. H. (1976). *Maternal-infant bonding.* St. Louis, MO: Mosby.

Kline, N. (1962). Drugs are the greatest practical advance in the history of psychiatry. *New Medical Material, 4,* 49.

Klink, M. E., & Quan, S. F. (1986, March). Sleep disorders in the elderly. *Drug Therapy,* 104–116.

Kobasa, S., Maddi, S., & Kahn, S. (1982). Hardiness and health: A prospective study. *Journal of Personality and Social Psychology, 42,* 168–177.

Kobasa, S. C., Maddi, S. R., Puccetti, M. C., & Zola, M. (1985). Relative effectiveness of hardiness, exercise, and social support as resources against illness. *Journal of Psychosomatic Research, 29,* 525–533.

Kohlberg, L. (1966). A cognitive-developmental analysis of children's sex-role concepts and attitudes. In E. E. Maccoby (Ed.), *The development of sex differences.* Palo Alto, CA: Stanford University Press.

Kohlberg, L. (1976). Moral stages and moralization. The cognitive-developmental approach. In T. Lickona (Ed.), *Moral development and behavior.* New York: Holt, Rinehart, & Winston.

Kohlberg, L. (1984). *Essays on moral development: Vol. 2. The psychology of moral development.* San Francisco: Harper & Row.

Kohler, W. (1925). *The mentality of apes.* New York: Harcourt Brace Jovanovich.

Kohut, H. (1977). *The restoration of the self.* New York: International Universities Press.

Kolb, B., & Whishaw, I. Q. (1985). *Fundamentals of neuropsychology.* 2nd ed. San Francisco: W. H. Freeman.

Kolb, L. (1973). *Modern clinical psychiatry* (8th ed.). Philadelphia: W. B. Saunders.

Kornetsky, C. (1986, August). *Effects of opiates and stimulants on brain stimulation: Implications for abuse.* Paper presented at the meeting of the American Psychological Association, Washington, DC.

Kosslyn, S. M. (1983). *Ghosts in the mind's machine.* New York: Norton.

Kossyln, S. (1986). A computational analysis of mental image generation: Evidence from functional dissociations in split-brain patients. *Journal of Experimental Psychology: General, 114*(3), 311–341.

Koten, J. (1984, January 19). Marketing: Coca-Cola turns to Pavlov. *Wall Street Journal,* p. 33.

Kozak, M. J., Foa, E. B., & McCarthy, P. R. (1987). Obsessive-compulsive disorder. In C. G. Last & M. Hersen (Eds.), *Handbook of anxiety disorders.* Elmsford, NY: Pergamon.

Kramer, B. A. (1987). Electroconvulsive therapy use in geriatric depression. *Journal of Nervous and Mental Disease, 175,* 233–235.

Kripke, D. F., & Simons, R. N. (1976). Average sleep, insomnia, and sleeping pill use. *Sleep Research, 5,* 110.

Kroger, W. S., & Fezler, W. D. (1976). *Hypnosis and behavior modification: Imagery conditioning.* Philadelphia: Lippincott.

Kübler-Ross, E. (1974). *Questions and answers on death and dying.* New York: Macmillan.

Kuhn, D. (1980). *On the development of developmental psychology.* Unpublished manuscript, Harvard University, Cambridge, MA.

Kuhn, M. (1987). Ethics and the elderly. In L. L. Cartensen & B. A. Edelstein (Eds.), Handbook of Clinical Gerontology. New York: Pergamon.

Kulik, J. A., Bangert-Drowns, R. L., & Kulik, C. C. (1984). The effectiveness of coaching for aptitude tests. *Psychological Bulletin, 95,* 179–188.

Kulik, J. A., Kulik, C. C., & Bangert-Drowns, R. L. (1985). Effectiveness of computer-based education in elementary schools. *Computers in Human Behavior, 1,* 59–74.

LaBerge, S. P. (1981, January). Lucid dreaming: Directing the action as it happens. *Psychology Today, 15,* 48–57.

LaBerge, S. P. (1985). *Lucid dreaming.* Los Angeles: Tarcher.

Labouvie-Vief, G. (1982). Dynamic development and mature autonomy: A theoretical prologue. *Human Development, 25.*

Labouvie-Vief, G. (1986, August). *Modes of knowing and life-span cognition.* Paper presented at the annual meeting of the American Psychological Association, Washington, DC.

Ladner, J. (1971). *Tomorrow's tomorrow: The black woman in America.* New York: Anchor Books.

Lamb, M. (1982, April). Second thoughts on first touch. *Psychology Today,* pp. 9–11.

Lamb, M. E. (1977). Father-infant and mother-infant interaction in the first year of life. *Child Development, 48,* 167–181.

Lamb, M. E. (Ed.). (1986). *The father's role: Applied perspectives.* New York: Wiley.

Lamb, M. E. (1987). *The father's role: Cross-cultural perspective.* Hillsdale, NJ: Erlbaum.

Lamb, M. E., Thompson, R. A., Gardner, W. P., Charnov, E. L., & Estes, D. (1984). Security of infantile attachment as assessed in the strange situation: Its study and biological interpretation. *The Behavioral and Brain Sciences, 7,* 121–171.

Lane, H. (1976). *The wild boy of Aveyron.* Cambridge, MA: Harvard University Press.

Lange, C. G. (1922). *The emotions.* Baltimore: Williams and Wilkins.

Langer, E. J., & Rodin, J. (1976). The effects of choice and enhanced personal responsibility for the aged: A field experimental study in an institutional setting. *Journal of Personality and Social Psychology, 34,* 191–198.

Langlois, J. (1981). *From the eye of the beholder to behavioral reality.* Paper presented at the Ontario Symposium, "Physical appearance, stigma, and social behavior." Toronto, Canada.

Lanyon, R. I., & Goodstein, L. D. (1982). *Personality and assessment* (2nd ed.). New York: Wiley Interscience.

LaPiere, R. (1934). Attitudes versus actions. *Social Forces, 13,* 230–237.

Lapsley, D. K., Enright, R. D., & Serlin, R. C. (1985). Toward a theoretical perspective on the legislation of adolescence. *Journal of Early Adolescence, 5,* 441–466.

Lashley, K. S. (1950). In search of the engram. In *Symposium of the Society for Experimental Biology* (Vol. 4). New York: Cambridge University Press.

Latané, B. (1981). The psychology of social impact. *American Psychologist, 36,* 343–356.

Latané, B., & Elman, D. (1970). The bystander and the thief. In B. Latané & J. Darley (Eds.), *The unresponsive bystander: Why doesn't he help?* New York: Appleton-Century-Crofts.

Latané, B., & Nida, S. A. (1981). Ten years of research on group size and helping. *Psychological Bulletin, 80,* 308–324.

Lazarus, R. S. (1984). On the primacy of cognition. *American Psychologist, 39,* 124–129.

Lazarus, R. S., & Folkman, S. (1984). *Stress, appraisal, and coping.* New York: Springer.

Leaf, A. (1973, September). Getting old. *Scientific American,* pp. 44–53.

Leahey, T. H., & Harris, R. J. (1985). *Human learning.* Englewood Cliffs, NJ: Prentice-Hall.

Leamer, L. (1986). *As time goes by.* New York: Harper & Row.

LeBoeuf, B. J., & Peterson, R. S. (1969). Social status and mating activity in elephant seals. *Science, 163,* 91–93.

LeBon, G. (1960). *The crowd: A study of the popular mind.* New York: Viking Press. (Original work published 1895.)

Lefkowitz, M. M., Eron, L. D., Walder, L. O., & Huesmann, L. R. (1972). Television violence and children's aggression: A follow-up study. In G. A. Comstock & E. A. Rubenstein (Eds.), *Television and social behavior* (Vol. 3). Washington, DC: U.S. Government Printing Office.

Leigh, G. H. (1982). Kinship interaction over the family life span. *Journal of Marriage and the Family, 44,* 197–208.

Lenneberg, E. H. (1962). Understanding language without the ability to speak: A case report. *Journal of Abnormal and Social Psychology, 65,* 419–425.

Lenneberg, E. H., Rebelsky, F. G., & Nichols, I. A. (1965). The vocalization of infants born to deaf and hearing parents. *Human Development, 8,* 23–37.

Lepper, M., Greene, D., & Nisbett, R. E. (1973). Undermining children's intrinsic interest with extrinsic rewards. *Journal of Personality and Social Psychology, 28,* 129–137.

Lepper, M. R. (1985). Microcomputers in education: Motivational and social issues. *American Psychologist, 40,* 1–19.

Lerner, M. J. (1982). The justice motive in human relations and the economic model of man: A radical analysis of facts and fictions. In V. J. Derlega & J. Grzelak (Eds.), *Cooperation and helping behavior: Theories and research.* New York: Academic Press.

Leventhal, H. (1970). Findings and theory in the study of fear communications. In L. Berkowitz (Ed.), *Advances in experimental social psychology* (Vol. 5). New York: Academic Press.

Leventhal, H., & Tomarken, A. J. (1986). Emotion: Today's problems. *Annual Review of Psychology, 37,* 565–610.

Leventhal, H., Zimmerman, R., & Gultmann, M. (1984). Compliance: A self-regulation perspective. In D. Gentry (Ed.), *Handbook of behavioral medicine.* New York: Guilford Press.

Leverant, R. (1986). MDMA reconsidered. *Journal of Psychoactive Drugs, 18,* 373–379.

Levine, M. A. (1975). *A cognitive theory of learning.* Hillsdale, NJ: Erlbaum.

Levinger, G. (1987). Introduction. Media violence and antisocial behavior. *Journal of Social Issues, 42,* the editor's page.

Levinson, D. J. (1978). *The seasons of a man's life.* New York: Knopf.

Levy, S. (1984). The process and outcome of "adjustment" in the cancer patient: A reply to Taylor. *American Psychologist, 39,* 1327.

Levy, S. M. (1985). *Behavior and cancer.* San Francisco: Jossey Bass.

Lewinsohn, P. M. (1987). The Coping with Depression course. In R. F. Muñoz (Ed.), *Depression prevention.* New York: Hemisphere.

Lewinsohn, P. M., Antonuccio, D. O., Steinmetz, J., & Teri, L. (1984). *The coping with depression course: A psychoeducational intervention for unipolar depression.* Eugene, OR: Castalia Publishing.

Lewinsohn, P. M., Munoz, R. F., Youngren, M. A., & Zeiss, A. M. (1986). *Control your depression.* New York: Prentice-Hall.

Lewis, C. S. (1960). *The four loves.* New York: Harcourt, Brace, & World.

Lewis, M., & Brooks-Gunn, J. (1979). *Social cognition and the acquisition of the self.* New York: Plenum.

Lewis, M., Feiring, C., McGuffog, C., & Jaskir, J. (1984). Predicting psychopathology in six-year-olds from early social relations. *Child Development, 55,* 123–136.

Lieberman, M. A., Yalom, I. D., & Miles, M. B. (1973). *Encounter groups: First facts.* New York: Basic Books.

Lindskold, S. (1986). GRIT: Reducing distrust through carefully introduced conciliation. In S. Worschel & W. G. Austin (Eds.), *Psychology of intergroup relations.* Chicago: Nelson-Hall.

Lindskold, S., Han, G., & Betz, B. (1986). The essential elements of communication in the GRIT strategy. *Personality and Social Psychology Bulletin, 12,* 179–185.

Linton, M. (1979, July). I remember it well. *Psychology Today,* pp. 80–87.

Lipschitz, A. (1987). Diagnosis and classification of anxiety disorders. In C. G. Last & M. Hersen (Eds.), *Handbook of anxiety disorders.* Elmsford, NY: Pergamon.

Lipsitz, J. (1983, October). Making it the hard way: Adolescents in the 1980s. Testimony presented at the Crisis Intervention Task Force, House Select Committee on Children, Youth, and Families, Washington, DC.

Lockheed, M. E., Nielsen, A., & Stone, M. K. (1983). *Sex differences in microcomputer literacy.* Paper presented at the National Educational Computer Conference, Baltimore.

Loehlin, J. C., & Nichols, R. C. (1976). *Heredity, environment, and personality: A study of 850 sets of twins.* Austin: University of Texas Press.

Loehlin, J. C., Willerman, L., & Horn, J. M. (in press). Human behavior genetics. *Annual Review of Psychology, 39.*

Loehr, F. (1976). *Diary after death.* Los Angeles: Religious Research Frontier Books.

Loftus, E. F. (1975). Spreading activation within semantic categories: Comments on Rosch's "Cognitive representations of semantic categories." *Journal of Experimental Psychology, 104,* 234–240.

Loftus, E. F. (1979). *Eyewitness testimony.* Cambridge, MA: Harvard University Press.

Loftus, E. F. (1980). *Memory.* Reading, MA: Addison-Wesley.

Logan, F. A. (1960). *Incentive.* New Haven: Yale University Press.

Logue, A. W. (1986). *Eating and drinking.* New York: W. H. Freeman.

Logue, A. W. (1987). A comparison of taste aversion learning in humans and other species: Evolutionary pressures in common. In R. C. Bolles & M. D. Beecher (Eds.), *Evolution and learning.* Hillsdale, NJ: Erlbaum.

Long, P. (1986, January). Medical mesmerism. *Psychology Today,* pp. 28–29.

Long, T., & Long, L. (1983). *Latchkey children.* New York: Penguin.

Lorenz, K. Z. (1965). *Evolution and modification of behavior.* Chicago: University of Chicago Press.

Lowy, L. (1981, August). *The older generation: What is due, what is owed?* Paper presented at the meeting of the American Psychological Association, New York.

Ludolph, P. (1982, August). *A reanalysis of the literature on multiple personality.* Paper presented at the American Psychological Association, Washington, DC.

Luria, A. R. (1968). *The mind of a mnemonist.* New York: Basic Books.

Lykken, D. T. (1981). A tremor in the blood: Uses and abuses of the lie detector. New York: McGraw-Hill.

Lykken, D. T. (1982). Research with twins: The concept of emergenesis. *Psychophysiology, 19,* 361–373.

Lynn, S. J., & Snodgrass, M. (1986, September). *Hypnotizability and music involvement.* Paper presented at the meeting of the Society for Clinical and Experimental Hypnosis, Chicago.

Lytle, L. (in press). Interactions of drugs and diets with behavior. *Annual Review of Pharmacology and Toxicology, 28.*

Maccoby, E. E. (1980). *Social development.* New York: Harcourt Brace Jovanovich.

Maccoby, E. E., & Jacklin, C. N. (1974). The psychology of sex differences. Palo Alto, CA: Stanford University Press.

Maccoby, E. E., & Martin, J. A. (1983). Socialization in the context of the family: Parent-child interaction. In P. H. Mussen (Ed.), *Handbook of child psychology* (4th ed., Vol. 4). New York: John Wiley.

MacDonald, D. I. (1986, August). *Cocaine use among adolescents and adults.* Bethesda, MD: Department of Health and Human Services.

MacDougall, J. M., Dembroski, T. M., & Dimsdale, J. E. (1985). Components of Type A, hostility, and anger-in: Further relationships to angiographic findings. *Health Psychology, 4,* 137–152.

Mace, F. C., Page, T. J., Ivancic, M. T., & O'Brien, S. (1986). Effectiveness of brief time-out with and without contingent delay: A comparative analysis. *Journal of Applied Behavior Analysis, 19,* 79–86.

Mackintosh, N. J. (1983). *Conditioning and associative learning.* New York: Oxford University Press.

Macmillan, R. L., & Brown, K. W. G. (1971). Cardiac arrest remembered. *Canadian Medical Association Journal, 104,* 889.

Maddi, S. (1986, August). *The great stress-illness controversy.* Paper presented at the meeting of the American Psychological Association, Washington, DC.

Mahler, M. (1979). *Separation-individuation.* London: Jason Aronson.

Mahoney, M. (1980). *Abnormal psychology.* New York: Harper & Row.

Maier, N. R. F. (1931). Reasoning in humans. *Journal of Comparative Psychology, 12,* 181–194.

Maier, S. F., & Laudenslager, M. (1985, August). Stress and health: Exploring the links. *Psychology Today,* pp. 44–49.

Malamuth, N. M., & Donnerstein, E. (Eds.). (1983). *Pornography and sexual aggression.* New York: Academic Press.

Mandler, G. (1984). *Mind and body.* New York: Norton.

Mandler, J. M. (1983). Representation. In P. H. Mussen (Ed.), *Handbook of child psychology* (4th ed., Vol. 3). New York: John Wiley.

Maratsos, M. (1983). Some current issues in the study of the acquisition of grammar. In P. H. Mussen (Ed.), *Handbook of child psychology* (4th ed., Vol. 3). New York: Wiley.

Marder, S. R., & May, P. R. A. (1986). Benefits and limitations of neuroleptics—and other forms of treatment—in schizophrenia. *American Journal of Psychotherapy, 15,* 357–369.

Marder, S. R., Van Putten, T., & Mintz, J. (1984). Costs and benefits of two doses of fluphenazine. *Archives of General Psychiatry, 41,* 1025–1029.

Margolin, G., Michelli, J., & Jacobson, N. (1988). Assessment of marital dysfunction. In A. S. Bellack & M. Hersen (Eds.), *Behavioral assessment.* Elmsford, NY: Pergamon.

Markides, K., & Martin, H. (1979). A causal model of life satisfaction among the elderly. *Journal of Gerontology, 34,* 86–93.

Marks, I. M. (1987). *Fears, phobias, and rituals.* New York: Oxford University Press.

Marlatt, G. A., Baer, J. S., Donovan, D. M., & Kirlahan, D. R. (in press). Addictive behaviors: Etiology and treatment. *Annual Review of Physiology, 39.*

Marx, M. H., & Hillix, W. A. (1987). *Systems and theories in psychology* (4th ed.). New York: McGraw-Hill.

Maslow, A. H. (1954). *Motivation and personality.* New York: Harper & Row.

Maslow, A. H. (1971). *The farther reaches of human nature.* New York: Viking.

Masters, J. C., Burish, T. G., Hollow, S. D., & Rimm, D. C. (1988). *Behavior therapy.* San Diego: Harcourt Brace Jovanovich.

Masters, J. C., & Smith, W. P. (1987). *Social comparison, social justice, and relative deprivation.* Hillsdale, NJ: Erlbaum.

Masters, W. H., & Johnson, V. (1966). *Human sexual response.* Boston: Little, Brown.

Matarazzo, J. D. (1979). Health psychology: APA's newest division. *The Health Psychologist, 1,* 1.

Matas, L., Arend, R. A., & Sroufe, L. A. (1978). Continuity in adaptation: Quality of attachment and later competence. *Child Development, 49,* 547–556.

Matlin, M. (1983). *Cognition.* New York: Holt, Rinehart, & Winston.

Matlin, M. W. (1983). *Perception.* Boston: Allyn and Bacon.

Maupin, E. (1962). Zen Buddhism: A psychological review. *Journal of Consulting Psychology, 26,* 362–378.

Mayer, J. D., & Bower, G. H. (1986). Learning and memory for personality prototypes. *Journal of Personality and Social Psychology, 51,* 473–492.

Mayer, W. (1983). Alcohol abuse and alcoholism: The psychologist's role in prevention, research, and treatment. *American Psychologist, 38,* 1116–1121.

McAdoo, H. P., & McAdoo, J. L. (Eds.). (1985). *Black children: Social, educational, and parental environments.* Beverly Hills, CA: Sage.

McClelland, D. C. (1955). Some social consequences of achievement motivation. In M. R. Jones (Ed.), *Nebraska Symposium on Motivation.* Lincoln, NE: University of Nebraska Press.

McClelland, D. C., Atkinson, J. W., Clark, R., & Lowell, E. L. (1953). *The achievement motive.* New York: Appleton-Century-Crofts.

McClelland, D. C., & Winter, D. G. (1969). *Motivating economic achievement.* New York: Appleton-Century-Crofts.

McConnell, J. V. (1962). Memory transfer through cannibalism in planarians. *Journal of Neuropsychiatry, 3* (Monograph supplement 1).

McConnell, J. V., Cutler, R. L., & McNeil, E. B. (1958). Subliminal stimulation: An overview. *American Psychologist, 13,* 230–242.

McDaniel, M. A., Einstein, G. O., Dunay, P. K., & Cobb, R. C. (in press). Encoding difficulty and memory: Toward a unifying theory. *Journal of Memory and Language.*

McDaniel, M. A., & Pressley, M. (1987). *Imagery and related mnemonic processes.* New York: Springer-Verlag.

McDougall, W. (1908). *Social psychology.* New York: G. Putnam & Sons.

McGinty, D. J., & Szymusiak, R. (in press). Neuronal unit activity patterns in behaving animals. *Annual Review of Psychology, 39.*

McGrath, J. (1984). *Groups: Interaction and Performance.* Englewood Cliffs, NJ: Prentice-Hall.

McGuire, W. J. (1985). Attitudes and attitude change. In G. Lindzey & E. Aronson (Eds.), *Handbook of social psychology* (3rd ed., Vol. 2). New York: Random House.

McNally, R. J. (1986). Behavioral treatment of a choking phobia. *Journal of Behavior Therapy and Experimental Psychiatry, 17,* 185–188.

McNeil, D. (1970). The development of language. In P. H. Mussen (Ed.), *Manual of child psychology* (3rd ed., Vol. 1). New York: Wiley.

McNeil, E. B. (1967). *The quiet furies.* Englewood Cliffs, NJ: Prentice-Hall.

McQuire, W. J. (1986). The myth of mass media effectiveness. In G. Comstock (Ed.), *Public communication and behavior* (Vol. 1). New York: Academic Press.

McWhirter, D. P., Reinsch, J. M., & Sanders, S. A. (in press). Homosexuality/heterosexuality. New York: Oxford University Press.

Meador, B. C., & Rogers, C. R. (1979). Person-centered psychotherapy. In R. J. Corsini (Ed.), *Current psychotherapies.* Itasca, IL: Peacock.

Medin, D. L. (1986). Comment on "Memory storage and retrieval processes in category learning." *Journal of Experimental Psychology: General, 115,* 373–381.

Mednick, S. A., Gabrielli, W. F., & Hutchings, B. (1984). Genetic influences on criminal convictions: Evidence from an adoption cohort. *Science, 224,* 891–894.

Medvedev, Z. A. (1974). The nucleic acids in development and aging. In B. L. Strehler (Ed.), *Advances in gerontological research* (Vol. 1). New York: Academic Press.

Meehl, P. E. (1962). Schizotaxia, schizotypy, schizophrenia. *American Psychologist, 17,* 827–838.

Meehl, P. E. (1986). Diagnostic taxa as open concepts. In T. Millon & G. L. Klerman (Eds.), *Contemporary directions in psychopathology.* New York: Guilford Press.

Meichenbaum, D. (1977). *Cognitive-behavior modification: An integrative approach.* New York: Plenum Press.

Meichenbaum, D., Turk, D., & Burstein, S. (1975). The nature of coping with stress. In I. Sarason & C. Spielberger (Eds.), *Stress and anxiety.* Washington, DC: Hemisphere Publishing.

Meltzoff, A. N. (1987, April). *Imitation by nine-month-old in immediate and deferred tests.* Paper presented at the biennial meeting of the Society for Research in Child Development, Baltimore.

Meltzoff, A. N., & Moore, M. K. (1977). Interpreting "imitative" responses in early infancy. *Science, 205,* 217–219.

Melzack, R. (1973). *The puzzle of pain.* London: Penguin.

Melzack, R., & Dennis, S. G. (1978). Neurophysiological foundations of pain. In R. A. Sternbach (Ed.), *The psychology of pain.* New York: Raven.

Mercer, J. R., & Lewis, J. F. (1978). *System of multicultural pluralistic assessment.* New York: Psychological Corporation.

Mervis, J. (1986, July). NIMH data point way to effective treatment. *APA Monitor, 17,* 1, 13.

Messick, S., & Jungeblut, A. (1981). Time and method in coaching for the SAT. *Psychological Bulletin, 89,* 191–216.

Messinger, J. C. (1971). Sex and repression in an Irish folk community. In D. S. Marshall & R. C. Suggs (Eds.), *Human sexual behavior: Variations in the ethnic spectrum.* New York: Basic Books.

Metternich, R. (1880). *Memoirs of Prince Metternich.* New York: Scribners.

Meyer, R. G., & Osborne, Y. V. H. (1982). *Case studies in abnormal behavior.* Boston: Allyn & Bacon.

Meyers, J. (1985). *Hemingway.* New York: Harper & Row.

Michaels, J. W., Bloomel, J. M., Brocato, R. M., Linkous, R. A., & Rowe, J. S. (1982). Social facilitation and inhibition in a natural setting. *Replications in Social Psychology, 2,* 21–24.

Milgram, S. (1963). Behavioral study of obedience. *Journal of Abnormal and Social Psychology, 67,* 371–378.

Milgram, S. (1965). Some conditions of obedience and disobedience to authority. *Human Relations, 18,* 56–76.

Milgram, S. (1974). *Obedience to authority.* New York: Harper & Row.

Milgram, S., Liberty, H. J., Toledo, R., & Wackenhut, J. (1986). Response to intrusion into waiting lines. *Journal of Personality and Social Psychology, 51,* 683–689.

Miller, A. G. (Ed.). (1982). *In the eye of the beholder: Contemporary issues in stereotyping.* New York: Praeger.

Miller, G. A. (1956). The magical number seven, plus or minus two: Some limits on our capacity for information processing. *Psychological Review, 63,* 81–97.

Miller, G. A. (1981). *Language and speech.* San Francisco: W. H. Freeman.

Miller, N. E. (1941). The frustration-aggression hypothesis. *Psychological Review, 48,* 337–442.

Miller, N. E. (1959). Liberalization of basic S-R concepts: Extension to conflict behavior, motivation, and social learning. In S. Koch (Ed.), *Psychology: A study of science.* New York: McGraw-Hill.

Miller, N. E. (1969). Learning of visceral and glandular responses. *Science, 163,* 434–445.

Miller, N. E. (1985, February). Rx: Biofeedback. *Psychology Today,* pp. 54–59.

Miller, N. E. (1985). The value of behavioral research on animals. *American Psychologist, 40,* 432–440.

Millon, T. (1986). On the past and future of the DSM-III: Personal recollections and projections. In T. Millon & G. L. Klerman (Eds.), *Contemporary directions in psychopathology.* New York: Guilford Press.

Millon, T., & Klerman, G. L. (Eds.). (1986). *Contemporary directions in psychopathology: Toward the DSM-IV.* New York: Guilford Press.

Milner, B., Corkin, S., & Teuber, H. L. (1968). Further analysis of the hippocampal amnesic syndrome: 14 year follow-up study of H. M. *Neuropsychologica, 6,* 215–234.

Mineka, S. (in press). A primate model of phobic fears. In H. Eysenck & I. Martin (Eds.), *Theoretical foundations of behavior therapy.* New York: Plenum.

Mineka, S., & Cook, M. (1986). Immunization against the observational conditioning of snake fear in rhesus monkeys. *Journal of Abnormal Psychology.*

Mintz, J. (1983). Integrating research evidence: A commentary on meta-analysis. *Journal of Consulting and Clinical Psychology, 51,* 71–75.

Minuchin, P. (1985). Families and individual development: Provocations from the field of family therapy. *Child Development, 56,* 289–302.

Minuchin, P. P., & Shapiro, E. K. (1983). The school as a context for social development. In P. H. Mussen (Ed.), *Carmichael's manual of child psychology* (4th ed., Vol. 4). New York: John Wiley.

Minuchin, S. (1974). *Families and family therapy.* Cambridge, MA: Harvard University Press.

Mischel, W. (1968). *Personality and assessment.* New York: Wiley.

Mischel, W. (1973). Toward a cognitive social learning reconceptualization of personality. *Psychological Review, 80,* 252–283.

Mischel, W. (1984). Convergences and challenges in the search for consistency. *American Psychologist, 39,* 351–364.

Mischel, W. (1986). *Personality* (4th ed.). New York: Holt, Rinehart, & Winston.

Mischel, W., & Baker, N. (1975). Cognitive transformations of reward objects through instructions. *Journal of Personality and Social Psychology, 31,* 254–261.

Mischel, W., Ebbesen, E. B., & Zeiss, A. R. (1972). Cognitive and attentional mechanisms in delay of gratification. *Journal of Personality and Social Psychology, 21,* 204–218.

Mischel, W., Peake, P. K., & Zeiss, A. R. (1984). *Longitudinal studies of delay behavior.* Unpublished manuscript, Stanford University, Stanford, CA.

Mishara, B. L. (1976, July 22). Suicide. *The Philadelphia Inquirer,* Section C, p. 1.

Miskin, M. (1987, February). *The neurobiological basis of memory.* Paper presented at Symposium on Memory and Aging, American Association for the Advancement of Science, Chicago.

Moates, D. R., & Schumacher, G. M. (1980). *An introduction to cognitive psychology.* Belmont, CA: Wadsworth.

Money, J. (1987). Sin, sickness, or status? Homosexual gender identity and psychoneuroendocrinology. *American Psychologist,* 384–399.

Money, J., & Ehrhardt, A. A. (1972). *Man and woman, boy and girl.* Baltimore: Johns Hopkins Press.

Monnier, M., & Hosli, L. (1965). Humoral regulation of sleep and wakefulness by hypnogenic and activating dialyzable factors. *Progress in Brain Research, 18,* 118–123.

Monroe, R. (1988). *Creative brainstorms.* New York: Irvington.

Montemayor, R., & Hanson, E. (1985). A naturalistic view of conflict between adolescents and their parents and siblings. *Journal of Early Adolescence, 5,* 23–30.

Moody, R. (1977). *Reflections on life after life.* New York: Bantam.

Mook, D. G. (1987). *Motivation.* New York: Norton.

Moore-Ede, M. C., Sulzman, F. M., & Fuller, C. A. (1982). *The clocks that time us.* Cambridge, MA: Harvard University Press.

Moscovici, S. (1985). Social influence and conformity. In G. Lindzey & E. Aronson (Eds.), *Handbook of social psychology* (3rd ed., Vol. 2). New York: Random House.

Motokawa, K., Taira, N., & Okuda, J. (1962). Spectral response of single units in the primate cortex. *Tohoku Journal of Experimental Medicine, 79,* 320–337.

Mountcastle, V. B. (1975). The view from within: Pathways to the study of perception. *Johns Hopkins Medical Journal, 136,* 109–131.

Mountcastle, V. B. (1986, August). *The parietal visual system and optic flow.* Paper presented at the annual meeting of the American Psychological Association, Washington, DC.

Moushegian, G. W. (1987). Personal communication. University of Texas at Dallas, Richardson, TX.

Mullen, B., Futrell, D., Stairs, D., Tice, D. M., Baumeister, R. F., Dawson, K. E., Riordan, C. A., Radloff, C. E., Goethals, G. R., Kennedy, J. G., & Rosenfeld, P. (1986). Newscasters' facial expressions and voting behavior of viewers: Can a smile elect a president? *Journal of Personality and Social Psychology, 51,* 291–295.

Munoz, R. F. (Ed.). (1987). *Depression prevention: Research directions.* New York: Hemisphere.

Murphy, S. (1986). Unpublished ethnographic data. Reported in Beck, J., & Morgan, P. A. (1986). Designer drug confusion: A focus on MDMA. *Journal of Drug Education, 16,* 297.

Murray, H. A. (1938). *Explorations in personality.* New York: Oxford University Press.

Mussen, P., Honzik, M., & Eichorn, D. (1982). Early adult antecedents of life satisfaction at age 70. *Journal of Gerontology, 37,* 316–322.

Myers, B. J. (1984). Mother-infant bonding: Rejoinder to Kennell and Klaus. *Developmental Review, 4,* 283–288.

Nagler, S., & Mirsky, A. F. (1985). Introduction: The Israeli high-risk study. *Schizophrenic Bulletin, 11,* 19–28.

Nathans, J., Thomas, D., & Hogness, D. S. (1986). Molecular genetics of human color vision: The genes encoding blue, green, and red pigments. *Science, 232,* 193–202.

Neill, W. T., & Westberry, R. L. (1987). Selective attention and the suppression of cognitive noise. *Journal of Experimental Psychology: Learning, Memory, and Cognition, 13,* 327–334.

Neisser, U. (1982). *Memory observed.* New York: W. H. Freeman.

Nelson, K. E. (1978). *Children's language* (Vol. 1). New York: Gardner Press.

Nemeth, C. J. (1986). Intergroup relations between majority and minority. In S. Worschel & W. G. Austin (Eds.), *Psychology of intergroup relations.* Chicago: Nelson-Hall.

Neuberg, S. L., & Fiske, S. T. (1986, August). *Motivational influences on impression formation: Outcome dependency, accuracy-driven attention, and individuating processes.* Paper presented at the meeting of the American Psychological Association, Washington, DC.

Neugarten, B. (1986). The aging society. In A. Pifer & L. Bronte (Eds.), *Our aging society: Paradox and promise.* New York: Norton.

Neugarten, B. L., & Neugarten, D. A. (1986). Age in the aging society. *Daedalus, 115,* 31–49.

Nicholls, J. G. (1984). Conceptions of ability and achievement motivation. In R. E. Ames & C. Ames (Eds.), *Motivation in education.* New York: Academic Press.

Norem, J. K., & Cantor, N. (1986). Anticipatory and post-hoc cushioning strategies: Optimism and defensive pessimism in "risky" situations. *Cognitive Therapy Research, 10,* 347–362.

Norris, P. (1987). Biofeedback, voluntary control, and human potential. *Journal of Biofeedback and Self-Regulation, 11,* 1–20.

Nottelman, E. D., Susman, E. J., Blue, J. H., Inoff-Germain, G., Dorn, L. D., Loriaux, D. L., Cutler, G. B., & Chrousos, G. P. (1987). Gonadal and adrenal hormone correlates of adjustment in early adolescence. In N. R. Learner & T. Foch (Eds.), *Biological-psychosocial interactions in early adolescence: A life-span perspective.* Hillsdale, NJ: Erlbaum.

Nottelmann, E. D., Susman, E. J., Inoff, G. E., Dorn, L. D., Cutler, G. B., Loriaux, D. L., & Chrousos, G. P. (1985, May). *Hormone level and adjustment and behavior during early adolescence.* Paper presented at the annual meeting of the American Association for the Advancement of Science, Los Angeles, CA.

Novlin, D., Robinson, B. A., Culbreth, L. A., & Tordoff, M. G. (1983). Is there a role for the liver in the control of food intake? *American Journal of Clinical Nutrition, 9,* 233–246.

Nowak, C. A. (1977). Does youthfulness equal attractiveness? In L. E. Troll, J. Israel, & K. Israel (Eds.), *Looking ahead: A woman's guide to the problems and joys of growing older.* Englewood Cliffs, NJ: Prentice-Hall.

Noyes, R., Crowe, R. R., Harris, E. L., Hamra, B. J., McChesney, L. M., & Chaudhry, D. R. (1986). Relationship between panic disorder and major depression. *Archives of General Psychiatry, 43,* 227–232.

O'Brien, E. J., & Myers, J. L. (1985). When comprehension difficulty improves memory for text. *Journal of Experimental Psychology: Learning, Memory, and Cognition, 11,* 12–21.

O'Leary, K. D. (Ed.). (in press). *Assessment of marital discord.* Hillsdale, NJ: Erlbaum.

O'Leary, K. D., & Wilson, G. T. (1987). *Behavior therapy* (2nd ed.). Englewood Cliffs, NJ: Prentice-Hall.

Olds, J.M. (1958). Self-stimulation experiments and differentiated rewards systems. In H. H. Jasper, L. D. Proctor, R. S. Knighton, W. C. Noshay, & R. T. Costello (Eds.), *Reticular formation of the brain.* Boston: Little, Brown.

Olds, J. M., & Milner, P. M. (1954). Positive reinforcement produced by electrical stimulation of the septal area and other areas of the rat brain. *Journal of Comparative and Physiological Psychology, 47,* 419–427.

Orne, M. T. (1975). Implications of laboratory research for the detection of deception. In N. Ansley (Ed.), *Legal admissibility of the polygraph.* Springfield, IL: Charles C. Thomas.

Orne, M. T. (1979). The use and misuse of hypnosis in court. *International Journal of Clinical and Experimental Hypnosis, 27,* 311–341.

Ornstein, R. E. (1972). *The psychology of consciousness.* San Francisco: W. H. Freeman.

Ornstein, R. E. (Ed.). (1973). *The nature of human consciousness.* New York: Viking.

Osgood, C. E. (1959). Suggestions for winning the real war with communism. *Journal of Conflict Resolution, 3,* 295–325.

Osgood, C. E. (1983). *Psycho-social dynamics and the prospects for mankind.* Unpublished manuscript, University of Illinois.

Owen, S. V., Froman, R. D., & Moscow, H. (1981). *Educational psychology.* Boston: Little, Brown.

Oyama, S. (1973). *A sensitive period for the acquisition of a second language.* Unpublished doctoral dissertation, Harvard University, Cambridge, MA.

Paivio, A. (1971). *Imagery and verbal processes.* New York: Holt, Rinehart, & Winston.

Paivio, A. (1986). *Mental representations: A dual coding approach.* New York: Oxford University Press.

Panksepp, J. (1986). The neurochemistry of behavior. *Annual Review of Psychology, 37,* 77–107.

Pardes, H. (1986). Neuroscience and psychiatry: Marriage or coexistence? *American Journal of Psychiatry, 143,* 1205–1212.

Parke, R. D., & Sawin, D. B. (1980). The family in early infancy. In F. Pederson (Ed.), *The father-infant relationship: Observational studies in a family context.* New York: Praeger.

Parker, J., & Gottman, J. (1985, April). *Making friends with an extraterrestrial: Conversational skills and friendship formation in young children.* Paper presented at the meeting of the Society for Research in Child Development, Toronto.

Parkin, A. J. (1984). Levels of processing, context, and facilitation of pronunciation. *Acta Psychologica, 55,* 19–29.

Parks, T. E., & Cross, R. G. (1986, October). Prime illusion. *Psychology Today,* pp. 6–8.

Parlee, M. B. (1979, April). The friendship bond: PT's survey report on friendship in America. *Psychology Today,* pp. 43–54, 113.

Parmalee, A. H., & Stern, E. (1972). Development of states in infants. In C. B. Clemente, D. P. Purura, & F. E. Mayer (Eds.), *Sleep and the maturing of the nervous system.* New York: Academic Press.

Pasnau, R. O. (1986). Response to the presidential address. Health care crisis: A campaign for action. *American Journal of Psychiatry, 143,* 955–958.

Patterson, G. R. (1982). *Coercive family processes.* Eugene, OR: Castalia Publications.

Patterson, G. R., & Stouthamer-Loeber, M. (1984). The correlation of family management practices and delinquency. *Child Development, 55,* 1299–1307.

Paul, G. L. (1966). *Insight versus desensitization in psychotherapy: An experiment in anxiety reduction.* Stanford, CA: Stanford University Press.

Paul, G. L. (1967). Strategy of outcome research in psychotherapy. *Journal of Consulting Psychology, 31,* 109–119.

Pavlov, I. P. (1927). *Conditioned reflexes* (F. V. Anrep, Trans. and Ed.). New York: Dover.

Pearce, J. M. (in press). *Introduction to animal cognition.* Hillsdale, NJ: Erlbaum.

Pedersen, S. A. (in press). A perspective on research concerning fatherhood. In P. Berman & S. A. Pedersen (Eds.), *Men's transition to parenthood.* Hillsdale, NJ: Erlbaum.

Penfield, W. (1947). Some observations on the cerebral cortex of man. *Proceedings of the Royal Society, 134,* 349.

Pennebaker, J. W. (1982). *The psychology of physical symptoms.* New York: Springer-Verlag.

Penner, S. G. (1987). Parental responses to grammatical and ungrammatical child utterances. *Child Development, 58,* 376–384.

Peplau, L. A., Miceli, M., & Morasch, B. (1982). Loneliness and self-evaluation. In L. A. Peplau & D. Perlman (Eds.), Loneliness: A sourcebook of current theory, research, and therapy. New York: Wiley.

Perls, F. (1969). *Gestalt therapy verbatim.* Lafayette, CA: Real People Press.

Perry, S., Cooper, A. M., & Michels, R. (1987). The psychodynamic formulation: Its purpose, structure, and clinical application. *American Journal of Psychiatry, 144,* 543–551.

Pert, A. B., & Snyder, S. H. (1973). Opiate receptor: Demonstration in nervous tissue. *Science, 179,* 1011–1014.

Pervin, L. A. (1986, August). *Person-environment congruence in the light of the person-situation controversy.* Paper presented at the meeting of the American Psychological Association, Washington, DC.

Pervin, L. A. (1987, August). *Current trends in personality theory.* Paper presented at the meeting of the American Psychological Association, New York.

Peskin, H. (1967). Pubertal onset and ego functioning. *Journal of Abnormal Psychology, 72,* 1–15.

Petersen, A. C. (1979, January). Can puberty come any faster? *Psychology Today,* pp. 45–56.

Petersen, A. C. (in press). Adolescent development. *Annual Review of Psychology, 39.*

Petersen, A. C., & Taylor, B. (1980). The biological approach to adolescence. In J. Adelson (Ed.), *Handbook of adolescent psychology.* New York: Wiley.

Pfaffman, C. (1977). Biological and behavioral substrates of the sweet tooth. In J. M. Weiffenbach (Ed.), *Taste and development.* Besthesda, MD: U.S. Department of Health, Education, and Welfare.

Phares, E. J. (1984). *Personality.* Columbus, OH: Charles E. Merrill.

Phillips, E. L. (1968). Achievement place: Token reinforcement procedures in a home-style rehabilitation setting for predelinquent boys. *Journal of Applied Behavior Analysis, 1,* 213–223.

Phillips, L. W. (1986). Behavior analysis in a case of "post-partum depression." *Journal of Behavior Therapy and Experimental Psychiatry, 17,* 101–104.

Piaget, J. (1960). *The child's conception of the world.* Totowa, NJ: Littlefield.

Piaget, J. (1967). The mental development of the child. In D. Elkind (Ed.), *Six psychological studies by Piaget.* New York: Random House.

Pihl, R. O., & Zacchia, C. (1986). Alcohol and aggression: A test of the affect-arousal hypothesis. *Aggressive Behavior, 12,* 367–375.

Piliavin, I. N., Rodin, J., & Piliavin, J. A. (1969). Good Samaritanism: An underground phenomenon? *Journal of Personality and Social Psychology, 13,* 289–299.

Pinker, S. (1984). *Language learnability and language development.* Cambridge, MA: Harvard University Press.

Pittman, T. S., & Heller, J. S. (1987). Social motivation. *Annual Review of Psychology, 38,* 461–489.

Plath, S. (1971). The bell jar. New York: Harper and Row.

Platt, J. J. (1986). *Heroin addiction* (2nd ed.). Malabar, FL: Kreiger.

Plomin, R. (1986). *Development, genetics, and psychology.* Hillsdale, NJ: Erlbaum.

Plomin, R. (1987, April). *Adoption studies: Nurture as well as nature.* Paper presented at the biennial meeting of the Society for Research and Child Development, Baltimore, MD.

Plomin, R., & DeFries, J. C. (1983). The Colorado Adoption Project. *Child Development, 54,* 276–289.

Plutchik, R. (1980). *Emotion: A psychoevolutionary synthesis.* New York: Harper & Row.

Pomeranz, B. (1984). Acupuncture and the endorphins. *Ethos, 10,* 385–393.

Popper, K. R., & Eccles, J. C. (1977). *The self and its brain.* Berlin: Springer-Verlag.

Posner, M. I. (1987, August). *Structure and function of selective attention.* Paper presented at the meeting of the American Psychological Association, New York.

Potts, G. R. (1979). The role of inference in memory for real and artificial information. In R. Revlin & R. E. Mayer (Eds.), *Human reasoning.* Washington, DC: V. H. Winston.

Premack, A. J., & Premack, D. (1972). Teaching language to an ape. *Scientific American, 227,* 92–99.

Prentice-Dunn, S., & Spivey, C. B. (1986). Extreme deindividuation in the laboratory: Its magnitude and subjective components. *Personality and Social Psychology Bulletin, 12,* 206–215.

Pressley, M., McDaniel, M. A., Turnure, J. E., Wood, E., & Ahmad, M. (1987). Generation and precision of elaboration: Effects on intentional and incidental learning. *Journal of Experimental Psychology: Learning, Memory, and Cognition, 13,* 291–300.

Pribram, K. H. (1986). The cognitive revolution and mind/brain issues. *American Psychologist, 41,* 507–520.

Price, L. H., Charney, D. S., Rubin, A. L., & Heninger, G. R. (1986). Adrenergic receptor function in depression: The cortisol response to yohimbine. *Archives of General Psychiatry, 43,* 849–858.

Prunell, M., Boada, J., Feria, M., & Benitez, M. A. (1987). Antagonism of the stimulant and depressant effects of ethanol in rats by naloxone. *Psychopharmacology, 92,* 215–218.

Pylyshyn, Z. W. (1973). What the mind's eye tells the mind's brain: A critique of mental imagery. *Psychological Bulletin, 80,* 1–24.

Quigley-Fernandez, B., & Tedeschi, J. T. (1978). The bogus pipeline as lie detector: Two validity studies. *Journal of Personality and Social Psychology, 36*, 247–256.

Randi, J. (1980). *Flim-flam!* New York: Lippincott.

Randi, J. (1986, August 29). Inquiry: Psychic tricks. *USA Today*, p. 9A.

Randolph, F. L., Lindenberg, R. E., & Menn, A. Z. (1987). Residential facilities for the mentally ill. *Community Mental Health Journal, 22*, 77–89.

Rapaport, D. (1967). On the psychoanalytic theory of thinking. In M. M. Gill (Ed.), *The collected papers of David Rapaport*. New York: Basic Books.

Raskin, M., Bali, L. R., & Peeke, H. V. (1980). Muscle biofeedback and transcendental meditation. *Archives of General Psychiatry, 37*, 93–97.

Ratcliffe, R., & McKoon, G. (1986). More on the distinction between episodic and semantic memories. *Journal of Experimental Psychology: Learning, Memory, and Cognition, 12*, 312–313.

Reed, G. S. (1987). Rules of clinical understanding in classical psychoanalysis and self-psychology: A comparison. *Journal of the American Psychoanalytic Association, 35*, 421–446.

Regier, D. A., Myers, J. K., Kramer, M., Robins, L. N., Blazer, D. G., Hough, R. L., Eaton, W. W., & Locke, B. Z. (1984). The NIMH epidemiologic catchment area program: Historical contact, major objectives, and study population characteristics. *Archives of General Psychiatry, 41*, 949–958.

Reisenzein, R. (1983). The Schachter theory of emotion: Two decades later. *Psychological Bulletin, 94*, 239–264.

Reiser, B. J., Black, J. B., & Abselson, R. P. (1985). Knowledge structures in the organization and retrieval of autobiographical memories. *Cognitive Psychology, 17*, 89–137.

Rescorla, R. A. (1967). Pavlovian conditioning and its proper control procedures. *Psychological Review, 54*, 71–80.

Rescorla, R. A. (1987). A Pavlovian analysis of goal-directed behavior. *American Psychologist, 42*, 119–130.

Rescorla, R. A. (in press). Behavioral studies of Pavlovian conditioning. *Annual Review of Neuroscience, 11*.

Rescorla, R. A., & Wagner, A. R. (1972). A theory of Pavlovian conditioning: Variations in the effectiveness of reinforcement and nonreinforcement. In A. Black & W. F. Prokasy (Eds.), *Classical conditioning II: Current research and theory*. New York: Appleton-Century-Crofts.

Revitch, E., & Schlesinger, L. B. (1978). Murder: Evaluation, classification, and prediction. In I. L. Kutash, S. B. Kutash, & L. B. Schlesinger (Eds.), *Violence*. San Francisco: Jossey-Bass.

Rich, C. L., Young, D., & Fowler, R. C. (1986). San Diego suicide study. *Archives of General Psychology, 43*, 577–582.

Richmond, J. B. (1979). *Healthy people: The surgeon general's report on health promotion and disease prevention* (DHEW Publication No. 79-55071). Washington DC: U.S. Government Printing Office.

Richter, C. P. (1957). On the phenomenon of sudden death in animals and man. *Psychosomatic Medicine, 19*, 191–198.

Riess, M., Kalle, R. J., & Tedeschi, J. T. (1981). Bogus pipeline attitude assessment, impression management, and misattribution in induced compliance setting. *Journal of Social Psychology, 115*, 247–258.

Roberts, D. E., & Maccoby, N. (1985). Effects of mass communications. In G. Lindzey & E. Aronson (Eds.), *Handbook of social psychology* (3rd ed., Vol. 2). New York: Random House.

Robins, L. N., Helzer, J. E., Weissman, M. M., Orvashcel, H., Gruenberg, E., Burke, J. D., & Regier, D. A. (1984). Lifetime prevalence of specific psychiatric disorders in three sites. *Archives of General Psychiatry, 41*, 949–958.

Robinson, F. P. (1961). *Effective study*. New York: Harper & Row.

Rodin, J. (1981). Current status of the internal-external hypothesis for obesity. *American Psychologist, 36*, 361–372.

Rodin, J. (1984, December). Interview: A sense of control. *Psychology Today*, pp. 38–45.

Rodin, J. (1987, August). *Hunger, taste, and mother: Biobehavioral determinants of eating and its disorders*. Paper presented at the meeting of the American Psychological Association, New York.

Rodin, J., & Langer, E. J. (1977). Long-term effects of a control-relevant intervention with the institutionalized aged. *Journal of Personality and Social Psychology, 35*, 897–902.

Roedder, D. L., Sternthal, B., & Calder, B. J. (1983). Attitude-behavior consistency in children's responses to television advertising. *Journal of Marketing Research, 20*, 337–349.

Rofe, Y. (1984). Stress and affiliation: A utility theory. *Psychological Review, 91*, 251–268.

Rogers, C. R. (1961). *On becoming a person*. Boston: Houghton-Mifflin.

Rogers, C. R. (1963). The actualizing tendency in relation to "motives" and consciousness. In M. R. Jones (Ed.), *Nebraska Symposium on Motivation*. Lincoln, NE: University of Nebraska Press.

Rogers, C. R. (1967). Carl R. Rogers. In E. G. Boring & G. Lindzey (Eds.), *A history of psychology in autobiography*. New York: Macmillan.

Rogers, C. R. (1974). In retrospect: Forty-six years. *American Psychologist, 29*, 115–123.

Rogers, C. R. (1980). *A way of being*. Boston: Houghton-Mifflin.

Romer, D., Gruder, C. L., & Lizzadro, T. (1986). A person-situation approach to altruistic behavior. *Journal of Personality and Social Psychology, 51*, 1001–1012.

Rosch, E. H. (1973). On the internal structure of perceptual and semantic categories. In T. E. Moore (Ed.), *Cognition and the acquisition of language*. New York: Academic Press.

Rosch, E. H. (1988). Coherence and categorization: A historical review. In F. Kessel (Ed.), *The development of language and language resources*. Hillsdale, NJ: Erlbaum.

Rose, D. S. (1986). "Worse than death": Psychodynamics of rape victims and the need for psychotherapy. *American Journal of Psychiatry, 143*, 817–824.

Rosenblith, J. F., & Sims-Knight, J. E. (1985). *In the beginning*. Monterey, CA: Brooks/Cole.

Rosenfeld, A. H. (1985, June). Depression: Dispelling despair. *Psychology Today*, pp. 28–34.

Rosenhan, D. L. (1973). On being sane in insane places. *Science, 179*, 250–258.

Rosenthal, D. (1963). *The Genain quadruplets*. New York: Basic Books.

Rosenthal, N. E., Sack, D. A., Gillin, J. C. Lewy, A. J., Goodwin, F. K., Davenport, Y., Mueller, P. S., Newsome, D. A., & Wehr, T. A. (1984). Seasonal affective disorder: A description of the syndrome and preliminary findings with light therapy. *Archives of General Psychiatry, 41*, 72–80.

Rosenthal, R., & Jacobsen, L. (1968). *Pygmalion in the classroom*. New York: Holt, Rinehart & Winston.

Ross, L. (1974). Obesity and externality. In S. Schachter & J. Rodin (Eds.), *Obese humans and rats*. Hillsdale, NJ: Erlbaum.

Ross, L. (1977). The intuitive psychologist and his shortcomings: Distortions in the attribution process. In L. Berkowitz (Ed.), *Advances in experimental psychology* (Vol. 10). New York: Academic Press.

Ross, M., & Sicoly, F. (1979). Egocentric biases in availability and attribution. *Journal of Personality and Social Psychology, 37*, 322–336.

Ross, R. T. (1986). Pavlovian second-order conditioned analgesia. *Journal of Experimental Psychology: Animal Behavior Processes, 12*, 32–39.

Ross, R. T., & LoLordo, V. M. (1987). Devaluation of the relation between Pavlovian occasion-setting and instrumental discriminative stimuli. *Journal of Experimental Psychology: Animal Behavior Processes, 13*, 3–16.

Rotenberg, C. T. (1987). Current psychoanalytic theory and practice: Can there by any one valid unitary approach? *The American Journal of Psychoanalysis, 47*, 41–50.

Rowland, N. E., & Antelman, S. M. (1976). Stress-induced hyperphagia and obesity in rats: A possible model for understanding human obesity. *Science, 191*, 310–312.

Rozin, E. (1982). The structure of cuisine. In L. M. Barker (Ed.), *The psychobiology of human food selection*. Westport, CT: AVI Publishing.

Rubenstein, C., & Shaver, P. (1982). *In search of intimacy*. New York: Delacorte Press.

Rubin, D. C. (1985, September). The subtle deceiver: Recalling our past. *Psychology Today*, pp. 38–46.

Rubin, D. C., & Kozin, M. (1984). Vivid memories. *Cognition, 16*, 81–95.

Rubin, E. H., Zorumski, C. F., & Guze, S. B. (1986). Somatoform disorders. In T. Millon & G. L. Klerman (Eds.), *Contemporary directions in psychopathology*. New York: Guilford Press.

Rubin, Z. (1970). Measurement of romantic love. *Journal of Personality and Social Psychology, 16*, 265–273.

Rubin, Z. (1979, October). Seeking a cure for loneliness. *Psychology Today*.

Rubin, Z. (1981, May). Does personality really change after 20? *Psychology Today*.

Rubin, Z., & Mitchell, C. (1976). Couples research as couples counseling. *American Psychologist, 31*, 17–25.

Rumelhart, D. E., & McClelland, J. L. (1986). *Parallel distributed processing: Explorations in the microstructure of cognition*. Cambridge, MA: MIT Press.

Rushton, J. P., Fulker, D. W., Neale, M. C., Nias, D. K. B., & Eysenck, H. J. (1986). Altruism and aggression: The heritability of individual differences. *Journal of Personality and Social Psychology, 50*, 1192–1198.

Sackheim, H. A. (1985, June). The case for ECT. *Psychology Today*, pp. 37–40.

Sackheim, H. A., Decina, P., Portnoy, P. N., & Mayitz, S. (1987). Studies of dosage, seizure threshold, and seizure duration in ECT. *Biological Psychiatry, 22*, 249–268.

Sagan, C. (1980). *Cosmos*. New York: Random House.

Santrock, J. W. (1987). *Life-span development* (2nd ed.). Dubuque, IA: Wm. C. Brown Publishers.

Santrock, J. W., & Bartlett, J. C. (1986). *Developmental psychology*. Dubuque, IA: Wm. C. Brown Publishers.

Santrock, J. W., & Warshak, R. A. (1986). Development, relationships, and legal/clinical considerations in father-custody families. In M. E. Lamb (Ed.), *The father's role: Applied perspectives*. New York: John Wiley.

Sapir, E. (1958). Language and environment. In D. G. Mandelbaum (Ed.), *Selected writings of Edward Sapir in language, culture, and personality*. Berkeley: University of California Press.

Sarason, I. G., & Sarason, B. R. (1987). *Abnormal psychology* (5th ed.). Englewood Cliffs, NJ: Prentice-Hall.

Sarbin, T. R. (1986, August). *The framework clash in hypnosis*. Paper presented at the annual meeting of the American Psychological Association, Washington, DC.

Saslow, C. (1982). *Basic research methods*. Reading, MA: Addison-Wesley.

Satir, V. (1964). *Conjoint family therapy*. Palo Alto, CA: Science and Behavior Books.

Saxe, L., Dougherty, D., & Cross, T. (1985). The validity of polygraph testing: Scientific analysis and public controversy. *American Psychologist, 40*, 355–366.

Scardamalia, M., Bereiter, C., & Goelman, H. (1982). The role of production factors in writing ability. In M. Nystrand (Ed.), *What writers know*. New York: Academic Press.

Scarr, S. (1975). Genetics and the development of intelligence. In F. D. Horowitz (Ed.), *Review of child development research* (Vol. 4). Chicago: University of Chicago Press.

Scarr, S. (1984, May). Interview. *Psychology Today*, pp. 59–63.

Scarr, S. (1986, August). *Child care dilemma: Infant care*. Paper presented at the meeting of the American Psychological Association, Washington, DC.

Scarr, S., & Weinberg, R. A. (1976). IQ test performance of black children adopted by white families. *American Psychologist, 31*, 726–739.

Scarr, S., & Weinberg, R. A. (1979). Nature and nurture strike (out) again. *Intelligence, 3*, 31–39.

Scarr, S., & Weinberg, R. A. (1983). The Minnesota Adoption Studies: Genetic differences and malleability. *Child Development, 54*, 260–267.

Schachter, S. (1971). Some extraordinary facts about obese humans and rats. *American Psychologist, 26*, 129–144.

Schachter, S., & Singer, J. E. (1962). Cognitive, social, and physiological determinants of emotional state. *Psychological Review, 69*, 379–399.

Schacter, D. L. (in press). Implicit memory: History and current status. *Journal of Experimental Psychology: Learning, Memory, and Cognition*.

Schaffer, H. R., & Emerson, P. E. (1964). The development of social attachments in infancy. *Monographs of the Society for Research in Child Development, 29* (3, Serial No. 94).

Schaie, K. W. (1984). The Seattle longitudinal study: A 21-year exploration of psychometric intelligence in adulthood. In K. W. Schaie (Ed), *Longitudinal studies of adult psychological development*. New York: Guilford Press.

Schank, R., & Abelson, R. (1977). *Scripts, plans, goals, and understanding*. Hillsdale, NJ: Erlbaum.

Scheff, T. J. (1966). *Being mentally ill: A sociological theory*. Chicago: Aldine.

Scheff, T. J. (1986). Accountability in psychiatric diagnosis: A proposal. In T. Millon & G. L. Klerman (Eds.), *Contemporary directions in psychopathology*. New York: Guilford Press.

Schneider, D. S., & Blankmeyer, B. L. (1983). Prototype salience and implicit personality theories. *Journal of Personality and Social Psychology, 44*, 712–722.

Schoenrade, P. A., Batson, C. D., Brandt, J. R., & Loud, R. E. (1986). Attachment, accountability, and motivation to benefit another not in distress. *Journal of Personality and Social Psychology, 51*, 557–563.

Schofield, J., & Pavelchak, M. (1985). The day after: The impact of a media event. *American Psychologist, 40*, 542–548.

Schulz, R., & Alderman, D. (1974). Clinical research and the stages of dying. *Omega, 5*, 137–143.

Schunk, D. H. (1983). Developing children's self-efficacy and skills: The roles of social comparative information and goal setting. *Contemporary Educational Psychology, 8*, 76–86.

Schuster, C. (1986, May 1). Statement to Congressional Subcommittee on Bills Relating to Designer Drugs.

Schwartz, G. F., Weingerger, D. A., & Singer, J. A. (1981). Cardiovascular differentiation of happiness, sadness, anger, and fear following imagery and exercise. *Psychosomatic Medicine, 43*, 343–364.

Schwartz, M. A., & Wiggins, O. P. (1986). Systems and structuring of meaning: Contributions to a biopsychosocial medicine. *American Journal of Psychiatry, 143*, 1213–1221.

Schwarzwald, J., Bizman, A., & Raz, M. (1983). The foot-in-door paradigm: Effects of second request size on donation probability and donor generosity. *Personality and Social Psychology Bulletin, 9*, 443–450.

Sears, D. O. (1983). The persistence of early political predispositions: The role of attitude objects and life stage. *Review of Personality and Social Psychology, 4*, 79–186.

Sears, R. R., & Feldman, S. S. (Eds.). (1973). *The seven ages of man*. Los Altos, CA: William Kaufman.

Segerberg, O. (1982). *Living to be 100: 1200 who did and how they did it*. New York: Charles Scribner & Sons.

Sekuler, R., Pantle, A., & Levinson, E. (1978). Physiological basis of motion perception. In R. Held, H. W. Leibowitz, & H. L. Teuber (Eds.), *Handbook of sensory physiology: Vol. 8. Perception*. Berlin: Springer-Verlag.

Seligman, M. E. P. (1970). On the generality of the laws of learning. *Psychological Review, 77*, 406–418.

Seligman, M. E. P. (1975). Helplessness: On depression, development and death. San Francisco: W. H. Freeman.

Selye, H. (1974). *Stress without distress*. Philadelphia: W. B. Saunders.

Selye, H. (1983). The stress concept: Past, present, and future. In C. L. Cooper (Ed.), *Stress research*. New York: Wiley.

Seymour, R. B., Wesson, D. R., & Smith, D. E. (1986). Editor's introduction. *Journal of Psychoactive Drugs, 18*, 287–289.

Shaver, P. (1986a, August). *Being lonely, falling in love: Perspectives from attachment theory*. Paper presented at the meeting of the American Psychological Association, Washington, DC.

Shaver, P. (1986b). Consciousness without the body. *Contemporary Psychology, 31*, 645–647.

Shaver, P., & Buhrmester, D. (1983). Loneliness, sex-role orientation, and group life: A social needs perspective. In P. B. Paulus (Ed.), *Basic group processes*. New York: Springer-Verlag.

Shaw, E. D., Stokes, P. E., Mann, J. J., & Manevitz, A. (1987). Effects of lithium carbonate on the memory and motor speed of bipolar outpatients. *Journal of Abnormal Psychology, 96*, 64–69.

Sheehy, G. (1976). *Passages*. New York: Dutton.

Sheingold, K., & Tenney, Y. J. (1982). Memory for a salient childhood event. In U. Niesser (Ed.), *Memory observed*. New York: W. H. Freeman.

Shekelle, R. B., Gayle, M., & Norusis, M. (1985). Type A behavior (Jenkins Activity Survey) and risk of coronary heart disease in the Aspirin Myocardial Infarction Study. *American Journal of Cardiology, 56*, 221–225.

Sheldon, W. H. (1954). *Atlas of men*. New York: Harper & Brothers.

Shepard, G. M. (1974). *The synaptic organization of the brain*. New York: Oxford University Press.

Shepard, R. N. (1967). Recognition memory for words, sentences, and pictures. *Journal of Verbal Learning and Verbal Behavior, 6*, 156–163.

Sherif, M., Harvey, O. J., White, B. J., Hood, W. R., & Sherif, C. W. (1961). *Intergroup cooperation and competition: The Robbers Cave experiment*. Norman, OK: University Book Exchange.

Shimoff, E., Matthews, B. A., & Catania, A. C. (1986). Human operant performance: Sensitivity and pseudosensitivity to contingencies. *Journal of the Experimental Analysis of Behavior, 46*, 149–157.

Shneidman, E. S. (1971). Suicide among the gifted. *Suicide and Life-threatening Behavior, 1*, 23–45.

Shostrum, E. L. (1967). *Man, the manipulator*. New York: Bantam Books.

Shotland, R. L. (1985, June). When bystanders just stand by. *Psychology Today*, pp. 50–55.

Showers, C. (1986, August). *The motivational consequences of negative thinking: Those who imagine the worst try harder*. Paper presented at the annual meeting of the American Psychological Association, Washington, DC.

Showers, C., & Cantor, N. (1985). Social cognition: A look at motivated strategies. *Annual Review of Psychology, 36*, 275–305.

Shuckit, M. A. (1986). Genetic and clinical problems of alcoholism and affective disorder. *American Journal of Psychiatry, 143*, 140–147.

Siegel, R. (1985). Treatment of cocaine abuse: Historical and contemporary perspectives. *Journal of Psychoactive Drugs, 17*, 1–9.

Siegel, R. K. (1980). The psychology of life after death. *American Psychologist, 35*, 911–931.

Siegel, R. K., & Jarvik, M. E. (1975). Drug-induced hallucinations in animals and man. In R. K. Siegel & L. J. West (Eds.), *Hallucinations*. New York: Wiley.

Siegel, S. (1983). Classical conditioning, drug tolerance, and drug dependence. In *Research advances in alcohol and drug problems* (Vol. 7). New York: Plenum.

Siegler, R. (1983). Information processing approaches to development. In P. H. Mussen (Ed.), *Handbook of child psychology* (4th ed., Vol. 2, No. 1). New York: Wiley.

Siffre, M. (1975). Six months alone in a cave. *National Geographic, 147*, 426–435.

Sigelman, C. K., Thomas, D. B., Sigelman, L., & Ribich, F. D. (1986). Gender, physical attractiveness, and electability: An experimental investigation of voter biases. *Journal of Applied Social Psychology, 16*, 229–248.

Sigelman, L., & Welch, S. (1984). Race, gender, and opinion toward black and female presidential candidates. *Public Opinion Quarterly, 2*, 465–475.

Silverman, N. N., & Corsini, R. J. (1984). Is it true what they say about Adler's individual psychology? *Teaching of Psychology, 11*, 188–189.

Silverman, W. H. (1986). Client-therapist cooperation in the treatment of compulsive handwashing behavior. *Journal of Behavior Therapy and Experimental Psychiatry, 17*, 39–42.

Simmons, R. G., & Blyth, D. A. (1987). *Moving into adolescence: The impact of pubertal change and school contexts.* Hawthorne, NY: Aldine.

Simon, N. G., & Whalen, R. E. (1986). Hormonal regulation of aggression: Evidence for a relationship among genotype, receptor binding, and behavioral sensitivity to androgen and estrogen. *Aggressive Behavior, 12*, 255–266.

Simpson, E. R. (in press). Action of ACTH on adrenal cortical cells. *Annual Review of Physiology, 50.*

Simpson, J. A., Campbell, B., & Berscheid, E. (1986). The association between love and marriage: Kephart(1967) twice revisited. *Personality and Social Psychology Bulletin, 12*, 363–372.

Singer, J. L. (1975). *The inner world of daydreaming.* New York: Harper & Row.

Singer, J. L. (1984). *The human personality.* San Diego: Harcourt Brace Jovanovich.

Singer, M. T. (1977). The Rorschach as a transaction. In M. A. Rickers-Orsiankina (Ed.), *Rorschach psychology.* Huntington, NY: Krieger.

Singh, N. N., & Millichamp, C. J. (1987). Independent and social play among profoundly mentally retarded adults. *Journal of Applied Behavior Analysis, 20*, 23–34.

Skinner, B. F. (1938). *The behavior of organisms: An experimental analysis.* New York: Appleton-Century-Crofts.

Skinner, B. F. (1948). *Walden II.* New York: Macmillan.

Skinner, B. F. (1953). *Science and human behavior.* New York: Macmillan.

Skinner, B. F. (1957). *Verbal behavior.* New York: Appleton-Century-Crofts.

Skinner, B. F. (1961). Teaching machines. *Scientific American, 205*, 90–102.

Skinner, B. F. (1976). *About behaviorism.* New York: Vintage.

Skinner, B. F. (1986, August). *Whatever happened to psychology as a science of behavior?* Paper presented at the meeting of the American Psychological Association, Washington, DC.

Skinner, B. F. (1987, August). *Dialogue with B. F. Skinner.* Meeting of the American Psychological Association, New York.

Skodak, M., & Skeels, H. M. (1949). A final follow-up study of one hundred adopted children. *Journal of Genetic Psychology, 75*, 85–125.

Slavin, R. (1983). When does cooperative learning increase student achievement? *Psychological Bulletin, 94*, 429–445.

Sloan, W. W., & Solano, C. H. (1984). The conversational styles of lonely males with strangers and roommates. *Personality and Social Psychology Bulletin, 10*, 293–301.

Slobin, D. (1972, July). Children and language: They learn the same all around the world. *Psychology Today,* pp. 71–76.

Small, I. F., Milstein, V., Miller, M. J., Malloy, F. W., & Small, J. G. (1986). Electroconvulsive treatment—indications, benefits, and limitations. *American Journal of Psychotherapy, 15*, 343–355.

Smith, D. E. (1986). Cocaine-alcohol abuse: Epidemiological, diagnostic, and treatment considerations. *Journal of Psychoactive Drugs, 18*, 117–129.

Smith, G. P., Gibbs, J., & Kulkosky, P. J. (1980). Relationships between brain gut peptides and neurons in the control of food intake.

Smith, J., Dixon, R. A., & Baltes, P. B. (in press). Expertise in life planning. In M. L. Commons, J. D. Sinnott, F. A. Richards, & C. Armon (Eds.), *Beyond Formal Operations II.* New York: Praeger.

Smith, M. L., Glass, G. V., & Miller, R. L. (1980). *The benefits of psychotherapy.* Baltimore: Johns Hopkins Press.

Smith, R. (1985). Recovery and tissue repair. *British Medical Bulletin, 41*, 295–301.

Smith, T. L. (1986). Biology as allegory [Review of *The nature of selection*]. *Journal of The Experimental Analysis of Behavior, 46*, 105–112.

Smyth, M. M., Morris, P. E., Levy, P. M., & Ellis, A. W. (in press). *Cognition in action.* Hillsdale, NJ: Erlbaum.

Snow, C. E. (1988). The development of conversation between mothers and babies. In M. B. Franklin & S. S. Barten (Eds.), *Child language: A reader.* New York: Oxford University Press.

Snyder, M. (1979). Self-monitoring processes. In L. Berkowitz (Ed.), *Advances in experimental social psychology* (Vol. 12). New York: Academic Press.

Snyder, M. (1981). Impression management. In L. S. Wrightsman & K. Deaux (Eds.), *Social psychology in the eighties* (3rd ed.). Monterey, CA: Brooks/Cole.

Snyder, M. (1987). *Public appearances/Private realities.* New York: W. H. Freeman.

Snyder, M., Berscheid, E., & Glick, P. (1985). Focusing on the exterior and the interior: Two investigations of the initiation of personal relationships. *Journal of Personality and Social Psychology, 48*, 1427–1439.

Snyder, M., & Ickes, W. (1985). Personality and social behavior. In G. Lindzey & E. Aronson (Eds.), *Handbook of social psychology* (3rd. ed., Vol. 2). New York: Random House.

Sober, E. (1984). *The nature of selection: Evolutionary theory in philosophical focus.* Cambridge, MA: MIT Press.

Soloman, R. L. (1980). The opponent-process theory of acquired motivation: The costs of pleasure and the benefits of pain. *American Psychologist, 35*, 691–712.

Soloman, R. L. (1986, May). *The costs of pleasure and the benefits of pain.* Paper presented at the meeting of the American Association for the Advancement of Science, Philadelphia.

Sophian, C. (1985). Perseveration and infants' search: A comparison of two- and three-location tasks. *Developmental Psychology, 21*, 187–194.

Spanos, N. P. (1986). Hypnotic behavior: A social-psychological interpretation of amnesia, analgesia, and "trance logic." *Behavioral and Brain Sciences, 9*, 449–502.

Spearman, C. (1927). The abilities of man. New York: Macmillan.

Spence, J. T., & Helmreich, R. L. (1978). *Masculinity and femininity: Their psychological dimensions.* Austin, TX: University of Texas Press.

Sperling, G. (1960). The information available in brief visual presentations. *Psychological Monographs, 74* (Whole No. 11).

Sperry, R. W. (1964). The great cerebral commissure. *Scientific American, 210*, 42–52.

Sperry, R. W. (1974). Lateral specialization in surgically separated hemispheres. In F. O. Schmitt & F. G. Worden (Eds.), *The neurosciences: Third study program.* Cambridge, MA: MIT Press.

Sperry, R. W. (1976). Mental phenomena as causal determinants in brain function. In G. G. Globus, G. Maxwell, & I. Savodnick (Eds.), *Consciousness and the brain.* New York: Plenum.

Sperry, R. W., & Gazzaniga, M. S. (1967). Language following surgical disconnection of the hemispheres. In C. H. Milikan & F. L. Darley (Eds.), *Brain mechanisms underlying speech and language.* New York: Grune & Stratton.

Spiegel, R., Koberle, S., & Allen, S. R. (1986). Significance of slow wave sleep: Considerations from a clinical viewpoint. *Sleep, 9*, 66–79.

Spielberger, C. D., & Grier, K. (1983). Unpublished manuscript, University of South Florida, Tampa.

Squire, L. R. (1986). Mechanisms of memory. *Science, 232*, 1612–1619.

Squire, L. R. (1987). *Memory and brain.* New York: Oxford University Press.

Sroufe, L. A. (1985). Attachment classification from the perspective of infant-caregiver relationships and infant temperament. *Child Development, 56*, 1–14.

Sroufe, L. A. (in press). The role of infant-caregiver attachment in development. In J. Belsky & T. M. Nezworski (Eds.), *Clinical implications of attachment.* Hillsdale, NJ: Erlbaum.

St. Jean, R. (1986). Hypnosis: Artichoke or onion? *Behavioral and Brain Sciences, 9*, 482.

Start, M. C. (1987). Enhancing social skills and self-perceptions of physically disabled adults. *Behavior Modification, 11*, 3–16.

Steele, C. M., & Southwick, L. (1985). Alcohol and social behavior I: The psychology of drunken excess. *Journal of Personality and Social Psychology, 48*, 18–34.

Steggles, S., Stam, H. J., Fehr, R., & Azcoin, P. (1987). Hypnosis and cancer. *American Journal of Clinical Hypnosis, 29*, 281–290.

Steinberg, L. (1986). Latchkey children and susceptibility to peer pressure: An ecological analysis. *Developmental Psychology, 22*, 433–439.

Steinberg, L. (1987). Impact of puberty on family relations: Effects of pubertal status and pubertal timing. *Developmental Psychology, 23*, 451–460.

Stern, D. N. (1974). Mother and infant at play. In M. Lewis & L. A. Rosenblum (Eds.), *The effect of the infant on the caregiver.* New York: Wiley.

Stern, J. S. (1984). Is obesity a disease of inactivity? In A. J. Stunkard & E. Stellar (Eds.), *Eating and its disorders.* New York: Raven Press.

Sternberg, R. J. (1985). *Beyond IQ.* New York: Cambridge University Press.

Sternberg, R. J. (1986). *Intelligence applied.* San Diego: Harcourt Brace Jovanovich.

Sternberg, R. J. (1986). A triangular theory of love. *Psychological Review, 93*, 119–135.

Sternberg, R. J. (1987, August). *The future of intelligence testing.* Paper presented at the meeting of the American Psychological Association, New York.

Sternberg, R. J., Conway, B. E., Ketron, J. L., & Berstein, M. (1981). People's conceptions of intelligence. *Journal of Personality and Social Psychology, 41*, 37–55.

Stilwell, R. G. (1984). Statement before the Committee on Armed Services, United States Senate. In *Polygraphs for counterintelligence purposes in the Department of Defense.* Washington, DC: U.S. Government Printing Office.

Stipek, D. J., & Hoffman, J. M. (1980). Children's achievement-related expectancies as a function of academic performance histories and sex. *Journal of Educational Psychology, 72*, 861–865.

Stone, G. C. (1986, August). *Beliefs and health: A research agenda.* Paper presented at the meeting of the American Psychological Association, Washington, DC.

Stoner, J. (1961). *A comparison of individual and group decisions, including risk.* Unpublished master's thesis, School of Industrial Management, Massachusetts Institute of Technology.

Straus, M. A., Gelles, R. J., & Steinmetz, S. K. (1980). *Behind closed doors.* Garden City, NJ: Anchor Books.

Strean, H. (Ed.). (1988). *Psychoanalytic technique.* New York: Haworth.

Streissguth, A. P., Martin, D. C., Barr, H. M., Sandman, B. M., Kirchner, G. L., & Darby, B. L. (1984). Intra-uterine alcohol and nicotine exposure: Attention and reaction time in 4-year-old children. *Developmental Psychology, 20,* 533–541.

Strupp, H. H. (1986, August). *Psychotherapy: Current trends.* Paper presented at the meeting of the American Psychological Association, Washington, DC.

Stuart, B. D., Hughes, C., Frank, E., Anderson, B., Kendall, K., & West, D. (1987). The aftermath of rape. *Journal of Nervous and Mental Disease, 175,* 90–94.

Stuart, R. B., & Jacobson, B. (1987). *Couple's therapy workbook.* Champaign, IL: Research Press.

Stuart, R. B., & Mitchell, C. (1980). Self-help groups in the control of obesity. In A. J. Stunkard (Ed.), *Obesity.* Philadelphia: W. B. Saunders.

Stunkard, A., Levine, H., & Fox, S. (1970). The management of obesity: Patient self-help and medical treatment. *Archives of Internal Medicine, 125,* 1067–1072.

Stunkard, A. J. (in press). The regulation of body weight and the treatment of obesity. In H. Weiner & A. Baum (Eds.), *Eating regulations and discontrol.* Hillsdale, NJ: Erlbaum.

Suedfeld, P., Ballard, E. J., Baker-Brown, G., & Borrie, R. A. (1986). Flow of consciousness in restricted environmental stimulation. *Imagination, Cognition, and Personality, 5,* 219–230.

Suedfeld, P., Ballard, E. J., & Murphy, M. (1983). Water immersion and flotation: From stress experiment to stress treatment. *Journal of Environmental Psychology, 3,* 147–155.

Suedfeld, P., Corteen, R. S., & McCormick, C. (1986). The role of integrative complexity in military leadership: Robert E. Lee and his opponents. *Journal of Applied Social Psychology, 16,* 498–507.

Sullivan, H. S. (1953). *The interpersonal theory of psychiatry.* New York: Norton.

Sutton, R. G., & Kessler, M. (1986). National study of the effects of clients' socioeconomic status on clinical psychologists' professional judgments. *Journal of Consulting and Clinical Psychology, 54,* 275–276.

Sweeney, C. A., Lynn, S. J., & Bellezza, F. S. (1986). Hypnosis, hypnotizability, and imagery-mediated learning. *International Journal of Clinical and Experimental Hypnosis, 34,* 29–36.

Symons, D. (1986, August). *If we're all Darwinians, what's the fuss about?* Paper presented at the meeting of the American Psychological Association, Washington, DC.

Symons, D. (in press). The evolutionary approach: Can Darwin's view of life shed light on human sexuality? In J. Geer & W. O'Donohue (Eds.), *Approaches and paradigms in human sexuality.* New York: Plenum.

Syvalahti, E. K. (1985). Drug treatment of insomnia. *Annals of Clinical Research, 17,* 265–272.

Szasz, T. (1965). *The ethics of psychoanalysis.* New York: Basic Books.

Szasz, T. (1977). *Psychiatric slavery: When confinement and coercion masquerade as cure.* New York: Free Press.

Tajfel, H. (1970). Experiments in intergroup discrimination. *Scientific American, 223,* 96–102.

Tajfel, H. (1978). The achievement of group differentiation. In H. Tajfel (Ed.), *Differentiation between social groups: Studies in the social psychology of intergroup relations.* London: Academic Press.

Tajfel, H. (Ed.). (1982). *Social identity and intergroup relations.* Cambridge: Cambridge University Press.

Tajfel, H., & Turner, J. C. (1986). The social identity theory of intergroup behavior. In S. Worschel & W. G. Austin (Eds.), *Psychology of intergroup relations.* Chicago: Nelson-Hall.

Tanner, J. M. (1962). *Growth at adolescence.* Oxford: Blackwell Scientific Publications.

Tarkenton, C. (1986, August). Pornography and violence. *APA Monitor,* pp. 8–9.

Tart, C. (1975). *Learning to use extrasensory perception.* Chicago: University of Chicago Press.

Tart, C. T. (1986). Enlarging our world of experience. *Contemporary Psychology, 31,* 508–509.

Tavris, C. (1982, November). Anger diffused. *Psychology Today,* pp. 25–35.

Tavris, C. (1984). *Anger: The misunderstood emotion.* New York: Simon & Schuster.

Teri, L., & Lewinsohn, P. M. (1986). Individual and group treatment of unipolar depression: Comparison of treatment outcome and identification of predictors of successful treatment outcome. *Behavior Therapy, 17,* 215–228.

Terman, L. M. (1925). *Genetic studies of genius: Vol. 1. Mental and physical traits of a thousand gifted children.* Stanford, CA: Stanford University Press.

Terrace, H. (1979). *Nim: A chimpanzee who learned sign language.* New York: Knopf.

Thigpen, C. H., & Cleckley, H. M. (1957). *Three faces of Eve.* New York: McGraw-Hill.

Thomas, A., & Chess, S. (1987). Temperament. In Goldsmith, H. H. (convener), Roundtable: What is temperament? *Four Approaches. Child Development, 58,* 505–529.

Thomas, A., Chess, S., & Birch, H. G. (1970). The origin of personality. *Scientific American, 223,* 102–109.

Thomas, C. B. (1983). Unpublished manuscript, The Johns Hopkins University, Baltimore, MD.

Thomas, J. C. (1974). An analysis of behavior in the hobbits-orcs problem. *Cognitive Psychology, 6,* 257–269.

Thompson, R. F. (1985). *The brain.* New York: W. H. Freeman.

Thoresen, C. E., Eagleston, J. R., Kirmil-Gray, K., & Bracke, P. E. (1985, August). *Exploring the Type A behavior pattern in children and adolescents.* Paper presented at the meeting of the American Psychological Association, Los Angeles.

Thurstone, L. L. (1938). *Primary mental abilities.* Chicago: University of Chicago Press.

Tinbergen, N. (1969). *The study of instinct.* New York: Oxford University Press.

Tolman, E. C. (1932). *Purposive behavior in animals and man.* New York: Appleton-Century-Crofts.

Tolman, E. C. (1948). Cognitive maps in rats and men. *Psychological Review, 55,* 189–208.

Tolman, E. C., Ritchie, B. F., & Kalish, D. (1946). Studies in spatial learning: I. Orientation and short-cut. *Journal of Experimental Psychology, 36,* 13–24.

Tomlinson-Keasey, C., Warren, L. W., & Elliott, J. E. (1986). Suicide among gifted women: A prospective study. *Journal of Abnormal Psychology, 95,* 123–130.

Triplett, N. (1898). The hynamogenci factors in pacemaking and competition. *American Journal of Psychology, 9,* 507–533.

Trivers, R. L. (1971). The evolution of reciprocal altruism. *Quarterly Review of Biology, 46,* 35–57.

Troll, L. E., & Bengston, V. L. (1982). Intergenerational relations throughout the life span. In B. B. Wolman (Ed.), *A handbook of developmental psychology.* Englewood Cliffs, NJ: Prentice-Hall.

Trudel, M. (1987, April). *A cross-lag analysis of associations between attachment and temperament during the third year.* Paper presented at the meeting of the Society for Research in Child Development, Baltimore.

Tsuang, M. (1976). Schizophrenia around the world. *Comparative Psychiatry, 17,* 477–481.

Tuchman-Duplessis, H. (1975). Drug effects on the fetus. *Monographs on drugs* (Vol. 2). Sydney: ADIS Press.

Tulving, E. (1972). Episodic and semantic memory. In E. Tulving & W. Donaldson (Eds.), *Origins of memory.* NY: Academic Press.

Tulving, E. (1983). *Elements of episodic memory.* New York: Oxford University Press.

Tulving, E. (1986). What kind of hypothesis is the distinction between episodic and semantic memory? *Journal of Experimental Psychology: Learning, Memory, and Cognition, 12,* 307–311.

Tulving, E. (1987, June). *Oh, my, how times have changed, or have they?* Paper presented at the Symposium on Varieties of Memory and Consciousness. Paper in honour of Endel Tulving. University of Toronto.

Turk, D. C., Rudy, T. E., & Salovey, P. (1984). Health protection: Attitudes and behaviors of LPN's, teachers, and college students. *Health Psychology, 3,* 189–210.

Turkinton, C. (1985, September). Three-pronged approach explores roots of mental illness. *APA Monitor,* pp. 10–11.

Turkle, S. (1984). *The second self.* Cambridge, MA: Harvard University Press.

Turnbull, C. (1972). *The mountain people.* New York: Simon & Schuster.

Tversky, A., & Kahneman, D. (1973). Availability: A heuristic for judging frequency and probability. *Cognitive Psychology, 5,* 207–232.

Tyack, D. (1976). Ways of seeing: An essay on the history of compulsory schooling. *Harvard Educational Review, 46,* 355–389.

United States Department of Health, Education, and Welfare. (1976). *The condition of education in the United States.* Washington, DC: U.S. Government Printing Office.

United States Department of Justice, Bureau of Justice Statistics (1983, October). *Report to the nation on crime and violence* (NJC-87068). Washington, DC: U.S. Government Printing Office.

Udolf, R. (1981). *Handbook of hypnosis for professionals.* New York: Van Nostrand Rheinhold.

Udry, J. R., & Morris, N. M. (1977). Human sexual behavior at different stages of the menstrual cycle. *Journal of Reproduction and Fertility, 51,* 419.

Upton, A. C. (1977). Pathology. In C. E. Finch & L. Hayflick (Eds.), *Handbook of the biology of aging.* New York: Van Nostrand Reinhold.

Vaillant, G. E. (1977). *Adaptation to life.* Boston: Little, Brown.

Vanltallie, T. B. (1984). The enduring storage capacity for fat: Implications for treatment of obesity. In A. J. Stunkard & E. Stellar (Eds.), *Eating and its disorders.* New York: Raven Press.

van Kammen, D. P., van Kammen, W. B., Mann, L. S., Seppala, T., & Linnoila, M. (1986). Dopamine metabolism in the cerebrospinal fluid of drug-free schizophrenic patients with and without cortical atrophy. *Archives of General Psychiatry, 43,* 978–983.

Vaughn, E., & Fisher, A. E. (1962). Male sexual behavior induced by intracranial electrical stimulation. *Science, 137,* 758–760.

Veroff, J. (1982). Assertive motivations: Achievement versus power. In A. J. Stewart (Ed.), *Motivation and society.* San Francisco: Jossey-Bass.

Vokey, J. R., & Read, J. D. (1985). Subliminal messages: Between the devil and the media. *American Psychologist, 40,* 1231–1239.

von Bekesy, G. (1960). Vibratory patterns of the basilar membrane. In E. G. Wever (Ed.), *Experiments in hearing.* New York: McGraw-Hill.

von Frisch, K. (1974). Decoding the language of the bee. *Science, 185,* 663–668.

Voss, J. F., Green, T. R., Post, T. A., & Penner, B. C. (1983). Problem solving skill in social sciences. In G. Power (Ed.), *The psychology of learning and motivation* (Vol. 17). New York: Academic Press.

Waddington, C. H. (1957). *The strategy of the genes.* London: Allen and Sons.

Wagenaar, W. A., Gideon, K., & Pleit-Kuper, A. (1984). *Acta Psychologica, 56,* 167–178.

Wagenwoord, J., & Bailey, R. (1978). *Men: A book for women.* New York: Avon Books.

Walker, L. J. (1987, August). *A longitudinal study of moral stages.* Paper presented at the meeting of the American Psychological Association, New York.

Wallace, R. K., & Benson, H. (1972). The physiology of meditation. *Scientific American, 226,* 85–90.

Wallach, H. (1987). Perceiving a stable environment when one moves. *Annual Review of Psychology, 38,* 1–27.

Wallach, M. A. (1985). Creative testing and giftedness. In F. D. Horowitz & M. O'Brien (Eds.), *The gifted and the talented.* Washington, DC: American Psychological Association.

Wallach, M. A., & Kogan, N. (1965). *Modes of thinking in young children.* New York: Holt, Rinehart, & Winston.

Wallerstein, J. S., & Kelly, J. B. (1980). *Surviving the breakup.* New York: Basic Books.

Walster, E., Aronson, E., Abrahams, D., & Rottman, L. (1966). Importance of physical attractiveness in dating behavior. *Journal of Personality and Social Psychology, 4,* 508–516.

Walter, V., & Affiliates. (1986). *The 16 P-F Test.* Champaign, IL: The Institute for Personality and Ability Testing.

Ward, W. M., Orne, E. C., Cook, M. R., & Orne, M. T. (1981). Meprobamate reduces accuracy of physiological detection of deception. *Science, 212,* 71–73.

Wasserman, G. S. (1978). *Color vision: An historical introduction.* New York: Wiley.

Waters, E., & Sroufe, L. A. (1983). Social competence as a developmental construct. *Developmental Review, 3,* 79–97.

Watson, D., & Clark, L. A. (1984). Negative affectivity: The disposition to experience aversive emotional states. *Psychological Bulletin, 96,* 465–490.

Watson, J. B. (1930). *Behaviorism.* Chicago: University of Chicago Press.

Watson, J. B., & Raynor, R. (1920). Emotional reactions. *Journal of Experimental Psychology, 3,* 1–14.

Weaver, T. M. (1986). Broken sleep. *American Journal of Nursing, 86,* 146–150.

Webb, L. J., DiClemente, C. C., Johnstone, E. E., Sanders, J. L., & Perley, R. A. (1981). *DSM-III training guide.* New York: Brunner/Mazel.

Webb, W. B. (1978). Sleep and dreams. *Annual Review of Psychology, 29,* 223–252.

Wechsler, D. (1949). *Wechsler Intelligence Scale for Children.* New York: Psychological Corporation.

Wechsler, D. (1955). *Wechsler Adult Intelligence Scale manual.* New York: Psychological Corporation.

Wechsler, D. (1967). *Wechsler Preschool and Primary Scale of Intelligence.* New York: Psychological Corporation.

Wechsler, D. (1972). "Hold" and "Don't Hold" tests. In S. M. Chown (Ed.), *Human aging.* New York: Penguin.

Wechsler, D. (1974). *Wechsler Intelligence Scale for Children—Revised.* New York: Psychological Corporation.

Wechsler, D. (1981). *Wechsler Adult Intelligence Scale—Revised.* New York: Psychological Corporation.

Wehr, T. A., Jacobsen, F. M., Sack, D. A., Arendt, J., Tamarkin, L., & Rosenthal, N. E. (1986). Time of day and suppression of melatonin are not critical for antidepressant effects. *Archives of General Psychiatry, 43,* 870–875.

Wehr, T. A., Wirz-Justice, A., Goodwin, F. K., Duncan, W., & Gillin, J. C. (1979). Phase advance of the circadian sleep-wake cycle as an anti-depressant. *Science, 206,* 710–713.

Weinberger, D. R., Berman, K. F., & Zec, R. F. (1986). Physiologic dysfunction of the dorsolateral prefrontal cortex in schizophrenia. *Archives of General Psychiatry, 43,* 114–124.

Weiner, H., & Baum, A. (Eds.). (in press). *Eating regulations and discontrol.* Hillsdale, NJ: Erlbaum.

Weinman, B., Sanders, R., Kleiner, R., & Wilson, S. (1970). Community-based treatment of chronic psychotics. *Community Mental Health Journal, 6,* 13–21.

Weinstein, N. D. (1984). Reducing unrealistic optimism about illness susceptibility. *Health Psychology, 3,* 431–457.

Weinstein, S. (1968). Intensive and extensive aspects of tactile sensitivity as a function of body part, sex, and laterality. In D. R. Kenshalo (Ed.), *The skin senses.* Springfield, IL: Thomas.

Weiss, R. S. (1973). *Loneliness: The experience of emotional and social isolation.* Cambridge, MA: MIT Press.

Weiten, W. (1983). *Psychology applied to modern life.* Monterey, CA: Brooks/Cole.

Wells, G. L., & Loftus, E. F. (Eds.). (1984). *Eyewitness testimony: Psychological perspectives.* New York: Cambridge University Press.

Wells, G. L., & Turtle, J. W. (1986). Eyewitness identification: The importance of lineup models. *Psychological Bulletin, 3,* 320–329.

Wender, P. H., Kety, S. S., Rosenthal, D., Schulsinger, F., Ortmann, J., & Lunde, I. (1986). Psychiatric disorders in the biological and adoptive families of adopted individuals with affective disorders. *Archives of General Psychiatry, 43,* 923–929.

West, M. (Ed.). (1988). The psychology of meditation. New York: Oxford University Press.

White, B. L. (1988). *Educating the infant and toddler.* Lexington, Mass.: Lexington Books.

White, M. A. (Ed.). (in press). *What curriculum for the information age?* Hillsdale, NJ: Erlbaum.

White, R. W. (1959). Motivation reconsidered: The concept of competence. *Psychological Review, 66,* 297–333.

White, R. W. (1976). *The enterprise of living* (2nd ed.). New York: Holt, Rinehart, & Winston.

White, S. H. (1985, April). *Risings and fallings of developmental psychology.* Paper presented at the biennial meeting of the Society for Research in Child Development, Toronto.

Whitehead, W. E., Burgio, K. L., & Engel, B. T. (1985). Biofeedback treatment of fecal incontinence in geriatric patients. *Journal of the American Geriatrics Society, 33,* 320–324.

Whitehurst, G. J. (1985, April). *The role of imitation in language learning by children with language delay.* Paper presented at the biennial meeting of the Society for Research in Child Development, Toronto.

Whorf, B. L. (1956). *Language, thought, and creativity.* New York: Wiley.

Williams, B. A. (1986). Reinforcement, choice, and response strength. In R. C. Atkinson, R. J. Hernstein, G. Lindzey, & R. D. Luce (Eds.), *Steven's handbook of experimental psychology* (2nd ed.). New York: Wiley.

Williams, R. B. (1986, August). Hostility, anger, and heart disease. *Drug Therapy,* pp. 40–48.

Williams, R. B., Barefoot, J. C., & Haney, T. L. (1986, March). *Type A behavior and angiographically documented coronary atherosclerosis in a sample of 2,289 patients.* Paper presented at the annual meeting of the American Psychosomatic Society, Baltimore.

Williams, R. (1987). Is there life after type A? In T. Field, P. McCabe, & N. Schneiderman (Eds.), *Stress and Coping across Development.* Hillsdale, NJ: Erlbaum.

Wilson, E. (Ed.). (1945). The crack-up. In *Uncollected pieces.* New York: New Directions.

Wilson, E. O. (1975). *Sociobiology: The new synthesis.* Cambridge, MA: Harvard University Press.

Winner, E. (1986, August). Where pelicans kiss seals. *Psychology Today,* pp. 24–35.

Wishnoff, R. (1978). Modeling effects of explicit and nonexplicit sexual stimuli on the anxiety and behavior of women. *Archives of Sexual Behavior, 7,* 455–461.

Wolfe, J. (1986). In the mind's eye. *The mind's eye.* New York: W. H. Freeman.

Wolff, P. H. (1987). *The development of behavioral states and the expression of emotions in early infancy.* Chicago: The University of Chicago Press.

Wolman, B. B. (1987). *The sociopathic personality.* New York: Brunner/Mazel.

Wolpe, J. (1958). *Psychotherapy by reciprocal inhibition.* Stanford, CA: Stanford University Press.

Wolpe, J. (1961). The systematic desensitization treatment of neuroses. *Journal of Mental and Nervous Disease, 132,* 189–203.

Wolpe, J. (1963). Behavior therapy in complex neurotic states. *British Journal of Psychiatry, 110,* 28–34.

Wolpe, J. (1986). Individualization: The categorical imperative of behavior therapy practice. *Journal of Behavior Therapy and Experimental Psychiatry, 17,* 145–153.

Wolpe, J., & Rachman, S. (1960). Psychoanalytic "evidence": A critique based on Freud's case of Little Hans. *Journal of Nervous and Mental Disease, 130,* 135–148.

Women's Medical Center. (1977). *Menopause.* Washington, DC: Women's Medical Center.

Wooden, K. (1981). *The children of Jonestown.* New York: McGraw-Hill.

Wooley, S. C., & Wooley, O. W. (1984). Should obesity be treated at all? In A. J. Stunkard & E. Stellar (Eds.), *Eating and its disorders.* New York: Raven Press.

Woolsey, T. A., & Van der Loos, H. (1970). The structural organization of layer IV in the somatosensory region (SI) of mouse cerebral cortex: The description of a cortical field composed of discrete cytoarchitectonic units. *Journal of Comparative Neurology, 17,* 205–242.

Woolsey, T. A., & Wann, J. R. (1976). Areal changes in mouse cortical barrels following vibrissal damage at different postnatal ages. *Journal of Comparative Neurology, 170,* 53–66.

Worobey, J., & Belsky, J. (1982). Employing the Brazelton Scale to influence mothering: An experimental comparison of three strategies. *Developmental Psychology, 18,* 736–743.

Worschel, S. (1986). The role of cooperation in reducing intergroup conflict. In S. Worschel & W. G. Austin (Eds.), *Psychology of intergroup relations.* Chicago: Nelson-Hall.

Worschel, S., & Austin, W. G. (Eds.). (1986). *Psychology of intergroup relations.* Chicago: Nelson-Hall.

Worschel, T., & Cooper J. (1979). *Understanding social psychology.* Homewood, IL: Dorsey Press.

Wright, J., & Koulack, D. (1987). Dreams and contemporary stress: A disruption-avoidance-adaptation model. *Sleep, 10,* 172–179.

Wyatt, R. J., Cutler, N. R., DeLisi, L. E., Jester, D. V., Kleinman, J. E., Luchins, D. J., Potkin, S. G., & Wingerger, D. R. (1982). Biochemical and morphological factors in the etiology of the schizophrenic disorders. In L. Grinspoon (Ed.), *The American Psychiatric Association annual review, Psychiatry.* Washington, DC: The American Psychiatric Press.

Yalom, I. D. (1975). *The theory and practice of group psychotherapy.* New York: Basic Books.

Yankelovich, D. (1974). *The new morality: A profile of American youth in the 1970s.* New York: McGraw-Hill.

Yankelovich, D., Skelly, F., & White, A. (1984). *Sex stereotypes and candidacy for high level political office.* New York: Yankelovich, Skelly, & White, Inc.

Yarmey, A. D. (1973). I recognize your face but I can't remember your name: Further evidence on the tip of the tongue phenomenon. *Memory and Cognition, 1,* 287–290.

Zajonc, R. B. (1965). Social facilitation. *Science, 149,* 269–274.

Zajonc, R. B. (1984). On the primacy of affect. *American Psychologist, 39,* 117–123.

Zanna, M. P., & Fazio, R. H. (1982). The attitude-behavior relation: Moving toward a third generation of research. In M. P. Zanna, E. T. Higgins, & C. P. Herman (Eds.), *Consistency in social behavior: The Ontario Symposium* (Vol. 2). Hillsdale, NJ: Erlbaum.

Zeiler, M. B. (1987). On optimal choice strategies. *Journal of Experimental Psychology: Animal Behavior Processes, 13,* 31–39.

Zeiss, A. M., & Lewinsohn, P. M. (1986, Fall). Adapting behavioral treatment of depression to meet the needs of the elderly. *Clinical Psychologist,* pp. 98–100.

Zelnick, M., & Kantner, J. F. (1977). Sexual and contraceptive experiences of young unmarried women in the United States, 1976 and 1971. *Family Planning Perspectives, 9,* 55–71.

Zelnick, M., & Kantner, J. F. (1980). Sexual activity, contraceptive use and pregnancy among metropolitan-area teenagers: 1971–1979. *Family Planning Perspectives, 12,* 230–237.

Zembar, M. J., & Naus, M. J. (1985, April). *The combined effects of knowledge base and mnemonic strategies in children's memory.* Paper presented at the biennial meeting of the Society for Research in Child Development, Toronto.

Zigler, E. (1987, April). *Child care for parents who work outside the home: Problems and solutions.* Paper presented at the biennial meeting of The Society for Research in Child Development, Baltimore.

Zigler, E. F. (1987, August). *Issues in mental retardation research.* Paper presented at the meeting of the American Pscyhological Association, New York.

Zigler, E., & Farber, E. A. (1985). Commonalities between the intellectual extremes: Giftedness and mental retardation. In F. D. Horowitz & M. O'Brien (Eds.), *The gifted and the talented.* Washington, DC: American Psychological Association.

Zimbardo, P., Haney, C., Banks, W., & Jaffe, D. (1972). *The psychology of imprisonment: Privation, power, and pathology.* Unpublished manuscript, Stanford University, Stanford, CA.

Zubin, J., & Money, J. (Eds.). (1973). *Contemporary sexual behavior.* Baltimore: Johns Hopkins University Press.

Zuckerman, M. (1979). *Sensation seeking.* Hillsdale, NJ: Erlbaum.

Credits

Photographs

Section Openers

Section One: © Kent Reno/Jeroboam, Inc.; **Section Two:** © Robert Livingston; **Section Three:** © R. Cadge Productions/The Image Bank, Chicago; **Section Four:** © Robert Frerck/Odyssey Productions; **Section Five:** © Paul Slaughter/The Image Bank, Chicago; **Section Six:** © Chris Gray/The Image Works; **Section Seven:** © Dennis J. Cipnic/Photo Researchers, Inc.

Chapter 1

Page 6: © Sovfoto; **page 10:** © Ellis Herwig/Stock, Boston; **page 14:** © Tom McHugh/Photo Researchers, Inc.; **1.1, counterclockwise from top left:** National Library of Medicine, *Dictionary of American Portraits*/Dover Publications, Inc. 1967, Harvard University Archives, Culver Pictures, Inc., Historical Pictures, Chicago, Courtesy of Albert Bandura, Courtesy of Herbert Simon, Courtesy of Roger Sperry, UPI/Bettmann Newsphotos, National Library of Medicine, Harvard University News Office, Culver Pictures, Inc., Culver Pictures, Inc.; **page 17, left:** © F. B. Grunzweig/Photo Researchers, Inc.; **page 17, left center:** © Bob Coyle; **page 17, right center:** NASA/Stock, Boston; **page 17, right:** © Frank Keillor/Jeroboam, Inc.; **page 20:** © Robert Eckert/EKM-Nepenthe; **page 22:** © Mimi Forsyth/Monkmeyer Press; **page 26:** © Bruce Kliewe/Jeroboam, Inc.; **page 29, top:** © Nubar Alexanian/Stock, Boston; **page 29, bottom:** © John Barr/Gamma-Liaison; **page 32:** NIH/Science Source/Photo Researchers, Inc.; **page 33:** © Billy E. Barnes/Jeroboam, Inc.

Chapter 2

Page 41: © Robert Frerck/Odyssey Productions; **2.1, left to right:** NASA/Science Source/Photo Researchers, Inc., © Patricia Caulfield/Photo Researchers, Inc., © Edith G. Haun/Stock, Boston, © 1972 Miguel Castro/Photo Researchers, Inc., © Cleo Freelance Photo, © Jane Lindblad/Photo Researchers, Inc.; **2.2:** © Regents of the University of California; **2.4:** National Library of Medicine; **2.9:** © Dr. Christopher Frederickson; **page 55:** © Harold V. Green/Valan Photos; **2.14:** © Lennart Nilsson, from *Behold Man,* Little, Brown and Company, Boston; **2.15:** © Floyd Bloom, Director of Preclinical Neuroscience and Endocrinology, Scripps Clinic and Research Foundations, La Jolla, CA.; **2.A:** © Lennart Nilsson, from *Behold Man,* Little, Brown and Company, Boston; **2.B:** © Norman E. Rosenthal, MD. Intramural Research Program, National Institute of Mental Health; **page 60:** © Patsy Davidson/The Image Works; **2.C:** from Lou, H., Henriksen, L., and Bruhn, P. Focal cerebral hypoperfusion in children with dysphasia and/or attention deficit disorder. *Archives of Neurology,* vol. 41, Aug. 1984, p. 827. **2.16:** © Lennart Nilsson, from *A Child Is Born,* Dell Publishing Co., New York; **2.23:** © Manfred Kage/Peter Arnold, Inc.; **2.25:** from the Penfield Papers, courtesy of Montreal Neurological Institute.

Chapter 3

Page 85: © Royl/Panographics; **page 87:** © Bob Coyle; **3.2b:** © Helmut Gritscher/Peter Arnold, Inc.; **3.2c:** © Douglas B. Nelson/Peter Arnold, Inc.; **3.3:** © Lennart Nilsson, from *Behold Man,* Little, Brown and Company, Boston; **3.8:** Courtesy of Munsell Color, Baltimore, MD.; **3.10a,b:** Fritz Goreau/LIFE Magazine © 1944 Time, Inc.; **3.17:** © The British Library; **3.18:** © Science Source/Photo Researchers, Inc.; **3.19–3.20c:** © Lennart Nilsson, from *Behold Man,* Little, Brown and Company, Boston; **3.22:** © 1988 M. C. Escher. c/o Cordon Art—Baarn—Holland; **3.23:** "A Kindly Man of Fearful Aspect," Kuniyoshi (late Edo era), Collection by Juzo Suzuki (from Museum of Fun Exhibition by Asahi Shimbun) 1979; **3.25:** © Billy E. Barnes/CLICK, Chicago; **3.28:** © Bob Coyle; **3.32b:** © Erich Hartmann/Magnum Photos; **3.33(left):** © Herman Eisenbeiss/Photo Researchers, Inc.; **3.33(right):** © Emilio Mercado/Jeroboam, Inc.; **3.35:** © Dr. Peter Thompson; **3.36:** REPRINTED FROM PSYCHOLOGY TODAY MAGAZINE, Copyright © 1976, American Psychological Association. Don Peterson, Photographer.

Chapter 4

4.2: © Picturepoint Ltd.; **4.4:** from DREAMSTAGE Scientific Catalog © 1977. J. Allan Hobson and Hoffmann-La Roche, Inc.; **4.6:** "Acorn Harvest" miniature from *Les Tres Riches Heures* of Jean duc de Berry, ca. 1413. THE GRANGER COLLECTION, New York; **4A:** © Michael Siffre from Bloom, Floyd et al.: *Brain, Mind and Behavior.* 1985 W. H. Freeman Company; **page 126, top:** © Leonard Lee Rue III/Monkmeyer Press; **page 126, bottom:** © Frank Siteman/Jeroboam, Inc.; **4.7:** © SCALA/Art Resource, Inc., New York; **4.9a–c:** Courtesy of Samuel LeBaron, Ph.D.; **page 137:** © Jerry Howard/Stock, Boston; **page 142:** © John T. Barr/Gamma-Liaison; **page 143, top:** © Jon Feingersh/Stock, Boston; **4.13a,b:** U.S. Drug Enforcement Administration; **4.13c:** © Owen Franken/Stock, Boston; **page 144:** © Jon Feingersh/Stock, Boston.

Chapter 5

Page 154: © Robert Frerck/Odyssey Productions; **page 158:** © Alan Carey/The Image Works; **page 160:** © Nicholas Sapieha/Stock, Boston; **5.9:** © Cleo Freelance Photography; **5.10:** Courtesy of B. F. Skinner; **page 166:** © Mimi Forsyth/Monkmeyer Press; **page 169:** © Ken Gaghan/Jeroboam, Inc.; **5.14:** REPRINTED FROM PSYCHOLOGY TODAY MAGAZINE Copyright © 1985, American Psychological Association. Roe DiBona, photographer; **5.15:** © Albert Bandura; **5.22:** Courtesy of Animal Behavior Enterprises, Inc.; **page 180:** © Tom McHugh/Photo Researchers, Inc.

Chapter 6

Page 186: © Bill Anderson/Monkmeyer Press; **page 187:** © Martin Rogers/Stock, Boston; **page 189:** © Frank Keillor/Jeroboam, Inc.; **page 190, top:** © Mimi Forsyth/Monkmeyer Press; **page 190, center:** © Ken Gaghan/Jeroboam, Inc.; **page 195:** © Max Winter/Stock, Boston; **page 197:** © Al Horvath/Panographics; **page 201a:** Bettmann Newsphotos; **page 201b:** © Ellis Herwig/Stock, Boston; **page 201c:** NASA; **page 201d:** © Howard Dratch/The Image Works; **page 202, top:** © MacDonald Photography/Panographics; **page 202, bottom:** © Lowell J. Georgia/Photo Researchers, Inc.; **page 204:** UPI/Bettmann Newsphotos; **page 205, top:** © James Shaffer; **page 205, bottom:** © Bob Coyle.

Chapter 7

Page 212: © Hugh Rogers/Monkmeyer Press; **page 217:** UPI/Bettmann Newsphotos; **page 218:** Historical Pictures Service, Chicago; **page 221:** © Dallas Morning News/Gamma-Liaison; **page 227:** © Billy E. Barnes/Stock, Boston; **7.14:** AP/Wide World Photos; **page 231:** © Gregory G. Dimijian/Photo Researchers, Inc.; **7A:** © Dr. R. Allen Gardner; **7B:** © Susan Kuklin; **page 236:** © Anthony Bannister/Earth Scenes; **page 240, top:** © Simon/Photo Researchers, Inc.; **page 240, center:** © George Holton/Photo Researchers, Inc.

Chapter 8

Page 245: © Owen Franken/Stock, Boston; **page 247:** © Billy E. Barnes/Jeroboam, Inc.; **8.5, top to bottom:** Historical Pictures Service, Chicago, Dictionary of American Portraits, Dover Publications, Inc. 1967, Culver Pictures, Inc., National Library of Medicine, Historical Pictures Service, Chicago, Historical Pictures Service, Chicago; **page 257, left:** UPI/Bettmann Newsphotos; **page 257, right:** Historical Pictures Service, Chicago; **page 259:** © Susan Yivisaker/Jeroboam, Inc.; **8A, 8B:** © Enrico Ferorelli/Dot, Inc.; **page 265:** © David Austen/Stock, Boston; **8D:** Sternberg, R. J. *Beyond IQ.* New York: Cambridge University Press, 1985; **8.9:** © Jill Cannefax/EKM-Nepenthe.

Chapter 9

9.1: Herb Gehr/Life Magazine, © 1947 Time Inc.; **9.2:** © Lennart Nilsson, from *Behold Man,* Little, Brown and Company, Boston; **9A(b):** © Dr. Ricardo Asche; **9.3, 9.4:** © Lennart Nilsson, from *Behold Man,* Little, Brown and Company, Boston; **page 289:** © Taeke Henstra, Petit Format/Photo Researchers, Inc.; **9.7:** Conel, J. L.: *Postnatal Development of the Human Cerebral Cortex. Vols I–VI,* 1939–1963. Harvard University Press.; **9.8:** © Martin Rogers/Stock, Boston; **9.10:** © Doug Goodman/Monkmeyer Press; **9.11a:** © Leonard Lee Rue III/Photo Researchers, Inc.; **9.11b:** © Mitch Reardon/Photo Researchers, Inc.; **9.11c:** © Allen Green/Photo Researchers, Inc.; **9.12:** courtesy of Harlow Primate Laboratory, University of Wisconsin; **9.14:** © Sybille Kalas; **page 300:** © Dennis Cox; **page 306:** © Timothy Strang; **page 310:** © Ken Gaghan/Jeroboam, Inc.; **page 321:** National Library of Medicine.

Chapter 10

Page 323: © Katrina Thomas/Photo Researchers, Inc.; **page 325:** © Cleo Freelance Photography; **page 326:** © George Goodwin/Monkmeyer Press; **page 330:** © Alan Carey/The Image Works; **page 331:** © Wernher Krutein/Jeroboam, Inc.; **page 342a:** © Owen Franken/Stock, Boston; **page 342b:** UPI/ Bettmann Newsphotos; **page 344:** © George Goodwin/Monkmeyer Press; **page 345:** courtesy of School of Medicine, University of California, San Diego; **page 346:** UPI/Bettmann Newsphotos; **page 351:** AP/Wide World Photos; **page 352:** © Bruce Kliewe/Jeroboam, Inc.

Chapter 11

Page 363, left, left center: courtesy of The Academy of Motion Picture Arts & Sciences; **page 363, right center:** AP/Wide World Photos; **page 363, right:** Historical Pictures Service, Chicago; **11.3:** Teitelbaum, Philip, Appetite, *Proceedings of the American Philosophical Society,* 1964, *108,* 467; **page 369:** © Owen Franken/Stock, Boston; **page 372, left:** © James L. Reynolds; **page 372, right:** © Howard Dratch/The Image Works; **page 373:** © Suzanne Wu/Jeroboam, Inc.; **page 377:** © Cleo Freelance Photography; **page 380, top:** © Bob Coyle; **page 380, top center:** © Anthony Mercieca/Photo Researchers, Inc.; **page 380, bottom center:** © Sven-Olof Lindblad/Photo Researchers, Inc., **page 380, bottom:** © Jill Cannefax/EKM-Nepenthe; **page 382:** © Robert V. Eckert/EKM-Nepenthe; **11.8:** courtesy of Harlow Primate Laboratory, University of Wisconsin; **11.10:** courtesy of Community Relations, University of British Columbia; **page 392:** © Lawrence Migdale/Photo Researchers, Inc.; **page 393:** courtesy of Dr. Sandra Graham; **page 394:** © Hugh Rogers/Monkmeyer Press.

Chapter 12

Page 399: © Robert Eckert/EKM-Nepenthe; **page 401:** © Dennis Budd Gray/Jeroboam, Inc.; **12.3, left and middle right:** © John T. Urban; **12.3, middle left and right:** © Paul Ekman; **12A:** © James Shaffer; **page 406:** © Richard Hutchings/Photo Researchers, Inc.; **page 407:** © L. S. Stepanowicz/Panographics; **12.6:** courtesy of Donald Dutton, Department of Psychology, University of British Columbia, Vancouver; **page 409:** © Terry E. Eller/Stock, Boston; **12.7a,b:** © Dr. Tiffany Field; **12.9a,b:** © Dr. A. Liepins/Photo Researchers, Inc.; **page 418, 422:** © Alan Carey/The Image Works; **page 426:** © Robert Frerck/Odyssey Productions.

Chapter 13

13.1: Historical Pictures Service, Chicago; **page 440, top left:** © Robert Eckert/EKM-Nepenthe; **page 440, top right:** © James Marshall/ Marshalplan; **page 440, bottom left:** © James Shaffer; **page 440, bottom center:** © Kit Hedman/ Jeroboam; **page 440, bottom right:** © Richard Hutchings/Photo Researchers, Inc.; **13.3:** © Jonathan T. Wright/Bruce Coleman, Inc.; **page 448:** courtesy of Walter Mischel; **13.4:** Picasso, Pablo, *Girl Before a Mirror. 1932.* Oil on canvas, 64 × 51¼″, Collection, The Museum of Modern Art, N.Y. Gift of Mrs. Simon Guggenheim; **13.6a:** Scala/Art Resource Inc., New York; **13.6b:** Academy of Fine Arts, Florence; **13.6c:** Picasso, Pablo. *The Actor, 1905.* Oil on canvas, H76 ⅜ in, W44 ⅛ in. The Metropolitan Museum of Art, Gift of Thelma Chrysler Foy, 1952; **13.10:** from "Thematic Apperception Test" by Henry A. Murray, Harvard University Press, 1943, President & fellows of Harvard College; **13.11a:** © Cary Wolinsky/Stock, Boston; **13.11b:** © Ken Gaghan/ Jeroboam, Inc.

Chapter 14

Page 472: UPI/Bettmann Newsphotos; **14.1:** AP/ Wide World Photos; **14A:** courtesy of The Academy of Motion Picture Arts and Sciences; **page 481:** © James L. Reynolds; **page 483:** © Alan Carey/The Image Works; **14.3:** © Gerald Martineau, 1975/ *Washington Post;* **page 488:** © Jack Spratt/The Image Works; **14.5:** © Grunnitus/Monkmeyer Press; **14C, 14D:** Monte S. Buchsbaum, M.D.; **page 500, top:** UPI/Bettmann Newsphotos; **page 500, bottom:** © Charles Gatewood/The Image Works.

Chapter 15

15.1: National Museum of Denmark; **15.2:** Historical Pictures Service, Chicago; **15.3:** Historical Pictures Service, Chicago; **page 515:** © Deke Simon/Real People Press; **page 518, top:** © L. S. Stepanowicz/Panographics; **page 518, bottom:** © Howard Dratch/The Image Works; **page 523:** courtesy of Albert Ellis; **page 526, bottom:** © Joseph Nettis/Photo Researchers, Inc.; **page 528:** © Mimi Forsyth/Monkmeyer Press; **page 537:** © Will McIntyre/Photo Researchers, Inc.

Chapter 16

Page 547: UPI/Bettmann Newsphotos; **page 548, left:** AP/Wide World Photos; **page 548, center and right:** © Y. Hemsey/Gamma-Liaison; **page 550:** © Ken Gaghan/Jeroboam, Inc.; **16.3:** © 1987 California Raisin Advisory Board; **page 554:** © Arthur Grace/Stock, Boston; **page 555:** © Bruce Kliewe/Jeroboam, Inc.; **page 559:** © Steve Hansen/ Stock, Boston; **page 561:** © Billy E. Barnes/Stock, Boston; **page 564:** © Ken Kaminsky/Panographics; **16.6:** © William Vandivert; **16.8, both:** courtesy of Philip G. Zimbardo, Stanford University; **16.9, both:** © 1965 by Stanley Milgram. From the film *Obedience,* distributed by the New York University Film Division and the Pennsylvania State University, PCR.

Chapter 17

Page 575, left: Bettmann Archives, Inc.; **page 575, center and right:** AP/Wide World Photos; **page 576, top:** © Frank Siteman/Jeroboam, Inc.; **17.1:** UPI/ Bettmann Archives, Inc.; **17.2a:** © Anthony Bannister/Earth Scenes; **17.2b:** © Chagnon/Antho-Photo; **page 581:** © Dave Schaefer/Jeroboam, Inc.; **page 582, top:** © Kent Reno/Jeroboam, Inc.; **page 582, bottom:** © MacDonald Photography/ Panographics; **17A:** © Harry Wilks/Stock, Boston; **17.4:** courtesy of The Academy of Motion Picture Arts and Sciences; **page 588, bottom left:** courtesy of The Academy of Motion Picture Arts and Sciences; **page 588, bottom center:** AP/Wide World Photos; **page 588, bottom right:** Movie Star News; **page 594:** © Alan Carey/The Image Works; **page 595:** © Al Horvath/Panographics; **page 596, top:** © Michael G. Edrington/The Image Works; **page 596, center:** © Michael Siluk/EKM-Nepenthe; **page 596, bottom:** © Jean-Marc Loubat/Photo Researchers, Inc.; **page 598:** © Alberto Garcia/ Gamma-Liaison; **page 600, top:** © Bob Daemmrich/ Stock, Boston; **page 600, center:** © Ferry/Gamma-Liaison; **page 600, bottom:** © Bill Gillette/Stock, Boston; **page 603:** © Cleo Freelance Photography; **page 604, bottom left:** UPI/Bettmann Newsphotos; **page 604, top left:** AP/Wide World Photos; **page 604, right:** UPI/Bettmann Newsphotos.

Illustrators

Catherine Twomey
Figures 2.3, 2.7, 2.12, 2.13, 2.24

Fineline Illustrations, Inc.
Figures 1.1, 1.2, 1.3, 4.A, 5.2, 5.17, 5.18, 6.1, 6.2, 6.4, 6.5, 6.6, 6.7, 6.11, 6.12, 6.A, 7.1, 7.2, 7.5, 7.8, 7.9, 7.10, 7.12, 7.13, TA 7.12, 8.1, 8.3, 8.5, 8.6, 8.7, 8.C, 9.9, 9.19, 9.20, 10.4, 10.8, 11.1, 11.11, 12.2, 12.4, 12.8, 13.5, 13.B, 14.B, 14.4, 14.6, 16.1, 16.2, 16.A, 16.7, 16.10, 17.3, 17.B, 17.6, 17.7

Line Art and Text

Chapter 1

Figure P.1: From Walter Pauk, *How To Study In College,* Third Edition. Copyright © 1984, Houghton-Mifflin Company. Used with permission. **Figures 1.4 and 1.5:** From Stapp, J., and R. Fulcher, "The Employment of APA Members," *American Psychologist,* vol. 36. Copyright © 1981 by the American Psychological Association. Reprinted by permission of the author.

Chapter 2

Figures 2.10, 2.17, and 2.18: From Johnson, Leland G., *Biology,* 2d ed. © 1983, 1987 Wm. C. Brown Publishers, Dubuque, Iowa. All Rights Reserved. Reprinted by permission. **Figure 2.11:** From Groves, Philip M., and Kurt Schlesinger, *Introduction to Biological Psychology,* 2d ed. © 1979, 1982 Wm. C. Brown Publishers, Dubuque, Iowa. All Rights Reserved. Reprinted by permission. **Figure 2.20:** From *Rand McNally Atlas of the Body and Mind.* © Mitchell Beazley Publishers, Ltd., 1976. Published in the U.S.A. by Rand McNally, 1976, p. 15. Rand McNally and Co., P.O. Box 7600, Chicago, IL 60680 USA. **Figure 2.21:** Reprinted with permission of Macmillan Publishing Company from *Physiology: A Regulatory Systems Approach* by Fleur L. Strand. Copyright © 1983 by Fleur L. Strand. **Figure 2.22:** From Gazzaniga, Michael S., Diane Steen, and Bruce Volpe, *Functional Neuroscience.* © 1979 Harper & Row, Publishers, Inc., New York, NY. **Figure 2.24:** From Van De Graaff, Kent M., *Human Anatomy Laboratory Textbook,* 2d ed. © 1981, 1984 Wm. C. Brown Publishers, Dubuque, Iowa. All Rights Reserved. Reprinted by permission. **Figure 2.26:** From Peele, T. L., *Neuroanatomical Basis for Clinical Neurology,* 2d ed. © 1961 McGraw-Hill Book Company, New York, NY. Reprinted by permission. **Figure 2.D:** From T. A. Woolsey and J. R. Wann, "Areal Changes in Mouse Cortical Barrels Following Vibrissal Damage at Different Postnatal Ages," in *Journal of Comparative Neurology, 170,* pp. 53–66. Copyright © by Alan R. Liss, Inc. Reprinted by permission. **Figure 2.27:** From *The Neurosciences: A Third Study Program,* edited by Schmitt and Worden, by permission of MIT Press, Cambridge, Mass. Copyright 1974 by the MIT Press, Cambridge, Mass. **Figure 2.28:** From Hole, John W., Jr., *Human Anatomy and Physiology,* 4th ed. © 1978, 1981, 1984, 1987 Wm. C. Brown Publishers, Dubuque, Iowa. All Rights Reserved. Reprinted by permission.

Chapter 3

Figures 3.4, 3.6, and 3.16: From Hole, John W., Jr., *Human Anatomy and Physiology,* 4th ed. © 1978, 1981, 1984, 1987 Wm. C. Brown Publishers, Dubuque, Iowa. All Rights Reserved. Reprinted by permission. **Figure 3.7:** From *Sensation and Perception,* 2nd ed., p. 203, by H. R. Schiffman. Copyright © 1982 by John Wiley and Sons, Inc. Reprinted by permission of John Wiley and Sons, Inc. **Figure 3.11:** Reprinted by permission from *Vision Research, 7,* pp. 519–537, by Tomita, T., Kaneko, A., Murakami, M., and E. Pautler. Copyright 1967, Pergamon Press, Ltd. **Figures 3.21 and 3.34:** From Fernald, Dodge L., and Peter S. Fernald, *Introduction to Psychology,* 5th ed. © 1985 Wm. C. Brown Publishers, Dubuque, Iowa. All Rights Reserved. Reprinted by permission. **Figure 3.24:** From Munsinger, Harry, *Fundamentals of Child Development,* 2d ed. © 1975 Holt, Rinehart and Winston, New York, NY. **Figure 3.26:** From *Sensation and Perception,* 2nd ed., p. 323, by H. R. Schiffman. Copyright © 1982 by John Wiley and Sons, Inc. Reprinted by permission of John Wiley and Sons, Inc. **Figure 3.27:** Reprinted from Wathen-Dunn, *Models for the Perception of Visual Form,* by permission of the MIT Press, Cambridge, Mass. **Figure 3.29:** From James J. Gibson, *The Perception of the Visual World,* p. 170. Copyright © 1950, renewed 1977 by Houghton-Mifflin Company. Used by permission.

Chapter 4

Figure 4.1: From *Epilepsy and the Functional Anatomy of the Human Brain*, by W. Penfield and H. Jasper. Copyright © 1954 by Little, Brown and Company. Reprinted by permission. **Figure 4.5:** From Berger, R. J., "The Sleep and Dream Cycle," in Kales, A., *Sleep: Physiology and Pathology*. Copyright © 1969 by J. B. Lippincott Company. Reprinted by permission **Figure 4.B:** From *Brain, Mind and Behavior* by Floyd E. Bloom, et al. Copyright © 1985 Educational Broadcasting Corporation. Reprinted with permission of W. H. Freeman and Company, New York, NY. **Figure 4.8:** Courtesy of Multimedia Entertainment, Inc. **Figure 4.11:** From "Effects of Transcendental Meditation vs. Resting . . ." by D. S. Holmes, S. Solomon, B. M. Cappo, and J. L. Greenberg, in *Journal of Personality and Social Psychology, 44,* 1248–1252. Copyright © 1983 by the American Psychological Association. Reprinted by permission of the author. **Figure 4.12:** From "Hallucinations" by Ronald K. Siegel, Alan D. Joselin, artist. © October/1977 by Scientific American, Inc. All rights reserved.

Chapter 5

Figures 5.3, 5.8, and 5.11: From Chance P., *Learning and Behavior,* 1979. Reprinted by permission of Wadsworth Publishing Company. **Figure 5.4:** From Morgan/King, *Introduction to Psychology.* Copyright © 1971 by McGraw-Hill Book Company. Reprinted by permission. **Figure 5.7:** From Dember, William N., James J. Jenkins, and Timothy Teyler, *General Psychology,* 2d ed. © 1984 Lawrence Erlbaum Associates, Inc., Hillsdale, NJ. Reprinted by permission of the publisher and author. **Figure 5.13:** From Guttman, N., and H. I. Kalish, "Discriminability and Stimulus Generalization," in *Journal of Experimental Psychology, 51,* p. 81. Copyright 1956 by the American Psychological Association. **Figure 5.16:** From A. Bandura, "Influence of Model's Reinforcement Contingencies on the Acquisition of Imitative Responses," in *Journal of Personality and Social Psychology, 1,* pp. 589–595. Copyright © 1965 by the American Psychological Association. Reprinted by permission of the author. **Figures 5.19 and 5.20:** From Tolman, E. C., Ritchie, B. F., and D. Kalish, "Studies in Spacial Learning: I. Orientation and Shortcut," in *Journal of Experimental Psychology, 36,* pp. 13–24. Copyright © 1946 by the American Psychological Association. **Figure 5.A:** From Gould, P., and R. White, *Mental Maps.* © 1974 Penguin Books, Ltd., United Kingdom. All Rights Reserved. **Figure 5.21:** From *Biology Today,* 2d ed. Copyright 1972, 1975 by Random House, Inc. Reprinted from CRM Books, a division of Random House, Inc.

Chapter 6

Figure 6.3: From Murdock, Bennet B., Jr., *Human Memory: Theory and Data.* © 1974 Lawrence Erlbaum Associates, Inc., Publishers. Reprinted by permission. **Figures 6.8 and 6.9:** From Bower, G. H., "Organizational Factors in Memory," *Cognitive Psychology, 1,* 18–46. Copyright 1970 by Academic Press. Reprinted by permission of the author and publisher. **Figure 6.10:** From Collins, A. M., and M. R. Quillian, "Retrieval Time from Semantic Memory," *Journal of Verbal Learning and Verbal Behavior, 3,* pp. 240–248. Copyright © 1969 by Academic Press. Reprinted by permission of the author and publisher. **Figure 6.11:** From Lachman, R., et al., *Cognitive Psychology and Information Processing.* © 1979 Lawrence Erlbaum Associates, Inc., Hillsdale, NJ. **Figure 6.13:** From Schank, P., and R. Abelson, *Scripts, Plans, Goals, and Understanding.* © 1976 Lawrence Erlbaum Associates, Inc., Publishers. Reprinted by permission. **Table 6–A:** From Rubin, D. C., and M. Kozin, "Vivid Memories," in *Cognition, 16,* pp. 81–95. © 1984 Associated Scientific Publishers, Amsterdam, The Netherlands.

Chapter 7

Figure 7.3: From Moates, Danny R., and Gary M. Schumacher, *An Introduction to Cognitive Psychology,* 1980. Reprinted by permission of Wadsworth Publishing Company. **Figure 7.4:** From Matlin, Margaret, *Cognition.* © 1983 Holt, Rinehart and Winston, New York, NY. **Figures 7.6 and 7.7:** From Lahey, Benjamin B., *Psychology: An Introduction,* 2d ed. © 1983, 1986 Wm. C. Brown Publishers, Dubuque, Iowa. All Rights Reserved. Reprinted by permission. **Figure 7.11:** From Hunt, Morton, *The Universe Within.* Copyright © 1982 by Morton Hunt. Reprinted by permission of Simon & Schuster, Inc. **Figure 7.15:** The Nobel Foundation 1974. **Figure 7.16:** From Brown, R., Cazden, C., and U. Bellugi-Klima, "The Child's Grammar From 1 to 111," in *Minnesota Symposium on Child Psychology,* Vol. 2, 1969, by J. P. Hill (ed.). Reprinted by permission of the University of Minnesota Press.

Chapter 8

Figure 8.2: Adapted from Sattler, Jerome M., *Assessment of Children's Intelligence and Special Abilities,* 2d ed. © 1982 Allyn and Bacon, Newton, MA. Reprinted by permission of the author. **Figure 8.6:** From Scarr, S., and R. A. Weinberg, "IQ test performance of black children adopted by white families," *American Psychologist, 31,* 726–736. Copyright 1976 American Psychological Association. Reprinted by permission of the author. **Figure 8.8:** Permission of J. C. Raven Limited. **Figure 8.10:** Source: J. P. Guilford, *The Nature of Human Intelligence.* © 1967 McGraw-Hill Book Company, New York, NY. **Excerpts, page 244:** From the *Los Angeles Times,* October 18, 1979 and May 25, 1982. Section IV Opening: From the Prologue by Carl Sandburg to *The Family of Man,* edited by Edward Steichen. Copyright © 1955, renewed 1983, The Museum of Modern Art. All Rights Reserved.

Chapter 9

Figure 9.A: Copyright 1984 Time, Inc. All rights reserved. Reprinted by permission from *Time.* **Figures 9.5 and 9.18:** From Santrock, John W., *Life-Span Development,* 2d ed. © 1983, 1986 Wm. C. Brown Publishers, Dubuque, Iowa. All Rights Reserved. Reprinted by permission. **Figure 9.6:** From *Human Embryology,* by Patten. Copyright 1933. Used with permission of McGraw-Hill Book Company. (Redrawn from Scammon.) **Figure 9.13:** From Harlow, H. F., and R. R. Zimmerman, "Affectional responses in the infant monkey," *Science, 130,* pp. 421–432. © 1959 American Association for the Advancement of Science. Reprinted by permission of the author and publisher. **Figure 9.15:** From Matas, Arend, and Sroufe, in *Child Development,* 1978, p. 551. Copyright © The Society for Research in Child Development, Inc. Reprinted by permission. **Figure 9.16:** From Lewis/Brooks-Gunn, in *Social Cognition and the Acquisition of the Self,* p. 64. Copyright 1979 Plenum Publishing Corporation. Reprinted by permission. **Figure 9.17:** From Santrock, John W., and Steven R. Yussen, *Child Development: An Introduction,* 3d ed. © 1978, 1982, 1987 Wm. C. Brown Publishers, Dubuque, Iowa. All Rights Reserved. Reprinted by permission. **Figure 9.B:** Joshua Nove/Dennie Palmer Wolf—Project Zero/Harvard University. **Figures 9.C, 9.E, and 9.F:** Reprinted with permission of Ellen Winner. **Figure 9.D:** From Golomb, Claire, *The Child's Invention of a Pictorial World: Studies in the Psychology of Child Art.* **Figure 9.G:** From Hyde, J. S., "Children's understanding of sexist language," *Developmental Psychology, 20,* p. 703. Copyright 1984 by the American Psychological Association. Reprinted by permission of the author.

Chapter 10

Figure 10.1: From Roche, A. F., "Secular Trends in Human Growth, Maturation, and Development," in *Monographs of the Society for Research in Child Development,* 1979, *44,* ser. #179, p. 20. Copyright © The Society for Research in Child Development, Inc. Reprinted by permission. **Figure 10.4:** Adapted from Blythe, D. A., R. Bulcroft, and R. G. Simmons, "The Impact of Puberty on Adolescence: A Longitudinal Study," in *Girls at Puberty,* by Jeanne Brooks-Gunn. Copyright 1981 by the Plenum Publishing Corporation. Reprinted by permission. **Figure 10.A:** Permission *Mad Magazine.* © 1985 by E. C. Publications, Inc. **Figure 10.5:** From Brown, B. B., and M. J. Lohr, "Peer group affiliation and adolescent self-esteem: An integration of ego identity and symbolic interaction theories," *Journal of Personality and Social Psychology, 52,* pp. 47–55. Copyright 1987 by the American Psychological Association. Reprinted by permission of the author. **Figures 10.6, 10.11, and 10.12:** From Santrock, John W., *Life-Span Development,* 2d ed. © 1983, 1986 Wm. C. Brown Publishers, Dubuque, Iowa. All Rights Reserved. Reprinted by permission. **Figure 10.7:** From Levinson, D. J., "Toward a conception of the adult life course," in N. J. Smelser and E. H. Erikson (Eds.), *Themes of Work and Love in Adulthood.* Copyright © 1980 Harvard University Press, Cambridge, MA. **Figure 10.8:** From Hultsch, D. F., and J. K. Plemons, "Life Events and Life Span Development," in *Life Span Development and Behavior,* Vol. 2, by P. B. Baltes and O. G. Brim. Copyright © 1979 by Academic Press. Reprinted by permission of the publisher and the author.

Chapter 11

Figure 11.1: Data (for diagram) based on Hierarchy of Needs in "A Theory of Human Motivation," from *Motivation and Personality,* Second Edition, by Abraham H. Maslow. Copyright © 1970 Abraham H. Maslow. **Figure 11.2:** Reprinted from Cannon, W. B., "Hunger and thirst," in C. Murchison, (Ed.), *The Foundations of Experimental Psychology,* 1928, With permission from Clark University Press. **Figure 11.4:** "Reprinted from 1961 *Nebraska Symposium on Motivation,* by permission of Nebraska Press. Copyright © 1961 by the University of Nebraska Press." **Figure 11.5:** Source: Langley, L. L., *Physiology of Man,* Toronto: Van Nostrand Reinhold Company, 1971, p. 576. Reprinted by permission of Wadsworth, Inc. **Figure 11.6:** From W. H. Masters, and V. E. Johnson, *Human Sexual Response,* 1966, Little, Brown, Boston. Reprinted by permission. **Figure 11.7:** From Darling, C. A., D. J. Kallen, and J. E. VanDusen, "Sex in Transition: 1900–1984," *Journal of Youth and Adolescence, 13,* 385–399. Copyright © 1984 Plenum Publishing Corporation. Reprinted by permission. **Figure 11.A:** From Jones, E. F., et al., "Teenage pregnancy in developed countries: Determinants and policy implications," *Family Planning Perspectives, 17,* 53–63. © 1985 Alan Guttmacher Institute, New York, NY. **Figure 11.11:** From Lepper, Mark, "Microcomputers in education," *American Psychologist, 40,* 1–9. Copyright 1985 by the American Psychological Association. **Figure 11.12:** From Lepper, M., D. Greene, and R. E. Nisbett, "Undermining Children's Intrinsic Interest with Extrinsic Rewards," in *Journal of Social Psychology,* p. 134. Copyright © 1973 by the American Psychological Association. Reprinted by permission of the author.

Chapter 12

Figure 12.5: Reprinted by permission of Elsevier Science Publishing Co., Inc., from "Cardiovascular Differentiation of Happiness, Sadness, Anger, and Fear Following Imagery and Exercise," by Gary Schwartz, et al., *Psychosomatic Medicine,* Vol. 43, pp. 349–352. Copyright 1981 by The American Psychosomatic Society, Inc. **Figure 12.8:** From Field, T. M., et al., "Discrimination and imitation of facial expressions by neonates," *Science,* 218, pp. 180–181, October 8, 1982. © 1982 American Association for the Advancement of Science. Reprinted by permission of the author and publisher.

Chapter 13

Figure 13.2: From *Psychology Applied to Modern Life,* by W. Weiten. Copyright © 1983 by Wadsworth, Inc. Reprinted by permission of Brooks/Cole Publishing Company, Monterey, California 93940. **Figure 13.A:** From Mischel, W., et al., "Cognitive and Attentional Mechanisms in Delay of Gratification," in *Journal of Personality and Social Psychology, 21,* pp. 204–218. Copyright © 1972 by the American Psychological Association. Reprinted by permission of the author. **Figure 13.5:** Data (for diagram) based on Hierarchy of Needs in "A Theory of Human Motivation," from *Motivation and Personality,* Second Edition, by Abraham H. Maslow. Copyright © 1970 Abraham H. Maslow. **Figure 13.B:** From *Man, The Manipulator* by Everett L. Shostrom. Copyright © 1967 by Abingdon Press. Used by permission. **Figure 13.8:** From Mischel, Walter, *Introduction to Personality,* 2d ed. © 1971 Holt, Rinehart and Winston, New York, NY.

Chapter 14

Figure 14.2: From *Abnormal Psychology.* Copyright © 1972 by Random House, Inc. Reprinted by permission of Random House, Inc. **Figure 14.4:** Reprinted with permission from *DSM-III Training Guide,* edited by L. J. Webb, C. C. DiClemente, E. E. Johnstone, J. L. Sanders, and R. A. Perley. New York: Brunner/Mazee, 1981, p. 87. **Figure 14.6:** Data from Gottesman, I. L., and J. Shields, *The Schizophrenic Puzzle.* © 1982 Cambridge University Press, New York, NY. **Figure 14.7:** From Goodstein, L. D., and J. F. Calhoun, *Understanding Abnormal Behavior,* 1982. Reprinted by permission of Random House, Inc.

Chapter 15

Figure 15.4: From Kendall, P., and J. Norton-Ford, *Clinical Psychology.* Copyright © 1982 by John Wiley and Sons, Inc. Reprinted by permission of John Wiley and Sons, Inc.

Chapter 16

Figure 16.1: From Mullen, B., et al., "Newscasters' facial expressions and voting behavior of viewers," *Journal of Personality and Social Psychology, 51,* p. 294. Copyright 1986 by the American Psychological Association. Reprinted by permission of the author. **Figure 16.2:** From Festinger, L., and J. Carlsmith, "Cognitive consequences of forced complicance," *Journal of Abnormal and Social Psychology, 58,* pp. 203–210. Copyright 1959 by the American Psychological Association. Reprinted by permission of the author. **Figure 16.A:** From Snyder, M., E. Berscheid, and P. Glick, "Focusing on the exterior and the interior: Two investigations of the initiation of personal relationships," *Journal of Personality and Social Psychology, 48,* pp. 1427–1439. Copyright 1985 by the American Psychological Association. Reprinted by permission of the author. **Figure 16.7:** From Zimbardo, P., C. Haney, W. Banks, and D. Jaffe, *The Psychology of Imprisonment: Privation, Power and Pathology.* Unpublished manuscript, Stanford University, 1972. Reprinted by permission of P. Zimbardo. **Figure 16.5:** From S. E. Asch, "Studies of independence and conformity: A minority of one against a unanimous majority," *Psychological Monographs, 90,* whole #416. Copyright 1956 by the American Psychological Association. **Figure 16.10:** From Milgram, Stanley, "Behavioral study of obedience," *Journal of Abnormal and Social Psychology, 67,* pp. 371–378. Copyright 1963 by the American Psychological Association. Reprinted by permission.

Chapter 17

Figure 17.6: From Kephart, W. M., "Some correlates of romantic love," *Journal of Marriage and the Family, 29,* pp. 470–474. © 1967 National Council on Family Relations, Minneapolis, MN. **Figure 17.8:** From Baron, Robert A., and Donn Byrne, *Social Psychology: Understanding Human Interaction,* 4th ed. © 1984 Allyn and Bacon, Inc., Needham, MA.

Name Index

Subject Index

665

Helplessness, learned, 493
Hemispheres, of brain, 65, 71–74
Heredity, and intelligence, 261–63
Hermaphrodite, 377
Heroin, 160
Hertz, 99
Heterosexuality, 381–82, 386
Heuristics, 220, 221
Hidden-observer theory, of hypnosis, 134
Hierarchical organization, 192–94
Hierarchy of motives, 365–66, 376
Hierarchy of needs, 453
Hindbrain, 64, 66
Hinduism, 136
Hippocampus, 66
Histrionic personality disorder, 499
H.M.S. *Beagle,* 41
Hobbits, and orcs, 218
Holistic orientation, to health, 425
Holmes-Rahe scale, 415, 416
Holophrase hypothesis, 237
Homeostasis, 364–65
Homeostatic imbalance theory, 348
Homo sapiens, 42, 371, 582
  and language, 231
Homosexuality, 382, 386
Hopi Indians, 409
Horizontal-vertical illusion, 112
Hormones, 76, 368, 375
  and brain processes, 377–78
  FSH. *See* Follicle stimulating hormone (FSH)
  GH. *See* Growth hormone (GH)
Hue, 93, 94
Humanistic approach, 12
Humanistic perspective, and personality, 450–56
Humanistic psychotherapies, 513–17, 525
Hunger, and motivation, 366–75, 376
Huntington's chorea, 57
Hypnagogic state, 123
Hypnosis, 133–36
  applications of, 135–36, 140
  theories of, 134–35
Hypochondriasis, 465, 485, 487
Hypomania, 465
Hypothalamus, 65, 66, 67, 77
Hypotheses, 17
Hypothetical-deductive reasoning, 326
Hysteria, 465

Iatmul, 265
Iconic images, 187
Id, 437
IDEAL, 218, 219, 220, 224
Identity, 331, 334
  authentic, 343
Idiot savants, 256
Ik, 578
Illusions, 112–14
Imagery, 195–96, 206–7
  eidetic, 195
Images, iconic and echoic, 187
Imaginary audience, 326
Immune system, and stress, 413–14, 424
Implicit memory, 199, 207
Implicit personality theory, 558
Imprinting, 297
Impulse, nerve, 53–54
Incentive conditions, 173
Incentives, 365, 376
Incest, 502
Independence, 299–300, 301, 331, 334
Independent variable, 25

Inderal, 411
Individual differences, 245
Individual traits, 458
Individuation, 559
  de-, 596
Induction, 133
Industrial psychology, 33
Industry, 312
Infancy, 289–300
  disorders, 479
  and life-cycle perspective, 335
Infant, and emotion, 410–11, 412
Infant development, 279–317
Infantile amnesia, 199
Inference, statistical, 613–16
Inferiority, 312
Infinite generativity, 229
Informational pressure, 598
Information processing, glandular, 76–78
Information processing perspective, 13
Information theory, 157
Infrared light, 88
Initiative, 311
Innate goodness, 281
Inner ear, 100
Insecure attachment, 298
Insight learning, 178
Insight therapies, 516
Insomnia, 128
Instinctive drift, 179–80
Instincts, 364, 376
Instruction, computer-assisted, 170–71
Insulin, 368, 372
Integration, and brain, 74–76
Integrity, 353
Intellect, 459
Intelligence, 174, 243–75
  componential, experiential, and contextual, 268–69
  defined, 244–45
  extremes of, 270–73
  and heredity and environment, 261–63
  and knowledge and process, 266–67
  measurement and nature of, 248–61
  triarchic theory of, 268–69, 270
Intelligence quotient (IQ), 244, 249, 250, 251–54, 263, 267–73. *See also* Intelligence
Interaction
  group, 596–98
  and newborn, 287–88
Interactionist approach, and abnormality, 475
Interference, proactive and retroactive, 198
Intergenerational relations, 344, 345
Intergroup relations, 600–604
International Health Exhibition, 248
Interneurons, 50
Interpersonal learning, 526
Interposition, 110
Interpretation, 512
Interviews, and questionnaires, 20–22
Intimacy, 339
Intrinsic motivation, 389–90
Introspection, 8
Introversion, 459
In vitro fertilization, 284
Iodopsin, 91
Ions, and axons, 53
IQ. *See* Intelligence quotient (IQ)
Iris, 89, 90
Irrational statements, 522
Isolation, 339
  emotional and social, 593

James-Lange theory of emotion, 403–6, 412
Jigsaw classroom, 602
Jnd. *See* Just noticeable difference (jnd)
Jogging, 345
Johns Hopkins University, 391
Judge, 455
Justice perspective, 333
Justification, effort, 551
Just noticeable difference (jnd), 87

K-ABC. *See* Kaufman Assessment Battery for Children (K-ABC)
Kaufman Assessment Battery for Children (K-ABC), 265
Keying, empirical, 464
Kindly Man of Fearful Aspect, A, 109
Kinesthetic senses, 105–7
Knowledge
  declarative and procedural, 189
  and intelligence, 266–67
  tacit, 268–69
Ku Klux Klan, 596
Kung, 577

Laboratory, 19
LAD. *See* Language acquisition device (LAD)
Language, 228–40
  and adolescence, 328–29
  and animals, 231–32
  and behavior and environment, 233–36
  biological basis of, 230–36
  culture, and cognition, 238–40
  development of, 236–38
  and *Homo sapiens,* 231
  sign, 234–35
  and thinking, 211–42
Language acquisition device (LAD), 230
Late adolescence, 322
Late adulthood, 335
  and aging, 345–54
Late childhood, 300, 335
Latency stage, 444, 446
Law of Effect, 162
Leader, 454
Leadership, 598–99
Learned helplessness, 493
Learning, 151–82
  and affective disorders, 492–93
  associative and cognitive, 262
  and behavior therapies, 517, 531
  biological factors in, 179–80
  and cognition, 149–275, 174–78
  defined, 153–54
  insight, 178
  interpersonal, 526
  observational, 172–73
  and personality, 446–50, 456
  place, 177
Learning set, 221
Lens, 89
Levels of processing view, of memory, 191
Lewinsohn approach, to depression treatment, 521
Librium, 142
Lie detector, 402, 404–5
Life, 86, 145
Life cycle, and development, 277–356
Life-cycle perspective, 334
Life-events framework, 341–42
Life expectancy, 346, 349
Light, 89–91

Light-dark cycles, 58–59, 124–26
Liking, 590
Limbic system, 66
Linear perspective, 110
Listening, active, 514
Lithium, 536
Little Hans, 442–43
Living to Be 100: 1200 Who Did and How They Did It, 347
Loafing, social, 596
Lobes, of brain, 68
Lobotomy, prefrontal, 538
Loci, method of, 206
Loneliness, 593–94
Lonely, and alone, 594
Longevity, 346–48, 349
Longitudinal study, 352
Long-term memory, 185, 186, 187, 189, 190, 194
Loudness, 99
Love, 585–94
LSD. *See* Lysergic acid diethylamide (LSD)
Lucid dreaming, 130, 131
Lysergic acid diethylamide (LSD), 143

Macaque, 65
Mad, 328–29
Magnetic resonance imaging (MRI), 62
Magnetism, animal, 134
Maier string problem, 223
Major depression, 488–89, 498, 503
Mammals, 65
Manipulation, 454–55
Man the Manipulator, 454–55
Mantra, 137
Man Who Could Work Miracles, The, 41
Maps, 174–77
Marathon groups, 528
Mardi Gras, 596
Marijuana, 26, 143, 144, 337
Masculinity, 312, 313, 444, 465
MA. *See* Mental age (MA)
Mask, 588
Maslow's approach, and personality, 452–54, 456
Maslow's hierarchy of motives, 365–66, 376
Masochism, 501
Matching, prototype, 217
Matching hypothesis, 588
Maze running, 175
MDMA, 143, 144, 145
MD. *See* Doctor of Medicine (MD)
Mean, 610
Mean length of utterance (MLU), 238
Median, 610
Medical model, and abnormality, 475
Meditation, 136–38, 140
Medium, 556, 557
Medulla, 64
Memory, 184–210
  and adulthood, 338
  autobiographical, 200–201
  and buzz, 217
  defined, 185
  episodic, 189
  flashbulb, 200–201
  implicit, 199, 207
  long-term, 185, 186, 187, 189, 190, 194
  neurobiological basis of, 205–6, 207
  and organization, 192–94
  and processing, 190, 191
  repisodic, 204, 207